Fourth Edition

Zoology

Stephen A. Miller

College of the Ozarks

John B. Harley

Eastern Kentucky University

WCB McGraw-Hill

Boston Burr Ridge, IL Dubuque, IA Madison, WI New York San Francisco St. Louis
Bangkok Bogotá Caracas Lisbon London Madrid
Mexico City Milan New Delhi Seoul Singapore Sydney Taipei Toronto

WCB/McGraw-Hill
A Division of the McGraw-Hill Companies

ZOOLOGY, FOURTH EDITION

 This book is printed on recycled paper.

1 2 3 4 5 6 7 8 9 0 QPD/QPD 9 3 2 1 0 9 8

ISBN 0–697–34555–6

Vice president and editorial director: *Kevin T. Kane*
Publisher: *Michael D. Lange*
Sponsoring editor: *Margaret J. Kemp*
Developmental editor: *Adora L. Pozolinski*
Marketing manager: *Thomas C. Lyon*
Senior project manager: *Peggy J. Selle*
Production supervisor: *Deborah Donner*
Designer: *K. Wayne Harms*
Photo research coordinator: *Lori Hancock*
Art editor: *Joyce Watters*
Compositor: *GTS Graphics, Inc.*
Typeface: *10/12 Goudy*
Printer: *Quebecor Printing Book Group/Dubuque, IA*

Cover image: *Animals/Animals/Gibb, M./OSF*
Cover design: *Ellen Pettengell*
Interior design: *Kathy Theis*

Library of Congress Cataloging–in–Publication Data

Miller, Stephen A.
    Zoology/ Stephen A. Miller, John P. Harley. — 4th ed.
        p.   cm.
    Includes index.
    ISBN 0–697–34555–6. — ISBN 0–07–115810–3 (International ed.)
    1. Zoology.   I. Harley, John P.   II. Title.
QL47.2.M55   1999
590-dc21

                           98-12999
                               CIP

www.mhhe.com

brief CONTENTS

CONTENTS

PART TWO
THE CONTINUITY OF ANIMAL LIFE 83

10 DESCRIPTIVE EMBRYOLOGY   133

PART THREE
EVOLUTION   151

11 EVOLUTION: A HISTORICAL PERSPECTIVE   152

12 EVOLUTION AND GENE FREQUENCIES   163

PART FOUR
BEHAVIOR AND ECOLOGY   177

13 ANIMAL BEHAVIOR   178

PART FIVE
ANIMAL-LIKE PROTISTS AND ANIMALIA 225

36 CIRCULATION, IMMUNITY, AND GAS EXCHANGE 605

37 NUTRITION AND DIGESTION 629

38 TEMPERATURE AND BODY FLUID REGULATION 655

39 REPRODUCTION AND DEVELOPMENT   677

preface

The preparation of the fourth edition of *Zoology* involved a careful evaluation of the features of previous editions that contributed to the understanding of zoology as an exciting and dynamic scientific field. Students and instructors continue to praise this text as the most readable general zoology text available. A text that is not read—despite the authority and detail of its content—is of little use to instructors and students of general zoology. Readability and integrity in content are the characteristics that we were committed to retaining and improving on in the fourth edition. We are grateful to all of the instructors and students who provided recommendations during the preparation of this new edition.

One of the biggest challenges in preparing a general zoology text is to publish a comprehensive volume that is both manageable in size and adaptable to the variety of approaches instructors use to teach zoology. This edition, like the third, has fewer than 700 pages of text and is full color. Many instructors have taken advantage of the full-color customization options, selecting only the chapters covered in their course.

Our efforts in the production of this edition involved improving the accuracy and clarity of all chapters and updating information. This edition contains the following **new** features: new and revised illustrations and photographs, new boxed readings, coverage of the most recently described phylum (Cycliophora), expanded and updated coverage of cladistics, chapter-by-chapter descriptions of Internet sites containing information related to chapter content, expanded coverage of the phylum Mollusca, and Wildlife Alerts. We believe that the Wildlife Alerts will be particularly valuable to students and instructors. The first Wildlife Alert introduces students to endangered species and threatened species classifications and to the extent of the species loss problem in the United States. Other Wildlife Alerts depict the plight of selected animal species and are scattered throughout the text to remind the reader of the impact that humans have had on animal populations. Some endangered species described are vertebrate species. Other descriptions are of animals like the Karner blue butterfly, the Iowa Pleistocene snail, and freshwater mussels. We hope that these Wildlife Alerts will increase student awareness of the need to preserve animal habitats and species.

Zoology is organized into six parts. We emphasize the interrelationships of all life-forms by covering the common life processes early in the text. Part One includes an introduction to zoology, as well as coverage of cellular chemistry, structure, and function. Part Two covers the basic biological concepts of molecular biology, genetics, and embryology. Part Three addresses evolution, and Part Four covers behavior and ecology. Evolutionary and ecological topics precede the survey of the animal phyla and the form and function sections of the text to emphasize the important foundation that they provide for all aspects of zoology.

Part Five is the survey of animals, emphasizing evolutionary relationships, aspects of animal organization that unite major animal phyla, and animal adaptations. Chapter 16 covers classification, organization, and phylogeny of animals. We have expanded the coverage of the principles of cladistics in chapter 16, and use cladograms to depict evolutionary relationships in chapters 17 to 31. Cladistic analysis has become increasingly important in animal systematics. While cladistic analysis has resulted in some nontraditional taxonomic groupings, beginning students need to be introduced to these methods. These chapters also include lists of phylum characteristics and full-color visuals. We cover the lesser-known invertebrate phyla in the form of Endpapers strategically placed between specific chapters to reflect the evolutionary relationships of the animals discussed in each chapter. Endpapers prevent the discussions of these animals from getting lost within lengthy chapters.

Part Six covers animal form and function using a comparative approach. This approach includes descriptions and full-color artwork that depict the evolutionary changes in the structure and function of selected organ systems. Part Six includes an appropriate balance between invertebrate and vertebrate descriptions.

SUPPLEMENTARY MATERIALS

Supplementary materials are available to assist instructors with their presentations and general course management.

1. An **Instructor's Manual/Test Item File,** prepared by Jane Aloi, provides examples of lecture/reading schedules for courses with various emphases. In addition, each chapter contains a detailed outline, purpose, objectives, key terms, summary, sources for audiovisual materials and computer software, and approximately 50 multiple-choice test questions.
2. **General Zoology Student Study Guide,** prepared by Jane Aloi and Gina Erickson, contains subject-by-subject summaries, questions, Web site addresses, and learning activities.
3. A set of 100 full-color acetate **transparencies** are available to supplement class-room lectures.
4. **General Zoology Laboratory Manual,** fourth edition, by Stephen A. Miller, is an excellent corollary to the text and incorporates many of the same learning aids. This edition offers enhanced coverage of the scientific method, a new exercise on cladistics, and activities in the survey of the animal phyla in Part Two that emphasize evolutionary relationships. A **Laboratory Resource Guide** is also available and contains additional

information about materials and procedures, and the answers to worksheet questions that accompany the lab exercises.

5. The **Customized Laboratory Manual.** Each lab manual exercise is also available individually as offprints, so students need buy only those exercises used in the laboratory. Contact your local sales representative for more details.

6. **Life Science Animations** is a series of five videotapes featuring more than 50 animations of key physiological processes spanning the breadth of concepts covered in a typical life science course. Of particular interest to professors teaching zoology are tape 3, *Animal Biology: Part I*, and tape 4, *Animal Biology, Part II*. These full-color animations enable the student to more fully and easily grasp such concepts as the formation of the myelin sheath, saltatory nerve conduction, signal integration, reflex arcs, and the organ of static equilibrium. (ISBNs 25050 and 25071)

7. **How to Study Science,** by Fred Drewes, offers students valuable tips on note-taking, how to interpret text figures, how to manage time, how to prepare for tests, and how to overcome "science anxiety." (ISBN 14474)

8. **The Life Science Living Lexicon CD-ROM,** by William Marchuk, provides comprehensive coverage of all the life science disciplines—biology, anatomy, physiology, botany, zoology, environmental science, and microbiology—by combining complete lexicon components:

   Overview of word construction and how to use the text material

   Glossary of common biological root words, prefixes, and suffixes

   Glossary of descriptive terms

   Glossary of common biological terms, organized by discipline

   Section describing the classification system

   in a powerful interactive CD-ROM with more than a thousand vivid illustrations and animations of key processes and systems—including histology micrographs and an interactive quizzing program. (ISBN 12133)

9. **Critical Thinking: A Collection of Readings,** by David J. Stroup and Robert D. Allen, is available for instructors who are working to integrate critical thinking into their curricula. This inexpensive text helps in the planning and implementation of programs intended to develop students' abilities to think logically and analytically. The book is a collection of articles that provide instruction and examples of current programs. The authors have included descriptions and evaluations of their personal experiences with incorporating critical thinking study in their coursework. (ISBN 14556)

ACKNOWLEDGMENTS

We wish to thank the reviewers who provided detailed criticism and analysis of the text during development. In the midst of their busy teaching and research schedules, they took time to read our manuscript and to offer constructive advice that greatly improved the final text.

REVIEWERS

Jane Aloi, *Saddleback College*

Beverly Burden, *Louisiana State – Shreveport*

Sarah Cooper, *Beaver College*

Tom Dale, *Kirtland Community College*

Elizabeth Desy, *Southwest State University*

Patricia Dooris, *Saint Leo College*

Peter Ducey, *State University of New York at Cortland*

Bruce Edinger, *Salem-Teikyo University*

DuWayne Englert, *Southern Illinois University*

Jim Goetze, *Laredo Community College*

Nels Granholm, *South Dakota State University*

Michael Hartman, *Haywood Community College*

William F. Hibschman, *Hartford Community College*

Karen Hickman, *University of Mary Hardin-Baylor*

Brian Hill, *Freed-Hardeman University*

Nathan Hovekamp, *Lenoir Community College*

Daniel Ippolito, *Anderson University*

Steve Landers, *Troy State University – Main Campus*

Virginia Lyons, *Trinity College*

Eddie Lunsford, *Tri-County Community College*

William Mathena, *Kaskaskia College*

Thomas Moon, *California University of Pennsylvania*

Eric V. Nelson, *Ohio Northern University*

Murray Paton Pendarvis, *Southeastern Louisiana University*

Neil Schanker, *College of the Siskiyous*

Fred Schindler, *Indian Hills Community College*

Amy C. Sprinkle, *Jefferson Community College – Southwest*

Mike Stokes, *Western Kentucky University*

John Tibbs, *University of Montana*

Dwina Willis, *Freed-Hardeman University*

Robert Yost, *Indiana Purdue University – Indianapolis*

The publication of a text requires the efforts of many people. We are grateful for the work of our colleagues at WCB/McGraw-Hill, who have shown extraordinary patience, skill, and commitment to this text. Marge Kemp, our sponsoring editor, and Kevin Kane, vice president and editorial director, have helped shape *Zoology* from its earliest planning stages. Our developmental editor, Adora Pozolinski, helped make the production of the fourth edition remarkably smooth. Adora kept us on schedule and the production moving in the plethora of directions that are nearly unimaginable to us. Peggy Selle served as our project manager. We are grateful for her skilled coordination of the many tasks with publishing this edition of *Zoology*.

Finally, but most importantly, we wish to extend appreciation to our families for their patience and encouragement. Janice A. Miller lived with this text through many months of planning and writing. She died suddenly 2 months before the first edition was released. Our wives, Carol A. Miller and Jane R. Harley, have been supportive throughout the revision process. We appreciate the sacrifices that our families have made during the writing and revision of this text. We dedicate this book to the memory of Jan and to our families.

Stephen A. Miller
John P. Harley

part ONE

SCIENCE, THE CELL, AND MOLECULAR BIOLOGY

One of the fundamental principles of modern biology is that processes occurring in organisms obey the laws of chemistry and physics, just as processes in nonliving systems do. The special properties of life arise because of the complex organization of organisms and the chemical processes that occur within them. Biologists must understand certain principles of chemistry to better analyze the organization and function of life on earth.

Another key to understanding life on our planet is recognizing the role of the cell as the fundamental organizational unit of life. As you learn more about cell function and structure, you will find that many cellular components and chemical processes are identical or very similar in cells from a variety of organisms. Recognition of these similarities at the cellular level provides an important unifying framework within which biologists approach the diversity of organisms.

All organisms require energy for maintenance, growth, and reproduction. Some organisms obtain energy by harnessing light energy from the sun (photosynthesis) and then producing materials they need. Other organisms, however, are not capable of using light energy in this way. They must use photosynthesizing organisms as sources of energy and materials.

Chapter 1 examines some of the underlying principles of zoology. Chapters 2 through 5 cover the biologically important concepts of chemistry, some basic characteristics of the cells that constitute organisms, and some of the energy relationships upon which animal life depends.

chapter 1

ZOOLOGY:
ITS PLACE IN SCIENCE

Concepts

1. The field of zoology is a subdiscipline of biology, the study of life.
2. All life shares a common genetic molecule (DNA), unit of organization (the cell), evolutionary forces, and environment (the earth).
3. Zoology, the study of animals, is a broad field with many subdisciplines.
4. The scientific method is a procedure that allows an investigator to objectively analyze biological occurrences.

Would You Like to Know . . .

1. the relationship between zoology and biology? (p. 3)

2. what fundamental molecule carries the genetic code for life? (p. 3)

3. the age of the earth? (p. 6)

4. why boa constrictors have remnants of pelvic appendages? (p. 6)

This chapter answers these and other useful questions.

This chapter contains evolutionary concepts, which are set off in this font.

What were your first experiences with **zoology** (Gr. *zoon*, animal + *logos*, to study), the study of animals? If your experiences were like those of many professional zoologists, your interests in zoology began at an early age with a fascination for animals (figure 1.1). These early interests in zoology probably came from petting and feeding domestic animals, and from observing animals in zoos, pet stores, and in the wild. Your questions regarding where these animals live and what they eat reflected a natural curiosity and a desire to learn.

As you matured, your curiosity probably did not lessen. Your ability to think critically and to solve difficult problems, however, matured. The questions that you now ask about animals reflect this maturity. Now you not only want to know where an animal lives and what it eats, you are also curious about the building blocks of animals, and how the properties of these building blocks explain characteristics of the entire organism. **①** In asking these kinds of questions, you are beginning to learn the relationship between zoology and **biology** (Gr. *bios*, life + *logos*, to study), the study of all life. Two goals of this text are to continue cultivating your natural curiosity and to provide the background that helps you understand the interrelationships of all life-forms. This text will help you to develop a framework for critical thinking that can be used to answer questions about life in general and animal life in particular.

A ONE-WORLD VIEW

In spite of life's diversity, a fundamental unity embraces all of the biological disciplines. As modern biology probes deeper into the secrets of life, it becomes clearer that all life shares a common genetic blueprint (in DNA); a common organizational unit (the cell); common evolutionary forces that influence the form, function, and habitat of the animal; and a common environment (the earth).

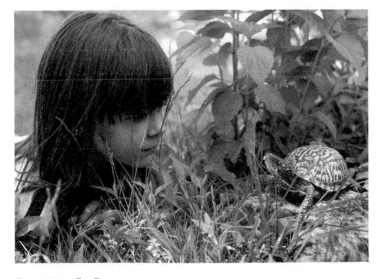

FIGURE 1.1

A Budding Zoologist. With zoological training, the natural curiosity of youth can mature into a framework for solving zoological problems as adults.

GENETIC UNITY

② All life is based on the fundamental molecule deoxyribonucleic acid (DNA). This molecule carries the genetic code for all proteins that make up the structural and functional components of life and is passed from generation to generation (figure 1.2). Understanding the structure of the DNA molecule has led to tremendous advances in the field of biology called "molecular biology." These advances have left no area of biology untouched. The fundamental importance of the DNA molecule in all aspects of biology should become clearer as you study later chapters.

THE FUNDAMENTAL UNIT OF LIFE

The cell is the fundamental unit of life. At the cellular level, biology transcends the boundaries that are sometimes constructed to organize life's diversity. A strong background in cell biology is required, whether you are studying animal biology (zoology), plant biology (botany), or any other subdiscipline of biology.

However, just as you can never view an animal apart from its cells, you fail to perceive the animal by focusing only on the cell. Cell interaction determines what animals look like, how they live, and frequently, when they die.

EVOLUTIONARY ONENESS AND THE DIVERSITY OF LIFE

Animals are united at all levels because of their common evolutionary origin and the shared forces that influenced their history. Evolutionary processes are remarkable for their relative simplicity, yet they have

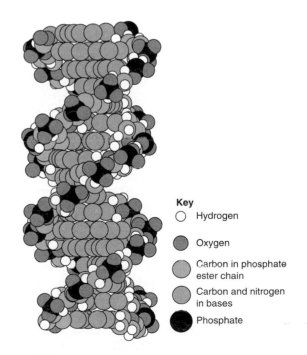

Key
○ Hydrogen
● Oxygen
● Carbon in phosphate ester chain
● Carbon and nitrogen in bases
● Phosphate

FIGURE 1.2

DNA, the Genetic Material of Life. This computer-generated model shows part of a DNA molecule.

(a)

(b)

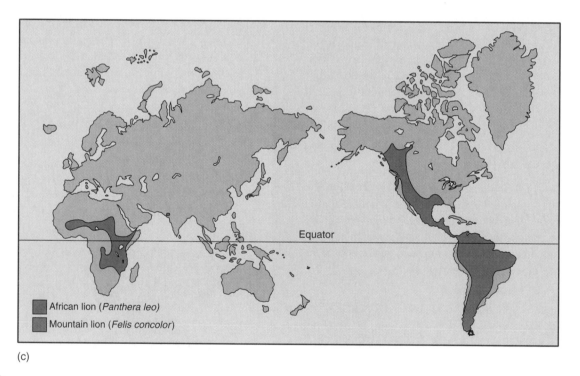

(c)

FIGURE 1.3

Biogeography as Evidence of Evolutionary Change. (*a*) An African lion (*Panthera leo*) has a similar ecological role as a (*b*) mountain lion (*Felis concolor*) of North and South America. Their similar form suggests a distant common ancestry. Obvious differences, however, result from millions of years of independent evolution. (*c*) Distribution of lions found in Africa and North and South America.

awesome effects on life-forms. Evolutionary processes have resulted in an estimated 4 to 30 million species of organisms living today. (Only 1.4 million species have been described.) Many more existed in the past and have become extinct.

The theory of organic evolution is the concept that populations of organisms change over time. Charles Darwin (1809–1882) published convincing evidence for his theory in *On the Origin of Species by Means of Natural Selection* in 1859. By 1900, most biologists were convinced that evolution occurs and that natural selection is a reasonable explanation of how it occurs.

Evidence of Evolution

Today, a wealth of evidence documents the basic premises of evolution. Nowhere is that evidence more convincing than in zoology.

Biogeography **Biogeography** is the study of the geographic distribution of plants and animals. Biogeographers attempt to explain why organisms are distributed as they are. Biogeographic studies show that life-forms in different parts of the world have distinctive evolutionary histories. For example, large

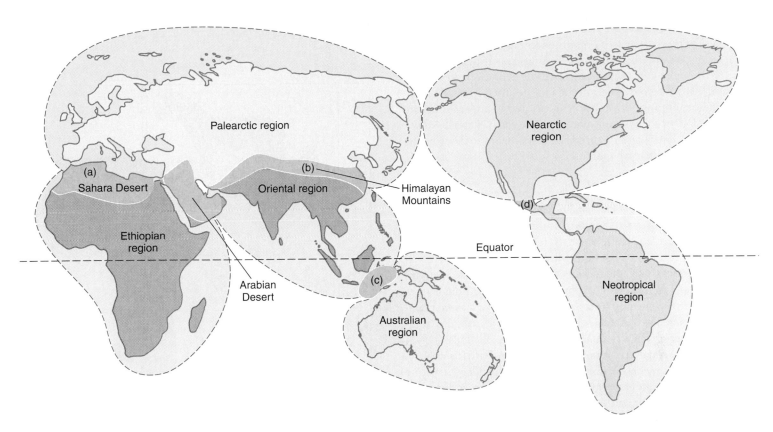

FIGURE 1.4

Biogeographic Regions of the World. Barriers, such as oceans, mountain ranges, and deserts, separate biogeographic regions of the world. (*a*) The Sahara and Arabian Deserts separate the Ethiopian and Palearctic regions, (*b*) the Himalayan Mountains separate the Palearctic and Oriental regions, (*c*) deep ocean channels separate the Oriental and Australian regions, and (*d*) the mountains of southern Mexico and Mexico's tropical lowlands separate the Nearctic and Neotropical regions.

areas of the world have similar climatic and geographic factors. Each of these geographic regions has distinctive plants and animals with particular roles in the environment. Compare the large meat-eating mountain lion (also called a cougar) of North America with the lion of Africa (figure 1.3). Their similar form suggests a distant common ancestry. Obvious differences, however, result from millions of years of independent evolution.

Recognizing that plants and animals in different parts of the world have distinctive evolutionary histories, biogeographers divide the world into six major biogeographic regions (figure 1.4). Each region has a characteristic group of plants and animals, and even though you may move from one region to another and experience similar climates, the different plants and animals encountered may make it seem as if you have entered another world.

Paleontology   Paleontology (Gr. *palaios*, old + *on*, existing + *logos*, to study), which is based on the study of the fossil record, provides some of the most direct evidence for evolution. **Fossils** (L. *fossilis*, to dig) are evidence of plants and animals that existed in the past and have become incorporated into the earth's crust (e.g., as rock or mineral) (figure 1.5). For fossilization to occur, sediments must quickly cover an organism to prevent scavenging and in a way that seals out oxygen and slows decomposition. Fossilization is most likely to occur in aquatic or

FIGURE 1.5

Paleontological Evidence of Evolutionary Change. Fossils, such as this trilobite (*Phacops rana*), are direct evidence of evolutionary change. Trilobites existed about 500 million years ago and became extinct about 250 million years ago. Fossils may form when an animal dies and is covered with sediments. Water dissolves calcium from hard body parts and replaces it with another mineral, forming a hard replica of the original animal. This process is called mineralization. This specimen is 6.5 cm long.

semiaquatic environments. The fossil record is, therefore, more complete for those groups of organisms living in or around water and for organisms with hard parts. This documentation provides some of the most convincing evidence for evolution. In spite of gaps in the fossil record, paleontology has resulted in nearly complete understanding of many evolutionary lineages (figure 1.6). ③ Paleontologists estimate that the earth is about 4.6 billion years old. They have also used the fossil record to describe the history of life on the earth (table 1.1).

Comparative Anatomy

A structure in one animal may resemble a structure in another animal because of a common evolutionary origin. **Comparative anatomy** is the subdiscipline of zoology that is fundamentally based on this relationship. Comparative anatomists study the structure of fossilized and living animals, looking for similarities that could indicate evolutionarily close relationships. Structures derived from common ancestry are **homologous** (Gr. *homolog* + *os*, agreeing) (i.e., having the same or a similar relation). Some examples of homology are obvious. For example, vertebrate appendages have a common arrangement of similar bones, even though the function of the appendages may vary (figure 1.7). Along with other evidence, this similarity in appendage structure indicates that the vertebrates evolved from a common ancestor.

Not all such similarities indicate homology. **Convergent evolution** occurs when two unrelated organisms adapt to similar conditions, resulting in superficial similarities in structure. For example, the wing of a bird and the wing of an insect are both adaptations for flight, but are not homologous (figure 1.8). Any similarities simply reflect the fact that, to fly, an animal must have a broad, flat gliding surface. Instead of being homologous, these structures are **analogous** (i.e., having a similar function but dissimilar origin).

Organisms often retain structures that have lost their usefulness. These structures are often poorly developed and are called **vestigial structures.** ④ For example, boa constrictors have minute remnants of hindlimb (pelvic) bones left over from appendages of their reptilian ancestors. Such remnants of once useful structures are clear indications of change—hence, evolution.

Molecular Biology

Recently, **molecular biology** has yielded a wealth of information on evolutionary relationships. Just as animals can have homologous structures, animals may also have homologous biochemical processes.

Ultimately, structure and function are based on the genetic blueprint found in all living animals: the DNA molecule. Related animals have similar DNA derived from their common ancestor. Because DNA carries the codes for proteins that make up each animal, related animals have similar proteins. With the modern laboratory technologies now available, zoologists can extract and analyze the structure of proteins from animal tissue, and compare the DNA of different animals. By looking for dissimilarities in the structure of related proteins and DNA, and by assuming relatively constant mutation rates, molecular biologists can estimate the elapsed time since divergence from a common ancestral molecule.

Biogeography, paleontology, comparative anatomy, and molecular biology have all generated impressive documentation of evolution since the initial studies of Darwin. The vast majority of

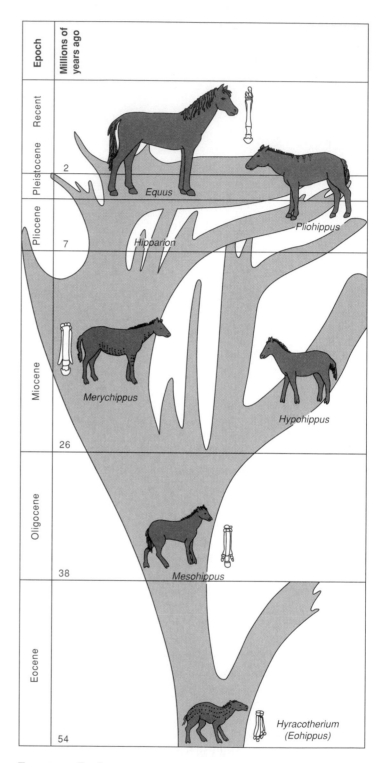

FIGURE 1.6

Reconstruction of an Evolutionary Lineage from Evidence in the Fossil Record. The fossil record allows horse evolution to be traced back about 60 million years. *Hyracotherium* (*Eohippus*) was a dog-sized animal with four prominent toes on each foot. A single middle digit of the toe and vestigial digits on either side of that remain in modern horses. About 17.7 million years ago, rapid evolutionary diversification resulted in the grazing lifestyle of modern horses. About 15 million years ago, 10–12 contemporaneous species of fossil horses lived in North America. Note that evolutionary lineages are seldom simple ladders of change. Instead, numerous evolutionary side branches often meet with extinction.

TABLE 1.1	THE HISTORY OF THE EARTH: GEOLOGICAL ERAS, PERIODS, AND MAJOR BIOLOGICAL EVENTS

ERA*	PERIOD	AGE AT BEGINNING OF THE PERIOD (MILLIONS OF YEARS)	MAJOR BIOLOGICAL EVENTS
CENOZOIC	Quaternary	0.01	Subtropical forests gave way to cooler forests and grassland areas.
CENOZOIC	Tertiary	65	Modern orders of mammals evolved. Humans evolved in the last 5 million years.
MESOZOIC	Cretaceous	135	Continental seas and swamps spread. Extinction of ancient birds and reptiles.
MESOZOIC	Jurassic	195	Climate warm and stable. High reptilian diversity. Birds first appeared.
MESOZOIC	Triassic	240	Climate warm. Extensive deserts. Dinosaurs replace mammal-like reptiles. First true mammals.
PALEOZOIC	Permian	285	Climate cold early, but then warmed. Mammal-like reptiles common. Widespread extinction of amphibians.
PALEOZOIC	Carboniferous	375	Warm and humid with extensive coal-producing swamps. Arthropods and amphibians common. First reptiles appeared.
PALEOZOIC	Devonian	420	Land high and climate cool. Freshwater basins developed. Fish diversified. Early amphibians appeared.
PALEOZOIC	Silurian	450	Extensive shallow seas. Warm climate. First terrestrial arthropods. First jawed fish.
PALEOZOIC	Ordovician	520	Shallow extensive seas. Climate warmed. Many marine invertebrates. Jawless fish widespread.
PALEOZOIC	Cambrian	570	Extensive shallow seas and warm climate. Trilobites and brachiopods common. Earliest vertebrates found late in the Cambrian.
PROTEROZOIC		2,000	Multicellular organisms appeared and flourished. Many invertebrates. Eukaryotic organisms appeared (1,500 million years ago). Oxygen accumulated in the atmosphere.
ARCHEAN		4,600	Prokaryotic life appeared (3,500 million years ago). Origin of the earth (4,600 million years ago).

*Note that the time scale in the Proterozoic and Archean eras is greatly compressed.

scientists have no doubt as to the reality of evolution. Evolutionary theory has impacted biology like no other single theory. It has impressed scientists with the fundamental unity of all of biology. As you progress through this text, you will continually be reminded of the unity that exists within life because of its common origin.

ENVIRONMENT AND WORLD RESOURCES

A common environment also unites life. In some parts of the world, the land is recovering from decades of abuse. You need only compare the polluted Lake Erie of the 1960s to the much cleaner lake of the 1990s. A lake once unfit for fishing and other recreational uses is now used extensively for these purposes. Tracts of land have been set aside for use as natural and wilderness areas. Many nonbiodegradable (not broken down by biological processes) substances have been taken out of the marketplace. These developments and others like them offer hope. Certainly, some societies are beginning to realize that all life shares a dependence on the earth's resources.

Even though there is hope, many societies have not abandoned those values that treat land, water, and air as commodities that can be bought and sold, or neglected and abused. The problems are most acute in the developing countries, which are striving to attain the same wealth as industrialized nations. In the process, the land suffers, population growth goes unchecked, toxic wastes are dumped, plant and animal species become extinct, and deserts and famine expand.

Governmental and private agencies (e.g., Worldwatch Institute) have undertaken large-scale evaluations of the environmental health of the world. The results of such studies deserve the serious attention of every concerned citizen.

Population

Global overpopulation is at the root of virtually all other environmental problems. Human population growth is expected to continue into the twenty-first century. Through the year 2000, most growth (92%) will be in less developed countries, where 5 billion out of a projected total of 6.35 billion humans will live. Since a high proportion of the population will be of childbearing age, growth could be even faster in the twenty-first century. As the human population grows, the disparity between the wealthiest and poorest nations is likely to increase.

World Resources

Human overpopulation is stressing world resources. Although new technologies continue to increase food production, most food is produced in industrialized countries that already have a high

(a)

(b)

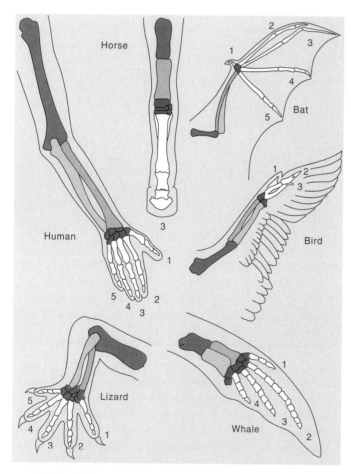

FIGURE 1.7

The Concept of Homology. The forelimbs of vertebrates evolved from an ancestral pattern. Even vertebrates as dissimilar as whales and bats have the same basic arrangement of bones. The digits (fingers) are numbered 1 (thumb) to 5 (little finger). Color coding indicates homologous bones.

FIGURE 1.8

The Concept of Analogy. The wings of (a) a bird and (b) an insect are analogous. They are specialized for a similar function, which coincidentally led to the flat, planing surfaces required for flight. Both kinds of wings arose independently and, therefore, are not homologous.

per-capita food consumption. Maximum oil production is expected to continue into the new millenium. Continued use of fossil fuels adds more carbon dioxide to the atmosphere, contributing to the greenhouse effect and global warming. Deforestation of large areas of the world results from continued demand for forest products and fuel. This trend contributes to the greenhouse effect, causes severe regional water shortages, and results in the extinc-

tion of many plant and animal species, especially in tropical forests. Forest preservation would result in the identification of new species of plants and animals that could be important human resources: new foods, drugs, building materials, and predators of pests (figure 1.9). Nature also has intrinsic value that is just as important as its provision of human resources. Recognition of this intrinsic worth provides important aesthetic and moral impetus for preservation.

Solutions

The problems just described have no easy solutions. Unless we deal with the problem of human overpopulation, however, solving the other problems will be impossible. The one certainty is that there is no time for delay. We must begin to work as a world community to prevent the spread of disease, famine, and other forms of suffering that accompany overpopulation. Bold and imaginative steps toward improved social and economic conditions and better resource management are needed.

(a)

(b)

FIGURE 1.9

Tropical Rain Forests: A Threatened World Resource. Tropical rain forest (a) before and (b) after clear-cutting and burning to make way for agriculture. These soils quickly become depleted and are abandoned for richer soils of adjacent forests. Loss of tropical forests results in extinction of many valuable forest species.

> ### Stop and Ask Yourself
>
> 1. What are four unifying themes of biology? Why is the study of each an important part of any biologist's training?
> 2. What is organic evolution?
> 3. How do each of the following contribute to the evidence for evolution: (a) biogeography, (b) paleontology, (c) mo-lec-u-lar biology, and (d) comparative anatomy?
> 4. What are the conclusions of studies on the environmental health of the world regarding (a) the earth's population in the year 2001, (b) resources for the year 2001, and (c) solutions for environmental problems?

WHAT IS ZOOLOGY?

Zoology is one of the broadest fields in all of science. The diversity of its subdisciplines reflects its breadth. These subdisciplines are based on particular functional, structural, or ecological interests that span many animal groups (table 1.2). Specializing in the biology of a particular group of animals is also possible (table 1.3). Given the size of some animal groups, further specialization is also common. For example, there are approximately 300,000 described (and many undescribed) species of beetles! One person cannot possibly be an expert in all areas of beetle biology. Therefore, he or she can specialize even further and become a beetle taxonomist, physiologist, or ecologist. Obviously, sharply defined boundaries do not separate the zoology subdisciplines, and the subdisciplines share much information.

THE CLASSIFICATION OF ANIMALS

Like all organisms, animals are named and classified into a hierarchy of relatedness. Although Karl von Linné (1707–1778) is primarily remembered for collecting and classifying plants, his system

TABLE 1.2	EXAMPLES OF SPECIALIZATIONS IN ZOOLOGY
SUBDISCIPLINE	**DESCRIPTION**
Anatomy	Study of the structure of entire organisms and their parts
Cytology	Study of the structure and function of cells
Ecology	Study of the interaction of organisms with their environment
Embryology	Study of the development of an animal from the fertilized egg to birth or hatching
Genetics	Study of the mechanisms of transmission of traits from parents to offspring
Histology	Study of tissues
Molecular biology	Study of subcellular details of animal structure and function
Parasitology	Study of animals that live in or on other organisms at the expense of the host
Physiology	Study of the function of organisms and their parts
Systematics	Study of the classification of, and the evolutionary interrelationships among, animal groups

TABLE 1.3	EXAMPLES OF SPECIALIZATIONS IN ZOOLOGY BY TAXONOMIC CATEGORIES
Entomology	Study of insects
Herpetology	Study of amphibians and reptiles
Ichthyology	Study of fishes
Mammalogy	Study of mammals
Ornithology	Study of birds
Protozoology	Study of protozoa

THE SCIENTIFIC METHOD

Science is knowledge obtained by observation. The usefulness of science is limited, therefore, to what we can detect with our senses or technological extensions of our senses. Science functions in the realm of matter and energy. The methods of science cannot be applied in areas of investigation involving other aspects of human experiences (e.g., matters of the mind or spirit). Trying to use science to either support or disprove nonscientific matters is a mistake (box 1.1). Scientific knowledge is neither inherently good nor bad. The same scientific knowledge that gave us nuclear medicine (e.g., radiation therapy for cancer victims) also brought us nuclear wastes. Although scientists and others use scientific knowledge to make ethical decisions, science itself is ethically neutral.

Science is based on observation; however, science is not without presuppositions. They are:

1. Nature is real. What we sense is reality.
2. Cause-and-effect relationships are consistent in nature—that is, the processes that shaped the world in the past are the same as those operating today and in the future. Stated another way, an experiment performed yesterday and repeated today should yield the same results both days.
3. Even though there is no perfect knowledge and no perfect observer, nature is understandable.

of naming—**binomial nomenclature**—has also been adopted for animals. A two-part name describes each kind of organism. The first part indicates the genus, and the second part indicates the species to which the organism belongs. Each kind of organism is recognized throughout the world by its two-part name. Above the species and genus levels, organisms are grouped into families, orders, classes, phyla, and kingdoms, based on a hierarchy of relatedness (figure 1.10). Organisms in the same species are more closely related than organisms in the same genus, and organisms in the same genus are more closely related than organisms in the same family, and so on.

FIGURE 1.10

Hierarchy of Relatedness. Classification of a housefly, horsefly, honeybee, and human.

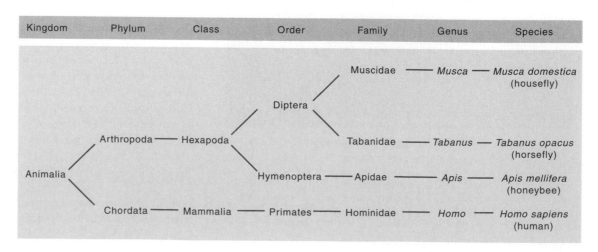

Kingdom	Phylum	Class	Order	Family	Genus	Species
				Muscidae — *Musca* —		*Musca domestica* (housefly)
			Diptera			
	Arthropoda — Hexapoda			Tabanidae — *Tabanus* —		*Tabanus opacus* (horsefly)
Animalia			Hymenoptera — Apidae —		*Apis* —	*Apis mellifera* (honeybee)
	Chordata — Mammalia —		Primates — Hominidae —		*Homo* —	*Homo sapiens* (human)

BOX 1.1 SCIENCE AND PSEUDOSCIENCE

The history of science has shown that science works well. In science, no questions should be avoided, and no concepts are sacred. The scientific community's inevitable scrutiny of a person's research provides a mechanism for exposing false statements and faulty methods. Science thrives on researchers pointing out errors in a current explanation, and proposing and testing an alternative hypothesis. Further testing eventually refutes the results of "bad science."

Pseudoscience is the representation of ideas or beliefs as scientific without scientific basis. Pseudoscience is usually more dangerous than bad science because its tenets are not open to testing and disproof, and because it is sometimes difficult to recognize. If the beliefs of a group are represented as scientific but are actually assumptions that are not open to testing, then they are the product of pseudoscience.

Pseudoscience should never be considered harmless fun because people unfamiliar with the scientific method find it difficult to distinguish science from pseudoscience. Hitler's claim of the superiority of his race, the use of extrasensory perception to solve crimes, psychic surgery, and many other manifestations of pseudoscience have wasted lives and millions of dollars. Unfortunately, our modern world seems obsessed with pseudoscience. A few of its manifestations are listed here. Can you think of others?

astrology	water witching	tea leaves
Bermuda Triangle	Loch Ness monster	"evil eye"
telepathy	ghosts	Ouija boards
precognition	pyramidology	perpetual motion
telekinesis	full moon criminality	psychics
remote viewing	palmistry	creationism
bleeding statues	numerology	UFOs

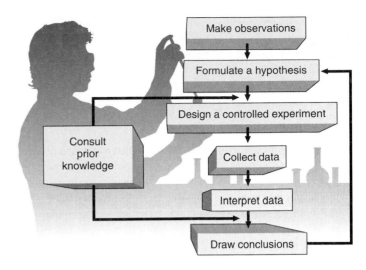

FIGURE 1.11

Steps of the Scientific Method. Application of the scientific method usually involves both sequential steps (center arrows and boxes) and repeating cycles of hypothesis formation, experimentation, and evaluation (side arrows and box).

processes is not as easy as it may seem. Knowing the right questions requires background information as well as a perceptive mind. Asking the proper questions frequently determines whether the data gathered can be used to formulate reliable answers.

Following the initial questioning, scientists attempt to formulate a reasonable explanation for the question—a **hypothesis.** To be useful, a hypothesis must be testable. Frequently, a hypothesis is so broad that it cannot be directly tested. Rather, some predictions of the hypothesis are tested. The simplest explanations that seem consistent with the evidence available are usually the ones most easily tested.

The hypothesis is tested by collecting data from further observations or from an experiment that has been designed. An experiment has three sets of **variables** (parameters that may change, either intentionally or through oversight). An **independent variable** is the parameter being tested in the experiment. A properly designed experiment should have a single independent variable. For example, in an experiment to determine how the length of daylight in a 24-hour period affects an animal's reproductive readiness, the length of daylight is the independent variable. A **dependent variable** is the parameter measured to determine the outcome of an experiment. In the example experiment already described, the condition of a female's ovaries and the frequency of mating attempts by males would be dependent variables. An experiment can have more than one dependent variable. A **controlled variable** is one that could influence the outcome of an experiment and thus must be held constant in all treatments through the use of a control group. A **control group** is treated the same as an experimental group, except that the independent variable being tested is omitted. A control is a basis for comparing the data from the experiment. Any differences in the results in the control and experimental groups must be a result of the independent variable being tested. Regardless of the outcome of an experiment, further testing is needed to back up any conclusions, and

These presuppositions are not provable, but past experience makes them reasonable assumptions.

Observation is the authority in science, but humans are the observers. Because science is a human activity, and because one person cannot observe everything, scientists must rely on the observations of others and accept those observations as valid or accurate. The methods used in observations must allow objective analysis. This objective process is often called the **scientific method** (figure 1.11). Traditionally, scientists take a series of steps to study natural occurrences. Some problems may be solved by designing experiments; detailed observations of processes or structures solve others. The scientific method is an objective process that helps ensure accurate observations. Because science is a human endeavor, human errors occur. Further, time and space considerations may influence observations. Therefore, the scientific method depends on many scientists repeating investigations to confirm or reject experiment results.

Traditionally, the scientific method involves asking questions based on a set of observations. Being able to look at nature and ask relevant questions regarding biological (or other)

the results must be communicated to other scientists. This communication may take the form of an article published in one of the hundreds of biological journals or a paper presented orally at one of the many gatherings of scientists throughout the world. Regardless of the vehicle chosen, these reports must include discussions of the hypothesis, the methodology, the results, and the conclusions. The results of any scientist's work are thus available for the scrutiny of others.

After repeated testing, scientists may assemble accepted and related hypotheses into a generalized statement that can be used in a predictive fashion and is called a **theory.** To a scientist, "theory" means something very different from the common use of the word as a conjecture or a guess. Scientists recognize that the details of what is known today will probably change with future research and that their knowledge is incomplete, as history has repeatedly shown. When scientists talk about the theory of evolu-

tion (or the theory of anything else), they are talking about a concept that data from years of research have supported. What scientists can never do, however, is claim that all of the details of evolutionary (or other) mechanisms have been determined. Thus, scientific theories are always provisional.

Stop and Ask Yourself

5. What is zoology? Why do most zoologists choose to specialize in a field within zoology?
6. What is binomial nomenclature?
7. What is a hypothesis?
8. What is a scientific theory? How is the word theory, used in this context, different from everyday usage?

SUMMARY

1. Biology, the study of life, has four themes that unify its divergent disciplines: (1) a common genetic molecule—DNA, (2) a common unit of organization—the cell, (3) a common evolutionary history, and (4) a common environment—the earth.
2. Evidence for evolution comes from the fields of biogeography, paleontology, comparative anatomy, and molecular biology.
3. All animals share a common environment. Human overpopulation has placed undue pressure on all of the earth's resources. Human values must change to successfully check deterioration of the environment.
4. Zoology is the study of animals. It is a broad field that requires zoologists to specialize.
5. Animals are classified into a hierarchical system of classification that uses a two-part name for every different kind of animal.
6. The scientific method is a system of thought and procedure that allows the investigator to objectively analyze an occurrence.

SELECTED KEY TERMS

binomial nomenclature (p. 10)
biology (p. 3)
convergent evolution (p. 6)
homologous (p. 6)
hypothesis (p. 11)
scientific method (p. 11)
theory (p. 12)
zoology (p. 3)

CRITICAL THINKING QUESTIONS

1. Zoologists need to consider the broader perspective that unites zoology with biology as a whole. Could this broader perspective also include the arts and humanities? Explain.
2. What is the difference between analogy and homology? In an evolutionary context, how could analogous structures arise?
3. Why is perfect objectivity impossible to attain in science?
4. Imagine that you have just gotten into your car and turned the key, but the engine did not start. Outline how you would use an objective, scientific approach to solve this problem. (Substitute another everyday problem, if you prefer.)

5. What are some current issues that involve both zoology and questions of ethics or public policy? What should be the role of zoologists in helping to resolve these issues?
6. A zoologist observed that a small beetle larva, *Psephenus herricki*, was found on rocks covered with unicellular algae in streams with rapid currents. The zoologist asked the following question: "Does the presence or absence of algae influence whether or not these beetle larvae are found on rocks?"
    a. Describe a testable hypothesis for investigating this question.
    b. Design an experiment to test your hypothesis.
    c. Identify the independent variable in your experiment.
    d. Identify the dependent variable(s) in your experiment.
    e. Identify the controlled variables in your experiment.

REFERENCES ON THE WORLD WIDE WEB

SCIENCE AND TECHNOLOGY

1. **Museum of Science, Boston, Massachusetts.**   This Web site allows you to explore many areas of science and the relationships between scientific disciplines. It also contains resources for prospective science teachers.
    http://www.mos.org/mos/homepage.html
2. **New Scientist.**   Science and technology news is the focus of this Web site. *Internet Magazine* called this the best Web site in 1995. A must-see site for amateur and professional scientists.
    http://www.newscientist.com/
3. **Science.**   At this site, you can explore a wide range of topics in all areas of science, including the environment, evolution, genetics, and the history of science. It contains interactive learning activities.
    http://www.sci.lib.uci.edu/SEP/life.html#5

BIOLOGY

4. **Biology.**   This site, maintained by California State University at Long Beach, provides a wide variety of biological images and activities. You can access numerous attractive photographs of animals and their environment. Click on "Global Campus and Biology."
    http://www.csulb.edu/gc

5. **Biology.** This site provides general information on the biological sciences.

    http://galaxy.tradewave.com/galaxy/Science/Biology.html

EVOLUTION AND GEOLOGICAL TIME

6. **Geological Time.** This Web site presents an excellent description of the geological time scale and the events that highlight major geological time periods.

    http://www.ucmp.berkeley.edu/exhibit/geology.html

ENVIRONMENT AND ECOLOGY

7. **Ecology.** This site provides information on many topics in environmental science and biodiversity.

    http://www.bio.uci.edu/academic/upgrad/resource.html#TOC25479

8. **Ecology.** This site provides general information on ecological topics and current ecological issues and developments.

    http://www.ecology.com/

9. **Biodiversity.** This site provides information on biodiversity studies from around the world.

    http://muse.bio.cornell.edu/taxonomy/general.html

10. **Women Working in Resource Conservation.** This site explains the role that women are playing in natural resource work. It is written by and for women.

    http://www.ets.uidaho.edu/winr/r

11. **Population Ecology.** This site provides on-line data, information on lecture courses, and the names of organizations, people, and journals involved in population ecology.

    http://www.gypsymoth.ento.vt.edu/~sharov/popechome/welcome.html

CAREERS IN BIOLOGY AND ZOOLOGY

The following sites all contain information on careers in biology and zoology:

12. http://www.primex.co.uk/iob/c18.html
13. http://www.furman.edu/~snyder/careers/careers.html
14. http://www.stfrancis.edu/ns/careers.html
15. http://shs.starkville.k12.ms.us/~biology/acareers.html

c h a p t e r 2

THE CHEMICAL BASIS OF ANIMAL LIFE

Concepts

1. Animals are made up of molecules, which are collections of atoms bound to one another. The life processes within an animal are based, to a large degree, on the chemical properties of atoms, ions, and molecules.
2. Carbon is the key element of organic molecules because it has unique physical and chemical characteristics.
3. Carbohydrates and lipids are principal sources of energy for most animals.
4. Proteins, nucleotides, and nucleic acids are large molecules that provide the basis for structure, function, information storage, energy transfer, and genetic regulation in animals.

Would You Like to Know . . .

1. what the four most common elements in most animals are? (p. 16)
2. what holds adjacent water molecules together? (p. 19)
3. why the type of fat called an oil is liquid at room temperature? (p. 23)

This chapter answers these and other useful questions.

Chemical processes are essential to everything that goes on within the body of an animal. Without these chemical processes, life as we know it could not exist. This chapter presents the chemistry you need to understand the basic chemical processes that enable animals to function in the environment as living entities.

Chemistry is the branch of science dealing with the composition of substances and reactions among these substances. In chemical reactions, bonds between atoms break or join to form different combinations of atoms or molecules. A knowledge of chemistry is essential for understanding the structure (**anatomy** [Gr. *ana*, again + *temnein*, to cut]) and function (**physiology** [Gr. *physis*, nature]) of animals because body functions involve chemical changes in structural units, such as cells. As interest in the chemistry of animals grew, and knowledge in this area expanded, a new subdivision of science called **biochemistry** ("the chemistry of life") emerged. Biochemistry is the study of the molecular basis of life.

ATOMS AND ELEMENTS: BUILDING BLOCKS OF ALL MATTER

Matter is anything that occupies space and has mass. It includes all of the solids, liquids, and gases in our environment, as well as those in bodies of all forms of life. **Mass** refers to the amount of matter in an object. Matter is composed of **elements,** chemical substances that ordinary chemical reactions cannot break down into simpler units. An element is designated by either a one- or two-letter abbreviation of its Arabic, English, German, or Latin name. For example, O is the symbol for the element oxygen, H stands for hydrogen, and Na is the symbol for sodium (from the Latin, *natrium*). Currently, scientists recognize 92 elements occurring in nature. ❶ Fifteen elements are found in large quantities in most animals, and four of these (carbon, hydrogen, oxygen, and nitrogen) account for the majority (97%) of an animal's body weight (table 2.1). The remaining 3% of an animal's weight consists primarily of calcium, phosphorus, and potassium. Elements present in trace amounts include sodium, sulfur, manganese, magnesium, copper, iodine, iron, and chlorine.

Elements are composed of units of matter called atoms. An **atom** (Gr. *atomos*, indivisible) is the smallest part of an element that can enter into a chemical reaction. Atoms vary in size, weight, and the diverse ways they interact with each other. For example, some atoms can combine with atoms like themselves or with dissimilar atoms; others lack this ability.

STRUCTURE OF ATOMS

Atoms have two main parts: a central core called a nucleus and the surrounding electron cloud (figure 2.1). The nucleus contains two major particles: the positively charged **protons (p^+)** and the uncharged **neutrons (n^0).** Surrounding the nucleus are negatively charged particles called **electrons (e^-).** Any one electron moves so rapidly around the nucleus that it cannot be found at any given

TABLE 2.1 NATURALLY OCCURRING ELEMENTS IN ANIMALS				
ELEMENT	SYMBOL	ATOMIC NUMBER	ATOMIC MASS	PERCENT WET WEIGHT OF BODY*
Oxygen	O	8	16	65
Carbon	C	6	12	19
Hydrogen	H	1	1	10
Nitrogen	N	7	14	3
Calcium	Ca	20	40	1
Phosphorus	P	15	31	1
Potassium	K	19	39	0.2
Sulfur	S	16	32	0.1
Sodium	Na	11	23	0.1
Chlorine	Cl	17	35	0.1
Magnesium	Mg	12	24	0.1
Manganese	Mn	25	55	0.1
Iron	Fe	26	56	0.1
Copper	Cu	29	64	0.1
Iodine	I	53	127	0.1

The first four elements (Oxygen, Carbon, Hydrogen, Nitrogen) are grouped as 97%; the remaining eleven elements are grouped as approximately 3%.

*Includes water.

point at any particular moment in time; therefore, its location is given as an electron cloud. Because the number of negatively charged electrons outside the nucleus is equal to the number of positively charged protons, the atom is electrically uncharged or neutral.

The number of protons and neutrons in a nucleus and the number and arrangement of electrons in the electron cloud determine an atom's chemical and physical properties. The **atomic number** of an element is the number of protons in the nucleus of one of its atoms. Elements are identified by their atomic number. For example, if an atom has one proton, it is hydrogen; if it has six, it is carbon; and if an atom has eight protons, it is oxygen.

Another measure of an atom is its atomic mass. The **atomic mass** is equal to the number of neutrons and protons in the atom's nucleus. Because carbon contains six protons and six neutrons, its atomic mass is 12 and is symbolized with a superscript preceding the element's symbol: ^{12}C (read "carbon-12"). Table 2.1 shows the atomic numbers and atomic masses of the more important elements in a typical animal.

Most naturally occurring elements are actually a mixture of slightly varying forms of that element. All atoms of a given element have the same number of protons in the nucleus, but some have different numbers of neutrons, and thus, different

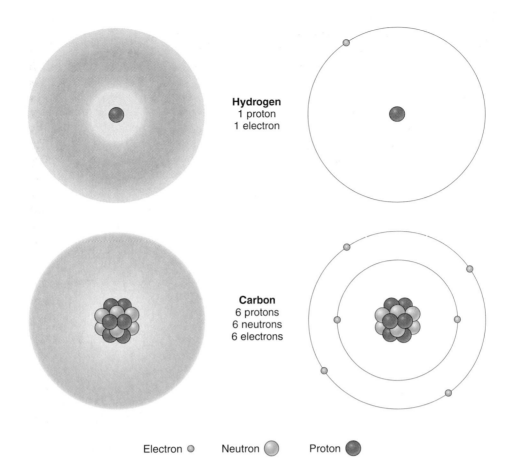

FIGURE 2.1

Structure of Hydrogen and Carbon Atoms. Both the shaded orange spheres on the left and the concentric circles on the right represent the electron orbitals and indicate probable electron positions. Both of these diagrams are extremely simplified. At this scale, the nucleus of these two representative atoms would only be an invisible dot, and the electrons would be too close to the nucleus.

atomic masses. These different forms with the same atomic number but different atomic masses are **isotopes.** For example, the most common form of carbon atom has six protons and six neutrons in the nucleus and an atomic mass of 12 (^{12}C). A carbon isotope with six protons and seven neutrons has an atomic mass of 13 (^{13}C), and a carbon isotope with six protons and eight neutrons has an atomic mass of 14 (^{14}C) (figure 2.2).

Some isotopes (e.g., ^{12}C and ^{13}C) are stable and do not break down. Other isotopes (e.g., ^{14}C) are unstable and tend to break down (decay or decompose) by periodically emitting small particles and energy. These unstable isotopes are **radioisotopes** (radioactive isotopes). Oxygen, iron, cobalt, iodine, and phosphorus are examples of elements that have radioactive isotopes.

ENERGY-LEVEL SHELLS

The electrons of an atom are distributed around its nucleus in orbitals called **energy-level shells** or **clouds of electrons** (figure 2.3). The location of these electrons in relation to the nucleus greatly influences the way atoms react with each other. Seven energy-level shells are possible. Each shell can hold only a certain number of electrons. The shell nearest the nucleus never has more than two electrons. The second and third shells can each have as many as eight electrons. Larger numbers fill the more distant shells. When the shell of an atom holds the maximum number of electrons possible, the shell is complete and stable. An atom with an incomplete, or unstable, outer shell tends to gain, lose, or share electrons with another atom. For example, an atom of sodium has eleven electrons arranged as illustrated in figure 2.3: two in the first shell, eight in the second shell, and one in the third shell. As a result of this arrangement, this atom tends to form chemical bonds with other atoms in which it loses the single electron from its outer shell. This leaves the second shell filled and the atom stable.

Stop and Ask Yourself

1. What is the relationship between matter and atoms of elements?

2. How are electrons, protons, and neutrons positioned within an atom?

3. What is the difference between atomic number and atomic mass?

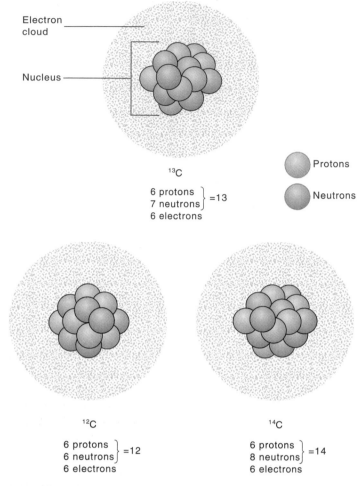

FIGURE 2.2

Isotopes—Variations on Normal Atomic Structure. The nuclei of these carbon isotopes differ in their number of neutrons, although each has six protons. ^{12}C has six neutrons, ^{13}C has seven neutrons, and ^{14}C has eight neutrons.

COMPOUNDS AND MOLECULES: AGGREGATES OF ATOMS

In addition to being an element, a substance can also be a compound. A **compound** is composed of atoms of two or more elements chemically united in fixed proportions. For example, water has two H atoms and one O atom. This composition does not change (i.e., a compound cannot be separated into its pure components—the atoms of the elements present—except by chemical methods).

When atoms interact chemically to form **molecules,** electrical forces called chemical bonds hold the atoms together. Three types of chemical bonds are covalent, hydrogen, and ionic.

COVALENT BONDS: SHARING ELECTRON PAIRS

When atoms share outer-shell electrons with other atoms, the chemical bond that forms is a **covalent bond** (the prefix *co-* indi-

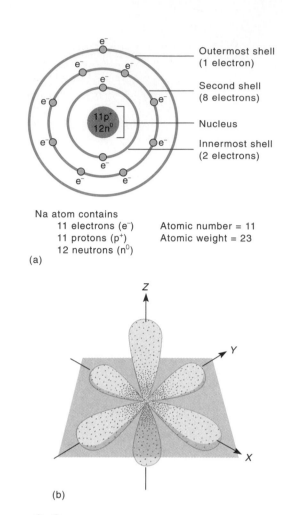

FIGURE 2.3

How Electrons Are Arranged in Atoms. (*a*) Sodium (Na) atom, showing its three energy-level shells. (*b*) In reality, electrons are not found in a definite location but travel rapidly in a three-dimensional space (X, Y, and Z planes) around the nucleus.

FIGURE 2.4

A Covalently Bonded Molecule—Hydrogen (H_2). A single covalent bond forms when two hydrogen atoms share a pair of electrons.

cates a shared condition) (figure 2.4). In covalent bonding, electrons are always shared in pairs. When a pair of electrons is shared (one from each molecule), a single bond forms (e.g., the hydrogen [H—H] molecule); when two pairs are shared, a double bond forms (e.g., the oxygen [O=O] molecule); and when three are shared, a triple bond forms (e.g., the nitrogen [N≡N] molecule).

In a molecule like H_2, the electrons spend as much time orbiting one nucleus as the other. Therefore, the distribution of charges is symmetrical, and the bond is called a **nonpolar covalent bond.** Because of this equal sharing, the molecule is electrically balanced, and the molecule as a whole is neutral.

In other molecules, such as H_2O, where two hydrogen atoms combine with one oxygen atom, the electrons spend more time orbiting the oxygen nucleus than the hydrogen nuclei. Because the electrical charge from the cloud of moving electrons is asymmetrical, the bond is called a **polar covalent bond.** Such a bond leaves the oxygen atom with a slightly negative charge and the hydrogens with a slightly positive charge, even though the entire mole-

FIGURE 2.5

Hydrogen Bonds and Water Droplets. Hydrogen bonds form when oxygen atoms of different water molecules weakly join by the attraction of the electronegative oxygen for the positively charged hydrogen. Because of the arrangement of electron orbitals and the bonding angles between oxygen and hydrogen, the molecule as a whole is polar (it carries a slight negative charge at one end and a slight positive charge at the other end). This polarity is responsible for many important properties of water.

cule is electrically neutral. The shape of the H_2O molecule reflects this polarity; rather than the linear arrangement H—O—H, the two hydrogens are at one end, a bit like the corners of a triangle. This shape and polarity can lead to the formation of another kind of chemical bond—the hydrogen bond.

HYDROGEN BONDS

In molecules in which hydrogen bonds to certain other atoms (e.g., O, N, or Fe), the hydrogen electron is drawn toward another atom, leaving a proton behind. As a result, the hydrogen atom gains a slight positive charge. The remaining proton is attracted to negatively charged atoms of, for example, oxygen in nearby molecules. When this happens, a weak attraction, called a **hydrogen bond,** forms. ② The hydrogen atom in one water molecule forms a hydrogen bond with the oxygen atom in another water molecule, and so forth, until many molecules bond (figure 2.5).

IONIC BONDS: OPPOSITES ATTRACT

When an atom either gains or loses electrons, it acquires an electrical charge and is called an **ion** (Gr. *ion*, going). If an atom loses one or more electrons, it becomes positively charged because more positively charged protons are now in the nucleus than negatively charged electrons surrounding the nucleus. This positive charge is shown as one or more "plus" signs. Conversely, if an atom gains one or more electrons, it becomes negatively charged, and this negative charge is shown as one or more "minus" signs. A positive ion is known as a cation, and a negative ion is an anion. Examples of cations are sodium (Na^+), potassium (K^+), hydrogen (H^+), calcium (Ca^{2+}), and iron (Fe^{3+}). Some anions are chloride (Cl^-), hydroxyl (OH^-), bicarbonate (HCO_3^-), sulfate (SO_4^{2-}), phosphate (PO_4^{3-}), and carboxyl (COO^-).

Ionic bonds form when an atom or group of atoms develops an electrical charge (because of an electron loss or gain) and attracts an atom or group of atoms with an opposite charge. Figure 2.6 shows how an ionic bond forms between sodium and chlorine to produce sodium chloride. When a sodium atom and chlorine atom come together, the sodium atom donates an electron to the

FIGURE 2.6

An Ionically Bonded Molecule—Table Salt (NaCl). In the formation of sodium chloride, an electron from the outermost shell transfers from the sodium atom to the chlorine atom, giving both atoms complete outermost shells. This transfer gives the sodium atom a net charge of +1 (sodium ion) and the chlorine atom a net charge of −1 (chloride ion). An ionic bond forms between the oppositely charged ions.

Sodium atom

11 protons
12 neutrons
11 electrons

Only 1 in
outer shell

Chlorine atom

17 protons
18 neutrons
17 electrons

Needs only 1
to complete
outer shell

Sodium ion

Full outer shell

Chlorine ion

Full outer shell

Sodium chloride (NaCl)

chlorine atom. This electron transfer changes the balance between the protons and electrons in each of the two atoms. The sodium atom ends up with one more proton than it has electrons, and the chlorine atom with one more electron than it has protons. The sodium atom is left with a net charge of +1 (Na^+), and the net charge of the chlorine atoms is −1 (Cl^-). These opposite charges attract each other and form the ionic bond.

ACIDS, BASES, AND BUFFERS

An **electrolyte** is any substance, such as sodium chloride (NaCl), that conducts electricity when in solution. Many fluids contain strong electrolytes that break down (ionize) into ions. Most acids and bases are electrolytes.

An **acid** is a substance that releases hydrogen ions (H^+) when dissolved in water. Because a hydrogen atom without its electron is only a proton, an acid can be described as a proton donor:

$$HCl \rightarrow H^+ + Cl^-$$

One molecule of hydrogen chloride dissolves in water to produce hydrochloric acid, which dissociates into one hydrogen ion and one chloride ion.

In contrast, a **base** (or alkali) is a substance that releases hydroxyl ions (OH^-) when dissolved in water:

$$NaOH \rightarrow Na^+ + OH^-$$

One molecule of sodium hydroxide dissolves in water to produce one sodium ion and one hydroxyl ion.

When a base dissolves in water, it removes free protons (H^+) from the water; therefore, it is a proton acceptor:

$$OH^- + H^+ \rightarrow H_2O$$

pH: MEASURING ACIDITY AND ALKALINITY

Hydrogen and hydroxyl ions often affect the chemical reactions involved with life processes. Therefore, the concentrations of these ions in body fluids are important. The higher the concentration of hydrogen ions (H^+), the more acidic the solution, and the higher the concentration of hydroxyl (OH^-) ions, the more basic (alkaline) the solution. A solution is neutral when the number of hydrogen ions equals the number of hydroxyl ions.

The **pH scale,** which runs from 0 to 14, measures acidity and alkalinity (table 2.2). Acidic solutions have a pH less than 7, and basic (alkaline) solutions have a pH above 7. A pH of 7 is neutral. Each whole number on the pH scale represents a tenfold

TABLE 2.2   THE RELATIONSHIP BETWEEN HYDROGEN ION (H^+) CONCENTRATION, HYDROXYL ION (OH^-) CONCENTRATION, AND pH

H^+ (HYDROGEN ION)	pH		EXAMPLES	OH^- (HYDROXYL ION)
$10^0 = 1$		0	Battery acid	$10^{-14} = 0.00000000000001$
$10^{-1} = 0.1$		1	Gastric (stomach) juice	$10^{-13} = 0.0000000000001$
$10^{-2} = 0.01$		2	Lemon juice	$10^{-12} = 0.000000000001$
$10^{-3} = 0.001$	Acidic	3	Grapefruit juice	$10^{-11} = 0.00000000001$
$10^{-4} = 0.0001$		4	Tomato juice	$10^{-10} = 0.0000000001$
$10^{-5} = 0.00001$		5	Coffee	$10^{-9} = 0.000000001$
$10^{-6} = 0.000001$		6	Urine, milk	$10^{-8} = 0.00000001$
$10^{-7} = 0.0000001$	Neutral	7	Distilled water	$10^{-7} = 0.0000001$
$10^{-8} = 0.00000001$		8	Seawater	$10^{-6} = 0.000001$
$10^{-9} = 0.000000001$		9	Baking soda	$10^{-5} = 0.00001$
$10^{-10} = 0.0000000001$		10	Milk of magnesia	$10^{-4} = 0.0001$
$10^{-11} = 0.00000000001$	Basic	11	Household ammonia	$10^{-3} = 0.001$
$10^{-12} = 0.000000000001$	(alkaline)	12	Household bleach	$10^{-2} = 0.01$
$10^{-13} = 0.0000000000001$		13	Oven cleaner	$10^{-1} = 0.1$
$10^{-14} = 0.00000000000001$		14	Lye	$10^0 = 1$

change (logarithmic) in acidity; therefore, a solution with a pH of 3 is 10 times more acidic than a solution with a pH of 4, and a pH of 9 is 10 times more basic than a pH of 8. Actually, the pH value is equal to the negative logarithm of the hydrogen ion concentration:

$$pH = -\log [H^+]$$

or

$$pH = \log(1/[H^+])$$

pH: Control with Buffers

Maintenance of a stable internal environment in an animal requires a relatively constant pH of the body fluids. Too much of a strong acid or base can destroy cell stability. Also, too sudden a change in pH may be destructive. The fluid systems of most animals contain chemical substances that help regulate the acid-base balance. These substances, called **buffers,** resist changes in pH by accepting H^+ ions when they are in excess and donating H^+ ions when they are depleted. The most important buffers are the bicarbonates, phosphates, and organic molecules, such as amino acids and proteins.

The carbonic acid–bicarbonate ion system is important in buffering the blood of many vertebrates:

$$H_2CO_3 \rightleftharpoons H^+ + HCO_3^-$$

Carbonic acid dissociates to form hydrogen ion and bicarbonate ion.

In this example, if H^+ ions are added to the system, they combine with HCO_3^- to form H_2CO_3 (the reaction goes to the left). This reaction removes H^+ ions and keeps the pH from changing. If excess OH^- ions are added, they react with the H^+ ions to form water, and more H_2CO_3 will ionize and replace the H^+ ions that were used (the reaction goes to the right). Again, pH stability is maintained.

Stop and Ask Yourself

8. What is an electrolyte? What is an acid? What is a base?
9. With respect to pH, what is a neutral solution?
10. What is the relationship between pH and H^+ ion concentration?
11. How do buffers function? Why are buffers important to animals?

The Molecules of Animals

The chemicals that enter into, or are produced by, metabolic reactions can be divided into two large groups: (1) **organic molecules,** which contain carbon atoms, and (2) **inorganic molecules,** which lack carbon atoms. (A few simple molecules containing carbon, such as CO_2, are considered for convenience to be inorganic.)

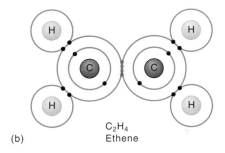

Figure 2.7

Carbon Bonding. (*a*) A single covalent bond joins two carbon atoms. The remaining three pairs of electrons are shared with hydrogen atoms in this molecule. (*b*) A double covalent bond joins two carbon atoms. In this case, only two pairs of electrons are shared with hydrogen atoms.

The most important characteristics of organic molecules depend on properties of the key element, carbon—the indispensable element for all life. The carbon atom has four electrons in its outer orbital; thus, it must share four additional electrons by covalent bonding with other atoms to fill its outer orbital with eight electrons. This unique bonding requirement enables carbon to bond with other carbon atoms to form chains and rings of varying lengths and configurations, as well as to bond with hydrogen and other atoms.

With only four electrons in the outer shell, carbon atoms can form covalent bonds to fill this shell. Adjacent carbon atoms may share one or two pairs of electrons. When they share one pair of electrons, a single covalent bond forms, leaving each carbon free to bond to as many as three other atoms (figure 2.7*a*). When adjacent carbon atoms share two pairs of electrons, a double covalent bond forms, leaving each carbon free to bond to only two additional atoms (figure 2.7*b*).

Hydrocarbons are organic molecules that contain only carbon and hydrogen, and most have their carbons bonded in a linear fashion. Hydrocarbons form the framework of all organic molecules.

The carbon chain or ring of many organic molecules provides a relatively inactive molecular "backbone," to which reactive groups or atoms attach. These functional groups of the molecule are responsible for the molecule's unique chemical properties and behavior. Figure 2.8 shows some of the more important functional groups.

—OH
Hydroxyl group

Carboxyl group

—NH$_2$
Amino group

C=O
Carbonyl group

Aldehyde group

Methyl group

Phosphate group

—SH
Sulfhydryl group

—S—S—
Disulfide group

FIGURE 2.8

Some Functional Groups of Organic Molecules. Functional groups confer distinctive properties to carbon compounds. The "unfilled" bond attaches to a carbon or other atom in the rest of the molecule.

The important groups of organic molecules in animals include carbohydrates, lipids, proteins, nucleotides, and nucleic acids. Each of these groups is now briefly discussed.

CARBOHYDRATES: STORED ENERGY AND STRUCTURAL SUPPORT

Carbohydrates are animals' major source of energy. Most animal cells have the chemical machinery to break down the energy-rich carbon-hydrogen (C—H) bonds in sugars and starches. Simple carbohydrates (e.g., monosaccharides) are composed of atoms of carbon, hydrogen, and oxygen.

Carbohydrates are classified according to their molecular structure. The simplest types with short carbon chains are **monosaccharides** (Gr. *monos*, single + *sakharon*, sugar) or sugars. As their name implies, monosaccharides taste sweet. Monosaccharides are the building blocks of more complex carbohydrate molecules. Four common monosaccharides in animals are glucose, fructose, glyceraldehyde, and dihydroxyacetone (figure 2.9).

Two monosaccharides can combine to form a **disaccharide** (*di*, two) (figure 2.10) by removing a molecule of water (dehydration synthesis). Disaccharides all have the same molecular formula, $C_{12}H_{22}O_{11}$. Compounds with the same molecular formula but different structure are **isomers.** Each isomer has unique properties. Examples of disaccharide isomers are sucrose, lactose, and maltose. Sucrose (table sugar) is a disaccharide formed by linking a molecule of glucose to a molecule of fructose. If a glucose molecule bonds to another monosaccharide, galactose, the resulting disaccharide is lactose (commonly called milk sugar). Maltose,

two joined glucose subunits, gives barley seeds a sweet taste. Beer brewers ferment barley into alcohol.

Other carbohydrates consist of many monosaccharides joined to form **polysaccharides** (*poly*, many) (figure 2.11). Glycogen, a major storage form for glucose in animals, is a polysaccharide. Because the number of glucose units within the glycogen molecule may vary, it is symbolized by the formula $(C_6H_{10}O_5)_n$, with n equal to the number of glucose units in the molecule. Other biologically important polysaccharides include chitin (a major component of the exoskeleton of insects and of crustaceans, such as lobsters and crabs), starch (a storage form of carbohydrate in plants), and cellulose (a woody structural component of the cell wall of plants).

LIPIDS: ENERGY, INTERFACES, AND SIGNALS

Unlike the other three groups of organic molecules, **lipids** are nonpolar organic molecules that are insoluble in polar water but soluble in nonpolar organic solvents, such as ether, alcohol, and chloroform. Phospholipids and cholesterol are lipids that are important constituents of cell membranes. The most common lipids in animals, however, are fats. Fats build cell parts and supply energy for cellular activities.

Lipid molecules are composed primarily of carbon, hydrogen, and oxygen atoms, although some may contain small amounts of phosphorus and nitrogen. They contain a much smaller proportion of oxygen than do carbohydrates, as the formula for the fat, tristearin, $C_{57}H_{110}O_6$, illustrates.

The building blocks of fat molecules are fatty acids and glycerol. Fatty acids contain long hydrocarbon chains bonded to carboxyl (—COOH) groups. Glycerol is a three-carbon alcohol, with each carbon bearing a hydroxyl (—OH) group. Three fatty acid molecules combine with one glycerol molecule by joining to each of the three carbon atoms in the glycerol backbone (figure 2.12). Because there are three fatty acids, the resulting fat molecule is called a triglyceride neutral fat, or triacylglycerol.

Glyceraldehyde   Dihydroxyacetone   Glucose   Fructose

FIGURE 2.9

Monosaccharides. Structural formulas of four simple sugars: glyceraldehyde and dihydroxyacetone have three carbons (i.e., they are trioses), and glucose and fructose have six carbons (i.e., they are hexoses). The functional groups are shaded. Note that glyceraldehyde and dihydroxyacetone, and glucose and fructose have the same ratio and number of atoms; thus, they are structural isomers of each other.

FIGURE 2.10

Disaccharides. Sucrose is ordinary table sugar, and lactose is the sugar in milk. Maltose is found in malt.

FIGURE 2.11

Polysaccharides. Cellulose, starch, and glycogen are all chains of glucose subunits, but they differ in structure. Notice that the glucose subunits of cellulose link differently than the glucose subunits of starch. Glycogen is also a glucose polymer, but is more highly branched than either cellulose or starch. Chitin is a polymer of acetylglucosamine units.

Although the glycerol portion of every fat molecule is the same, there are many kinds of fatty acids and, therefore, many kinds of fats. Fatty acid molecules differ in the length of their carbon chains and in the ways the carbon atoms combine. The most common are even-numbered chains of 14 to 20 carbons. In some cases, the carbon atoms join by single carbon-carbon bonds, and each carbon atom binds to as many hydrogen atoms as possible. This type of fatty acid is saturated (figure 2.13a). Other fatty acids have one or more double bonds between carbon atoms and are unsaturated because the double bonds replace some of the hydrogen atoms, and therefore, the fatty acids contain fewer than the max-

imum number of hydrogen atoms (figure 2.13b). Fatty acids with one double bond are monounsaturated, and those with numerous double bonds are polyunsaturated.

Unsaturated fats have low melting points because their chains bend at the double bonds and the fat molecules cannot align closely with one another, which would lead to solidification. **3** Consequently, the fat may be fluid at room temperature. A liquid fat is called an oil. Most plant fats are unsaturated. Animal fats, in contrast, are often saturated and occur as hard or solid fats.

A phospholipid molecule is similar to a fat molecule in that it contains a glycerol portion and fatty acid chains. However, the

FIGURE 2.12

Triglycerides. A triglyceride is a fat molecule consisting of a glycerol molecule bonded to three fatty acid molecules. Beef fat, with three stearic acids, is shown.

FIGURE 2.13

Fatty Acids. Structural formulas for (*a*) saturated (stearic) and (*b*) unsaturated (oleic) fatty acids. Note the double bond in the carbon backbone of oleic acid.

phospholipid has only two fatty acid chains. Phosphate (PO_4^{3-}) and nitrogen-containing groups replace the third chain. The polar phosphate and nitrogen groups are soluble in water (hydrophilic) and form the "head" of the molecule; the insoluble (nonpolar, hydrophobic) fatty acid portion forms the "tail." Phospholipids are the major structural components of cell membranes because of this tendency to be soluble at one end and insoluble at the other.

Steroids are naturally occurring, lipid-soluble molecules composed of four fused carbon rings that provide a somewhat rigid structure (figure 2.14). Three of the rings are six-sided, and the fourth is five-sided. The four rings contain a total of 17 carbons. Cholesterol is an important biologically active steroid, as are vitamin D and hormones of the adrenal gland (e.g., aldosterone), the ovaries (e.g., estrogen), and the testes (e.g., testosterone).

PROTEINS: THE BASIS OF LIFE'S DIVERSITY

In animals, **proteins** are structural material, energy sources, protection against disease in higher animals, chemical messengers (hormones), and receptors on cell membranes. Some proteins play important roles in metabolic reactions by acting as biological catalysts called enzymes. They enter and speed up specific chemical reactions without being used up themselves. (Chapter 4 discusses enzymes in more detail.)

Proteins always contain atoms of carbon, hydrogen, nitrogen, oxygen, and sometimes, sulfur. The individual building blocks of proteins are **amino acids.** Amino acids always contain an amino group (—NH_2), a carboxyl group (—COOH), a hydrogen atom, and a functional group, designated R, all bonded to a central carbon atom:

$$H_2N-\overset{\overset{\textstyle R}{|}}{\underset{\underset{\textstyle H}{|}}{C}}-COOH$$

The nature of the R group linked to the central carbon atom determines the identity and unique chemical properties of each amino acid. Twenty different amino acids commonly occur in animals. Covalent bonds called **peptide bonds** link individual amino acids in chains. In the formation of a peptide bond, the carboxyl group of one amino acid bonds to the amino group of another

FIGURE 2.14

Steroids. Structures of two common steroids, showing the backbone of one five-carbon ring and three six-carbon rings. Cholesterol affects the fluidity of membranes. Testosterone is a male hormone in mammals that is responsible for the development and maintenance of secondary sexual characteristics, and for the maturation and functioning of sex organs.

amino acid, with the elimination of water (a dehydration synthesis reaction), as follows:

When two amino acids bond, they form a unit called a dipeptide; three bonded amino acids form a tripeptide. When many amino acids bond, they form a chain called a polypeptide.

In different proteins, the chain of amino acids can vary from fewer than 50 to more than 2,000 amino acids. Each type of protein contains a specific number and kind of amino acids arranged in a particular sequence. The protein molecule may be coiled and folded, or it may interact with other protein molecules to form a unique three-dimensional structure. Different kinds of protein molecules have different shapes related to their particular functions in life processes.

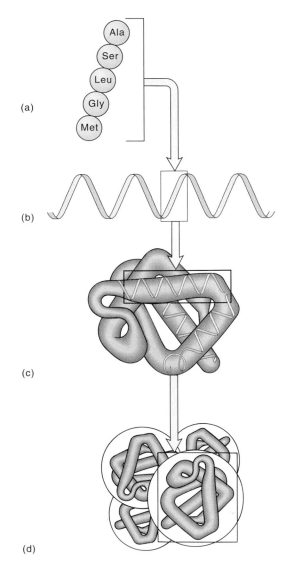

FIGURE 2.15

Levels of Protein Structure. (*a*) Primary structure is the protein's linear sequence of amino acids. (*b*) The repeating configurations in the structure of the amino acids determine secondary structure. (*c*) The three-dimensional folding of the secondary structure determines tertiary structure. (*d*) The three-dimensional arrangement of more than one polypeptide gives some proteins their quaternary structure.

A protein molecule has several different levels of structure. The primary structure is the linear sequence of amino acids in the polypeptide chains comprising the molecule (figure 2.15*a*). The secondary structure of a protein is a repeating pattern of bonds (often hydrogen bonds) between amino acids, and it commonly takes the shape of an alpha helix or pleated sheet (figure 2.15*b*). The tertiary structure results from the helix folding into a three-dimensional shape (figure 2.15*c*). In some instances, two protein chains join to form a larger protein, the shape of which is called the quaternary structure (figure 2.15*d*).

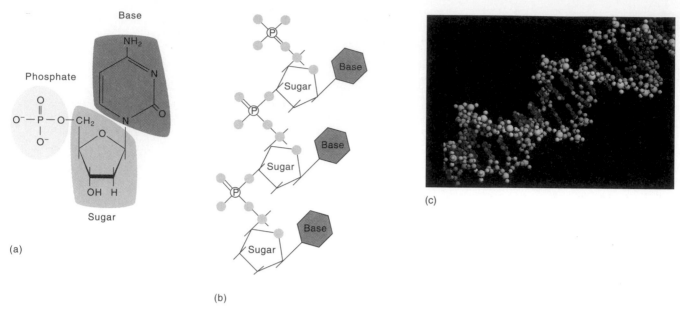

(a)

(b)

(c)

FIGURE 2.16

Nucleotides. (*a*) A nucleotide has a phosphate group, a ribose or deoxyribose sugar, and a nitrogen-containing base. Each of the five types of bases has a slightly different chemical composition. DNA uses four of the five, while RNA uses a different set of four. (*b*) A single-stranded DNA molecule consists of many nucleotide monomers joined to form a long chain. (*c*) In this computer-generated model, two single-stranded chains twist about each other to form the double-stranded (helix) DNA molecule.

NUCLEOTIDES AND NUCLEIC ACIDS: INFORMATION STORAGE, CHEMICAL MESSENGERS, AND ENERGY TRANSFER

Small organic compounds called nucleotides are essential to life. Each **nucleotide** is composed of three substances: (1) a nitrogen-containing organic base, (2) a five-carbon sugar (ribose or deoxyribose), and (3) phosphate (figure 2.16).

Adenosine phosphates and nucleotide coenzymes are nucleotides. Adenosine phosphates are small molecules that function as chemical messengers within and between cells, and as energy transfer molecules. An example of a chemical messenger is cyclic adenosine monophosphate (cAMP). Adenosine triphosphate (ATP) is a nucleotide that functions as an energy carrier, and is discussed in detail in chapter 4.

Nucleotide coenzymes, such as NAD^+ and FAD, play an important role in energy transfer within the cell and are discussed in detail in chapter 5.

Nucleic acids are large single- or double-stranded chains of nucleotide subunits. The two nucleic acids are **deoxyribonucleic** acid (**DNA**) and **ribonucleic acid (RNA).** DNA makes up the chromosomes in the cell's nucleus, can replicate itself, and contains the genetic (hereditary) information of the cell. RNA may be present in either the nucleus or the cytoplasm (the part of the cell outside the nucleus) and carries information between the DNA and the cellular sites of protein synthesis. Chapters 8 and 9 examine nucleic acids in more detail.

Stop and Ask Yourself

12. What is a typical carbohydrate? What is one function of a carbohydrate in an animal?

13. What is a lipid? Where would you find lipids in an animal?

14. What is the difference between a fat and an oil? How are fats used in animals?

15. What is a peptide bond?

16. What is a nucleotide? What are several functions of nucleotides in animals?

ENDANGERED SPECIES

WILDLIFE ALERT—AN OVERVIEW OF THE PROBLEMS

Extinction has been the fate of most plant and animal species. It is a natural process that will continue. In recent years, however, the threat to the welfare of wild plants and animals has increased dramatically—mostly as a result of habitat destruction. Tropical rain forests, the most threatened areas on the earth, have been reduced to 44% of their original extent. In certain areas, such as Ecuador, forest coverage has been reduced by 95%. This decrease in habitat has resulted in tens of thousands of extinctions. Accurately estimating the number of extinctions is impossible in areas like rain forests, where taxonomists have not even described most species. We are losing species that we do not know exist, and we are losing resources that could lead to new medicines, foods, and textiles. Other causes of extinction include climate change, pollution, and invasions from foreign species. Habitats other than rain forests—grasslands, marshes, deserts, and coral reefs—are also being seriously threatened.

No one knows how many species living today are close to extinction. Table 1 lists the 10 species that the World Wildlife Fund has designated closest to extinction. As of 1998, the U.S. Fish and Wildlife Service lists 432 animal and 529 plant species on its endangered or threatened species lists. An **endangered species** is in imminent danger of extinction throughout its range (where it lives). A **threatened species** is likely to become endangered in the near future. Figure 1 shows the number of endangered and threatened species in different regions of the United States. Clearly, much work is needed to improve these alarming statistics.

In the chapters that follow, you will learn that saving species requires more than preserving a few remnant individuals. It requires a large diversity of genes within species groups to promote species survival in changing environments. This genetic diversity requires large populations of plants and animals.

Preservation of endangered species depends on a multifaceted conservation plan that includes the following components:

1. A global system of national parks to protect large tracts of land and wildlife corridors that allow movement between natural areas

2. Protected landscapes and multiple-use areas that allow controlled private activity but also retain value as a wildlife habitat

3. Zoos and botanical gardens to save species whose extinction is imminent

TABLE 1   THE WORLD WILDLIFE FUND'S 10 MOST ENDANGERED SPECIES

COMMON NAME	SCIENTIFIC NAME	STATUS
Tiger	*Panthera tigris*	Southeast Asia. Fewer than six thousand remain. Endangered due to habitat loss and poaching.
Black rhino	*Diceros bicornis*	Africa. Fewer than two thousand remain. Endangered due to poaching for horn.
Giant panda	*Ailuropoda melanoleuca*	China. Fewer than one thousand remain. Endangered due to habitat loss and poaching.
Asiatic black bear	*Ursus thibetanus*	Asia. Endangered due to habitat loss and poaching.
Himalayan yew (conifer)	*Taxus wallichiana*	Asia and Middle East. Endangered due to deforestation and collecting for medicinal purposes.
Atlantic bluefin tuna	*Thunnus thynnus*	Western Atlantic Ocean. Population has declined 80% in the last 20 years. Endangered due to overfishing.
Hawksbill sea turtle	*Eretomochelys imbricata*	Tropical reef habitats. Endangered due to poaching for "tortoise shell" and very low reproductive rates.
Saiga antelope	*Saiga tatarica*	Mongolia and Russia. Endangered due to poaching for antelope horn used in ancient medicines.
Egyptian tortoise	*Testudo kelinmanni*	Middle East. Endangered due to overcollection for pet markets and medicines.
Red and blue lory (parrot)	*Eos histrio*	Indonesian islands. Fewer than three thousand remain. Endangered due to overcollection for pet markets.

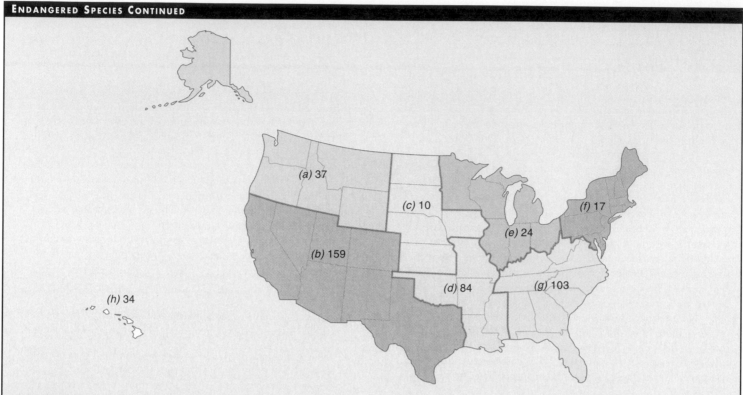

FIGURE 1

Map Showing Approximate Numbers of Endangered and Threatened Animals in the United States. Because the ranges of some animals overlap two or more regions, the sum of all numbers is greater than the sum of all endangered and threatened animals. (*a*) Northwest region, including Alaska. (*b*) Southwest region. (*c*) Great Plains region. (*d*) Mississippi Valley region. (*e*) Great Lakes region. (*f*) Northeast region. (*g*) Southeast region. (*h*) Hawaii.

"Wildlife Alerts" are at the end of selected chapters of this text to be a continuing reminder of the peril that an unprecedented number of species around the world face. Endangered or threatened species from a diverse group of animal phyla are highlighted. You can find much more information on endangered species on the World Wide Web. Check the following Web sites:

http://www.nceet.snre.umich.edu/EndSpp/Endangered.html
http://www.fws.gov/~r9endspp/endspp.html

SUMMARY

1. Matter is anything that has mass and occupies space. The most important particles of matter are protons, neutrons, and electrons, all of which associate to form atoms. The nucleus of an atom contains the protons and neutrons; electrons orbit around the nucleus.

2. The distribution of electrons in an atom's outermost shell largely determines the atom's chemical nature. Atoms tend to lose or gain electrons until the outer shell stabilizes.

3. Atoms react with other atoms to form molecules. Chemical bonds hold atoms together. A covalent bond results from the sharing of one or more pairs of electrons. A hydrogen bond forms from the attraction of the partial positive charge of a hydrogen atom of one water molecule to the partial negative charge of an oxygen atom of another water molecule. An ionic bond results from the attraction of opposite charges.

4. An acid releases hydrogen ions (protons) when dissolved in water. A base releases hydroxyl ions (accepts protons) when dissolved in water.

5. The pH scale measures a solution's alkalinity or acidity by indicating the concentration of free hydrogen ions in water. The fluid systems of most animals contain buffers that help regulate acid-base balance.

6. Simple carbohydrates are made of carbon, hydrogen, and oxygen, and are important energy sources for most animals. Carbohydrates are classified as monosaccharides, disaccharides, or polysaccharides, according to the number of sugars they contain.

7. Lipids are molecules containing many more C—H bonds than carbohydrates. Fats and oils are familiar lipids. Lipids can store large amounts of energy in an organism's body.

8. Proteins are large, complex molecules composed of smaller structural units called amino acids. Peptide bonds link amino acids in chains called polypeptides.

9. Nucleic acids are very large molecules composed of bonded units called nucleotides. The two nucleic acids are deoxyribonucleic acid (DNA) and ribonucleic acid (RNA). Nucleic acids carry the hereditary messages and regulate protein synthesis. Two other nucleotides are the adenosine phosphates (cAMP and ATP) that function as energy transfer molecules within and between cells, and the nucleotide coenzymes (NAD^+ and FAD) that play a role in energy transfer within the cell.

SELECTED KEY TERMS

atom (p. 16)   isomer(p. 22)
atomic mass (p. 16)   mass (p. 16)
atomic number (p. 16)   matter (p. 16)
buffers (p. 21)   neutrons (p. 16)
carbohydrates (p. 22)   pH scale (p. 20)
disaccharide (p. 22)   proteins (p. 24)
electrons (p. 16)   protons (p. 16)
elements (p. 16)   steroids (p. 24)
ion (p. 19)

CRITICAL THINKING QUESTIONS

1. Given the major elements of which all living organisms are composed, is it likely that the earth's surface could have been the major chemical "breadbasket" for the origin of life? Explain.

2. What is meant by the statement, "Evolution resulted in carbon-based life"?

3. Why should a zoologist who studies animal life also be interested in the properties of chemical bonds?

4. The major biological molecules are polymers—long chains of subunits. Why are linear polymers so common in living animals?

5. Why are all forms of life composed of, and affected by, the same elements?

REFERENCES ON THE WORLD WIDE WEB

1. **General Chemistry.**   This Web site contains helpful information on various introductory chemistry topics, such as atomic structure and chemical bonds.
    http://www.satech.net.au/~rowanb/chem

2. **Amino Acids.**   This site lists the 20 different amino acids, presents their structure, and discusses their abbreviations.
    http://www.chemie.fu-berlin.de/chemistry/bio/amino-acids.html

3. **Chemist's Art Gallery.**   This site consists of a series of visualizations and animations of various chemicals and chemical processes.
    http://www.csc.fi/lul/chem/graphics.html

4. **Large Molecule Review.**   This site does an excellent job of reviewing the carbohydrates, lipids, proteins, and nucleic acids.
    http://esg-www.mit.edu:8001/esgbio/lm/lmdir.html

5. **The pH Factor.**   This site includes explanations of pH, acids, and bases.
    http://www.miamisci.org/pH/default.html

6. **Theory of Atoms in Molecules: Introduction.**   This site covers the structure of the atom.
    http://www.chemistry.mcmaster.ca/faculty/bader/aim/

7. **Table of Isotopes.**   This site contains current information on isotopes.
    http://isotopes.lbl.gov/isotopes/toi.html

8. **Chemistry Review.**   The chapters that follow are from a hypertextbook. They cover chemical bonds, pH, structural models, and basic organic functional groups.
    http://esg-www.mit.edu:8001/esgbio/chem/review.html
    http://esg-www.mit.edu:8001/esgbio/chem/review.html#chembonds
    http://esg-www.mit.edu:8001/esgbio/chem/review.html#pH
    http://esg-www.mit.edu:8001/esgbio/chem/models.html
    http://esg-www.mit.edu:8001/esgbio/chem/functionalgroups.html

9. The chapters that follow are from a hypertextbook. They cover lipids, sugars, and nucleic and amino acids.
    http://esg-www.mit.edu:8001/esgbio/lm/lipids.html
    http://esg-www.mit.edu:8001/esgbio/lm/sugars.html
    http://esg-www.mit.edu:8001/esgbio/lm/proteins/aa/aminoacids.html
    http://esg-www.mit.edu:8001/esgbio/lm/nucleicacids/nucleicacids.html

CELLS, TISSUES, ORGANS, AND ORGAN SYSTEMS OF ANIMALS

Concepts

1. Cells are the basic organizational units of life.
2. Eukaryotic cells exhibit a considerable degree of internal organization, with a dynamic system of membranes forming internal compartments termed organelles.
3. The structure and function of a typical cell usually applies to all animals.
4. Different cell types organize into structural and functional units called tissues, organs, and organ systems.

Would You Like to Know . . .

1. what the functional unit of life is? (p. 32)
2. why most cells are so small? (p. 34)
3. why most higher animals need cholesterol? (p. 35)
4. what the "fingerprints" of a cell are? (p. 38)
5. why red blood cells can burst when placed in distilled water? (p. 39)
6. how cells "drink" water? (p. 42)
7. why mitochondria are the "power generators" of the cell? (p. 46)
8. if cells have a skeleton? (p. 47)

This chapter answers these and other useful questions.

This chapter contains evolutionary concepts, which are set off in this font.

Because all animals are made of cells, the cell is as fundamental to an understanding of zoology as the atom is to an understanding of chemistry. In the hierarchy of biological organization, the cell is the simplest organization of matter that exhibits the properties of life (figure 3.1). Some organisms are single celled; others are multicellular. An animal has a body composed of many kinds of specialized cells. A division of labor among cells allows specialization into higher levels of organization (tissues, organs, and organ systems). Yet, everything that an animal does is ultimately happening at the cellular level.

This chapter presents an overview of the structure and function of a "generalized" animal cell. Chapters 4 and 5 examine how cells exchange and utilize matter and energy with their surroundings.

WHAT ARE CELLS?

1 Cells are the functional units of life, in which all of the chemical reactions necessary for the maintenance and reproduction of life take place. They are the smallest independent units of life. Structurally speaking, cells are either prokaryotic or eukaryotic. All **prokaryotes** ("before nucleus") are independent, single-celled organisms (e.g., bacteria). The word *prokaryote* describes cells in which DNA is localized in a region but is not bound by a membrane. Table 3.1 summarizes some of the more salient characteristics of a prokaryotic cell.

All **eukaryotes** ("true nucleus") have cells with a membrane-bound nucleus containing DNA (box 3.1). In addition, eukaryotic cells contain many other structures called **organelles** ("little organs") that perform specific functions. Eukaryotic cells also have a

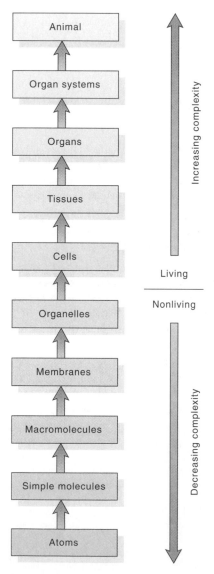

FIGURE 3.1

Structural Hierarchy in a Multicellular Animal. At each level, function depends on the structural organization of that level and those below it.

TABLE 3.1	COMPARISON OF PROKARYOTIC AND EUKARYOTIC CELLS	
COMPONENT	PROKARYOTE	EUKARYOTE
Cell wall	Present	Absent in animals (present in plants)
Centrioles and microtubule-organizing center	Absent	Present in animals (absent in plants)
Chloroplasts	Present in some cells	Present in some cells
Genetic material	Single circular chromosome of DNA	Arranged in multiple chromosomes; DNA associated with protein
Cilia (9 + 2)	Absent	Present in some cells
Cytoskeleton	Absent	Present
Endoplasmic reticulum	Absent	Present
Flagellum	Often present	Present in some cells
Glycocalyx	Absent	Present
Golgi apparatus	Absent	Present
Lysosomes	Absent	Present
Mitochondria	Absent	Present
Nucleus	Absent	Present
Plasma membrane	Present	Present
Ribosomes	Present	Present
Vacuoles	Present	Present
Vesicles	Present	Present

BOX 3.1   THE ORIGIN OF EUKARYOTIC CELLS

The first cells were most likely very simple prokaryotic forms. Radiometric dating indicates that the earth is 4 to 5 billion years old and that prokaryotes may have arisen more than 3.5 billion years ago. Eukaryotes are thought to have first appeared about 1.5 billion years ago.

The eukaryotic cell might have evolved when a large anaerobic (living without oxygen) amoeboid prokaryote ingested small aerobic (living with oxygen) bacteria and stabilized them instead of digesting them. This idea is known as the **endosymbiont hypothesis** (figure 1a) and was first proposed by Lynn Margulis, a biologist at Boston University. (**Symbiosis** is an intimate association between two organisms of different species.) According to this hypothesis, the aerobic bacteria developed into mitochondria, which are the sites of aerobic respiration and most energy conversion in eukaryotic cells. The possession of these mitochondria-like endosymbionts conferred the advantage of aerobic respiration on the host.

Flagella (whiplike structures) may have arisen through the ingestion of prokaryotes similar to spiral-shaped bacteria called spirochetes. Ingestion of prokaryotes that resembled present-day cyanobacteria could have led to the endosymbiotic development of chloroplasts in plants.

Another hypothesis for the evolution of eukaryotic cells proposes that the prokaryotic cell membrane invaginated (folded inward) to enclose copies of its genetic material (figure 1b). This invagination resulted in the formation of several double-membrane-bound entities (organelles) in a single cell. These entities could then have evolved into the eukaryotic mitochondrion, nucleus, and chloroplasts.

Although the exact mechanism for the evolution of the eukaryotic cell will never be known with certainty, the emergence of the eukaryotic cell led to a dramatic increase in the complexity and diversity of life-forms on the earth. At first, these newly formed eukaryotic cells existed only by themselves. Later, however, some probably evolved into multicellular organisms in which various cells became specialized into tissues, which, in turn, led to the potential for many different functions. These multicellular forms then adapted to life in a great variety of environments.

FIGURE 1
Two Hypotheses on the Evolution of the Eukaryotic Cell. (a) Endosymbiont hypothesis. (b) Membrane invagination hypothesis. A prokaryotic cell (1) duplicates its genetic material (genome) (2) The plasma membrane then invaginates to form double-membrane-bound organelles, and the individual genomes separate from each other (3) The nuclear genome eventually enlarges, while the other organelle genomes lose many of their genes, resulting in a eukaryotic cell (4) *Redrawn from T. Uzzell and C. Spolsky, "Origin of the Eukaryotic Cell,"* American Scientist *62:334–343, copyright 1974 Sigma Xi, The Scientific Research Society. Used by permission.*

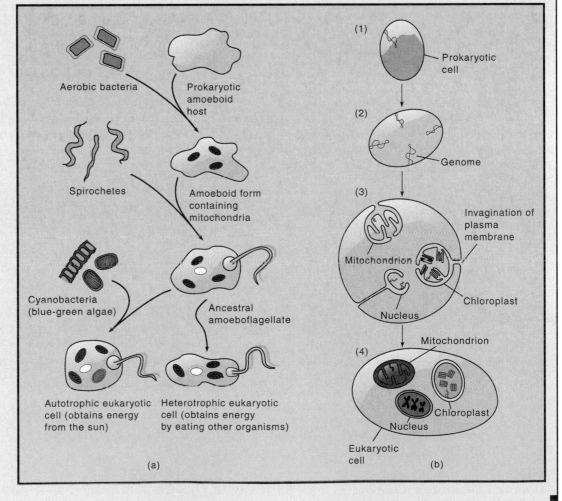

network of specialized structures called filaments and tubules organized into the cytoskeleton, which gives shape to the cell and allows intracellular movement.

All eukaryotic cells have three basic parts (table 3.1):

1. The **plasma membrane** is the outer boundary of the cell. It separates the internal metabolic events from the environment and allows them to proceed in organized, controlled ways. The plasma membrane also has specific receptors for external molecules that alter the cell's function.
2. **Cytoplasm** (Gr. *kytos*, hollow vessel + *plasm*, fluid) is the portion of the cell outside the nucleus. The semifluid portion of the cytoplasm is called the cytosol. Suspended within the cytosol are the organelles.
3. The **nucleus** (pl., nuclei) is the cell control center. It contains the chromosomes and is separated from the cytoplasm by its own nuclear envelope. The nucleoplasm is the semifluid material in the nucleus.

Because cells vary so much in form and function, no "typical" cell exists. However, to help you learn as much as possible about cells, figure 3.2 shows an idealized version of a eukaryotic cell and most of its component parts.

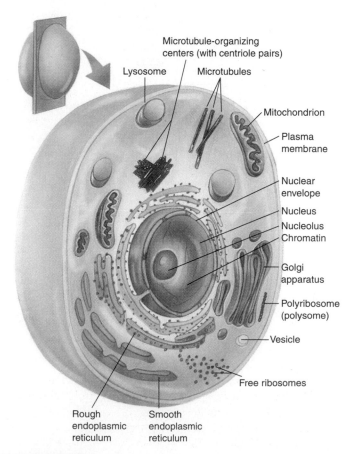

FIGURE 3.2

A Generalized Animal Cell. Understanding of the structures in this cell is based mainly on electron microscopy. The sizes of some organelles and structures are exaggerated to show detail.

1. What are the three basic parts of the cell?
2. What is the difference between cytoplasm and cytosol?
3. How do nucleoplasm and cytoplasm differ?

WHY ARE MOST CELLS SMALL?

Most cells are small and can be seen only with the aid of a microscope (box 3.2). (Exceptions include the eggs of most vertebrates [fishes, amphibians, reptiles, and birds] and some long nerve cells.) One reason for the smallness of cells is that the ratio of the volume of the cell's nucleus to the volume of its cytoplasm must not be so small that the nucleus, the cell's major control center, cannot control the cytoplasm.

Another aspect of cell volume works to limit cell size. As the radius of a cell lengthens, cell volume increases more rapidly than cell surface area (figure 3.3). The need for nutrients and the rate of waste production are proportional to cell volume. The cell takes up nutrients and eliminates wastes through its surface plasma membrane. If cell volume becomes too large, the surface-area-to-volume ratio is too small for an adequate exchange of nutrients and wastes.

CELL MEMBRANES

The plasma membrane surrounds the cell. Other membranes inside the cell enclose some organelles and have properties similar to the plasma membrane.

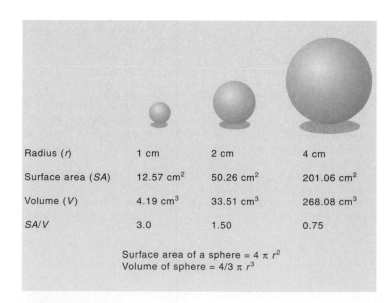

Radius (r)	1 cm	2 cm	4 cm
Surface area (SA)	12.57 cm^2	50.26 cm^2	201.06 cm^2
Volume (V)	4.19 cm^3	33.51 cm^3	268.08 cm^3
SA/V	3.0	1.50	0.75

Surface area of a sphere = $4 \pi r^2$
Volume of sphere = $4/3 \pi r^3$

FIGURE 3.3

The Relationship between Surface Area and Volume. As the radius of a sphere increases, its volume increases more rapidly than its surface area. (SA/V = surface area to volume ratio.)

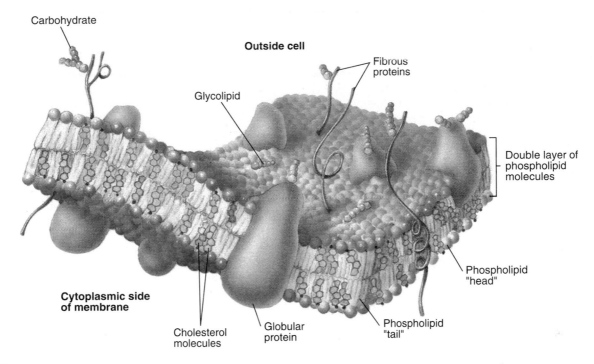

Carbohydrate

Outside cell

Glycolipid

Fibrous proteins

Double layer of phospholipid molecules

Phospholipid "head"

Cytoplasmic side of membrane

Cholesterol molecules

Globular protein

Phospholipid "tail"

FIGURE 3.4

Fluid-Mosaic Model of Membrane Structure. Intrinsic globular proteins may protrude above or below the lipid bilayer and may move about in the membrane. Peripheral proteins attach to either the inner or outer surfaces.

STRUCTURE OF CELL MEMBRANES

In 1972, S. Jonathan Singer and Garth Nicolson developed the fluid-mosaic model of membrane structure. According to this model, a membrane is a double layer (bilayer) of proteins and phospholipids, and is fluid rather than solid. The phospholipid bilayer forms a fluid "sea" in which specific proteins float like icebergs (figure 3.4). Being fluid, the membrane is in a constant state of flux—shifting and changing, while retaining its uniform structure. The word mosaic refers to the many different kinds of proteins dispersed in the phospholipid bilayer.

The following are important points of the fluid-mosaic model:

1. The phospholipids have one polar end and one nonpolar end. The polar ends are oriented on one side toward the outside of the cell and into the fluid cytoplasm on the other side, and the nonpolar ends face each other in the middle of the bilayer. The "tails" of both layers of phospholipid molecules attract each other and are repelled by water (they are hydrophobic, "water dreading"). As a result, the polar spherical "heads" (the phosphate portion) are located over the cell surfaces (outer and inner) and are "water attracting" (they are hydrophilic).

2. ③ Cholesterol is present in the plasma membrane and organelle membranes of eukaryotic cells. The cholesterol molecules are embedded in the interior of the membrane and help to make the membrane less permeable to water-soluble substances. In addition, the relatively rigid structure of the cholesterol molecules helps to stabilize the membrane (figure 3.5).

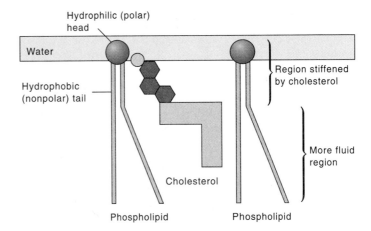

Hydrophilic (polar) head

Water

Hydrophobic (nonpolar) tail

Region stiffened by cholesterol

More fluid region

Cholesterol

Phospholipid

Phospholipid

FIGURE 3.5

The Arrangement of Cholesterol between Lipid Molecules of a Lipid Bilayer. Cholesterol stiffens the outer lipid bilayer and causes the inner region of the bilayer to become slightly more fluid. Only half the lipid bilayer is shown; the other half is a mirror image.

3. The membrane proteins are individual molecules attached to the inner or outer membrane surface (peripheral proteins) or embedded in it (intrinsic proteins) (*see figure 3.4*). Some intrinsic proteins are links to sugar-protein markers on the cell surface. Other intrinsic proteins help to move ions or molecules across the membrane, and still others attach the membrane to the cell's inner scaffolding (the cytoskeleton) or to various molecules outside the cell.

3.2   MICROSCOPES—WINDOWS INTO THE CELL

Despite the very small size of most cells, knowledge of cell structure and function has accumulated through the use of various techniques. One technique is **microscopy**—the use of several types of microscopes to peer into the innermost parts of a cell.

The **light microscope (LM)** relies on the bending (refraction) of light rays. Light rays pass through the center of a curved lens. The farther they are from the center, the more they bend (figure 1a). The compound microscope used in most zoology laboratories contains at least two of these lenses (figure 1b,e). All the rays eventually converge through the lens system onto one focal point—the eye(s). Specific stains are often used to highlight certain structures. Unfortunately, these staining procedures kill the cell. However, living cells can be observed through the phase contrast microscope. In this type of light microscopy, small differences in the way different parts of the cell refract light are converted to larger variations in brightness. In the dark-field microscope, living cells can be observed by making the field surrounding the specimen appear black while the specimen itself is brightly illuminated. The best light microscopes magnify images approximately two thousand times.

In the **transmission electron microscope (TEM),** an electron beam focuses on a thin section or slice of the cell by means of electromagnets (figure 1c,f). After passing through the cell, the electron beam travels through more magnetic lenses, which magnify the image and project it onto either a fluorescent screen or photographic film. Magnifications of several hundred thousand times are possible with the TEM.

The **scanning electron microscope (SEM)** is used to study surfaces rather than thin sections of cells (figure 1d,g). SEM photomicrographs, with their three-dimensional quality, reveal remarkable details of the surface of cells or other objects. Surfaces to be studied are first covered with a very thin layer of metal, such as gold. In the SEM, electron beams scan the surface of the specimen, driving off electrons from the atoms of the metal surface—called secondary

electrons. The pattern of these scattered secondary electrons is then detected on a cathode-ray tube like that in a television set. Maximum magnifications of the SEM are usually around twenty thousand times.

The **scanning tunneling microscope (STM)** was invented in the 1980s and can achieve magnifications of over 100 million. This magnification allows viewing of atoms on the surface of a solid. The electrons surrounding the surface atoms tunnel or project a very short distance from the surface. The STM has a needle probe with a point so sharp that often only one atom is at its tip. The probe is lowered toward the surface of the specimen until its electron cloud just touches the surface atoms. When a small voltage is applied between the tip and specimen, electrons flow through a narrow channel in the electron clouds. The arrangement of atoms on the surface of the specimen is determined by moving the probe tip back and forth over the surface. As the tip follows the surface contours, a computer records and analyzes the motion to create an accurate, three-dimensional image of the surface atoms. The surface map can be either displayed on a computer screen or plotted on paper. The microscope's inventors, Gerd Binnig and Heinrich Rohrer, shared the 1986 Nobel Prize in Physics for their work. Interestingly, another recipient of the prize was Ernst Ruska, the inventor of the first transmission electron microscope.

(a)

(b)

FIGURE 1

Types of Microscopes and Their Images (Sperm Cells). (a) Focusing of light rays. (b) Compound light microscope. (c) Transmission electron microscope. (d) Scanning electron microscope. Three images of human sperm from the three different types of microscopes: (e) a compound light microscope (LM ×400), (f) a transmission electron microscope (TEM ×18,000), and (g) a scanning electron microscope (SEM ×5,000). *Thomas D. Brock,* Biology of Microorganisms, *3e., © 1979, p. 774, 775. Adapted by permission of Prentice Hall, Englewood Cliffs, New Jersey.*

Electron gun
(cathode)

Anode

Path of electrons

Magnetic condenser
lens

Specimen

Magnetic objective
lens

Intermediate lens

Intermediate image
Magnetic projection
lens

Final image
on fluorescent screen
or photographic film

(c)

Electron gun
(cathode)

Anode

Path of electrons

First magnetic lens

Scanning generator

Second magnetic lens

Secondary electron
collector

Amplifier

Specimen

Cathode ray
tube
(television
screen)

Final image

(d)

(e)

(f)

(g)

4. When carbohydrates unite with proteins, they form glyco-proteins, and when they unite with lipids, they form glyco-lipids on the surface of a plasma membrane. Surface carbohydrates and portions of the proteins and lipids make up the **glycocalyx** ("cell coat") (figure 3.6).   ④ The complexly arranged and distinctively shaped groups of sugar molecules of the glycocalyx act as a molecular "fingerprint" for each cell type. The glycocalyx is necessary for cell-to-cell recognition and the behavior of certain cells, and is a key component in coordinating cell behavior in animals.

Stop and Ask Yourself

4. What do the terms fluid and mosaic refer to in the fluid-mosaic model of an animal cell membrane?

5. What is the function of the glycocalyx?

6. What is the function of the following in the plasma membrane: (*a*) cholesterol, (*b*) phospholipid, and (*c*) protein?

FUNCTIONS OF CELL MEMBRANES

Cell membranes (1) regulate material moving into and out of the cell, and from one part of the cell to another; (2) separate the inside of the cell from the outside; (3) separate various organelles within the cell; (4) provide a large surface area on which specific chemical reactions can occur; (5) separate cells from one another; and (6) are a site for receptors containing specific cell identification markers that differentiate one cell type from another.

The ability of the plasma membrane to let some substances in and keep others out is called **selective permeability** (L. *permeare* or *per*, through + *meare*, pass) and is essential for maintaining cellular homeostasis. **Homeostasis** (Gr. *homeo*, always the same + *stasis*, standing) is the maintenance of a relatively constant internal environment despite fluctuations in the external environment. However, before you can fully understand how substances pass into and out of cells and organelles, you must know how the molecules of those substances move from one place to another.

MOVEMENT ACROSS MEMBRANES

Molecules can cross membranes in a number of ways, both by using their own energy and by relying on an outside energy source. Table 3.2 summarizes the various kinds of transmembrane movement, and the sections that follow discuss them in more detail.

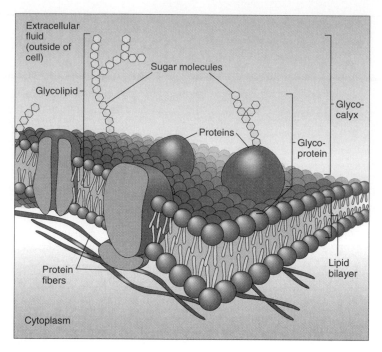

FIGURE 3.6

The Glycocalyx, Showing the Glycoproteins and Glycolipids. Note that all of the attached carbohydrates are on the outside of the plasma membrane.

SIMPLE DIFFUSION

Molecules move randomly (due to spontaneous molecular motion) from areas where they are highly concentrated to areas of lower concentration, until they are evenly distributed in a state of dynamic equilibrium. This process is **simple diffusion** (L. *diffundre*, to spread). Simple diffusion accounts for most of the short-distance transport of substances moving into and out of cells. Figure 3.7 shows the diffusion of sugar particles away from a sugar cube placed in water.

FACILITATED DIFFUSION

Polar molecules (not soluble in lipids) may diffuse through protein channels (pores) in the lipid bilayer (figure 3.8). The protein channels offer a continuous pathway for specific molecules to move across the plasma membrane so that they never come into contact with the hydrophobic layer or the membrane's polar surface.

Large molecules and some of those not soluble in lipids require assistance in passing across the plasma membrane. These molecules use **facilitated diffusion,** which, like simple diffusion, requires no energy input. To pass across the membrane, a molecule temporarily binds with a carrier (transport) protein in the plasma membrane and is transported from an area of higher concentration to one of lower concentration (figure 3.9).

TABLE 3.2	DIFFERENT TYPES OF MOVEMENT ACROSS PLASMA MEMBRANES	
TYPE OF MOVEMENT	**DESCRIPTION**	**EXAMPLE IN THE BODY OF A FROG**
Simple diffusion	No cell energy is needed. Molecules move "down" a concentration gradient. Molecules spread out randomly from areas of higher concentration to areas of lower concentration until they are distributed evenly in a state of dynamic equilibrium.	A frog inhales air containing oxygen, which moves into the lungs and then diffuses into the bloodstream.
Facilitated diffusion	Carrier (transport) proteins in a plasma membrane temporarily bind with molecules and help them pass across the membrane. Other proteins form channels through which molecules move across the membrane.	Glucose in the gut of a frog combines with carrier proteins to pass through the gut cells into the bloodstream.
Osmosis	Water molecules diffuse across selectively permeable membranes from areas of higher concentration to areas of lower concentration.	Water molecules move into a frog's red blood cell when the concentration of water molecules outside the blood cell is greater than it is inside.
Filtration	Hydrostatic pressure forces small molecules across selectively permeable membranes from areas of higher pressure to areas of lower pressure.	A frog's blood pressure forces water and dissolved wastes into the kidney tubules during urine formation.
Active transport	Specific carrier proteins in the plasma membrane bind with molecules or ions to help them cross the membrane against a concentration gradient. Energy is required.	Sodium ions move from inside the neurons of the sciatic nerve of a frog (the sodium-potassium pump) to the outside of the neurons.
Endocytosis	The bulk movement of material into a cell by formation of a vesicle.	
Pinocytosis	The plasma membrane encloses small amounts of fluid droplets (in a vesicle) and takes them into the cell.	The kidney cells of a frog take in fluid to maintain fluid balance.
Phagocytosis	The plasma membrane forms a vesicle around a solid particle or other cell and draws it into the phagocytic cell.	The white blood cells of a frog engulf and digest harmful bacteria.
Receptor-mediated endocytosis	Extracellular molecules bind with specific receptor proteins on a plasma membrane, causing the membrane to invaginate and draw molecules into the cell.	The intestinal cells of a frog take up large molecules from the inside of the gut.
Exocytosis	The movement of material out of a cell. A vesicle (with particles) fuses with the plasma membrane and expels particles or fluids from the cell across the plasma membrane.	The sciatic nerve of a frog releases a chemical (neurotransmitter).

OSMOSIS

The diffusion of water across a selectively permeable membrane from an area of higher concentration to an area of lower concentration is **osmosis** (Gr. *osmos*, pushing). Osmosis is just a special type of diffusion, not a different method (figure 3.10).

The term **tonicity** (Gr. *tonus*, tension) refers to the relative concentration of solutes in the water inside and outside the cell. For example, in an **isotonic** (Gr. *isos*, equal + *tonus*, tension) solution, the solute concentration is the same inside and outside a red blood cell (figure 3.11a). The concentration of water molecules is also the same inside and outside the cell. Thus, water molecules move across the plasma membrane at the same rate in both directions, and there is no net movement of water in either direction.

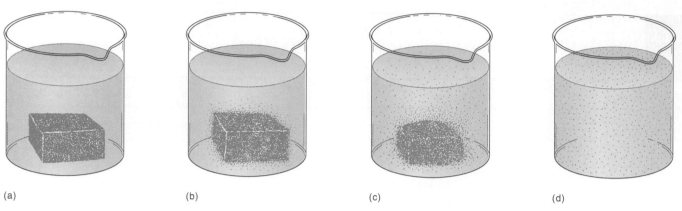

(a)   (b)   (c)   (d)

FIGURE 3.7

Simple Diffusion. When a sugar cube is placed in water (a), it slowly dissolves (b) and disappears. As this happens, the sugar molecules diffuse from a region where they are more concentrated to a region (c) where they are less concentrated. Even distribution of the sugar molecules throughout the water is diffusion equilibrium (d).

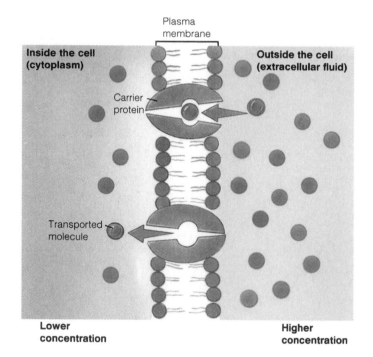

FIGURE 3.8

Transport Proteins. Molecules can move into and out of cells through integrated protein channels (pores) in the plasma membrane without using energy.

FIGURE 3.9

Facilitated Diffusion and Carrier (Transport) Proteins. Some molecules move across the plasma membrane with the assistance of carrier proteins that transport the molecules down their concentration gradient, from a region of higher concentration to one of lower concentration. A carrier protein alternates between two configurations, moving a molecule across a membrane as the shape of the protein changes. The rate of facilitated diffusion depends on how many carrier proteins are available in the membrane and how fast they can move their specific molecule.

In a **hypertonic** (Gr. *hyper*, above) solution, the solute concentration is higher outside the red blood cell than inside. Because the concentration of water molecules inside the cell is higher than outside, water moves out of the cell, which shrinks (figure 3.11*b*). This condition is called crenation in red blood cells.

In a **hypotonic** (Gr. *hypo*, under) solution, the solute concentration is lower outside the red blood cell than inside. Con-

versely, the concentration of water molecules is higher outside the cell than inside.   ⑤   As a result, water moves into the cell, which swells and may burst (figure 3.11*c*).

Selectively permeable membrane

● Water molecule
○ Sugar molecule

(a)   (b)

Time

FIGURE 3.10

Osmosis. (*a*) A selectively permeable membrane separates the beaker into two compartments. Initially, compartment 1 contains sugar and water molecules, and compartment 2 contains only water molecules. Due to molecular motion, water moves down the concentration gradient (from compartment 2 to compartment 1) by osmosis. The sugar molecules remain in compartment 1 because they are too large to pass across the membrane. (*b*) At osmotic equilibrium, the number of water molecules in compartment 1 does not increase.

Isotonic (no net change in water movement)

Hypertonic (water diffuses outward)

Hypotonic (water diffuses inward)

FIGURE 3.11

Effect of Salt Concentration on Cell Volumes. (*a*) An isotonic solution with the same salt concentration inside and outside the cell has no effect on the size of the red blood cell. (*b*) A hypertonic (high salt) solution causes water to leave the red blood cell, which shrinks. (*c*) A hypotonic (low salt) solution results in an inflow of water, causing the red blood cell to swell. Arrows indicate direction of water movement. (Scanning electron micrographs SEMs ×18,000.)

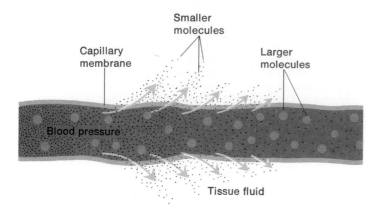

FIGURE 3.12

Filtration. The high blood pressure in the capillary forces small molecules through the capillary membrane. Larger molecules cannot pass through the small openings in the capillary membrane and remain in the capillary. Arrows indicate the direction of small molecule movement.

FILTRATION

Filtration is a process that forces small molecules across selectively permeable membranes with the aid of hydrostatic (water) pressure (or some other externally applied force, such as blood pressure). For example, in the body of an animal such as a frog, filtration is evident when blood pressure forces water and dissolved molecules through the permeable walls of small blood vessels called capillaries (figure 3.12). In filtration, large molecules, such as proteins, do not pass through the smaller membrane pores. Filtration also takes place in the kidneys when blood pressure forces water and dissolved wastes out of the blood vessels and into the kidney tubules in the first step in urine formation.

Stop and Ask Yourself

7. How does diffusion occur in an animal cell?

8. What is osmosis? How does it differ from diffusion?

9. What is the difference between simple diffusion and facilitated diffusion?

10. What is the purpose of facilitated diffusion? What is the purpose of filtration?

ACTIVE TRANSPORT

Active-transport processes move molecules and other substances across a selectively permeable membrane against a concentration gradient—that is, from an area of lower concentration to one of higher concentration. This movement against the concentration gradient requires ATP energy.

The active-transport process is similar to facilitated diffusion, except that the carrier protein in the plasma membrane must use energy to move the molecules against their concentration gradient (figure 3.13).

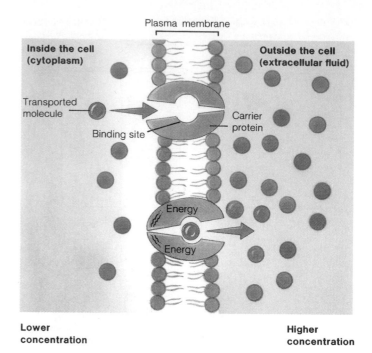

FIGURE 3.13

Active Transport. During active transport, a molecule combines with a carrier protein whose shape is altered as a result of the combination. This change in configuration, along with energy, helps move the molecule across the plasma membrane against a concentration gradient.

One active-transport mechanism, the sodium-potassium pump, helps maintain the high concentrations of potassium ions and low concentrations of sodium ions inside nerve cells that are necessary for transmission of electrical impulses. Another active-transport mechanism, the calcium pump, keeps the calcium concentration hundreds of times lower inside the cell than outside.

ENDOCYTOSIS

Another process by which substances move across the plasma membrane is endocytosis. **Endocytosis** (Gr. *endon,* within) involves bulk movement of materials across the plasma membrane, rather than movement of individual molecules. The three forms of endocytosis are pinocytosis, phagocytosis, and receptor-mediated endocytosis.

⑥ **Pinocytosis** ("cell drinking," from Gr. *pinein,* to drink + *cyto,* cell) is nonspecific uptake of small droplets of extracellular fluid. Any small solid dissolved in the fluid is also taken into the cell. Pinocytosis occurs when a small portion of the plasma membrane indents (invaginates). The open end of the invagination seals itself off, forming a small vesicle. This tiny vesicle detaches from the plasma membrane and moves into the cytoplasm (figure 3.14*a*).

Phagocytosis ("cell eating," from Gr. *phagein,* to eat + *cyto,* cell) is similar to pinocytosis, except that the cell takes in solid material rather than liquid. Commonly, an organelle called a lyso-

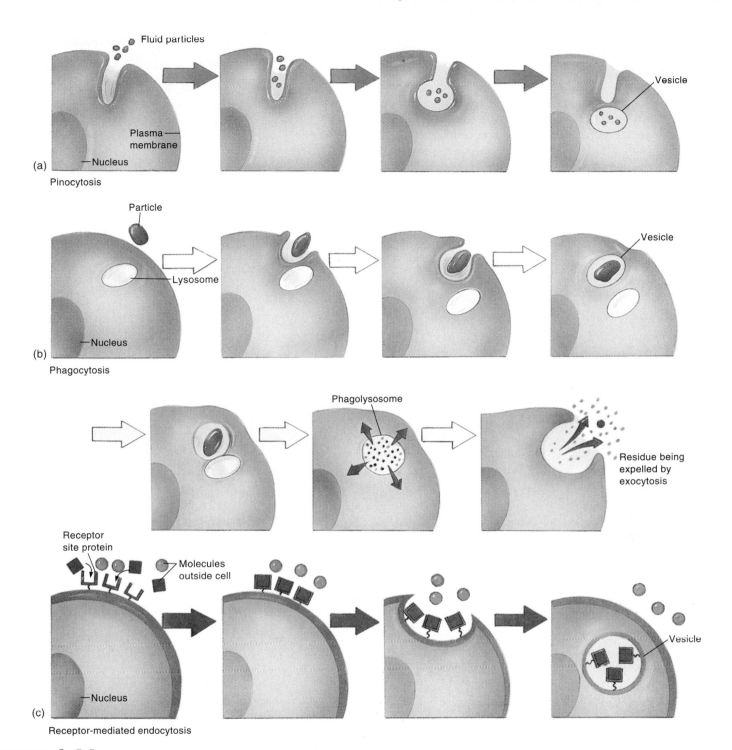

FIGURE 3.14

Endocytosis and Exocytosis. (*a*) Pinocytosis. A cell takes in small fluid particles and forms a vesicle. (*b*) Phagocytosis. A cell takes in a solid particle and forms a vesicle. A lysosome combines with a vesicle, forming a phagolysosome. Lysosomal enzymes digest the particle. The vesicle can also fuse with the plasma membrane and release its contents by exocytosis. (*c*) In receptor-mediated endocytosis, a specific molecule binds to a receptor protein, inducing the formation of a vesicle.

some (*see page 46*) combines with the vesicle to form a **phagolysosome** ("digestion vacuole"), and lysosomal digestive enzymes break down the vesicle's contents (figure 3.14*b*).

Receptor-mediated endocytosis involves a specific receptor protein on the plasma membrane that "recognizes" an extra-cellular molecule and binds with it (figure 3.14*c*). This reaction somehow stimulates the membrane to indent and create a vesicle containing the selected molecule. A variety of important molecules (such as cholesterol) are brought into cells in this manner.

EXOCYTOSIS

An organelle known as the Golgi apparatus (described in a later section) packages proteins and other molecules that the cell produces into vesicles for secretion. In the process of **exocytosis** (Gr. *exo,* outside), these secretory vesicles fuse with the plasma membrane and release their contents into the extracellular environment (figure 3.14*b*). This process adds new membrane material, which replaces the plasma membrane lost during endocytosis.

> ### Stop and Ask Yourself
>
> 11. How do active transport and facilitated diffusion across plasma membranes differ?
> 12. What is the difference between endocytosis and exocytosis?
> 13. How does receptor-mediated endocytosis occur?
> 14. Where does an active-transport process occur in an animal?

CYTOPLASM, ORGANELLES, AND CELLULAR COMPONENTS

Many cell functions that are performed in the cytoplasmic compartment result from the activity of specific structures called organelles. Table 3.3 summarizes the structure and function of these organelles, and the sections that follow discuss them in more detail.

CYTOPLASM

The cytoplasm of a cell has two distinct parts: (1) The **cytomembrane system** consists of well-defined structures, such as the endoplasmic reticulum, Golgi apparatus, vacuoles, and vesicles. (2) The fluid **cytosol** suspends the structures of the cytomembrane system and contains various dissolved molecules.

RIBOSOMES: PROTEIN WORKBENCHES

Ribosomes are non-membrane-bound structures that are the sites for protein synthesis. They contain almost equal amounts of protein and a special kind of ribonucleic acid called ribosomal RNA (rRNA). Chapter 9 discusses the role of ribosomes in protein synthesis. Some ribosomes attach to the endoplasmic reticulum (see next section), and some float freely in the cytoplasm. Whether ribosomes are free or attached, they usually cluster in groups connected by a strand of another kind of ribonucleic acid called messenger RNA (mRNA). These clusters are called polyribosomes or polysomes (*see figure 3.2*).

(a)   Rough endoplasmic reticulum

(b)   Smooth endoplasmic reticulum

FIGURE 3.15

Endoplasmic Reticulum (ER). (*a*) Ribosomes coat rough ER. Notice the double membrane and the lumen (space) between each membrane. (*b*) Smooth ER lacks ribosomes.

ENDOPLASMIC RETICULUM: PRODUCTION AND TRANSPORT

The **endoplasmic reticulum (ER)** is a complex, membrane-bound labyrinth of flattened sheets, sacs, and tubules that branches and spreads throughout the cytoplasm. The ER is continuous from the nuclear envelope to the plasma membrane (*see figure 3.2*) and is a series of channels that helps various materials circulate throughout the cytoplasm. It also is a storage unit for enzymes and other proteins and a point of attachment for ribosomes. ER with attached ribosomes is rough ER (figure 3.15*a*), and ER without attached ribosomes is smooth ER (figure 3.15*b*). Smooth ER is the site for lipid production, detoxification of a wide variety of organic molecules, and storage of calcium ions in muscle cells. Most cells contain both types of ER, although the relative proportion varies among cells.

TABLE 3.3	STRUCTURE AND FUNCTION OF CELLULAR COMPONENTS	
COMPONENT	**STRUCTURE/DESCRIPTION**	**FUNCTION**
Centriole	Located within microtuble-organizing center; contains nine triple microtubules	Forms basal body of cilia and flagella; functions in mitotic spindle formation
Chloroplast	Organelle that contains chlorophyll and is involved in photosynthesis	Traps, transforms, and uses light energy to convert carbon dioxide and water into glucose and oxygen
Chromosome	Made up of nucleic acid (DNA) and protein	Controls heredity and cellular activities
Cilia, flagella	Threadlike processes	Cilia and flagella move small particles past fixed cells and are a major form of locomotion in some cells
Cytomembrane system	The endoplasmic reticulum, Golgi apparatus, vacuoles, vesicles	Organelles, functioning as a system, to modify, package, and distribute newly formed proteins and lipids
Cytoplasm	Semifluid enclosed within plasma membrane; consists of fluid cytosol, organelles, and other structures	Dissolves substances; houses organelles and vesicles
Cytoskeleton	Interconnecting microfilaments and micro-tubules; flexible cellular framework	Assists in cell movement; provides support; site for binding of specific enzymes
Cytosol	Fluid part of cytoplasm; enclosed within plasma membrane; surrounds nucleus	Houses organelles; serves as fluid medium for meta-bolic reactions
Endoplasmic reticulum (ER)	Extensive membrane system extending throughout the cytoplasm from the plasma membrane to the nuclear envelope	Storage and internal transport; rough ER is a site for attachment of ribosomes; smooth ER makes lipids
Golgi apparatus	Stacks of disklike membranes	Sorts, packages, and routes cell's synthesized products
Lysosome	Membrane-bound sphere	Digests materials
Microfilament	Rodlike structure containing the protein actin	Gives structural support and assists in cell movement
Microtubule	Hollow, cylindrical structure	Assists in movement of cilia, flagella, and chromosomes; transport system
Microtubule-organizing center	Cloud of cytoplasmic material that contains centrioles	Dense site in the cytoplasm that gives rise to large numbers of microtubules with different functions in the cytoskeleton
Mitochondrion	Organelle with double, folded membranes	Converts energy into a form the cell can use
Nucleolus	Rounded mass within nucleus; contains RNA and protein	Preassembly point for ribosomes
Nucleus	Spherical structure surrounded by a nuclear envelope; contains nucleolus and DNA	Contains DNA that controls cell's genetic program and metabolic activities
Plasma membrane	The outer bilayered boundary of the cell; composed of protein, cholesterol, and phospholipid	Protection; regulation of material movement; cell-to-cell recognition
Ribosome	Contains RNA and protein; some are free, and some attach to ER	Site of protein synthesis
Vacuole	Membrane-surrounded, often large, space in the cytoplasm	Storage site of food and other compounds; also pumps water out of a cell (e.g., contractile vacuole)
Vesicle	Small, membrane-surrounded space; contains enzymes or secretory products	Site of intracellular digestion, storage, or transport

Cisternae

(a)

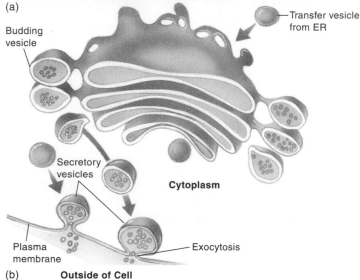

Transfer vesicle from ER

Budding vesicle

Secretory vesicles

Cytoplasm

Plasma membrane

Exocytosis

(b)   **Outside of Cell**

FIGURE 3.16

Golgi Apparatus. (*a*) The Golgi apparatus consists of a stack of cisternae. Notice the curved nature of the cisternae. (*b*) The Golgi apparatus stores, sorts, packages, and secretes cell products. Secretory vesicles move from the Golgi apparatus to the plasma membrane and fuse with it, releasing their contents to the outside of the cell via exocytosis.

GOLGI APPARATUS: PACKAGING, SORTING, AND EXPORT

The **Golgi apparatus** or **complex** (named for Camillo Golgi, who discovered it in 1898) is a collection of membranes associated physically and functionally with the ER in the cytoplasm (figure 3.16*a*; *see also figure 3.2*). It is composed of flattened stacks of membrane-bound cisternae (sing., cisterna; closed spaces serving as fluid reservoirs). The Golgi apparatus sorts, packages, and secretes proteins and lipids.

Proteins that ribosomes synthesize are sealed off in little packets called transfer vesicles. Transfer vesicles pass from the ER to the Golgi apparatus and fuse with it (figure 3.16*b*). In the Golgi apparatus, the proteins are concentrated and chemically modified. One function of this chemical modification seems to be

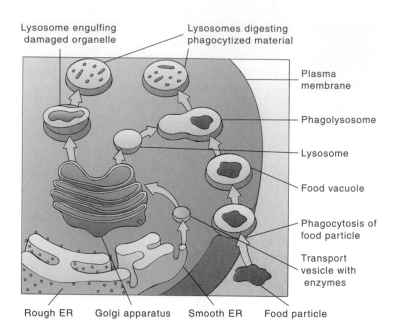

Lysosome engulfing damaged organelle

Lysosomes digesting phagocytized material

Plasma membrane

Phagolysosome

Lysosome

Food vacuole

Phagocytosis of food particle

Transport vesicle with enzymes

Rough ER   Golgi apparatus   Smooth ER   Food particle

FIGURE 3.17

Lysosome Formation and Function. Lysosomes arise from the Golgi apparatus and fuse with vesicles that have engulfed foreign material to form digestive vesicles (phagolysosomes). These vesicles function in the normal recycling of cell constituents.

to mark and sort the proteins into different batches for different destinations. Eventually, the proteins are packaged into secretory vesicles, which are released into the cytoplasm close to the plasma membrane. When the vesicles reach the plasma membrane, they fuse with it and release their contents to the outside of the cell by exocytosis. Golgi apparatuses are most abundant in cells that secrete chemical substances (e.g., pancreatic cells secreting digestive enzymes and nerve cells secreting neurotransmitters). As noted in the next section, the Golgi apparatus also produces lysosomes.

LYSOSOMES: DIGESTION AND DEGRADATION

Lysosomes (Gr. *lyso*, dissolving + *soma*, body) are membrane-bound spherical organelles that contain enzymes called acid hydrolases, which are capable of digesting organic molecules (lipids, proteins, nucleic acids, and polysaccharides) under acidic conditions. The enzymes are synthesized in the ER, transported to the Golgi apparatus for processing, and then secreted by the Golgi apparatus in the form of lysosomes or as vesicles that fuse with lysosomes (figure 3.17). Lysosomes fuse with phagocytic vesicles, thus exposing the vesicle's contents to lysosomal enzymes.

Cells can also selectively digest portions of their own cytoplasm or organelles and then reuse the digested materials when they are returned to the cytoplasm.

(a)

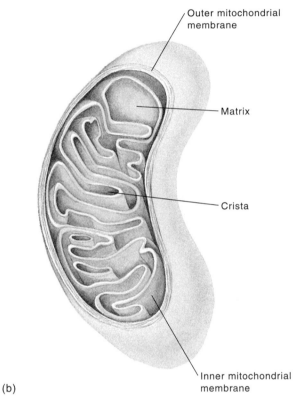

Outer mitochondrial
membrane

Matrix

Crista

Inner mitochondrial
membrane

(b)

FIGURE 3.18

Mitochondrion. (*a*) Mitochondrial membranes, cristae, and matrix (TEM ×36,300). The matrix contains DNA, ribosomes, and enzymes. (*b*) A "typical" mitochondrion.

MITOCHONDRIA: POWER GENERATORS

Mitochondria (sing., *mitochondrion*) are double-membrane-bound organelles that are spherical to elongate in shape. A small space separates the outer membrane from the inner membrane. The inner membrane folds and doubles in on itself to form incomplete partitions called cristae (sing., crista; figure 3.18). The cristae increase the surface area available for the chemical reactions that trap usable energy for the cell. The space between the cristae is the matrix. The matrix contains ri-

Endoplasmic
reticulum
  Ribosome

Plasma
membrane

Microtubule
Intermediate
filament
    Microfilament

Mitochondrion

Polyribosome

FIGURE 3.19

The Cytoskeleton. Model of the cytoskeleton, showing the three-dimensional arrangement of the microtubules, intermediate filaments, and microfilaments.

bosomes, circular DNA, and other material.   **7** Because they convert energy to a usable form, mitochondria are frequently called the "power generators" of the cell. Mitochondria usually multiply when a cell needs to produce more energy. Chapter 5 covers cellular energy production in more detail.

CYTOSKELETON: MICROTUBULES, INTERMEDIATE FILAMENTS, AND MICROFILAMENTS

8 In most cells, the microtubules, intermediate filaments, and microfilaments form the flexible cellular framework called the **cytoskeleton** ("cell skeleton") (figure 3.19). This latticed framework extends throughout the cytoplasm, connecting the various organelles and cellular components.

Microtubules are hollow, slender, cylindrical structures in animal cells. Each microtubule is made of spiraling subunits of globular proteins called tubulin subunits (figure 3.20*a*). Microtubules function in the movement of organelles, such as secretory vesicles, and in chromosome movement during division of the cell nucleus. They are also part of a transport system within the cell. For example, in nerve cells, they help move materials through the

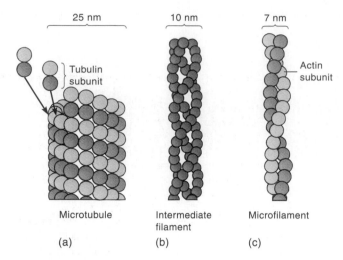

FIGURE 3.20

Three Major Classes of Protein Fibers Making Up the Cytoskeleton of Eukaryotic Cells. (*a*) Microtubules consist of globular protein subunits (tubulins) linked in parallel rows. (*b*) Intermediate filaments in different cell types are composed of different protein subunits. (*c*) The protein actin is the key subunit in microfilaments.

long nerve processes. Microtubules are an important part of the cytoskeleton in the cytoplasm, and they are involved in the overall shape changes that cells undergo during periods of specialization.

Intermediate filaments are a chemically heterogeneous group of protein fibers, the specific proteins of which can vary with cell type (figure 3.20*b*). These filaments help to maintain cell shape and the spatial organization of organelles, as well as promote mechanical activities within the cytoplasm.

Microfilaments are solid strings of protein (actin) molecules (figure 3.20*c*). Actin microfilaments are most highly developed in muscle cells as myofibrils, which help muscle cells to shorten or contract. Actin microfilaments in nonmuscle cells provide mechanical support for various cellular structures and help form contractile systems responsible for some cellular movements (e.g., amoeboid movement in some protozoa).

CILIA AND FLAGELLA: MOVEMENT

Cilia (sing., cilium; L. "eyelashes") and **flagella** (sing., flagellum; L. "small whips") are elongated appendages on the surface of some cells by which the cells, including many unicellular organisms, propel themselves. In stationary cells, cilia or flagella move material over the cell's surface.

Although flagella are 5 to 20 times as long as cilia and move somewhat differently, cilia and flagella have a similar structure. Both are membrane-bound cylinders that enclose a matrix. In this matrix is an **axoneme** or **axial filament,** which consists of nine pairs of microtubules arranged in a circle around two central tubules (figure 3.21). This is called a 9 + 2 pattern of microtubules. Each microtubule pair (a doublet) also has pairs of dynein (protein) arms projecting toward a neighboring doublet and spokes extending toward the central pair of microtubules. Cilia and flagella move as a result of the microtubule doublets sliding along one another.

FIGURE 3.21

Internal Structure of Cilia and Flagella. In cross section, the arms extend from each microtubule doublet toward a neighboring doublet, and spokes extend toward the central paired microtubules. The dynein arms push against the adjacent microtubule doublet to bring about movement.

In the cytoplasm at the base of each cilium or flagellum lies a short, cylindrical **basal body,** also made up of microtubules and structurally identical to the centriole. The basal body controls the growth of microtubules in cilia or flagella. The microtubules in the basal body form a 9 + 0 pattern: nine sets of three with none in the middle.

CENTRIOLES AND MICROTUBULE-ORGANIZING CENTERS

The specialized nonmembranous regions of cytoplasm near the nucleus are the **microtubule-organizing centers.** These centers of dense material give rise to a large number of microtubules with different functions in the cytoskeleton. For example, one type of center gives rise to the **centrioles** (*see figure 3.2*) that lie at right angles to each other. Each centriole is composed of nine triplet microtubules that radiate from the center like the spokes of a wheel. The centrioles are duplicated preceding cell division, are involved with chromosome movement, and help organize the cytoskeleton.

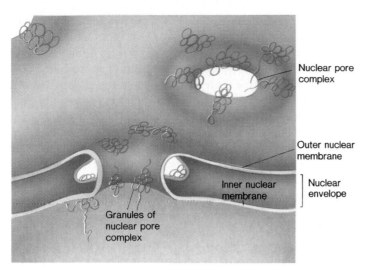

FIGURE 3.22

Nuclear Envelope. An artist's interpretation of pore structure, showing how the pore spans the two-layered nuclear envelope. The protein granules around the edge and in the center govern what passes through the pores.

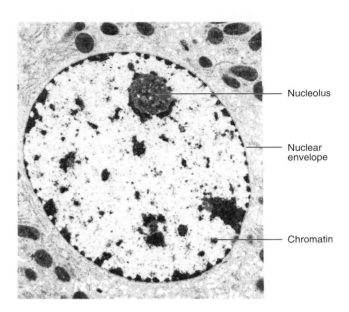

FIGURE 3.23

Nucleus. The nucleolus, chromatin, and nuclear envelope are visible in this nucleus (TEM ×16,000).

VACUOLES: CELL MAINTENANCE

Vacuoles are membranous sacs that are part of the cytomembrane system. Vacuoles occur in different shapes and sizes and have various functions. For example, some single-celled organisms (e.g., protozoa) and sponges have contractile vacuoles that collect water and pump it to the outside to maintain the organism's internal environment (*see figure 17.11*). Other protozoa and sponges have vacuoles for storing food (*see figure 18.5*).

THE NUCLEUS: INFORMATION CENTER

The nucleus contains the DNA and is the control and information center for the eukaryotic cell. It has two major functions. The nucleus directs chemical reactions in cells by transcribing genetic information from DNA into RNA, which then translates this specific information into proteins (e.g., enzymes) that determine the cell's specific activities. The nucleus also stores genetic information and transfers it during cell division from one cell to the next, and from one generation of organisms to the next.

NUCLEAR ENVELOPE: GATEWAY TO THE NUCLEUS

The **nuclear envelope** is a membrane that separates the nucleus from the cytoplasm that is continuous with the endoplasmic reticulum at a number of points. Over three thousand nuclear pores penetrate the surface of the nuclear envelope (figure 3.22). These pores allow materials to enter and leave the nucleus, and give the nucleus direct contact with the endoplasmic reticulum (*see figure 3.2*). Nuclear pores are not simply holes in the nuclear envelope; each is composed of an ordered array of globular and filamentous granules, probably proteins. These granules form the nuclear pore complex, which governs the transport of molecules into and out of the nucleus. The size of the pores prevents DNA from leaving the nucleus but permits RNA to be moved out.

CHROMOSOMES: GENETIC CONTAINERS

The nucleoplasm is the inner mass of the nucleus. In a nondividing cell, it contains genetic material called **chromatin.** Chromatin consists of a combination of DNA and protein, and is the uncoiled, tangled mass of **chromosomes** ("colored bodies") containing the hereditary information in segments of DNA called genes. During cell division, each chromosome coils tightly, which makes the chromosome visible when viewed through a light microscope.

NUCLEOLUS: PREASSEMBLY POINT FOR RIBOSOMES

The **nucleolus** (pl., nucleoli) is a non-membrane-bound structure in the nucleoplasm that is present in nondividing cells (figure 3.23). Two or three nucleoli form in most cells, but some cells (e.g., amphibian eggs) have thousands. Nucleoli are preassembly points for ribosomes and usually contain proteins and RNA in many stages of synthesis and assembly. Assembly of ribosomes is completed after they leave the nucleus through the pores of the nuclear envelope.

TISSUES

In an animal, individual cells differentiate during development to perform special functions as aggregates called tissues. A **tissue** (Fr. *tissu*, woven) is a group of similar cells specialized for the performance of a common function. Animal tissues are classified as epithelial, connective, muscle, or nervous.

EPITHELIAL TISSUE: MANY FORMS AND FUNCTIONS

Epithelial tissue exists in many structural forms. In general, it either covers or lines something and typically consists of renewable sheets of cells that have surface specializations adapted for their specific roles. Usually, a basement membrane separates epithelial tissues from underlying, adjacent tissues. Epithelial tissues absorb (e.g., the lining of the small intestine), transport (e.g., kidney tubules), excrete (e.g., sweat glands), protect (e.g., the skin), and contain nerve cells for sensory reception (e.g., the taste buds in the tongue). The size, shape, and arrangement of epithelial cells are directly related to these specific functions.

Epithelial tissues are classified on the basis of shape and the number of layers present. Epithelium can be simple, consisting of only one layer of cells, or stratified, consisting of two or more stacked layers (figure 3.24e). Individual epithelial cells can be flat (squamous epithelium; figure 3.24a), cube shaped (cuboidal epithelium; figure 3.24b), or columnlike (columnar epithelium; figure 3.24c). The cells of pseudostratified ciliated columnar epithelium possess cilia and appear stratified or layered, but they are not; hence, the prefix pseudo. They look layered because their nuclei are at two or more levels within cells of the tissues (figure 3.24d).

CONNECTIVE TISSUE: CONNECTION AND SUPPORT

Connective tissues support and bind. Unlike epithelial tissues, connective tissues are distributed throughout an extracellular matrix. This matrix frequently contains fibers that are embedded in a ground substance with a consistency anywhere from liquid to solid. To a large extent, the nature of this extracellular material determines the functional properties of the various connective tissues.

Connective tissues are of two general types, depending on whether the fibers are loosely or densely packed. In **loose connective tissue** strong, flexible fibers of the protein collagen are interwoven with fine, elastic, and reticular fibers, giving loose connective tissue its elastic consistency and making it an excellent binding tissue (e.g., binding the skin to underlying muscle tissue) (figure 3.24g). In **fibrous connective tissue,** the collagen fibers are densely packed and may lie parallel to one another, creating very strong cords, such as tendons (which connect muscles to bones or to other muscles) and ligaments (which connect bones to bones) (figure 3.24h).

Adipose tissue is a type of loose connective tissue that consists of large cells that store lipid (figure 3.24f). Most often, the cells accumulate in large numbers to form what is commonly called fat.

Cartilage is a hard yet flexible tissue that supports such structures as the outer ear and forms the entire skeleton of such animals as sharks and rays (figure 3.24i–k). Cells called chondrocytes lie within spaces called lacunae that are surrounded by a rubbery matrix that chondroblasts secrete. This matrix, along with the collagen fibers, gives cartilage its strength and elasticity.

Bone cells (osteocytes) also lie within lacunae, but the matrix around them is heavily impregnated with calcium phosphate, making this kind of tissue hard and ideally suited for its functions of support and protection (figure 3.24l). Chapter 32 covers the structure and function of bone in more detail.

Blood is a connective tissue in which a fluid called plasma suspends specialized red and white blood cells plus platelets (figure 3.24m). Blood transports various substances throughout the body of animals. Chapter 36 covers blood in more detail.

MUSCLE TISSUE: MOVEMENT

Muscle tissue allows movement. Chapter 32 discusses the details of this contractile process. The three kinds of muscle tissue are smooth muscle, skeletal muscle, and cardiac muscle (figure 3.24o–q).

NERVOUS TISSUE: COMMUNICATION

Nervous tissue is composed of several different types of cells: Impulse-conducting cells are called neurons (figure 3.24n); cells involved with protection, support, and nourishment are called neuroglia; and cells that form sheaths and help protect, nourish, and maintain cells of the peripheral nervous system are called peripheral glial cells. Chapter 33 discusses nervous tissue in more detail.

FIGURE 3.24

Tissue Types. (*a*) **Simple squamous epithelium** consists of a single layer of tightly packed, flattened cells with a disk-shaped central nucleus (LM ×250). **Location:** Air sacs of the lungs, kidney glomeruli, lining of heart, blood vessels, and lymphatic vessels. **Function:** Allows passage of materials by diffusion and filtration.

(*b*) **Simple cuboidal epithelium** consists of a single layer of tightly packed, cube-shaped cells. Notice the cell layer indicated by the arrow (LM ×250). **Location:** Kidney tubules, ducts and small glands, and surface of ovary. **Function:** Secretion and absorption.

(*c*) **Simple columnar epithelium** consists of a single layer of elongated cells. The arrow points to a specialized goblet cell that secretes mucus (LM ×400). **Location:** Lines digestive tract, gallbladder, and excretory ducts of some glands. **Function:** Absorption, enzyme secretion.

(*d*) **Pseudostratified ciliated columnar epithelium.** A tuft of cilia tops each columnar cell, except for goblet cells (LM ×500). **Location:** Lines the bronchi, uterine tubes, and some regions of the uterus. **Function:** Propels mucus or reproductive cells by ciliary action.

(*e*) **Stratified squamous epithelium** consists of many layers of cells (LM ×67). **Location:** Lines the esophagus, mouth, and vagina. Keratinized variety lines the surface of the skin. **Function:** Protects underlying tissues in areas subject to abrasion.

(*f*) **Adipose tissue** cells (adipocytes) contain large fat droplets that push the nuclei close to the plasma membrane. The arrow points to a nucleus (LM ×250). **Location:** Around kidneys, under skin, in bones, within abdomen, and in breasts. **Function:** Provides reserve fuel (lipids), insulates against heat loss, and supports and protects organs.

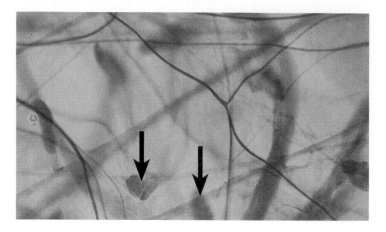

(g) **Loose connective tissue** contains numerous fibroblasts (arrows) that produce collagenous and elastic fibers (LM ×250). **Location:** Widely distributed under the epithelia of the human body. **Function:** Wraps and cushions organs.

(h) **Fibrous connective tissue** consists largely of tightly packed collagenous fibers (LM ×250). The arrow points to a fibroblast. **Location:** Dermis of the skin, submucosa of the digestive tract, and fibrous capsules of organs and joints. **Function:** Provides structural strength.

(i) **Hyaline cartilage** cells are located in lacunae (arrow) surrounded by intercellular material containing fine collagenous fibers (LM ×250). **Location:** Forms embryonic skeleton; covers ends of long bones; and forms cartilage of nose, trachea, and larynx. **Function:** Support and reinforcement.

(j) **Elastic cartilage** contains fine collagenous fibers and many elastic fibers in its intercellular material (LM ×250). **Location:** External ear, epiglottis. **Function:** Maintains a structure's shape while allowing great flexibility.

(k) **Fibrocartilage** contains many large, collagenous fibers in its intercellular material (×195). The arrow points to a fibroblast. **Location:** Intervertebral disks, pubic symphysis, and disks of knee joint. **Function:** Absorbs compression shock.

(l) **Bone (osseous) tissue.** Bone matrix is deposited in concentric layers around osteonic canals (LM ×160). **Location:** Bones. **Function:** Supports, protects, provides lever system for muscles to act on, stores calcium and fat, and forms blood cells.

(m) **Blood** is a type of connective tissue. It consists of red blood cells, white blood cells, and platelets suspended in an intercellular fluid (plasma) (LM ×640). **Location:** Within blood vessels. **Function:** Transports oxygen, carbon dioxide, nutrients, wastes, hormones, minerals, vitamins, and other substances.

(n) **Nervous tissue.** Neurons in nervous tissue transmit electrical signals to other neurons, muscles, or glands (LM ×450). **Location:** Brain, spinal cord, and nerves. **Function:** Transmits electrical signals from sensory receptors to the spinal cord or brain, and from the spinal cord or brain to effectors (muscles and glands).

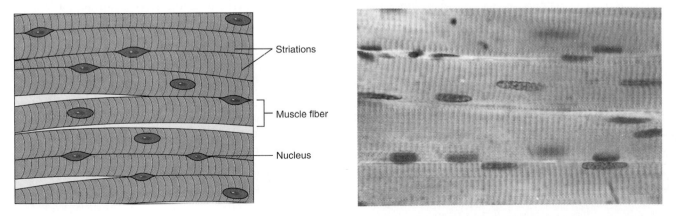

(o) **Skeletal muscle tissue** is composed of striated muscle fibers (cells) that are long and cylindrical, and contain many peripheral nuclei (LM ×250). **Location:** In skeletal muscles attached to bones. **Function:** Voluntary movement, locomotion.

(p) **Smooth muscle tissue** is formed of spindle-shaped cells, each containing a single nucleus (arrow) (LM ×250). Cells are arranged closely to form sheets. Smooth muscle tissue is not striated. **Location:** Mostly in the walls of hollow organs. **Function:** Moves substances or objects (food-stuffs, urine, a baby) along internal passageways; involuntary control.

(q) **Cardiac muscle tissue** consists of striated cells, each containing a single nucleus and specialized cell junctions called intercalated disks (arrow) that allow ions (action potentials) to move quickly from cell to cell (LM ×400). **Location:** The walls of the heart. **Function:** As the walls of the heart contract, cardiac muscle tissue propels blood into the circulation; involuntary control.

ORGANS

Organs (Gr. *organnon,* an independent part of the body) are the functional units of an animal's body that are made up of more than one type of tissue. Examples include the heart, lungs, liver, spleen, and kidneys.

ORGAN SYSTEMS

The next higher level of structural organization in animals is the organ system. An **organ system** (Gr. *systema,* being to-gether) is an association of organs that together perform an overall function. The organ systems in higher vertebrate ani-mals are the integumentary, skeletal, muscular, nervous, en-docrine, circulatory, lymphatic, respiratory, digestive, urinary,

and reproductive systems. Chapters 32 through 39 discuss these systems in detail.

The highest level of organization in an animal body is the organismic level. All parts of the animal body function with one another to contribute to the total organism—a living entity or individual.

Stop and Ask Yourself

19. What is a tissue?
20. What are some functions of epithelial tissue? Where would these tissues be in a higher animal?
21. How are epithelial tissues classified?
22. What are the different types of connective tissue?

ENDANGERED SPECIES

WILDLIFE ALERT—THE EAST AFRICAN BLACK RHINOCEROS (*Diceros bicornis michaeli*)

VITAL STATISTICS

Classification: Phylum Chordata, class Mammalia, order Perissodactyla

Range: Eastern and southern Africa

Habitat: Brushy plains and scrub habitat

Number remaining: Fewer than two thousand

Status: Endangered

NATURAL HISTORY AND ECOLOGICAL STATUS

The African black rhino is one of five species of rhinoceroses and one of two species in Africa (figure 1). The black rhino male reaches a height at the shoulders of about 1.6 m and a weight of about 1,350 kg (figure 2). Its natural life span is about 40 years. It is a browser and uses a unique prehensile (fingerlike) upper lip to grasp twigs and leaves. This upper lip distinguishes the black rhino from the other African rhino, the white rhino, which lacks the prehensile lip and is also larger than the black rhino. The color difference implied by the common names of the two rhinos is misleading, as both are gray. The names probably arose from the color of the mud caked on individuals after wallowing in mud.

Male black rhinos have relatively poor eyesight but keen senses of smell and hearing. They are territorial and solitary, except during breeding. This territoriality and aggressive behavior have given them a reputation for being short-tempered. Males mark territories by dung heaps, which probably advertise their presence to females. Mating can occur anytime but is usually more common during rainy periods. Gestation lasts about 17 months, and offspring weigh about 34 kg. Offspring are weaned after about 2 years and are mature in about 7 years. Mature females mate about once every 3 years.

Black rhinoceros populations have decreased alarmingly in recent decades—down 96% since 1970. Twenty years ago, the number of black rhinos was estimated at sixty-five thousand. Today, fewer than two thousand black rhinos remain. In the wild, mature black rhinos have no natural enemies, although the young are prey of hyenas and lions. Poaching is the primary cause of their demise, although habitat destruction has also contributed to the population decline. Rhino horns, which are actually not true horns with a bony core, are comprised of hairlike keratin fibers cemented together. The front horn can be 1 m long, and the rear horn is about 20 cm long. Oriental cultures use ground rhino horn as a medicinal powder, although its medical value has never been demonstrated. The use of rhino horns for dagger handles, a symbol of wealth in Yemen and other Middle Eastern countries, is the reason for most poaching.

Protection afforded by national parks, including the use of high-voltage fences, seems to be improving the chances for the survival of the African black rhino. Zoos in North America are playing an important role in preserving some of the genetic diversity of these animals. If conditions improve in eastern Africa, the captive animals may one day be used to strengthen the genetic stock of the natural populations.

FIGURE 1   Approximate Distribution of the African Black Rhinoceros.

FIGURE 2   The African Black Rhinoceros (*Diceros bicornis michaeli*)

SUMMARY

1. All animal cells have three basic parts: the nucleus, cytoplasm, and plasma membrane.

2. Cell membranes, composed mainly of phospholipids and proteins, allow certain materials to move across them. This quality is called selective permeability. The fluid-mosaic model is based on knowledge of the plasma membrane.

3. Some molecules use their own energy to pass across a cell membrane from areas of higher concentration to areas of lower concentration. Examples of these passive processes are simple diffusion, facilitated diffusion, osmosis, and filtration.

4. Active transport across cell membranes requires energy from the cell to move substances from areas of lower concentration to areas of higher concentration. Additional processes that move molecules across membranes are endocytosis and exocytosis. Three types of endocytosis are pinocytosis, phagocytosis, and receptor-mediated endocytosis.

5. The cytoplasm of a cell has two parts. The cytomembrane system consists of well-defined structures, such as the endoplasmic reticulum, Golgi apparatus, vacuoles, and vesicles. The aqueous part consists of the fluid cytosol.

6. Ribosomes are the sites of protein synthesis.

7. The endoplasmic reticulum (ER) is a series of channels that transports, stores enzymes and proteins, and provides a point of attachment for ribosomes. The two types of ER are smooth and rough.

8. The Golgi apparatus aids in the synthesis and secretion of glycoproteins, as well as processing and modifying other materials (e.g., enzymes).

9. Lysosomes digest nutrients and clean away dead or damaged cell parts.

10. Mitochondria convert energy in food molecules to a form the cell can use.

11. Microtubules, intermediate filaments, and microfilaments make up the cytoskeleton of the cell. The cytoskeleton functions in transport, support, and the movement of structures in the cell, such as organelles and chromosomes.

12. Cilia and flagella are appendages on the surface of some cells and function in movement.

13. Centrioles assist in cell division and help move chromosomes during cell division.

14. Vacuoles are membranous sacs that are part of the cytomembrane system.

15. The nucleus of a cell contains DNA, which controls the cell's genetic program and other metabolic activities.

16. The nuclear envelope contains many pores that allow material to enter and leave the nucleus.

17. The chromosomes in the nucleus have DNA organized into genes, which are specific DNA sequences that control and regulate cell activities.

18. The nucleolus is a preassembly point for ribosomes.

19. Tissues are groups of cells with a common structure and function. The four types of tissues are epithelial, connective, muscle, and nervous.

20. An organ is composed of more than one type of tissue. An organ system is an association of organs.

SELECTED KEY TERMS

centrioles (p. 48)
cytomembrane system (p. 44)
cytoplasm (p. 34)
cytoskeleton (p. 47)
endoplasmic reticulum (ER) (p. 44)
epithelial tissue (p. 50)
Golgi apparatus (p. 44)

homeostasis (p. 38)
lysosomes (p. 46)
microtubule-organizing center (p. 48)
mitochondria (p. 47)
nucleolus (p. 49)
nucleus (p. 34)

CRITICAL THINKING QUESTIONS

1. Why is the mitochondrion called the "power generator" of the cell?

2. One of the larger facets of modern zoology can be described as "membrane biology." What common principles unite the diverse functions of membranes?

3. Why is the current model of the plasma membrane called the "fluid-mosaic" model? What is the fluid, and in what sense is it fluid? What makes up the mosaic?

4. If you could visualize osmosis, seeing the solute and solvent particles as individual entities, what would an osmotic gradient look like?

5. Why can some animal cells transport materials against a concentration gradient? Could animals survive without this capability?

REFERENCES ON THE WORLD WIDE WEB

1. **Cells Alive.** This site contains video microscopy of living cells, such as bacteria, protozoa, and parasites, and also has three-dimensional animations of cells.
http://www.comet.chv.va.us/quill/

2. **The Dictionary of Cell Biology.** This site contains a comprehensive dictionary related to cytology, histology, and molecular biology.
http://www.mblab.gla.ac.uk/~julian/Dict.html

3. **Cell Biology Directory.** This site is the cell biology directory of the MIT hypertext program.
http://esg-www.MIT.EDU:8001/esgbio/cbdir.html

4. **Prokaryotic and Eukaryotic Cells.** This site compares and contrasts eukaryotic and prokaryotic cells.
http://esg-www.MIT.EDU:8001/esgbio/cb/prok_euk.html

5. **Cell Basics.** This site discusses life, the cell theory, cell size, and cell composition.
http://esg-www.MIT.EDU:8001/esgbio/cb/cellbasics.html

6. **Cell Organelles.** Included at this site are electron micrographs of plant and animal cells.
http://esg-www.MIT.EDU:8001/esgbio/cb/org/organelles.html

7. **The Cytoskeleton.** This site provides a description and discussion of the function of the cytoskeleton.
http://esg-www.MIT.EDU:8001/esgbio/cb/cytoskeleton.html

8. **Cell Membranes.** This site discusses the structure and function of cell membranes.
http://esg-www.MIT.EDU:8001/esgbio/cb/membranes/intro.html

9. **Cell Membrane Structure.** This site describes the fluid-mosaic model of membrane structure.
http://esg-www.MIT.EDU:8001/esgbio/cb/membranes/structure.html

10. **Cell Biology Self-Quiz.**   A series of multiple-choice questions at this site offers a review.

    http://esg-www.MIT.EDU:8001/esgbio/cb/sq.html

11. **Cell Biology Self Quiz II.**   Short-answer essay questions and practical cell biology problems are at this site.

    http://esg-www.MIT.EDU:8001/esgbio/cb/problems.html

12. **Histology.**   This site is a histological index and includes light and electron micrographs.

    http://med-amsa.bu.edu/Anat-AADS/Histology.html

13. **University of Wisconsin Medical School Histology Home Page.** This site is an excellent review of histological specimens.

    http://www.anatomy.wisc.edu/histology/histo.html

14. **Medical Matrix.**   This is an outstanding collection of histology micrographs.

    http://www.slackinc.com/matrix/BASIC/HISTOLOGY.HTML

15. **Cellular Transport.**   This site describes the mechanisms of cellular transport. Examples include diffusion, active transport, and the sodium-potassium ATPase pump.

    http://esg-www.MIT.EDU:8001/esgbio/cb/membranes/transport.html

16. **Course Tutorial on Cell Biology.**   This site is an excellent tutorial on basic cell biology.

    http://lenti.med.umn.edu:80/~mwd/cell_www/cell.html

17. **Relationship between Cells, Tissues, Organs, and Organ Systems.** This site provides information on how cells, tissues, and organs interact.

    http://www.sd30.bc.ca/html/relation.html

18. **How the Scanning Electron Microscope Works.**   This site explains how the SEM works.

    http://dekalb.dc.peachnet.edu/~pgore/students/w96/joshbond/symb.htm

19. **Receptors.**   Various membrane receptors and transport processes are discussed at this site.

    http:esg-www.mit.edu:8001/esgbio/cb/membranes/transport.html

20. **Microvision.**   This site provides the user with beautiful light and electron micrographs.

    http://www.pbrc.hawaii.edu/~kunkel/

chapter

④

ENERGY AND ENZYMES:
LIFE'S DRIVING AND CONTROLLING FORCES

Concepts

1. Energy drives all life processes in a cell. Energy is the capacity to do work. It can exist in two forms: Kinetic energy is actively involved in doing work, and potential energy is stored for future use.
2. The cell obtains energy by utilizing chemical fuel and by obeying the first and second laws of thermodynamics.
3. The speed of a chemical reaction depends on the activation energy necessary to initiate it. Catalysts reduce the amount of activation energy necessary to initiate a chemical reaction and, therefore, speed up the reaction. Cells use specialized proteins and nucleic acids (RNA) called enzymes as biological catalysts.
4. Any factor (e.g., temperature, pH, and other chemicals) that alters an enzyme's shape affects the enzyme's activity. Cofactors are metal ions or organic molecules that facilitate enzyme activity. Specific cofactors that are nonprotein organic molecules are called coenzymes.
5. ATP is the universal energy currency of all cells.

Would You Like to Know . . .

① what a food chain is? (p. 60)

② what work is? (p. 60)

③ how an animal accomplishes biological work? (p. 60)

④ how the shape of an enzyme can be compared with a handshake? (p. 62)

⑤ what the energy currency of all animal life is? (p. 64)

This chapter answers these and other useful questions.

This chapter contains evolutionary concepts, which are set off in this font.

An animal's use of the sun's radiant energy begins with photosynthetic plants (and certain microorganisms) "capturing" that energy and converting it to chemical energy in the form of carbohydrates. Because plants capture the sun's energy, they are **primary producers.** A **primary consumer** is a plant-eating animal, or herbivore (L. *herba*, grass + *vorare*, to devour), that obtains organic molecules by eating producers or their products. Primary consumers use the energy in organic molecules to carry out all of their cellular activities, including the synthesis of complex organic molecules. ❶ Primary consumers are preyed on by other animals, the **secondary consumers,** and so on, in what is termed a **food chain.** As each organism dies, its constituents are broken down by digestion or by various **decomposers,** such as bacteria and fungi. This producer-consumer-decomposer sequence in a food chain represents a flow of both energy and matter in an ecosystem. An **ecosystem** is an array of organisms and their physical environment, all interacting through a one-way flow of energy and a cycling of materials (figure 4.1).

Nutrients are continuously being broken down to provide the energy necessary for life. In fact, life is a constant flow of energy that an animal or plant channels to do the work of living. This "living chemistry" is called metabolism. **Metabolism** (Gr. *metaballein*, to change) is the total of all the chemical reactions occurring in a cell. It involves the acquisition and use of energy in stockpiling, breaking down, assembling, and eliminating substances to ensure the maintenance, growth, and reproduction of the organisms. Metabolism consists of synthetic processes called **anabolism** (Gr. *anabole*, building up) and degrading processes called **catabolism** (Gr. *katabole*, breaking down). This chapter focuses on what energy is, how an animal uses it, and how enzymes control metabolism. Chapter 5 presents the network of chemical reactions for the flow of energy through an animal.

WHAT IS ENERGY?

Energy is the capacity to do work. ❷ **Work** is the transfer of energy. Energy can also be transformed. For example, a plant can transform solar (radiant) energy into chemical energy (*see figure 4.1*). The plant can then be burned in a steam generator and the energy transformed into the energy of motion (e.g., the turning of a wheel). Energy has many forms: the heat from a furnace, the sound of a jet plane, the electric current that lights a bulb, the radioactivity in a heart pacemaker, or the pull of a magnet.

Energy exists in two states: kinetic and potential. **Kinetic energy** is the energy of motion (e.g., a thundering waterfall). **Potential energy** is stored energy (e.g., a giant boulder poised on a pinnacle). In a living animal, energy in chemical bonds is a form of potential energy. ❸ Animals use the bond energy in organic molecules to accomplish biological work. Much of the work an animal performs involves the transformation of potential energy to kinetic energy in its cells.

The most convenient way to measure energy is in terms of heat production. This is why the study of energy is called **thermodynamics** (Gr. *therme*, heat + *dynamis*, power). The most commonly employed unit for measuring heat in an animal is the **kilocalorie**

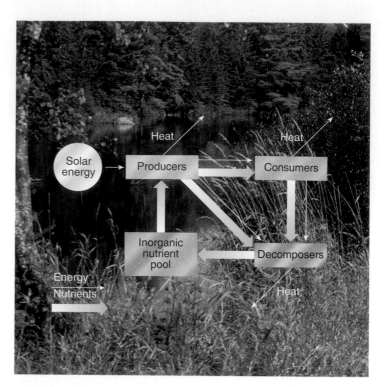

FIGURE 4.1

The Sun's Radiant Energy Sustains Virtually All Organisms. This figure represents the flow of energy and materials through an ecosystem. Notice that chemical nutrients cycle, but energy flows through the system because all the energy derived from the sun eventually dissipates as heat.

(kcal) or nutritional **Calorie** (notice the large "C"). A kilocalorie is the amount of heat necessary to raise 1 kg of water 1° C and is equal to 1,000 calories. A reasonable daily intake of energy for an average person is approximately 2,000 to 2,500 kcal. A **calorie** (notice the small "c") is the amount of heat it takes to raise the temperature of 1 g (1 cc) of water 1° C (usually from 14.5 to 15.5° C).

Stop and Ask Yourself

1. How would you define metabolism?
2. What is energy? What is work?
3. What is the difference between kinetic and potential energy?
4. What defines a primary producer? What defines a secondary consumer?

THE LAWS OF ENERGY TRANSFORMATIONS

Two laws of thermodynamics govern energy transformations. The **first law of thermodynamics,** sometimes called the law of energy conservation, states that energy can neither be created nor destroyed, only transformed. What this means is that energy can change from one form to another (e.g., electrical energy passes

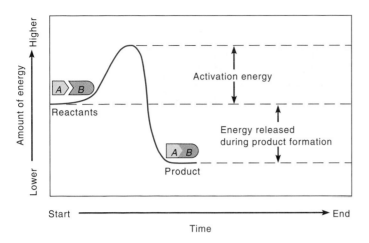

FIGURE 4.2

Energy Diagram. Before a chemical reaction occurs, energy must be supplied to destabilize existing chemical bonds. This energy is called activation energy.

through a hot plate to produce heat energy) or can be transformed from potential to kinetic energy (e.g., a squirrel eats a nut and then uses this energy to climb a tree), but it can never be lost or created. Thus, the total amount of energy in the universe remains constant.

The **second law of thermodynamics** states that all objects in the universe tend to become more disordered and that the total amount of disorder in the universe is continually increasing. The measure of this degree of disorganization is called **entropy.** Consider this simple illustration: When natural gas burns in a stove, the potential chemical energy stored in the bonds of the gas molecules is converted to light (the blue flame) and heat. Some of the heat energy can be used to boil water on the stove, and some is dissipated into the kitchen, where it is no longer available to do work. This unusable energy represents increased entropy.

ACTIVATION ENERGY

Most chemical reactions require an input of energy to start (e.g., a match is lit, and the heat energy is used to start wood burning in a fireplace). At the chemical level, input energy must break existing chemical bonds before new bonds can form. In thermodynamics, this input energy is called activation energy (figure 4.2).

In a reaction with a net release of energy, the reactant contains more energy than the products. In other words, the amount of this excess energy (called "free energy") released into the environment is greater than the activation energy required to initiate the reaction. These reactions occur spontaneously and are called **exergonic** (L. *ex*, out + Gr. *ergon*, work) (figure 4.3*a*). In contrast, a chemical reaction in which the product contains more energy than the reactants requires a greater input of energy from the environment than is released (figure 4.3*b*). Because these reactions do not occur spontaneously, they are called **endergonic** (Gr. *endon*, within + *ergon*, work).

The amount of reactant substance(s) converted to product substance(s) in a given period of time is the reaction rate. The

(a) An exergonic reaction

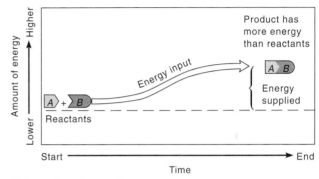

(b) An endergonic reaction

FIGURE 4.3

Exergonic and Endergonic Reactions. (*a*) In an exergonic reaction, the products have less energy than the reactant, and excess energy is released to the environment. (*b*) In an endergonic reaction, the product of the reaction contains more energy than the reactants, so energy input is needed for the reaction to occur.

reaction rate of an exergonic reaction does not depend on how much energy the reaction releases, but on the amount of activation energy required for the reaction to begin. The larger the activation energy of a chemical reaction, the more slowly the reaction occurs, because at a given temperature, fewer molecules succeed in overcoming the initial energy hurdle. However, activation energies are not fixed. For example, when certain chemical bonds are stressed, they may break more easily. Affecting a chemical bond in a way that lowers the activation energy of a reaction is **catalysis.** Any substance that performs catalysis is called a catalyst. A **catalyst** (Gr. *kata*, down + *lysis*, a loosening) is a substance that accelerates the rate of a chemical reaction (or allows it to proceed at a lower environmental temperature) by decreasing the activation energy, without itself being used up in the reaction (figure 4.4). In cells, catalysts are almost always protein enzymes.

Stop and Ask Yourself

5. What is the difference between an exergonic and endergonic chemical reaction?

6. What is activation energy?

7. What are the first and second laws of thermodynamics?

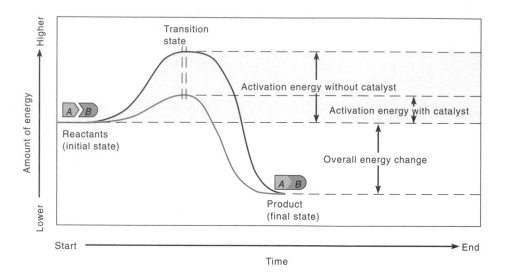

FIGURE 4.4

Function of a Catalyst. Catalysts lower the amount of activation energy required to initiate a chemical reaction. As a result, at the same temperature, the reaction moves to completion much more quickly.

FIGURE 4.5

Enzymes. Enzyme action is like an induced fit. Substrate molecules A and B fit into the active site of enzyme C, forming an enzyme-substrate complex A and B react to form the new compound AB. AB is released from the enzyme, and the enzyme recycles.

ENZYMES: BIOLOGICAL CATALYSTS

Most enzymes are proteins; some (**ribozymes**) are nucleic acids (RNA). Enzymes have enormous catalytic power; they greatly enhance the rate at which specific chemical reactions take place. The metabolism of an animal is organized and controlled specifically at the points where catalysis takes place. Therefore, one of the most important foundations in all of biology is that life is a series of chemical processes that enzymes regulate. An **enzyme** (Gr. *enzymos*, leavened) is a biological catalyst that can accelerate a specific chemical reaction by lowering the required activation energy but is unaltered in the process. In other words, the same reaction would have occurred to the same degree in the absence of the catalyst, but it would have progressed at a much slower rate. Because it is unaltered, the enzyme can be used over and over.

An enzyme is extremely selective for the reaction it will catalyze. The reactants of enzymatic reactions are called **substrates.** The precise "fit" between an enzyme and its specific substrate is crucial to cell metabolism. For example, cellular concentrations of many reactants must be kept at low levels to avoid undesirable side reactions. At the same time, concentrations must remain high enough for the required reactions to occur at a rate compatible with life. As presented in chapter 5, metabolism proceeds under these seemingly conflicting conditions because enzymes channel molecules into and through specific chemical pathways. With the exception of the several digestive enzymes that were the first to be discovered (e.g., pepsin and trypsin), all enzyme names end with the suffix ase and are named after their substrate.

ENZYME STRUCTURE

Enzymes are three-dimensional globular protein molecules or nucleic acids with at least one surface region having a crevice or pocket. This crevice occupies only a small portion of the enzyme's surface and is known as the enzyme's active site (figure 4.5). This site is shaped so that a substrate molecule (or several substrate molecules, depending on the reaction) fits into it in a very specific way and is held in place by weak chemical forces, such as hydrogen bonds. Binding of the substrate to the enzyme changes the enzyme's shape, a phenomenon called **induced fit.** ④ Induced fit is like a clasping handshake. The active site's embrace of the substrate brings chemical groups of the active site into positions that

(a)

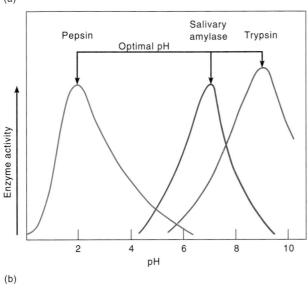

(b)

FIGURE 4.6

How the Environment Affects Enzymes. (a) Effect of temperature on enzyme activity. (b) Effect of pH on three different enzymes.

enhance their ability to work on the substrate and to catalyze the chemical reaction. When the reaction is complete, the product (new compound) of the catalyzed reaction is released, and the enzyme resumes its initial conformation (shape), ready to catalyze another chemical reaction.

ENZYME FUNCTION

When a substrate molecule binds to an enzyme's active site, an **enzyme-substrate complex (ES)** forms (*see figure 4.5*). This is the essential first step in enzyme catalysis and can be summarized as follows:

$$\text{Enzyme + substrate} \rightleftharpoons \text{enzyme-substrate complex}$$
$$\rightleftharpoons \text{products + enzyme}$$

Once the unstable, high-energy ES forms, amino acid side groups of the enzyme are placed against certain bonds of the substrate.

These side groups stress or distort the substrate bonds, lowering the activation energy needed to break the bonds. The bonds break, releasing the substrate, which now reacts to produce the final product and release the enzyme.

FACTORS AFFECTING ENZYME ACTIVITY

Any condition that alters the three-dimensional shape of an enzyme also affects the enzyme's activity. Two factors that affect enzyme activity are temperature and pH.

As presented in chapter 2, the shape of a protein or nucleic acid is determined largely by its hydrogen bonds (*see figure 2.15*). Temperature changes easily disrupt hydrogen bonds. For example, most higher vertebrates, such as birds and mammals, have enzymes that function best within a relatively narrow temperature range (between 35 and 40° C) (figure 4.6a). Below 35° C, the bonds that determine protein shape are not flexible enough to permit the shape change necessary for substrate to fit into a reactive site. Above 40° C, the bonds are too weak to hold the protein in proper position and to maintain its shape. When proper shape is lost, the enzyme is, in essence, destroyed; this loss of shape is called **denaturation.**

Most enzymes also have a pH optimum, usually between 6 and 8 (figure 4.6b). For example, when the pH is too low, the H^+ ions combine with the R groups of the enzyme's amino acids, reducing their ability to bind with substrates. Acidic environments can also denature enzymes not adapted to such conditions. Some enzymes, however, function at a low pH. For example, pepsin (the enzyme found in the stomach of mammals) has an optimal pH of approximately 2. Pepsin functions at such a low pH because it has an amino acid sequence that maintains its ionic and hydrogen bonds, even in the presence of large numbers of H^+ ions (low pH). Conversely, trypsin is active in the more basic medium (pH 9) found in the small intestine of mammals. Overall, the pH optimum of an enzyme reflects the pH of the body fluid in which the enzyme is found.

Stop and Ask Yourself

8. What is an enzyme? What is a substrate?
9. How are enzymes named?
10. What is the structure of an enzyme?
11. How do enzymes function?
12. How do temperature, pH, and other factors affect enzyme function?

COFACTORS AND COENZYMES

Cofactors are metal ions, such as Ca^{2+}, Mg^{2+}, Mn^{2+}, Cu^{2+}, and Zn^{2+}. Many enzymes must use these metal ions to change a nonfunctioning active site to a functioning one. In these enzymes, the attachment of a cofactor changes the shape of the protein and allows it to combine with its substrate (figure 4.7a). The cofactors of other enzymes participate in the temporary bonds between the

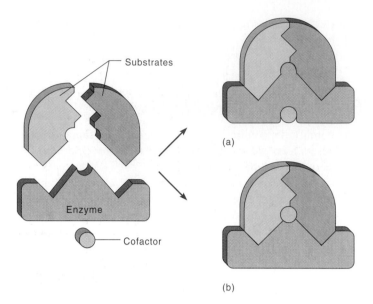

FIGURE 4.7

Cofactors. (*a*) The cofactor changes the conformation of the active site, permitting a better fit between the enzyme and the substrate. (*b*) The cofactor participates in the temporary bonding between the active site of the enzyme and the substrate.

enzyme and its substrate when the enzyme-substrate complex forms (figure 4.7*b*).

Coenzymes are nonprotein, organic molecules that participate in enzyme-catalyzed reactions, often by transporting electrons, in the form of hydrogen atoms, from one enzyme to another. Many vitamins (e.g., niacin and riboflavin) function as coenzymes or are used to make coenzymes. Just as a taxi transports people around a city, so coenzymes transport energy, in the form of hydrogen atoms, from one enzyme to another.

One of the most important coenzymes in the cell is the hydrogen acceptor **nicotinamide adenine dinucleotide (NAD⁺)**, which is made from a B vitamin. When NAD⁺ acquires a hydrogen atom from an enzyme, it reduces to NADH (figure 4.8). The electron of the hydrogen atom contains energy that the NADH molecule then carries. For example, when various foods are oxidized in the cell, the cell strips electrons from the food molecules and transfers them to NAD⁺, which reduces to NADH.

ATP: THE CELL'S ENERGY CURRENCY

⑤ The major energy currency of all cells is a nucleotide called **adenosine triphosphate (ATP).** Because ATP plays a central role as the energy currency in all organisms, it must have appeared early in the history of life.

The ability of ATP to store and release energy stems from the molecule's structure. Each ATP molecule has three subunits: (1) adenine, an organic molecule composed of two carbon-nitrogen rings; (2) ribose, a five-carbon sugar; and (3) three phosphate groups

Oxidized form   Reduced form

FIGURE 4.8

Nicotinamide Adenine Dinucleotide (NAD): Oxidized (NAD⁺) and Reduced (NADH) Forms. When NAD is reduced, one electron attaches to the nitrogen atom at position 1. The second electron attaches to a carbon atom at position 4 and is accompanied by a hydrogen ion.

FIGURE 4.9

Structural Formula for Adenosine Triphosphate, or ATP. The ATP molecule is the primary energy currency of the cell. It consists of an adenine portion, the sugar ribose, and three phosphates. The wavy lines (tildes) connecting the last two phosphates represent high-energy chemical bonds that can quickly release energy.

in a linear chain (figure 4.9). The covalent bond connecting these phosphates is indicated by the "tilde" symbol ($\sim$) and is a high-energy bond. However, the energy is not localized in the bond itself; it is a property of the entire molecule and is simply released as the phosphate bond breaks. These bonds have a low activation energy (*see figure 4.4*) and break easily. The breaking of one bond releases about 7.3 kcal (7,300 calories) per mole of ATP as follows:

$$\text{ATP} + \text{H}_2\text{O} \rightarrow \text{ADP} + \text{P}_i + \text{energy (7.3 kcal/mole)}$$

The energy from ATP is sufficient to drive most of the cell's endergonic reactions. In a typical energy reaction, only the outermost of the two high-energy bonds breaks (is hydrolyzed). When

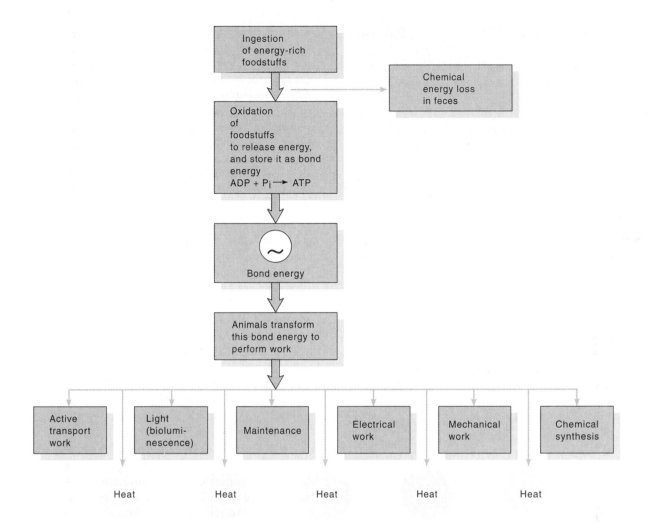

FIGURE 4.10

Some Energy Utilization Pathways in Animals. Notice that heat is lost in every transformation.

this happens, ATP becomes **ADP (adenosine diphosphate).** In some cases, ADP is hydrolyzed to **AMP (adenosine monophosphate)** as follows:

$$ADP + H_2O \rightarrow AMP + P_i + energy \ (7.3 \ kcal/mole)$$

Cells contain a reservoir of ADP and phosphate (P_i). As long as a cell is living, ATP is constantly being cleaved into ADP plus phosphate to drive the cell's many energy-requiring processes, enabling the animal to perform biological work (figure 4.10). However, ATP cannot be stored for long. Once formed, ATP lasts only a few seconds before it is used to perform biological work. Thus, cells constantly recycle ADP. With the energy derived from foodstuffs and from stored fats and starches, ADP and phosphate recombine to form ATP, with 7.3 kcal of energy per mole contributed to each newly formed high-energy phosphate bond.

HOW CELLS CONVERT ENERGY: AN OVERVIEW

Within their cells, animals make ATP in two ways: substrate-level phosphorylation and chemiosmosis. As noted earlier, ATP formation from ADP and phosphate requires the input of energy (the same 7.3 kcal released when ATP is hydrolyzed). To get this energy, the reaction is coupled with an exergonic reaction (figure 4.11a). An enzyme transfers a phosphate group to ADP from a substrate with a phosphate bond even more easily broken than that of ATP (i.e., the energy from the exergonic reaction is greater than the energy input necessary to drive ATP synthesis). The generation of ATP by coupling strongly exergonic reactions with ATP synthesis from ADP and phosphate is called **substrate-level phosphorylation.** Substrate-level phosphorylation probably appeared very early in the history of organisms because (1) organisms' initial

(a) Substrate-level
    phosphorylation

Mitochondrion

High H$^+$
concentration

Low H$^+$
concentration

ATP Synthetase

ADP + P$_i$

H$^+$

ATP

Proton
pump

NADH

H$^+$

NAD$^+$

Outer compartment
of mitochondrion

Inner compartment
of mitochondrion

(b) Chemiosmosis

FIGURE 4.11

ATP Generation. (*a*) Substrate-level phosphorylation. In this example, a phosphate group is transferred from an enzyme-substrate complex to ADP to form ATP. This reaction takes place because the high-energy bond of the substrate has higher energy than the phosphate bonds of ADP. (*b*) Chemiosmosis occurs as hydrogen ions cross from one side of a membrane to the other, generating a proton gradient across the membrane. When protons move back across the membrane through special channels, their passage generates ATP from ADP and P$_i$.

use of carbohydrates as an energy source is accomplished by substrate-level phosphorylation; (2) the mechanism for substrate-level phosphorylation is present in most living animal cells; and (3) substrate-level phosphorylation is one of the most fundamental of all ATP-generating reactions.

Although substrate-level phosphorylation may be the oldest method of generating ATP, far more ATP is generated from another process, called **chemiosmosis** (figure 4.11*b*). Organisms possess transmembrane channels in their mitochondrial membranes that can pump protons. These proton pumps use a flow of electrons to induce a shape change in the protein, which, in turn, causes protons to move out of the inner compartment of a mitochondrion. As the proton (H$^+$) concentration in the outer compartment of the mitochondrion becomes greater than that of the inside compartment, the outer protons are driven across the membrane by an electrical-chemical proton gradient. As protons move down this gradient between outer and inner mitochondrial compartments, they induce the formation of ATP from ADP, phosphate, and the enzyme ATP synthetase.

The electrons that drive the electron transport system involved in chemiosmosis are obtained from chemical bonds of food molecules in all organisms and from photosynthesis in plants. This electron-stripping process is called **cellular respiration,** or **aerobic respiration** because free oxygen is needed. Basically, aerobic respiration is the oxidation of food molecules to obtain energy and is the subject of chapter 5.

Biologists have been questioning what biological molecules do for approximately one hundred years. Chapter 5 presents some facts on how these molecules function via enzymes. **Enzymes have evolved for over 3 billion years, and they have a great deal to teach us.** Happily, the number of lessons is probably finite, for we already see examples of enzyme molecules, unrelated by evolution, but with almost identically arranged working parts. Chapter 5 clarifies what enzymes are telling us about the universality of energy-harvesting pathways and animal life.

Stop and Ask Yourself

13. What three component parts make up the ATP molecule?

14. Why doesn't ATP accumulate in a cell?

15. What is substrate-level phosphorylation? What is chemiosmosis?

16. How do cofactors function? How do coenzymes function?

SUMMARY

1. Energy is the capacity to do work. Kinetic energy is the energy that is actively engaged in doing work, whereas potential energy is stored energy. Animals convert potential energy into kinetic energy to perform biological work, which is the transfer of energy.

2. The first law of thermodynamics states that the amount of energy in the universe is fixed and that energy cannot be created or destroyed. However, energy can be converted from one form to another.

3. The second law of thermodynamics states that the randomness or disorder in the universe is increasing. This process is called entropy.

4. The speed of a chemical reaction depends on the amount of activation energy required to break existing bonds. Catalysis is the chemical process of increasing the reaction rate by lowering the amount of activation energy required to initiate the reaction. Enzymes are the biological catalysts of cells.

5. Enzymes have a specific three-dimensional shape, with one or more reactive sites that bind substrates. Cells contain many different enzymes, each of which catalyzes a different chemical reaction.

6. Factors such as temperature, pH, substrate concentration, cofactors, and coenzymes can affect the reaction rate of an enzyme.

7. Cells focus their energy resources on the manufacture of ATP from ADP and phosphate, a process that require cells to supply 7.3 kcal/mole of energy, which it obtains from electrons stripped from foodstuffs. Mitochondrial membranes are the main site of ATP production. Cells use ATP to drive endergonic reactions and accomplish biological work.

8. Chemical energy is harvested via either substrate-level phosphorylation or chemiosmosis. In substrate-level phosphorylation, a phosphate group is transferred from an enzyme-substrate complex to ADP by coupling an endergonic reaction to a highly exergonic one. In chemiosmosis, electrons are transported to an electron transport system in the mitochondrial membrane. In the process, a gradient of H^+ ions (protons) is established that powers ATP synthesis.

SELECTED KEY TERMS

anabolism (p. 60)
catabolism (p. 60)
catalysis (p. 61)
catalyst (p. 61)
ecosystem (p. 60)
endergonic (p. 61)

energy (p. 60)
entropy (p. 61)
enzyme (p. 62)
enzyme-substrate complex (ES) (p. 63)
exergonic (p. 61)

CRITICAL THINKING QUESTIONS

1. Does the living state of an animal violate the second law of thermodynamics? In other words, how does an animal maintain a high degree of organization, even though the universal trend is toward disorganization?

2. Why are the two laws of thermodynamics called laws, whereas the central organizing concept of biology—evolution—is called a theory?

3. Living organisms are constantly transforming energy via many different mechanisms. Give several examples in animals where one form of energy is transformed into another form.

4. As you read this statement, you are losing energy. At the risk of losing even more, describe what this means with respect to entropy.

5. Why is ATP the major energy-carrying molecule in all organisms?

REFERENCES ON THE WORLD WIDE WEB

1. **Animated GIFs and Protein Chemistry.** At this site, you can encounter the three-dimensional structure of an enzyme with its substrate bound to the active site.
http://www2.ucsc.edu/people/straycat/cpa.html

2. The chapters that follow are from the 8001 hypertextbook. They cover chemical energetics, enzyme mechanics, enzyme kinetics, feedback inhibition, and solving feedback regulation problems.
http://esg-www.mit.edu:8001/esgbio/eb/chem/energetics.html
http://esg-www.mit.edu:8001/esgbio/eb/structure.html
http://esg-www.mit.edu:8001/esgbio/eb/kinetics/intro.html
http://esg-www.mit.edu:8001/esgbio/eb/feedback

chapter 5

HOW ANIMALS HARVEST ENERGY STORED IN NUTRIENTS

Concepts

1. All animals harvest energy from nutrients to fuel their metabolism with energy from ATP. The catabolic processes involved include glycolysis, fermentation, and aerobic respiration.
2. Glycolysis is a specific metabolic pathway that does not require oxygen and involves chemical reactions that transfer chemical energy by rearranging the chemical bonds of glucose to form molecules of pyruvate and to generate two usable molecules of ATP.
3. Animals that live in an anaerobic (low in oxygen) environment utilize fermentation to transfer the electrons and associated hydrogen produced in glycolysis to another atom or molecule. Molecules other than oxygen (e.g., NAD^+) are electron acceptors.
4. In aerobic respiration, the Krebs cycle completes the breakdown of pyruvate to carbon dioxide, water, and H^+ (protons). In the mitochondrion, electrons from hydrogen (H) atoms are channeled to the inner mitochondrial membrane to drive proton pumps and to generate ATP by way of the electron transport chain and chemiosmosis.
5. Fats and proteins can also be nutrients for animals. These molecules break down to intermediates that are eventually fed into the Krebs cycle.

Would You Like to Know . . .

1. how the first organisms obtained energy in the absence of oxygen? (p. 70)
2. why an inefficient method of harvesting energy has persisted through eons of time? (p. 70)
3. how glycolysis is a metabolic memory of an animal's evolutionary past? (p. 72)
4. why animals store excess energy in the form of fat? (p. 74)
5. how cells are thrifty, expedient, and responsive in their metabolism? (p. 76)

This chapter answers these and other useful questions.

This chapter contains evolutionary concepts, which are set off in this font.

Chapter 4 discussed how animals require a constant supply of energy to perform biological work. The energy-rich molecule ATP usually provides this energy (*see figure 4.9*). All animals can generate ATP by breaking down organic nutrients (carbohydrates, fats, and proteins). The energy released is used to join ADP and phosphate (P_i) to form ATP.

In animals, the breakdown of organic nutrients, such as glucose, begins in a step-by-step series of chemical reactions called glycolysis. The end product of glycolysis (pyruvate) is then further broken down either in the presence of free oxygen (**aerobic**)—a process called aerobic respiration—or in the absence of free oxygen (**anaerobic**)—a process called fermentation.

Figure 5.1 provides an overview of the catabolic metabolism involved in ATP production. Note that glycolysis and fermentation (anaerobic processes) take place in the cytoplasm of a cell and that aerobic respiration takes place in the mitochondrion.

Glycolysis and fermentation occur in the cytoplasm because during eukaryotic cell evolution, the enzymes that catalyze each reaction remained dissolved in the cytoplasm and did not localize in membranous organelles. ❶ This implies an origin prior to the evolution of complex organelles. These reactions are also older in an evolutionary sense than aerobic respiration because they could have occurred in the earliest primitive environment of earth before the atmosphere contained free oxygen.

This chapter presents some of the fundamental biological principles that underlie glycolysis, aerobic respiration, and fermentation in animal cells.

GLYCOLYSIS: THE FIRST PHASE OF NUTRIENT METABOLISM

Glycolysis (Gr. *glykys*, sweet + *lyein*, to loosen) is the initial sequence of catabolic chemical reactions that almost all cells use to break the six-carbon glucose molecule into two molecules of a three-carbon compound called pyruvate (pyruvic acid) with the net production of two molecules of ATP (figure 5.2). For each molecule of glucose that enters the glycolytic pathway, four molecules of ATP form. However, because two ATP molecules are used to rearrange the glucose molecule to form new six-carbon compounds, the net energy yield from glycolysis is only two ATP molecules. Although glycolysis does not efficiently harvest all the available energy from glucose, it was the only way most organisms could harvest energy and generate ATP molecules for hundreds of millions of years during the anaerobic stages of early life on earth.

EVOLUTIONARY PERSPECTIVE ON GLYCOLYSIS

If glycolysis is such an inefficient method of harvesting energy, why has it persisted? ❷ One reason might be that evolution is a slow, incremental process involving change based on past events. When glycolysis first evolved, the cells possessing it had a competitive advantage

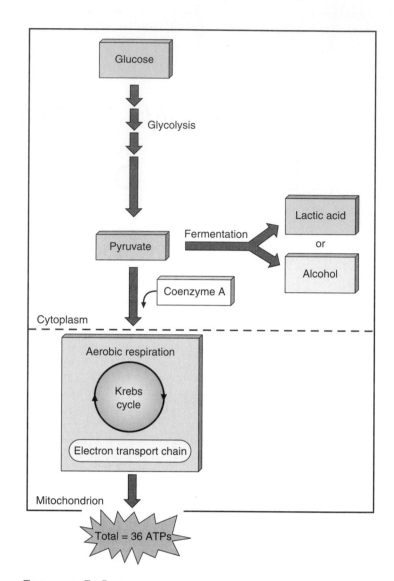

FIGURE 5.1

Overview of the Catabolic Pathways (Glycolysis, Fermentation, Aerobic Respiration) That Generate ATP Molecules. Glycolysis begins in the cytoplasm and causes glucose to be broken down to pyruvate. In the absence of free oxygen, pyruvate undergoes fermentation instead of entering the Krebs cycle. The first step in aerobic respiration is the conversion of pyruvate to a high-energy intermediate by the addition of coenzyme A. The Krebs cycle removes electrons and passes them to the electron transport chain by way of carrier molecules. Both of these processes take place in the mitochondrion. From start (glycolysis) to finish, the aerobic pathway typically has a net energy yield of 36 ATP molecules.

over those that did not. The biochemistry of contemporary organisms indicates that only those organisms capable of glycolysis survived the early competition of life on earth. Obviously, later evolutionary changes in catabolism built on this success. During this building process, glycolysis was not discarded but used as a stepping stone for the evolution of another process for the complete breakdown of glucose. Just as an artist adds successive layers

FIGURE 5.2

Glycolysis. In the reactions of glycolysis, glucose is rearranged, split into two three-carbon (3-C) intermediates, then rearranged further to yield two molecules of pyruvate. Along the way, four ATP and two NADH molecules are produced. However, since two ATPs are used in the initial steps of glycolysis, the net yield is only two ATP molecules.

of paint to obtain a final painting, so evolution added another layer of chemical reactions (aerobic respiration) onto the foundation layer (glycolysis) to produce an efficient method of harvesting energy. ③ Looking at glycolysis in another way, all forms of animal life (including humans) carry on glycolysis within their cells—a metabolic memory of an animal's evolutionary past.

Stop and Ask Yourself

1. What is the difference between aerobic and anaerobic respiration?
2. Where does glycolysis take place in a cell? Where does aerobic respiration take place?
3. What is the net energy yield in ATP molecules from glycolysis?
4. What is the evolutionary significance of glycolysis?

THE NATURE OF ELECTRON TRANSFERS

Much of the flow of energy through cells involves the transfer of electrons from one molecule to another. This electron transfer is called an **oxidation-reduction reaction,** or **redox reaction.** The molecule that gives up electrons is oxidized; thus, **oxidation** is the loss of electrons. The molecule that accepts electrons is reduced; thus, **reduction** is the gain of electrons. Oxidation-reduction reactions always occur together.

FERMENTATION: "LIFE WITHOUT OXYGEN"

Fermentation (L. *fermentum,* leaven) is either an evolutionary bypass that some organisms use to keep glycolysis functioning under anaerobic conditions or, more likely, a biochemical remnant that evolved very early in the history of life, when the earth's atmosphere contained little or no oxygen. As with glycolysis, the ubiquity of fermentation is strong evidence for the common descent of organisms from primitive cells in which glycolysis and fermentation first appeared and still persist.

In fermentation, the hydrogen atoms that glycolysis generates are donated to organic molecules as follows:

$$\text{Pyruvate} + \text{NADH} \rightarrow \text{reduced compound} + \text{NAD}^+$$

The reduced compound can be an organic acid in lactate fermentation (e.g., lactic acid) or an alcohol in alcoholic fermentation (e.g., ethanol; figure 5.3).

The important point to remember about fermentation is that glucose is not completely degraded, so considerable unusable energy still remains in the products. Beyond the two ATP molecules formed during glycolysis, no more ATP is produced. Fermentation serves only to regenerate NAD^+ (the oxidized form of NADH).

Two types of organisms can carry out fermentation: obligative anaerobic and facultative anaerobic ones. Obligative anaerobic organisms include certain types of bacteria that survive only in the complete absence of molecular oxygen. Facultative anaerobic organisms and tissues include certain bacteria, yeasts, and cells (e.g., animal muscle) that can ferment nutrients when oxygen is absent to generate some ATP by providing NAD^+ for glycolysis.

FIGURE 5.3

Fermentation. Fermentation regenerates NAD^+, which is needed to drive glycolysis to ultimately obtain ATP. The boxed hydrogens indicate the hydrogen ions donated by reduced NADH and where the donated hydrogen ions end up after fermentation is complete. (*a*) The pathway from pyruvate to ethanol is called alcoholic fermentation and is catalyzed by specific microbial enzymes. (*b*) The pathway from pyruvate to lactate (lactic acid). Certain animal cells, deprived of oxygen, temporarily carry out lactic acid fermentation.

FIGURE 5.4

The Electron Carrier Flavin Adenine Dinucleotide (FAD). The equation illustrates the oxidized form of FAD being reduced to $FADH_2$. The reactive sites are shaded, and the rest of the molecule is indicated by R.

FAD
Oxidized form

FADH$_2$
Reduced form

Facultative anaerobic organisms and tissues carry out more efficient energy harvesting when oxygen is present—hence, the term facultative (not obligative).

Stop and Ask Yourself

5. Why has glycolysis persisted through time, even though it is inefficient?
6. How is fermentation a link to the past?
7. How does fermentation occur?
8. What type of organism carries out fermentation?

AEROBIC RESPIRATION: THE MAJOR SOURCE OF ATP

As already noted, the anaerobic generation of ATP through glycolysis and fermentation is relatively inefficient. The end product of glycolysis (pyruvate) still contains a great deal of potential bond energy that can be harvested by further oxidation. The evolution of aerobic respiration in microorganisms and in the mitochondria of eukaryotic cells became possible only after free oxygen had accumulated in the earth's atmosphere as a result of photosynthesis. The addition of an oxygen-requiring stage to the energy-harvesting mechanisms provided cells with a more powerful and efficient way of extracting energy from nutrient molecules. Indeed, without mitochondria's large-scale ATP production, life would have to be at a "snail's pace," and most animals present on earth today would never have evolved.

In aerobic respiration, the pyruvate that glycolysis produces is shunted into a metabolic pathway called the Krebs cycle or **citric acid cycle;** the NADH goes to the electron transport chain. During this aerobic metabolism, free oxygen accepts electrons and reduces to H_2O as follows:

$$\text{Pyruvate} + O_2 \rightarrow CO_2 + H_2O + 34\text{ATP} + \text{heat energy}$$

During this reaction, 34 molecules of ATP are produced for each molecule of pyruvate consumed.

As in glycolysis, aerobic respiration is organized into a number of reactions, each catalyzed by a specific enzyme and organized into the **Krebs cycle** and the electron transport chain. The Krebs cycle, named after Hans Krebs (who began working out its details in the 1930s), is a series of reactions in which the pyruvate from glycolysis is oxidized to CO_2. Two electron carriers, nicotinamide adenine dinucleotide (NAD) (*see figure 4.8*) and **flavin adenine dinucleotide (FAD)** (figure 5.4), act as hydrogen acceptors and reduce to NADH and $FADH_2$. During this phase of the cycle, three molecules of CO_2 are generated from each pyruvate molecule, and some energy is harvested in the form of ATP (figure 5.5). Most of the remaining energy is in the form of NADH and $FADH_2$. These two molecules are shuttled into the **electron transport chain.** In this chain, the reduced NADH and $FADH_2$ are oxidized, and their electrons are passed along a series of oxidation-reduction reactions to the final acceptor, oxygen (figure 5.6).

As previously mentioned, in eukaryotic cells, aerobic respiration takes place in the mitochondria. The Krebs cycle occurs in the mitochondrial matrix (figure 5.7). The enzymes used to catalyze these reactions are dissolved in the fluid matrix. (In prokaryotic cells, the enzymes occur in the cytoplasm.) The proteins (cytochromes) that bring about the reactions of the electron transport chain are bound to the inner mitochondrial membrane, which is arranged in numerous folds called cristae (sing., crista). (In prokaryotes, cytochromes are bound to the plasma membrane.) Pyruvate, oxygen, ADP, and inorganic phosphate (P_i) continuously diffuse into the mitochondrial matrix. In turn, the end products of aerobic metabolism—ATP, CO_2, and H_2O—diffuse outward into the cytoplasm.

THE ENERGY SCORE FOR AEROBIC RESPIRATION: A BALANCE SHEET

The eukaryotic cell obtains a net gain of 36 ATP molecules from the breakdown of each glucose molecule (table 5.1). Glycolysis produces four ATP molecules, but two are used in the glycolytic reactions. The two molecules of NADH formed during glycolysis yield six ATP molecules, but two are used in the reactions that transport the NADH electrons across the inner mitochondrial membrane into the matrix to enter the Krebs cycle. One molecule of NADH is produced for each pyruvate that is converted to acetyl-coenzyme A, and one molecule of CO_2 is released as acetyl-coenzyme A enters the Krebs cycle. Two more ATP molecules are produced in the Krebs cycle, as well as six NADH and two $FADH_2$ molecules. The six NADH from the Krebs cycle and two NADH from the entry of acetyl-coenzyme A into the cycle yield 24 ATP molecules, and the oxidation of the two molecules of $FADH_2$ produced during the Krebs cycle yields four more molecules of ATP. The net gain from all of these reactions is 36 molecules of ATP. As

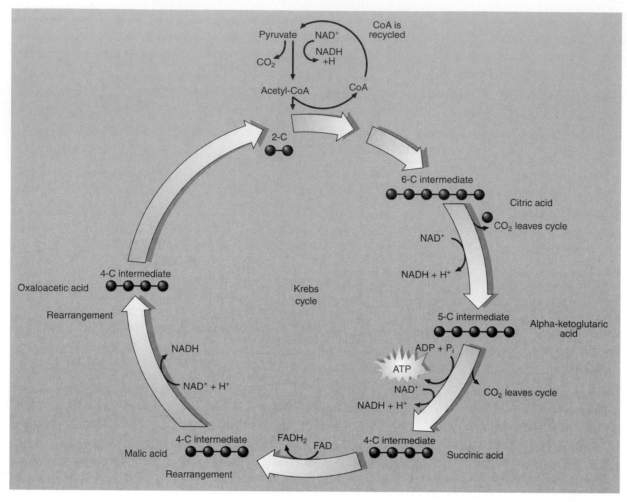

FIGURE 5.5

The Krebs Cycle. For each pyruvate molecule that enters the Krebs cycle by way of acetyl-CoA, two CO_2, one ATP, three NADH, and one $FADH_2$ molecules form. Each of these events occurs twice for each glucose molecule broken down into two molecules of pyruvate.

table 5.1 illustrates, the electron transport chain is more efficient than glycolysis at producing ATP for cell activities. Glycolysis, however, can produce ATP in anaerobic conditions, which the Krebs cycle and electron transport chain cannot.

METABOLISM OF FATS AND PROTEINS: ALTERNATIVE FOOD MOLECULES

Even though the catabolism of glucose is the most common metabolic pathway in cells, animals also consume fats and proteins, which may be used to harvest energy. Recall from chapter 2 that fats built from long-chain fatty acids and glycerol are triglycerides. The initial catabolism of a fat begins with the digestion of the triglycerides (by way of an enzyme called a lipase) to glycerol and three fatty acid molecules (figure 5.8). The glycerol is phosphorylated and can enter the glycolytic pathway at the level of glyceraldehyde 3-phosphate. The free fatty acids move into the mitochondrion, where their carbons are removed, two at a time, to form acetyl-coenzyme A plus additional NADH and $FADH_2$. The acetyl-

coenzyme A is then oxidized by the Krebs cycle, and the NADH and $FADH_2$ that are produced are oxidized via the electron transport chain. ④ Interestingly, 1 g of fat provides about 2.5 times more ATP energy than does either 1 g of carbohydrate or protein because the number of hydrogen atoms per unit weight of fat is greater than in carbohydrates or protein. This is why many animals store energy in the form of fat in adipose tissue (*see figure 3.24f*).

Animals initially digest proteins to yield individual amino acids. Some of these are distributed throughout the body and used to synthesize new proteins. Other amino acids are transported in the blood or extracellular fluid and comprise the amino acid pool. If needed for fuel, these amino acids can be further degraded by removal of the amine group to yield ammonia. This process is called a **deamination reaction:**

$$R-\overset{\displaystyle |}{\underset{\displaystyle NH_2}{CH}}-COOH + H_2O \longrightarrow R-\overset{\displaystyle O}{\overset{\displaystyle \|}{C}}-COOH + NH_3 + H_2$$

Amino acid Water Keto acid Ammonia Hydrogen

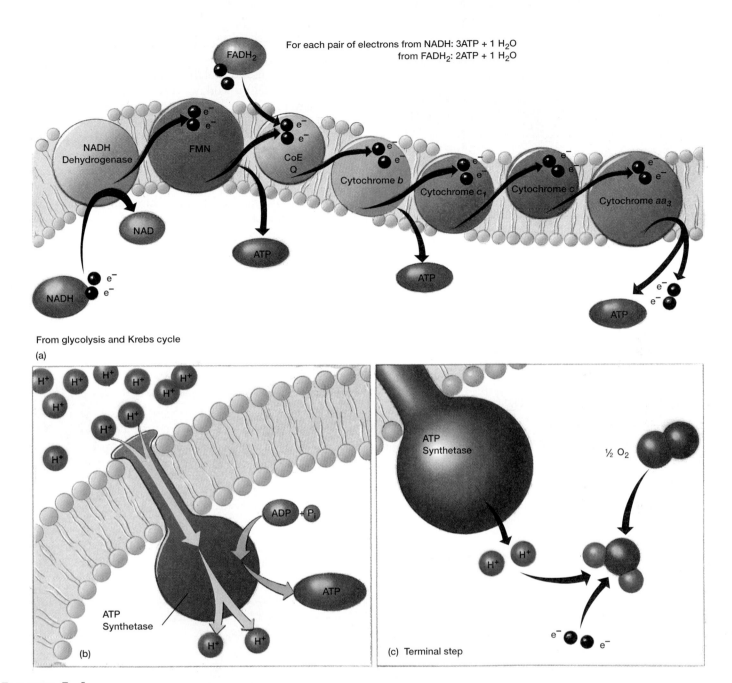

For each pair of electrons from NADH: 3ATP + 1 H_2O
from FADH₂: 2ATP + 1 H_2O

FIGURE 5.6

Electron Transport Chain and Oxidative Phosphorylation. (a) Electrons from NADH and FADH₂ generated in glycolysis and the Krebs cycle are passed along electron-carrier molecules (colored circles) in the electron transport chain by way of oxidation-reduction reactions. (b) The energy released along the way is captured in the high-energy phosphate bonds of ATP by way of oxidative phosphorylation. (c) When the electrons reach the end of the chain, an oxygen molecule accepts the electrons and combines with hydrogen to generate a water molecule.

In deamination, an oxygen atom replaces an amine group to form a keto acid. The keto acid can then be funneled into the Krebs cycle (figure 5.8). Eventually, the carbon skeleton of the amino acid is dismantled and oxidized to CO_2. On the average, 1 g of protein yields about the same amount of energy (about 4 kcal) as does 1 g of glucose. The ammonia produced from the complete catabolism of an amino acid is highly toxic and must be excreted. Chapter 38 discusses the various ways in which different animals rid their bodies of toxic wastes.

CONTROL OF METABOLISM

Cells are very efficient. They do not waste energy by making more of a substance than they need. For example, if a certain amino acid is overabundant in the amino acid pool, the anabolic pathway that synthesizes that amino acid from an intermediate in the Krebs cycle is turned off. The most common mechanism for this control uses **end-product (feedback) inhibition.** In end-product inhibition, the end product of the

FIGURE 5.7

Mitochondrial Architecture. Reactions of the Krebs cycle occur in the mitochondrial matrix. Molecular complexes that are an integral part of the inner membrane carry out the reactions in the electron transport chain.

anabolic pathway inhibits the enzyme that catalyzes a key step in the pathway.

Cells can also control their catabolism. For example, if a cell (e.g., a muscle cell) is working very hard and its ATP concentration begins to decrease, aerobic respiration increases. When ATP is sufficient to meet demand, aerobic respiration slows, sparing valuable organic molecules for other necessary functions. ⑤ As with anabolism, control is based on regulating enzyme activity at strategic points in the catabolic pathway. As a result, cells are thrifty, expedient, and responsive in their metabolism.

One of the main controlling points in aerobic respiration is the enzyme phosphofructokinase. By controlling how fast or slow this single enzyme functions, a cell can either speed or slow the entire metabolic process. Phosphofructokinase is an enzyme with receptor sites for specific inhibitors and activators. ATP inhibits it, and either ADP or AMP stimulates it. Phosphofructokinase is sensitive to the energy needs of the cell and the ratio of ATP to ADP or AMP (figure 5.9). If ATP begins to accumulate, this enzyme shuts down glycolysis. If ADP or AMP begins to accumulate,

FIGURE 5.8

Catabolism of Various Food Molecules. While only certain molecules can feed directly into the Krebs cycle (e.g., acetyl-CoA), proteins, carbohydrates, and fats can also be broken down into constituent parts and used as fuel for respiration. The dashed arrows indicate that the system also works in anabolic (synthetic) reactions.

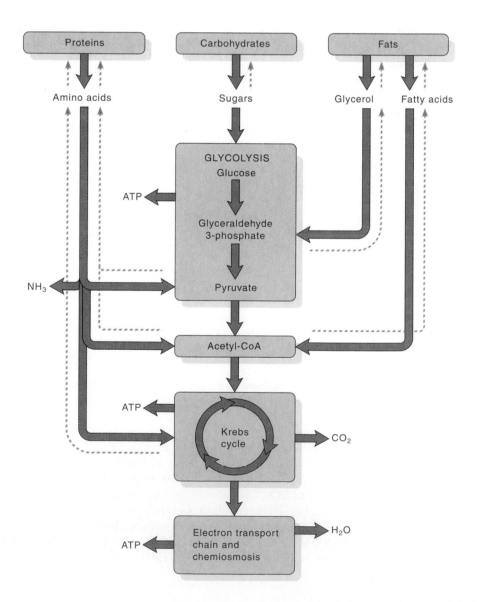

TABLE 5.1	APPROXIMATE ATP YIELD FROM THE COMPLETE AEROBIC OXIDATION OF ONE MOLECULE OF GLUCOSE		
PROCESS	ATP PRODUCED	NADH, FADH$_2$ PRODUCED	ATP USED
Glycolysis	4 ATP	2 NADH	−2 ATP
Entrance of NADH to Krebs cycle		2 NADH	−2 ATP
Krebs cycle	2 ATP	6 NADH, 2 FADH$_2$	
Electron transport chain:			
3 ATP for each of 2 NADH generated via glycolysis	6 ATP		
3 ATP for each of 8 NADH generated via Krebs cycle and entrance to the cycle	24 ATP		
2 ATP for each of 2 FADH$_2$ generated via Krebs cycle	4 ATP		
Total	40 ATP		−4 ATP
Net ATP	36 ATP		

FIGURE 5.9

Control of Cellular Respiration. The enzyme phosphofructokinase responds to activators and inhibitors to regulate the rate of glycolysis and the Krebs cycle. ADP and AMP stimulate the enzyme, but ATP and citric acid inhibit it.

phosphofructokinase becomes active and turns on the glycolytic pathway. Citric acid in the cytoplasm also inhibits phosphofructokinase. This control pathway helps synchronize the rates of glycolysis and the Krebs cycle. For example, when citric acid begins to accumulate, glycolysis slows down, reducing the supply of acetyl-coenzyme A to the Krebs cycle. Conversely, if citric acid consumption increases, glycolysis accelerates and meets the needed demand for more acetyl-coenzyme A.

THE METABOLIC POOL

The degradative chemical reactions (catabolism) of glycolysis and the Krebs cycle do more than just harvest energy for ATP production in animals. They also constitute a metabolic pool that supplies materials for synthesis (anabolism) of many important cellular components (*see figure 5.8*). Overall, the balance between catabolism and anabolism is what maintains homeostasis in the cell and, in turn, the whole animal. For example, gly-

colysis and the Krebs cycle are open systems. An open system has a two-way flow of materials into and out of it. Various compounds enter the pathways at different points so that carbohydrates, fats, and proteins can all be oxidized. At the same time, some of the intermediates of these pathways can be withdrawn from the energy-harvesting machinery and used in synthesis reactions. Thus, the products of glycolysis and the Krebs cycle are all part of a metabolic pool whereby materials are either added or withdrawn.

Stop and Ask Yourself

9. How many ATP molecules are produced during complete aerobic metabolism of one molecule of glucose?

10. How does the flow of electrons generate ATP molecules?

11. How do fats serve as an alternative food molecule?

12. What is end-product (feedback) inhibition?

ENDANGERED SPECIES

WILDLIFE ALERT 3—THE KARNER BLUE BUTTERFLY (*Lycaeides melissa samuelis*)

VITAL STATISTICS

Classification: Phylum Arthropoda, class Hexapoda, order Lepidoptera

Range: New England to the Great Lakes Region (historical), Western Great Lakes Region (current)

Habitat: Sand plains, oak savannas, or pine barrens in association with wild lupine

Number remaining: Less than 1% of its population in 1900

Status: Endangered

NATURAL HISTORY AND ECOLOGICAL STATUS

The male Karner blue butterfly is silvery or dark blue with a narrow black margin on the upper surface of the wing (figure 1). The female has grayish brown wings with a dark border and orange bands.

The Karner blue butterfly lives in sand plains, oak savannas, or pine barrens. These habitats are patchily distributed across the northeastern and midwestern parts of the United States (figure 2). They consist of grassland areas with scattered trees and are maintained in their natural state by periodic disturbances from fire. Without fire disturbance, shrub and tree vegetation soon overruns these habitats. These grassy islands are the home of a plant called wild lupine (*Lupinus perennis*), which is the sole food source for caterpillars of the Karner blue butterfly.

FIGURE 1   Male Karner Blue Butterfly (*Lycaeides melissa samuelis*).

FIGURE 2   Approximate Distribution of Karner Blue Butterfly (*Lycaeides melissa samuelis*).

In the spring, Karner blue eggs, which have overwintered, hatch, and the larvae feed on wild lupine. By the end of May, the larvae have grown and pupate. Adults emerge and mate, and the females lay eggs on or near wild lupine. Eggs quickly hatch, and the larvae feed, grow, and pupate. By the end of July, the second generation of adults emerges and mates. This generation of females lays eggs among the plant litter near wild lupine. These eggs remain dormant until the following April. After August, no adults or larvae of the Karner blue butterfly are found.

The endangered status of the Karner blue butterfly is a result of habitat loss. As humans develop land, they quickly bring fires under control. Fire control allows a wild lupine habitat to overgrow with shrubs and trees, making it no longer suitable for wild lupine or the Karner blue butterfly. Habitat loss is devastating for a species, especially if habitat distribution is patchy. Patchy distribution does not provide corridors for movement and dispersal to new areas. When a patch of habitat is lost, the species present in that patch usually have no place to go. Even when patches of habitat are not entirely lost, but simply broken up by human development, dispersal within the habitat may be nearly impossible. The construction of roads, buildings, and off-road vehicle trails presents formidable obstacles for a species as fragile and specialized as the Karner blue butterfly.

This example vividly illustrates an organism's dependence on habitat preservation. The struggle of the Karner blue butterfly is a subtle reminder that something is wrong in our treatment of the land. Protecting pine barrens and oak savannas will improve the chances for survival of wild lupine, the Karner blue butterfly, and other species specialized for life in these fragile habitats.

SUMMARY

1. During glycolysis, glucose breaks down anaerobically to yield two molecules of pyruvate, which are processed further in aerobic respiration. Glycolysis harvests chemical energy by rearranging the chemical bonds of glucose to form two pyruvate molecules and two molecules of ATP.

2. Organisms living in anaerobic environments require a mechanism to dispose of the hydrogen and associated electrons produced in glycolysis. The electrons can be donated to a number of other compounds in a process called fermentation.

3. Each pyruvate molecule formed during glycolysis loses a carbon dioxide molecule and combines with coenzyme A to form acetyl-coenzyme A. Coenzyme A transfers the acetyl group to the Krebs cycle. During one turn of the cycle, the equivalents of the acetyl group's two carbons are removed in the form of carbon dioxide. Some ATP is also produced. During the process, NAD^+ and FAD accept electrons and become NADH and $FADH_2$. They carry these electrons to the electron transport chain.

4. The electron transport chain produces most of the energy harvested during aerobic respiration. The oxidation of one molecule of glucose results in the net production of 36 ATP molecules.

5. Many other metabolic pathways feed into glycolysis and the Krebs cycle from the metabolic pool, enabling cells to use many organic compounds in addition to glucose as food sources to generate usable energy to perform biological work.

6. End-product inhibition helps regulate metabolism and maintain homeostasis within organisms.

SELECTED KEY TERMS

aerobic (p. 70)
anaerobic (p. 70)
deamination reaction (p. 74)
electron transport chain (p. 73)
end-product (feedback)
  inhibition (p. 75)

fermentation (p. 72)
flavin adenine dinucleotide
  (FAD) (p. 73)
glycolysis (p. 70)

CRITICAL THINKING QUESTIONS

1. The aerobic metabolism of glucose generates exactly the same chemical end products and the same amount of energy as when glucose is burned. However, when a cell "burns" glucose, it does so in many small steps. Why has evolution divided glucose catabolism into so many small steps?

2. In anaerobic catabolism of glucose, further conversions of pyruvate to lactate do not yield any more usable energy. What, then, is the advantage of these conversions?

3. Why is anaerobic respiration wasteful and potentially harmful to an animal?

4. Diverse organisms, such as dogs and yeasts, have certain enzymes in common and even share similar metabolic pathways. What are the implications of these similarities in terms of evolution?

5. When an animal cell contains more than enough ATP to carry out its functions, the excess ATP signals a slowing down of the respiratory chain by decreasing the production of acetyl-coenzyme A. When ATP levels fall below what is required for cellular functions, the increased ADP signals increased breakdown of glucose. What general metabolic phenomenon do these relationships demonstrate?

REFERENCES ON THE WORLD WIDE WEB

1. **Design-It-Yourself Glycolysis.** This site covers the different steps in glycolysis.
    http://bmbwww.leeds.ac.uk/designs/diygly/home.htm

2. **Carbohydrate Metabolism: The Energetics of Carbohydrate Metabolism.** A brief discussion of the energetics of carbohydrate metabolism, as well as information on endergonic and exergonic reactions, hydrolysis, and ATP formation in cells, is presented at this site.
    http:wizard.pharm.wayne.edu/biochem/energy.html

3. **Carbohydrate Metabolism: Introductory Metabolism Module.** This site presents an introduction to carbohydrate metabolism.
    http://www.prm.unisa.edu.au/h&p2carb.htm

4. **Metabolism: Introduction.** This site provides information on the metabolism of cells.
    http://medtstgo.ucdavis,edu/endo/lecture/metintro.htm

5. **Glycolysis.** This site provides a brief outline of the reactions involved in glycolysis.
    http://www.prim.unisa.edu.au/h&p2carb.htm#glycolysis

6. **Anaerobic Glycolysis.** The conditions by which anaerobic glycolysis occurs are discussed at this site.
    http://www.prim.unisa.edu.au/h&p2carb.htm#gly_anaer

7. **Aerobic Metabolism of Glucose.** This site discusses the aerobic metabolism of glucose.
    http://www.prim.unisa.edu.au/h&p2carb.htm#glyc_

8. **Citric Acid Cycle and Electron Transport Chain.** An introduction to the citric acid cycle and the electron transport chain is presented at this site.
    http://www.prim.unisa.edu.au/h&p2cac.htm#intro

9. **Protein Metabolism.** This site presents an introduction to protein metabolism.
    http://www.prm.unisa.edu.au/h&p2ptn.htm#intro

10. **Fatty Acid Oxidation: Alternative Oxidation Pathways.** This site offers a discussion of the alternative oxidation pathway.
    http://web.indstate.edu/thcme/mwking/fatox.html#alternative

SUGGESTED READINGS

BOOKS

Alberts, B., Bray, D., Lewis, J., Raff, M., Roberts, K., and Watson, J. 1994. *Molecular Biology of the Cell*. 3d ed. New York: Garland.

Atkins, P. 1984. *The Second Law*. New York: W. H. Freeman.

Atkins, P. W. 1987. *Molecules*. New York: W. H. Freeman.

Avers, C. J. 1986. *Molecular Cell Biology*. Reading, Mass.: Addison-Wesley.

Baker, J. J. W., and Allen, G. E. 1981. *Matter, Energy, and Life*. 4th ed. Reading, Mass.: Addison-Wesley.

Becker, W. M. 1977. *Energy and the Living Cell: An Introduction to Bioenergetics*. New York: Harper & Row.

Becker, W., Reece, J., and Poenie, M. 1996. *The World of the Cell*. Menlo Park, Calif.: Benjamin Cummings.

Blum, H. F. 1962. *Time's Arrow and Evolution*. New York: Harper & Row.

Brown, L. R., Durning, A., Flavin, C., Heise, L., Jacobson, J., Postel, S., Renner, M., Shea, C. P., and Starke, L. 1989. *State of the World*. New York: W. W. Norton.

Calvin, M., and Pryor, W. A. 1973. *Organic Chemistry of Life: Readings from Scientific American*. New York: W. H. Freeman.

Carson, R. 1962. *Silent Spring*. Burlington: Houghton Mifflin.

Cristensen, H. N., and Cellarius, R. A. 1972. *Introduction to Bioenergetics: Thermodynamics for the Biologist*. Philadelphia: W. B. Saunders.

Danpier, W. C. 1966. *A History of Science and Its Relation to Philosophy and Religion*. New York: Cambridge University Press.

DeDuve, C. 1986. *A Guided Tour of the Living Cell*, vols. 1 and 2. New York: Scientific American Books.

Fersht, A. 1985. *Enzyme Structure and Mechanism*. 2d ed. New York: W. H. Freeman.

Gould, S.J. 1980. *The Panda's Thumb: More Reflections in Natural History*. New York: W. W. Norton.

Henderson, L. S. 1958. *The Fitness of the Environment*. Boston: Beacon Press.

Kuhn, T. S. 1970. *Structure of Scientific Revolutions*. Chicago: University of Chicago Press.

Lehninger, A. L. et al. 1993. *Principles of Biochemistry*. New York: Worth.

Lodish, H., Baltimore, D., Berk, A., Zipursky, S., Matsudaira, P., and Darnell, J. 1995. *Molecular Cell Biology*. 3d. ed. New York: Scientific American Books.

Moore, J. 1993. *Science As a Way of Knowing: The Foundation of Modern Biology*. Cambridge, Mass.: Harvard University Press.

Rodella, T. D. et al. 1989. *Through the Molecular Maze*. Los Altos, Calif.: W. Kaufmann Press.

Sayre, A. 1975. *Rosalind Franklin and DNA*. New York: W. W. Norton.

Schrodinger, E. 1967. *What Is Life?* and *Mind and Matter*. New York: Cambridge University Press.

Stryer, L. 1988. *Biochemistry*. 3d ed. New York: W. H. Freeman.

Thomas, L. 1974. *The Lives of a Cell*. New York: Viking Press.

U.S. Government Printing Office. 1983. *The Global 2000 Report to the President: Entering the Twenty-First Century, vols. 1–3*. Washington, D.C.: U.S. Government Printing Office.

Watson, J. D. 1968. *The Double Helix*. New York: Signet Books.

Wolfe, S. 1995. *Introduction to Molecular and Cellular Biology*. Belmont, Calif.: Wadsworth.

ARTICLES

Armbruster, P., and Munzenberg, G. 1989. Creating superheavy elements. *Scientific American*, May.

Bingham, R. 1982. On the life of Mr. Darwin. *Science '82* 3(3): 82.

Bretscher, M. S. 1985. The molecules of the cell membrane. *Scientific American*, October.

Bretscher, M. S. 1987. How animal cells move. *Scientific American*, December.

Capaldi, R. A. 1974. A dynamic model of cell membranes. *Scientific American*, March.

DeDuve, C. 1996. The birth of complex cells. *Scientific American*, April.

DeDuve, C. 1983. Microbodies in the living cell. *Scientific American*, May.

Diamond, J. 1991. The search for life on earth. *Natural History*, April.

Dickerson, E. 1980. Cytochrome *c* and the evolution of energy metabolism. *Scientific American*, March.

Doolittle, R. 1985. Proteins. *Scientific American*, October.

Eiseley, L. C. 1956. Charles Darwin. *Scientific American*, February.

———. 1959. Alfred Russel Wallace. *Scientific American*, February.

Feldman, G., and Steinberger, G. 1991. The number of families of matter. *Scientific American*, February.

Frieden, E. 1972. The chemical elements of life. *Scientific American*, July.

Glover, D. 1993. The centrosome. *Scientific American*, June.

Gould, S. J. 1980. Wallace's fatal flaw. *Natural History* 89: 26.

Greider, C., and Blackburn, E. 1996. Telomeres, telomerase and cancer. *Scientific American*, February.

Hinkle, P. C., and McCarthy, R. E. 1978. How cells make ATP. *Scientific American*, March.

Jacobson, K., Sheets, E., and Sinson, R. 1995. Revisiting the fluid-mosaic model of membranes. *Scientific American*, June.

Karplus, M., and McCammon, A. 1986. The dynamics of proteins. *Scientific American*, April.

Koshland, D. E. 1973. Protein shape and biological control. *Scientific American*, October.

Kraut, J. 1988. How do enzymes work? *Science* 242: 533–39.

Krebs, H. A. 1970. The history of the tricarboxylic acid cycle. *Perspectives in Biology and Medicine* 14: 154–70.

Leninger, A. L. 1961. How cells transform energy. *Scientific American*, September.

Levine, M. H., Stammers, D., and Stuart, D. 1978. Structure of pyruvate kinase and similarities with other enzymes: Possible implications for protein taxonomy and evolution. *Nature* 271: 626–30.

Luria, S. E. 1975. Colicins and the energetics of cell membranes. *Scientific American*, December.

McCarty, R. E. 1980. H-ATPase in oxidative and photosynthetic phosphorylation. *BioScience* 35: 27–30.

McPherson, A. 1989. Macromolecular crystals. *Scientific American*, March.

Mitchell, P. 1979. Klein's respiratory chain concept and its chemiosmotic consequences. *Science* 206: 1148–59.

Nauenberg, M., Stroud, C., and Yeazell, J. 1994. The classical limit of an atom. *Scientific American*, June.

Paabo, Svante. 1993. Ancient DNA. *Scientific American*, November.

Phillips, D. C. 1966. The three-dimensional structure of an enzyme molecule. *Scientific American*, November.

Porter, K., and Tucker, J. 1981. The ground substance of the living cell. *Scientific American*, March.

Racker, E. 1980. From Pasteur to Mitchell, a hundred years of bioenergetics. *Federation Proceedings* 39: 210–15.

Rebek, J. 1994. Synthetic self-replicating molecules. *Scientific American*, July.

Richards, F. 1991. The protein folding problem. *Scientific American*, January.

Rothman, J. E. 1985. The compartmental organization of the Golgi apparatus. *Scientific American*, September.

Rothman, J., and Orci, L. 1996. Budding vesicles in living cells. *Scientific American*, March.

Satir, B. 1975. The final steps in secretion. *Scientific American*, October.

———. 1974. How cilia move. *Scientific American*, October.

Schulman, R. G. 1983. NMR spectroscopy of living cells. *Scientific American*, January.

Sharon, N. 1980. Carbohydrates. *Scientific American*, November.

———. 1974 Glycoproteins. *Scientific American*, May.

Singer, S. J., and Nicolson, G. 1972. The fluid-mosaic model of the structure of cell membranes. *Science* 175: 720–31.

Slayman, C. 1985. Proton chemistry and the ubiquity of proton pumps. *BioScience* 35: 16–17.

Staehelin, L. A., and Hull, B. E. 1978. Junctions between living cells. *Scientific American*, May.

Staff writers. 1991. The 23rd environmental quality index. *National Wildlife* 29(2): 33–40.

Stossel, T. 1994. The machinery of cell crawling. *Scientific American*, September.

Todorov, I. 1990. How cells maintain stability. *Scientific American*, December.

Upton, A. C. 1982. The biological affects of low-level ionizing radiation. *Scientific American*, February.

Weber, K., and Osborn, M. 1985. The molecules of the cell matrix. *Scientific American*, October.

Weinberg, C., and Williams, R. 1990. Energy from the sun. *Scientific American*, September.

Weinberg, R. A. 1985. The molecules of life. *Scientific American*, October.

Welch, W. 1993. How cells respond to stress. *Scientific American*, May.

Zewail, A. 1990. The birth of molecules. *Scientific American*, December.

part TWO

THE CONTINUITY OF ANIMAL LIFE

The ability to reproduce is a fundamental property of living organisms. All organisms age and eventually die. For the species, however, reproduction provides a means of potentially increasing the size of a population and results

in continual replacement of aging individuals with young, vigorous ones. In addition, sexual reproduction produces individuals with new genetic combinations, which increases genetic diversity and makes long-term survival of the species more likely. Sexual reproduction also leads to individual variation—and variation is the foundation of evolution.

Reproductive processes involve specific activities of individual cells. In unicellular organisms (protists), one individual divides to produce two individuals. Most animals produce individual reproductive cells, such as eggs and sperm. Specific genetic mechanisms transmit characteristics from one generation to the next. Each offspring has a new set of genes that is somewhat different from each of the parent's.

An animal's genetic makeup is expressed through developmental processes and continues throughout life in the form of growth, maturation, and aging. Developmental processes are also involved in the continual replacement of body cells, in healing of injuries, and in specific responses to infection and disease. However, developmental processes gone awry, such as in abnormal growth, can be life threatening.

Chapters 6 through 10 present the cell division mechanisms involved in animal reproduction and development, and the means by which genetic information is transmitted and expressed.

chapter 6

CELL DIVISION

Concepts

1. The cell cycle consists of four phases: G_1, a period of normal metabolism; S, the phase of DNA replication; G_2, a brief period of structural preparation; and mitosis (nuclear division) and cytokinesis (cytoplasmic division). G_1, S, and G_2 are referred to as interphase, and mitosis and cytokinesis are known as the mitotic phase (M).

2. Mitosis ensures an orderly and accurate distribution of chromosomes during the cell cycle and is divided into four phases: prophase, metaphase, anaphase, and telophase. Cytokinesis often begins during late anaphase or early telophase, and soon after mitosis ends, two daughter cells are evident.

3. Meiosis is a special type of cell division that reduces the chromosome number by half. Meiosis allows for the random distribution of one member of each pair of parental chromosomes to the offspring.

4. Gamete formation involves meiosis and the formation of specialized reproductive cells called sperm and eggs.

Would You Like to Know . . .

1 why in cell division, DNA untwists, unzips, rezips, and retwists? (p. 85)

2 the length of a DNA molecule in a human cell? (p. 86)

3 how cell division is related to a motion picture? (p. 87)

4 what is happening to a cell that makes it look like someone tied a cord around it and pulled the rope tight? (p. 89)

This chapter answers these and other useful questions.

This chapter contains evolutionary concepts, which are set off in this font.

Reproduction is essential to life. Each organism exists solely because its ancestors succeeded in producing progeny that could themselves develop, survive, and reach reproductive age. Reproduction at the level of the organism ranges from the simplest fission of unicellular organisms (asexual reproduction) to the complicated processes involved in the sexual reproduction of higher animals. At the molecular level, reproduction involves the cell's unique capacity to manipulate large amounts of DNA and DNA's ability to replicate itself.

The cellular capacity to manipulate large amounts of DNA (the information-carrying molecule) emerged more than a billion years ago among the ancestors of modern-day eukaryotes. This capacity was based on two occurrences: (1) the "packaging" of DNA and its associated proteins into compact structures called chromosomes, and (2) the development of an apparatus that could move the chromosomes. Eukaryotic cell division evolved as a result of these two developments.

One of the most intriguing activities of a cell is its ability to reproduce itself by cell division. In some cases, an entire new organism is reproduced, as when the unicellular protozoan called *Amoeba proteus* divides to form duplicate offspring. In other cases, cell division enables a multicellular organism, such as yourself, to grow and develop from a single cell. In fact, even after you are fully grown, cell division continues to function in renewal and repair to maintain homeostasis.

DNA controls cell division. What is most remarkable about this control is the faithfulness with which genetic programs pass from one generation to the next. A cell preparing to undergo cell division first copies all of its genes and then allocates them equally to its two daughter cells. The key to biological inheritance—the bridge to the next generation—is in this division process.

MITOSIS, CYTOKINESIS, AND THE CELL CYCLE: AN OVERVIEW

Cell division occurs in all animals. Cells divide in two basic stages: **Mitosis** is division of the nucleus, and **cytokinesis** (Gr. *kytos*, hollow vessel + *kinesis*, motion) is division of the cytoplasm. However, cell division is just one phase in the life history of a cell. Between divisions (interphase), the cell must grow and carry out its various metabolic processes. The **cell cycle** is that period from the time a cell is produced until it completes mitosis (figure 6.1).

The cell cycle is a dynamic process with four consecutive phases that can be expressed as follows:

$$G_1 \rightarrow S \rightarrow G_2 \rightarrow M$$

The G_1 (first growth or gap) phase represents the early growth phase of the cell. In many organisms, this phase occupies the major portion of the cell's life span. During the S (DNA synthesis) phase, growth continues, but this phase also involves DNA replication, whereby the cell synthesizes a replica of the **genome** (the total genetic constitution of an organism). The G_2 (second growth or gap) phase prepares the cell for genomic separation. It includes replication of the mitochondria and other organelles,

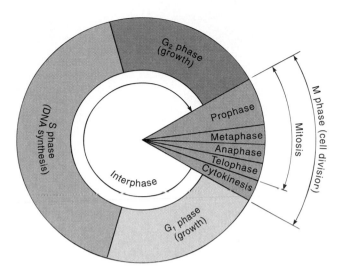

FIGURE 6.1

Life Cycle of a Eukaryotic Cell. During the G_1 phase, cell components are synthesized and metabolism occurs, often resulting in cell growth. During the S (synthesis) phase, the chromosomes replicate, resulting in two identical copies called sister chromatids. During the G_2 phase, metabolism and growth continue until the mitotic phase is reached. This drawing is generalized, and the length of different stages varies greatly from one cell to the next. *Source: Stuart Ira Fox,* Human Physiology, *4th ed., copyright © 1993 Wm. C. Brown Communications, Inc., Dubuque, Iowa.*

synthesis of microtubules and protein that will make up the mitotic spindle fibers, and chromosome condensation. The M (mitotic) phase is characterized by assembly of the microtubules, their binding to the chromosomes, separation of the replicated chromosomes, reformation of nuclear membranes in daughter cells, and cytokinesis. Cytokinesis usually begins late in mitosis, when the cytoplasm of the cell divides to create two daughter cells.

INTERPHASE: REPLICATING THE HEREDITARY MATERIAL

Often erroneously described as a resting period between cell divisions, **interphase** (L. *inter*, between) (includes the G_1, S, and G_2 phases) is actually a period of great metabolic activity that typically occupies about 90% of the total cell cycle. It is the period during which the normal activities of the cell take place. Interphase also sets the stage for cell division because DNA replication is completed during the S phase of interphase.

Before a cell divides, the DNA in its nucleus must produce an exact copy of itself. This process is called replication because the double-stranded DNA makes a replica, or duplicate, of itself. Replication is essential to ensure that each daughter cell receives the same genetic material as is present in the parent cell.

Replication begins with the strands of DNA untwisting (figure 6.2). A DNA helicase enzyme breaks the weak hydrogen bonds joining the purine and pyrimidine bases, and the DNA molecule begins to "unzip" itself. As soon as new bonds form, the untwisted strands begin to twist again.   ① Apparently, the

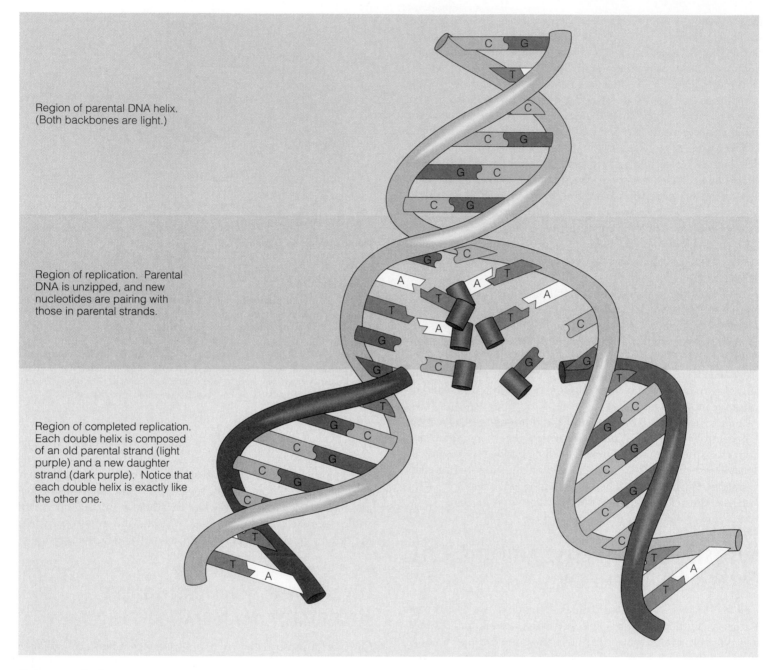

Region of parental DNA helix.
(Both backbones are light.)

Region of replication. Parental
DNA is unzipped, and new
nucleotides are pairing with
those in parental strands.

Region of completed replication.
Each double helix is composed
of an old parental strand (light
purple) and a new daughter
strand (dark purple). Notice that
each double helix is exactly like
the other one.

FIGURE 6.2

DNA Replication. When a DNA strand replicates, a group of enzymes separate the strands, and previously unattached nucleotides (that have accumulated in the nucleus) diffuse and pair up with appropriate bases. Another enzyme links the new bases to form new strands identical to the parental DNA molecule. In each new double helix, one strand is conserved from the parent, and one is formed anew.

untwisting, unzipping, rezipping, and retwisting occur sequentially and ensure that each newly formed double helix is exactly like the other one. The final result is a pair of **sister chromatids** (figure 6.3). A **chromatid** is a copy of a chromosome produced by replication. Each chromatid attaches to its other copy, or sister, at a point of constriction called a centromere. The **centromere** is a specific DNA sequence of about 220 nucleotides and has a specific location on any given chromosome. Bound to each centromere is a

disk of protein called a **kinetochore,** which eventually is an attachment site for the microtubules of the mitotic spindle.

After replication, the chromosomes are fully extended. ❷ For example, the total length of the DNA strands in the nucleus of a human cell is greater than the length of the entire human body, but the strands are too thin to be seen with the light microscope. As the cell cycle moves into the G_2 phase, however, the chromosomes begin condensation. During condensation, each

FIGURE 6.3

Duplicated Chromosomes. Each parental chromosome replicates to make two genetically identical sister chromatids attached at a region called the centromere.

sister chromatid becomes coiled and supercoiled into a very tightly compacted structure, which can now be seen with the light microscope and is called a chromosome. During the G₂ phase, the cell also begins to assemble the structures that it will later use to move the chromosomes to opposite poles (ends) of the cell. For example, centrioles replicate, and there is extensive synthesis of alpha and beta tubulins, which are the proteins that make up the microtubules *(see figure 3.20)*.

PHASES OF MITOSIS

Mitosis is divided into four phases: prophase, metaphase, anaphase, and telophase. ❸ In a dividing cell, however, the process is actually continuous, with each phase smoothly flowing into the next phase. There are no start and stop positions; the phases make up a continuum (figure 6.4). If you were to watch a film on mitosis, you would see that each drawing in figure 6.4 is merely a single frame of a continuous, changing drama.

PROPHASE: FORMATION OF THE MITOTIC SPINDLE

The first phase of mitosis, **prophase** (Gr. *pro*, before + phase), begins when chromosomes become visible with the light microscope as threadlike structures. (The term mitosis refers to this emergence; it comes from the Greek, *mitos*, which means thread.) By the beginning of prophase, the chromatids are well folded; the nucleoli and nuclear envelope begin to break up, and their components are resorbed into the endoplasmic reticulum (figure 6.5a). The spindle microtubules assemble between the separating centrioles, and the two centriole pairs move apart.

By the end of prophase, the centriole pairs are at opposite poles of the cell. Their position at the poles determines the direction in which the cell divides. The centrioles also radiate an array of microtubules called **asters** (L. *aster*, little star), which brace each centriole against the plasma membrane, mechanically stiffening the point of microtubular attachment. Between the centrioles, the microtubules form a spindle of fibers that extends from pole to pole. The asters, spindle, centrioles, and microtubules are collectively called the **mitotic spindle** (or mitotic apparatus).

As prophase continues, a second group of microtubules grows out from the kinetochore to the poles of the cell. These

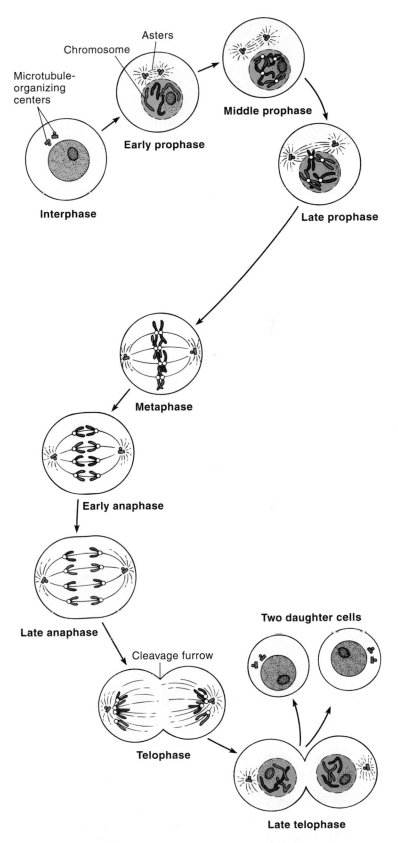

FIGURE 6.4

Continuum of Mitosis and Cytokinesis. Mitosis is a continuous process during which the nuclear parts of a cell divide into two equal portions.

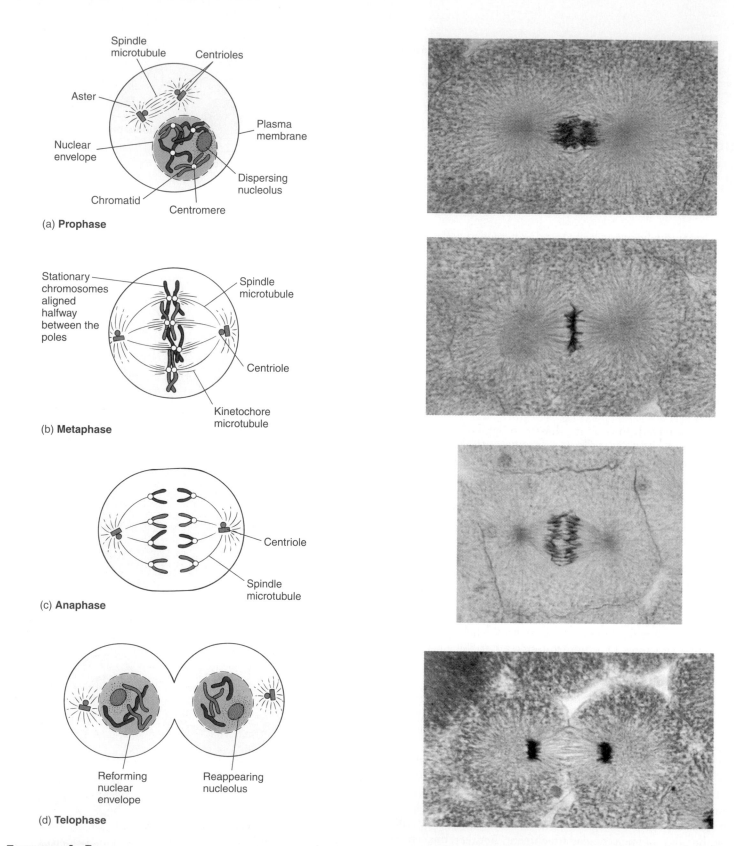

(a) **Prophase**

Spindle microtubule
Centrioles
Aster
Plasma membrane
Nuclear envelope
Dispersing nucleolus
Chromatid
Centromere

(b) **Metaphase**

Stationary chromosomes aligned halfway between the poles
Spindle microtubule
Centriole
Kinetochore microtubule

(c) **Anaphase**

Centriole
Spindle microtubule

(d) **Telophase**

Reforming nuclear envelope
Reappearing nucleolus

FIGURE 6.5

Stages of Mitosis. (*a*) During prophase, the nucleoli disappear, and the sister chromatids fold into discrete chromosomes. In the cytoplasm, the centrioles move apart, and the mitotic spindle begins to form. (*b*) At metaphase, the centriole pairs are now at opposite poles of the cell. The chromatids (replicated chromosomes) line up in the center of the cell, arranged so that their centromeres all lie in one plane. (*c*) Anaphase begins when the shortening of the mitotic spindles pulls the chromatids apart. (*d*) At telophase, daughter nuclei begin to form at the two poles of the cell, where the chromosomes have gathered. (Light photomicrographs at right are whitefish mitosis at ×315.)

kinetochore microtubules connect each sister chromatid to the poles of the spindle.

METAPHASE: ALIGNMENT OF CHROMOSOMES

As the dividing cell moves into **metaphase** (Gr. *meta*, after + phase), the chromatids (replicated chromosomes) begin to align in the center of the cell, along the spindle equator (figure 6.5*b*). With the help of the microtubules attached to the individual kinetochores, the chromatids form a neat array in the center of the cell, with each centromere equidistant from each pole of the cell.

Toward the end of metaphase, the centromeres divide and detach the two sister chromatids from each other, although the chromatids remain aligned next to each other. After the centromeres divide, the sister chromatids are considered full-fledged chromosomes (called daughter chromosomes).

ANAPHASE: MOVEMENT OF THE DAUGHTER CHROMOSOMES

Of all the phases of mitosis, **anaphase** (Gr. *ana*, back again + phase) takes the least time (figure 6.5*c*). The shortening of the microtubules in the mitotic spindle pulls each daughter chromosome apart from its copy (the sister chromatid to which it had been attached) and toward its respective pole. When the chromosomes move to the poles, they can appear straight, V-shaped, or J-shaped, depending on the location of the centromere region. Anaphase ends when all the daughter chromosomes have moved to the poles of the cell. Each pole now has a complete, identical set of chromosomes.

TELOPHASE: REFORMATION OF NUCLEI

Telophase (Gr. *telos*, end + phase) begins once the daughter chromosomes arrive at the opposite poles of the cell. During telophase, the mitotic spindle disassembles (figure 6.5*d*). The alpha and beta tubulin monomers from the microtubules now build the cytoskeleton of the new cells. A nuclear envelope reforms around each set of chromosomes, which begin to uncoil for gene expression. One of the first genes to be expressed is the rRNA gene, which results in the reappearance of the nucleolus. The cell also begins to pinch in the middle. Mitosis is over, but cell division is not.

CYTOKINESIS: PARTITIONING THE CYTOPLASM

The final phase of cell division is cytokinesis, in which the cytoplasm divides (figure 6.6). Cytokinesis usually starts sometime during late anaphase or early telophase and is not as precise as nuclear division. Before cytokinesis, the two newly formed nuclei still share the same cytoplasmic compartment but are at opposite ends of the cell. A contracting belt of microfilaments called the

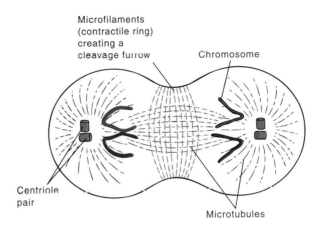

FIGURE 6.6

Cytokinesis. Spatial relationship between the contractile ring of microfilaments and the microtubules of the mitotic spindle.

contractile ring pinches the plasma membrane to begin cell separation. The ring lies midway between the two spindle poles and asters, and the microfilaments of the ring link to the inner surface of the plasma membrane, so their contractile activity pulls the cell surface inward. ❹ The cleavage furrow, located where the pinching occurs, looks as though a cord was tied around the circumference of the cell and pulled tight. Two new, genetically identical daughter cells form, each about half the size of the original parent cell.

CONTROL OF THE CELL CYCLE

One of the most exciting areas of cell biology is the study of cell cycle control. Converging lines of evidence have led to a "universal model" specifying that cell division follows the same biochemical pathway in all eukaryotic cells—from yeasts to humans (figure 6.7*a*). Most of the details center on the enzyme cdc2 kinase, which has changed little in its structure, and none in its function, during a billion years of evolution. This enzyme is one part of a protein complex called the maturation-promoting factor (MPF). Once activated, MPF plays a role in most of the events of the cell cycle, such as (1) condensation of chromosomes, (2) reorganization of cell structure, (3) breakdown of the nuclear envelope, and (4) segregation of the chromosomes into daughter cells during mitosis. In addition, MPF initiates the M and S phases.

Evidence indicates that events in the nucleus do not control the cell cycle. Instead, an autonomous oscillator—a set of chemical reactions in the cytoplasm—controls cell division with the regularity of a clock.

The basic mechanism of this control involves cyclin proteins activating and inactivating MPF. During interphase, cyclin accumulates until the rate of MPF activation by cyclin exceeds the rate of cyclin destruction by an inactivase enzyme—the concentration of which is assumed to be constant (figure 6.7*b*). As a consequence, active MPF accumulates, leading to a series of modifications of other mitotic substrates. MPF activity also induces

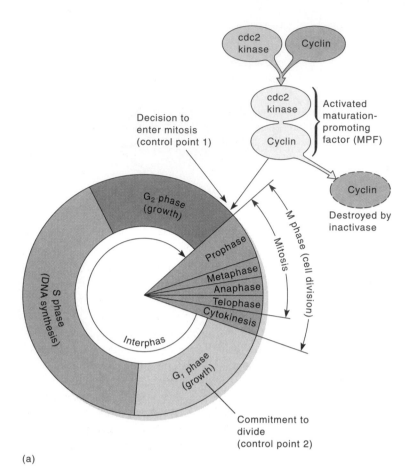

MEIOSIS: THE BASIS OF SEXUAL REPRODUCTION

The vast majority of animals do not simply divide in half to reproduce, as do single cells, but instead undergo sexual reproduction. Sexual reproduction requires a genetic contribution from two different sex cells. Egg and sperm cells are specialized sex cells called **gametes** (Gr. *gamete*, wife; *gametes*, husband). In animals, a male gamete (sperm) unites with a female gamete (egg) during fertilization to form a single cell called a **zygote** (Gr. *zygotos*, yoked together). The fusion of gametes is called **syngamy** (Gr. *gamos*, marriage). The zygote is the first cell of the new animal. Each of the two gametes contributes half of the genetic information to the zygote.

To maintain a constant and stable number of chromosomes in the next generation, animals that reproduce sexually must produce gametes with half the chromosome number of their ordinary body cells (called **somatic cells**). All of the cells in the body, except for the egg and sperm cells, have the diploid (2*N*) number of chromosomes. A diploid set of chromosomes contains a species-specific number of chromosome pairs. The chromosomes are in pairs because each cell contains one chromosome of each type from one parent and another chromosome of each type from the other parent. Humans have 46 total chromosomes (2*N*), comprising 23 chromosome pairs.

A type of cell division called **meiosis** (Gr. *meiosis*, dimunition) occurs in specialized cells of the ovaries and testes and reduces the number of chromosomes to half the diploid (2*N*) number. The resulting cells (eggs and sperm) are said to be haploid (*N*), or have the haploid number of chromosomes. Haploid cells have only one of each type of chromosome (only one member of each pair of chromosomes found in diploid cells). The nuclei of the two gametes combine during fertilization and restore the diploid number.

Meiosis begins after the G$_2$ phase in the cell cycle—after DNA replication (*see figure 6.2*). Two successive nuclear divisions, designated meiosis I and meiosis II, take place. Each division has a prophase, metaphase, anaphase, and telophase. The mitotic spindles function in meiosis just as they do in mitosis. Mitosis results in two identical daughter cells, each with the same number of chromosomes as the parent cell, whereas the two nu-

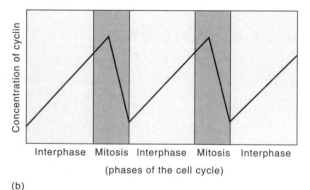

FIGURE 6.7

Control of the Cell Cycle. (*a*) This "universal model" shows how mitosis may be regulated at two control points. At control point 1, cyclin accumulates during interphase and, at a critical concentration, associates with cdc2 kinase to form a complex (maturation-promoting factor), which triggers mitosis (M) and activates enzymes (inactivases) that destroy cyclin. (*b*) As cyclin is destroyed, the cyclin-destroying enzymes become inactive. Thus, cyclin accumulates once again. Cyclin is also thought to highly regulate passage through control point 2 (the time when a cell becomes committed to divide).

cyclin destruction, and cyclin disappearance results in the inactivase destabilizing MPF. The interphase structures are then reestablished, and cyclin begins accumulating and initiates the next mitotic cycle.

clear divisions of meiosis result in four daughter cells, each with half the number of chromosomes as the parent cell. Moreover, these daughter cells are not genetically identical. Like mitosis, meiosis is a continuous process, and biologists divide it into the phases that follow only for convenience.

THE FIRST MEIOTIC DIVISION: PROPHASE I TO TELOPHASE I

During interphase, each chromosome has already replicated to form two sister chromatids joined at their centromeres (*see figure 6.3*). In prophase I, DNA folds more and more tightly, and becomes visible under a light microscope (figure 6.8a). Because a cell has a copy of each type of chromosome from each original parent cell, it contains the diploid number of chromosomes. The chromosomes of each homologous pair contain the same genes in the same order along the length of the chromosome. **Homologous chromosomes** (homologues) carry genes for the same traits, are the same length, and have a similar staining pattern, making them identifiable as matching pairs. During prophase I, homologous chromosomes line up side-by-side in a process called **synapsis** (Gr. *synapsis*, conjunction), forming a **tetrad** of chromatids (also called a bivalent). The tetrad thus contains the two homologous chromosomes, each with its copy, or sister chromatid (figure 6.9). A network of protein and RNA is laid down between the sister chromatids of the two homologous chromosomes. This network holds the sister chromatids in a precise union so that each gene is directly across from its sister gene on the homologous chromosome. An analogy is zipping up a zipper. Within this complex, portions of the DNA helix of each chromatid unwind (*see figure 6.2*), and single strands of DNA pair with their complementary member from the other homologue.

Synapsis also initiates a series of events called **crossing-over,** whereby the nonsister chromatids of the two homologous chromosomes in a tetrad exchange DNA segments (figure 6.9). This process effectively redistributes genetic information among the paired homologous chromosomes and produces new combinations of genes on the various chromatids in homologous pairs. Thus, each chromatid ends up with new combinations of instructions for a variety of traits. Crossing-over is a form of **genetic recombination** and is a major source of genetic variation in a population of a given species. Chapter 8 discusses it in more detail.

The point of crossing-over can be seen under the light microscope as an X-shaped structure called a **chiasma** (pl., chiasmata; Gr. cross) (figure 6.9a). A chiasma indicates that two nonsister chromatids of paired homologous chromosomes have exchanged parts. Apparently, the continued attachment of nonsister chromatids at chiasmata plays a role in aligning homologues at the spindle equator during metaphase I.

In metaphase I, the microtubules form a spindle apparatus just as in mitosis (*see figures 6.4 and 6.5*). However, unlike mitosis, where homologous chromosomes do not pair, each pair of homologues lines up in the center of the cell, with centromeres on each side of the spindle equator.

When all chromosome pairs are in the center of the cell, all those inherited from one parent do not necessarily line up on the same side as those inherited from the other parent. For example, with only three homologues, any of the alignments shown in figure 6.10 are as likely as any other. As a consequence, each gamete receives a different combination of paternal and maternal chromosomes. This random alignment of chromosomes at metaphase I is another major source of genetic variation in sexually reproducing animals.

Anaphase I begins when homologous chromosomes separate and begin to move toward each pole (*see figure 6.8a*). Because the replicated chromosomes of each homologous pair are moving in opposite directions, each daughter cell will receive one replicated chromosome from each homologous pair. No centromere division occurs in the first meiotic division; thus, each of these chromosomes still consists of two chromatids and is called a **dyad** (Gr. *dyas*, two). Each pole of the cell now has just one complete set of replicated chromosomes: one member of each homologous pair. Because the orientation of each pair of homologous chromosomes in the center of the cell is random (figure 6.10), the specific chromosomes that each pole receives from each pair of homologues are also random.

Meiotic telophase I is similar to mitotic telophase in that the parent cell divides into two daughter cells via cytokinesis (*see figure 6.6*). During this phase, nuclear envelopes appear around the chromosome sets, the nucleoli reappear, and the spindle fibers disappear. The transition to the second nuclear division is called interkinesis. Cells proceeding through interkinesis do not replicate their DNA. After a varying time period, meiosis II occurs.

THE SECOND MEIOTIC DIVISION: PROPHASE II TO TELOPHASE II

The second meiotic division (meiosis II) resembles an ordinary mitotic division (*see figure 6.8b*), except the number of chromosomes has been reduced by half. The phases are prophase II, metaphase II, anaphase II, and telophase II. During prophase II, the spindle apparatus appears, and the replicated chromosomes line up on the spindle equator during metaphase II. During anaphase II, centromeres finally divide, and the sister chromatids separate to become individual chromosomes, maintaining the haploid number that was produced during anaphase I. At the end of telophase II and cytokinesis, the final products of these two divisions of meiosis are four new "division products." In most animals, each of these "division products" is haploid and may function directly as a gamete (sex cell).

Stop and Ask Yourself

6. What are gametes?
7. What is synapsis?
8. What is the importance of crossing-over?
9. In meiosis, why don't sister chromatids part during anaphase I?
10. What happens during the second meiotic division?

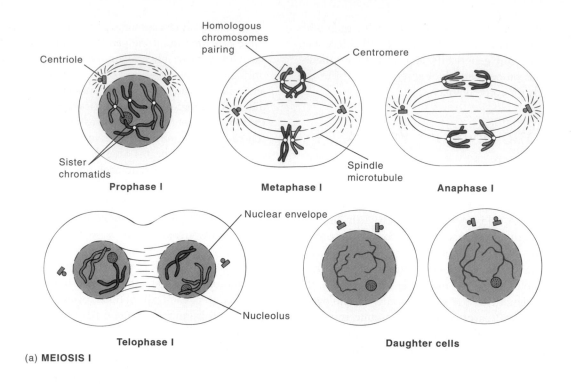

Centriole

Homologous chromosomes pairing

Centromere

Sister chromatids

Prophase I

Metaphase I

Spindle microtubule

Anaphase I

Nuclear envelope

Nucleolus

Telophase I

Daughter cells

(a) **MEIOSIS I**

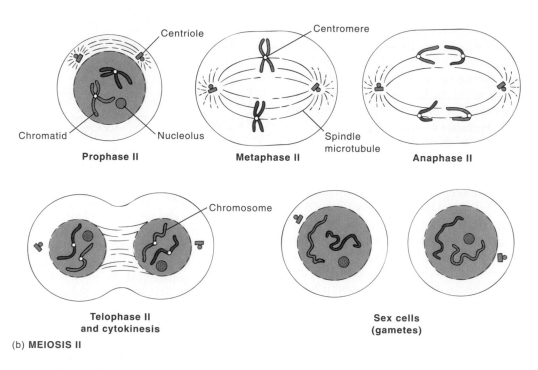

Centriole

Centromere

Chromatid

Nucleolus

Prophase II

Metaphase II

Spindle microtubule

Anaphase II

Chromosome

Telophase II and cytokinesis

Sex cells (gametes)

(b) **MEIOSIS II**

Figure 6.8

Meiosis and Cytokinesis. (a) Stages in the first meiotic division. (b) Stages in the second meiotic division.

Gamete Formation

During the life cycle of most animals, some diploid cells undergo meiosis and haploid gametes form in a process called **gametogene-** **sis.** In the testes of the male, the type of gametogenesis that produces sperm is called spermatogenesis; in the ovaries of the female, the production of ova (eggs) is called oogenesis.

SPERMATOGENESIS

Spermatogenesis produces mature sperm as follows (figure 6.11*a*):

1. Spermatogenesis begins in unspecialized germ cells called spermatogonia (sing., spermatogonium). The spermatogonium enlarges and becomes a primary spermatocyte.
2. A primary spermatocyte undergoes meiosis (meiotic division I) and produces two smaller secondary spermatocytes.

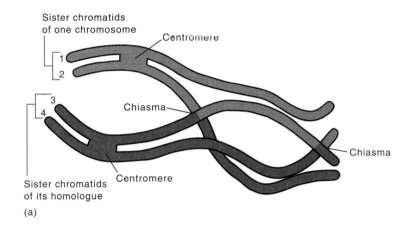

Sister chromatids of one chromosome

Centromere

1
2

3
4

Chiasma

Chiasma

Centromere

Sister chromatids of its homologue

(a)

(b)

FIGURE 6.9

Synapsis and Crossing-Over. (*a*) Crossing-over and the location of chiasmata, where nonsister chromatids remain temporarily attached. (*b*) The same chromosomes diagrammatically separated to show the result of crossing-over.

3. Both secondary spermatocytes undergo a second meiotic division (meiotic division II) to form spermatids. (Notice that each primary spermatocyte gives rise to four spermatids, each with the haploid number of chromosomes.)
4. The spermatids develop into mature sperm (spermatozoa) without undergoing any further cell division.

OOGENESIS

Oogenesis, the maturation of ova (sing., ovum) or eggs, differs from spermatogenesis in several ways and proceeds as follows (figure 6.11*b*):

1. Oogenesis begins in unspecialized germ cells called oogonia (sing., oogonium), which undergo mitosis.
2. An oogonium develops and grows into a primary oocyte, which contains the diploid number of chromosomes. The primary oocyte undergoes a first meiotic division to produce two daughter cells of unequal size.
3. The larger of the daughter cells is the secondary oocyte. It contains almost all of the primary oocyte's food-rich cytoplasm, which provides nourishment for the developing ovum.
4. The smaller of the two daughter cells is a first polar body and is essentially only a nucleus. It may divide again, but eventually, it degenerates.
5. In some animals, if the secondary oocyte is fertilized, it begins a second meiotic division, producing a haploid ovum, and another tiny polar body forms. This second polar body is also destined to disintegrate. When the haploid sperm and ovum nuclei merge (syngamy), the ovum becomes a zygote. Notice that in oogenesis, each primary oocyte gives rise to only one functional gamete instead of four as in spermatogenesis.

Stop and Ask Yourself

11. What are the main steps in spermatogenesis? What are the main steps in oogenesis?
12. How do oogenesis and spermatogenesis differ?

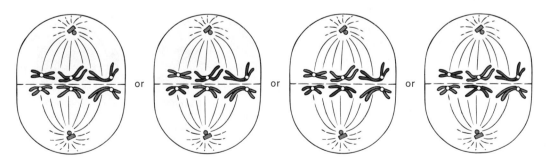

FIGURE 6.10

Chance Alignment of Paired Homologous Chromosomes during Metaphase I of Meiosis. Which member of a pair of chromosomes faces which pole of the cell is random. For some pairs, the maternal chromosome may face "north," while for the other pairs, the maternal chromosome may face "south."

(a) **Spermatogenesis**

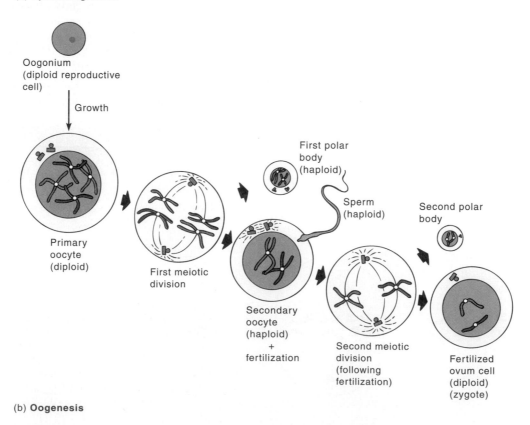

(b) **Oogenesis**

FIGURE 6.11

Gametogenesis. (*a*) Spermatogenesis is a meiotic process that involves two successive divisions. (*b*) In oogenesis, meiosis is complete following fertilization of the secondary oocyte.

ENDANGERED SPECIES

WILDLIFE ALERT 4—KIRTLAND'S WARBLER (*DENDROICA KIRTLANDII*)

VITAL STATISTICS

Classification: Phylum Chordata, class Aves, order Passeriformes

Range: Northern lower peninsula of Michigan

Habitat: Stands of jack-pine between 5 and 20 ft high

Number remaining: 400

Status: Endangered

NATURAL HISTORY AND ECOLOGICAL STATUS

Kirtland's warbler is a small bird that breeds in Michigan (figure 1) and winters in the Bahamas and other Caribbean islands. It is blue-gray with a yellow breast and black streaks on its back. The male has a black mask (figure 2). Kirtland's warbler feeds on insects, pine pitch, grass, and berries.

During its reproductive period in late spring and early summer, the loud, nearly constant singing of Kirtland's warbler can be heard over distances of 0.5 km. Kirtland's warbler nests on the ground in jack-pine stands that are larger than 80 acres and that have trees between 5 and 20 ft tall. A jack-pine stand achieves this status 9 to 13 years after fire destroys an earlier stand. Kirtland's warblers abandon older tree stands because the jack-pines become too tall for lower branches to form protective cover below the trees. Each female pro-

FIGURE 2   Male Kirtland's Warbler (*Dendroica kirtlandii*).

duces four or five eggs, and both parents take responsibility for feeding the young chicks. By September, all birds are ready for the migration to the Caribbean.

Fire control and habitat destruction are the major threats to Kirtland's warbler. This bird's very specific habitat requirements mean that changes in the jack-pine habitat interrupt nesting activities. Jack-pine reproduction depends on fire because fire opens jack-pine cones for seed release. Human fire-control measures have prevented the burning of old jack-pine forests and the subsequent reestablishment of the younger forests that Kirtland's warbler needs for its reproductive activities.

Cowbirds have also been a significant threat to Kirtland's warbler. Cowbirds are often called nest parasites because they lay their eggs in the nest of other birds and do not rear their young. Parents in the host nest incubate the cowbird eggs along with their own. Because cowbird eggs develop quickly and hatch early into large chicks, cowbird chicks usually are fed most often. Cowbird chicks often push host chicks from the nest. Unfortunately, cowbirds' parasitism of Kirtland's warbler nests has contributed to this warbler's endangered status.

Finally, zoologists do not know much about the overwintering conditions that Kirtland's warbler faces. Of the eight hundred to nine hundred birds that leave Michigan in the fall for the Caribbean, only about four hundred return the following spring.

Extensive efforts are underway to save Kirtland's warbler. Cutting, burning, and planting are restoring jack-pine habitats. Careful monitoring of human development, control of human intrusion into jack-pine forests during the breeding season, and cowbird control measures may provide for the recovery of this species.

Michigan

FIGURE 1   Breeding Range of Kirtland's Warbler (*Dendroica kirtlandii*).

SUMMARY

1. The replication of DNA and its subsequent allocation to daughter cells during mitosis involves a number of phases, collectively called the cell cycle. The cell cycle is that period from the time a cell is produced until it completes mitosis.

2. Mitosis maintains the parental number of chromosome sets in each daughter nucleus. It separates the sister chromatids of each (replicated) chromosome for distribution to daughter nuclei.

3. Interphase represents about 90% of the total cell cycle.

4. The first phase of mitosis is prophase, during which the mitotic spindle forms. At the end of prophase, the nuclear envelope disintegrates, and microtubules attach each of the sister chromatids to the two poles of the cell.

5. The second phase of mitosis is metaphase. During this phase, the replicated chromosomes align along the spindle equator in the center of the cell.

6. The third phase of mitosis is anaphase, during which the centromeres joining the sister chromatids divide. Microtubules then pull the sister chromatids to opposite poles of the cell.

7. The final phase of mitosis is telophase, during which the mitotic spindle disassembles, the nuclear envelope reforms, and the chromosomes unfold in the nucleoplasm.

8. A belt of microfilaments and microtubules pinches most cells undergoing cytokinesis in two.

9. The cell cycle (mitosis) is highly regulated. During interphase, cyclin accumulates and associates with the cdc2 enzyme to form maturation-promoting factor (MPF). MPF triggers mitosis and activates enzymes that degrade cyclin. As cyclin is destroyed, MPF disappears, and the cyclin-degrading enzymes become inactive. Thus, cyclin accumulates once again to start another cell division.

10. Meiosis is a special form of nuclear division during gamete formation in most eukaryotes. It consists of a single replication of the chromosomes and two nuclear divisions that result in four daughter cells, each with half the original number of chromosomes.

11. In the life cycle of most animals, certain diploid cells undergo gametogenesis to form haploid gametes (sperm in males and eggs in females). Fusion of a sperm and an egg nucleus at fertilization produces a new diploid cell (zygote), which undergoes mitosis and cytokinesis to develop into a new individual.

SELECTED KEY TERMS

anaphase (p. 89)
cell cycle (p. 85)
crossing-over(p. 91)
cytokinesis (p. 85)
interphase (p. 85)
meiosis (p. 90)
metaphase (p. 89)
mitosis (p. 85)
prophase (p. 87)
telophase (p. 89)

CRITICAL THINKING QUESTIONS

1. Humans are diploid organisms and are biased in favor of diploidy over haploidy. What are the biological advantages of having diploid cells? Do haploid organisms have some advantages?

2. If the function of meiosis were only to make haploid cells from a diploid cell, this could be accomplished in a single cell division; that is, canceling chromosome replication and separating homologous chromosomes would produce two haploid gametes from each diploid cell. What important aspect of meiosis would this simple procedure be omitting?

3. Is reproduction life's death-defying escape from inevitable destruction? Explain.

4. Which do you think evolved first—meiosis or mitosis? Why? What do you think may have been some of the stages in the evolution of one from the other?

5. How do new genetic combinations arise during meiosis?

REFERENCES ON THE WORLD WIDE WEB

1. **Mitosis.** This site contains a brief discussion of the stages of mitosis.
   http://esg-www.mit.edu:8001/esgbio/cb/mitosis.html

2. **Cell Division: Binary Fission and Mitosis.** This site provides a detailed description of cell division.
   http://www.emc.maricopa.edu/bio/bio181/BIOBK/BioBookmito.html

3. **Meiosis and Genetic Recombination.** This site is a section from the Mendelian genetics chapter of the 8.001 hypertextbook.
   http://esg-www.mit.edu:8001/esgbio/mg/meiosis.html

chapter 7

INHERITANCE PATTERNS

Concepts

1. Modern genetics began with the work of Gregor Mendel. The principles that he described explain the inheritance patterns of many animal traits, including dominance, segregation, and independent assortment.
2. Rapid developments in twentieth-century genetics have expanded on the work of Gregor Mendel. Geneticists have discovered that (*a*) many alternative forms of a gene may exist in a population, (*b*) these alternative forms may interact in different ways, (*c*) interactions among many gene pairs determine some traits, and (*d*) the environment influences gene expression.

Would You Like to Know . . .

1. why modern genetics is so important to zoology and modern society? (p. 98)

2. how an Augustinian monk got started crossing garden peas? (p. 98)

3. why some traits have many expressions? (p. 103)

4. why some traits, such as height, show a range of variation, while other traits show an all-or-none expression? (p. 104)

5. how the environment influences the expression of some genes? (p. 105)

This chapter answers these and other useful questions.

This chapter contains evolutionary concepts, which are set off in this font.

Genetics (Gr. *gennan,* to produce) is the study of how biological information is transmitted from one generation to the next, and of how this information is expressed in an organism. Humans have been aware for centuries that certain traits pass from parents to offspring and have used that knowledge in selective breeding of domesticated plants and animals.

The importance of genetics to modern societies, however, surpasses anything that ancient animal breeders could have imagined. Modern genetics began with the work of Gregor Mendel (1822–1884). Since then, geneticists have been performing crosses, characterizing the genetic material (DNA), and investigating the functions of DNA.

The genetics revolution has had a tremendous effect on biology. Genetics can explain why offspring are, in some ways, similar to their parents, whereas in other ways, they are very different. Genetic mechanisms also help explain how species change over time. Genetic and evolutionary themes are interdependent in biology, and biology without either would be unrecognizable from its present form. ① Emerging genetic technologies are also presenting society with moral and ethical issues regarding what, if any, limits should be placed on genetic manipulations. The benefits of genetic technologies include mass production of hormones and antibodies, increased agricultural production, and the replacement of defective genes.

Even though genetic technologies hold great promise for the future, their possible negative effects must also be considered. Science is ethically neutral (*see chapter 1*). Thus, society must deal with questions about the effects of genetically engineered bacteria and other organisms on the environment, the use of genetically engineered organisms for waging war, what kinds of genetic manipulations may be performed on humans, and cloning.

In light of these concerns, the next three chapters examine genetics. This chapter covers many of the genetic principles that can be traced back to the beginnings of modern genetics. Chapter 8 explores the chromosomal basis of inheritance. Chapter 9 looks at modern concepts of genes and gene functions, and some of the modern technologies that allow gene manipulation.

THE BIRTH OF MODERN GENETICS

Gregor Mendel (figure 7.1) was born in 1822 in an area of Europe now known as the Czech Republic. He was the son of a farmer and grew up learning about the cultivation and propagation of crop plants. Mendel entered an Augustinian monastery in Brunn (Brno, Czech Republic) and became a priest at age 25. He was then given the opportunity to study physics, mathematics, and natural sciences at the University of Vienna in Austria. Mendel completed his studies in Vienna in 1854 and returned to Brunn, where he began teaching.

In 1857, Mendel began experiments with the garden pea, *Pisum sativum.* He was not the first scientist to study inheritance; however, his approach was unique. ② Mendel selected an experimental organism whose pollination could be easily controlled and chose seven clearly defined traits to study. He carried his crosses through multiple generations and approached his experi-

FIGURE 7.1

Gregor Mendel (1822–1884): The Father of Genetics. Gregor Mendel's work with garden peas, although unappreciated during his time, was rediscovered and confirmed in 1900. This rediscovery marks the beginning of modern genetics.

ments as a mathematician, as well as a biologist. Mendel published his work in 1866, but his contemporaries did not recognize the importance of his conclusions. Mendel died in 1884. The rediscovery and confirmation of his writings in 1900 propelled genetics into the twentieth century.

Stop and Ask Yourself

1. What is genetics?
2. Why is a basic understanding of genetics an important part of any zoologist's training?
3. In what way was Mendel's approach to the study of genetics unique?

MENDELIAN INHERITANCE PATTERNS

The fruit fly, *Drosophila melanogaster,* is a classic tool for studying inheritance patterns. Its utility stems from its ease of handling, short life cycle, and easily recognized characteristics.

Studies of any fruit fly trait always make comparisons to a wild-type fly. If a fly has a characteristic similar to that found in wild flies, it is said to have the wild-type expression of that trait. (In the examples that follow, wild-type wings lay over the back at rest and extend past the posterior tip of the body, and wild-type eyes are red.) Numerous mutations from the wild-type body form, such as vestigial wings (reduced, shriveled wings) and sepia (dark brown) eyes have been described (figure 7.2).

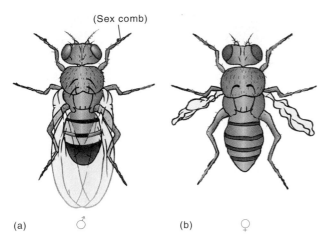

FIGURE 7.2

Distinguishing Sexes and Phenotypes of *Drosophila melanogaster*.
(*a*) Male with wild-type wings and wild-type eyes. (*b*) Female with
vestigial wings and sepia eyes. In contrast to the female, the posterior
aspect of the male's abdomen has a wide, dark bank and a rounded tip.

SEGREGATION

During gamete formation, units of inheritance in each parent are
incorporated into separate gametes. These units of inheritance are
called **genes** (Gr. *genos*, race). During anaphase I of meiosis, homologous chromosomes move toward opposite poles of the cell,
and the resulting gametes have only one member of each chromosome pair. Genes carried on one member of a pair of homologous
chromosomes end up in one gamete, and genes carried on the
other member are segregated into a different gamete. Mendel's
principle of segregation states that pairs of hereditary factors are
distributed between gametes during gamete formation. (Mendel,
of course, knew nothing of the cellular basis of gamete formation.)
Fertilization results in the random combination of gametes and
brings homologous chromosomes together again.

A cross of wild-type fruit flies with flies having vestigial
wings illustrates Mendel's principle of segregation. (The flies come
from stocks that have been inbred for generations to ensure that
they breed true for wild-type wings or vestigial wings.) The offspring (progeny) of this cross have wild-type wings and are the
first generation of offspring, or the first filial (F_1) generation (figure 7.3). If these flies are allowed to mate with each other, their
progeny are the second filial (F_2) generation. Approximately a
fourth of these F_2 generation of flies have vestigial wings, and
three-fourths have wild wings (figure 7.3). Note that the vestigial
characteristic, although present in the parental generation, disappears in the F_1 generation and reappears in the F_2 generation. In
addition, the ratio of wild-type flies to vestigial-winged flies in the
F_2 generation is approximately 3:1. Reciprocal crosses, which involve the same characteristics but a reversal of the sexes of the individuals introducing a particular expression of the trait into the
cross, yield similar results.

From his experiments, Mendel concluded that heritable
"factors" (genes) determine traits. Genes that determine the expression of a particular trait can exist in alternative forms called

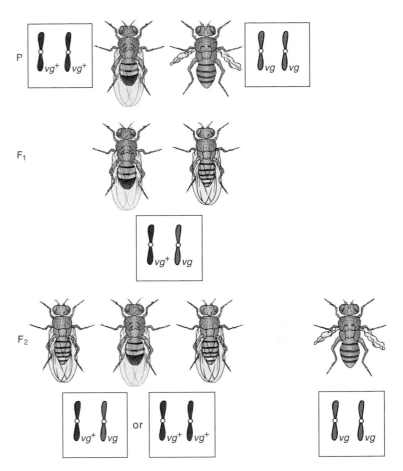

FIGURE 7.3

Cross Involving a Single Trait. Cross between parental flies (P) with
wild-type (vg^+) wings and vestigial (vg) wings, carried through two
generations (F_1 and F_2).

alleles (Gr. *allelos*, each other). In the fruit-fly cross, the vestigial
allele is present in the F_1 generation, and even though it is masked
by the wild-type allele for wing shape, it retains its uniqueness because it is expressed again in some members of the F_2 generation.
Mendel defined **dominant** factors as those that can hide the expression of another factor; **recessive** factors are those whose expression can be masked. In the fruit-fly example, the wild-type
allele is dominant because it can mask the expression of the vestigial allele, which is therefore recessive.

The visual expression of alleles may not always indicate the
underlying genetic makeup of an organism. This visual expression
is the **phenotype,** and the genetic makeup is the **genotype.** In the
example, the flies of the F_1 generation have the same phenotype as
one of the parents, but they differ genotypically because they carry
both a dominant and recessive allele. They are hybrids, and because this cross concerns only one pair of genes and a single trait,
it is a **monohybrid cross** (Gr. *monos*, one + L. *hybrida*, offspring of
two kinds of parents).

An organism is **homozygous** (L. *homo*, same + Gr. *zygon*,
paired) if it carries two identical genes for a given trait and **heterozygous** (Gr. *heteros*, other) if the genes are different. Thus, in the
example, all members of the parental generation are homozygous

because only true-breeding flies are crossed. All members of the F_1 generation are heterozygous.

Crosses are often diagrammed using a letter or letters descriptive of the trait in question. The first letter of the description of the dominant allele commonly is used. In fruit flies, and other organisms where all mutants are compared with a wild-type, the symbol is taken from the allele that was derived by a mutation from the wild condition. A superscript "+" next to the symbol represents the wild-type allele. A capital letter means that the mutant allele being represented is dominant, and a lowercase letter means that the mutant allele being represented is recessive. Thus, the original fruit-fly cross can be represented as follows:

	Wild-type	Vestigial
P generation	$vg^+ \, vg^+$ $\times$	$vg \, vg$
F1 generation	$vg^+ \, vg$	

Matings of the F_1 flies resulted in a ratio of three wild-type flies to one vestigial fly in the F_2 generation. Mendel recognized that a 3:1 ratio would result when two alleles, each present in a separate gamete, combined randomly at fertilization (*see chapter 6*).

Geneticists use the Punnett square to help predict the results of crosses. Figure 7.4 illustrates the use of a **Punnett square** to predict the results of the cross of two F_1 flies. The first step is to determine the kinds of gametes that each parent produces. One of the two axes of a square is designated for each parent, and the different kinds of gametes each parent produces are listed along the appropriate axis. Combining gametes in the interior of the square shows the results of random fertilization. As figure 7.4 indicates, the F_1 flies are heterozygous, with one wild-type allele and one vestigial allele. The two phenotypes of the F_2 generation are shown inside the Punnett square and are in a 3:1 ratio.

The **phenotypic ratio** expresses the results of a cross according to the relative numbers of progeny in each visually distinct class (e.g., 3 wild-type : 1 vestigial). The Punnett square has thus explained in another way the F_2 results in figure 7.3. It also shows that F_2 individuals may have one of three different genotypes. The **genotypic ratio** expresses the results of a cross according to the relative numbers of progeny in each genotypic category (e.g., 1 vg^+vg^+ : 2 vg^+vg : 1 $vgvg$). A 3:1 phenotypic ratio and a 1:2:1 genotypic ratio are typical results of monohybrid crosses. Crosses rarely result in exact phenotypic or genotypic ratios. Instead, the results approximate the expected ratios and generally approach the expected values as more progeny are produced.

Mendel's principle of segregation explains how members of a pair of genes are distributed into separate gametes. Fertilization restores the paired (diploid) condition. Analysis of a large number of progeny from these fertilizations demonstrates the predictable phenotypic and genotypic ratios.

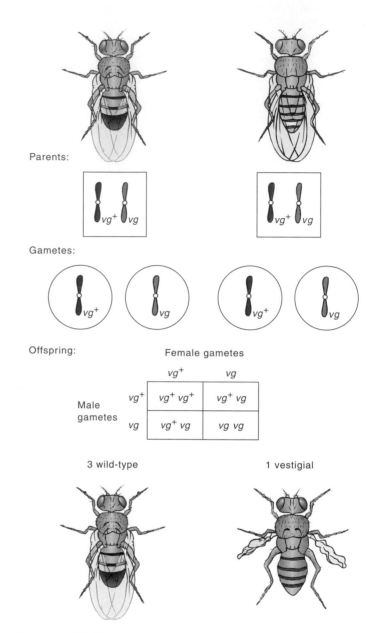

FIGURE 7.4

Use of a Punnett Square. A Punnett square helps predict the results of a cross. The kinds of gametes that each member of a cross produces are determined and placed along the axes of a square. Combining gametes in the interior of the square shows the results of mating: a phenotypic ratio of three flies with wild-type wings (vg^+) to one fly with vestigial wings (vg).

INDEPENDENT ASSORTMENT

In his crosses, Mendel also followed two pairs of characteristics. Similar crosses are made using flies with vestigial wings and sepia eyes, and flies that are wild for these characteristics. Sepia eyes are dark brown, and wild-type eyes are red. Figure 7.5 shows the results of crosses carried through two generations.

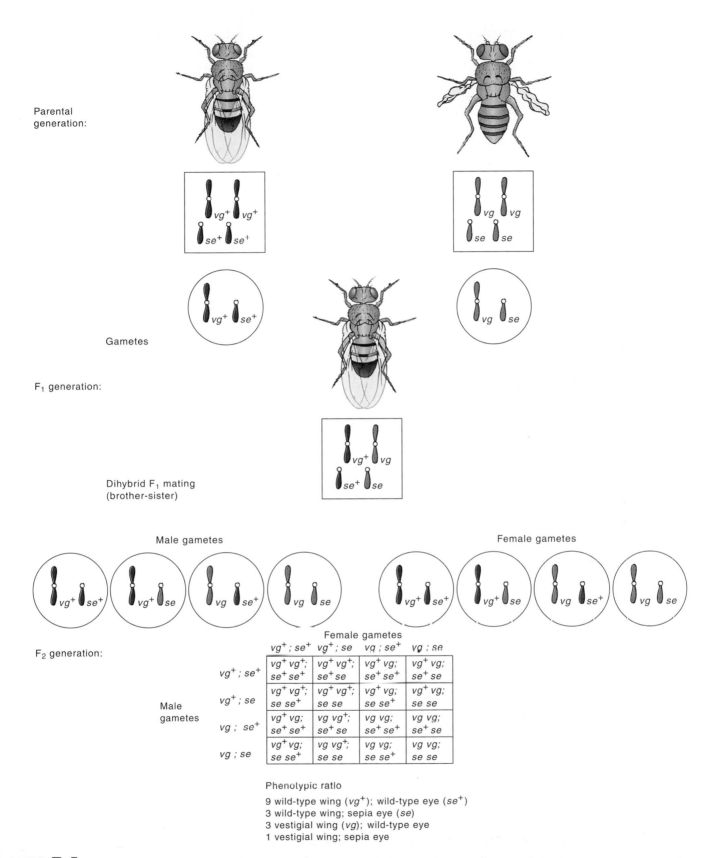

Parental generation:

Gametes

F₁ generation:

Dihybrid F₁ mating (brother-sister)

Male gametes   Female gametes

F₂ generation:

Female gametes

	$vg^+ ; se^+$	$vg^+ ; se$	$vg ; se^+$	$vg ; se$
$vg^+ ; se^+$	$vg^+ vg^+;$ $se^+ se^+$	$vg^+ vg^+;$ $se^+ se$	$vg^+ vg;$ $se^+ se^+$	$vg^+ vg;$ $se^+ se$
$vg^+ ; se$	$vg^+ vg^+;$ $se se^+$	$vg^+ vg^+;$ $se se$	$vg^+ vg;$ $se se^+$	$vg^+ vg;$ $se se$
$vg ; se^+$	$vg^+ vg;$ $se^+ se^+$	$vg vg^+;$ $se^+ se$	$vg vg;$ $se^+ se^+$	$vg vg;$ $se^+ se$
$vg ; se$	$vg^+ vg;$ $se se^+$	$vg vg^+;$ $se se$	$vg vg;$ $se se^+$	$vg vg;$ $se se$

Male gametes (row labels on left side of table)

Phenotypic ratio

9 wild-type wing (vg^+); wild-type eye (se^+)
3 wild-type wing; sepia eye (se)
3 vestigial wing (vg); wild-type eye
1 vestigial wing; sepia eye

FIGURE 7.5

Constructing a Punnett Square for a Cross Involving Two Characteristics. Note that every gamete has one allele for each trait and that all combinations of alleles for each trait are represented.

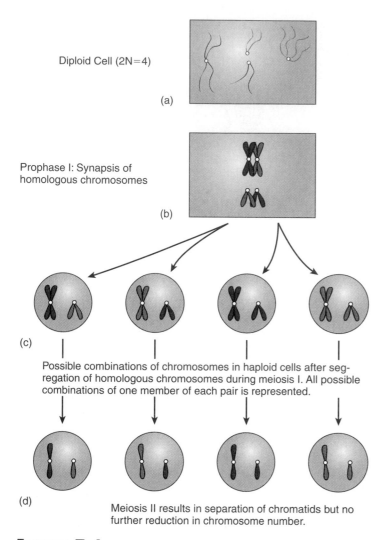

Diploid Cell (2N=4)

(a)

Prophase I: Synapsis of
homologous chromosomes

(b)

(c)

Possible combinations of chromosomes in haploid cells after segregation of homologous chromosomes during meiosis I. All possible
combinations of one member of each pair is represented.

(d)

Meiosis II results in separation of chromatids but no
further reduction in chromosome number.

FIGURE 7.6

Independent Assortment of Chromosomes during Meiosis. Color
distinguishes maternal and paternal chromosomes. Similar size and
shape indicate homologous chromosomes. (a) This cell has a diploid
(2N) chromosome number of four. (b) During the first meiotic division, one homologous pair of chromosomes (and hence, the genes this
pair carries) is segregated without regard to the movements of any
other homologous pair. (c) Thus, all combinations of large and small
chromosomes in the cells are possible at the end of meiosis I.
(d) Meiosis II simply results in the separation of chromatids without
further reduction in chromosome number. Most organisms have more
than two pairs of homologous chromosomes in each cell. As the
number of homologous pairs increases, the number of different kinds
of gametes also increases.

Note that flies in the parental generation are homozygous
for the traits in question and that each parent produces only one
kind of gamete. Gametes have one allele for each trait. Because
each parent produces only one kind of gamete, fertilization results
in offspring heterozygous for both traits. The F$_1$ flies have the
wild-type phenotype; thus, wild-type eyes are dominant to sepia
eyes. The F$_1$ flies are hybrids, and because the cross involves two
pairs of genes and two traits, it is a **dihybrid cross** (Gr. *di*, two +
L. *hybrida*, offspring of two kinds of parents).

Gregor Mendel recognized the 9:3:3:1 ratio as what would
be expected if genes obeyed certain probability laws. He concluded that, during gamete formation, the distribution of genes
determining one trait did not influence how genes determining
the other trait were distributed. In the example, this means that
an F$_1$ gamete with a *vg*$^+$ gene for wing condition may also have either the *se* or *se*$^+$ gene for eye color, as the F$_1$ gametes of figure 7.5
show. Note that all combinations of the eye color and wing condition genes are present, and that all combinations are equally
likely. This illustrates Mendel's **principle of independent assortment,** which states that, during gamete formation, pairs of factors
segregate independently of one another.

The events of meiosis explain Mendel's principle of independent assortment (*see figure 6.8*). Cells produced during meiosis have one member of each homologous pair of chromosomes.
Independent assortment simply means that when homologous
chromosomes line up at metaphase I and then segregate, the behavior of one pair of chromosomes does not influence the behavior of any other pair (figure 7.6; *see also figure 6.10*). After meiosis,
maternal and paternal chromosomes are distributed randomly
among cells.

Accurately determining all possible gametes that participants in a cross produce is critical when doing genetics problems.
Remember that (1) all gametes must have one (and only one) allele for each trait, and (2) all possible combinations of alleles for
the traits being considered must be represented in the gametes.

TESTING PHENOTYPES

The wild-type flies in the F$_2$ generation of the monohybrid cross
had two different genotypes. How can the genotype of any one
wild-type fly be determined? One way is by carrying out a **testcross,** which involves crossing the phenotypically dominant fly to
a fly that shows the recessive phenotype. (Remember that any organism that shows a recessive trait is homozygous for that trait.)
Testcross results differ depending on whether the phenotypically
dominant fly is homozygous or heterozygous. A testcross with a fly
homozygous for a dominant trait always yields phenotypically
dominant offspring. A testcross with a fly heterozygous for a dominant trait always yields a 1:1 ratio of phenotypically dominant to
phenotypically recessive offspring (table 7.1).

Stop and Ask Yourself

4. What is Mendel's principle of segregation? What events
    of meiosis does this principle reflect?

5. What is Mendel's principle of independent assortment?
    What events of meiosis does it reflect?

6. How would you define the following terms: (a) homozy-
    gous, (b) heterozygous, (c) phenotype, (d) genotype, and
    (e) allele?

7. What is a testcross?

TABLE 7.1	A Comparison of the Results of a Testcross of Heterozygous and Homozygous Dominant Flies

Dominant Phenotype (Wild-Type Wings)

If homozygous (vg^+vg^+)	If heterozygous (vg^+vg)
Testcross: $vgvg \times vg^+vg^+$	$vgvg \times vg^+vg$
Gametes: vg vg^+	vg vg^+,vg
Offspring: vg^+vg all wild-type wings	$vg^+vg, vgvg$ 1 wild-type wings: 1 vestigial wings

TABLE 7.2	Genotypes and Phenotypes in the ABO Blood Groups

Genotype(s)	Phenotype
I^AI^A, I^Ai	A
I^BI^B, I^Bi	B
I^AI^B	A and B
ii	O

Other Inheritance Patterns

The traits considered thus far have been determined by two genes, where one allele is dominant to a second. In this section, you learn that there are often many alleles in a population, that not all traits are determined by an interaction between a single pair of dominant or recessive genes, and that various internal and external environmental factors can affect the phenotype.

Multiple Alleles

Two genes, one carried on each chromosome of a homologous pair, determine traits in one individual. ③ A population, on the other hand, may have many different alleles with the potential to contribute to the phenotype of any member of the population. These are called **multiple alleles.** As chapters 12 to 14 explain, the diversity of alleles in a population supplies the phenotypic variation on which evolution can act.

Genes for a particular trait are at the same position on a chromosome. The gene's position on the chromosome is called its **locus** (L. *loca*, place). Numerous human loci have multiple alleles. Three alleles, symbolized I^A, I^B, and i, determine the familiar ABO blood types. Table 7.2 shows the combinations of alleles that determine a person's phenotype. Note that i is recessive to I^A and to I^B. I^A and I^B, however, are neither dominant nor recessive to each other. When I^A and I^B are present together, both are expressed.

Multiple alleles also determine the Rh blood type. Scientists discovered during World War II that matching ABO blood types did not always ensure a successful transfusion. They found that another blood cell trait, first discovered in the rhesus monkey, was responsible for transfusion rejections when the ABO blood type was matched. The Rh system is inherited as if it is determined by two alleles, with Rh positive being dominant to Rh negative. In fact, the system is much more complex. It now appears that more than 30 alleles determine the Rh phenotype!

Incomplete Dominance and Codominance

Incomplete dominance is an interaction between two alleles that are expressed more or less equally, and the heterozygote is different from either homozygote. For example, in cattle, the alleles for red coat color and for white coat color interact to produce an intermediate coat color called roan. Because neither the red nor the white allele is dominant, uppercase letters and a prime or a superscript are used to represent genes. Thus, red cattle are symbolized RR, white cattle are symbolized $R'R'$, and roan cattle are symbolized RR'.

Codominance occurs when the heterozygote expresses the phenotypes of both homozygotes. Thus, in the ABO blood types, the I^AI^B heterozygote expresses both alleles.

Another example of codominance is the inheritance of sickle-cell anemia. Sickle-cell anemia arose in Africa as a result of a mutation in the genes coding for one of the proteins making up the hemoglobin molecule. The normal allele is symbolized Hb^A, and the sickle-cell allele is symbolized Hb^S. When present in the homozygous condition, the sickle-cell allele results in severe sickling (having a crescent shape) of red blood cells, and the anemia that results is usually fatal. Even though the Hb^S allele is detrimental in the homozygous state, it is much less dangerous when heterozygous. Heterozygotes have about equal numbers of Hb^A and Hb^S hemoglobin molecules in their red blood cells, and sickling only develops under oxygen stress. The anemia is not only less severe, but heterozygotes are less susceptible to infections by the organism that causes malaria. Prior to malarial control programs in Africa, heterozygotes had a better chance of surviving than either homozygote!

Crosses involving incomplete dominance and codominance are analyzed in exactly the same manner as the previous crosses discussed. Mendelian rules are obeyed, but the results are interpreted differently. For example, figure 7.7 shows how a cross between a roan bull and a roan cow is analyzed. In this case, the 1:2:1 genotypic ratio is also the phenotypic ratio.

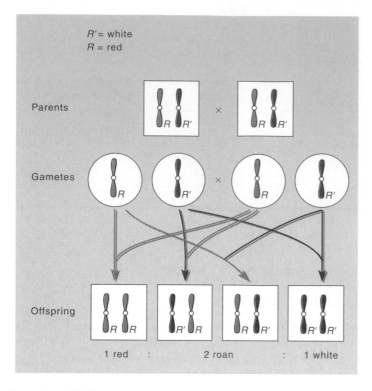

FIGURE 7.7

Incomplete Dominance. A cross between a roan bull and a roan cow results in a 1:2:1 ratio of red:roan:white. This phenotypic ratio is also the genotypic ratio (1 *RR*: 2 *RR′*: 1 *R′R′*).

QUANTITATIVE TRAITS: POLYGENES

In all traits considered thus far, genes produced discrete variations in phenotypes. Distinguishing a vestigial-winged fruit fly from a wild-type winged fruit fly, or a person with type A blood from a person with type O blood, is easy. Such traits display discontinuous variation. Many other traits, however, vary by small increments and must be categorized by some kind of quantitative measure (e.g., weight or height must be measured). Traits such as height, skin color, weight, and intelligence display continuous variation over a range of phenotypes. ④ Such traits are often determined by an interaction of multiple loci, where each locus adds a small increment to a phenotype. A mating between tall and short individuals (figure 7.8*a*) produces offspring intermediate in height (figure 7.8*b*). A mating between two individuals that are heterozygous at each locus produces a range of phenotypes (figure 7.8*c*). Plotting the frequency of each phenotype in the phenotypic range produces the bell-shaped distribution common in polygenic inheritance in a population (figure 7.8*d*). Because distinguishing between phenotypes requires quantitative measurements, traits like these are often called **quantitative traits.** Similarly, the participation of multiple loci in determining these traits prompts the use of the term **polygenes** when referring to the genes involved.

The steplike transitions between phenotypes seen in figure 7.8*d* become smaller as more loci are added to a cross. As discussed in the next section, no genes are isolated from external and inter-

FIGURE 7.8

How Polygenic Inheritance Can Produce Continuous Variation. Assume three loci are involved with the determination of height, and assume that each gene designated with a prime adds 13 cm to a base height of 120 cm. (*a*) Grandparents showing the two phenotypic extremes. (*b*) Offspring in the next generation are intermediate in height. (*c*) A mating between one member of that second generation and a person of similar stature could produce offspring that are very tall, very short, or anywhere between those extremes. (The numbers in the Punnett square were derived by multiplying 13 by the number of primed alleles in a cell and adding that product to 120 cm.) (*d*) Note in the bar graph that the distribution between extremes approaches a normal (bell-shaped) curve. Slight environmental variations would smooth the steplike transitions from one phenotypic class to another.

nal environments. Environmental conditions often influence the degree to which genes are expressed, and therefore, they make transitions between phenotypes of quantitative traits smoother.

ENVIRONMENTAL EFFECTS AND GENE EXPRESSION

Your genetic makeup is not necessarily a set of blueprints that dictates your final form, like the blueprints of a building dictate the final form of a home. For most traits, the outcome of a set of genetic instructions is the product of a genotype interacting with the environment. **5** The genotype establishes a more or less fixed potential; whether or not that potential is realized depends on important environmental influences. For example, nutritional factors may influence whether or not animals achieve their genetic potential regarding physical or mental stature.

Environmental effects on gene expression in animals can be manipulated experimentally by maintaining animals of identical genotypes in different environments and observing the environmental effect on the phenotype. The environment influences numerous traits in the fruit fly. For example, the temperature at which cultures are maintained affects the number of facets (lenses) in certain compound eye mutants.

Stop and Ask Yourself

8. What are multiple alleles?
9. Define the term locus.
10. What are polygenes?
11. How do quantitative inheritance patterns explain the occurrence of continuous variation in some traits?
12. What human traits do you think are influenced by environmental factors?

SUMMARY

1. Genetics is the study of how biological information is transmitted from one generation to the next. During the last 20 years, genetic research has influenced both science and society.
2. Gregor Mendel worked with garden peas and concluded that pairs of factors (genes) determine traits and that one gene may be dominant to another (the recessive gene). These genes pass unaltered from parents to offspring.
3. Mendel's principle of segregation states that pairs of genes are distributed between gametes during gamete formation when homologous chromosomes are distributed to different gametes during meiosis.
4. Mendel's principle of independent assortment states that, during gamete formation, pairs of genes segregate independently of one another. This is a result of meiotic processes in which members of one homologous pair of chromosomes are not influenced by the movements of any other pair of chromosomes.
5. Populations may have many alternative expressions of a gene at any locus. Human traits, like the ABO and Rh blood groups, are traits determined by multiple alleles.
6. Incomplete dominance is an interaction between two alleles in which the alleles contribute more or less equally to the phenotype. The heterozygote is intermediate between the parental extremes.
7. Codominance is an interaction between two alleles in which both alleles are expressed in the heterozygote.
8. Quantitative traits vary by small increments, displaying continuous variation. These traits are the result of genes at many loci (polygenes) adding small increments of expression to a phenotype.
9. The environment influences the degree to which a genotype is expressed.

SELECTED KEY TERMS

alleles (p. 99)
dominant (p. 99)
genes (p. 99)
genetics (p. 98)
genotype (p. 99)

phenotype (p. 99)
principle of independent assortment (p. 102)
principle of segregation (p. 99)
quantitative traits (p. 104)
recessive (p. 99)

CRITICAL THINKING QUESTIONS

1. A wild-type fruit fly, which had one vestigial-winged parent, is crossed with a vestigial-winged fruit fly. Use a Punnett square to predict the phenotypic and genotypic ratios in the offspring of this cross. What is this cross called?
2. A vestigial-winged, wild-eyed fruit fly is crossed with a wild-winged, sepia-eyed fruit fly. At least one parent of both of these flies had vestigial wings and sepia eyes. Use a Punnett square to predict the phenotypic ratio expected in the offspring of this cross.
3. Supply the genotypes, as completely as possible, for the parents and progeny of the following crosses:
   a. wild-type wing; sepia eye × wild-type wing; wild-type eye = 3 wild-type wing; sepia eye : 1 vestigial wing; sepia eye : 3 wild-type wing; wild-type eye : 1 vestigial wing; wild-type eye
   b. wild-type wing; sepia eye × wild-type wing; wild-type eye = 1 wild-type wing; sepia eye : 1 wild-type wing; wild-type eye
   c. vestigial wing; wild-type eye × wild-type wing; sepia eye = all wild-type wing; wild-type eye
   d. vestigial wing; wild-type eye × wild-type wing; sepia eye = 1 vestigial wing; wild-type eye : 1 vestigial wing; sepia eye : 1 wild-type wing; sepia eye : 1 wild-type wing; wild-type eye
4. The following progeny are the result of a cross between two fruit flies. Unfortunately, the phenotypes of the parental flies were not recorded. Formulate a hypothesis regarding the genotypes of the parental flies. (Hint: Consider the ratio between wing phenotypes separately from eye phenotypes in formulating your hypothesis.)
   Progeny:
   293 wild-type wing; wild-type eye
   310 wild-type wing; sepia eye
   97 vestigial wing; wild-type eye
   100 vestigial wing; sepia eye
5. Do you think that Mendel's conclusions regarding assortment of genes for two traits would have been any different if he had used traits encoded by genes carried on the same chromosome? Explain.
6. Explain why the phenotypic range of polygenic traits shows a gradual transition between phenotypes rather than the stair-step transitions figure 7.8d shows.

7. Design an experiment to determine whether or not an environmental factor, such as temperature, light, or nutritional state, influences a particular trait in fruit flies. Why are environmental effects on gene expression more difficult to investigate in humans than in fruit flies?

8. In guinea pigs, black fur is dominant over white fur. How could an animal breeder test whether a black guinea pig is homozygous or heterozygous?

9. To observe the laws of chance, toss a dime and a quarter simultaneously 10 times, and count the number of head-head, head-tail, and tail-tail combinations. How close are your results to a 1:2:1 ratio? Now toss the coins 90 times more for a total of 100 tosses. How close are your new results to a 1:2:1 ratio? Explain the difference.

References on the World Wide Web

1. **Mendel Web.**   This site is a resource for teachers and students interested in classical genetics, data analysis, and the history and literature of science. It includes Mendel's original paper (written in German) and an English translation of the paper.

   http://www.netspace.org/MendelWeb/

2. **Rupert's Genetic Page.**   This site includes links to a genetics glossary, references on various genetics topics, information on the human genome project, and health topics.

   http://www.cybergate.com/~maliobor/genetic.htm

3. **Genetics.**   This site includes information on the human genome project and links to sites dealing with the genetics of particular animal groups.

   http://www.ornl.gov/TechResources/human_genome/genetics.html

4. **Drosophila.**   Students interested in the genetics of the fruit fly will find this site interesting. It includes information on fruit fly inheritance, photographs, and movies.

   http://cbbridges.harvard.edu:7081/

chapter

8

CHROMOSOMES AND GENE LINKAGE

Concepts

1. The genetic material is organized into chromosomes, although during interphase only diffuse chromatin is visible. Chromosomes may be represented differently in males and females. However, the number of chromosomes is constant for a given species.
2. Genes that are on the same chromosome (linked) tend to be inherited together. Inheritance patterns differ, depending on whether genes are linked on sex chromosomes or on autosomes, and on the distance between linked genes. Linkage relationships help determine the position of loci on chromosomes.
3. Human pedigree analysis allows geneticists to determine how a trait is inherited.
4. Chromosome number and structure can change. The phenotypic consequences of such changes depend on the amount of genetic material lost or duplicated.

Would You Like to Know . . .

1 why the numbers of males and females in the world are approximately equal? (p. 108)

2 why some traits, such as color blindness, are more common in males than in females? (p. 111)

3 how "sex checks" of Olympic athletes are carried out? (p. 112)

4 whether or not females can express pattern baldness? (p. 113)

5 what causes genetic diseases, such as Down syndrome? (p. 114)

This chapter answers these and other useful questions.

This chapter contains evolutionary concepts, which are set off in this font.

Can you imagine compacting a mass of thread into a ball that is 10,000 times smaller than the length of the original thread? Imagine unwinding the thread again, mixing it with 45 other similar lengths of thread, and repeating the process. For those of us who have problems keeping knots out of extension cords and garden hoses, the task seems Herculean! Yet, a similar feat is done every time a human cell divides. The formation of human chromosomes involves compacting 46 microscopic threads of DNA and protein, whose total length is about 1 m, into a single cell. This packaging must be precise so that the DNA and protein can be dispersed in the nucleus of the cell after division is completed, and so the genes the chromosomes carry continue to function normally. This chapter describes chromosomes, how genes are arranged on chromosomes, and how these arrangements influence patterns of inheritance.

EUKARYOTIC CHROMOSOMES

Several years before Mendel's death, Friedrich Schneider (1831–1890) and Walther Flemming (1843–1905) described darkly staining nuclear threads, now called chromosomes. Around the turn of the century, Edouard van Beneden (1849–1922) announced that the number of chromosomes was usually constant in each cell of an organism. The only exception occurred during gamete formation, when the number of chromosomes was reduced by half. These discoveries were quickly followed by those of Thomas Hunt Morgan (1866–1945) and his co-workers, who showed that genes occur in linear arrays on chromosomes.

Since these early studies, research has shown that metaphase chromosomes consist of two chromatids joined at the centromere (*see figure 6.3*). Chromosomes of most animals exist in homologous pairs, which carry genes that code for the same traits and are visually similar. Chromosome size, centromere position, and staining patterns help geneticists recognize homologous pairs.

ORGANIZATION OF DNA AND PROTEIN

Chromatin consists of DNA and histone proteins. Research over the past 20 years has begun to explain how this association of DNA and protein helps with the complex jobs of packing DNA into chromosomes and regulating DNA activity.

There are five different histone proteins. Pairs of four of these proteins form a core particle. DNA wraps in a coil around the proteins, a combination called a **nucleosome** (figure 8.1*a, b*). The fifth histone, sometimes called the linker protein, is not needed to form the nucleosome but may help anchor the DNA to the core and promote the winding of the chain of nucleosomes into a cylinder (*figure 8.1c*). Further folding and the addition of protective proteins result in the formation of chromosomes during mitosis and meiosis.

Many geneticists originally believed that histone proteins simply facilitated the packing of DNA into chromosomes. Further research showed, however, that histone proteins are very similar among different species. For example, histones of peas are almost identical to those of cows. Absence of change in a protein over evolutionary time usually indicates a function so critical to life that mutation is not tolerated. Evidence is now accumulating that histones do much more than package DNA. They are also involved with regulating gene function. When DNA is loosely associated with core histones, associated genes are active; and when DNA is tightly bound to core histones, genes are inactive. (The 10 nm configuration in figure 8.1*c* shows the loosely associated state, and the 30 nm configuration shows the tightly bound state.)

Not all chromatin is equally active. Some human genes, for example, are active only after adolescence. In other cases, entire chromosomes may not function in particular cells. Inactive portions of chromosomes produce dark banding patterns with certain staining procedures and are **heterochromatic regions,** whereas active portions of chromosomes are **euchromatic regions.**

SEX CHROMOSOMES AND AUTOSOMES

In the early 1900s, attention turned to the cell to find a chromosomal explanation for determination of maleness or femaleness. Some of the evidence for a chromosomal basis for sex determination came from work with the insect *Protenor*. One darkly staining chromosome of *Protenor*, called the X chromosome, is represented differently in males and females. All somatic (body) cells of males have one X chromosome (XO), and all somatic cells of females have two X chromosomes (XX). Similarly, half of all sperm contain a single X, and half contain no X, while all female gametes contain a single X. This pattern suggests that fertilization involving an X-bearing sperm will result in a female offspring and that fertilization involving a sperm with no X chromosome will result in a male offspring. As figure 8.2 illustrates, this sex determination system explains the approximately 50:50 ratio of females to males in this insect species. Chromosomes that are represented differently in females than in males and function in sex determination are **sex chromosomes.** Chromosomes that are alike and not involved in determining sex are **autosomes** (Gr. *autus*, self + *soma*, body).

The system of sex determination described for *Protenor* is called the X-O system. It is the simplest system for determining sex because it involves only one kind of chromosome. Many other animals (e.g., humans and fruit flies) have an X-Y system of sex determination. In the X-Y system, males and females have an equal number of chromosomes, but the male is usually XY, and the female is XX. (In birds, the sex chromosomes are designated Z and W, and the female is ZW.) The sex chromosomes may look quite different and carry different genes; however, they function during meiosis as a homologous pair. ❶ This mode of sex determination also results in approximately equal numbers of male and female offspring:

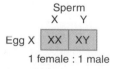

1 female : 1 male

The number of X chromosomes, or the presence of a Y chromosome, is not the only genetic factor that determines sex. An individual's XO or XY status is often referred to as his or her "chromosomal sex." Genes that are not a part of sex chromosomes can influence, and even reverse, the chromosomal sex of some animals.

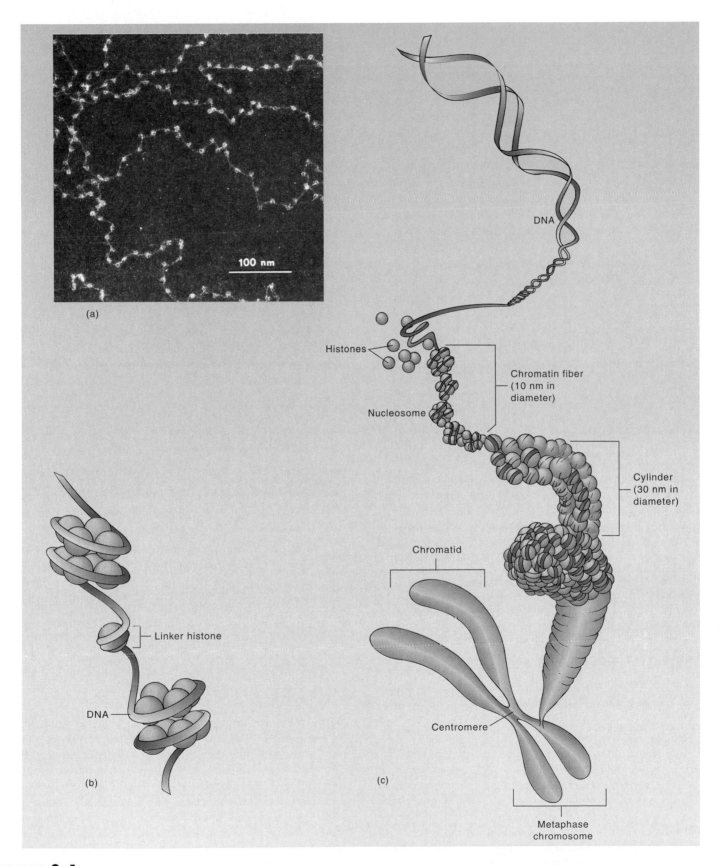

FIGURE 8.1

Organization of Eukaryotic Chromosomes. (*a*) Electron micrograph of a strand of chromatin. Nucleosomes appear as beads arranged sequentially on a thread of DNA. (*b*) A nucleosome consists of four pairs of histone proteins wound by a strand of DNA. Linker histone proteins are associated with DNA between adjacent nucleosomes. (*c*) The nucleosome/DNA chain winds into a cylinder, which then undergoes folding. When chromatin is active, nucleosomes are loosely associated with DNA, and the chromatin is found in the 10 nm in diameter form.

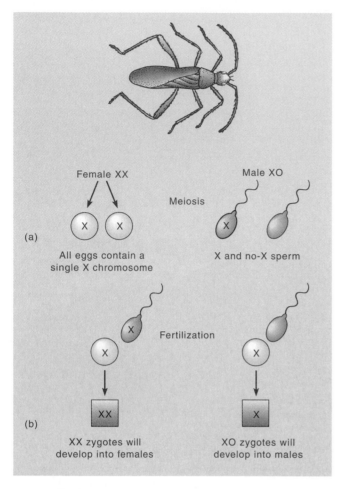

FIGURE 8.2

XO-System of Sex Determination for the Insect *Protenor*. (*a*) In females, all cells except gametes possess two X chromosomes. During meiosis, homologous X chromosomes segregate, and all eggs contain one X chromosome. Males possess one X chromosome per cell. Meiosis results in half of all sperm cells having one X, and half of all sperm cells having no X. (*b*) Fertilization results in half of all offspring having one X chromosome (males), and half of all offspring having two X chromosomes (females).

TABLE 8.1	CHROMOSOME NUMBERS OF SELECTED ANIMALS	
COMMON NAME	SCIENTIFIC NAME	NUMBER OF CHROMOSOMES (2N)
Fruit fly	*Drosophila melanogaster*	8
Frog	*Rana pipiens*	26
Honeybee	*Apis mellifera*	32
Hydra	*Hydra vulguria attenuata*	32
Cat	*Felis domesticus*	38
Rat	*Rattus norvegicus*	42
Human	*Homo sapiens sapiens*	46
Chimpanzee	*Pan troglodytes*	48
Dog	*Canis familiaris*	78
Chicken	*Gallus domesticus*	78
Carp	*Cyprinus carpio*	104

Stop and Ask Yourself

1. What is the difference between chromatin and chromosomes? What is a nucleosome?

2. Why are the numbers of males and females in human offspring approximately equal?

3. What condition has one set (*N*) of chromosomes? What condition has more than two sets of chromosomes (3*N*, 4*N*, etc.)?

NUMBER OF CHROMOSOMES

Even though the number of chromosomes is constant within a species, chromosome number varies greatly among species (table 8.1).

Chromosomes are present in sets, with the number in a set being characteristic of each kind of animal and expressed as "*N*." *N* identifies the number of different kinds of chromosomes. Most animals have two sets, or 2*N* chromosomes. This is the **diploid** (Gr. *di*, two + *eoides*, doubled) condition. Some animals have only one set, or *N* chromosomes (like gametes) and are **haploid** (Gr. *hapl*, single) (e.g., male honeybees and some rotifers).

Very few animals (e.g., brine shrimp, snout beetles, some flatworms, and some sow bugs) have more than the diploid number of chromosomes, a condition called **polyploidy** (Gr. *polys*, more). The upset in numbers of sex chromosomes apparently interferes with reproductive success. Asexual reproduction often accompanies polyploidy.

LINKAGE RELATIONSHIPS

Within a few years of the rediscovery of Mendel's work, William Bateson and R. C. Punnett discovered that certain traits of the pea seemed to violate the principle of independent assortment in that they observed altered ratios in progeny from what they thought was a dihybrid cross. Bateson and Punnett suggested that a physical connection between the genes could explain the results. Geneticists now know that many genes are carried on the same chromosome and are **linked genes.** Because they tend to be inherited together, these genes belong to a **linkage group,** which is the functional definition of a chromosome. Genes on the same chromosome are carried together to one pole of the cell during anaphase I of meiosis and do not assort independently, although the chromosomes do. Linked genes, however, are not linked forever because crossing-over can occur (*see figure 6.9*). In crossing-over, parts of homologous chromosomes can be exchanged and genetic variability among offspring can increase during meiosis.

AUTOSOMAL LINKAGE

Genes linked to autosomal chromosomes tend to be inherited together, and the pattern of inheritance is similar in both males and females. Occasionally, genes are so closely linked that they are always inherited together. This is called **complete linkage.** More often, however, some crossing-over between linked genes results in **incomplete linkage.**

Crossing-over of linked genes occurs during prophase I of meiosis and is also called recombination. Exactly where recombination occurs along a chromosome is random, but not accidental. A complex of proteins, called the synaptonemal complex, helps homologous chromosomes pair in a gene-to-gene fashion, and proteins within that complex are apparently responsible for snipping and rejoining homologous chromosomes. If chromatid fragments from homologous chromosomes rejoin after snipping, crossing-over has occurred (*see figure* 6.9). Geneticists have analyzed rates of crossing-over between linked genes to map the position of genes on chromosomes (figure 8.3).

SEX LINKAGE

Genes linked on sex chromosomes do not necessarily influence traits dealing with sexual characteristics, and inheritance patterns for sex-linked genes are different from those for autosomally linked genes.

X Linkage

Females usually have two X chromosomes, and males usually have a single X chromosome. Therefore, females have two genes for each trait. Males, however, have only one gene and are **hemizygous** for X-linked traits. Genes in the hemizygous state are always expressed, regardless of whether they are dominant or recessive, because there is no allele on a homologous chromosome with which to interact.

In crosses involving X linkage, the genes involved are carried only on the X chromosome. These genes are customarily represented by an "X" to symbolize the X chromosome and superscript letters to symbolize the gene (e.g., X^a or X^A). A "Y" designates the other sex chromosome; it does not have a superscript since the Y chromosome does not carry genes homologous to those on the X chromosome.

The following example illustrates important considerations when working with crosses involving X linkage. A recessive, X-linked allele produces the white eye color in the fruit fly, *Drosophila*. Note that the two crosses in figure 8.4 involve white-eyed flies and red-eyed (wild-type) flies in the parental generation. The results of the two crosses illustrate how X linkage can affect the F_1 flies. In cross A, the male introduces the white eye allele, and in cross B, the female introduces the white eye allele. The results of a cross differ, depending on the sex of the parent that in-

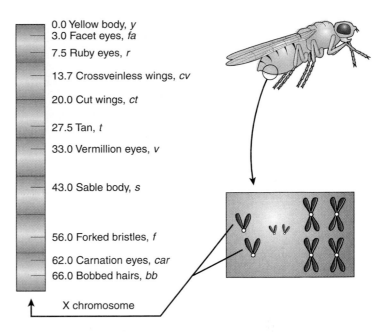

FIGURE 8.3

Partial Map of the X Chromosome of *Drosophila melanogaster*. Map units are shown to the right of the chromosome, along with the name of the locus and its abbreviation.

troduces the mutant gene. Therefore, it is important in crosses involving X linkage to keep track of the sex and phenotype of parents and offspring.

X-linked, recessive traits are expressed in male offspring because the male Y chromosome does not carry an allele to mask the recessive gene. If the mother is heterozygous (a carrier), she will not show the trait, but approximately half of her sons will (figure 8.4; cross A, F_2 and cross B, F_2). Male offspring always receive the X chromosome from their mother and the Y chromosome from their father, and thus, X-linked traits tend to be passed to males from their mothers.

As illustrated in cross A, X-linked recessive genes are often expressed in males of alternate generations. A father who shows a recessive, X-linked trait passes the gene to all of his daughters. The daughters are then carriers and may pass the gene to half of their sons.

❷ X-linked, recessive traits are expressed more frequently in males than in females. For a female offspring to show an X-linked trait, her father must show the trait and her mother must at least be a carrier (cross B, F_2), or the gene in question must be dominant.

Genes carried on the X chromosome determine many human traits. One of these is red-green color blindness. Another, less common trait is hemophilia, or "bleeder's disease."

The Lyon Hypothesis

The unequal numbers of X chromosomes in males and females present an interesting question. Why is it that females, with two Xs, do not produce twice the amount of X-linked gene products

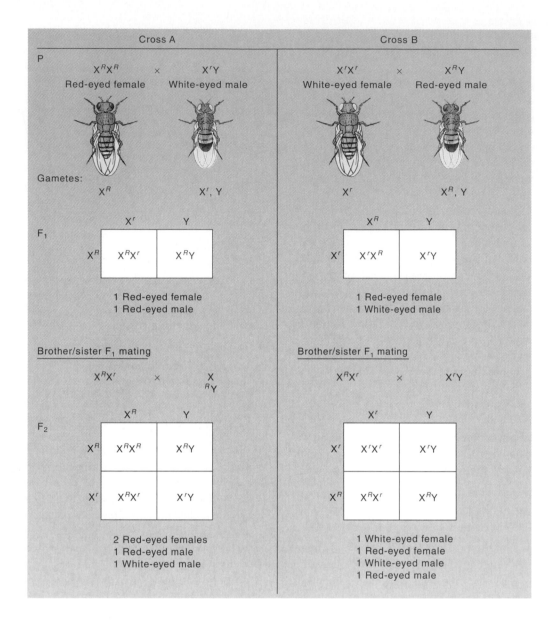

FIGURE 8.4

Patterns of Inheritance of X-linked Traits. Crosses A and B are reciprocal crosses because they differ only in regard to the sex of the parent that introduces a trait (white eye) into the cross. These crosses illustrate several important considerations for working with crosses involving X linkage. X^R = red eye allele; X^r = white eye allele.

that males do? Another interesting and related observation is that females, known to be heterozygous for an X-linked, recessive trait, occasionally express the recessive allele! Mary Lyon's work with mice explained both of these observations.

In 1961, Lyon suggested that at an early stage of development, one of the two X chromosomes present in mammalian body cells, except in some ovarian tissues, is inactivated. Much earlier, Murray L. Barr (1908–) had discovered a densely staining patch of chromatin present in cell nuclei of females but not males. Lyon suggested that each **Barr body** is really an X chromosome that has become entirely inactive, or heterochromatic. This X inactivation occurs early in development, and the X that is inactivated is determined by chance. Because inactivation is random, an occasional female, known to be heterozygous, may express a recessive

X-linked trait (figure 8.5a). ❸ Barr bodies are used in diagnosing certain diseases involving sex chromosome abnormalities, and they have also been used to check the sex of athletes competing in Olympic events that are open to only one sex (figure 8.5b). The procedure involves staining and examining cells scraped from inside the mouth.

Y Linkage

Y linkage is rare because the Y chromosome is small and carries few genes except those determining maleness. The pattern of transmission for Y-linked traits, when they occur, is relatively easy to diagnose. Y-linked traits are passed from a father to all of his sons because all sons must receive their father's Y chromosome.

(a)

(b1)

(b2)

FIGURE 8.5

X Inactivation. (*a*) X inactivation occurs early in development. Coat color in calico cats is an X-linked trait, and the calico coat occurs only in heterozygous females. The orange patches on this cat are made up of cells descended from cells in which the black allele was inactivated. The black patches consist of cells descended from cells in which the orange allele was inactivated. (*b*) A Barr body marks an inactivated X chromosome. Normally, one X chromosome is inactivated in the cells of a female mammal. A normal male cell (*b1*) has no Barr body, and a normal female cell (*b2*) has one Barr body (arrow). (*b1 and b2*) *From Wilson and Foster*, Williams Textbook of Endocrinology *7th ed. © W.B. Saunders 1985.*

SEX-INFLUENCED TRAITS

Autosomally determined traits can also be expressed differently in the two sexes. These **sex-influenced traits** are mentioned briefly in this section on sex linkage because inheritance patterns can superficially resemble patterns for X-linked traits. Consider, for example, the hypothetical family history in figure 8.6, showing a distribution of pattern baldness. As with X-linked traits, a majority of those affected with baldness are males. However, unlike X linkage, the transmission can be (as is the case in figure 8.6) from father to son. Gene physiology, rather than gene transmission, explains the preponderance of affected males. The gene for pattern baldness acts as a dominant gene in males because of high levels of testosterone, the male sex hormone. ➍ Females, on the other hand, express the trait only when the gene is homozygous because female testosterone levels are low.

When the gene is expressed, it results in extreme thinning of hair, but not complete baldness. Because the dominance relationships of the two alleles are not fixed, upper- and lowercase letters cannot be used to symbolize alleles.

Stop and Ask Yourself

4. What is a linkage group?

5. What accounts for a male with a single, recessive, X-linked allele usually showing the recessive trait?

6. What accounts for females heterozygous for an X-linked trait showing either the dominant or recessive phenotype?

7. What is the difference between sex-linked traits and sex-influenced traits?

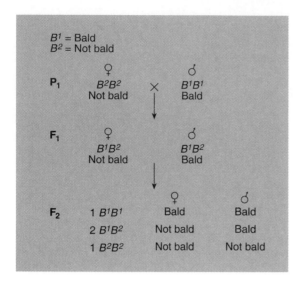

B^1 = Bald
B^2 = Not bald

		♀		♂	
P_1		B^2B^2	×	B^1B^1	
		Not bald		Bald	

		♀		♂
F_1		B^1B^2		B^1B^2
		Not bald		Bald

		♀		♂
F_2	1 B^1B^1	Bald		Bald
	2 B^1B^2	Not bald		Bald
	1 B^2B^2	Not bald		Not bald

FIGURE 8.6

Expression of a Sex-Influenced Trait. Pattern baldness is the result of a gene that is dominant in males and recessive in females.

CHANGES IN CHROMOSOME NUMBER AND STRUCTURE

The genetic material of a cell can change, and these changes increase genetic variability and help increase the likelihood of survival in changing environments. One kind of genetic rearrangement—recombination—has already been discussed. Crossing-over permits linked genes to recombine and experience different genetic environments. Larger, cytologically visible changes include changes in chromosome number and structure.

DETECTING NUMBER AND STRUCTURE CHANGES

Biologists use modern tissue culture techniques to obtain large numbers of rapidly dividing cells so that they can examine chromosomes of humans and other animals. Preparing and examining slides and photographs of metaphase chromosomes is called **karyotyping** (Gr. *karyo*, nucleus + *typos*, image) (figure 8.7). In karyotyping, a small quantity of blood taken from a subject or from the umbilical vein of a fetus is cultured in a medium that promotes the rapid division of certain white blood cells. The cells are killed, applied to a slide, and stained. Well-spread metaphase chromosomes are analyzed by computer-aided techniques or photographed. Images of homologous chromosomes are arranged in order of decreasing size, by centromere position, and by banding patterns, and then numbered 1 to 22, plus X and Y (figure 8.7*b*). Arranging the chromosomes in numbered homologous pairs allows biologists to detect changes in the expected structure and number of the chromosomes. Karyotyping is used to diagnose changes in chromosome numbers and chromosome structure in both fetuses and postnatal individuals.

Checking the number of Barr bodies present in cheek epithelial cells detects changes in the number of X chromosomes. The number of Barr bodies is always one less than the number of X chromosomes. Therefore, a female with no Barr bodies is XO, a female with two Barr bodies is XXX, and a male with one or more Barr bodies has two or more Xs as well as a Y.

VARIATION IN NUMBER

Changes in chromosome number may involve entire sets of chromosomes, as in polyploidy, which was discussed earlier. **Aneuploidy** (Gr. *a*, without), on the other hand, involves the addition or deletion of one or more chromosomes, not entire sets. The addition of one chromosome to the normal 2N chromosome number (2N + 1) is a trisomy (Gr. *tri*, three + ME *some*, a group of), and the deletion of a chromosome from the normal 2N chromosome number (2N − 1) is a monosomy (Gr. *monos*, single).

Errors during meiosis usually cause aneuploidy. **Nondisjunction** occurs when a homologous pair fails to segregate during meiosis I or when chromatids fail to separate at meiosis II (figure 8.8). Gametes produced are either deficient in one chromosome or have an extra chromosome. If one of these gametes is involved in fertilization with a normal gamete, the monosomic or trisomic condition results.

⑤ Trisomy 21, or Down syndrome, is a human trisomy involving chromosome number 21. Symptoms include short and broad hands, short stature, mental retardation, heart problems, and shortened life expectancy. Maternal age and possibly paternal age are important factors in the frequency of nondisjunction of these, and possibly other, chromosomes. Women between the ages of 35 and 39 are 7 times more likely to have a Down syndrome child than women ages 15 to 19. The frequency increases to 20 times for 40- to 45-year-old women, and to 50 times for women over 45. This is an important consideration for couples who, for various reasons, delay having children. Other aneuploid variations usually result in severe consequences involving mental retardation and sterility.

VARIATION IN STRUCTURE

The cell has a variety of protective and repair systems to make DNA a remarkably stable molecule. However, DNA structure does change. Cytologically invisible changes are point mutations, which are discussed in chapter 9. Other changes may involve breaks in chromosomes. After breaking, pieces of chromosomes may be lost, or they may reattach, but not necessarily in their original position. The result is a chromosome that may have a different sequence of genes, multiple copies of genes, or missing genes. All of these changes can occur spontaneously. Various environmental agents, such as ionizing radiation and certain chemicals, can also induce these changes.

Translocations involve transfers of genetic material between nonhomologous chromosomes and may take a number of forms. The most common form involves a single break in each of two chromosomes and an exchange of broken pieces (figure 8.9*a*). Because translocations involve shifting, not deleting or adding,

(a)

(b)

FIGURE 8.7

Karyotyping. (*a*) Karyotypes are routinely prepared from human white blood cells. Similar determinations can be made from samples of fetal blood drawn from an umbilical vein, from cells of the amniotic fluid bathing a fetus, or from samples of certain extraembryonic membranes (the chorion) surrounding a fetus. (Chorion sampling is relatively simple and has an advantage in that it can be performed at an earlier stage of development than sampling amniotic fluid.) Fetal tissues are sampled only in individuals with a significant risk for a disease, since all sampling procedures pose some risk to the fetus. (*b*) Human karyotype.

genetic material, they may not be too serious for the individual. The translocation can, however, cause chromosome defects when gametes form (duplications and deletions).

In some instances, translocations are associated with certain phenotypic abnormalities. A form of Down syndrome, called translocation Down, results from the bottom third of chromosome

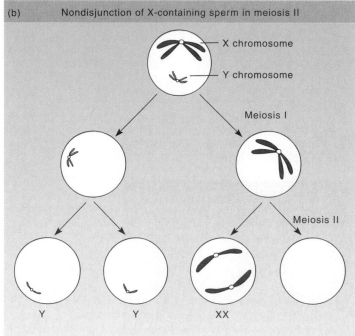

FIGURE 8.8

Results of Primary and Secondary Nondisjunction in Sperm Formation. (*a*) Primary nondisjunction occurs in meiosis I and results in both the X and Y chromosomes ending up in one secondary spermatocyte. A normal second meiotic division results in half of all sperm having both X and Y chromosomes. The other half of all sperm lack any sex chromosomes. (*b*) Secondary nondisjunction occurs after a normal first meiotic division. Failure of the chromatids of the X chromosomes, for example, to separate in the second division means that a fourth of the sperm will have no sex chromosomes, a fourth will have two X chromosomes, and half will have one Y chromosome (from the normal separation of Y chromatids).

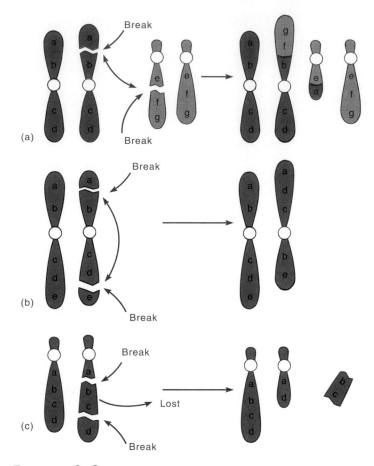

FIGURE 8.9

Common Kinds of Changes in Chromosome Structure. (*a*) Translocations involve transfers of genetic material between nonhomologous chromosomes. (*b*) Inversions occur when a region of a chromatid is flip-flopped, resulting in gene order changes. (*c*) Deletions result from the loss of a segment of a chromosome.

21 being translocated to another chromosome (most often chromosome 14). The gamete could end up with both the normal chromosome 21 and a portion of chromosome 21 being carried on chromosome 14. When fertilization occurs, the zygote contains three copies of some of the genes carried on chromosome 21. A translocation that results in the movement of an arm of human chromosome 22 to chromosome 9 is the first chromosome abnormality associated with a form of cancer. Myeloid leukemia is a malignancy of blood-forming tissues (bone marrow) that causes a proliferation of certain white blood cells.

Inversions involve two breaks in a chromosome, followed by the broken ends rejoining, with the central segment flip-flopped (figure 8.9*b*). The amount of DNA is not changed, but the order of some genes is reversed. Usually, the phenotypic effects are not serious.

Deletions usually result from two breaks in a chromosome and the loss of the intervening chromosome segment (figure 8.9*c*).

The effects of deletions increase in severity as the lost sections become larger. A human genetic disease, called Cri-du-chat (Fr., cry of the cat), results from a loss of part of chromosome 5. Symptoms include a very small head, wide-set eyes, mental retardation, and a catlike cry.

Duplications occur when portions of chromosomes are present in multiple copies. Duplications are difficult to detect in humans, although they probably exist. They are known in many experimental organisms. The effects of duplications are probably less severe than for deletions. In fact, duplicated regions of chromosomes are believed to have had important evolutionary consequences. Because the duplicated genes are extra copies, they are not required for expression of the phenotype. Mutations of duplicated genes may be tolerated and may even prove beneficial.

Stop and Ask Yourself

8. What procedure is used in karyotyping?
9. What is aneuploidy, and how is it likely to occur?
10. How would you describe the following kinds of chromosome rearrangements: (*a*) translocations, (*b*) inversions, (*c*) deletions, and (*d*) duplications?

SUMMARY

1. Eukaryotic chromosomes are complexly coiled associations of DNA and histone proteins.
2. Histone proteins help package DNA in the cell and have important gene regulation functions.
3. The presence or absence of certain chromosomes that are represented differently in males and females determine the sex of an animal. The X-Y system of sex determination is most common.
4. Numbers of chromosomes are constant for a given species. Although some examples of haploidy and polyploidy are cited, diploidy is most common in animals.
5. Genes carried on the same chromosome are linked because they tend to be inherited together.
6. Crossing-over (recombination) results in parts of homologous chromosomes being exchanged during meiosis.
7. X-linked traits show up more frequently in males than females because males are hemizygous for any X-linked gene and show the trait regardless of whether a dominant or a recessive gene determines the trait.
8. Y-linked traits are transmitted exclusively from father to son.
9. Chromosome size, banding patterns, and centromere position can identify particular chromosomes in microscopic preparations.
10. Aneuploidy occurs when one or more, but not entire sets of, chromosomes are added to or deleted from a genome. Aneuploidy results from nondisjunction during the first or second meiotic division. Changes in chromosome number almost always result in severe phenotypic consequences.
11. Changes in chromosome structure include translocations, inversions, deletions, and duplications. The severity of the phenotypic effect depends on the amount of genetic material lost or duplicated.

SELECTED KEY TERMS

aneuploidy (p. 114)
autosomes (p. 108)
chromatin (p. 108)
diploid (p. 110)
haploid (p. 110)
hemizygous (p. 111)

karyotyping (p. 114)
linked genes (p. 110)
nondisjunction (p. 114)
polyploidy (p. 110)
sex chromosomes (p. 108)
translocation (p. 114)

CRITICAL THINKING QUESTIONS

1. Coat color in cats is determined by X-linked alleles, such that black (X^B) is dominant to orange (X^b). Calico cats, however, display patches of orange and black, and they are almost always female. Explain how the Lyon hypothesis can account for these observations.
2. Nondisjunction during the formation of a human sperm may result in XX, YY, XY, or no X- or Y-containing sperm, depending on when nondisjunction occurs. Diagram the meiotic events that could result in each of these sperm. Assuming that each sperm fertilized a normal egg, how many Barr bodies would be present in the resulting zygotes?
3. How would the inheritance pattern for an X-linked, dominant trait be different from that of an X-linked, recessive trait?
4. In recent years, many couples have delayed starting a family until both partners have established a career. What factors should young couples consider before making their decision about when to start a family?
5. Explain why it is important that all regions of chromosomes are not continually active.

REFERENCES ON THE WORLD WIDE WEB

1. **Genetics Jump Station.** This site provides links to journals, other publications, institutes, and news groups dealing with genetics topics.
   http://www.frn.bbsrc.ac.uk/gm/lab/docs/genetics.html
2. **A World of Genetics Societies.** This site provides links to genetics societies concerned with human genetics and medical genetics. It also provides links to educational sites and sites describing careers in genetics.
   http://www.faseb.org/genetics/
3. **Online Mendelian Inheritance in Man.** This site includes a catalog of human genes and genetic disorders. It provides text, images, references, and a map of human chromosomes.
   http://www3.ncbi.nlm.nih.gov/Omim/
4. **The Human Gene Map.** This map allows you to browse human chromosomes. A certain gene is featured on each chromosome, and text material describes the disease conditions associated with that gene.
   http://www.ncbi.nlm.nih.gov/science96/

chapter 9

MOLECULAR GENETICS:
ULTIMATE CELLULAR CONTROL

Concepts

1. Deoxyribonucleic acid (DNA) is the genetic material of the cell. Its double helix structure suggests how it is able to replicate itself and how it can code for the sequences of amino acids that make proteins.
2. Protein synthesis involves two processes. Transcription is the production of a messenger RNA (mRNA) molecule that is complementary to a gene in DNA. Translation is the assembly of proteins at ribosomes based on the genetic information in the transcribed mRNA.
3. Substantial evidence indicates that gene activity changes. The mechanisms for gene regulation in eukaryotic organisms are complex and well understood for only a few genes.
4. Point mutations can drastically alter proteins. Some mutations occur spontaneously; however, various chemicals and radiation can increase mutation rates.
5. Modern genetic technologies manipulate DNA. Recombinant DNA techniques are used to insert DNA into bacteria to produce large quantities of a desired protein. Gene insertion is the introduction of copies of desired genes into an organism lacking those genes.

Would You Like to Know . . .

1. what the "master molecule of life," DNA, looks like? (p. 120)
2. how DNA replicates itself for distribution to daughter cells during cell division? (p. 121)
3. how DNA codes for protein? (p. 123)
4. why genes coding for some proteins (e.g., hormones) are active at some times in your life but not at others? (p. 125)
5. why most mutations are harmful? (p. 127)
6. what happens when a mutation occurs? (p. 127)
7. what biologists are doing in recombinant DNA experiments? (p. 128)
8. what diseases may soon be treatable using gene therapy? (p. 131)

This chapter answers these and other useful questions.

This chapter contains evolutionary concepts, which are set off in this font.

Everyone has a unique combination of physical and personality traits. Many of these characteristics are traceable to genetic differences, and genetic differences are manifested in the kinds of proteins present in each individual. Some of these proteins contribute to observable traits, such as eye color, hair color, and height. Many other proteins contribute to individual uniqueness in more subtle, but just as important, ways. These proteins are enzymes (*see chapter 4*) that regulate rates of chemical reactions in organisms. Within certain environmental limits, you are who you are by the proteins that you synthesize!

This chapter explores the biochemical answers to such questions as: What is a gene? How do genes control the expression of traits? How are gene activities controlled over the life of an organism? Much of the thrust of modern genetics revolves around questions such as these.

DNA: THE GENETIC MATERIAL

Twentieth-century biologists realized that a molecule that serves as the genetic material must have certain characteristics to explain the properties of life. First, the genetic material must be able to code for the sequence of amino acids in proteins and control protein synthesis. Second, it must be able to replicate (produce an exact copy of) itself prior to cell division so that daughter cells receive complete sets of genetic instructions. Third, the genetic material must be in the nucleus of eukaryotic cells. (The participation of the nucleus in fertilization and the chromosomal basis of heredity were described in the early 1900s.) Fourth, it must be able to change over time to account for evolutionary change. Only one molecule, DNA (deoxyribonucleic acid), fulfills all of these requirements.

THE DOUBLE HELIX MODEL

Two kinds of molecules participate in protein synthesis. By the early 1900s, scientists knew that both molecules are in the nucleus and that both are based on a similar building block, the nucleotide, giving them their name—nucleic acids. One of these molecules, **deoxyribonucleic acid** or **DNA,** is the genetic material, and the other, **ribonucleic acid** or **RNA,** is produced in the nucleus and moves to the cytoplasm, where it participates in protein synthesis. The study of how the information stored in DNA codes for RNA and protein is **molecular genetics.**

Nucleic Acid Structure

DNA and RNA are large molecules made up of subunits called nucleotides (figure 9.1). A nucleotide consists of a nitrogen-containing organic base, either in the form of a double ring (**purine**) or a single ring (**pyrimidine**). Nucleotides also contain a pentose (five-carbon) sugar and a phosphate ($-PO_4$) group. DNA and RNA molecules, however, differ in several ways. Both DNA and RNA contain the purine bases adenine and guanine, and the

FIGURE 9.1

Components of Nucleic Acids. (*a*) The nitrogenous bases in DNA and RNA. (*b*) Nucleotides form by attaching a nitrogenous base to the 1′ carbon of a pentose sugar and attaching a phosphoric acid to the 5′ carbon of the sugar. (Carbons of the sugar are numbered with primes to distinguish them from the carbons of the nitrogenous base.) The sugar in DNA is deoxyribose, and the sugar in RNA is ribose. In ribose, a hydroxyl group ($-OH$) would replace the hydrogen shaded yellow.

pyrimidine base cytosine. The second pyrimidine in DNA, however, is thymine, whereas in RNA it is uracil. A second difference in DNA and RNA involves the sugar present in the nucleotides. The pentose of DNA is deoxyribose, and in RNA it is ribose. A third important difference between DNA and RNA is that DNA is a double-stranded molecule and RNA is single stranded, although it may fold back on itself and coil.

The key to understanding the function of DNA is knowing how nucleotides link into a three-dimensional structure. James Watson (1928–), a U.S. biologist, and Francis Crick (1916–), a British biophysicist, propelled research on DNA structure into a new era. ❶ They proposed that the DNA molecule is ladder-like, with the rails of the ladder consisting of alternating sugar-phosphate groups (figure 9.2a). The phosphate of a nucleotide attaches at the fifth (5′) carbon of deoxyribose. Adjacent nucleotides attach to one another by a covalent bond between the phosphate of one nucleotide and the third (3′) carbon of deoxyri-

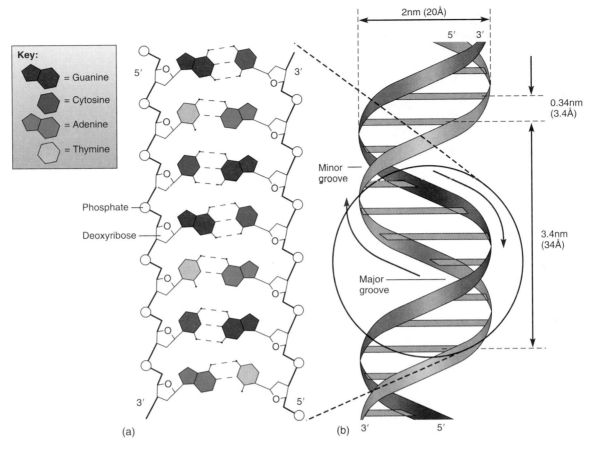

FIGURE 9.2

Structure of DNA. (*a*) Nucleotides of one strand of nucleic acid join by linking the phosphate of one nucleotide to the 3′ carbon of an adjacent nucleotide. Dashed lines between the nitrogenous bases indicate hydrogen bonds. Three hydrogen bonds are between cytosine and guanine, and two are between thymine and adenine. The antiparallel orientation of the two strands is indicated by using the 3′ and 5′ carbons at the ends of each strand. (*b*) Three-dimensional representation of DNA. The antiparallel nature of the strands is indicated by the curved arrows.

bose. The pairing of nitrogenous bases between strands holds the two strands together. Adenine (a purine) is hydrogen bonded to its complement, thymine (a pyrimidine), and guanine (a purine) is hydrogen bonded to its complement, cytosine (a pyrimidine) (figure 9.2b). Each strand of DNA is oriented such that the 3′ carbons of deoxyribose in one strand are oriented in the opposite directions from the 3′ carbons in the other strand. The strands' terminal phosphates are, therefore, at opposite ends, and the DNA molecule is thus said to be **antiparallel** (Gr. *anti*, against + *para*, beside + *allelon*, of one another). The entire molecule is twisted into a right-handed helix, with one complete spiral every 10 base pairs (figure 9.2b). This description of DNA is accurate for DNA from nearly all organisms.

DNA REPLICATION IN EUKARYOTES

2 In the late 1950s, Matthew Meselson and Franklin Stahl elegantly demonstrated an important aspect of DNA replication. They showed that each DNA strand is a template for a new strand because the pairing requirements between purine and pyrimidine bases dictate the positioning of nucleotides in a new strand. Thus, each new DNA molecule contains one strand from the old DNA molecule and one newly synthesized strand. Because half of the old molecule is conserved in the new molecule, DNA replication is said to be semiconservative.

DNA replication in eukaryotic cells occurs in many chromosomes simultaneously, involves numerous enzymes, and requires the production of histone proteins that associate with the DNA in chromatin (*see figure 8.1*). Once enzymes have separated the strands, DNA replication begins simultaneously at many sites along the strands. The replication units, which are the DNA segments copied at each initiation site, are called replicons (figure 9.3). Two new strands are synthesized simultaneously, going in both directions from the initiation site of a replicon. DNA polymerases—the enzymes that assemble nucleotides into DNA strands—copy an existing strand, beginning at the 3′ end and working toward the 5′ end. Because the replicated strand is complementary to the old strand, the new DNA strands are synthesized from their 5′ end to their 3′ end.

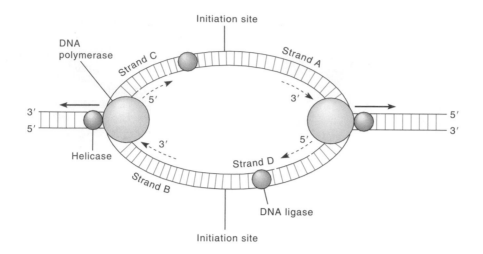

FIGURE 9.3

DNA Replication. Replication begins simultaneously at many initiation sites along the length of a chromosome. The DNA associated with each initiation site is called a replicon. Notice that synthesis of strands A and B is continuous from the initiation site, and that synthesis of strands C and D is discontinuous from the initiation site. Strands C and D are produced in fragments because DNA polymerase can only produce new DNA strands in the 5′ to 3′ direction. Helicase enzymes aid in the untwisting of the double helix during replication, and DNA ligase enzymes join DNA fragments produced during replication. Replication is bidirectional from the initiation site. Dashed arrows indicate the direction of DNA elongation. Solid arrows indicate the bidirectional progress of replication.

Stop and Ask Yourself

1. How are the nucleotides of DNA and RNA similar? How are they different?
2. Why is the DNA molecule antiparallel?
3. Why is DNA replication semiconservative?
4. What is the function of DNA polymerases?

GENES IN ACTION

In the 1930s, George Beadle and Edward Tatum studied the important relationship between genes and enzymes. Their research culminated in the one-gene/one-enzyme hypothesis, stating that one gene codes for one specific enzyme. This hypothesis has been revised as scientists have learned more about proteins and today is known as the **one-gene/one-polypeptide theory.**

This early work indicated to later researchers that the genetic material must carry instructions for protein synthesis. A gene can be defined as a sequence of bases in DNA that codes for the synthesis of one polypeptide, and genes must somehow transmit their information from the nucleus to the cytoplasm, where protein synthesis occurs. The **central dogma** of molecular genetics describes the relationship among the steps from DNA to the production of a protein (figure 9.4). The synthesis of an RNA molecule is called **transcription** (L. *trans*, across + *scriba*, to write), and the decoding of the message at the ribosome is called **translation** (L. *trans*, to transfer + *latere*, to remain hidden).

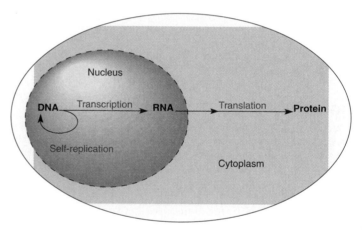

FIGURE 9.4

Central Dogma. Transcription involves the production of messenger RNA (mRNA) from DNA in the nucleus. Messenger RNA carries the transcribed code from the nucleus to the cytoplasm, where translation occurs. Translation is the decoding of the message in mRNA and the production of a protein.

THREE MAJOR KINDS OF RNA

Each of the three major kinds of RNA has a specific role in protein synthesis and is produced in the nucleus from DNA. **Messenger RNA (mRNA)** is a linear strand that carries a set of genetic instructions for synthesizing proteins to the cytoplasm. **Transfer RNA (tRNA)** picks up amino acids in the cytoplasm, carries them to ribosomes, and helps position them for incorporation into a polypeptide. **Ribosomal RNA (rRNA),** along with proteins, makes up ribosomes.

Second position

First position	U	C	A	G	Third position
U	UUU ⎫ Phe UUC ⎭ UUA ⎫ Leu UUG ⎭	UCU ⎫ UCC ⎪ Ser UCA ⎪ UCG ⎭	UAU ⎫ Tyr UAC ⎭ UAA ⎫ STOP UAG ⎭	UGU ⎫ Cys UGC ⎭ UGA STOP UGG Trp	U C A G
C	CUU ⎫ CUC ⎪ Leu CUA ⎪ CUG ⎭	CCU ⎫ CCC ⎪ Pro CCA ⎪ CCG ⎭	CAU ⎫ His CAC ⎭ CAA ⎫ Gln CAG ⎭	CGU ⎫ CGC ⎪ Arg CGA ⎪ CGG ⎭	U C A G
A	AUU ⎫ AUC ⎪ Ile AUA ⎭ AUG Met	ACU ⎫ ACC ⎪ Thr ACA ⎪ ACG ⎭	AAU ⎫ Asn AAC ⎭ AAA ⎫ Lys AAG ⎭	AGU ⎫ Ser AGC ⎭ AGA ⎫ Arg AGG ⎭	U C A G
G	GUU ⎫ GUC ⎪ Val GUA ⎪ GUG ⎭	GCU ⎫ GCC ⎪ Ala GCA ⎪ GCG ⎭	GAU ⎫ Asp GAC ⎭ GAA ⎫ Glu GAG ⎭	GGU ⎫ GGC ⎪ Gly GGA ⎪ GGG ⎭	U C A G

Ala	=	Alanine	Leu =	Leucine
Arg	=	Arginine	Lys =	Lysine
Asn	=	Aparagine	Met =	Methionine
Asp	=	Aspartic acid	Phe =	Phenylalanine
Cys	=	Cysteine	Pro =	Proline
Gin	=	Glutamine	Ser =	Serine
Glu	=	Glutamic acid	Thr =	Threonine
Gly	=	Glycine	Trp =	Tryptophan
His	=	Histidine	Tyr =	Tyrosine
Ile	=	Isoleucine	Val =	Valine

FIGURE 9.5

Genetic Code. Sixty-four messenger RNA codons are shown here. The first base of the triplet is on the left side of the figure, the second base is at the top, and the third base is on the right side. The abbreviations for amino acids are also shown. In addition to coding for the amino acid methionine, the AUG codon is the initiator codon. Three codons—UAA, UAG, and UGA—do not code for an amino acid but act as a signal to stop protein synthesis.

THE GENETIC CODE

DNA must code for the 20 different amino acids found in all organisms. ③ The information-carrying capabilities of DNA reside in the sequence of nitrogenous bases. The genetic code is a sequence of three bases—a triplet code. Figure 9.5 shows the genetic code as reflected in the mRNA that will be produced from DNA. Each three-base combination is a **codon,** and close examination of figure 9.5 reveals that more than one codon can specify the same amino acid because there are 64 possible codons, but only 20 amino acids. This characteristic of the code is referred to as **degeneracy.** Usually, when the first two bases are determined, the amino acid is determined. Note that not all codons code for an amino acid. The base sequences UAA, UAG, and UGA are all stop signals. As a period indicates the end of a sentence, a stop codon indicates where polypeptide synthesis should end. The base sequence AUG codes for the amino acid methionine, which is a start signal.

The genetic code is a universal code because of its remarkable constancy in virtually all life-forms. Exceptions to the code have been found only in the DNA of mitochondria and a few single-celled organisms.

TRANSCRIPTION

The central dogma indicates that the genetic information in DNA is not translated directly into proteins, but is first transcribed into mRNA. Transcription involves numerous enzymes that unwind a region of a DNA molecule, initiate and end mRNA synthesis, and modify the mRNA after transcription is complete. Unlike DNA replication, only one or a few genes are exposed, and only one of the two DNA strands is transcribed (figure 9.6).

One of the important enzymes of this process is RNA polymerase. After a section of DNA is unwound, RNA polymerase recognizes a specific sequence of DNA nucleotides called the promoter. RNA polymerase attaches at the promoter and begins joining ribose nucleotides, which are complementary to the 3′ end of the DNA strand. As in replication, the new nucleotide sequence (which now will be RNA) is formed in the 5′ to 3′ direction. In RNA, the same complementary bases in DNA are paired, except that in RNA, the base uracil replaces the base thymine as a complement to adenine. Thus, everywhere adenine occurs in the DNA being transcribed, uracil is the complementary base added to the mRNA strand.

Newly transcribed mRNA, called the primary transcript, must be modified before leaving the nucleus to carry out protein synthesis. Some base sequences in newly transcribed mRNA do not code for proteins. In eukaryotic organisms, noncoding regions called introns interrupt the base sequences that code for proteins, called exons. RNA splicing involves cutting out introns so that the mRNA coding region can be read continuously at the ribosome.

TRANSLATION

Translation is protein synthesis at the ribosomes in the cytoplasm, based on the genetic information in the transcribed mRNA.

Amino Acids and tRNA

Another type of RNA, called transfer RNA (tRNA), is important in the translation process. It brings the different amino acids coded for by the mRNA into alignment so that a polypeptide can be made. Transfer RNA is frequently represented as a two-dimensional cloverleaf (figure 9.7a), although the molecule actually undergoes helical twisting (figure 9.7b). Complementary pairing of bases across the molecule maintains tRNA's configuration. The

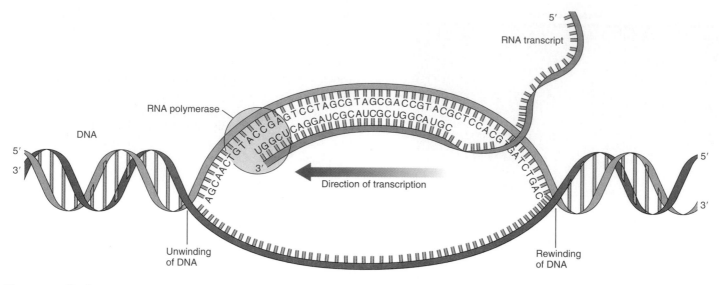

FIGURE 9.6

Transcription. Transcription involves the production of a messenger RNA molecule that is complementary to the coding strand of the DNA segment. Note that transcription is similar to DNA replication in that the molecule is synthesized in the 5′ to 3′ direction.

shape of tRNA has important functional implications. The presence of some unusual bases (i.e., other than adenine, thymine, cytosine, guanine, or uracil) disrupts the normal base pairing and forms loops in the molecule. The center loop (the "anticodon loop") has a sequence of three unpaired bases called the **anticodon.** During translation, pairing of the mRNA codon with its complementary anticodon of tRNA appropriately positions the amino acid that tRNA carries.

Ribosomes, mRNA, and Peptide Bonds

Ribosomes, the sites of protein synthesis, consist of large and small subunits that organize the pairing between the codon and the anticodon. Several sites on the ribosome are binding sites for mRNA and tRNA. At the initiation of translation, mRNA binds to a small, separate ribosomal subunit. Attachment of the mRNA requires that the initiation codon (AUG) of mRNA be aligned with the P (peptidyl) site of the ribosome. A tRNA with a complementary anticodon for methionine binds to the mRNA, and a large subunit joins, forming a complete ribosome.

Polypeptide formation can now begin. Another site, the A (aminoacyl) site, is next to the P site. A second tRNA, whose anticodon is complementary to the codon in the A site, is positioned. Two tRNA molecules with their attached amino acids are now side-by-side in the P and A sites (figure 9.8). This step requires enzyme aid and energy, in the form of guanine triphosphate (GTP). An enzyme (peptidyl transferase), which is actually a part of the larger ribosomal subunit, breaks the bond between the amino acid and tRNA in the P site, and catalyzes the formation of a peptide bond between that amino acid and the amino acid in the A site. (ATP previously conferred the energy for this reaction to the bond between the amino acid and tRNA.)

The mRNA strand then moves along the ribosome a distance of one codon. This step requires more enzymatic action and more energy from GTP. The tRNA with two amino acids attached to it that was in the A site is now in the P site. A third tRNA can now enter the exposed A site. This process continues until the entire mRNA has been translated, and a polypeptide chain has been synthesized. Often, many ribosomes translate a single mRNA strand simultaneously. Translation ends when a termination codon (e.g., UAA) is encountered. Proteins called release factors, as well as the hydrolysis of GTP to GDP + P_i, are involved in release of the ribosome from the mRNA.

In spite of the complexities of translation, the process is very rapid. Approximately 20 peptide bonds form every second. An average-sized protein can be synthesized in about 15 seconds at a cost of four high-energy bonds per peptide bond.

POSTTRANSLATIONAL MODIFICATIONS

Proteins synthesized in the translation process have a variety of destinations in an animal. Some are secreted from a cell, some are incorporated into lysosomes, some make up components of membranes, and some make up the cell's structural framework. Others act as enzymes. Most proteins are synthesized as preproteins. Preproteins have a sequence of amino acids attached at one end that helps direct them to their destination.

Protein synthesis often occurs on ribosomes on the surface of the rough endoplasmic reticulum (ER; *see figure 3.15*). The positioning of ribosomes on the ER allows preproteins to move into the ER as the protein is being translated. Once the preprotein or a portion of it is through the membrane, amino acids that do not contribute to the finished protein are cleaved from the molecule, and when the translation is finished, the protein can be moved to the Golgi apparatus for packaging into a secretory vesicle or a lysosome.

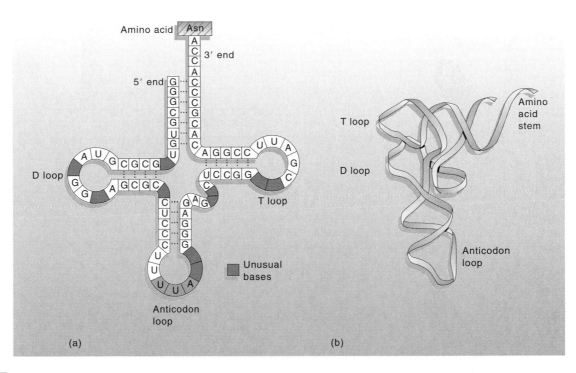

FIGURE 9.7

Structure of Transfer RNA. (*a*) Diagrammatic representation of the secondary structure of transfer RNA (tRNA). An amino acid attaches to the 3′ end of the molecule. The ACC base sequence at this end of the molecule is present in all tRNAs. The "t loop" helps position tRNA at the ribosome. The anticodon is the sequence of three bases that pairs with the codon in mRNA, thus positioning the amino acid that tRNA carries. Other aspects of tRNA structure position the tRNA in the enzyme that attaches the correct amino acid to the tRNA. (*b*) More accurate representation of tRNA, showing its three-dimensional folding.

Stop and Ask Yourself

5. The genetic code is a degenerate code. What does this mean?

6. How does a primary transcript differ from the mRNA molecule that leaves the nucleus?

7. What is the anticodon?

8. What is the role of the following in protein synthesis: (*a*) A site, (*b*) P site, and (*c*) preprotein?

CONTROL OF GENE EXPRESSION IN EUKARYOTES

The gene control processes that function in prokaryotic organisms are well understood. Genes of prokaryotes usually link into functional units called operons. Operons consist of **structural genes,** which are genes that code for the desired end product, and **regulator genes,** which control transcription of the structural genes. Similar regulatory genes exist in eukaryotic organisms. The control of gene function in eukaryotic organisms is very complex, and details of gene regulation are well known for only a few genes.

4 Many genes are functional only during particular stages in the life history of an animal. Consider, for example, the changes that humans go through only during puberty. Other genes are turned on and off more frequently. Aldosterone, for example, is a steroid hormone produced in the cortex (outer region) of the adrenal gland. This hormone functions at the kidney to promote reabsorption of sodium from the urine and secretion of potassium into the urine. Aldosterone enters kidney cells by diffusion, combines with a cytoplasmic receptor, and enters the nucleus to alter gene activity.

Cytological evidence indicates that gene activity changes throughout the life of an animal cell and that changes in gene activity may alter chromosome structure. In addition, most animals have far more DNA in the nuclei of their cells than codes for all of their proteins. Some of this extra DNA may consist of regulatory genes.

MUTATIONS

Genetic material must account for evolutionary change. Mutations are changes in the structure of genes and chromosomes. Chapter 8 discusses changes in chromosome number and cytologically visible changes in structure. **Point mutations** are changes in nucleotide sequences and may result from the replacement, addition, or deletion of nucleotides. Mutations are always random events.

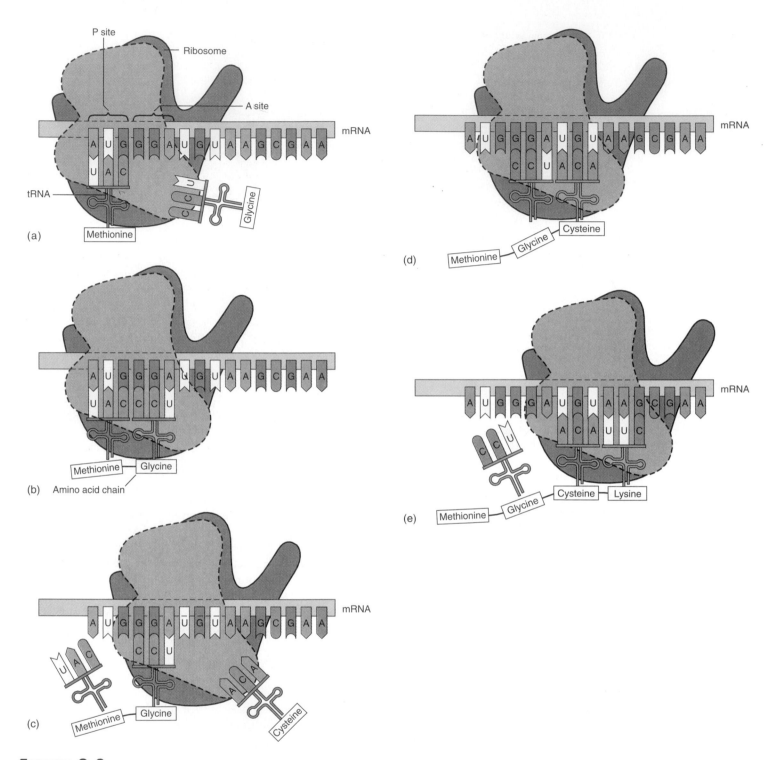

FIGURE 9.8

Events of Translation. (*a*) Translation begins when a methionine tRNA associates with the P site of the smaller ribosomal subunit and the initiation codon of mRNA associated with that subunit. The larger ribosomal subunit attaches to the small subunit/tRNA complex. (*b*) A second tRNA carrying the next amino acid enters the A site. A peptide bond forms between the two amino acids, freeing the first tRNA in the P site. (*c*) The mRNA, along with the second tRNA and its attached dipeptide, moves the distance of one codon. The first tRNA is discharged, leaving its amino acid behind. The second tRNA is now in the P site, and the A site is exposed and ready to receive another tRNA-amino acid. (*d*) A second peptide bond forms. (*e*) This process continues until an mRNA stop signal is encountered.

Although certain environmental factors may change mutation rates, predicting what genes will be affected or what the nature of the change will be is impossible. ⑤ Some mutations may be unnoticed or even beneficial. However, the consequences of genetic changes are usually negative because they disturb the structure of proteins that are the products of millions of years of evolution.

KINDS OF POINT MUTATIONS

Animals are protected from the negative effects of base changes when the changes occur in the third position of a DNA triplet. Because the first two bases of a DNA triplet code for many amino acids, the third base can vary and not change the amino acid specified. Thus, roughly 30% of all single base changes will never manifest themselves in altered protein structure and are "silent" mutations.

⑥ On the other hand, base changes in the first or second position of a DNA code, and sometimes base changes in the third position, result in the substitution of one amino acid for another. Sickle-cell anemia (*see chapter 7*) reduces the ability of hemoglobin to carry oxygen and causes affected red blood cells to get stuck in, and clog, capillary beds. These dramatic changes in circulatory physiology result from a single base substitution in one of the polypeptides of hemoglobin. Valine (GUG) is substituted for glutamic acid (GAG) at one position. Mutations that result in single amino acid changes are missense mutations.

Mutations that produce the most severe changes in protein structure are the result of the addition or deletion of a base. These mutations are called frameshift mutations because adding or deleting a base causes all codons after the change to be misread. This kind of change is likely to create a useless protein (figure 9.9).

Point of nucleotide
insertion in (b) and (c)
↓

(a) 5′ A U G | C C A | U A C | U G G | U A A 3′
        Met   Pro   Tyr   Trp   STOP

(b) 5′ A U G | C C A | U C A | C U G | G U A 3′
        Met   Pro   Ser   Ser   Val

(c) 5′ A U G | C C A | U A A | C U G | G U A 3′
        Met   Pro   STOP   Ser   Val

FIGURE 9.9

Frameshift Mutations. Segment of mRNA, showing how insertion of a nucleotide can cause frameshift mutations. (*a*) Normal mRNA base sequence. (*b*) The insertion of "C" deletes the stop signal and alters the sequence of amino acids following the point of insertion. (*c*) The insertion of "A" creates a stop signal in the middle of a gene, causing premature termination.

CAUSES OF MUTATIONS

Although various environmental agents increase mutation rates, mutations are not unique to the modern world. They have occurred throughout the history of life on earth. Many mutations are spontaneous because they have no obvious cause. Many of these are a result of base-pairing errors during replication, which result in a substitution of one base pair for another.

A variety of mutagenic agents affect mutation rates. Thousands of chemicals used in industry and in science laboratories are suspected mutagens. Some of these chemicals, such as 5-bromodeoxyuridine, have structures similar to normal DNA bases, but may pair differently during replication and cause a base substitution. Other chemicals change the structure of certain bases. Nitrous acid (HNO_2), a powerful mutagen, converts adenine to a guaninelike compound, and after replication, an A-T base pair would be changed to a G-C base pair.

Electromagnetic radiation (ultraviolet light, X rays, and gamma rays) and nuclear radiation (alpha and beta particles, protons, and neutrons) are also mutagenic. Ultraviolet light from the sun, for example, easily penetrates the outer epidermal cell layers and can cause base substitutions in DNA of cells in the germinal layers of the epidermis. These changes are a primary cause of skin cancer.

Fortunately, cells have DNA repair mechanisms, so that damage is often repaired without detrimental effects. Repair mechanisms involve enzyme systems that detect a base change by comparing the altered strand to the complementary strand and cut out and replace the altered base.

Stop and Ask Yourself

9. What evidence indicates that many genes are active only at certain times?
10. What are (*a*) "silent" mutations, (*b*) missense mutations, and (*c*) frameshift mutations?
11. How does the double helix of DNA protect against the negative effects of point mutations?

APPLICATIONS OF GENETIC TECHNOLOGIES

Technologies that have allowed scientists to understand life are now being applied to manipulate life. Most scientists and many laypersons would agree that these technologies have great potential for improving the quality of life on earth. For example, scientists can now assay individuals for some genetic abnormalities before birth, detect some abnormalities hidden in the genome of prospective parents, control fertilization, and manipulate DNA (figure 9.10). However, numerous ethical considerations

(a)

(b)

(c)

(d)

(e)

FIGURE 9.10

Manipulation of DNA. (*a*) Preparation of an electrophoretic gel for the analysis of nucleic acids. (*b*) Analysis of gel electrophoresis results and determination of DNA base sequences. (*c*) Hybridoma cells to be used in the production of monoclonal antibodies are stored at −34° C (−94° F). (*d*) Purification of a product by column chromatography. (*e*) Interferon production in a large fermenter.

accompany the use of these technologies. The remainder of this chapter focuses on two applications of genetic technologies and briefly discusses ethical dilemmas that each application presents.

RECOMBINANT DNA

⑦ **Recombinant DNA** techniques involve the incorporation of human, or other, DNA into bacteria or other host cells in hopes that the cells will become factories for the desired protein. For example, most of the growth hormone used to treat dwarfism is now produced using recombinant DNA techniques.

Recombinant DNA techniques differ, depending on whether interest is in producing a protein of prokaryotic or eu-

karyotic origin. Either case, however, requires a vector to incorporate foreign DNA into the bacteria. One kind of vector is a plasmid. Plasmids are small, extrachromosomal circles of DNA that occur naturally in bacteria. They replicate independently from a bacterial chromosome, can be isolated by gel electrophoresis, and can be incorporated back into bacteria using a calcium-enriched medium. Because plasmids are self-replicating, many copies of an engineered plasmid are present in each bacterial cell. Isolating prokaryotic DNA for transfer involves cutting the DNA into fragments using restriction enzymes. The same kind of enzyme is used to cleave plasmids (figure 9.11*a*). When plasmid DNA and DNA fragments are mixed, and an enzyme called DNA ligase is added, the fragments and the plasmid DNA

FIGURE 9.11

Recombinant DNA. (*a*) These techniques involve cutting plasmid DNA and donor DNA with restriction enzymes. This process leaves the ends of DNA fragments with complementary base sequences. (The electron micrograph shows a cleaved plasmid and a fragment of host DNA.) (*b*) Ligase enzymes join plasmid and host fragments. (*c*) The plasmid, now containing host DNA, is introduced into bacteria. (Note the recombined plasmid lying next to the bacterium in the electron micrograph.)

may join (figure 9.11*b*). The plasmids can then be reincorporated into bacteria (figure 9.11*c*).

After incorporating DNA into bacteria, the investigator must find the bacterial copies that contain the plasmids with the desired gene. Not all plasmids will have incorporated the desired gene, and not all bacteria will have incorporated plasmids. If the plasmid has genes that convey resistance to an antibiotic, culturing bacteria on a medium containing that antibiotic will select for bacteria containing the plasmid. Out of those bacteria that survive, only a few will have the desired gene. One technique for isolating these bacteria involves isolating mRNA from a cell culture

actively synthesizing the desired protein and incorporating a radioactive label into that mRNA. The mRNA has a base sequence complementary to the desired gene, and hybridization (bonding) between mRNA and DNA can be induced. This procedure is done by transferring bacterial colonies to special filter paper, treating the filter paper with alkali to separate DNA strands, and flooding the filter paper with labeled mRNA. The filter paper is then placed on photographic film, and the hybridized DNA/mRNA exposes the film, identifying the bacterial colony containing the desired gene. Bacteria from that colony can be cultured, and their protein product recovered.

BOX 9.1 TRANSGENIC ANIMALS

Although recombinant DNA technology was pioneered in bacteria, it is now being applied to animals. When an animal cell receives a foreign gene, and then an individual develops from the engineered cell, the resulting organism is termed **transgenic** (L. *trans*. through + *genes*). The altered cell can be from an oocyte or fertilized egg of a sexually reproducing animal.

Because transgenic animals can produce large quantities of valuable drugs, they may revolutionize the pharmaceutical industry. For example, in Edinburgh, Scotland, a flock of sheep now exists that is a direct descendant of one ewe (a female sheep) named Ethel. When Ethel was a fertilized egg, she received a human gene for factor VIII. Factor VIII is a blood protein that animals and humans need for blood to clot. If it is absent, hemophilia results. As a result of the inserted human gene for factor VIII, Ethel and her progeny now produce large amounts of factor VIII in their milk. This valuable protein need only

be separated from the sheep's milk to supply enough clotting factor for all of the hemophiliacs in the world.

Transgenic goats have been similarly engineered to secrete tissue-plasminogen activator (t-PA) in their milk (figure 1). Tissue-plasminogen activator dissolves blood clots in the treatment of heart attacks and arterial blockages. Transgenic mice that contain the gene for breast cancer have been engineered, enabling scientists to study this human disease in an animal model. Other transgenic mice lack an immune system (have severe combined immune deficiency [SCID]) and are now models for studying such human diseases as acquired immunodeficiency syndrome (AIDS), muscular dystrophy, and diabetes. Pig embryos injected with human hemoglobin genes develop into transgenic pigs that synthesize human hemoglobin. Current plans are to purify human hemoglobin and use it as a blood substitute.

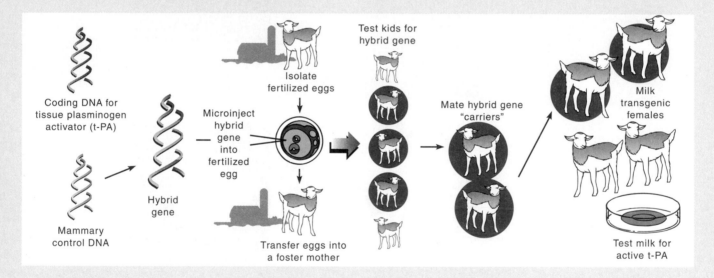

FIGURE 1 **How to Put t-PA into Goat's Milk.** Circled goats symbolize those goats found to carry the t-PA gene.

Techniques for incorporating eukaryotic DNA into plasmids are slightly different. They begin by isolating mRNA rather than DNA because mRNA from a cell undergoing protein synthesis will not have intron base sequences. An enzyme called reverse transcriptase produces DNA from the mRNA. This DNA, called complementary DNA (cDNA), can be incorporated into plasmids and into bacteria in the usual fashion. Culturing these bacteria can result in large quantities of protein at relatively low cost.

The Controversy

Recombinant DNA technologies can provide supplies of valuable proteins and useful bacteria. Concerns regarding the application of these technologies, however, center around recombinant organisms that eventually need to be tested outside the laboratory. Even

though scientists may take precautions to ensure that bacteria will have little chance of harming the environment, many people have concerns about the uncontrolled proliferation of engineered organisms. Thus, even though guidelines for laboratory applications have been relaxed, guidelines for field tests are stringent.

GENE INSERTION

Gene insertion is introducing copies of desired genes into an organism that lacks those genes (box 9.1). In human applications, gene insertion, or gene therapy, has been used to insert normal genes into a patient with defective genes. In other applications, it could involve the insertion of genes for disease resistance, faster growth, or increased size into plant or animal stocks.

FIGURE 9.12

Genetic Treatment for SCID. A blood sample is drawn from the umbilical cord of a SCID newborn. Stem cells are isolated and incubated with retroviruses containing the ADA gene. After the ADA gene is incorporated into the stem cells, the stem cells are allowed to multiply and then are reinjected into the infant. The hope is that genetically altered cells will take over the production of T lymphocytes, resulting in a permanent supply of ADA.

A recent attempt at human gene therapy illustrates the basic strategy of gene insertion. SCID (severe combined immune deficiency) represents a group of diseases that affects one in 100,000 infants. Affected individuals have essentially no immune system, and they often die from otherwise mild childhood infections.

In one form of SCID, a group of white blood cells, called T lymphocytes, lacks the ability to produce an enzyme called adenosine deaminase (ADA). This enzyme breaks down chemicals that destroy T lymphocytes. In the absence of ADA, T lymphocytes are destroyed, and the immune system does not function. Treatment for this form of SCID has involved receiving injections of ADA, isolated from cattle, twice each week for the life of the individual.

In 1993, Donald Kohn and his colleagues at Children's Hospital in Los Angeles attempted a genetic cure for this disease in three SCID newborns (figure 9.12). They used recombinant DNA techniques to isolate and clone the normal ADA gene, and then inserted the ADA gene into specially engineered viruses called retroviruses. Retroviruses can insert DNA into a human cell, but they do not damage the cell. When the three SCID infants were born, T lymphocyte precursor cells (stem cells) were isolated from their umbilical cords. Stem cells normally reside in the bone marrow and divide throughout life to produce T lymphocytes and other blood cells. These stem cells were incubated with the retroviruses, and then they were injected into the infants with the hope that transformed cells would make their way into the bone marrow and begin producing T lymphocytes capable of ADA synthesis.

These attempts at a genetic cure for SCID have been encouraging. The follow-up studies show that the T lymphocyte descendants of the stem cells treated at the birth of these children

are producing ADA. While these children still receive weekly ADA injections, doctors are slowly decreasing the quantity of enzyme injected and are closely monitoring the amount of circulating ADA. ADA injections may soon be unnecessary.

⑧ Gene therapies are being designed for other diseases. Genetic diseases like cystic fibrosis and hypercholesterolemia may soon be treated in a fashion similar to the SCID treatment. Cancers—such as melanoma, neuroblastoma, and brain tumors—and AIDS may also be treatable by genetically altering immune cells that are targeted at these diseased cells or by creating immune cells that are resistant to infection by HIV and other viruses.

The Controversy

Undoubtedly, gene insertion will become a reality; it has tremendous potential for good. Ethical concerns regard decision-making processes involved with these manipulations. Some individuals question whether humans should alter the human genome. Others simply wonder who will be trusted to make decisions about what genes are "good" and what genes are "bad."

Stop and Ask Yourself
12. How are the following used in recombinant DNA techniques: (*a*) restriction enzymes, (*b*) plasmids, (*c*) DNA ligase, and (*d*) reverse transcriptase?
13. What is gene insertion? How is gene insertion being used in the treatment of SCID patients?

SUMMARY

1. Deoxyribonucleic acid (DNA) is the hereditary material of the cell. Ribonucleic acid (RNA) participates in protein synthesis.

2. Nucleotides are nucleic acid building blocks. Nucleotides consist of a nitrogenous (purine or pyrimidine) base, a phosphate, and a pentose sugar.

3. DNA consists of a double helix in which the sugar-phosphate groups form the rails of the helix and nitrogenous bases pair across the molecule, held by hydrogen bonds.

4. DNA replication is semiconservative. During replication, the DNA strands separate, and each strand is a template for a new strand. Half of the old molecule is conserved in each new molecule.

5. A gene is a series of nucleotides of DNA that code for a single polypeptide.

6. Protein synthesis is a result of two processes. Transcription involves the production of a messenger RNA molecule from a DNA molecule. Translation involves the movement of messenger RNA to the cytoplasm, where transfer RNA and ribosomes link amino acids in a proper sequence to produce a polypeptide.

7. Proteins are often produced as preproteins. Sequences of amino acids attached at one end of the protein help direct proteins to their destination.

8. Cytological evidence indicates that gene activity changes throughout the life of an animal cell. The details of gene regulation in eukaryotes are well known for only a few genes.

9. Point mutations are changes in nucleotide sequences in DNA. Mutations can occur spontaneously, although a variety of mutagenic agents, such as various chemicals and electromagnetic and nuclear radiation, affect mutation rates.

10. Recombinant DNA techniques involve the incorporation of human, or other, DNA into bacteria or other cells in hopes that the cell will produce a desired protein. Gene insertion involves the introduction of desired genes into an organism that lacks those genes.

SELECTED KEY TERMS

anticodon (p. 124)
antiparallel (p. 121)
codon (p. 123)
deoxyribonucleic acid (DNA) (p. 120)
messenger RNA (mRNA) (p. 122)
molecular genetics (p. 120)

point mutations (p. 125)
regulator genes (p. 125)
ribonucleic acid (RNA) (p. 120)
ribosomal RNA (rRNA) (p. 122)
structural genes (p. 125)
transcription (p. 122)
transfer RNA (tRNA) (p. 122)
translation (p. 122)

CRITICAL THINKING QUESTIONS

1. Matthew Meselson and Franklin Stahl found that DNA replication is semiconservative. Explain the results they would have had in their experiments if replication were conservative (that is, if replication resulted in one entirely new molecule and conserved the parent molecule).

2. In a zoology laboratory experiment, you analyze the DNA from your own white blood cells. You determine that 15% of the nucleotide bases it contains is thymine. What percentage of the bases is cytosine?

3. Explain why degeneracy in the genetic code lessens the impact of mutations that result in base substitutions. Does degeneracy also lessen the impact of frameshifts? Explain.

4. Given that most mutations are recessive and usually do not show up in natural populations, explain why zoos are concerned with the loss of genetic diversity by excessive inbreeding within the confines of the zoo.

5. Imagine that you are a prospective parent in the year 2010. A genetic counselor tells you and your spouse that you both carry a rare recessive gene that could result in a severely deformed child. The chance of this trait showing up in your child is one in four. You have four choices:

   a. You may decide not to have a child.
   b. You may adopt a child.
   c. You may take your chances with nature.
   d. You may have corrective genes inserted into your own (your spouse's) ovum, which would then undergo in vitro fertilization with your spouse's (your) sperm. You can then be confident of having a normal child.

   Which option would you choose? Why? Which aspects of the decision are "scientific" and which are "nonscientific"?

REFERENCES ON THE WORLD WIDE WEB

1. **Fly Base.**   This site is a database of genetic and molecular data for the fruit fly, *Drosophila melanogaster*.
   http://flybase.bio.indiana.edu

2. **The *Drosophila* Virtual Library.**   This Web site lists fruit fly mutants, publications, and genetic data, and gives examples of current research involving the fruit fly.
   http://www.leland.stanford.edu/~ger/drosophila.html

3. **MIT Biology Hypertextbook.**   This site has information on all areas of biology, including medical genetics, molecular genetics, and immunology. It has an excellent presentation on the methodologies involved with recombinant DNA.
   http://esg-www.mit.edu:8001/esgbio/

4. **Cell and Molecular Biology Online.**   This resource for cellular and molecular biologists provides links to information on publications, careers, laboratory methods, educational resources, current research, and three-dimensional graphics.
   http://www.tiac.net/users/pmgannon/

5. **Cancer Web.**   This site, maintained by the National Cancer Institute, provides answers to commonly asked questions about gene therapy and cancer.
   http://www.graylab.ac.uk/cancernet/600718.html

10

DESCRIPTIVE EMBRYOLOGY

Concepts

1. Embryology is the study of an animal's development from the fertilized egg to the formation of all major organ systems. Descriptive embryology describes developmental stages of an animal, and experimental embryology examines the cellular controls for development.
2. Development of a new animal begins with a sperm fertilizing an egg. Fertilization events help ensure successful fertilization, help prevent multiple fertilization, and help prepare the egg for development.
3. Developmental patterns of different animals have important common themes. Some unique developmental patterns arise from differences in yolk distribution in animal eggs.
4. Echinoderm development illustrates how eggs with very little, evenly distributed yolk may develop.
5. Amphibian development illustrates how a moderate amount of unevenly distributed yolk influences development.
6. The embryos of reptiles, birds, and mammals require adaptations for long developmental periods in terrestrial environments.

Would You Like to Know . . .

1. why, although millions are produced, only one sperm usually penetrates an egg during fertilization? (p. 135)

2. why echinoderms (sea stars and sea urchins) are often used to study animal development? (p. 138)

3. why frog eggs are darkly pigmented on top and lightly pigmented on the bottom? (p. 140)

4. what a chicken egg contains? (p. 143)

This chapter answers these and other useful questions.

This chapter contains evolutionary concepts, which are set off in this font.

How is the complexity of form and function in adult animals explained? Can all of this complexity arise from a single egg? Most biologists of the seventeenth and eighteenth centuries believed in **preformation,** the concept that gametes contain miniaturized versions of all of the elements present in the adult.

In the mid-eighteenth century, the competing theory of **epigenesis** (Gr. *epi,* on + L. *genesis,* birth) gained in popularity. Biologists who favored this theory maintained that the egg contains the material from which the embryo is gradually built—much like a carpenter builds a building from lumber, nails, bricks, and mortar. During the fourth century B.C., Aristotle described the essence of this theory, which depended on an unexplained "creative principle" to direct the assembly.

In separate experiments, Wilhelm Roux (1888) and Hans Driesch (1892) set out to determine whether epigenesis or preformation was correct. Both allowed a fertilized egg to divide to the two-cell stage. Roux, using amphibian embryos (frogs, toads, salamanders), killed one of the two cells with a hot needle. Driesch, using echinoderm embryos (sea stars, sea urchins, sea cucumbers), completely separated the divided cells. An entire animal developing from a single cell would support epigenesis. A portion of the animal developing would favor preformation. What was the result? Interestingly, Roux described the formation of a half embryo that he called a "hemiembryo" (figure 10.1*a*), and Driesch found that each cell retained the potential to develop into an entire organism (figure 10.1*b*). Biologists now know that Driesch was the more correct of the two and that the killed cell, still attached to Roux's developing amphibian embryo, probably altered the development of the untreated cell.

This episode in history marks an important turning point in **embryology** (Gr. *embryo,* to be full + *logos,* discourse), the study of animal development from the fertilized egg to the formation of all major organ systems. Early studies were descriptive in nature, documenting stages in embryological development. Such material is the subject of this chapter. The works of Roux, Driesch, and others were the beginning of experimental embryology (or developmental biology). Developmental biologists use the tools of molecular biology (*see chapter 9*) to investigate the genetic controls of development.

FERTILIZATION

Different animals use a variety of mechanisms to bring opposite sexes together and to induce the release of eggs and/or sperm. Similarly, once gametes have been released, different mechanisms increase the likelihood of fertilization.

For fertilization to occur, a sperm must penetrate the gel coat of an egg, which consists of protein, or protein and polysaccharide (mucopolysaccharide). To penetrate this coating, the sperm of most animals possess enzymes called sperm lysins. These enzymes may be associated with a specialized organelle at the head of the sperm, called the **acrosome,** or with the plasma membrane of the sperm's anterior tip. When a sperm contacts the gel coat, the acrosome releases lysins that dissolve a pathway for the sperm (figure 10.2). In humans, even 80 million sperm per ejaculation

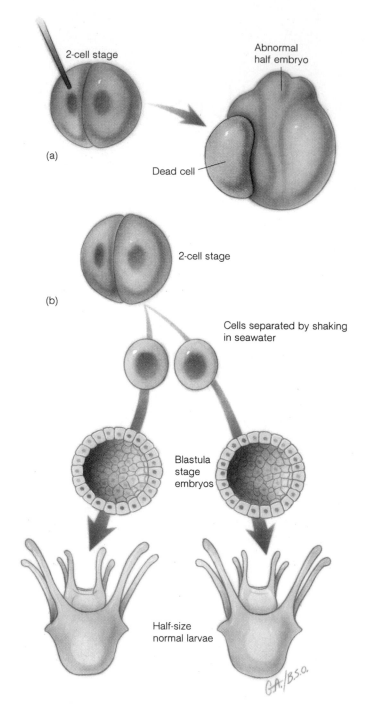

FIGURE 10.1

Experiments of Wilhelm Roux and Hans Driesch. (*a*) Wilhelm Roux produced a "hemiembryo" by killing one blastomere of a two-celled amphibian embryo. (*b*) Driesch found that separating cells of a two-celled echinoderm embryo resulted in the development of two small, but otherwise normal, larvae.

often mean reduced fertility because sperm lysins from many sperm are required to dissolve the gel coat of an egg. The acrosome of some species reorganizes into an acrosomal process after releasing lysins (figure 10.3). Just outside the egg plasma membrane is the vitelline layer (or zona pellucida). Egg binding proteins (bindins) on the surface of the acrosomal process bind to sperm at-

(a)

(b)

(c)

(d)

FIGURE 10.2

Fertilization of Sea Urchin Eggs. (*a*) Sperm contacting the egg surface. (*b*) Microvilli of the egg plasma membrane beginning to enfold the head of the sperm (SEM ×7,500). (*c,d*) Completion of sperm penetration (SEMs ×4,800; ×7,125). The fertilization membrane was removed before photomicrographs (*c*) and (*d*) were taken. (*Reprinted with permission from M. J. Tegner, "Sea Urchin Sperm: Eggs Instraction Studied with The Electron Microscope," Science, 179:685, February 1973. Copyright 1973 American Association for the Advancement of Science.*)

tachment molecules on the vitelline layer of the egg plasma membrane (figure 10.4). Acrosomal and egg plasma membranes then fuse. Other parts of the sperm (e.g., the mitochondria, centrioles, and flagellum) may or may not enter the egg, depending on the species involved.

EGG ACTIVATION

The fusion of acrosomal and egg membranes is the beginning of egg activation. Egg activation is a series of biochemical changes in the egg that ensures the completion of fertilization and initiates embryonic development. Biologists have extensively studied the events of egg activation in echinoderms, and some of the findings of that work are discussed here.

Membrane and Cortical Events

Some of the earliest changes in the zygote occur at the plasma membrane and in the outer region of the cell cytoplasm (called the cortex). ① These early changes ensure fertilization by only a single sperm. Single-sperm fertilization is important because multiple fertilization usually results in genetic imbalances and a nonviable embryo.

After contact by sperm, microvilli from the plasma membrane of the ovum wrap around a single sperm. Contraction of microfilaments in the egg's cytoplasm then draws the sperm into the egg (*see figures 10.2 and 10.3*).

A second series of events defends against multiple fertilization. Within milliseconds of penetration by a sperm, ionic changes

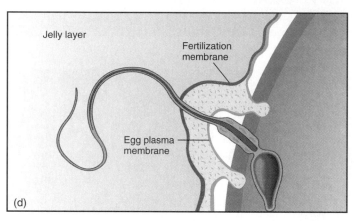

FIGURE 10.3

Fertilization of Echinoderm Eggs. (*a*) Acrosomal process contacts the vitelline membrane. (*b*) Sperm lysins create a hole in the vitelline membrane. Changes in the permeability of the plasma membrane to sodium ions initiate changes in the membrane that permit only a single sperm to enter. (*c*) Cortical granules discharge, and the vitelline membrane begins to rise off the egg plasma membrane. (*d*) The fertilization membrane forms.

make the plasma membrane unresponsive to other sperm and initiate the formation of a protective envelope around the egg, called the **fertilization membrane.**

The fertilization membrane forms as granules in the cortex discharge into the region between the egg plasma membrane and the vitelline layer (*see figure 10.3c*). The cortical granules release enzymes that loosen the vitelline layer's contact with the plasma membrane. The granules allow water to enter the space between the vitelline layer and the egg plasma membrane, causing the vitelline layer to lift off the egg. Proteins of the cortical granules thicken and strengthen the vitelline layer. All of these reactions are completed in 1 to 2 minutes following fertilization.

Other important changes occur in the egg cortex. After sperm penetration, the cortical layer thickens, and rotational and sliding movements of the outer egg cytoplasm begin. In amphibians, these cortical changes result in the formation of a **gray crescent** on the egg, opposite the point of sperm penetration. The gray crescent has an important influence on later development.

METABOLIC AND NUCLEAR EVENTS

Prior to nuclear fusion (called syngamy; *see chapter 6*), other nuclear events usually occur. Postfertilization changes help prepare the zygote for the ensuing mitotic divisions. Ionic changes raise the intra-

cellular pH and initiate changes in zygote physiology. DNA replication occurs, and in most species investigated, rates of protein synthesis increase. Rapid protein synthesis following fertilization meets the needs of new cells for enzymes and structural proteins that make up the mitotic spindle and contribute to chromosome structure. Little mRNA is synthesized in the zygote. Instead, existing maternal (egg) mRNA is activated, and it directs the formation of the bulk of the proteins synthesized in early stages of embryonic development. This influence is called maternal dominance.

The region of the egg referred to as the **animal pole** contains less yolk, more mitochondria, and more ribosomes, and is more metabolically active than the opposite, **vegetal pole** of the egg.

Stop and Ask Yourself

1. How do descriptive and experimental embryology differ?
2. What is the role of each of the following in fertilization: (*a*) acrosome, (*b*) egg binding proteins, (*c*) fertilization membrane, and (*d*) bindin receptors?
3. What membrane and cortical events occur during egg activation? What is their purpose?
4. How do the animal and vegetal poles of an egg differ?

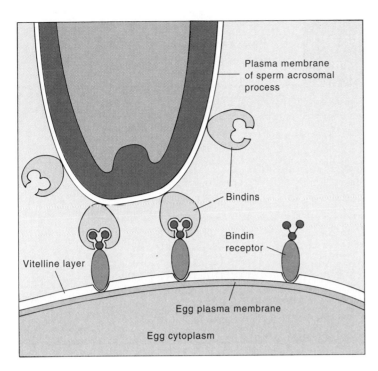

FIGURE 10.4

Sperm-Egg Adhesion Is Mediated by Species-Specific Macromolecules. Schematic drawing of bindin proteins covering the surface of the acrosomal process of a sea urchin sperm. The bindin proteins bind to specific bindin receptor molecules (a carbohydrate) associated with the vitelline layer of the egg. (Bindin proteins and receptors are drawn disproportionately large.)

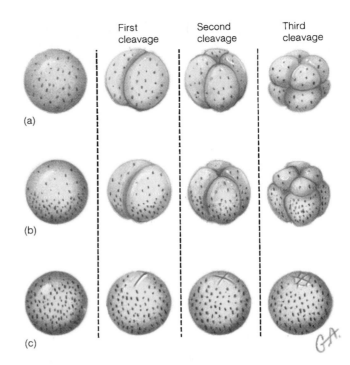

FIGURE 10.5

Early Cleavage Patterns. (*a*) Holoblastic cleavage of an embryo containing a small quantity of evenly distributed yolk results in uniformly sized blastomere (e.g., a sea urchin). (*b*) Holoblastic cleavage of an embryo containing moderate to large quantities of unevenly distributed yolk results in unequal blastomeres (e.g., an amphibian). (*c*) Meroblastic cleavage occurs when large quantities of yolk prevent the embryo from dividing completely (e.g., a reptile or bird).

EMBRYONIC DEVELOPMENT, CLEAVAGE, AND EGG TYPES

Billions of cells that make up adult animals arise from the zygote. **Cleavage** refers to cell divisions that occur during embryonic development, and the cells that cleavage produces are **blastomeres** (Gr. *blasto*, sprout + *mero*, part). The first cell division of the zygote results in two daughter cells. These blastomeres divide in synchrony, producing a four-celled embryo. As more blastomeres are produced, divisions become asynchronous. Throughout early embryology, the embryo does not increase in overall size. Instead, blastomeres become smaller, and the proportion of DNA to cytoplasm increases.

QUANTITY AND DISTRIBUTION OF YOLK

Egg sizes, cleavage patterns, and the length of embryonic periods of animal species are related to differences in the quantity and distribution of yolk in an egg. Yolk, a mixture of proteins, lipids, and glycogen, is the food reserve for the developing embryo. Animals with relatively small amounts of yolk—for example, echinoderms (sea stars and their relatives) and amphibians (frogs and their relatives)—often have larval stages that begin to feed after a brief period of embryological development during which yolk is entirely absorbed. Some animals with longer periods of embryologi-

cal development (reptiles and birds) provide embryos with larger quantities of yolk. Other animals with long periods of embryological development (eutherian, or placental, mammals and some sharks) provide nourishment to embryos through a placenta or some other modification of the female reproductive tract.

CLEAVAGE PATTERNS

The relative size of the blastomeres that result from cleavage and the rate of cleavage show how yolk influences cleavage patterns. Eggs with evenly distributed yolk usually have cleavage patterns that result in uniformly sized blastomeres. Eggs with unevenly distributed yolk have cleavage patterns that result in unequal blastomeres.

Cleavages that completely divide an egg are **holoblastic** (Gr. *holo*, whole + *blasto*, sprout). If cleavages cannot completely divide the embryo because of large quantities of yolk, the cleavages are **meroblastic** (Gr. *mero*, part). These embryos develop around, or on top of, the yolk (figure 10.5).

Other cleavage patterns result from differences in the orientation of the mitotic spindle during mitosis, and the degree to which the fate of early blastomeres is predetermined. Developmental differences are thought to reflect differences in the evolutionary history of the animal groups that possess them. For example, the pattern of cleavage where blastomeres are oriented directly over one another is characteristic of the evolutionary lineage leading to the echinoderms and chordates. Another pattern of cleavage, where an upper tier of blastomeres is twisted out of line with a lower tier of blastomeres, is characteristic of the lineage leading to the annelids (segmented worms) and arthropods (insects and their relatives). Chapter 21 compares cleavage patterns as well as other developmental differences in these two evolutionary lineages.

THE PRIMARY GERM LAYERS AND THEIR DERIVATIVES

Tissues and organs of animals arise from layers, or blocks, of embryonic cells called **primary germ layers.** Their development from a nondescript form in the early embryo to their form in late embryonic through adult stages is called **differentiation.** One layer, **ectoderm** (Gr. *ektos*, outside + *derm*, skin), gives rise to the outer body wall. **Endoderm** (Gr. *endo*, within) forms the inner lining of the digestive cavity. **Mesoderm** (Gr. *meso*, in the middle) gives rise to tissues between ectoderm and endoderm. Undifferentiated mesoderm (called **mesenchyme**) develops into muscles, blood and blood vessels, skeletal elements, and other connective tissues (table 10.1).

Stop and Ask Yourself

5. How does yolk influence cleavage patterns?
6. How do holoblastic and meroblastic cleavages differ?
7. What tissue is derived from each of the following germ layers: (*a*) ectoderm, (*b*) endoderm, and (*c*) mesoderm?
8. What is mesenchyme?

ECHINODERM EMBRYOLOGY

Biologists have studied echinoderm embryology extensively. ❷ Echinoderms are easily maintained in laboratories, and the ease with which mature sperm and eggs are obtained makes them convenient models to illustrate principles of early animal development.

The eggs of echinoderms have relatively little yolk, and the yolk is evenly distributed throughout the egg (figure 10.6 *a*). Cleavages are holoblastic and result in similarly sized blastomeres (figure 10.6*b–d*). In just a few hours, a solid ball of small cells, called the **morula** (L. *morum*, mulberry) is produced (figure 10.6*e*).

As cell division continues, cells pull away from the interior of the embryo. A fluid-filled cavity, the **blastocoel,** forms, and the cells form a single layer around the cavity. The embryo is now a hollow sphere called a **blastula** (figure 10.6*f*). In sea urchins, development through the blastula stage takes place within the fertilization membrane. When the cells of the blastula develop cilia, the blastula breaks out of the fertilization membrane and begins to swim. Late in the blastula stage, groups of cells break free of the animal end of the embryo and position themselves within the blastocoel. These cells, called primary mesenchyme, will form skeletal elements (called spicules) of the embryo.

The next series of events in echinoderm embryology is **gastrulation.** The first sign of gastrulation is the invagination of cells at a point in the vegetal half of the embryo (figure 10.6*g*). The

TABLE 10.1	THE PRIMARY GERM LAYERS AND THEIR DERIVATIVES IN VERTEBRATES
GERM LAYER	DERIVATIVE
Ectoderm	Nervous tissue
	Epidermis of the skin
	Sensory organs
Endoderm	Gut tract lining
	Digestive glands
	Respiratory tract lining
Mesoderm	Connective tissues
	Circulatory system
	Bones, tendons, ligaments
	Dermis of the skin
	Excretory structures
	Reproductive structures
	Muscle

point of invagination is the **blastopore,** which will eventually form the anal opening of the larva. During invagination, an embryonic gut, the **archenteron** (Gr. *archeo*, ancient + *enteron*, gut), elongates and reduces the size of the blastocoel (figure 10.6*h*).

During gastrulation, the embryo also begins to lengthen and assumes a pyramidal shape. Although adult echinoderms do not have head and tail ends, larvae have a preferred direction of movement. The end of an animal that meets the environment during locomotion is called the anterior end and is where the head of most animals is located. The opposite end is the posterior end. The shape changes that occur during gastrulation establish the anteroposterior axis of the embryo.

Finally, a body cavity, or coelom, forms from outpockets of the archenteron, and the gut breaks through the anterior body wall. The opening thus produced is the mouth.

The cell movements that begin in gastrulation result from groups of cells changing their shapes simultaneously. Contractile microfilaments mediate these shape changes (*see figure 3.20*). These precise, coordinated changes transform a single-layered sphere of cells into an embryo with several layers of cells. The progressive development of an animal's form that begins in gastrulation is **morphogenesis.** In the sea urchin, these changes produce a pluteus larva that swims freely in the sea and feeds on even smaller plants and animals (figure 10.6*i*).

Stop and Ask Yourself

9. What changes in an echinoderm egg lead to the formation of the blastula?
10. How does the archenteron of an echinoderm gastrula form? What is the fate of the blastopore?
11. What is morphogenesis?

FIGURE 10.6

Stages in the Development of an Echinoderm. (*a*) Unfertilized egg. (*b*) The first two cleavages occur along the animal/vegetal axis. (*c*) The third cleavage occurs at right angles to the previous cleavages, midway between animal and vegetal poles. An eight-cell stage with approximately equal blastomeres results. (*d,e*) Subsequent cleavages result in the formation of the morula. (*f*) The blastula—a hollow sphere whose walls are a single cell layer thick. (*g*) Gastrulation begins with invagination at a point on the surface of the blastula. (*h*) As gastrulation continues, the archenteron enlarges. (*i*) The pluteus. This scanning electron micrograph (×200) shows the pyramidal shape of the larva. Spicules form, and the gut track is complete. Note the presence of cilia for locomotion. (*a–h* photomicrographs are ×400.)

VERTEBRATE EMBRYOLOGY

Early stages of vertebrate (animals with a vertebral column or "backbone") development are similar to those described for echinoderms. The differences are the result of longer developmental periods and, for some vertebrates, adaptations for development on land.

THE CHORDATE BODY PLAN

Vertebrates are members of the phylum Chordata, and certain structures characterize all chordates. The endpoint of the study of vertebrate embryology is the point at which most of these characteristic structures have formed (figure 10.7).

(a)

(b)

FIGURE 10.7

Chordate Body Plan. The development of all chordates involves the formation of a neural tube, the notochord, pharyngeal slits or pouches, and a postanal tail. Derivatives of all three primary germ layers are present. (*a*) Side view. (*b*) Cross section.

The chordate nervous system develops from ectoderm, and is dorsal and tubular. The first evidence of a developing nervous system is the formation of the neural tube. Nervous tissue proliferates anteriorly into a brain.

The notochord is the primary axial structure in all chordate embryos, as well as many adults. It is flexible, yet supportive, and lies just beneath the neural tube. The notochord is mesodermal in origin and consists of vacuolated cells packed into a connective tissue sheath.

In addition to the notochord and the dorsal tubular nerve cord, all chordates possess pharyngeal slits or pouches and a postanal tail at some point in their life history.

AMPHIBIAN EMBRYOLOGY

Most amphibians lay eggs in watery environments, and the eggs are fertilized as the female releases them (figure 10.8*a*). Frog eggs have a pigmented animal pole. Because the vegetal pole is heavily laden with yolk, the eggs rotate in their jelly coats so that the less dense, darkly pigmented animal pole is oriented up (figure 10.8*b*). This rather simple series of events has interesting adaptive significance. Amphibian eggs usually develop with little care or protection from the parents. ❸ The pigmentation helps camouflage developing embryos from predators. When viewed from below, the light color of the vegetal end of floating eggs blends with the sky above. When viewed from above, the dark color of the animal end blends with the bottom of the pond, lake, or stream. The dark pigment of the animal pole also absorbs heat from the sun, and the warming may promote development.

FIGURE 10.8

Fertilization of Amphibian Eggs. (*a*) In frogs, eggs are released and fertilized when the male (the smaller frog) mounts and grasps the female. This positioning is called amplexus. The male fertilizes the eggs as the female releases them. (*b*) The egg of a frog shortly after fertilization has a jellylike coat. Note the darkly pigmented animal pole at the top and the yolk-laden vegetal pole at the bottom (×6).

Initial Cleavages

The first cleavage of the amphibian embryo, like that of echinoderms, is longitudinal. It begins at the animal pole and divides the gray crescent in half. Because of the large amount of yolk in the vegetal end of the egg, cleavages are slower there than in the animal end. The amphibian morula, therefore, consists of many small cells at the animal end of the embryo and fewer, larger cells at the vegetal end of the embryo (figures 10.9*a,b* and 10.10*a–e*). The amphibian blastula forms in much the same way as the echinoderm blastula, except that the yolky vegetal cells cause the blastocoel to form in the animal half of the embryo (figure 10.10; *see also figure 10.9b*). Unlike that of echinoderms, the blastula wall of amphibians has multiple cell layers.

(a)

(b)

(c)

(d)

(e)

(f)

FIGURE 10.9

Frog Development. (*a*) Eight-cell stage. (*b*) Early blastula stage. (*c*) Late gastrula (yolk plug) stage. Note the circular blastopore with yolk protruding from within the embryo. (*d*) Neural groove stage. (Photomicrographs *a-d* are ×6.) (*e*) Tadpole of the American bullfrog, *Rana catesbeiana*. (*f*) Tadpole of the American bullfrog undergoing metamorphosis. Note the presence of both legs and tail.

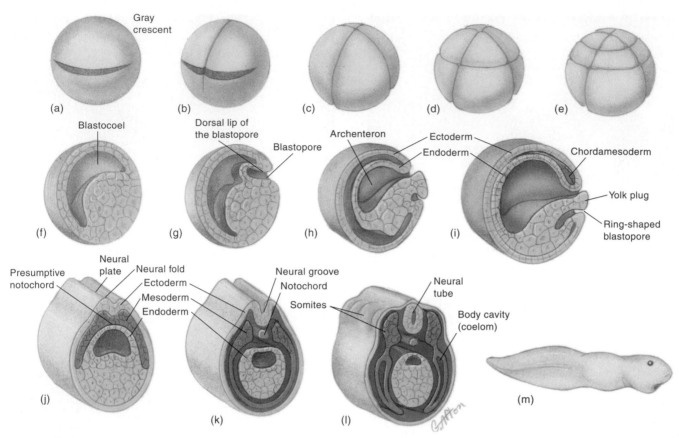

FIGURE 10.10

Stages in the Development of a Frog. (*a–c*) Early cleavages. The gray crescent is shown in (*a*). The first and second cleavages usually begin at the animal pole and are at right angles to one another. The second cleavage begins before the first cleavage is completed. (*d*) The third cleavage is horizontal. Because of the dense, yolky cytoplasm at the vegetal pole, this third cleavage occurs closer to the animal pole and results in unequal blastomeres. (*e*) Morula. (*f*) Blastula. Note the blastocoel near the animal pole and the multiple cell layers of the blastula. (*g,h*) Gastrulation. Involution begins as cells move into the interior of the embryo, forming a slitlike blastopore. The blastopore extends to the sides and toward the vegetal pole. Ectodermal cells spread into a thin layer over the surface of the embryo, gradually covering the vegetal end. The ends of the blastopore join, forming a yolk plug, and the blastopore eventually closes. (*i*) Chordamesoderm begins forming the notochord and spreads laterally. (*j,k*) The embryo lengthens during gastrulation, and when gastrulation is complete, nerve cord formation begins. The neural plate develops, its edges upfold, and the neural tube forms. (*l*) The mesoderm proliferates, forming somites. Mesoderm along the sides of the embryo splits, forming the body cavity, or coelom. (*m*) The larval stage, or tadpole, gradually uses up the yolk stored in endodermal cells and begins to feed.

Gastrulation

The cells of the blastula that will develop into specific structures are grouped on the surface of the blastula. During gastrulation, some of these cells move into the interior of the embryo. Embryologists use dyes or carbon particles to mark the surface of the blastula and then follow the movements of these cells during gastrulation. Embryonic cells are designated according to their future development by "presumptive notochord," "presumptive endoderm," and so forth.

The first sign that gastrulation is beginning is the formation of a groove between the gray crescent and the vegetal region of the embryo. This groove is the slitlike blastopore. The animal-pole margin of the blastopore is the dorsal lip of the blastopore. Cells at the bottom of the groove move to the interior of the embryo, and the groove spreads transversely (figure 10.10g). This groove is similar to that which occurs during echinoderm blasto-

pore formation. In amphibians, however, superficial cells begin to roll over the dorsal lip of the blastopore in a process called **involution** (to curl inward). Cells spread from the animal pole toward the blastopore and replace those moving into the interior of the embryo. In the process, the ends of the slitlike blastopore continue to spread transversely and downward toward the vegetal pole until one end of the slit meets and joins the opposite end of the slit. A ringlike blastopore now surrounds the protruding, yolk-filled cells near the vegetal end of the embryo (*see figure 10.9c*). These protruding cells are called the **yolk plug** (figure 10.10h,i). Eventually, the lips of the blastopore contract to completely enclose the yolk. The blastopore is said to have "closed."

During the closing of the blastopore, two other movements occur. First, the spreading of cells from the animal pole toward the dorsal lip of the blastopore and the rolling of cells into the blastopore form the archenteron. As these mesodermal and endodermal cells roll into the interior of the embryo, the archenteron becomes larger, and the blastocoel becomes smaller (figure 10.10g–i). Because the large, yolk-filled cells of the vegetal end are less active in these movements, they ultimately make up the floor of the gut tract. Second, gastrulation results in a spreading and thinning of ectodermal cells toward the blastopore. In addition, ectoderm spreads over the entire embryo, a process called **epiboly.**

Mesoderm Formation

Some of the last cells to roll over the dorsal lip into the blastopore are presumptive notochord and presumptive mesoderm (figure 10.10i). Initially, these cells make up the dorsal lining of the archenteron near the blastopore. Later, they detach from the endoderm and move to a position between the endoderm and ectoderm in the region of the dorsal lip of the blastopore. This mesoderm, called **chordamesoderm,** spreads anteriorly (the embryo is now beginning to elongate) between ectoderm and endoderm. Chordamesoderm will differentiate into notochord (figure 10.10j,k). Lateral to the notochord, mesoderm spreads and thickens along the sides of the embryo. These thickenings, called **somites,** are visible externally as a row of bumps on either side of the embryo (figure 10.10l). As mesoderm continues to spread ventrally, it splits to form the body cavity (coelom) and the mesodermal lining of the body wall and gut.

Neural Tube Formation

During late gastrulation, external changes along the upper surface of the embryo begin to form the neural tube—a process called **neurulation.** After gastrulation is complete, an oval-shaped area on the dorsal side (the future backside) of the embryo marks the presumptive neural tube. This region is the neural plate. Microfilaments in neural plate cells flatten and thicken the neural plate. The edges of the neural plate roll up and over the midline of the neural plate. These longitudinal ridges, called neural folds, meet dorsally to form the neural tube (figure 10.10j; *see also figure 10.9d*). The portion of the neural tube that will become the brain is the last to close.

With further development of the mesoderm, the amphibian embryo gradually takes on the form of a tadpole larva. Yolk in cells lining the floor of the gut is gradually depleted, and the larva begins feeding on algae and other plant material (figure 10.10m; *see also figure 10.9e,f*).

DEVELOPMENT IN TERRESTRIAL ENVIRONMENTS

Reptiles (class Reptilia), birds (class Aves), and mammals (class Mammalia) develop on land rather than in the water. Embryos that develop on land require protection from desiccation, which a series of extraembryonic membranes provides. The longer developmental periods of these animals reflect their lack of independent larval stages. (Larval stages, such as those of amphibians, allow individuals to achieve increased complexity in spite of short embryonic periods.)

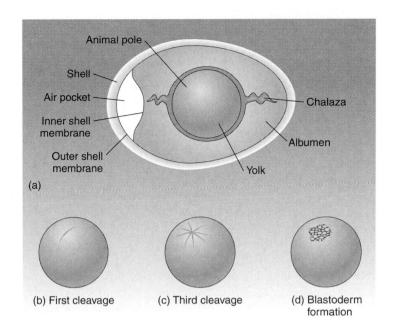

(a)

(b) First cleavage (c) Third cleavage (d) Blastoderm formation

FIGURE 10.11

Structure and Early Development of the Chicken Egg. (*a*) Egg and egg membranes. Albumen is an accessory food source, and along with egg membranes, protects the embryo and prevents it from drying. (*b*) The first cleavage cannot pass through the massive yolk. (*c*) Third cleavage. (*d*) Blastoderm formation at the animal end of the egg.

AVIAN EMBRYOLOGY

Chicken development can be used to model the development of birds and reptiles. ❹ What is commonly referred to as the "egg" of a chicken is, in reality, the true egg, plus a variety of membranes that protect the egg. The yellow portion of the chicken egg is the single cell produced in the chicken ovary. This egg is released into the oviduct, where fertilization may occur. Following fertilization, membranes and fluids collect around the egg (figure 10.11a). A vitelline membrane covers the surface of the true egg. The "white" consists of water and a protein called albumen. This watery environment protects the egg from mechanical damage and drying. Albumen is a source of nutrients (in addition to the yolk of the egg) and is eventually consumed during development. Two denser strands of albumen (called chalazas) attach to the inside of the shell and to the egg, and suspend the egg in the center of the watery albumen. The shell is made of calcium carbonate impregnated with protein. Thousands of tiny pores (40 to 50 μm in diameter) in the shell permit gas exchange between the embryo and the outside. On the inside of the shell are two shell membranes. An air pocket forms between these membranes at the rounded end of the shell. The air pocket enlarges during development, as air moves through pores in the shell to replace water loss. As hatching approaches, the chick penetrates the air pocket with its beak, the lungs inflate, and the chick begins to breathe from the air sac, while still exchanging gases across vascular extraembryonic membranes.

Early Cleavages and Gastrulation

Cleavage of the chicken egg is meroblastic (figure 10.11*b–d*). A small disk of approximately sixty thousand cells at the animal end of the egg develops and is the **blastoderm.** The blastoderm is raised off the yolk, leaving a fluid-filled space analogous to the blastocoel of the amphibian blastula. Proliferation and movement of blastoderm cells sort the cells into two layers. The **epiblast** (Gr. *epi,* upon + *blast,* sprout) is the outer layer of cells, and the **hypoblast** (Gr. *hypo,* below) is the inner layer (figure 10.12*a–c*). The movements of blastoderm cells are the beginning of gastrulation. The female reproductive tract releases the egg at about this time.

A medial, linear invagination, called the **primitive streak,** gradually extends anteriorly (figure 10.12*d*). A depression, called Henson's node, forms at the anterior margin of the primitive streak and marks the beginning of an inward migration of epiblast cells, comparable to involution of the amphibian gastrula. The primitive streak is, therefore, analogous to the dorsal lip of the blastopore. This migration occurs during a dramatic posterior movement of Henson's node. Migrating cells form mesoderm, what is left of the epiblast on the surface of the embryo is the ectoderm, and the hypoblast forms the endodermal lining of the gut tract. The three germ layers are now arranged above the surface of the yolk.

Following gastrulation, notochordal cells separate from the overlying neural ectoderm, and the neural tube forms as described earlier for the amphibian embryo. In addition, mesoderm, which originally formed as solid blocks of cells, organizes into somites and splits to form the coelom.

The embryo lifts off the yolk when the margins of the embryo grow downward and meet below the embryo (figure 10.12*e*). A connection between the embryo and the yolk is retained and is called the yolk stalk. Blood vessels develop in the yolk stalk and carry nutrients from the yolk to the embryo.

The Development of Extraembryonic Membranes

Extraembryonic membranes of amniotes include the yolk sac, the amnion, the chorion, and the allantois (figure 10.13). Reptiles and birds have a large quantity of yolk that becomes enclosed by a **yolk sac.** The yolk sac develops from a proliferation of the endoderm and mesoderm around the yolk. The yolk sac is highly vascular and distributes nutrients to the developing embryo.

Following the neural tube stage, the ectoderm and mesoderm on both sides of the embryo lift off the yolk and grow dorsally over the embryo. As these membranes meet dorsally, they fuse and form an inner **amnion** and an outer **chorion.** The amnion encloses the embryo in a fluid-filled sac. This amniotic cavity protects against shock and drying. The chorion is nearer the shell, becomes highly vascular, and aids in gas exchange.

Development in a closed environment presents a problem of waste disposal. Accumulation of nitrogenous waste products in

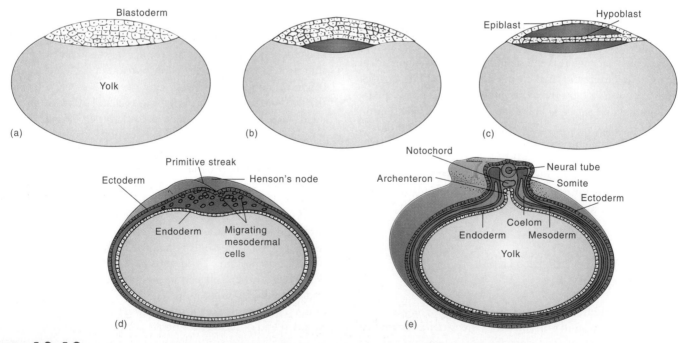

FIGURE 10.12

Gastrulation in the Chick Embryo. (*a,b*) Meroblastic cleavage results in blastoderm formation. (*c*) Cells of the blastoderm rise off the yolk and rearrange into two layers—epiblast and hypoblast. (*d*) Gastrulation results from the migration of epiblast cells into a longitudinal groove called the primitive streak. These migrating cells form mesoderm and endoderm, and cells remaining in the epiblast form ectoderm. (*e*) The embryo lifts off the yolk when the margins of the embryo grow downward and meet below the embryo.

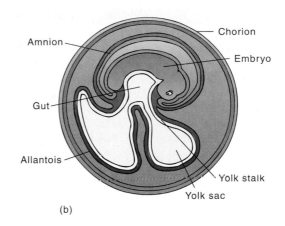

(a)   (b)

FIGURE 10.13

Formation of Extraembryonic Membranes. (*a*) The embryo lifts off the yolk as the hypoblast proliferates around the yolk to form the yolk sac. The amnion begins forming before the allantois. (*b*) Amnion folds fuse above the embryo, enclosing the embryo in the amnion and forming a continuous chorion on the inside of the shell. The allantois increases in size as uric acid accumulates. The yolk is absorbed and metabolized as the embryo grows.

the embryo, or unconfined in the shell, would be lethal for the embryo. The immediate breakdown product of proteins is highly toxic ammonia. This ammonia is converted to a less toxic form, uric acid, which is excreted and stored in the **allantois,** a ventral outgrowth of the gut tract. Uric acid is a semisolid, and thus, little water is wasted. The allantois gradually enlarges during development to occupy the region between the amnion and the chorion. In addition, the allantois becomes highly vascular and functions with the chorion in gas exchange.

THE FATE OF MESODERM

Following gastrulation in birds, reptiles, and mammals, all three primary germ layers have formed. Of the three layers, the fate of mesoderm is the most complex. Mesoderm forms all of the supportive tissues of vertebrates, including connective tissues (bone, cartilage, and blood) and muscle. These supportive tissues are frequently associated with derivatives of other primary germ layers. For example, the inner lining of the gut is endodermal, but mesodermally derived structures, such as smooth muscle, blood, and blood vessels, make up the bulk of that system.

Stop and Ask Yourself

12. How would you define involution, epiboly, yolk plug, and chordamesoderm?

13. What are the initial phases of mesoderm formation in amphibians?

14. How does a chicken egg provide a suitable environment for terrestrial development?

ENDANGERED SPECIES

WILDLIFE ALERT 5—FAT POCKETBOOK MUSSEL (*Potamilus capax*)

VITAL STATISTICS

Classification: Phylum Mollusca, class Bivalvia, order Lamellibranchia
Range: Upper Mississippi River
Habitat: Shallow, stable, sandy, or gravelly substrates of freshwater rivers
Number Remaining: Unknown
Status: Endangered

NATURAL HISTORY AND ECOLOGICAL STATUS

The fat pocketbook mussel lives in the sand, mud, and fine-gravel bottoms of large rivers in the upper Mississippi River drainage (figure 1). It buries itself, leaving the posterior margin of its shell and mantle exposed so that its siphons can accommodate the incurrent

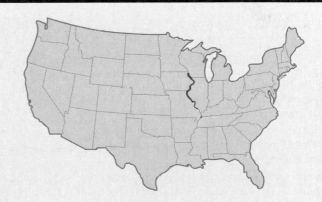

FIGURE 1   Distribution of the fat pocketbook mussel (*Potamilus capax*).

and excurrent water that circulates through its mantle cavity. The fat pocketbook mussel is a filter feeder, and like other members of its family (Unionidae), it produces glochidia larvae (*see figure 21.15c*). Sperm released by a male are taken into the female's mantle cavity. Eggs are fertilized and develop into glochidia larvae in the gills of the female. Females release glochidia, which live as parasitic hitchhikers on fish gills. The freshwater drum (*Aplodinotus grunniens*) is probably the primary host fish. After a short parasitic existence, the young clams drop to the substrate, where they may live up to 50 years.

The fat pocketbook mussel (figure 2) is one of the more than 60 freshwater mussels that the U.S. Fish and Wildlife Service lists as threatened or endangered. The problems that freshwater mussels face stem from economic exploitation, habitat destruction, pollution, and invasion of a foreign mussel.

The pearl-button industry began harvesting freshwater mussels in the late 1800s. In the early 1900s, 196 pearl-button factories were operating along the Mississippi River. After harvesting and cleaning, bivalve shells were drilled to make buttons (figure 3). In 1912, this industry produced more than $6 million in buttons. Since that year, however, the harvest has declined.

In the 1940s, plastic buttons replaced pearl buttons, but mussel harvesters soon discovered a new market for freshwater bivalve shells. Small pieces of mussel shell placed into pearl oysters are a nucleus for the formation of a cultured pearl. A renewed impetus for

FIGURE 3   Shell of a freshwater mussel after having been drilled to make pearl buttons.

harvesting freshwater mussels in the 1950s resulted in overharvesting. In 1966, harvesters took 3,500 tons of freshwater mussels.

Habitat destruction, pollution, and invasion by the zebra mussel also threaten freshwater mussels (*see box 21.1*). Freshwater mussels require shallow, stable, sandy or gravelly substrates, although a few species prefer mud. Channelization for barge traffic and flood control purposes has destroyed many mussel habitats. Siltation from erosion has replaced stable substrates with soft, mucky river bottoms. A variety of pollutants, especially agricultural runoff containing pesticides, also threaten mussel conservation. In addition, the full impact of the recently introduced zebra mussel (*Dreissena polymorpha*) on native mussels has yet to be determined. However, the zebra mussel has the unfortunate habit of using native mussel shells as a substrate for attachment. They can cover a native mussel so densely that the native mussel cannot feed.

The gloomy outlook is lightened with a few rays of hope. Recently, researchers from Southwest Missouri State University unexpectedly found an apparently healthy, reproducing population of the fat pocketbook mussel in Southeast Missouri.

FIGURE 2   Fat pocketbook mussel (*Potamilus capax*).

SUMMARY

1. Embryology is the study of animal development from the fertilized egg to the formation of all major organ systems. Descriptive embryologists document these changes. Experimental embryologists study the cellular controls of development.

2. Fertilization is the process by which the union of two gametes forms a diploid zygote. A variety of mechanisms have evolved to ensure fertilization.

3. Contact with sperm activates the egg. Changes in the egg cytoplasm ensure that a single sperm penetrates the egg and that the cell is metabolically ready for mitosis.

4. The quantity and distribution of yolk influence cleavage patterns. Eggs that contain little yolk divide into equal-sized blastomeres. Eggs that contain larger amounts of yolk either do not divide completely or divide into unequal blastomeres.

5. One of the goals of embryology is the description of the formation and fates of the primary germ layers: ectoderm, endoderm, and mesoderm.

6. Echinoderm development is representative of the development of a zygote that contains little yolk. Cleavages are holoblastic and equal. Gastrulation occurs by invagination of the blastula. Mesoderm and the coelom form from simple outpockets of the archenteron.

7. Frog eggs have a large amount of unequally distributed yolk. As a result, their cleavage is holoblastic and unequal. The blastocoel forms near the animal pole, and gastrulation occurs by involution. Chordamesoderm forms between ectoderm and endoderm, and develops into somites, coelomic linings, and the notochord. Changes in the ectoderm include the formation of the neural tube.

8. The development of reptiles, birds, and mammals shows adaptations for living on land, including the formation of extraembryonic membranes.

9. The initial cleavages of a chicken egg result in the formation of a disk of cytoplasm, the blastoderm, at the animal end of the embryo. Gastrulation involves cells migrating toward a medial longitudinal groove, called the primitive streak.

SELECTED KEY TERMS

allantois (p. 145)
amnion (p. 144)
blastula (p. 138)
chorion (p. 144)
differentiation (p. 138)
ectoderm (p. 138)

embryology (p. 134)
endoderm (p. 138)
gastrulation (p. 138)
mesoderm (p. 138)
morula (p. 138)

CRITICAL THINKING QUESTIONS

1. In what sense is fertilization a random event? Do you think random fertilization is adaptive for a species? Explain.

2. What mechanisms prevent fertilization of an egg by more than one sperm? Why is this important?

3. Practical applications often follow quickly on the heels of basic research. How could basic research into the process of fertilization be applied to problems of contraception and infertility?

4. Evaluate the following statement: "The primary differences between early cleavages of most animal embryos are the result of the quantity and distribution of yolk."

5. The eggs of many terrestrial vertebrates are protected by a shell and have large quantities of yolk. Why do most mammalian eggs lack these features?

REFERENCES ON THE WORLD WIDE WEB

1. **Magnetic Resonance Image Microscopy of Embryos.**   This site provides images of mouse and human embryos at various stages of development.
   http://wwwcivm.mc.duke.edu/civmPeople/smithBR/brs.html

2. **Embryo Development.**   This site provides images of embryos, representations of developmental stages, and descriptions of developmental processes.
   http://www.med.upenn.edu/embryo_project/embryo.html

3. **Wadsworth's Wonderful Worms.**   This site, sponsored by Robert Wood Johnson Medical School, presents research information, images, cartoons, and a quiz on the developmental biology of the nematode, *Caenorhabditis elegans.*
   http://rigel.umdnj.edu/

4. **Bill Wasserman's Developmental Biology Page.**   This site provides links to general information on fruitfly, mammal, and sea urchin developmental biology.
   http://www.luc.edu/depts/biology/dev.htm

5. **Amphibian Embryology.**   This site is a tutorial on amphibian embryology. Click on an icon to learn more about particular stages of development.
   http://www.library.wisc.edu:80/guides/Biology/demo/frog2/welcome.html

6. **Virtual Library—Developmental Biology.**   This site provides educational resources on many topics in developmental biology.
   http://sbd.bio.purdue.edu/other/VL_DB_EducaRes.html

7. **Human Embryology.**   Click on a human developmental stage to learn more about that stage of development.
   http://viseembryo.ucsf.edu/

8. **Urchin Web.**   This site provides links to sea urchin publications, researchers, educational resources, and information on sea urchin molecular biology.
   http://www-leland.stanford.edu/~hkibak/urchinweb.html

SUGGESTED READINGS
BOOKS

Balinsky, B. 1982. *An Introduction to Embryology.* 6th ed. Philadelphia: W. B. Saunders.

Cohen, J. 1977. *Reproduction.* London: Butterworths.

Cummings, M. R. 1993. *Human Heredity.* 3d ed. St. Paul: West Publishing.

Cummings, S., ed. 1996. *Current Perspectives in Genetics: Insights and Applications in Molecular, Classical, and Human Genetics.* Minneapolis: West Publishing.

Dunn, L. C. 1965. *A Short History of Genetics.* New York: McGraw-Hill.

Ehrlich, P. R., and Feldman, S. S. 1977. *The Race Bomb: Skin Color, Prejudice, and Intelligence.* New York: Quandrangle.

Ferraris, J. D., and Palumbi, S. R., eds. 1996. *Molecular Zoology: Advances, Strategies, and Protocols.* New York: Wiley-Liss.

Gilbert, S. 1988. *Developmental Biology.* 2d ed. Sunderland, Mass.: Sinauer Associates.

Giudice, G. 1986. *The Sea Urchin Embryo: A Developmental Biological System.* New York: Springer-Verlag.

Hopper, A. F., and Hart, N. H. 1985. *Foundations of Animal Development.* 2d ed. Boston: Oxford University Press.

Iltis, H. 1966. *Life of Mendel.* New York: Haffner.

John, P. C. L., ed. 1985. *The Cell Cycle.* New York: Cambridge University Press.

Karp, B., and Berrill, N. J. 1981. *Development.* 2d ed. New York: McGraw-Hill.

Keller, E. F. 1983. *A Feeling for the Organism: The Life and Work of Barbara McClintock.* San Francisco: W. H. Freeman.

Klug, W. S., and Cummings, M. R. 1994. *Concepts of Genetics.* 4th ed. Columbus, Ohio: Charles E. Merrill.

Krimsky, S. 1982. *The Social History of the Recombinant DNA Controversy.* Cambridge, Mass.: MIT Press.

Levitan, M. 1988. *Textbook of Human Genetics.* 3d ed. New York: Oxford University Press.

Lewin, B. 1994. *Genes.* 5th ed. New York: John Wiley & Sons.

Lewis, R. 1997. *Human Genetics: Concepts and Applications.* 2d ed. Dubuque, Iowa: Wm. C. Brown Publishers.

Margulis, L., and Sagan, D. 1986. *Origins of Sex: Three Billion Years of Genetic Recombination.* New Haven, Conn.: Yale University Press.

Old, R. W., and Primrose, S. B. 1994. *Principles of Gene Manipulation: An Introduction to Genetic Engineering.* Oxford: Blackwell Science.

Rothwell, N. 1988. *Understanding Genetics.* New York: Oxford University Press.

Russell, P. J. 1996. *Genetics*, 4th ed. New York: HarperCollins.

Saunders, J. W., Jr. 1982. *Developmental Biology*. New York: Macmillan.

Slack, J. M. W. 1983. *From Egg to Embryo: Determinative Events in Early Development*. Cambridge: Cambridge University Press.

Stern, C., and Sherwood, E. R., eds. 1966. *The Origin of Genetics, A Mendel Source Book*. San Francisco: W. H. Freeman. (Contains translations of Mendel's classic papers as well as other papers by early geneticists.)

Suzuki, D. T., Griffiths, A. J. F., Miller, J. H., and Lewontin, R. C. 1989. *An Introduction to Genetic Analysis*. 4th ed. San Francisco: W H. Freeman.

Tamarin, R. H. 1996. *Principles of Genetics*. 5th ed. Dubuque, Iowa: Wm. C. Brown Publishers.

Trinkaus, J. P. 1984. *Cells into Organs*. 2d ed. Englewood Cliffs, N.J.: Prentice-Hall.

Weaver, R. F., and Hedrick, P. W. 1997. *Genetics*. 3d ed. Dubuque, Iowa: Wm. C. Brown Publishers.

Zimmerman, A. M., and Forer, A. 1981. *Mitosis/Cytokinesis*. New York: Academic Press.

ARTICLES

Beams, S. W., and Kessel, R. G. 1976. Cytokinesis: A comparative study of cytoplasm division in animal cells. *American Scientist* 64: 279–90.

Beardsley, T. 1988. Sex switch: The gene determining maleness in human embryos is found. *Scientific American,* March.

Belmont, L., and Marolla, F. A. 1973. Birth order, family size, and intelligence. *Science* 182: 1096–101.

Benditt, J. 1988. Genetic skeleton. *Scientific American,* July.

Bouchard, T. J., Jr., and McGue, M. 1981. Familial studies of intelligence: A review. *Science* 212: 1055–59.

Cech, T. R. 1986. RNA as an enzyme. *Scientific American,* November.

Chandley, A. C. 1988. Meiosis in man. *Trends in Genetics* 4: 79–83.

Cooke, J. 1988. The early embryo and the formation of body pattern. *American Scientist* 76: 3535–42.

De Duve, C. 1988. The second genetic code. *Nature* 333: 117–18.

D'Eustachio, P., and Ruddle, R. H. 1983. Somatic cell genetics and gene families. *Science* 220: 919.

Diamond, J. 1989. Blood, genes, and malaria. *Natural History,* February.

Donelson, D. E., and Turner, M. J. 1985. How the trypanosome changes its coat. *Scientific American,* February.

Doolittle, R. F. 1985. Proteins. *Scientific American,* October.

Edelman, G. M. 1989. Topobiology. *Scientific American,* May.

Epel, D. 1980. Fertilization. *Endeavour* 4: 26.

———. 1977. The program of fertilization. *Scientific American,* November.

Friedmann, T. 1989. Progress toward human gene therapy. *Scientific American,* June.

Fuchs, F. 1980. Genetic amniocentesis. *Scientific American,* June.

Gerhart, J., Black, S., Scharf, S., Gimlich, R., Vincent, J. P., Danilchik, M., Rowning, B., and Roberts, J. 1986. Amphibian early development. *BioScience* 36: 541–49.

Gould, M., and Stephano, J. L. 1987. Electrical responses of eggs to acrosomal protein similar to those induced by sperm. *Science* 235: 1654–57.

Gould, S. J. 1983. Sex and size. *Natural History,* August.

———. 1980. Down's syndrome. *Natural History,* September.

Greider, C. W., and Blackburn, E. H. 1996. Telomeres, telomerase and cancer. *Scientific American,* February.

Grunstein, M. 1992. Histones as regulators of genes. *Scientific American,* October.

Haseltine, W. 1997. Discovering genes for new medicine. *Scientific American,* March.

Inoue, S. 1981. Cell division and the mitotic spindle. *Journal of Cell Biology* 91: 132s–37s.

John, B. 1976. Myths and mechanisms of meiosis. *Chromosoma* 54: 295–325.

Laskey, R. A. 1988. A role for the nuclear envelope in controlling DNA replication within the cell cycle. *Nature* 332: 546–48.

Macalpine, I., and Hunter, R. 1969. Porphyria and King George III. *Scientific American,* July.

Marx, J. L. 1985. Putting the human genome on the map. *Science* 229: 150.

———. 1989. Detecting mutations in human genes. *Science* 243: 737–38.

———. 1991. A "mitey" theory for gene jumping. *Science* 253: 1092.

———. 1991. Getting a jump on gene transfer in *Drosophila. Science* 253: 1093.

Mazia, D. 1974. The cell cycle. *Scientific American,* January.

McIntosh, J. R., and McDonald, K. L. 1989. The mitotic spindle. *Scientific American,* October.

McKnight, S. L. 1991. Molecular zippers in gene regulation. *Scientific American,* April.

McKusick, V. A. 1981. The mapping of human chromosomes. *Scientific American,* April.

Metz, C. 1978. Sperm and egg receptors involved in fertilization. *Current Topics in Developmental Biology* 12: 107–19.

Murray, A. W., and Kirschner, M. W. 1991. What controls the cell cycle. *Scientific American,* March.

Murray, A. W., and Szostak, J. W. 1987. Artificial chromosomes. *Scientific American,* November.

Murray, J. 1988. How the leopard gets its spots. *Scientific American,* March.

Pardee, A. B. 1978. Animal cell cycle. *Annual Review of Biochemistry* 47: 715–50.

Patterson, D. 1987. The causes of Down syndrome. *Scientific American,* August.

Ptashne, M. 1989. How gene activators work. *Scientific American,* January.

Radman, M., and Wagner, R. 1989. The high fidelity of DNA duplication. *Scientific American,* August.

Rahn, H., Ar, A., and Paganelli, V. 1979. How bird eggs breathe. *Scientific American,* February.

Roberts, L. 1988. Chromosomes: The ends in view. *Science* 240: 982–83.

———. 1988. The race for the cystic fibrosis gene. *Science* 240: 141–44.

Silberner, J. 1985. Off-on switch for cell division found. *Science News,* 24 August.

Sloboda, R. D. 1980. The role of microtubules in cell structure and cell division. *American Scientist* 68: 290–98.

Special focus: Genetic engineering. 1984. *American Biology Teacher* 46(8) and 46(9).

Stahl, F. 1987. Genetic recombination. *Scientific American*, February.

Steitz, J. A. 1988. "Snurps." *Scientific American*, June.

Takahashi, H. 1995. Molecular biological clocks. *American Scientist* 83(2): 158–65.

Tjian, R. 1995. Molecular machines that control genes. *Scientific American*, February.

Turnbull, A. 1988. Woman enough for the games? *New Scientist* 119: 61–5.

Vaughan, C. 1988. Second thoughts on second genetic code. *Science News* 133: 341.

Verma, I. M. 1990. Gene therapy. *Scientific American*, November.

Wassaman, P. M. 1987. The biology and chemistry of fertilization. *Science* 235: 553–60.

———. 1988. Fertilization in mammals. *Scientific American*, December.

Weintraub, H. M. 1990. Antisense RNA and DNA. *Scientific American*, January.

Weiss, R. 1989. Genetic testing possible before conception. *Science News* 136(21): 326.

White, R., and Lalouel, J. 1988. Chromosome mapping with DNA markers. *Scientific American*, February.

Winkler, M. 1988. Translational regulation in sea urchin eggs. *BioEssays* 8: 157–61.

Yanieshevsky, R. M., and Stein, G. H. 1981. Regulation of the cell cycle in eukaryotic cells. *International Review of Cytology* 69: 223–59.

Zeidler, J. P. 1988. Automated chromosome analysis. *Nature* 334: 635.

part THREE

EVOLUTION

All organisms have an evolutionary history and a future that evolutionary forces will influence. Evolution is a major unifying theme in biology because it helps us understand the life-shaping processes that all species experience.

Charles Darwin and Alfred Russel Wallace conducted groundbreaking studies of evolution in the nineteenth century. Their historical work is an important introduction to evolutionary theory. Chapter 11 explores the work of these and other pioneer evolutionary biologists. Since these early studies, our knowledge of genetics—in particular the principles of population genetics—has greatly influenced evolutionary theory. Chapter 12 examines these genetic ideas, along with the questions of direction and rate of change.

Part Three ends with chapter 12, but coverage of evolution does not end there. Even though organisms experience common evolutionary processes, evolution has resulted in a great diversity of animal life. An important goal of Part Five of this book is to present the diversity of animal life from an evolutionary perspective.

chapter

11

EVOLUTION:
A HISTORICAL PERSPECTIVE

Concepts

1. Organic evolution is the change of a species over time.
2. Although the concept of evolution is very old, Charles Darwin formulated the modern explanation of how change occurs. Darwin began gathering his evidence of evolution during a worldwide mapping expedition on the HMS *Beagle* and spent the rest of his life formulating and defending his ideas.
3. Darwin's theory of evolution by natural selection, although modified from its original form, is still a highly regarded account of how evolution occurs.
4. Modern evolutionary theorists apply principles of genetics, ecology, and geographic and morphological studies when investigating evolutionary mechanisms.
5. Adaptation may refer to either a process of evolutionary change or to the result of a change. In the latter sense, an adaptation is a structure or a process that increases an animal's potential to survive and reproduce in specific environmental conditions.

Would You Like to Know . . .

1 whether the idea of evolutionary change originated with Charles Darwin? (p. 153)

2 what circumstances led Charles Darwin to become a naturalist on the HMS *Beagle*? (p. 154)

3 how Charles Darwin's experiences in South America convinced him that evolution occurs? (p. 156)

4 what prompted Charles Darwin to publish his work in 1859, 23 years after returning from his voyage on the HMS *Beagle*? (p. 159)

5 why geography is important for biologists? (p. 159)

This chapter answers these and other useful questions.

Questions of earth's origin and life's origin have been on the minds of humans since prehistoric times, when accounts of creation were passed orally from generation to generation. For many people, these questions centered around concepts of purpose. Religious and philosophical writings help provide answers to such questions as: Why are we here? What is human nature really like? How do we deal with our mortality?

Many of us are also concerned with other, very different, questions of origin: How old is the planet earth? How long has life been on earth? How did life arise on earth? How did a certain animal species come into existence? Answers for these questions come from a different authority—that of scientific inquiry.

This chapter presents the history of the study of organic evolution, and introduces the **theory of evolution by natural selection. Organic evolution** (L. *evolutus*, unroll), according to Charles Darwin, is "descent with modification." This simply means that species change over time. Evolution by itself does not imply any particular lineage or any particular mechanism, and virtually all scientists agree that the evidence for change in organisms over long time periods is overwhelming *(see chapter 1)*. Further, most scientists agree that natural selection, the mechanism for evolution that Charles Darwin outlined, is one explanation of how evolution occurs. In spite of the scientific certainty of evolution and an acceptance of a general mechanism, much is still to be learned about the details of evolutionary processes. Scientists will be debating these details for years to come (box 11.1).

PRE-DARWINIAN THEORIES OF CHANGE

(1) The idea of evolution did not originate with Charles Darwin. Some of the earliest references to evolutionary change are from the ancient Greeks. The philosophers Empedocles (495–435 B.C.) and Aristotle (384–322 B.C.) described concepts of change in living organisms over time. Georges-Louis Buffon (1707–1788) spent many years studying comparative anatomy. His observations of structural variations in particular organs of related animals, and especially his observations of vestigial structures *(see chapter 1)*, convinced him that change must have occurred during the history of life on earth. Erasmus Darwin (1731–1802), a physician and the grandfather of Charles Darwin, was intensely interested in questions of origin and change. He believed in the common ancestry of all organisms.

LAMARCK: AN EARLY PROPONENT OF EVOLUTION

Jean Baptiste Lamarck (1744–1829) was a distinguished French zoologist. His contributions to zoology include important studies of animal classification. Lamarck, however, is remembered more for a theory of how change occurs. He believed that species are not constant and that existing species were derived from preexisting species.

Lamarck's rather elaborate explanation for evolutionary change involved a theory that was widely accepted in the early 1800s called the **theory of inheritance of acquired characteristics.** Lamarck believed that organisms develop new organs or modify existing organs as environmental problems present themselves. In other words, organs change as the need arises. Lamarck illustrated this point with the often-quoted example of the giraffe. He contended that ancestral giraffes had short necks, much like those of any other mammal. Straining to reach higher branches during browsing resulted in their acquiring higher shoulders and longer necks. These modifications, produced in one generation, were passed on to the next generation. Lamarck went on to state that the use of any organ resulted in that organ becoming highly developed and that disuse resulted in degeneration. Thus, the evolution of highly specialized structures, such as vertebrate eyes, could be explained.

Lamarck published his theory in 1802 and defended it in the face of social and scientific criticism. Society in general was unaccepting of the ideas of evolutionary change, and evidence for evolution had not been developed thoroughly enough to convince most scientists. Thus, Lamarck was criticized in his day more for advocating ideas of evolutionary change than for the mechanism he proposed for that change. Today, he is criticized for defending a mechanism of inheritance and evolutionary change that is now known to lack reasonable supporting evidence. For a change to be passed on to the next generation, it must be based on genetic changes in the germ cells. Changes in the giraffes' necks, as envisioned by Lamarck, could not be passed on because they did not originate as changes in the genetic material. Even though Lamarck's mechanism of change was incorrect, he should be remembered for his steadfastness in promoting the idea of evolutionary change and for his other accomplishments in zoology.

Stop and Ask Yourself

1. What is organic evolution?
2. What contributions did Buffon make to the concept of evolution?
3. What is the theory of inheritance of acquired characteristics? How did Lamarck use it to explain evolution?

DARWIN'S EARLY YEARS AND HIS JOURNEY

Charles Robert Darwin (1809–1882) was born on February 12, 1809. His father, like his grandfather, was a physician. During Darwin's youth in Shrewsbury, England, his interests centered around dogs, collecting, and hunting birds—all popular pastimes in wealthy families of nineteenth-century England. These activities captivated him far more than the traditional education he received at boarding school. At the age of 16 (1825), he entered medical school in Edinburgh, Scotland. For 2 years, he enjoyed the company of the school's well-established scientists. Darwin, however, was not interested in a career in medicine because he could not bear the sight of pain. This prompted his father to

BOX 11.1   THE ORIGIN OF LIFE ON EARTH—LIFE FROM NONLIFE

Geologists estimate from radioisotope dating that the earth is approximately 4.6 billion years old. The oldest fossils are of cyanobacteria that come from 3.5-billion-year-old rocks (stromatolites) from Australia and South Africa. Thus, it took no more than 1 to 1.5 billion years for life to originate.

In trying to explain how life may have arisen, scientists first needed to know the conditions that existed on the earth after its formation. In 1929, J. B. S. Haldane described the atmosphere of primordial earth as a reducing atmosphere (with little free oxygen present) containing primarily hydrogen, water, ammonia, and methane. In 1953, Stanley Miller and Harold Urey constructed a reaction vessel in which they duplicated the atmosphere Haldane described. They heated the mixture to 80° C and provided the atmosphere with an electrical spark to simulate lightning. Over the course of a week, they removed samples from their system and found a variety of common amino acids and other organic acids.

The previous scenario for the origin of the first organic compounds, although once widely accepted, is under increasing scrutiny. Recent evidence suggests that carbon dioxide and nitrogen gas, not methane and ammonia, were the major components of the earth's primitive atmosphere. These conditions are much less favorable for the formation of organic compounds using the Miller/Urey apparatus.

Scientists have begun to look for new explanations of the origin of the first organic chemicals and at older explanations, which are being revived. One of these is that life may have begun deep in the oceans, in underwater hot springs called hydrothermal vents. These vents could have supplied the energy and raw materials for the origin and survival of early life-forms. A group of bacteria, called archaebacteria, that tolerate temperatures up to 120° C and seem to have undergone less evolutionary change than any other living species supports this vent hypothesis.

Another explanation for the origin of the earth's first organic molecules is that they came from outer space. Astronomers are detecting an increasing diversity of organic compounds (such as amino acids and other hydrocarbons) in meteorites that have collided with the earth. Investigations of the most recent pass-by of Halley's comet revealed that comets may be relatively rich in organic compounds. Even though many scientists think that the first organic compounds could have come from space, no microbial life-forms have been detected in space, and conditions in outer space are incompatible with life as we know it.

A second step in the origin of life must have been the hooking together of early organic molecules into the polymers of living organisms: polypeptides, polynucleotides, and carbohydrates. Organic molecules may have become isolated in tidepools or freshwater ponds, and as water was lost through evaporation, condensation reactions could have occurred. Alternatively, reacting molecules may have been concentrated by adsorption on the surfaces of clay or iron pyrite particles, where polymerization could occur.

The final steps in the origin of life are the subject of endless speculations. In some way, organic molecules were surrounded by a membranelike structure, self-replication occurred, and DNA became established as the genetic material. A "chicken-or-the-egg" paradox emerges if DNA was the first genetic material. DNA codes for proteins, yet proteins are required for DNA replication, transcription, and translation. Thomas R. Cech and Sidney Altman suggested a possible way around this paradox in the early 1980s. They discovered a certain type of RNA that acts like an enzyme, cutting and splicing itself into a functional molecule. The first organisms could have been vesicles of self-replicating RNA molecules. Other scientists think that proteins may have been the first genetic material and that DNA was established as the code-carrying molecule secondarily. No self-replicating proteins, however, have been found.

The nutrients produced in the primordial environment would have limited early life. If life were to continue, another source of nutrients was needed. Photosynthesis, which is the production of organic molecules using solar energy and inorganic compounds, probably freed living organisms from a dwindling supply of nutrients. The first photosynthetic organisms probably used hydrogen sulfide as a source of hydrogen for reducing carbon dioxide to sugars. Later, water served this same purpose, and oxygen liberated by photosynthetic reactions began to accumulate in the atmosphere. Earth and its atmosphere slowly began to change. Ozone in the upper atmosphere began to filter ultraviolet radiation from the sun, the reducing atmosphere slowly became an oxidizing atmosphere, and at least some living organisms began to utilize oxygen. About 420 million years ago, enough protective ozone had built up to make life on land possible. Ironically, the change from a reducing atmosphere to an oxidizing atmosphere also meant that life could no longer arise abiotically.

---

suggest that he train for the clergy in the Church of England. With this in mind, Charles enrolled at Christ's College in Cambridge and graduated with honors in 1831. This training, like the medical training he received, was disappointing for Darwin. Again, his most memorable experiences were those with Cambridge scientists. During his stay at Cambridge, Darwin developed a keen interest in collecting beetles and made valuable contributions to beetle taxonomy.

VOYAGE OF THE HMS *Beagle*

2 One of his Cambridge mentors, a botanist by the name of John S. Henslow, nominated Darwin to serve as a naturalist on a mapping expedition that was to travel around the world. Darwin was commissioned as a naturalist on the HMS *Beagle*, which set sail on December 27, 1831 on a 5-year voyage (figure 11.1). Darwin helped with routine seafaring tasks and made numerous collec-

FIGURE 11.1

Voyage of the *HMS Beagle*. Charles Darwin served as a naturalist on a 5-year mapping expedition. Darwin's observations, especially those on the Galápagos Islands, were the basis for his theory of evolution by natural selection.

tions, which he sent to Cambridge. The voyage gave him ample opportunity to explore tropical rain forests, fossil beds, the volcanic peaks of South America, and the coral atolls of the South Pacific. Most importantly, Darwin spent 5 weeks on the **Galápagos Islands,** a group of volcanic islands 900 km off the coast of Ecuador. Some of his most revolutionary ideas came from his observations of plant and animal life on these islands. At the end of the voyage, Darwin was just 27 years old. He spent the rest of his life examining specimens, rereading notes, making new observations, and preparing numerous publications. His most important publication, *On the Origin of Species by Means of Natural Selection,* was published in 1859 and revolutionized biology.

EARLY DEVELOPMENT OF DARWIN'S IDEAS OF EVOLUTION

The development of Darwin's theory of evolution by natural selection was a long, painstaking process. Darwin had to become

convinced that change occurs over time. Before leaving on his voyage, Darwin accepted the prevailing opinion that the earth and its inhabitants had been created 6,000 years ago and had not changed since. Because his observations during his voyage suggested that change does occur, he realized that 6,000 years could not account for the diversity of modern species if they arose through gradual change. Once ideas of change were established in Darwin's thinking, it took about 20 years of study to conceive, and thoroughly document, the mechanism by which change occurs. Darwin died without knowing the genetic principles that support his theory.

GEOLOGY

Darwin began his voyage by reading Charles Lyell's (1779–1875) *Principles of Geology.* In this book, Lyell developed the ideas of another geologist, James Hutton, into the theory of **uniformitarianism.** His theory was based on the idea that the forces of wind, rain, rivers, volcanoes, and geological uplift shape the earth today, just as they have in the past. Lyell and Hutton contended that it was these forces, not catastrophic events, that shaped the face of the earth over hundreds of millions of years. This book planted two important ideas in Darwin's mind: (1) the earth could be much older than 6,000 years, and (2) if the face of the earth changed gradually over long periods, could not living forms also change during that time?

Fossil Evidence

Once the HMS *Beagle* reached South America, Darwin spent time digging in the dry riverbeds of the pampas (grassy plains) of Argentina. He found the fossil remains of an extinct hippopotamus-like animal, now called *Toxodon*, and fossils of a horselike animal, *Thoantherium*. Both of these fossils were from animals that were clearly different from any other animal living in the region. Modern horses were in South America, of course, but Spanish explorers had brought these horses to the Americas in the 1500s. The fossils suggested that horses had been present and had become extinct long before the 1500s. Darwin also found fossils of giant armadillos and giant sloths. Except for their large size, these fossils were very similar to forms Darwin found living in the region.

Fossils were not new to Darwin. They were popularly believed to be the remains of animals that perished in catastrophic events, such as Noah's flood. ③ In South America, however, Darwin understood them to be evidence that the species composition of the earth had changed. Some species became extinct without leaving any descendants. Others became extinct, but not before giving rise to new species.

Galápagos Islands

On its trip up the western shore of South America, the HMS *Beagle* stopped at the Galápagos Islands, which are named after the large tortoises that inhabit them (Sp. *galápago*, tortoise). The tortoises weigh up to 250 kg, have shells up to 1.8 m in diameter, and live for 200 to 250 years. The islands' governor pointed out to Darwin that the shapes of the tortoise shells from different parts of Albemarle Island differed. Darwin noticed other differences as well. Tortoises from the drier regions had longer necks than tortoises from wetter habitats (figure 11.2). In spite of their differences, the tortoises were quite similar to each other and to the tortoises on the mainland of South America.

How could these overall similarities be explained? Darwin reasoned that the island forms were derived from a few ancestral animals that managed to travel from the mainland, across 900 km of ocean. (Because the Galápagos Islands are volcanic and arose out of the seabed, no land connection with the mainland ever existed. One modern hypothesis is that tortoises floated from the mainland on mats of vegetation that regularly break free from coastal riverbanks during storms.) Without predators on the islands, tortoises gradually increased in number.

Darwin also explained some of the differences that he saw. In dryer regions, where vegetation was sparse, tortoises with

(a)

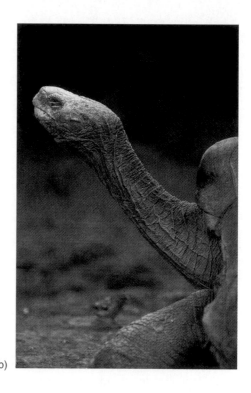

(b)

Figure 11.2

Galápagos Tortoises. (*a*) Shorter-necked subspecies of *Geochelone elephantopus* live in moister regions and feed on low-growing vegetation. (*b*) Longer-necked subspecies live in drier regions and feed on high-growing vegetation.

longer necks would be favored because they could reach higher to get food. In moister regions, tortoises with longer necks would not necessarily be favored, and the shorter-necked tortoises could survive.

Darwin made similar observations of a group of dark, sparrowlike birds. Although he never studied them in detail, Darwin noticed that the Galápagos finches bore similarities suggestive of common ancestry. Scientists now think that Galápagos finches also descended from an ancestral species that originally inhabited the mainland of South America. The chance arrival of a few finches, in either single or multiple colonization events, probably set up the first bird populations on the islands. Early finches encountered many different habitats, all empty of other birds and predators. Ancestral finches, probably seed eaters, multiplied rapidly and filled the seed-bearing habitats most attractive to them. Fourteen species of finches arose from this ancestral group, including one species found on small Cocos Island northeast of the Galápagos Islands. Each species is adapted to a specific habitat on the islands. The most obvious difference between these finches relates to dietary adaptations and is reflected in the size and shape of their bills. The finches of the Galápagos Islands provide an example of **adaptive radiation**—the formation of new forms from an ancestral species, usually in response to the opening of new habitats (figure 11.3).

Darwin's experiences in South America and the Galápagos Islands convinced him that animals change over time. It took the remaining years of his life for Darwin to formulate and document his ideas, and to publish a description of the mechanism of evolutionary change.

THE THEORY OF EVOLUTION BY NATURAL SELECTION

On his return to England in 1836 and for the next 17 years, Darwin worked diligently on the notes and specimens he had collected and made new observations. He was particularly interested in the obvious success of breeders in developing desired variations in plant and animal stocks (figure 11.4). He wondered if this artificial selection of traits could have a parallel in the natural world.

Initially, Darwin was unable to find a natural process similar to artificial selection. However, in 1838, he read an essay by Thomas Malthus (1766–1834) entitled *Essay on the Principle of Population*. Malthus believed that the human population has the potential to increase geometrically. However, because resources cannot keep pace with the increased demands of a burgeoning population, population-restraining factors, such as poverty, wars, plagues, and famine, begin to have an influence. Darwin realized that a similar struggle to survive occurs in nature. This struggle, when viewed over generations, could be a means of **natural selection.** Traits that were detrimental for an animal would be eliminated by the failure of the animal containing them to reproduce.

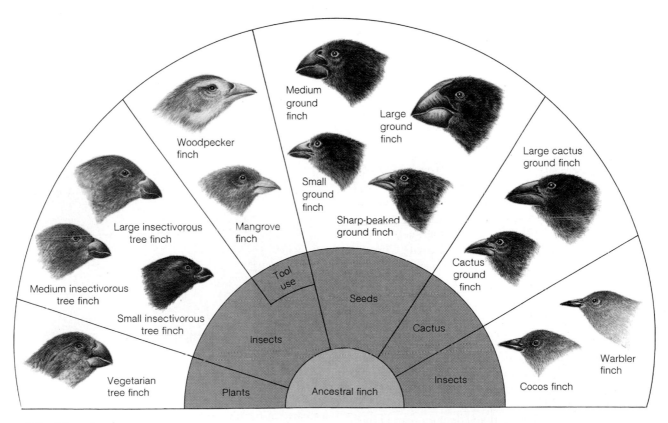

FIGURE 11.3
Adaptive Radiation of the Galápagos Finches. Ancestral finches from the South American mainland colonized the Galápagos Islands. Open habitats and few predators promoted the radiation of finches into 14 different species.

Natural Selection

By 1844 Darwin had formulated, but not yet published, his ideas on natural selection. The essence of his theory is as follows:

1. All organisms have a far greater reproductive potential than is ever realized. For example, a female oyster releases about 100,000 eggs with each spawning, a female sea star releases about 1 million eggs each season, and a female robin may lay four fertile eggs each season. What if all of these eggs were fertilized and developed to reproductive adults by the following year? A half million female sea stars (half of the million eggs would produce females and half would produce males), each producing another million eggs, repeated over just a few generations would soon fill up the oceans! Even the adult female robins, each producing four more robins, would result in unimaginable resource problems in just a few years.
2. Inherited variations arise by random mutation. Seldom are any two individuals exactly alike. Some of these genetic variations may confer an advantage to the individual possessing them. In other instances, variations may be harmful to an individual. In still other instances, particular variations may be neither helpful nor harmful. (These are said to be neutral.) These variations can be passed on to offspring.
3. Because resources are limited, existence is a constant struggle. Many more offspring are produced than resources can support; therefore, many individuals die. Darwin reasoned that the individuals that die are those with the traits (variations) that make survival and successful reproduction less likely. Traits that promote successful reproduction are said to be adaptive.
4. Adaptive traits are perpetuated in subsequent generations. Because organisms with maladaptive traits are less likely to reproduce, the maladaptive traits become less frequent in a population and eventually are eliminated.

With these ideas, Darwin formulated a theory that explained how the tortoises and finches of the Galápagos Islands changed over time (figure 11.5). In addition, Darwin's theory explained how some animals, such as the ancient South American horses, could become extinct. What if a group of animals is faced with a new environment to which it is ill-adapted? Climatic changes, food shortages, and other environmental stressors could lead to extinction.

Adaptation

Adaptation occurs when a change in a phenotype increases an animal's chance of successful reproduction. It is likely to be expressed when an organism encounters a new environment and may result in the evolution of multiple new groups if an environment can be exploited in different ways. No terms in evolution have been more laden with confusion than adaptation and fitness or adaptedness. Adaptation is sometimes used to refer to a process of change in evolution. That use of the term is probably less confusing than when it is used to describe the result of the process of

(a)

(b)

Figure 11.4

Artificial Selection. The artificial selection of domestic fowl has resulted in the diverse varieties seen today. Breeders perpetuated the variations they desired by allowing only certain offspring to breed. (*a*) Bearded white Polish fowl. (*b*) Jungle fowl.

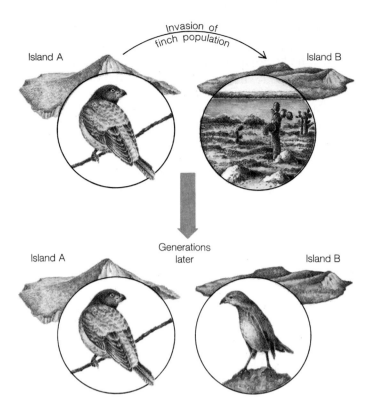

FIGURE 11.5

Natural Selection in Galápagos Finches. Natural selection of finches on the Galápagos Islands resulted in changes in bill shape. In this illustration, tree-feeding birds on island A invade island B. The relatively treeless habitats of island B select against birds most adapted to living in trees, and individuals that can exploit seeds on the ground in low-growing vegetation are more likely to survive and reproduce. Subsequent generations of finches on island B show ground-feeding bill characteristics.

change. In this text, adaptations are defined as characteristics that increase the potential of an organism or species to successfully reproduce in a specified environment. In a similar fashion, adaptedness or fitness is a measure of the capacity for successful reproduction in a given environment.

Not every characteristic is an adaptation to some kind of environmental situation. Some have erroneously concluded that if a structure is now performing a specific function, it must have arisen for that purpose and is, therefore, an adaptation. An extreme extension of this incorrect view is that evolutionary adaptations lead to perfection.

ALFRED RUSSEL WALLACE

Alfred Russel Wallace (1823–1913) was an explorer of the Amazon Valley and led a zoological expedition to the Malay Archipelago, which is an area of great biogeographical importance. Wallace, like Darwin, was impressed with evolutionary change and had read the writings of Thomas Malthus on human populations. In the midst of a bout with malarial fever (*see box 17.2*), he synthesized a theory of evolution similar to Darwin's theory of evolution by natural selection. After writing the details of his

theory, Wallace sent his paper to Darwin for criticism. ④ Darwin recognized the similarity of Wallace's ideas and prepared a short summary of his own theory. Both Wallace's and Darwin's papers were published in the *Journal of the Proceedings of the Linnean Society* in 1859. Darwin's insistence on having Wallace's ideas presented along with his own shows Darwin's integrity. Darwin then shortened a manuscript he had been working on since 1856 and published it as *On the Origin of Species by Means of Natural Selection* in November 1859. The 1,250 copies prepared in the first printing sold out the day the book was released.

In spite of the similarities in the theories of Wallace and Darwin, there were also important differences. Wallace, for example, believed that every evolutionary modification was a product of selection and, therefore, had to be adaptive for the organism. Darwin, on the other hand, admitted that natural selection may not explain all evolutionary changes. He did not insist on finding adaptive significance for every modification. Further, unlike Darwin, Wallace stopped short of attributing human intellectual functions and the ability to make moral judgments to evolution. On both of these matters, Darwin's ideas are closer to the views of most modern scientists.

Wallace's work motivated Darwin to publish his own ideas. The theory of natural selection, however, is usually credited to Charles Darwin. Darwin's years of work and massive accumulations of evidence led even Wallace to attribute the theory to Darwin. Wallace wrote to Darwin in 1864:

> I shall always maintain [the theory of evolution by natural selection] to be actually yours and yours only. You had worked it out in details I had never thought of years before I had a ray of light on the subject.

Stop and Ask Yourself

4. How did the following contribute to Charles Darwin's formulation of the theory of natural selection: (*a*) uniformitarianism, (*b*) South American fossils, and (*c*) Galápagos tortoises?

5. What are four elements of the theory of evolution by natural selection?

EVOLUTIONARY THOUGHT AFTER DARWIN

The most significant changes in evolutionary thought began in the 1930s and have continued to the present. The combination of population genetics with Darwinian evolutionary theory is called the **modern synthesis** or **neo-Darwinism.**

BIOGEOGRAPHY

⑤ In the tradition of Darwin and Wallace, biologists of the period of modern synthesis recognized the importance of geography in explaining the evolution and the distribution of plants and animals (*see chapter 1; figures 1.3 and 1.4*). One of the distribution patterns that biogeographers try to explain is how similar groups of organisms can live in places separated by seemingly impenetrable barriers. Recall that Darwin was struck by the presence of fossil horses in South America. This distribution was puzzling because modern horses were introduced to America from Europe. Could the fossil horses have arisen in America, migrated to Europe, and then became extinct in America? Biogeographers also try to explain why plants and animals, separated by geographical barriers, are often very different in spite of similar environments. For example, evolution may take different directions in different parts of the world; therefore, major predators in Africa and America might be expected to differ if they had no common ancestry. Finally, biogeographers try to explain why oceanic islands, such as the Galápagos, often have relatively few, but unique, resident species. They try to document island colonization and subsequent evolutionary events, which may be very different from evolutionary events in ancestral, mainland groups.

Modern evolutionary biologists recognize the importance of geological events, such as volcanic activity, the movement of great landmasses, climatic changes, and geological uplift (mountain building), in creating or removing barriers to the movements of plants and animals. As scientists learn more about earth's geologic history, they understand more about animal distribution patterns and factors that played important roles in animal evolution. Only in understanding how the surface of the earth came to its present form can we understand its inhabitants (box 11.2).

Biogeographical information can be applied to the study of contemporary environmental problems. Prehistoric removal of geographic barriers allowed species from one region of the world to invade other regions, sometimes dramatically changing species composition. Invading species tend to be highly competitive, with high reproductive potential, and have been important agents of extinction in regions that they invade. For example, during the Pliocene and Miocene epochs (about 10 million years ago), the Central American land bridge formed between North and South America (*see box 11.2*). Many species of plants and animals used this land bridge to move between continents. Information from the study of past events is now being applied to predict the effect of the removal of geographical barriers on native populations. For example, the proposed sea-level canal across Panama could bring an interchange of species between the Atlantic and Pacific Oceans, causing extinction of many fishes and other animals. In addition, the canal could introduce the voracious coral predator, *Acanthaster planci* (the crown-of-thorns sea star), into the Caribbean region.

Evolution is one of the major unifying themes in biology because it helps explain both the similarities and diversity of life. In chapter 1, you learned of the sources of evidence for evolution: Biogeography gives evidence of prehistoric climates, habitats, and animal distribution patterns; paleontology provides evidence of animals that existed in the past; comparative anatomy leads to the description of homologous structures; and molecular biology provides evidence of relatedness of animals based on their biochemical similarities. This evidence leaves little doubt that evolution has occurred in the past, and this chapter describes the historical development of a theory that accounts for how evolution occurs. Chapter 12 examines how the principles of population genetics have affected scientific concepts of the mechanism of evolution.

Stop and Ask Yourself

6. What is modern synthesis or neo-Darwinism?
7. What are some of the distribution patterns that biogeographers attempt to explain?
8. How has the discovery of continental drift influenced the understanding of evolution?

 BOX 11.2   CONTINENTAL DRIFT

It seems remarkable, but the earth's largest landmasses are moving—about 1 cm a year! The 1960s revolutionized geology as **continental drift** became an accepted theory.

During the Permian period (about 250 million years ago), all of earth's landmasses united into a single continent called Pangaea (figure 1*a*). Soon after, Pangaea began to break up, as the huge crustal plates moved apart. Approximately 200 million years ago, there were two great continents. The northern continent was Laurasia, and the southern continent was Gondwana (figure 1*b*). Seventy million years ago, Gondwana broke apart, followed later by the breakup of Laurasia (figure 1*c*).

Movement of these crustal plates continues today. Their study is known as **plate tectonics.** During these movements, new crustal material is thrust up from the ocean floor along the mid-Atlantic ridge and flows in both directions from that ridge. The mid-Atlantic ridge runs from the Falkland Islands, at its southern end, to Iceland, at its northern end. As the huge crusts move away from each other in the Atlantic, old crustal material sinks back into the earth in deep oceanic trenches in the Pacific Ocean. Earthquakes along the western coast of North America and the eastern coast of Asia are evidence of these movements.

Continental drift has important implications for biogeographers and paleontologists. It explains why some fossils have a worldwide distribution. Land organisms in existence when all continents were united as Pangaea had access to most of the landmasses of the world. This explains why some fossils are similar in all parts of the world, such as the fossils that Charles Darwin found in South America that were very similar to animals living in Africa. Were it not for continental drift, this pattern would be difficult to explain.

Continental drift also explains how differences in organisms may develop. Continental drift created oceanic barriers that sepa-

rated populations of plants and animals when continents separated. Evolution then proceeded independently in each biogeographical region and resulted in species characteristic of that region.

FIGURE 1 **Continental Drift.** (a) About 250 million years ago, the continents of the earth joined in a single landmass that geologists call Pangaea. (b) About 200 million years ago, Pangaea broke into the northern (Laurasia) and southern (Gondwana) continents. (c) This breakup was followed, about 70 million years ago, by the separation of continents in the Southern Hemisphere, and later, by the separation of continents in the Northern Hemisphere. (d) Present position of continents. Note the complementary outlines of the eastern coast of South America and the western coast of Africa. The collision of India with Eurasia (c)

Summary

1. Organic evolution is the change of a species over time.

2. Ideas of evolutionary change can be traced back to the ancient Greeks.

3. Jean Baptiste Lamarck was an eighteenth-century proponent of evolution and proposed a mechanism—inheritance of acquired characteristics—to explain it.

4. Charles Darwin saw impressive evidence for evolutionary change while on a mapping expedition on the HMS *Beagle*. The theory of uniformitarianism, South American fossils, and observations of tortoises and finches on the Galápagos Islands convinced Darwin that evolution occurs.

5. After returning from his voyage, Darwin began formulating his theory of evolution by natural selection. In addition to his experiences

on his voyage, later observations of artificial selection and Malthus' theory of human population growth helped shape his theory.

6. Darwin's theory of natural selection includes the following elements: (a) All organisms have a greater reproductive potential than is ever attained; (b) inherited variations arise by mutation; (c) in a constant struggle for existence, those organisms that are least suited to their environment die; (d) the adaptive traits present in the survivors tend to be passed on to subsequent generations, and the nonadaptive traits tend to be lost.

7. Adaptation may refer to a process of change or a result of change. An adaptation is a characteristic that increases an organism's potential to survive and reproduce in a given environment.

8. Not all evolutionary changes are adaptive; nor do all evolutionary changes lead to perfect solutions to environmental problems.

9. Alfred Russel Wallace outlined a theory similar to Darwin's but never accumulated significant evidence documenting his theory.

10. Modern evolutionary theorists apply principles of genetics, ecological theory, and geographic and morphological studies to solving evolutionary problems.

11. The study of biogeography provides information on how similar groups of organisms can live in widely separated areas, accounts for the importance of geological events in the evolution of plants and animals, and helps scientists predict the effects of removal of geographical barriers on extant populations.

SELECTED KEY TERMS

adaptation (p. 158)
continental drift (p. 160)
Galápagos Islands (p. 155)
modern synthesis (p. 159)
natural selection (p. 157)
neo-Darwinism (p. 159)

organic evolution (p. 153)
theory of evolution by natural
  selection (p. 153)
theory of inheritance of
  acquired characteristics (p. 153)
uniformitarianism (p. 155)

CRITICAL THINKING QUESTIONS

1. Chapter 1 discusses the scientific method. Review that discussion and then (a) outline a hypothesis and design a test of "inheritance of acquired characteristics," and (b) define what is meant by the word theory in the theory of evolution by natural selection.

2. Assuming that you have already studied chapter 9, describe the implications of inheritance of acquired characteristics for the central dogma of molecular genetics (see figure 9.4).

3. Review the definition of adaptation in the sense of a result of evolutionary change. Imagine that two deer, A and B, are identical twins. A hunter shoots deer A before it has a chance to reproduce. Deer B is not shot and goes on to reproduce. According to the definition of adaptation, is deer B more fit for its environment than deer A? Why or why not?

4. Why is the stipulation of "a specified environment" included in the definition of adaptation?

5. Imagine that you could go back in time and meet simultaneously with Charles Darwin and Gregor Mendel. Construct a dialogue in which you explain to both the effect of their ideas on each other's theory and their theories on modern biology. Include their responses and questions throughout the dialogue.

REFERENCES ON THE WORLD WIDE WEB

1. **Evolution and Behavior.** This site provides answers to frequently asked questions related to many topics on evolution. It provides book reviews, information on contemporary and historical evolutionary scientists, and perspectives on evolution and religion.
   http://ccp.uchicago.edu/~jyin/evolution.html

2. **Charles Robert Darwin.** This site lists the geneology of Charles Darwin and links to other Darwin sites.
   http://www.Geocities.com/heartland/3479/Darwin.html

3. **Charles Robert Darwin.** This site provides a biography of Charles Darwin and a history of evolutionary thought. It provides links to the papers of Darwin and Wallace and to the controversies surrounding evolutionary theory.
   http://spruce.evansville.edu/~a122/darwin.html

4. **The Talk, Origins Archive.** This site provides a discussion of Darwin's theory and traces the history of scientists' acceptance of evolution.
   http://www.talkorigins.org/faqs/modern-synthesis.html

5. **Charles Darwin Research Station: Galápagos.** This site provides information on the Charles Darwin Research Station, including research being conducted, news on the status of tortoise and other island populations, and volunteer and employment opportunities.
   http://www.polaris.net/~jpinson/welcome.html

EVOLUTION AND GENE FREQUENCIES

Concepts

1. In modern genetic theory, organic evolution is a change in the frequency of alleles in a population.
2. The principles of modern genetics help biologists understand how variation arises. This variation increases the chances of a population's survival in changing environments.
3. Population genetics is the study of events occurring in gene pools. The Hardy-Weinberg theorem helps scientists understand the circumstances under which evolution occurs. Evolution is a result of (a) genetic drift or neutral selection, (b) gene flow, (c) mutations that introduce new genes into populations, or (d) natural selection.
4. Balanced polymorphism occurs when two or more body forms are maintained in a population without a range of phenotypes between them.
5. The fundamental unit of classification is the species, and the process by which new species form is speciation.
6. Speciation requires reproductive isolation.
7. Different organisms, as well as structures within organisms, evolve at different rates. Evolution may also proceed in jumps, rather than at a constant pace.
8. Molecular biologists study DNA and proteins to uncover evolutionary relationships.

Would You Like to Know . . .

This chapter answers these and other useful questions.

Natural selection can be envisioned as operating in two ways, and both are important perspectives on evolution. One way (e.g., the focus of chapter 11) looks at characteristics of individual animals. When a bird acquires an adaptation through natural selection that permits it to feed more efficiently on butterflies, the trait is described in terms of physical characteristics (e.g., bill shape) or inherited behaviors. This description of natural selection recognizes that natural selection must act in the context of living organisms.

The organism, however, must be viewed as a vehicle that permits the phenotypic expression of genes. This chapter examines the second way that natural selection operates—on the gene. Birds and butterflies are not permanent—they die. The genes they carry, however, are potentially immortal. The result of natural selection (and evolution in general) is reflected in how common, or how rare, specific genes are in a group of animals that are interbreeding—and, therefore, sharing genes. Individuals of the same species that occupy a given area at the same time and share a unique set of genes are a **population.**

A more precise definition of organic evolution is a change in the frequency of alleles in a population. The frequency of an allele in a population is the abundance of that particular allele in relation to the sum of all alleles at that locus. Another way to express the same idea is that organic evolution is a change in the total genetic makeup of a population (the **gene pool**). This chapter examines evolution from the perspective of changes in gene pools and covers some of the mechanisms by which evolution occurs, as well as processes by which new species arise.

The Modern Synthesis: A Closer Look

An understanding of the modern synthesis comes from studying genetics because it explains why variations among individuals exist and how they pass to future generations. Genetic variation is important in evolution because some variations may confer an advantage to individuals, leading to natural selection. The potential for genetic variation in individuals of a population is unlimited. Even the relatively simple principles of inheritance that Gregor Mendel described provide for remarkable variation. Crossing-over, multiple alleles, and mutations add to this variation. The result is that no two individuals, except identical twins, are genetically identical. Chance combinations of genes are likely to result in some individuals being better able to survive and reproduce in a given environment than others.

Must Evolution Happen?

Evolution is central to biology, but is evolution always occurring in a particular population? Sometimes, the rate of evolution is slow, and sometimes, it is rapid. But are there times when evolution does not occur at all? ❶ The answer to this question lies in the theories of **population genetics,** the study of the genetic events in gene pools.

The Hardy-Weinberg Theorem

In 1908, English mathematician Godfrey H. Hardy and German physician Wilhelm Weinberg independently derived a mathematical model describing what happens to the frequency of alleles in a population over time. Their combined ideas became known as the Hardy-Weinberg theorem. It states that the mixing of alleles at meiosis and their subsequent recombination do not alter the frequencies of the alleles in future generations, if certain assumptions are met. Stated another way, if certain assumptions are met, evolution will not occur because the allelic frequencies will not change from generation to generation, even though the specific mixes of alleles in individuals may vary.

The assumptions of the Hardy-Weinberg theorem are as follows:

1. The population size must be large. Large size ensures that gene frequency will not change by chance alone.
2. Mating within the population must be random. Every individual must have an equal chance of mating with any other individual in the population. Expressed in a slightly different way, the choice of a mate must not be based on similarity or dissimilarity in a given trait. If this condition is not fulfilled, then some individuals are more likely to reproduce than others, and natural selection may occur.
3. Individuals cannot migrate into, or out of, the population. Migration may introduce new genes into the gene pool, or add or delete copies of existing genes.
4. Mutations must not occur. If they do, mutational equilibrium must exist. Mutational equilibrium is when mutation from the wild-type allele to a mutant form is balanced by mutation from the mutant form back to the wild type. In either case, no new genes are introduced into the population from this source.

These assumptions must be met if allelic frequencies are not changing—that is, if evolution is not occurring. Clearly, these assumptions are restrictive, and few, if any, real populations meet them. ❷ This means that most populations are evolving. The Hardy-Weinberg theorem, however, does provide a useful theoretical framework for examining changes in gene frequencies in populations (box 12.1)

The next section explains how, when the assumptions are not met, evolutionary change occurs.

Stop and Ask Yourself

1. What is a gene pool?
2. What are the four assumptions of the Hardy-Weinberg theorem?
3. Are the Hardy-Weinberg assumptions realistic for animal populations?
4. What conclusion can be drawn from the Hardy-Weinberg theorem?

BOX	12.1	GENETIC EQUILIBRIUM

To illustrate the Hardy-Weinberg theorem, consider a hypothetical population that meets all of the assumptions listed on p. 164. In this population, a particular autosomal locus has two alleles: allele A has a frequency of 0.8 [$f(A) = 0.8$], and allele a has a frequency of 0.2 [$f(a) = 0.2$]. Stated another way, in this population, 80% of the genes for this locus are allele A, and 20% are allele a. For the purpose of the example, assume dominance; however, it is irrelevant to the Hardy-Weinberg theorem.

Because random mating is assumed, the genotypic and phenotypic frequencies of the next generation can be determined using a Punnett square type of analysis (figure 1). Since dominance is assumed, the phenotypic frequencies of the F_1 generation are:

$$f(\text{phenotype } A) = 0.64 + 0.32 = 0.96$$
$$f(\text{phenotype } a) = 0.04$$

Gene frequencies of the F_1 generation are determined by adding the frequency of each homozygote to half the frequency of the heterozygote. (The frequency of an allele in the heterozygote is reduced by half because heterozygotes contain only a single copy of each allele.)

	$f(\text{allele } A)$	$f(\text{allele } a)$
AA individuals	0.64	0
Aa individuals	½(0.32) = 0.16	½(0.32) = 0.16
aa individuals	0	0.04
Overall frequency	0.80	0.20

Note that the overall frequency of each allele in the F_1 generation has not changed from that assumed for the parental generation. This example illustrates that, if the assumptions of the Hardy-Weinberg theorem are met, gene frequency does not change from generation to generation. In other words, **Hardy-Weinberg equilibrium** is achieved, and evolution does NOT occur!

$$f(AA) = 0.64, \; f(Aa + aA) = 0.32, \; f(aa) = 0.04$$
$$(p + q)^2 = p^2 + 2pq + q^2 = 1$$

FIGURE 1   Genotypic Frequencies. Determining the genotypic frequencies of offspring from allelic frequencies in a parental generation. This analysis assumes random mating and that each allele is equally likely to be incorporated into a viable gamete. The frequency of each allele in a sperm or egg is simply the frequency of that allele in the parental population. Allelic frequencies are often represented by p and q, and genotypic frequencies can be found by expanding the binomial $(p + q)^2$.

The Hardy-Weinberg theorem can be stated in general mathematical terms. Given a locus with two interacting alleles, if p = the frequency of one allele, and q = the frequency of a second allele, then $p + q = 1$. The frequency of genotypes in the next generation is found by algebraically expanding the binomial equation $(p + q)^2 = p^2 + 2pq + q^2 = 1$.

EVOLUTIONARY MECHANISMS

Evolution is neither a creative force working for progress nor a dark force sacrificing individuals for the sake of the group. It is neither moral nor immoral. It has neither a goal nor a mind to conceive a goal. Such goal-oriented thinking is said to be teleological. Evolution is simply a result of some individuals in a population surviving and being more effective at reproducing than others in the population, leading to changes in gene frequencies. This section examines some of the situations when the Hardy-Weinberg assumptions are not met—situations in which gene frequencies change from one generation to the next and evolution occurs.

POPULATION SIZE, GENETIC DRIFT, AND NEUTRAL SELECTION

3 Chance often plays an important role in the perpetuation of genes in a population, and the smaller the population, the more

significant chance may be. Fortuitous circumstances, such as a chance encounter between reproductive individuals, may promote reproduction. Some traits of a population survive, not because they convey increased fitness, but because they happen to be in gametes involved in fertilization. Chance events influencing the frequencies of genes in populations result in **genetic drift.** Because gene frequencies are changing independently of natural selection, genetic drift is often called **neutral selection.**

The process of genetic drift is analogous to flipping a coin. The likelihood of getting a head or a tail is equal. The 50:50 ratio of heads and tails is most likely in a large number of tosses. In only 10 tosses, for example, the ratio may be a disproportionate 7 heads and 3 tails. Similarly, the chance of one or the other of two equally adaptive alleles being incorporated into a gamete, and eventually into an individual in a second generation, is equal. Gamete sampling in a small population may show unusual proportions of alleles in any one generation of gametes because meiotic events, like tossing a coin, are random. Assuming that both alleles have equal fitness, these unusual proportions are reflected in the genotypes of the next generation. These chance events may result in a particular allele increasing or decreasing in frequency (figure 12.1a). In small populations, inbreeding is also common. Genetic drift and inbreeding are likely to reduce genetic variation within a population.

If a mutation introduces a new allele into a population and that allele is no more or less adaptive than existing alleles, genetic drift may permit the new allele to become established in the population (figure 12.1b), or the new allele may be lost because of genetic drift. The likelihood of genetic drift occurring in small populations suggests that a Hardy-Weinberg equilibrium will not occur.

Two special cases of genetic drift have influenced the genetic makeup of some populations. When a few individuals from a parental population colonize new habitats, they seldom carry a representative sample of the gene pool from which they came. The new colony that emerges from the founding individuals is likely to have a distinctive genetic makeup with far less variation than the larger population. This form of genetic drift is the **founder effect.**

An often-cited example of the founder effect concerns the genetic makeup of the Dunkers of eastern Pennsylvania. They emigrated from Germany to the United States early in the eighteenth century, and for religious reasons, have not married outside their sect. Examination of certain traits (e.g., ABO blood type) in their population reveals very different gene frequencies from the Dunker populations of Germany. These differences are attributed to the chance absence of certain genes in the individuals who founded the original Pennsylvania Dunker population.

A similar effect can occur when the number of individuals in a population is drastically reduced. For example, cheetah populations in South and East Africa are endangered. Their depleted populations have reduced genetic diversity to the point that even if populations are restored, they will have only a remnant of the original gene pool. This form of genetic drift is called the **bottleneck effect** (figure 12.2). A similar example concerns the northern elephant seal, which was hunted to near extinction in the late 1800s (figure 12.3). Legislation to protect the seal was enacted in 1922, and now the population is greater than 100,000 individuals. In spite of this relatively large number, genetic variability in the population is low.

The effects of bottlenecks are somewhat controversial. The traditional interpretation is that decreases in genetic diversity make populations less likely to withstand environmental stress and more susceptible to extinction. That is, a population with high genetic diversity is more likely to have some individuals with a combination of genes that allows them to withstand environmental changes. In the case of the cheetah, recent evidence indicates that this cat's current problems may be more a result of lions and spotted hyenas preying on cheetah cubs than low genetic diversity. Most evolutionary biologists agree, however, that over evolutionary time frames, high genetic diversity makes extinction less likely.

Gene Flow

The Hardy-Weinberg theorem assumes that no individuals enter a population from the outside (immigrate) and that no individuals

FIGURE 12.1

Genetic Drift. (a) Genetic diversity may be lost as a result of genetic drift. Assume that alleles a and A are equally adaptive. Allele a might be incorporated into gametes more often than A, or it could be involved in more fertilizations. In either case, the frequency of a increases and the frequency of A decreases because of random events operating at the level of gametes. (b) A new, equally adaptive, allele may become established in a population as a result of genetic drift. In this example, the allele (A') substitutes for an existing allele (A). The same mechanisms could also account for the loss of the newly introduced allele or the establishment of A' as a third allele.

leave a population (emigrate). Immigration or emigration upsets the Hardy-Weinberg equilibrium, resulting in changes in gene frequency (evolution). Changes in gene frequency from migration of individuals are **gene flow.** Although some natural populations do not have significant gene flow, most populations do.

Mutation

Mutations are changes in the structure of genes and chromosomes (see chapters 8 and 9). The Hardy-Weinberg theorem assumes that no mutations occur or that mutational equilibrium exists. Mutations, however, are a fact of life. Most importantly, mutations are the origin of all new genes and a source of variation that may prove adaptive for an animal. Mutation counters the loss of

(a)

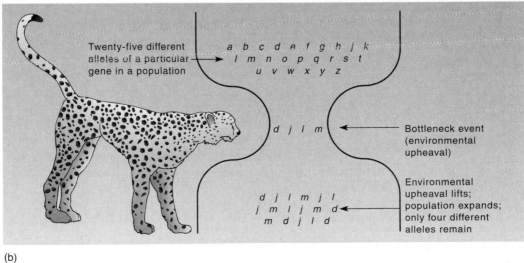

(b)

FIGURE 12.2

Bottleneck Effect. (*a*) Human activities have endangered cheetahs (*Acinonyx jubatus*) of South and East Africa. (*b*) Severe reduction in the original population has caused a bottleneck effect. Even if the population size recovers, genetic diversity has been significantly reduced.

FIGURE 12.3

Bottleneck Effect. The northern elephant seal (*Mirounga angustirostris*) was severely overhunted in the late 1800s. Even though its population numbers are now increasing, its genetic diversity is low.

genetic material from natural selection and genetic drift, and increases the likelihood that variations will be present that allow a group to survive future environmental shocks.

Mutations are random events, and the likelihood of a mutation is not affected by the mutation's usefulness. Organisms cannot filter harmful genetic changes from advantageous changes before they occur. The effects of mutations vary enormously. Most are deleterious. Some may be neutral or harmful in one environment and help an organism survive in another environment.

Mutational equilibrium is when a mutation from the wild-type allele to a mutant form is balanced by mutation from the mutant back to the wild type. This has the same effect on allelic frequency as if no mutation occurred. Mutational equilibrium rarely exists, however. **Mutation pressure** is a measure of the tendency for gene frequencies to change through mutation.

NATURAL SELECTION REEXAMINED

The theory of natural selection remains preeminent in modern biology. Natural selection occurs whenever some phenotypes are more successful at leaving offspring than other phenotypes. The tendency for natural selection to occur—and upset Hardy-Weinberg equilibrium—is **selection pressure.** Although natural selection is simple in principle, it is diverse in actual operation.

Modes of Selection

For certain traits, many populations have a range of phenotypes, characterized by a bell-shaped curve that shows that phenotypic extremes are less common than the intermediate phenotypes. Natural selection may affect a range of phenotypes in three ways.

Directional selection occurs when individuals at one phenotypic extreme are at a disadvantage compared to all other individuals in the population (figure 12.4*a*). In response to this selection, the deleterious gene(s) decreases in frequency, and all

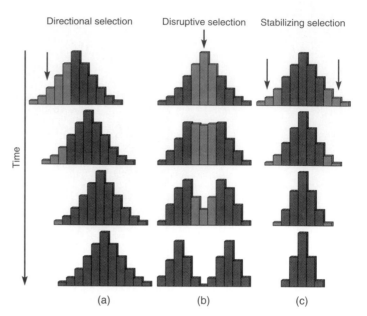

FIGURE 12.4

Modes of Selection. (*a*) Directional selection occurs when individuals at one phenotypic extreme are selected against. It shifts phenotypic distribution toward the advantageous phenotype. (*b*) Disruptive selection occurs when an intermediate phenotype is selected against. It produces distinct subpopulations. (*c*) Stabilizing selection occurs when individuals at both phenotypic extremes are selected against. It narrows both ends of the range. Arrows indicate selection against one or more phenotypes. The X-axis of each graph indicates the range of phenotypes for the trait in question.

other genes increase in frequency. Directional selection may occur when a mutation gives rise to a new gene, or when the environment changes to select against an existing phenotype.

Industrial melanism, a classic example of directional selection, occurred in England during the Industrial Revolution. Museum records and experiments document how environmental changes affected selection against one phenotype of the peppered moth, *Biston betularia*.

In the early 1800s, a gray form made up about 99% of the peppered moth population. That form still predominates in nonindustrial northern England and Scotland. In industrial areas of England, a black form replaced the gray form over a period of about 50 years. In these areas, the gray form made up only about 5% of the population, and 95% of the population was black. The gray phenotype, previously advantageous, had become deleterious.

The nature of the selection pressure was understood when investigators discovered that birds prey more effectively on moths resting on a contrasting background. Prior to the Industrial Revolution, gray moths were favored because they blended with the bark of trees on which they rested. The black moth contrasted with the lighter, lichen-covered bark and was easily spotted by birds (figure 12.5*a*). Early in the Industrial Revolution, however, factories used soft coal, and spewed soot and other pollutants into the air. Soot covered the tree trunks and killed the lichens where the moths rested. Bird predators now could easily pick out gray moths against the black background of the tree trunk, while the black form was effectively camouflaged (figure 12.5*b*).

(a)   (b)

FIGURE 12.5

Directional Selection of the Peppered Moth, _Biston betularia._ Each photo shows two forms of the moth: black and gray. (_a_) Prior to the Industrial Revolution, bird predators easily spotted the black form of moth, and the gray form was camouflaged. (_b_) In industrial regions after the Industrial Revolution, selection was reversed because soot now covered the bark of trees where moths rested. Note how clearly the gray form is seen, whereas the black form is almost invisible.

In the 1950s, the British Parliament enacted air pollution standards that have reduced soot in the atmosphere. As expected, the gray form of the moth has experienced a small but significant increase in frequency.

Another form of natural selection involves circumstances selecting against individuals of an intermediate phenotype (figure 12.4_b_). **4 Disruptive selection** produces distinct subpopulations. Consider, for example, what could happen in a population of snails with a range of shell colors between white and dark brown and living in a marine tidepool habitat with two background colors. The sand, made up of pulverized mollusc shells, is white, and rock outcroppings are brown. In the face of shorebird predation, what phenotypes are going to be most common? Although white snails may not actively select a white background, those present on the sand are less likely to be preyed on than intermediate phenotypes on either sand or rocks. Similarly, brown snails are less likely to be preyed on than intermediate phenotypes on either substrate. Thus, disruptive selection could produce two distinct subpopulations, one white and one brown.

When both phenotypic extremes are deleterious, a third form of natural selection—**stabilizing selection**—narrows the phenotypic range (figure 12.4_c_). During long periods of environmental constancy, new variations that arise, or new combinations of genes that occur, are unlikely to result in more fit phenotypes than the genes that have allowed a population to survive for thousands of years, especially when the new variations are at the extremes of the phenotypic range.

A good example of stabilizing selection is the horseshoe crab (_Limulus_), which lives along the Atlantic coast of the United States (_see figure 23.8_). Comparison of the fossil record with living forms indicates that this body form has changed little over 200 million years. Apparently, the combination of characteristics

present in this group of animals is adaptive for the horseshoe crab's environment.

Neutralist/Selectionist Controversy

Most biologists recognize that both natural selection and neutral selection occur, but may not be equally important in all circumstances. For example, during long periods when environments are relatively constant, and stabilizing selection is acting on phenotypes, neutral selection may operate at the molecular level. Certain genes could be randomly established in a population. Occasionally, however, the environment shifts, and directional or disruptive selection begins to operate, resulting in gene frequency changes (often fairly rapid).

The relative importance of neutral selection and natural selection in natural populations is debated and is an example of the kind of debates among evolutionists. These debates concern the mechanics of evolution and are the foundations of science. They lead to experiments that will ultimately present a clearer understanding of evolution.

BALANCED POLYMORPHISM AND HETEROZYGOTE SUPERIORITY

Polymorphism occurs in a population when two or more distinct forms exist without a range of phenotypes between them. **Balanced polymorphism** (Gr. _poly,_ many + _morphe,_ form) occurs when different phenotypes are maintained at relatively stable frequencies in the population and may resemble a population in which disruptive selection operates.

Sickle-cell anemia (_see chapters 7 and 9_) results from a change in the structure of the hemoglobin molecule. Some of the red blood cells of persons with the disease are misshapen, reducing their ability to carry oxygen. In the heterozygous state, the quantities of normal and sickled cells are roughly equal. Sickle-cell heterozygotes occur in some African populations with a frequency as high as 0.4. The maintenance of the sickle-cell heterozygotes and both homozygous genotypes at relatively unchanging frequencies makes this trait an example of a balanced polymorphism.

Why hasn't natural selection eliminated such a seemingly deleterious gene? The sickle-cell gene is most common in regions of Africa that are heavily infested with the malarial parasite, *Plasmodium falciparum*. Sickle-cell heterozygotes are less susceptible to malarial infections; if infected, they experience less severe symptoms than do homozygotes without sickled cells. Individuals homozygous for the normal allele are at a disadvantage because they experience more severe malarial infections, and individuals homozygous for the sickle-cell allele are at a disadvantage because they suffer from the severe anemia that the sickle cells cause. The heterozygotes, who usually experience no symptoms of anemia, are more likely to survive than either homozygote. This system is also an example of heterozygote superiority—when the heterozygote is more fit than either homozygote. Heterozygote superiority can lead to balanced polymorphism because perpetuation of the alleles in the heterozygous condition maintains both alleles at a higher frequency than would be expected if natural selection acted only on the homozygous phenotypes.

Stop and Ask Yourself

5. What is neutral selection? Why are the effects of neutral selection more likely to show up in small populations, or in fringe groups of larger populations?

6. Why are mutations important to evolution?

7. How would you define the terms directional selection, disruptive selection, and stabilizing selection? Which is more likely in a time of climatic change?

Species and Speciation

Taxonomists classify organisms according to their similarities and differences (*see chapters 1 and 16*). The fundamental unit of classification is the species. Unfortunately, formulating a universally applicable definition of species is difficult. According to a biological definition, a **species** is a group of populations in which genes are actually, or potentially, exchanged through interbreeding.

Although concise, this definition has problems associated with it. Taxonomists often work with morphological characteristics, and the reproductive criterion must be assumed based on morphological and ecological information. Also, some organisms do not reproduce sexually. Obviously, other criteria need to be applied in these cases. Another problem concerns fossil material. Paleontologists describe species of extinct organisms, but how can they test the reproductive criterion? Finally, populations of similar

organisms may be so isolated from each other that gene exchange is geographically impossible. To test a reproductive criterion, biologists can transplant individuals to see if mating can occur, but mating of transplanted individuals does not necessarily prove what would happen if animals were together in a natural setting.

Rather than trying to establish a definition of a species that solves all these problems, it is probably better to simply understand the problems associated with the biological definition. In describing species, taxonomists use morphological, physiological, embryological, behavioral, molecular, and ecological criteria, realizing that all of these have a genetic basis.

⑤ **Speciation** is the formation of new species. A requirement of speciation is that subpopulations are prevented from interbreeding. This is called **reproductive isolation.** When subpopulations are reproductively isolated, natural selection and genetic drift can result in evolution taking a different course in each subpopulation. Reproductive isolation can occur in different ways.

Premating isolation prevents mating from taking place. For example, impenetrable barriers, such as rivers or mountain ranges, may separate subpopulations. Other forms of premating isolation are more subtle. If courtship behavior patterns of two animals are not mutually appropriate, mating does not occur. Similarly, individuals with different breeding periods or that occupy different habitats are unable to breed with each other.

Postmating isolation prevents successful fertilization and development, even though mating may have occurred. For example, conditions in the reproductive tract of a female may not support the sperm of another individual, which prevents successful fertilization. Postmating isolation also occurs because hybrids are usually sterile (e.g., the mule produced from a mating of a male donkey and a mare is a sterile hybrid). Mismatched chromosomes cannot synapse properly during meiosis, and any gametes produced are not viable. Other kinds of postmating isolation include developmental failures of the fertilized egg or embryo.

Allopatric Speciation

Allopatric (Gr. *allos*, other + *patria*, fatherland) **speciation** occurs when subpopulations become geographically isolated from one another. For example, a mountain range or river may permanently separate members of a population. Adaptations to different environments or neutral selection in these separate populations may result in members not being able to mate successfully with each other, even if experimentally reunited. Many biologists believe that allopatric speciation is the most common kind of speciation (figure 12.6).

The finches that Darwin saw on the Galápagos Islands are a classic example of allopatric speciation, as well as adaptive radiation (*see chapter 11*). Adaptive radiation occurs when a number of new forms diverge from an ancestral form, usually in response to the opening of major new habitats.

Fourteen species of finches evolved from the original finches that colonized the Galápagos Islands. Ancestral finches, having emigrated from the mainland, probably were distributed among a few of the islands of the Galápagos. Populations became isolated

(a)

(b)

FIGURE 12.6

Allopatric Speciation. Allopatric speciation can occur when a geographic barrier divides a population. (*a*) In this hypothetical example, a population of freshwater fish in a river drainage system is divided into three subpopulations: A, A_1, and A_2. Genetic exchanges may occur between A and A_1, and between A_1 and A_2. Exchanges are less common between A and A_2. (*b*) A rise in the level of the ocean forces the breakup of A_1 and makes A and A_2 separate populations. Genetic drift and different selection pressures in the two populations may eventually result in the formation of species B and C.

on various islands over time, and though the original population probably displayed some genetic variation, even greater variation arose. The original finches were seed eaters, and after their arrival, they probably filled their preferred habitats rapidly. Variations

within the original finch population may have allowed some birds to exploit new islands and habitats where no finches had been. Mutations changed the genetic composition of the isolated finch populations, introducing further variations. Natural selection favored the retention of the variations that promoted successful reproduction.

The combined forces of isolation, mutation, and natural selection allowed the finches to diverge into a number of species with specialized feeding habits (*see figure 11.3*). Of the 14 species of finches, 6 have beaks specialized for crushing seeds of different sizes. Others feed on flowers of the prickly pear cactus or in the forests on insects and fruit.

PARAPATRIC SPECIATION

Another form of speciation, called **parapatric** (Gr. *para*, beside) **speciation,** occurs in small, local populations, called **demes.** For example, all of the frogs in a particular pond or all of the sea urchins in a particular tidepool make up a deme. Individuals of a deme are more likely to breed with one another than with other individuals in the larger population, and because they experience the same environment, they are subject to similar selection pressures. Demes are not completely isolated from each other because individuals, developmental stages, or gametes can move among demes of a population. On the other hand, the relative isolation of a deme may mean that its members experience different selection pressures than other members of the population. If so, speciation can occur. Although most evolutionists theoretically agree that parapatric speciation is possible, no certain cases are known. Parapatric speciation is therefore considered of less importance in the evolution of animal groups than allopatric speciation.

SYMPATRIC SPECIATION

A third kind of speciation, called **sympatric** (Gr. *sym*, together) **speciation,** occurs within a single population. Even though organisms are sympatric, they still may be reproductively isolated from one another. Many plant species are capable of producing viable forms with multiple sets of chromosomes. Such events could lead to sympatric speciation among groups in the same habitat. While sympatric speciation in animals is uncommon, it has been documented in two species of bats and several species of insects and fish.

Stop and Ask Yourself

8. Why is reproductive isolation necessary for speciation to occur?

9. What form of premating isolation is likely to promote allopatric speciation?

10. What is postmating isolation? What are three forms it can take?

11. What are sympatric, parapatric, and allopatric speciation?

RATES OF EVOLUTION

Charles Darwin perceived evolutionary change as occurring gradually over millions of years. This concept, called **phyletic gradualism,** has been the traditional interpretation of the tempo, or rate, of evolution.

Some evolutionary changes, however, happen very rapidly. Studies of the fossil record show that many species do not change significantly over millions of years. These periods of stasis (Gr. *stasis*, standing still), or equilibrium, are interrupted when a group encounters an ecological crisis, such as a change in climate or a major geological event. Over the next 10,000 to 100,000 years, a variation that previously was selectively neutral or disadvantageous might now be advantageous. Alternatively, geological events might result in new habitats becoming available. (Events that occur in 10,000 to 100,000 years are almost instantaneous in an evolutionary time frame.) This geologically brief period of change "punctuates" the previous million or so years of equilibrium and eventually settles into the next period of stasis. In this model, stabilizing selection characterizes the periods of stasis, and directional or disruptive selection characterizes the periods of change (figure 12.7). Long periods of stasis interrupted by brief periods of change is called the **punctuated equilibrium model** of evolution.

Biologists have observed such rapid evolutionary changes in small populations. Examples include the rapid pesticide and antibiotic resistance that insect pests and bacteria acquire. In addition, in a series of studies over a 20-year period, Peter R. Grant has shown that natural selection results in rapid morphological changes in the bills of Galápagos finches. A long, dry period from the middle of 1976 to early January 1978 resulted in birds with larger, deeper bills. Early in this dry period, birds quickly consumed smaller, easily cracked seeds. As they were forced to turn to larger seeds, birds with weaker bills were selected against, resulting in a measurable change in the makeup of the finch population of the island Daphne Major.

One advantage of the punctuated equilibrium model is its explanation for the fossil record not always showing transitional stages between related organisms. Gradualists attribute the absence of transitional forms to fossilization being an unlikely event; thus, many transitional forms disappeared without leaving a fossil record. Since punctuated equilibrium involves rapid changes in small, isolated populations, preservation of intermediate forms in the fossil record is even less likely. The rapid pace (geologically speaking) of evolution resulted in apparent "jumps" from one form to another.

MOLECULAR EVOLUTION

Many evolutionists study changes in animal structure and function that are observable on a large scale—for example, changes in the shape of a bird's bill or in the length of an animal's neck. All evolutionary change, however, results from changes in the base sequences in DNA and amino acids in proteins. ⑥ Molecular evolutionists investigate evolutionary relationships among organ-

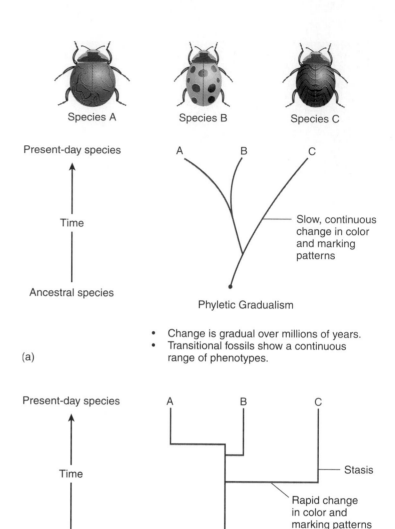

(a)

(b)

FIGURE 12.7

Rates of Evolution. A comparison of phyletic gradualism and punctuated equilibrium in three hypothetical beetle species. (*a*) In the phyletic gradualism model of evolution, changes are gradual over long time periods. Note that this tree implies a gradual change in color and marking patterns in the three beetle species. (*b*) In the punctuated equilibrium model of evolution, rapid periods of change interrupt long periods of stasis. This tree implies that the color and marking patterns in the beetles changed rapidly and did not change significantly during long periods of stabilizing selection (stasis).

isms by studying DNA and proteins. For example, cytochrome *c* is a protein present in the cellular respiration pathways in all eukaryotic organisms (table 12.1). Organisms that other research has shown to be closely related have similar cytochrome *c* molecules. That cytochrome *c* has changed so little during hundreds of millions of years suggests that mutations of the cytochrome *c* gene are nearly always detrimental, and are selected against. Because it has changed so little, cytochrome *c* is said to have been conserved evolutionarily.

TABLE 12.1	AMINO ACID DIFFERENCES IN CYTOCHROME c FROM DIFFERENT ORGANISMS
ORGANISMS	**NUMBER OF VARIANT AMINO ACID RESIDUES**
Cow and sheep	0
Cow and whale	2
Horse and cow	3
Rabbit and pig	4
Horse and rabbit	5
Whale and kangaroo	6
Rabbit and pigeon	7
Shark and tuna	19
Tuna and fruit fly	21
Tuna and moth	28
Yeast and mold	38
Wheat and yeast	40
Moth and yeast	44

Not all proteins are conserved as rigorously as cytochrome c. Although variations in highly conserved proteins can help establish evolutionary relationships among distantly related organisms, less conserved proteins are useful for looking at relationships among more closely related animals. Because some proteins are conserved and others are not, the best information regarding evolutionary relationships requires comparing as many proteins as possible in any two species.

GENE DUPLICATION

Recall that most mutations are selected against. Sometimes, however, an extra copy of a gene is present. One copy may be modified, but as long as the second copy furnishes the essential protein,

the organism is likely to survive. Gene duplication, the accidental duplication of a gene on a chromosome, is one way that extra genetic material can arise (*see chapter 8*).

Vertebrate hemoglobin and myoglobin are believed to have arisen from a common ancestral molecule. Hemoglobin carries oxygen in red blood cells, and myoglobin is an oxygen storage molecule in muscle. The ancestral molecule probably carried out both functions. However, about 1 billion years ago, gene duplication followed by mutation of one gene resulted in the formation of two polypeptides: myoglobin and hemoglobin. Further gene duplications over the last 500 million years probably explain why most vertebrates, other than primitive fishes, have hemoglobin molecules consisting of four polypeptides.

MOSAIC EVOLUTION

As discussed earlier, rates of evolution can vary both in populations and in molecules and structures. A species is a mosaic of different molecules and structures that have evolved at different rates. Some molecules or structures are conserved in evolution; others change more rapidly. The basic design of a bird provides a simple example. All birds are easily recognizable as birds because of highly conserved structures, such as feathers, bills, and a certain body form. Particular parts of birds, however, are less conservative and have a higher rate of change. Wings have been modified for hovering, soaring, and swimming. Similarly, legs have been modified for wading, swimming, and perching. These are examples of **mosaic evolution.**

Stop and Ask Yourself

12. How do phyletic gradualism and punctuated equilibrium models of evolution differ?

13. How can amino acid sequencing and DNA base sequencing provide evidence of evolutionary relationships?

14. What does it mean to say that cytochrome c is an evolutionarily conserved protein?

SUMMARY

1. Organic evolution is a change in the frequency of alleles in a population.

2. Unlimited genetic variation, in the form of new alleles and new combinations of alleles, increases the chances that a population will survive future environmental changes.

3. Population genetics is the study of events occurring in gene pools. The Hardy-Weinberg theorem states that, if certain assumptions are met, gene frequencies of a population remain constant from generation to generation.

4. The assumptions of the Hardy-Weinberg theorem, when not met, define circumstances under which evolution will occur: (a) Fortu-

itous circumstances may allow only certain alleles to be carried into the next generation. Such chance variations in allelic frequencies are called genetic drift or neutral selection. (b) Allelic frequencies may change as a result of individuals immigrating into, or emigrating from, a population. (c) Mutations are the source of new genetic material for populations. Mutational equilibrium rarely exists, and thus, mutations usually result in changing allelic frequencies. (d) The tendency for allelic frequencies to change, due to differing fitness, is called selection pressure.

5. Selection may be directional, disruptive, or stabilizing.

6. Balanced polymorphism occurs when two or more body forms are maintained in a population. Heterozygote superiority can lead to balanced polymorphism.

7. According to a biological definition, a species is a group of populations within which there is potential for exchange of genes. Significant problems are associated with the application of this definition.

8. Speciation requires reproductive isolation. Speciation may occur sympatrically, parapatrically, or allopatrically, although most speciation events are believed to be allopatric.

9. Premating isolation prevents mating from occurring. Postmating isolation prevents the development of fertile offspring, if mating has occurred.

10. Phyletic gradualism is a model of evolution that depicts change as occurring gradually, over millions of years. Punctuated equilibrium is a model of evolution that depicts long periods of stasis interrupted by brief periods of relatively rapid change.

11. The study of rates of molecular evolution helps establish evolutionary interrelationships among organisms.

12. A mutation may modify a duplicated gene, which then may serve a function other than its original role.

13. A species is a mosaic of different molecules and structures that have evolved at differing rates.

SELECTED KEY TERMS

Hardy-Weinberg equilibrium
  (p. 165)
neutral selection (p. 165)
phyletic gradualism (p. 172)
population genetics (p. 164)

punctuated equilibrium model
  (p. 172)
reproductive isolation (p. 170)
speciation (p. 170)
species (p. 170)

CRITICAL THINKING QUESTIONS

1. Can natural selection act on variations that are not inherited? (Consider, for example, deformities that arise from contracting a disease.) If so, what is the effect of that selection on subsequent generations?

2. In what way does overuse of antibiotics and pesticides increase the likelihood that these chemicals will eventually become ineffective? This is an example of which one of the three modes of natural selection?

3. What are the implications of the "bottleneck effect" for wildlife managers who try to help endangered species, such as the whooping crane, recover from near extinction?

4. What does it mean to think of evolutionary change as being goal-oriented? Explain why this way of thinking is wrong.

5. Imagine that two species of butterflies resemble one another closely. One of the species (the model) is distasteful to bird predators, and the other species (the mimic) is not. How could directional selection have resulted in the mimic species evolving a resemblance to the model species?

REFERENCES ON THE WORLD WIDE WEB

1. **Modern Synthesis.**   This site provides information on how ideas from modern genetics and evolutionary theory work together to provide information on the causes and results of evolutionary change.
     http://www.talkorigins.org/faqs/modern-synthesis.html

2. **Punctuated Equilibrium.**   This site provides a complete history of the observations and ideas that led to the punctuated equilibrium model of evolution, as well as a detailed description of the model and the reasons why it is important—especially to paleontologists. The site also explains common misconceptions regarding the punctuated equilibrium model.
     http://www.talkorigins.org/faqs/punc-eq.html

3. **Origins of Humankind.**   A wealth of information regarding human origins is available at this site.
     http://www.dealsonline.com/origins/help.htm

4. **The Fossil Evidence for Human Evolution in China.**   This site documents early human evolution in China. It provides maps, photographs of fossil remains, and full-length articles.
     http://www.cruzio.com/~cscp/index.htm

5. **Fossil Hominids.**   This site provides a summary of current thinking about human evolution and refutes creationist claims regarding human origins.
     http://www.talkorigins.org/faqs/fossil-hominids.html

6. **Biology and Evolutionary Theory.**   This site provides a wealth of information on evolutionary theory. It introduces evolutionary theory at a basic level, provides evidence for evolution, and presents the modern synthesis of evolution and genetics.
     http://www.talkorigins.org/origins/faqs-evolution.html

SUGGESTED READINGS
BOOKS

Ayala, F. J. 1982. *Population and Evolutionary Genetics: A Primer.* Menlo Park, Calif.: Benjamin Cummings.

Bowler, P. 1984. *Evolution: The History of an Idea.* Berkeley, Calif.: University of California Press.

Darwin, C. 1894. *On the Origin of Species.* Reprint. 1975. Cambridge: Cambridge University Press.

Dodson, E. O., and Dodson, P. 1985. *Evolution: Process and Product.* Belmont, Calif.: Wadsworth.

Eldredge, N., and Cracraft, J. 1980. *Phylogenetic Patterns and the Evolutionary Process: Method and Theory in Comparative Biology.* New York: Columbia University Press.

Endler, J. A. 1986. *Natural Selection in the Wild.* Princeton, N.J.: Princeton University Press.

Futuyma, D. J. 1986. *Evolutionary Biology.* 2d ed. Sunderland: Sinauer Associates.

Godfrey, L. R. 1985. *What Darwin Began.* Boston: Allyn and Bacon.

Grant, P. R. 1986. *Ecology and Evolution of Darwin's Finches.* Princeton, N.J.: Princeton University Press.

Hecht, M. K., Wallace, B., and Prance, G. T., eds. 1967–1988. *Evolutionary Biology,* vols. 1–22. New York: Plenum Press.

Mayr, E. 1982. *The Growth of Biological Thought: Diversity, Evolution, and Inheritance.* Cambridge: Harvard University Press.

Menard, H. W. 1986. *The Ocean of Truth: A Personal History of Global Tectonics.* Princeton, N.J.: Princeton University Press.

Otte, D., and Endler, J. A. eds. 1989. *Speciation and Its Consequences.* Sunderland: Sinauer Associates.

Ridley, M. 1996. *Evolution.* 2d ed. Cambridge, Mass.: Blackwell Science.

Smith, J. M. 1989. *Evolutionary Genetics.* New York: Oxford University Press.

Smith, J. M. ed. 1982. *Evolution Now: A Century after Darwin*. New York: W. H. Freeman.

Stebbins, G. L. 1982. *Darwin to DNA, Molecules to Humanity*. New York: W. H. Freeman.

Volpe, E. P. 1985. *Understanding Evolution*. 5th ed. Dubuque, Iowa: Wm. C. Brown Publishers.

ARTICLES

Allegre, C. J., and Schneider, S. H. 1994. The evolution of the earth. *Scientific American*, October.

Altman, S. A. 1989. The monkey and the fig. *American Scientist* 77(3): 256–63.

Alvarez, W., and Asaro, F. 1990. What caused the mass extinction? An extraterrestrial impact. *Scientific American*, October.

Amato, I. 1987. Tics in the tocks of molecular clocks: Comparing the DNA, RNA and proteins of different species may reveal the entire tree of life, but obstacles are emerging. *Science News* 131: 74–75.

Briggs, D. E. G. 1991. Extraordinary fossils. *American Scientist* 79(2): 130–41.

Callagan, C. A. 1987. Instances of observed speciation. *The American Biology Teacher* 49(1): 34–36.

Carson, H. L. 1987. The process whereby species originate. *BioScience* 37: 715–20.

Cherfas, J. 1991. Ancient DNA: Still busy after death. *Science* 253: 1354–56.

Ciochon, R. L., and Larick, R. L. 1996. The African emergence and early Asian dispersals of the genus *Homo*. *American Scientist* 84(6): 538–51.

Courtillot, V. E. 1990. What caused the mass extinction? A volcanic eruption. *Scientific American*, October.

Coyne, J. A., and Barton, N. H. 1988. What do we know about speciation? *Nature* 331: 485–86.

Dalziel, I. W. D. 1995. Earth before Pangea. *Scientific American*, January.

Dawkins, R. 1995. God's utility function. *Scientific American*, November.

DeDuve, C. 1995. The beginnings of life on earth. *American Scientist* 83(5): 428–37.

DeDuve, C. 1996. The birth of complex cells. *Scientific American*, April.

Drosei, M. L., Fortey, R., and Li, X. 1996. The Ordovician radiation. *American Scientist* 84(2): 122–31.

Erwin, D. E. 1996. The mother of mass extinctions. *Scientific American*, July.

Finchel, T., and Finlay, B. J. 1994. The evolution of life without oxygen. *American Scientist* 82 (1): 22–29.

Freedman, W. L. 1992. The expansion rate and size of the universe. *Scientific American*, November.

Gould, S. J. 1994. The evolution of life on the earth. *Scientific American*, October.

Grant, P. R. 1991. Natural selection and Darwin's finches. *Scientific American*, October.

Herbert, S. 1986. Darwin as a geologist. *Scientific American*, May.

Hogan, C. J. 1996. Primordial deuterium and the big bang. *Scientific American*, December.

Horgan, J. 1991. In the beginning . . . *Scientific American*, February.

Horgan, J. 1995. The new social darwinists. *Scientific American*, October.

Jermeij, G. J. 1991. When biotas meet: Understanding biotic interchange. *Science* 253: 1099–1104.

Joyce, G. F. 1992. Directed molecular evolution. *Scientific American*, December.

Kirshner, R. P. 1994. The earth's elements. *Scientific American*, October.

Lewontin, R. C. 1978. Adaptation. *Scientific American*, September.

Linde, A. 1994. The self-reproducing inflationary universe. *Scientific American*, November.

Mark, R. 1996. Architecture and evolution. *American Scientist*, 84(4): 383–89.

May, R. R. 1987. The evolution of ecological systems. *Scientific American*, September.

Milner, R. 1995. Charles Darwin: The last portrait. *Scientific American*, November.

Myers, N. 1985. The ends of the lines. *Natural History* 94: 2–6.

Peebles, J. E., Schramm, D. N., Turner, E. L., and Kron, R. G. 1994. The evolution of the universe. *Scientific American*, October.

Ramos, V. A. 1989. The birth of southern South America. *American Scientist* 77(5): 444–59.

Rebek, J. 1994. Synthetic self-replicating molecules. *Scientific American*, July.

Ross, P. E. 1992. Eloquent remains. *Scientific American*, May.

Ruthen, R. 1993. Adapting to complexity. *Scientific American*, January.

Ryan, M. J. 1990. Signals, species, and sexual selection. *American Scientist* 78(1): 46–52.

Sheldon, P. 1988. Making the most of evolution diaries. New Scientist 117: 52–54.

Taylor, S. R., and McLennan, S. M. 1996. The evolution of the continental crust. *Scientific American*, January.

Weinberg, S. 1994. Life in the universe. *Scientific American*, October.

York, D. 1993. The earliest history of the earth. *Scientific American*, January.

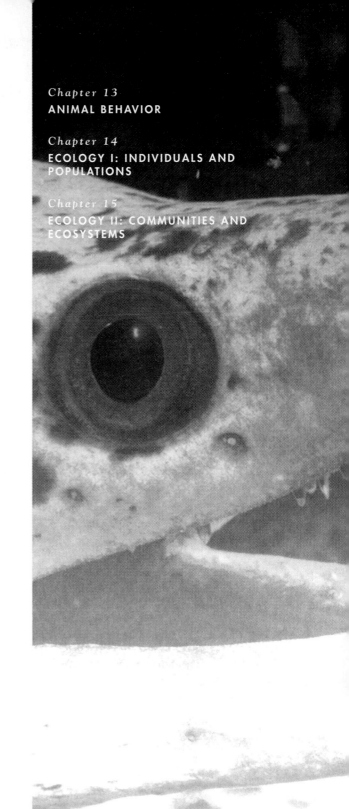

$part$ FOUR

BEHAVIOR AND ECOLOGY

Chapter 1 stresses unity and diversity. All life is unified at molecular, cellular, and evolutionary levels. A fundamental unity also exists at an environmental level. All living organisms are partners in the use of the earth's resources. In

particular, humans have a responsibility to see that the resources of this planet are preserved for all organisms in all generations. Only through studying the interactions of organisms with one another, and with the physical attributes of their environment, will this goal be realized. Even in our "enlightened" generation, waste and misuse are unbridled. In many ways, our technologies have permitted abusive practices unheard of by previous generations. Scientists, theologians, and philosophers must lead the way in protecting our fragile ecosystems.

Part Four (chapters 13 through 15) explores behavioral interactions among organisms and interactions between organisms and their environment. Many relationships are complex, and zoologists can fully understand organisms only in the context of populations, communities, and ecosystems.

chapter 13

ANIMAL BEHAVIOR

Concepts

1. Behavior refers to the varied activities that an animal performs during its lifetime. Internal physiological conditions, environmental stimuli, and social situations influence specific behavioral responses.
2. Proximate factors that influence the behavior of an animal include genetics, developmental experiences, and the current environment, including photoperiod, season, and temperature. The nervous and endocrine systems of the animal mediate these effects.
3. The ultimate factor that influences the behavior of an animal is natural selection. Animals that possess certain traits are more successful at surviving and reproducing.
4. Two key problems that face each animal are finding food and a place to live.
5. The evolution of various social systems, in which animals live in groups, affects many aspects of their behavior.

Would You Like to Know . . .

1. if an earthworm placed on a hook feels any pain? (p. 179)
2. how tadpoles know how to swim? (p. 179)
3. how baby chicks know how to follow their mother? (p. 180)
4. how a trainer teaches an animal to do tricks? (p. 181)
5. how a fly processes information from its environment and feeds? (p. 183)
6. how male moths detect the presence of females who are ready to mate? (p. 185)
7. what decisions hummingbirds make while finding and visiting flower patches? (p. 185)
8. why some animals eat only a limited number of foods and others eat many different foods? (p. 186)
9. why some animals live in groups and others live alone? (p. 187)

This chapter answers these and other useful questions.

This chapter contains evolutionary concepts, which are set off in this font.

Animal behavior refers to the activities animals perform during their lifetime, including locomotion, feeding, breeding, capture of prey, avoidance of predators, and social behavior. Animals send signals, respond to signals or stimuli, carry out maintenance behavior, make choices, and interact with one another. This chapter examines some of these aspects of animal behavior.

FOUR APPROACHES TO ANIMAL BEHAVIOR

Naturalists and philosophers have observed animal behavior for centuries. Only in the last century, however, has there been significant progress in understanding this behavior.

One approach to the study of animal behavior is **comparative psychology.** Comparative psychologists emphasize studies of the genetic, neural, and hormonal bases of animal behavior. Psychologists conduct experimental studies, in both laboratory and field settings, that relate to animal learning and to the development of behavior. They explore how animals receive information, and the processes and nature of the behavior patterns constituting the animals' responses to their surroundings.

Ethology (Gr. *ethologica*, depicting character) is the study of animal behavior that focuses on evolution and the natural environment. The leaders of this approach have been Konrad Lorenz, Niko Tinbergen, and Karl von Frisch, who were awarded the Nobel Prize in Physiology or Medicine in 1973. Ethologists observe the behavior of a variety of animals in their natural environments and study the behavior of closely related species to consider the evolution and origin of certain behavior patterns. Ethologists rarely deal with learning and are interested instead in animal communication, mating behavior, and social behavior.

Behavioral ecology emphasizes the ecological aspects of animal behavior. Predator-prey interactions, foraging strategies, reproductive strategies, habitat selection, intraspecific and interspecific competition, and social behavior are topics of interest to behavioral ecologists.

Sociobiology is the study of the evolution of social behavior. It combines many aspects of ethology and behavioral ecology. Sociobiologists emphasize the importance of natural selection on individuals living in groups.

PROXIMATE AND ULTIMATE CAUSES

Behavioral scientists frequently ask, "Why do animals do what they do?" More immediate ecological and physiological causes of behavior, such as eating to satisfy hunger, are called proximate causes. Another level of causation in behavior occurs on the evolutionary time scale and is that of ultimate causes. For example, a display not only attracts a mate, but also increases the likelihood of passing genetic information to the next generation.

ANTHROPOMORPHISM

Anthropomorphism (Gr. *anthropos*, man + *morphe*, form) is the application of human characteristics to anything not human. In observations of animals, assigning human feelings to animal behavior is not likely to be accurate, especially with invertebrate animals. Consider the example of placing an earthworm on a fishhook. Does the fishhook hurt the earthworm, causing it to writhe in pain? Both of the descriptive words, hurt and pain, are based on human experience and conscious awareness.   ❶ A better explanation that reduces the anthropomorphic interpretation is that placing the earthworm on the hook stimulates certain receptors which generate nerve impulses that travel along reflex neural circuits. The impulses stimulate muscles that allow the worm to wriggle in an attempt to escape from the hook. This explanation more closely describes what has been observed and does not attempt to suggest what the earthworm "feels."

DEVELOPMENT OF BEHAVIOR

Development of a normal behavior pattern requires the genes that code for the formation of the structures and organs involved in the behavior. For example, in vertebrates, normal locomotion movements will not occur without proper development and growth of the limbs. This process requires some interaction with the animal's environment because proper nourishment, water balance, and other factors must be maintained for normal development.

MATURATION

Some behavior patterns appear only after a specific developmental stage or time. During **maturation,** performance of the behavior pattern improves as parts of the nervous system and other structures complete development.   ❷ A classic example is tail movement in frog embryos that are near hatching. While still in the egg membranes, they start moving their tails as they would if they were swimming, and movement coordination improves with time. These improved movements are due to maturation, not practice or experience.

INSTINCT/LEARNING INTERACTIONS

In recent years, many behavioral scientists have concluded that both instinct and learning are important in animal behavior. Interaction of inherited (i.e., instinctive) and learned components shapes a number of behavior patterns. For example, young bobcats raised in isolation without the chance to catch live prey did not attack a white rat placed with them, unless the rat tried to escape. At first, their attacks were not efficient, but after some experience, they were seizing prey by the neck and rapidly killing them. Apparently, learning refines inherited components of this behavior.

Under normal conditions, the learning or experiences occur during play with littermates.

Another example involving instinctive and learned components to behavior is the nut-cracking behavior of squirrels. Squirrels gnaw and pry to open a nut. Inexperienced squirrels are not efficient; they gnaw and pry at random on the nut. Experienced squirrels, however, gnaw a furrow on the broad side, then wedge their lower incisors into the furrow and crack the nut open (figure 13.1).

IMPRINTING

During **imprinting,** a young animal develops an attachment toward another animal or object (figure 13.2*a*). The attachment usually forms only during a specific critical period soon after hatching or birth and is not reversible (figure 13.2*b*). Imprinting is a rapid learning process that apparently occurs without reinforcement.

Konrad Lorenz (1903–1989) conducted experiments with geese in which he allowed the geese to imprint on him (figure 13.2*c*). The goslings followed him as though he was their mother. ③ In nature, many species of birds in which the young follow the parent soon after birth use imprinting so that the young can identify with or recognize their parent(s). They can then be led successfully to the nest or to water. Both visual and auditory cues are important in imprinting systems.

(a)

(b)

FIGURE 13.1

Instinctive and Learned Behavior. Nut-cracking behavior in squirrels involves instinctive and learned components. (*a, b*) An inexperienced squirrel has opened this hazelnut, as evidenced by the many random gnawing marks. (*c, d*) An experienced squirrel has efficiently cracked open this hazelnut by gnawing and prying on the broad side of the nut. *Courtesy of Prof. Dr. Eibl-Eibesfeldt.*

(c)

FIGURE 13.2

Imprinting in Young Birds. (*a*) Circular arena apparatus for imprinting the young duckling on its "mother" (a stuffed model). (*b*) The critical period for imprinting is most likely 13 to 16 hours after hatching. (*c*) Imprinted geese following Konrad Lorenz.

LEARNING

Learning produces changes in the behavior of an individual that are due to experience. Learning is adaptive because it allows an animal to respond quickly to changes in its environment. Once an animal learns something, its behavioral choices increase.

An animal's ability to learn may correlate with the predictability of certain characteristics of its environment. Where certain changes in the habitat occur regularly and are predictable, the animal may rapidly respond to a stimulus with an unmodified instinctive behavior. An animal would not necessarily benefit from learning in this situation. However, where certain environmental changes are unpredictable and cannot be anticipated, an animal may modify its behavioral responses through learning or experience. This modification is adaptive because it allows an animal to not only change its response to fit a given situation, but also to improve its response to subsequent, similar environmental changes.

Several different categories of learning have been identified, ranging from habituation (the simplest form of learning) to insight learning (the most complex form) that involves cognitive processes.

HABITUATION

Habituation is the simplest and perhaps most common type of behavior in many different animals. Habituation involves a waning or decrease in response to repeated or continuous stimulation. Simply, an animal learns not to respond to stimuli in its environment that are constant and probably relatively unimportant. By habituating to unimportant stimuli, an animal conserves energy and time that are better spent on other important functions. For example, after time, birds learn to ignore scarecrows that previously caused them to flee. Squirrels in a city park adjust to the movements of humans and automobiles. If the stimulus is withheld, then the response returns rapidly. Habituation does not involve any conditioning. Habituation is believed to be controlled through the central nervous system and should be distinguished from sensory adaptation. Sensory adaptation involves repeated stimulation of receptors until they stop responding. For example, if you enter a room with an unusual odor, your olfactory sense organs soon stop responding to these odors.

CLASSICAL CONDITIONING

Classical conditioning is a type of learning documented by Russian physiologist, Ivan Pavlov (1849–1936). In his classic experiment on the salivary reflex in dogs, Pavlov presented food right after the sound of a bell (figure 13.3). After a number of such presentations, the dogs were conditioned—they associated the sound of the bell with food. It was then possible to elicit the dog's usual response to food—salivation—with just the sound of the bell. The food was a positive reinforcement for salivating behavior, but responses could also be conditioned using negative reinforcement.

Classical conditioning is very common in the animal kingdom. For example, birds learn to avoid certain brightly colored

FIGURE 13.3

Apparatus Pavlov Used to Demonstrate Classical Conditioning. If a bell rings just before a dog is given food, the dog soon begins to associate the stimulus with the food and becomes conditioned to salivate with the ringing of the bell alone.

caterpillars that have a noxious taste. Because birds associate the color pattern with the bad taste, they may also avoid animals with a similar color pattern.

INSTRUMENTAL CONDITIONING

In **instrumental conditioning** (also known as trial-and-error learning), the animal learns while carrying out certain searching actions, such as walking and moving about. For example, if the animal finds food during these activities, the food reinforces the behavior, and the animal associates the reward with the behavior. If this association is repeated several times, the animal learns that the behavior leads to reinforcement.

A classic example of instrumental conditioning is that of a rat in a "Skinner box," developed by B. F. Skinner (1904–1990), a prominent psychologist (figure 13.4). When placed in the box, the rat begins to explore. It moves all about the box and, by accident, eventually presses a lever and is rewarded with a food pellet. Because food rewards are provided each time the rat presses the lever, the rat associates the reward with the behavior. Through repetition, the rat learns to press the lever right away to receive the reward. In this type of learning, the animal is instrumental in providing its own reinforcement.

4 In instrumental conditioning, providing the reinforcement (food) whenever the animal comes close to the lever and continuing to supply reinforcement when the animal touches the lever "shapes" the behavior. Finally, the animal learns to press the lever to obtain food.

Young animals' attempts to learn new motor patterns often involve instrumental conditioning. A young bird learning to fly or a young mammal at play may improve coordination of certain movements or behavior patterns by practice during these activities.

FIGURE 13.4

Instrumental Conditioning in a Skinner Box. The rat, through random movements, accidentally presses the lever and receives a reward. Through repetition, the rat associates the behavior of pressing the lever with the reward.

LATENT LEARNING

Latent learning, sometimes called exploratory learning, involves making associations without immediate reinforcement or reward. The reward is not obvious. An animal is apparently motivated, however, to learn about its surroundings. For example, if a rat is placed in a maze that has no food or reward, it explores the maze, although rather slowly. If food or another reward is provided, the rat quickly runs the maze. Apparently, previous learning of the maze had occurred but remained latent, or hidden, until an obvious reinforcement was provided. Latent learning allows an animal to learn about its surroundings as it explores. Knowledge about an animal's home area may be important for its survival, perhaps enabling it to escape from a predator or capture prey.

INSIGHT LEARNING

In **insight learning,** the animal uses cognitive or mental processes to associate experiences and solve problems. The classic example is the work of Wolfgang Kohler (1887–1967) on chimpanzees that were trained to use tools to obtain food rewards (figure 13.5a). One chimpanzee was given some bamboo poles that could be joined to make a longer pole, and some bananas were hung from the ceiling. Once the chimp formed the longer pole, it used the pole to knock the bananas to the cage floor. Kohler believed that the animal used insight learning to get the bananas.

In addition, Jane van Lawick-Goodall (1934–) has observed chimpanzees in the wild using tools to accomplish various tasks. For example, they use crumpled leaves as a sponge for drinking water (figure 13.5b).

Stop and Ask Yourself

1. What are four ways to study animal behavior?
2. How would you differentiate proximate and ultimate causation?
3. Why is anthropomorphism a problem when describing the behavior of animals?
4. What happens during the maturation of a behavior pattern?
5. What is the interaction between inherited and learned components of behavior?
6. What are some functions of imprinting in animals?
7. What are the five categories of learning? Give an example of each kind.

CONTROL OF BEHAVIOR

Internal mechanisms (proximate causes) that include the nervous system and the endocrine system regulate animal behavior. These systems receive information from the external environment via the sensory organs, process that information involving the brain and the endocrine glands, and initiate responses in terms of motor patterns or changes in the operations of internal organs. In general, the nervous system mediates more specific and rapid responses, while the endocrine system monitors slower, more general responses.

NERVOUS SYSTEM

Chapter 33 provides details of the structure of the nervous systems found in animals, and how the various parts function. The goal here is to examine the ways in which the nervous system is involved in behavior. One key role for the nervous system is to act as a **stimulus filter.** Stimuli from many sources continuously bom-

(a)   (b)

FIGURE 13.5

Insight Learning in Chimpanzees. (*a*) This chimpanzee (*Pan troglodytes*) puts two sticks together and stands on stacked boxes to reach the bananas suspended from the ceiling. (*b*) This chimpanzee uses a crumpled leaf as a sponge for drinking water.

bard each organism. The sensory organs and central nervous system of the animal block incoming stimuli that are unimportant or irrelevant. The information that passes through the sensory filters is then sorted and processed within the nervous system to ensure appropriate responses.

5 The manner in which blowflies feed illustrates how the nervous system mediates behavior (figure 13.6). The blowfly has special sensory receptors on its feet. As the fly moves around and encounters different substrates, the receptors can detect the presence of certain sugars. The information from the feet is processed in the fly's nervous system and results in the extension of the proboscis, which, in turn, stimulates the oral taste receptors, and the fly begins to feed. How does the fly know when to stop feeding? Without some feedback mechanism, the fly could continue to consume the sugar solution until it burst! Receptors in the blowfly's foregut (the first stop for the incoming food in the fly's digestive system), send a message to the fly's brain when the foregut swells sufficiently. The message is relayed to the nerves that control the feeding response, halting further intake of the sugar solution.

Another example of how the nervous system regulates behavior concerns the control of aggressive behavior in rhesus monkeys. In one study, researchers identified the dominant male monkey in a group of four to six animals and then surgically implanted electrodes into the monkey's brain regions involved in either eliciting or inhibiting aggressive behavior. Mild electrical stimulation to the monkey's brain produced either aggressive or passive behaviors, depending on which electrode sent the message. The other monkeys in the group also could be trained to press a lever whenever the dominant monkey became aggressive.

Pressing the lever sent a message to the brain of the dominant male that inhibited his aggression.

ENDOCRINE SYSTEM

In animals, the endocrine system is closely interrelated with the nervous system. Many receptors located on neurons in the brain or central nervous system are specialized for receiving input from hormones. In addition, the brain communicates with the

FIGURE 13.6

Blowfly Feeding. Blowflies (*Lucilia* spp.) detect food with their feet, resulting in proboscis extension and feeding.

endocrine system via neurons, such as the connections between the hypothalamus and pituitary gland of vertebrates (*see chapter 35*). Other endocrine glands (e.g., the adrenals and gonads) are located throughout the body of the organism. **Hormones,** the products from the endocrine glands, affect behavior in two major ways: organizational effects and activational effects.

Organizational effects of hormones occur during development and are particularly important for sex differentiation. These effects involve the presence of hormones and critical time periods during which the developmental pathways for specific brain regions and developing gonadal tissues are influenced to become either female- or malelike. The major effect is such that at about the middle of gestation in most male mammalian embryos (e.g., guinea pigs, monkeys), the testes produce a surge of male hormone (testosterone). This organizes both other developing tissues and certain regions of the brain. In the absence of a testosterone surge, female embryos develop more femalelike characteristics in terms of external anatomy and brain regions important for sex differences. Genes normally turn on the production and release of testosterone in the tissues of the developing animal, but sometimes, the testosterone comes from an external source.

In cattle, a female embryo is masculinized if her twin is a male fetus. When his system turns on and releases testosterone during gestation, some of that hormone crosses over to affect the developing female. The result is a freemartin, a sterile heifer that exhibits a number of malelike behavior patterns. In humans, some hormone treatments that used to be given to pregnant women who were in danger of losing their fetus resulted in masculinization of female embryos because the hormones injected as a medical treatment were converted to and acted like testosterone within the embryo.

Activational effects of hormones occur when an external stimulus triggers a hormonally mediated response by the organism. Many male fishes change color patterns when their territory boundary is threatened; the color change is a prelude to potentially aggressive behavior to defend the territory. Many animals, including domestic cats, roosters, and mice, lose their aggressive fighting ability after castration (removal of the gonads). The gonads are the source of testosterone, which stimulates particular brain receptors to produce aggression.

COMMUNICATION

Communication is the transfer of information from one animal to another. It requires a sender and receiver that are mutually adapted to each other. The animal acting as the sender must send a clear signal to the receiver. Communication can occur within species (intraspecific) or between species (interspecific). Intraspecific communication in animals is especially important for reproductive success. Examples of interspecific communication include warning signals, such as the rattle of a rattlesnake's tail and the skunk's presentation of its hindquarters and tail.

Animals use a variety of modalities for communication, including visual, auditory, tactile, and chemical signals. Natural se-

lection has influenced the characteristics of a signal system. Animals have evolved combinations of signals that may be more effective than any single signal.

VISUAL COMMUNICATION

Visual communication is important to many animals because a large amount of information can be conveyed in a short time. Most animals (e.g., cephalopod molluscs, arthropods, and most vertebrates other than mammals) with well-developed eyes have color vision. Many fishes, reptiles, and birds exhibit brilliant color patterns that usually have a signaling function. Most mammals have plain, darker colors and lack color vision because they are nocturnal, as were their probable ancestors—nocturnal insectivores. Primates are a notable exception in that they have both color vision and colorful displays.

A visual signal may be present at all times, as are the bright facial markings of a male mandrill. The signal may be hidden or located on a less exposed part of an animal's body, and then suddenly presented. Some lizards, such as green anoles, can actually change their color through activities of pigment cells in the skin.

Visual signals have some disadvantages in that various objects in the environment may block the line of sight, and/or the signals may be difficult to see over a long distance. Also, the signals are usually not effective at night and may be detected by predators.

ACOUSTIC COMMUNICATION

Arthropods and vertebrates commonly use acoustic or sound communication. These animals must expend energy to produce sounds, but sounds can be used during night or day. Sound waves also have the advantage of traveling around objects, and may be produced or received while an animal is in the open or concealed. Sounds can carry a large amount of information because of the many possible variations in frequency, duration, volume, and tone.

Acoustic communication systems are closely adapted to the environmental conditions in which they are used and the function of the signal. For example, tropical forest birds produce low-frequency calls that pass easily through dense vegetation. Many primates in tropical forests produce sounds that travel over long distances. Other examples include the calls of territorial birds that sit on a high perch to deliver the signal more effectively and the alarm calls of many small species of birds. Some of the more complex acoustic signals that have been studied are birdsong and human speech.

TACTILE COMMUNICATION

Tactile communication refers to the communication between animals in physical contact with each other. The antennae of many invertebrates and the touch receptors in the skin of vertebrates function in tactile communication (*see figure 34.14*). Some examples of tactile communication are birds preening the feathers of other birds and primates grooming each other (figure 13.7).

FIGURE 13.7

Tactile Communication. A subordinant male (left) chacma baboon (*Papio ursinus*) grooms a dominant male (right).

CHEMICAL COMMUNICATION

Chemical communication is another common mode of communication. Unicellular organisms with chemoreceptors can recognize members of their own species. Chemical signals are well-developed in insects, fishes, salamanders, and mammals. Advantages of chemical signals are that they (1) usually provide a simple message that can last for hours or days; (2) are effective night or day; (3) can pass around objects; (4) may be transported over long distances; and (5) take relatively little energy to produce. Disadvantages of chemical signals are that they cannot be changed quickly and are slow to act.

Chemicals that are synthesized by one organism and that affect the behavior of another member of the same species are called **pheromones.** Olfactory receptors in the receiving animal usually detect chemical signals. Many animals mark their territories by depositing odors that act as chemical signals to other animals of the same species. For example, many male mammals mark specific points in their territories with pheromones that warn other males of their presence in the area. The same pheromones may also attract females that are in breeding condition.

Differences in the chemical structure of pheromones may be directly related to their function. Pheromones used for marking territories and attracting mates usually last longer because of their higher molecular weights. Airborne signals have lower molecular weights and disperse easily. **6** For example, the sex attractant pheromones of female moths who are ready to mate are airborne, and males several kilometers away can detect them.

BEHAVIORAL ECOLOGY

Behavioral ecologists investigate how animals find their way about (orientation and navigation), how they find a place to live (habitat selection), what foods they select to eat (foraging behavior), and the ways in which behavior can influence population biology.

Stop and Ask Yourself

8. Why are stimulus filters in the nervous system important?
9. How would you separate organizational and activational effects of hormones on behavior?
10. What differences would you expect between the communication system of animals that are active at night versus those that are active in the daytime?
11. What are the advantages of chemical communication?

HABITAT SELECTION

Habitat selection refers to the animal's choice of a place to live. Two types of factors affect where animals of a particular species live. First are the animal's physiological tolerance limits, which are set by evolution and may involve temperature, humidity, water salinity, and other environmental parameters. Within those constraints, a second set of psychological factors are important: Animals make choices about where to reside based on available food resources, nest sites, lack of predators, and past experience. For example, woodland deer mice may be constrained to live in forests rather than fields because they cannot tolerate the high temperatures in the field environment (figure 13.8). Within the forest, they may prefer (choose to live in) areas with larger trees (e.g., oak or beech) because these trees provide more food in the form of acorns and beechnuts, in addition to better shelter and more nest sites.

FORAGING BEHAVIOR

All animals must consume food to survive. For most organisms, a large portion of their daily routine involves finding and consuming food. The process of locating food resources is called **foraging behavior.** Animals face the following choices:

1. What items should be included in the diet?
2. Given that food is not often distributed evenly in the environment, but occurs in patches or clumps, what path should an animal take between patches, and how should it locate new patches of food?
3. As the food in a patch is depleted, when should the animal depart from that location and seek another patch of food?

7 Hummingbirds and various species of bees that visit clumps of flowers to obtain nectar must make each of these decisions. Owls that forage for small rodents in different habitats, including fields and forests, must make similar decisions.

Although animals do not calculate their personal energy budgets as they forage, there are energy costs and gains in finding and consuming food. These considerations include energy needed to search for food, energy used to pursue or handle the food, and energy required to digest the food. If the animal is to survive, then the energy gain from digesting a particular set of food items must

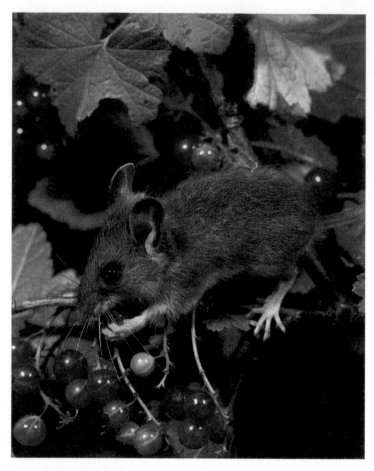

FIGURE 13.8

Habitat Selection in Deer Mice. Deer mice inhabit a variety of habitats. *Peromyscus maniculatus* (shown here) lives in forests, often nesting in trees.

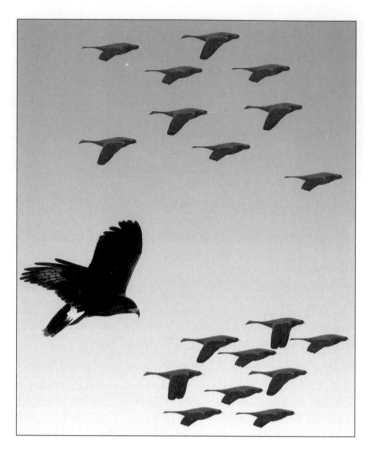

FIGURE 13.9

Group Living. A flock of birds reacts to a bird of prey by forming a tight group, reducing the chances of the predator singling out any particular individual.

exceed the costs. Thus, a praying mantis must expend energy to locate a moth, to strike the moth, to remove the moth's wings, to consume the moth's body, and finally, to digest the meal. The mantis will survive if the energy derived from digesting the moth is greater than these costs. This is particularly true if extra energy is needed for searching for a mate or laying eggs.

Specialists and Generalists

Some animals are **specialists** with respect to diet and habitat selection. Evolution has resulted in these animals being very efficient at utilizing a particular resource. The koala, an Australian marsupial, eats the leaves of only certain species of eucalyptus trees. ⑧ Its digestive system is adapted to derive energy from the leaves of these trees more efficiently than are the digestive systems of other animals. Although being a specialist means successfully exploiting a particular resource, it is also risky. If a plant disease invades and kills trees of the eucalyptus species that form the koalas' diet, koalas may not be able to survive.

At the other end of the continuum are **generalists,** animals capable of eating a variety of foods or living in a variety of habitats. These animals can survive under a wide range of conditions.

Humans are a good example of a generalist species. So, too, are some pest species, like European starlings, introduced into the United States a century ago and now living in almost every available type of habitat. The disadvantage for generalists is that almost everywhere they eat and live, they face competition from other organisms, something that specialists often avoid.

SOCIAL BEHAVIOR

Social behavior typically refers to any interactions among members of the same species, but it also applies to animals of different species, excluding predator-prey interactions.

LIVING IN GROUPS

Animal populations are often organized into groups. A group of animals may form an aggregation for some simple purpose, such as feeding, drinking, or mating. Several *Drosophila* flies on a piece of rotting fruit is an example of an aggregation. A true animal **society** is a stable group of individuals of the same species that maintains a cooperative social relationship. This association typically extends beyond the level of mating and taking care of young.

Social behavior has evolved independently in many species of animals; invertebrates as well as vertebrates have complex social organizations.

⑨ One major benefit of belonging to a group may be that it offers protection against predators (figure 13.9). There is safety in numbers, and predator detection may be enhanced by having several group members on alert to warn against an intruder. Also, cooperative hunting and capture of prey increase the feeding efficiency of predators. Living in social groups is also advantageous in some instances due to the ability to gain protection from the elements (e.g., huddling together in cold weather) and during the processes of mate finding and rearing of young. In many species, most notably the social insects, living in groups has resulted in the evolutionary division of labor, with specific individuals performing specialized tasks (e.g., defense, food procurement, feeding of young).

A disadvantage of group living may be competition for resources. Other disadvantages include the diseases and parasites that may spread more rapidly in group-living animals, and interference between individuals with regard to reproduction and rearing of young. The value of group living depends on the species and behaviors involved.

FIGURE 13.10

Agonistic Behavior. A baboon (*Comopithecus hamadryas*) exhibits a threat display toward other members of the troop.

AGONISTIC BEHAVIOR, TERRITORIES, AND DOMINANCE HIERARCHIES

A society of animals usually has some maintenance of social structure and spacing of group members. Agonistic behavior, in which one animal is aggressive or attacks another animal, which responds by either returning the aggression or submitting, is often responsible for these patterns. In rare cases, agonistic behavior is lethal, but usually, animals are not killed or even severely injured. In many species, males vent much of their aggression in the form of threat displays. Displays typically involve signals that warn other males of an intention to defend an area or territory (figure 13.10). Although agonistic behavior may seem antisocial, it maintains the social order. It is especially important in the maintenance of territories and dominance hierarchies.

A territorial animal uses agonistic behavior to defend a site or area against certain other individuals. The site is known as the animal's **territory,** and competing individuals are excluded from it. Many male birds and mammals occupy a breeding territory for part of the year. A male actively defends his area against other males, so that he can attract a female and court her without interference from other males. In addition to being a location for attracting a mate and rearing young, territories may contain a food supply or provide shelter to avoid predators and unfavorable climate.

In **dominance hierarchies,** a group of animals is organized so that some members of the group have greater access to resources, such as food or mates, than do others. Those near the top of the order have first choice of resources, whereas those near the bottom go last and may do without if resources are in short supply. An example of a dominance hierarchy is the "pecking order" of chickens in a pen. When chickens are placed together, they fight among themselves until a linear hierarchy of dominance is established. Higher-ranked chickens are among the first to eat and may peck lower-ranked chickens. Once the hierarchy is set, peaceful coexistence is possible. Occasional fights will occur if a bird tries to move up in the order.

Dominance hierarchies exist in many vertebrate groups, the most common being in the form of linear relationships, although triangular relationships may form. In baboons, the strongest male is usually highest in the rank order. But sometimes, older males may form coalitions to subdue a stronger male and lead the troop.

ALTRUISM

In **altruism,** an individual gives up or sacrifices some of its own reproductive potential to benefit another individual. For example, one individual of a group of crows gives an alarm call to warn other individuals of the group of an approaching predator, even though the call may attract the predator to the sender of the signal. How did such behavior evolve? Are normal natural selection processes at work here?

To be successful in a biological sense, an animal must produce as many young as possible, thereby passing its genes to succeeding generations. However, genes can be passed on by aiding a relative and its young because they probably share some genes. In terms of reproductive potential or output, an individual may theoretically pass more genes to the next generation by aiding the survival of relatives than it would rearing its own young.

A well-known example of altruism occurs in societies of hymenopteran insects, such as honeybees. The male drones are haploid, and the female workers and queen are diploid, resulting in a genetic asymmetry. Diploid workers share, on the average, three-fourths of their genes with their full sisters. If they reproduced, they would share only half of their genes with hypothetical offspring. Thus, female honeybees may have more genes in common with their sisters than they would with their own offspring. The workers may pass more genes to the next generation by helping their mother produce more full sisters, some of whom may become reproductive queens, than if they produce their own young.

William Hamilton (1936–) proposed the idea of **kin selection** to explain how selection acting on related animals can affect the fitness of an individual. In this way, a gene that a particular individual carries may pass to the next generation through a related animal. An individual's fitness is therefore based on the genes it passes on, as well as those common genes its relatives pass on. A genetically based tendency to be altruistic could therefore be passed on by the individual carrying it or by a relative who also carries it. Obviously, for kin selection to work, individuals of a group must be able to identify relatives, as can small groups of primates and social insects.

Summary

1. Animal behavior includes the many activities of an animal during its lifetime. Four approaches to the study of animal behavior are comparative psychology, ethology, behavioral ecology, and sociobiology.

2. Natural selection influences animal behavior just as it does other animal characteristics. Certain behavioral traits that allow animals to survive and reproduce are favored.

3. Certain behavior patterns require time for maturation, during which performance of the behavior improves as parts of the nervous system and other structures complete development.

4. Many behavior patterns require an interaction of instinctive and learned components for efficient performance. In some instances, an animal may inherit a disposition to learn a specific behavior. Also, an animal may learn certain behavior patterns only during a specific sensitive period early in life.

5. Through learning, an animal can adjust quickly to changes in its environment. Learning is adaptive for animals in an environment where changes are not predictable. The types of learning known to occur in animals include habituation, classical conditioning, instrumental conditioning, latent learning, and insight learning.

6. The nervous system regulates behavior through sensory reception of information from the environment, processing and storing of that information, and mediating appropriate motor responses.

7. Hormonal effects on behavior may either be organizational, affecting developmental processes such as sexual differentiation, or activational, involving more immediate behavioral responses, such as aggression.

8. Communication in animals requires the use of clear signals by one animal and their reception by another. Visual, acoustic, tactile, and chemical signals are important channels in communication systems.

9. Animals have evolved mechanisms for guiding their selection of foods and of habitats in which to live and reproduce.

10. Many animal species live in groups that provide various benefits. Groups range from simple aggregations to more complex social organizations, or societies.

11. Agonistic behavior in the form of attacks or threat displays is important in spacing the members of a species or establishing and defending a territory. In some instances, a dominance hierarchy may rank members in order from the most dominant individual to the most subordinate individual. Once the hierarchy is established, agonistic behavior is reduced in the group.

12. In some societies, one individual sacrifices its reproductive potential to help another individual. Altruism may be a result of kin selection, in which aiding one's relatives enhances the spreading of genes shared with relatives.

Selected Key Terms

behavioral ecology (p. 179)
classical conditioning (p. 181)
comparative psychology (p. 179)
dominance hierarchies (p. 187)
ethology (p. 179)
foraging behavior (p. 185)
habitat selection (p. 185)
habituation (p. 181)

imprinting (p. 180)
insight learning (p. 182)
instrumental conditioning (p. 181)
latent learning (p. 182)
maturation (p. 179)
sociobiology (p.179)
territory (p. 187)

Critical Thinking Questions

1. How can you distinguish between classical and instrumental conditioning? What are some examples of each that might occur in nature?

2. How is kin selection related to natural selection?

3. Will a seagull incubate an infertile chicken egg placed in her nest? Explain your answer.

4. An advertisement for Boone Trail Nugget Company features a hiker eating a bowl of cereal on a mountaintop. Upon what type of learning does this type of advertisement rely? Explain your answer.

5. What habitat features would a rattlesnake examine when looking for a place to live?

REFERENCES ON THE WORLD WIDE WEB

1. **Animal Behavior.** This site provides links to animal behavior Web sites, including teacher resources and laboratory activities, societies and organizations, book reviews, electronic journals, and news groups.

   http://www.wam.und.edu/~jaguar/behavior/behavior.html

2. **Evolution and Behavior.** This Web site provides information on evolution and links to the Animal Behavior Society.

   http://ccp.uchicago.edu/~jyin/evolution.html

3. **Animal Behavior Society.** Information at this Web site includes documents on the value of the study of animal behavior, lists of institutions with departments specializing in animal behavior, educa-tional activities, the Animal Behavior Society newsletter, research reports, and interesting "news scoops" about animal behavior.

   http://www.cisab.indiana.edu/animal_behavior.html

4. **Center for Integrative Study of Animal Behavior.** Programs in animal behavior, research articles, computer archives for the study of animal behavior, and articles from *Animal Behavior Bulletin* are featured at this site.

   http://www.cisab.indiana.edu/index.html

5. **Internet Animal Behavior.** This site provides a wealth of information on animal behavior societies, resources, programs, mailing lists, and research results.

   http://cricket.unl.edu/NBBG/InterAB.html

ECOLOGY I:
INDIVIDUALS AND POPULATIONS

Concepts

1. Ecology is the study of the relationships of organisms to their environment and to other organisms. In part, it involves the study of how abiotic factors, such as energy, temperature, moisture, light, and soils, influence individuals.
2. Ecology also involves the study of populations. Populations grow, and population density, the carrying capacity of the environment, and interactions among members of the same population regulate growth.
3. Ecology also involves the study of individuals interacting with members of their own and other species. Herbivory, predator-prey interactions, competition for resources, and other kinds of interactions influence the makeup of animal populations.

Would You Like to Know . . .

1. whether some animals can tolerate colder temperatures than others in the same species? (p. 192)
2. why deer hunters in northern climates shoot larger animals than hunters in the south? (p. 193)
3. whether bears really hibernate? (p. 193)
4. why some animals never need to drink water? (p. 194)
5. how an animal can tell that winter is coming and that it is time to accumulate food reserves? (p. 194)
6. how long a bird, like a robin, tends to live? (p. 195)
7. why mosquitoes appear so quickly after a few days of rain? (p. 197)
8. why predators usually do not hunt their prey to extinction? (p. 197)
9. why a parasite usually does not kill its host? (p. 198)

This chapter answers these and other useful questions.

This chapter contains evolutionary concepts, which are set off in this font.

All animals have certain requirements for life. In searching out these requirements, animals come into contact with members of their own species and other species. The resulting interactions mold the lives of the animals involved. Sometimes, these interactions are obvious and even violent, such as between predator and prey. Other interactions may occur without the participants seeing each other. This chapter examines the multitude of interactions of animals with their environment and other animals.

ANIMALS AND THEIR ABIOTIC ENVIRONMENT

An animal's **habitat** (environment) includes all living (biotic) and nonliving (abiotic) characteristics of the area in which the animal lives. Abiotic characteristics of a habitat include availability of oxygen and inorganic ions, light, temperature, and current or wind velocity. Physiological ecologists who study abiotic influences have found that animals live within a certain range of values, called the **tolerance range,** for any environmental factor. At either limit of the tolerance range, one or more essential functions cease. A certain range of values within the tolerance range, called the **range of optimum,** defines the conditions under which an animal is most successful (figure 14.1).

Combinations of abiotic factors are necessary for an animal to survive and reproduce. When one of these is out of an animal's tolerance range, it becomes a **limiting factor.** For example, even though a stream insect may have the proper substrate for shelter, adequate current to bring in food and aid in dispersal, and the

proper ions to ensure growth and development, inadequate supplies of oxygen make life impossible.

Often, an animal's response to an abiotic factor is to orient itself with respect to it; such orientation is called **taxis.** For example, a response to light is called phototaxis. If an animal favors well-lighted environments and moves toward a light source, it is displaying positive phototaxis. If it prefers low light intensities and moves away from a light source, it displays negative phototaxis.

❶ Physiological ecologists have found that tolerance ranges often change in response to altered environmental conditions (e.g., changes in season). Catfish maintained at 25° C have a tolerance range for temperature that is 2 to 3° C lower than catfish maintained at 30° C. Such changes in tolerance ranges are called **acclimation.**

ENERGY

Energy is the ability to do work. For animals, work includes everything from foraging for food to moving molecules around within cells. To supply their energy needs, animals ingest other organisms; that is, animals are **heterotrophic** (Gr. *hetero,* other + *tropho,* feeder). **Autotrophic** (Gr. *autos,* self + *tropho,* feeder) organisms (e.g., plants) carry on photosynthesis or other carbon-fixing activities that supply their food source. An accounting of an animal's total energy intake and a description of how that energy is used and lost is an **energy budget** (figure 14.2).

The total energy contained in food an animal eats is the gross energy intake. Some food is undigested, and some food that is digested is not absorbed into the bloodstream. Energy in unab-

FIGURE 14.1

Tolerance Range of an Animal. Plotting changes in an environmental factor versus some index of success (perhaps egg production, longevity, or growth) shows an animal's tolerance range. The graphs that result are often, though not always, bell-shaped. The range of optimum is the range of values of the factor within which success is greatest. The range of tolerance and range of optimum may vary, depending on an animal's stage of life, health, and activity.

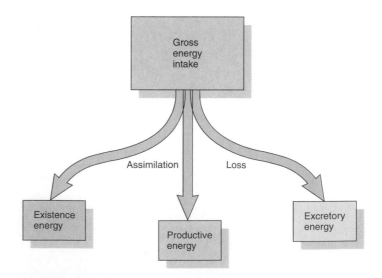

FIGURE 14.2

Energy Budgets of Animals. The gross energy intake of an animal is the sum of energy lost in excretory pathways plus energy assimilated for existence and productive functions. The relative sizes of the boxes in this diagram are not necessarily proportional to the amount of energy devoted to each function. An animal's gross energy intake, and thus, the amount of energy devoted to productive functions, depends on various internal and external factors (e.g., time of year and reproductive status).

sorbed and undigested food is lost in the feces. Other food may be absorbed but later lost to excretion in urine or perspiration. Energy lost in feces and through excretion is excretory energy.

The remainder of gross energy intake is absorbed and is available for cell work. Some of this energy supports minimal maintenance activities, such as pumping blood, exchanging gases, supporting repair processes, and maintaining nervous, sensory, and endocrine functions. In addition, animals must have energy for necessary activities, such as catching food, escaping predators, and finding shelter. The energy devoted to minimal maintenance and necessary activities is existence energy.

Any energy left after existence and excretory functions can be devoted to growth, mating, nesting, and caring for young. The portion of gross energy intake that exceeds excretory and existence energies is productive energy. Survival requires that individuals acquire enough energy to supply these productive functions. Favorable energy budgets are sometimes difficult to attain, especially in temperate regions where winter often makes food supplies scarce.

TEMPERATURE

An animal expends part of its existence energy in regulating body temperature. Temperature influences the rates of chemical reactions in animal cells (metabolic rate) and affects the animal's overall activity. The body temperature of an animal seldom remains constant because of an inequality between heat loss and heat gain. Heat energy can be lost to objects in an animal's surroundings as infrared and heat radiation, to the air around the animal through convection, and as evaporative heat. On the other hand, heat is gained from solar radiation, infrared and heat radiation from objects in the environment, and relatively inefficient metabolic activities that generate heat as a by-product of cellular functions. Thermoregulatory needs influence many habitat requirements, such as the availability of food, water, and shelter.

Body size and metabolic rates are interrelated. In a particular taxonomic category, smaller animals have higher rates of metabolism than do larger animals. For example, the metabolic rate of a mouse is more than 20 times higher per gram of tissue than the metabolic rate of an elephant. The reason for this relationship between size and metabolic rate is not entirely clear. A traditional explanation is that small animals have a higher surface-area-to-volume ratio, and thus, as body size increases, there is relatively less body surface over which heat is lost (figure 14.3). This explanation, however, is less than satisfactory. Ectotherms (animals that use external heat sources for regulation of body temperature), whose rate of heat loss is less influenced by body size, show the same relationship of metabolic rate to body mass as endotherms (animals that use internal heat sources for regulation of body temperature).

The surface-area explanation, however, probably does explain another observation. ❷ Members of a species living in cold climates tend to be larger than members of the same species in warm climates. The smaller surface area per unit of body mass of large animals reduces heat loss compared to smaller animals of the same species.

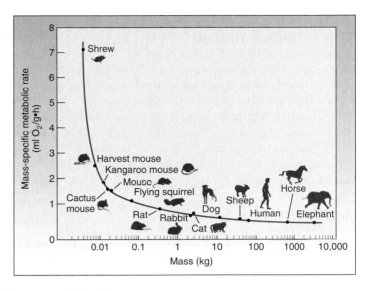

FIGURE 14.3

Effects of Body Size on Metabolic Rate for Some Mammals. Metabolic rate is expressed in milliliters of oxygen consumed per gram of body weight per hour. Note that the X-axis has a logarithmic scale to compress the difference between the weights of the shrew and the elephant. Metabolic rates and body size are inversely related.

Animal Inactivity

When food becomes scarce, or when animals are not feeding for other reasons, they are subject to starvation. This problem is especially severe for small endotherms, whose metabolic rates are high and whose energy reserves are small. Under these circumstances, metabolic activities may decrease dramatically.

Torpor is a time of decreased metabolism and lowered body temperature in daily activity cycles. Hummingbirds and bats must feed almost constantly when they are active. Their body temperature and metabolic rate drop dramatically during daily periods of inactivity. A lower metabolic rate conserves energy and allows hummingbirds and bats to survive periods when they do not feed. At the end of a period of torpor, metabolic activity and body temperature rise quickly.

Hibernation is a time of decreased metabolism and lowered body temperature that may last for weeks or months. True hibernation occurs in small mammals, such as rodents, shrews, and bats. The set point of a hibernator's thermoregulatory center drops to about 20° C, but thermoregulation is not suspended. This maintenance of thermoregulation distinguishes hibernation from the winter inactivity of ectotherms. Snakes, for example, overwinter in retreats that are unlikely to experience freezing temperatures. In an unusually cold winter, however, animals may freeze to death because they have no internal thermoregulatory abilities.

Winter sleep occurs in some larger animals. Large energy reserves sustain these mammals through periods of winter inactivity. ❸ Body temperatures do not drop substantially, and sleeping animals can wake and become active very quickly— as any rookie zoologist probing around the den of a sleeping bear quickly learns!

Aestivation is a period of inactivity in some animals that must withstand extended periods of drying. The animal usually enters a burrow as its environment begins to dry. It generally does not eat or drink and emerges again after moisture returns. Aestivation is common in many invertebrates. For example, some arthropods enter the substrate of drying ponds and streams, and remain inactive until the pond or stream fills with water again. The Australian burrowing frog (*Cyclorana alboguttatus; see figure 28.15b*) and the chuckwalla (*Sauromalus obesus; see figure 29.9*) are vertebrates that live in dry habitats and withstand seasonal droughts by aestivating.

MOISTURE

All life processes occur in the watery environment of the cell. Water is lost in urine and feces, during gas exchange, and through evaporation from body surfaces, and it must be replaced if life is to continue. Animals display numerous adaptations to lower or reduce the impact of water loss. Some animals reduce water loss by producing essentially dry feces. Others produce a concentrated urine and utilize excretory products that can be excreted in semisolid form. Controlling evaporative water loss involves a difficult set of compromises between water conservation and evaporative cooling. Often, environments that require water conservation also require cooling. The nocturnal (night-active) lifestyle of many desert animals is apparently an adaptation to reduce the need for evaporative cooling in a hot environment. Some animals, such as camels, can tolerate water losses of 25 to 40% of their total body weight (*see box 38.1*).

Animals acquire water from food, drink, and metabolism. Metabolic water is water produced as a by-product of cellular metabolism. ④ Numerous arthropods, and some mammals, have such efficient water conservation mechanisms that metabolic water is sufficient for replacing water loss. For example, flour beetles (*Tribolium* spp.) that spend their entire lives in containers of dry flour survive on water from cellular metabolism.

Aquatic animals also face water-regulation problems. Maintaining proper ion and water balances in freshwater environments involves conserving ions that tend to be lost to the environment and countering the osmotic influx of water into animal tissues. The problem in marine environments is just the opposite. Seawater is hypertonic to the tissues of many marine animals. As on land, water tends to be lost to the environment, and ions tend to accumulate in body tissues.

LIGHT

Light conditions also influence animals. A photoperiod is the length of the light period in a 24-hour day and is an accurate index of seasonal change. As spring approaches and the period of daylight increases, birds enter their breeding condition. Lengthening daylight hours indicate that conditions will soon be suitable for producing and rearing offspring. ⑤ Similarly, the changing photoperiod in autumn indicates that food supplies will soon dwindle. This change may be an important cue to stockpile food reserves or to find a suitable wintering site.

Light also influences cycles of daily activity, called **circadian** (L. *circa*, about + *diem*, day) **rhythms.** Many people have experienced air travel to different time zones and the accompanying upset in timing of daily activities. This upset, commonly known as "jet lag," is a result of our innate (biological) clock telling us it is time for one activity (e.g., sleep) and external cues (e.g., daylight) telling us it is time for another (daytime) activity. Similar problems result from a change between "day shift" and "night shift" at a job. Recent research indicates that the photoperiod is responsible for resetting our biological clocks so the new time of activity can seem normal.

Many animals have circadian rhythms. Freshwater and marine invertebrates have daily patterns of migration between the upper and lower levels of a water column. Many stream invertebrates (e.g., mayfly and stonefly naiads and caddisfly larvae) have periods of activity at dawn and dusk. Terrestrial animals are either diurnal or nocturnal. Biological clocks that are probably influenced by the photoperiod control these cycles of activity.

Many animals have marked phototactic responses that help them find appropriate habitats. For example, many invertebrates living in the substrates of lakes and streams are negatively phototactic. Their daily activities are thus directed away from light sources and into sheltering substrates.

GEOLOGY AND SOILS

Soils reflect an area's geological and biological history, and affect animal life directly and indirectly. Soils are homes for a large variety of protozoa, nematodes, earthworms, arthropods, and vertebrates, such as salamanders, snakes, and moles. Soil characteristics, such as texture, amount of organic matter, fertility, and water-holding ability, directly influence the number and kinds of animals living in or on the soil. Soils also have obvious effects on the kinds of plants that grow in an area. This indirectly influences animal life because all animals, regardless of whether they live in or on top of the soil, ultimately depend on plants for their food.

Stop and Ask Yourself

1. The tolerance range of a certain fish for dissolved oxygen is between 5 and 14 parts per million oxygen. What does this mean?

2. What is a shift in the tolerance range of an organism for a particular environmental factor called?

3. What are three avenues of energy expenditure that contribute to the dissipation of gross energy intake?

4. Why is the photoperiod a more reliable indicator of seasonal change than temperature?

POPULATIONS

Populations are groups of individuals of the same species that occupy a given area at the same time and have unique attributes, including growth rate, age structure, sex ratio, and mortality rate.

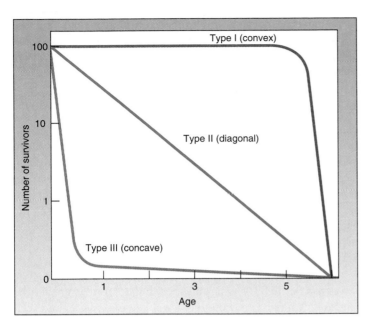

FIGURE 14.4

Survivorship. Survivorship curves are a plot of number of survivors (usually a logarithmic plot) versus age. Type I curves apply to populations in which individuals are likely to live out their potential life span. Type II curves apply to populations in which mortality rates are constant throughout age classes. Type III curves apply to populations in which mortality rates are highest for the youngest cohorts.

POPULATION GROWTH

Animal populations change over time as a result of birth, death, and dispersal. One way to characterize a population with regard to the death of individuals is with survivorship curves (figure 14.4). The Y-axis of a survivorship graph is a logarithmic plot of numbers of survivors, and the X-axis is a linear plot of age. There are three kinds of survivorship curves. Individuals in type I (convex) populations survive to an old age, then die rapidly. Environmental factors are relatively unimportant in influencing mortality, and most individuals live their potential life span. Some human populations approach type I survivorship. Individuals in type II (diagonal) populations have a constant probability of death throughout their lives. The environment has an important influence on death and is no harsher on the young than on the old. Populations of birds and rodents often have type II survivorship curves. Individuals in type III (concave) populations experience very high juvenile mortality. Those reaching adulthood, however, have a much lower mortality rate. Fishes and many invertebrates display type III survivorship curves.

Mortality in natural populations is often high. In birds, for example, each cohort—a group of individuals all hatched at the same time—commonly experiences greater than 50% mortality each year. ⑥ The potential life span of the American robin, for example, is 11 years; however, the average robin probably lives only 1.4 years.

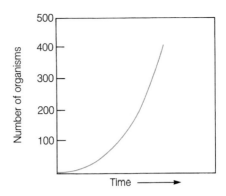

FIGURE 14.5

Exponential Growth. The number of organisms (Y-axis) is plotted on an arithmetic scale, resulting in a curve with an increasing slope.
Source: Leland G. Johnson, Biology, 2d Ed. Copyright © 1987 Wm. C. Brown Communications, Inc. Dubuque, Iowa.

Exponential Growth

The potential for population growth can be demonstrated in the laboratory under conditions that provide abundant resources and space. For example, a few fruit flies in a large culture jar containing abundant food reproduce rapidly. One female fruit fly lays more than 50 eggs. Reproductive adults develop in about 14 days, with approximately equal numbers of male and female offspring. For each female that began the population, 50 flies are expected 2 weeks later. Each female in the second generation produces 50 more flies after 2 more weeks, and so on. In other words, the population is experiencing **exponential growth,** shown in figure 14.5 in an arithmetic plot. Rather than increasing by adding a constant number of individuals to the population in every generation, the population increases by the same ratio per unit time.

All populations do not display the same capacity for growth. Such factors as the number of offspring produced, the likelihood of survival to reproductive age, the duration of the reproductive period, and the length of time it takes to reach maturity all influence reproductive potential. The capacity of a population to increase maximally is called its **biotic potential** or **intrinsic rate of growth.** It is symbolized by *r* and defined as the rate of population increase under optimal conditions.

Logistic Population Growth

Exponential growth cannot occur indefinitely. In some years, for example, American robin populations are larger than in other years; on average, however, robin populations are relatively constant. The constraints that climate, food, space, and other environmental factors place on a population are called **environmental resistance.** The population size that a particular environment can support is the environment's **carrying capacity** and is symbolized by *K*. In these situations, growth curves assume a sigmoid, or flattened **S**, shape (figure 14.6*a*). Logistic population growth results when environmental resistance limits exponential growth.

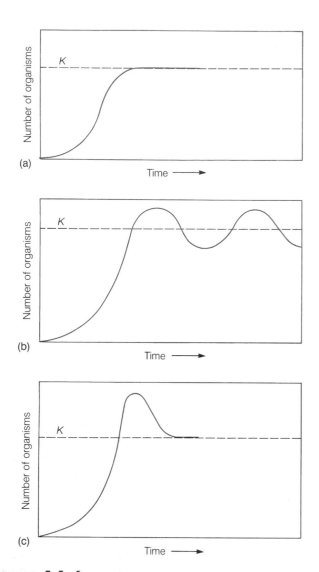

FIGURE 14.6

Logistic Population Growth. Logistic growth curves reflect limited resources placing an upper limit on population size. (*a*) At carrying capacity (*K*), population growth levels off, creating an **S**-shaped curve. (*b,c*) During its exponential growth phase, a population may overshoot carrying capacity because demand on resources may lag behind population growth. When that happens, numbers may cycle on either side of *K* (*b*), or form a **J**-shaped curve (*c*).

The effects of environmental resistance are often not instantaneous. For example, a field of grain may support a large population of young field mice, but as mice mature and acquire larger appetites, resources may dwindle. Increasing populations, therefore, may exceed the carrying capacity. Eventually, increased death rate will cause the population to decrease to, or go below, *K*. Growth curves may thus fluctuate around *K*, or assume a **J** shape (figure 14.6*b,c*).

POPULATION REGULATION

The conditions that an animal must meet to survive are unique for every species. What many species have in common, however, is that population density and competition impact populations in predictable ways. In addition, unstable environmental conditions may prevent animal populations from ever reaching the carrying capacity of the environment.

Population Density

Density-independent factors influence the number of animals in a population without regard to the number of individuals per unit space (density). For example, weather conditions often limit populations. An extremely cold winter with little snow cover may devastate a population of lizards sequestered beneath the litter of the forest floor. Regardless of the size of the population, a certain percentage of individuals will freeze to death. Human activities, such as construction and deforestation, often affect animal populations in a similar fashion.

Density-dependent factors are more severe when population density is high (or sometimes very low) than they are at other densities. Animals often use territorial behavior, song, and scent marking to tell others to look elsewhere for reproductive space. These actions become more pronounced as population density increases and are thus density dependent. Other density-dependent factors include competition for resources, disease, predation, and parasitism.

Intraspecific Competition

Competition occurs when animals utilize similar resources and in some way interfere with each other's procurement of those resources. Competition among members of the same species, called **intraspecific competition,** is often intense because the resource requirements of individuals of a species are nearly identical. Intraspecific competition may occur without individuals coming into direct contact. (The "early bird that gets the worm" may not actually see later arrivals.) In other instances, the actions of one individual directly affect another. Territorial behavior and the actions of socially dominant individuals are examples of direct interference.

r and K Selection

In some instances, the logistic-growth model accurately characterizes a population. Populations whose size tends to evolve toward their carrying capacity are said to be **K-selected.** Density-dependent factors regulate these populations, which are found in relatively predictable environments. *K*-selected populations tend to be made up of long-lived, slowly maturing species. Reproductive rates are relatively low, and the young may receive substantial parental care. *K*-selection is responsible for most populations of large mammals.

At the opposite extreme are populations that are prevented from achieving their carrying capacity. When natural selection promotes rapid population growth, ecologists say that the population is *r*-selected. Regulation through *r* selection involves density-independent factors like climate. Individuals may occupy marginally adequate habitats and reproduce very quickly when conditions permit. One female produces many young, and developmental stages mature quickly with little parental care. Efficient dispersal systems distribute eggs, young, or adults. In other words, the biotic potential of individuals with *r*-selected traits has been maximized during evolution.   **7** A mosquito population that increases rapidly a few days after a rainy period is a familiar example of *r* selection (table 14.1).

TABLE 14.1	CHARACTERISTICS OF *r* VERSES *K* SELECTION
r-Selected Traits	**K-Selected Traits**
Early maturation that increases reproductive potential	Late maturation that avoids risks of breeding
Many, smaller young produced	Fewer, larger young produced
Short life spans (often less than 1 year)	Longer life spans
Less parental care of offspring	More parental care, which increases individual offspring's chances of survival
Uncrowded conditions that require little competition for resources	Crowding that nearly always results in intense competition for resources

---

Stop and Ask Yourself

5. What does the survivorship curve of a type III population look like?

6. What growth-limiting factor(s) are taken into consideration in logistic growth calculations?

7. What is the difference between density-independent and density-dependent population regulation? Give examples of each.

8. Are environmental factors, such as weather, very important, moderately important, or unimportant in determining survivorship of juvenile stages in *r*-selected species?

INTERSPECIFIC INTERACTIONS

Members of other species can affect all characteristics of a population. Interspecific interactions include herbivory, predation, competition, coevolution, and symbiosis. These artificial categories that zoologists create, however, rarely limit animals. Animals often do not interact with other animals in only one way. The nature of interspecific interactions may change as an animal matures, or as seasons or the environment changes.

HERBIVORY

Animals that feed on plants by cropping portions of the plant, but usually not killing the plant, are herbivores. Some are grazers (e.g., cattle and bison), which means that they feed on grasses and other herbaceous vegetation. Browsers (e.g., deer and rabbits) feed on the leaves and twigs of woody plants. Other forms of herbivory include frugivory (feeding on fruits), seed eating, nectar and sap feeding, and pollen eating.

PREDATION

Predators are animals that feed by killing and eating other organisms. Predators influence the distribution and abundance of prey populations, and conversely, the distribution and abundance of prey influence predator populations. For example, the lake trout (*Salvelinus namaycush*) is the only freshwater fish whose native distribution included virtually all of North America but never crossed the narrow Bering Strait into Siberia. In contrast, lake trout have crossed larger expanses of ocean to the freshwater systems of islands in northern Canada. Predation by the Pacific sea lamprey (*Entosphenus* spp.) has probably prevented the movement of lake trout to Siberian freshwater systems (figure 14.7). The decline of lake trout in the Great Lakes after the opening of the Welland Canal allowed the Atlantic sea lamprey (*Petromyzon* spp.) to move into the Great Lakes (*see box 27.1*) supports this explanation.

Interactions between predators and prey are complex, and many characteristics of the environment affect them.   **8** Coexistence of predator and prey apparently requires a habitat that allows prey to take refuge when their numbers are small. Under these conditions, predator populations decline, but some survive by finding other sources of food.

INTERSPECIFIC COMPETITION

When members of different species compete for resources, one species may be forced to move or become extinct, or the two species may share the resource and coexist.

Competitive Exclusion

The **competitive exclusion principle** has influenced the thinking of ecologists for over 50 years. It states that two species with exactly the same requirements for food, habitat, nest sites, and other conditions of life cannot coexist.

Numerous laboratory investigations and observations in nature, however, have failed to document the universality of the competitive exclusion principle. Part of the reason for this failure is that two species rarely have identical requirements for food, space, and other conditions of life.

Competitive exclusion apparently did occur in the citrus groves of southern California. California red scale is an insect pest of citrus trees. A wasp parasite of scale insects, called the golden-naveled scalesucker, lays its eggs under the scalelike citrus pest, and larvae feed on and eventually kill the scale insect. In hopes of more efficient pest control, a second scalesucker, the Lingnan scalesucker, was introduced to southern California from China. The Lingnan scalesucker outcompeted the golden-naveled scalesucker, and within 2 years, completely replaced the native species at some plots.

FIGURE 14.7

Predator/Prey Interactions. Distribution of lake trout (shown in lighter green) (*Salvelinus namaycush*) in North America before the construction of the Welland Canal. Purple areas show the distribution of sea lampreys (*Entosphenus* and *Petromyzon* species). *From C.C. Lindsey, "Problems in Zoology of the Lake Trout,* Salvelinus namaycush," *Journal of Fisheries Research Board of Canada, 21:977–994, 1964. Used by permission.*

Coexistence

Most studies have shown that competing species can coexist. Coexistence can occur when species utilize resources in slightly different ways and when the effects of interspecific competition are less severe than the effects of intraspecific competition. Robert MacArthur studied five species of warblers that all used the same caterpillar prey. Warblers partitioned their spruce tree habitats by dividing a tree into preferred regions for foraging. Although foraging regions overlapped, competition was limited, and the five species coexisted (figure 14.8).

Competing species can divide resources in many ways. Partitioning, however, cannot occur indefinitely because the total quantity of any resource is limited. If individuals in a population cannot obtain enough of a resource to support reproduction, then similarities between species become important limiting factors, and competitive exclusion may occur.

COEVOLUTION

The evolution of ecologically related species is sometimes coordinated such that each species exerts a strong selective influence on the other. This is **coevolution.**

Coevolution may occur when species are competing for the same resource or during predator-prey interactions. In the evolution of predator-prey relationships, for example, natural selection favors the development of protective characteristics in prey species. Similarly, selection favors characteristics in predators that allow them to become better at catching and immobilizing prey. Predator-prey relationships coevolve when a change toward greater predator efficiency is countered by increased elusiveness of prey. If evolutionary rates are balanced, neither species wins this evolutionary "arms race." If not balanced, then one species becomes extinct, and another species takes its place. Evidence documenting the development of predator-prey relationships through coevolution, however, is scanty.

Coevolution is obvious in the relationships between some flowering plants and their animal pollinators (figure 14.9). Early land plants were dependent on wind and rain to achieve pollination. Cross-pollination became more likely when insects, birds, or bats began carrying pollen from one flower to another. Plants that display adaptations for attracting specific pollinators, or animals that display adaptations for extracting pollen and nectar from specific plants, are demonstrating the results of coevolution.

Flowers attract pollinators with a variety of elaborate olfactory and visual adaptations. Insect-pollinated flowers are usually yellow or blue because insects see these wavelengths of light best. In addition, petal arrangements often provide perches for pollinating insects. Flowers pollinated by hummingbirds, on the other hand, are often tubular and red. Hummingbirds have a poor sense of smell but see red very well. The long beak of hummingbirds is an adaptation that allows them to reach far into tubular flowers. Their hovering ability means that they have no need for a perch. One particularly striking example of coevolution between a hummingbird and a flowering plant occurs in the tropics. *Ensifera ensifera* is a hummingbird with an extremely long bill (in excess of 8 cm). It feeds almost exclusively on passion flowers, which store their nectar deep within tubular flowers. The structure of the flower excludes virtually all other nectar-feeding animals, limiting competition for the hummingbird and reducing the chances of cross-pollination with other plant species.

SYMBIOSIS

Some of the best examples of adaptations arising through coevolution come from two different species living in continuing, intimate associations, called **symbiosis** (Gr. *sym*, together + *bio*, life). Such interspecific interactions influence the species involved in dramatically different ways. In some instances, one member of the association benefits, and the other is harmed. In other cases, life without the partner would be impossible for both.

Parasitism

Parasitism is a common form of symbiosis in which one organism lives in or on a second organism, called a host. ⑨ The host usually survives at least long enough for the parasite to complete one or more life cycles.

The relationships between a parasite and its host(s) are often complex. Some parasites have life histories involving multiple hosts. The definitive or final host is the host that harbors the sexual stages of the parasite. A fertile female in a definitive host may produce and release hundreds of thousands of eggs in its lifetime. Each egg gives rise to an immature stage that may be a parasite of

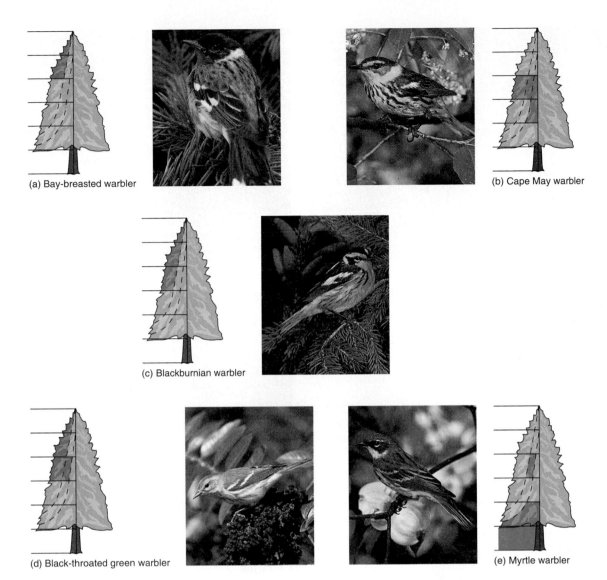

FIGURE 14.8

Coexistence of Competing Species. Robert MacArthur found that five species of warblers (*a–e*) coexisted by partitioning spruce trees into preferred foraging regions (shown in dark green). (*a*) Bay-breasted warbler (*Dendroica castanea*). (*b*) Cape May warbler (*D. tigrina*). (*c*) Blackburnian warbler (*D. fusca*). (*d*) Black-throated green warbler (*D. virens*). (*e*) Myrtle warbler (*D. coronata*).

a second host. This second host is called an intermediate host, and asexual reproduction may occur in this host. Some life cycles may have more than one intermediate host and more than one immature stage. For the life cycle to be completed, the final immature stage must have access to a definitive host. The likelihood that a particular egg will mature into a reproductive adult is usually remote. Producing large numbers of eggs is one of many parasitic adaptations that help ensure that a few individuals will eventually complete the life cycle. In any symbiotic relationship, however, the parasite is only half of the story. Hosts may evolve mechanisms that help them resist parasitic infections. Many examples of coevolutionary interactions between host and parasite are cited in Part Five of this text.

Parasitoids are animals that deposit eggs or other developmental stages on another animal. As immatures develop, they live off host tissues and eventually kill the host. Because the death of the host is the usual outcome, parasitoids combine features of parasite and predator. For example, ichneumonid wasps lay eggs on or in other insects. The larvae feed on the host's tissues during larval development, eventually killing the host.

Commensalism

Commensalism is a symbiotic relationship in which one member of the relationship benefits, and the second is neither helped nor harmed. The distinction between parasitism and commensalism is

FIGURE 14.9

Coevolution. Flowers and their pollinators have coevolved for millions of years. Typical hummingbird-pollinated flowers are red and produce large amounts of nectar. As a hummingbird feeds on the nectar with its long, thin bill, its head contacts the flower parts involved in pollination. Cost's hummingbird (*Calypte costae*) is shown here.

somewhat difficult to apply in natural situations. Whether or not the host is harmed often depends on such factors as the host's nutritional state. Thus, symbiotic relationships may be commensalistic in some situations and parasitic in others. One example of a commensalistic relationship involves *Entamoeba gingivalis*, a common amoeba that lives in the mouth of humans. Although often associated with tooth decay, it does not cause tooth or gum decay. One host passes it to another by direct contact. Hosts provide commensals with food, transportation (a relationship called phoresis), or shelter.

Mutualism

Mutualism is a symbiotic relationship that benefits both members. Examples of mutualism abound in the animal kingdom. Clownfish and sea anemones live together in close association. The anemones protect the clownfish, which, in turn, provide some food to the anemones (figure 14.10*a*). Another example of mutualism is the cleaning of one animal by other animals. In cleaning mutualism, small fishes or invertebrates may swim into the mouth of larger fishes to remove ectoparasites. Characteristic markings and behavior identify cleaner species, which enjoy relative safety in the mouths of predatory species, such as barracudas and groupers (figure 14.10*b*).

Coevolution may occur in any symbiotic relationship. A host species that has a long history of association with a particular parasite may evolve greater resistance to the parasite. Similarly, extremely virulent parasites may kill their host before the parasite has a chance to reproduce. Thus, lower pathogenicity on the part of the parasite is advantageous for most parasites. Commensalistic or mutualistic symbiotic relationships, therefore, tend to be long-standing.

(a)

(b)

FIGURE 14.10

Mutualism. (*a*) Mutualistic relationship between a clownfish (*Amphiprion perideraion*) and a sea anemone. The clownfish provides the anemone with scraps of its food, and the anemone provides the clownfish with protection. Mucus that does not elicit discharge of the anemone's stinging organelles (called nematocysts) apparently covers the clownfish. (*b*) Cleaning symbiosis is a common mutualistic relationship between marine animals. Two gobies are cleaning this Nassau grouper (*Epinephelus striatus*).

Commensalism or mutualism, however, is not a guaranteed outcome for all symbiotic relationships. It may be advantageous for a parasite to kill or weaken its host if perpetuation of a parasite species requires that a host be eaten. For example, certain acanthocephalans are larval parasites of freshwater crustaceans called amphipods and adult parasites of mallard ducks. Mallards acquire infections by eating amphipods. When infected by acanthocephalan larvae, amphipod behavior changes dramatically. Their usual negative phototaxis reverses so that they leave the bottom sub-

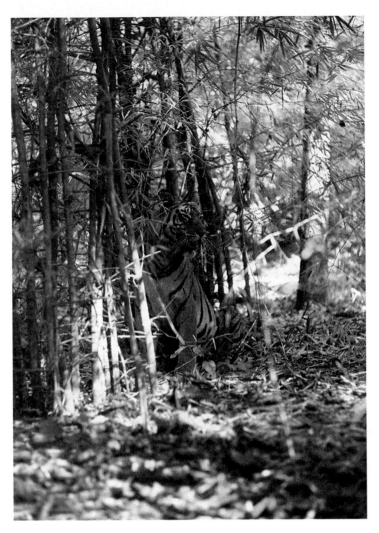

FIGURE 14.11

Camouflage. The color pattern of this tiger (*Panthera tigris*) provides effective camouflage that helps when stalking prey.

strates of a lake or river, and swim near the surface, where they are easy prey for mallard ducks.

OTHER INTERSPECIFIC ADAPTATIONS

Interspecific interactions have shaped many other characteristics of animals. For example, predator-prey systems have led to some unusual adaptations, (e.g., coloration patterns) in either predator or prey species.

Camouflage

Camouflage occurs when an animal's color patterns help hide the animal, or a developmental stage, from another animal. **Cryptic coloration** (L. *crypticus*, hidden) is a type of camouflage that occurs when an animal takes on color patterns in its environment to blend in with the surroundings. Some prey animals are camouflaged to prevent predators from seeing them. For example, the Arctic hare acquires a white coat at its fall molt to blend in with its snowy background. In the spring, however, when the snow melts and exposes bare ground, another molt produces a brown coat.

Countershading is a kind of camouflage common in frog and toad eggs. These eggs are darkly pigmented on top and lightly pigmented on the bottom (*see figure 10.8*). When a bird or other predator views the eggs from above, the dark of the top side hides the eggs from detection against the darkness below. On the other hand, when fish view the eggs from below, the light undersurface blends with the bright air-water interface. Similar countershading occurs in many fish species.

Predators use camouflage to avoid detection by prey. The rufous-red coat overlaid with black stripes that breaks up the outline of a tiger in the forests of India, China, and Persia successfully hides the tiger as it stalks its prey (figure 14.11). Prey species, in turn, use camouflage to avoid detection by predators. Decorator crabs mask themselves with algae and other concealing organisms to blend in with their environment.

Aposematic Coloration and Mimicry

Some animals that protect themselves by being dangerous or distasteful to predators advertise their condition by conspicuous coloration that clearly signals predators to stay away. Certain dendrobatid frogs of Central and South America have toxic secretions in their skin and are brightly colored to warn potential predators (*see box 28.1*). The sharply contrasting white stripe(s) of a skunk and bright colors of poisonous snakes give similar messages. These color patterns are examples of warning or **aposematic coloration** (Gr. *apo*, away from + *sematic*, sign).

Resembling conspicuous animals may also be advantageous. **Mimicry** (L. *mimus*, to imitate) is when a species resembles one, or sometimes more than one, other species and gains protection by the resemblance. **Batesian mimicry** is when one species, called the mimic, resembles a second species, called the model, that is protected by aposematic coloration. One of the many examples of Batesian mimicry are flies belonging to the family Syrphidae. Different species of this family are often given the wary respect that bees and wasps command. Some of the flies are setose (hairy) with yellow and black bands, similar to bees. Other syrphid flies lack setae and are uniformly black, similar to many wasps. Like bees, syrphid flies usually hover around flowers, but they neither bite nor sting. It is easy to distinguish syrphid flies from bees and wasps: All flies have one pair of wings, and bees and wasps have two pairs.

A second form of mimicry, called **Müllerian mimicry,** is when the model and the mimic are both distasteful. A predator does not have to taste both of the species involved to encounter the distasteful form (figure 14.12).

FIGURE 14.12

Müllerian Mimicry. These six species of *Heliconius* are all distasteful to bird predators. A bird that consumes any member of the six species is likely to avoid all six species in the future.

Stop and Ask Yourself

9. What is competitive exclusion? Under what circumstances is coexistence of competing species possible?

10. What is parasitism? How does it differ from commensalism and mutualism? What is coevolution?

11. How might coevolution of parasites and their hosts lead to mutualism?

12. Under what circumstances might it be advantageous for parasites to kill their hosts?

13. What is cryptic coloration? Give an example

14. What is mimicry? What are two forms it can take?

ENDANGERED SPECIES

WILDLIFE ALERT 6—THE IOWA PLEISTOCENE SNAIL *(Discus macclintocki)*

VITAL STATISTICS

Classification: Phylum Mollusca, class Gastropoda, order Pulmonata
Range: Northeast Iowa and northwest Illinois
Habitat: Leaf litter around cave entrances and fissures where ground temperatures remain below 50° C
Number remaining: Unknown
Status: Endangered

NATURAL HISTORY AND ECOLOGICAL STATUS

The Iowa Pleistocene snail is small (8 mm in diameter) with a brown or greenish white shell (figure 1). It lives on the north-facing slope of cool, moist hillsides. It is often found in leaf litter around cave entrances and fissures, where ice persists long into the spring and ground temperatures remain below 50° C all summer. Its habitat is called an "algific talus slope." This snail feeds on the fallen leaves of birch, maple, and dogwood trees. During the winter, it burrows underground and becomes dormant. Breeding begins in March and continues until August. An individual snail lays two to six eggs in the leaf litter, and the eggs hatch in 28 days. A snail lives 5 to 7 years.

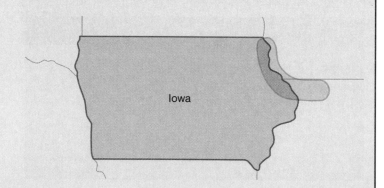

FIGURE 1   Iowa Pleistocene Snail *(Discus macclintocki).*

FIGURE 2   Distribution of Iowa Pleistocene Snail *(Discus macclintocki).*

The Iowa Pleistocene snail is a victim of habitat destruction and climate change. About 75% of this snail's original habitat has been destroyed since 1850. Agriculture, road construction, rock quarrying, and sinkhole filling have all contributed to the decline in snail populations. The long-term cause of the decline of this species is the warming of the climate. This snail is a relic of the Ice Age, and its survival would be much more likely if glacial conditions returned.

Today, these snails are found at only about 20 locations in Iowa and Illinois (figure 2). Landowners and conservation agencies in these states are working together to conserve this snail's habitat.

SUMMARY

1. Many abiotic factors influence where an animal may live. Animals have a tolerance range and a range of optimum for environmental factors.

2. Energy for animal life comes from consuming autotrophs or other heterotrophs. It is expended in excretory, existence, and productive functions.

3. Temperature, water, light, and soils are important environmental factors that influence animal lifestyles.

4. Animal populations change in size over time. Change can be characterized using survivorship curves.

5. Animal populations grow exponentially until the carrying capacity of the environment is achieved, at which point environmental resistance restricts population growth.

6. Density-independent and density-dependent mechanisms regulate populations. Population control mechanisms may prevent some populations from achieving their carrying capacity.

7. Interspecific interactions influence animal populations. These interactions include herbivory, predator-prey interactions, interspecific competition, coevolution, symbiosis, and mimicry.

SELECTED KEY TERMS

autotrophic (p. 192)
carrying capacity (p. 195)
coevolution (p. 198)
energy budget (p. 192)
exponential growth (p. 195)

habitat (p. 192)
heterotrophic (p. 192)
limiting factor (p. 192)
mimicry (p. 201)
symbiosis (p. 198)

CRITICAL THINKING QUESTIONS

1. Explain how a 5 part per million level of dissolved oxygen might be a limiting factor for a fish in the summer but completely suitable for that same fish in the winter.

2. Compare the survivorship curves for human populations of developed and developing countries.

3. Assuming a starting population of five males and five females, a doubling time of 1 month, and no mortality, how many generations would it take a hypothetical population to achieve 10,000 individuals?

4. Why do you think that winter inactivity of many small mammals takes the form of hibernation, whereas winter inactivity in larger mammals is in the form of winter sleep?

5. Are most parasites K-selected or r-selected? Explain.

REFERENCES ON THE WORLD WIDE WEB

1. **Population Ecology.** This site provides links to population ecology information, including people, organizations, meetings, journals, electronic papers, and ecological models.
   http://www.gypsymoth.edu/~sharov/popechrom/welcome.html

2. **Conservation Ecology.** This is an online electronic journal published by the Ecological Society of America.
   http://www.consecol.org//

3. **Ecoweb.** This site contains a wealth of information on all ecological topics and has links to numerous ecology sites, environmental chat lines, and mailing lists.
   http://ecosys.drdr.virginia.edu/EcoWeb.html

4. **EE-Link.** This site is a source of information on endangered species of the United States. It provides species lists sorted by region and taxonomic group, and information on natural history, laws, treaties, and periodicals.
   http://www.nceet.snre.umich.edu/EndSpp/Endangered.html

5. **Endangered Species.** The U.S. Fish and Wildlife Service maintains information on endangered species. This site provides answers to frequently asked questions, information on the Endangered Species Act, and species lists.
   http://www.fws.gov/~r9endspp/endspp.html

6. **WWF's 1994 10 Most Endangered List.** This site describes the World Wildlife Fund's 10 most endangered species, including the factors that threaten each species.
   http://envirolink.org/arrs/endangered.html

ECOLOGY II:
COMMUNITIES AND ECOSYSTEMS

Concepts

1. All populations living in an area make up a community. Communities have unique attributes that ecologists can characterize.
2. Communities and their physical surroundings are called ecosystems. Energy flowing through an ecosystem does not cycle. Energy that comes into an ecosystem must support all organisms living there before it is lost as heat. Nutrients and water, on the other hand, cycle through an ecosystem, and organisms reuse them.
3. The earth can be divided into ecosystem types according to characteristic plants, animals, and physical factors.
4. Concepts of community and ecosystem ecology provide a basis for understanding many ecological problems, including human population growth, pollution, and resource depletion.

Would You Like to Know . . .

1. why we have an energy crisis? (p. 207)

2. why predators, such as hawks and eagles, are relatively uncommon, but other kinds of animals, such as robins and rabbits, are often numerous? (p. 211)

3. where many of the atoms that make up your body tissues were in the years before you were born? (p. 211)

4. one of the earliest natural applications of solar power? (p. 213)

5. whether the earth's current human population can be supported for many years to come? (p. 221)

6. why predators are often the first to feel the effects of poisons released into the environment? (p. 222)

This chapter answers these and other useful questions.

All populations living in an area make up a **community.** If you take off your shoes to explore the animals living in streams, you enter a foreign environment. However, you may have some ideas about what you will find because ecologists have shown that community interactions, even in very different communities, have common themes.

Communities cannot be considered apart from their physical environment. Communities and their physical environments are called **ecosystems,** and by studying ecosystems, ecologists discover how physical surroundings influence communities. A stream community, for example, depends on supplies of carbon, phosphorus, nitrogen, water, and energy. At the same time, however, populations alter their physical environment. Stream animals may reshape the stream by digging into its banks or by moving its substrate. Even in the act of dying, a stream animal changes the characteristics of its environment by contributing organic matter to the streambed.

This chapter examines the interactions in communities and ecosystems. The principles that explain these interactions can help you understand many of today's environmental problems.

COMMUNITY STRUCTURE AND DIVERSITY

Communities are not just random mixtures of species; instead, they have a unique organization. Most communities have certain members that have overriding importance in determining community characteristics. For example, a stream community may have a large population of rainbow trout that helps determine the makeup of certain invertebrate populations on which the trout feed. Species that are responsible for establishing community characteristics are called **dominant species.**

Keystone species are species on which several other species depend. Removal of a keystone species would cause the death of the dependent species. Beavers, for example, construct dams that create a habitat that supports many aquatic species.

Cycles of activity also characterize communities. Stream invertebrates are most active around sunset and sunrise. In other communities, some animals are nocturnal (night active). Nocturnal animals may avoid predators and the hot, dry conditions of the daylight hours. Most birds (except owls), on the other hand, are diurnal (day active) and are dependent on keen vision for gathering food and avoiding predators. Other patterns of activity may follow the seasons, or conditions of temperature and moisture. Daily, seasonal, or other cycles of activity are called a community's temporal structure.

Many communities also have a spatial structure, which is most obvious in the layering that occurs in a forest or a lake. Most photosynthesis occurs in the upper layers of forests and lakes. Animals feeding on this plant life must live in or visit these upper regions. Eventually, organic matter falls to the forest floor or lake bottom, where it supports other organisms.

The variety of animals present in a community, called the **community (species) diversity** or richness, also reflects community structure. Forces of nature and human activities influence community diversity. Factors that promote high diversity include a wide variety of resources, high productivity, climatic stability, moderate levels of predation, and moderate levels of disturbance from outside the community. Pollution often reduces the species diversity of ecosystems.

THE ECOLOGICAL NICHE

The **ecological niche** is an important concept of community structure. The niche of any species includes all the attributes of an animal's lifestyle: where it looks for food, what it eats, where it nests, and what conditions of temperature and moisture it requires. Measuring and plotting the tolerance ranges of an animal for environmental factors allows the construction of a multidimensional image that describes how an animal functions in a community (figure 15.1). Theoretically, competition results when the niches of two species overlap. Although niches overlap in many communities, the effect is minimized as communities mature. Niche overlap may be reduced if a common resource is divided in specific ways. This mechanism is called niche diversification.

Although the niche concept is difficult to quantify, it is valuable for perceiving community structure. It illustrates that community members tend to complement each other in resource use. They tend to partition resources rather than compete for them. The niche concept is also helpful for visualizing the role of an animal in the environment.

COMMUNITY STABILITY

As with individuals, communities are born and they die. Between those events is a time of continual change. Some changes in the life of a community are not permanent. These include the next generation replacing the current one and seasonal fluctuations in the abundance of some animals. Other changes, however, are permanent and directional. Some permanent changes are the result of climatic or geological events. Members of the community are responsible for others. The latter are important for understanding community structure and diversity.

The dominant members of a community often change a community in predictable ways in a process called **succession** (L. *successio,* to follow). Communities may begin in areas nearly devoid of life. For example, geological events, such as the retreat of a glacier, may form a deep, nutrient-poor lake. This lake, however, will not remain in its early postglacial condition forever. Nutrients that can support new life wash into the lake from surrounding hillsides. The first community to become established in an area is called the **pioneer community.** Death, decay, and additional nutrients from the shore provide the raw materials that further enrich the lake. Animals (e.g., lake trout) that require deep, cold water can no longer survive, and

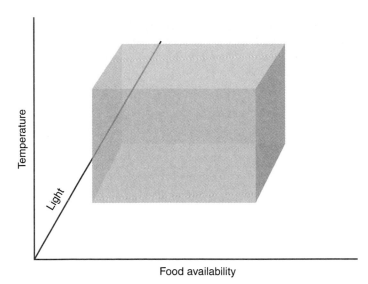

FIGURE 15.1

The Niche as a Multidimensional Space. The niche of an animal includes all aspects of the animal's lifestyle. In this graph, three characteristics of a niche are plotted on a separate axis: food availability, the tolerance range for temperature, and the tolerance range for light. Adding other dimensions, such as food size, rainfall, and reproductive requirements, would better portray the complete niche.

species that live in warmer, shallower waters replace them. Over thousands of years, the lake fills with organic matter and inorganic sediments. Eventually, what was once a lake transforms into a marsh, then a field, and finally a forest. Each successional stage is called a **seral stage,** and the entire successional sequence is a **sere** (ME *seer,* to wither). Succession occurs because the dominant life-forms of a sere gradually make the area less favorable for themselves, but more favorable for organisms of the next successional stage.

The final community (the forest in this example) is the **climax community.** It is different from the seral stages that preceded it because it can tolerate its own reactions. Accumulation of the products of life and death no longer make the area unfit for the individuals living there. Climax communities usually have complex structure and high species diversity. Species of climax communities tend to be *K*-selected. The stability of a climax community generally depends on a stable environment, although moderate, short-lived disturbances are tolerated.

Succession in an area that did not previously support a community is called primary succession. Examples include the establishment of a community on a newly exposed stretch of sandy beach or a new volcanic island (figure 15.2*a*). Succession also may occur in areas that previously supported a community, but where some outside disturbance (e.g., fire) upset the previous community. This kind of succession, called secondary succession, occurs more rapidly than primary succession because some organisms are already living there (figure 15.2*b,c*).

ECOSYSTEMS

This section emphasizes two important facts.   ① First, energy on this planet is not recyclable. Although energy constantly comes to the earth from the sun, once used, energy stored in the earth's energy reserves can never be reused. Second, everything else comes from the planet. Eventually, materials return to the earth for reuse by future generations.

TROPHIC STRUCTURE

An ecosystem must have enough energy to support the activities of all organisms living there. This energy enters an ecosystem as sunlight and is incorporated into the chemical bonds of the molecules within living and decaying tissues (*see figure 4.1*). The sum of all living and decaying tissues in an ecosystem is the **biomass** (Gr. *bios,* life + ME *masse,* to knead). Sooner or later, the energy in the biomass is lost from an ecosystem as heat.

The sequence of organisms through which energy moves in an ecosystem is a **food chain.** One relatively simple food chain might look like the following:

grass → grazing insects → shrews → owls

Complexly interconnected food chains, called **food webs,** that involve many kinds of organisms are more realistic (figure 15.3). Because food webs can be complex, it is convenient to group organisms according to the form of energy used. These groupings are called **trophic levels.**

Producers

Producers (autotrophs) obtain nutrition (complex organic compounds) from inorganic materials and an energy source. They form the first trophic level of an ecosystem. The most familiar producers are green plants. They are called **photoautotrophs** (Gr. *photos,* light + *autos,* self + *trophe,* to feed). Their energy source is the sun, and they convert energy to food through the reactions of photosynthesis. Photosynthesis transforms less than 1% of the sunlight reaching the earth's atmosphere. The rest is reflected

(a)

(c)

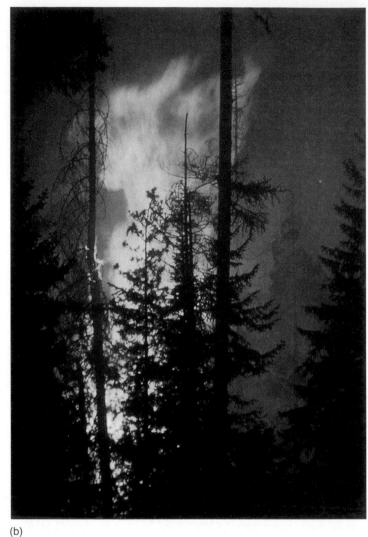

(b)

FIGURE 15.2

Succession. (a) Primary succession on a sand dune. Beach grass is the first species to become established. It stabilizes the dune so that shrubs, and eventually trees, can grow. (b,c) Secondary succession after fires in Yellowstone National Park. The lodgepole pine shown here is a fire-dependent species—that is, the maintenance of a healthy forest of lodgepole pine requires periodic burning (every 60 to 100 years).

back into space by the atmosphere (30%), absorbed by the atmosphere (20%), or absorbed by the earth (50%). The total amount of energy that producers fix is called **gross primary production.** A portion of gross primary production is used for maintenance needs of the producers. The rest, called **net primary production,** is available to other trophic levels.

Producers in a few ecosystems obtain energy other than from the sun and are called **chemolithoautotrophs** (Gr. *chemeai*, to alloy metals + *lithos*, stone + *autos*, self + *trophe*, to feed). They oxidize inorganic compounds to obtain energy. (box 15.1).

Consumers

Other trophic levels are made up of consumers (heterotrophs). Consumers eat other organisms to obtain energy. Herbivores (primary consumers) eat producers. Some carnivores (secondary consumers) eat herbivores, and other carnivores (tertiary consumers) eat the carnivores that ate the herbivores. Consumers also include scavengers that feed on large chunks of dead and decaying organic matter. Scavengers include earthworms and vultures.

Blue whale

Sperm whale

Other toothed whales

Humpback whale

Right whale

Sei whale

Fin whale

Minke whale

Leopard seal

Carnivorous zooplankton

Weddell seal

Squid

Copepods and other herbivorous zooplankton

King and emperor penguins

Crabeater seal

Other penguins

Elephant seal

Phytoplankton, (diatoms), microplankton, and bacteria

Ocean fish

Krill

Albatrosses and petrels

Ross and fur seal

Light, circulation, temperature, and nutrients

Protozoa

Echinodermata

Other birds

Detritus

Crustacea

Bacteria and protozoa

Mollusca

Macroalgae

Other bottom-dwelling animals

L. O'Keefe

Primary production and heterotrophy

Higher trophic levels

FIGURE 15.3

Food Webs. An Antarctic food web. Small crustaceans called krill support nearly all life in Antarctica. Six species of baleen whales, 20 species of squid, over 100 species of fish, 35 species of birds, and 7 species of seals eat krill. Krill feed on algae, protozoa, other small crustaceans, and various larvae. To appreciate the interconnectedness of food webs, trace the multiple paths of energy from light (lower left), through krill, to the leopard seal.

BOX 15.1 HYDROTHERMAL VENT COMMUNITIES

A 1977 Woods Hole Oceanographic Institute expedition to the Galápagos Rift in the Pacific Ocean made what some have called the oceanographic discovery of the century (figure 1a). The rift (an opening made by splitting) is over 2,700 m (over 1.5 mi) below the surface and part of an extensive midoceanic ridge system that develops where the tectonic plates of the earth's crust move apart (*see box 11.2*). In such places, a flow of lava (magma) occasionally emerges, and **hydrothermal vents** spew out hot water rich in hydrogen sulfide and other minerals.

One unusual finding of the expedition was that the life of a vent community is based not on the "rain" of material that the producers in the surface zones generate, but on a rich community of chemolithotrophic bacteria that derive all of the energy they need from the oxidation of inorganic compounds, such as hydrogen sulfide. They live in total darkness because the vents are far below the level of light penetration.

The expedition also noted that clams, crabs, polychaete annelids, and one species (*Riftia pachyptila*) of pogonophoran covered the substrate around each vent (figure 1b). Like other pogonophorans (tube worms), *Riftia* is nourished in part by the endosymbiotic bacteria found in its trophosome (*see endpaper 2*). These bacteria can oxidize hydrogen sulfide to sulfate and reduce carbon dioxide to organic compounds, which nourish both the symbiont and host. The worms' two kinds of hemoglobin carry oxygen and hydrogen sulfide. This chemical bonding keeps these two molecules from reacting in an unproductive fashion before they are delivered to the bacteria. They also protect the host's tissue from the toxic hydrogen sulfide. These vent communities are among the few on earth that do not depend on solar energy for life.

(a)

(b)

FIGURE 1 **Hydrothermal Vent Communities.** (a) The Galápagos Rift is the site of an extensive ocean-bottom community living on inorganic nutrients issuing from hydrothermal vents. (b) Life around these hydrothermal vents in the Galápagos Rift. Tube worms and crabs can be seen close to the vent.

Decomposers

Feeding at any consumer level is never 100% efficient. If herbivores crop 20% of net primary production, 80% is left behind. Eventually, this primary production dies. Thanks to the decomposers, however, leftovers do not accumulate. Decomposers break down dead organisms and feces. Bacteria and fungi perform most of the decomposition by digesting organic matter extracellularly and absorbing the products of digestion. They are said to be saprophytic.

Efficiencies

The efficiency with which the animals of a trophic level convert food into new biomass depends on the nature of the food (figure 15.4). Much of the production of a forest is tied up in inedible, or undigestible, cellulose. On the other hand, a greater proportion of a grassland is available for herbivores. Carnivores are more efficient at assimilation than herbivores because most of a herbivore's biomass is digestible. Further, the efficiency with which

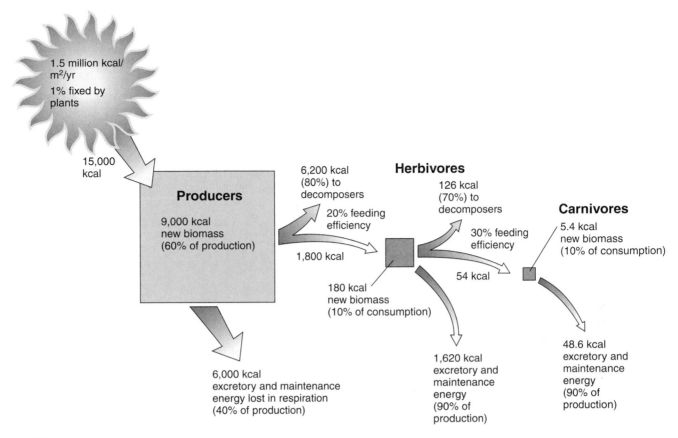

FIGURE 15.4

Energy Flow through Ecosystems. Approximately 1.5 million kcal of radiant energy strike a square meter of the earth's surface each year. Plants convert less than 1% (15,000 kcal/m²/yr) into chemical energy. Of this, approximately 60% is converted into new biomass, and 40% is lost in respiration. The herbivore trophic level harvests approximately 20% of net primary production, and decomposers get the rest. Of the 1,800 kcal moving into the herbivore trophic level, 10% (180 kcal) is converted to new biomass, and 90% (1,620 kcal) is lost in respiration. Carnivores harvest about 30% of the herbivore biomass, and 10% of that is converted to carnivore biomass. At subsequent trophic levels, harvesting efficiencies of about 30% and new biomass production of about 10% can be assumed. All of these percentages are approximations. Absolute values depend on the nature of the primary production (e.g., forest versus grassland) and characteristics of the herbivores and carnivores (e.g., ectothermic versus endothermic).

an animal converts food into new biomass depends on maintenance requirements of the animals involved. Biomass conversion efficiency averages 10%, although efficiencies range from less than 1% for herbivorous endotherms to 35% for carnivorous ectotherms.

Ecological Pyramids

Ecological pyramids express the relationships between trophic levels in a graphic form. A **pyramid of numbers** shows the numbers of individuals at each trophic level of an ecosystem, a **pyramid of biomass** represents the biomass at each trophic level, and a **pyramid of energy** represents the amount of energy tied up in each trophic level (figure 15.5). All of these pyramids have the same shape. The area devoted to each level of the pyramid generally decreases from the producer to the highest consumer levels. ❷ Thus, predators (e.g., hawks and eagles) are much less common than animals such as squirrels and rabbits.

The trophic level concept is useful for visualizing what happens to energy in ecosystems. In real ecosystems, however, trophic levels are difficult to describe. While most producers function only at the first trophic level, most animals function at more than one trophic level. Herbivores often consume insects when they graze, and carnivores move back and forth between secondary and tertiary consumer levels.

CYCLING

Did you ever wonder where the calcium atoms in your bones were 100 or even 100 million years ago? ❸ Perhaps they were in the bones of an ancient reptile or in the sediments of prehistoric seas. Unlike energy, all matter is cycled from nonliving reservoirs to living systems and then back to nonliving reservoirs. Matter moves through ecosystems in **biogeochemical cycles.**

■ Tertiary consumer	15
■ Secondary consumer	100
■ Primary consumer	1.5×10^4
■ Producer	7.2×10^{10}

(a) Pyramid of numbers

0.1
0.66
1.25
17.7

(b) Pyramid of biomass

0.1
1.2
26.8
280

(c) Pyramid of energy

FIGURE 15.5

Ecological Pyramids for Data from an Experimental Pond. (*a*) Pyramid of numbers (individuals/m²). (*b*) Pyramid of biomass (dry g/m²). This figure represents a relatively long time interval. In open-water systems, instantaneous producer biomass is often less than herbivore biomass because producers are small and reproduce rapidly, and consumers are large and live longer. (*c*) Pyramid of energy (dry mg/m²).

Nutrient Cycling

A nutrient is any element essential for life. Approximately 97% of living matter is made of oxygen, carbon, nitrogen, and hydrogen. Gaseous cycles involving these elements use the atmosphere or oceans as a reservoir. Elements such as sulfur, phosphorus, and calcium are less abundant in living tissues than those with gaseous cycles, but they are no less important in sustaining life. The nonliving reservoir for these nutrients is the earth, and the cycles involving these elements are called sedimentary cycles.

Carbon Cycle   Carbon is plentiful on the earth and is rarely a limiting factor. The reservoir for carbon is carbon dioxide (CO_2) in the atmosphere or water. Carbon enters the reservoir when organic matter is oxidized to CO_2. CO_2 is released to the atmosphere or water where autotrophs incorporate it into organic compounds. In aquatic systems, some of the CO_2 combines with water to form carbonic acid ($CO_2 + H_2O \rightleftharpoons H_2CO_3$). Because this reaction is reversible, carbonic acid can supply CO_2 to aquatic plants for photosynthesis when CO_2 levels in the water decrease. Carbonic acid can also release CO_2 to the atmosphere.

Some of the carbon in aquatic systems is tied up as calcium carbonate ($CaCO_3$) in the shells of molluscs and skeletons of echinoderms. Accumulations of mollusc shells and echinoderm skeletons have resulted in limestone formations that are the bedrock of much of the United States. Geological uplift, volcanic activities, and weathering returns much of this carbon to the earth's surface and the atmosphere.

A large supply of carbon is also tied up in fossil fuels. During the 65 million years of the Carboniferous period (which ended about 280 million years ago), organic matter accumulated in peat bogs. Incomplete decomposition and conditions of high temperature and pressure converted this carbon to coal, natural gas, and oil. Since the beginning of the Industrial Revolution (1760), humans have been burning fossil fuels and returning large quantities of this carbon to the atmosphere as CO_2 (figure 15.6).

Nitrogen Cycle   Nitrogen is an essential component of proteins, nucleic acids, and ATP. The reservoir for this nitrogen is the atmosphere, which is about 78% nitrogen (figure 15.7). Gaseous nitrogen, however, is not directly available to most plants. Instead, plants require nitrogen as ammonia (NH_3) or nitrate (NO_3^-). Plants can remove these forms of nitrogen from the soil or water and incorporate them into protein. Animals, of course, get their nitrogen by eating plants or other animals. When animals metabolize proteins and amino acids, they excrete nitrogen as ammonia, urea, or uric acid. The latter two are readily converted to the ammonium ion (NH_4^+). Bacteria convert ammonia and the ammonium ion, in turn, into nitrate and nitrite (NO_2^-) in an energy-yielding reaction called nitrification. Plants then take up nitrites and nitrates and incorporate them into proteins.

In another part of the nitrogen cycle, the nitrogen in nitrates returns to the air as gaseous nitrogen (N_2). Denitrifying bacteria live in anaerobic environments and use nitrates as a source of oxygen for cellular respiration. Denitrifying bacteria are offset by nitrogen fixation. Nitrogen-fixing bacteria (in association with leguminous plants such as soybeans) and cyanobacteria (blue-green algae) convert gaseous nitrogen to nitrates.

Other components of the nitrogen cycle include the industrial production of nitrates, the conversion by lightning of N_2 to nitrates, and volcanic activities that release nitrates from the earth's crust.

Other Nutrient Cycles   Phosphorus is an essential component of DNA, RNA, ATP, and vertebrate skeletons. Its cycle involves a sedimentary reservoir that contains about 0.000003% phosphorus. Animals acquire phosphorus in their diet, and phosphorus returns to the soil in excretion and decay. Mining operations remove phosphates from the soil for the production of fertilizers and detergents. Overuse of these can promote algal growth in rivers and lakes. Algal overgrowth leads to increased decomposition, oxygen depletion, and the early death of waterways.

Sulfur is found in elemental form in the earth's crust and as sulfate (SO_2) in the atmosphere. It is an essential component of amino acids but is rarely limiting. Animals acquire sulfur from plants, which extract it from the soil. Decaying plants and animals produce hydrogen sulfide and sulfate, and return sulfur to the soil. The burning of high-sulfur coal also sends sulfate into the atmosphere.

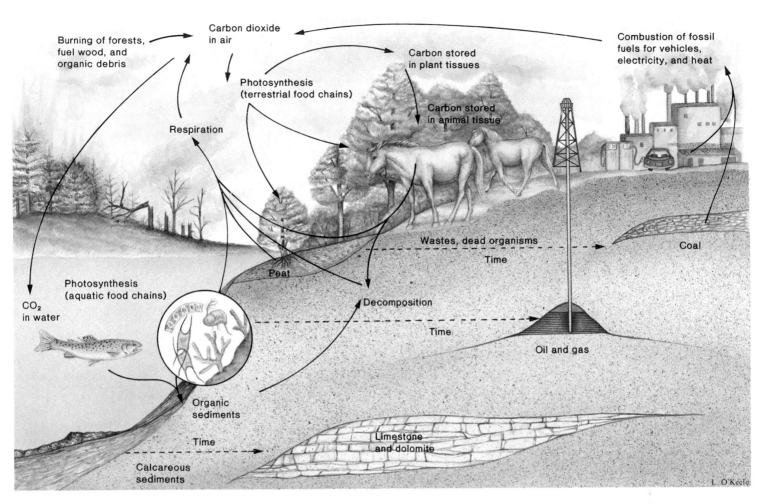

FIGURE 15.6

Carbon Cycle. Carbon cycles between its reservoir in the atmosphere, living organisms, fossil fuels, and limestone bedrock.

Calcium is essential for muscle contraction, bone formation, nerve impulse conduction, and many other animal functions. The reservoir for calcium is the earth's crust (limestone beds) and the oceans. Animals acquire calcium in food and water, and return it to the soil in death, decay, and excretion.

Human activities disrupt biogeochemical cycles. For example, the mining of phosphates for fertilizers increases the rate at which phosphates are lost through terrestrial runoff to ocean depths. Activities such as these can lead to serious shortages of some nutrients.

Water Cycling

Water has one of the most basic of all cycles. Water moves between land, oceans, and the atmosphere. Oceans contain 97% of the earth's water, and water that evaporates from oceans eventually falls as rain, snow, ice, or fog. Evaporation from soil or leaves returns some water that falls on land to the atmosphere. Other water is temporarily absorbed in the soil. Rain that does not evaporate or contribute to groundwater runs off into lakes and streams. Eventually, streams make their way to rivers, and rivers to oceans.

In completing its cycle, water is a powerful force. It sculpts the land, transports nutrients to the sea, and powers electric generators. ④ The water cycle, called the **hydrological cycle,** is one of the earliest forms of solar power because it is powered entirely by sun-induced evaporation from the oceans.

Stop and Ask Yourself

5. What is the source of energy for individuals at the producer trophic level? What is the source of energy for individuals at the secondary consumer trophic level?

6. Approximately what portion of the energy intake at one trophic level is converted into biomass at that trophic level? What happens to the rest of the energy?

7. What is the main reservoir for carbon in the carbon cycle?

8. What do nitrogen-fixing bacteria do?

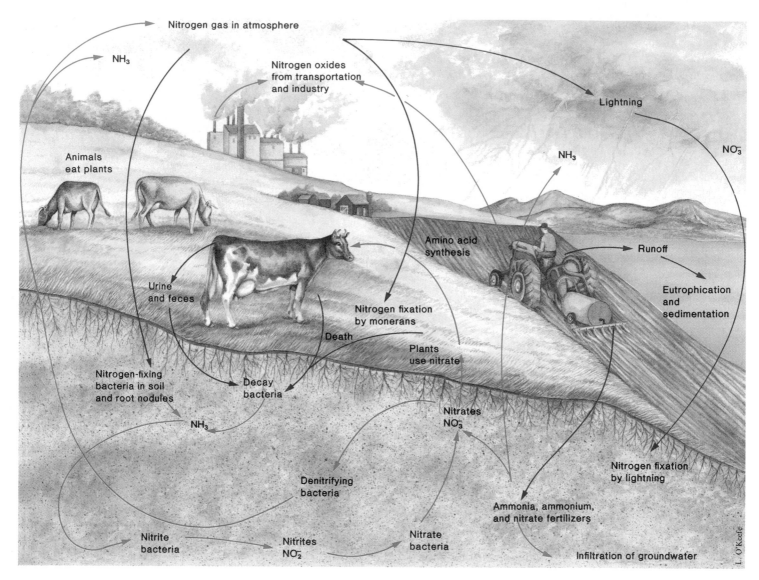

FIGURE 15.7

Nitrogen Cycle. Nitrogen cycles between its reservoir in the atmosphere and living organisms. Nitrogen fixation converts gaseous nitrogen to nitrogen in nitrates. Red arrows show the pathways by which nitrogen accumulates as ammonia in the soil. Blue arrows show the conversion of ammonia to nitrites, nitrates, and eventually, nitrogen gas.

ECOSYSTEMS OF THE EARTH

Characteristic plants, animals, and physical factors divide the earth into ecosystem types. Terrestrial ecosystems are divided into distinctive associations of plant and animal populations called **biomes** (figure 15.8). Biomes have certain geographical boundaries, but different parts of the world with similar climatic and geographical features have similar biome types. Aquatic ecosystems are subdivided into freshwater and marine ecosystems, each of which is further subdivided.

TERRESTRIAL ECOSYSTEMS

Tundra exists in two forms in North America. Arctic tundra occurs in the far northern reaches of North America (figure 15.9). For most of the year, snow and ice cover it. A short summer provides only about 60 days during which mosses, lichens, grasses, and shrubs can grow. No trees occur here. Precipitation is a scanty 25 cm/year, yet the summer soils are wet and boggy. Just below the surface of the ground is a permanently frozen subsoil called permafrost. Productivity is low. The animal life of arctic

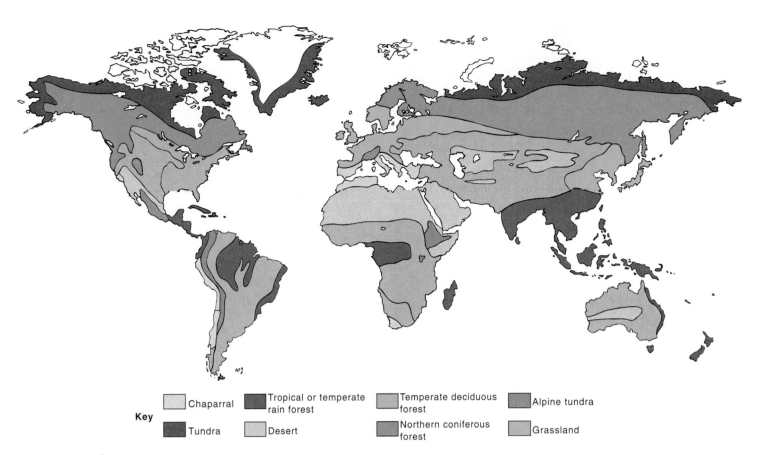

FIGURE 15.8

Biomes of the World. Biomes are distinctive associations of plant and animal populations that climatic and geographical features dictate.

tundra consists of rodents, musk oxen, caribou, owls, foxes, and weasels.

Alpine tundra occurs in mountains, above the altitude at which trees grow. Widely fluctuating temperatures, moderate precipitation, grasses, and shrubs characterize this ecosystem.

Northern coniferous forests are characterized by cool summers, cold winters, short (130-day) growing seasons, and moderate precipitation (40 to 100 cm/year). Most of the precipitation comes in the form of heavy winter snows. Soils are acidic and relatively infertile. Plants characteristic of the northern coniferous forests are spruce, fir, and pine. Because coniferous forests are "evergreen," some limited primary production can occur on warmer winter days. Pine needles that accumulate on the forest floor are slow to decompose, and fire is important in promoting seed germination and release of nutrients locked in the pine needles. The diversity of animals in northern coniferous forests is not great, although population sizes can be large. Insects abound in the summer months, and other residents include snowshoe hares, lynx, wolves, caribou, and moose (figure 15.10).

Temperate deciduous forests occur in regions with moderate climate and well-defined summer and winter seasons. Precipitation ranges from 75 to 150 cm/year, and soils are relatively fertile. Deciduous trees, which lose their leaves in fall, dominate these forests. Decomposition of fallen leaves enriches forest soils. Vertical stratification of temperate deciduous forests is well developed, with most production occurring in the tops of the trees (the forest canopy). Insects are the most common herbivores, and white-tailed deer are the largest herbivores (figure 15.11). Carnivores of temperate deciduous forests include wolves and mountain lions, although the numbers and distributions of these carnivores today are greatly reduced.

The **grasslands** of North America are called prairies. Similar ecosystems in South America and Africa are called tropical savannas. A few scattered trees may be present in grasslands, but grasses, such as big and little bluestem, predominate. The nature of the vegetation of a grassland depends on the amount of moisture. Moist prairies in North America are called tall-grass prairies, and drier prairies are called short-grass prairies. As in northern coniferous forests, fire plays a role in maintaining grasslands by

FIGURE 15.9

Biomes—Arctic Tundra. Mosses, lichens, grasses, and shrubs dominate arctic tundra. Animal life includes rodents, caribou (*Rangifer caribou*, shown here), musk oxen, owls, weasels, and arctic foxes.

FIGURE 15.10

Biomes—Northern Coniferous Forests. Spruce and fir trees dominate northern coniferous forests. Animal life includes snowshoe hares, wolves, and moose (*Alces americanus*, shown here).

killing trees and shrubs that recover from disturbance slowly. Because much of the primary production of a grassland dies each year, organic matter accumulates quickly in grassland soils. The fertile soils of the prairies of North America have been exploited for agricultural purposes, and few tracts of virgin prairie remain.

Because most of their primary production is edible, grasslands support large populations of herbivores, such as numerous insects and bison (figure 15.12).

Chaparral occurs in relatively dry (30 to 75 cm of rain per year) areas of the world, including the southwestern United States. Most precipitation comes during the winter, and temperatures fluctuate between 13 and 23° C. Plants of the chaparral are low and shrubby, and have tough, waxy leaves. Animals include insects, rodents, rabbits, lizards, snakes, and mule deer (figure 15.13). The chaparral is another ecosystem in which fire is an important regulator of plant and animal populations.

Deserts occur around the world between the latitudes of 30° N and 30° S. Rainfall is less than 25 cm/year. Temperatures fluctuate widely; they are high during daylight hours and low at nighttime. Plants of very hot deserts are predominantly cacti and desert shrubs. Sagebrush characterizes cooler deserts. Animals of the desert include birds, rodents, reptiles, numerous insects, and other arthropods (figure 15.14). The evolution of desert animals has involved delicate compromises between the needs for evaporative cooling and water-based excretion, and the need to conserve water.

Tropical rain forests are found, among other places, in the equatorial regions of Central America and northern South Amer-

FIGURE 15.12

Biomes—Grasslands. Grasses such as bluestem dominate North American grasslands and once provided abundant food for grazing animals, such as bison *(Bison bison)*.

FIGURE 15.11

Biomes—Temperate Deciduous Forests. Temperate deciduous forests provide beautiful landscapes in the fall. Animal life includes white-tailed deer *(Odocoileus virginianus)*.

ica. Their temperatures fluctuate between 20 and 25° C, and rainfall approaches 200 cm/year. Because of the high moisture, high temperatures, and the 12-month growing season, nutrients cycle rapidly. Soils of tropical rain forests are relatively poor in nutrients because most of the nutrients are tied up in organisms. Life-forms of tropical rain forests are diverse. Trees are broad-leaved and non-deciduous, and the forest is highly stratified. A nearly complete forest canopy creates a densely shaded forest floor. The rich diversity of plant life creates diverse food and habitat resources for animals. The stable temperatures and high humidity create ideal conditions for both soft- and hard-bodied ectothermic animals; therefore, populations of annelids, arthropods, amphibians, and reptiles abound (figure 15.15).

AQUATIC ECOSYSTEMS

Aquatic environments are divided into freshwater and marine ecosystems, both of which have diverse habitats.

FIGURE 15.13

Biomes—Chaparral. Chaparral occurs in the southwestern United States. It is characterized by low, shrubby vegetation and animals such as mule deer *(Odocoileus hemionus,* shown here), rodents, rabbits, and many reptiles.

FIGURE 15.14

Biomes—Deserts. Cacti and desert shrubs dominate deserts. Desert animal life includes birds, rodents, and numerous species of reptiles and arthropods, such as this giant hairy desert scorpion (*Hadrurus arizonensis*).

Freshwater Ecosystems

Freshwater ecosystems are classified according to water flow. **Lotic ecosystems** include brooks, streams, and rivers in which water is flowing. Attached aquatic plants and algae provide some of the primary production of streams. However, most of the primary production for lotic ecosystems comes from surrounding terrestrial habitats as runoff during rains and autumn leaf falls. Because most lotic ecosystems are relatively shallow and have long shorelines, terrestrial production is more than adequate to supply energy needs. Lotic ecosystems typically have high oxygen levels. Water flowing over rocks, logs, and other objects causes turbulence that oxygenates the water. Numerous aquatic insects and other invertebrates divide resources. Some shred larger pieces of plant matter. Others, such as blackfly larvae and caddisfly larvae, filter floating microscopic debris from the water. Predators include numerous species of fish, as well as insects, such as stonefly larvae and dobsonfly larvae.

Current is probably the most important physical factor in lotic habitats. Some animals are strong swimmers, capable of negotiating rapids and waterfalls. Others retreat from the current by living on or in the substrate. The latter are called **benthic** (Gr. *benthos*, depth of the sea) **animals.** Many stream insects display adaptations for living in moving water. Adaptations include streamlining, flattening, and ballasting themselves with pebbles (figure 15.16).

Lentic ecosystems, including lakes and ponds, have standing water. Vertical stratification of lakes is common, especially in temperate regions. In the summer, the upper regions (the epilimnion) of a lake warm quickly. Because the deeper water (the hypolimnion) is cool, and because cool water is denser than warm

FIGURE 15.15

Biomes—Tropical Rain Forests. Tropical rain forests have a great variety of plant and animal species. The forest's interior is dark and moist, and is the last refuge on earth for many animals, such as this morpho butterfly (*Morpho achillaena*).

water, mixing between upper and lower levels of the water column is prevented. Photosynthesis (and thus oxygen production) occurs only in the upper levels of a lake because water filters light with increasing depth. The main reactions occurring in the depths of a lake are those of decomposition. The deepest parts of a lake are often depleted of oxygen in the summer. In the fall, however, the surface waters cool, and winds cause mixing of the entire water column in what is called turnover. In the winter, the water again becomes layered under the ice, but winds and temperature changes cause another turnover in the spring.

In contrast to lotic ecosystems, a much greater share of the production for lentic ecosystems occurs in the body of water. Most of this production is from microscopic algae floating near the surface. Organisms that swim or float in surface waters and are at the mercy of wind, waves, and current are a part of the **planktonic**

FIGURE 15.16

Lotic Ecosystems. Stream insects display a great variety of adaptations for living in moving water. This mayfly nymph (*Siphlonisca aerodromia*) shows streamlining and flattening, which allow the insect to maintain itself in strong currents.

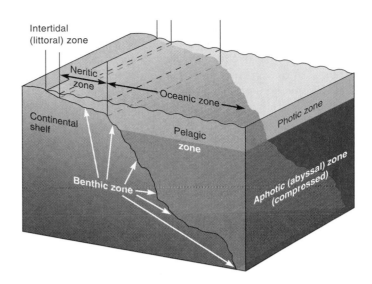

FIGURE 15.17

Marine Ecosystems. Diagrammatic section of an ocean, showing the distribution of major marine ecosystems.

(Gr. *planktos,* to wander) community. Deep, cold lakes that are nutrient-poor and relatively unproductive are oligotrophic. Shallow, warm, nutrient-rich lakes are highly productive and are eutrophic. Succession in a lake, called **eutrophication,** was described earlier. Adding nutrients to a lake from fertilizers and other sources greatly increases the rate of eutrophication.

Other freshwater ecosystems include wet grassland areas called marshes, wet woodland areas called swamps, and peat bogs. They occur where the water table is near the surface of the land. Freshwater wetlands are important as hatcheries and rearing grounds for wildlife.

Marine Ecosystems

The most important physical characteristic that distinguishes marine ecosystems from freshwater ecosystems is the salinity of the water. Marine ecosystems have water containing a mixture of salts, which make up 3.5% of the mass of a quantity of seawater. This section briefly examines five marine ecosystems: estuaries, intertidal (littoral) zones, neritic zones, oceanic zones, and coral reefs.

Estuaries occur where freshwater meets seawater, and the salinity of seawater is diluted. Estuaries are productive because freshwater streams carry nutrients into the estuary, and tidal currents bring nutrients from the ocean. The primary producers in estuaries include plankton, larger attached aquatic vegetation, and emergent vegetation, such as cordgrass. Herbivores and decomposers feed on this production, and find refuge in it. Estuarine ecosystems are nursery grounds for many marine fishes, molluscs, and crustaceans. They are also important feeding grounds for wading and swimming birds.

Humans have drained and filled estuaries to develop subdivisions and condominiums, and have excavated estuaries to harbor pleasure boats. Estuaries have also been polluted by oil explorations and drilling. Acid rain threatens their productivity. In recent years, these activities have been slowed, but not stopped.

Intertidal (littoral) zones extend from the splash zone of ocean waves to the low tide marks (figure 15.17). These regions are subject to the actions of both waves and tides (figure 15.18). In the splash zone, most water comes from splashing waves, and snails like the periwinkles (*Littorina* spp.) dominate.

Animals use a variety of strategies to survive during low tide. More motile animals, such as fish and some crabs, move in and out of intertidal zones with the tides. Other animals, such as amphipods, isopods, ghost crabs, and numerous polychaetes, burrow beneath the sand and mud of the intertidal areas. A shovelful of intertidal sand and mud reveals thousands of hidden residents. Yet other inhabitants of the intertidal zone are in tidal pools. Small basins in the rock may be completely submerged at high tide, but exposed at low tide. Water trapped in tidepools by ebbing tides supports a rich animal life, including numerous echinoderms, barnacles, limpets, and chitons. Attached animals withstand periods of exposure by closing their shells to avoid drying.

Neritic ecosystems consist of relatively shallow water that extends from the littoral zone to the edge of the continental shelves. Oceanic currents bring nutrient-rich bottom waters to the surface, where they stimulate photosynthesis by planktonic algae (phytoplankton). In some communities, attached algae, such as the vast kelp beds of the north Pacific, are locally important in contributing to primary production. Animals that live in or on the substrate include crabs, sponges, echinoderms, corals, and polychaetes. These animals inhabit the benthic zone. The pelagic zone is the water above the substrate. Swimming and planktonic animals inhabit this zone. Animal members of the plankton (zooplankton) include the numerous crustaceans and larval stages of barnacles, echinoderms, and polychaetes. Neritic zones support some of the largest vertebrate predators and provide food for human consumption.

Oceanic ecosystems extend from the continental shelves into the relatively unproductive open ocean. Virtually all primary production in the open ocean occurs in the upper waters, a region called the photic zone. Phytoplankton again forms the base of the food web. The aphotic (abyssal) zone below 200 m is always dark. Life at these depths is dependent on production from the surface waters drifting to great depths. (The vent communities of the ocean floor are an exception that was described earlier; *see box 15.1.*) Animals found at these great depths may have luminescent organs that serve as searchlights, lures for prey, and sexual attractants.

In some parts of the world, upwelling zones provide the highest productivity of all marine ecosystems. In these areas (e.g., off the coasts of California and Peru), surface currents carry water away from the shore, and nutrient-rich water rises from the depths to take its place. Nutrients in this water promote high rates of primary production, supporting some of the world's greatest fisheries.

Coral reefs are one of the most highly productive ecosystems in the world. They are associations of stony corals (phylum Cnidaria, class Anthozoa) and algae (called coralline algae and zooxanthellae). Reefs form over thousands of years in warm, clear, relatively shallow waters. The greatest depth at which they can grow is between 50 and 60 m. Below this depth, light is insufficient to support the growth of the zooxanthellae necessary for reef formation (*see box 18.2*).

Stop and Ask Yourself

9. What are the physical characteristics, dominant plants, and dominant animals of northern coniferous forests?

10. What are the physical characteristics, dominant plants, and dominant animals of tropical rain forests?

11. What is the source of most nutrients entering lotic ecosystems?

12. What is a definition for the following terms: (*a*) benthic animals, (*b*) planktonic, (*c*) intertidal (littoral) zone, (*d*) neritic ecosystem, and (*e*) oceanic ecosystem?

FIGURE 15.18

Marine Ecosystems—The Intertidal Zone. Many members of the intertidal zone survive periods of low tide in water trapped in tidepools. These tidepools make rich habitats for exploration.

ECOLOGICAL PROBLEMS

In the last few hundred years, humans have attempted to provide for the needs and wants of a growing human population. In the search for longer and better lives, however, humans have lost a sense of being a part of the world's ecosystems. Now that you have studied some general ecological principles, it should be easier to understand many of the ecological problems.

HUMAN POPULATION GROWTH

An expanding human population is the root of most environmental problems. Human populations, like those of other animals, tend to grow exponentially. The earth, like any ecosystem on it, has a carrying capacity and a limited supply of resources. When human populations achieve that carrying capacity, populations should stabilize. If they do not stabilize in a fashion that limits human misery, then war, famine, and/or disease is sure to take care of the problem.

5 What is the earth's carrying capacity? The answer is not simple. In part, it depends on the desired standard of living and on whether or not resources are distributed equally among all populations. Currently, the earth's population stands at 5.8 billion people. Virtually all environmentalists agree that number is too high if all people are to achieve the affluence of developed countries.

Unless intense efforts are made to curb population growth, world populations could double in the next 50 years. Looking at the age characteristics of world populations helps to explain why human populations will grow rapidly. The **age structure** of a population shows the proportion of a population that is in prereproductive, reproductive, and postreproductive classes. Age structure is often represented by an age pyramid. Figure 15.19 shows an age pyramid for a developed country and for a developing country. In developing countries, the age pyramid has a broad base, indicating high birthrates. As in many natural populations, high infant mortality offsets these high birthrates. However, what happens when developing countries begin accumulating technologies that reduce prereproductive mortality and prolong the life of the elderly? Unless reproductive practices change, a population explosion occurs. Unfortunately, cultural practices change slowly, and there has been a reluctance to use modern birth control practices.

In developed countries, population growth is slower, and the proportion of the population in each reproductive class is balanced. Birthrates in the United States have decreased in recent years because of the use of modern birth control practices. In spite of decreased birthrate, the U.S. population, now at about 265 million, is still growing. Immigration is currently the biggest factor influencing population growth in the United States. If 2 million legal and illegal immigrants arrive per year, then the U.S. population may increase to 500 million by 2050. Given the current standard of living, even 200 million people living in the United States is too many. Homelessness, hunger, resource depletion, and pollution all stem from trying to support too many people at the current standard of living.

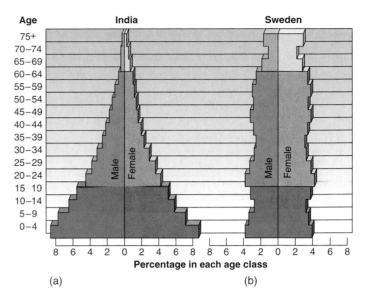

FIGURE 15.19

Human Age Pyramids. (a) In developing countries, a greater proportion of the population is in the prereproductive age classes. High mortality in that age class compensates for high birthrates. As technologies reduce infant mortality and prolong the life span of the elderly, populations increase rapidly. (b) In developed countries, the age structure is more rectangular because of reduced mortality in all age classes. Age classes are divided into prereproductive (lower), reproductive (middle), and postreproductive (upper) cohorts. *Source: Robert Leo Smith,* The Ecology of Man, *2d ed., copyright 1976 Harper & Row, 1976.*

POLLUTION

Pollution is any detrimental change in an ecosystem. Most kinds of pollution are the results of human activities. Large human populations and demands for increasing goods and services compound pollution problems. Previous sections on ecosystem productivity and nutrient cycling in this chapter should clarify why these problems exist.

Water pollution takes many forms. Industries generate toxic wastes, heat, and plastics, some of which will persist for centuries. Every household in the world generates human wastes for disposal. All too often, industrial and human wastes find their ways into groundwater, streams, lakes, and oceans. When they do, water becomes unfit for human consumption and unfit for wildlife.

Air pollution also presents serious problems. Burning fossil fuels releases sulfur dioxide and nitrogen oxides into the atmosphere. Sulfur dioxide and water combine to produce sulfuric acid, which falls as **acid deposition.** Acid deposition lowers the pH of lakes, often many kilometers from the site of sulfur dioxide production. Carbon dioxide released in burning fuels is accumulating in the atmosphere, causing the **greenhouse effect.** Carbon dioxide reflects solar radiation back to the earth. This reflection of solar radiation is predicted to cause an increase in world temperature, polar ice caps to melt, and ocean levels to rise. The release of chlorinated fluorocarbons from aerosol cans, air conditioners, and refrigerators contributes to the depletion of the earth's ultraviolet filter—the atmospheric ozone layer. As a result, the incidence of skin cancer is likely to increase.

When wastes and poisons enter food webs, organisms at the highest trophic levels usually suffer the most. ⑥ Tiny amounts of a toxin incorporated into primary production can quickly build up as carnivores feed on herbivores that have concentrated toxins in their tissues. This problem is especially severe when the material is not biodegradable (not broken down by biological processes). The accumulation of matter in food webs is called **biological magnification.**

RESOURCE DEPLETION AND BIODIVERSITY

Other environmental problems arise because humans have been too slow to realize that an ecosystem's energy is used only once. When a quantity of energy is lost to outer space as heat, it is gone from the earth forever.

As with energy, human populations are also squandering other resources. Overgrazing and deforestation have led to the spread of deserts. Exploitation of tropical rain forests has contributed to the extinction of many plant and animal species.

The variety of living organisms in an ecosystem is called **biodiversity.** No one knows the number of species in the world. About 1.4 million species have been described, but taxonomists estimate that there are 4 to 30 million more. Much of this unseen, or unnoticed, biodiversity is unappreciated for the free services it performs. Forests hold back flood waters and recycle CO_2 and nutrients. Insects pollinate crops and control insect pests, and subterranean organisms promote soil fertility through decomposition. Many of these undescribed species would, when studied, provide new food crops, petroleum substitutes, new fibers, and pharmaceuticals. All of these functions require not

just remnant groups but large, healthy populations. Large populations promote the genetic diversity required for surviving environmental changes. When genetic diversity is lost, it is lost forever. Heroic attempts to save endangered species come far too late. Even when they succeed, they salvage only a tiny portion of an original gene pool.

The biodiversity of all natural areas of the world is threatened. Acid rain, pollution, urban development, and agriculture know no geographic or national boundaries. The main threats to biological diversity arise from habitat destruction by expanding human populations. Humans are either directly or indirectly exploiting about 40% of the earth's net primary production. Often, this involves converting natural areas to agricultural uses, frequently substituting less efficient crop plants for native species. Habitat loss displaces thousands of native plants and animals.

Some of the most important threatened natural areas include tropical rain forests, coastal wetlands, and coral reefs. Of these, tropical rain forests have probably received the most attention. Tropical rain forests cover only 7% of the earth's land surface, but they contain more than 50% of the world's species. Tropical rain forests are being destroyed rapidly, mostly for agricultural production. About 76,000 km^2 (an area larger than Costa Rica) is being cleared each year (*see figure 1.9*). At current rates of destruction, most tropical rain forests will be gone in the twenty-first century. According to some estimates, 17,500 rain forest species are lost each year. Clearing of tropical rain forests achieves little because the thin, nutrient-poor soils of tropical rain forests are exhausted within 2 years (figure 15.20). Sadly, rain forests are a nonrenewable resource. Seeds of rain forest plants germinate rapidly, but seedlings are unprotected on sterile, open soils. Even if a forest were able to become reestablished, it would take many centuries to return to a climax rain forest.

The problems of threatened biodiversity have solutions, but none of the solutions is quick and easy. First, more money needs to be appropriated for training taxonomists and ecologists, and for supporting their work. Second, all countries of the world need to realize that biodiversity, when preserved and managed properly, is a source of economic wealth. Third, the world needs a system of international ethics that values natural diversity for the beauty it brings to human lives. Anything short of these steps will surely lead to severe climatic changes and mass starvation.

FIGURE 15.20

Tropical Deforestation. Severe erosion quickly followed the removal of the tropical rain forest on these slopes in Madagascar.

Stop and Ask Yourself

13. What is an age pyramid? How do age pyramids help predict future population trends?

14. What is acid deposition? What kinds of pollutants contribute to its formation?

15. Why are chlorinated fluorocarbons thought to contribute to skin cancer?

16. Why do poisons in the food web often affect higher trophic levels most severely?

Summary

1. All populations living in an area make up a community.
2. Dominant members, cycles of activity, and the variety of organisms present characterize communities.
3. Organisms have roles in their community. The niche concept helps ecologists visualize those roles.
4. Communities often change in predictable ways. Successional changes often lead to a stable climax community.
5. Energy that supports ecosystem reactions is not recyclable. Energy that is fixed by producers is eventually lost as heat.
6. Unlike energy, nutrients and water cycle through ecosystems. Cycles involve movements of material from nonliving reservoirs in the atmosphere or the earth to biological systems and back to the reservoirs again.
7. The earth is divided into ecosystem types according to characteristic plants, animals, and physical factors. Terrestrial ecosystems are called biomes. Aquatic ecosystems are subdivided into freshwater and marine ecosystems.
8. Human population growth is the root of most environmental problems. Trying to support too many people at the standard of living present in developed countries has resulted in air and water pollution and resource depletion.
9. Pollution and resource depletion are important environmental problems that threaten life. Human activities are reducing the biodiversity of the world.

Selected Key Terms

biodiversity (p. 222)
biogeochemical cycles (p. 211)
biomes (p. 214)
community (p. 206)
ecological niche (p. 206)
ecosystems (p. 206)

food webs (p. 207)
net primary production (p. 208)
photoautotrophs (p. 207)
succession (p. 206)
trophic levels (p. 207)

Critical Thinking Questions

1. What is the usefulness of the ecological niche concept?
2. Which of the following would be a more energetically efficient strategy for supplying animal protein for human diets? Explain your answers.
   a. Feeding people beef raised in feedlots on grain, or feeding people beef that has been raised in pastures.
   b. Feeding people sardines and herrings, or processing sardines and herrings into fishmeal that is subsequently used to raise poultry, which is used to feed people.
3. Explain why the biomass present at one trophic level of an ecosystem decreases at higher trophic levels.
4. What is the role of fire in grassland and coniferous forest ecosystems? Should fires on lands that the U.S. Park Service manages be allowed to burn themselves out?
5. Why are wetlands and estuaries important ecosystems?

References on the World Wide Web

1. **Biodiversity and Biological Collections Web Server.**   This site provides a journal, announcements, news, and access to ecological newsletters. It also provides ecological information organized by animal taxonomic group.

   http://muse.bio.cornell.edu/

2. **The Association for Tropical Biology.**   This site provides links to meeting announcements, publications, and a table of contents for recent issues of the journal *Biotropica*.

   http://ecolog.ums/edu/atb/

3. **Ecological Society of America.**   This site presents news, environmental policy updates, a newsletter, ESA press releases, and membership information.

   http://www.sdsc.edu/~ESA/ESA.html

4. **Green Web Directory.**   This site, maintained by the World Wildlife Fund, provides links to environmental Internet sites and the capability to search for information by topic. Links to information on climate and climate change, water resources, endangered species, and other ecological topics are also provided.

   http://www.panda.org/index/netindex.htm

5. **Kennedy Space Center (KSC) Ecological Resources Home Page.** This site provides highlights of ecological programs of the Kennedy Space Center.

   http://atlas.ksc.nasa.gov/env.html

6. **National Wildlife Federation.**   This site, maintained by the National Wildlife Federation, provides an environmental hotline and presents information on pending legislation concerning environmental issues. It also provides classroom activities and games for kids.

   http://www.nwf.org/nwf/

7. **Great Lakes Natural Resource Center.**   This site provides information on environmental issues regarding the Great Lakes.

   http://greatlakes.nwf.org/glnrc.htm

8. **Aquatic Ecology Page.**   This site provides information on organizations that focus on aquatic ecology. Links to other sites can be used to look up information on particular aquatic animals.

   http://www2.netdoor.com/~pinky/aquatic.htm

9. **North American Benthological Society (NABS).**   This site is maintained by NABS and answers the question, "What is benthos"? It provides links to recent papers that NABS members have published, tutorials, and conservation topics.

   http://www.inhs.uiuc.edu/nabs/nabs.htm

10. **U.S. Census Bureau.**   This site provides the latest U.S. census statistics, news, and economic indicators.

    http://www.census.gov/

11. **Statistics.**   This site provides links to the latest world and U.S. population statistics.

    http://www.magpage.com/~davidson/stats.html

Suggested Readings
Books

Alcock, J. 1989. *Animal Behavior.* Sunderland, Mass.: Sinauer Associates.

Brewer, R. 1994. *The Science of Ecology.* 2d ed. Philadelphia: Saunders College Publishing.

Hunt, C. E. 1988. *Down by the River: The Impact of Federal Water Projects and Policies on Biological Diversity.* Washington, D.C.: Island Press.

Kennedy, I. R. 1988. *Acid Soil and Acid Rain*. Champaign, Ill.: Research Studies Press.

Krebs, C. J. 1985. *Ecology: The Experimental Analysis of Distribution and Abundance*. New York: Harper & Row.

Manning, A., and Partridge, L. 1992. *An Introduction to Animal Behaviour*. New York: Cambridge University Press.

Norton, B. G. 1988. *The Preservation of Species: The Value of Biological Diversity*. Princeton, Mass.: Princeton University Press.

Shair, H. N., Barr, G. A., and Hofer, M. A. 1991. *Developmental Psychology: New Methods and Changing Concepts*. New York: Oxford University Press.

Trivers, R. 1985. *Social Evolution*. Menlo Park, Calif.: Benjamin Cummings.

Wilson, E. O. 1975. *Sociobiology: The New Synthesis*. Cambridge, Mass.: Belknap Press.

Wilson, E. O., ed. 1988. *Biodiversity*. Washington, D.C.: National Academy Press.

ARTICLES

Axelrod, R., and Hamilton, W. D. 1981. The evolution of cooperation. *Science* 211: 1390–96.

Bertness, M. D. 1992. The ecology of a New England salt marsh. *American Scientist* 80(3): 260–68.

Bongaarts, J. 1994. Can the growing human population feed itself? *Scientific American*, March.

Bray, F. 1994. Agriculture for developing nations. *Scientific American*, July.

Charlson, R. J. 1994. Sulfate aerosol and climatic change. *Scientific American*, February.

Dasgupta, P. S. 1995. Population, poverty and the local environment. *Scientific American*, February.

Denny, M. 1995. Survival in the surf zone. *American Scientist* 83(2): 166–73.

Edmunds. P. J. 1996. Ten days under the sea. *Scientific American*, October.

Energy for planet earth. 1990. *Scientific American*, September (special issue).

Fingeman, M., ed. 1988. Energetics and animal behavior (a symposium). *American Zoologist* 28(3): 813–938.

Gould, J., and Marler, P. 1987. Learning by instinct. *Scientific American*, January.

Greenspan, R. J. 1995. Understanding the genetic construction of behavior. *Scientific American*, April.

Harden, G. 1986. Cultural carrying capacity: A biological approach to human problems. *BioScience* 36: 599–607.

Hedin, L., and Likens, G. 1996. Atmospheric dust and acid rain. *Scientific American*, December.

Hoagland, W. 1995. Solar energy. *Scientific American*, September.

Holloway, M. 1991. Soiled shores. *Scientific American*, October.

Holloway, M. 1993. Sustaining the Amazon. *Scientific American*, July.

Holloway, M. 1994. Nurturing nature. *Scientific American*, April.

Jones, R. D., and Wigley, T. M. L. 1990. Global warming trends. *Scientific American*, August.

Koslow, J. A. 1997. Seamounts and the ecology of deep-sea fisheries. *American Scientist* 85(2): 168–76.

Kusler, J. A., Mitsch, W. J., and Larson, J. S. 1994. Wetlands. *Scientific American*, January.

Lanham, D. A. 1995. The industrial ecology of the 21st century. *Scientific American*, September.

Lucky, R. W. 1995. What technology alone cannot do. *Scientific American*, September.

Managing planet earth. 1989. *Scientific American*, September (special issue).

May, R. M. 1992. How many species inhabit the earth? *Scientific American*, October.

Moore, J. A. 1985. Science as a way of knowing: Human ecology. *American Zoologist* 25: 483.

Nicol, S. J., and de la Mare, W. 1993. Ecosystem management and the Antarctic krill. *American Scientist* 81(1): 36–47.

Nordhaus, W. D. 1994. Expert opinion on climatic change. *American Scientist* 82(1): 45–51.

Norman, D. A. 1995. Designing the future. *Scientific American*, September.

Page, R. E. 1989. Genetic specialists, kin recognition, and nepotism in honeybee colonies. *Nature* 338: 576–79.

Pearce, D., Adger, N., Maddison, D., and Moran, D. 1995. Debt and the environment. *Scientific American*, June.

Peterson, D. H., Cayan, D., Dileo-Stevens, J., Nobel, M., and Dettinger, M. 1995. The role of climate in estuarine variability. *American Scientist* 83(1): 58–67.

Plucknett, D. L., and Winkelman, D. L. 1995. Technology for sustainable agriculture. *Scientific American*, September.

Prosterman, R. L., Hanstad, T., and Ping, L. 1996. Can China feed itself? *Scientific American*, November.

Repetto, R. 1990. Deforestation in the tropics. *Scientific American*, April.

Repetto, R. 1992. Accounting for environmental assets. *Scientific American*, June.

Robison, B. H. 1995. Light in the ocean's midwaters. *Scientific American*, July.

Romme, W. H., and Despain, D. G. 1989. The Yellowstone fires. *Scientific American*, November.

Rutzler, K., and Feller, I. C. 1996. Caribbean mangrove swamps. *Scientific American*, March.

Scheller, R. H., and Axel, R. 1984. How genes control an innate behavior. *Scientific American*, March.

Schindler, D. W. 1988. Effects of acid rain on freshwater ecosystems. *Science* 239: 149–57.

Schneider, D. 1997. The rising seas. *Scientific American*, March.

Scott, J. M., Csuti, B., Jacobi, J. D., and Estes, J. E. 1987. Species richness: A geographic approach to protecting future biological diversity. *BioScience* 37: 782–788.

Terborgh, J. 1992. Why American songbirds are vanishing. *Scientific American*, May.

Trivers, R. L. 1971. The evolution of reciprocal altruism. *Quarterly Review Biology* 46: 35.

Vitousek, P. M., D'Antonio, C. M., Loope, L. L., and Westbrooks, R. 1996. Biological invasions as global environmental changes. *American Scientist* 84(5): 468–78.

Wallace, A. 1988. Mechanisms of coexistence. *Nature* 333: 597.

part FIVE

ANIMAL-LIKE PROTISTS AND ANIMALIA

One person can never fully appreciate the amazing diversity in the animal kingdom. Zoologists, therefore, must specialize and study particular animal groups. Knowledge of all aspects of animal biology is invaluable because it

reveals the delicate balances in nature and gives clues to how to preserve those balances. Furthermore, as zoologists learn more about animal groups, information that directly affects human welfare emerges. For example, from research on the nervous systems of squid and cockroaches comes much of what is known about nerve cells and many human nervous disorders. In spite of the work of generations of zoologists, many questions about animals remain unanswered. Many species, especially in the tropics, have not been described. Some species may hold keys to unlocking the secrets of cancer, AIDS, and other diseases. Other species may provide insight into managing world resources.

Chapters 16 to 31 present an overview of the known animal-like protists and animal phyla. Specifically, chapter 16 is an introduction to animal taxonomy, which is the study of the naming of organisms and their evolutionary relationships, and to the basic organization of animal bodies. Chapter 17 then covers the animal-like protists, and chapters 18 to 31 survey the animal phyla. These chapters are the beginning of an exciting journey into the diversity of the animal kingdom. Perhaps one of these chapters will captivate your attention, and you will join the thousands of zoologists who spend their lives studying a portion of the animal kingdom.

ANIMAL CLASSIFICATION, PHYLOGENY, AND ORGANIZATION

Concepts

1. Order in nature allows systematists to name animals and discern evolutionary relationships among them.
2. Traditional grouping resulted in the classification of organisms into five kingdoms. Recent information from molecular studies has challenged this concept with three major evolutionary lineages: Eubacteria, Archaea, and Eukarya.
3. Animal systematists use a variety of methods to discern evolutionary relationships. Evolutionary systematics and phylogenetic systematics (cladistics) are two widely used approaches to the study of evolutionary relationships.
4. Animal relationships are represented by branching evolutionary-tree diagrams.
5. Animal body plans can be categorized according to how cells are organized into tissues and how body parts are distributed within and around an animal.

Would You Like to Know . . .

1   why zoologists use scientific names, rather than common names, for the animals they study? (p. 228)

2   why zoology courses often cover such organisms as *Amoeba* and *Paramecium* when these organisms are not really animals? (p. 230)

3   why evolutionary-tree diagrams can be misleading? (p. 233)

4   why sedentary animals, such as sea anemones, do not have heads and tails? (p. 234)

5   why body cavities are advantageous to animals that possess them? (p. 236)

This chapter answers these and other useful questions.

This chapter contains evolutionary concepts, which are set off in this font.

Biologists have identified approximately 1.4 million species, more than three-fourths of which are animals. Many zoologists spend their lives grouping animals according to shared characteristics. These groupings reflect the order found in living systems that is a natural consequence of shared evolutionary processes. Often, the work of these zoologists involves describing new species and placing them into their proper relationships with other species. Obviously, much work remains in discovering and classifying the world's 4 to 30 million undescribed species.

Rarely do zoologists describe new taxa above the species level (*see figure 1.10*). In 1995, however, R. M. Kirstensen and P. Funch of the University of Copenhagen described a new animal species—*Symbion pandora*—on the mouthparts of lobsters. This species is so different that it has been assigned to a new phylum— the broadest level of animal classification (figure 16.1). The description of this new phylum, Cycliophora, is a remarkable event that brings the total number of recognized animal phyla to 36 (*see endpaper 4*). This chapter describes the principles that zoologists use as they group and name animals.

CLASSIFICATION OF ORGANISMS

One of the characteristics of modern humans is our ability to communicate with a spoken language. Language not only allows us to communicate, but also helps us encode and classify concepts, objects, and organisms that we encounter. To make sense out of life's diversity, we need more than just names for organisms. A pot-

FIGURE 16.1

The Most Recently Described Phylum. Systematists group animals according to evolutionary relationships. Usually, the work of systematists results in newly described species (or species for which new information has been uncovered) being placed in higher taxonomic categories along with previously studied species. They rarely describe new higher taxonomic groups because finding an organism so different from any previously known organism is unlikely. *Symbion pandora* (shown here) was discovered in 1995 and was distinctive enough for the description of an entirely new phylum, Cycliophora. The individuals shown here are covering the mouth parts of a lobster and are about 0.3 mm long.

pourri of over a million animal names is of little use to anyone. To be useful, a naming system must reflect the order and relationships that arise from evolutionary processes. The study of the kinds and diversity of organisms and the evolutionary relationships among them is called **systematics** (Gr. *systema*, system + *ikos*, body of facts) or **taxonomy** (Gr. *taxis*, arrangement + L. *nominalis*, belonging to a name). These studies result in the description of new species and the organization of animals into groups (taxa) based on degree of evolutionary relatedness. (Some biologists distinguish between systematics and taxonomy, preferring to think of taxonomy as the work involved with the original description of species, and systematics as the assignment of species into evolutionary groups. This text does not make this distinction because of the extensive overlap between the two tasks.) **Nomenclature** (L. *nominalis*, belonging to a name + *calator*, to call) is the assignment of a distinctive name to each species.

A TAXONOMIC HIERARCHY

The modern classification system is rooted in the work of Karl von Linné (Carolus Linnaeus) (1707–1778). His binomial system (*see chapter 1*) is still used today. Von Linné also recognized that different species could be grouped into broader categories based on shared characteristics. Any grouping of animals that shares a particular set of characteristics forms an assemblage called a **taxon**. For example, a housefly (*Musca domestica*), although obviously unique, shares certain characteristics with other flies (the most important of these being a single pair of wings). Based on these similarities, all true flies form a logical, more inclusive taxon. Further, all true flies share certain characteristics with bees, butterflies, and beetles. Thus, these animals form an even more inclusive taxon. They are all insects.

Von Linné recognized five taxa. Modern taxonomists use those five and have added three others. The taxa are arranged hierarchically (from broad to specific): **domain, kingdom, phylum, class, order, family, genus,** and **species** (table 16.1). (Domain,

TABLE 16.1	TAXONOMIC CATEGORIES OF A HUMAN AND A DOG	
TAXON	HUMAN	DOMESTIC DOG
Domain	Eukarya	Eukarya
Kingdom	Animalia	Animalia
Phylum	Chordata	Chordata
Class	Mammalia	Mammalia
Order	Primates	Carnivora
Family	Hominidae	Canidae
Genus	*Homo*	*Canis*
Species	*sapiens*	*familiaris*

the broadest taxonomic category, was added recently, is not yet universally accepted, and is discussed in a later section.)

Even though von Linné did not accept evolution, many of his groupings reflect evolutionary relationships. Morphological similarities between two animals have a genetic basis and are the result of a common evolutionary history. Thus, in grouping animals according to shared characteristics, von Linné grouped them according to their evolutionary relationships. Ideally, members of the same taxonomic group are more closely related to each other than to members of different taxa (see figure 1.10).

Above the species level, the definitions of what constitutes a particular taxon are not precise. (The species concept is discussed in chapter 12.) Disagreements as to whether two species should be grouped in the same taxon or different taxa are common.

NOMENCLATURE

Do you call certain freshwater crustaceans crawdads, crayfish, or crawfish? Do you call a common sparrow an English sparrow, a barn sparrow, or a house sparrow? ① The binomial system of nomenclature brings order to a chaotic world of common names. Common names have two problems. First, they vary from country to country, and from region to region within a country. Some species have literally hundreds of different common names. Biology transcends regional and nationalistic boundaries, and so must the names of what biologists study. Second, many common names refer to taxonomic categories higher than the species level. Most different kinds of pillbugs (class Crustacea, order Isopoda) or most different kinds of crayfish (class Crustacea, order Decapoda) cannot be distinguished from a superficial examination. A common name, even if you recognize it, often does not specify a particular species.

The binomial system of nomenclature is universal and clearly indicates the level of classification involved in any description. No two kinds of animals have the same binomial name, and every animal has only one correct name, as required by the *International Code of Zoological Nomenclature*, thereby avoiding the confusion that common names cause. The genus of an animal begins with a capital letter, the species designation begins with a lowercase letter, and the entire scientific name is italicized or underlined because it is derived from Latin or is latinized. Thus, the scientific name of humans is written *Homo sapiens*. When the genus is understood, the binomial name can be abbreviated *H. sapiens*.

MOLECULAR APPROACHES TO ANIMAL SYSTEMATICS

In recent years, molecular biological techniques (see chapter 9) have provided important information for taxonomic studies. The relatedness of animals is reflected in the gene products (proteins) animals produce and in the genes themselves (the sequence of nitrogenous bases in DNA). Related animals have DNA derived from a common ancestor. Genes and proteins of related animals, therefore, are more similar than genes and proteins from distantly related animals. By comparing the sequence of amino acids in proteins, or the sequence of nitrogenous bases in DNA or RNA, and

assuming a relatively constant mutation rate (referred to as a molecular clock), taxonomists can estimate the time elapsed since divergence from a common ancestor. Sequencing the nuclear DNA and the mitochondrial DNA of animals has become commonplace. Mitochondrial DNA is useful in taxonomic studies because mitochondria have their own genetic systems and are inherited cytoplasmically. That is, mitochondria are transmitted from parent to offspring through the egg cytoplasm and can be used to trace maternal lineages. Using mitochondrial DNA involves relatively small quantities of DNA that change at a relatively constant rate. As you will see in the next section, the sequencing of ribosomal RNA has been used extensively in studying taxonomic relationships.

Molecular techniques have provided a wealth of new information useful to animal taxonomists. These techniques, however, will not replace traditional taxonomic methods. The molecular clocks used to determine rates of evolutionary change have provided important information that helps fill in time gaps in the fossil record. Molecular clocks, however, apparently run at different rates, depending on whether one is looking at the sequence of amino acids in proteins, the sequence of bases in DNA from organelles like mitochondria, the sequence of bases in nuclear DNA, or data from different evolutionary lineages. Molecular and traditional methods of investigation will probably always be used to complement each other in taxonomic studies.

KINGDOMS OF LIFE

In 1969, Robert H. Whittaker described a system of classification that distinguished between kingdoms according to cellular organization and mode of nutrition (figure 16.2a). According to this system, members of the kingdom **Monera** are the bacteria and the cyanobacteria. They are distinguished from all other organisms by being prokaryotic (see table 3.1). Members of the kingdom **Protista** are eukaryotic and consist of single cells or colonies of cells. This kingdom includes *Amoeba, Paramecium,* and many others. Members of the kingdom **Plantae** are eukaryotic, multicellular, and photosynthetic. Plants have walled cells and are usually nonmotile. Members of the kingdom **Fungi** are also eukaryotic and multicellular. They also have walled cells and are usually nonmotile. Mode of nutrition distinguishes fungi from plants. Fungi digest organic matter extracellularly and absorb the breakdown products. Members of the kingdom **Animalia** are eukaryotic and multicellular, and they usually feed by ingesting other organisms or parts of other organisms. Their cells lack walls and they are usually motile.

In recent years, new information has challenged the five-kingdom classification system. For the first 2 billion years of life on the earth, the only living forms were prokaryotic microbes. Fossil evidence from this early period is scanty; however, molecular studies of variations in base sequences (see chapter 9) of ribosomal RNA from more than two thousand organisms are providing evidence of relationships rooted within this 2-billion-year period. The emerging picture is that the five previously described kingdoms do not represent distinct evolutionary lineages.

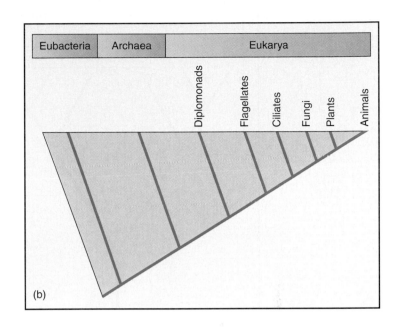

FIGURE 16.2

Classification of Organisms. (*a*) In 1969, Robert H. Whittaker described a five-kingdom classification system based on cellular organization and mode of nutrition. (*b*) Recent studies of ribosomal RNA indicate that a grouping into three domains more accurately portrays early evolutionary relationships.

Ribosomal RNA is excellent for studying the evolution of early life on earth. It is an ancient molecule, and it is present and retains its function in virtually all organisms. In addition, ribosomal RNA changes very slowly. This slowness of change, called **evolutionary conservation,** indicates that the protein-producing machinery of a cell can tolerate little change and still retain its vital function. Evolutionary conservation of this molecule means that closely related organisms (recently diverged from a common ancestor) are likely to have similar ribosomal RNAs. Distantly related organisms are expected to have ribosomal RNAs that are less similar, but the differences are small enough that the relationships to some ancestral molecule are still apparent.

Molecular systematists compare the base sequences in ribosomal RNA of different organisms to find the number of positions in the RNAs where bases are different. They enter these data into computer programs and examine all possible relationships among the different organisms. The systematists then decide which arrangement of the organisms best explains the data.

Studies of ribosomal RNA have led systematists to the conclusions that all life shares a common ancestor and that there are three major evolutionary lineages (figure 16.2*b*). Each of these lineages is called a domain. The domain thus supersedes the kingdom as the broadest taxonomic grouping. The **Archaea** are prokaryotic microbes that live in extreme environments, such as high-temperature rift valleys on the ocean floor, or high-salt or acidic environments. All members of the Archaea inhabit anaerobic environments. These environments may reflect the conditions on the earth at the time of life's origin. The Archaea are the most primitive life-forms known. Ancient archaeans gave rise to two other domains of organisms: Eubacteria

and Eukarya. The **Eubacteria** are true bacteria and are prokaryotic microorganisms. The **Eukarya** include all eukaryotic organisms. Interestingly, the Eukarya diverged more recently than the Eubacteria from the Archaea. Thus, the Eukarya are more closely related than the Eubacteria to the Archaea.

The Eukarya arose about 1.5 billion years ago. The photosynthetic accumulation of oxygen in the atmosphere probably resulted in the production of ozone, which shielded the planet from deadly ultraviolet light. The Eukarya then underwent a late, but rapid, evolutionary diversification into the modern lineages of protists, fungi, plants, and animals.

Many biologists find the relatively close relationships of all eukaryotic organisms depicted in this taxonomic scheme strange and unsettling. The relationships depicted in figure 16.2*b* not only are new but also are based on cellular characteristics, rather than the whole-organism characteristics that taxonomists traditionally use. As a result, many questions remain to be answered before zoologists accept this system of higher taxonomy.

One of these questions involves how to deal with the eukaryotic kingdom lineages. Should the Animalia, Fungi, and Plantae still be considered kingdoms? Most zoologists would answer, "Yes." If so, molecular studies indicate that the separate protist lineages shown in figure 16.2*b* should also be elevated to kingdom status. Questions such as this make systematics a lively and challenging field of study, and future editions of this text will almost certainly contain taxonomic revisions that center around the relationships within the Eukarya.

This text is primarily devoted to the animals. Chapter 17, however, covers the animal-like protists (protozoa). The inclusion

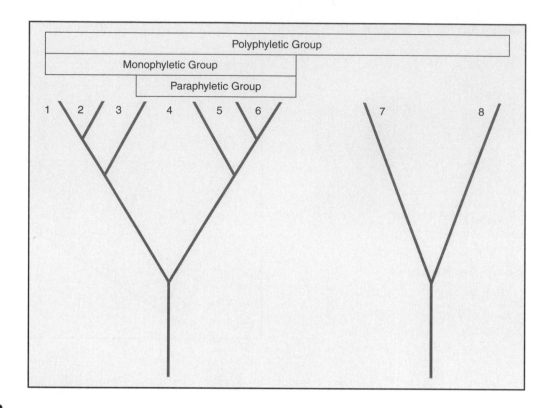

FIGURE 16.3

Evolutionary Groups. An assemblage of species 1–8 is a polyphyletic group because species 1–6 have a different ancestor than species 7 and 8. An assemblage of species 3–6 is a paraphyletic group because species 1 and 2 share the same ancestor as 3–6, but they have been left out of the group. An assemblage of species 1–6 is a monophyletic group because it includes all of the descendants of a single ancestor.

of protozoa is part of a tradition that originated with an old two-kingdom classification system.   ② Animal-like protists (e.g., *Amoeba* and *Paramecium*) were once considered a phylum (Protozoa) in the animal kingdom, and general zoology courses usually include them.

Stop and Ask Yourself

1. What does it mean to say that a classification system is hierarchical?

2. Why are common names inadequate for scientific purposes?

3. How has molecular biology contributed to understanding animal systematics?

4. What source of evidence has resulted in a reevaluation of the kingdoms of life that R.H. Whittaker described? What is the nature of that reevaluation?

ANIMAL SYSTEMATICS

The goal of animal systematics is to arrange animals into groups that reflect evolutionary relationships. Ideally, these groups should include a single ancestral species and all of its descendants. Such a group is called a **monophyletic group** (figure 16.3). In searching out monophyletic groups, taxonomists look for animal attributes called characters, that indicate relatedness. A **character** is virtually anything that has a genetic basis and that can be measured—from an anatomical feature to a sequence of nitrogenous bases in DNA or RNA. **Polyphyletic groups** have members that can be traced to separate ancestors. Since each group should have a single ancestor, a polyphyletic group reflects insufficient knowledge of the group.

A **paraphyletic group** includes some, but not all, members of a lineage. Paraphyletic groups also result when knowledge of the group is insufficient (*see figure 16.3*).

As in any human endeavor, disagreements have arisen in animal systematics. These disagreements revolve around methods of investigation and whether or not data may be used in describing distant evolutionary relationships. Three contemporary schools of systematics exist: evolutionary systematics, numerical taxonomy, and phylogenetic systematics (cladistics).

Evolutionary systematics is the oldest of the three approaches. It is sometimes called the "traditional approach," although it has certainly changed since the beginnings of animal systematics. A basic assumption of evolutionary systematists is that organisms closely related to an ancestor will resemble that ancestor more closely than they resemble distantly related organisms.

Two kinds of similarities between organisms are recognized: homologies and analogies (*see also the discussion of homology and analogy in chapter 1*). Homologies are resemblances that result

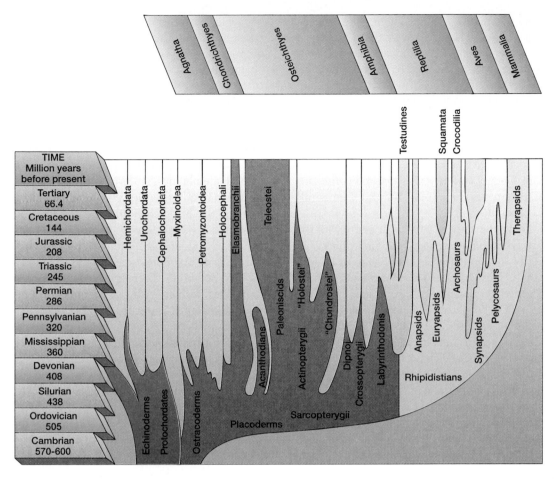

FIGURE 16.4

Phylogenetic Tree Showing Vertebrate Phylogeny. A phylogenetic tree derived from evolutionary systematics depicts the degree of divergence since branching from a common ancestor, which is indicated by the time periods on the vertical axis. The width of the branches indicates the number of recognized genera for a given time period. Note that this diagram shows the birds (Aves) as being closely related to the reptiles (Reptilia), and both groups as having class-level status.

from common ancestry and are useful in classifying animals. An example is the similarity in the arrangement of bones in the wing of a bird and the arm of a human (*see figure 1.7*). Analogies are resemblances that result from organisms adapting under similar evolutionary pressures. The latter process is sometimes called convergent evolution. Analogies do not reflect common ancestry and are not used in animal taxonomy. The similarity between the wings of birds and insects is an analogy.

Evolutionary systematists often portray the results of their work on phylogenetic trees, where organisms are ranked according to their evolutionary relationships. Figure 16.4 is a phylogenetic tree showing vertebrate evolutionary relationships, as well as time scales and relative abundance of animal groups. These diagrams reflect judgments made about rates of evolution and the relative importance of certain key characters (e.g., feathers in birds).

Numerical taxonomy emerged during the 1950s and 1960s and represents the opposite end of the spectrum from evolutionary systematics. The founders of numerical taxonomy believed that the criteria for grouping taxa had become too arbitrary and vague. They tried to make taxonomy more objective. Numerical

taxonomists use mathematical models and computer-aided techniques to group samples of organisms according to overall similarity. They do not attempt to distinguish between homologies and analogies. Numerical taxonomists admit that analogies exist. They contend, however, that telling one from the other is sometimes impossible and that the numerous homologies used in data analysis overshadow the analogies. A second major difference between evolutionary systematics and numerical taxonomy is that numerical taxonomists limit discussion of evolutionary relationships to closely related taxa. Numerical taxonomy is the least popular of the three taxonomic schools; however, all taxonomists use the computer programs that numerical taxonomists developed.

Phylogenetic systematics (cladistics) is a third approach to animal systematics. The goal of cladistics is similar to that described for evolutionary systematics—the generation of hypotheses of genealogical relationships among monophyletic groups of organisms. Cladists contend, however, that their methods are more open to analysis and testing, and thus are more scientific, than those of evolutionary systematists.

As do evolutionary systematists, cladists differentiate between homologies and analogies. They believe, however, that homologies of recent origin are most useful in phylogenetic studies. Characters that all members of a group share are referred to as **symplesiomorphies** (Gr. *sym*, together + *plesio*, near + *morphe*, form). These characters are homologies that may indicate a shared ancestry, but they are useless in describing relationships within the group.

To decide what character is ancestral for a group of organisms, cladists look for a related group of organisms, called an **outgroup,** that is not included in the study group. Figure 16.5 shows a hypothetical lineage for five taxa. Notice that taxon 5 is the outgroup for taxa 1–4. Character A is symplesiomorphic (ancestral) for the outgroup and the study group.

Characters that have arisen since common ancestry with the outgroup are called **derived characters** or **synapomorphies** (Gr. *syn*, together + *apo*, away + *morphe*, form). Taxa 1–4 in figure 16.5 share derived character B. This character separates taxa 1–4 from the outgroup. Similarly, derived characters C and D arose more recently than character B. Closely related taxa 1 and 2 share character C. Closely related taxa 3 and 4 share character D. Taxa that share a certain synapomorphy form a subset called a **clade** (Gr. *klados*, branch). Taxa 1 and 2 form a clade characterized by C.

The hypothetical lineage shown in figure 16.5 is called a **cladogram.** Cladograms depict a sequence in the origin of derived characters. A cladogram is interpreted as a family tree depicting a hypothesis regarding monophyletic lineages. New data in the form of newly investigated characters or reinterpretation of old data are used to test the hypothesis the cladogram describes.

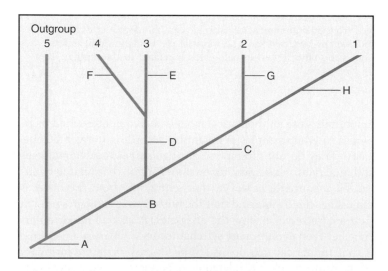

FIGURE 16.5

Interpreting Cladograms. This hypothetical cladogram shows five taxa (1–5) and the characters (A–H) used in deriving the taxonomic relationships. Character A is symplesiomorphic for the entire group. Taxon 5 is the outgroup because it shares only that ancestral character with taxa 1–4. All other characters are more recently derived. What single character is a synapomorphy for taxa 1 and 2, separating them from all other taxa?

Figure 16.6 is a cladogram depicting the evolutionary relationships among the vertebrates. The tunicates and cephalochordates are an outgroup for the entire vertebrate lineage. Derived characters are listed on the right side of the cladogram. Notice that extraembryonic membranes is a synapomorphy used to define the clade containing the reptiles, birds, and mammals. These extraembryonic membranes are shared character for these groups and are not present in any of the fish taxa or the amphibians. Distinguishing between reptiles, birds, and mammals requires looking at characters that are even more recently derived than extraembryonic membranes. A derived character, the shell, distinguishes turtles from all other members of the clade; skull characters distinguish the lizard/crocodile/bird lineage from the mammal lineage; and hair, mammary glands, and endothermy is a unique mammalian character combination. Note that a synapomorphy at one level of taxonomy may be a symplesiomorphy at a different level of taxonomy. Extraembryonic membranes is a synapomorphic character within the vertebrates that distinguishes the reptile/bird/mammal clade. It is symplesiomorphic for reptiles, birds, and mammals because it is ancestral for the clade and cannot be used to distinguish among members of these three groups.

Zoologists widely accept cladistics. This acceptance has resulted in some nontraditional interpretations of animal phylogeny. A comparison of figures 16.4 and 16.6 shows one example of different interpretations derived through evolutionary systematics and cladistics. Generations of taxonomists have assigned class-level status (Aves) to birds. Reptiles also have had class-level status (Reptilia). Cladistic analysis has shown, however, that birds are more closely tied by common ancestry to the alligators and crocodiles than to any other group. According to the cladistic interpretation, birds and crocodiles should be assigned to a group that reflects this close common ancestry. Birds would become a subgroup within a larger group that included both birds and reptiles. Crocodiles would be depicted more closely related to the birds than they would be to snakes and lizards. Traditional evolutionary systematists maintain that the traditional interpretation is still correct because it takes into account the greater importance of key characters of birds (e.g., feathers and endothermy) that make the group unique. Cladists support their position by pointing out that the designation of "key characters" involves value judgments that cannot be tested.

As debates between cladists and evolutionary systematists continue, knowledge of evolutionary relationships among animals will become more complete. Debates like these are the fuel that force scientists to examine and reexamine old assumptions. Animal systematics is certain to be a lively and exciting field in future years.

The chapters that follow are a survey of the animal kingdom. The organization of these chapters reflects the traditional taxonomy that makes most zoologists comfortable. Cladograms are usually included in "Further Phylogenetic Considerations" at the end of most chapters, and any different interpretations of animal phylogeny implicit in these cladograms are discussed.

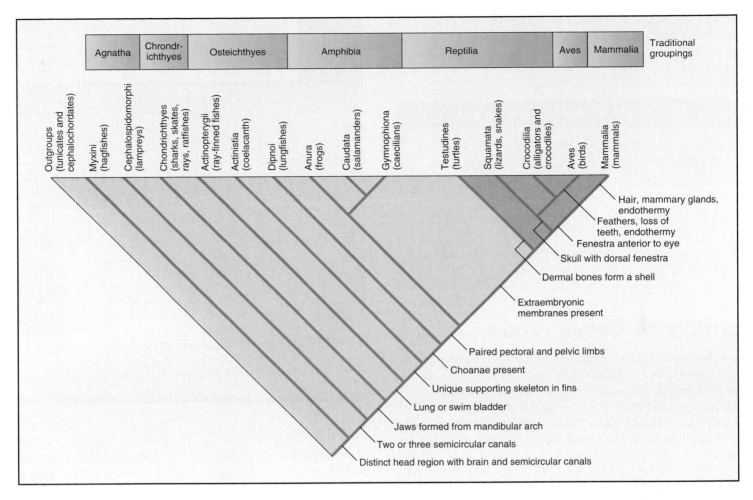

FIGURE 16.6

Cladogram Showing Vertebrate Phylogeny. A cladogram is constructed by identifying points at which two groups diverged. Animals that share a branching point are included in the same taxon. Notice that timescales are not given or implied. The relative abundance of taxa is also not shown. Notice that this diagram shows the birds and crocodilians sharing a common branch, and that these two groups are more closely related to each other than either is to any other group of animals.

EVOLUTIONARY RELATIONSHIPS AND TREE DIAGRAMS

Although evolutionary-tree diagrams can help clarify evolutionary relationships and timescales, they are often a source of misunderstanding because they illustrate relationships among levels of classification above the species (*see figure 16.6*). ③ Depicting phyla or classes as ancestral is misleading because evolution occurs in species groups (populations), not at higher taxonomic levels. Also, even though phyla or classes are depicted as ancestral, modern representatives of these "ancestral phyla" have had just as long an evolutionary history as animals in other taxonomic groups that may have descended from the common ancestor. All modern representatives of any group of animals should be visualized at the tips of a "tree branch," and they may be very different from ancestral species. Zoologists use modern representatives to help visualize general characteristics of an ancestral species, but never to specify details of the ancestor's structure, function, or ecology.

In addition to these problems of interpretation, evolutionary trees often imply a ladderlike progression of increasing complexity. This is misleading because evolution has often resulted in reduced complexity and body forms that are evolutionary failures. In many cases, evolution does not lead to phenotypes that permit survival under changing conditions, and extinction occurs. Further, the common representation of a phylogeny as an inverted cone, or a tree with a narrow trunk and many higher branches, is often misleading. This implies that evolution is a continuous process of increasing diversification. The fossil records show that this is often wrong. For example, 20 to 30 groups of echinoderms (sea stars and their relatives) are in the fossil record, but there are only 5 modern groups. This evolutionary lineage, like many others, underwent rapid initial evolutionary diversification. After the initial diversification, extinction—not further diversification—was the rule. Contemporary paleontologist Stephen J. Gould uses the term contingency to refer to rapid evolutionary explosion followed by a high likelihood of extinction.

In spite of these problems, tree diagrams persist in scientific literature and are used in this text. As long as you keep their limitations in mind, they can help you visualize evolutionary relationships.

PATTERNS OF ORGANIZATION

One of the most strikingly ordered series of changes in evolution is reflected in body plans in the animal kingdom and the protists. Evolutionary changes in animal body plans might be likened to a road map through a mountain range. What is most easily depicted are the starting and ending points and a few of the "attractions" along the route. What cannot be seen from this perspective are the tortuous curves and grades that must be navigated and the extra miles that must be traveled to chart back roads. Evolutionary changes do not always mean "progress" and increased complexity. Evolution frequently results in backtracking, in failed experiments, and in inefficient or useless structures. Evolution results in frequent dead ends, even though the route to that dead end may be filled with grandeur. The account that follows is a look at patterns of animal organization. As far as evolutionary pathways are concerned, this account is an inexplicit road map through the animal kingdom. On a grand scale, it portrays evolutionary trends, but it does not depict an evolutionary sequence.

SYMMETRY

The bodies of animals and protists are organized into almost infinitely diverse forms. Within this diversity, however, are certain patterns of organization. The concept of symmetry is fundamental to understanding animal organization. **Symmetry** describes how the parts of an animal are arranged around a point or an axis (table 16.2).

Asymmetry, which is the absence of a central point or axis around which body parts are equally distributed, characterizes most protists and many sponges (figure 16.7). Asymmetry cannot be said to be an adaptation to anything or advantageous to an organism. Asymmetrical organisms do not develop complex communication, sensory, or locomotor functions. Clearly, however, protists and animals whose bodies consist of aggregates of cells have flourished.

A sea anemone can move along a substrate, but only very slowly. How does it gather food? How does it detect and protect it-

TABLE 16.2	ANIMAL SYMMETRY
TERM	MEANING
Asymmetry	The arrangement of body parts without a central axis or point (e.g., the sponges).
Bilateral symmetry	The arrangement of body parts such that a single plane passing between the upper and lower surfaces and through the longitudinal axis divides the animal into right and left mirror images (e.g., the vertebrates).
Radial symmetry	The arrangement of body parts such that any plane passing through the oral-aboral axis divides the animal into mirror images (e.g., the cnidarians). Radial symmetry can be modified by the arrangement of some structures in pairs, or other combinations, around the central axis (e.g., biradial symmetry in the ctenophorans and some anthozoans, and pentaradial symmetry in the echinoderms).

self from predators? For this animal, a blind side would leave it vulnerable to attack and cause it to miss many meals. The sea anemone, as is the case for most sedentary animals, has sensory and feeding structures uniformly distributed around its body. ④ Sea anemones do not have distinct head and tail ends. Instead, one point of reference is the end of the animal that possesses the mouth (the oral end), and a second point of reference is the end opposite the mouth (the aboral end). Animals such as the sea anemone are radially symmetrical. **Radial symmetry** is the arrangement of body parts such that any plane passing through the central oral-aboral axis divides the animal into mirror images (figure 16.8). Radial symmetry is often modified by the arrangement of some structures in pairs, or in other combinations, around the central oral-aboral axis. The paired arrangement of some structures in radially symmetrical animals is called biradial symmetry. The arrangement of structures in fives around a radial animal is called pentaradial symmetry.

Although the sensory, feeding, and locomotor structures in radially symmetrical animals could never be called "simple," they are not comparable to the complex sensory, locomotor, and feeding structures in many other animals. The evolution of such complex structures in radially symmetrical animals would require repeated distribution of specialized structures around the animal.

Bilateral symmetry is the arrangement of body parts such that a single plane, passing between the upper and lower surfaces and through the longitudinal axis of an animal, divides the animal into right and left mirror images (figure 16.9). Bilateral symmetry is characteristic of active, crawling, or swimming animals. Because bilateral animals move primarily in one direction, one end of the

FIGURE 16.7

Asymmetry. Sponges display a cell-aggregate organization, and as this brown volcano sponge (*Hemectyon ferox*) shows, many are asymmetrical.

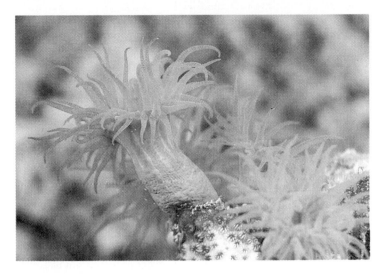

FIGURE 16.8

Radial Symmetry. Planes that pass through the oral-aboral axis divide radially symmetrical animals, such as this tube coral polyp (*Tubastraea, sp*), into equal halves. Certain arrangements of internal structures modify the radial symmetry of sea anemones.

animal is continually encountering the environment. The end that meets the environment is usually where complex sensory, nervous, and feeding structures evolve and develop. These developments result in the formation of a distinct head and are called **cephalization** (Gr. *kephale*, head). Cephalization occurs at an animal's anterior end. Posterior is opposite anterior; it is the animal's tail end. Other important terms of direction and terms describing body planes and sections apply to bilateral animals. These terms are for locating body parts relative to a point of reference or an imaginary plane passing through the body (tables 16.2 and 16.3; figure 16.9).

OTHER PATTERNS OF ORGANIZATION

In addition to body symmetry, other patterns of animal organization are recognizable. In a broad context, these patterns may reflect evolutionary trends. As explained earlier, however, these trends are not exact sequences in animal evolution.

The Unicellular (Cytoplasmic) Level of Organization

Organisms whose bodies consist of single cells or cellular aggregates display the unicellular level of organization. Unicellular body plans are characteristic of the Protista. Some zoologists prefer to use the designation "cytoplasmic" to emphasize that all living functions are carried out within the confines of a single plasma membrane. Unicellular organization is not "simple." All unicellular organisms must provide for the functions of locomotion, food acquisition, digestion, water and ion regulation, sensory perception, and reproduction in a single cell.

Cellular aggregates (colonies) consist of loose associations of cells that exhibit little interdependence, cooperation, or coordination of function—therefore, cellular aggregates cannot be

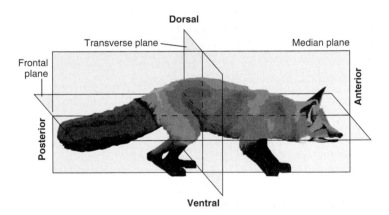

FIGURE 16.9

Bilateral Symmetry. Planes and terms of direction useful in locating parts of a bilateral animal. A bilaterally symmetrical animal, such as this fox, has only one plane of symmetry. An imaginary median plane is the only plane through which the animal could be cut to yield mirror-image halves.

considered tissues (*see chapter 3*). In spite of the absence of interdependence, these organisms show some division of labor. Some cells may be specialized for reproductive, nutritive, or structural functions.

Diploblastic Organization

Cells are organized into tissues in most animal phyla. **Diploblastic** (Gr. *diplóos*, twofold + *blaste*, to sprout) organization is the simplest, tissue-level organization (figure 16.10). Body parts are organized into layers derived from two embryonic tissue layers. Ectoderm gives rise to the epidermis, the outer layer of the body wall. Endoderm gives rise to the gastrodermis, the tissue that lines

TABLE 16.3	TERMS OF DIRECTION	
TERM	**DESCRIPTION**	
Aboral	The end opposite the mouth	
Oral	The end containing the mouth	
Anterior	The head end; usually the end of a bilateral animal that meets its environment	
Posterior	The tail end	
Caudal	Toward the tail	
Cephalic	Toward the head	
Distal	Away from the point of attachment of a structure on the body (e.g. the toes are distal to the knee)	
Proximal	Toward the point of attachment of a structure on the body (e.g., the hip is proximal to the knee)	
Dorsal	The back of an animal; usually the upper surface; synonymous with posterior for animals that walk upright	
Ventral	The belly of an animal; usually the lower surface; synonymous with anterior for animals that walk upright	
Inferior	Below a point of reference (e.g., the mouth is inferior to the nose in humans)	
Superior	Above a point of reference (e.g., the neck is superior to the chest)	
Lateral	Away from the plane that divides a bilateral animal into mirror images	
Medial (median)	On or near the plane that divides a bilateral animal into mirror images	

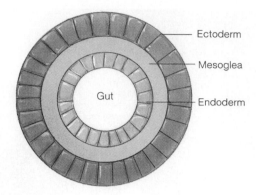

FIGURE 16.10

Diploblastic Body Plan. Diploblastic animals have tissues derived from ectoderm and endoderm. Between these two layers is a noncellular mesoglea.

the gut. A third embryological layer is sandwiched between the ectoderm and endoderm. This layer is mesoderm, which gives rise to supportive, contractile, and blood cells. Most triploblastic animals have an organ-system level of organization. Tissues are organized to form excretory, nervous, digestive, reproductive, circulatory, and other systems. Triploblastic animals are usually bilaterally symmetrical (or have evolved from bilateral ancestors) and are relatively active.

Triploblastic animals are organized into several subgroups based on the presence or absence of a body cavity and, for those that possess one, the kind of body cavity present. A body cavity is a fluid-filled space in which the internal organs can be suspended and separated from the body wall. ⑤ Body cavities are advantageous because they

1. Provide more room for organ development.
2. Provide more surface area for diffusion of gases, nutrients, and wastes into and out of organs.
3. Provide an area for storage.
4. Often act as hydrostatic skeletons.
5. Provide a vehicle for eliminating wastes and reproductive products from the body.
6. Facilitate increased body size.

Of these, the hydrostatic skeleton deserves further comment. Body-cavity fluids give support, while allowing the body to remain flexible. Hydrostatic skeletons can be illustrated with a water-filled balloon, which is rigid yet flexible. Because the water in the balloon is incompressible, squeezing one end causes the balloon to lengthen. Compressing both ends causes the middle of the balloon to become fatter. In a similar fashion, body-wall muscles, acting on coelomic fluid, are responsible for movement and shape changes in many animals.

the gut cavity. Between the epidermis and the gastrodermis is a noncellular layer called mesoglea. In some diploblastic organisms, cells occur in the mesoglea, but they are always derived from ectoderm or endoderm.

The cells in each tissue layer are functionally interdependent. The gastrodermis consists of nutritive (digestive) and muscular cells, and the epidermis contains epithelial and muscular cells. The feeding movements of *Hydra* or the swimming movements of a jellyfish are only possible when groups of cells cooperate, showing tissue-level organization.

Triploblastic Organization

Animals described in chapters 19 to 31 are **triploblastic** (Gr. *treis,* three + *blaste,* to sprout); that is, their tissues are derived from three embryological layers. As with diploblastic animals, ectoderm forms the outer layer of the body wall, and endoderm lines

The Triploblastic Acoelomate Pattern
Triploblastic animals whose mesodermally derived tissues form a relatively solid mass of cells between ectodermally and endodermally derived tissues are called **acoelomate** (Gr. *a,* without + *kilos,* hollow) (figure 16.11a). Some cells between the ectoderm and endoderm of acoelomate ani-

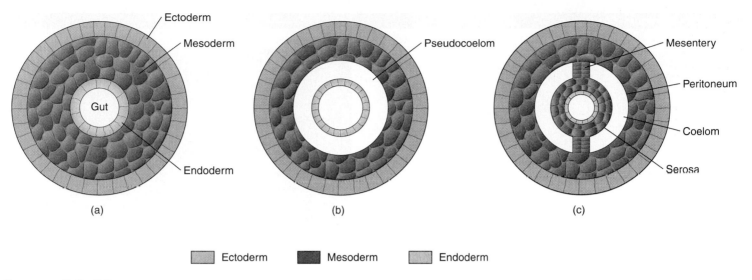

Ectoderm   Mesoderm   Endoderm

FIGURE 16.11

Triploblastic Body Plans. Triploblastic animals have tissues derived from ectoderm, mesoderm, and endoderm. (*a*) Triploblastic acoelomate pattern. (*b*) Triploblastic pseudocoelomate pattern. Note the absence of mesodermal lining on the gut track. (*c*) Triploblastic coelomate pattern. Mesodermally derived tissues completely surround the coelom.

mals are loosely organized cells called parenchyma. Parenchymal cells are not specialized for a particular function.

The Triploblastic Pseudocoelomate Pattern

A **pseudocoelom** (Gr. *pseudes*, false) is a body cavity not entirely lined by mesoderm (figure 16.11*b*). No muscular or connective tissues are associated with the gut tract, no mesodermal sheet covers the inner surface of the body wall, and no membranes suspend organs in the body cavity. Embryologically, the pseudocoelom is derived from the blastocoel of the embryo (*see chapter 10*).

The Triploblastic Coelomate Pattern

A **coelom** is a body cavity completely surrounded by mesoderm (figure 16.11*c*). A thin mesodermal sheet, the peritoneum, lines the inner body wall and is continuous with the serosa, which lines the outside of visceral organs. The peritoneum and the serosa are continuous, and suspend visceral structures in the body cavity. These suspending sheets are called mesenteries. Having mesodermally derived

tissues, such as muscle and connective tissue, associated with internal organs enhances the function of virtually all internal body systems. The chapters that follow show many variations on the triploblastic coelomate pattern.

Stop and Ask Yourself

9. How would you distinguish between radial symmetry and bilateral symmetry? Why is radial symmetry advantageous for sedentary animals?
10. Why does cephalization usually accompany bilateral symmetry?
11. What kinds of tissue form from the mesoderm?
12. What advantages do body cavities confer to coelomate animals?

ENDANGERED SPECIES

WILDLIFE ALERT 7: OZARK BIG-EARED BAT (*PLECOTUS TOWNSENDII INGENS*)

VITAL STATISTICS

Classification: Phylum Chordata, class Mammalia, order Chiroptera
Range: Oklahoma and Arkansas
Habitat: Limestone caves of Oklahoma and Arkansas
Status: Endangered
Number remaining: Fewer than two thousand

NATURAL HISTORY AND ECOLOGICAL STATUS

The Ozark big-eared bat is medium-sized with a wingspan of 78 to 96 mm and a mass of 7 to 12 g. It is light to dark brown, and its long ears and facial glands are distinctive (figure 1). It lives year-round in limestone caves found in hardwood forests of Oklahoma and Arkansas (figure 2). Its distribution once included Missouri, but it is now extirpated from that state.

(a)

(b)

FIGURE 1   The Ozark Big-Eared Bat *(Plecotus townsendii ingens)*. *(a)* Note the large ears used in echolocation. *(b)* A group of bats roosting in a cave.

In the winter, the bat hibernates in cold caves, where the temperature varies between 2.5 and 9.5° C. In the spring, it moves to warmer (15 to 18° C) maternity caves to rear young. Copulation occurs in the fall and winter after a ritualized courtship that includes vocalizations and head-nuzzling displays. Sperm are stored in the female reproductive tract until ovulation and delayed fertilization in the spring. A 2- to 3-month gestation follows fertilization. Like most bats, the Ozark big-eared bat is nocturnal and finds its food by echolocation. It feeds on lepidopterans (moths and butterflies), dipterans (flies), and coleopterans (beetles).

The current endangered status of the Ozark big-eared bat is primarily due to disturbance of its cave roosting-sites. When humans enter hibernation caves, they arouse the bats, whose metabolic rate increases. A single arousal can expend 10 to 30 days of fat reserves. This can result in death by starvation because the bats have little extra fat reserve. Disturbance of maternity caves often results in direct mortality. Destruction of cave roosting-sites and predation at the cave entrance by house cats, raccoons, bobcats, and other animals has caused significant mortality.

Concerns over the endangered status of the Ozark big-eared bat prompted the U.S. Fish and Wildlife Service to establish the Sequoyah/Oklahoma Bat Cave National Wildlife Refuge. In other ar-

eas, fenced cave entrances—to keep humans and domestic animals out of the caves but to allow bats access—are helping to prevent further population declines.

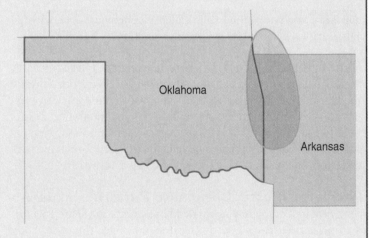

FIGURE 2   Distribution of Ozark Big-Eared Bat *(Plecotus townsendii ingens)*.

SUMMARY

1. Systematics is the study of the evolutionary history and classification of organisms. The binomial system of classification originated with von Linné and is used throughout the world in classifying organisms.

2. Organisms are classified into broad categories called kingdoms. The five-kingdom classification system used in recent years is being challenged as new information regarding evolutionary relationships among the monerans and protists is discovered.

3. The three modern approaches to systematics are evolutionary systematics, numerical taxonomy, and phylogenetic systematics (cladistics). The ultimate goal of systematics is to establish evolutionary

relationships in monophyletic groups. Evolutionary systematists use homologies and rank the importance of different characteristics in establishing evolutionary relationships. These taxonomists take into consideration differing rates of evolution in taxonomic groups. Phylogenetic systematists (cladists) look for shared, derived characteristics that can be used to investigate evolutionary relationships. Cladists do not attempt to weigh the importance of different characteristics. Wide acceptance of cladistic methods has resulted in some nontraditional taxonomic groupings of animals.

4. Evolutionary-tree diagrams are useful for depicting evolutionary relationships, but their limitations must be understood.

5. The bodies of animals are organized into almost infinitely diverse forms. Within this diversity, however, are certain patterns of organi-

zation. Symmetry describes how the parts of an animal are arranged around a point or an axis.

6. Other patterns of organization reflect how cells associate into tissues, and how tissues organize into organs and organ systems.

SELECTED KEY TERMS

bilateral symmetry (p. 234)   kingdom (p. 227)
class (p. 227)   order (p. 227)
coelom (p. 237)   phylum (p. 227)
family (p. 227)   radial symmetry (p. 234)
genus (p. 227)   species (p. 227)

CRITICAL THINKING QUESTIONS

1. In one sense, the animal classification system above the species level is artificial. In another sense, however, it is real. Explain this paradox.

2. Give proper scientific names to six hypothetical animal species. Assume that you have three different genera represented in your group of six. Be sure your format for writing scientific names is correct.

3. Describe hypothetical synapomorphies that would result in an assemblage of one order and two families (in addition to the three genera and six species from question 2).

4. Construct a cladogram, similar to that shown in figure 16.6, using your hypothetical animals from questions 2 and 3. Make drawings of your animals.

5. Describe the usefulness of evolutionary-tree diagrams in zoological studies. Describe two problems associated with their use.

REFERENCES ON THE WORLD WIDE WEB

1. **The Tree of Life.**   This site is a must for anyone interested in information on the classification and phylogeny of animals. Its navigator provides the ability to search for phylogenetic information on a wide range of animal groups. It provides links to other biological information on the Internet.

   http://phylogeny.arizona.edu/tree/phylogeny.html

2. **BIOSIS.**   BIOSIS is an Internet resource guide to animal taxa, animal diversity, amazing animals, and mailing lists. Search for information by animal group categories or subject categories.

   http://www.york.biosis.org/zrdocs/zoolinfo/grp_all.htm

3. **Metazoa: Systematics.**   This site provides information on animal systematics and shows evolutionary-tree diagrams.

   http://www.ucmp.berkeley.edu/phyla/metazoaasy.html

4. **Journey into Phylogenetic Systematics.**   This is a must-visit site for anyone interested in animal phylogenetics. It provides an introduction to cladistics, cladistic methods, and implications of cladistic studies.

   http://www.ucmp.berkeley.edu/clad.clad4.html

5. **Taxonomy Resources.**   This site, maintained by the National Center of Biotechnology Information, provides information on systematics and molecular genetics.

   http://www3.ncbi.nlm.nih.gov/Taxonomy/taxpage2.html

6. **Taxonomy: The System and Practice of Naming Organisms.**   This site provides an introduction to taxonomic principles.

   http://cope.ummz.isa.umich.edu/research/darwin.html

chapter 17

ANIMAL-LIKE PROTISTS:
THE PROTOZOA

Concepts

1. The kingdom Protista is a polyphyletic group with origins in ancestral Archaea.
2. Protozoa display unicellular or colonial organization. All functions must be carried out within the confines of a single plasma membrane.
3. According to the most widely accepted classification scheme, the seven protozoan phyla are Sarcomastigophora, Labyrinthomorpha, Apicomplexa, Microspora, Acetospora, Myxozoa, and Ciliophora.
4. Certain members of these phyla have had, and continue to have, important influences on human health and welfare.

Would You Like to Know . . .

1 whether all protozoan phyla trace back to a single Archaean ancestor? (p. 242)

2 whether some protozoa should be considered single cells, multicellular organisms, or both? (p. 242)

3 what causes "red tides"? (p. 246)

4 what protozoan causes one form of dysentery in humans? (p. 249)

5 what protozoan has caused more deaths in armies throughout history than actual combat? (p. 251)

6 why sandboxes should always be covered when not in use? (p. 252)

7 what group of protozoa includes the most complex of all protists? (p. 253)

This chapter answers these and other useful questions.

This chapter contains evolutionary concepts, which are set off in this font.

EVOLUTIONARY PERSPECTIVE

Where are your "roots"? Although most people are content to go back into their family tree several hundred years, scientists look back millions of years to the origin of all life-forms. The fossil record indicates that virtually all protist and animal phyla living today were present during the Cambrian period, about 550 million years ago (*see table 1.1*). Unfortunately, fossil evidence of the evolutionary pathways that gave rise to these phyla is scant. Instead, scientists gather evidence by examining the structure and function of living species. The "Evolutionary Perspective" sections in chapters 17 to 31 present hypotheses regarding the origin of protist and animal phyla. These hypotheses seem reasonable to most zoologists; however, they are untestable, and alternative interpretations are in the scientific literature.

Ancient members of the Archaea were the first living organisms on this planet. The Archaea gave rise to the kingdom Protista (also called Protoctista) about 1.5 billion years ago. The endosymbiont hypothesis is one of a number of explanations of how this could have occurred (*see box 3.1*). ❶ Most scientists agree that the protists probably arose from more than one ancestral Archaean group. Depending on the classification system, zoologists recognize between 7 and 45 phyla of protists. These phyla represent numerous evolutionary lineages. Groups of organisms believed to have had separate origins are said to be **polyphyletic** (Gr. *polys*, many + *phylon*, race). Some protists are plantlike because they are primarily autotrophic (they produce their own food). Others are animal-like because they are primarily heterotrophic (they feed on other organisms). This chapter covers seven phyla of protists commonly called the protozoa (figures 17.1, 17.2).

LIFE WITHIN A SINGLE PLASMA MEMBRANE

Protozoa (Gr. *proto*, first + *zoa*, animal) display unicellular (cytoplasmic) organization, which does not necessarily imply that they are simple organisms. ❷ Often, they are more complex than any particular cell in higher organisms. In some protozoan phyla, individuals group to form colonies, associations of individuals that are not dependent on one another for most functions. Protozoan colonies, however, can become complex, with some individuals becoming so specialized that differentiating between a colony and a multicellular organism becomes difficult.

MAINTAINING HOMEOSTASIS

Organelles that are similar to the organelles of other eukaryotic cells carry out specific functions in protozoa (figure 17.3; *see also figure 3.2*). Some protozoan organelles, however, reflect specializations for unicellular lifestyles.

A regular arrangement of microtubules, called the **pellicle,** underlies the plasma membrane of many protozoa. The pellicle is rigid enough to maintain the shape of the protozoan, but it is also flexible.

FIGURE 17.1

A Protozoan. *Naegleria fowleri,* the cause of primary amebic meningoencephalitis in humans. The facelike structures attack and engulf food sources (SEM ×600).

The cytoplasm of a protozoan is differentiated into two regions. The portion of the cytoplasm just beneath the pellicle is called **ectoplasm** (Gr. *ectos,* outside + *plasma,* to form). It is relatively clear and firm. The inner cytoplasm, called **endoplasm** (Gr. *endon,* within), is usually granular and more fluid. The conversion of cytoplasm between these two states is important in one kind of protozoan locomotion and is discussed later in the chapter.

Most marine protozoa have solute concentrations similar to that of their environments. Freshwater protozoa, however, must regulate the water and solute concentrations of their cytoplasm. Water enters freshwater protozoa by osmosis because of higher solute concentrations in the protozoan than in the environment. **Contractile vacuoles** remove this excess water (figure 17.3). In some protozoa, contractile vacuoles form by coalescence of smaller vacuoles. In others, the vacuoles are permanent organelles that collecting tubules radiating into the cytoplasm fill. Contracting microfilaments (*see figure 3.20*) have been implicated in the emptying of contractile vacuoles.

Most protozoa absorb dissolved nutrients by active transport or ingest whole or particulate food through endocytosis (*see figure 3.14*). Some protozoa ingest food in a specialized region analogous

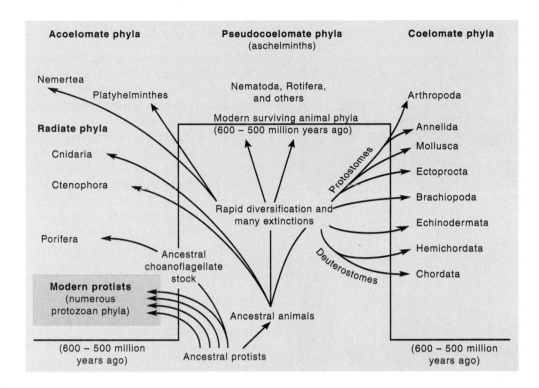

FIGURE 17.2

Animal-like Protists: The Protozoa. A generalized evolutionary tree depicting the major events and possible lines of descent for the protozoa (shaded in orange).

to a mouth, called the **cytopharynx.** Digestion and transport of food occurs in **food vacuoles** that form during endocytosis. Enzymes and acidity changes mediate digestion. Food vacuoles fuse with enzyme-containing lysosomes and circulate through the cytoplasm, distributing the products of digestion. After digestion is complete, the vacuoles are called **egestion vacuoles.** They release their contents by exocytosis, sometimes at a specialized region of the plasma membrane or pellicle called the **cytopyge.**

Because protozoa are small, they have a large surface area in proportion to their volume (*see figure 3.3*). This high surface-area-to-volume ratio facilitates two other maintenance functions: gas exchange and excretion. Gas exchange involves acquiring oxygen for cellular respiration and eliminating the carbon dioxide produced as a by-product. Excretion is the elimination of the nitrogenous by-products of protein metabolism, which, in protozoa, is primarily ammonia. Both gas exchange and excretion occur by diffusion across the plasma membrane.

REPRODUCTION

Both asexual and sexual reproduction occur among the protozoa. One of the simplest and most common forms of asexual reproduction is **binary fission.** In binary fission, mitosis produces two nuclei that are distributed into two similar-sized individuals when the cytoplasm divides. During cytokinesis, some organelles duplicate to ensure that each new protozoan has the needed organelles to continue life. Depending on the group of protozoa, cytokinesis may be longitudinal or transverse (figures 17.4 and 17.5).

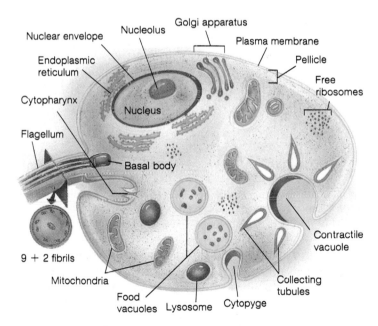

FIGURE 17.3

A Protozoan Protist. This drawing of a stylized protozoan with a flagellum illustrates the basic protozoan morphology. *From: "A LIFE OF INVERTEBRATES"* © *1979 W. D. Russell-Hunter.*

Other forms of asexual reproduction are common. During **budding,** mitosis is followed by the incorporation of one nucleus into a cytoplasmic mass that is much smaller than the parent cell. **Multiple fission** or **schizogony** (Gr. *schizein,* to split) is when a

Figure 17.4

Asexual Reproduction in Protozoa. Binary fission begins with mitosis. Cytoplasmic division (cytokinesis) divides the organelles between the two cells and results in two similarly sized protozoa. Binary fission is (*a*) longitudinal in some protozoa (e.g., mastigophorans) and (*b*) transverse in other protozoa (e.g., ciliates).

large number of daughter cells form from the division of a single protozoan. Schizogony begins with multiple mitotic divisions in a mature individual. When a certain number of nuclei has been produced, cytoplasmic division results in the separation of each nucleus into a new cell.

Sexual reproduction requires gamete formation and the subsequent fusion of gametes to form a zygote. In most protozoa, the sexually mature individual is haploid. Gametes are produced by mitosis, and meiosis follows union of the gametes. Ciliated protozoa are an exception to this pattern. Specialized forms of sexual reproduction are covered as individual protozoan groups are discussed.

Symbiotic Life-styles

Many protozoa have symbiotic lifestyles. **Symbiosis** (Gr. *syn*, with + *bios*, life) is an intimate association between two organisms. For many protozoa, these interactions involve a form of symbiosis called **parasitism,** in which one organism lives in or on a second organism, called a **host.** The host is harmed but usually survives, at least long enough for the parasite to complete one or more life cycles.

The relationships between a parasite and its host(s) are often complex. Some parasites have life histories involving multiple hosts. The **definitive host** harbors the sexual stages of the parasite. The sexual stages may produce offspring that enter another host, called an **intermediate host,** where they reproduce asexually. Some life cycles require more than one intermediate host and more than one immature stage. For the life cycle to be complete, the final, asexual stage must have access to a definitive host.

Other kinds of symbiosis involve relationships that do not harm the host. **Commensalism** is a symbiotic relationship in which one member of the relationship benefits, and the second member is neither benefited nor harmed. **Mutualism** is a symbiotic relationship in which both species benefit.

Protozoan Taxonomy

Zoologists who specialize in the study of protozoa are called **protozoologists.** Most protozoologists now regard the protozoa as a subkingdom, consisting of seven separate phyla within the kingdom Protista. These are the phylum Sarcomastigophora, consisting of flagellates and amoebae with a single type of nucleus; the phyla Labyrinthomorpha, Apicomplexa, Microspora, Acetospora, and Myxozoa, consisting of either saprozoic or parasitic species; and the phylum Ciliophora, containing ciliated protozoa with two types of nuclei. The classification of this subkingdom into phyla is based primarily on types of nuclei, mode of reproduction, and mechanism of locomotion (table 17.1). These taxa are discussed further later in this chapter. Overall, the number of protozoan species exceeds 38,000.

Stop and Ask Yourself

1. Ancestral members of what group of organisms gave rise to the protozoa?
2. What is the function of the following structures: (*a*) pellicle, (*b*) contractile vacuoles, (*c*) cytopharynx, and (*d*) egestion vacuoles?
3. What are three forms of asexual reproduction in protozoa?
4. Why do most protozoa produce gametes by mitosis rather than by meiosis?

(a)   (b)   (c)   (d)

FIGURE 17.5

Binary Fission of the Ciliate, *Stentor coeruleus*. (*a,b*) Fission includes the division of some surface features—in this case, cilia modified into a bandlike structure called a membranelle (M). F designates the frontal field. The arrow in (*b*) shows the beginning of a fission furrow. (*c,d*) Fission is completed by division of the cytoplasm. (SEMs ×250.)

TABLE 17.1	SUMMARY OF PROTOZOAN CLASSIFICATION

Kingdom Protista (pro-tees′ta) Single-celled eukaryotes.

Subkingdom Protozoa (pro″to-zo′ah) Animal-like protistans.

Phylum Sarcomastigophora (sar″ko-mas-ti-gof′o-rah)
Protozoa that possess flagella, pseudopodia, or both for locomotion and feeding; single type of nucleus. About 18,000 species.

  Subphylum Mastigophora (mas″ti-gof′o-rah)
One or more flagella for locomotion; autotrophic, heterotrophic, or saprozoic.

    Class Phytomastigophorea (fi″to-mas-ti-go-for′ah)
Chloroplasts usually present; mainly autotrophic, some heterotrophic. *Euglena, Volvox, Chlamydomonas*.

    Class Zoomastigophorea (zo″o-mas-ti-go-for′ah)
Lack chloroplasts; heterotrophic or saprozoic. *Trypanosoma, Trichonympha, Trichomonas, Giardia, Leishmania*.

  Subphylum Sarcodina (sar″ko-din′ah)
Pseudopodia for movement and food gathering; naked or with shell or test; mostly free living.

    Superclass Rhizopoda (ri-zop′o-dah)
Lobopodia, filopodia, reticulopodia, or no distinct pseudopodia. *Amoeba, Entamoeba, Naegleria, Arcella, Difflugia*; foraminiferans (*Gumbelina*). About 4,000 species.

    Superclass Actinopoda (ak″ti-nop′o-dah)
Spherical, planktonic; axopodia supported by microtubules; includes marine radiolarians with siliceous tests and freshwater heliozoans (*Actinophrys*). About 3,000 species.

  Subphylum Opalinata (op″ah-li-not′ah)
Cylindrical; covered with cilia. *Opalina, Zelleriella*.

Phylum Labyrinthomorpha (la″brinth-o-mor′fa)
Trophic stage as ectoplasmic network with spindle-shaped or spherical, nonamoeboid cells; saprozoic and parasitic on algae and seagrass; mostly marine and estuarine. *Labyrinthula*.

Phylum Apicomplexa (a″pi-kom-plex′ah)
Parasitic with an apical complex used for penetrating host cells; cilia and flagella lacking, except in certain reproductive stages. The gregarines (*Monocystis*), coccidians (*Eimeria, Isospora, Sarcocystis, Toxoplasma*), *Plasmodium*. About 5,500 species.

Phylum Microspora (mi″cro-spor′ah)
Unicellular spores; intracellular parasites in nearly all major animal groups. The microsporeans (*Nosema*). About 850 species.

Phylum Acetospora (ah-sēt-o-spor′ah)
Multicellular spore; all parasitic in invertebrates. The acetosporans (*Paramyxa, Haplosporidium*).

Phylum Myxozoa (mix″o-zoo′ah)
Spores of multicellular origin; all parasitic. The myxozoans (*Myxosoma*). About 1,250 species.

Phylum Ciliophora (sil″i-of′or-ah)
Protozoa with simple or compound cilia at some stage in the life history; heterotrophs with a well-developed cytostome and feeding organelles; at least one macronucleus and one micronucleus present. *Paramecium, Stentor, Euplotes, Vorticella, Balantidium*. About 9,000 species.

Phylum Sarcomastigophora

With over 18,000 described species, Sarcomastigophora (sar″ko-mas-ti-gof′o-rah) (Gr. *sarko*, fleshy + *mastigo*, whip + *phoros*, to bear) is the largest protozoan phylum and has the following characteristics:

1. Unicellular or colonial
2. Locomotion by flagella, pseudopodia, or both
3. Autotrophic, saprozoic, or heterotrophic
4. Single type of nucleus
5. Sexual reproduction (usually)

Subphylum Mastigophora: Flagellar Locomotion

Members of the subphylum Mastigophora (mas″ti-gof′o-rah) use flagella in locomotion. Flagella may produce two-dimensional, whiplike movements or helical movements that push or pull the protozoan through its aquatic medium.

Class Phytomastigophorea

The subphylum Mastigophora has two classes. Members of the class Phytomastigophorea (fi″to-mas-ti-go-for′ah) (Gr. *phytos*, plant) possess chlorophyll and one or two flagella. Phytomastigophoreans produce a large portion of the food in marine food webs. Much of the oxygen in aquatic habitats comes from photosynthesis by these marine organisms.

Marine phytomastigophoreans include the dinoflagellates (figure 17.6). Dinoflagellates have one flagellum that wraps around the organism in a transverse groove. The primary action of this flagellum causes the organism to spin on its axis. A second flagellum is a trailing flagellum that pushes the organism forward. In addition to chlorophyll, many dinoflagellates contain xanthophyll pigments, which give them a golden brown color. At times, dinoflagellates become so numerous that they color the water. Several genera, such as *Gymnodinium*, have representatives that produce toxins. ❸ Periodic "blooms" of these organisms are called "red tides" and result in fish kills along the continental shelves. Humans who consume tainted molluscs or fish may die. The Bible reports that the first plague Moses visited upon the Egyptians was a blood-red tide that killed fish and fouled water. Indeed, the Red Sea is probably named after these toxic dinoflagellate blooms.

Euglena is a freshwater phytomastigophorean (figure 17.7). Each chloroplast has a **pyrenoid,** which synthesizes and stores polysaccharides. If cultured in the dark, euglenoids feed by absorption and lose their green color. Some euglenoids (e.g., *Peranema*) lack chloroplasts and are always heterotrophic.

Euglena orients toward light of certain intensities. A pigment shield (**stigma**) covers a photoreceptor at the base of the flagellum. The stigma permits light to strike the photoreceptor from only one direction, allowing *Euglena* to orient and move in relation to a light source.

Figure 17.6

Class Phytomastigophorea: Dinoflagellates. Two species of dinoflagellates—*Peridinium* in the upper left and *Ceratium* in the lower half. The transverse grooves in the center of each dinoflagellate are the location for one of the two flagella (SEM ×800).

Euglenoid flagellates are haploid and reproduce by longitudinal binary fission (*see figure 17.4a*). Sexual reproduction in these species is unknown.

Volvox is a colonial flagellate consisting of up to 50,000 cells embedded in a spherical, gelatinous matrix (figure 17.8a). Individual cells possess two flagella, which cause the colony to roll and turn gracefully through the water (figure 17.8b).

Although most *Volvox* cells are relatively unspecialized, reproduction depends on certain specialized cells. Asexual reproduction occurs in the spring and summer when certain cells withdraw to the watery interior of the parental colony and form daughter colonies. When the parental colony dies, it ruptures and releases daughter colonies.

Sexual reproduction in *Volvox* occurs during autumn. Some species are **dioecious** (having separate sexes); other species are **monoecious** (having both sexes in the same colony). In autumn, specialized cells differentiate into macrogametes or microgametes. Macrogametes are large, filled with nutrient reserves, and nonmotile. Microgametes form as a packet of flagellated cells that leaves the parental colony and swims to a colony containing macrogametes. The packet then breaks apart, and syngamy occurs between macro- and microgametes. The zygote, an overwintering stage, secretes a resistant wall around itself and is released when the parental colony dies. Because the parental colony consists of haploid cells, the zygote must undergo meiosis to reduce the chromosome number from the diploid zygotic condition. One of the products of meiosis then undergoes repeated mitotic divisions to form a colony consisting of just a few cells. The other products of meiosis degenerate. This colony is released from the protective zygotic capsule in the spring.

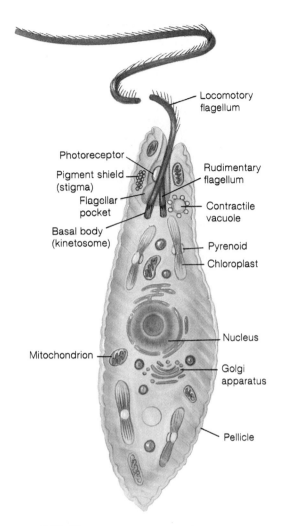

FIGURE 17.7

Phytomastigophorean Anatomy: The Structure of *Euglena.* Note the large, well-organized chloroplasts. The photoreceptor allows the organism to swim toward light. The organism is about 50 μm long.

(a)

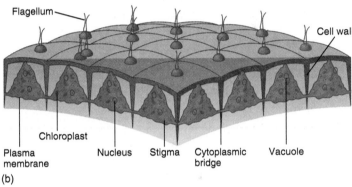

(b)

FIGURE 17.8

Class Phytomastigophorea: *Volvox,* a Colonial Flagellate. (*a*) A *Volvox* colony, showing asexually produced daughter colonies (LM ×400). (*b*) An enlargement of a portion of the colony wall.

CLASS ZOOMASTIGOPHOREA

Members of the class Zoomastigophorea (zo″o-mas-ti-go-for′ah) (Gr. *zoion*, animal) lack chloroplasts and are heterotrophic. Some members of this class are important parasites of humans (box 17.1).

One of the most important species of zoomastigophoreans is *Trypanosoma brucei.* This species is divided into three subspecies: *T. b. brucei, T. b. gambiense,* and *T. b. rhodesiense,* often referred to as the *Trypanosoma brucei* complex. The first of these three subspecies is a parasite of nonhuman mammals of Africa. The latter two cause sleeping sickness in humans. Tsetse flies (*Glossina* spp.) are intermediate hosts and vectors of all three subspecies. When a tsetse fly bites an infected human or mammal, it picks up parasites in addition to its meal of blood. Trypanosomes multiply asexually in the gut of the fly for about 10 days, then migrate to the salivary glands. While in the fly, trypanosomes transform, in 15 to 35 days, through a number of body forms. When the infected tsetse fly bites another vertebrate host, the parasites travel with salivary secre-

tions into the blood of a new definitive host. The parasites multiply asexually in the new host and again transform through a number of body forms. Parasites may live in the blood, lymph, spleen, central nervous system, and cerebrospinal fluid (figure 17.9).

When trypanosomes enter the central nervous system, they cause general apathy, mental dullness, and lack of coordination. "Sleepiness" develops, and the infected individual may fall asleep during normal daytime activities. Death results from any combination of the previous symptoms, as well as from heart failure, malnutrition, and other weakened conditions. If detected early, sleeping sickness is curable. However, if an infection has advanced to the central nervous system, recovery is unlikely.

SUBPHYLUM SARCODINA: PSEUDOPODIA AND AMOEBOID LOCOMOTION

Members of the subphylum Sarcodina (sar″ko-din′ah) are the amoebae (sing., amoeba). When feeding and moving, they form temporary cell extensions called **pseudopodia** (sing., pseudopodium) (Gr. *pseudes*, false + *podion*, little foot). Pseudopodia

GIARDIASIS: "BACKPACKER'S DISEASE" IN THE ROCKY MOUNTAINS

Many of the pristine rivers, streams, and lakes in the Rocky Mountains now harbor the mastigophorean *Giardia lamblia* (figure 1). *Giardia* can inhabit the intestine of humans, and wild and domestic animals. In the intestine, the parasites multiply by binary fission and thickly carpet the intestinal wall. Because the parasites are so numerous, a person or animal can shed millions of *Giardia* cysts in the feces. If a human or animal infected by the parasite defecates close to a body of water, the durable cysts can infect someone else who drinks the water even 2 to 3 months later. Dogs, cattle, beavers, deer, bear, and other *Giardia* hosts add to the reservoir of contaminated feces and have helped to create the current situation.

In animals and humans, *Giardia* causes the disease **giardiasis,** commonly called "backpacker's disease." Giardiasis is exceedingly unpleasant and usually involves severe diarrhea and painful intestinal cramps that can last for days or weeks. Antiparasitic drugs can quickly cure the disease. However, the best advice is to avoid giardiasis in the first place by not drinking water from wilderness streams or lakes.

FIGURE 1   *Giardia lamblia* (SEM ×1,000). The organism is 12 to 15 μm long.

(a)

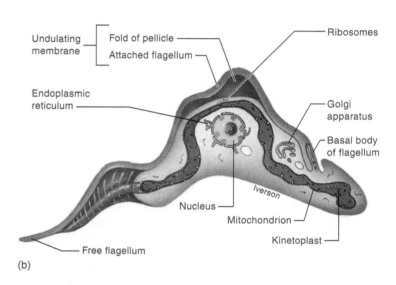

(b)

FIGURE 17.9

Class Zoomastigophorea: The Life Cycle of *Trypanosoma brucei.* (*a*) When a tsetse fly feeds on a vertebrate host, trypanosomes enter the vertebrate's circulatory system (first arrow on right) with the fly's saliva. Trypanosomes multiply in the vertebrate's circulatory and lymphatic systems by binary fission. When another tsetse fly bites this vertebrate host again, trypanosomes move into the gut of the fly and undergo binary fission. Trypanosomes then migrate to the fly's salivary glands, where they are available to infect a new host. (*b*) Structure of the flagellate, *Trypanosoma brucei rhodesiense*. This flagellate is about 25 μm long.

exist in a variety of forms. **Lobopodia** (sing., lobopodium) (Gr. *lobos*, lobe) are broad cell processes containing ectoplasm and endoplasm and are used for locomotion and engulfing food (figure 17.10*a*). **Filopodia** (sing., filopodium) (L. *filum*, thread) contain ectoplasm only and provide a constant two-way streaming that delivers food in a conveyor-belt fashion (figure 17.10*b*). **Reticulopodia** (sing., reticulopodium) (L. *reticulatus*, netlike) are similar to filopodia, except that they branch and rejoin to form a netlike se-

(a)

FIGURE 17.10

Variations in Pseudopodia. (*a*) Lobopodia of *Amoeba* contain both ectoplasm and endoplasm and are used for locomotion and engulfing food. (*b*) Filopodia of a shelled amoeba contain ectoplasm only and provide constant two-way streaming that delivers food particles to this protozoan in a conveyor-belt fashion. (*c*) Reticulopodia are similar to filopodia except that they branch and rejoin to form a netlike series of cell extensions. They occur in foraminiferans such as *Globigerina*. (*d*) Axopodia on the surface of a heliozoan such as *Actinosphaerium* deliver food to the central cytoplasm.

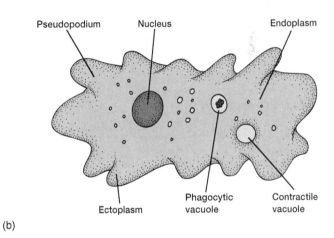

(b)

FIGURE 17.11

Subphylum Sarcodina: Class Lobosea. (*a*) *Amoeba proteus*, showing blunt lobopodia (LM ×160). (*b*) Anatomy of *Amoeba proteus*.

ries of cell extensions (figure 17.10*c*). **Axopodia** (sing., axopodium) (L. *axis*, axle) are thin, filamentous, and supported by a central axis of microtubules. The cytoplasm covering the central axis is adhesive and movable. Food caught on axopodia can be delivered to the central cytoplasm of the amoeba (figure 17.10*d*).

SUPERCLASS RHIZOPODA, CLASS LOBOSEA

The most familiar amoebae belong to the superclass Rhizopoda (ri-zop′o-dah), class Lobosea (lo-bo′sah) (Gr. *lobos*, lobe), and the genus *Amoeba* (figure 17.11). These amoebae are naked (they have no test or shell) and are normally found on shallow-water substrates of freshwater ponds, lakes, and slow-moving streams, where they feed on other protists and bacteria. They engulf food by phagocytosis, a process that involves the cytoplasmic changes described earlier for amoeboid locomotion (*see figure 3.14*). In the process, food is incorporated into food vacuoles. Binary fission occurs when an amoeba reaches a certain size limit. As with other amoebae, no sexual reproduction is known to occur.

Other members of the class Lobosea possess a test or shell. **Tests** are protective structures that the cytoplasm secretes. They may be calcareous (made of calcium carbonate), proteinaceous (made of protein), siliceous (made of silica [SiO_2]), or chitinous (made of chitin—a polysaccharide [*see figure 2.11*]). Other tests may be composed of sand or other debris cemented into a secreted matrix. Usually, one or more openings in the test allow pseudopo-

dia to be extruded. *Arcella* is a common freshwater, shelled amoeba. It has a brown, proteinaceous test that is flattened on one side and domed on the other. Pseudopodia project from an opening on the flattened side. *Difflugia* is another common freshwater, shelled amoeba (figure 17.12). Its test is vase shaped and is composed of mineral particles embedded in a secreted matrix.

Most amoebae are symbiotic; a few are pathogenic. ❹ For example, *Entamoeba histolytica* causes one form of dysentery in humans. Inflammation and ulceration of the lower intestinal tract and a debilitating diarrhea that includes blood and mucus characterize dysentery. Amoebic dysentery is a worldwide problem that plagues humans in crowded, unsanitary conditions.

A significant problem in the control of *Entamoeba histolytica* is that an individual can be infected and contagious without experiencing symptoms of the disease. Amoebae live in the folds of the intestinal wall, feeding on starch and mucoid secretions. They pass from one host to another in the form of cysts transmitted by fecal contamination of food or water. After ingestion by a new host, amoebae leave their cysts and take up residence in the host's intestinal wall.

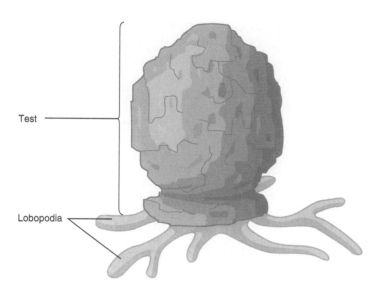

FIGURE 17.12

Subphylum Sarcodina. *Difflugia oblongata*, a common freshwater, shelled amoeba. The test consists of cemented mineral particles.

FIGURE 17.13

Subphylum Sarcodina: Foraminiferan Test (*Polystomella*). As this foraminiferan grows, it secretes new, larger chambers that remain attached to older chambers, making this protozoan look like a tiny snail (LM ×63).

SUPERCLASS ACTINOPODA: FORAMINIFERANS, HELIOZOANS, AND RADIOLARIANS

Foraminiferans (commonly called forams) are primarily a marine group of amoebae. Foraminiferans possess reticulopodia and secrete a test that is primarily calcium carbonate. As foraminiferans grow, they secrete new, larger chambers that remain attached to the older chambers (figure 17.13). Test enlargement follows a symmetrical pattern that may result in a straight chain of chambers or a spiral arrangement that resembles a snail shell. Many of these tests become relatively large; for example, "Mermaid's pennies," found in Australia, may be several centimeters in diameter.

Foram tests are abundant in the fossil record since the Cambrian period. They make up a large component of marine sediments, and their accumulation on the floor of primeval oceans resulted in limestone and chalk deposits. The white cliffs of Dover in England are one example of a foraminiferan-chalk deposit. Oil geologists use fossilized forams to identify geologic strata when taking exploratory cores.

Heliozoans are aquatic amoebae that are either planktonic or live attached by a stalk to some substrate. (The plankton of a body of water consists of those organisms that float freely in the water.) Heliozoans are either naked or enclosed within a test that contains openings for axopodia (figure 17.14*a*).

Radiolarians are planktonic marine and freshwater amoebae. They are relatively large; some colonial forms may reach several centimeters in diameter. They possess a test (usually siliceous) of long, movable spines and needles or of a highly sculptured and ornamented lattice (figure 17.14*b*). When radiolarians die, their tests drift to the ocean floor. Some of the oldest known fossils of eukaryotic organisms are radiolarians.

PHYLUM LABYRINTHOMORPHA

The very small phylum Labyrinthomorpha (la"brinth-o-mor'fa) consists of protozoa with spindle-shaped, nonamoeboid, vegetative cells. In some genera, amoeboid cells use a typical gliding motion to move within a network of mucous tracks. Most members are marine, and either saprozoic or parasitic on algae or seagrass. Several years ago, *Labyrinthula* killed most of the "eel grass" (a grasslike marine flowering plant) on the Atlantic coast, starving many ducks that feed on the grass.

Stop and Ask Yourself

5. How and when does sexual reproduction occur in *Volvox*?
6. How do trypanosomes gain entry to human hosts?
7. What mechanism explains amoeboid locomotion?
8. How is *Entamoeba histolytica* transmitted among humans? How is *Giardia lamblia* transmitted among humans?

PHYLUM APICOMPLEXA

Members of the phylum Apicomplexa (a"pi-kom-plex'ah) (L. *apex*, point + *com*, together, + *plexus*, interweaving) are all parasites. Characteristics of the phylum include:

1. Apical complex for penetrating host cells
2. Single type of nucleus
3. No cilia and flagella, except in certain reproductive stages
4. Life cycles that typically include asexual (schizogony, sporogony) and sexual (gametogony) phases

Axopodium—

(a)

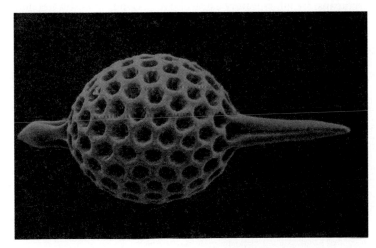

(b)

FIGURE 17.14

Subphylum Sarcodina: Heliozoan and Radiolarian Tests. (*a*) *Actinosphaerium sol* has a spherical body covered with fine, long axopodia made of numerous microtubules and surrounded by streaming cytoplasm. Following phagocytosis by an axopodium, waves of cytoplasmic movement carry trapped food particles into the main body of this protozoan (LM ×450). (*b*) The radiolarian *Spaerostylus* is typically spherical with a highly sculptured test (LM ×480).

CLASS SPOROZOEA

The most important species in the phylum Apicomplexa are members of the class Sporozoea (spor"o-zo'e). The class name derives from most sporozoeans producing a resistant spore or oocyst following sexual reproduction. Some members of this class, including *Plasmodium* and coccidians, cause a variety of diseases in domestic animals and humans.

Although the life cycles of sporozoeans vary considerably, certain generalizations are possible. Many are intracellular parasites, and their life cycles have three phases. **Schizogony** is multiple fission of an asexual stage in host cells to form many more (usually asexual) individuals, called merozoites, that leave the host cell and infect many other cells. (Schizogony to produce merozoites is also called **merogony.**)

Some of the merozoites undergo **gametogony,** which begins the sexual phase of the life cycle. The parasite forms either microgametocytes or macrogametocytes. Microgametocytes undergo multiple fission to produce biflagellate microgametes that emerge from the infected host cell. The macrogametocyte develops directly into a single macrogamete. A microgamete fertilizes a macrogamete to produce a zygote that becomes enclosed and is called an oocyst.

The zygote undergoes meiosis, and the resulting cells divide repeatedly by mitosis. This process, called **sporogony,** produces many rodlike sporozoites in the oocyst. Sporozoites infect the cells of a new host after the new host ingests and digests the oocyst, or sporozoites are otherwise introduced (e.g., by a mosquito bite).

One sporozoean genus, *Plasmodium*, causes malaria and has a long history. Accounts of the disease go back as far as 1550 B.C. ⑤ Malaria contributed significantly to the failure of the Crusades during the medieval era, and along with typhus, has devastated more armies than has actual combat. Recently (since the early 1970s), malaria has resurged throughout the world. Over 100 million humans are estimated to annually contract the disease.

The *Plasmodium* life cycle involves vertebrate and mosquito hosts (figure 17.15). Schizogony occurs first in liver cells and later in red blood cells, and gametogony also occurs in red blood cells. A mosquito takes in gametocytes during a meal of blood, and the gameotocytes subsequently fuse. The zygote penetrates the gut of the mosquito and transforms into an oocyst. Sporogony forms haploid sporozoites that may enter a new host when the mosquito bites the host.

The symptoms of malaria recur periodically and are called paroxysms (box 17.2). Chills and fever correlate with the maturation of parasites, the rupture of red blood cells, and the release of toxic metabolites.

Four species of *Plasmodium* are the most important human malarial species. *P. vivax* causes malaria in which the paroxysms recur every 48 hours. This species occurs in temperate regions and has been nearly eradicated in many parts of the world. *P. falciparum* causes the most virulent form of malaria in humans. Paroxysms are more irregular than in the other species. *P. falciparum* was once worldwide, but is now mainly tropical and subtropical in distribution. It remains one of the greatest killers of humanity, especially in Africa. *P. malariae* is worldwide in distribution and causes malaria

Figure 17.15

Phylum Apicomplexa: The Life Cycle of *Plasmodium*. Schizogony (merogony) occurs in liver cells and, later, in the red blood cells (RBCs) of humans. Gametogony occurs in RBCs. During a blood meal, the mosquito takes in micro- and macrogametes, which fuse to form zygotes. Zygotes penetrate the gut of the mosquito and form oocysts. Meiosis and sporogony form many haploid sporozoites that may enter a new host when the mosquito bites the host.

with paroxysms that recur every 72 hours. *P. ovale* is the rarest of the four human malarial species and is primarily tropical in distribution.

Other members of the class Sporozoea also cause important diseases. Coccidiosis is primarily a disease of poultry, sheep, cattle, and rabbits. Two genera, *Isospora* and *Eimeria*, are particularly important parasites of poultry. Yearly losses to the U.S. poultry industry from coccidiosis have approached $35 million. Another coccidian, *Cryptosporidium*, has become more well known with the advent of AIDS since it causes chronic diarrhea in AIDS patients. Toxoplasmosis is a disease of mammals, including humans, and birds. Sexual reproduction of *Toxoplasma* occurs primarily in cats. Infections occur when oocysts are ingested with food contaminated by cat feces, or when meat containing encysted merozoites is eaten raw or poorly cooked. Most infections in humans are asymptomatic, and once infected, an effective immunity develops. However, if a woman is infected near the time of pregnancy, or during pregnancy, congenital toxoplasmosis may develop in a fetus. Congenital toxoplasmosis is a major cause of stillbirths and spontaneous abortions. Fetuses that survive frequently show signs of mental retardation and epileptic seizures. Congenital toxoplasmosis has no cure. Toxoplasmosis also ranks high among the opportunistic diseases afflicting AIDS patients. ❻ Steps to avoid

infections by *Toxoplasma* include keeping stray and pet cats away from children's sandboxes; using sandbox covers; and awareness, on the part of couples considering having children, of the potential dangers of eating raw or very rare pork, lamb, and beef.

PHYLUM MICROSPORA

Members of the phylum Microspora (mi″cro-spor′ah), commonly called microsporidia, are small, obligatory intracellular parasites. Included in this phylum are several species that parasitize beneficial insects. *Nosema bombicus* parasitizes silkworms (figure 17.16), causing the disease **pebrine,** and *N. apis* causes serious dysentery (foul brood) in honeybees. These parasites have a possible role as biological control agents for insect pests. For example, the U.S. Environmental Protection Agency has approved and registered *N. locustae* for use in residual control of rangeland grasshoppers. Recently, four microsporidian genera have been implicated in secondary infections of immunosuppressed and AIDS patients.

PHYLUM ACETOSPORA

Acetospora (ah-sēt-o-spor′ah) is a relatively small phylum that consists exclusively of obligatory extracellular parasites characterized by spores lacking polar caps or polar filaments. The acetosporeans (e.g., *Haplosporidium*) primarily are parasitic in the cells, tissues, and body cavities of molluscs.

PHYLUM MYXOZOA

The phylum Myxozoa (myx″o-zoo′ah), commonly called myxosporeans, are all obligatory extracellular parasites in freshwater and marine fish. They have a resistant spore with one to six coiled polar filaments. The most economically important myxosporean is *Myxosoma cerebralis,* which infects the nervous system and auditory organs of trout and salmon, causing whirling or tumbling disease.

Stop and Ask Yourself

9. What is an apical complex? What is it used for?
10. What is schizogony?
11. Members of which protozoan genus have caused the most human suffering since antiquity?
12. What are the three stages in the life cycle of *Plasmodium*?
13. How are infections of *Toxoplasma* acquired?
14. What are the dangers of toxoplasmosis for a fetus?
15. What are the four most important sporozoean parasites and the diseases they cause?
16. What is one economically important disease caused by a microsporidian?
17. What group of animals do myxosporeans usually parasitize?

BOX 17.2 MALARIA CONTROL—A GLIMMER OF HOPE

The quotation that follows is from *The Lake Regions of Central Africa* by Sir Richard Burton (1821–1890). Sir Burton was an adventurer whose visits to the Far East and Africa brought him into contact with the greatest killer of humanity, *Plasmodium falciparum*.

> *The approach of malignant fever is very insidious. An attack begins mostly with an ordinary chill, attended by no unusual or marked symptoms. Sometimes the patient has had a light chill a day or two before this, which he has neglected. Sometimes he has felt slightly unwell for ten or fourteen days; has complained of loss of appetite and general weakness; but as these symptoms are not very marked, they are very apt to be overlooked, especially with newcomers.*
>
> *The real attack may begin with a chill or with a fever, but its effects are, in either case, at once evident in a peculiarly yellow skin and haggard countenance. In fever there is profuse perspiration, a rush of blood to the head, high and irregular pulse, and general prostration. Sometimes the body is hot, but dry. Thirst is urgent, but the stomach rejects whatever is drunk.*
>
> *If the paroxysm [sudden attack] of fever returns, it is with renewed force, and the third attack is commonly fatal. Before death the patient becomes insensible; there is violent vomiting, which is, in fact, regurgitation of ingesta, mixed with green and yellow fluid. Immediately after the chill, and even before this has passed off, the urine becomes dark red or black. The pulse is very irregular, the breathing slow and finally the patient sinks away into a state of coma, and dies without a struggle.*

Malaria is still a fact of life—especially in Africa. Nearly 300 million people are afflicted annually, and a third of them die. The fight against this disease has centered on two fronts: elimination of the mosquito species known to carry *Plasmodium* parasites and treatment of infected persons with antimalarial drugs. In the fight against mosquitoes, DDT (dichloro-diphenyl-trichloroethane) was employed successfully in the 1950s and 1960s. Its use greatly reduced the incidence of malaria by the middle 1960s. Mosquito-control programs, however, began to lose their effectiveness, largely because mosquitoes evolved resistance to DDT. DDT has also been found to be a highly persistent pesticide. It retains its toxicity for many years and can build up to lethal levels in aquatic and terrestrial environments. Its use became less effective and more expensive—both in economic and environmental terms. Other pesticides are now being used, but mosquito resistance is becoming a problem with these pesticides, too.

Even more serious is the worldwide development of resistance by *Plasmodium* parasites to antimalarial drugs, such as chloroquine.

As bleak as this picture sounds, scientists and health officials are optimistic that malaria will eventually be conquered. Recent advancements in molecular biology and immunology are being employed in the development of antimalarial vaccines. Some vaccines are now being tested. Researchers have found that the complexity of the disease presents special problems in vaccine development. Not only does each *Plasmodium* species require a separate vaccine, but each stage of the life cycle of a single species requires a separate immunological vaccine component.

PHYLUM CILIOPHORA

7 The phylum Ciliophora (sil"i-of′or-ah) includes some of the most complex protozoa (*see table 17.1*). Ciliates are widely distributed in freshwater and marine environments. A few ciliates are symbiotic. Characteristics of the phylum Ciliophora include:

1. Cilia for locomotion and for the generation of feeding currents in water
2. Relatively rigid pellicle and more or less fixed shape
3. Distinct cytostome (mouth) structure
4. Dimorphic nuclei, typically a larger macronucleus and one or more smaller micronuclei

CILIA AND OTHER PELLICULAR STRUCTURES

Cilia are generally similar to flagella, except that they are much shorter, more numerous, and widely distributed over the surface of the protozoan (figure 17.17). Ciliary movements are coordinated so that ciliary waves pass over the surface of the ciliate. Many ciliates can reverse the direction of ciliary beating and the direction of cell movement.

Basal bodies (kinetosomes) of adjacent cilia are interconnected with an elaborate network of fibers that are believed to anchor the cilia and give shape to the organism.

Some ciliates have evolved specialized cilia. Cilia may cover the outer surface of the protozoan. They may join to form **cirri,** which are used in movement. Alternatively, cilia may be lost from large regions of a ciliate.

Trichocysts are pellicular structures primarily used for protection. They are rodlike or oval organelles oriented perpendicular to the plasma membrane. In *Paramecium*, they have a "golf tee" appearance. The pellicle can discharge trichocysts, which then remain connected to the body by a sticky thread (figure 17.18).

NUTRITION

Some ciliates, such as *Paramecium*, have a ciliated oral groove along one side of the body (*see figure 17.17*). Cilia of the oral groove sweep small food particles toward the cytopharynx, where a food vacuole forms. When the food vacuole reaches an upper size limit, it breaks free and circulates through the endoplasm.

Some free-living ciliates prey upon other protists or small animals. Prey capture is usually a case of fortuitous contact. The

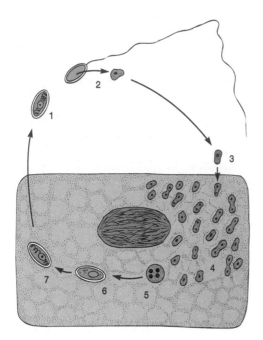

FIGURE 17.16

Phylum Microspora: The Microsporean *Nosema bombicus*, Which Is Fatal to Silkworms. The cell of a silkworm infected with *N. bombicus* is shown here. *(1)* A typical spore with one coiled filament. *(2)* When ingested, the spore extrudes the filament, which is used in locomotion. *(3)* The parasite enters an epithelial cell in the silkworm intestine and *(4)* divides many times to form small amoebae that eventually fill the cell and kill it. *(5–7)* During this phase, some of the amoebae with four nuclei become spores. Silkworms are infected by eating leaves contaminated with the feces of infected

ciliate *Didinium* feeds principally on *Paramecium*, a prey that is bigger than itself. *Didinium* forms a temporary opening that can greatly enlarge to consume its prey (figure 17.19).

Suctorians are ciliates that live attached to their substrate. They possess tentacles whose secretions paralyze prey, often ciliates or amoebae. The tentacles digest an opening in the pellicle of the prey, and prey cytoplasm is drawn into the suctorian through tiny channels in the tentacle. The mechanism for this probably involves tentacular microtubules (figure 17.20).

GENETIC CONTROL AND REPRODUCTION

Ciliates have two kinds of nuclei. A large, polyploid **macronucleus** regulates daily metabolic activities. One or more smaller **micronuclei** are the genetic reserve of the cell.

Ciliates reproduce asexually by transverse binary fission and, occasionally, by budding. Budding occurs in suctorians and results in the formation of ciliated, free-swimming organisms that attach to the substrate and take the form of the adult.

Ciliates reproduce sexually by **conjugation** (figure 17.21). The partners involved are called conjugants. Many species of cili-

(a)

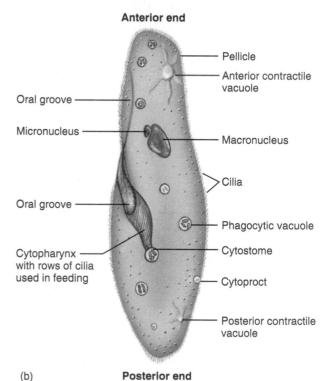

(b)

FIGURE 17.17

Phylum Ciliophora. *(a)* The ciliate, *Paramecium sonneborn*. This paramecium is 40 μm in length. Note the oral groove near the middle of the body that leads into the cytopharynx (SEM ×1,600). *(b)* The structure of a typical ciliate such as *Paramecium*.

ates have numerous mating types, not all of which are mutually compatible. Initial contact between individuals is apparently random, and sticky secretions of the pellicle facilitate adhesion. Ciliate plasma membranes then fuse and remain that way for several hours.

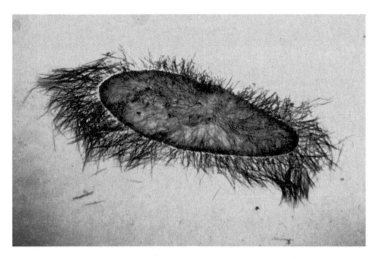

FIGURE 17.18

Discharged Trichocysts of *Paramecium*. Each trichocyst transforms itself into a long, sticky, proteinaceous thread when discharged (LM ×150).

FIGURE 17.19

A Single-Celled Hunter and Its Prey. The juglike *Didinium* (left) swallowing a slipper-shaped *Paramecium* (right) (SEM ×550).

FIGURE 17.20

Suctorian (*Tokophrya* spp.) Feeding. The knobbed tip of a tentacle holds a ciliate (right). Tentacles discharge enzymes that immobilize the prey and dissolve the pellicle. Pellicles of tentacle and prey fuse, and the tentacle enlarges and invaginates to form a feeding channel. Prey cytoplasm moves down the feeding channel and incorporates into endocytic vacuoles at the bottom of the tentacle (LM ×181).

SYMBIOTIC CILIATES

Most ciliates are free living; however, some are commensalistic or mutualistic, and a few are parasitic. *Balantidium coli* is an important parasitic ciliate that lives in the large intestines of humans, pigs, and other mammals. At times, it is a ciliary feeder; at other times, it produces proteolytic enzymes that digest host epithelium, causing a flask-shaped ulcer. (Its pathology resembles that of *Entamoeba histolytica*.) *B. coli* is passed from one host to another in cysts that form as feces begin to dehydrate in the large intestine. Fecal contamination of food or water is the most common form of transmission. Its distribution is potentially worldwide, but it is most common in the Philippines.

Large numbers of different species of ciliates also inhabit the rumen of many ungulates (hoofed animals). These ciliates contribute to the digestive processes of their hosts.

FURTHER PHYLOGENETIC CONSIDERATIONS

Protozoa probably originated about 1.5 billion years ago. Although known fossil species exceed 30,000, they are of little use in investigations of the origin and evolution of the various protozoan groups. Only protozoa with hard parts (tests) have left much of a fossil record, and only the foraminiferans and radiolarians have well-established

The macronucleus does not participate in the genetic exchange that follows. Instead, the macronucleus breaks up during or after micronuclear events, and reforms from micronuclei of the daughter ciliates.

After separation, the exconjugants undergo a series of nuclear divisions to restore the nuclear characteristics of the particular species, including the formation of a macronucleus from one or more micronuclei. Cytoplasmic divisions that form daughter cells accompany these events.

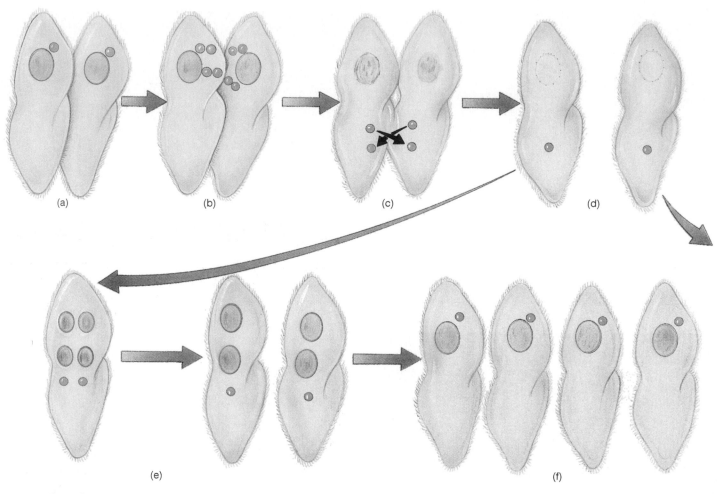

FIGURE 17.21

Conjugation in *Paramecium*. (*a*) Random contact brings individuals of opposite mating types together. (*b*) Meiosis results in four haploid pronuclei. (*c*) Three pronuclei and the macronucleus degenerate. Mitosis and mutual exchange of pronuclei is followed by fusion of pronuclei. (*d–f*) Conjugants separate. Nuclear divisions that restore nuclear characteristics of the species follow. Cytoplasmic divisions may accompany these events.

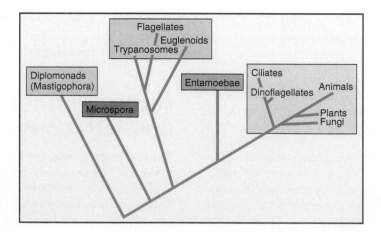

FIGURE 17.22

Cladogram Showing the Evolutionary Relationships of Protozoa and Other Eukaryotes Based on 18S Ribosomal RNA Sequence Comparisons. This cladogram suggests that evolution along the nuclear line of descent was not continuous but instead occurred in major epochs (an epoch is a particular time period marked by distinctive features and events). Five major evolutionary radiations (colored boxes) are apparent for the protozoa. The Mastigophora (e.g., *Giardia*) and Microspora (e.g., *Nosema*) are modern relatives of the earliest major eukaryotic cell lines. Following the development of these protozoa, the other groups of protozoa radiated off the nuclear line of descent.

fossil records in Precambrian rocks. Recent evidence from the study of base sequences in ribosomal RNA indicates that each of the seven protozoan phyla probably had separate origins and that each is sufficiently different from the others to warrant elevating all of these groups to phylum status, as this chapter has (figure 17.22). Additional modifications to the present scheme of protozoan classification are continually being proposed as the results of new ultrastructural and molecular studies are published. For example, in 1993, T. Cavalier-Smith proposed that the protozoa be elevated to kingdom status with 18 phyla. Whether protozoologists will accept this new classification, however, remains to be determined.

Stop and Ask Yourself

18. What are four characteristics of the phylum Ciliophora?
19. How do ciliates use trichocysts?
20. What occurs during conjugation in *Paramecium*?
21. Why is it difficult to find protozoan fossils?

SUMMARY

1. The kingdom Protista is a polyphyletic group that arose about 1.5 billion years ago from the Archaea. The evolutionary pathways leading to modern protozoa are uncertain.

2. Protozoa are both single cells and entire organisms. Organelles specialized for the unicellular lifestyle carry out many protozoan functions.

3. Many protozoa live in symbiotic relationships with other organisms, often in a host-parasite relationship.

4. Members of the phylum Sarcomastigophora possess pseudopodia and/or one or more flagella.

5. Members of the class Phytomastigophorea are photosynthetic and include the genera *Euglena* and *Volvox*. Members of the class Zoomastigophorea are heterotrophic and include *Trypanosoma*, which causes sleeping sickness.

6. Amoebae use pseudopodia for feeding and locomotion.

7. Members of the subphylum Sarcodina include the freshwater genera *Amoeba*, *Arcella*, and *Difflugia*, and the symbiotic genus *Entamoeba*. Foraminiferans and radiolarians are common marine amoebae.

8. Members of the phylum Apicomplexa are all parasites. The phylum includes *Plasmodium* and *Toxoplasma*, which cause malaria and toxoplasmosis, respectively. Many apicomplexans have a three-part life cycle involving schizogony, gametogony, and sporogony.

9. The phylum Microspora consists of small protozoa that are intracellular parasites of every major animal group. They are transmitted from one host to the next as a spore, the form from which the group obtains its name.

10. The phylum Acetospora contains protozoa that produce spores lacking polar capsules. These protozoa are primarily parasitic in molluscs.

11. The phylum Myxozoa consists entirely of parasitic species, usually found in fishes. One to six polar filaments characterize the spore.

12. The phylum Ciliophora contains some of the most complex of all protozoa. Its members possess cilia, a macronucleus, and one or more micronuclei. Mechanical coupling of cilia coordinates their movements, and cilia can be specialized for different kinds of locomotion. Ciliates reproduce sexually by conjugation. Diploid ciliates undergo meiosis of the micronuclei to produce haploid pronuclei that two conjugants can exchange.

13. Precise evolutionary relationships are difficult to determine for the protozoa. The fossil record is sparse, and what does exist is not particularly helpful in deducing relationships. However, ribosomal RNA sequence comparisons indicate that each of the seven protozoan phyla probably had separate origins.

SELECTED KEY TERMS

ectoplasm (p. 242)
endoplasm (p. 242)
giardiasis (p. 248)
macronucleus (p. 254)
micronuclei (p. 254)
multiple fission (schizogony)
  (p. 243)

pellicle (p. 242)
protozoa (p. 242)
protozoologists (p. 244)
trichocysts (p. 253)

CRITICAL THINKING QUESTIONS

1. If knowing for certain the evolutionary pathways that gave rise to protozoa and animal phyla is impossible, is it worth constructing hypotheses about those relationships? Why or why not?

2. In what ways are protozoa similar to animal cells? In what ways are they different?

3. If sexual reproduction is unknown in *Euglena*, how do you think this lineage of organisms has survived through evolutionary time? (Recall that sexual reproduction provides the genetic variability that allows species to adapt to environmental changes.)

4. The use of DDT has been greatly curtailed for ecological reasons. In the past, it has proven to be an effective malaria deterrent. Many organizations would like to see this form of mosquito control resumed. Do you agree or disagree? Explain your reasoning.

5. If you were traveling out of country and were concerned about contracting amoebic dysentery, what steps could you take to prevent acquiring the disease? How would the precautions differ if you were going to a country where malaria is a problem?

REFERENCES ON THE WORLD WIDE WEB

1. **Protozoa.**   This site presents a collection of medically important parasites.

    http://www2.life.sci.qut.edu.au/darben/protozoa.htm

2. **The Parasitology Quiz Page.**   This site provides a quiz and a review of the protozoa and other parasites.

    http://www2.life.sci.qut.edu.au/darben/paraquiz.htm

3. **Parasites and Parasitological Resources.**   This site is maintained by Ohio State University and contains many slides and life cycles of the protozoa.

    http://www.biosci.ohio-state/edu/~zoology/parasite/home.html

4. **Invertebrates: Electronic Zoo.** This site links with a variety of sites containing information about such invertebrates as the protozoa.

    http://netvet.wustl.edu/invert.html

5. **Protozoa.** Various lectures on different protozoan groups are at this site.

    http://www.cbs.umn.edu/class/biol/1106/protozoa.htm

6. **Protozoan News.** This site contains news about different protozoa.

    http://www.protozoa.com/

7. **Protozoa As Parasites.** This site describes protozoa as parasites of animals (including humans), prevention and control of protozoa, and protozoan life cycles.

    http://www.agnic.nal.usda.gov/cc/d_1823.html

8. **Protozoa.** The American Museum of Natural History maintains this site on protozoa.

    http://amnh.org/exhibition/expedition/treasures/glass_protozoa/protozoa.html

c h a p t e r

18

MULTICELLULAR AND TISSUE LEVELS OF ORGANIZATION

Outline

Concepts

1. How multicellularity originated in animals, and whether the animal kingdom is monophyletic, diphyletic, or polyphyletic, are largely unknown.
2. Animals whose bodies consist of aggregations of cells, but whose cells do not form tissues, are in the phylum Porifera, as well as some lesser known phyla.
3. Animals that show diploblastic, tissue-level organization are in the phyla Cnidaria and Ctenophora.
4. Members of the phylum Cnidaria are important in zoological research because of their relatively simple organization and their contribution to coral reefs.

Would You Like to Know . . .

1. how multicellularity could have arisen in the animal kingdom? (p. 260)
2. how natural sponges are prepared for use in cleaning applications? (p. 265)
3. the value of the intricate branching canal systems to a sponge? (p. 265)
4. whether cells of a sponge body communicate with one another? (p. 266)
5. how soft-bodied cnidarians support themselves? (p. 270)
6. why you should avoid touching blue, gas-filled floats washed up on beaches of temperate and tropical waters? (p. 273)
7. which jellyfish you should avoid when swimming in coastal waters? (p. 273)
8. what organisms form coral reefs? (p. 276)

This chapter answers these and other useful questions..

This chapter contains evolutionary concepts, which are set off in this font.

Evolutionary Perspective

Animals with multicellular and tissue levels of organization have captured the interest of scientists and laypersons alike. A description of some members of the phylum Cnidaria, for example, could fuel a science fiction writer's imagination:

> From a distance I was never threatened, in fact I was infatuated with its beauty. A large, inviting, bright blue float lured me closer. As I swam nearer I could see that hidden from my previous view was an infrastructure of tentacles, some of which dangled nearly nine meters below the water's surface! The creature seemed to consist of many individuals and I wondered whether or not each individual was the same kind of being because, when I looked closely, I counted eight different body forms!
>
> I was drawn closer and the true nature of this creature was painfully revealed. The beauty of the gas-filled float hid some of the most hideous weaponry imaginable. When I brushed against those silky tentacles I experienced the most excruciating pain. Had it not been for my life vest, I would have drowned. Indeed, for some time, I wished that had been my fate.

Swimmers of tropical waters who have come into contact with *Physalia physalis*, the Portuguese man-of-war, know that this fictitious account rings true (figure 18.1). In organisms such as *Physalia physalis*, cells are grouped, specialized for various functions, and interdependent. This chapter covers three animal phyla whose multicellular organization varies from a loose association of cells to cells organized into two distinct tissue layers. These phyla are the Porifera, Cnidaria, and Ctenophora (figure 18.2).

Origins of Multicellularity

Multicellular life has been a part of the earth's history for approximately 550 million years. Although this seems a very long time, it represents only 10% of the earth's geological history. Multicellular life arose quickly in the 100 million years prior to the Precambrian/Cambrian boundary, in what scientists view as an evolutionary explosion. These evolutionary events resulted not only in the appearance of all of the animal phyla recognized today, but also 15 to 20 animal groups that are now extinct. Since this initial evolutionary explosion, most of the history of multicellular life has been one of extinction.

The evolutionary events leading to multicellularity are shrouded in mystery. ❶ Many zoologists believe that multicellularity could have arisen as dividing cells remained together, in the fashion of many colonial protists. Although variations of this hypothesis exist, they are all treated here as the **colonial hypothesis** (figure 18.3*a*).

A second proposed mechanism is called the **syncytial hypothesis** (figure 18.3*b*). A syncytium is a large, multinucleate cell. The formation of plasma membranes in the cytoplasm of a syncytial

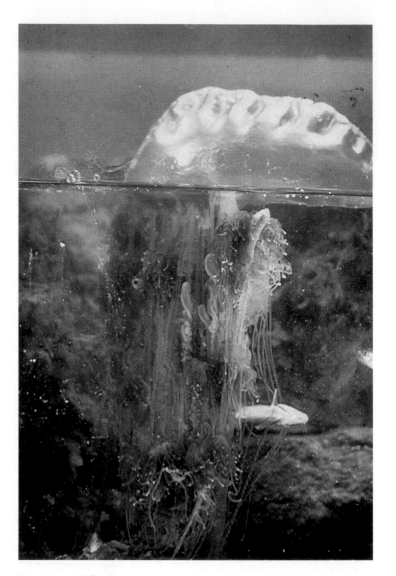

Figure 18.1

Physalia physalis, **the Portuguese Man-of-War.** The bluish float is about 12 cm long, and the nematocyst-laden tentacles can be up to 9 m long. Nematocysts are lethal to small vertebrates and dangerous to humans. Note the fish that the tentacles have captured. Digestion will eventually leave only the fish's skeletal remains.

protist could have produced a small, multicellular organism. Both the colonial and syncytial hypotheses are supported by the colonial and syncytial organization that occurs in some protist phyla.

Animal Origins

A fundamental question concerning animal origins is whether animals are monophyletic (derived from a single ancestor), diphyletic (derived from two ancestors), or polyphyletic (derived from many ancestors). The view that animals are polyphyletic is attractive to a growing number of zoologists. The nearly simultaneous appearance

FIGURE 18.2

Evolutionary Relationships of the Poriferans and the Radiate Phyla. Members of the phylum Porifera are derived from ancestral protozoan stocks independently of other animal phyla. The radiate animals (shaded in orange) include members of the phyla Cnidaria and Ctenophora. This figure shows a diphyletic origin of the animal kingdom in which sponges arise from the protists separate from other animals. Other interpretations of sponge origins are discussed in the text.

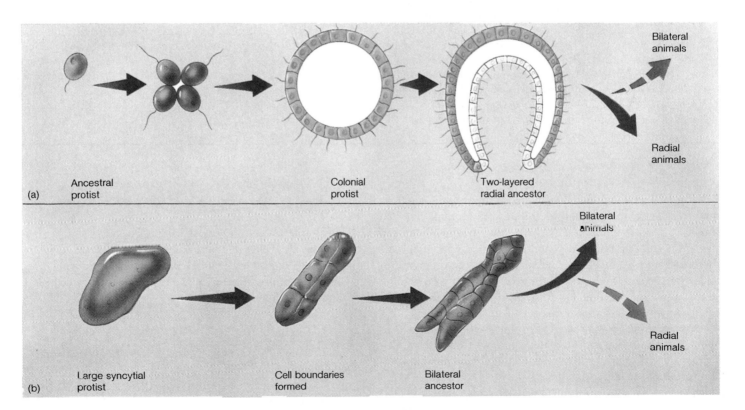

FIGURE 18.3

Two Hypotheses Regarding the Origin of Multicellularity. (*a*) The colonial hypothesis. Multicellularity may have arisen when cells that a dividing protist produced remained together. Cell invagination could have formed a second cell layer. This hypothesis is supported by the colonial organization of some Sacromastigophora. (The colonial protist and the two-layered radial ancestor are shown in sectional views.) (*b*) The syncytial hypothesis. Multicellularity could have arisen when plasma membranes formed within the cytoplasm of a large, multinucleate protist. Multinucleate, bilateral ciliates support this hypothesis.

BOX 18.1   ANIMAL ORIGINS—THE CAMBRIAN EXPLOSION

The geological timescale (*see table 1.1*) is marked by significant geological and biological events, including the origin of the earth about 4.6 billion years ago, the origin of life about 3.5 billion years ago (*see box 11.1*), the origin of eukaryotic life-forms about 1.5 billion years ago (*see box 3.1*), and the origin of animals about 0.6 billion years ago. The latter event marks the beginning of the Cambrian period. Animals originated relatively late in the history of the earth—in only the last 10% of the earth's history. During a geologically brief 100-million-year period, all modern animal phyla (along with other animals that are now extinct) evolved. This rapid origin and diversification of animals is often referred to as "the Cambrian explosion."

Scientists have asked important questions about this explosion since Charles Darwin. Why did it occur so late in the history of the earth? The origin of multicellularity seems a relatively simple step compared to the origin of life itself. Why do no fossil records document the series of evolutionary changes during the evolution of the animal phyla? Why did animal life evolve so quickly? Paleontologists continue to search the fossil records for answers to these questions.

One interpretation regarding the absence of fossils during this important 100-million-year period is that early animals were soft-bodied and simply did not fossilize. Fossilization of soft-bodied animals is less likely than fossilization of hard-bodied animals, but it does occur. Conditions that promote fossilization of soft-bodied animals include very rapid covering by sediments that creates an anoxic environment that discourages decomposition. In fact, fossil beds containing soft-bodied animals have been known for many years.

The Ediacara fossil formation, which contains the oldest known animal fossils, consists exclusively of soft-bodied forms. Although named after a site in Australia, the Ediacara formation is worldwide in distribution and dates to Precambrian times. This 700-million-year-old formation gives few clues to the origin of modern animals, however, because paleontologists believe it represents an evolutionary experiment that failed. It contains no ancestors of modern animal phyla.

A slightly younger fossil formation containing animal remains is the Tommotian formation—named after a locale in Russia. It dates to the very early Cambrian period, and it also contains only soft-bodied forms. At one time, the animals present in these fossil beds were assigned to various modern phyla, including the Porifera and Cnidaria, but most paleontologists now agree that all Tommotian fossils represent unique body forms that arose early in the Cambrian period and disappeared before the end of the period, leaving no descendants in the modern animal phyla.

A third fossil formation containing soft-bodied animals provides evidence of the results of the Cambrian explosion. This fossil formation, called the Burgess Shale, is in Yoho National Park in the Canadian Rocky Mountains of British Columbia. Shortly after the Cambrian explosion, mud slides rapidly buried thousands of marine animals under conditions that favored fossilization. These fossil beds provide evidence of virtually all of the 32 phyla described in this text, plus about 20 other animal body forms that are so different from any modern animals that they cannot be assigned to any one of the modern phyla (figure 1). These unassignable animals include a large swimming predator called *Anomalocaris* and a soft-bodied, detritus- or algae-eating animal called *Wiwaxia*. The Burgess Shale formation also has fossils of many extinct representatives of modern phyla. For example, a well-known Burgess Shale animal called *Sidneyia* is a representative of a previously unknown group of arthropods (insects, spiders, mites, crabs).

of all animal phyla in fossils from the Precambrian/Cambrian boundary is difficult to explain if animals are monophyletic. If animals are polyphyletic, more than one explanation of the origin of multicellularity could be possible, and more than one body form could be ancestral. Conversely, the impressive similarities in animal cellular organization support the view that all or most animals are derived from a single ancestor. For example, asters (*see figure 6.4*) form during mitosis in most animals, certain cell junctions are similar in all animal cells, most animals produce flagellated sperm, and the proteins that accomplish movement are similar in most animal cells. These common features are difficult to explain, assuming polyphyletic origins. If you assume one or two ancestral lineages, then only one or two hypotheses regarding the origin of multicellularity can be correct (box 18.1).

PHYLUM PORIFERA

The Porifera (po-rif'er-ah) (L. *porus*, pore + *fera*, to bear), or sponges, are primarily marine animals consisting of loosely organized cells (figure 18.4; table 18.1). The approximately nine thousand species of sponges vary in size from less than a centimeter to a mass that would fill your arms.

Characteristics of the phylum Porifera include:

1. Asymmetrical or radially symmetrical
2. Three cell types: pinacocytes, mesenchyme cells, and choanocytes
3. Central cavity, or a series of branching chambers, through which water circulates during filter feeding
4. No tissues or organs

Fossil formations like the Burgess Shale show that evolution cannot always be thought of as a slow progression. The Cambrian explosion involved rapid evolutionary diversification, followed by the extinction of many unique animals. Why was this evolution so rapid? No one really knows. Many zoologists believe that it was be-cause so many ecological niches were available with virtually no competition from existing species. Will zoologists ever know the evolutionary sequences in the Cambrian explosion? Perhaps an-other ancient fossil bed of soft-bodied animals from 600-million-year-old seas is awaiting discovery.

FIGURE 1   The Burgess Shale. An artist's reconstruction of the Burgess Shale. The Burgess Shale contained numerous unique forms of animal life, as well as representatives of most animal phyla described in this textbook. A trilobite is in the lower left. Tall sponges are on the right and left in the foreground. *Sidneyia* is on the seafloor in the middle foreground and in the middle left.

CELL TYPES, BODY WALL, AND SKELETONS

In spite of their relative simplicity, sponges are more than colonies of independent cells. As in all animals, sponge cells are specialized for particular functions. This organization is often referred to as division of labor.

Thin, flat cells, called **pinacocytes,** line the outer surface of a sponge. Pinacocytes may be mildly contractile, and their con-traction may change the shape of some sponges. In a number of sponges, some pinacocytes are specialized into tubelike, contrac-tile **porocytes,** which can regulate water circulation (figure 18.5*a*). Openings through porocytes are pathways for water mov-ing through the body wall.

Just below the pinacocyte layer of a sponge is a jellylike layer called the **mesohyl** (Gr. *meso,* middle + *hyl,* matter). Amoeboid cells called **mesenchyme cells** move about in the mesohyl and are specialized for reproduction, secreting skeletal elements, trans-porting and storing food, and forming contractile rings around openings in the sponge wall.

Below the mesohyl and lining an inner chamber(s) are choanocytes, or collar cells. **Choanocytes** (Gr. *choane,* funnel + *cyte,* cell) are flagellated cells that have a collarlike ring of mi-crovilli surrounding a flagellum. Microfilaments connect the microvilli, forming a netlike mesh within the collar. The flagellum creates water currents through the sponge, and the collar filters microscopic food particles from the water (figure 18.5*b*). The

(a)

(b)

FIGURE 18.4

Phylum Porifera. Many sponges are brightly colored with hues of red, orange, green, or yellow. *(a)* *Verongia* sp. *(b)* *Axiomella* sp.

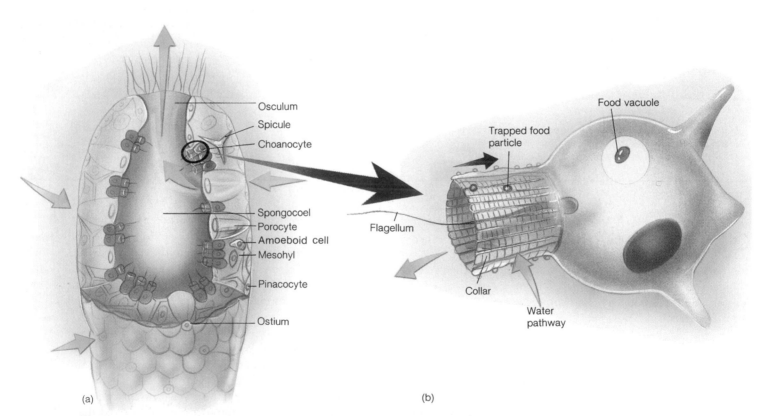

(a)

Osculum

Spicule

Choanocyte

Spongocoel

Porocyte

Amoeboid cell

Mesohyl

Pinacocyte

Ostium

(b)

Food vacuole

Trapped food particle

Flagellum

Collar

Water pathway

FIGURE 18.5

Morphology of a Simple Sponge. *(a)* In this example, pinacocytes form the outer body wall, and mesenchyme cells and spicules are in the mesohyl. Porocytes that extend through the body wall form ostia. *(b)* Choanocytes are cells with a flagellum surrounded by a collar of microvilli that traps food particles. Food moves toward the base of the cell, where it is incorporated into a food vacuole and passed to amoeboid mesenchyme cells, where digestion takes place. Blue arrows show water flow patterns. The brown arrow shows the direction of movement of trapped food particles.

TABLE 18.1	CLASSIFICATION OF THE PORIFERA

Phylum Porifera (po-rif′er-ah)*
The animal phylum whose members are sessile and either asymmetrical or radially symmetrical; body organized around a system of water canals and chambers; cells not organized into tissues or organs. Approximately 9,000 species.

Class Calcarea (kal-kar′e-ah)
Spicules composed of calcium carbonate; spicules are needle shaped or have three or four rays; ascon, leucon, or sycon body forms; all marine. Calcareous sponges. *Grantia* (*Scypha*), *Leucosolenia*.

Class Hexactinellida (hex-act″in-el′id-ah)
Spicules composed of silica and usually six rayed; spicules often fused into an intricate lattice; cup or vase shaped; sycon or leucon body form; found at 450 to 900 m depths in tropical West Indies and eastern Pacific. Glass sponges. *Euplectella* (Venus flowerbasket).

Class Demospongiae (de-mo-spun′je-e)
Brilliantly colored sponges with needle-shaped or four-rayed siliceous spicules or spongin or both; leucon body form; up to 1 m in height and diameter. Includes one family of freshwater sponges, Spongillidae, and the bath sponges. *Cliona*, *Spongilla*.

*The class Sclerospongiae has been recently abandoned and its members assigned to Calcarea and Demospongiae.

FIGURE 18.6

Sponge Spicules. Photomicrograph of a variety of sponge spicules (×150).

presence of choanocytes in sponges suggests an evolutionary link between the sponges and a group of protists called choanoflagellates. This link is discussed further at the end of this chapter.

Sponges are supported by a skeleton that may consist of microscopic needlelike spikes called **spicules.** Spicules are formed by amoeboid cells, are made of calcium carbonate or silica, and may take on a variety of shapes (figure 18.6). ❷ Alternatively, the skeleton may be made of **spongin** (a fibrous protein made of collagen), which is dried, beaten, and washed until all cells are removed to produce a commercial sponge. The nature of the skeleton is an important characteristic in sponge taxonomy.

WATER CURRENTS AND BODY FORMS

The life of a sponge depends on the water currents that choanocytes create. Water currents bring food and oxygen to a sponge and carry away metabolic and digestive wastes. Methods of food filtration and circulation reflect the body forms in the phylum. Zoologists have described three sponge body forms.

The simplest and least common sponge body form is the **ascon** (figure 18.7a). Ascon sponges are vaselike. Ostia are the outer openings of porocytes and lead directly to a chamber called the spongocoel. Choanocytes line the spongocoel, and their flagellar movements draw water into the spongocoel through the ostia. Water exits the sponge through the osculum, which is a single,

large opening at the top of the sponge.

In the **sycon** body form, the sponge wall appears folded (figure 18.7b). Water enters a sycon sponge through openings called dermal pores. Dermal pores are the openings of invaginations of the body wall, called incurrent canals. Pores in the body wall connect incurrent canals to radial canals, and the radial canals lead to the spongocoel. Choanocytes line radial canals (rather than the spongocoel), and the beating of choanocyte flagella moves water from the ostia, through incurrent and radial canals, to the spongocoel, and out the osculum.

Leucon sponges have an extensively branched canal system (figure 18.7c). Water enters the sponge through ostia and moves through branched incurrent canals, which lead to choanocyte-lined chambers. Canals leading away from the chambers are called excurrent canals. Proliferation of chambers and canals has resulted in the absence of a spongocoel, and often, multiple exit points (oscula) for water leaving the sponge.

❸ In complex sponges, an increased surface area for choanocytes results in large volumes of water being moved through the sponge and greater filtering capabilities. Although the evolutionary pathways in the phylum are complex and incompletely described, most pathways have resulted in the leucon body form.

MAINTENANCE FUNCTIONS

Sponges feed on particles that range in size from 0.1 to 50 μm. Their food consists of bacteria, microscopic algae, protists, and other suspended organic matter. The prey are slowly drawn into the sponge and consumed. Large populations of sponges play an important role in reducing turbidity of coastal waters. A single leucon sponge, 1 cm in diameter and 10 cm high, can filter in excess of 20 liters of water every day! Recent investigations have discovered that a few sponges are carnivorous. These deep-water sponges (*Asbestopluma*) can capture small crustaceans using spicule-covered filaments.

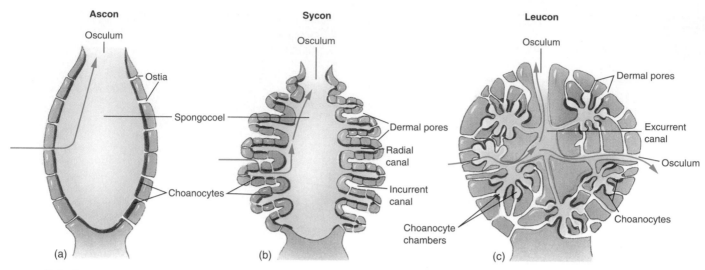

FIGURE 18.7

Sponge Body Forms. (*a*) An ascon sponge. Choanocytes line the spongocoel in ascon sponges. (*b*) A sycon sponge. The body wall of sycon sponges appears folded. Choanocytes line radial canals that open into the spongocoel. (*c*) A leucon sponge. The proliferation of canals and chambers results in the loss of the spongocoel as a distinct chamber. Multiple oscula are frequently present. Blue arrows show the direction of water flow.

Choanocytes filter small, suspended food particles. Water passes through their collar near the base of the cell and then moves into a sponge chamber at the open end of the collar. Suspended food is trapped on the collar and moved along microvilli to the base of the collar, where it is incorporated into a food vacuole (*see figure 18.5b*). Digestion begins in the food vacuole by lysosomal enzymes and pH changes. Partially digested food is passed to amoeboid cells, which distribute it to other cells.

Filtration is not the only way that sponges feed. Pinacocytes lining incurrent canals may phagocytize larger food particles (up to 50 μm) (*see figure 3.14*). Sponges also may absorb by active transport nutrients dissolved in seawater.

Because of extensive canal systems and the circulation of large volumes of water through sponges, all sponge cells are in close contact with water. Thus, nitrogenous waste (principally ammonia) removal and gas exchange occur by diffusion.

Sponges do not have nerve cells to coordinate body functions. Most reactions result from individual cells responding to a stimulus. For example, water circulation through some sponges is at a minimum at sunrise and at a maximum just before sunset because light inhibits the constriction of porocytes and other cells surrounding ostia, keeping incurrent canals open. ④ Other reactions, however, suggest some communication among cells. For example, the rate of water circulation through a sponge can drop suddenly without any apparent external cause. This reaction can be due only to choanocytes ceasing activities more or less simultaneously, and implies some form of internal communication. The nature of this communication is unknown. Amoeboid cells transmitting chemical messages and ion movement over cell surfaces are possible control mechanisms.

REPRODUCTION

Most sponges are monoecious (both sexes occur in the same individual) but do not usually self-fertilize because individual sponges produce eggs and sperm at different times. Certain choanocytes lose their collars and flagella and undergo meiosis to form flagellated sperm. Other choanocytes (and amoeboid cells in some sponges) probably undergo meiosis to form eggs. Eggs are retained in the mesohyl of the parent. Sperm cells exit one sponge through the osculum and enter another sponge with the incurrent water. Sperm are trapped by choanocytes and incorporated into a vacuole. The choanocytes lose their collar and flagellum, become amoeboid, and transport sperm to the eggs.

In most sponges, early development occurs in the mesohyl. Cleavage of a zygote results in the formation of a flagellated larval stage. (A **larva** is an immature stage that may undergo a dramatic change in structure before attaining the adult body form.) The larva breaks free, and water currents carry the larva out of the parent sponge. After no more than 2 days of a free-swimming existence, the larva settles to the substrate and begins to develop into the adult body form (figure 18.8*a,b*).

Asexual reproduction of freshwater and some marine sponges involves the formation of resistant capsules, called **gemmules,** containing masses of amoeboid cells. When the parent sponge dies in the winter, it releases gemmules, which can survive both freezing and drying (figure 18.8*c,d*). When favorable conditions return in the spring, amoeboid cells stream out of a tiny opening, called the micropyle, and organize into a sponge.

Some sponges possess remarkable powers of regeneration. Portions of a sponge that are cut or broken from one individual regenerate new individuals.

Parenchymula larva

Amphiblastula larva

(a)

(b)

Micropyle

Amoeboid cells

Spicule

(c)

(d)

FIGURE 18.8

Development of Sponge Larval Stages. (a) Most sponges have a parenchymula larva (0.2 mm). Flagellated cells cover most of the larva's outer surface. After the larva settles and attaches, the outer cells lose their flagella, move to the interior, and form choanocytes. Interior cells move to the periphery and form pinacocytes. (b) Some sponges have an amphiblastula larva (0.2 mm), which is hollow and has half of the larva composed of flagellated cells. On settling, the flagellated cells invaginate into the interior of the embryo and form choanocytes. Nonflagellated cells overgrow the choanocytes and form the pinacocytes. (c) Gemmules (0.9 mm) are resistant capsules containing masses of amoeboid cells. Gemmules are released when a parent sponge dies (e.g., in the winter), and amoeboid cells form a new sponge when favorable conditions return. (d) Scanning electron micrograph of a gemmule of the freshwater sponge *(Dosilia brouni)*. It is 0.5 mm in diameter and covered with a shell of spicules and spongin.

Stop and Ask Yourself

1. How do the colonial and syncytial hypotheses account for the origin of multicellularity?

2. What evidence supports the idea that the kingdom Animalia is polyphyletic?

3. What are three kinds of cells found in the Porifera, and what are their functions?

4. What is the path of water circulating through (a) an ascon sponge, (b) a sycon sponge, and (c) a leucon sponge?

PHYLUM CNIDARIA (COELENTERATA)

Members of the phylum Cnidaria (ni-dar'e-ah) (Gr. *knide*, nettle) possess radial or biradial symmetry. Biradial symmetry is a modification of radial symmetry in which a single plane, passing through a central axis, divides the animal into mirror images. It results from the presence of a single or paired structure in a basically radial animal and differs from bilateral symmetry in that dorsal and ventral surfaces are not differentiated. Radially symmetrical animals have no anterior or posterior ends. Thus, terms of direction are based on the position of the mouth opening. The end of the animal that contains the mouth is the oral end, and the opposite end is the aboral end. Radial symmetry is advantageous for sedentary animals because sensory receptors are evenly distributed around the body. These organisms can respond to stimuli from all directions.

The Cnidaria include over nine thousand species, are mostly marine, and are important in coral reef ecosystems (table 18.2).

Characteristics of the phylum Cnidaria include:

1. Radial or biradial symmetry
2. Diploblastic, tissue-level organization
3. Gelatinous mesoglea between the epidermal and gastrodermal tissue layers
4. Gastrovascular cavity
5. Nervous system in the form of a nerve net
6. Specialized cells, called cnidocytes, used in defense, feeding, and attachment

THE BODY WALL AND NEMATOCYSTS

Cnidarians possess diploblastic, tissue-level organization (*see figure 16.10*). Cells organize into tissues that carry out specific functions, and all cells are derived from two embryological layers. The ectoderm of the embryo gives rise to an outer layer of the body

TABLE 18.2	CLASSIFICATION OF THE CNIDARIA

Phylum Cnidaria (ni-dar'e-ah)
Radial or biradial symmetry, diploblastic organization, a gastrovascular cavity, and cnidocytes. Over 9,000 species.

Class Hydrozoa (hi″dro-zo'ah)
Cnidocytes present in the epidermis; gametes produced epidermally and always released to the outside of the body; no wandering mesenchyme cells in mesoglea; medusae usually with a velum; many polyps colonial; mostly marine with some freshwater species. *Hydra, Obelia, Gonionemus, Physalia.*

Class Scyphozoa (si″fo-zo'ah)
Medusa prominent in the life history; polyp small; gametes gastrodermal in origin and released into the gastrovascular cavity; cnidocytes present in the gastrodermis as well as epidermis; medusa lacks a velum; mesoglea with wandering mesenchyme cells of epidermal origin; marine. *Aurelia.*

Class Cubozoa (ku″bo-zo'ah)
Medusa prominent in life history; polyp small; gametes gastrodermal in origin; medusa cuboidal in shape with tentacles that hang from each corner of the bell; marine. *Chironex.*

Class Anthozoa (an″tho-zo'ah)
Colonial or solitary polyps; medusae absent; cnidocytes present in the gastrodermis; gametes gastrodermal in origin; gastrovascular cavity divided by mesenteries that bear nematocysts; internal biradial or bilateral symmetry present; mesoglea with wandering mesenchyme cells; marine. Anemones and corals. *Metridium.*

wall, called the **epidermis,** and the inner layer of the body wall, called the **gastrodermis,** is derived from endoderm (figure 18.9). Cells of the epidermis and gastrodermis differentiate into a number of cell types for protection, food gathering, coordination, movement, digestion, and absorption. Between the epidermis and gastrodermis is a jellylike layer called **mesoglea.** Cells are present in the middle layer of some cnidarians, but they have their origin in either the epidermis or the gastrodermis.

One kind of cell is characteristic of the phylum. Epidermal and/or gastrodermal cells called **cnidocytes** produce structures called nematocysts, which are used for attachment, defense, and feeding. A **nematocyst** is a fluid-filled, intracellular capsule enclosing a coiled, hollow tube (figure 18.10). A lidlike operculum caps the capsule at one end. The cnidocyte has a modified cilium, called a cnidocil. Stimulation of the cnidocil forces open the operculum, discharging the coiled tube—as you would evert a sweater sleeve that had been turned inside out.

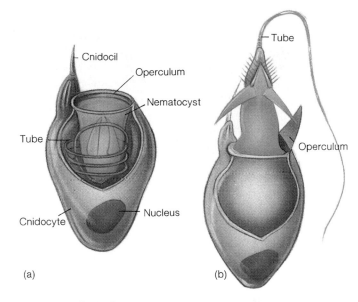

FIGURE 18.9

Body Wall of a Cnidarian (Class Anthozoa). Cnidarians are diploblastic (two tissue layers). The epidermis is derived embryologically from ectoderm, and the gastrodermis is derived embryologically from endoderm. Between these layers is mesoglea. *Source: After Bullock and Horridge.*

FIGURE 18.10

Cnidocyte Structure and Nematocyst Discharge. (*a*) A nematocyst develops in a capsule in the cnidocyte. The capsule is capped at its outer margin by an operculum (lid) that is displaced upon discharge of the nematocyst. The triggerlike cnidocil is responsible for nematocyst discharge. (*b*) A discharged nematocyst. When the cnidocil is stimulated, a rapid (osmotic) influx of water causes the nematocyst to evert, first near its base, and then progressively along the tube from base to tip. The tube revolves at enormous speeds as the nematocyst is discharged. In nematocysts armed with barbs, the advancing tip of the tube is aided in its penetration of the prey as barbs spring forward from the interior of the tube and then flick backward along the outside of the tube.

Zoologists have described nearly 30 kinds of nematocysts. Nematocysts used in food gathering and defense may discharge a long tube armed with spines that penetrates the prey. The spines have hollow tips that deliver paralyzing toxins. Other nematocysts contain unarmed tubes that wrap around prey or a substrate. Still other nematocysts have sticky secretions that help the animal anchor itself. Six or more kinds of nematocysts may be present in one individual.

ALTERNATION OF GENERATIONS

Most cnidarians possess two body forms in their life histories (figure 18.11). The **polyp** is usually asexual and sessile. It attaches to a substrate at the aboral end, and has a cylindrical body, called the column, and a mouth surrounded by food-gathering tentacles. The **medusa** (pl., medusae) is dioecious and free swimming. It is shaped like an inverted bowl, and tentacles dangle from its margins. The mouth opening is centrally located facing downward, and the medusa swims by gentle pulsations of the body wall. The mesoglea is more abundant in a medusa than in a polyp, giving the former a jellylike consistency.

MAINTENANCE FUNCTIONS

The gastrodermis of all cnidarians lines a blind-ending **gastrovascular cavity.** This cavity functions in digestion, the exchange of respiratory gases and metabolic wastes, and the discharge of gametes. Food, digestive wastes, and reproductive stages enter and leave the gastrovascular cavity through the mouth.

The food of most cnidarians consists of very small crustaceans, although some cnidarians feed on small fish (*see figure 18.1*). Nematocysts entangle and paralyze prey, and contractile cells in the tentacles cause the tentacles to shorten, which draws food toward the mouth. As food enters the gastrovascular cavity, gastrodermal gland cells secrete lubricating mucus and enzymes, which reduce food to a soupy broth. Certain gastrodermal cells, called nutritive-muscular cells, phagocytize partially digested food and incorporate it into food vacuoles, where digestion is completed. Nutritive-muscular cells also have circularly oriented contractile fibers that help move materials into or out of the gastrovascular cavity by peristaltic contractions. During peristalsis,

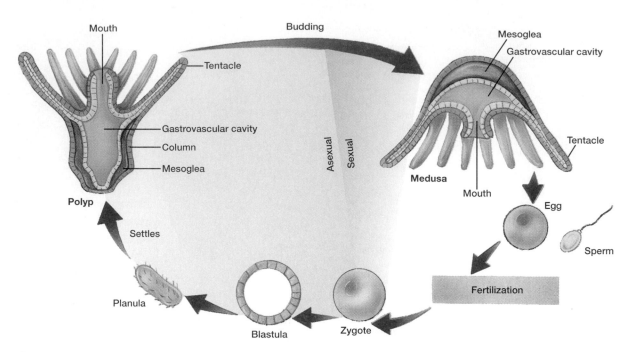

FIGURE 18.11

Generalized Cnidarian Life Cycle. This figure shows alternation between medusa and polyp body forms. Dioecious medusae produce gametes that may be shed into the water for fertilization. Early in development, a ciliated planula larva forms. After a brief free-swimming existence, the planula settles to the substrate and forms a polyp. Budding of the polyp produces additional polyps and medusa buds. Medusae break free of the polyp and swim away. The polyp or medusa stage of many species is either lost or reduced, and the sexual and asexual stages have been incorporated into one body form.

ringlike contractions move along the body wall, pushing contents of the gastrovascular cavity ahead of them, expelling undigested material through the mouth.

⑤ Cnidarians derive most of their support from the buoyancy of water around them. In addition, a hydrostatic skeleton aids in support and movement. A **hydrostatic skeleton** is water or body fluids confined in a cavity of the body and against which contractile elements of the body wall act. In the Cnidaria, the water-filled gastrovascular cavity acts as a hydrostatic skeleton. Certain cells of the body wall, called epitheliomuscular cells, are contractile and aid in movement. When a polyp closes its mouth (to prevent water from escaping) and contracts longitudinal epitheliomuscular cells on one side of the body, the polyp bends toward that side. If these cells contract while the mouth is open, water escapes from the gastrovascular cavity, and the polyp collapses. Contraction of circular epitheliomuscular cells causes constriction of a part of the body and, if the mouth is closed, water in the gastrovascular cavity is compressed, and the polyp elongates.

Polyps use a variety of forms of locomotion. They may move by somersaulting from base to tentacles and from tentacles to base again, or move in an inchworm fashion, using their base and tentacles as points of attachment. Polyps may also glide very slowly along a substrate while attached at their base or walk on their tentacles.

Medusae move by swimming and floating. Water currents and wind are responsible for most horizontal movements. Vertical movements are the result of swimming. Contractions of circular and radial epitheliomuscular cells cause rhythmic pulsations of the bell and drive water from beneath the bell, propelling the medusa through the water.

Cnidarian nerve cells have been of interest to zoologists for many years because they may be the most primitive nervous elements in the animal kingdom. By studying these cells, zoologists may gain insight into the evolution of animal nervous systems. Nerve cells are located below the epidermis, near the mesoglea, and interconnect to form a two-dimensional nerve net. This net conducts nerve impulses around the body in response to a localized stimulus. The extent to which a nerve impulse spreads over the body depends on stimulus strength. For example, a weak stimulus applied to a polyp's tentacle may cause the tentacle to be retracted. A strong stimulus at the same point may cause the entire polyp to withdraw.

Sensory structures of cnidarians are distributed throughout the body and include receptors for perceiving touch and certain chemicals. More specialized receptors are located at specific sites on a polyp or medusa.

Because cnidarians have large surface-area-to-volume ratios (*see figure 3.3*), all cells are a short distance from the body surface, and oxygen, carbon dioxide, and nitrogenous wastes exchange by diffusion.

REPRODUCTION

Most cnidarians are dioecious. Sperm and eggs may be released into the gastrovascular cavity or to the outside of the body. In some instances, eggs are retained in the parent until after fertilization.

A blastula forms early in development, and migration of surface cells to the interior fills the embryo with cells that will eventually form the gastrodermis. The embryo elongates to form a ciliated, free-swimming larva, called a **planula.** The planula attaches to a substrate, interior cells split to form the gastrovascular cavity, and a young polyp develops (*see figure 18.11*).

Medusae nearly always form by budding from the body wall of a polyp, and polyps may form other polyps by budding. Buds may detach from the polyp, or they may remain attached to the parent to contribute to a colony of individuals. Variations on this general pattern are discussed in the survey of cnidarian classes that follows.

Stop and Ask Yourself

5. What are the three layers of the cnidarian body wall?
6. What is a nematocyst? What are several functions of nematocysts?
7. How would you characterize the nervous organization of cnidarians?
8. What is a hydrostatic skeleton? How does this function in cnidarians?

CLASS HYDROZOA

Hydrozoans (hi″dro-zo′anz) are small, relatively common cnidarians. The vast majority are marine, but this is the one cnidarian class with freshwater representatives. Most hydrozoans have life cycles that display alternation of generations; however, in some, the medusa stage is lost, while in others, the polyp stage is very small.

Three features distinguish hydrozoans from other cnidarians: (1) nematocysts are only in the epidermis; (2) gametes are epidermal and released to the outside of the body rather than into the gastrovascular cavity; and (3) the mesoglea never contains amoeboid mesenchyme cells (*see table 18.2*).

Most hydrozoans have colonial polyps in which individuals may be specialized for feeding, producing medusae by budding, or defending the colony. In *Obelia*, a common marine cnidarian, the planula develops into a feeding polyp, called a **gastrozooid**

(gas′tra-zo′oid) (figure 18.12). The gastrozooid has tentacles, feeds on microscopic organisms in the water, and secretes a skeleton of protein and chitin, called the perisarc, around itself.

Growth of an *Obelia* colony results from budding of the original gastrozooid. Rootlike processes grow into and horizontally along the substrate. They anchor the colony and give rise to branch colonies. The entire colony has a continuous gastrovascular cavity, body wall, and perisarc, and is a few centimeters high. Gastrozooids are the most common type of polyp in the colony; however, as an *Obelia* colony grows, gonozooids are produced. A **gonozooid** (gon′o-zo′oid) is a reproductive polyp that produces medusae by budding. *Obelia's* small medusae form on a stalklike structure of the gonozooid. When medusae mature, they break free of the stalk and swim out an opening at the end of the gonozooid. Medusae reproduce sexually to give rise to more colonies of polyps.

Gonionemus is a hydrozoan in which the medusa stage predominates (figure 18.13*a*). It lives in shallow marine waters, where it often clings to seaweeds by adhesive pads on its tentacles. The biology of *Gonionemus* is typical of most hydrozoan medusae. The margin of the *Gonionemus* medusa projects inward to form a shelflike lip, called the velum. A velum is present on most hydrozoan medusae but is absent in all other cnidarian classes. The velum concentrates water expelled from beneath the medusa to a smaller outlet, creating a jet-propulsion system. The mouth is at the end of a tubelike **manubrium** that hangs from the medusa's oral surface. The gastrovascular cavity leads from the inside of the manubrium into four radial canals that extend to the margin of the medusa. An encircling ring canal connects the radial canals at the margin of the medusa (figure 18.13*b*).

In addition to a nerve net, *Gonionemus* has a concentration of nerve cells, called a nerve ring, that encircles the margin of the medusa. The nerve ring coordinates swimming movements. Embedded in the mesoglea around the margin of the medusa are sensory structures called statocysts. A **statocyst** consists of a small sac surrounding a calcium carbonate concretion called a statolith. When *Gonionemus* tilts, the statolith moves in response to the pull of gravity. This initiates nerve impulses that may change the animal's swimming behavior.

Gonads of *Gonionemus* medusae hang from the oral surface, below the radial canals. *Gonionemus* is dioecious and sheds gametes directly into seawater. A planula larva develops and attaches to the substrate, eventually forming a polyp (about 5 mm tall). The polyp reproduces by budding to make more polyps and medusae.

Hydra is a common freshwater hydrozoan that hangs from the underside of floating plants in clean streams and ponds. *Hydra* lacks a medusa stage and reproduces both asexually by budding from the side of the polyp and sexually. Hydras are somewhat unusual hydrozoans because sexual reproduction occurs in the polyp stage. Testes are conical elevations of the body surface that form from mitosis of certain epidermal cells, called

FIGURE 18.12

***Obelia* Structure and Life Cycle.** *Obelia* alternates between polyp and medusa stages. An entire polyp colony stands about 1 cm tall. A mature medusa is about 1 mm in diameter, and the planula is about 0.2 mm long. Unlike *Obelia*, the majority of colonial hydrozoans have medusae that remain attached to the parental colony, and release gametes or larval stages through the gonozooid. The medusae often degenerate and may be little more than gonadal specializations in the gonozooid.

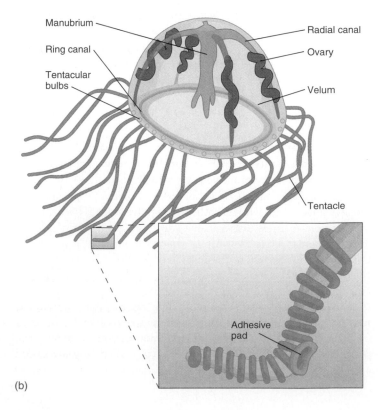

(a)

(b)

FIGURE 18.13

A Hydrozoan Medusa. (*a*) A *Gonionemus* medusa. (*b*) Structure of *Gonionemus*.

interstitial cells. Sperm form by meiosis in the testes. Mature sperm exit the testes through temporary openings. Ovaries also form from interstitial cells. One large egg forms per ovary. During egg formation, yolk is incorporated into the egg cell from gastrodermal cells. As ovarian cells disintegrate, a thin stalk of tissue attaches the egg to the body wall. After fertilization and early development, epithelial cells lay down a resistant chitinous shell. The embryo drops from the parent, overwinters, hatches in the spring, and develops into an adult.

Large oceanic hydrozoans belong to the order Siphonophora. These colonies are associations of numerous polypoid and medusoid individuals. Some polyps, called dactylozooids, possess a single, long (up to 9 m) tentacle armed with cnidocytes for capturing prey. Other polyps are specialized for digesting prey. Various medusoid individuals form swimming bells, sac floats, oil floats, leaflike defensive structures, and gonads.

Physalia physalis, commonly called the Portuguese man-of-war, is a large, colonial siphonophore. It lacks swimming capabilities and moves at the mercy of wind and waves. **6** Its cnidocyte-laden dactylozooids are lethal to small vertebrates and dangerous to humans.

Class Scyphozoa

Members of the class Scyphozoa (si″fo-zo′ah) are all marine and are "true jellyfish" because the dominant stage in their life history is the medusa (figure 18.14). Unlike hydrozoan medusae, scyphozoan medusae lack a velum, the mesoglea contains amoeboid mesenchyme cells, cnidocytes occur in the gastrodermis as well as the epidermis, and gametes are gastrodermal in origin *(see table 18.2)*.

Many scyphozoans are harmless to humans; others can deliver unpleasant and even dangerous stings. For example, *Mastigias quinquecirrha*, the so-called stinging nettle, is a common Atlantic scyphozoan whose populations increase in late summer and become hazardous to swimmers (figure 18.14*a*). **7** A rule of thumb for swimmers is to avoid helmet-shaped jellyfish with long tentacles and fleshy lobes hanging from the oral surface.

Aurelia is a common scyphozoan in both Pacific and Atlantic coastal waters of North America (figure 18.14*b*). The margin of its medusa has a fringe of short tentacles and is divided by notches. The mouth of *Aurelia* leads to a stomach with four gastric pouches, which contain cnidocyte-laden gastric filaments. Radial canals lead from gastric pouches to the margin of the bell. In *Aurelia*, but not all scyphozoans, the canal system is extensively branched and leads to a ring canal around the margin of the medusa. Gastrodermal cells of all scyphozoans possess cilia to continuously circulate seawater and partially digested food.

Aurelia is a plankton feeder. At rest, it sinks slowly in the water and traps microscopic animals in mucus on its epidermal surfaces. Cilia carry this food to the margin of the medusa. Four fleshy lobes, called oral lobes, hang from the manubrium and scrape food from the margin of the medusa (figure 18.15*a*). Cilia on the oral lobes carry food to the mouth.

(a)

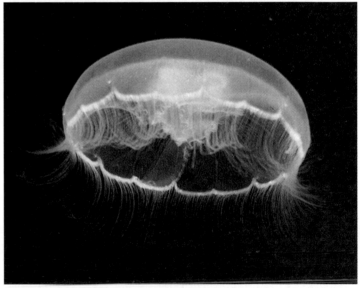

(b)

FIGURE 18.14

Representative Scyphozoans. *(a) Mastigias quinquecirrha. (b) Aurelia* sp.

In addition to sensory receptors on the epidermis, *Aurelia* has eight specialized structures, called rhopalia, in the notches at the margin of the medusa. Each **rhopalium** consists of sensory structures surrounded by rhopalial lappets. Two sensory pits (presumed to be olfactory) are associated with sensory lappets. A statocyst and photoreceptors, called ocelli, are associated with rhopalia (figure 18.15*b*). *Aurelia* displays a distinct negative phototaxis, coming to the surface at twilight and descending to greater depths during bright daylight.

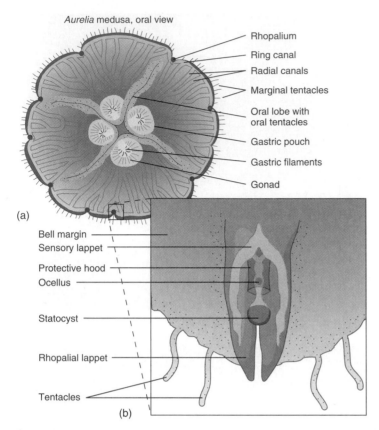

Aurelia medusa, oral view

- Rhopalium
- Ring canal
- Radial canals
- Marginal tentacles
- Oral lobe with oral tentacles
- Gastric pouch
- Gastric filaments
- Gonad

(a)

- Bell margin
- Sensory lappet
- Protective hood
- Ocellus
- Statocyst
- Rhopalial lappet
- Tentacles

(b)

FIGURE 18.15

Structure of a Scyphozoan Medusa. (*a*) Internal structure of *Aurelia*. (*b*) A section through a rhopalium of *Aurelia*. Each rhopalium consists of two sensory (olfactory) lappets, a statocyst, and a photoreceptor called an ocellus. (*b*) *Source: After L. H. Hyman,* Biology of the Invertebrates, *copyright 1940 McGraw-Hill Publishing Co.*

Scyphozoans are dioecious. *Aurelia*'s eight gonads are in gastric pouches, two per pouch. Gametes are released into the gastric pouches. Sperm swim through the mouth to the outside of the medusa. In some scyphozoans, eggs are fertilized in the female's gastric pouches, and early development occurs there. In *Aurelia*, eggs lodge in the oral lobes, where fertilization and development to the planula stage occurs.

The planula develops into a polyp called a **scyphistoma** (figure 18.16). The scyphistoma lives a year or more, during which time budding produces miniature medusae, called **ephyrae.** Repeated budding of the scyphistoma results in ephyrae being stacked on the polyp—as you might pile saucers on top of one another. After ephyrae are released, they gradually attain the adult form.

CLASS CUBOZOA

The class Cubozoa (ku″bo-zo′ah) was formerly classified as an order in the Scyphozoa. The medusa is cuboidal, and tentacles hang

from each of its corners. Polyps are very small and, in some species, are unknown. Cubozoans are active swimmers and feeders in warm tropical waters. Some possess dangerous nematocysts (figure 18.17).

CLASS ANTHOZOA

Members of the class Anthozoa (an″tho-zo′ah) are colonial or solitary, and lack medusae. They include anemones and stony and soft corals. Anthozoans are all marine and are found at all depths.

Anthozoan polyps differ from hydrozoan polyps in three respects: (1) the mouth of an anthozoan leads to a pharynx, which is an invagination of the body wall that leads into the gastrovascular cavity; (2) mesenteries (membranes) that bear cnidocytes and gonads on their free edges divide the gastrovascular cavity into sections; and (3) the mesoglea contains amoeboid mesenchyme cells (*see table 18.2*).

Externally, anthozoans appear to show perfect radial symmetry. Internally, the mesenteries and other structures convey biradial symmetry to members of this class.

Sea anemones are solitary, frequently large, and colorful (figure 18.18*a*). Some attach to solid substrates, some burrow in soft substrates, and some live in symbiotic relationships (figure 18.18*b*). The polyp attaches to its substrate by a pedal disk (figure 18.19). An oral disk contains the mouth and hollow, oral tentacles. At one or both ends of the slitlike mouth is a siphonoglyph, which is a ciliated tract that moves water into the gastrovascular cavity to maintain the hydrostatic skeleton.

Mesenteries are arranged in pairs. Some attach at the body wall at their outer margin and to the pharynx along their inner margin. Other mesenteries attach to the body wall but are free along their entire inner margin. Openings in mesenteries near the oral disk permit water to circulate between compartments the mesenteries set off. The free lower edges of the mesenteries form a trilobed mesenterial filament. Mesenterial filaments bear cnidocytes, cilia that aid in water circulation, gland cells that secrete digestive enzymes, and cells that absorb products of digestion. Threadlike acontia at the ends of mesenterial filaments bear cnidocytes. Acontia subdue live prey in the gastrovascular cavity and can be extruded through small openings in the body wall or through the mouth when an anemone is threatened.

Muscle fibers are largely gastrodermal. Longitudinal muscle bands are restricted to the mesenteries. Circular muscles are in the gastrodermis of the column. When threatened, anemones contract their longitudinal fibers, allowing water to escape from the gastrovascular cavity. This action causes the oral end of the column to fold over the oral disk, and the anemone appears to collapse. Reestablishment of the hydrostatic skeleton depends on gradual uptake of water into the gastrovascular cavity via the siphonoglyphs.

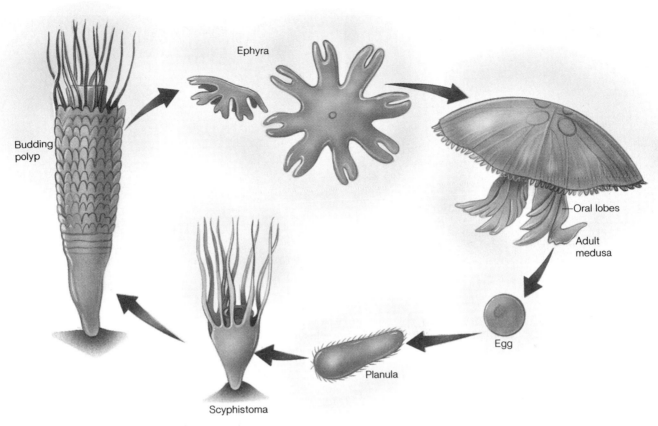

FIGURE 18.16

Aurelia **Life History.** *Aurelia* is dioecious, and like all scyphozoans, the medusa (10 cm) predominates in the organism's life history. The planula (0.3 mm) develops into a polyp called a scyphistoma (4 mm), which produces young medusae, or ephyrae, by budding.

FIGURE 18.17

Class Cubozoa. The sea wasp, *Chironex fleckeri*. The medusa is cuboidal, and tentacles hang from the corners of the bell. *Chironex fleckeri* has caused more human suffering and death off Australian coasts than the Portuguese man-of-war has in any of its home waters. Death from heart failure and shock is not likely unless the victim is stung repeatedly.

(a)

(b)

FIGURE 18.18

Representative Sea Anemones. *(a)* Giant sea anemone *(Anthopleura xanthogrammica)*. Symbiotic algae give this anemone its green color. *(b)* This sea anemone *(Calliactis parasitical)* lives in a mutualistic relationship with a hermit crab *(Eupargurus)*. Hermit crabs lack a heavily armored exoskeleton over much of their bodies and seek refuge in empty snail shells. When this crab outgrows its present home, it will take its anemone with it to a new snail (whelk) shell. This anemone, riding on the shell of the hermit crab, has an unusual degree of mobility. In turn, the anemone's nematocysts protect the crab from predators.

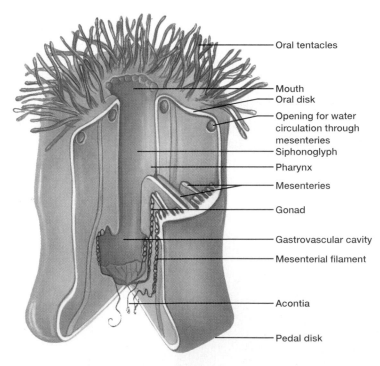

- Oral tentacles
- Mouth
- Oral disk
- Opening for water circulation through mesenteries
- Siphonoglyph
- Pharynx
- Mesenteries
- Gonad
- Gastrovascular cavity
- Mesenterial filament
- Acontia
- Pedal disk

FIGURE 18.19

Class Anthozoa. Structure of the anemone, *Metridium* sp.

Anemones have limited locomotion. They glide on their pedal disk, crawl on their side, and walk on their tentacles. When disturbed, some "swim" by thrashing their body or tentacles. Some anemones float using a gas bubble held within folds of the pedal disk.

Anemones feed on invertebrates and fishes. Tentacles capture prey and draw it toward the mouth. Radial muscle fibers in the mesenteries open the mouth to receive the food.

Anemones show both sexual and asexual reproduction. In asexual reproduction, a piece of pedal disk may break away from the polyp and grow into a new individual in a process called pedal laceration. Alternatively, longitudinal or transverse fission may divide one individual into two, with missing parts being regenerated. Unlike other cnidarians, anemones may be either monoecious or dioecious. In monoecious species, male gametes mature earlier than female gametes so that self-fertilization does not occur. This is called **protandry** (Gr. *protos*, first + *andros*, male). Gonads occur in longitudinal bands behind mesenterial filaments. Fertilization may be external or within the gastrovascular cavity. Cleavage results in the formation of a planula, which develops into a ciliated larva that settles to the substrate, attaches, and eventually forms the adult.

Other anthozoans are corals. ⑧ Stony corals form coral reefs (box 18.2) and, except for lacking siphonoglyphs, are

BOX 18.2 | CORAL REEFS

Not all corals build coral reefs. Those that do not are called soft corals and often live at great depths in cold seawater. Stony corals are reef-building species. Coral reefs are built as calcium carbonate exoskeletons of one generation of stony corals are secreted on the exoskeletons of preceding generations. It requires millions of years for massive reefs, such as those found in warm, shallow waters of the Indian Ocean, the south Pacific Ocean, and the Caribbean Sea, to develop (figure 1). Reef formation requires constantly warm (20° C), shallow (less than 90 m) water and constant salinity near 3.5%.

Most reef-building activities are the result of stony corals living in a mutualistic relationship (*see chapter 17*) with a group of dinoflagellate protists called **zooxanthellae** (*see figure 18.20*). Stony corals depend on photosynthetic activities of zooxanthellae as a prin-

cipal source of carbohydrates. Predatory activities are mainly a source of protein for polyps. Zooxanthellae also promote exceptionally high rates of calcium deposition. As zooxanthellae carry on photosynthesis, they remove carbon dioxide (CO_2) from the polyp's environment. Associated pH changes induce the precipitation of dissolved $CaCO_3$ as aragonite (coral limestone). The 90 m depth limit for reef building is believed to correspond to the limits to which sufficient light penetrates to support dinoflagellate photosynthesis.

Certain algae, called **coralline algae,** live outside the coral organisms and create their own calcium carbonate masses. These algae contribute to the reef by cementing together larger coral formations.

Reefs can extend hundreds of meters below the ocean's surface; however, only the upper and outer layer includes coral animals and algae. Most of the reef formation consists of exoskeletons of previous generations of stony corals. (The depth of the reef mass is evidence of changing oceanic levels during glacial periods and of the subsidence of the ocean floor.) In addition to the outer layer of photosynthetic and cnidarian life-forms, the reef supports a host of other organisms, including fishes, molluscs, arthropods, echinoderms, soft corals, and sponges. The exceptionally high productivity of reef communities depends on the ability of reef organisms to recycle nutrients rather than to lose them to the ocean floor.

There are three types of coral reefs: (1) Fringing reefs are built up from the sea bottom so close to a shoreline that no navigable channel exists between the shoreline and the reef. This reef formation frequently creates a narrow, shallow lagoon between the reef and the shore. Surging water creates frequent breaks and irregular channels through these reefs. (2) Barrier reefs are separated from shore by wide, deep channels. The Great Barrier Reef of Australia is 1,700 km long with a channel 20 to 50 m deep and up to 48 km wide. (The Great Barrier Reef actually consists of a number of different reef forms, including barrier reefs.) (3) Atolls are circular reefs that enclose a lagoon in the open ocean. One hypothesis regarding their origin, first described by Charles Darwin, is that atolls built up around islands that later sank.

FIGURE 1   **Coral Reefs.** A fringing reef surrounding Hoskyn Islands off the coast of Australia.

similar to the anemones. Their common name derives from a cuplike calcium carbonate exoskeleton that epithelial cells secrete around the base and the lower portion of the column (figure 18.20). When threatened, polyps retract into their protective exoskeletons. Sexual reproduction is similar to that of anemones, and asexual budding produces other members of the colony.

The colorful octacorallian corals are common in warm waters. They have eight pinnate (featherlike) tentacles, eight mesenteries, and one siphonoglyph. The body walls of members of a colony are connected, and mesenchyme cells secrete an internal skeleton of protein or calcium carbonate. Sea fans, sea pens, sea whips, red corals, and organ-pipe corals are members of this group (figure 18.21).

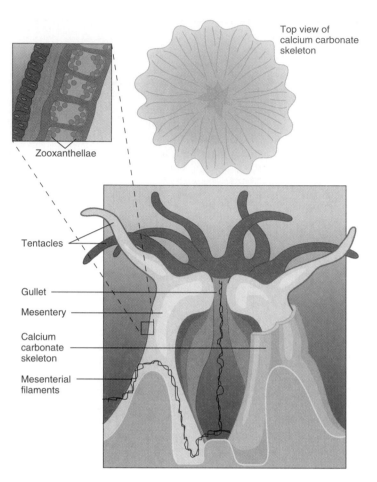

Top view of calcium carbonate skeleton

Zooxanthellae

Tentacles

Gullet

Mesentery

Calcium carbonate skeleton

Mesenterial filaments

FIGURE 18.20

Class Anthozoa. A stony coral polyp in its calcium carbonate skeleton (longitudinal section).

Stop and Ask Yourself

9. What hydrozoan has well-defined alternation of generations? What hydrozoan has reduced alternation of generations?

10. What kinds of sensory structures occur in cnidarians?

11. How do the following fit into the life history of a scyphozoan: (*a*) scyphistoma, (*b*) ephyra, and (*c*) planula?

12. What is protandry? How does it apply to the Anthozoa?

Phylum Ctenophora

Animals in the phylum Ctenophora (ti-nof'er-ah) (Gr. *kteno*, comb + *phoros*, to bear) are called sea walnuts or comb jellies (table 18.3). The approximately 90 described species are all marine (figure 18.22a). Most ctenophorans have a spherical form, although several groups are flattened and/or elongate.

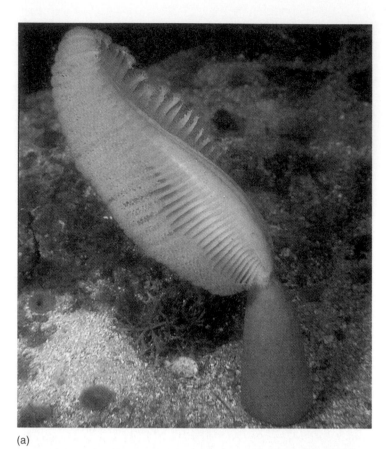

(a)

(b)

FIGURE 18.21

Representative Octacorallian Corals. (*a*) Fleshy sea pen (*Ptilosaurus gurneyi*). (*b*) Purple sea fan (*Gorgonia ventalina*).

Characteristics of the phylum Ctenophora include:

1. Diploblastic, tissue-level organization
2. Biradial symmetry
3. Gelatinous mesoglea between the epidermal and gastrodermal tissue layers

TABLE 18.3	CLASSIFICATION OF THE CTENOPHORA

Phylum Ctenophora (ti-nof′er-ah)
The animal phylum whose members are biradially symmetrical, diploblastic, usually ellipsoid or spherical in shape, possess colloblasts, and have meridionally arranged comb rows.
   Class Tentaculata (ten-tak′u-lah-tah)
   With tentacles that may or may not be associated with sheaths, into which the tentacles can be retracted. *Pleurobranchia.*
   Class Nuda (nu′dah)
   Without tentacles; flattened; a highly branched gastrovascular cavity. *Beroë.*

(a)

4. Gastrovascular cavity
5. Nervous system in the form of a nerve net
6. Adhesive structures called colloblasts
7. Eight rows of ciliary bands, called comb rows, for locomotion

   Pleurobranchia has a spherical or ovoid, transparent body about 2 cm in diameter. It occurs in the colder waters of the Atlantic and Pacific Oceans (figure 18.22b). *Pleurobranchia*, like most ctenophorans, has eight meridional bands of cilia, called **comb rows,** between the oral and aboral poles. Comb rows are locomotor structures that are coordinated through a statocyst at the aboral pole. *Pleurobranchia* normally swims with its aboral pole oriented downward. The statocyst detects tilting, and the comb rows adjust the animal's orientation. Two long, branched tentacles arise from pouches near the aboral pole. Tentacles possess contractile fibers that retract the tentacles, and adhesive cells, called **colloblasts,** that capture prey (figure 18.22c).
   Ingestion occurs as the tentacles wipe the prey across the mouth. The mouth leads to a branched gastrovascular canal system. Some canals are blind; however, two small anal canals open to the outside near the apical sense organ. Thus, unlike the cnidarians, ctenophores have an anal opening. Some undigested wastes are eliminated through these canals, and some are probably also eliminated through the mouth (*see figure 18.22b*).
   Pleurobranchia is monoecious, as are all ctenophores. Two bandlike gonads are associated with the gastrodermis. One of these is an ovary, and the other is a testis. Gametes are shed through the mouth, fertilization is external, and a slightly flattened larva develops.

FURTHER PHYLOGENETIC CONSIDERATIONS

The evolutionary position of the phyla covered in this chapter is subject to debate. If the animal kingdom is polyphyletic, then all phyla could have had separate origins, although scientists who believe in multiple origins agree that the number of independent origins is probably small. Some zoologists believe the animal

FIGURE 18.22

Phylum Ctenophora. (*a*) The ctenophore *Mnemiopsis* sp. Ctenophorans are well known for their bioluminescence. Light-producing cells are in the walls of their digestive canals, which are beneath comb rows. (*b*) The structure of *Pleurobranchia* sp. The animal usually swims with the oral end forward or upward. (*c*) Colloblasts consist of a hemispherical sticky head that connects to the core of the tentacle by a straight filament. A contractile spiral filament coils around the straight filament. Straight and spiral filaments prevent struggling prey from escaping.

kingdom to be at least diphyletic, with the Porifera being derived separately from all other phyla. The similarity of poriferan choanocytes and choanoflagellate protists suggests evolutionary ties between these groups. Many other zoologists believe that the sponges have a common, although remote, ancestry with other animals. The amoeboid and flagellated cells in sponges and higher animals support this view. One thing that nearly everyone agrees upon, however, is that the Porifera are evolutionary "dead ends." They gave rise to no other animal phyla.

If two origins are assumed, the origin of the nonporiferan lineage is also debated. One interpretation is that the ancestral animal was derived from a radially symmetrical ancestor, which, in turn, may have been derived from a colonial flagellate similar in form to *Volvox* (see figure 17.8). If this is true, then the radiate phyla (Cnidaria and Ctenophora) could be closely related to that ancestral group. Other zoologists contend that bilateral symmetry is the ancestral body form and that a bilateral ancestor gave rise to both the radiate phyla and bilateral phyla. In this interpretation, the radiate phyla are further removed from the base of the evolutionary tree.

Figure 18.23 shows the probable evolutionary relationships of the cnidarian classes. The classical interpretation is that primitive Hydrozoa were the ancestral radial animals and that the medusoid body form is the primitive body form. This ancestry is suggested by the medusa being the adult body form in the Hydrozoa and the only body form in some trachyline hydrozoans. The polyp may have evolved secondarily as a larval stage. In the evolution of the other three orders, septa appeared—dividing the gastrovascular cavity—and gonads became endodermal in origin. The Scyphozoa and Cubozoa are distinguished from the Anthozoa by the evolutionary reduction of the polyp stage in the former classes and the loss of the medusa stage in the latter class. The Scyphozoa and Cubozoa are distinguished from each other by budding of the polyp (Scyphozoa) and the cuboidal shape of the medusa (Cubozoa).

The relationships of the Ctenophora to any other group of animals are uncertain. The Ctenophora and Cnidaria share important characteristics, such as radial (biradial) symmetry, diploblastic organization, nerve nets, and gastrovascular cavities.

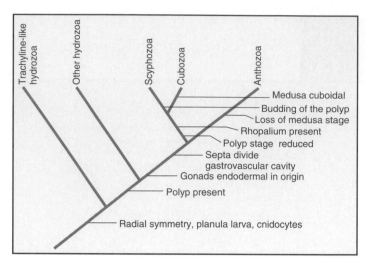

FIGURE 18.23

Cladogram Showing Cnidarian Taxonomy. Selected synapomorphic characters are shown. Most zoologists believe hydrozoans to be ancestral to other cnidarians.

In spite of these similarities, differences in adult body forms and embryological development make it difficult to derive the Ctenophora from any group of cnidarians. Relationships between the Cnidaria and Ctenophora are probably distant.

Stop and Ask Yourself

13. What characteristics do the Ctenophora and the Cnidaria share?
14. What are colloblasts?
15. How do ctenophores use statocysts and comb rows to maintain an upright position in the water?
16. Why are the sponges considered evolutionary "dead ends"?

SUMMARY

1. Although the origin of multicellularity in animals is unknown, the colonial hypothesis and the syncytial hypothesis are explanations of how animals could have arisen. Whether the animal kingdom had origins in one, two, or many ancestors is debated.

2. Animals in the phylum Porifera are the sponges. Cells of sponges are specialized to create water currents, filter food, produce gametes, form skeletal elements, and line the sponge body wall.

3. Sponges circulate water through their bodies to bring in food and oxygen and to carry away wastes and reproductive products. Evolution has resulted in most sponges having complex canal systems and large water-circulating capabilities.

4. Members of the phylum Cnidaria are radially or biradially symmetrical and possess diploblastic, tissue-level organization. Cells are specialized for food gathering, defense, contraction, coordination, digestion, and absorption.

5. Hydrozoans differ from other cnidarians in having ectodermal gametes, mesoglea without mesenchyme cells, and nematocysts only in their epidermis. Most hydrozoans have well-developed polyp and medusa stages.

6. The class Scyphozoa contains the jellyfish. The polyp stage of scyphozoans is usually very small.

7. Members of the class Cubozoa live in warm, tropical waters. Some possess dangerous nematocysts.

8. The Anthozoa lack the medusa stage. They include sea anemones and corals.

9. Members of the phylum Ctenophora are biradially symmetrical and diploblastic. Bands of cilia, called comb rows, characterize the ctenophores.

10. Zoologists debate whether or not the Porifera had a common origin with other animals. The Cnidaria and Ctenophora are distantly related phyla. Within the Cnidaria, the ancient hydrozoans are believed to be the stock from which modern hydrozoans and other cnidarians evolved.

SELECTED KEY TERMS

choanocytes (p. 263)

cnidocytes (p. 268)

epidermis (p. 268)

gastrodermis (p. 268)

gastrovascular cavity (p. 269)

hydrostatic skeleton (p. 270)

medusa (p. 269)

mesoglea (p. 268)

polyp (p. 269)

statocyst (p. 271)

CRITICAL THINKING QUESTIONS

1. If most animals are derived from a single ancestral stock, and if that ancestral stock was radially symmetrical, would the colonial hypothesis or the syncytial hypothesis of animal origins be more attractive to you? Explain.

2. Colonies are defined in chapter 16 as "loose associations of independent cells." Why are sponges considered to have surpassed that level of organization? In your answer, compare a sponge with a colonial protist like *Volvox*.

3. Evolution is often viewed as a continuous process of increasing diversification of body forms and species. What evidence in early animal evolution contradicts this viewpoint?

4. Most sponges and sea anemones are monoecious, yet separate individuals usually reproduce sexually. Why is this advantageous for these animals? What ensures that sea anemones do not self-fertilize?

5. Do you think that the polyp stage or the medusa stage predominated in the ancestral cnidarian? Support your answer. What implications does your answer have when interpreting the evolutionary relationships among the cnidarian classes?

REFERENCES ON THE WORLD WIDE WEB

1. **Porifera: Fossil Record.**   The fossil history, life history, ecology, systematics, and morphology of sponges are described at this site.
   http://www.ucmp.berkeley.edu/porifera/poriferafr.html

2. **Introduction to Porifera.**   This site describes the evolutionary history, life history, and ecology of the sponges.
   http://www.ucmp.berkeley.edu/porifera/porifera.html

3. **Guide to Sponge Collection and Identification.**   This site provides a sponge identification guide, taxonomic listings, a glossary, and instructions for preparing sponges for identification.
   http://www2.tcd.ie/People/Bernard.Picton/porifera/sponge_guide.html

4. **Carnivorous Sponge.**   This site describes the recent discovery of a carnivorous, crustacean-eating sponge.
   http://outcast.gene.com/ae/WN/SU/carniverous_sponge.html

5. **Cnidaria WWW Server.**   Many aspects of cnidarian biology are described here—from body structure to molecular evolution.
   http://128.200.5.5/

6. **Introduction to Cnidaria.**   This site provides information on the fossil record, life history, ecology, systematics, and morphology of cnidarians.
   http://www.ucmp.berkeley.edu/cnidaria/cnidaria.html

7. **Corals and Coral Reefs.**   This site provides information on reef biology, including classification, habitat, distribution, physical characteristics, life history, and conservation.
   http://www.bev.net/education/SeaWorld/coral_reefs/introcr.html

8. **Coral Forest.**   This presentation on the biology of coral reefs includes information on threats to coral reefs and possible solutions to conservation problems. It also provides maps of coral reef distribution, suggestions for teachers, a photo gallery, and many links to other web sites concerning reef biology.
   http://www.blacktop.com/coralforest/index

9. **Keys to Marine Invertebrates of the Woods Hole Region.** This site provides links to taxonomic keys to the Porifera and Cnidaria.
   http://www.mbl.edu/html/BB/keys/KEYScontents.html

SOME LESSER-KNOWN INVERTEBRATES:
MESOZOA AND PLACOZOA

THREE MULTICELLULAR PHYLA OF UNCERTAIN AFFINITIES

The Mesozoa and Placozoa are small groups of animals that most of us will never encounter outside of textbook descriptions and illustrations. Even though these phyla are of uncertain evolutionary affinities, some zoologists consider the placozoan body form to be similar to that present in (at least one group of) the first animals.

THE MESOZOAN PHYLA: ORTHONECTIDA AND RHOMBOZOA

The Mesozoa (mez″o-zo′ah) (Gr. *mesos*, middle + *zoin*, animal) include two phyla, Orthonectida and Rhombozoa (figure 1). These two phyla have approximately one hundred species. As larvae and/or adults, mesozoans are parasites of other marine invertebrates (brittle stars, bivalved molluscs, and cephalopod molluscs). They consist of 20 to 30 cells arranged in two layers: an inner layer of reproductive cells and an outer layer of ciliated cells. Mesozoans are dioecious (sexes are separate) with complex life histories involving both sexual and asexual cycles.

PHYLUM PLACOZOA

Members of the phylum Placozoa (plak″o-zo′ah) (Gr. *plak,* flattened + *zoin,* animal) are small (2 to 5 mm) marine organisms. The phylum's one species, *Tricoplax adhaerens,* was first described in the 1800s, largely forgotten, and then rediscovered in the 1960s on algae from the Red Sea. *Tricoplax* consists of two epithelial layers with fiber cells (possibly locomotor in function) between them. The upper epithelium consists of flagellated cells and transparent spheres of fatty material. The lower epithelium consists of flagellated cylinder cells and gland cells of nutritive function (figure 2). When *Tricoplax* feeds, it forms a temporary, ventral digestive cavity by raising its body off the substrate and secreting enzymes into the cavity. The similarity of this animal to a hypothetical ancestor proposed in the syncytial hypothesis of animal origins causes some zoologists to wonder if this group could be closely related to the first animals.

FIGURE 1
The Mesozoans.
(*a*) *Rhopalura* (0.5 mm), an orthonectid parasite of clams.
(*b*) *Pseudicyema* (1.0 mm), a rhombozoan parasite of cuttlefish.

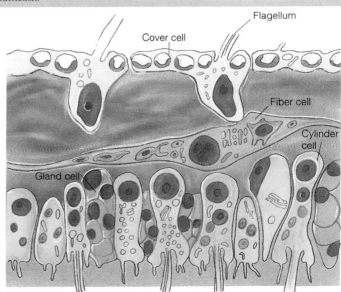

FIGURE 2 **Phylum Placozoa.** *Tricoplax adhaerens* consists of two epithelial layers with fiber cells sandwiched between.

The Triploblastic, Acoelomate Body Plan

Concepts

1. The acoelomates are represented by the phyla Platyhelminthes, Nemertea, and Gastrotricha. These phyla are phylogenetically important because they are transitional between radial animals and the more complex bilateral animals. Three important characteristics appeared initially in this group: bilateral symmetry, a true mesoderm that gives rise to muscles and other organs, and a nervous system with a primitive brain and nerve cords.
2. Acoelomates lack a body cavity because the mesodermal mass completely fills the area between the outer epidermis and digestive tract.
3. The phylum Platyhelminthes is a large group of dorsoventrally flattened animals commonly called the flatworms.
4. Members of the class Turbellaria are mostly free-living. Representatives of the classes Monogenea, Trematoda, and Cestoidea are parasitic.
5. The phylum Nemertea (proboscis or ribbon worms) contains predominantly marine, elongate, burrowing worms with digestive and vascular systems.
6. The gastrotrichs are members of a small phylum (Gastrotricha) of free-living and freshwater species that inhabit the space between bottom sediments.
7. Acoelomates may have evolved from a primitive organism resembling a modern turbellarian.

Would You Like to Know . . .

1. what biological advances appear in flatworms? (p. 286)
2. what sexual maturity in a larval body form is called? (p. 286)
3. how turbellarians catch, ingest, and digest their food? (p. 288)
4. why monoecious animals exchange sperm? (p. 290)
5. how monogenetic flukes got their name? (p. 291)
6. how parasites called "flukes" got their name? (p. 291)
7. which trematodes are dangerous human parasites? (p. 293)
8. why *Fasciola hepatica* is called the sheep liver fluke? (p. 293)
9. how 10 m long tapeworms feed, even though they lack a mouth and digestive tract? (p. 294)

This chapter answers these and other useful questions.

This chapter contains evolutionary concepts, which are set off in this font.

EVOLUTIONARY PERSPECTIVE

1 Members of the phyla Platyhelminthes, Nemertea, and Gastrotricha are the first animals to exhibit bilateral symmetry and a body organization more complex than that of the cnidarians. All of the animals covered in this chapter are triploblastic (have three primary germ layers), acoelomate (without a coelom), and classified into three phyla: The phylum Platyhelminthes includes the flatworms (figure 19.1) that are either free living (e.g., turbellarians) or parasitic (e.g., flukes and tapeworms); the phylum Nemertea includes a small group of elongate, unsegmented, soft-bodied worms that are mostly marine and free-living; and the phylum Gastrotricha includes members that inhabit the space between bottom sediments.

The evolutionary relationship of the major phylum in this chapter (Platyhelminthes) to other phyla is controversial. One interpretation is that the triploblastic acoelomate body plan is an important intermediate between the radial, diploblastic plan and the triploblastic coelomate plan. The flatworms would thus represent an evolutionary side branch from a hypothetical triploblastic acoelomate ancestor. Evolution from radial ancestors could have involved a larval stage that became sexually mature in its larval body form. **2** Sexual maturity in a larval body form is called **paedomorphosis** (Gr. *pais*, child + *morphe*, form) and has occurred many times in animal evolution.

Other zoologists envision the evolution of the triploblastic, acoelomate plan from a bilateral ancestor. Primitive acoelomates, similar to flatworms, would have preceded the radiate phyla, and the radial, diploblastic plan would be secondarily derived.

FIGURE 19.1

Flatworms: Animals with Primitive Organ Systems. The marine tiger flatworm *(Prostheceraeus bellustriatus)* shows brilliant markings and bilateral symmetry. This flatworm inhabits the warm, shallow waters around the Hawaiian Islands and is about 25 mm long.

The recent discovery of a small group of worms (Lobatocercebridae, Annelida) that shows both flatworm and annelid characteristics (annelids are a group of coelomate animals, such as the earthworm) suggests that the acoelomate body plan is a secondary characteristic. In this case, the flatworms would represent a side branch that resulted from the loss of a body cavity (figure 19.2).

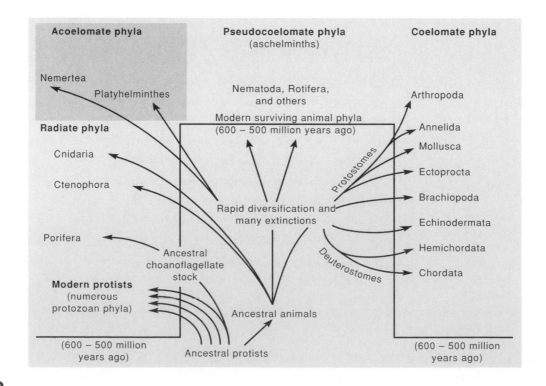

FIGURE 19.2

Acoelomate Phyla. A generalized evolutionary tree depicting the major events and possible lines of descent for the acoelomates (shaded in orange).

PHYLUM PLATYHELMINTHES

The phylum Platyhelminthes (plat″e-hel-min′thez) (Gr. *platys*, flat + *helmins*, worm) contains over 20,000 animal species. Flatworms range in adult size from 1 mm or less to 25 m (*Taeniarhynchus saginatus*; see p. 297), in length. Their mesodermally derived tissues include a loose tissue called **parenchyma** (Gr. *parenck*, anything poured in beside) that fills spaces between other more specialized tissues, organs, and the body wall. Depending on the species, parenchyma may provide skeletal support, nutrient storage, motility, reserves of regenerative cells, transport of materials, structural interactions with other tissues, modifiable tissue for morphogenesis, oxygen storage, and perhaps other functions yet to be determined. This is the first phylum covered that has an organ-system level of organization—a significant evolutionary advancement over the tissue level of organization. The phylum is divided into four classes (table 19.1): (1) the Turbellaria consists of mostly free-living flatworms, whereas the (2) Monogenea, (3) Trematoda, and (4) Cestoidea contain solely parasitic species.

Characteristics of the phylum Platyhelminthes include:

1. Usually flattened dorsoventrally, triploblastic, acoelomate, bilaterally symmetrical
2. Unsegmented worms (members of the class Cestoidea are strobilated)
3. Incomplete gut usually present; gut absent in Cestoidea
4. Somewhat cephalized, with an anterior cerebral ganglion and usually longitudinal nerve cords
5. Protonephridia as excretory/osmoregulatory structures
6. Hermaphroditic; complex reproductive systems

CLASS TURBELLARIA: THE FREE-LIVING FLATWORMS

Members of the class Turbellaria (tur″bel-lar′e-ah) (L. *turbellae*, a commotion + *aria*, like) are mostly free-living bottom dwellers in freshwater and marine environments, where they crawl on stones, sand, or vegetation. Turbellarians are named for the turbulence that their beating cilia create in the water. Over three thousand species have been described. Turbellarians are predators and scavengers. The few terrestrial turbellarians known live in the humid tropics and subtropics. Although most turbellarians are less than 1 cm long, the terrestrial, tropical ones may reach 60 cm in length. Coloration is mostly in shades of black, brown, and gray, although some groups display brightly colored patterns.

Body Wall

As in the Cnidaria, the ectodermal derivatives include an epidermis that is in direct contact with the environment (figure 19.3). Some epidermal cells are ciliated, and others contain microvilli. A basement membrane of connective tissue separates the epidermis from mesodermally derived tissues. An outer layer of circular muscle and an inner layer of longitudinal muscle lie beneath the basement membrane. Other muscles are located dorsoventrally and

TABLE 19.1	CLASSIFICATION OF THE PLATYHELMINTHES

Phylum Platyhelminthes (plat″e-hel-min′thez)
Flatworms; bilateral acoelomates. Over 20,000 species.

Class Turbellaria (tur″bel-lar′e-ah)
Mostly free-living and aquatic; external surface usually ciliated; predaceous; possess rhabdites, protrusible proboscis, frontal glands, and many mucous glands; mostly hermaphroditic. *Convoluta, Notoplana, Dugesia.* Over 3,000 species.

Class Monogenea (mon″oh-gen′e-ah)
Monogenetic flukes; mostly ectoparasites on vertebrates (usually on fishes; occasionally on turtles, frogs, copepods, squids); one life-cycle form in only one host; bear opisthaptor. *Disocotyle, Gyrodactylus, Polystoma.* About 1,100 species.

Class Trematoda (trem″ah-to′dah)
Trematodes; all are parasitic; several holdfast devices present; have complicated life cycles involving both sexual and asexual reproduction. Over 10,000 species.

> **Subclass Aspidogastrea**
> Mostly endoparasites of molluscs; possess large opisthaptor; most lack an oral sucker. *Aspidogaster, Cotylaspis, Multicotyl.* About 32 species.

> **Subclass Digenea**
> Adults endoparasites in vertebrates; at least two different life-cycle forms in two or more hosts; have oral sucker and acetabulum. *Schistosoma, Fasciola, Clonorchis.* About 1,350 species.

Class Cestoidea (ses-toid′e-ah)
All parasitic with no digestive tract; have great reproductive potential; tapeworms. About 3,500 species.

> **Subclass Cestodaria**
> Body not subdivided into proglottids; larva in crustaceans, adult in fishes. *Amphilina, Gyrocotyle.* About 15 species.

> **Subclass Eucestoda**
> True tapeworms; body divided into scolex, neck, and strobila; strobila composed of many proglottids; both male and female reproductive systems in each proglottid; adults in digestive tract of vertebrates. *Protocephalus, Taenia, Echinococcus, Taeniarhynchus, Diphyllobothrium.* About 1,000 species.

obliquely between the dorsal and ventral surfaces. Between the longitudinal muscles and the gastrodermis are the loosely organized parenchymal cells.

The innermost tissue layer is the endodermally derived gastrodermis. It consists of a single layer of cells that comprise the digestive cavity. The gastrodermis secretes enzymes that aid in digestion, and it absorbs the end products of digestion.

On the ventral surface of the body wall are several types of glandular cells of epidermal origin. **Rhabdites** are rodlike cells that swell and form a protective mucous sheath around the body, possibly in response to attempted predation or desiccation. **Adhesive glands** open to the epithelial surface and produce a chemical that attaches part of the turbellarian to a substrate. **Releaser glands** secrete a chemical that dissolves the attachment as needed.

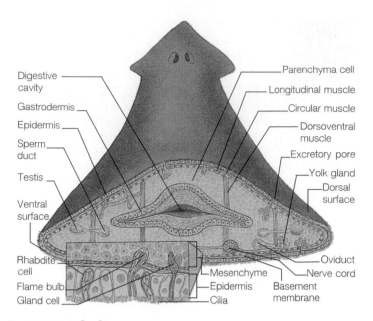

FIGURE 19.3

Phylum Platyhelminthes: Class Turbellaria. Cross section through the body wall of a sexually mature turbellarian (the planarian, *Dugesia*), showing the relationships of the various body structures.

Locomotion

Turbellarians are the first group of bilaterally symmetrical animals. Bilateral symmetry is usually characteristic of animals with an active lifestyle. Turbellarians are primarily bottom dwellers that glide over the substrate. They move using cilia and muscular undulations. As they move, turbellarians lay down a sheet of mucus that aids in adhesion and helps the cilia gain traction. The densely ciliated ventral surface and the flattened body of turbellarians enhance the effectiveness of this locomotion.

Digestion and Nutrition

Some marine turbellarians lack the digestive cavity characteristic of other turbellarians (figure 19.4a). This blind cavity varies from a simple, unbranched chamber (figure 19.4b) to a highly branched system of digestive tubes (figure 19.4d,e). Other turbellarians have digestive tracts that are lobed (figure 19.4c). From an evolutionary perspective, highly branched digestive systems are an advancement that results in more gastrodermis closer to the sites of digestion and absorption, reducing the distance nutrients must diffuse. This aspect of digestive tract structure is especially important in some of the larger turbellarians and partially compensates for the absence of a circulatory system.

The turbellarian pharynx functions as an ingestive organ. It varies in structure from a simple, ciliated tube to a complex organ developed from the folding of muscle layers. In the latter, the free end of the tube lies in a pharyngeal sheath and can project out of the mouth when feeding (figure 19.5).

❸ Most turbellarians, such as the common planarian, are carnivores and feed on small, live invertebrates or scavenge on larger, dead animals; some are herbivores and feed on algae that

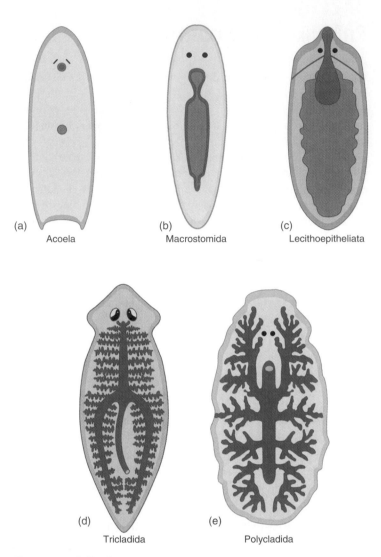

FIGURE 19.4

Digestive Systems in Some Orders of Turbellarians. (*a*) No pharynx and digestive cavity. (*b*) A simple pharynx and straight digestive cavity. (*c*) A simple pharynx and unbranched digestive cavity. (*d*) A branched digestive cavity. (*e*) An extensively branched digestive cavity in which the branches reach almost all parts of the body.

they scrape from rocks. Sensory cells (chemoreceptors) on their heads help them detect food from a considerable distance.

Food digestion is partially extracellular. Pharyngeal glands secrete enzymes that help break down food into smaller units that can be taken into the pharynx. In the digestive cavity, phagocytic cells engulf small units of food, and digestion is completed in intracellular vesicles.

Exchanges with the Environment

The turbellarians do not have respiratory organs; thus, respiratory gases (CO_2 and O_2) are exchanged by diffusion through the body wall. Most metabolic wastes (e.g., ammonia) are also removed by diffusion through the body wall.

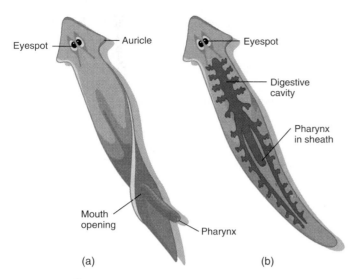

FIGURE 19.5

The Turbellarian Pharynx. A planarian turbellarian with its pharynx (*a*) extended in the feeding position and (*b*) retracted within the pharyngeal sheath.

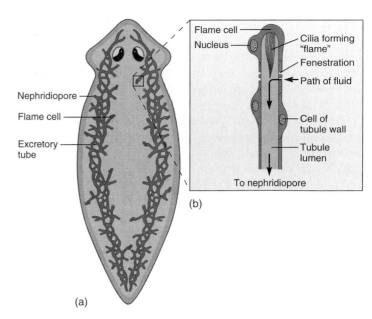

FIGURE 19.6

Protonephridial System in a Turbellarian. (*a*) The protonephridial system lies in the parenchyma and consists of a network of fine tubules that run the length of the animal on each side and open to the surface by minute nephridiopores. (*b*) Numerous, fine side branches from the tubules originate in the parenchyma in enlargements called flame cells. Small black arrows indicate the direction of fluid movement.

In marine environments, invertebrates are often in osmotic equilibrium with their environment. In freshwater, invertebrates are hypertonic to their aquatic environment and thus must regulate the osmotic concentration (water and ions) of their body tissues. The evolution of osmoregulatory structures in the form of protonephridia enabled turbellarians to invade freshwater.

Protonephridia (Gr. *protos*, first + *nephros*, kidney) (sing., protonephridium) are networks of fine tubules that run the length of the turbellarian, along each of its sides (figure 19.6*a*). Numerous, fine side branches of the tubules originate in the parenchyma as tiny enlargements called **flame cells** (figure 19.6*b*). Flame cells (so named because, in the living organism, they resemble a candle flame) have numerous cilia that project into the lumen of the tubule. Slitlike fenestrations (openings) perforate the tubule wall surrounding the flame cell. The beating of the cilia drives fluid down the tubule, creating a negative pressure in the tubule. As a result, fluid from the surrounding tissue is sucked through the fenestrations into the tubule. The tubules eventually merge and open to the outside of the body wall through a minute opening called a **nephridiopore.**

Nervous System and Sense Organs

The most primitive type of flatworm nervous system, found in worms in the order Acoela (e.g., *Convoluta* spp.), is a subepidermal nerve plexus (figure 19.7*a*). This plexus resembles the nerve net of cnidarians. A statocyst in the anterior end functions as a mechanoreceptor (a receptor excited by pressure) that detects the turbellarian's body position in reference to the direction of gravity. Some turbellarians have a more centralized nerve net with cerebral ganglia (figure 19.7*b*). The nervous system of most other turbellarians, such as the planarian *Dugesia*, consists of a subepidermal nerve net and several pairs of long nerve cords (figure 19.7*c*). Lateral branches called commissures (points of union)

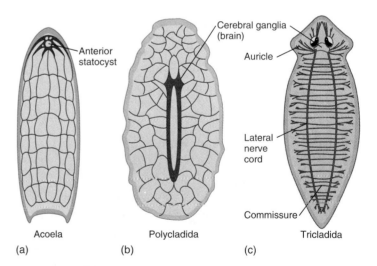

FIGURE 19.7

Nervous Systems in Three Orders of Turbellaria. (*a*) *Convoluta* has a nerve net with a statocyst. (*b*) The nerve net in a turbellarian in the order Polycladida has cerebral ganglia and two lateral nerve cords. (*c*) The cerebral ganglia and nerve cords in the planarian, *Dugesia*.

connect the nerve cords. Nerve cords and their commissures give a ladderlike appearance to the turbellarian nervous system. Neurons are organized into sensory (going to the primitive brain), motor (going away from the primitive brain), and association (connecting) types—an important evolutionary advance with respect to the nervous system. Anteriorly, the nervous tissue concentrates into a pair of cerebral ganglia (sing., ganglion) called a primitive brain.

Turbellarians respond to a variety of stimuli in their external environment. Many tactile and sensory cells distributed over the body detect touch, water currents, and chemicals. **Auricles** (sensory lobes) may project from the side of the head (figure 19.7c). Chemoreceptors that aid in food location are especially dense in these auricles.

Most turbellarians have two simple eyespots called **ocelli** (sing., ocellus) (*see figure 19.5*). These ocelli orient the animal to the direction of light. (Most turbellarians are negatively phototropic and move away from light.) Each ocellus consists of a cuplike depression lined with black pigment. Photoreceptor nerve endings in the cup are part of the neurons that leave the eye and connect with a cerebral ganglion.

Reproduction and Development

Many turbellarians reproduce asexually by transverse fission. Fission usually begins as a constriction behind the pharynx (figure 19.8). The two (or more) animals that result from fission are called **zooids** (Gr., *zoon*, living being or animal), and they regenerate missing parts after separating from each other. Sometimes, the zooids remain attached until they have attained a fairly complete degree of development, at which time they detach as independent individuals.

Turbellarians are monoecious, and reproductive systems arise from the mesodermal tissues in the parenchyma. Numerous paired testes lie along each side of the worm and are the site of sperm production. Sperm ducts (vas deferens) lead to a seminal vesicle (a sperm storage organ) and a protrusible penis (figure 19.9). The penis projects into a genital chamber.

The female system has one to many pairs of ovaries. Oviducts lead from the ovaries to the genital chamber, which opens to the outside through the genital pore.

④ Even though turbellarians are monoecious, reciprocal sperm exchange between two animals is usually the rule. This cross-fertilization ensures greater genetic diversity than does self-fertilization. During cross-fertilization, the penis of each individual is inserted into the copulatory sac of the partner. After copulation, sperm move from the copulatory sac to the genital chamber and then through the oviducts to the ovaries, where fertilization occurs. Yolk may either be directly incorporated into the egg during egg formation, or yolk cells may be laid around the zygote as it passes down the female reproductive tract past the vitellaria (yolk glands).

Eggs are laid with or without a gel-like mass. A hard capsule called a **cocoon** (L., *coccum*, eggshell) encloses many turbellarian eggs. These cocoons attach to the substrate by a stalk and contain several embryos per capsule. Two kinds of capsules are laid. Summer capsules hatch in 2 to 3 weeks, and immature animals emerge. Autumn capsules have thick walls that can resist freezing and drying, and hatch after overwintering.

Development of most turbellarians is direct—a gradual series of changes transforms embryos into adults. A few turbellarians have a free-swimming stage called a **Müller's larva.** It has ciliated extensions for feeding and locomotion. The larva eventually settles to the substrate and develops into a young turbellarian.

Stop and Ask Yourself

1. What are several general characteristics of the phylum Platyhelminthes?
2. What is a cocoon? What is a Müller's larva? What is a zooid?
3. How does a turbellarian move, feed, and reproduce?

FIGURE 19.8

Asexual Reproduction in a Turbellarian. (*a*) Just before division and (*b*) just after. The posterior zooid soon develops a head, pharynx, and other structures. (*c,d*) Later development.

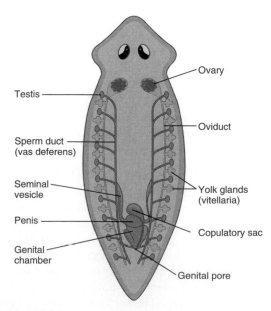

FIGURE 19.9

Triclad Turbellarian Reproductive System. Note that this single individual has both male and female reproductive organs.

CLASS MONOGENEA

⑤ Monogenetic flukes are so named because they have only one generation in their life cycle; that is, one adult develops from one egg. Monogeneans are mostly external parasites (ectoparasites) of freshwater and marine fishes, where they attach to the gill filaments and feed on epithelial cells, mucus, or blood. A large, posterior attachment organ called an opisthaptor facilitates attachment (figure 19.10). Adult monogeneans produce and release eggs that have one or more sticky threads that attach the eggs to the fish gill. Eventually, a ciliated larva called an **oncomiracidium** hatches from the egg and swims to another host fish, where it attaches by its opisthaptor and develops into an adult.

CLASS TREMATODA

⑥ The approximately eight thousand species of parasitic flatworms in the class Trematoda (trem"ah-to'dah) (Gr. *trematodes,* perforated form) are collectively called **flukes,** which describes their wide, flat shape. Almost all adult flukes are parasites of vertebrates, whereas immature stages may be found in vertebrates or invertebrates, or encysted on plants. Many species are of great economic and medical importance.

Most flukes are flat and oval to elongate, and range from less than 1 mm to 6 cm in length (figure 19.11). They feed on host cells and cell fragments. The digestive tract includes a mouth and muscular, pumping pharynx. Posterior to the pharynx, the digestive tract divides into two blind-ending, variously branched pouches called cecae (sing., cecum). Some flukes supplement their feeding by absorbing nutrients across their body wall.

Body-wall structure is similar for all flukes and represents an evolutionary adaptation to the parasitic way of life. The epidermis consists of an outer layer called the **tegument** (figure 19.12), which forms a syncytium (a continuous layer of fused cells). The outer zone of the tegument consists of an organic layer of proteins and carbohydrates called the glycocalyx. The glycocalyx aids in the transport of nutrients, wastes, and gases across the body wall, and protects the fluke against enzymes and the host's immune system. Also found in this zone are microvilli that facilitate nutrient exchange. Cytoplasmic bodies that contain the nuclei and most of

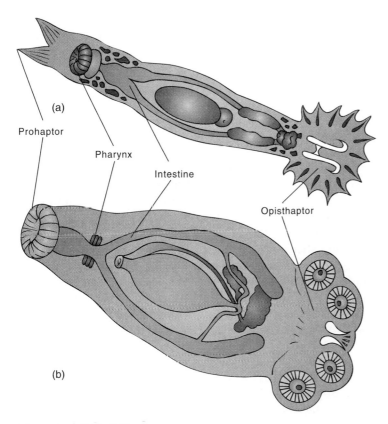

FIGURE 19.10

Class Monogenea. Two monogeneid trematodes. (*a*) *Gyrodactylus.* (*b*) *Sphyranura.* Note the opisthaptors by which these ectoparasites cling to the gills of their fish hosts. Both of these monogenea are about 1 cm long.

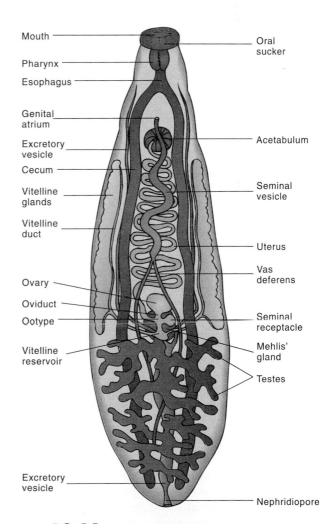

FIGURE 19.11

Generalized Fluke (Digenetic Trematode). Note the large percentage of the body devoted to reproduction. The Mehlis' gland is a conspicuous feature of the female reproductive tract; its function in trematodes is uncertain.

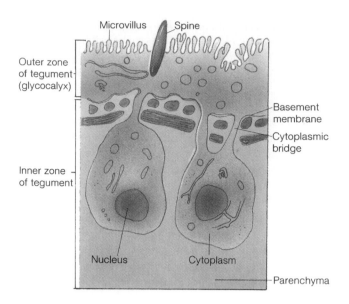

FIGURE 19.12

Trematode Tegument. The fine structure of the tegument of a fluke. The tegument is an evolutionary adaptation that is highly efficient at absorbing nutrients and for protection.

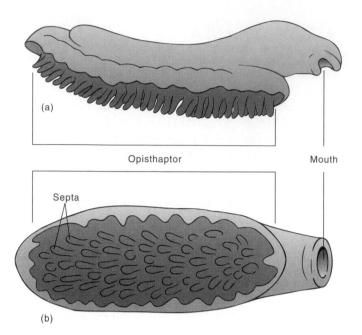

FIGURE 19.13

Class Trematoda: Subclass Aspidogastrea. A representative aspidogastrean fluke. (*a*) Lateral and (*b*) ventral views show the large opisthaptor and numerous septa. These flukes are about 3 mm long.

the organelles lie below the basement membrane. Slender cell processes called cytoplasmic bridges connect the cytoplasmic bodies with the outer zone of the tegument.

Subclass Aspidogastrea

Subclass Aspidogastrea consists of a small group of flukes that are primarily internal parasites (endoparasites) of molluscs. A large, oval holdfast organ called the **opisthaptor** covers the entire ventral surface of the animal and characterizes all aspidogastreans. (figure 19.13). The opisthaptor is an extremely strong attachment organ, and ridges or septa usually subdivide it. The oral sucker, characteristic of most other trematode mouths, is absent. The life cycle of aspidogastreans may involve only one host (a mollusc) or two hosts. In the latter case, the final host is usually a vertebrate (fishes or turtles) that becomes infected by ingesting a mollusc that contains immature aspidogastreans.

Subclass Digenea

The vast majority of all flukes belong to the subclass Digenea (Gr. *di*, two + *genea*, birth). In this subclass, at least two different forms, an adult and one or more larval stages, develop—a characteristic from which the name of the subclass was derived. Because digenetic flukes require at least two different hosts to complete their life cycles, these animals possess the most complex life cycles in the entire animal kingdom. As adults, they are all endoparasites in the bloodstreams, digestive tracts, ducts of the digestive organs, or other visceral organs in a wide variety of vertebrates that serve as definitive, or final, hosts. The one or more intermediate hosts (the hosts that harbor immature stages) may harbor several differ-

ent larval stages. The adhesive organs are two large suckers. The anterior sucker is the **oral sucker** and surrounds the mouth. The other sucker, the **acetabulum,** is located ventrally on the middle portion of the body (*see figure 19.11*).

The eggs of digenetic trematodes are oval and usually have a lidlike hatch called an **operculum** (figure 19.14*a*). When an egg reaches freshwater, the operculum opens, and a ciliated larva called a **miracidium** (pl., miracidia) swims out (figure 19.14*b*). The miracidium swims until it finds a suitable first intermediate host (a snail) to which it is chemically attracted. The miracidium penetrates the snail, loses its cilia, and develops into a **sporocyst** (figure 19.14*c*). (Alternately, the miracidium may remain in the egg and hatch after a snail eats it.) Sporocysts are baglike and contain embryonic cells that develop into either **daughter sporocysts,** or **rediae** (sing., redia) (figure 19.14*d*). At this point in the life cycle, asexual reproduction first occurs. From a single miracidium, hundreds of daughter sporocysts, and in turn, hundreds of rediae can form by asexual reproduction. Embryonic cells in each daughter sporocyst or redia produce hundreds of the next larval stage, called **cercariae** (sing., cercaria) (figure 19.14*e*). (This phenomenon of producing many cercariae is called polyembryony. It greatly enhances the chances that one cercaria will further the life cycle.) A cercaria has a digestive tract, suckers, and a tail. Cercariae leave the snail and swim freely until they encounter a second intermediate or final host, which may be a vertebrate, invertebrate, or plant. The cercaria penetrates this host and encysts as a **metacercaria** (pl., metacercariae) (figure 19.14*f*). When the definitive host eats the second intermediate host, the metacercaria excysts and develops into an adult (figure 19.14*g*).

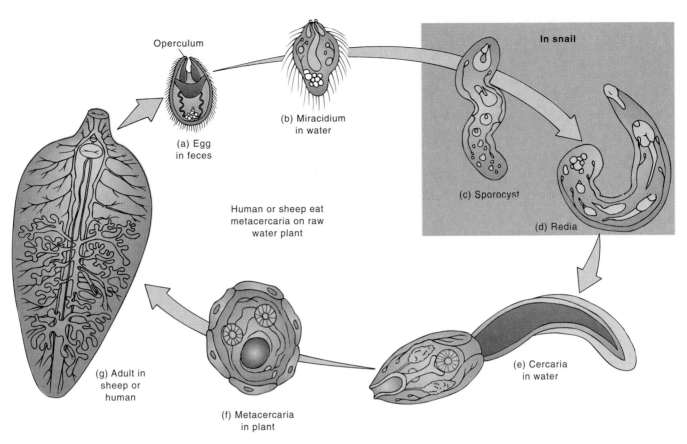

Operculum

(a) Egg
in feces

(b) Miracidium
in water

In snail

(c) Sporocyst

(d) Redia

Human or sheep eat
metacercaria on raw
water plant

(e) Cercaria
in water

(g) Adult in
sheep or
human

(f) Metacercaria
in plant

FIGURE 19.14

Class Trematoda: Subclass Digenea. The life cycle of the digenetic trematode, *Fasciola hepatica* (the common liver fluke). The adult is about 30 mm long and 13 mm wide. The cercaria is about 0.5 mm long.

Some Important Trematode Parasites of Humans

7 The Chinese liver fluke, *Clonorchis sinensis,* is a common parasite of humans in Asia, where over 30 million people are infected. The adult lives in the bile ducts of the liver, where it feeds on epithelial tissue and blood (figure 19.15a). The adults release embryonated eggs into the common bile duct. The eggs make their way to the intestine and are eliminated with feces (figure 19.15b). The miracidia are released when a snail ingests the eggs. Following the sporocyst and redial stages, cercariae emerge into the water. If a cercaria contacts a fish (the second intermediate host), it penetrates the epidermis of the fish, loses its tail, and encysts. The metacercaria develops into an adult in a human who eats raw or poorly cooked fish, a delicacy in Asian countries and gaining in popularity in the Western world.

8 *Fasciola hepatica* is called the sheep liver fluke (*see figure 19.14*a) because it is common in sheep-raising areas and uses sheep or humans as its definitive host. The adults live in the bile duct of the liver. Eggs pass via the common bile duct to the intestine, from which they are eliminated. Eggs deposited in freshwater hatch, and the miracidia must locate the proper species of snail. If a snail is found, miracidia penetrate the snail's soft tissue and develop into sporocysts that develop into rediae and give rise to cercariae. After the cercariae emerge from the snail, they encyst on aquatic vegetation. Sheep or other animals become infected when they graze on the aquatic vegetation. Humans may become infected with *Fasciola hepatica* by eating a freshwater plant called watercress that contains the encysted metacercaria.

Schistosomes are blood flukes with vast medical significance. The impact these flukes have had on history is second only to that of *Plasmodium* (malaria; *see box 17.2*). They infect over 200 million people throughout the world. Infections are most common in Africa (*Schistosoma haematobium* and *S. mansoni*), South and Central America (*S. mansoni*), and Southeast Asia (*S. japonicum*). The adult dioecious worms live in the human bloodstream (figure 19.16a). The male fluke is shorter and thicker than the female, and the sides of the male body curve under to form a canal along the ventral surface (schistosoma means "split body"). The female fluke is long and slender, and is carried in the canal of the male (figure 19.16b). Copulation is continuous, and the female produces thousands of eggs over her lifetime. Each egg contains a spine that mechanically aids it in moving through host tissue until it is eliminated in either the feces or urine (figure 19.16c). Unlike other flukes, schistosome eggs lack an operculum. The miracidium escapes through a slit that develops in the egg when the egg reaches freshwater (figure 19.16d). The miracidium seeks via chemotaxis a snail (figure 19.16e), penetrates it, and develops into a sporocyst, then daughter sporocysts, and finally forked-tailed cercariae (figure 19.16f). There is no redial generation. The

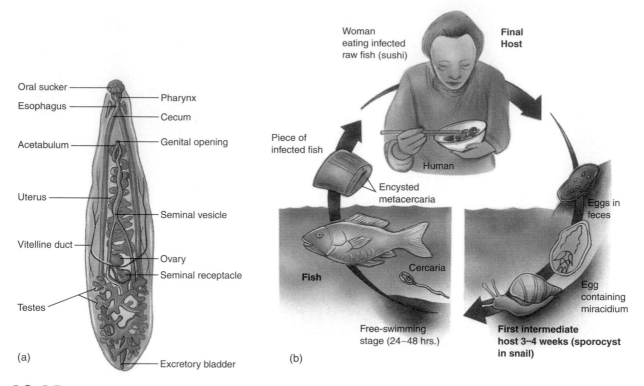

FIGURE 19.15

Chinese Liver Fluke, *Clonorchis sinensis.* (*a*) Dorsal view. (*b*) Life cycle. The adult worm is 10 to 25 mm long and 1 to 5 mm wide.

cercariae leave the snail and penetrate the skin of a human (figure 19.16g). Anterior glands that secrete digestive enzymes aid penetration. Once in a human, the cercariae lose their tails and develop into adults in the intestinal veins, skipping the metacercaria stage (box 19.1).

Stop and Ask Yourself

4. What is unique about the trematode tegument?
5. What is the function of an opisthaptor?
6. What is the major difference between the life cycle of a monogenean and that of a digenean fluke?
7. Define each of the following: (*a*) miracidium, (*b*) sporocyst, (*c*) redia, (*d*) cercaria, (*e*) metacercaria, and (*f*) operculum.

CLASS CESTOIDEA: THE TAPEWORMS

The most highly specialized class of flatworms are members of the class Cestoidea (ses-toid'e-ah) (Gr. *kestos,* girdle + *eidos,* form), commonly called either tapeworms or cestodes. All of the approximately 3,500 species are endoparasites that usually reside in the vertebrate digestive system. Their color is often white with shades of yellow or gray. Adult tapeworms range from 1 mm to 25 m in length.

Two unique adaptations to a parasitic lifestyle characterize tapeworms: ⑨ (1) Tapeworms lack a mouth and digestive tract in all of their life-cycle stages; they absorb nutrients directly across their body wall. (2) Most adult tapeworms consist of a long series of repeating units called **proglottids.** Each proglottid contains a complete set of reproductive structures.

As with most endoparasites, adult tapeworms live in a very stable environment. The vertebrate intestinal tract has very few environmental variations that would require the development of great anatomical or physiological complexity in any single tapeworm body system. The physiology of the tapeworm's host maintains the tapeworm's homeostasis (internal constancy). In adapting to such a specialized environment, tapeworms have lost some of the structures believed to have been present in ancestral turbellarians. Tapeworms are, therefore, a good example of evolution not always resulting in greater complexity.

Subclass Cestodaria

Representatives of the subclass Cestodaria are all endoparasites in the intestine and coelom of primitive fishes. Zoologists have identified about 15 species. They possess some digenetic trematode features in that only one set of both reproductive systems is present in each animal, some bear suckers, and their bodies are not divided into proglottids like other cestodes. Yet, the absence of a digestive system, the presence of larval stages similar to those of cestodes, and the presence of parenchymal muscle cells, which are

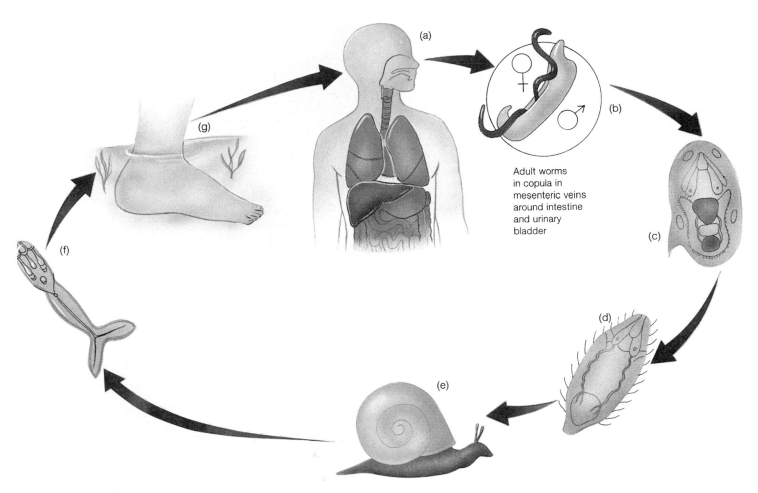

FIGURE 19.16

Representative Life Cycle of a Schistosome Fluke. The cycle begins in a human (*a*) when the female fluke lays eggs (*b,c*) in the thin-walled, small vessels of the large or small intestine (*S. mansoni* and *S. japonicum*) or urinary bladder (*S. haematobium*). Secretions from the eggs weaken the walls, and the blood vessels rupture, releasing eggs into the intestinal lumen or urinary bladder. From there, the eggs leave the body. If they reach fresh water, the eggs hatch into ciliated, free-swimming larvae called miracidia (*d*). A miracidium burrows into the tissues of an aquatic snail (*e*), losing its cilia in the process, and develops into a sporocyst, then daughter sporocysts. Eventually, forked-tailed larvae (cercariae) are produced (*f*). After the cercariae leave the snail, they actively swim about. If they encounter human skin (*g*), they attach to it and release tissue-degrading enzymes. The larvae enter the body and migrate to the circulatory system, where they mature. They end up at the vessels of the intestines or urinary bladder, where sexual reproduction takes place, and the cycle begins anew. The adult worms are 10 to 20 mm long.

not present in any other platyhelminth, all suggest strong phylogenetic affinities with other cestodes.

Subclass Eucestoda

Almost all of the cestodes belong to the subclass Eucestoda and are called true tapeworms. They represent the ultimate degree of specialization of any parasitic animal. The body is divided into three regions (figure 19.17*a*). At one end is a hold-fast structure called the **scolex** that contains circular or leaflike suckers and sometimes a rostellum of hooks (figure 19.17*b*). With the scolex, the tapeworm firmly anchors itself to the intestinal wall of its definitive vertebrate host. No mouth is present.

Posteriorly, the scolex narrows to form the neck. Transverse constrictions in the neck give rise to the third body region, the **strobila** (Gr. *strobilus*, a linear series) (pl., strobilae). The strobila consists of a series of linearly arranged proglottids, which function

BOX 19.1   SWIMMER'S ITCH

An interesting phase of schistosome biology concerns cercarial dermatitis or "swimmer's itch." Cercariae of species that normally infect birds (waterfowl and shorebirds) and other vertebrates, especially certain mammals (e.g., muskrats and mink), attempt to penetrate the skin of humans. In doing so, they sensitize the area of attack, resulting in itchy rashes. Because humans are not suitable definitive hosts for these cercariae, the flukes do not enter the bloodstream and mature, but perish after penetrating the skin. One of the most common causative agents of marine swimmer's itch on both the east and west coasts of North America is a blood parasite of seagulls, the cercariae of which develop in a common mudflat snail.

(a)

(b)

FIGURE 19.17

Class Cestoidea: A Tapeworm. (*a*) The scolex, neck, and proglottids of the pork tapeworm, *Taenia solium*. The adult worm attains a length of 2 to 7 m. Included is a detailed view of a mature proglottid with a complete set of male and female reproductive structures. (*b*) The scolex of the cestode *Taenia solium* (SEM ×100). Notice the rostellum with two circles of hooks.

primarily as reproductive units. As a tapeworm grows, new proglottids are added in the neck region, and older proglottids are gradually pushed posteriorly. As they move posteriorly, proglottids mature and begin producing eggs. Thus, anterior proglottids are said to be immature, those in the midregion of the strobila are mature, and those at the posterior end that have accumulated eggs are gravid (L. *gravida*, heavy, loaded, pregnant).

The outer body wall of tapeworms consists of a tegument similar in structure to that of trematodes (*see figure 19.12*). It plays a vital role in nutrient absorption because tapeworms have no digestive system. The tegument even absorbs some of the host's own enzymes to facilitate digestion.

With the exception of the reproductive systems, the body systems of tapeworms are reduced in structural complexity. The nervous system consists of only a pair of lateral nerve cords that arise from a nerve mass in the scolex and extend the length of the

strobila. A protonephridial system also runs the length of the tapeworm (*see figure 19.6*).

Tapeworms are monoecious, and most of their physiology is devoted to producing large numbers of eggs. Each proglottid contains a complete set of male and female reproductive organs (figure 19.17*a*). Numerous testes are scattered throughout the proglottid and deliver sperm via a duct system to a copulatory organ called a cirrus. The cirrus opens through a genital pore, which is an opening shared with the female system. The male system of a proglottid matures before the female system, so that copulation usually occurs with another mature proglottid of the same tapeworm or with another tapeworm in the same host. As previously mentioned, the avoidance of self-fertilization leads to hybrid vigor.

A single pair of ovaries in each proglottid produce eggs. Sperm stored in a seminal receptacle fertilize eggs as the eggs move through the oviduct. Vitelline cells from the vitelline gland are then dumped onto the eggs in the ootype. The ootype is an expanded region of the oviduct that shapes capsules around the eggs. The ootype is also surrounded by the Mehlis' gland, which aids in the formation of the egg capsule. Most tapeworms have a blind-ending uterus, where eggs accumulate (figure 19.17a). As eggs accumulate, the reproductive organs degenerate; thus, gravid proglottids can be thought of as "bags of eggs." Eggs are released when gravid proglottids break free from the end of the tapeworm and pass from the host with the feces. In a few tapeworms, the uterus opens to the outside of the worm, and eggs are released into the host's intestine. Because proglottids are not continuously lost, adult tapeworms usually become very long.

Some Important Tapeworm Parasites of Humans

One medically important tapeworm of humans is the beef tapeworm, *Taeniarhynchus saginatus* (figure 19.18). Adults live in the small intestine and may reach lengths of 25 m. About 80,000 eggs per proglottid are released as proglottids break free of the adult worm. As an egg develops, it forms a six-hooked (hexacanth) larva called the **onchosphere.** As cattle (the intermediate host) graze in pastures contaminated with human feces, they ingest oncospheres (or proglottids). Digestive enzymes of the cattle free the oncospheres, and the larvae use their hooks to bore through the intestinal wall into the bloodstream. The bloodstream carries the larvae to skeletal muscles, where they encyst and form a fluid-filled bladder called a **cysticercus** (pl., cysticerci) or **bladder worm.** When a human eats infected meat (termed "measly beef") that is raw or improperly cooked, the cysticercus is released from the meat, the scolex attaches to the human intestinal wall, and the tapeworm matures.

A closely related tapeworm, *Taenia solium* (the pork tapeworm), has a life cycle similar to that of *Taeniarhynchus saginatus,* except that the intermediate host is the pig. The strobila has been reported as being 10 m long, but 2 to 3 m is more common. The pathology is more serious in the human than in the pig. Gravid proglottids frequently release oncospheres before the proglottids have had a chance to leave the small intestine of the human host. When these larvae hatch, they move through the intestinal wall, enter the bloodstream, and are distributed throughout the body, where they eventually encyst in human tissue as cysticerci. The disease that results is called **cysticercosis** and can be fatal if the cysticerci encyst in the brain.

The broad fish tapeworm, *Diphyllobothrium latum,* is relatively common in the northern parts of North America and in the Great Lakes area of the United States. This tapeworm has a scolex with two longitudinal grooves (bothria; sing., bothrium) that act as hold-fast structures (figure 19.19). The adult worm may attain a length of 10 m and shed up to a million eggs a day. Many proglottids release eggs through uterine pores. When eggs are deposited in freshwater, they hatch, and ciliated larvae called **coracidia** (sing., coracidium) emerge. These coracidia swim about until small crustaceans called copepods ingest them. The larvae shed their cili-

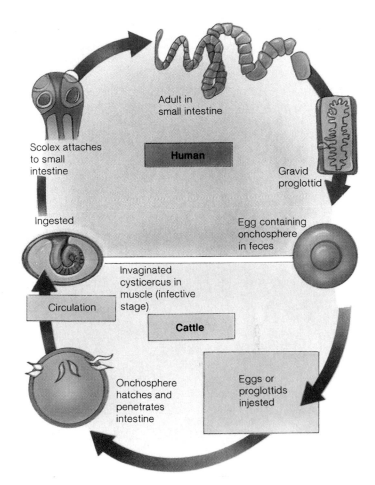

FIGURE 19.18

Life Cycle of the Beef Tapeworm, *Taeniarhynchus saginatus.* Adult worms may attain a length of 25 m. *Source: Redrawn from Centers for Disease Control, Atlanta, GA.*

ated coats in the copepods and develop into **procercoid larvae.** When fish eat the copepods, the procercoids burrow into the muscle of the fish and become **plerocercoid larvae.** Larger fishes that eat smaller fishes become similarly infected with plerocercoids. When humans (or other carnivores) eat infected, raw, or poorly cooked fishes, the plerocercoids attach to the small intestine and grow into adult worms.

Stop and Ask Yourself

8. What is a proglottid? What is a scolex? What is a strobila?
9. How do tapeworms obtain nutrients?
10. What is the life cycle of a typical tapeworm?
11. Define each of the following: (a) coracidium, (b) cysticercus, (c) procercoid larva, and (d) plerocercoid larva.

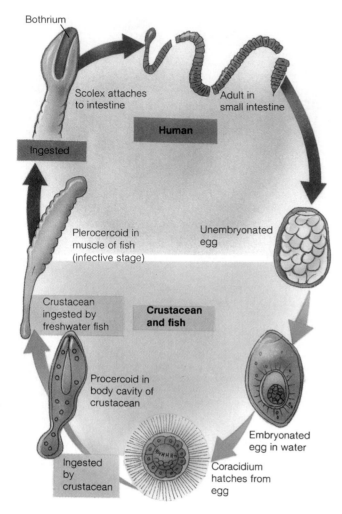

FIGURE 19.19

Life Cycle of the Broad Fish Tapeworm, *Diphyllobothrium latum.*
Adult worms may be 3 to 10 m long. *Source: Redrawn from Centers for Disease Control, Atlanta, GA.*

PHYLUM NEMERTEA

Most of the approximately nine hundred species of nemerteans (nem-er'te-ans) (Gr. *Nemertes*, a Mediterranean sea nymph; the daughter of Nereus and Doris) are elongate, flattened worms found in marine mud and sand. Due to a long proboscis, nemerteans are commonly called proboscis worms. Adult worms range in size from a few millimeters to several centimeters in length. Most nemerteans are pale yellow, orange, green, or red. Characteristics of the phylum Nemertea include:

1. Triploblastic, acoelomate, bilaterally symmetrical, unsegmented worms possessing a ciliated epidermis containing mucous glands
2. Complete digestive tract with an anus
3. Protonephridia
4. Cerebral ganglion, longitudinal nerve cords, and transverse commissures

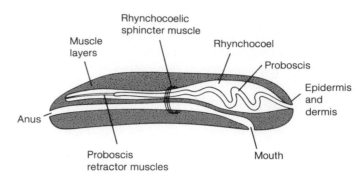

FIGURE 19.20

Phylum Nemertea. Longitudinal section of a nemertean, showing the tubular gut and proboscis. *Source: Modified from Turbeville and Ruppert, 1983, Zoomorphology, 103:103, Copyright 1983, Springer-Verlag, Heidelberg, Germany.*

5. Closed circulatory system
6. Body musculature organized into two or three layers

The most distinctive feature of nemerteans is a long proboscis held in a sheath called a **rhynchocoel** (figure 19.20). The proboscis may be tipped with a barb called a stylet. Carnivorous species use the proboscis to capture annelid (segmented worms) and crustacean prey.

Unlike the platyhelminths, nemerteans have a complete one-way digestive tract. They have a mouth for ingesting food and an anus for eliminating digestive wastes. This enables mechanical breakdown of food, digestion, absorption, and feces formation to proceed sequentially in an anterior to posterior direction—a major evolutionary innovation found in all higher bilateral animals.

Another major innovation found in all higher animals evolved first in the nemerteans—a circulatory system consisting of two lateral blood vessels and, often, tributary vessels that branch from lateral vessels. However, no heart is present, and contractions of the walls of the large vessels propel blood. Blood does not circulate but simply moves forward and backward through the longitudinal vessels. Blood cells are present in some species. This combination of blood vessels with their capacity to serve local tissues and a one-way digestive system with its greater efficiency at processing nutrients allows nemerteans to grow much larger than most flatworms.

Nemerteans are dioecious. Male and female reproductive structures develop from parenchymal cells along each side of the body. External fertilization results in the formation of a helmet-shaped, ciliated **pilidium larva.** After a brief free-swimming existence, the larva develops into a young worm that settles to the substrate and begins feeding.

When they move, adult nemerteans glide on a trail of mucus. Cilia and peristaltic contractions of body muscles provide the propulsive forces.

PHYLUM GASTROTRICHA

The gastrotrichs (gas-tro-tri'ks) (Gr. *gastros*, stomach + *trichos*, hair) are members of a small phylum of about five hundred free-

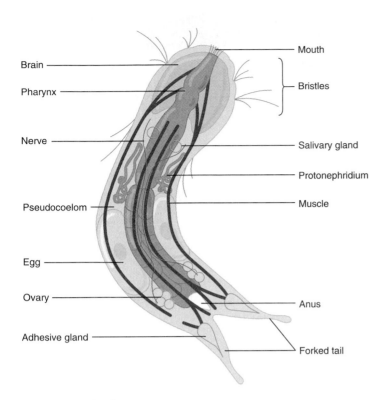

FIGURE 19.21

Phylum Gastrotricha. The internal anatomy of a freshwater gastrotrich. This animal is about 3 mm long.

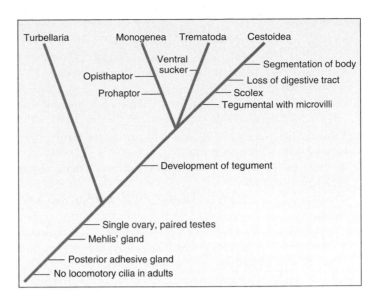

FIGURE 19.22

Cladogram Showing Evolutionary Relationships among the Classes of Platyhelminthes. The absence of synapomorphies for the Turbellaria suggests that the ancestral platyhelminth was itself a turbellarian and that some member of that class was ancestral to the three living parasitic groups. *Source: Data from D. R. Brooks,* Journal of Parasitology, *1989, pp. 606–616.*

living marine and freshwater species that inhabit the space between bottom sediments. They range from 0.01 to 4 mm in length. Gastrotrichs use cilia on their ventral surface to move over the substrate. The phylum contains a single class divided into two orders.

The dorsal cuticle often contains scales, bristles, or spines, and a forked tail is often present (figure 19.21). A syncytial epidermis is beneath the cuticle. Sensory structures include tufts of long cilia and bristles on the rounded head. The nervous system includes a brain and a pair of lateral nerve trunks. The digestive system is a straight tube with a mouth, a muscular pharynx, a stomach-intestine, and an anus. The action of the pumping pharynx allows ingestion of microorganisms and organic detritus from the bottom sediment and water. Digestion is mostly extracellular. Adhesive glands in the forked tail secrete materials that anchor the animal to solid objects. Paired protonephridia occur in freshwater species, rarely in marine ones. Gastrotrich protonephridia, however, are morphologically different from those found in other acoelomates. Each protonephridium possesses a single flagellum instead of the cilia found in flame cells.

Most of the marine species reproduce sexually and are hermaphroditic. Most of the freshwater species reproduce asexually by parthenogenesis; the females can lay two kinds of unfertilized eggs. Thin-shelled eggs hatch into females during favorable environmental conditions, whereas thick-shelled resting eggs can

withstand unfavorable conditions for long periods before hatching into females. There is no larval stage; development is direct, and the juveniles have the same form as the adults.

FURTHER PHYLOGENETIC CONSIDERATIONS

Zoologists who believe that the platyhelminth body form is central to animal evolution envision an ancestral flatworm similar to a turbellarian. Figure 19.22 is a cladogram emphasizing the uniqueness of the tegument as a synapomorphy (a shared, evolutionarily derived character used to describe common descent among two or more species) uniting the Monogenea, Trematoda, and Cestoidea.

More conclusive evidence links the parasitic flatworms to ancient, free-living ancestors. The free-living and parasitic ways of life probably diverged in the Cambrian period, 600 million years ago. The first flatworm parasites were probably associated with primitive molluscs, arthropods, and echinoderms. They must have acquired the vertebrate hosts and complex life cycles described in this chapter much later.

The gastrotrichs show some distant relationships to the acoelomates. For example, many gastrotrichs lack a body cavity, and are monoecious and small, and their ventral cilia may have been derived from the same ancestral sources as those of the turbellarian flatworms.

SUMMARY

1. The free-living platyhelminths, members of the class Turbellaria, are small, bilaterally symmetrical, acoelomate animals with some cephalization.

2. Most turbellarians move entirely by cilia and are predators and scavengers. Digestion is initially extracellular and then intracellular.

3. Protonephridia are present in many flatworms and are involved in osmoregulation. A primitive brain and nerve cords are present.

4. Turbellarians are monoecious with the reproductive systems adapted for internal fertilization.

5. The monogenetic flukes (class Monogenea) are mostly ectoparasites of fishes.

6. The class Trematoda is divided into two subclasses (Aspidogastrea and Digenea), and most are external or internal parasites of vertebrates. A gut is present, and most of these flukes are monoecious.

7. Cestodes, or tapeworms, are gut parasites of vertebrates. They are structurally more specialized than flukes, having a scolex with attachment organs, a neck region, and a strobila, which consists of a chain of segments (proglottids) budded off from the neck region. A gut is absent, and the reproductive system is repeated in each proglottid.

8. Nemerteans are similar to platyhelminths but can be much larger. They prey on other invertebrates, which they capture with a unique proboscis. They have a one-way digestive tract and a blood-vascular system, and the sexes are separate.

9. Gastrotrichs are microscopic, aquatic animals with a head, neck, and trunk. Numerous adhesive glands are present. The group is generally hermaphroditic, although males are rare and female parthenogenesis is common in freshwater species.

SELECTED KEY TERMS

acetabulum (p. 292)

cercariae (p. 292)

coracidia (p. 297)

procercoid larvae (p. 297)

rediae (p. 292)

sporocyst (p. 292)

CRITICAL THINKING QUESTIONS

1. Describe the morphological and developmental similarities and differences between nemerteans and turbellarians.

2. How do parasitic flatworms evade their host's immune system?

3. How could a zoologist document the complex life cycle of a digenetic trematode?

4. Describe some of the key features of acoelomate animals.

REFERENCES ON THE WORLD WIDE WEB

1. **Platyhelminthes: Trematodes.** Photos of trematodes that infect humans are at this site.
   http://www2.life.sci.qut.edu.au/darben/trematod.htm

2. **Platyhelminthes: Cestodes.** Photos of some of the medically important cestodes are at this site.
   http://www.2.life.sci.qut.edu.au/darben/cestode.htm

3. **Phylum Platyhelminthes.** This site contains a wealth of information on flatworm biology.
   http://www.oit.itd.umich.edu/biol/platyhelminthes.shtml

4. **Introduction to the Platyhelminthes.** Many interesting facts on flatworm biology are at this site.
   http://www.ucmp.berkeley.edu/pl.es/es.html

5. **Phylum Platyhelminthes.** This site presents a general lecture on flatworms.
   http://biology.unm.edu/~nio404/platyhelminthes.html

6. **Class Turbellaria.** Some interesting facts on the turbellaria are at this site.
   http://oz.plymouth.edu/~1ts/invertebrates/turbellaria.html

chapter 20

THE PSEUDOCOELOMATE BODY PLAN:
ASCHELMINTHS

Concepts

1. The aschelminths comprise seven phyla: Rotifera, Kinorhyncha, Nematoda, Nematomorpha, Acanthocephala, Loricifera, and Priapulida. Because most of these phyla have had a separate evolutionary history, this grouping is mostly one of convenience.
2. The major unifying aschelminth feature is a pseudocoelom. The pseudocoelom is a type of body cavity that develops from the blastocoel (the primitive cavity in the embryo) and is not fully lined by mesoderm, as in the true coelomates. In the pseudocoelomates, the muscles and other structures of the body wall and internal organs are in direct contact with fluid in the pseudocoelom.
3. Other common aschelminth features include a complete digestive tract, a muscular pharynx, constant cell numbers (eutely), protonephridia, a cuticle, and adhesive glands.

Would You Like to Know . . .

1. why worms molt? (p. 303)
2. how rotifers got their name? (p. 304)
3. in what animal the reproductive organ called a penis first developed? (p. 305)
4. what are some of the most abundant animals on earth? (p. 306)
5. why roundworms move in an undulating, wavelike fashion? (p. 307)
6. why all nematodes are round? (p. 308)
7. what is the most common roundworm parasite in the United States? (p. 310)
8. why you should not eat improperly cooked pork products? (p. 311)
9. what causes the disease elephantiasis? (p. 311)
10. what causes heartworm disease in dogs? (p. 311)
11. why horsehair worms were thought to arise from horses' tails? (p. 312)
12. how spiny-headed worms got their name? (p. 313)

This chapter answers these and other useful questions.

This chapter contains evolutionary concepts, which are set off in this font.

EVOLUTIONARY PERSPECTIVE

The seven different phyla grouped for convenience as the **aschelminths** (Gr. *askos*, bladder + *helmins*, worm) are very diverse animals. They have obscure phylogenetic affinities, and their fossil record is meager. Two hypotheses have been proposed for their phylogeny. The first hypothesis contends that the phyla are related based on the presence of the following structures: a pseudocoelom, a cuticle, a muscular pharynx, and adhesive glands. The second hypothesis contends that the various aschelminth phyla are not related to each other; thus, they are probably polyphyletic. The absence of any single unique feature found in all groups strongly suggests independent evolution of each phylum. The similarities among the living aschelminths may simply be the result of convergent evolution as these various animals adapted to similar environments.

The correct phylogeny may actually be something between the two hypotheses. All phyla are probably distantly related to each other based on the few anatomical and physiological features they share (figures 20.1, 20.2). True convergent evolution may have also produced some visible analogous similarities, but each phylum probably arose from a common acoelomate ancestor and diverged very early in evolutionary history (figure 20.3). Such an ancestor might have been a primitive, ciliated, acoelomate turbellarian (*see figure 19.4a*), from which it would follow that the first ancestor was ciliated, acoelomate, marine, and probably monoecious, and lacked a cuticle.

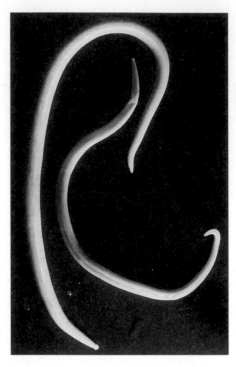

FIGURE 20.1

Roundworm Characteristics: A Fluid-Filled Body Cavity and a Complete Digestive System. *Ascaris lumbriocoides* inhabits the intestines of both pigs and humans. Male ascarid worms measure 15 to 31 cm in length and are smaller than females (20 to 35 cm in length). Males also have a curved posterior end.

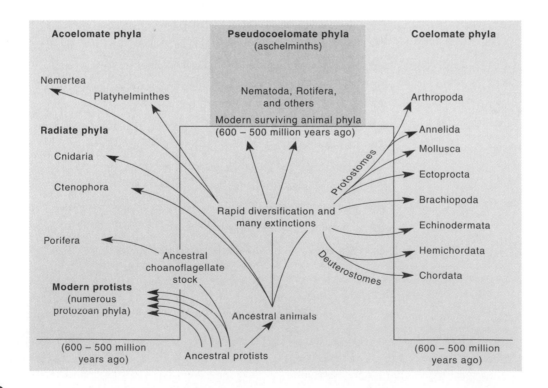

FIGURE 20.2

Pseudocoelomate Phyla. A generalized evolutionary tree depicting the major events and possible lines of descent for the pseudocoelomates (shaded in orange).

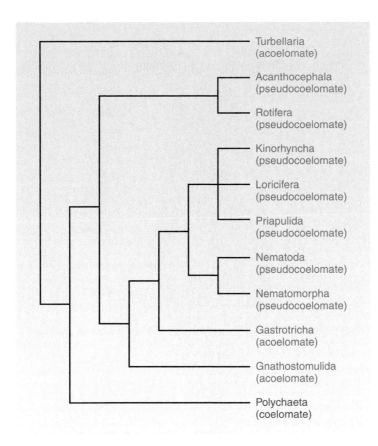

FIGURE 20.3

Cladogram of the Seven Pseudocoelomate (Aschelminth) Phyla.
For comparative purposes, one coelomate (Polychaeta) and three
acoelomates (Turbellaria, Gastrotricha, and Gnathostomulida) phyla
are included. Notice that in this cladogram the Kinorhyncha, Loricifera, and Priapulida are closely related, the Acanthocephala and
Rotifera are closely related, and the Nematoda and Nematomorpha
are closely related. Thus, the pseudocoelomates comprise two main
clades and a minor clade: comprising the Acanthocephala + Rotifera
defined principally by a syncytial epidermis, an intracytoplasmic lam-
ina, and sperm with anterior flagella; and a major clade composed of
two subclades—Loricifera + Priapulida + Kinorhyncha and Nematoda + Nematomorpha—defined principally by an extracellular cuticle that is molted. This consensus cladogram permits, but does not
require, a polyphyletic origin of the pseudocoelom. *Source: Data from Robert
L. Wallace, Claudia Ricci, and Giulio Melone, Invertebrate Biology, 1996, pp. 104–12.*

GENERAL CHARACTERISTICS

The aschelminths are the first assemblage of animals to possess a
distinct body cavity, but it lacks the peritoneal linings and membranes, called mesenteries, found in more advanced animals. As a
result, the various internal (visceral) organs lie free in the cavity.
Such a cavity is called a pseudocoelom or **pseudocoel** (*see figure
16.11b*), and the animals are called **pseudocoelomates.** The
pseudocoelom is often fluid filled or may contain a gelatinous substance with mesenchyme cells, serves as a cavity for circulation,
aids in digestion, and acts as an internal hydrostatic skeleton that
functions in locomotion.

Most aschelminths (the acanthocephalans and nematomorphs are exceptions) have a complete tubular digestive tract
that extends from an anterior mouth to a posterior anus. This
complete digestive tract was first encountered in the nemerteans
(*see figure 19.20*) and is characteristic of almost all other higher
animals. It permits, for the first time, the mechanical breakdown of
food, digestion, absorption, and feces formation to proceed sequentially and continually from an anterior to posterior direction—an evolutionary advancement over the blind-ending digestive system.
Most aschelminths also have a specialized muscular pharynx that
is adapted for feeding.

Many aschelminths show **eutely** (Gr. *euteia*, thrift), a condition in which the number of cells (or nuclei in syncytia) is constant both for the entire animal and for each given organ in all the
animals of that species (box 20.1). For example, the number of
body (somatic) cells in all adult *Caenorhabditis elegans* nematodes
is 959, and the number of cells in the pharynx of every worm in
the species is precisely 80.

Most aschelminths are microscopic, although some grow to
over a meter in length. They are bilaterally symmetrical, unsegmented, triploblastic, and cylindrical in cross section. Most aschelminths have an osmoregulatory system of protonephridia (*see
figure 19.6*). This system is best developed in freshwater forms, in
which osmotic problems are the greatest. No separate blood or gas
exchange systems are present. Some cephalization is evident, with
the anterior end containing a primitive brain, sensory organs, and
a mouth. The vast majority of aschelminths are dioecious. Both
reproductive systems are relatively uncomplicated; life cycles are
usually simple, except in parasites. Cilia are generally absent from
the external surface, but a thin, tough, external cuticle is present.
The **cuticle** (L. *cutis*, skin) may bear spines, scales, or other forms
of ornamentation that protect the animal and are useful to taxonomists.   ① Some aschelminths shed this cuticle in a process called
molting or **ecdysis** (Gr. *ekdysis*, to strip off) in order to grow. Beneath
the cuticle is a syncytial epidermis that actively secretes the cuticle.
Several longitudinal muscle layers lie beneath the epidermis.

BOX 20.1   AN APPLICATION OF EUTELY

The science of aging is called **gerontology** (Gr. *gerontos*, old man).
The eutelic characteristic of aschelminths makes them excellent
research animals for studies on aging because (1) none of the cells
of aschelminths are being continually renewed; (2) aschelminths
cannot repair cells; and (3) a specific number of cells is present, and
their exact lineage is known. In a eutelic animal, cellular longevity
appears to be a simple, measurable parameter, and the onset of aging can be easily studied. Some of the characteristics of aging that
have been studied in these animals include the progressive disorganization of muscle and nerve cells, mitochondrial degeneration, decrease in cellular motility, accumulation of age pigments, and
increase in specific gravity.

(a)

(b)

FIGURE 20.4

Phylum Rotifera. (*a*) A rotifer, *Brachionus* (LM ×150). (*b*) Internal anatomy of a typical rotifer, *Philodina*. This rotifer is about 2 mm long.

Most aschelminths are freshwater animals; only a few live in marine environments. The nematomorphs and acanthocephalans, and many of the nematodes are parasitic. The rest of the aschelminths are mostly free-living; some rotifers are colonial.

PHYLUM ROTIFERA

2 The rotifers (ro-tif′ers) (L. *rota*, wheel + *fera*, to bear) derive their name from the characteristic ciliated organ, the **corona** (Gr. *krowe*, crown), around lobes on the head of these animals (figure 20.4*a*). The cilia of the corona do not beat in synchrony; instead, each cilium is at a slightly earlier stage in the beat cycle than the next cilium in the sequence. A wave of beating cilia thus appears to pass around the periphery of the ciliated lobes and gives the impression of a pair of spinning wheels. (Interestingly, the rotifers were first called "wheel animalicules.")

Rotifers are small animals (0.1 to 3 mm in length) that are abundant in most freshwater habitats; a few (less than 10%) are marine. The approximately two thousand species are divided into

three classes (table 20.1). The body has approximately a thousand cells, and the organs are eutelic. Rotifers are usually solitary, free-swimming animals, although some colonial forms are known. Others occur between grains of sand.

Characteristics of the phylum Rotifera include:

1. Triploblastic, bilateral, unsegmented, pseudocoelomate
2. Complete digestive system, regionally specialized
3. Anterior end often has a ciliated organ called a corona
4. Posterior end with toes and adhesive glands
5. Well-developed cuticle
6. Protonephridia with flame cells
7. Males generally reduced in number or absent; parthenogenesis common

EXTERNAL FEATURES

An epidermally secreted cuticle covers a rotifer's external surface. In many species, the cuticle thickens to form an encasement called a **lorica** (L. *corselet*, a loose-fitting case). The cuticle or lor-

TABLE 20.1	CLASSIFICATION OF THE ROTIFERA

Phylum Rotifera (ro-tif′er-ah)

A ciliated corona surrounding a mouth; muscular pharynx (mastax) present with jawlike features; nonchitinous cuticle; parthenogenesis is common; both freshwater and marine species. About 2,000 species.

Class Seisonidea (sy″son-id′e-ah)
A single genus of marine rotifers that are commensals of crustaceans; large and elongate body with reduced corona. *Seison.* Only 2 species.

Class Bdelloidea (Digononta) (del-oid′e-ah)
Anterior end retractile and bearing two trochal disks; mastax adapted for grinding; paired ovaries; cylindrical body; males absent. *Adineta, Philodina, Rotaria.* About 590 species.

Class Monogononta (mon″o-go-non′tah)
Rotifers with one ovary; mastax not designed for grinding; produce mictic and amictic eggs. Males appear only sporadically. *Conochilus, Collotheca, Notommata.* About 1,400 species.

ica provides protection and is the main supportive element, although fluid in the pseudocoelom also provides hydrostatic support. The epidermis is syncytial; that is, no plasma membranes are between nuclei.

The head contains the corona, mouth, sensory organs, and brain (figure 20.4b). The corona surrounds a large, ciliated area called the buccal field. The trunk is the largest part of a rotifer, and is elongate and saclike. The anus occurs dorsally on the posterior trunk. The posterior narrow portion is called the foot. The terminal portion of the foot usually bears one or two toes. At the base of the foot are many pedal glands whose ducts open on the toes. Secretions from these glands aid in temporary attachment of the foot to a substratum.

FEEDING AND THE DIGESTIVE SYSTEM

Most rotifers feed on small microorganisms and suspended organic material. The coronal cilia create a current of water that brings food particles to the mouth. The pharynx contains a unique structure called the **mastax** (jaws). The mastax is a muscular organ that grinds food. The inner walls of the mastax contain several sets of jaws called trophi (figure 20.4b). The trophi vary in morphological detail, and taxonomists use them to distinguish species.

From the mastax, food passes through a short, ciliated esophagus to the ciliated stomach. Salivary and digestive glands secrete digestive enzymes into the pharynx and stomach. Complete extracellular digestion and absorption of food occur in the stomach. In some species, a short, ciliated intestine extends posteriorly and becomes a cloacal bladder, which receives water from the protonephridia and eggs from the ovaries, as well as digestive waste. The cloacal bladder opens to the outside via an anus at the junction of the foot with the trunk.

OTHER ORGAN SYSTEMS

All visceral organs lie in a pseudocoelom filled with fluid and interconnecting amoeboid cells. Protonephridia that empty into the cloacal bladder function in osmoregulation. Rotifers, like other pseudocoelomates, exchange gases and dispose of nitrogenous wastes across body surfaces. The nervous system is composed of two lateral nerves and a bilobed, ganglionic brain on the dorsal surface of the mastax. Sensory structures include numerous ciliary clusters and sensory bristles concentrated on either one or more short antennae or the corona. One to five photosensitive eyespots may be on the head.

REPRODUCTION AND DEVELOPMENT

Some rotifers reproduce sexually, although several types of parthenogenesis occur in most species. Smaller males appear only sporadically in one class (Monogononta), and no males are known in another class (Bdelloidea). In the class Seisonidea, fully developed males and females are equally common in the population. Most rotifers have a single ovary and an attached syncytial vitellarium, which produces yolk that is incorporated into the eggs. The ovary and vitellarium often fuse to form a single germovitellarium (figure 20.4b). After fertilization, each egg travels through a short oviduct to the cloacal bladder and out its opening.

In males, the mouth, cloacal bladder, and other digestive organs are either degenerate or absent. A single testis produces sperm that travel through a ciliated vas deferens to the gonopore. ③ Male rotifers typically have an eversible penis that injects sperm, like a hypodermic needle, into the pseudocoelom of the female (hypodermic impregnation).

In one class (Seisonidea), the females produce haploid eggs that must be fertilized to develop into either males or females. In another class (Bdelloidea), all females are parthenogenetic and produce diploid eggs that hatch into diploid females. The third class (Monogononta) produces two different types of eggs, (figure 20.5). **Amictic** (Gr. *a*, without + *miktos*, mixed or blended; thin-shelled summer eggs) eggs are produced by mitosis, are diploid, cannot be fertilized, and develop directly into amictic females. Thin-shelled, **mictic** (Gr. *miktos*, mixed or blended) eggs are haploid. If the mictic egg is not fertilized, it develops parthenogenetically into a male; if fertilized, mictic eggs secrete a thick, heavy shell and become dormant or resting winter eggs. Dormant eggs always hatch with melting snows and spring rains into amictic females, which begin a first amictic cycle, building up large populations quickly. By early summer, some females have begun to produce mictic eggs, males appear, and dormant eggs are produced. Another amictic cycle, as well as the production of more dormant eggs, occurs before the yearly cycle is over. Winds or birds often disperse dormant eggs, accounting for the unique distribution patterns of many rotifers. Most females lay either amictic or mictic eggs, but not both. Apparently, during oocyte development, the physiological condition of the female determines whether her eggs will be amictic or mictic.

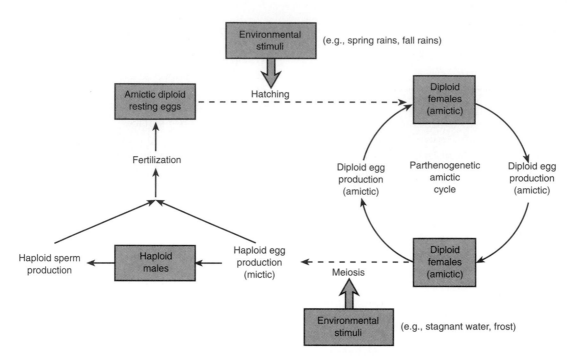

FIGURE 20.5

Life Cycle of a Monogonont Rotifer. Dormant, diploid, resting eggs hatch in response to environmental stimuli (e.g., melting snows and spring rains) to begin a first amictic cycle. Other environmental stimuli (e.g., population density, stagnating water) later stimulate the production of haploid mictic eggs that lead to the production of dormant eggs that carry the species through the summer (e.g., when the pond dries up). The autumn rains initiate a second amictic cycle. Frost stimulates the production of mictic eggs again and the eventual dormant resting eggs that allow the population of rotifers to overwinter.

Stop and Ask Yourself

1. How do the cilia of a rotifer beat?
2. What are some external features on a rotifer?
3. How do rotifers feed? How do they reproduce?
4. How do mictic and amictic rotifer eggs differ?

PHYLUM KINORHYNCHA

Kinorhynchs (kin″o-rink′es) are small (less than 1 mm long), elongate, bilaterally symmetrical worms found exclusively in marine environments, where they live in mud and sand. Because they have no external cilia or locomotor appendages, they simply burrow through the mud and sand with their snout. In fact, the phylum takes its name (Kinorhyncha, Gr. *kinein*, motion + *rhynchos*, snout) from this method of locomotion. The phylum Kinorhyncha contains about 150 known species.

The body surface of a kinorhynch is devoid of cilia and is composed of 13 or 14 definite units called **zonites** (figure 20.6). The head, represented by zonite 1, bears the mouth, an oral cone, and spines. The neck, represented by zonite 2, contains spines called **scalids** and plates called **placids.** The head can be retracted into the neck. The trunk consists of the remaining 11 or 12 zonites and terminates with the anus. Each trunk zonite bears a pair of lateral spines and one dorsal spine.

The body wall consists of a cuticle, epidermis, and two pairs of muscles: dorsolateral and ventrolateral. The pseudocoelom is large and contains amoeboid cells.

A complete digestive system is present, consisting of a mouth, buccal cavity, muscular pharynx, esophagus, stomach, intestine (where digestion and absorption take place), and anus. Most kinorhynchs feed on diatoms, algae, and organic matter.

A pair of protonephridia is in zonite 11. The nervous system consists of a brain and single ventral nerve cord with a ganglion (a mass of nerve cells) in each zonite. Some species have eyespots and sensory bristles. Kinorhynchs are dioecious with paired gonads. Several spines that may be used in copulation surround the male gonopore. The young hatch into larvae that do not have all of the zonites. As the larvae grow and molt, the adult morphology appears. Once adulthood is attained, molting no longer occurs.

PHYLUM NEMATODA

④ Nematodes (nem-a-to′des) (Gr. *nematos*, thread) or roundworms are some of the most abundant animals on earth—some 5 billion may be in every acre of fertile garden soil. Zoologists estimate that the number of roundworm species ranges from 16,000 to 500,000. Roundworms feed on every conceivable source of organic matter—from rotting substances to the living tissues of other invertebrates, vertebrates, and plants (box 20.2). They range in size from microscopic to several meters long.

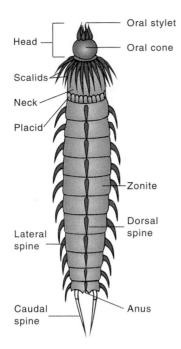

Head —

Oral stylet

Oral cone

Scalids —

Neck —

Placid —

Zonite

Lateral spine —

Dorsal spine

Caudal spine

Anus

FIGURE 20.6

Phylum Kinorhyncha. External anatomy of an adult kinorhynch (dorsal view).

BOX 20.2   THE ECOLOGY OF SOIL NEMATODES

Nematodes are incredibly abundant and diverse in soils. Some are parasitic on the roots of various plants, where they do considerable damage. Their large reproductive potential is generated at the expense of the plants on whose tissues they feed. The result is millions of dollars worth of damage to garden, truck farm, woody, and ornamental plants.

The vast majority of soil nematodes, however, are free-living. They move between soil particles and are important in soil ecology. For example, some nematodes feed voraciously on soil bacteria and fungi, helping to control the populations of these microorganisms. Other nematodes feed, in turn, on these microbial feeders and also play an important role in biological control. Still other nematodes are eminently important in the entire process of decomposition. Many of these species are omnivorous or saprophytic (eat decomposing organic matter). Soil arthropods, some fungi, and earthworms feed on the abundant soil nematodes. Overall, nematodes are essential to the energy flow and nutrient cycling in soil ecosystems.

Many nematodes are parasites of plants or animals; others are free-living in marine, freshwater, or soil habitats. Some nematodes play an important role in recycling nutrients in soils and bottom sediments.

Except in their sensory structures, nematodes lack cilia, a characteristic they share with arthropods. Also in common with some arthropods, the sperm of nematodes is amoeboid. Zoologists recognize two classes of nematodes (table 20.2).

Characteristics of the phylum Nematoda include:

1. Triploblastic, bilateral, vermiform (resembling a worm in shape; long and slender), unsegmented, pseudocoelomate
2. Body round in cross section and covered by a layered cuticle; molting usually accompanies growth in juveniles
3. Complete digestive tract; mouth usually surrounded by lips bearing sense organs
4. Most with unique excretory system comprised of one or two renette cells or a set of collecting tubules
5. Body wall has only longitudinal muscles

EXTERNAL FEATURES

A typical nematode body is slender, elongate, cylindrical, and tapered at both ends (figure 20.7*a,b*). Much of the success of nematodes is due to their outer, noncellular, collagenous cuticle (figure 20.7*c*) that is continuous with the foregut, hindgut, sense organs, and parts of the female reproductive system. The cuticle may be smooth, or it may contain spines, bristles, papillae (small, nipple-like projections), warts, or ridges, all of which are of taxonomic significance. Three primary layers make up the cuticle: cortex, matrix layer, and basal layer. The cuticle maintains internal hy-

drostatic pressure, provides mechanical protection, and in parasitic species of nematodes, resists digestion by the host. The cuticle is usually molted four times during maturation.

Beneath the cuticle is the epidermis, or hypodermis, which surrounds the pseudocoelom (figure 20.7*d*). The epidermis may be syncytial, and its nuclei are usually in the four epidermal cords (one dorsal, one ventral, and two lateral) that project inward. The longitudinal muscles are the principal means of locomotion in nematodes. ⑤ Contraction of these muscles results in undulatory waves that pass from the anterior to posterior end of the animal, creating characteristic thrashing movements. Nematodes lack

TABLE 20.2   CLASSIFICATION OF THE NEMATODES

Phylum Nematoda (nem-a-to′dah)

Nematodes, or roundworms. About 16,000 species have been described to date.

Class Secernentea (Phasmidea) (ses-er-nen′te-ah)
Paired glandular or sensory structures called phasmids in the tail region; similar pair of structures (amphids) poorly developed in anterior end; excretory system present; both free-living and parasitic species. *Ascaris, Enterobius, Rhabditis, Turbatrix, Necator, Wuchereria*. About 5,000 described species.

Class Adenophorea (Aphasmidia) (a-den″o-for′e-ah)
Phasmids absent; most free-living, but some parasitic species occur. *Dioctophyme, Trichinella, Trichuris*. About 3,000 species.

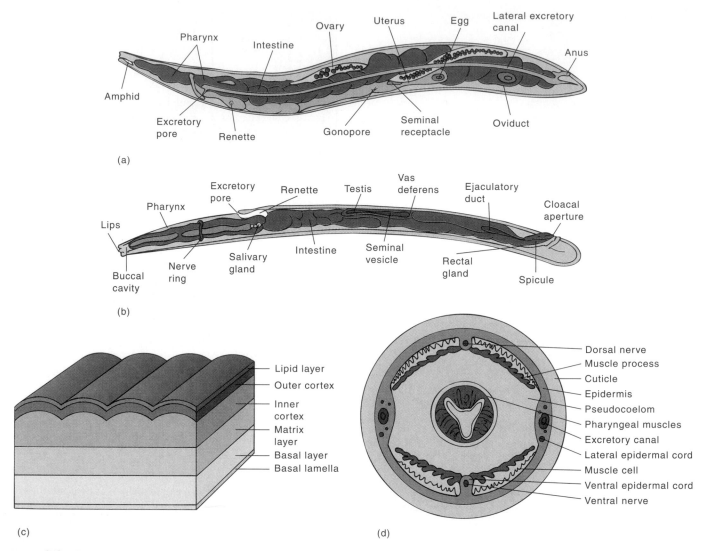

FIGURE 20.7

Phylum Nematoda. Internal anatomical features of an (*a*) female and (*b*) male *Rhabditis*. (*c*) Section through a nematode cuticle, showing the various layers. (*d*) Cross section through the region of the muscular pharynx of a nematode. The hydrostatic pressure in the pseudocoelom maintains the rounded body shape of a nematode and also collapses the intestine, which helps move food and waste material from the mouth to the anus.

circular muscles and therefore cannot crawl as do worms with more complex musculature.

Some nematodes have lips surrounding the mouth, and some species bear spines or teeth on or near the lips. In others, the lips have disappeared. Some roundworms have head shields that afford protection. Sensory organs include amphids, phasmids, or ocelli. **Amphids** are anterior depressions in the cuticle that contain modified cilia and function in chemoreception. **Phasmids** are near the anus and also function in chemoreception. The presence or absence of these organs determines the taxonomic class to which nematodes belong (*see table 20.2*). Paired ocelli (eyes) are present in aquatic nematodes.

INTERNAL FEATURES

The nematode pseudocoelom is a spacious, fluid-filled cavity that contains the visceral organs and forms a hydrostatic skeleton. ⑥ All nematodes are round because the body muscles contracting against the pseudocoelomic fluid generate an equal outward force in all directions (figure 20.7*d*).

FEEDING AND THE DIGESTIVE SYSTEM

Depending on the environment, nematodes are capable of feeding on a wide variety of foods; they may be carnivores, herbivores, om-

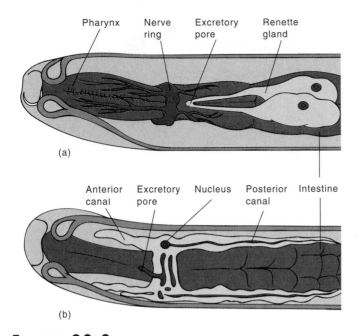

FIGURE 20.8

Nematode Excretory Systems. (*a*) Glandular, as in *Rhabditis*. (*b*) Tubular, as in *Ascaris*.

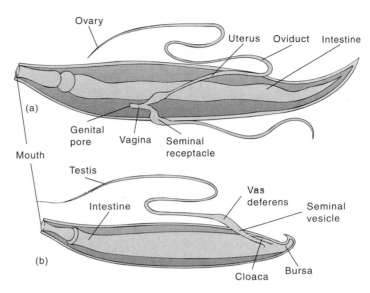

FIGURE 20.9

Nematode Reproductive Systems. The reproductive systems of an (*a*) female and (*b*) male nematode, such as *Ascaris*. The sizes of the reproductive systems are exaggerated to show details.

nivores, or saprobes (saprotrophs) that consume decomposing organisms, or parasitic species that feed on blood and tissue fluids of their hosts.

Nematodes have a complete digestive system consisting of a mouth, which may have teeth, jaws, or stylets (sharp, pointed structures); buccal cavity; muscular pharynx; long, tubular intestine where digestion and absorption occur; short rectum; and anus. Hydrostatic pressure in the pseudocoelom and the pumping action of the pharynx push food through the alimentary canal.

OTHER ORGAN SYSTEMS

Nematodes accomplish osmoregulation and excretion of nitrogenous waste products (ammonia, urea) with two unique systems. The glandular system is in aquatic species and consists of ventral gland cells, called **renettes,** posterior to the pharynx (figure 20.8*a*). Each gland absorbs wastes from the pseudocoelom and empties them to the outside through an excretory pore. Parasitic nematodes have a more advanced system, called the tubular system, that develops from the renette system (figure 20.8*b*). In this system, the renettes unite to form a large canal, which opens to the outside via an excretory pore.

The nervous system consists of an anterior nerve ring (*see figure 20.7b*). Nerves extend anteriorly and posteriorly; many connect to each other via commissures. Certain neuroendocrine secretions are involved in growth, molting, cuticle formation, and metamorphosis.

REPRODUCTION AND DEVELOPMENT

Most nematodes are dioecious and dimorphic, with the males being smaller than the females. The long, coiled gonads lie free in the pseudocoelom.

The female system consists of a pair of convoluted ovaries (figure 20.9*a*). Each ovary is continuous with an oviduct whose proximal end is swollen to form a seminal receptacle. Each oviduct becomes a tubular uterus; the two uteri unite to form a vagina that opens to the outside through a genital pore.

The male system consists of a single testis, which is continuous with a vas deferens that eventually expands into a seminal vesicle (figure 20.9*b*). The seminal vesicle connects to the cloaca. Males are commonly armed with a posterior flap of tissue called a bursa. The bursa aids the male in the transfer of sperm to the female genital pore during copulation.

After copulation, hydrostatic forces in the pseudocoelom (*see figure 20.7*d) move each fertilized egg to the gonopore (genital pore). The number of eggs produced varies with the species; some nematodes produce only several hundred, whereas others may produce hundreds of thousands daily. Some nematodes give birth to larvae (ovoviviparity). External factors, such as temperature and moisture, influence the development and hatching of the eggs. Hatching produces a larva (some parasitologists refer to it as a juvenile) that has most adult structures. The larva (juvenile) undergoes four molts, although in some species, the first one or two molts may occur before the eggs hatch.

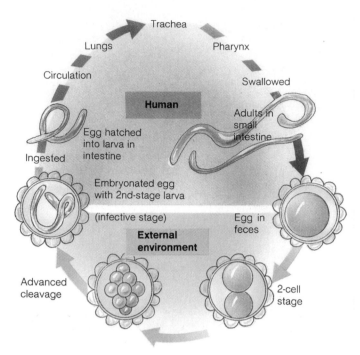

FIGURE 20.10

Life Cycle of *Ascaris lumbricoides.* (See text for details.) *Source: Redrawn from Centers for Disease Control, Atlanta, GA.*

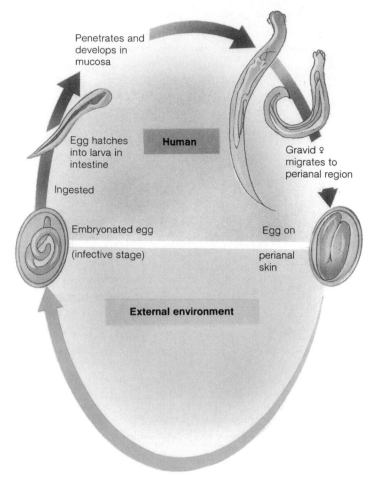

FIGURE 20.11

Life Cycle of *Enterobius vermicularis.* (See text for details.) *Source: Redrawn from Centers for Disease Control, Atlanta, GA.*

SOME IMPORTANT NEMATODE PARASITES OF HUMANS

Parasitic nematodes show a number of evolutionary adaptations to their way of life. These include a high reproductive potential, life cycles that increase the likelihood of transmission from one host to another, an enzyme-resistant cuticle, resistant eggs, and encysted larvae. Nematode life cycles are not as complicated as those of cestodes or trematodes because only one host is usually involved. Discussions of the life cycles of five important human parasites follow.

Ascaris lumbricoides: *The Giant Intestinal Roundworm of Humans*

As many as 800 million people throughout the world may be infected with *Ascaris lumbricoides*. Adult *Ascaris* (Gr. *askaris*, intestinal worm) live in the small intestine of humans. They produce large numbers of eggs that exit with the feces (figure 20.10). A first-stage larva develops rapidly in the egg, molts, and matures into a second-stage larva, the infective stage. When a human ingests embryonated eggs, they hatch in the intestine. The larvae penetrate the intestinal wall and are carried via the circulation to the lungs. They molt twice in the lungs, migrate up the trachea, and are swallowed. The worms attain sexual maturity in the intestine, mate, and begin egg production.

Enterobius vermicularis: *The Human Pinworm*

7 Pinworms (*Enterobius*; Gr. *enteron*, intestine + *bios*, life) are the most common roundworm parasites in the United States. Adult *Enterobius vermicularis* become established in the lower region of the large intestine. At night, gravid females migrate out of the cecum to the perianal area, where they deposit eggs containing a first-stage larva (figure 20.11). When humans ingest these eggs, the eggs hatch. The larvae molt four times in the small intestine and migrate to the large intestine. Adults mate, and females soon begin egg production.

Necator americanus: *The New World Hookworm*

The New World or American hookworm, *Necator americanus* (L. *necator*, killer), is found in the southern United States. The

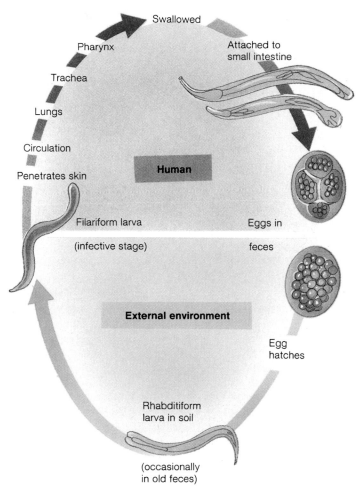

FIGURE 20.12

Life Cycle of Necator americanus. (See text for details.) *Source: Redrawn from Centers for Disease Control, Atlanta, GA.*

adults live in the small intestine, where they hold onto the intestinal wall with teeth and feed on blood and tissue fluids (figure 20.12). Individual females may produce as many as 10,000 eggs daily, which pass out of the body in the feces. An egg hatches on warm, moist soil and releases a small rhabditiform larva. It molts and becomes the infective filariform larva. Humans become infected when the filariform larva penetrates the skin, usually between the toes. (Outside defecation and subsequent walking barefoot through the immediate area maintains the life cycle in humans.) The larva burrows through the skin to reach the circulatory system. The rest of its life cycle is similar to that of *Ascaris* (see figure 20.10).

Trichinella spiralis: *The Porkworm*

Adult *Trichinella* (Gr. *trichinos*, hair) *spiralis* live in the mucosa of the small intestine of humans and other omnivores (e.g., the pig). In the intestine, adult females give birth to young larvae that then enter the circulatory system and are carried to skeletal (striated) muscles of the same host (figure 20.13). The young larvae encyst in the skeletal muscles and remain infective for many years. The disease this nematode causes is called **trichinosis.** Another host must ingest infective meat (muscle) to continue the life cycle. ❽ Humans most often become infected by eating improperly cooked pork products. Once ingested, the larvae excyst in the stomach and make their way to the small intestine, where they molt four times and develop into adults.

Wuchereria spp.: *The Filarial Worms*

In tropical countries, over 250 million humans are infected with filarial (L. *filium*, thread) worms. Two examples of human filarial worms are *Wuchereria bancrofti* and *W. malayi.* These elongate, threadlike nematodes live in the lymphatic system, where they block the vessels. Because lymphatic vessels return tissue fluids to the circulatory system, when the filarial nematodes block these vessels, fluids and connective tissue tend to accumulate in peripheral tissues. ❾ This fluid and connective tissue accumulation causes the enlargement of various appendages, a condition called **elephantiasis** (figure 20.14).

In the lymphatic vessels, filarial nematode adults copulate and produce larvae called **microfilariae** (figure 20.15). The microfilariae are released into the bloodstream of the human host and migrate to the peripheral circulation at night. When a mosquito feeds on a human, it ingests the microfilariae. The microfilariae migrate to the mosquito's thoracic muscles, where they molt twice and become infective. When the mosquito takes another meal of blood, the mosquito's proboscis injects the infective third-stage larvae into the blood of the human host. The final two molts take place as the larvae enter the lymphatic vessels.

A filarial worm prevalent in the United States is *Dirofilaria immitis,* a parasite of dogs. ❿ Since the adult worms live in the heart and large arteries of the lungs, the infection is called **heartworm disease.** Once established, these filarial worms are difficult to eliminate, and the condition can be fatal. Prevention with heartworm medicine is thus advocated for all dogs.

Stop and Ask Yourself

5. What is the function of the nematode cuticle?

6. What are some internal structures of nematodes? What are some external structures?

7. What are the two types of excretory systems in nematodes?

8. What are the life cycles of the following human parasites: *(a) Ascaris, (b) Enterobius, (c) Necator, (d) Trichinella,* and *(e) Wuchereria?*

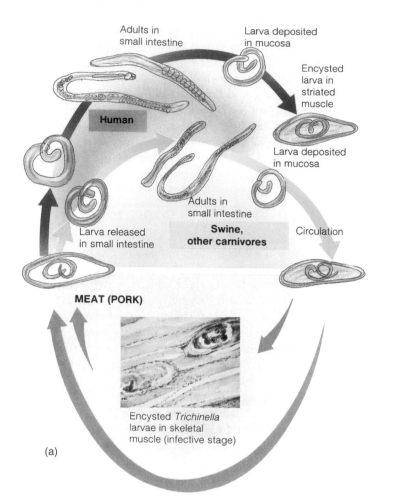

(a)

Encysted *Trichinella* larvae in skeletal muscle (infective stage)

(b)

FIGURE 20.13

Life Cycle of *Trichinella spiralis*. (*a*) (See text for details.) (*b*) An enlargement of the insert in (*a*), showing two encysted larvae in skeletal muscle (LM ×450). (*a*) *Source: Redrawn from Centers for Disease Control, Atlanta, GA.*

PHYLUM NEMATOMORPHA

Nematomorphs (nem″a-to-mor′fs) (Gr. *nema*, thread + *morphe*, form) are a small group (about 250 species) of elongate worms commonly called either **horsehair worms** or **Gordian worms.** ⑪ The hairlike nature of these worms is so striking that they were formerly thought to arise spontaneously from the hairs of a horse's tail in drinking troughs or other stock-watering places. The adults are free-living, but the juveniles are all parasitic in arthropods. They have a worldwide distribution and can be found in both running and standing water.

The nematomorph body is extremely long and threadlike and has no distinct head (figure 20.16). The body wall has a thick cuticle, a cellular epidermis, longitudinal cords, and a muscle layer of longitudinal fibers. The nervous system contains an anterior nerve ring and a vental cord.

Nematomorphs have separate sexes; two long gonads extend the length of the body. After copulation, the eggs are deposited in water. A small larva with a protrusible proboscis armed with spines hatches from the egg. Terminal stylets are also present on the proboscis. The larva must quickly enter an arthropod (e.g., a beetle, cockroach) host, either by penetrating the host or by being eaten. Lacking a digestive system, the larva feeds by absorbing material directly across its body wall. Once mature, the worm leaves its host only when the arthropod is near

FIGURE 20.14

Elephantiasis Caused by the Filarial Worm, *Wuchereria bancrofti*. It takes years for elephantiasis to advance to the degree shown in this photograph.

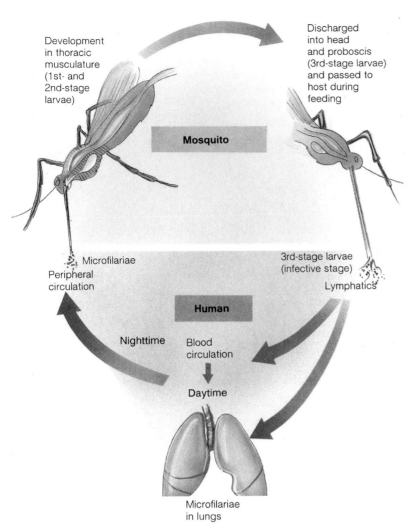

FIGURE 20.15

Life Cycle of *Wuchereria* spp. (See text for details.) *Source: Redrawn from Centers for Disease Control, Atlanta, GA.*

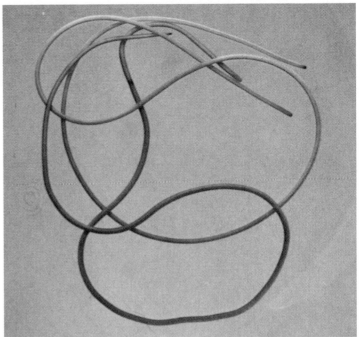

FIGURE 20.16

Phylum Nematomorpha. Photomicrograph of two adult worms, each about 25 cm long. These worms tend to twist and turn upon themselves, giving the appearance of complicated knots—thus, the name "Gordian worms." (Legend has it that King Gordius of Phrygia tied a formidable knot—the Gordian knot—and declared that whoever might undo it would be the ruler of all Asia. No one could accomplish this until Alexander the Great cut through it with his broadsword.)

water. Sexual maturity is attained during the free-living adult phase of the life cycle.

Phylum Acanthocephala

Adult acanthocephalans (a-kan"tho-sef'a-lans) (Gr. *akantha*, spine or thorn + *kephale*, head) are endoparasites in the intestinal tract of vertebrates (especially fishes). Two hosts are required to complete the life cycle. The juveniles are parasites of crustaceans and insects. Acanthocephalans are generally small (less than 40 mm long), although one important species, *Macracanthorhynchus hirudinaceus*, that occurs in pigs can be up to 80 cm long. The body of the adult is elongate and composed of a short anterior proboscis, a neck region, and a trunk (figure 20.17*a*). ⑫ The proboscis is covered with recurved spines (figure 20.17*b*); hence, the name "spiny-headed worms." The retractible proboscis provides the means of attachment in the host's intestine. Females are always larger than males, and zoologists have identified about a thousand species.

A living syncytial tegument that has been adapted to the parasitic way of life covers the body wall of acanthocephalans. A glycocalyx (*see figure 3.6*) consisting of mucopolysaccharides and glycoproteins covers the tegument and protects against host enzymes and immune defenses. No digestive system is present; acanthocephalans absorb food directly through the tegument from the host by specific membrane transport mechanisms and pinocytosis. Protonephridia may be present. The nervous system is composed of a ventral, anterior ganglionic mass from which anterior and posterior nerves arise. Sensory organs are poorly developed.

The sexes are separate, and the male has a protrusible penis. Fertilization is internal, and eggs develop in the pseudocoelom. The biotic potential of certain acanthocephalans is great; for example, a gravid female *Macroacanthorhynchus hirudinaceus* may contain up to 10 million embryonated eggs. The eggs pass out of the host with the feces and must be eaten by certain insects (e.g., cockroaches or grubs [beetle larvae]) or by aquatic crustaceans (e.g., amphipods, isopods, ostracods). Once in the invertebrate, the larva emerges from the egg and is now called an **acanthor.** It burrows through the gut wall and lodges in the hemocoel, where it develops into an **acanthella** and, eventually, into a **cystacanth.** When a mammal, fish, or bird eats the intermediate host the cystacanth excysts and attaches to the intestinal wall with its spiny proboscis.

(a)

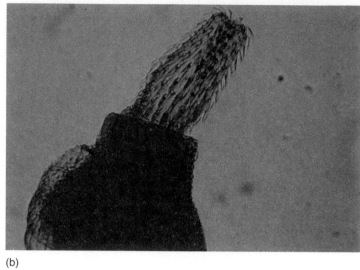

(b)

FIGURE 20.17

Phylum Acanthocephala. *(a)* Dorsal view of an adult male. *(b)* The proboscis of a spiny-headed worm (LM ×50).

Stop and Ask Yourself

9. Why are nematomorphs called horsehair worms or Gordian worms?
10. What is the life cycle of a nematomorph?
11. What is unique about the tegument of an acanthocephalan?
12. What is the life cycle of an acanthocephalan?

PHYLUM LORICIFERA

The phylum Loricifera (lor′a-sif-er-ah) (L. *lorica*, clothed in armor + *fero*, to bear) is a recently described animal phylum. Its first members were identified and named in 1983. Loriciferans live in spaces between marine gravel. A characteristic species is *Nanalori-* *cus mysticus*. It is a small, bilaterally symmetrical worm with a spiny head called an **introvert,** a thorax, and an abdomen surrounded by a lorica (figure 20.18). Loriciferans can retract both the introvert and thorax into the anterior end of the lorica. The introvert bears eight oral stylets that surround the mouth. The lorical cuticle is periodically molted. A pseudocoelom is present and contains a short digestive system, brain, and several ganglia. Loriciferans are dioecious with paired gonads. Zoologists have described about 14 species.

PHYLUM PRIAPULIDA

The priapulids (pri′a-pyu-lids) (Gr. *priapos*, phallus + *ida*, pleural suffix; from *Priapos*, the Greek god of reproduction, symbolized by the penis) are a small group (only 16 species) of marine worms found in cold waters. They live buried in the mud and sand of the seafloor, where they feed on small annelids and other invertebrates.

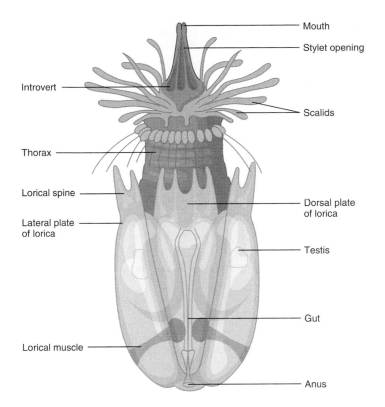

FIGURE 20.18

Phylum Loricifera. Dorsal view of the anatomy of an adult male *Nanaloricus.*

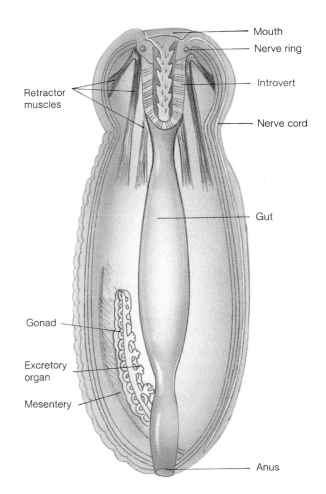

FIGURE 20.19

Phylum Priapulida. Internal anatomy of the priapulid, *Priapulus caudatus,* with the introvert withdrawn into the body.

The priapulid body is cylindrical in cross section and ranges in length from 2 mm to about 8 cm (figure 20.19). The anterior part of the body is an introvert (proboscis), which priapulids can draw into the longer, posterior trunk. The introvert functions in burrowing, and spines surround it. A thin cuticle that bears spines covers the muscular body, and the trunk bears superficial annuli. A straight digestive tract is suspended in a large pseudocoelom that acts as a hydrostatic skeleton. In some species, the pseudocoelom contains amoeboid cells that probably function in gas transport. The nervous system consists of a nerve ring around the pharynx and a single midventral nerve cord. The sexes are separate but not superficially distinguishable. A pair of gonads is suspended in the pseudocoelom and shares a common duct with the protonephridia. The duct opens near the anus, and gametes are shed into the sea. Fertilization is external, and the eggs eventually sink to the bottom, where the larvae develop into adults. The cuticle is repeatedly molted throughout life. The most commonly encountered species is *Priapulus caudatus.*

FURTHER PHYLOGENETIC CONSIDERATIONS

The aschelminths are clearly a diverse assemblage of animals. Despite the common occurrence of a cuticle, pseudocoelom, muscu-

lar pharynx, and adhesive glands, no distinctive features occur in every phylum.

The rotifers have certain features in common with the acoelomates. The protonephridia of rotifers closely resemble those of some freshwater turbellarians, and zoologists generally believed that rotifers originated in freshwater habitats. Both flatworms and rotifers have separate ovaries and vitellaria. Rotifers probably had their origins from the earliest acoelomates and may have had a common bilateral, metazoan ancestor.

The kinorhynchs, acanthocephalans, loriciferans, and priapulids all have a spiny anterior end that can be retracted; thus, they are probably related. Loriciferans and kinorhynchs appear to be most closely related.

The affinities of the nematodes to other phyla are vague. No other living group is believed to be closely related to these worms. Nematodes probably evolved in freshwater habitats and then colonized the oceans and soils. The ancestral nematodes may have been sessile, attached at the posterior end, with the anterior end protruding upward into the water. The nematode cuticle, feeding structures, and food habits probably preadapted these worms for parasitism. In fact, free-living species could become parasitic without substantial anatomical or physiological changes.

Nematomorphs may be more closely related to nematodes than to any other group by virtue of both groups being cylindrical in shape, having a cuticle, and being dioecious and sexually dimorphic. However, because the larval form of some nematomorphs resembles priapulids, the exact affinity to the nematodes is questionable.

Stop and Ask Yourself

13. What are the characteristics of a typical loriciferan?
14. How can a typical priapulan be described?
15. What evidence indicates that the individual aschelminth phyla exhibit diverse phylogenetic relationships?

Summary

1. The aschelminths are seven phyla grouped for convenience. Most have a well-defined pseudocoelom, a constant number of body cells or nuclei (eutely), protonephridia, and a complete digestive system with a well-developed pharynx. No organs are developed for gas exchange or circulation. A cuticle that may be molted covers the body. Only longitudinal muscles are often present in the body wall.

2. The phylogenetic affinities among the seven phyla and with other phyla are uncertain.

3. The majority of rotifers inhabit freshwater. The head of these animals bears a unique ciliated corona used for locomotion and food capture. Males are smaller than females and unknown in some species. Females may develop parthenogenetically.

4. Kinorhynchs are minute worms living in marine habitats. Their bodies are comprised of 13 zonites, which have cuticular scales, plates, and spines.

5. Nematodes live in aquatic and terrestrial environments. Many are parasitic and of medical and agricultural importance. They are all elongate, slender, and circular in cross section. Two sexes are present.

6. Nematomorpha are threadlike and free-living in freshwater. They lack a digestive system.

7. Acanthocephalans are also known as spiny-headed worms because of their spiny proboscis. All are endoparasites in vertebrates.

8. The phylum Loricifera was described in 1983. These microscopic animals have a spiny head and thorax, and live in gravel in marine environments.

9. The phylum Priapulida contains only 16 known species of cucumber-shaped, wormlike animals that live buried in the bottom sand and mud in marine habitats.

Selected Key Terms

amictic eggs (p. 305)
aschelminths (p. 302)
corona (p. 304)
cuticle (p. 303)

eutely (p. 303)
mastax (p. 305)
mictic eggs (p. 305)
zonites (p. 306)

Critical Thinking Questions

1. Discuss how the structure of the body wall places limitations on shape changes in nematodes.

2. What characteristics set the Nematomorpha apart from the Nematoda? What characteristics do the Nematomorpha share with the Nematoda?

3. In what respects are the kinorhynchs like nematodes? How are they like rotifers?

4. How are nematodes related to the rotifers?

5. What environmental factors appear to trigger the production of mictic females in monogonont rotifers?

References on the World Wide Web

1. **Rotifers Systematics Database.** At this site is information on the reproduction, diet, and morphology of rotifers, as well as a labeled image of rotifer anatomy.
   http://www.mmtlc.utep.edu/BIO/INFO.HTML

2. **Parasites and Parasitology Resources.** Most of the roundworms that infect humans can be found at this site.
   http://www.biosci.ohio-state.edu/~zoology/parasites

3. **Introduction to the Aschelminth Phyla.** This site contains many scanning electron microscope images of microscopic nematodes.
   http://www.ucmp.berkeley.edu/aschelminthes/aschelminthes.html

4. **Nematodes.** This site presents an overview of nematode life cycles.
   http://www.mcs.dundee.ac.uk:8080/~sanderso/nems.html

MOLLUSCAN SUCCESS

Concepts

1. Triploblastic animals are often assembled into two groups—the protostomes and deuterostomes—based on certain developmental features.
2. Molluscs have a coelom, as well as a head-foot, visceral mass, mantle, and mantle cavity. Most also have a radula.
3. Members of the class Gastropoda are the snails and slugs. They include the only terrestrial molluscs. Torsion and shell coiling modify their bodies.
4. Clams, oysters, mussels, and scallops are members of the class Bivalvia. They are all aquatic filter feeders and often burrow in soft substrates or attach to hard substrates.
5. The class Cephalopoda includes the octopuses, squids, cuttlefish, and nautili. They are the most complex of all invertebrates and are adapted for predatory lifestyles.
6. Other molluscs include members of the classes Scaphopoda (tooth shells), Monoplacophora, Aplacophora (solenogasters), and Polyplacophora (chitons). Members of these classes are all marine.
7. Zoologists debate the exact relationship of molluscs to other animal phyla. Specializations of molluscs have obscured evolutionary relationships among molluscan classes.

Would You Like to Know . . .

1. what characteristics identify molluscs? (p. 320)
2. how coiling of a snail's shell affects the arrangement of the snail's internal organs? (p. 323)
3. how a snail extends its tentacles? (p. 324)
4. how a pearl forms? (p. 326)
5. how a clam feeds? (p. 326)
6. how some bivalves burrow through limestone and coral? (p. 329)
7. what invertebrate preys on whales? (p. 331)
8. what molluscs have the most advanced nervous and sensory functions among invertebrates? (p. 332)

This chapter answers these and other useful questions.

This chapter contains evolutionary concepts, which are set off in this font.

EVOLUTIONARY PERSPECTIVE

Octopuses, squids, and cuttlefish (the cephalopods) are some of the invertebrate world's most adept predators. Predatory lifestyles have resulted in the evolution of large brains (by invertebrate standards), complex sensory structures (by any standards), rapid locomotion, grasping tentacles, and tearing mouthparts. In spite of these adaptations, cephalopods rarely make up a major component of any community. Once numbering about 9,000 species, the class Cephalopoda now includes only about 550 species (figure 21.1).

Zoologists do not know why the cephalopods have declined so dramatically. Vertebrates may have outcompeted cephalopods because the vertebrates were also making their appearance in prehistoric seas, and some vertebrates acquired active, predatory lifestyles. Alternatively, the cephalopods may have declined simply because of random evolutionary events.

This has not been the case for all molluscs. Overall, this group has been very successful. If success is measured by numbers of species, the molluscs are twice as successful as vertebrates! The vast majority of the nearly 100,000 living species of molluscs belongs to two classes: Gastropoda, the snails and slugs; and Bivalvia, the clams and their close relatives.

Molluscs are triploblastic, as are all the remaining animals covered in this text. In addition, they are the first animals described in this text that possess a coelom, although the coelom of molluscs is only a small cavity (the pericardial cavity) surrounding the heart and gonads. A coelom is a body cavity that arises in mesoderm and is lined by a sheet of mesoderm called the peritoneum *(see figure 16.11c)*.

RELATIONSHIPS TO OTHER ANIMALS

Comparative embryology is the study of similarities and differences in early development of animals. Events in embryology of animals may be similar because of shared ancestry; however, similarities in development can also reflect adaptations of distantly related, or unrelated, species to similar environments. Comparative embryologists, therefore, have the difficult task of sorting homologous developmental sequences from analogous developmental sequences *(see chapter 1)*. This difficulty is well illustrated in the attempt to determine the phylogenetic relationships of the molluscs to other phyla. The phyla described in the chapters that follow are divided into two large groups, and many of the reasons for this separation stem from comparative embryology. Although there are exceptions to the generalizations that follow, most zoologists are convinced that these two groups are true evolutionary assemblages (figure 21.2).

Protostomes include animals in the phyla Mollusca, Annelida, Arthropoda, and others. Figure 21.3*a–d* shows the developmental characteristics that unite these phyla. One characteristic is the pattern of the early cleavages of the zygote. In spiral cleavage, the mitotic spindle is oriented obliquely to the animal/vegetal axis of a cell *(see chapters 6 and 10)*. For example, division of the four-celled embryo produces an eight-celled embryo in which the up-

FIGURE 21.1

Phylum Mollusca. The phylum Mollusca includes nearly 100,000 living species, including members of the class Cephalopoda—some of the invertebrate world's most adept predators. A member of the genus *Octopus* is shown here.

per tier of cells is twisted out of line with the lower cells. A second characteristic common to many protostomes is that early cleavage is determinate, meaning that the fate of cells is established very early in development. If blastomeres of a two- or four-celled embryo are separated, none develops into a complete organism. A third characteristic is reflected in the term protostome (Gr. *protos*, first + *stoma*, mouth). The blastopore, which forms during an embryonic process called gastrulation *(see chapter 10)*, usually remains open and forms the mouth. Other attributes of many protostomes include a top-shaped larva, called a **trochophore larva,** and a pattern of coelom and mesoderm formation, called schizocoelous, in which the mesoderm splits to form the coelom.

The other group, the **deuterostomes,** includes animals in the phyla Echinodermata, Hemichordata, Chordata, and others. Figure 21.3*e–h* shows the developmental characteristics that unite these phyla. Radial cleavage occurs when the mitotic spindle is oriented perpendicularly to the animal/vegetal axis of a cell and results in blastomeres oriented directly over one another. Cleavage is indeterminate, meaning that the fate of blastomeres is determined late in embryology, and if blastomeres are separated, they can develop into entire individuals. In deuterostomes (Gr. *deutero*, second + *stoma*, mouth), either the blastopore forms the anus, or the blastopore closes, and the anus forms in the region of the blastopore. Mesoderm and coelom formation also differ from that of protostomes. The mesoderm pinches off as pouches of the gut, and the coelom forms inside the mesodermal pouches. This method of coelom formation is called enterocoelous. A kidney-bean-shaped larva, called a dipleurula, is sometimes present in deuterostomes. There is, however, no single kind of deuterostome larval stage.

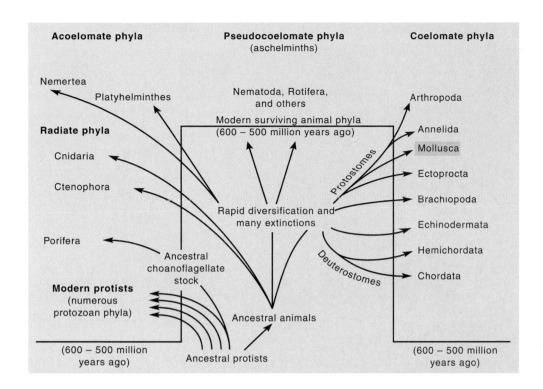

FIGURE 21.2

Evolutionary Relationships of the Molluscs. Molluscs (shaded in orange) share certain developmental characteristics with annelids, arthropods, ectoprocts, and brachiopods. These groups are placed into a larger assemblage called the protostomes. This chapter discusses the developmental characteristics that protostomes share.

ORIGIN OF THE COELOM

A number of hypotheses focus on the origin of the coelom. These hypotheses influence how zoologists picture the evolutionary relationships among triploblastic phyla.

The schizocoel hypothesis (Gr. *schizen*, to split + *koilos*, hollow) is patterned after the method of mesoderm development and coelom formation in many protostomes (figure 21.3*a*), in which all mesoderm is derived from a particular ectodermal cell of the blastula. Mesoderm derived from this cell fills the area between ectoderm and endoderm. The coelom arises from a splitting of this mesoderm. If the coelom formed in this way during evolution, mesodermally derived tissues would have preceded the coelom, implying that a triploblastic, acoelomate (flatworm) body form could be the forerunner of the coelomate body form (*see figure 16.11a*).

The enterocoel hypothesis (Gr. *enteron*, gut + *koilos*, hollow) suggests that the coelom may have arisen as outpocketings of a primitive gut tract. This hypothesis is patterned after the method of coelom formation in deuterostomes (other than vertebrates; *see figure 21.3b*). The implication of this hypothesis is that mesoderm and the coelom formed from the gut of a diploblastic animal. If this is true, the triploblastic, acoelomate body form would have been secondarily derived by mesoderm filling the body cavity of a coelomate animal.

Unfortunately, zoologists may never know which, if either, of these hypotheses is accurate. Some zoologists believe that the coelom may have arisen more than once in different evolutionary lineages, in which case, more than one explanation could be correct.

MOLLUSCAN CHARACTERISTICS

Molluscs range in size and body form from the giant squid, measuring 18 m in length, to the smallest garden slug, less than 1 cm long. In spite of this diversity, the phylum Mollusca (mol-lus'kah) (L. *molluscus*, soft) is not difficult to characterize (table 21.1).

Characteristics of the phylum Mollusca include:

1. Body of two parts: head-foot and visceral mass
2. Mantle that secretes a calcareous shell and covers the visceral mass
3. Mantle cavity functions in excretion, gas exchange, elimination of digestive wastes, and release of reproductive products
4. Bilateral symmetry
5. Protostome characteristics, including trochophore larvae, spiral cleavage, and schizocoelous coelom formation
6. Coelom reduced to cavities surrounding the heart, nephridia, and gonads
7. Open circulatory system in all but one class (Cephalopoda)
8. Radula usually present and used in scraping food

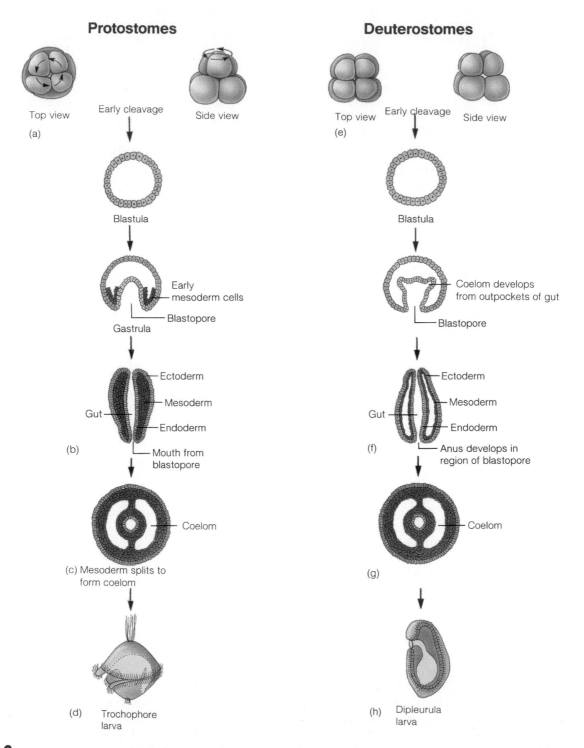

FIGURE 21.3

Developmental Characteristics of Protostomes and Deuterostomes. Protostomes are characterized by (*a*) spiral and determinate cleavage, (*b*) a mouth that forms from an embryonic blastopore, (*c*) schizocoelous coelom formation, and (*d*) a trochophore larva. Deuterostomes are characterized by (*e*) radial and indeterminate cleavage, (*f*), an anus that forms in the region of the embryonic blastopore, and (*g*) enterocoelous coelom formation. A dipleurula larva is present in some echinoderms; however, this larval stage (*h*) is often absent in other deuterostomes.

① The body of a mollusc has three main regions—the head-foot, the visceral mass, and the mantle (figure 21.4). The **head-foot** is elongate with an anterior head, containing the mouth and certain nervous and sensory structures, and an elongate foot, used for attachment and locomotion. The **visceral mass** contains the organs of digestion, circulation, reproduction, and excretion and is positioned dorsal to the head-foot.

The **mantle** of a mollusc usually attaches to the visceral mass, enfolds most of the body, and may secrete a shell that overlies the mantle. The shell of a mollusc is secreted in three layers

TABLE 21.1	CLASSIFICATION OF THE MOLLUSCA

Phylum Mollusca (mol-lus′kah)
The coelomate animal phylum whose members possess a head-foot, visceral mass, mantle, and mantle cavity. Most molluscs also possess a radula and a calcareous shell. Nearly 100,000 species.

Class Caudofoveata (kaw′do-fo″ve-a″ta)
Wormlike molluscs with a cylindrical, shell-less body and scale-like, calcareous spicules; lack eyes, tentacles, statocysts, crystalline style, foot, and nephridia. Deep-water, marine burrowers. *Chaetoderma.* Approximately 70 species.

Class Aplacophora (a″pla-kof′o-rah)
Shell, mantle, and foot lacking; wormlike; head poorly developed; burrowing molluscs. Marine. *Neomenia.* Approximately 250 species.

Class Polyplacophora (pol″e-pla-kof′o-rah)
Elongate, dorsoventrally flattened; head reduced in size; shell consisting of eight dorsal plates. Marine, on rocky intertidal substrates. *Chiton.*

Class Monoplacophora (mon″o-pla-kof′o-rah)
Molluscs with a single arched shell; foot broad and flat; certain structures serially repeated. Marine. *Neopilina.*

Class Scaphopoda (ska-fop′o-dah)
Body enclosed in a tubular shell that is open at both ends; tentacles used for deposit feeding; no head. Marine. *Dentalium.* Over 300 species.

Class Bivalvia (bi′val″ve-ah)
Body enclosed in a shell consisting of two valves, hinged dorsally; no head or radula; wedge-shaped foot. Marine and freshwater. *Anodonta, Mytilus, Venus.* Approximately 30,000 species.

Class Gastropoda (gas-trop′o-dah)
Shell, when present, usually coiled; body symmetry distorted by torsion; some monoecious species. Marine, freshwater, terrestrial. *Nerita, Orthaliculus, Helix.* Over 35,000 species.

Class Cephalopoda (sef′ah-lop″o-dah)
Foot modified into a circle of tentacles and a siphon; shell reduced or absent; head in line with the elongate visceral mass. Marine. *Octopus, Loligo, Sepia, Nautilus.*

This taxonomic listing reflects a phylogenetic sequence. The discussions that follow, however, begin with molluscs that are familiar to most students.

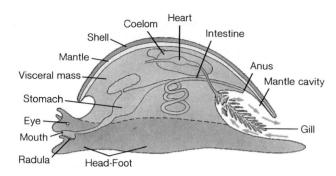

FIGURE 21.4

Molluscan Body Organization. All molluscs possess three features unique to the phylum. The head-foot is a muscular structure usually used for locomotion and sensory perception. The visceral mass contains organs of digestion, circulation, reproduction, and excretion. The mantle is a sheet of tissue that enfolds the rest of the body and secretes the shell. Blue arrows indicate the flow of water through the mantle cavity.

Between the mantle and the foot is a space called the **mantle cavity.** The mantle cavity opens to the outside and functions in gas exchange, excretion, elimination of digestive wastes, and release of reproductive products.

The mouth of most molluscs possesses a rasping structure called a **radula,** which consists of a chitinous belt and rows of posteriorly curved teeth (figure 21.6). The radula overlies a fleshy, tonguelike structure supported by a cartilaginous **odontophore.** Muscles associated with the odontophore permit the radula to be protruded from the mouth. Muscles associated with the radula move the radula back and forth over the odontophore. Food is scraped from a substrate and passed posteriorly to the digestive tract.

Stop and Ask Yourself

1. What characteristics unite the protostomes? What characteristics unite the deuterostomes?

2. Why does the schizocoel hypothesis of the origin of the coelom suggest that coelomate animals evolved from triploblastic animals?

3. What are the three regions of the body of a generalized mollusc? What are the functions of these three regions?

4. What are the functions of the molluscan mantle cavity?

CLASS GASTROPODA

The class Gastropoda (gas-trop′o-dah) (Gr. *gaster,* gut + *podos,* foot) includes the snails, limpets, and slugs. With over 35,000 living species (*see table 21.1*), Gastropoda is the largest and most varied molluscan class. Its members occupy a wide variety of marine, freshwater, and terrestrial habitats. Most people give gastropods little thought unless they encounter *Helix pomatia* (escargot) in a French restaurant or are pestered by garden slugs and snails. One

(figure 21.5). The outer layer of the shell is called the periostracum. Mantle cells at the mantle's outer margin secrete this protein layer. The middle layer of the shell, called the prismatic layer, is the thickest of the three layers and consists of calcium carbonate mixed with organic materials. Cells at the mantle's outer margin also secrete this layer. The inner layer of the shell, the nacreous layer, forms from thin sheets of calcium carbonate alternating with organic matter. Cells along the entire epithelial border of the mantle secrete the nacreous layer. Nacre secretion thickens the shell.

important impact of gastropods on humans is that gastropods are intermediate hosts for some medically important trematode parasites of humans (*see chapter 19*).

TORSION

One of the most significant modifications of the molluscan body form in the gastropods occurs early in gastropod development.

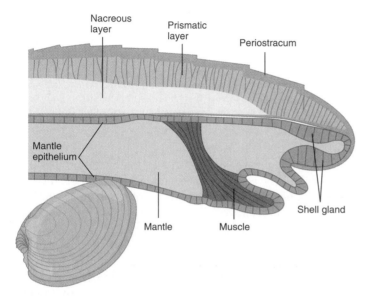

FIGURE 21.5

Molluscan Shell and Mantle. A transverse section of a bivalve shell and mantle shows the three layers of the shell and the portions of the mantle responsible for shell secretion.

Torsion is a 180°, counterclockwise twisting of the visceral mass, mantle, and mantle cavity. Torsion positions the gills, anus, and openings from the excretory and reproductive systems just behind the head and nerve cords, and twists the digestive tract into a U shape (figure 21.7).

The adaptive significance of torsion is speculative; however, three advantages are plausible. First, without torsion, withdrawal into the shell would proceed with the foot entering first and the more vulnerable head entering last. With torsion, the head enters the shell first, exposing the head less to potential predators. In some snails, a proteinaceous covering, called an **operculum,** on the dorsal, posterior margin of the foot enhances protection. When the gastropod draws the foot into the mantle cavity, the operculum closes the opening of the shell, thus preventing desiccation when the snail is in drying habitats. A second advantage of torsion concerns an anterior opening of the mantle cavity that allows clean water from in front of the snail to enter the mantle cavity, rather than water contaminated with silt stirred up by the snail's crawling. The twist in the mantle's sensory organs around to the head region is a third advantage of torsion because it makes the snail more sensitive to stimuli coming from the direction in which it moves.

Note in figure 21.7*d* that, after torsion, the anus and nephridia empty dorsal to the head and create potential fouling problems. However, a number of evolutionary adaptations seem to circumvent this problem. Various modifications allow water and the wastes it carries to exit the mantle cavity through notches or openings in the mantle and shell posterior to the head. Some gastropods undergo detorsion, in which the embryo undergoes a full 180° torsion and then untwists approximately 90°. The mantle cavity thus opens on the right side of the body, behind the head.

FIGURE 21.6

Radular Structure. (*a*) The radular apparatus lies over the cartilaginous odontophore. Muscles attached to the radula move the radula back and forth over the odontophore. (*b*) Micrograph of radular teeth arrangement of the marine snail, *Nerita.* Tooth structure is an important taxonomic characteristic for zoologists who study molluscs. (*a*) *From: "A LIFE OF INVERTEBRATES" © 1979 W. D. Russel-Hunter.*

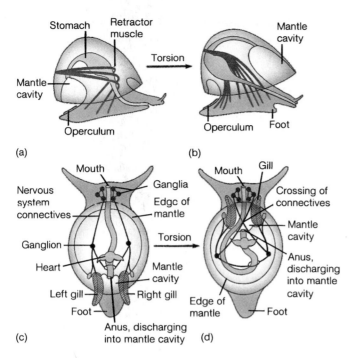

FIGURE 21.7

Torsion in Gastropods. (*a*) A pretorsion gastropod larva. Note the posterior opening of the mantle cavity and the untwisted digestive tract. (*b*) After torsion, the digestive tract is looped, and the mantle cavity opens near the head. The foot is drawn into the shell last, and the operculum closes the shell opening. (*c*) A hypothetical adult ancestor, showing the arrangement of internal organs prior to torsion. (*d*) Modern adult gastropods have an anterior opening of the mantle cavity and the looped digestive tract. *Redrawn from L. Hyman, The Invertebrates, Volume VI. Copyright © 1967 McGraw-Hill, Inc. Used by permission.*

SHELL COILING

The earliest fossil gastropods had a shell that was coiled in one plane. This arrangement is not common in later fossils, probably because growth resulted in an increasingly cumbersome shell. (Some modern snails, however, have secondarily returned to this shell form.)

Most modern snail shells are asymmetrically coiled into a more compact form, with successive coils or whorls slightly larger than, and ventral to, the preceding whorl (figure 21.8*a*).

❷ This pattern leaves less room on one side of the visceral mass for certain organs, which means that organs that are now single were probably paired ancestrally. This asymmetrical arrangement of internal organs is described further in the descriptions of particular body systems.

LOCOMOTION

Nearly all gastropods have a flattened foot that is often ciliated, covered with gland cells, and used to creep across the substrate (figure 21.8*b*). The smallest gastropods use cilia to propel themselves over a mucous trail. Larger gastropods use waves of muscular contraction that move over the foot. The foot of some

(a)

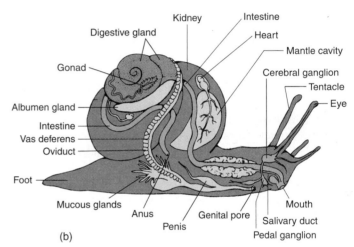

(b)

FIGURE 21.8

Gastropod Structure. (*a*) A land (pulmonate) gastropod (*Orthaliculus*). (*b*) Internal structure of a generalized gastropod.

gastropods is modified for clinging, as in abalones and limpets, or for swimming, as in sea butterflies and sea hares.

FEEDING AND DIGESTION

Most gastropods feed by scraping algae or other small, attached organisms from their substrate. Others are herbivores that feed on larger plants, scavengers, parasites, or predators.

The anterior portion of the digestive tract may be modified into an extensible proboscis, which contains the radula. This structure is important for some predatory snails that must extract animal flesh from hard-to-reach areas. The digestive tract of gastropods, like that of most molluscs, is ciliated. Food is trapped in mucous strings and incorporated into a mucoid mass called the **protostyle,** which extends to the stomach and is rotated by cilia. A digestive gland in the visceral mass releases enzymes and acid into the stomach, and food trapped on the protostyle is freed and digested. Wastes form fecal pellets in the intestine.

OTHER MAINTENANCE FUNCTIONS

Gas exchange always involves the mantle cavity. Primitive gastropods had two gills; modern gastropods have lost one gill because of coiling. Some gastropods have a rolled extension of the mantle, called a **siphon,** that serves as an inhalant tube. Burrowing species extend the siphon to the surface of the substrate to bring in water. Gills are lost or reduced in land snails (pulmonates), but these snails have a richly vascular mantle for gas exchange between blood and air. Mantle contractions help circulate air and water through the mantle cavity.

Gastropods, like most molluscs, have an **open circulatory system.** During part of its circuit around the body, blood leaves the vessels and directly bathes cells in tissue spaces called sinuses. Molluscs typically have a heart consisting of a single, muscular ventricle and two auricles. Most gastropods have lost one member of the pair of auricles because of coiling (*see figure 21.8b*).

In addition to transporting nutrients, wastes, and gases, the blood of molluscs acts as a hydraulic skeleton. A **hydraulic skeleton** consists of blood confined to tissue spaces for support. A mollusc uses its hydraulic skeleton to extend body structures by contracting muscles distant from the extending structure. ③ For example, snails have sensory tentacles on their heads, and if a tentacle is touched, retractor muscles can rapidly withdraw it. However, no antagonistic muscles exist to extend the tentacle. The snail slowly extends the tentacle by contracting distant muscles to squeeze blood into the tentacle from adjacent blood sinuses.

The nervous system of primitive gastropods is characterized by six ganglia located in the head-foot and visceral mass. In primitive gastropods, torsion twists the nerves that link these ganglia. The evolution of the gastropod nervous system has resulted in the untwisting of nerves and the concentration of nervous tissues into fewer, larger ganglia, especially in the head (*see figure 21.8b*).

Gastropods have well-developed sensory structures. Eyes may be at the base or at the end of tentacles. They may be simple pits of photoreceptor cells or consist of a lens and cornea. Statocysts are in the foot. Osphradia are chemoreceptors in the anterior wall of the mantle cavity that detect sediment and chemicals in inhalant water or air. The osphradia of predatory gastropods help detect prey.

Primitive gastropods possessed two nephridia. In modern species, the right nephridium has disappeared, probably because of shell coiling. The nephridium consists of a sac with highly folded walls and connects to the reduced coelom, the pericardial cavity. Excretory wastes are derived largely from fluids filtered and secreted into the coelom from the blood. The nephridium modifies this waste by selectively reabsorbing certain ions and organic molecules. The nephridium opens to the mantle cavity or, in land snails, on the right side of the body adjacent to the mantle cavity and anal opening. Aquatic gastropod species excrete ammonia because they have access to water in which toxic ammonia is diluted. Terrestrial snails must convert ammonia to a less-toxic form—uric acid. Because uric acid is relatively insoluble in water and less toxic, it can be excreted in a semisolid form, which helps conserve water.

REPRODUCTION AND DEVELOPMENT

Many marine snails are dioecious. Gonads lie in spirals of the visceral mass (*see figure 21.8b*). Ducts discharge gametes into the sea for external fertilization.

Many other snails are monoecious, and internal, cross-fertilization is the rule. Copulation may result in mutual sperm transfer, or one snail may act as the male and the other as the female. A penis has evolved from a fold of the body wall, and portions of the female reproductive tract have become glandular and secrete mucus, a protective jelly, or a capsule around the fertilized egg. Some monoecious snails are protandric in that testes develop first, and after they degenerate, ovaries mature.

Eggs are shed singly or in masses for external fertilization. Internally fertilized eggs are deposited in gelatinous strings or masses. The large, yolky eggs of terrestrial snails are deposited in moist environments, such as forest-floor leaf litter, and a calcareous shell may encapsulate them. In marine gastropods, spiral cleavage results in a free-swimming trochophore larva that develops into another free-swimming larva with foot, eyes, tentacles, and shell, called a **veliger larva.** Sometimes, the trochophore is suppressed, and the veliger is the primary larva. Torsion occurs during the veliger stage, followed by settling and metamorphosis to the adult.

GASTROPOD DIVERSITY

The largest group of gastropods is the subclass Prosobranchia. Its 20,000 species are mostly marine, but a few are freshwater or terrestrial. Most members of this subclass are herbivores or deposit feeders; however, some are carnivorous. Some carnivorous species inject venom into their fish, mollusc, or annelid prey with a radula modified into a hollow, harpoonlike structure. Prosobranch gastropods include most of the familiar marine snails and the abalone. This subclass also includes the heteropods. These animals are voracious predators, which have very small shells or no shells. The foot is modified into an undulating "fin" that propels the animal through the water (figure 21.9a).

Members of the subclass Opisthobranchia include sea hares, sea slugs, and their relatives (figure 21.9b). They are mostly marine and include fewer than two thousand species. The shell, mantle cavity, and gills are reduced or lost in these animals, but they are not defenseless. Many acquire undischarged nematocysts from their cnidarian prey, which they use to ward off predators. The pteropods have a foot modified into thin lobes for swimming.

The subclass Pulmonata contains about 17,000 predominantly freshwater or terrestrial species (*see figure 21.8*). These snails are mostly herbivores and have a long radula for scraping plant material. The mantle cavity of pulmonate gastropods is highly vascular and serves as a lung. Air or water moves in or out of the opening of the mantle cavity, the **pneumostome.** In addi-

(a)

(b)

(c)

FIGURE 21.9

Variations in the Gastropod Body Form. *(a)* Subclass Prosobranchia. This heteropod *(Carinaria)* is a predator that swims upside down in the open ocean. Its body is nearly transparent. The head is at the left, and the shell is below and to the right. Heteropoda is a superfamily of proso-branchs comprised of open-ocean, swimming snails with a finlike foot and reduced shell. *(b)* Subclass Opisthobranchia. Colorful nudibranchs have no shell or mantle cavity. The projections on the dorsal surface are used in gas exchange. In some nudibranchs, the dorsal projections are armed with nematocysts for protection. Nudibranchs prey on sessile animals, such as soft corals and sponges. *(c)* Subclass Pulmonata. Terrestrial slugs like this one *(Ariolimax columbianus)* lack a shell. Note the opening to the lung (pneumostome).

tion to typical freshwater or terrestrial snails, the pulmonates in-clude terrestrial slugs (figure 21.9c).

CLASS BIVALVIA

With close to 30,000 species, the class Bivalvia (bi′val″ve-ah) (L. *bis,* twice + *valva,* leaf) is the second largest molluscan class. This class includes the clams, oysters, mussels, and scallops *(see table 21.1).* A sheetlike mantle and a shell consisting of two valves (hence, the class name) cover these laterally compressed animals. Many bivalves are edible, and some form pearls. Because most bivalves are filter feeders, they are valuable in removing bac-teria from polluted water.

SHELL AND ASSOCIATED STRUCTURES

The two convex halves of the shell are called **valves.** Along the dorsal margin of the shell is a proteinaceous hinge and a series of tongue-and-groove modifications of the shell, called teeth, that prevent the valves from twisting (figure 21.10). The oldest part of the shell is the **umbo,** a swollen area near the shell's anterior mar-gin. Although bivalves appear to have two shells, embryologically, the shell forms as a single structure. The shell is continuous along its dorsal margin, but the mantle, in the region of the hinge, se-cretes relatively greater quantities of protein and relatively little calcium carbonate. The result is an elastic hinge ligament. The elasticity of the hinge ligament opens the valves when certain muscles relax.

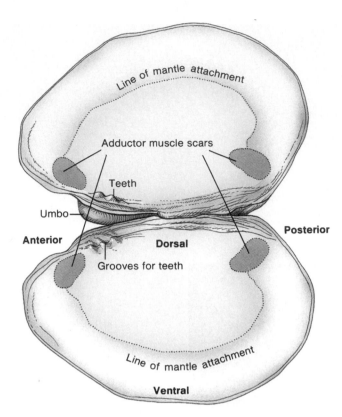

FIGURE 21.10

Inside View of a Bivalve Shell. The umbo is the oldest part of the bivalve shell. As the bivalve grows, the mantle lays down more shell in concentric lines of growth.

Adductor muscles at either end of the dorsal half of the shell close the shell. Anyone who has tried to force apart the valves of a bivalve mollusc knows the effectiveness of these muscles. This is important for bivalves because their primary defense against predatory sea stars is to tenaciously refuse to open their shell. Chapter 25 explains how sea stars have adapted to meet this defense strategy.

The bivalve mantle attaches to the shell around the adductor muscles and near the shell margin. ④ If a sand grain or a parasite lodges between the shell and the mantle, the mantle secretes nacre around the irritant, gradually forming a pearl. The Pacific oysters, *Pinctada margaritifera* and *Pinctada mertensi*, form the highest-quality pearls.

GAS EXCHANGE, FILTER FEEDING, AND DIGESTION

Bivalve adaptations to sedentary, filter-feeding lifestyles include the loss of the head and radula and, except for a few bivalves, the expansion of cilia-covered gills. Gills form folded sheets (lamellae), with one end attached to the foot and the other end attached to the mantle. The mantle cavity ventral to the gills is the inhalant region, and the cavity dorsal to the gills is the exhalant region (figure 21.11a). Cilia move water into the mantle cavity

FIGURE 21.11

Lamellibranch Gill of a Bivalve. (*a*) Blue arrows indicate incurrent and excurrent water currents. Food is filtered as water enters water tubes through pores in the gills. (*b*) Cross section through a portion of a gill. Water passing through a water tube is in close proximity to blood. Water and blood exchange gases in the water tubes. Blue arrows show the path of water. Black arrows show the path of blood.

through an incurrent opening of the mantle. Sometimes, this opening is at the end of a siphon, which is an extension of the mantle. A bivalve buried in the substrate can extend its siphon to the surface and still feed and exchange gases. Water moves from the mantle cavity into small pores in the surface of the gills, and from there, into vertical channels in the gills, called water tubes. In moving through water tubes, blood and water are in close proximity, and gases exchange by diffusion (figure 21.11b). Water exits the bivalve through a part of the mantle cavity at the dorsal aspect of the gills, called the suprabranchial chamber, and through an excurrent opening in the mantle (figure 21.11a).

⑤ The gills trap food particles brought into the mantle cavity. Zoologists originally thought that cilia action was responsible for the trapping. However, the results of a recent study indicate that cilia and food particles have little contact. The

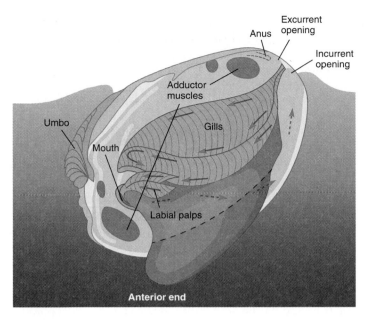

FIGURE 21.12

Bivalve Feeding. Solid blue arrows show the path of food particles after the gills filter them. Dashed blue arrows show the path of particles that the gills and the labial palps reject.

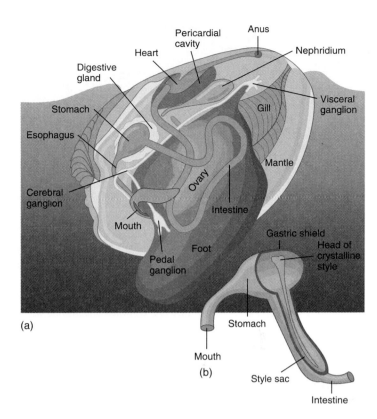

FIGURE 21.13

Bivalve Structure. (a) Internal structure of a bivalve. (b) Bivalve stomach, showing the crystalline style and associated structures.

OTHER MAINTENANCE FUNCTIONS

In bivalves, blood flows from the heart to tissue sinuses, nephridia, gills, and back to the heart (figure 21.14). The mantle is an additional site for oxygenation. In some bivalves, a separate aorta delivers blood directly to the mantle. Two nephridia are below the pericardial cavity (the coelom). Their duct system connects to the coelom at one end and opens at nephridiopores in the anterior region of the suprabranchial chamber (*see figure 21.13*).

The nervous system of bivalves consists of three pairs of interconnected ganglia associated with the esophagus, the foot, and the posterior adductor muscle. The margin of the mantle is the principal sense organ. It always has sensory cells, and it may have sensory tentacles and photoreceptors. In some species (e.g., scallops), photoreceptors are in the form of complex eyes with a lens and a cornea. Other receptors include statocysts near the pedal ganglion and an osphradium in the mantle, beneath the posterior adductor muscle.

REPRODUCTION AND DEVELOPMENT

Most bivalves are dioecious. A few are monoecious, and some of these species are protandric. Gonads are in the visceral mass, where they surround the looped intestine. Ducts of these gonads open directly to the mantle cavity or by the nephridiopore to the mantle cavity.

food-trapping mechanism is unclear, but once food particles are trapped, cilia move them to the gills' ventral margin. Cilia along the ventral margin of the gills then move food toward the mouth (figure 21.12). Cilia covering leaflike **labial palps** on either side of the mouth also sort filtered food particles. Cilia carry small particles into the mouth and move larger particles to the edges of the palps and gills. This rejected material, called pseudofeces, falls, or is thrown, onto the mantle, and a ciliary tract on the mantle transports the pseudofeces posteriorly. Water rushing out when valves are forcefully closed washes pseudofeces from the mantle cavity.

The digestive tract of bivalves is similar to that of other molluscs (figure 21.13a). Food entering the esophagus entangles in a mucoid food string, which extends to the stomach and is rotated by cilia lining the digestive tract. A consolidated mucoid mass, the **crystalline style,** projects into the stomach from a diverticulum, called the style sac (figure 21.13b). Enzymes for carbohydrate and fat digestion are incorporated into the crystalline style. Cilia of the style sac rotate the style against a chitinized **gastric shield.** This abrasion and acidic conditions in the stomach dislodge enzymes. The mucoid food string winds around the crystalline style as it rotates, which pulls the food string farther into the stomach from the esophagus. This action and the acidic pH in the stomach dislodge food particles in the food string. Further sorting separates fine particles from undigestible coarse materials. The latter are sent on to the intestine. Partially digested food from the stomach enters a digestive gland for intracellular digestion. Cilia carry undigested wastes in the digestive gland back to the stomach and then to the intestine. The intestine empties through the anus near the excurrent opening, and excurrent water carries feces away.

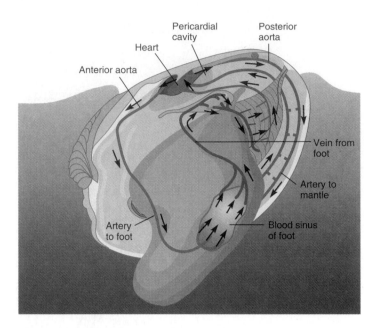

FIGURE 21.14

Bivalve Circulation. Blood flows (black arrows) from the single ventricle of the heart to tissue sinuses through anterior and posterior aortae. Blood from tissue sinuses flows to the nephridia, to the gills, and then to the auricles of the heart. In all bivalves, the mantle is an additional site for oxygenation. In some bivalves, a separate aorta delivers blood to the mantle. This blood returns directly to the heart. The ventricle of bivalves is always folded around the intestine. Thus, the pericardial cavity (the coelom) encloses the heart and a portion of the digestive tract.

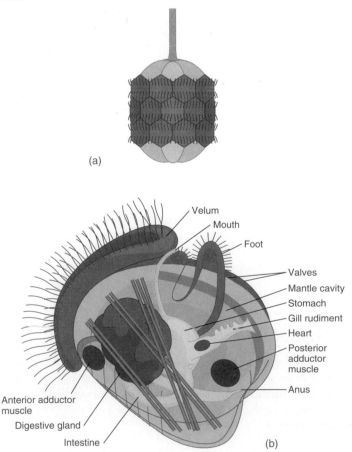

Most bivalves exhibit external fertilization. Gametes exit through the suprabranchial chamber of the mantle cavity and the exhalant opening. Development proceeds through trochophore and veliger stages (figure 21.15a,b). When the veliger settles to the substrate, it assumes the adult form.

Most freshwater bivalves brood their young. Fertilization occurs in the mantle cavity by sperm brought in with inhalant water. Some brood their young in maternal gills through reduced trochophore and veliger stages. Young clams are shed from the gills. Others brood their young to a modified veliger stage called a **glochidium,** which is parasitic on fishes (figure 21.15c). These larvae possess two tiny valves, and some species have toothlike hooks. Larvae exit through the exhalant aperture and sink to the substrate. Most die. If a fish contacts a glochidium, however, the larva attaches to the gills, fins, or another body part and begins to feed on host tissue. The fish forms a cyst around the larva. The mantles of some freshwater bivalves have elaborate modifications that present a fishlike lure to entice predatory fish. When a fish attempts to feed on the lure, the bivalve ejects glochidia onto the fish (figure 21.16). After several weeks of larval development, during which a glochidium begins acquiring its adult structures, the miniature clam falls from its host and takes up its filter-feeding lifestyle. The glochidium is a dispersal stage for an otherwise sedentary animal and is usually harmless to the fish.

BIVALVE DIVERSITY

Bivalves live in nearly all aquatic habitats. They may completely or partially bury themselves in sand or mud, attach to solid sub-

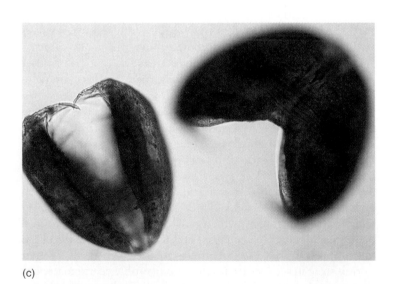

(c)

FIGURE 21.15

Larval Stages of Bivalves. (a) Trochophore larva (0.4 mm) of *Yoldia limatula*. (b) Veliger (0.5 mm) of an oyster. (c) Glochidium (1.0 mm) of a freshwater clam. Note the tooth used to attach to fish gills.

FIGURE 21.16

Class Bivalvia. This photograph shows a modification of the mantle of a freshwater bivalve (*Lampsilis reeviana*) into a lure. The edge of the bivalve shell is shown in the lower right corner of the photograph. When a fish approaches and bites at the lure, glochidia are released onto the fish.

strates, or bore into submerged wood, coral, or limestone (box 21.1).

The mantle margins of burrowing bivalves are frequently fused to form distinct openings in the mantle cavity (siphons). This fusion helps to direct the water washed from the mantle cavity during burrowing and helps keep sediment from accumulating in the mantle cavity.

Some surface-dwelling bivalves attach to the substrate either by proteinaceous strands called byssal threads, which a gland in the foot secretes, or by cementation to the substrate. The common marine mussel, *Mytilus*, uses the former method, while oysters employ the latter.

Boring bivalves live beneath the surface of limestone, clay, coral, wood, and other substrates. 6 Boring begins when the larvae settle to the substrate, and the anterior margin of their valves mechanically abrades the substrate. Acidic secretions from the mantle margin that dissolve limestone sometimes accompany physical abrasion. As the bivalve grows, it is often imprisoned in its rocky burrow because the most recently bored portions of the burrow are larger in diameter than portions bored earlier.

Stop and Ask Yourself

5. What three advantages does torsion confer on gastropods?
6. What is a hydraulic skeleton?
7. How do bivalves discourage predatory sea stars?
8. How do bivalves feed?

(a)

(b)

FIGURE 21.17

Class Cephalopoda. (*a*) Chambered nautilus (*Nautilus*). (*b*) A cuttlefish (*Sepia*).

CLASS CEPHALOPODA

The class Cephalopoda (sef'ah-lop"o-dah) (L. *cephalic*, head + Gr. *podos*, foot) includes the octopuses, squids, cuttlefish, and nautili (figure 21.17; *see table 21.1*; *see figure 21.1*). They are the most complex molluscs and, in many ways, the most complex invertebrates. The anterior portion of their foot has been modified into a circle of tentacles or arms used for prey capture, attachment, locomotion, and copulation (figure 21.18). The foot is also incorporated into a

BOX 21.1 THE ZEBRA MUSSEL—ANOTHER BIOLOGICAL INVASION

About one hundred years ago, a bird fancier released a few starlings in New York City's Central Park. Today, the starling is the most common bird in the United States. In 1866, the gypsy moth was transported from Europe to the New England states. It proliferated at the expense of North American forests. Today, these European invaders are joined by another exotic species, the zebra mussel (*Dreissena polymorpha*). The invasion of the zebra mussel, like the others before it, has been costly, both economically and ecologically for much of North America.

The zebra mussel is actually one of about 120 exotic invaders of the Great Lakes. The invasion began in 1985 or 1986, when larval mussels were picked up in freshwater ports of Europe as cargo ships filled their ballast tanks with freshwater. The larvae were released when ballast tanks were emptied into the Great Lakes. Within 3 or 4 years, the mussel spread into Lakes Erie, Ontario, Huron, and southern Lake Michigan. By June 1991, the mussels were reported in the Illinois River, and the mussel today threatens much of the Mississippi River drainage basin.

Many of the problems associated with zebra mussels are a result of their high reproductive potential. A single female may release 40,000 eggs. Their veliger larval stages may drift in the plankton for up to 5 weeks and be carried long distances by water currents. When larvae settle on a hard substrate, they attach by tough byssal threads. They grow to a length of about 2 cm, and densities of 200 individuals/m^2 are common (figure 1).

Economic problems associated with zebra mussels result from their settling on, and clogging, water intake pipes. Detroit Edison officials reported 700,000 mussels/m^2 on a single water intake screen. In December 1988, mussels and ice shards blocked water intake to the Detroit Edison plant, which resulted in power outages throughout Detroit. It cost the company $250,000 to restore electricity to the city. Detroit Edison officials spent $6 million on a new intake system that they hope will reduce the fouling problems. Throughout the Great Lakes, an estimated $2 billion will be spent cleaning and refitting pipes in Great Lakes port cities through the 1990s.

Zebra mussels also threaten the ecology of freshwater ecosystems. They are very efficient filter feeders and are expected to disrupt freshwater food webs. As larvae settle and encrust hard substrates, they may disrupt the spawning ground of game fish such as walleyed

FIGURE 1 **An Exotic Invader.** The zebra mussel (*Dreissena polymorpha*) invaded U.S. fresh waters and is threatening native bivalves and other

pike. The Mississippi River drainage basin is a particular concern. The Mississippi River and its tributaries contain the highest diversity of clams in the world. Some of these clams are endangered species. The valves of a native clam make an excellent substrate for zebra mussel attachment. The native clam can be so densely covered that feeding is impossible.

While research efforts are underway to monitor the spread of the zebra mussel and to search for its "Achilles' heel," a larger question looms in the background: "Are more invaders on the way?" One study of the ballast water of 55 cargo ships revealed that 17 species of animals were still alive in each ship by the time the ships arrived in North American freshwaters. Estimates of the number of individuals alive per species ranged between 10,000 and 8 billion! A relatively simple, partial solution to the problem of ballast-water invaders is to require ships to dump ballast water from foreign, freshwater ports into the open ocean and replace it with seawater. Seawater kills most freshwater organisms, and freshwater kills most marine organisms.

---

funnel associated with the mantle cavity and used for jetlike locomotion. The molluscan body plan is further modified in that the cephalopod head is in line with the visceral mass. Cephalopods have a highly muscular mantle that encloses all of the body except the head and tentacles. The mantle acts as a pump to bring large quantities of water into the mantle cavity.

SHELL

Ancestral cephalopods probably had a conical shell. The only living cephalopod that possesses an external shell is the nautilus (*see figure 21.17a*). Septa subdivide its coiled shell. As the nautilus

grows, it moves forward, secreting new shell around itself and leaving an empty septum behind. Only the last chamber is occupied. When formed, these chambers are fluid filled. A cord of tissue called a siphuncle, perforates the septa, absorbing fluids by osmosis and replacing them with metabolic gases. The amount of gas in the chambers is regulated to alter the buoyancy of the animal.

In all other cephalopods, the shell is reduced or absent. In cuttlefish, the shell is internal and laid down in thin layers, leaving small, gas-filled spaces that increase buoyancy. Cuttlefish shell, called cuttlebone, is used to make powder for polishing and is fed to pet birds to supplement their diet with calcium. The shell of a squid is reduced to an internal, chitinous structure called the pen.

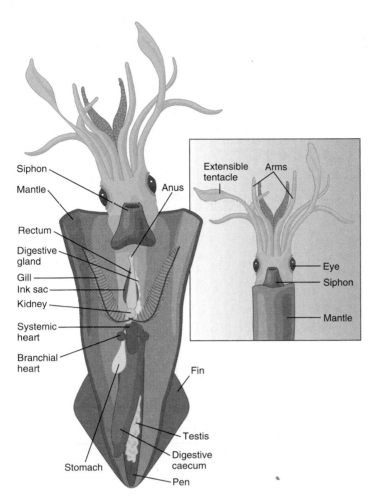

FIGURE 21.18

Internal Structure of the Squid, *Loligo*. The shell of most cephalopods is reduced or absent, and the foot is modified into a funnel and a circle of tentacles and/or arms that encircle the head. The inset shows the undissected anatomy of the squid.

In addition, squid also have cartilaginous plates in the mantle wall, neck, and head that support the mantle and protect the brain. The shell is absent in octopuses.

LOCOMOTION

As predators, cephalopods depend on their ability to move quickly using a jet-propulsion system. The mantle of cephalopods contains radial and circular muscles. When circular muscles contract, they decrease the volume of the mantle cavity and close collarlike valves to prevent water from moving out of the mantle cavity between the head and the mantle wall. Water is thus forced out of a narrow funnel. Muscles attached to the funnel control the direction of the animal's movement. Radial mantle muscles bring water into the mantle cavity by increasing the cavity's volume. Posterior fins act as stabilizers in squid and also aid in propulsion and steering in cuttlefish. "Flying squid" (family Onycoteuthidae) have been clocked at speeds of 30 km/hr. Octopuses are more sedentary

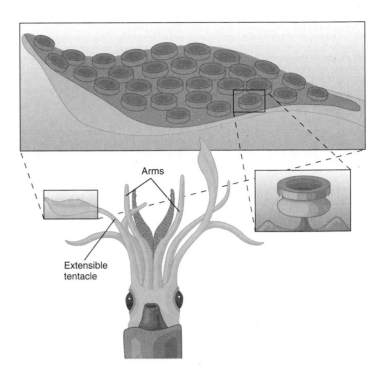

FIGURE 21.19

Cephalopod Tentacle. Cephalopods use suction cups for prey capture and as holdfast structures.

animals. They may use jet propulsion in an escape response, but normally, they crawl over the substrate using their tentacles. In most cephalopods, the use of the mantle in locomotion coincides with the loss of an external shell, since a rigid external shell would preclude the jet-propulsion method of locomotion described.

FEEDING AND DIGESTION

Cephalopods locate their prey by sight and capture prey with tentacles that have adhesive cups. In squid, the margins of these cups are reinforced with tough protein and sometimes possess small hooks (figure 21.19).

All cephalopods have jaws and a radula. The jaws are powerful, beaklike structures for tearing food, and the radula rasps food, forcing it into the mouth cavity.

Cuttlefish and nautili feed on small invertebrates on the ocean floor. Octopuses are nocturnal hunters and feed on snails, fish, and crustaceans. Octopuses have salivary glands that inject venom into prey. Squid feed on fishes and shrimp, which they kill by biting across the back of the head. ⑦ Giant squid even prey upon the young of sperm whales—just as adult sperm whales prey upon the young of giant squid.

The digestive tract of cephalopods is muscular, and peristalsis (coordinated muscular waves) replaces ciliary action in moving food. Most digestion occurs in a stomach and a large cecum. Digestion is primarily extracellular, with large digestive glands supplying enzymes. An intestine ends at the anus, near the funnel, and exhalant water carries wastes out of the mantle cavity.

OTHER MAINTENANCE FUNCTIONS

Cephalopods, unlike other molluscs, have a **closed circulatory system.** Blood is confined to vessels throughout its circuit around the body. Capillary beds connect arteries and veins, and exchanges of gases, nutrients, and metabolic wastes occur across capillary walls. In addition to having a heart consisting of two auricles and one ventricle, cephalopods have contractile arteries and structures called branchial hearts. The latter are at the base of each gill and help move blood through the gill. These modifications increase blood pressure and the rate of blood flow—necessary for active animals with relatively high metabolic rates. Large quantities of water circulate over the gills at all times. Cephalopods exhibit greater excretory efficiency because of the closed circulatory system. A close association of blood vessels with nephridia allows wastes to filter and secrete directly from the blood into the excretory system.

8 The cephalopod nervous system is unparalleled in any other invertebrate. Cephalopod brains are large, and their evolution is directly related to cephalopod predatory habits and dexterity. The brain forms by a fusion of ganglia. Large areas are devoted to controlling muscle contraction (e.g., swimming movements and sucker closing), sensory perception, and functions such as memory and decision making. Research on cephalopod brains has provided insight into human brain functions.

The eyes of octopuses, cuttlefish, and squids are similar in structure to vertebrate eyes (figure 21.20). (This similarity is an excellent example of convergent evolution.) In contrast to the vertebrate eye, nerve cells leave the eye from the outside of the eyeball, so that no blind spot exists. (The blind spot of the vertebrate eye is a region of the retina where no photoreceptors exist because of the convergence of nerve cells into the optic nerve. When light falls on the blind spot, no image is perceived.) Like many aquatic vertebrates, cephalopods focus by moving the lens back and forth. Cephalopods can form images, distinguish shapes, and discriminate some colors. The nautiloid eye is less complex. It lacks a lens, and the interior is open to seawater: thus, it acts as a pinhole camera.

Cephalopod statocysts respond to gravity and acceleration, and are in cartilages next to the brain. Osphradia are present only in *Nautilus.* Tactile receptors and additional chemoreceptors are widely distributed over the body.

Cephalopods have pigment cells called **chromatophores.** When tiny muscles attached to these pigment cells contract, the chromatophores quickly expand and change the color of the animal. Color changes, in combination with ink discharge, function in alarm responses. In defensive displays, color changes may spread in waves over the body to form large, flickering patterns. Color changes may also help cephalopods to blend with their background. The cuttlefish, *Sepia,* can even make a remarkably good impression of a checkerboard background. Color changes are also involved with courtship displays. Some species combine chromatophore displays with bioluminescence.

All cephalopods possess an ink gland that opens just behind the anus. Ink is a brown or black fluid containing melanin and other chemicals. Discharged ink confuses a predator, allowing the

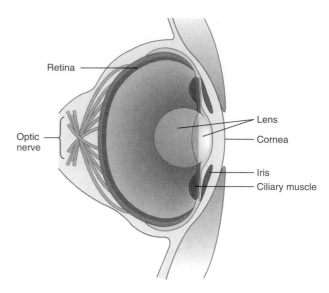

FIGURE 21.20

Cephalopod Eye. The eye is immovable in a supportive and protective socket of cartilages. It contains a rigid, spherical lens. An iris in front of the lens forms a slitlike pupil that can open and close in response to varying light conditions. Note that the optic nerve comes off the back of the retina.

cephalopod to escape. For example, *Sepiola* reacts to danger by darkening itself with chromatophore expansion prior to releasing ink. After ink discharge, *Sepiola* changes to a lighter color again to assist its escape.

REPRODUCTION AND DEVELOPMENT

Cephalopods are dioecious with gonads in the dorsal portion of the visceral mass. The male reproductive tract consists of testes and structures for encasing sperm in packets called **spermatophores.** The female reproductive tract produces large, yolky eggs and is modified with glands that secrete gel-like cases around eggs. These cases frequently harden on exposure to seawater.

One tentacle of male cephalopods, called the **hectocotylus,** is modified for spermatophore transfer. In *Loligo* and *Sepia,* the hectocotylus has several rows of smaller suckers capable of picking up spermatophores. During copulation, male and female tentacles intertwine, and the male removes spermatophores from his mantle cavity. The male inserts his hectocotylus into the mantle cavity of the female and deposits a spermatophore near the opening to the oviduct. Spermatophores have an ejaculatory mechanism that frees sperm from the baseball-bat-shaped capsule. Eggs are fertilized as they leave the oviduct, and are deposited singly or in stringlike masses. They usually attach to some substrate, such as the ceiling of an octopus's den. Octopuses clean developing eggs of debris with their arms and squirts of water.

Cephalopods develop in the confines of the egg membranes, and the hatchlings are miniature adults. Young are never cared for after hatching.

CLASS POLYPLACOPHORA

The class Polyplacophora (pol″e-pla-kof′o-rah) (Gr. *polys,* many + *plak,* plate + *phoros,* to bear) contains the chitons. Chitons are common inhabitants of hard substrates in shallow marine water. Early Native Americans ate chitons. Chitons have a fishy flavor but are tough to chew and difficult to collect.

Chitons have a reduced head, a flattened foot, and a shell that divides into eight articulating dorsal valves (figure 21.21*a*). A muscular mantle that extends beyond the margins of the shell and foot covers the broad foot (figure 21.21*b*). The mantle cavity is restricted to the space between the margin of the mantle and the foot. Chitons crawl over their substrate in a manner similar to gastropods. The muscular foot allows chitons to securely attach to a substrate and withstand strong waves and tidal currents. When chitons are disturbed, the edges of the mantle tightly grip the substrate, and foot muscles contract to raise the middle of the foot, creating a powerful vacuum that holds the chiton in place. Articulations in the shell allow chitons to roll into a ball when dislodged from the substrate.

A linear series of gills is in the mantle cavity on each side of the foot. Water currents that cilia on the gills create enter below the anterior mantle margins and exit posteriorly. The digestive, excretory, and reproductive tracts open near the exhalant area of the mantle cavity, and exhalant water carries products of these systems away.

Most chitons feed on attached algae. A chemoreceptor, the subradular organ, extends from the mouth to detect food, which the radula rasps from the substrate. Mucus traps food, which then enters the esophagus by ciliary action. Extracellular digestion occurs in the stomach, and wastes move on to the intestine (figure 21.21*c*).

The nervous system is ladderlike, with four anteroposterior nerve cords and numerous transverse nerves. A nerve ring encircles the esophagus. Sensory structures include osphradia, tactile receptors on the mantle margin, chemoreceptors near the mouth, and statocysts in the foot. In some chitons, photoreceptors dot the surface of the shell.

Sexes are separate in chitons. External fertilization and development result in a swimming trochophore that settles and metamorphoses into an adult without passing through a veliger stage.

CLASS SCAPHOPODA

Members of the class Scaphopoda (ska-fop′o-dah) (Gr. *skaphe,* boat + *podos,* foot) are called tooth shells or tusk shells. The over three hundred species are all burrowing marine animals that inhabit moderate depths. Their most distinctive characteristic is a conical shell that is open at both ends. The head and foot project from the wider end of the shell, and the rest of the body, including the mantle, is greatly elongate and extends the length of the shell

(a)

(b)

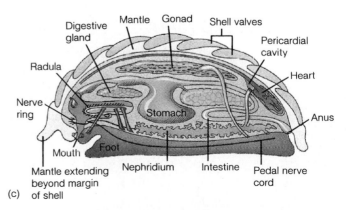

(c)

FIGURE 21.21

Class Polyplacophora. (*a*) Dorsal view of a chiton. Note the shell consisting of eight valves and the mantle extending beyond the margins of the shell. (*b*) Ventral view of a chiton. The mantle cavity is the region between the mantle and the foot. Arrows show the path of water moving across gills in the mantle cavity. (*c*) Internal structure of a chiton.

FIGURE 21.22

Class Scaphopoda. This conical shell is open at both ends. In its living state, the animal is mostly buried, with the apex of the shell projecting into the water.

(figure 21.22). Scaphopods live mostly buried in the substrate with head and foot oriented down and with the apex of the shell projecting into the water above. Incurrent and excurrent water enters and leaves the mantle cavity through the opening at the apex of the shell. Functional gills are absent, and gas exchange occurs across mantle folds. Scaphopods have a radula and tentacles, which they use in feeding on foraminiferans. Sexes are separate, and trochophore and veliger larvae are produced.

CLASS MONOPLACOPHORA

Members of the class Monoplacophora (mon″o-pla-kof′o-rah) (Gr. *monos*, one + *plak*, plate + *phoros*, to bear) have an undivided, arched shell; a broad, flat foot; and serially repeated pairs of gills and foot-retractor muscles. They are dioecious; however, nothing is known of their embryology. This group of molluscs was known only from fossils until 1952, when a limpetlike monoplacophoran, named *Neopilina*, was dredged up from a depth of 3,520 m off the Pacific coast of Costa Rica (figure 21.23).

CLASS CAUDOFOVEATA

Members of the class Caudofoveata (kaw′do-fo″ve-a″ta) (L. *cauda*, tail + *fovea*, small pit) are wormlike molluscs that range in size from 2 mm to 14 cm and live in vertical burrows on the deep-sea floor. They have scalelike spicules on the body wall and lack the following typical molluscan characteristics: shell, crystalline style, statocysts, foot, and nephridia. Zoologists have described approximately 70 species, but little is known of their ecology.

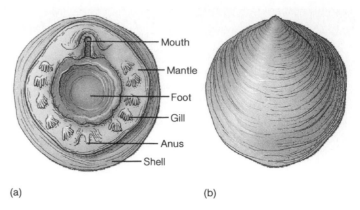

FIGURE 21.23

Class Monoplacophora. (*a*) Ventral and (*b*) dorsal views of *Neopilina*.

FIGURE 21.24

Class Aplacophora. Scanning electron micrograph of the solenogaster, *Meiomenia*. Flattened, spinelike, calcareous spicules cover the body. The ventral groove shown here may form from a rolling of the mantle margins. *Meiomenia* is approximately 2 mm long.

CLASS APLACOPHORA

Members of the class Aplacophora (a″pla-kof′o-rah) (Gr. *a*, without + *plak*, plate + *phoros*, to bear) are called solenogasters (figure 21.24). The approximately 250 species of these cylindrical molluscs lack a shell and crawl on their ventral surface. Their nervous system is ladderlike and reminiscent of the flatworm body form, causing some to suggest that this group may be closely related to the ancestral molluscan stock. One small group of aplacophorans contains burrowing species that feed on microorganisms and detritus, and possess a radula and nephridia. Most aplacophorans, however, lack nephridia and a radula, are surface dwellers on corals and other substrates, and are carnivores, frequently feeding on cnidarian polyps.

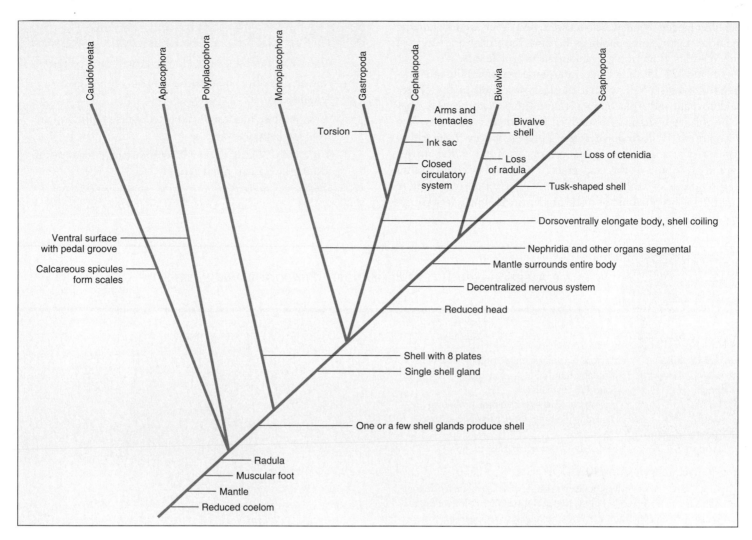

FIGURE 21.25

Molluscan Phylogeny. Cladogram showing possible evolutionary relationships among the molluscs.

FURTHER PHYLOGENETIC CONSIDERATIONS

Fossil records of molluscan classes indicate that the phylum is over 500 million years old. Although molluscs have protostome affinities, zoologists do not know the exact relationship of this phylum to other animal phyla. The discovery of *Neopilina* (class Monoplacophora) in 1952 seemed to revolutionize ideas regarding the position of the molluscs in the animal phyla. The most striking feature of *Neopilina* is a segmental arrangement of gills, excretory structures, and nervous system. Because annelids and arthropods (*see chapters 22 to 24*) also have a segmental arrangement of body parts, monoplacophorans were considered a "missing link" between other molluscs and the annelid-arthropod evolutionary line. This idea was further supported by molluscs, annelids, and arthropods sharing certain protostome characteristics (*see figure 21.3a*), and chitons also showing a repetition of some body parts.

Most zoologists now agree that the segmentation in some molluscs is very different from that of annelids and arthropods. Although information on the development of the serially repeating structures in *Neopilina* is not available, no serially repeating structure in any other mollusc develops in an annelid-arthropod fashion. Segmentation is probably not an ancestral molluscan characteristic. Many zoologists now believe that molluscs diverged from ancient triploblastic stocks independent of any other phylum. Other zoologists maintain that, in spite of the absence of annelid-like segmentation in molluscs, protostomate affinities still tie the molluscs to the annelid-arthropod line. Whichever is the case, the relationship of the molluscs to other animal phyla is distant.

The diversity of body forms and lifestyles in the phylum Mollusca is an excellent example of adaptive radiation. Molluscs probably began in Precambrian times as slow-moving, marine, bottom dwellers. The development of unique molluscan features allowed them to diversify relatively quickly. By the end of the Cambrian period, some were filter feeders, some were burrowers, and others were swimming predators. Later, some molluscs became terrestrial and invaded many habitats, from tropical rain forests to arid deserts.

Figure 21.25 shows one interpretation of molluscan phylogeny. Zoologists believe that the lack of a shell in the classes Caudofoveata and Aplacophora is a primitive character. All other molluscs have a shell or are derived from shelled ancestors. The multipart shell distinguishes the Polyplacophora from other classes. Other selected synapomorphies, discussed earlier in this chapter, are noted in the cladogram. There are, of course, other interpretations of molluscan phylogeny. The extensive adaptive radiation of this phylum has made higher taxonomic relationships difficult to discern.

Stop and Ask Yourself

13. What molluscs have eight dorsal, articulating plates?
14. How would you characterize members of the class Scaphopoda?
15. What mollusc has serially repeated pairs of gills and an undivided, arched shell?
16. What is the significance of *Neopilina* in hypotheses concerning molluscan phylogeny?

ENDANGERED SPECIES

WILDLIFE ALERT 8—RED HILLS SALAMANDER (*PHAEOGNATHUS HUBRICHTI*)

VITAL STATISTICS

Classification: Phylum Chordata, class Amphibia, order Caudata, family Plethodontidae
Range: Southern Alabama
Habitat: Burrows on the slopes of moist, cool ravines shaded by an overstory of hardwood trees
Number remaining: Unknown
Status: Endangered throughout its range

NATURAL HISTORY AND ECOLOGICAL STATUS

The Red Hills salamander is a fairly large, terrestrial salamander that grows to about 255 mm in length (figure 1). Its body color is gray to brownish without distinct markings. Sexual activity peaks in the spring, and eggs are deposited within the burrow system. There is no aquatic larval stage. Adults reach sexual maturity in 2 to 3 years and have a sexual longevity of 2 to 5 years.

The range of the Red Hills salamander is restricted to a narrow belt of two geological formations in southern Alabama (figure 2). This salamander inhabits burrows on the slopes of moist, cool

FIGURE 2   Range of Red Hills Salamander in Alabama.

ravines shaded by an overstory of hardwood trees. These areas are underlain by a subsurface siltstone stratum containing many crevices, root tracings, and solution channels that the salamander uses. The topsoil habitat is typically sandy loam.

Primary threats to this species include its restricted range, loss of habitat, a low reproductive rate, and a limited capability for dispersal. Of the approximately 63,000 acres of remaining habitat, about 60% is currently owned or leased by paper companies that primarily use a clear-cutting system of forest management. This technique, along with the mechanical preparation of the site for logging, appears to completely destroy the habitat for the Red Hills salamander.

Needed management activities include: acquisition of major habitats, conservation agreements and easements to maintain the viability of remaining populations, continued research on biological and management-related questions, and care in the planning of forestry operations.

FIGURE 1   Red Hills Salamander (*Phaeognathus hubrichti*).

ANNELIDA:
THE METAMERIC BODY FORM

Concepts

1. Members of the phylum Annelida are the segmented worms. Zoologists debate the relationships of annelids to lower triploblastic animals.
2. Metamerism has important influences on virtually every aspect of annelid structure and function.
3. Members of the class Polychaeta are annelids that have adapted to a variety of marine habitats. Some live in or on marine substrates; others live in burrows or are free-swimming. Parapodia and numerous, long setae characterize the polychaetes.
4. Members of the class Oligochaeta live in freshwater and terrestrial habitats. They lack parapodia and have fewer, short setae.
5. The class Hirudinea contains the leeches. They are predators in freshwater, marine, and terrestrial environments. Body-wall musculature and the coelom are modified from the pattern found in the other annelid classes. These differences influence locomotor and other functions of leeches.
6. The ancient polychaetes are probably the ancestral stock from which modern polychaetes, oligochaetes, and leeches evolved.

Would You Like to Know . . .

1. what worm is the basis of a great communal feast? (p. 340)
2. what metamerism is? (p. 340)
3. how fanworms use their fans? (p. 344)
4. why the blood of some marine worms is green? (p. 344)
5. why swarming of epitokes is advantageous for some marine worms? (p. 347)
6. why an earthworm is so difficult to extract from its burrow? (p. 348)
7. why leeches are predators, not parasites? (p. 351)
8. why earthworms live in soil around deciduous vegetation? (p. 354)

This chapter answers these and other useful questions.

This chapter contains evolutionary concepts, which are set off in this font.

EVOLUTIONARY PERSPECTIVE

At the time of the November full moon on islands near Samoa in the South Pacific, natives rush about preparing for one of their biggest yearly feasts. In just one week, the sea will yield a harvest that can be scooped up in nets and buckets. Worms by the millions transform the ocean into what one writer called "vermicelli soup!" Celebrants gorge themselves on worms that have been cooked or wrapped in breadfruit leaves. ❶ The Samoan palolo worm (*Eunice viridis*) spends its entire adult life in coral burrows at the sea bottom. Each November, one week after the full moon, this worm emerges from its burrow, and specialized body segments devoted to sexual reproduction break free and float to the surface, while the rest of the worm is safe on the ocean floor. The surface water is discolored as gonads release their countless eggs and sperm. The natives' feast is short-lived, however; these reproductive swarms last only 2 days and do not recur for another year.

The Samoan palolo worm is a member of the phylum Annelida (ah-nel'i-dah) (L. *annellus*, ring). Other members of this phylum include countless marine worms (figure 22.1), the soil-building earthworms, and predatory leeches (table 22.1).

Characteristics of the phylum Annelida include:

1. Body metameric, bilaterally symmetrical, and wormlike
2. Protostome characteristics include spiral cleavage, trochophore larvae (when larvae are present), and schizocoelous coelom formation
3. Paired, epidermal setae
4. Closed circulatory system
5. Dorsal suprapharyngeal ganglia and ventral nerve cord(s) with ganglia
6. Metanephridia (usually) or protonephridia

RELATIONSHIPS TO OTHER ANIMALS

Annelids are protostomes (*see figure 21.3*). Protostome characteristics, such as spiral cleavage, a mouth derived from an embryonic blastopore, schizocoelous coelom formation, and trochophore larvae are present in most members of the phylum (figure 22.2). (Certain exceptions are discussed later.) This diverse phylum, like most other phyla, originated at least as early as Precambrian times, more than 600 million years ago. Unfortunately, little evidence documents the evolutionary pathways that resulted in the first annelids.

A number of hypotheses account for annelid origins. These hypotheses are tied into hypotheses regarding the origin of the coelom (*see chapter 21*). If a schizocoelous origin of the coelom is correct, as many zoologists believe, then the annelids evolved from ancient flatworm stock. On the other hand, if an enterocoelous coelom origin is correct, then annelids evolved from ancient diploblastic animals, and the triploblastic, acoelomate body may have been derived from a triploblastic, coelomate ancestor. The recent discovery of a worm, *Lobatocerebrum*, that shares annelid and flatworm characteristics has lent support to the enterocoelous origin hypothesis. *Lobatocerebrum* is classified as an annelid based on the presence of

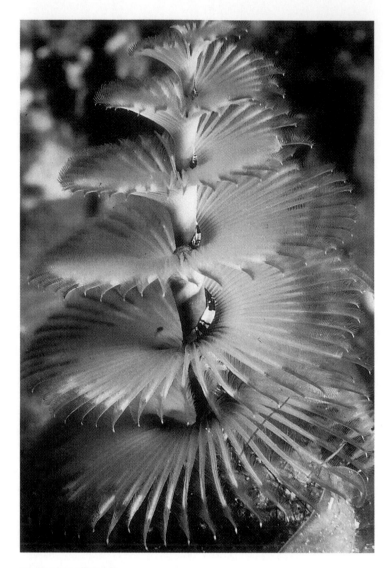

FIGURE 22.1

Phylum Annelida. The phylum Annelida includes about nine thousand species of segmented worms. Most of these are marine members of the class Polychaeta. The fanworm (*Sriro branchus*) is shown here. The fan of this tube-dwelling polychaete is specialized for feeding and gas exchange.

certain segmentally arranged excretory organs, an annelid-like body covering, a complete digestive tract, and an annelid-like nervous system. However, it has a ciliated epidermis and is acoelomate like flatworms. Some zoologists believe that *Lobatocerebrum* illustrates how the triploblastic, acoelomate design could have been derived from the annelid lineage.

METAMERISM AND TAGMATIZATION

Earthworm bodies are organized into a series of ringlike segments. What is not externally obvious, however, is that the body is divided internally as well. ❷ Segmental arrangement of body parts in an animal is called **metamerism** (Gr. *meta*, after + *mere*, part).

TABLE 22.1 CLASSIFICATION OF THE PHYLUM ANNELIDA

Phylum Annelida (ah-nel'i-dah)
The phylum of triploblastic, coelomate animals whose members are metameric (segmented), elongate, and cylindrical or oval in cross section. Annelids have a complete digestive tract; paired, epidermal setae; and a ventral nerve cord. The phylum is divided into three classes.

Class Polychaeta (pol″e-kēt'ah)
The largest annelid class; mostly marine; head with eyes and tentacles; parapodia bear numerous setae; monoecious or dioecious; development frequently involves a trochophore larval stage. *Nereis, Arenicola, Sabella.* More than 5,300 species.

Class Oligochaeta (ol″i-go-kēt'ah)
Few setae and no parapodia; no distinct head; monoecious with direct development; primarily freshwater or terrestrial. *Lumbricus, Tubifex.* Over 3,000 species.

Class Hirudinea (hi'ru-din″e-ah)
Leeches; bodies with 34 segments; each segment subdivided into annuli; anterior and posterior suckers present; monoecious with direct development; parapodia absent; setae reduced or absent. Freshwater, marine, and terrestrial. *Hirudo.* Approximately 500 species.

Metamerism profoundly influences virtually every aspect of annelid structure and function, such as the anatomical arrangement of organs that are coincidentally associated with metamerism. For example, the compartmentalization of the body has resulted in each segment having its own excretory, nervous, and circulatory structures. Two related functions are probably the primary adaptive features of metamerism: flexible support and efficient locomotion. These functions depend on the metameric arrangement of the coelom and can be understood by examining the development of the coelom and the arrangement of body-wall muscles.

During embryonic development, the body cavity of annelids arises by a segmental splitting of a solid mass of mesoderm that occupies the region between ectoderm and endoderm on either side of the embryonic gut tract. Enlargement of each cavity forms a double-membraned septum on the anterior and posterior margin of each coelomic space and dorsal and ventral mesenteries associated with the digestive tract (figure 22.3).

Muscles also develop from the mesodermal layers associated with each segment. A layer of circular muscles lies below the epidermis, and a layer of longitudinal muscles, just below the circular muscles, runs between the septa that separate each segment. In addition, some polychaetes have oblique muscles, and the leeches have dorsoventral muscles.

One advantage of the segmental arrangement of coelomic spaces and muscles is the creation of hydrostatic compartments,

FIGURE 22.2
Evolutionary Relationships of the Annelida. Annelids (shaded in orange) are protostomes with close evolutionary ties to the arthropods.

FIGURE 22.3

Development of Metameric, Coelomic Spaces in Annelids.
(*a*) A solid mesodermal mass separates ectoderm and endoderm in early embryological stages. (*b*) Two cavities in each segment form from the mesoderm splitting on each side of the endoderm (schizocoelous coelom formation). (*c*) These cavities spread in all directions. Enlargement of the coelomic sacs leaves a thin layer of mesoderm applied against the outer body wall (the parietal peritoneum) and the gut tract (the visceral peritoneum), and dorsal and ventral mesenteries form. Anterior and posterior expansion of the coelom in adjacent segments forms the double-membraned septum that separates annelid metameres.

which allow a variety of advantageous locomotor and supportive functions not possible in nonmetameric animals that utilize a hydrostatic skeleton. Each segment can be controlled independently of distant segments, and muscles can act as antagonistic pairs within a segment. The constant volume of coelomic fluid provides a hydrostatic skeleton against which muscles operate. Resultant localized changes in the shape of groups of segments provide the basis for swimming, crawling, and burrowing.

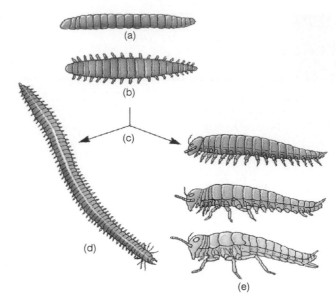

FIGURE 22.4

Possible Origin of Annelids and Arthropods. Possible sequence in the evolution of the annelid/arthropod line from a hypothetical worm-like ancestor. (*a*) Wormlike prototype. (*b*) Paired, metameric appendages develop. (*c*) Divergence of the annelid and arthropod lines. (*d*) Paired appendages develop into parapodia of ancestral polychaetes. (*e*) Extensive tagmatization results in specializations characteristic of the arthropods. A head is a sensory and feeding tagma, a thorax is a locomotor tagma, and an abdomen contains visceral organs.

A second advantage of metamerism is that it lessens the impact of injury. If one or a few segments are injured, adjacent segments, set off from injured segments by septa, may be able to maintain nearly normal functions, which increases the likelihood that the worm, or at least a part of it, will survive the trauma.

A third advantage of metamerism is that it permits the modification of certain regions of the body for specialized functions, such as feeding, locomotion, and reproduction. The specialization of body regions in a metameric animal is called **tagmatization** (Gr. *tagma*, arrangement). Although it is best developed in the arthropods, some annelids also display tagmatization. (The arthropods include animals such as insects, spiders, mites, ticks, and crayfish.)

Virtually all zoologists agree that, because of similarities in the development of metamerism in the two groups, annelids and arthropods are closely related. Other common features include triploblastic coelomate organization, bilateral symmetry, a complete digestive tract, and a ventral nerve cord. As usual, fossil evidence documenting ancestral pathways that led from a common ancestor to the earliest representatives of these two phyla is scant. Zoologists are confident that the annelids and arthropods evolved from a marine, wormlike, bilateral ancestor that possessed metameric design. Figure 22.4 depicts a sequence of evolutionary changes that may have given rise to these two phyla.

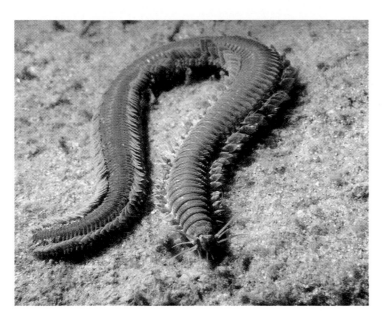

FIGURE 22.5

Class Polychaeta. External structure of *Nereis virens*. Note the numerous parapodia.

Stop and Ask Yourself

1. What are two hypotheses regarding the origin of the phylum Annelida?
2. What is metamerism? What is tagmatization?
3. What are three advantages of metameric organization?
4. What other phylum is closely related to the annelids?

CLASS POLYCHAETA

Members of the class Polychaeta (pol″-e-kēt′ah) (Gr. *polys*, many + *chaite*, hair) are mostly marine, and are usually between 5 and 10 cm long (*see table 22.1*). With more than 5,300 species, Polychaeta is the largest of the annelid classes. Polychaetes have adapted to a variety of habitats. Many live on the ocean floor, under rocks and shells, and within the crevices of coral reefs. Other polychaetes are burrowers and move through their substrate by peristaltic contractions of the body wall. A bucket of intertidal sand normally yields vast numbers and an amazing variety of these burrowing annelids. Other polychaetes construct tubes of cemented sand grains or secreted organic materials. Mucus-lined tubes serve as protective retreats and feeding stations.

EXTERNAL STRUCTURE AND LOCOMOTION

In addition to metamerism, the most distinctive feature of polychaetes is the presence of lateral extensions called **parapodia** (Gr. *para*, beside + *podion*, little foot) (figure 22.5). Chitinous rods support the parapodia, and numerous setae project from the parapodia, giving them their class name. **Setae** (L. *saeta*, bristle) are bristles secreted from invaginations of the distal ends of parapodia. They aid locomotion by digging into the substrate and also hold a worm in its burrow or tube.

The **prostomium** (Gr. *pro*, before + *stoma*, mouth) of a polychaete is a lobe that projects dorsally and anteriorly to the mouth and contains numerous sensory structures, including eyes, antennae, palps, and ciliated pits or grooves, called nuchal organs. The first body segment, the **peristomium** (Gr. *peri*, around), surrounds the mouth and bears sensory tentacles or cirri.

The epidermis of polychaetes consists of a single layer of columnar cells that secrete a protective, nonliving **cuticle.** Some polychaetes have epidermal glands that secrete luminescent compounds.

Various species of polychaetes are capable of walking, fast crawling, or swimming. To do so, the longitudinal muscles on one side of the body act antagonistically to the longitudinal muscles on the other side of the body so that undulatory waves move along the length of the body from the posterior end toward the head. The propulsive force is the result of parapodia and setae acting against the substrate or water. Parapodia on opposite sides of the body are out of phase with one another. When longitudinal muscles on one side of a segment contract, the parapodial muscles on that side also contract, stiffening the parapodium and protruding the setae for the power stroke (figure 22.6*a*). As a polychaete changes from a slow crawl to swimming, the period and amplitude of undulatory waves increase (figure 22.6*b*).

Burrowing polychaetes push their way through sand and mud by contractions of the body wall or by eating their way through the substrate. In the latter, polychaetes digest organic matter in the substrate, and eliminate absorbed and undigestible materials via the anus.

FEEDING AND THE DIGESTIVE SYSTEM

The digestive tract of polychaetes is a straight tube that mesenteries and septa suspend in the body cavity. The anterior region of the digestive tract is modified into a proboscis that special protractor muscles and coelomic pressure can evert through the mouth. Retractor muscles bring the proboscis back into the peristomium. In some, when the proboscis is everted, paired jaws are opened and may be used for seizing prey. Predatory polychaetes may not leave their burrow or coral crevice. When prey approaches a burrow entrance, the worm quickly extends its anterior portion, everts the proboscis, and pulls the prey back into the burrow. Some polychaetes have poison glands at the base of the jaw. Other polychaetes are herbivores and scavengers, and use jaws for tearing food. Deposit-feeding polychaetes (e.g., *Arenicola*, the lugworm) extract organic matter from the marine sediments they ingest. The digestive tract consists of a pharynx that, when everted, forms the proboscis; a storage sac, called a crop; a grinding gizzard; and a long, straight intestine. These are similar to digestive organs of earthworms (*see figure 22.13*). Organic matter is digested extracellularly, and the inorganic particles are passed through the intestine and released as "castings."

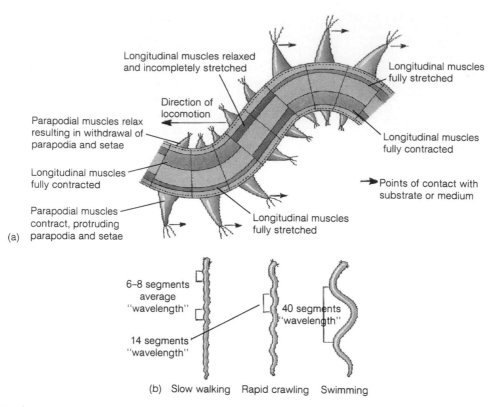

(b)   Slow walking   Rapid crawling   Swimming

FIGURE 22.6

Polychaete Locomotion. (*a*) Dorsal view of a primitive polychaete, showing the antagonism of longitudinal muscles on opposite sides of the body and the resultant protrusion and movement of parapodia. (*b*) Both the period and amplitude of locomotor waves increase as a polychaete changes from a "slow walk" to a swimming mode. *From: "A LIFE OF INVERTEBRATES" © 1979 W. D. Russell-Hunter.*

Many sedentary and tube-dwelling polychaetes are filter feeders. They usually lack a proboscis but possess other specialized feeding structures. Some tube dwellers, called fanworms, possess radioles that form a funnel-shaped fan. ❸ Cilia on the radioles circulate water through the fan, trapping food particles. Trapped particles are carried along a food groove at the axis of the radiole. During transport, a sorting mechanism rejects the largest particles and transports the finest particles to the mouth. Another filter feeder, *Chaetopterus*, lives in a U-shaped tube and secretes a mucous bag that collects food particles, which may be as small as 1 μm. The parapodia of segments 14 through 16 are modified into fans that create filtration currents. When full, the entire mucous bag is ingested.

Elimination of digestive waste products can be a problem for tube-dwelling polychaetes. Those that live in tubes that open at both ends simply have wastes carried away by water circulating through the tube. Those that live in tubes that open at one end must turn around in the tube to defecate, or they may use ciliary tracts along the body wall to carry feces to the tube opening.

Polychaetes that inhabit substrates rich in dissolved organic matter can absorb as much as 20 to 40% of their energy requirements across their body wall as sugars and other organic compounds. This method of feeding occurs in other animal phyla, too, but rarely accounts for more than 1% of their energy needs.

GAS EXCHANGE AND CIRCULATION

Respiratory gases of most annelids simply diffuse across the body wall, and parapodia increase the surface area for these exchanges. In many polychaetes, parapodial gills further increase the surface area for gas exchange.

Polychaetes have a closed circulatory system. Oxygen is usually carried in combination with molecules called respiratory pigments, which are usually dissolved in the plasma rather than contained in blood cells. ❹ Blood may be colorless, green, or red, depending on the presence and/or type of respiratory pigment.

Contractile elements of polychaete circulatory systems consist of a dorsal aorta that lies just above the digestive tract and propels blood from rear to front, and a ventral aorta that lies ventral to the digestive tract and propels blood from front to rear. Running between these two vessels are two or three sets of segmental vessels that receive blood from the ventral aorta and break into capillary beds in the gut and body wall. Capillaries coalesce again into segmental vessels that deliver blood to the dorsal aorta (figure 22.7).

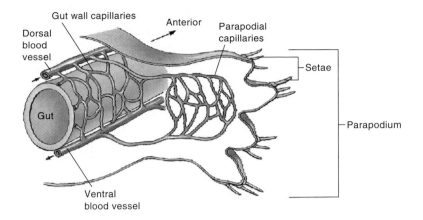

FIGURE 22.7

Circulatory System of a Polychaete.   Cross section through the body and a parapodium. In the closed circulatory system shown here, blood passes posterior to anterior in the dorsal vessel and anterior to posterior in the ventral vessel. Capillary beds interconnect dorsal and ventral vessel.

NERVOUS AND SENSORY FUNCTIONS

Nervous systems are similar in all three classes of annelids. The annelid nervous system includes a pair of suprapharyngeal ganglia, which connect to a pair of subpharyngeal ganglia by circumpharyngeal connectives that run dorsoventrally along either side of the pharynx. A double ventral nerve cord runs the length of the worm along the ventral margin of each coelomic space, and a paired segmental ganglion is in each segment. The double ventral nerve cord and paired segmental ganglia may fuse to varying extents in different taxonomic groups. Lateral nerves emerge from each segmental ganglion, supplying the body-wall musculature and other structures of that segment (figure 22.8a).

Segmental ganglia coordinate swimming and crawling movements in isolated segments. (Anyone who has used portions of worms as live fish bait can confirm that the head end—with the pharyngeal ganglia—is not necessary for coordinated movements.) Each segment acts separately from, but is closely coordinated with, neighboring segments. The subpharyngeal ganglia help mediate locomotor functions requiring coordination of distant segments. The suprapharyngeal ganglia probably control motor and sensory functions involved with feeding, and sensory functions associated with forward locomotion.

In addition to small-diameter fibers that help coordinate locomotion, the ventral nerve cord also contains giant fibers involved with escape reactions (figure 22.8b). For example, a harsh stimulus, such as a fishhook, at one end of a worm causes rapid withdrawal from the stimulus. Giant fibers are approximately 50 μm in diameter and conduct nerve impulses at 30 m/second (as opposed to 0.5 m/second in the smaller, 4 μm diameter annelid fibers).

Polychaetes have various sensory structures. Two to four pairs of eyes are on the surface of the prostomium. They vary in complexity from a simple cup of receptor cells to structures made up of a cornea, lens, and vitreous body. Most polychaetes react negatively to increased light intensities. Fanworms, however, re-

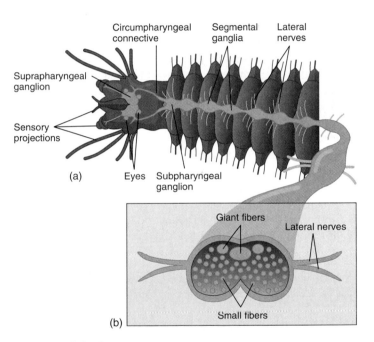

FIGURE 22.8

Nervous System of a Polychaete. (a) Connectives link suprapharyngeal and subpharyngeal ganglia. Segmental ganglia and lateral nerves occur along the length of the worm. (b) Cross section of the ventral nerve cord, showing giant fibers.

act negatively to decreasing light intensities. If shadows cross them, fanworms retreat into their tubes. This response is believed to help protect fanworms from passing predators. Nuchal organs are pairs of ciliated sensory pits or slits in the head region. Nerves from the suprapharyngeal ganglia innervate nuchal organs, which are thought to be chemoreceptors for food detection. Statocysts are in the head region of polychaetes, and ciliated tubercles, ridges, and bands, all of which contain receptors for tactile senses, cover the body wall.

EXCRETION

Annelids excrete ammonia, and because ammonia diffuses readily into the water, most nitrogen excretion probably occurs across the body wall. Excretory organs of annelids are more active in regulating water and ion balances, although these abilities are limited. Most marine polychaetes, if presented with extremely diluted seawater, cannot survive the osmotic influx of water and the resulting loss of ions. The evolution of efficient osmoregulatory abilities has allowed only a few polychaetes to invade freshwater.

The excretory organs of annelids, like those of many invertebrates, are called nephridia. Annelids have two types of nephridia. A protonephridium consists of a tubule with a closed bulb at one end and a connection to the outside of the body at the other end. Protonephridia have a tuft of flagella in their bulbular end that drives fluids through the tubule (figure 22.9a; see also figure 19.6). Some primitive polychaetes possess paired, segmentally arranged protonephridia that have their bulbular end projecting through the anterior septum into an adjacent segment and the opposite end opening through the body wall at a nephridiopore.

Most polychaetes possess a second kind of nephridium, called a metanephridium. A **metanephridium** consists of an open, ciliated funnel, called a nephrostome, that projects through an anterior septum into the coelom of an adjacent segment. At the opposite end, a tubule opens through the body wall at a nephridiopore or, occasionally, through the intestine (figure 22.9b,c). There is usually one pair of metanephridia per segment, and tubules may be extensively coiled, with one portion dilated into a bladder. A capillary bed is usually associated with the tubule of a metanephridium for active transport of ions between the blood and the nephridium (figure 22.9d).

Some polychaetes also have chloragogen tissue associated with the digestive tract. This tissue functions in amino acid metabolism in all annelids and is described further in a later section.

REGENERATION, REPRODUCTION, AND DEVELOPMENT

All polychaetes have remarkable powers of regeneration. They can replace lost parts, and some species have break points that allow worms to sever themselves when a predator grabs them. Lost segments are later regenerated.

Some polychaetes reproduce asexually by budding or by transverse fission; however, sexual reproduction is much more common. Most polychaetes are dioecious. Gonads develop as masses of gametes and project from the coelomic peritoneum. Primitively, gonads occur in every body segment, but most polychaetes have gonads limited to specific segments. Gametes are shed into the coelom, where they mature. Mature female worms are often packed with eggs. Gametes may exit worms by entering nephrostomes of metanephridia and exiting through the nephridiopore, or they may be released, in some polychaetes, after the

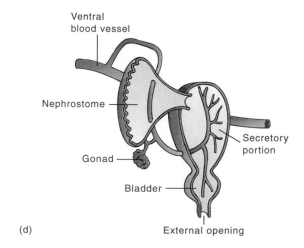

FIGURE 22.9

Annelid Nephridia. (a) Protonephridium. The bulbular ends of this nephridium contain a tuft of flagella that drives wastes to the outside of the body. In primitive polychaetes, a gonoduct (coelomoduct) carries reproductive products to the outside of the body. (b) Metanephridium. An open ciliated funnel (the nephrostome) drives wastes to the outside of the body. (c) In modern annelids, the gonoduct and the nephridial tubules undergo varying degrees of fusion. (d) Nephridia of modern annelids are closely associated with capillary beds for secretion, and nephridial tubules may have an enlarged bladder. From: "A LIFE OF INVERTEBRATES" © 1979 W. D. Russell-Hunter.

worm ruptures. In these cases, the adult soon dies. Only a few polychaetes have separate gonoducts, a condition believed to be primitive (*see figure 22.9a–c*).

Fertilization is external in most polychaetes, although a few species copulate. A unique copulatory habit has been reported in *Platynereis megalops* from Woods Hole, Massachusetts. Toward the end of their lives, male and female worms cease feeding, and their intestinal tracts begin to degenerate. At this time, gametes have accumulated in the body cavity. During sperm transfer, male and female worms coil together, and the male inserts his anus into the mouth of the female. Because the digestive tracts of the worms have degenerated, sperm transfer directly from the male's coelom to the egg-filled coelom of the female. This method ensures fertilization of most eggs, after which the female sheds eggs from her anus. Both worms die soon after copulation.

Epitoky is the formation of a reproductive individual (an epitoke) that differs from the nonreproductive form of the species (an atoke). Frequently, an epitoke has a body that is modified into two body regions. Anterior segments carry on normal maintenance functions, and posterior segments are enlarged and filled with gametes. The epitoke may have modified parapodia for more efficient swimming.

This chapter begins with an account of the reproductive swarming habits of *Eunice viridis* (the Samoan palolo worm) and one culture's response to those swarms. Similar swarming occurs in other species, usually in response to changing light intensities and lunar periods. The Atlantic palolo worm, for example, swarms at dawn during the first and third quarters of the July lunar cycle.

⑤ Zoologists believe that swarming of epitokes accomplishes at least three things. First, because nonreproductive individuals remain safe below the surface waters, predators cannot devastate an entire population. Second, external fertilization requires that individuals become reproductively active at the same time and in close proximity to one another. Swarming ensures that large numbers of individuals are in the right place at the proper time. Third, swarming of vast numbers of individuals for brief periods provides a banquet for predators. However, because vast numbers of prey are available for only short periods during the year, predator populations cannot increase beyond the limits of their normal diets. Therefore, predators can dine gluttonously and still leave epitokes that will yield the next generation of animals.

Spiral cleavage of fertilized eggs may result in planktonic trochophore larvae that bud segments anterior to the anus. Larvae eventually settle to the substrate (figure 22.10). As growth proceeds, newer segments continue to be added posteriorly. Thus, the anterior end of a polychaete is the oldest end. Many other polychaetes lack a trochophore and display direct development or metamorphosis from another larval stage.

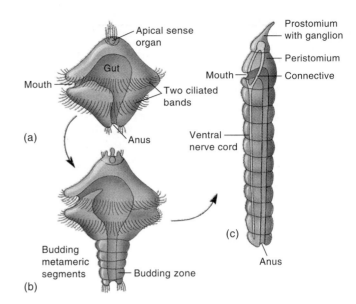

FIGURE 22.10

Polychaete Development. (*a*) Trochophore. (*b*) A later planktonic larva, showing the development of body segments. As more segments develop, the larva settles to the substrate. (*c*) Juvenile worm. *From: "A LIFE OF INVERTEBRATES" © 1979 W. D. Russell-Hunter.*

Stop and Ask Yourself

5. How is the body wall of a polychaete involved with crawling movement?
6. What is the function of giant nerve fibers in polychaetes?
7. What is epitoky? Why is it advantageous for some polychaetes?

CLASS OLIGOCHAETA

The class Oligochaeta (ol″ı-go-kēt′ah) has over three thousand species found throughout the world in freshwater and terrestrial habitats (*see table 22.1*). A few oligochaetes are estuarine, and some are marine. Aquatic species live in shallow water, where they burrow in mud and debris. Terrestrial species live in soils with high organic content and rarely leave their burrows. In hot, dry weather, they may retreat to depths of 3 m below the surface. Soil-conditioning habits of earthworms are well known (box 22.1). *Lumbricus terrestris* is commonly used in zoology laboratories because of its large size. It was introduced to the United States from northern Europe and has flourished. Common native species like *Eisenia foetida* and various species of *Allolobophora* are smaller.

BOX	22.1	SOIL CONDITIONING BY EARTHWORMS

Earthworms have had an inestimable impact on the development of earth's soil. For the past 100 million years, earthworms have evolved with deciduous vegetation. Leaf fall and the death of land plants have provided a massive food source for earthworms and other soil-inhabiting organisms. The excrement, death, and decay of these soil organisms build the organic constituents of soils, and earthworm burrowing aerates the soil and improves drainage.

In typical grassland and woodland soils, earthworms reach populations of hundreds of animals per square meter. They often dominate the invertebrate biomass (the total mass of invertebrate animals) in a region. Earthworms ingest soil as they feed on organic matter and as they burrow through the soil. Charles Darwin estimated that 15 tons of soil per acre per year passed through earthworm bodies. Recent, more accurate estimates of earthworm populations give even more impressive tillage figures of nearly 40 tons per acre per year!

Earthworms are surface feeders that pull leaf fragments and other plant debris into their burrows at night. Of the plant matter that earthworms ingest, less than 10% is incorporated into worm tissues. The rest passes through the digestive tract, is incorporated into castings (fecal material and soil), and is released deeper in the soil. Earthworm castings are also rich in ammonia, which is a form of nitrogen that some plants can use.

Earthworms are vegetation shredders in soils. Shredding vegetation and incorporating it into fecal material increases the surface area of plant matter by several orders of magnitude and hastens its eventual decomposition by bacteria and fungi. Researchers have demonstrated the role of shredders in the breakdown of plant litter by soil animals. Leaf-filled nylon bags were buried in the soil. Some bags had a 0.5 mm mesh size, which excluded all earthworms and other large invertebrates. Other bags had a mesh size of 7 mm, which allowed all invertebrates to enter. The rate of breakdown of leaf litter was reduced by approximately two-thirds in the small-mesh bags.

EXTERNAL STRUCTURE AND LOCOMOTION

Oligochaetes (Gr. *oligos*, few + *chaite*, hair) have setae, but fewer than are found in polychaetes (thus, the derivation of the class name). Oligochaetes lack parapodia because parapodia and long setae would interfere with their burrowing lifestyles, although they do have short setae on their integument. The prostomium consists of a small lobe or cone in front of the mouth and lacks sensory appendages. A series of segments in the anterior half of an oligochaete is usually swollen into a girdlelike structure called the **clitellum** that secretes mucus during copulation and forms a cocoon (figure 22.11). As in the polychaetes, a nonliving, secreted cuticle covers the body.

Oligochaete locomotion involves the antagonism of circular and longitudinal muscles in groups of segments. Neurally controlled waves of contraction move from rear to front.

Segments bulge and setae protrude when longitudinal muscles contract, providing points of contact with the burrow wall. In front of each region of longitudinal muscle contraction, circular muscles contract, causing the setae to retract, and the segments to elongate and push forward. Contraction of longitudinal muscles in segments behind a bulging region pulls those segments forward. Thus, segments move forward relative to the burrow as waves of muscle contraction move anteriorly on the worm (figure 22.12).

Burrowing is the result of coelomic hydrostatic pressure being transmitted toward the prostomium. As an earthworm pushes its way through the soil, it uses expanded posterior segments and

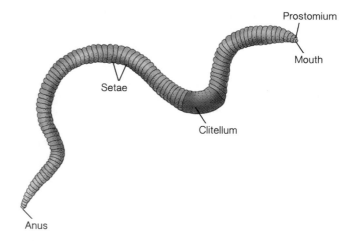

FIGURE 22.11

Class Annelida. External structures of the earthworm, *Lumbricus terrestris*.

protracted setae to anchor itself to its burrow wall.   ⑥ Any person pursuing fishing worms experiences the effectiveness of this anchor when trying to extract a worm from its burrow. Contraction of circular muscles transforms the prostomium into a conical wedge, 1 mm in diameter at its tip. Contraction of body-wall muscles generates coelomic pressure that forces the prostomium through the soil. During burrowing, earthworms swallow considerable quantities of soil.

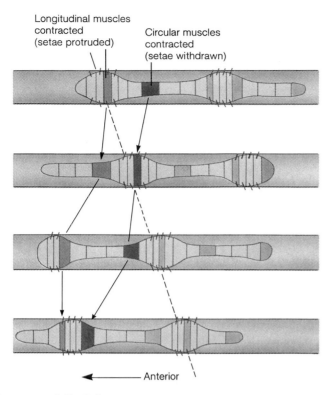

FIGURE 22.12

Earthworm Locomotion. Arrows designate activity in specific segments of the body, and broken lines indicate regions of contact with the substrate. *From: "A LIFE OF INVERTEBRATES" © 1979 W. D. Russell-Hunter.*

FEEDING AND THE DIGESTIVE SYSTEM

Oligochaetes are scavengers and feed primarily on fallen and decaying vegetation, which they drag into their burrows at night. The digestive tract of oligochaetes is tubular and straight (figure 22.13). The mouth leads to a muscular pharynx. In the earthworm, pharyngeal muscles attach to the body wall. The pharynx acts as a pump for ingesting food. The mouth pushes against food, and the pharynx pumps the food into the esophagus. The esophagus is narrow and tubular, and frequently expands to form a stomach, crop, or gizzard; the latter two are common in terrestrial species. A crop is a thin-walled storage structure, and a gizzard is a muscular, cuticle-lined grinding structure. Calciferous glands are evaginations of the esophageal wall that rid the body of excess calcium absorbed from food. They also help regulate the pH of body fluids. The intestine is a straight tube and is the principal site of digestion and absorption. A dorsal fold of the lumenal epithelium called the typhlosole substantially increases the surface area of the intestine (figure 22.14). The intestine ends at the anus.

GAS EXCHANGE AND CIRCULATION

Oligochaete respiratory and circulatory functions are as described for polychaetes. Some segmental vessels expand and may be contractile. In the earthworm, for example, expanded segmental vessels surrounding the esophagus propel blood between dorsal and ventral blood vessels and anteriorly in the ventral vessel toward the mouth. Even though these are sometimes called "hearts," the

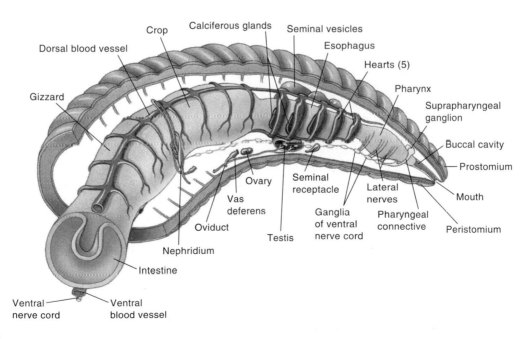

FIGURE 22.13

Earthworm Structure. Lateral view of the internal structures in the anterior third of an earthworm.

Longitudinal muscles
Circular muscles
Chloragogen cells
Coelomic lining
Typhlosole
Epidermis

Dorsal blood vessel
Muscular wall of intestine
Nephridium
Cuticle

Setae
Coelom
Ventral blood vessel
Ventral nerve cord
Subneural blood vessel

Nephridiopore
Nephrostome
Gland cell

FIGURE 22.14

Earthworm Cross Section. The nephrostomes shown here would actually be associated with the next anterior segment.

main propulsive structures are the dorsal and ventral vessels (*see* figure 22.13). Branches from the ventral vessel supply the intestine and body wall.

NERVOUS AND SENSORY FUNCTIONS

The ventral nerve cords and all ganglia of oligochaetes have undergone a high degree of fusion. Other aspects of nervous structure and function are essentially the same as those described earlier for polychaetes. As with polychaetes, giant fibers mediate escape responses. An escape response results from the stimulation of either the anterior or posterior end of a worm. An impulse conducted to the opposite end of the worm initiates the formation of an anchor, and longitudinal muscles contract to quickly pull the worm away from the stimulus.

Oligochaetes lack well-developed eyes, which is not surprising, given their subterranean lifestyle. Animals living in perpetual darkness often do not have well-developed eyes. Other oligochaetes have simple pigment-cup ocelli, and all have a "dermal light sense" that arises from photoreceptor cells scattered over the dorsal and lateral surfaces of the body. Scattered photoreceptor cells mediate a negative phototaxis in strong light (evidenced by movement away from the light source) and a positive phototaxis in weak light (evidenced by movement toward the light source).

Oligochaetes are sensitive to a wide variety of chemical and mechanical stimuli. Receptors for these stimuli are scattered over the body surface, especially around the prostomium.

EXCRETION

Oligochaetes use metanephridia for excretion and for ion and water regulation. As with polychaetes, funnels of metanephridia are associated with the segment just anterior to the segment containing the tubule and the nephridiopore. Nitrogenous wastes include ammonia and urea. Oligochaetes excrete copious amounts of very dilute urine, although they retain vital ions, which is important for organisms living in environments where water is plentiful but essential ions are limited.

Oligochaetes (as well as other annelids) possess chloragogen tissue that surrounds the dorsal blood vessel and lies over the dorsal surface of the intestine (*see figure 22.14*). **Chloragogen tissue** acts similarly to the vertebrate liver. It is a site of amino acid metabolism. Chloragogen tissue deaminates amino acids and converts ammonia to urea. It also converts excess carbohydrates into energy-storage molecules of glycogen and fat.

REPRODUCTION AND DEVELOPMENT

All oligochaetes are monoecious and exchange sperm during copulation. One or two pairs of testes and one pair of ovaries are located on the anterior septum of certain anterior segments. Both the sperm ducts and the oviducts have ciliated funnels at their proximal ends to draw gametes into their respective tubes.

Testes are closely associated with three pairs of **seminal vesicles,** which are sites for maturation and storage of sperm prior to their release. **Seminal receptacles** receive sperm during copulation. A pair of very small ovisacs, associated with oviducts, are sites for the maturation and storage of eggs prior to egg release (figure 22.15).

During copulation of *Lumbricus,* two worms line up facing in opposite directions, with the ventral surfaces of their anterior ends in contact with each other. This orientation lines up the clitellum of one worm with the genital segments of the other worm. A mucous sheath that the clitellum secretes envelops the anterior halves of both worms and holds the worms in place. Some species also have penile structures and genital setae that help maintain contact between worms. In *Lumbricus,* the sperm duct releases sperm, which travel along the external, ventral body wall in sperm grooves formed when special muscles contract. Muscular contractions along this groove help propel sperm toward the openings of the seminal receptacles. In other oligochaetes, copulation results in the alignment of sperm duct and seminal receptacle openings, and sperm transfer is direct. Copulation lasts 2 to 3 hours, during which both worms give and receive sperm.

Following copulation, the clitellum forms a cocoon for the deposition of eggs and sperm. The cocoon consists of mucoid and

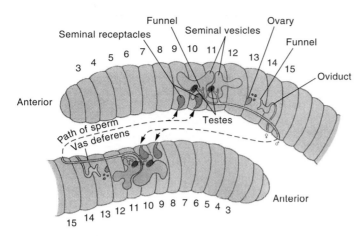

FIGURE 22.15

Earthworm Reproduction. Mating earthworms, showing arrangements of reproductive structures and the path sperm take during sperm exchange (shown by arrows).

chitinous materials that encircle the clitellum. The clitellum secretes a food reserve, albumen, into the cocoon, and the worm begins to back out of the cocoon. Eggs are deposited in the cocoon as the cocoon passes the openings to the oviducts, and sperm are released as the cocoon passes the openings to the seminal receptacles. Fertilization occurs in the cocoon, and as the worm continues backing out, the ends of the cocoon are sealed, and the cocoon is deposited in moist soil.

Spiral cleavage is modified, and no larva forms. Hatching occurs in one to a few weeks, depending on the species, when young worms emerge from one end of the cocoon.

Freshwater oligochaetes also reproduce asexually. Asexual reproduction involves transverse division of a worm, followed by regeneration of missing segments.

Stop and Ask Yourself

8. How does an earthworm move across a substrate? How does an earthworm burrow?

9. What is the function of each of the following: (a) calciferous glands, (b) the typhlosole, and (c) chloragogen tissue?

10. How would you describe the method of sperm transfer and egg deposition in earthworms?

11. In what way is oligochaete development different from polychaete development?

CLASS HIRUDINEA

The class Hirudinea (hi'ru-din"e-ah) (L. *hirudin,* leech) contains approximately 500 species of leeches (*see table 22.1*). Most leeches are freshwater; others are marine or completely terrestrial. Leeches prey on small invertebrates or feed on body fluids of vertebrates (box 22.2).

EXTERNAL STRUCTURE AND LOCOMOTION

Leeches lack parapodia and head appendages. Setae are absent in most leeches. In a few species, setae occur only on anterior segments. Leeches are dorsoventrally flattened and taper anteriorly. They have 34 segments, but the segments are difficult to distinguish externally because they have become secondarily divided. Several secondary divisions, called **annuli,** are in each true segment. Anterior and posterior segments are usually modified into suckers (figure 22.16).

Modifications of body-wall musculature and the coelom influence patterns of leech locomotion. The musculature of leeches is more complex than that of other annelids. A layer of oblique muscles is between the circular and longitudinal muscle layers. In addition, dorsoventral muscles are responsible for the typical leech flattening. The leech coelom has lost its metameric partitioning. Septa are lost, and connective tissue has invaded the coelom, resulting in a series of interconnecting sinuses.

These modifications have resulted in altered patterns of locomotion. Rather than being able to utilize independent coelomic compartments, the leech has a single hydrostatic cavity and uses it in a looping type of locomotion. Figure 22.17 describes the mechanics of this locomotion. Leeches also swim using undulations of the body.

FEEDING AND THE DIGESTIVE SYSTEM

Many leeches feed on body fluids or the entire bodies of other invertebrates. Some feed on blood of vertebrates, including human blood. ⑦ Leeches are sometimes called parasites; however, the association between a leech and its host is relatively brief. Therefore, describing leeches as predatory is probably more accurate. Leeches are also not species specific, as are most parasites. (Leeches are, however, class specific. That is, a leech that preys on a turtle may also prey on an alligator, but probably would not prey on a fish or a frog.)

The mouth of a leech opens in the middle of the anterior sucker. In some leeches, the anterior digestive tract is modified into a protrusible proboscis, lined inside and outside by a cuticle. In others, the mouth is armed with three chitinous jaws. While feeding, a leech attaches to its prey by the anterior sucker and either extends its proboscis into the prey or uses its jaws to slice

BOX 22.2   LEECHES AND SCIENCE

At first mention of the word leech, most thoughts turn to the medicinal leech, *Hirudo medicinalis* (figure 1), and the practice of bloodletting. In past centuries, various illnesses have been attributed to "bad blood," and bloodletting was common. Medicinal leeches were used in bloodletting because when they feed, they ingest seven to eight times their weight in blood—one of the biggest meals in the animal kingdom. After such a meal, the leech may not feed again for a year.

The writings of Galen, an early Greek physician, document the use of leeches in bloodletting during the second century. The practice was common through the early nineteenth century. The medicinal leech and medicine became almost synonymous. Physicians themselves were sometimes (respectfully) referred to as "leeches." During the late nineteenth and early twentieth century, the use of leeches in medicine declined. Now, however, the medicinal leech is again being used in medicine to remove excess blood from tissues after plastic surgery or after reattachment of amputated appendages. If the excess blood is not removed, blood accumulating in tissues of postoperative patients often slows the regrowth of capillary beds and can cause tissues to die.

Researchers are also using leeches to investigate the physiology of nervous systems. Leeches are good research subjects because their nervous system is simpler than that of many other animals that show system-level organization, and because the nerve cells of all animals share similar physiological properties. Leech nerve cells secrete certain chemicals, such as serotonin, that help regulate all aspects of leech feeding—from finding prey to ingesting blood. Organisms such as leeches may hold the keys to discovering the roles of essentially identical chemicals in the nervous systems of other animals.

FIGURE 1   The Medicinal Leech, *Hirudo medicinalis.*

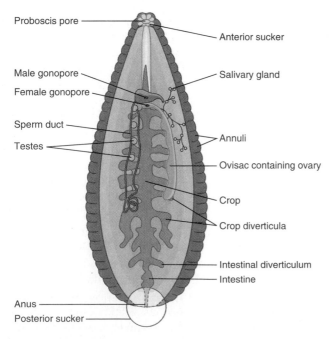

FIGURE 22.16

Internal Structure of a Leech. Annuli subdivide each true segment. Septa do not subdivide the coelom.

Labels: Proboscis pore, Anterior sucker, Male gonopore, Salivary gland, Female gonopore, Sperm duct, Annuli, Testes, Ovisac containing ovary, Crop, Crop diverticula, Intestinal diverticulum, Intestine, Anus, Posterior sucker

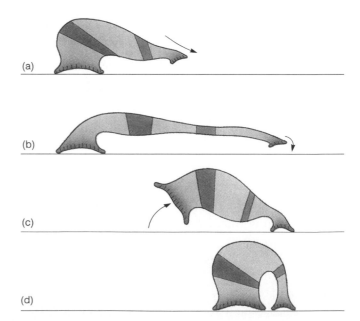

FIGURE 22.17

Leech Locomotion. *(a,b)* Attachment of the posterior sucker causes reflexive release of the anterior sucker, contraction of circular muscles, and relaxation of longitudinal muscles. This muscular activity compresses fluids in the single hydrostatic compartment, and the leech extends. *(c,d)* Attachment of the anterior sucker causes reflexive release of the posterior sucker, the relaxation of circular muscles, and the contraction of longitudinal muscles, causing body fluids to expand the diameter of the leech. The leech shortens, and the posterior sucker again attaches. *From: "A LIFE OF INVERTEBRATES" © 1979 W. D. Russell-Hunter.*

through host tissues. Salivary glands secrete an anticoagulant called hirudin that prevents blood from clotting.

Behind the mouth is a muscular pharynx that pumps body fluids of the prey into the leech. The esophagus follows the pharynx and leads to a large stomach with lateral cecae. Most leeches ingest large quantities of blood or other body fluids and gorge their stomachs and lateral cecae, increasing their body mass 2 to 10 times. After engorgement, a leech can tolerate periods of fasting that may last for months. The digestive tract ends in a short intestine and anus (*see figure 22.16*).

GAS EXCHANGE AND CIRCULATION

Leeches exchange gases across the body wall. Some leeches retain the basic annelid circulatory pattern, but in most leeches, it is highly modified, and coelomic sinuses replace vessels. Coelomic fluid has taken over the function of blood and, except in two orders, respiratory pigments are lacking.

NERVOUS AND SENSORY FUNCTIONS

The leech nervous system is similar to that of other annelids. Ventral nerve cords are unfused, except at the ganglia. The suprapharyngeal and subpharyngeal ganglia and the pharyngeal connectives all fuse into a nerve ring that surrounds the pharynx. Ganglia at the posterior end of the animal fuse in a similar way.

A variety of epidermal sense organs are widely scattered over the body. Most leeches have photoreceptor cells in pigment cups (2 to 10) along the dorsal surface of the anterior segments. Normally, leeches are negatively phototactic, but when searching for food, the behavior of some leeches changes, and they become positively phototactic, which increases the likelihood of contacting prey that happen to pass by.

Hirudo medicinalis, the medicinal leech, has a well-developed temperature sense, which helps it detect the higher body temperature of its mammalian prey. Other leeches are attracted to extracts of prey tissues.

All leeches have sensory cells with terminal bristles in a row along the middle annulus of each segment. These sensory cells, called sensory papillae, are of uncertain function but are taxonomically important.

EXCRETION

Leeches have 10 to 17 pairs of metanephridia, one per segment in the middle segments of the body. Their metanephridia are highly modified and possess, in addition to the nephrostome and tubule, a capsule believed to be involved with the production of coelomic fluid. Chloragogen tissue proliferates through the body cavity of most leeches.

REPRODUCTION AND DEVELOPMENT

All leeches reproduce sexually and are monoecious. None are capable of asexual reproduction or regeneration. They have a single pair of ovaries and from four to many testes. Leeches have a clitellum that includes three body segments. The clitellum is present only in the spring, when most leeches breed.

Sperm transfer and egg deposition usually occur in the same manner as described for oligochaetes. A penis assists sperm transfer between individuals. A few leeches transfer sperm by expelling a spermatophore from one leech into the integument of another, a form of hypodermic impregnation. Special tissues within the integument connect to the ovaries by short ducts. Cocoons are deposited in the soil or are attached to underwater objects. There are no larval stages, and the offspring are mature by the following spring.

FURTHER PHYLOGENETIC CONSIDERATIONS

Figure 22.18 shows a traditional interpretation of the evolutionary relationships within the Annelida, with the phylum divided into the three classes discussed in this chapter. According to this traditional interpretation, the ancestral polychaetes gave rise to modern polychaetes through adaptive radiation and a group of annelids that invaded freshwater. This freshwater invasion required the ability to regulate the salt and water content of body fluids. The oligochaetes are assumed to have evolved from this group, and some of these early oligochaetes are believed to have given rise to the Hirudinea.

Recent cladistic analysis of the phylum Annelida has cast a shadow on this traditional interpretation. These studies suggest that the phylum Annelida is not a monophyletic grouping and that the polychaetes arose from a metameric ancestor independently of the oligochaetes and leeches. The oligochaetes and leeches form a single clade, and share important characteristics, including the presence of a clitellum. Notice in figure 22.18 that no synapomorphies (derived characteristics) are unique to the oligochaetes. Instead, the oligochaetes are defined by the absence of leech characteristics. These facts support the conclusion that the oligochaetes and leeches should be combined into a single group—Clitellata. If these conclusions are true, then the Polychaeta, Clitellata, Arthropoda (*see chapters 23 and 24*), and Pogonophora (*see endpaper 2*) probably all had their origins in an ancestral metameric species, and the phylum name "Annelida" should be abandoned.

Adding to the uncertainty regarding annelid systematics has been the discovery of microscopic marine annelids grouped as "Archiannelida." Like *Lobatocerebrum*, described earlier in the chapter, these annelids lack a coelom, setae, and some other annelid characteristics. The group is poorly known, and its

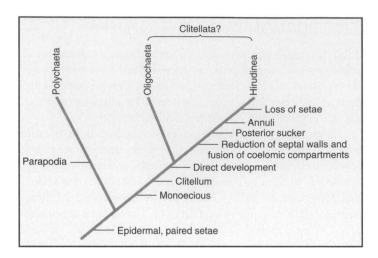

FIGURE 22.18

Annelid Phylogeny. Cladogram illustrating traditional interpretations of the evolutionary relationships of the three annelid classes. The ancestors of the annelids and arthropods were metameric coelomate animals in the protostome lineage. Paired epidermal setae are diagnostic of the phylum. The polychaetes were the first modern annelids to be derived from the ancestral annelids. The oligochaetes and leeches were derived from a second major lineage of annelids. Note that the absence of derived characters distinguishes the oligochaetes from the leeches. Some zoologists believe that these animals should be grouped into a single class, Clitellata (note the question mark in the cladogram).

taxonomic relationships to other annelids are not established. Some of these worms appear to be close to an ancestral form; others are probably derived from the polychaete lineage. When more work on these annelids has been completed, the picture of evolu-

tionary relationships among the annelid groups may be substantially different from current ideas.

The traditional interpretations of later annelid evolution are probably still accurate. The evolutionary history of the polychaetes is a story of impressive adaptive radiation into the variety of body forms and habits described earlier in this chapter. A few polychaetes adapted to freshwater environments. During the Cretaceous period, approximately 100 million years ago, oligochaetes invaded moist, terrestrial environments. This period saw the climax of the giant land reptiles, but more importantly, it was a time of proliferation of flowering plants. ⑧ The reliance of modern oligochaetes on deciduous vegetation can be traced back to their ancestors' exploitation of this food resource. A few oligochaetes secondarily invaded marine environments. Some of the early freshwater oligochaetes gave rise to the leeches. As with the oligochaetes, the leeches colonized marine and terrestrial habitats from freshwater.

Stop and Ask Yourself

12. How is basic annelid metamerism modified in leeches?
13. How do leeches use the body-wall musculature and the body cavity in locomotion?
14. How is leech reproduction similar to oligochaete reproduction? How is reproduction by members of these two classes different?
15. What are the phylogenetic relationships of the annelid classes?

SUMMARY

1. The origin of the Annelida is largely unknown. A diagnostic characteristic of the annelids is metamerism.
2. Metamerism allows efficient utilization of separate coelomic compartments as a hydrostatic skeleton for support and movement. Metamerism also lessens the impact of injury and makes tagmatization possible.
3. Members of the class Polychaeta are mostly marine and possess parapodia with numerous setae. Locomotion of polychaetes involves the antagonism of longitudinal muscles on opposite sides of the body, which creates undulatory waves along the body wall and causes parapodia to act against the substrate.
4. Polychaetes may be predators, herbivores, scavengers, or filter feeders.
5. The nervous system of polychaetes usually consists of a pair of suprapharyngeal ganglia, subpharyngeal ganglia, and double ventral nerve cords that run the length of the worm.
6. Polychaetes have a closed circulatory system. Respiratory pigments dissolved in blood plasma carry oxygen.
7. Polychaetes use either protonephridia or metanephridia in excretion.
8. Most polychaetes are dioecious, and gonads develop from coelomic

epithelium. Fertilization is usually external. Epitoky occurs in some polychaetes.
9. Development of polychaetes usually results in a planktonic trochophore larva that buds off segments near the anus.
10. The class Oligochaeta includes primarily freshwater and terrestrial annelids. Oligochaetes possess few setae, and they lack a head and parapodia.
11. Oligochaetes are scavengers that feed on dead and decaying vegetation. Their digestive tract is tubular and straight, and frequently has modifications for storing and grinding food, and for increasing the surface area for secretion and absorption.
12. Oligochaetes use metanephridia for excretion and for ion and water regulation. Chloragogen tissue is a site for urea formation from protein metabolism, and for synthesis and storage of glycogen and fat.
13. Oligochaetes are monoecious and exchange sperm during copulation.
14. Members of the class Hirudinea are the leeches. Complex arrangements of body-wall muscles and the loss of septa influence patterns of locomotion.

15. Leeches are predatory and feed on body fluids, the entire bodies of other invertebrates, and the blood of vertebrates.

16. Leeches are monoecious, and reproduction and development occur as in oligochaetes.

17. The segmented worms have been included in a single phylum, Annelida, comprised of three classes: Polychaeta, Oligochaeta, and Hirudinea. Recent cladistic analysis indicates that the polychaetes had an origin separate from the oligochaetes and leeches. If this is true, the phylum name "Annelida" should be abandoned.

SELECTED KEY TERMS

chloragogen tissue (p. 350)
clitellum (p. 348)
epitoky (p. 347)
metamerism (p. 340)
metanephridium (p. 346)
parapodia (p. 343)
peristomium (p. 343)
prostomium (p. 343)
tagmatization (p. 342)

CRITICAL THINKING QUESTIONS

1. What evidence links the annelids and arthropods in the same evolutionary line?

2. Distinguish between a protonephridium and a metanephridium. Name a class of annelids whose members may have protonephridia. What other phylum have we studied whose members also had protonephridia? Do you think that metanephridia would be more useful for a coelomate or an acoelomate animal? Explain.

3. In what annelid groups are septa between coelomic compartments lost? What advantages does this loss give each group?

4. What differences in nephridial structure might you expect in freshwater and marine annelids?

5. Few polychaetes have invaded freshwater. Can you think of a reasonable explanation for this?

REFERENCES ON THE WORLD WIDE WEB

1. **Annelid Worm Biodiversity Resources.** This site is a guide to information on annelids and current annelid research. It provides research resources, information on systematics, and news relating to the Annelida.
   http://muse.bio.cornell.edu/~worms/annelid.html

2. **Introduction to the Annelida.** This site is an introduction to the Annelida. It contains information on annelids in the fossil record and annelid life histories, systematics, and morphology.
   http://www.ucmp.berkeley/annelida/annelida.html

3. **BIOSIS Annelida.** A great deal of general information on annelids and specific information on the annelid classes can be found here.
   http://www.york.biosis.org/zrdocs/soolinfo/grp_worm.html

4. **The Burrow.** This site is for those interested in raising worms as a money-making venture. It contains information on earthworm breeding and using worms in composting.
   http://gnv.fdt.net/~windle

5. **FAQ about Earthworms.** This site contains photographs of earthworms and cocoons, answers to frequently asked questions about earthworms, and a description of earthworm sampling techniques.
   http://res.agr.ca/lond/pmrc/faq/earthwor.html

6. **Introduction to the Polychaeta.** This site provides an introduction to the polychaete fossil record. It has information on life histories, ecology, and systematics.
   http://www.ucmp.berkeley.edu/annelida/polyintro.html

7. **Chaetozone.** This site provides a polychaete newsletter and polychaete research news.
   gopher://muse.bio.cornell.edu/11/newsletters/chaetozone

8. **Leeches.** This site provides interesting information on the use of leeches in anticoagulant research. In addition, it answers many frequently asked questions about leeches.
   http://www.biopharm-leeches.com/index.html

SOME LESSER-KNOWN INVERTEBRATES:
POSSIBLE ANNELID RELATIVES

THREE PHYLA OF LIKELY ANNELID RELATIVES: THE ECHIURA, POGONOPHORA, AND SIPUNCULA

The coelomate phyla Echiura, Pogonophora, and Sipuncula comprise fewer than six hundred protostome species that may be annelid relatives. They probably branched off from various points along the annelid-arthropod lineage.

PHYLUM ECHIURA: THE SPOON WORMS

The echiurans (ek-e-yur'ans) (Gr. *echis*, serpent + *oura*, tail) consist of about 130 species of marine animals that have a worldwide distribution. Echiurans usually live in shallow waters, where they either burrow in mud or sand, or live protected in rock crevices. Only a thin cuticle covers the soft body. As a result, the animals keep to the safety of their burrows or crevices, even when feeding. An echiuran feeds by sweeping organic material into its spatula-shaped proboscis that contains a ciliated gutter (figure 1). Echiurans can extend the proboscis for a considerable distance, but they can never retract it into the body. Echiurans are sometimes called spoon worms because of the spatulate nature of the proboscis. Individual echiurans are from 15 to 50 cm in length, but the extensible proboscis may increase their length up to 2 m.

All echiurans are dioecious, and sexual dimorphism is extreme in some species. The eggs or sperm do not complete their development in the single ventral gonad but are released into the coelom. After they mature, special collecting organs release them into the seawater, where fertilization occurs, giving rise to free-swimming trochophore larvae. The early development of echiurans is similar to that of annelids with spiral cleavage. However, later development diverges from the annelid pattern in that no segmentation occurs.

FIGURE 1   **Phylum Echiura.** Internal structure of an echiuran. The muscular body wall surrounds the large coelom, containing a long, coiled intestine. A simple closed circulatory system is present, as well as a ventral nerve cord that extends into the proboscis, several pairs of metanephridia, and a pair of anal sacs that empty into the anus at the end of the worm. Gas exchange occurs through the body wall and proboscis.

FIGURE 2 **Phylum Pogonophora.** Giant red pogonophorans (*Riftia*) inside their tubes.

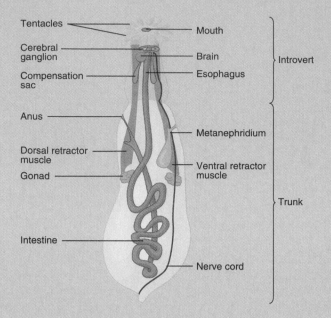

FIGURE 3 **Phylum Sipuncula.** Anatomy of a typical sipunculan. The body is composed of an anterior introvert and a posterior trunk. When the introvert is extended, the anterior portion, with its ciliated tentacles, surrounds the mouth. The long, U-shaped intestine is arranged in a spiral coil. Anteriorly, the intestine ends at an anus that opens to the outside, near the introvert. A large pair of metanephridia is in the anterior trunk. The anterior nervous system is annelid-like, with a supraesophageal brain and a ventral nerve cord that runs the length of the trunk.

of the body. These bacteria fix carbon dioxide into organic compounds that both the host and symbiont can use.

Little is known about pogonophoran reproduction and development. In general, the sexes are separate, and sperm are packaged into spermatophores before a male releases them. The mechanism of fertilization is unknown. After fertilization, a solid blastula develops following radial cleavage.

PHYLUM POGONOPHORA: THE POGONOPHORANS, OR BEARD WORMS

The pogonophorans (po"go-nof'or-ans) (Gr. *pogon*, beard + *phora*, bearing) or beard worms are a group of about 120 species of tube-dwelling marine worms distributed throughout the world's oceans, especially along the continental slopes and in oceanic rifts. They are named for a thick tuft of white or reddish tentacles (*see box 15.1*).

The slender, delicate body is protected in a secreted chitinous tube consisting of a series of rings, to which the worm adds as it grows (figure 2). The tubes are embedded in soft marine sediments in cold, deep (over 100 m), nutrient-poor waters. They range in length from about 10 cm to over 2 m.

Pogonophorans have no mouth or digestive tract. Nutrient uptake is via the outer cuticle and from the endosymbiotic bacteria that pogonophorans harbor in the posterior part (trophosome)

PHYLUM SIPUNCULA: THE SIPUNCULANS, OR PEANUT WORMS

The sipunculans (si-pun'kyu-lans) (Gr. L. *sipunculus*, little siphon) or peanut worms (because of their peanut shape when disturbed) consist of about 350 species of unsegmented, coelomate, burrowing worms found in oceans throughout the world. These worms live in mud, sand, or any protected retreat. Their burrows may be mucus lined, but sipunculans do not construct true tubes as do pogonophorans. They range in length from about 2 mm to 75 cm (figure 3).

Sipunculans are dioecious. Gonads attach to the coelomic wall and liberate their gametes into the coelom. After maturity, the gametes escape into the seawater via the metanephridia. Fertilization is external, cleavage is spiral, and development is either direct (no larva), or it may produce a free-swimming trochophore larva. The larva eventually settles to the bottom and grows into an adult. In a few species, asexual reproduction can also occur by transverse fission—the posterior part of the parent constricts to give rise to a new individual.

THE ARTHROPODS:
BLUEPRINT FOR SUCCESS

Concepts

1. Arthropods have been successful in almost all habitats on the earth. Some ancient arthropods were the first animals to live most of their lives in terrestrial environments.
2. Metamerism with tagmatization, a chitinous exoskeleton, and metamorphosis have contributed to arthropod success.
3. Members of the subphylum Trilobitomorpha are extinct arthropods that were a dominant life-form in the oceans between 345 and 600 million years ago.
4. The bodies of members of the subphylum Chelicerata are divided into two regions and have chelicerae. The class Merostomata contains the horseshoe crabs. The class Arachnida contains the spiders, mites, ticks, and scorpions. Some ancient arachnids were among the earliest terrestrial arthropods, and modern arachnids have numerous adaptations for terrestrial life. The class Pycnogonida contains the sea spiders.
5. Animals in the subphylum Crustacea have biramous appendages and two pairs of antennae. The class Branchiopoda includes the fairy shrimp, brine shrimp, and water fleas. The class Malacostraca includes the crabs, lobsters, crayfish, and shrimp. The classes Copepoda and Cirripedia include the copepods and barnacles, respectively.

Would You Like to Know . . .

1. what is the most abundant animal? (p. 360)
2. how an arthropod grows within the confines of a rigid exoskeleton? (p. 362)
3. how arthropods were preadapted for terrestrialism? (p. 366)
4. why some spiders go ballooning? (p. 368)
5. what two spiders found in the United States are dangerous to humans? (p. 368)
6. what causes the bite of a chigger to itch so badly? (p. 370)
7. what mite lives in the hair follicles of most readers of this text? (p. 370)
8. what crustaceans colonize the hulls of ships? (p. 377)

This chapter answers these and other useful questions.

This chapter contains evolutionary concepts, which are set off in this font.

Evolutionary Perspective

What animal species has the greatest number of individuals? ① The answer can only be an educated guess; however, many zoologists would argue that one of the many species of small (1 to 2 mm) crustaceans, called copepods, that drift in the open oceans must have this honor. Copepods have been very successful, feeding on the vast photosynthetic production of the open oceans (figure 23.1). After only 20 minutes of towing a plankton net behind a slowly moving boat (at the right location and during the right time of year), you can collect over 3 million copepods—enough to solidly pack a 2-gallon pail! Copepods are food for fish, such as herring, sardines, and mackerel, as well as for whale sharks and the largest mammals, the blue whale and its relatives. Humans benefit from copepod production by eating fish that feed on copepods. (Unfortunately, we use only a small fraction of the total food energy in these animals. In spite of half of the earth's human inhabitants lacking protein in their diet, humans process most of the herring and sardines caught into fish meal, which is then fed to poultry and hogs. In eating the poultry and hogs, we lose over 99% of the original energy present in the copepods!)

Copepods are one of many groups of animals belonging to the phylum Arthropoda (ar"thrah-po'dah) (Gr. *arthro*, joint + *podos*, foot). Crayfish, lobsters, spiders, mites, scorpions, and insects are also arthropods. Zoologists have described about 1 million species of arthropods, and recent studies estimate that 30 to 50 million species may yet be undescribed. In this chapter and chapter 24, you will discover the many ways in which some arthropods are considered among the most successful of all animals.

Characteristics of the phylum Arthropoda include:

1. Metamerism modified by the specialization of body regions for specific functions (tagmatization)
2. Chitinous exoskeleton that provides support and protection, and is modified to form sensory structures
3. Paired, jointed appendages
4. Growth accompanied by ecdysis or molting
5. Ventral nervous system
6. Coelom reduced to cavities surrounding gonads and sometimes excretory organs
7. Open circulatory system in which blood is released into tissue spaces (hemocoel) derived from the blastocoel
8. Complete digestive tract
9. Metamorphosis often present; reduces competition between immature and adult stages

Classification and Relationships to Other Animals

As discussed in chapter 22, arthropods and annelids are closely related. Shared protostome characteristics, such as schizocoelous

FIGURE 23.1

The Most Abundant Animal? Copepods, such as *Calanus* sp (shown here), are abundant in the oceans of the world and form important links in oceanic food webs.

coelom formation and the development of the mouth from the blastopore, as well as other common characteristics, such as the presence of a paired ventral nerve cord and metamerism, are evidence of a common ancestry (figure 23.2).

Zoologists, however, disagree about the evolutionary relationships among the arthropods. Many zoologists believe that it is not one phylum, but three. These ideas are discussed at the end of chapter 24. The arthropods are treated in this text as members of a single phylum. Living arthropods are divided into three subphyla: Chelicerata, Crustacea, and Uniramia. All members of a fourth subphylum, Trilobita, are extinct (table 23.1). This chapter examines Trilobita, Chelicerata, and Crustacea, and chapter 24 covers the Uniramia.

Metamerism and Tagmatization

Three aspects of arthropod biology have contributed to their success. One of these is metamerism. Metamerism of arthropods is most evident externally because the arthropod body is often composed of a

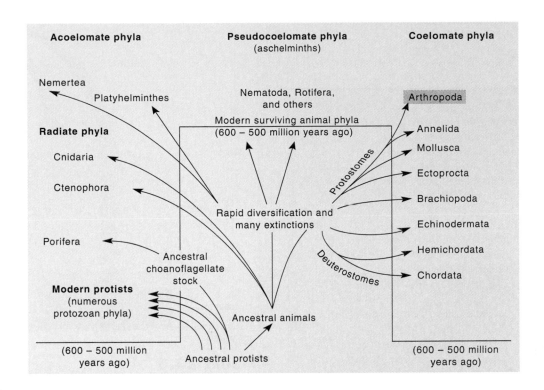

FIGURE 23.2

Evolutionary Relationships of the Arthropods. Arthropods (shaded in orange) are protostomes with close evolutionary ties to the annelids. A paired ventral nerve cord and metamerism in both groups are evidence of common ancestry.

series of similar segments, each bearing a pair of appendages (*see figure 22.4e*). Internally, however, septa do not divide the body cavity of arthropods, and most organ systems are not metamerically arranged. The reason for the loss of internal metamerism is speculative; however, the presence of metamerically arranged hydrostatic compartments would be of little value in the support or locomotion of animals enclosed by an external skeleton (discussed in the next section).

As discussed in chapter 22, metamerism permits the specialization of regions of the body for specific functions. This regional specialization is called tagmatization. In arthropods, body regions, called tagmata (sing., tagma), are specialized for feeding and sensory perception, locomotion, and visceral functions.

THE EXOSKELETON

An external, jointed skeleton, called an **exoskeleton** or **cuticle,** encloses arthropods. The exoskeleton is often cited as the major reason for arthropod success. It provides structural support, protection, impermeable surfaces for prevention of water loss, and a system of levers for muscle attachment and movement.

The exoskeleton covers all body surfaces and invaginations of the body wall, such as the anterior and posterior portions of the gut tract. It is nonliving and is secreted by a single layer of epidermal cells (figure 23.3). The epidermal layer is sometimes called the hypodermis because, unlike other epidermal tissues, it is cov-

ered on the outside by exoskeleton, rather than being directly exposed to air or water.

The exoskeleton has two layers. The epicuticle is the outermost layer. Made of a waxy lipoprotein, it is impermeable to water and a barrier to microorganisms and pesticides. The bulk of the exoskeleton is below the epicuticle and is called the procuticle. (In crustaceans, the procuticle is sometimes called the endocuticle.) The procuticle is composed of **chitin,** a tough, leathery polysaccharide, and several kinds of proteins (*see figure 2.11*). The procuticle hardens through a process called sclerotization and sometimes by impregnation with calcium carbonate. Sclerotization is a tanning process in which layers of protein are chemically cross-linked with one another—hardening and darkening the exoskeleton. In insects and most other arthropods, this bonding occurs in the outer portion of the procuticle. The exoskeleton of crustaceans hardens by sclerotization and by the deposition of calcium carbonate in the middle regions of the procuticle. Some proteins give the exoskeleton resiliency. Distortion of the exoskeleton stores energy for such activities as flapping wings and jumping. The inner portion of the procuticle does not harden.

Hardening in the procuticle provides armorlike protection for arthropods, but it also necessitates a variety of adaptations to allow arthropods to live and grow within their confines. Invaginations of the exoskeleton form firm ridges and bars for muscle attachment. Another modification of the exoskeleton is the

TABLE 23.1	CLASSIFICATION OF THE PHYLUM ARTHROPODA

Phylum Arthropoda (ar″thrah-po′dah)
Animals that show metamerism with tagmatization, a jointed exoskeleton, and a ventral nervous system.

Subphylum Trilobitomorpha (tri″lo-bit″o-mor′fah)
Marine, all extinct; lived from Cambrian to Carboniferous periods; bodies divided into three longitudinal lobes; head, thorax, and abdomen present; one pair of antennae and biramous appendages.

Subphylum Chelicerata (ke-lis′er-ah″tah)
Body usually divided into prosoma and opisthosoma; first pair of appendages piercing or pincerlike (chelicerae) and used for feeding.

Class Merostomata (mer′o-sto″mah-tah)
Marine, with book gills on opisthosoma. Two subclasses: Eurypterida, a group of extinct arthropods called giant water scorpions, and Xiphosura, the horseshoe crabs. *Limulus*.

Class Arachnida (ah-rak′nĭ-dah)
Mostly terrestrial, with book lungs, tracheae, or both; usually four pairs of walking legs in adults. Spiders, scorpions, ticks, mites, harvestmen, and others.

Class Pycnogonida (pik″no-gon′ĭ-dah)
Reduced abdomen; no special respiratory or excretory structures; four to six pairs of walking legs; common in all oceans. Sea spiders.

Subphylum Crustacea (krus-tās′e-ah)
Most aquatic, head with two pairs of antennae, one pair of mandibles, and two pairs of maxillae; biramous appendages.

Class Remipedia (re-mi-pe′de-ah)
A single species of cave-dwelling crustaceans from the Bahamas; body with approximately 30 segments that bear uniform, biramous appendages.

Class Cephalocarida (sef″ah-lo-kar′ĭ-dah)
Small (3 mm) marine crustaceans with uniform, leaflike, triramous appendages.

Class Branchiopoda (brang″ke-o-pod′ah)
Flattened, leaflike appendages used in respiration, filter feeding, and locomotion; found mostly in freshwater. Fairy shrimp, brine shrimp, clam shrimp, water fleas.

Class Malacostraca (mal-ah-kos′trah-kah)
Appendages possibly modified for crawling, feeding, swimming. Lobsters, crayfish, crabs, shrimp, isopods (terrestrial).

Class Copepoda (ko″pe-pod′ah)
Maxillipeds modified for feeding and antennae modified for swimming. Copepods.

Class Cirripedia (sir″ĭ-pēd′e-ah)
Sessile as adults, marine, and enclosed by calcium carbonate valves. Barnacles.

Subphylum Uniramia (yu″ne-ram′e-ah)
Head with one pair of antennae and usually one pair of mandibles; all appendages uniramous. Insects and their relatives (*see chapter 24*).

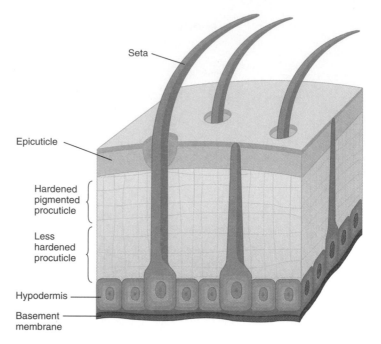

FIGURE 23.3

Arthropod Exoskeleton. The epicuticle is made of a waxy lipoprotein and is impermeable to water. Calcium carbonate deposition and/or sclerotization harden the outer layer of the procuticle. Chitin, a tough, leathery polysaccharide, and several kinds of proteins make up the bulk of the procuticle. The hypodermis secretes the entire exoskeleton.

formation of joints. A flexible membrane, called an articular membrane, is present in regions where the procuticle is thinner and less hardened (figure 23.4). Other modifications of the exoskeleton include sensory receptors, called sensilla, in the form of pegs, bristles, and lenses, and modifications of the exoskeleton that permit gas exchange.

2 Growth of an arthropod would be virtually impossible unless the exoskeleton were periodically shed, such as in the molting process called **ecdysis** (Gr. *ekdysis*, getting out). Ecdysis is divided into four stages: (1) Enzymes, secreted from hypodermal glands, begin digesting the old procuticle to separate the hypodermis and the exoskeleton (figure 23.5a,b); (2) new procuticle and epicuticle are secreted (figure 23.5c,d); (3) the old exoskeleton splits open along predetermined ecdysal lines when the animal stretches by air or water intake; pores in the procuticle secrete additional epicuticle (figure 23.5e); and (4) finally, calcium carbonate deposits and/or sclerotization harden the new exoskeleton (figure 23.5f). During the few hours or days of the hardening process, the arthropod is vulnerable to predators and remains hidden. The nervous and endocrine systems control all of these changes; the controls are discussed in more detail later in the chapter.

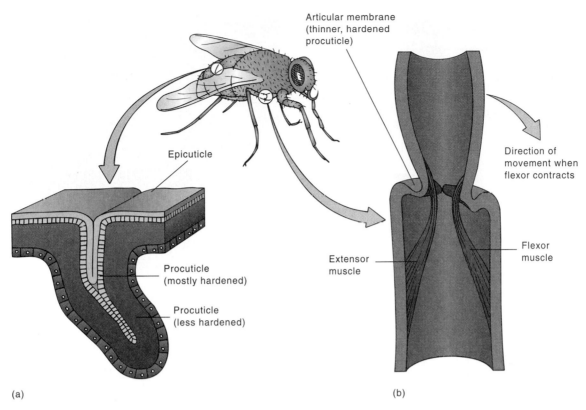

Articular membrane
(thinner, hardened
procuticle)

Epicuticle

Procuticle
(mostly hardened)

Procuticle
(less hardened)

Direction of
movement when
flexor contracts

Flexor
muscle

Extensor
muscle

(a)

(b)

FIGURE 23.4

Modifications of the Exoskeleton. (*a*) Invaginations of the exoskeleton result in firm ridges and bars when the procuticle in the region of the invagination remains thick and hard. These are muscle attachment sites. (*b*) Regions where the procuticle is thinned are flexible and form membranes and joints. *From: "A LIFE OF INVERTEBRATES" © 1979 W. D. Russell-Hunter.*

METAMORPHOSIS

A third characteristic that has contributed to arthropod success is a reduction of competition between adults and immature stages because of metamorphosis. Metamorphosis is a radical change in body form and physiology as an immature stage, usually called a larva, becomes an adult. The evolution of arthropods has resulted in an increasing divergence of body forms, behaviors, and habitats between immature and adult stages. Adult crabs, for example, usually prowl the sandy bottoms of their marine habitats for live prey or decaying organic matter, whereas larval crabs live and feed in the plankton. Similarly, the caterpillar that feeds on leafy vegetation eventually develops into a nectar-feeding adult butterfly or moth. Having different adult and immature stages means that the stages do not compete with each other for food or living space. In some arthropod and other animal groups, larvae also serve as the dispersal stage.

SUBPHYLUM TRILOBITOMORPHA

Members of the subphylum Trilobitomorpha (tri″lo-bit″o-mor′fah) (Gr. *tri*, three + *lobos*, lobes) were a dominant form of life in the oceans from the Cambrian period (600 million years

ago) to the Carboniferous period (345 million years ago). They crawled along the substrate feeding on annelids, molluscs, and decaying organic matter. The trilobite body was oval, flattened, and divided into three longitudinal regions (figure 23.6). All body segments articulated so that the trilobite could roll into a ball to protect its soft ventral surface. Most fossilized trilobites are found in this position. Trilobite appendages consisted of two lobes or rami, and are called **biramous** (L. *bi*, twice + *ramus*, branch) **appendages.** The inner lobe was a walking leg, and the outer lobe bore spikes or teeth that may have been used in digging or swimming or as gills in gas exchange.

Stop and Ask Yourself

1. What are the four subphyla of arthropods?
2. What three aspects of structure and function have been important in arthropod success?
3. How does metamorphosis reduce competition between adult and immature forms?
4. In what way is the name trilobite descriptive of that group of animals?

(a)

(b)
- Epicuticle
- Procuticle
- New epicuticle
- Molting gel
- Hypodermis

(c)

(d)
- Molting gel
- New epicuticle and procuticle
- Hypodermis

(e)

(f)
- Shed epicuticle and procuticle
- Secretory pores for new epicuticle

FIGURE 23.5

Events of Ecdysis. (*a,b*) During preecdysis, the hypodermis detaches from the exoskeleton, and the space between the old exoskeleton and the hypodermis fills with a fluid called molting gel. (*c,d*) The hypodermis begins secreting a new epicuticle, and a new procuticle forms as the old procuticle is digested. The products of digestion are incorporated into the new procuticle. Note that the new epicuticle and procuticle are wrinkled beneath the old exoskeleton to allow for increased body size after ecdysis. (*e*) Ecdysis occurs when the animal swallows air or water, and the exoskeleton splits along predetermined ecdysal lines. The animal pulls out of the old exoskeleton. (*f*) After ecdysis, the new exoskeleton hardens by calcium carbonate deposition and/or sclerotization, and pigments are deposited in the outer layers of the procuticle. Additional material is added to the epicuticle.

SUBPHYLUM CHELICERATA

One arthropod lineage, the subphylum Chelicerata (ke-lis′er-ah″tah) (Gr. *chele*, claw + *ata*, plural suffix), includes familiar animals, such as spiders, mites, and ticks, and less familiar animals, such as horseshoe crabs and sea spiders. These animals have two tagmata. The **prosoma** or **cephalothorax** is a sensory, feeding, and locomotor tagma. It usually bears eyes, but unlike other arthropods, never has antennae. Paired appendages attach to the prosoma. The first pair, called **chelicerae,** are often pincerlike or chelate, and are most often used in feeding. They may also be

FIGURE 23.6

Trilobite Structure. The trilobite body had three longitudinal sections (thus, the subphylum name). It was also divided into three tagmata. A head, or cephalon, bore a pair of antennae and eyes. The trunk, or thorax, bore appendages for swimming or walking. A series of posterior segments formed the pygidium, or tail.

specialized as hollow fangs or for a variety of other functions. The second pair, called **pedipalps,** are usually sensory but may also be used in feeding, locomotion, or reproduction. Paired walking legs follow pedipalps. Posterior to the prosoma is the **opisthosoma,** which contains digestive, reproductive, excretory, and respiratory organs.

CLASS MEROSTOMATA

Members of the class Merostomata (mer′o-sto″mah-tah) are divided into two subclasses. The Xiphosura are the horseshoe crabs, and the Eurypterida are the giant water scorpions (figure 23.7). The latter are extinct, having lived from the Cambrian period (600 million years ago) to the Permian period (280 million years ago).

Only four species of horseshoe crabs are living today. One species, *Limulus polyphemus,* is widely distributed in the Atlantic Ocean and the Gulf of Mexico (figure 23.8*a*). Horseshoe crabs scavenge sandy and muddy substrates for annelids, small molluscs, and other invertebrates. Their body form has remained virtually unchanged for over 200 million years, and they were cited in chapter 12 as an example of stabilizing selection.

A hard, horseshoe-shaped carapace covers the cephalothorax of horseshoe crabs. The chelicerae, pedipalps, and first three pairs of walking legs are chelate and are used for walking and food handling. The last pair of appendages has leaflike plates at their tips and are used for locomotion and digging (figure 23.8*b*).

The opisthosoma of a horseshoe crab includes a long, unsegmented telson. If wave action flips a horseshoe crab over, the crab arches its opisthosoma dorsally, which helps it to roll to its side

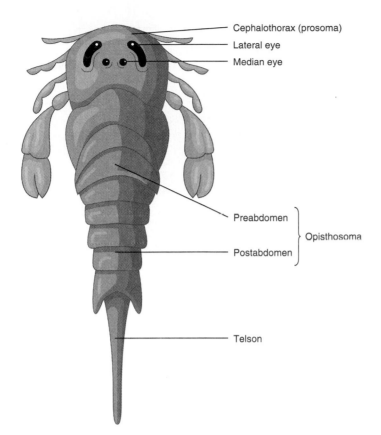

FIGURE 23.7

Class Merostomata. A eurypterid, *Euripterus remipes*.

(a)

and flip right side up again. The first pair of opisthosomal appendages cover genital pores and are called genital opercula. The remaining five pairs of appendages are **book gills.** The name is derived from the resemblance of these platelike gills to the pages of a closed book. Gases are exchanged between the blood and water as blood circulates through the book gills. Horseshoe crabs have an open circulatory system, as do all arthropods. Blood circulation in horseshoe crabs is similar to that described later in this chapter for arachnids and crustaceans.

Horseshoe crabs are dioecious. During reproductive periods, males and females congregate in intertidal areas. The male mounts the female and grasps her with his pedipalps. The female excavates shallow depressions in the sand, and as she sheds eggs into the depressions, the male fertilizes them. Fertilized eggs are covered with sand and develop unattended.

CLASS ARACHNIDA

Members of the class Arachnida (ah-rak′nĭ-dah) (Gr. *arachne*, spider) are some of the most misrepresented members of the animal kingdom. Their reputation as fearsome and grotesque creatures is vastly exaggerated. The majority of spiders, mites, ticks, scorpions, and related forms are either harmless or very beneficial to humans.

Most zoologists believe that arachnids arose from the eurypterids and were early terrestrial inhabitants. The earliest fossils

(b)

FIGURE 23.8

Class Merostomata. (*a*) Dorsal view of the horseshoe crab, *Limulus polyphemus.* (*b*) Ventral view.

of aquatic scorpions date from the Silurian period (405 to 425 million years ago), fossils of terrestrial scorpions date from the Devonian period (350 to 400 million years ago), and fossils of all other arachnid groups are present by the Carboniferous period (280 to 345 million years ago).

③ Water conservation is a major concern for any terrestrial organism, and their relatively impermeable exoskeleton preadapted ancestral arachnids for terrestrialism. **Preadaptation** is when a structure present in members of a species proves useful in promoting reproductive success when an individual encounters new environmental situations. Later adaptations included evolution of efficient excretory structures, internal surfaces for gas exchange, appendages modified for locomotion on land, and greater deposition of wax in the epicuticle.

Form and Function

Most arachnids are carnivores. They hold small arthropods with their chelicerae while enzymes from the gut tract pour over the prey. Partially digested food is then taken into the mouth. Others inject enzymes into prey through hollow chelicerae (e.g., spiders) and suck partially digested animal tissue. The gut tract of arachnids is divided into three regions. The anterior portion is the foregut, and the posterior portion is the hindgut. Both develop as infoldings of the body wall and are lined with cuticle. A portion of the foregut is frequently modified into a pumping pharynx, and the hindgut is frequently a site of water reabsorption. The midgut between the foregut and hindgut is noncuticular and lined with secretory and absorptive cells. Lateral diverticula increase the area available for absorption and storage.

Arachnids use coxal glands and/or Malpighian tubules for excreting nitrogenous wastes. **Coxal glands** are paired, thin-walled, spherical sacs bathed in the blood of body sinuses. Nitrogenous wastes are absorbed across the wall of the sacs, transported in a long, convoluted tubule, and excreted through excretory pores at the base of the posterior appendages. Arachnids that are adapted to dry environments possess blind-ending diverticula of the gut tract that arise at the juncture of the midgut and hindgut. These tubules, called **Malpighian tubules,** absorb waste materials from the blood, and empty them into the gut tract. Excretory wastes are then eliminated with digestive wastes. The major excretory product of arachnids is uric acid. As discussed in chapter 38, uric acid excretion is advantageous for terrestrial animals because uric acid is excreted as a semisolid with little water loss.

Gas exchange also occurs with minimal water loss because arachnids have few exposed respiratory surfaces. Some arachnids possess structures, called **book lungs,** that are assumed to be modifications of the book gills in the Merostomata. Book lungs are paired invaginations of the ventral body wall that fold into a series of leaflike lamellae (figure 23.9). Air enters the book lung through a slitlike opening and circulates between lamellae. Respiratory gases diffuse between the blood moving among the lamellae and the air in the lung chamber. Other arachnids possess a series of branched, chitin-lined tubules that deliver air directly to body tis-

FIGURE 23.9

Arachnid Book Lung. Air and blood moving on opposite sides of a lamella of the lung exchange respiratory gases by diffusion. Figure 23.12 shows the location of book lungs in spiders.

sues. These tubule systems, called **tracheae** (sing., trachea), open to the outside through openings called **spiracles** along the ventral or lateral aspects of the abdomen. (Tracheae are also present in insects but had a separate evolutionary origin. Aspects of their physiology are described in chapter 24.)

The circulatory system of arachnids, like that of most arthropods, is an open system in which a dorsal contractile vessel (usually called the dorsal aorta or "heart") pumps blood into tissue spaces. In arthropods, the coelom is reduced to cavities surrounding the gonads and sometimes the coxal glands. Large tissue spaces, or sinuses, are derived from the blastocoel and are called the **hemocoel.** Blood bathes the tissues and then returns to the dorsal aorta through openings in the aorta called ostia. Arachnid blood contains the dissolved respiratory pigment hemocyanin and has amoeboid cells that aid in clotting and body defenses.

The nervous system of all arthropods is ventral and, in ancestral arthropods, must have been laid out in a pattern similar to that of the annelids (*see figure 22.8a*). With the exception of scorpions, the nervous system of arachnids is centralized by fusion of ganglia.

The body of an arachnid has a variety of sensory structures. Most mechanoreceptors and chemoreceptors are modifications of the exoskeleton, such as projections, pores, and slits, together with sensory and accessory cells. Collectively, these receptors are called **sensilla.** For example, setae are hairlike, cuticular modifications that may be set into membranous sockets. Displacement of a seta initiates a nerve impulse in an associated nerve cell (figure 23.10a). Vibration receptors are very important to some arach-

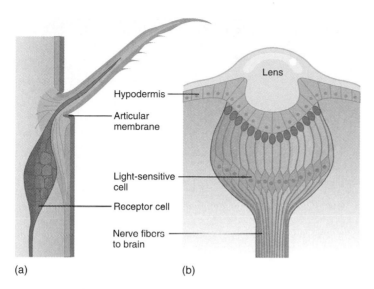

(a)   (b)

FIGURE 23.10

Arthropod Seta and Eye (Ocellus). (*a*) A seta is a hairlike modification of the cuticle set in a membranous socket. Displacement of the seta initiates a nerve impulse in a receptor cell (sensillum) associated with the base of the seta. (*b*) The lens of this spider eye is a thickened, transparent modification of the cuticle. Below the lens and hypodermis are light-sensitive sensillae with pigments that convert light energy into nerve impulses.

nids. Spiders that use webs to capture prey, for example, determine both the size of the insect and its position on the web by the vibrations the insect makes while struggling to free itself. The chemical sense of arachnids is comparable to taste and smell in vertebrates. Small pores in the exoskeleton are frequently associated with peglike, or other, modifications of the exoskeleton, and allow chemicals to stimulate nerve cells. Arachnids possess one or more pairs of eyes, which they use primarily for detecting movement and changes in light intensity (figure 23.10*b*). The eyes of some hunting spiders probably form images.

Arachnids are dioecious. Paired genital openings are on the ventral side of the second abdominal segment. Sperm transfer is usually indirect. The male often packages sperm in a spermatophore, which is then transferred to the female. Courtship rituals confirm that individuals are of the same species, attract a female to the spermatophore, and position the female to receive the spermatophore. In some taxa (e.g., spiders), copulation occurs, and sperm is transferred via a modified pedipalp of the male. Development is direct, and the young hatch from eggs as miniature adults. Many arachnids tend their developing eggs and young during and after development.

Order Scorpionida

Members of the order Scorpionida (skor″pe-ah-ni′dah) are the scorpions (figure 23.11*a*). They are common from tropical to warm temperate climates. Scorpions are secretive and nocturnal, hiding during most daylight hours under logs and stones.

Scorpions have small chelicerae that project anteriorly from the front of the carapace (figure 23.11*b*). A pair of enlarged,

(a)

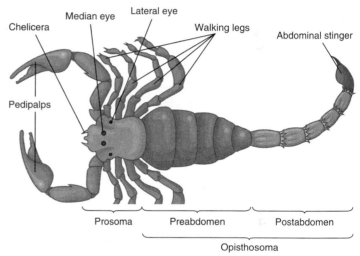

(b)

FIGURE 23.11

Order Scorpionida. (*a*) A scorpion captures its prey using chelate pedipalps. Venom from its sting paralyzes the prey prior to feeding. This Kenyan scorpion (*Pardinus*) is eating a cricket. (*b*) External anatomy of a scorpion.

chelate pedipalps is posterior to the chelicerae. The opisthosoma is divided. An anterior preabdomen contains the slitlike openings to book lungs, comblike tactile and chemical receptors called pectines, and genital openings. The postabdomen (commonly called the tail) is narrower than the preabdomen and is curved dorsally and anteriorly over the body when aroused. At the tip of the postabdomen is a sting. The sting has a bulbular base that contains venom-producing glands and a hollow, sharp, barbed point. Smooth muscles eject venom during stinging. Only a few scorpions have venom that is highly toxic to humans. Species in the genera *Androctonus* (northern Africa) and *Centuroides* (Mexico, Arizona, and New Mexico) have been responsible for human deaths. Other scorpions from the southern and southwestern areas of North America give stings comparable to wasp stings.

FIGURE 23.12

External Structure of a Spider. (*a*) Dorsal view. (*b*) Ventral view.
Sources: (a) After Sherman and Sherman. (b) After the Kastons.

FIGURE 23.13

Order Araneae. Members of the family Araneidae, the orb weavers, produce some of the most beautiful and intricate spider webs. Many species are relatively large, like this garden spider—*Argiope*. A web is not a permanent construction. When webs become wet with rain or dew, or when they age, they lose their stickiness. The entire web, or at least the spiraled portion, is then eaten and replaced.

Prior to reproduction, male and female scorpions have a period of courtship that lasts from 5 minutes to several hours. Male and female scorpions face each other and extend their abdomens high into the air. The male seizes the female with his pedipalps, and they repeatedly walk backward and then forward. The lower portion of the male reproductive tract forms a spermatophore that is deposited on the ground. During courtship, the male positions the female so that the genital opening on her abdomen is positioned over the spermatophore. Downward pressure of the female's abdomen on a triggerlike structure of the spermatophore releases sperm into the female's genital chamber.

Most arthropods are **oviparous;** females lay eggs that develop outside the body. Many scorpions and some arthropods are **ovoviviparous;** development is internal, although large, yolky eggs provide all the nourishment for development. Some scorpions, however, are **viviparous,** meaning that the mother provides nutrients to nourish the embryos. Eggs develop in diverticula of the ovary that are closely associated with diverticula of the digestive tract. Nutrients pass from the digestive tract diverticula to the developing embryos. Development requires up to 1.5 years, and 20 to 40 young are brooded. After birth, the young crawl onto the mother's back, where they remain for up to a month.

Order Araneae

With about 34,000 species, the order Araneae (ah-ran′a-e) is the largest group of arachnids (figure 23.12). The prosoma of spiders bears chelicerae with poison glands and fangs. Pedipalps are leglike and, in males, are modified for sperm transfer. The dorsal, anterior margin of the carapace usually has six to eight eyes.

A slender, waistlike pedicel attaches the prosoma to the opisthosoma. The abdomen is swollen or elongate and contains openings to the reproductive tract, book lungs, and tracheae. It also has six to eight conical projections, called spinnerets, that are associated with silk glands. The protein that forms silk is emitted as a liquid, but hardens as it is drawn out. Spiders produce several kinds of silk, each with its own use. In addition to webs for capturing prey (figure 23.13), silk is used to line retreats, to lay a safety line that fastens to the substrate to interrupt a fall, and to wrap eggs into a case for development. Air currents catch silk lines that young spiders produce and disperse them. ④ Silk lines have carried spiders at great altitudes for hundreds of kilometers. This is called ballooning.

Most spiders feed on insects and other arthropods that they hunt or capture in webs. A few (e.g., tarantulas or "bird spiders") feed on small vertebrates. Spiders bite their prey to paralyze them and then sometimes wrap prey in silk. They puncture the prey's body wall and inject enzymes. The spider's pumping stomach then sucks predigested prey products into the spider's digestive tract. The venom of most spiders is harmless to humans. ⑤ Black widow spiders (*Lactrodectus*) and brown recluse spiders (*Loxosceles*) are exceptions, since their venom is toxic to humans (box 23.1).

BOX 23.1 | A FEARSOME TWOSOME

The fearsome reputation of spiders is vastly exaggerated. All spiders have poison glands and fangs (modifications of chelicerae) that they use to immobilize prey. Most spider venom, however, is not dangerous to humans. Only about 20 species of spiders have bites considered dangerous to humans. Of these, only two are found in North America.

The black widow spider (*Latrodectus mactans*) is found throughout the United States and southern Canada (figure 1*a*). The black widow's venom is a neurotoxin. Its bite is not particularly painful, but symptoms can be severe and include abdominal and leg pain, high cerebrospinal fluid pressure, nausea, muscular spasms, and respiratory paralysis. Since an antivenom is available, human deaths are rare.

The brown recluse spider (*Loxosceles reclusa*) is common in the midwestern United States (figure 1*b*). Its venom is a hemolytic toxin. The effects of a brown recluse's bite are initially confined to the site of the bite and consist of localized tissue death and ulceration. The ulceration, however, quickly spreads to adjacent tissues and creates a large ulcer that is slow to heal. Human deaths from brown recluse bites are likewise rare since an antivenom is available.

Of these two species of spiders, the brown recluse is probably more likely to have encounters with humans. The black widow is usually in the wild—under rocks and logs, in brush piles, and in other natural areas. Its distinctive marking—a ventral red hourglass pattern on a shiny black body—is easy to recognize. The brown recluse, on the other hand, lives closely with humans and domestic animals. It is nocturnal, secretive, and may go unnoticed. During the winter months, the brown recluse is relatively inactive. While the brown recluse is drab-looking, compared to the black widow, a distinctive violin-shaped mark on the dorsal aspect of the prosoma is clearly visible. In the midwestern United States, most human dwellings have had or will have brown recluse spiders in residence. Pesticide spraying helps to control these spiders, but the spiders' reclusive habits and inactive periods mean that the sprays do not always reach their intended targets.

The best advice concerning these two species of spiders is to learn to recognize them, and to shake out shoes, boots, and other articles of clothing that have not been recently worn. These spiders, like all of their relatives, have exaggerated reputations—but the key to a peaceful coexistence is to respect the spiders' venomous bites.

(a)

(b)

FIGURE 1   **Two Venomous Spiders.** (*a*) A black widow spider (*Lactrodectus mactans*) is recognized by its shiny black body with the red hourglass pattern on the ventral surface of its opisthosoma. (*b*) A brown recluse spider (*Loxosceles reclusa*) is recognized by the dark brown, violin-shaped mark on the dorsal aspect of its prosoma.

Mating of spiders involves complex behaviors that include chemical, tactile, and/or visual signals. Females deposit chemicals called pheromones on their webs or bodies to attract males. (Pheromones are chemicals that one individual releases into the environment to create a behavioral change in another member of the same species.) A male may attract a female by plucking the strands of a female's web. The pattern of plucking is species specific and helps identify and locate a potential mate and prevents the male spider from becoming the female's next meal. The tips of a male's pedipalps possess a bulblike reservoir with an ejaculatory duct and a penislike structure called an embolus. Prior to mating, the male fills the reservoir of his pedipalps by depositing sperm on a small web and then collecting sperm with his pedipalps. During mating, the pedipalp is engorged with blood, the embolus is inserted into the female's reproductive opening, and sperm are discharged. The female deposits up to 3,000 eggs in a silken egg case, which she then seals and attaches to webbing, places in a retreat, or carries with her.

Order Opiliones

Members of the order Opiliones (o′pi-le″on-es) are the harvestmen or daddy longlegs. The prosoma broadly joins to the opisthosoma, and thus, the body appears ovoid. Legs are very long and slender. Many harvestmen are omnivores (they feed on a variety of plant and animal material), and others are strictly predators. They seize prey with their pedipalps and ingest prey as described for other arachnids. Digestion is both external and internal. Sperm transfer is direct, as males have a penislike structure. Females have a tubular ovipositor that projects from a sheath at the time of egg laying. Females deposit hundreds of eggs in damp locations on the ground.

Order Acarina

Members of the order Acarina (ak′ar-i″nah) are the mites and ticks. Many are ectoparasites (parasites on the outside of the body) on humans and domestic animals. Others are free-living in both terrestrial and aquatic habitats. Of all arachnids, acarines have had the greatest impact on human health and welfare.

Mites are 1 mm or less in length. The prosoma and opisthosoma are fused and covered by a single carapace. An anterior projection called the capitulum carries mouthparts. Chelicerae and pedipalps are variously modified for piercing, biting, anchoring, and sucking, and adults have four pairs of walking legs.

Free-living mites may be herbivores or scavengers. Herbivorous mites, such as spider mites, damage ornamental and agricultural plants. Scavenging mites are among the most common animals in soil and in leaf litter. These mites include some pest species that feed on flour, dried fruit, hay, cheese, and animal fur (figure 23.14).

Parasitic mites usually do not permanently attach to their hosts, but feed for a few hours or days and then drop to the ground. One mite, the notorious chigger or red bug (*Trombicula*), is a parasite during one of its larval stages on all groups of terrestrial vertebrates. **6** A larva enzymatically breaks down and sucks host skin, causing local inflammation and intense itching at the site of the bite. The chigger larva drops from the host and then molts to the next immature stage, called a nymph. Nymphs eventually molt to adults, and both nymphs and adults feed on insect eggs.

A few mites are permanent ectoparasites. **7** The follicle mite, *Demodex folliculorum*, is common (but harmless) in hair follicles of most of the readers of this text. Itch mites cause scabies in humans and other animals. *Sarcoptes scabei* is the human

FIGURE 23.14

Order Acarina. *Dermatophagoides farinae* (×200) is common in homes and grain storage areas. It is believed to be a major cause of dust allergies.

itch mite. It tunnels in the epidermis of human skin, where females lay about 20 eggs each day. Secretions of the mites irritate the skin, and infections are acquired by contact with an infected individual.

Ticks are ectoparasites during their entire life history. They may be up to 3 cm in length, but are otherwise similar to mites. Hooked mouthparts are used to attach to their hosts and to feed on blood. The female ticks, whose bodies are less sclerotized than those of males, expand when engorged with blood. Copulation occurs on the host, and after feeding, females drop to the ground to lay eggs. Eggs hatch into six-legged immatures called seed ticks. Immatures feed on host blood and drop to the ground for each molt. Some ticks transmit diseases to humans and domestic animals. For example, *Dermacentor andersoni* transmits the bacteria that cause Rocky Mountain spotted fever and tularemia, and *Ixodes scapularis* transmits the bacteria that cause Lyme disease (figure 23.15).

Other orders of arachnids include whip scorpions, whip spiders, pseudoscorpions, and others.

CLASS PYCNOGONIDA

Members of the class Pycnogonida (pik″no-gon′i-dah) are the sea spiders. All are marine and are most common in cold waters (figure 23.16). Pycnogonids live on the ocean floor and frequently feed on cnidarian polyps and ectoprocts. Some sea spiders feed by sucking prey tissues through a proboscis. Others tear at prey with their chelicerae.

Pycnogonids are dioecious. Gonads are U-shaped, and branches of the gonads extend into each leg. Gonopores are on one of the pairs of legs. As the female releases eggs, the male fertilizes them, and the fertilized eggs are cemented into spherical masses and attached to a pair of elongate appendages of the male, called ovigers, where they are brooded until hatching.

(a)

(b)

FIGURE 23.15

Order Acarina. (*a*) *Ixodes scapularis*, the tick that transmits the bacteria that cause Lyme disease. (*b*) The adult (shown here) is about the size of a sesame seed, and the nymph is the size of a poppy seed. People walking in tick-infested regions should examine themselves regularly and remove any ticks found on their skin because ticks can transmit diseases, such as Rocky Mountain spotted fever, tularemia, and Lyme disease.

Stop and Ask Yourself

5. How are the members of the subphylum Chelicerata characterized?

6. What are book lungs? What animals have them?

7. What characteristic of arachnids preadapted them for terrestrial environments?

8. What are three ways that spiders use silk?

FIGURE 23.16

Class Pycnogonida. Sea spiders are often found in intertidal regions feeding on cnidarian polyps. This male sea spider (*Nymphon gracile*) is carrying eggs on ovigers.

SUBPHYLUM CRUSTACEA

Some members of the subphylum Crustacea (krus-tās'e-ah) (L. *crustaceus*, hard shelled), such as crayfish, shrimp, lobsters, and crabs, are familiar to nearly everyone. Many others are lesser-known but very common taxa. These include copepods, cladocerans, fairy shrimp, isopods, amphipods, and barnacles. Except for some isopods and crabs, crustaceans are all aquatic.

Crustaceans differ from other living arthropods in two ways. They have two pairs of antennae, whereas all other arthropods have one pair or none. In addition, crustaceans possess biramous appendages, each of which consists of a basal segment, called the **protopodite,** with two rami (distal processes that give the appendage a Y shape) attached. The medial ramus is the **endopodite,** and the lateral ramus is the **exopodite** (figure 23.17). Trilobites had similar structures, which may be evidence that the trilobites were ancestral to the crustaceans.

CLASS MALACOSTRACA

Malacostraca (mal-ah-kos'trah-kah) (Gr. *malakos*, soft + *ostreion*, shell) is the largest class of crustaceans. It includes crabs, lobsters, crayfish, shrimp, mysids, shrimplike krill, isopods, and amphipods.

The order Decapoda (dek-i-pod'ah) is the largest order of crustaceans and includes shrimp, crayfish, lobsters, and crabs. Shrimp have a laterally compressed, muscular abdomen and pleopods for swimming. Lobsters, crabs, and crayfish are adapted to crawling on the surface of the substrate (figure 23.18). The abdomen of crabs is greatly reduced and is held flexed beneath the cephalothorax.

Crayfish illustrate general crustacean structure and function. They are convenient to study because of their relative abundance and large size. The body of a crayfish is divided into

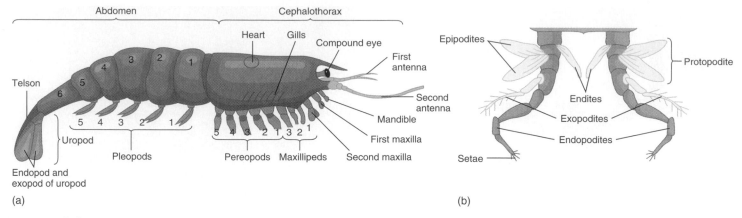

FIGURE 23.17

Crustacean Body Form. (*a*) External anatomy of a crustacean. (*b*) Pair of appendages, showing the generalized biramous structure. A protopodite attaches to the body wall. An exopodite (a lateral ramus) and an endopodite (a medial ramus) attach at the end of the protopodite. In modern crustaceans, both the distribution of appendages along the length of the body and the structure of appendages are modified for specialized functions.

FIGURE 23.18

Order Decapoda. The lobsters, shrimp, crayfish, and crabs comprise the largest crustacean order. The lobster, *Homarus americanus*, is shown here.

two regions. A cephalothorax is derived from developmental fusion of a sensory and feeding tagma (the head) with a locomotor tagma (the thorax). The exoskeleton of the cephalothorax extends laterally and ventrally to form a shieldlike carapace. The abdomen is posterior to the cephalothorax, has locomotor and visceral functions, and in crayfish, takes the form of a muscular "tail."

Paired appendages are present in both body regions (figure 23.19). The first two pairs of cephalothoracic appendages are the first and second antennae. The third through fifth pairs of appendages are associated with the mouth. During crustacean evolution, the third pair of appendages became modified into chewing or grinding structures called **mandibles.** The fourth and fifth pairs of appendages, called **maxillae,** are for food handling. The second maxilla bears a gill and a thin, bladelike structure, called a scaphognathite (gill bailer), for circulating water over the gills. The sixth through the eighth cephalothoracic ap-

pendages are called maxillipeds and are derived from the thoracic tagma. They are accessory sensory and food-handling appendages. Each also bears a gill. Appendages 9 to 13 are thoracic appendages called periopods (walking legs). The first periopod, known as the cheliped, is enlarged and chelate (pincherlike) and used in defense and capturing food. All but the last pair of appendages of the abdomen are called pleopods (swimmerets) and used for swimming. In females, developing eggs attach to pleopods, and the embryos are brooded until after hatching. In males, the first two pairs of pleopods are modified into gonopods (claspers) used for sperm transfer during copulation. The abdomen ends in a median extension called the telson. The telson bears the anus and is flanked on either side by flattened, biramous appendages of the last segment, called uropods. The telson and uropods make an effective flipperlike structure used in swimming and in escape responses.

All crustacean appendages, except the first antennae, have presumably evolved from an ancestral biramous form, as evidenced by their embryological development, in which they arise as simple two-branched structures. (First antennae develop as uniramous appendages and later acquire the branched form. The crayfish and their close relatives are unique in having branched first antennae.) Structures, such as the biramous appendages of a crayfish, whose form is based on a common ancestral pattern and that have similar development in the segments of an animal, are said to be **serially homologous.**

Crayfish prey upon other invertebrates, eat plant matter, and scavenge dead and dying animals. The foregut includes an enlarged stomach, part of which is specialized for grinding. A digestive gland secretes digestive enzymes and absorbs products of digestion. The midgut extends from the stomach and is often called the intestine. A short hindgut ends in an anus and is important in water and salt regulation (figure 23.20*a*).

As previously described, the gills of a crayfish attach to the bases of some cephalothoracic appendages. Gills are in a branchial (gill) chamber, the space between the carapace and the lateral

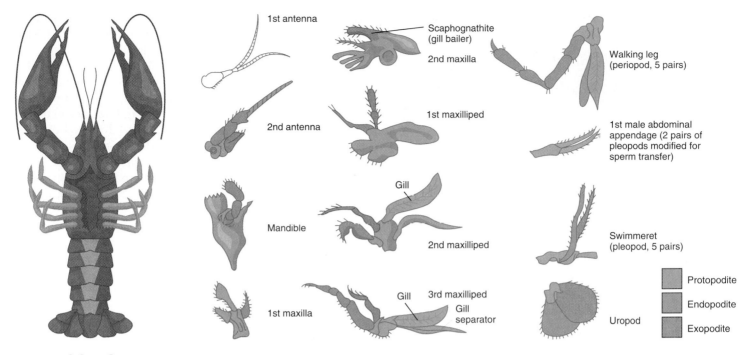

1st antenna

Scaphognathite
(gill bailer)

2nd maxilla

Walking leg
(periopod, 5 pairs)

2nd antenna

1st maxilliped

1st male abdominal
appendage (2 pairs of
pleopods modified for
sperm transfer)

Gill

Mandible

2nd maxilliped

Swimmeret
(pleopod, 5 pairs)

Gill

3rd maxilliped

Gill
separator

1st maxilla

Uropod

Protopodite

Endopodite

Exopodite

FIGURE 23.19

Crayfish Appendages. Ventral view of a crayfish, with appendages removed and arranged in sequence. Homologies regarding the structure of appendages are color coded. The origin and homology of the first antennae are uncertain.

body wall (figure 23.20b). The beating of the scaphognathite of the second maxilla drives water anteriorly through the branchial chamber. Oxygen and carbon dioxide are exchanged between blood and water across the gill surfaces, and a respiratory pigment, hemocyanin, carries oxygen in blood plasma.

Circulation in crayfish is similar to that of most arthropods. Dorsal, anterior, and posterior arteries lead away from a muscular heart. Branches of these vessels empty into sinuses of the hemocoel. Blood returning to the heart collects in a ventral sinus and enters the gills before returning to the pericardial sinus, which surrounds the heart (figure 23.20b).

Crustacean nervous systems show trends similar to those in annelids and arachnids. Primitively, the ventral nervous system is ladderlike. Higher crustaceans show a tendency toward centralization and cephalization. Crayfish have supraesophageal and subesophageal ganglia that receive sensory input from receptors in the head and control the head appendages. The ventral nerves and segmental ganglia fuse, and giant neurons in the ventral nerve cord function in escape responses (figure 23.20a). When nerve impulses are conducted posteriorly along giant nerve fibers of a crayfish, powerful abdominal flexor muscles of the abdomen contract alternately with weaker extensor muscles, causing the abdomen to flex (the propulsive stroke) and then extend (the recovery stroke). The telson and uropods form a paddlelike "tail" that propels the crayfish posteriorly.

In addition to antennae, the sensory structures of crayfish include compound eyes, simple eyes, statocysts, chemoreceptors,

proprioceptors, and tactile setae. Chemical receptors are widely distributed over the appendages and the head. Many of the setae covering the mouthparts and antennae are chemoreceptors used in sampling food and detecting pheromones. A single pair of statocysts is at the bases of the first antennae. A statocyst is a pitlike invagination of the exoskeleton that contains setae and a group of cemented sand grains called a statolith. Crayfish movements move the statolith and displace setae. Statocysts provide information regarding movement, orientation with respect to the pull of gravity, and vibrations of the substrate. Because the statocyst is cuticular, it is replaced with each molt. Sand is incorporated into the statocyst when the crustacean is buried in sand. Other receptors involved with equilibrium, balance, and position senses are tactile receptors on the appendages and at joints. When a crustacean is crawling or resting, stretch receptors at the joints are stimulated. Crustaceans detect tilting from changing patterns of stimulation. These widely distributed receptors are important to crustaceans that lack statocysts.

Crayfish have compound eyes mounted on movable eyestalks. The lens system consists of 25 to 14,000 individual receptors called ommatidia. Compound eyes also occur in insects, and their structure and function are discussed in chapter 24. Larval crustaceans have a single, median photoreceptor consisting of a few sensilla. These simple eyes, called ocelli, allow larval crustaceans to orient toward or away from the light, but do not form images. Many larvae are planktonic and use their ocelli to orient toward surface waters.

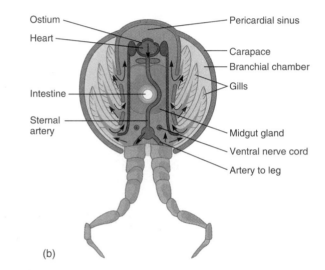

FIGURE 23.20

Internal Structure of a Crayfish. (*a*) Lateral view of a male. In the female, the ovary is in the same place as the testis of the male, but the gonoducts open at the base of the third periopods. (*b*) Cross section of the thorax in the region of the heart. In this diagram, gills are shown attached higher on the body wall than they actually occur to show the path of blood flow (arrows) through them.

The endocrine system of a crayfish controls functions such as ecdysis, sex determination, and color change. Endocrine glands release chemicals called hormones into the blood, where they circulate and cause responses at certain target tissues. In crustaceans, endocrine functions are closely tied to nervous functions. Nervous tissues that produce and release hormones are called neurosecretory tissues. X-organs are neurosecretory tissues in eyestalks of crayfish. Associated with each X-organ is a sinus gland that accumulates and releases the secretions of the X-organ. Other glands, called Y-organs, are not directly associated with nervous tissues. They are near the bases of the maxillae. Both the X-organ and the Y-organ control ecdysis. The X-organ produces molt-inhibiting hormone, and the sinus gland releases it. The target of this hormone is the Y-organ. As long as molt-inhibiting hormone is present, the Y-organ is inactive. Certain conditions prevent release of molt-inhibiting hormone, and the Y-organ releases ecdysone hormone, leading to molting (*see figure 35.5*). (These "certain conditions" are often complex and species specific. They include factors

such as nutritional state, temperature, and photoperiod.) Other hormones that facilitate molting have also been described. These include, among others, a molt-accelerating factor.

Androgenic glands in the cephalothorax of males mediate another endocrine function. (Females possess rudiments of these glands during development, but the glands never mature.) Normally, androgenic hormone(s) promotes the development of testes and male characteristics, such as gonopods. Removal of androgenic glands from males results in the development of female sex characteristics, and if androgenic glands are experimentally implanted into a female, she develops testes and gonopods.

Hormones probably regulate many other crustacean functions. Some that have been investigated include the development of female brooding structures in response to ovarian hormones, the seasonal regulation of ovarian functions, and the regulation of heart rate and body color changes by eyestalk hormones.

The excretory organs of crayfish are called antennal glands (green glands) because they are at the bases of the second antennae and are green in living crayfish. In other crustaceans, they are called maxillary glands because they are at the base of the second maxillae. They are structurally similar to the coxal glands of arachnids and presumably had a common evolutionary origin. Excretory products form by filtration of blood. Ions, sugars, and amino acids are reabsorbed in the tubule before the diluted urine is excreted. As with most aquatic animals, ammonia is the primary excretory product. However, crayfish do not rely solely on the antennal glands to excrete ammonia. Ammonia also diffuses across thin parts of the exoskeleton. Even though it is toxic, ammonia is water soluble, and water rapidly dilutes it. All freshwater crustaceans face a continual influx of freshwater and loss of ions. Thus, the elimination of excess water and the reabsorption of ions become extremely important functions. Gill surfaces are also important in ammonia excretion and water and ion regulation (osmoregulation).

Crayfish, and all other crustaceans except the barnacles, are dioecious. Gonads are in the dorsal portion of the thorax, and gonoducts open at the base of the third (females) or fifth (males) periopods. Mating occurs just after a female has molted. The male turns the female onto her back and deposits nonflagellated sperm near the openings of the female's gonoducts. Fertilization occurs after copulation, as the eggs are shed. The eggs are sticky and securely fasten to the female's pleopods. Fanning movements of the pleopods over the eggs keeps the eggs aerated. The development of crayfish embryos is direct, with young hatching as miniature adults. Many other crustaceans have a planktonic, free-swimming larva called a nauplius (figure 23.21*a*). In some, the nauplius develops into a miniature adult. Crabs and their relatives have a second larval stage called a zoea (figure 23.21*b*). When all adult features are present, except sexual maturity, the immature is called the postlarva.

Two other orders of malacostracans have members familiar to most humans. Members of the order Isopoda (i'so'pod'ah) include "pillbugs." Isopods are dorsoventrally flattened, may be either aquatic or terrestrial, and scavenge decaying plant and animal material. Some have become modified for clinging to and feeding on other animals. Terrestrial isopods live under rocks and logs and in leaf litter (figure 23.22*a*). Members of the

(a)

(b)

FIGURE 23.21

Crustacean Larvae. (a) Nauplius larva of a barnacle (0.5 mm). (b) Zoea larvae (1 mm) of a crab (*Pachygrapsus crassipes*).

order Amphipoda (am-fi-pod'ah) have a laterally compressed body that gives them a shrimplike appearance. Amphipods move by crawling or swimming on their sides along the substrate. Some species are modified for burrowing, climbing, or jumping (figure 23.22b). Amphipods are scavengers, and a few species are parasites.

CLASS BRANCHIOPODA

Members of the class Branchiopoda (brang″ke-o-pod'ah) (Gr. *branchio*, gill + *podos*, foot) primarily live in freshwater. All branchiopods possess flattened, leaflike appendages used in respiration, filter feeding, and locomotion.

(a)

(b)

FIGURE 23.22

Orders Isopoda and Amphipoda. (a) Some isopods roll into a ball when disturbed or threatened with drying—thus, the name "pillbug." (b) This amphipod (*Orchestoidea californiana*) spends some time out of the water hopping along beach sands—thus, the name "beachhopper."

Fairy shrimp and brine shrimp comprise the order Anostraca (an-ost'ra-kah). Fairy shrimp usually live in temporary ponds that spring thaws and rains form. Eggs are brooded, and when the female dies, and the temporary pond begins to dry, the embryos become dormant in a resistant capsule. Embryos lay on the forest floor until the pond fills again the following spring, at which time they hatch into nauplius larvae. Animals, wind, or water currents may carry the embryos to other locations. Their short and uncertain life cycle is an adaptation to living in ponds that dry up. The vulnerability of these slowly swimming and defenseless crustaceans probably explains why they live primarily in temporary ponds, a habitat that contains few larger predators. Brine shrimp also form resistant embryos. They live in salt lakes and ponds (e.g., the Great Salt Lake in Utah).

Members of the order Cladocera (kla-dos'er-ah) are called water fleas (figure 23.23). A large carapace covers their bodies, and they swim by repeatedly thrusting their second antennae downward to create a jerky, upward locomotion. Females reproduce parthenogenetically (without fertilization) in spring and summer, and can rapidly populate a pond or lake. Eggs are brooded in an egg case beneath the carapace. At the next molt, the egg case is released and either floats or sinks to the bottom of the pond or lake. In response to decreasing temperature, changing photoperiod, or decreasing food supply, females produce eggs that develop parthenogenetically into males. Sexual reproduction produces resistant "winter eggs" that overwinter and hatch in the spring.

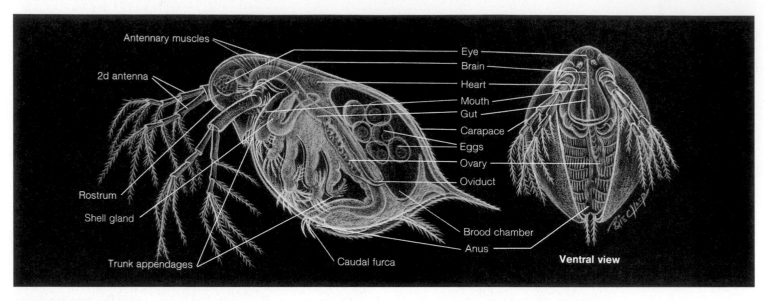

FIGURE 23.23

Class Branchiopoda. The structure of a cladoceran water flea (*Daphnia*). Lateral and ventral views (2mm).

(a)

(b)

FIGURE 23.24

Class Cirripedia. (*a*) Internal structure of a stalkless (acorn) barnacle. (*b*) Stalked (gooseneck) barnacles (*Lepas*).

CLASS COPEPODA

Members of the class Copepoda (ko″pe-pod′ah) (Gr. *kope*, oar + *podos*, foot) include some of the most abundant crustaceans (*see* figure 23.1). There are both marine and freshwater species. Copepods have a cylindrical body and a median ocellus that develops in the nauplius stage and persists into the adult stage. The first antennae (and the thoracic appendages in some) are modified for swimming, and the abdomen is free of appendages. Most copepods are planktonic and use their second maxillae for filter feeding. Their importance in marine food webs was noted in the "Evolu-

tionary Perspective" that opens this chapter. A few copepods live on the substrate, a few are predatory, and others are commensals or parasites of marine invertebrates, fishes, or marine mammals.

CLASS CIRRIPEDIA

Members of the class Cirripedia (sir″ĭ-ped′e-ah), the barnacles, are sessile and highly modified as adults (figure 23.24*a*). They are exclusively marine and include about one thousand species. Most barnacles are monoecious. The planktonic nauplius of barnacles is followed by a planktonic larval stage, called a cypris larva, which

---

BOX | **23.2** | SACCULINA: A HIGHLY MODIFIED PARASITE

Barnacles of the order Rhizocephala are parasites. Many are very similar to free-living barnacles, but others, such as *Sacculina*, are some of the most highly modified of all animal parasites. Not only do adults not look like barnacles, they are difficult to recognize as animals and more closely resemble a fungus. Larval stages, however, disclose the true identity of this parasite.

The life cycle of *Sacculina* begins when a cypris larva attaches by its first antennae to a seta on a limb of a crab. The larva moves to a membranous area and bores through the crab exoskeleton. Once inside the body, the larva loses its exoskeleton, and dedifferentiated cells move through the blood to the midgut. The parasite then grows throughout the hemocoel and branches into a mycelium-like mass of parasite tissue. When the crab molts, a brood sac (externa) containing the parasite's eggs forms in the flexed abdomen of the crab—in the same position that the female crabs normally brood their own young (figure 1).

Early research indicated that all crabs parasitized by *Sacculina* were females. Later, investigators found the *Sacculina* also parasitizes males and transforms them into females by destroying the androgenic gland! Just as experimental removal of the androgenic glands transforms males into females, so does parasitization.

The crab cares for the parasite's brood sac as if it were its own. Fertilization occurs when a male cypris larva introduces sperm-forming tissue into the parasite's brood sac. Nauplius larvae are released from the brood sac, and they metamorphose into cypris larvae. Parasitism prevents further molting by the crab, results in sterility, and usually causes the crab's death.

FIGURE 1   **The Brood Sac (Externa) of a Rhizocephalan.** This crab (*Carcinus muenus*) is parasitized by the rhizocephalan (*Sacculina carcini*). Notice the parasitic externa beneath the crab's abdomen, which contains eggs of the parasite.

---

has a bivalved carapace. Cypris larvae attach to the substrate by their first antennae and metamorphose to adults. In the process of metamorphosis, the abdomen is reduced, and the gut tract becomes U-shaped. Thoracic appendages are modified for filtering and moving food into the mouth. Calcareous plates cover the larval carapace in the adult stage.

8 Barnacles attach to a variety of substrates, including rock outcroppings, ship bottoms, whales, and other animals. Some barnacles attach to their substrate by a stalk (figure 23.24b). Others are nonstalked and are called acorn barnacles. Barnacles that colonize ship bottoms reduce both ship speed and fuel efficiency. Much time, effort, and money have been devoted to research on keeping ships free of barnacles.

Some barnacles have become highly modified parasites (box 23.2). The evolution of parasitism in barnacles is probably a logical consequence of living attached to other animals.

FURTHER PHYLOGENETIC CONSIDERATIONS

As this chapter indicates, the arthropods have been very successful. This is evidenced by diverse body forms and lifestyles of copepods, crabs, lobsters, crayfish, and barnacles, which are an example of adaptive radiation. Few aquatic environments are without some crustaceans.

The subphylum Chelicerata is a very important group of animals from an evolutionary standpoint, even though they are less numerous in terms of numbers of species and individuals than are many of the crustacean groups. Their arthropod exoskeleton and the evolution of excretory and respiratory systems that minimize water loss resulted in ancestral members of this subphylum becoming some of the first terrestrial animals. Chelicerates, however, are not the only terrestrial arthropods. In terms of numbers of species and numbers of individuals, chelicerates are dwarfed in terrestrial environments by the fourth arthropod lineage—the insects and their relatives. This lineage and the evolutionary relationships within the entire phylum are the subject of chapter 24.

Stop and Ask Yourself

9. What evidence supports the hypothesis that trilobites were ancestral to the crustaceans?

10. What structures of a crayfish are serially homologous? What does this mean?

11. What are neurosecretory tissues? How are they involved in regulating crustacean metamorphosis?

12. What crustaceans belong to the class Branchiopoda and reproduce by parthenogenesis?

SUMMARY

1. Arthropods and annelids are closely related animals. Living arthropods are divided into three subphyla: Chelicerata, Crustacea, and Uniramia. All members of a fourth subphylum, Trilobitomorpha, are extinct.

2. Arthropods have three distinctive characteristics: they are metameric and display tagmatization, they possess an exoskeleton, and many undergo metamorphosis during development.

3. Members of the extinct subphylum Trilobitomorpha had oval, flattened bodies that consisted of three tagmata and three longitudinal lobes. Appendages were biramous.

4. The subphylum Chelicerata has members whose bodies are divided into a prosoma and an opisthosoma. They also possess a pair of feeding appendages called chelicerae.

5. The horseshoe crabs and the giant water scorpions belong to the class Merostomata.

6. The class Arachnida includes spiders, mites, ticks, scorpions, and others. Their exoskeleton partially preadapted the arachnids for their terrestrial habitats.

7. The sea spiders are the only members of the class Pycnogonida.

8. The subphylum Crustacea contains animals characterized by two pairs of antennae and biramous appendages. All crustaceans, except for some isopods, are primarily aquatic.

9. The class Malacostraca includes the crabs, lobsters, crayfish, shrimp, isopods, and amphipods. This is the largest crustacean class in terms of numbers of species and contains the largest crustaceans.

10. Members of the class Branchiopoda have flattened, leaflike appendages. Examples are fairy shrimp, brine shrimp, and water fleas.

11. Members of the class Copepoda include the copepods.

12. The class Cirrepedia contains the barnacles, which are sessile filter feeders.

SELECTED KEY TERMS

biramous appendages (p. 363)
chelicerae (p. 364)
ecdysis (p. 362)
exoskeleton or cuticle (p. 361)
hemocoel (p. 366)

mandibles (p. 372)
oviparous (p. 368)
ovoviviparous (p. 368)
serially homologous (p. 372)
viviparous (p. 368)

CRITICAL THINKING QUESTIONS

1. What is tagmatization, and why is it advantageous for metameric animals?

2. Explain how, in spite of being an armorlike covering, the exoskeleton permits movement and growth.

3. Why is the arthropod exoskeleton often cited as the major reason for arthropod success?

4. Explain why excretory and respiratory systems of ancestral arachnids probably preadapted these organisms for terrestrial habitats.

5. Barnacles are very successful arthropods. What factors do you think are responsible for the evolution of their highly modified body form?

REFERENCES ON THE WORLD WIDE WEB

1. **Kevin's Trilobite Home Page.** This site contains information on the trilobites, including photographs, drawings, updates on trilobite conferences, and literature.
   http://www.alberta.ca/~kbrett/Trilobites.html

2. **Spiders (Arachnida).** Learn about common spiders in northwest Europe at this site. It contains general information, photographs, and links to other arachnid sites on the Internet.
   http://www.xs4all.nl/~ednieuw/spiders/spidhome.htm

3. **Arachnology.** Many links to information on arachnids are found here. Learn about arachnid societies, scientists, taxonomy, paleontology, and myths. This site also provides links to photographs of arachnids.
   http://dns.ufsia.ac.be/Arachnology/Arachnology.html

4. **BIOSIS Arachnida.** This site provides links to information on the paleontology, taxonomy, life history, and ecology of members of most arachnid groups.
   http://www.york.biosis.org/zrdocs/zoolinfo/grp_arac.htm

5. **BIOSIS Crustacea.** This site provides links to information on the paleontology, taxonomy, life history, and ecology of members of most crustacean groups.
   http://www.york.biosis.org/zrdocs/zoolinfo/grp_crus.htm

6. **Crustacean Neuroscience.** Find many crustacean links at this site.
   http://wwwzoo.kfunigruz.ac.at/cruties.html

7. **The Crustacean Society.** This site contains information on The Crustacean Society plus many links to information on the crustaceans.
   http://www.lam.mus.ca.us/~tcs/

8. **Crayfish Home Page.** This site contains links to information on crayfish phylogeny, threatened species, diseases, and recipes.
   http://www.utexas.edu/depts/tnhc/.www/crayfish/crayhome.html

9. **Crustacea.** Find general information on crustacean taxonomy, collecting, and preservation, as well as a key to higher crustacean taxa at this site.
   http://rivers.oscs.montana.edu/dlg/aim/crustac.html

chapter 24

THE HEXAPODS AND MYRIAPODS:
TERRESTRIAL TRIUMPHS

Concepts

1. Flight, along with other arthropod characteristics, has resulted in insects becoming the most abundant and diverse group of terrestrial animals.
2. The myriapods include members of the classes Diplopoda, Chilopoda, Pauropoda, and Symphyla.
3. Members of the class Hexapoda (Insecta) are characterized by three pairs of legs, and they usually have wings.
4. Adaptations for living on land are reflected in many aspects of insect structure and function.
5. Insects have important effects on human health and welfare.
6. Some zoologists believe that the arthropods should be divided into three phyla: the Chelicerata, Crustacea, and Uniramia.

Would You Like to Know . . .

1. why insects have been so successful on land? (p. 380)
2. what animals first invaded terrestrial habitats? (p. 381)
3. how fast the wings of a midge (a small fly) beat? (p. 385)
4. how far you could leap if, relative to body size, you could jump the same distance as a flea? (p. 386)
5. what an insect sees? (p. 388)
6. how insects communicate over long distances? (p. 389)
7. how the social organization in a honeybee hive is regulated? (p. 392)

This chapter answers these and other useful questions.

This chapter contains evolutionary concepts, which are set off in this font.

EVOLUTIONARY PERSPECTIVE

By almost any criterion, the insects have been enormously successful. Zoologists have described approximately 750,000 species, and some estimate that the number of insect species may be as high as 30 million! Most of the undescribed species are in tropical rain forests. Since just the described insect species comprise 75% of all living species, the total number of described and undescribed insect species dwarfs all other kinds of living organisms. Although freshwater and parasitic insect species are numerous, the success of insects has largely been due to their ability to exploit terrestrial habitats (figure 24.1).

During the late Silurian and early Devonian periods (about 400 million years ago), terrestrial environments were largely uninhabited by animals. Low-growing herbaceous plants and the first forests were beginning to flourish, and enough ozone had accumulated in the upper atmosphere to filter ultraviolet radiation from the sun. Animals with adaptations that permitted life on land had a wealth of photosynthetic production available, and unlike in marine habitats, faced little competition from other animals for resources. However, the problems associated with terrestrial life were substantial. Support and movement outside of a watery environment were difficult on land, as were water, ion (electrolyte), and temperature regulation.

A number of factors contributed to insect dominance of terrestrial habitats. The exoskeleton preadapted the insects for life on land. Not only is the exoskeleton supportive, but the evolution of a waxy epicuticle enhanced the exoskeleton's water-conserving properties. The evolution of flight also played a big role in insect success. The ability to fly allowed insects to use widely scattered food resources, to invade new habitats, and to escape unfavorable environments. These factors—along with desiccation-resistant eggs, metamorphosis, high

FIGURE 24.1

Class Hexapoda. Insects were early inhabitants of terrestrial environments. The exoskeleton and the evolution of flight have contributed to the enormous success of this group of arthropods.

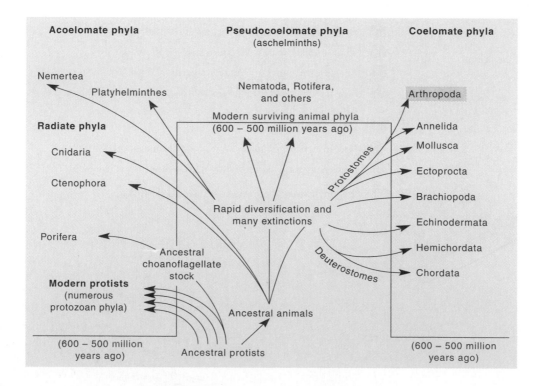

FIGURE 24.2

Evolutionary Relationships of the Arthropods. Arthropods (shaded in orange) are protostomes that are closely related to the annelids. Members of the subphylum Uniramia are the subject of this chapter.

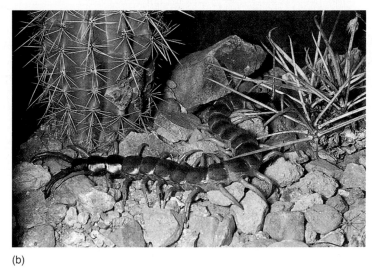

(a)

(b)

FIGURE 24.3

Myriapods. *(a)* A woodland millipede *(Ophyiulus pilosus)*. *(b)* A centipede *(Scolopendra heros)*.

reproductive potential, and diversification of mouthparts and feeding habits—permitted insects to become the dominant class of organisms on the earth.

The insects make up one of five classes in the subphylum Uniramia (table 24.1; figure 24.2). The four noninsect classes (discussed next) are grouped into a convenient, nontaxonomic category called the **myriapods** (Gr. *myriad*, ten thousand + *podus*, foot).

CLASS DIPLOPODA

The class Diplopoda (dip'lah-pod'ah) (Gr. *diploos*, twofold + *podus*, foot) contains the millipedes. ❷ Ancestors of this group appeared on land during the Devonian period and were among the first terrestrial animals. Millipedes have 11 to 100 trunk segments derived from an embryological and evolutionary fusion of primitive metameres. An obvious result of this fusion is the occurrence of two pairs of appendages on each apparent trunk segment. Each segment is actually the fusion of two segments. Fusion is also reflected internally by two ganglia, two pairs of ostia, and two pairs of tracheal trunks per apparent segment. Most millipedes are round in cross section, although some are more flattened (figure 24.3a).

Millipedes are worldwide in distribution and are nearly always found in or under leaf litter, humus, or decaying logs. Their epicuticle does not contain much wax; therefore, their choice of habitat is important to prevent desiccation. Their many legs, simultaneously pushing against the substrate, help millipedes bulldoze through the habitat. Millipedes feed on decaying plant matter using their mandibles in a chewing or scraping fashion. A few millipedes have mouthparts modified for sucking plant juices.

Millipedes roll into a ball when faced with desiccation or when disturbed. Many also possess repugnatorial glands that pro-

duce hydrogen cyanide, which repels other animals. Hydrogen cyanide is not synthesized and stored as hydrogen cyanide because it is caustic and would destroy millipede tissues. Instead, a precursor compound and an enzyme mix as they are released from separate glandular compartments. Repellants increase the likelihood that the millipede will be dropped unharmed and decrease the chances that the same predator will try to feed on another millipede.

Male millipedes transfer sperm to female millipedes with modified trunk appendages, called gonopods, or in spermatophores. Eggs are fertilized as they are laid and hatch in several weeks. Immatures acquire more legs and segments with each molt until they reach adulthood.

CLASS CHILOPODA

Members of the class Chilopoda (ki"lah-pod'ah) (Gr. *cheilos*, lip + *podus*, foot) are the centipedes. Most centipedes are nocturnal and scurry about the surfaces of logs, rocks, or other forest-floor debris. Like millipedes, most centipedes lack a waxy epicuticle and therefore require moist habitats. Their bodies are flattened in cross section, and they have a single pair of long legs on each of their 15 or more trunk segments. The last pair of legs is usually modified into long sensory appendages.

Centipedes are fast-moving predators (figure 24.3b). Food usually consists of small arthropods, earthworms, and snails; however, some centipedes feed on frogs and rodents. Poison claws (modified first-trunk appendages called maxillipeds) kill or immobilize prey. Maxillipeds, along with mouth appendages, hold the prey as mandibles chew and ingest the food. Most centipede venom is essentially harmless to humans, although many centipedes have bites that are comparable to wasp stings; a few human deaths have been reported from large, tropical species.

TABLE 24.1

CLASSIFICATION OF THE SUBPHYLUM UNIRAMIA*

Phylum Arthropoda (ar″thra-po′dah)
Animals with metamerism and tagmatization, a jointed exoskeleton, and a ventral nervous system.
 Subphylum Uniramia (u″ne-ram′e-ah) (L. *unis*, one + *ramis*, branch)
 Head with one pair of antennae and usually one pair of mandibles; all appendages uniramous.
  Class Diplopoda (dip″lah-pod′ah)
  Two pairs of legs per apparent segment; body usually round in cross section. Millipedes.
  Class Chilopoda (ki″lah-pod′ah)
  One pair of legs per segment; body oval in cross section; poison claws. Centipedes.
  Class Pauropoda (por″o-pod′ah)
  Small (0.5 to 2 mm), soft-bodied animals; 11 segments; nine pairs of legs; live in leaf mold. Pauropods.
  Class Symphyla (sim-fi′lah)
  Small (2 to 10 mm); long antennae; centipede-like; 10 to 12 pairs of legs; live in soil and leaf mold. Symphylans.
  Class Hexapoda (hex″sah-pod′ah)**
  Three pairs of legs; usually two pairs of wings; body with head, thorax, and abdomen; mandibulate mouthparts variously adapted. Insects.
   Subclass Apterygota (ap-ter-i-go′tah)
   Primitively wingless insects; pregenital abdominal appendages; ametabolous metamorphosis; indirect sperm transfer.
    Order Collembola (col-lem′bo-lah)
    Antennae with four to six segments; compound eyes absent; abdomen with six segments, most with springing appendage on fourth segment; inhabit soil and leaf litter. Springtails.
    Order Protura (pro-tu′rah)
    Minute, with cone-shaped head; antennae, compound eyes, and ocelli absent; abdominal appendages on first three segments; inhabit soil and leaf litter. Proturans.
    Order Diplura (dip-lu′rah)
    Head with many segmented antennae; compound eyes and ocelli absent; cerci multisegmented or forcepslike; inhabit soil and leaf litter. Diplurans.
    Order Thysanura (thi-sa-nu′rah)
    Tapering abdomen; flattened; scales on body; terminal cerci; long antennae. Silverfish.
   Subclass Pterygota (ter-i-go′tah)
   Insects descendant from winged ancestors; no pregenital abdominal appendages; direct sperm transfer.
    Superorder Exopterygota (eks-op-ter-i-go′tah)
    Paurometabolous (or hemimetabolous) metamorphosis; wings develop as external wing pads.
    Order Ephemeroptera (e-fem-er-op′ter-ah)
    Elongate abdomen with two or three tail filaments; two pairs of membranous wings with many veins; forewings triangular; short, bristlelike antennae. Mayflies.
    Order Odonata (o-do-nat′ah)
    Elongate, membranous wings with netlike venation; abdomen long and slender; compound eyes occupy most of head. Dragonflies, damselflies.
    Order Phasmida (fas′mi-dah)
    Body elongate and sticklike; wings reduced or absent; some tropical forms are flattened and leaflike. Walking sticks, leaf insects.

*Selected orders of insects are described.

**Most entomologists now use the term *Hexapoda* as the inclusive class name. The term *Insecta* is used in a more restricted sense to refer to ectognathous hexapods (those whose mouthparts are more or less exposed). This text commonly uses the term *insect* to refer to hexapods in general.

Centipede reproduction may involve courtship displays in which the male lays down a silk web using glands at the posterior tip of the body. He places a spermatophore in the web, which the female picks up and introduces into her genital opening. Eggs are fertilized as they are laid. A female may brood and guard eggs by wrapping her body around the eggs, or they may be deposited in the soil. Young are similar to adults except that they have fewer legs and segments. Legs and segments are added with each molt.

CLASSES PAUROPODA AND SYMPHYLA

Members of the class Pauropoda (por″o-pod′ah) (Gr. *pauros*, small + *podus*, foot) are soft-bodied animals with 11 segments. These animals live in forest-floor litter, where they feed on fungi, humus, and other decaying organic matter. Their very small size and thin, moist exoskeleton allow gas exchange across the body surface and diffusion of nutrients and wastes in the body cavity.

Order Orthoptera (or·thop'ter-ah)
Forewing long, narrow, and leathery; hindwing broad and membranous; chewing mouthparts. Grasshoppers, crickets, katydids.
Order Mantodea (man·to'deah)
Prothorax long; prothoracic legs long and armed with strong spines for grasping prey; predators. Mantids.
Order Blattaria (blat·tar'eah)
Body oval and flattened; head concealed from above by a shieldlike extension of the prothorax. Cockroaches.
Order Isoptera (i·sop'ter-ah)
Workers white and wingless; front and hindwings of reproductives of equal size; reproductives and some soldiers may be sclerotized; abdomen broadly joins thorax; social. Termites.
Order Dermaptera (der·map'ter-ah)
Elongate; chewing mouthparts; threadlike antennae; abdomen with unsegmented forcepslike cerci. Earwigs.
Order Phthiraptera (fthi·rap'ter-ah)
Small, wingless ectoparasites of birds and mammals; body dorsoventrally flattened; white. Sucking and chewing lice.
Order Hemiptera (hem·ip'ter-ah)
Proximal portion of forewing sclerotized, distal portion membranous; sucking mouthparts arise ventrally on anterior margin of head. True bugs.
Order Homoptera (ho·mop'ter-ah)
Wings entirely membranous; mouthparts arise ventrally on posterior margin of head (hypognathous). Cicadas, leafhoppers, aphids, whiteflies, scale insects.
Order Thysanoptera (thi·sa·nop'ter-ah)
Small bodied; sucking mouthparts; wings narrow and fringed with long setae; plant pests. Thrips.
Superorder Endopterygota (en·dop·ter·i·go'tah)
Holometabolous metamorphosis; wings develop internally during pupal stage.
Order Neuroptera (neu·rop'ter-ah)
Wings membranous; hindwings held rooflike over body at rest. Lacewings, snakeflies, antlions, dobsonflies.
Order Coleoptera (ko·le·op'ter-ah)
Forewings sclerotized, forming covers (elytra) over the abdomen; hindwings membranous; chewing mouthparts; the largest insect order. Beetles.
Order Trichoptera (tri·kop'ter-ah)
Mothlike with setae-covered antennae; chewing mouthparts; wings covered with setae and held rooflike over abdomen at rest; larvae aquatic and often dwell in cases that they construct. Caddis flies.
Order Lepidoptera (lep·i·dop'ter-ah)
Wings broad and covered with scales; mouthparts formed into a sucking tube. Moths, butterflies.
Order Diptera (dip'ter-ah)
Mesothoracic wings well developed; metathoracic wings reduced to knoblike halteres; variously modified but never chewing mouthparts. Flies.
Order Siphonaptera (si·fon·ap'ter-ah)
Laterally flattened, sucking mouthparts; jumping legs; parasites of birds and mammals. Fleas.
Order Hymenoptera (hi·men·op'ter-ah)
Wings membranous with few veins; well-developed ovipositor, sometimes modified into a sting; mouthparts modified for biting and lapping; social and solitary species. Ants, bees, wasps.

Members of the class Symphyla (sim-fi'lah) (Gr. *sym*, same + *phyllos*, leaf) are small arthropods (2 to 10 mm in length) that occupy soil and leaf mold, superficially resemble centipedes, and are often called garden centipedes. They lack eyes and have 12 leg-bearing trunk segments. The posterior segment may have one pair of spinnerets or long, sensory bristles. Symphylans normally feed on decaying vegetation; however, some species are pests of vegetables and flowers.

Stop and Ask Yourself

1. What probably accounts for the insects' dominance on land?
2. What classes of arthropods are collectively called the myriapods?
3. How would you characterize members of the following classes: (*a*) Diplopoda, (*b*) Chilopoda, (*c*) Pauropoda, and (*d*) Symphyla?
4. How do millipedes discourage predators?

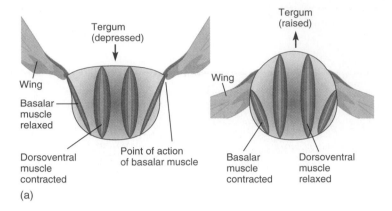

(a)

FIGURE 24.4

External Structure of a Generalized Insect. Insects are characterized by a body divided into head, thorax, and abdomen; three pairs of legs; and two pairs of wings.

CLASS HEXAPODA

Members of the class Hexapoda (hex″sah-pod′ah) (Gr. *hexa,* six + *podus,* feet) are, in terms of numbers of species and individuals, the most successful land animals. Order-level classification varies, depending on the authority consulted. Table 24.1 shows one system. In spite of obvious diversity, common features make insects easy to recognize. Many insects have wings and one pair of antennae, and virtually all adults have three pairs of legs.

EXTERNAL STRUCTURE AND LOCOMOTION

The body of an insect is divided into three tagmata: head, thorax, and **abdomen** (figure 24.4). The head bears a single pair of antennae, mouthparts, compound eyes, and zero, two, or three ocelli. The thorax consists of three segments. They are, from anterior to posterior, the **prothorax,** the **mesothorax,** and the **metathorax.** One pair of legs attaches along the ventral margin of each thoracic segment, and a pair of wings, when present, attaches at the dorsolateral margin of the mesothorax and metathorax. Wings have thickened, hollow veins for increased strength. The thorax also contains two pairs of spiracles, which are openings to the tracheal system. Most insects have 10 or 11 abdominal segments, each of which has a lateral fold in the exoskeleton that allows the abdomen to expand when the insect has gorged itself or when it is full of mature eggs. Each abdominal segment has a pair of spiracles. Also present are genital structures used during copulation and egg deposition, and sensory structures called cerci. Gills are present on abdominal segments of certain immature aquatic insects.

Insect Flight

Insects move in diverse ways. From an evolutionary perspective, however, flight is the most important form of insect locomotion. Insects were the first animals to fly. One of the most popular hypotheses on the origin of flight states that wings may have evolved from rigid, lateral outgrowths of the thorax that probably protected the legs or spiracles. Later, these fixed lobes could have been used in glid-

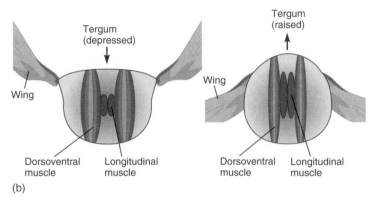

(b)

FIGURE 24.5

Insect Flight. (*a*) Muscle arrangements for the direct or synchronous flight mechanism. Note that muscles responsible for the downstroke attach at the base of the wings. (*b*) Muscle arrangements for the indirect or asynchronous flight mechanism. Muscles changing the shape of the thorax cause wings to move up and down.

ing from the top of tall plants to the forest floor. The ability of the wing to flap, tilt, and fold back over the body probably came later.

Another requirement for flight was the evolution of limited thermoregulatory abilities. Thermoregulation is the ability to maintain body temperatures at a level different from environmental temperatures. Relatively high body temperatures, perhaps 25° C or greater, are needed for flight muscles to contract rapidly enough for flight.

Some insects use a **direct** or **synchronous flight** mechanism, in which muscles acting on the bases of the wings contract to produce a downward thrust, and muscles attaching dorsally and ventrally on the exoskeleton contract to produce an upward thrust (figure 24.5*a*). The synchrony of direct flight mechanisms depends on the nerve impulse to the flight muscles that must precede each wingbeat.

Other insects use an **indirect** or **asynchronous flight** mechanism. Muscles act to change the shape of the exoskeleton for both upward and downward wing strokes. Dorsoventral muscles pulling the dorsal exoskeleton (tergum) downward produce the upward wing thrust. The downward thrust occurs when longitudinal muscles contract and cause the exoskeleton to arch upward (figure 24.5*b*). The resilient properties of the exoskeleton enhance

BOX	24.1	HOW INSECTS FLY—SECRETS REVEALED

When conventional laws of aerodynamics are applied to investigating insect flight, they reveal that insect lift forces are insufficient for flight. According to these principles, insects should not be able to fly. Obviously, however, insects do fly. Where does the extra lift come from? Recently, Charles Ellington and his coworkers at the University of Cambridge found the answer. They used hawkmoths (*Manduca sexta*) tethered in a stream of air, smoke particles to reveal air movements, video equipment, and a giant, computer-controlled hawkmoth with a wingspan greater than 1 m to investigate how air flows around the wings during insect flight.

Small streams of smoke particles carried over the wings of a flying hawkmoth revealed a vortex or cylinder of air that curled up from the front edge of the wing during the downstroke. The vortex then spiraled toward the tip of the wing with a velocity equal to the wing-stroke velocity. As it moved toward the wingtip, the vortex enlarged. This vortex creates a low-pressure area above the wing that sucks the top of the wing upward, providing lift to keep the insect airborne (figure 1).

The vortex that a 10 cm hawkmoth creates is very small. The researchers used the mechanical model to investigate the exact place and moment at which a vortex is created. Colored smoke particles released from the leading edge of the wing demonstrated precise air movement patterns within the vortex. The vortex originates at the beginning of the downstroke at the base of the wing. Elevation of the front edge of the wing helps to create lift, and the vortex moving toward the tip of the wing helps prevent the insect from stalling and crashing to the ground. (Stalling can be duplicated by tilting the forward margin of a paper airplane wing to provide extreme lift but a very short flight.) Thus, the vortex created during insect flight results in low pressure on the upper surface of the wing and a delay in the threatened stall that the upward tilt of the front margin of the wing creates.

Many insects are adept fliers. Others are awkward and inefficient.

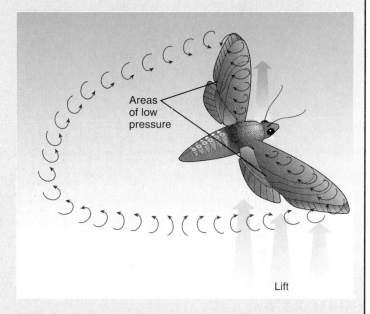

FIGURE 1   **Insect Flight.** The downstroke of a wing creates vortices (red arrows) at the base of the wing's leading margin. The vortices enlarge and move toward the tip of the wing during the downstroke. These moving vortices create low pressure on the upper surface of the wing that increases lift (blue arrows), and they stabilize the insect's tendency to stall from the upward tilt of the wing's front margin.

As this account demonstrates, our initial perceptions of natural phenomena are often inadequate, and further investigation can yield valuable lessons. Studies of insect flight may help us better understand bird flight and perhaps provide aerodynamic lessons that influence how we humans construct our own flying machines.

the power and velocity of these strokes. During a wingbeat, the thorax is deformed, storing energy in the exoskeleton. At a critical point midway into the downstroke, stored energy reaches a maximum, and at the same time, resistance to wing movement suddenly decreases. The wing then "clicks" through the rest of the cycle, using energy stored in the exoskeleton. Asynchrony of this flight mechanism arises from the lack of one-to-one correspondence between nerve impulses and wingbeats. ❸ A single nerve impulse can result in approximately 50 cycles of the wing, and frequencies of 1,000 cycles per second (cps) have been recorded in some midges! The asynchrony between wingbeat and nerve impulses is dependent on flight muscles being stretched during the "click" of the thorax. The stretching of longitudinal flight muscles during the upward beat of the wing initiates the subsequent contraction of these muscles. Similarly, stretching during the downward beat of the wing initiates subsequent contraction of dorsoventral flight muscles. Indirect flight muscles are frequently called **fibrillar flight muscles.**

Simple flapping of wings is not enough for flight. The tilt of the wing must be controlled to provide lift and horizontal propulsion. In most insects, muscles that control wing tilting attach to sclerotized plates at the base of the wing (box 24.1).

Other Forms of Locomotion

Insects walk, run, jump, or swim across the ground or other substrates. When they walk, insects have three or more legs on the ground at all times, creating a very stable stance. When they run, fewer than three legs may be in contact with the ground. A fleeing cockroach (order Blattaria) reaches speeds of about 5 km/hour, although it seems much faster when trying to catch one. The apparent speed is the result of their small size and ability to quickly change directions. Jumping insects, such as grasshoppers (order Orthoptera), usually have long, metathoracic legs in which leg musculature is enlarged to generate large, propulsive forces. Energy for a flea's (order Siphonaptera) jump is stored as elastic

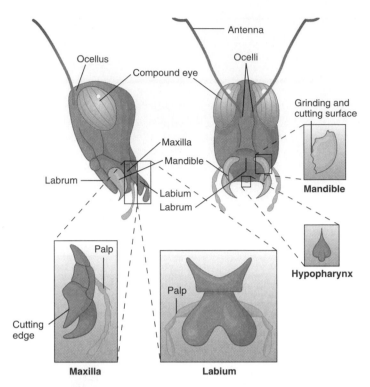

FIGURE 24.6

Head and Mouthparts of a Grasshopper. All mouthparts except the labrum are derived from segmental appendages. The labrum is a sensory upper lip. The mandibles are heavily sclerotized and used for tearing and chewing. The maxillae have cutting edges and a sensory palp. The labium forms a sensory lower lip. The hypopharynx is a sensory, tonguelike structure.

FIGURE 24.7

Specialization of Insect Mouthparts. The mouthparts of insects are often highly specialized for specific feeding habits. For example, the sucking mouthparts of a butterfly consist of modified maxillae that coil when not in use. Mandibles, labia, and the labrum are reduced in size. A portion of the anterior digestive tract is modified as a muscular pump for drawing liquids through the mouthparts.

energy of the exoskeleton. Muscles that flex the legs distort the exoskeleton. A catch mechanism holds the legs in this "cocked" position until special muscles release the catches and allow the stored energy to quickly extend the legs. This action hurls the flea

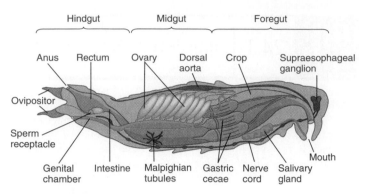

FIGURE 24.8

Internal Structure of a Generalized Insect. Salivary glands produce enzymes but may be modified for the secretion of silk, anticoagulants, or pheromones. The crop is an enlargement of the foregut and stores food. The proventriculus is a grinding and/or straining structure at the junction of the midgut and hindgut. Gastric cecae secrete digestive enzymes. The intestine and the rectum are modifications of the hindgut that absorb water and the products of digestion.

for distances that exceed 100 times its body length.   ④ A comparable distance for a human long jumper would be the length of two football fields (*see figure 32.23*)!

NUTRITION AND THE DIGESTIVE SYSTEM

The diversity of insect feeding habits parallels the diversity of insects themselves. Figure 24.6 shows the head and mouthparts of an insect such as a grasshopper or cockroach. An upper, liplike structure is called the labrum. It is sensory, and unlike the remaining mouthparts, is not derived from segmental, paired appendages. Mandibles are sclerotized, chewing mouthparts. The maxillae often have cutting surfaces and bear a sensory palp. The **labium** is a sensory lower lip. All of these aid in food handling. Variations on this plan are specializations for sucking or siphoning plant or animal fluids (figure 24.7). The digestive tract, as in all arthropods, consists of a foregut, a midgut, and a hindgut (figure 24.8). Enlargements for storage and diverticula that secrete digestive enzymes are common.

GAS EXCHANGE

Gas exchange with air requires a large surface area for the diffusion of gases. In terrestrial environments, these surfaces are also avenues for water loss. Respiratory water loss in insects, as in some arachnids, is reduced through the invagination of respiratory surfaces to form highly branched systems of chitin-lined tubes, called tracheae.

Tracheae open to the outside of the body through spiracles, which usually have some kind of closure device to prevent excessive water loss. Spiracles lead to tracheal trunks that branch, eventually giving rise to smaller branches, the tracheoles. Tracheoles end intracellularly and are especially abundant in metabolically active tissues, such as flight muscles. No cells are more than 2 or 3 μm from a tracheole (figure 24.9).

Most insects have ventilating mechanisms that move air into and out of the tracheal system. For example, contracting flight muscles alternately contract and expand the larger tracheal

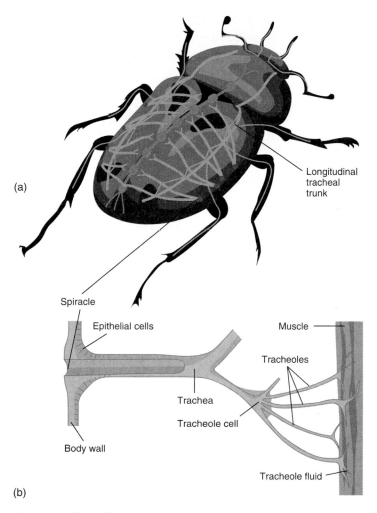

(a)

Longitudinal
tracheal
trunk

Spiracle

Epithelial cells

Muscle

Tracheoles

Trachea

Tracheole cell

Body wall

Tracheole fluid

(b)

FIGURE 24.9

Tracheal System of an Insect. (*a*) Major tracheal trunks. (*b*) Tracheoles end in cells, and the terminal portions of tracheoles are fluid filled.

trunks and thereby ventilate the tracheae. In some insects, carbon dioxide that metabolically active cells produce is sequestered in the hemocoel as bicarbonate ions (HCO_3^-). As oxygen diffuses from the tracheae to the body tissues, and is not replaced by carbon dioxide, a vacuum is created that draws more air into the spiracles. This process is called passive suction. Periodically, the sequestered bicarbonate ions are converted back into carbon dioxide, which escapes through the tracheal system. Other insects contract abdominal muscles in a pumplike fashion to move air into and out of their tracheal systems.

CIRCULATION AND TEMPERATURE REGULATION

The circulatory system of insects is similar to that described for other arthropods, although the blood vessels are less well developed. Blood distributes nutrients, hormones, and wastes, and amoeboid blood cells participate in body defense and repair mechanisms. Blood is not important in gas transport.

As described earlier, thermoregulation is a requirement for flying insects. Virtually all insects warm themselves by basking in the sun or resting on warm surfaces. Because they use external heat sources in temperature regulation, insects are generally considered ectotherms. Other insects (e.g., some moths, alpine bumblebees, and beetles) can generate heat by rapid contraction of flight muscles, a process called shivering thermogenesis. Metabolic heat generated in this way can raise the temperature of thoracic muscles from near 0 to 30° C. Because some insects rely to a limited extent on metabolic heat sources, they have a variable body temperature and are sometimes called heterotherms. Insects are also able to cool themselves by seeking cool, moist habitats. Honeybees can cool a hive by beating their wings at the entrance of the hive, thus circulating cooler outside air through the hive.

Stop and Ask Yourself

5. How can you recognize an arthropod as being an insect?
6. Why was the evolution of thermoregulatory abilities an important step in the evolution of flight?
7. What is indirect or asynchronous flight?
8. What are the functions of the circulatory system of insects?

NERVOUS AND SENSORY FUNCTIONS

The nervous system of insects is similar to the pattern described for annelids and other arthropods (*see figure 24.8*). The supraesophageal ganglion is associated with sensory structures of the head. Connectives join the supraesophageal ganglion to the subesophageal ganglion, which innervates the mouthparts and salivary glands and has a general excitatory influence on other body parts. Segmental ganglia of the thorax and abdomen fuse to various degrees in different taxa. Insects also possess a well-developed visceral nervous system that innervates the gut tract, reproductive organs, and heart.

Research has demonstrated that insects are capable of some learning and have a memory. For example, bees (order Hymenoptera) instinctively recognize flowerlike objects by their shape and ability to absorb ultraviolet light, which makes the center of the flower appear dark. If a bee is rewarded with nectar and pollen, it learns the odor of the flower. Bees that feed once at artificially scented feeders choose that odor in 90% of subsequent feeding trials. Odor is a very reliable cue for bees because it is more constant than color and shape. Wind, rain, and herbivores may damage the latter.

Sense organs of insects are similar to those found in other arthropods, although they are usually specialized for functioning on land. Mechanoreceptors perceive physical displacement of the body or of body parts. Setae are distributed over the mouthparts, antennae, and legs (*see figure 23.10a*). Touch, air movements, and vibrations of the substrate can displace setae. Stretch receptors at the joints, on other parts of the cuticle, and on muscles monitor posture and position.

Hearing is a mechanoreceptive sense in which airborne pressure waves displace certain receptors. All insects can respond to pressure waves with generally distributed setae; others have specialized receptors. For example, **Johnston's organs** are in the base of the antennae of most insects, including mosquitoes and midges (order Diptera). Long setae that vibrate when certain frequencies of sound strike them cover the antennae of these insects. Vibrating setae move the antenna in its socket, stimulating sensory cells. Sound waves in the frequency range of 500 to 550 cycles per second (cps) attract and elicit mating behavior of male mosquitoes (*Aedes aegypti*). These waves are in the range of sounds that the wings of females produce. **Tympanal (tympanic) organs** are in the legs of crickets and katydids (order Orthoptera), in the abdomen of grasshoppers (order Orthoptera) and some moths (order Lepidoptera), and in the thorax of other moths. Tympanal organs consist of a thin, cuticular membrane covering a large air sac. The air sac acts as a resonating chamber. Just under the membrane are sensory cells that detect pressure waves. Grasshopper tympanal organs can detect sounds in the range of 1,000 to 50,000 cps. (The human ear can detect sounds between 20 and 20,000 cps.) Bilateral placement of tympanal organs allows insects to discriminate the direction and origin of a sound.

Insects use chemoreception in feeding, selection of egg-laying sites, mate location, and sometimes, social organization. Chemoreceptors are usually abundant on the mouthparts, antennae, legs, and ovipositors, and take the form of hairs, pegs, pits, and plates that have one or more pores leading to internal nerve endings. Chemicals diffuse through these pores and bind to and excite nerve endings.

All insects are capable of detecting light and may use light in orientation, navigation, feeding, or other functions. **Compound eyes** are well developed in most adult insects. They are similar in structure and function to those of other arthropods, although zoologists debate their possible homology (common ancestry) with those of crustaceans, horseshoe crabs, and trilobites. Compound eyes consist of a few to 28,000 receptors, called **ommatidia,** that fuse into a multifaceted eye. The outer surface of each ommatidium is a lens and is one facet of the eye. Below the lens is a crystalline cone. The lens and the crystalline cone are light-gathering structures. Certain cells of an ommatidium, called retinula cells, have a special light-collecting area, called the rhabdom. The rhabdom converts light energy into nerve impulses. Pigment cells surround the crystalline cone, and sometimes the rhabdom, and prevent the light that strikes one rhabdom from reflecting into an adjacent ommatidium (figure 24.10).

⑤ Although many insects form an image of sorts, the concept of an image has no real significance for most species. The compound eye is better suited for detecting movement. Movement of a point of light less than 0.1° can be detected as light successively strikes adjacent ommatidia. For this reason, bees are attracted to flowers blowing in the wind, and predatory insects select moving prey. Compound eyes detect wavelengths of light that the human eye cannot detect, especially in the ultraviolet end of the spectrum. In some insects, compound eyes also detect polarized light, which may be used for navigation and orientation.

Ocelli consist of 500 to 1,000 receptor cells beneath a single cuticular lens (*see figure 23.10b*). Ocelli are sensitive to changes in light intensity and may be important in the regulation of daily rhythms.

EXCRETION

The primary insect excretory structures are the Malpighian tubules and the rectum. Malpighian tubules end blindly in the hemocoel and open to the gut tract at the junction of the midgut and the hindgut. Microvilli cover the inner surface of their cells. Various ions are actively transported into the tubules, and water passively follows. Uric acid is secreted into the tubules and then into the gut tract, as are amino acids and ions (figure 24.11). In the rectum, water, certain ions, and other materials are reabsorbed, and the uric acid is eliminated.

As described in chapter 23, excretion of uric acid is advantageous for terrestrial animals because it minimizes water loss. There is, however, an evolutionary trade-off. The conversion of primary nitrogenous wastes (ammonia) to uric acid is energetically costly. Nearly half of the food energy a terrestrial insect consumes may be used to process metabolic wastes! In aquatic insects, ammonia simply diffuses out of the body into the surrounding water.

CHEMICAL REGULATION

The endocrine system controls many physiological functions of insects, such as cuticular sclerotization, osmoregulation, egg maturation, cellular metabolism, gut peristalsis, and heart rate. As in all arthropods, ecdysis is under neuroendocrine control. In insects, the subesophageal ganglion and two endocrine glands—the corpora allata and the prothoracic glands—control these activities.

Neurosecretory cells of the subesophageal ganglion manufacture ecdysiotropin. This hormone travels in neurosecretory cells to a structure called the corpora cardiaca. The corpora cardiaca then releases thoracotropic hormone, which stimulates the prothoracic gland to secrete ecdysone. Ecdysone initiates the reabsorption of the inner portions of the procuticle and the formation of the new exoskeleton. Chapter 35 discusses these events further (*see figure 35.6*). Other hormones are also involved in ecdysis. The recycling of materials absorbed from the procuticle, changes in metabolic rates, and pigment deposition are a few of probably many functions that hormones control.

In immature stages, the corpora allata produces and releases small amounts of juvenile hormone. The amount of juvenile hormone circulating in the hemocoel determines the nature of the next molt. Large concentrations of juvenile hormone result in a molt to a second immature stage, intermediate concentrations result in a molt to a third immature stage and low concentrations result in a molt to the adult stage. Decreases in the level of circulating juvenile hormone also lead to the degeneration of the prothoracic gland so that, in most insects, molts cease once adulthood is reached. Interestingly, after the final molt, the level of juvenile hormone increases again, but now it promotes the development of accessory sexual organs, yolk synthesis, and the egg maturation.

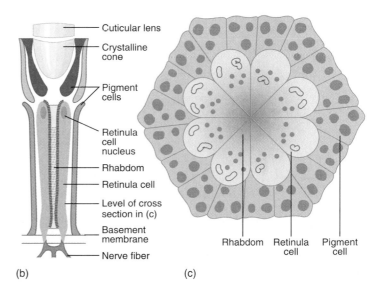

(a)   (b)   (c)

FIGURE 24.10

Compound Eye of an Insect. (*a*) Compound eye of *Drosophila* (SEM ×300). Each facet of the eye is the lens of a single sensory unit called an ommatidium. (*b*) Structure of an ommatidium. The lens and the crystalline cone are light-gathering structures. Retinula cells have light-gathering areas, called rhabdoms. Pigment cells prevent light in one ommatidium from reflecting into adjacent ommatidia. In insects that are active at night, the pigment cells are often migratory, and pigment can be concentrated around the crystalline cone. In these insects, low levels of light from widely scattered points can excite an ommatidium. (*c*) Cross section through the rhabdom region of an ommatidium.

Pheromones are chemicals an animal releases that cause behavioral or physiological changes in another member of the same species. Zoologists have described many different insect uses of pheromones (table 24.2). Pheromones are often so specific that the stereoisomer (chemical mirror image) of the pheromone may be ineffective in initiating a response. ⑥ Wind or water may carry pheromones several kilometers, and a few pheromone molecules falling on a chemoreceptor of another individual may be enough to elicit a response.

Stop and Ask Yourself

9. What evidence indicates that bees are capable of learning?

10. Compound eyes are particularly well suited for what visual function?

11. What are the endocrine functions that regulate ecdysis in insects?

12. What are pheromones? What are three kinds of functions they serve in insects?

REPRODUCTION AND DEVELOPMENT

One of the reasons for insects' success is their high reproductive potential. Reproduction in terrestrial environments, however, has its risks. Temperature, moisture, and food supplies vary with the season. Internal fertilization requires highly evolved copulatory structures because gametes dry quickly on exposure to air. In addition, mechanisms are required to bring males and females together at appropriate times.

Complex interactions between internal and external environmental factors regulate sexual maturity. Internal regulation includes interactions between endocrine glands (primarily the corpora allata) and reproductive organs. External regulating factors may include the quantity and quality of food. For example, the eggs of mosquitoes (order Diptera) do not mature until after the female takes a meal of blood, and the number of eggs produced is proportional to the quantity of blood ingested. Many insects use the photoperiod (the relative length of daylight and darkness in a 24-hour period) for timing reproductive activities because it indicates seasonal changes. Population density, temperature, and humidity also influence reproductive activities.

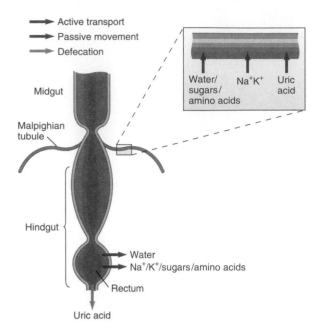

FIGURE 24.11

Insect Excretion. Malpighian tubules remove nitrogenous wastes from the hemocoel. Various ions are actively transported across the outer membranes of the tubules. Water follows these ions into the tubules and carries amino acids, sugars, and some nitrogenous wastes along passively. Some water, ions, and organic compounds are reabsorbed in the basal portion of the Malpighian tubules and the hindgut; the rest are reabsorbed in the rectum. Uric acid moves into the hindgut and is excreted.

TABLE 24.2	FUNCTIONS OF INSECT PHEROMONES

Sex pheromones—Excite or attract members of the opposite sex; accelerate or retard sexual maturation. Example: Female moths produce and release pheromones that attract males.

Caste-regulating pheromones—Used by social insects to control the development of individuals in a colony. Example: The amount of "royal jelly" fed a female bee larva determines whether the larva will become a worker or a queen.

Aggregation pheromones—Produced to attract individuals to feeding or mating sites. Example: Certain bark beetles aggregate on pine trees during an attack on a tree.

Alarm pheromones—Warn other individuals of danger; may cause orientation toward the pheromone source and elicit a subsequent attack or flight from the source. Example: A sting from one bee alarms other bees in the area, who are are likely to attack.

Trailing pheromones—Laid down by foraging insects to help other members of a colony identify the location and quantity of food found by one member of the colony. Example: Ants often trail on a pheromone path to and from a food source. The pheromone trail is reinforced each time an ant travels over it.

A few insects, including silverfish (order Thysanura) and springtails (order Collembola) have indirect fertilization. The male deposits a spermatophore that the female picks up later. Most insects have complex mating behaviors for locating and recognizing a potential mate, for positioning a mate for copulation, or for pacifying an aggressive mate. Mating behavior may involve pheromones (moths, order Lepidoptera), visual signals (fireflies, order Coleoptera), and auditory signals (cicadas, order Homoptera; and grasshoppers, crickets, and katydids, order Orthoptera). Once other stimuli have brought the male and female together, tactile stimuli from the antennae and other appendages help position the insects for mating.

Abdominal copulatory appendages of the male usually transfer the sperm to an outpocketing of the female reproductive tract, the sperm receptacle (*see figure 24.8*). Eggs are fertilized as they leave the female and are usually laid near the larval food supply. Females may use an **ovipositor** to deposit eggs in or on some substrate.

Insect Development and Metamorphosis

Insect evolution has resulted in the divergence of immature and adult body forms and habits. For insects in the superorder Endopterygota (*see table 24.1*), immature stages, called **larval instars,** are a time of growth and accumulation of reserves for the transition to adulthood. The adult stage is associated with reproduction and dispersal. In these orders, insects tend to spend a greater part of their lives in juvenile stages. The developmental patterns of insects reflect degrees of divergence between immatures and adults and are classified into three (or sometimes four) categories.

In insects that display **ametabolous** (Gr. *a*, without + *metabolos*, change) **metamorphosis,** the primary differences between adults and larvae are body size and sexual maturity. Both adults and larvae are wingless. The number of molts in the ametabolous development of a species varies, and unlike most other insects, molting continues after sexual maturity. Silverfish (order Thysanura) have ametabolous metamorphosis.

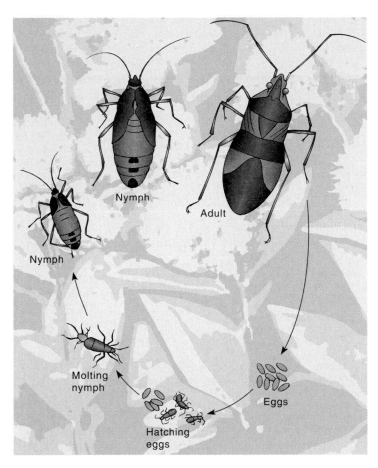

FIGURE 24.12

Paurometabolous Development of the Milkweed Bug, Oncopeltus fasciatus (Order Hemiptera). Eggs hatch into nymphs. Note the gradual increase in nymph size and the development of external wing pads. In the adult stage, the wings are fully developed, and the insect is sexually mature.

Paurometabolous (Gr. *pauros*, small) **metamorphosis** involves a species-specific number of molts between egg and adult stages, during which immatures gradually take on the adult form. The external wings develop (except in those insects, such as lice, that have secondarily lost wings), adult body size and proportions are attained, and the genitalia develop during this time. Immatures are called **nymphs.** Grasshoppers (order Orthoptera) and milkweed bugs (order Hemiptera) show paurometabolous metamorphosis (figure 24.12).

Some zoologists use an additional classification for insects that have a series of gradual changes in their development, but whose immature form is much different from the adult form usually due to the presence of gills (e.g., mayflies, order Ephemeroptera;

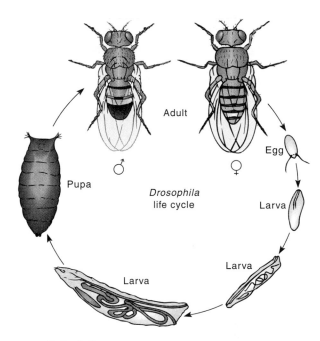

FIGURE 24.13

Holometabolous Development of the Fruit Fly, *Drosophila melanogaster* (Order Diptera). The egg hatches into a larva that is different in form and habitat from the adult. After a certain number of larval instars, the insect pupates. During the pupal stage, all adult characteristics form.

dragonflies, order Odonata). This kind of development is called **hemimetabolous** (Gr. *hemi*, half) **metamorphosis,** and the immatures are aquatic and called **naiads** (L. *naiad*, water nymph).

In **holometabolous** (Gr. *holos*, whole) **metamorphosis,** immatures are called larvae because they are very different from the adult in body form, behavior, and habitat (figure 24.13). The number of larval instars is species specific, and the last larval molt forms the **pupa.** The pupa is a time of apparent inactivity but is actually a time of radical cellular change, during which all characteristics of the adult insect develop. A protective case may enclose the pupal stage. The last larval instar (e.g., moths, order Lepidoptera) constructs a **cocoon** partially or entirely from silk. The **chrysalis** (e.g., butterflies, order Lepidoptera) and **puparium** (e.g., flies, order Diptera) are the last larval exoskeletons and are retained through the pupal stage. Other insects (e.g., mosquitoes, order Diptera) have pupae that are unenclosed by a larval exoskeleton, and the pupa may be active. The final molt to the adult stage usually occurs within the cocoon, chrysalis, or puparium, and the adult then exits, frequently using its mandibles to open the cocoon or other enclosure. This final process is called emergence or eclosion.

BOX 24.2   COMMUNICATION IN HONEYBEES

Zoologists have studied honeybees' exploitation of food sources for decades, but its study still offers important challenges. One area of research concerns the extent to which honeybees communicate the location of food to other bees. A worker bee that returns to a hive laden with nectar and pollen stimulates other experienced workers to leave the hive and visit productive pollen and nectar sources. Inexperienced workers are also recruited to leave the hive and search for nectar and pollen, but stronger stimuli are needed to elicit their searching behavior. In the darkness of the hive, the incoming bee performs what researchers have described as a round dance and a waggle dance. Throughout the dancing, other workers contact the dancing bee with their antennae and mouthparts, sensing the odors associated with pollen, nectar, and other objects in the vicinity of the incoming bee's food source. During the dance, the incoming bee moves first in a semicircle to the left, then in a straight course to the starting point. Next, she follows a semicircle to the right, and then another straight course to the starting point. During the linear parts of the dance, the bee waggles her abdomen. These stimuli apparently encourage inexperienced workers to leave the hive and begin searching for food. As described in the text, their search relies heavily on olfaction, and pollen and nectar similar to what the dancing bee brought back to the hive tend to attract workers.

The round and waggle dances may also convey information on location of a food source. Biologists have found that the dance contains information regarding the direction and distance of a food source from the hive. The angle that the waggle dance makes with the vertical of the comb approximates the angle between the sun and the food source (figure 1). Similarly, the number of straight line runs per unit time, the duration of sounds made during the dance, and the

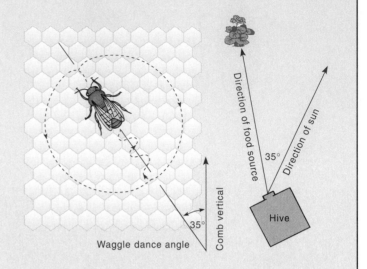

FIGURE 1   **Insect Communication.**   The waggle dance of the honeybee. *From:* "A LIFE OF INVERTEBRATES" © *1979 W. D. Russell-Hunter.*

number of waggles during the dance vary with the distance of the food source from the hive.

These observations indicate that bees communicate information regarding distance, direction, and kind of food to other bees after a foraging trip. Thus, the exploitation of pollen and nectar is a very efficient process and is evidence of the highly evolved nature of the honeybee colony.

INSECT BEHAVIOR

Insects have many complex behavior patterns. Most of these are innate (genetically programmed). For example, a newly emerged queen in a honeybee hive will search out and try to destroy other queen larvae and pupae in the hive. This behavior is innate because no experiences taught the potential queen that her survival in the hive required the death or dispersal of all other potential queens. Similarly, no experience taught her how queen-rearing cells differ from the cells containing worker larvae and pupae. Some insects are capable of learning and remembering, and these abilities play important roles in insect behavior.

Social Insects

Social behavior has evolved in many insects and is particularly evident in those insects that live in colonies (box 24.2). Usually, different members of the colony are specialized, often structurally as well as behaviorally, for performing different tasks. Social behavior is most highly evolved in the bees, wasps, and ants (order Hymenoptera) and in termites (order Isoptera). Each kind of individual in an insect colony is called a **caste.** Often, three or

four castes are present in a colony. Reproductive females are referred to as queens. Workers may be sterile males and females (termites) or sterile females (order Hymenoptera) and support, protect, and maintain the colony. Their reproductive organs are often degenerate. Reproductive males inseminate the queen(s) and are called kings or drones. Soldiers are usually sterile and may possess large mandibles to defend the colony.

Honeybees (order Hymenoptera) have three of these castes in their colonies (figure 24.14). A single queen lays all the eggs. Workers are female, and they construct the comb out of wax that they produce. They also gather nectar and pollen, feed the queen and drones, care for the larvae, and guard and clean the hive. These tasks are divided among workers according to age. Younger workers take care of jobs around the hive, and older workers forage for nectar and pollen. Except for those that overwinter, workers live for about one month. Drones develop from unfertilized eggs, do not work, and are fed by workers until they leave the hive to attempt mating with a queen.

7 A pheromone that the queen releases controls the honeybee caste system. Workers lick and groom the queen and other workers. In so doing, they pick up and pass to other workers a caste-

(a)   (b)   (c)

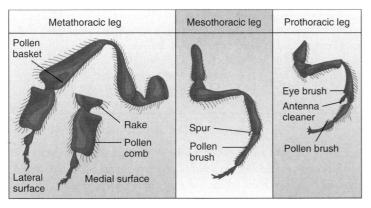

(d)

FIGURE 24.14

Honeybees (Order Hymenoptera). Honeybees have a social organization consisting of three castes. Eye size and overall body size distinguish the castes. (*a*) A worker bee. (*b*) A drone bee. (*c*) A queen bee marked with blue to identify her. (*d*) The inner surface of metathoracic legs have setae, called the pollen comb, that remove pollen from the mesothoracic legs and the abdomen. Pollen is then compressed into a solid mass by being squeezed in a pollen press and moved to a pollen basket on the outer surface of the leg, where the pollen is carried. The mesothoracic legs gather pollen from body parts. The prothoracic legs of a worker bee clean pollen from the antennae and body.

regulating pheromone. This pheromone inhibits the workers from rearing new queens. As the queen ages, or if she dies, the amount of caste-regulating pheromone in the hive decreases. As the pheromone decreases, workers begin to feed the food for queens ("royal jelly") to several female larvae developing in the hive. This food contains chemicals that promote development of queen characteristics. The larvae that receive royal jelly develop into queens, and as they emerge, the new queens begin to eliminate each other until only one remains. The queen that remains goes on a mating flight and returns to the colony, where she lives for several years.

The evolution of social behavior involving many individuals leaving no offspring and sacrificing individuals for the perpetuation of the colony has puzzled evolutionists for many years. It may be explained by the concepts of kin selection and altruism, which are discussed in chapter 13.

INSECTS AND HUMANS

Only about 0.5% of insect species adversely affect human health and welfare (box 24.3). Many others have provided valuable services and commercially valuable products, such as wax, honey, and silk, for thousands of years. Insects are responsible for the pollination of approximately 65% of all plant species. Insects and flowering plants have coevolutionary relationships that directly benefit humans. The annual value of insect-pollinated crops is estimated at $19 billion per year in the United States.

Insects are also agents of biological control. The classic example of one insect regulating another is the vedalia (lady bird) beetles' control of cottony-cushion scale. The scale insect, *Icerya purchasi*, was introduced into California in the 1860s. Within 20 years, the citrus industry in California was virtually destroyed. The vedalia beetle (*Vedalia cardinalis*) was brought to the United States in 1888 and 1889 and cultured on trees infested with scale. In just a few years, the scale was under control, and the citrus industry began to recover.

Many other insects are also beneficial. Soil-dwelling insects play important roles in aeration, drainage, and turnover of soil, and they promote decay processes. Other insects serve important roles in food webs. Insects are used in teaching and research, and have contributed to advances in genetics, population ecology, and physiology. Insects have also given endless hours of pleasure to those who collect them and enjoy their beauty.

Some insects, however, are parasites and vectors of disease. Parasitic insects include head, body, and pubic lice (order Anoplura); bedbugs (order Hemiptera); and fleas (order Siphonaptera). Other insects transmit disease-causing microorganisms, nematodes, and flatworms. Insect-transmitted diseases, such as malaria, yellow fever, bubonic plague, encephalitis, leishmaniasis, and typhus, have changed the course of history (*see box 17.2*).

Other insects are pests of domestic animals and plants. Some reduce the health of domestic animals and the quality of animal products. Insects feed on crops and transmit plant diseases, such as Dutch elm disease, potato virus, and asters yellow. Annual lost revenue from insect damage to crops or insect-transmitted diseases in the United States is approximately $5 billion.

FURTHER PHYLOGENETIC CONSIDERATIONS

A fundamental question regarding arthropod evolution concerns whether or not the arthropod taxa represent fundamentally different evolutionary lineages. Many zoologists believe that the living arthropods should be divided into three separate phyla: Chelicerata, Crustacea, and Uniramia. A polyphyletic origin of these groups implies convergent evolution of remarkably similar arthropodan features in all three (or at least two of three) phyla. Although evidence exists for dual origins of tracheae, mandibles, and compound eyes, many zoologists believe that convergence in all other arthropod traits is unlikely.

This text assumes a monophyletic origin of the arthropods. Given this assumption, the phylogenetic relationships within the

BOX 24.3   "KILLER BEES?"

The "African bee," *Apis mellifera scutellata,* is common in most parts of Africa. It is a small bee and is adapted to warm climates with extended dry seasons. In its home range, it has many enemies, including humans and birds. Aggressive behavior and frequent swarming have allowed colonies to escape predation and survive drought.

In 1956, a few *Apis mellifera scutellata* queens were imported to Brazil in hopes of breeding these queens with local stocks to create bees better adapted to tropical climates than were the local bees. (Bees of the Americas were imported from Europe in the 1600s.) A few of these queens escaped captivity and hybridized with local bees. (Referring to the hybridized bees as "African bees," "Africanized bees," or "killer bees" is inaccurate. Their reputation as "killers" has been exaggerated. Most authorities now refer to hybridized bees as Brazilian bees.) Many of the qualities that allowed the African bee to succeed in Africa allowed these Brazilian bees to spread 150 to 300 km/year. Their frequent swarming and their ability to nest in relatively open shelters gave them a distinct selective advantage over the

bees imported from Europe many years earlier. By 1969, Brazilian bees had spread to Argentina; by 1973, to Venezuela; and by early 1980, they had crossed the Panama Canal. Mexico presented few barriers to their spread, and they have now crossed the border into the southwestern United States. How far will Brazilian bees ultimately spread? An educated guess requires looking at the distribution of the African bee in Africa. African bees cannot overwinter outside of tropical regions. Similarly, the Brazilian bee will likely be limited to the warmer latitudes.

The primary implications of the spread of Brazilian bees have less to do with threats to human health than to the health of the beekeeping industry. Wearing protective clothing is one way to deal with the unpleasant temperament of these bees. More formidable problems associated with the culture of these bees include their tendency to swarm and their lower productivity. To a beekeeper, swarming means the loss of bees and a lowered honey production. Frequent swarming makes profitable beekeeping almost impossible.

Arthropoda are also debated. Members of all four subphyla are present in the fossil record from the early Paleozoic era, and there currently are no known fossils of arthropods from Precambrian times. The fossil record, therefore, is of little help in discovering the evolutionary relationships among the arthropod subphyla. Zoologists must rely on comparative anatomy, comparative embryology, and molecular studies to investigate these relationships.

Central to the questions surrounding arthropod phylogeny are two important issues. One issue is whether or not the biramous limbs of crustaceans and trilobites are homologous. Homology of these appendages would imply that the trilobites were closely related to the crustaceans; therefore, many zoologists view the trilobites as an important ancestral group. It is possible to envision crustaceans, and possibly the arachnids, arising from the trilobites, but envisioning a similar origin for the myriapods and insects is more difficult. A second important issue is whether or not the mandibles of uniramians and crustaceans are homologous. Superficially, the mandibles of members of these groups are structurally similar and have similar functions. Muscle arrangements and methods of articulation, however, are different enough that many zoologists doubt that these appendages are homologous. Discussions of arthropod phylogeny also center around the origins and possible homologies of arthropod compound eyes, tracheal systems, and Malpighian tubules.

Depending on how these issues have been interpreted, a number of hypotheses regarding the relationships of the arthropod subphyla have been presented. Figure 24.15 shows two of these

hypotheses. Figure 24.15*a,* depicts the Uniramia and the Crustacea as being closely related. This hypothesis emphasizes possible homologies between the mandibles, compound eyes, and other structures of these two groups. Figure 24.15*b* shows the Uniramia diverging independently of the Chelicerata and Crustacea. The latter two subphyla are depicted as being closely related to the trilobites. This figure implies that the mandibles of the crustaceans and uniramians are not homologous and that the biramous appendages of the crustaceans and trilobites are homologous.

Questions regarding the evolutionary relationships within the arthropods are difficult to answer. These questions will probably remain unanswered until new fossils are discovered or data from molecular studies provide more information on ancestral arthropods.

Stop and Ask Yourself

13. What is the sequence of changes in the life history of a holometabolous insect?

14. What are three castes in a honeybee hive, and how is the caste system regulated?

15. What is the nature of the debate regarding arthropod phylogeny?

FIGURE 24.15

Two Interpretations of Arthropod Phylogeny. Systematists have proposed a number of interpretations of arthropod phylogeny. Two interpretations are shown here. Only a few of the many characters used in establishing the relationships are shown. (*a*) Many zoologists think that the crustaceans and uniramians are closely related. Evidence for this hypothesis comes from possible homologies of mandibles, ommatidia of compound eyes, and other characters. (*b*) Other zoologists believe that the uniramians are more distantly related to other arthropods and that primitive uniramous appendages, and mandibles that are not homologous to those of crustaceans, distinguish the uniramians from the arthropods.

SUMMARY

1. During the Devonian period, insects began to exploit terrestrial environments. Flight, the exoskeleton, and metamorphosis are probably keys to insect success.

2. Myriapods include four classes of arthropods. Members of the class Diplopoda (the millipedes) are characterized by apparent segments bearing two pairs of legs. Members of the class Chilopoda (the centipedes) are characterized by a single pair of legs on each of their 15 segments and a body that is flattened in cross section. The class Pauropoda contains soft-bodied animals that feed on fungi and decaying organic matter in forest-floor litter. Members of the class Symphyla are centipede-like arthropods that live in soil and leaf mold, where they feed on decaying vegetation.

3. Animals in the class Hexapoda are characterized by a head with one pair of antennae, compound eyes, and ocelli; a thorax with three pairs of legs and usually two pairs of wings; and an abdomen that is free of appendages except terminal sensory (cerci) and reproductive (ovipositor) structures.

4. Insect flight involves either a direct (synchronous) flight mechanism or an indirect (asynchronous) flight mechanism.

5. Mouthparts of insects are adapted for chewing, piercing, and/or sucking, and the gut tract may be modified for pumping, storage, digestion, and water conservation.

6. In insects, gas exchange occurs through a tracheal system.

7. The insect nervous system is similar to that of other arthropods. Sensory structures include tympanal organs, compound eyes, and ocelli.

8. Malpighian tubules transport uric acid to the digestive tract. Conversion of nitrogenous wastes to uric acid conserves water but is energetically expensive.

9. Hormones regulate many insect functions, including ecdysis and metamorphosis. Pheromones are chemicals emitted by one individual that alter the behavior of another member of the same species.

10. Insect adaptations for reproduction on land include resistant eggs, external genitalia, and behavioral mechanisms that bring males and females together at appropriate times.

11. Metamorphosis of an insect may be ametabolous, paurometabolous, hemimetabolous, or holometabolous. Neuroendocrine and endocrine secretions control metamorphosis.

12. Insects show both innate and learned behavior.

13. Many insects are beneficial to humans, and a few are parasites and/or transmit diseases to humans or agricultural products. Others attack cultivated plants and stored products.

14. Zoologists continue to debate whether the arthropods represent a monophyletic group or a polyphyletic group.

SELECTED KEY TERMS

ametabolous metamorphosis (p. 390)
caste (p. 392)
direct or synchronous flight (p. 384)
hemimetabolous metamorphosis (p. 391)
holometabolous metamorphosis (p. 391)

indirect or asynchronous flight (p. 384)
larval instars (p. 390)
nymphs (p. 391)
paurometabolous metamorphosis (p. 391)
pupa (p. 391)

CRITICAL THINKING QUESTIONS

1. What problems are associated with living and reproducing in terrestrial environments? Explain how insects overcome these problems.

2. List as many examples as you can of how insects communicate with each other. In each case, what is the form and purpose of the communication?

3. In what way does holometabolous metamorphosis reduce competition between immature and adult stages? Give specific examples.

4. What role does each stage play in the life history of holometabolous insects?

5. Some biologists think that the arthropods are a polyphyletic group. What does that mean? What would polyphyletic origins require in terms of the origin of the exoskeleton and its derivatives?

REFERENCES ON THE WORLD WIDE WEB

1. **Introduction to the Myriapoda.** This site contains information on the biology and paleontology of the Chilopoda, Diplopoda, Symphyla, and Pauropoda.

   http://www.ucmp.berkeley.edu/arthropoda/uniramia/myriapoda.html

2. **Introduction to the Uniramia.** This site contains information on the fossil record, life history, ecology, systematics, and morphology of all the uniramian anthropods.

   http://www.ucmp.berkeley.edu/arthropoda/uniramia/uniramia.html

3. **The Virtual Insectary.** This site has information on insect foods and habitats, as well as many images of insects.

   http://www.vt.edu:10021/forestry/wildlife/stein/insects.html

4. **Forensic Entomology Homepage.** Learn how insects can help to solve crimes.

   http://www.uio.no/~mostarke/forens_ent/forensic_entomology.html

5. **Iowa State Entomology Index of Internet Resources.** This resource is a directory and search engine of insect-related sources on the Internet. Find information on beekeeping, entomology meetings, and insect collections. Hear insect sounds, and see insect images.

   http://www.public.iastate.edu/~entomology/ResourceList.html

6. **FETCH 21.** This resource provides links to information for anyone interested in forest insects, as well as other economically important insects.

   http://www.forestry.ubc.ca/fetch21/fetch21/FETCH21.html

7. **Iowa State University's Tasty Insect Recipes.** Learn to cook banana worm bread, bug blox, and chocolate chirpie chip cookies. Insects can be nutritious and delicious!

   http://www.ent.iastate.edu/Misc/InsectsAsFood.html

8. **Fon's Bug World.** This site for insect enthusiasts includes insect art, photographs, and links to museums and other entomology sites.

   http://www.sirius.com/~fonzilla/insect.htm

9. **Beetles.** Here is a site devoted entirely to beetles. In addition to seeing photographs, you learn how beetles fly and navigate.

   http://www.source.at/beetles/

10. **Entomoloy.** This site provides entomology links and information on meetings, jobs, publications, movies, and graduate schools.

    http://www.colstate.edu/Depts/Entomology/WWWVL-Entomology.htm

11. **Entomology Interest Page.** Learn about the use of insects in education, entertainment, business, landscaping, and recreation at this site.

    http://www.netgate.net/~ddc/entomol/index.html

12. **University of Florida Book of Insect Records.** This site is an insect record book. What insect is the fastest flier? What insect has the most spectacular mating habits? What insect has the smallest eggs? Learn answers to these and many other questions by visiting this site.

    http://gnv.ifas.ufl.edu/~tjw/recbk.htm

Some Lesser-Known Invertebrates:
Possible Arthropod Relatives

Three Phyla of Uncertain Affiliation: The Onychophora, Pentastomida, and Tardigrada

Animals in the phyla Onychophora, Pentastomida, and Tardigrada show a combination of arthropod and nonarthropod characteristics.

Phylum Onychophora: The Onychophorans, or Velvet or Walking Worms

The onychophorans (on-e-kof'o-rans) (Gr. *onyx*, claw + *pherein*, to bear), also known as velvet or walking worms, are free-living terrestrial animals that live in certain humid, tropical regions. Their ancestors have been considered an evolutionary transition between annelids and arthropods because of their many similarities to both phyla. These interesting worms may live up to 6 years. Zoologists have described more than one hundred species, with *Peripatus* being the best-known genus.

Onychophorans usually come out at night and move by using their unjointed legs to crawl (figure 1). Most species are predaceous and feed on small invertebrates. To capture fast-moving prey, onychophorans secrete an adhesive slime (that their adhesive gland produces) from their oral papillae. Some species can eject a stream of slime with enough force to strike a prey animal 50 cm away. The slime hardens immediately, entangling the prey, which is then masticated with the mandibles and sucked into the mouth.

The sexes are separate, and fertilization is internal. Onychophorans are either oviparous or viviparous. The oviparous species lay large, yolky eggs, each enclosed in a shell, in moist places; cleavage is spiral. The viviparous species retain the embryos in the uterus.

(a)

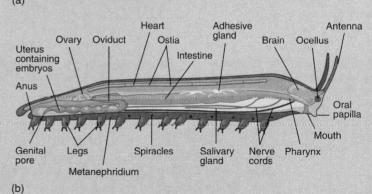

(b)

FIGURE 1 **Phylum Onychophora.** *(a) Peripatus. (b)* Lateral view of the internal anatomy of a female. The anterior end consists of two large antennae and a ventral mouth. Oral papillae and clawlike mandibles analogous to those of arthropods surround the mouth. The legs vary in number from 14 to 43 pairs; each leg has a pair of terminal claws. Small scales cover large and small tubercles that are arranged in rings or bands over the entire body surface.

399

FIGURE 2   **Phylum Pentastomida.** Close-up of the hooks pentastomids use to attach to their hosts. Note the mouth between the middle hooks (arrow). When feeding, a pentastomid grasps the host tissue with its clawed legs, inflicting a wound. It then uses its mouth to suck blood and tissue fluid out of the wound.

FIGURE 3   **Phylum Tardigrada.** The tardigrade, *Macrobiotus tonolli* (SEM ×1080). The body is elongate, cylindrical, and unsegmented, and has four pairs of unsegmented legs with claws. A proteinaceous cuticle covers the entire body and is periodically molted.

PHYLUM PENTASTOMIDA: THE PENTASTOMIDS, OR TONGUE WORMS

The pentastomids (pen-tah-stom'ids) (Gr. *pente*, five + *stoma*, mouth), or tongue worms, are all endoparasitic in the lungs or nasal passageways of carnivorous vertebrates (figure 2). Ninety percent of pentastomid hosts are reptiles (e.g., snakes, lizards, crocodiles). There are about 90 species; two of the more well-known genera are *Linguatula* and *Raillietiella*.

Pentastomids are dioecious, and females are larger than males. Gonads are unpaired, and gonopores open to the outside. Male and female pentastomids mate in the final host. Following internal fertilization, females lay millions of shelled eggs, which pass out in the host's nasal secretions, saliva, or feces. If one of a variety of vertebrate intermediate hosts eats the eggs, the larvae develop. The larva has four to six arthropod-like jointed appendages. When a final host eats the intermediate host, digestive enzymes free the larva, and it migrates up the esophagus to the lungs, trachea, or nasal sinuses. Just as in the arthropods, pentastomids possess a brain and ventral nerve cord with ganglia and a hemocoel.

PHYLUM TARDIGRADA: THE TARDIGRADES, OR WATER BEARS

The tardigrades (tar-di-gra'ds) (L. *tardus*, slow + *gradus*, step) are commonly called water bears because of their body shape and legs and the way they lumber over aquatic vegetation (figure 3). These small animals (less than 1 mm in length) live in marine interstitial areas, in freshwater detritus, and in the water film on terrestrial lichens, liverworts, and mosses. There are about five hundred species; the most common genera are *Echiniscus*, *Echiniscoides*, and *Macrobiotus*.

Tardigrades are dioecious, with a single gonad dorsal to the midgut. A single oviduct or sperm duct empties into a gonopore. Fertilization is internal. The female lays several dozen ornate eggs. After about 2 weeks, a juvenile hatches from the egg, molts, and develops into an adult. In some moss-dwelling species, males are rare or have never been observed, and parthenogenic reproduction presumably occurs.

Tardigrades (as well as nematodes and many rotifers) can enter a period of suspended animation termed cryptobiosis (Gr. *kryptos*, hidden + *bios*, life). This ability offers great survival benefit to these animals, which live in habitats where conditions can suddenly become adverse. If a tardigrade begins to dry out (desiccate), it contracts into a shape that produces an ordered packing of organs and tissues to minimize the mechanical damage that the desiccation causes. Overall metabolism slows. Rehydration reverses these events. Interestingly, repeated periods of cryptobiosis can extend a life span of approximately 1 year to 60 to 70 years.

THE ECHINODERMS

Concepts

1. Echinoderms are a part of the deuterostome evolutionary lineage. They are characterized by pentaradial symmetry, a calcium carbonate internal skeleton, and a water-vascular system.
2. Although many classes of echinoderms are extinct, living echinoderms are divided into six classes: (1) Asteroidea, sea stars; (2) Ophiuroidea, brittle stars and basket stars; (3) Echinoidea, sea urchins and sand dollars; (4) Holothuroidea, sea cucumbers; (5) Crinoidea, sea lilies and feather stars; and (6) Concentricycloidea, sea daisies.
3. Pentaradial symmetry of echinoderms probably developed during the evolution of sedentary lifestyles, in which echinoderms used the water-vascular system in suspension feeding. Later, evolution resulted in some echinoderms becoming more mobile, and the water-vascular system came to be used primarily in locomotion.

Would You Like to Know . . .

1. what evidence links echinoderms and chordates to a common evolutionary pathway? (p. 402)
2. why most sea stars have five arms, rather than four or six? (p. 403)
3. how a sea star opens the shell of a clam? (p. 405)
4. how brittle stars use their snakelike arms? (p. 407)
5. what sea urchins use to chew through rock and coral? (p. 409)
6. how sea cucumbers "spill their insides" for a predator or a collector? (p. 411)
7. what is the most recently discovered class of living echinoderms? (p. 412)
8. what was the original function of the water-vascular system? (p. 412)

This chapter answers these and other useful questions.

This chapter contains evolutionary concepts, which are set off in this font.

EVOLUTIONARY PERSPECTIVE

If you could visit 400-million-year-old Paleozoic seas, you would see representatives of nearly every phylum studied in the previous eight chapters of this text. In addition, you would observe many representatives of the phylum Echinodermata (i-ki′na-dur″ma-tah) (Gr. *echinos*, spiny + *derma*, skin + *ata*, to bear). Many ancient echinoderms attached to their substrate and probably lived as filter feeders—a feature found in only one class of modern echinoderms (figure 25.1). Today, the relatively common sea stars, sea urchins, sand dollars, and sea cucumbers represent this phylum. In terms of numbers of species, echinoderms may seem to be a declining phylum. Fossil records indicate that about 12 of 18 classes of echinoderms have become extinct. That does not mean, however, that living echinoderms are of minor importance. Members of three classes of echinoderms have flourished and often make up a major component of the biota of marine ecosystems (table 25.1).

Characteristics of the phylum Echinodermata include:

1. Calcareous endoskeleton in the form of ossicles that arise from mesodermal tissue
2. Adults with pentaradial symmetry and larvae with bilateral symmetry
3. Water-vascular system composed of water-filled canals used in locomotion, attachment, and/or feeding
4. Complete digestive tract that may be secondarily reduced
5. Hemal system derived from coelomic cavities
6. Nervous system consisting of a nerve net, nerve ring, and radial nerves

RELATIONSHIPS TO OTHER ANIMALS

❶ Most zoologists believe that echinoderms share a common ancestry with hemichordates and chordates because of the deuterostome characteristics that they share *(see figure 21.3)*: an anus that develops in the region of the blastopore, a coelom that forms from outpockets of the embryonic gut tract (vertebrate chordates are an exception), and radial, indeterminate cleavage. Unfortunately, no known fossils document a common ancestor for these phyla or demonstrate how the deuterostome lineage was derived from ancestral diploblastic or triploblastic stocks (figure 25.2).

Although echinoderm adults are radially symmetrical, most zoologists believe that echinoderms evolved from bilaterally symmetrical ancestors. Evidence for this relationship includes bilaterally symmetrical echinoderm larval stages and extinct forms that were not radially symmetrical.

ECHINODERM CHARACTERISTICS

The approximately seven thousand species of living echinoderms are exclusively marine and occur at all depths in all oceans. Modern echinoderms have a form of radial symmetry, called **pentaradial symmetry,** in which body parts are arranged in fives, or a

FIGURE 25.1

Phylum Echinodermata. This feather star (*Comanthina*) uses its highly branched arms in filter feeding. Although this probably reflects the original use of echinoderm appendages, most modern echinoderms use arms for locomotion, capturing prey, and scavenging the substrate for food.

TABLE 25.1	CLASSIFICATION OF THE PHYLUM ECHINODERMATA

Phylum Echinodermata (i-ki′na-dur″ma-tah)
The phylum of triploblastic, coelomate animals whose members are pentaradially symmetrical as adults and possess a water-vascular system and an endoskeleton covered by epithelium. Pedicellaria often present.

> **Class Crinoidea** (krin-oi′de-ah)
> Free-living or attached by an aboral stalk of ossicles; flourished in the Paleozoic era. Approximately 230 living species. Sea lilies, feather stars.
>
> **Class Asteroidea** (as″te-roi′de-ah)
> Rays not sharply set off from central disk; ambulacral grooves with tube feet; suction disks on tube feet; pedicellariae present. Sea stars. About 1,500 species.
>
> **Class Ophiuroidea** (o-fe-u-roi′de-ah)
> Arms sharply marked off from the central disk; tube feet without suction disks. Brittle stars. Over 2,000 species.
>
> **Class Concentricycloidea** (kon-sen″tri-si-kloi′de-ah)
> Two concentric water-vascular rings encircle a disklike body; no digestive system; digest and absorb nutrients across their lower surface; internal brood pouches; no free-swimming larval stage. Sea daisies.
>
> **Class Echinoidea** (ek″i-noi′de-ah)
> Globular or disk shaped; no rays; movable spines; skeleton (test) of closely fitting plates. Sea urchins, sand dollars. Approximately 1,000 species.
>
> **Class Holothuroidea** (hol″o-thu-roi′de-ah)
> No rays; elongate along the oral-aboral axis; microscopic ossicles embedded in a muscular body wall; circumoral tentacles. Sea cucumbers. Approximately 1,500 species.

This listing reflects a phylogenetic sequence; however, the discussion that follows begins with the echinoderms that are familiar to most students.

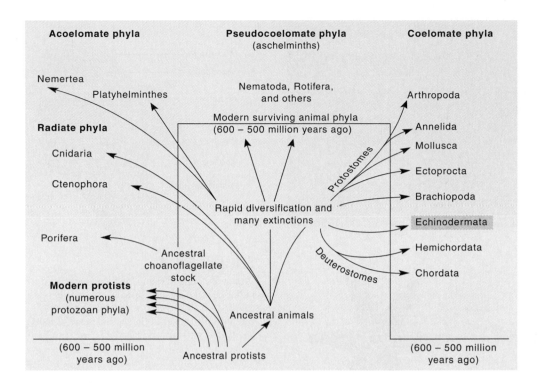

FIGURE 25.2

Evolutionary Relationships of the Echinoderms. The echinoderms (shaded in orange) diverged from the deuterostomate lineage at least 600 million years ago. Although modern echinoderms are pentaradially symmetrical, the earliest echinoderms were probably bilaterally symmetrical.

multiple of five, around an oral-aboral axis (figure 25.3a). Radial symmetry is adaptive for sedentary or slowly moving animals because it allows a uniform distribution of sensory, feeding, and other structures around the animal. Some modern mobile echinoderms, however, have secondarily returned to a basically bilateral form.

The echinoderm skeleton consists of a series of calcium carbonate plates called ossicles. These plates are derived from mesoderm, held in place by connective tissues, and covered by an epidermal layer. If the epidermal layer is abraded away, the skeleton may be exposed in some body regions. The skeleton is frequently modified into fixed or articulated spines that project from the body surface.

2 The evolution of the skeleton may be responsible for the pentaradial body form of echinoderms. The joints between two skeletal plates represent a weak point in the skeleton (figure 25.3b). By not having weak joints directly opposite one another, the skeleton is made stronger than if the joints were arranged opposite each other.

The **water-vascular system** of echinoderms is a series of water-filled canals, and their extensions are called tube feet. It originates embryologically as a modification of the coelom and is ciliated internally. The water-vascular system includes a ring canal that surrounds the mouth (figure 25.4). The ring canal usually opens to the outside or to the body cavity through a stone canal and a sievelike plate, called the madreporite. The madreporite may serve as an inlet to replace water lost from the water-vascular system and may help equalize pressure differences between the water-vascular system and the outside. Tiedemann bodies are

swellings often associated with the ring canal. They are believed to be the site for production of phagocytic cells, called coelomocytes, whose functions are described later in this chapter. Polian vesicles are sacs that are also associated with the ring canal and function in fluid storage for the water-vascular system.

Five (or a multiple of five) radial canals branch from the ring canal. Radial canals are associated with arms of star-shaped echinoderms. In other echinoderms, they may be associated with the body wall and arch toward the aboral pole. Many lateral canals branch off each radial canal and end at the tube feet.

Tube feet are extensions of the canal system and usually emerge through openings in skeletal ossicles (see figure 25.3a). Internally, tube feet usually terminate in a bulblike, muscular ampulla. When an ampulla contracts, it forces water into the tube foot, which then extends. Valves prevent the backflow of water from the tube foot into the lateral canal. A tube foot often has a suction cup at its distal end. When the foot extends and contacts solid substrate, muscles of the suction cup contract and create a vacuum. In some taxa, tube feet have a pointed or blunt distal end. These echinoderms may extend their tube feet into a soft substrate to secure contact during locomotion or to sift sediment during feeding.

The water-vascular system has other functions in addition to locomotion. As is discussed at the end of this chapter, the original function of water-vascular systems was probably feeding, not locomotion. In addition, the soft membranes of the water-vascular system permit diffusion of respiratory gases and nitrogenous wastes across the body wall.

(a)

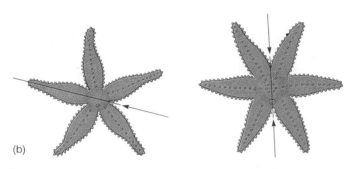

(b)

FIGURE 25.3

Pentaradial Symmetry. (*a*) Echinoderms exhibit pentaradial symmetry, in which body parts are arranged in fives around an oral-aboral axis. Note the madreporite between the bases of the two arms in the foreground and the tube feet on the tips of the upturned arm. (*b*) Comparison of hypothetical penta- and hexaradial echinoderms. The five-part organization may be advantageous because joints between skeletal ossicles are never directly opposite one another, as they would be with an even number of parts. Having joints on opposite sides of the body in line with each other (arrows) could make the skeleton weaker.

A **hemal system** consists of strands of tissue that encircle an echinoderm near the ring canal of the water-vascular system and run into each arm near the radial canals (*see figure 25.4*). The hemal system has been likened to a vestigial circulatory system; however, its function is largely unknown. It may aid in the transport of large molecules, hormones, or coelomocytes, which are cells that engulf and transport waste particles within the body.

CLASS ASTEROIDEA

The sea stars make up the class Asteroidea (as″te-roi′de-ah) (Gr. *aster*, star + *oeides*, in the form of) and include about 1,500 species (box 25.1). They often live on hard substrates in marine environ-

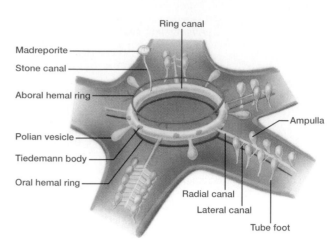

FIGURE 25.4

Water-Vascular System of a Sea Star. The ring canal gives rise to radial canals that lead into each arm. It opens to the outside or to the body cavity through a stone canal that ends at a madreporite on the aboral surface. Polian vesicles and Tiedemann bodies are often associated with the ring canal.

ments, although some species also live in sandy or muddy substrates. Sea stars may be brightly colored with red, orange, blue, or gray. *Asterias* is an orange sea star common along the Atlantic coast of North America and is frequently studied in introductory zoology laboratories.

Sea stars have five arms that radiate from a central disk. The oral opening, or mouth, is in the middle of one side of the central disk. It is normally oriented downward, and movable oral spines surround it. Movable and fixed spines project from the skeleton and roughen the aboral surface. Thin folds of the body wall, called **dermal branchiae,** extend between ossicles and function in gas exchange (figure 25.5). In some sea stars, the aboral surface has numerous pincherlike structures called **pedicellariae,** which clean the body surface of debris and have protective functions. Pedicellariae may be attached on a movable spine, or they may be immovably fused to skeletal ossicles.

A series of ossicles in the arm form an **ambulacral groove** that runs the length of the oral surface of each arm. The ambulacral groove houses the radial canal, and paired rows of tube feet protrude through the body wall on either side of the ambulacral groove. Tube feet of sea stars move in a stepping motion. Alternate extension, attachment, and contraction of tube feet move sea stars across their substrate. The nervous system coordinates the tube feet so that all feet move the sea star in the same direction; however, the tube feet do not move in unison. The suction disks of tube feet are effective attachment structures, allowing sea stars to maintain their position, or move from place to place, in spite of strong wave action.

BOX 25.1 | A THORNY PROBLEM FOR AUSTRALIA'S BARRIER REEF

The crown-of-thorns sea star (*Acanthaster planci*) is a common inhabitant of the South Pacific. Adults have a diameter of about 0.5m and 13 to 16 arms (figure 1). Their common name is derived from their large, venomous spines that can cause swelling, pain, and nausea in humans.

The crown-of-thorns sea star has become a problem in the waters off Australia and other South Pacific coasts. It feeds on coral polyps, and in one day, a single individual can extract polyps from $0.1m^2$ of reef. Over the last 20 years, the crown-of-thorns sea star has experienced a dramatic population increase. Thousands of sea stars move slowly along a reef, leaving a white, almost sterile, limestone coral skeleton in their trail. They have seriously damaged over 500 km^2 of Australia's Great Barrier Reef.

One or more hypotheses may explain why there is a problem now, when these sea stars and coral polyps have coexisted for millions of years. Some believe that the population increase in sea stars may be partially due to the destruction of sea star predators—in particular, the giant triton gastropods. Tritons are valued for their beautiful shells, and blasting to create shipping channels has disrupted their habitat. Pesticides and other pollutants are also believed to be destroying predators of crown-of-thorns larvae. Another hypothesis suggests that the apparent increase in the sea star population may be a natural fluctuation in population size.

The reefs of the South Pacific are a source of economic wealth in the form of fisheries and tourism; therefore, the proliferation of crown-of-thorns sea stars has been the subject of intense study and control efforts. The Australian government has spent in excess of $3 million and has not yet achieved satisfactory control. Control measures have included scuba divers injecting formaldehyde into adult crown-of-thorns sea stars, the erection of wire fences to divert sea star populations from reefs, and the use of computers to predict

FIGURE 1   The Crown-of-Thorns Sea Star (*Acanthaster planci*). This sea star is feeding on coral (*Pocillopora*).

movements of colonies and local population explosions. One of the difficulties in these control efforts stems from sea star larvae being planktonic and widely dispersed by oceanic currents.

The original relationship between crown-of-thorns sea stars, coral polyps, and possibly, sea star predators is an interesting example of a balanced predator-prey relationship. What is unfortunate is that humans often do not appreciate such balances until they have been altered.

MAINTENANCE FUNCTIONS

Sea stars feed on snails, bivalves, crustaceans, polychaetes, corals, detritus, and a variety of other food items. The mouth opens to a short esophagus and then to a large stomach that fills most of the coelom of the central disk. The stomach is divided into two regions. The larger, oral stomach, sometimes called the cardiac stomach, receives ingested food (figure 25.6). It joins the smaller, aboral stomach, sometimes called the pyloric stomach. The aboral (pyloric) stomach gives rise to ducts that connect to secretory and absorptive structures called pyloric ceca. Two pyloric ceca extend into each arm. A short intestine leads to rectal ceca (uncertain functions) and to a nearly nonfunctional anus, which opens on the aboral surface of the central disk.

Some sea stars ingest whole prey, which are digested extracellularly within the stomach. Undigested material is expelled through the mouth. Many sea stars feed on bivalves by forcing the valves apart. (Anyone who has tried to pull apart the valves of a bivalve shell can appreciate that this is a remarkable accomplishment.) ③ When a sea star feeds on a bivalve, it wraps itself around the bivalve's ventral margin. Tube feet attach to the outside of the shell, and the body-wall musculature forces the valves apart. (This is possible because the sea star changes tube feet when the muscles of engaged tube feet begin to tire.) When the valves are opened about 0.1 mm, increased coelomic pressure everts the oral (cardiac) portion of the sea star's stomach into the bivalve shell. Digestive enzymes are released, and partial digestion occurs in the bivalve shell. This digestion further weakens

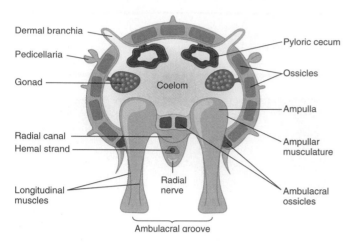

FIGURE 25.5

Body Wall and Internal Anatomy of a Sea Star. A cross section through one arm of a sea star shows the structures of the water-vascular system and the tube feet extending through the ambulacral groove.

the bivalve's adductor muscles, and the shell eventually opens completely. Partially digested tissues are taken into the aboral (pyloric) portion of the stomach, and into the pyloric ceca for further digestion and absorption. After feeding and initial digestion, the sea star retracts the stomach, using stomach retractor muscles.

Gases, nutrients, and metabolic wastes are transported in the coelom by diffusion and by the action of ciliated cells lining the body cavity. Gas exchange and excretion of metabolic wastes (principally ammonia) occur by diffusion across dermal branchiae, tube feet, and other membranous structures. A sea star's hemal system consists of strands of tissue that encircle the mouth near the ring canal, extend aborally near the stone canal, and run into the arms near radial canals (*see figure 25.4*).

The nervous system of sea stars consists of a nerve ring that encircles the mouth and radial nerves that extend into each arm. Radial nerves lie within the ambulacral groove, just oral to the radial canal of the water-vascular system and the radial strands of the hemal system (*see figure 25.5*). Radial nerves coordinate the functions of tube feet. Other nervous elements are in the form of a nerve net associated with the body wall.

Most sensory receptors are distributed over the surface of the body and tube feet. Sea stars respond to light, chemicals, and various mechanical stimuli. They often have specialized photoreceptors at the tips of their arms. These are actually tube feet that lack suction cups but have a pigment spot surrounding a group of ocelli.

REGENERATION, REPRODUCTION, AND DEVELOPMENT

Sea stars are well known for their powers of regeneration. They can regenerate any part of a broken arm. In a few species, an entire starfish can be regenerated from a broken arm if the arm con-

(a)

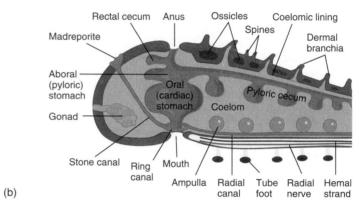

(b)

FIGURE 25.6

Digestive Structures in a Sea Star. A mouth leads to a large oral (cardiac) stomach and an aboral (pyloric) stomach. Pyloric ceca extend into each arm. (*a*) Aboral view. (*b*) Lateral view through central disk and one arm.

tains a portion of the central disk. Regeneration is a slow process, taking up to 1 year for complete regeneration. Asexual reproduction involves dividing the central disk, followed by regeneration of each half.

Sea stars are dioecious, but sexes are indistinguishable externally. Two gonads are present in each arm and enlarge to nearly fill an arm during the reproductive periods. Gonopores open between the bases of each arm.

The embryology of echinoderms has been studied extensively because of the relative ease of inducing spawning and maintaining embryos in the laboratory. External fertilization is the rule. Because gametes cannot survive long in the ocean, maturation of gametes and spawning must be coordinated if fertilization is to take place. The photoperiod (the relative length of light and dark in a 24-hour period) and temperature are environmental factors used to coordinate sexual activity. In addition, gamete release by one individual is accompanied by the release of spawning pheromones, which induce other sea stars in the area to spawn, increasing the likelihood of fertilization.

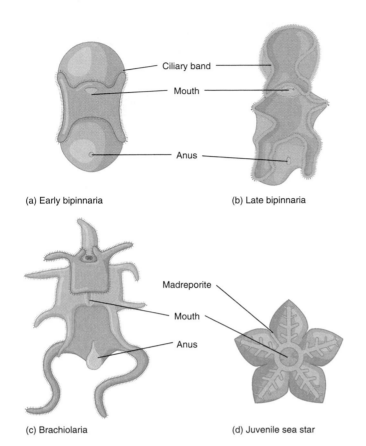

(a) Early bipinnaria

Ciliary band

Mouth

Anus

(b) Late bipinnaria

Madreporite

Mouth

Anus

(c) Brachiolaria

(d) Juvenile sea star

FIGURE 25.7

Development of a Sea Star. Later embryonic stages are ciliated and swim and feed in the plankton. In a few species, embryos develop from yolk stored in the egg during gamete formation. Following blastula and gastrula stages, larvae develop. (*a*) Early bipinnaria larva (0.5 mm). (*b*) Late bipinnaria larva (1 mm). (*c*) Brachiolaria larva (1 mm). (*d*) Juvenile sea star (1 to 2 mm).

Chapter 10 covers the early stages of echinoderm embryology in detail. Embryos are planktonic, and cilia are used in swimming (figure 25.7). After gastrulation, bands of cilia differentiate, and a bilaterally symmetrical larva, called a bipinnaria larva, forms. The larva usually feeds on planktonic protists. The development of larval arms results in a brachiolaria larva, which settles to the substrate, attaches, and metamorphoses into a juvenile sea star.

Stop and Ask Yourself

1. Why do many zoologists believe that ancestral echinoderms were bilaterally symmetrical?
2. What are the functions of the water-vascular system?
3. How does a sea star feed on a clam?
4. How is the nervous tissue arranged in a sea star?

CLASS OPHIUROIDEA

The class Ophiuroidea (o-fe-u-roi'de-ah) (Gr. *ophis*, snake + *oura*, tail + *oeides*, in the form of) includes the basket stars and the brittle stars. With over two thousand species, this is the most diverse group of echinoderms. Ophiuroids, however, are often overlooked because of their small size and their tendency to occupy crevices in rocks and coral or to cling to algae.

The arms of ophiuroids are long and, unlike those of asteroids, are sharply set off from the central disk, giving the central disk a pentagonal shape. Brittle stars have unbranched arms, and most range in size from 1 to 3 cm (figure 25.8*a*). Basket stars have arms that branch repeatedly (figure 25.8*b*). Neither dermal branchiae nor pedicellariae are present in ophiuroids. The tube feet of ophiuroids lack suction disks and ampullae, and contraction of muscles associated with the base of a tube foot extends the tube foot. Unlike the sea stars, the madreporite of ophiuroids is on the oral surface.

The water-vascular system of ophiuroids is not used for locomotion. Instead, the skeleton is modified to permit a unique form of grasping and movement. Superficial ossicles, which originate on the aboral surface, cover the lateral and oral surfaces of each arm. The ambulacral groove—containing the radial nerve, hemal strand, and radial canal—is thus said to be "closed." Ambulacral ossicles are in the arm, forming a central supportive axis. ❹ Successive ambulacral ossicles articulate with one another and are acted upon by relatively large muscles to produce snakelike movements that allow the arms to curl around a stalk of algae or to hook into a coral crevice. During locomotion, the central disk is held above the substrate, and two arms pull the animal along, while other arms extend forward and/or trail behind the animal.

MAINTENANCE FUNCTIONS

Ophiuroids are predators and scavengers. They use their arms and tube feet in sweeping motions to collect prey and particulate matter, which are then transferred to the mouth. Some ophiuroids are filter feeders that wave their arms and trap plankton on mucus-covered tube feet. Trapped plankton is passed from tube foot to tube foot along the length of an arm until it reaches the mouth.

The mouth of ophiuroids is in the center of the central disk, and five triangular jaws form a chewing apparatus. The mouth leads to a saclike stomach. There is no intestine, and no part of the digestive tract extends into the arms.

The coelom of ophiuroids is reduced and is mainly confined to the central disk, but it still serves as the primary means for the distribution of nutrients, wastes, and gases. Coelomocytes aid in the distribution of nutrients and the expulsion of particulate wastes. Ammonia is the primary nitrogenous waste product, and it is lost by diffusion across tube feet and membranous sacs, called **bursae,** that invaginate from the oral surface of the central disk. Slits in the oral disk, near the base of each arm, allow cilia to move water into and out of the bursae (figure 25.9).

(a)

(b)

FIGURE 25.8

Class Ophiuroidea. (*a*) This brittle star (*Ophiopholis aculeata*) uses its long, snakelike arms for crawling along its substrate and curling around objects in its environment. (*b*) Basket stars have five highly branched arms. They wave the arms in the water and with the mucus-covered tube feet capture planktonic organisms.

REGENERATION, REPRODUCTION, AND DEVELOPMENT

Like sea stars, ophiuroids can regenerate lost arms. If a brittle star is grasped by an arm, the contraction of certain muscles may sever and cast off the arm—hence the common name brittle star. This process, called autotomy (Gr. *autos*, self + *tomos*, to cut), is used in escape reactions. The ophiuroid later regenerates the arm. Some species also have a fission line across their central disk. When an ophiuroid splits into halves along this line, two ophiuroids regenerate.

Ophiuroids are dioecious. Males are usually smaller than females, who often carry the males. The gonads are associated with each bursa, and gametes are released into the bursa. Eggs may be shed to the outside or retained in the bursa, where they are fertilized and held through early development. Embryos are protected in the bursa and are sometimes nourished by the parent. A

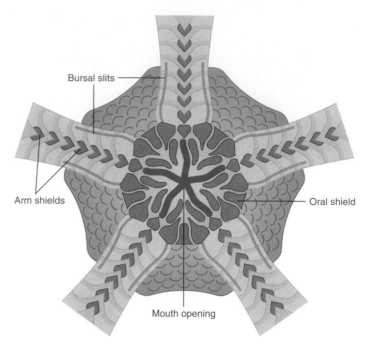

FIGURE 25.9

Class Ophiuroidea. Oral view of the disk of the brittle star, *Ophiomusium*. *Redrawn from L. Hyman, The Invertebrates, Volume IV. Copyright © 1959 McGraw-Hill, Inc. Used by permission.*

larval stage, called an ophiopluteus, is planktonic. Its long arms bear ciliary bands used to feed on plankton, and it undergoes metamorphosis before sinking to the substrate.

CLASS ECHINOIDEA

The sea urchins, sand dollars, and heart urchins make up the class Echinoidea (ek″i-noi′-de-ah) (Gr. *echinos*, spiny + *oeides*, in the form of). The approximately one thousand species are widely distributed in nearly all marine environments. Sea urchins are specialized for living on hard substrates, often wedging themselves into crevices and holes in rock or coral (figure 25.10*a*). Sand dollars and heart urchins usually live in sand or mud, and burrow just below the surface (figure 25.10*b*). They use tube feet to catch organic matter settling on them or passing over them. Sand dollars often live in dense beds, which favors efficient reproduction and feeding.

Sea urchins are rounded, and their oral end is oriented toward the substrate. Their skeleton, called a test, consists of 10 closely fitting plates that arch between oral and aboral ends. Five ambulacral plates have openings for tube feet, and alternate with five interambulacral plates, which have tubercles for the articulation of spines. The base of each spine is a concave socket, and muscles at its base move the spine. Spines are often sharp and sometimes hollow and contain venom dangerous to swimmers. The pedicellariae of sea urchins have either two or three jaws and connect to the body wall by a relatively long stalk (figure 25.11*a*). They clean the body of debris and capture planktonic larvae, which provide an extra source of food. Pedicellariae of some sea urchins contain venom sacs and are grooved or hollow to inject venom into a predator, such as a sea star.

(a)

(b)

FIGURE 25.10

Class Echinoidea. (*a*) A sea urchin (*Strongylocentrotus*) (*b*) Sand dollars are specialized for living in soft substrates, where they are often partially buried.

The water-vascular system is similar to that of other echinoderms. Radial canals run along the inner body wall between the oral and the aboral poles. Tube feet possess ampullae and suction cups, and the water-vascular system opens to the outside through many pores in one aboral ossicle that serves as a madreporite.

Echinoids move by using spines for pushing against the substrate and tube feet for pulling. Sand dollars and heart urchins use spines to help burrow in soft substrates. ⑤ Some sea urchins burrow into rock and coral to escape the action of waves and strong currents. They form cup-shaped depressions and deeper burrows, using the action of their chewing Aristotle's lantern, which is described next.

MAINTENANCE FUNCTIONS

Echinoids feed on algae, bryozoans, coral polyps, and dead animal remains. Oral tube feet surrounding the mouth manipulate food. A chewing apparatus, called **Aristotle's lantern,** projects from the

(a)

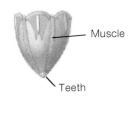

(b)

FIGURE 25.11

Internal Anatomy of a Sea Urchin. (*a*) Sectional view. (*b*) Aristotle's lantern is a chewing structure consisting of about 35 ossicles and associated muscles.

mouth (figure 25.11*b*). It consists of about 35 ossicles and attached muscles and cuts food into small pieces for ingestion. The mouth cavity leads to a pharynx, an esophagus, and a long, coiled intestine that ends aborally at the anus.

Echinoids have a large coelom, and coelomic fluids are the primary circulatory medium. Small gills, found in a thin membrane surrounding the mouth, are outpockets of the body wall and are lined by ciliated epithelium. Gas exchange occurs by diffusion across this epithelium and across the tube feet. Ciliary currents, changes in coelomic pressure, and the contraction of muscles associated with Aristotle's lantern move coelomic fluids into and out of gills. Excretory and nervous functions are similar to those described for asteroids.

REPRODUCTION AND DEVELOPMENT

Echinoids are dioecious. Gonads are on the internal body wall of the interambulacral plates. During breeding season, they nearly fill the spacious coelom. One gonopore is in each of five ossicles, called genital plates, at the aboral end of the echinoid, although the sand dollars usually have only four gonads and gonopores. Gametes are shed into the water, and fertilization is external. Development eventually results in a pluteus larva that spends several months in the plankton and eventually undergoes metamorphosis to the adult (*see figure 10.6*).

FIGURE 25.12

Class Holothuroidea. A sea cucumber (*Parastichopus californicus*).

CLASS HOLOTHUROIDEA

The class Holothuroidea (hol″o-thu-roi′de-ah) (Gr. *holothourion*, sea cucumber + *oeides*, in the form of) has approximately 1,500 species, whose members are commonly called sea cucumbers. Sea cucumbers are found at all depths in all oceans, where they crawl over hard substrates or burrow through soft substrates (figure 25.12).

Sea cucumbers have no arms, and they are elongate along the oral-aboral axis. They lie on one side, which is usually flattened as a permanent ventral side, giving them a secondary bilateral symmetry. Tube feet surrounding the mouth are elongate and referred to as tentacles. Most adults range in length between 10 and 30 cm. Their body wall is thick and muscular, and lacks protruding spines or pedicellariae. Beneath the epidermis is the dermis, a thick layer of connective tissue with embedded ossicles. Sea cucumber ossicles are microscopic and do not function in determining body shape. Larger ossicles form a calcareous ring that encircles the oral end of the digestive tract, serving as a point of attachment for body wall muscles (figure 25.13). Beneath the dermis is a layer of circular muscles overlying longitudinal muscles. The body wall of sea cucumbers, when boiled and dried, is known as trepang in Asian countries. It may be eaten as a main-course item or added to soups as flavoring and a source of protein.

The madreporite of sea cucumbers is internal, and the water-vascular system is filled with coelomic fluid. The ring canal encircles the oral end of the digestive tract and gives rise to one to

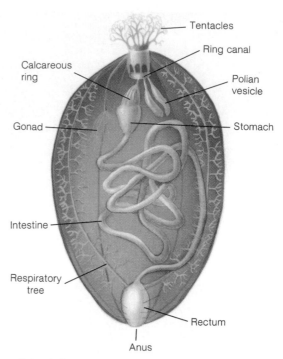

FIGURE 25.13

Internal Structure of a Sea Cucumber, *Thyone*. The mouth leads to a stomach supported by a calcareous ring. The calcareous ring is also the attachment site for longitudinal retractor muscles of the body. Contractions of these muscles pull the tentacles into the anterior end of the body. The stomach leads to a looped intestine. The intestine continues to the rectum and anus. (The anterior portion of the digestive tract is displaced aborally in this illustration.)

ten Polian vesicles. Five radial canals and the canals to the tentacles branch from the ring canal. Radial canals and tube feet, with suction cups and ampullae, run between the oral and aboral poles. The side of a sea cucumber resting on the substrate contains three of the five rows of tube feet, which are primarily used for attachment. The two rows of tube feet on the upper surface may be reduced in size or may be absent.

Sea cucumbers are mostly sluggish burrowers and creepers, although some swim by undulating their body from side to side. Locomotion using tube feet is inefficient because the tube feet are not anchored by body wall ossicles. Locomotion more commonly results from contractions of body-wall muscles that produce wormlike, locomotor waves that pass along the length of the body.

MAINTENANCE FUNCTIONS

Most sea cucumbers ingest particulate organic matter using their tentacles. Mucus covering the tentacles traps food as the tentacles sweep across the substrate or are held out in seawater. The digestive tract consists of a stomach; a long, looped intestine; a rectum; and an anus (figure 25.13). Sea cucumbers thrust tentacles into the mouth to wipe off trapped food. During digestion, coelomocytes move across the intestinal wall, secrete enzymes to aid in digestion, and engulf and distribute the products of digestion.

The coelom of sea cucumbers is large, and the cilia of the coelomic lining circulate fluids throughout the body cavity, distributing respiratory gases, wastes, and nutrients. The hemal system of sea cucumbers is well developed, with relatively large sinuses and a network of channels containing coelomic fluids. Its primary role is food distribution.

Respiratory trees are a pair of tubes that attach at the rectum and branch throughout the body cavity of sea cucumbers. The pumping action of the rectum circulates water into these tubes. When the rectum dilates, water moves through the anus into the rectum. Contraction of the rectum, along with contraction of an anal sphincter, forces water into the respiratory tree. Water exits the respiratory tree when tubules of the tree contract. Respiratory gases and nitrogenous wastes move between the coelom and seawater across these tubules.

The nervous system of sea cucumbers is similar to that of other echinoderms but has additional nerves supplying the tentacles and pharynx. Some sea cucumbers have statocysts, and others have relatively complex photoreceptors.

Casual examination suggests that sea cucumbers are defenseless against predators. Many sea cucumbers, however, produce toxins in their body walls that discourage predators. Other sea cucumbers can evert tubules of the respiratory tree, called Cuverian tubules, through the anus. These tubules contain sticky secretions and toxins capable of entangling and immobilizing predators. ❻ In addition, contractions of the body wall may result in expulsion of one or both respiratory trees, the digestive tract, and the gonads through the anus. This process, called evisceration, is a defensive adaptation that may discourage predators. Regeneration of lost parts follows.

REPRODUCTION AND DEVELOPMENT

Sea cucumbers are dioecious. They possess a single gonad, located anteriorly in the coelom, and a single gonopore near the base of the tentacles. Fertilization is usually external, and embryos develop into planktonic larvae. Metamorphosis precedes settling to the substrate. In some species, a female's tentacles trap eggs as the eggs are released. After fertilization, eggs are transferred to the body surface, where they are brooded. Although rare, coelomic brooding also occurs. Eggs are released into the body cavity, where fertilization (by an unknown mechanism) and early development occur. The young leave through a rupture in the body wall. Sea cucumbers can also reproduce by transverse fission, followed by regeneration of lost parts.

Stop and Ask Yourself

9. What structural features of sea cucumbers result in their having a secondary bilateral symmetry?
10. How is the water-vascular system of sea cucumbers modified for feeding?
11. What is a respiratory tree?
12. How does a sea cucumber defend itself against predators?

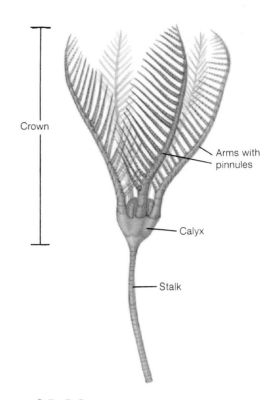

FIGURE 25.14
Class Crinoidea. A sea lily (*Ptilocrinus*).

CLASS CRINOIDEA

Members of the class Crinoidea (krin-oi″de-ah) (Gr. *krinon*, lily + *oeides*, in the form of) include the sea lilies and the feather stars. They are the most primitive of all living echinoderms and are very different from any covered thus far. Approximately 630 species are living today; however, an extensive fossil record indicates that many more were present during the Paleozoic era, 200 to 600 million years ago.

Sea lilies attach permanently to their substrate by a stalk (figure 25.14). The attached end of the stalk bears a flattened disk or rootlike extensions that are fixed to the substrate. Disklike ossicles of the stalk appear to be stacked on top of one another and are held together by connective tissues, giving a jointed appearance. The stalk usually bears projections, or cirri, arranged in whorls. The unattached end of a sea lily is called the crown. The aboral end of the crown attaches to the stalk and is supported by a set of ossicles, called the **calyx.** Five arms also attach at the calyx. They are branched, supported by ossicles, and bear smaller branches (pinnules)—giving them a featherlike appearance. Tube feet are in a double row along each arm. Ambulacral grooves on the arms lead toward the mouth. The mouth and anus open onto the upper (oral) surface.

Feather stars are similar to sea lilies, except they lack a stalk and are swimming and crawling animals (figure 25.15). The aboral end of the crown bears a ring of rootlike cirri, which cling when the animal is resting on a substrate. Feather stars swim by raising and lowering the arms, and they crawl over substrate by pulling with the tips of the arms.

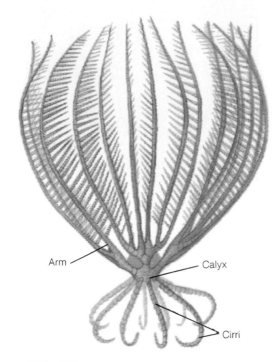

FIGURE 25.15
Class Crinoidea. A feather star (*Neometra*).

MAINTENANCE FUNCTIONS

Circulation, gas exchange, and excretion in crinoids are similar to these functions in other echinoderms. In feeding, however, crinoids use outstretched arms for suspension feeding. A planktonic organism that contacts a tube foot is trapped, and cilia in ambulacral grooves carry it to the mouth. Although this method of feeding is different from how other modern echinoderms feed, it probably reflects the original function of the water-vascular system.

Crinoids lack the nerve ring found in most echinoderms. Instead, a cup-shaped nerve mass below the calyx gives rise to radial nerves that extend through each arm and control the tube feet and arm musculature.

REPRODUCTION AND DEVELOPMENT

Crinoids, like other echinoderms, are dioecious. Gametes form from germinal epithelium in the coelom and are released through ruptures in the walls of the arms. Some species spawn in seawater, where fertilization and development occur. Other species brood embryos on the outer surface of the arms. Metamorphosis occurs after larvae attach to the substrate. Like other echinoderms, crinoids can regenerate lost parts.

CLASS CONCENTRICYCLOIDEA

The class Concentricycloidea (kon-sen″tri-si-kloi′de-ah) (ME *consentrik*, having a common center + Gr. *kykloeides*, like a circle) contains a single described species, known as the sea daisy.

FIGURE 25.16
Class Concentricycloida. A preserved sea daisy (*Xyloplax medusiformis*). This specimen is 3 mm in diameter.

⑦ Sea daisies have been recently discovered on debris in deep oceans (figure 25.16). They lack arms and are less than 1 cm in diameter. The most distinctive features of this species are the two circular water-vascular rings that encircle the disklike body. The inner of the two rings probably corresponds to the ring canal of members of other classes because it has Polian vesicles attached. The outer ring contains tube feet and ampullae, and probably corresponds to the radial canals of members of other classes. Sea daisies lack an internal digestive system. Instead, a thin membrane, called a velum, covers the surface of the animal applied to the substrate (e.g., decomposing wood) and digests and absorbs nutrients. Internally, five pairs of brood pouches hold embryos during development. No free-swimming larval stages are apparent. The mechanism for fertilization is unknown.

FURTHER PHYLOGENETIC CONSIDERATIONS

As mentioned earlier, most zoologists believe that echinoderms evolved from bilaterally symmetrical ancestors. Radial symmetry probably evolved during the transition from active to more sedentary lifestyles; however, the oldest echinoderm fossils, about 600 million years old, give little direct evidence of how this transition occurred.

Ancient fossils do give clues regarding the origin of the water-vascular system and the calcareous endoskeleton. Of all living echinoderms, the crinoids most closely resemble the oldest fossils. ⑧ Because crinoids use their water-vascular system for suspension feeding, filter feeding, rather than locomotion was probably the original function of the water-vascular system. As do crinoids, early echinoderms probably assumed a mouth-up position and attached aborally. They may have used arms and tube feet to capture food and move it to the mouth. The calcium carbonate endoskeleton may have evolved to support extended filtering arms and to protect these sessile animals.

Many modern echinoderms are more mobile. This free-living lifestyle is probably secondarily derived, as is the mouth-down orientation of most echinoderms. The mouth-down position is advantageous for predatory and scavenging lifestyles. Similarly, changes in the water-vascular system, such as the evolution of ampullae, suction disks, and feeding tentacles, can be interpreted as adaptations for locomotion and feeding in a more mobile lifestyle. The idea that the free-living lifestyle is secondary is reinforced by the observation that some echinoderms, such as the irregular echinoids and the holothuroids, have bilateral symmetry imposed upon a pentaradial body form.

The evolutionary relationships among the echinoderms are not clear. Numerous fossils date into the Cambrian period, but no interpretation of the evolutionary relationships among living and extinct echinoderms is definitive. Figure 25.17 shows one interpretation of the evolutionary relationships among extant (with living members) echinoderm classes. Most taxonomists agree that the echinoids and holothuroids are closely related. Whether the ophiuroids are more closely related to the echinoid/holothuroid lineage or the asteroid lineage is debated. The position of the Concentricycloidea in echinoderm phylogeny is highly speculative, and figure 25.17 does not show it.

Stop and Ask Yourself

13. What is the function of the stalk, calyx, and cirri in crinoids?
14. How is the function of the crinoid water-vascular system different from that of other echinoderms?
15. How do the water-vascular systems and feeding mechanisms of sea daisies differ from those of other echinoderms?
16. What could account for the evolution of the calcium carbonate endoskeleton of echinoderms?

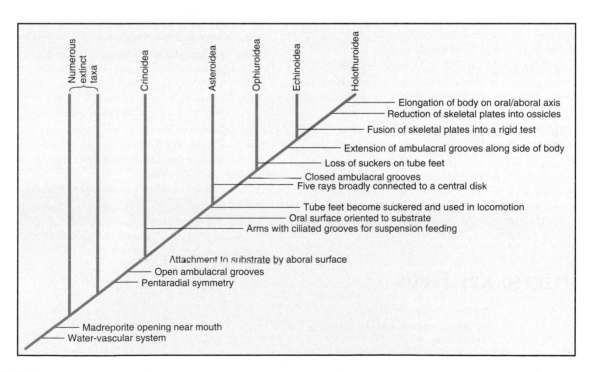

FIGURE 25.17

Echinoderm Phylogeny. The evolutionary relationships among echinoderms are not clear. This interpretation shows a relatively distant relationship between the Asteroidea and Ophiuroidea. Some taxonomists interpret the five-rayed body form as a synapomorphy that links these two groups to a single ancestral lineage. The position of the Concentricycloidea is highly speculative and is not shown here.

SUMMARY

1. Echinoderms, chordates, and other deuterostomes share a common, but remote, ancestry. Modern echinoderms were probably derived from bilaterally symmetrical ancestors.

2. Echinoderms are pentaradially symmetrical, have an endoskeleton of interlocking calcium carbonate ossicles, and have a water-vascular system that is used for locomotion, food gathering, attachment, and exchanges with the environment.

3. Members of the class Asteroidea are the sea stars. They are predators and scavengers, and their arms are broadly joined to the central disk. Sea stars are dioecious, and external fertilization results in the formation of planktonic bipinaria and brachiolaria larvae. Sea stars also have remarkable powers of regeneration.

4. The brittle stars and basket stars make up the class Ophiuroidea. Arms are sharply set off from the central disk. Ophiuroids are dioecious. Externally fertilized eggs may either develop in the plankton, or they may be brooded.

5. The class Echinoidea includes the sea urchins, heart urchins, and sand dollars. They have a specialized chewing structure, called Aristotle's lantern. External fertilization results in a planktonic pluteus larva.

6. Members of the class Holothuroidea include the sea cucumbers. They rest on one side and are elongate along their oral-aboral axis. Their body wall contains microscopic ossicles. Many sea cucumbers eviscerate themselves when disturbed. Sea cucumbers are dioecious, and fertilization and development are external.

7. The class Crinoidea contains the sea lilies and feather stars. They are oriented oral side up and use arms and tube feet in suspension feeding. Crinoids are dioecious, and fertilization and development are external.

8. The class Concentricycloidea contains one recently discovered species that lives on wood and other debris in deep water.

9. Radial symmetry of echinoderms probably evolved during a transition to a sedentary, filter-feeding lifestyle. The water-vascular system and the calcareous endoskeleton are probably adaptations for that lifestyle. The evolution of a more mobile lifestyle has resulted in the use of the water-vascular system for locomotion and in the assumption of a mouth-down position.

SELECTED KEY TERMS

ambulacral groove (p. 404)
Aristotle's lantern (p. 409)
dermal branchiae (p. 404)
pedicellariae (p. 404)

pentaradial symmetry (p. 402)
respiratory trees (p. 411)
tube feet (p. 403)
water-vascular system (p. 403)

CRITICAL THINKING QUESTIONS

1. What is pentaradial symmetry, and why is it adaptive for echinoderms?

2. Why do zoologists think that pentaradial symmetry was not present in the ancestors of echinoderms?

3. Compare and contrast the structure and function of the water-vascular systems of asteroids, ophiuroids, echinoids, holothuroids, and crinoids.

4. In which of the groups in question 3 is the water-vascular system probably most similar in form and function to an ancestral condition? Explain your answer.

5. What physical process is responsible for gas exchange and excretion in all echinoderms? What structures facilitate these exchanges in each echinoderm class?

REFERENCES ON THE WORLD WIDE WEB

1. **Enchinodermata.** This site provides links to a variety of information on the echinoderms.
   http://york.biosis.org/zrdocs/zoolinfo/grp_ech.htm

2. **Introduction to the Echinoderms.** This site provides information on the echinoderm fossil record, life histories, systematics, and morphology. It also provides links to sites that focus on each of the echinoderm classes.
   http://www.ucmp.berkeley.edu/echinodermata/echinodermata.html

3. **The CAS Echinoderm Webpage.** This site provides information on echinoderm taxonomy and on the echinoderm collection of the California Academy of Science. It also provides links to other echinoderm sites.
   http://www.calacademy.org/research/izg/echinoderm/

4. **The Echinoderm Newsletter.** This newsletter, prepared by the National Museum of Natural History, provides information on echinoderm conferences and publications, and also gives addresses of echinoderm biologists.
   http://www.nmnh.si.edu/gopher-menus/TheEchinodermNewsletter.html

5. **Phylum Echinodermata.** This site provides taxonomic keys for four classes of living echinoderms other than Crinoidea.
   http://www.mbl.edu/html/KEYS/INVERTS/18intro.html

SOME LESSER-KNOWN INVERTEBRATES: THE LOPHOPHORATES, ENTOPROCTS, CYCLIOPHORES, AND CHAETOGNATHS

THE LOPHOPHORATES: BRACHIOPODA, ECTOPROCTA (BRYOZOA), AND PHORONIDA

Three of the phyla (Brachiopoda, Ectoprocta [Bryozoa], and Phoronida) discussed in this endpaper share one major anatomical feature—the **lophophore** (Gr. *lophos*, crest or tuft + *phorein*, to bear). The lophophore is a circumoral (around the mouth) body region characterized by a circular or U-shaped ridge, with either one or two rows of ciliated, hollow tentacles (figure 1). An anus always opens outside of the lophophore. The lophophore is a food-collecting organ and a surface for gas exchange. Sensory cells receptive to chemicals and touch are concentrated on its tentacles. The lophophore can usually be extended for feeding or withdrawn for protection.

All lophophorates are sessile or sedentary filter feeders that have a U-shaped digestive tract—a feature common in sedentary animals—and live in a secreted chitinous or calcareous tube. As in deuterostomes, these phyla have radial cleavage in embryonic stages and a coelom that is divided into compartments. As in protostomes, however, the embryonic mouth forms in the region of the blastopore. Recent molecular biological studies involving the sequencing of ribosomal DNA, however, suggest that the lophophorates are protostomes.

PHYLUM BRACHIOPODA: THE BRACHIOPODS, OR LAMPSHELLS

The brachiopods (brak-i-op'ods) (Gr. *brachion*, arm + *podos*, foot) bear a superficial resemblance to the bivalve molluscs because they have a bivalved, calcareous and/or chitinous shell that a mantle secretes and that encloses nearly all of the body. However, unlike the left and right valves in molluscs, the brachiopods have dorsal and ventral valves. In addition, molluscs filter with their gills, whereas brachiopods use a lophophore. Brachiopods are commonly called lampshells because they resemble ancient Roman oil lamps.

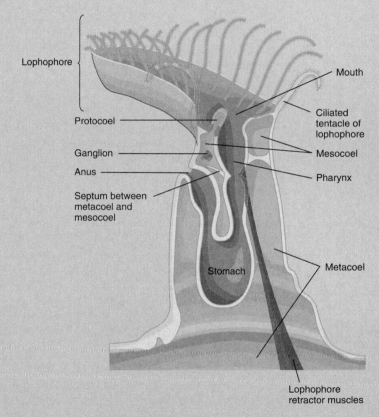

FIGURE 1 Lophophorate Structure. Longitudinal section through the body of a lophophorate with the lophophore extended.

Brachiopods are exclusively marine; most species live from the tidal zone to the edge of the continental shelves (about 200 m deep). The phylum contains about three hundred living species. In the Articulata, the valves are composed primarily of calcium carbonate and have a hinge with interlocking teeth (figure 2a). The Inarticulata have unhinged valves that are composed primarily of calcium phosphate and held together only by muscles. Most members of both classes have a stalked pedicel that usually attaches to a hard surface. Some, such as *Lingula*, have a muscular pedicel used for burrowing and anchoring in mud or sand.

(a)   (b)

FIGURE **2**   **Phylum Brachiopoda.** *(a)* Articulata brachiopod opened to show the two attached valves. *(b)* Internal anatomy of an articulate brachiopod.

The large, horseshoe-shaped lophophore in the anterior mantle cavity bears long, ciliated tentacles used in respiration and feeding (figure 2*b*). The cilia set up water currents that carry food particles (mainly organic detritus and algae) between the valves and over the lophophore into the mouth.

A solitary, dioecious brachiopod reproduces sexually by releasing gametes from multiple gonads into the metacoel and discharging them into the water by the nephridia. Fertilization is usually external, and the nonfeeding, ciliated, free-swimming larva is planktonic before settling and developing into an adult. Development is similar to that of deuterostomes, with radial, mostly equal, holoblastic cleavage, and enterocoelous coelom formation. In the Inarticulata, the juvenile resembles a small brachiopod with a coiled pedicel in the mantle cavity. There is no metamorphosis; when the juvenile settles to the bottom, the pedicel attaches to a solid object, and adult existence begins.

PHYLUM ECTOPROCTA (BRYOZOA): MOSS ANIMALS

The ectoprocts (ek′to-proks) (Gr. *ektos*, outside + *proktos*, anus) or bryozoans superficially resemble hydroids or corals. Bryozoa (Gr. *bryon*, moss + *zoon*, animal) means moss animals and refers to the mosslike appearance of the colonies. The name ectoprocta refers to the position of the anus outside the ring of tentacles. The approximately four thousand living species of pseudocoelomate ectoprocts belong to three classes. All species are aquatic (both freshwater and marine) and less than 1.5 mm in length.

Each body, or zooid, has a circular or horseshoe-shaped lophophore and is covered with a thin cuticle that encloses a calcified exoskeleton (*see figure 1*). The feeding body (lophophore, digestive tract, muscles, nerves) is called the polypide, the exoskeleton plus body wall (epidermis) is the cystid, and the secreted, nonliving part (exskeleton) is the zooecium (Gr. *zoo*, animal + *oceus*, house). Ectoprocts have an eversible lophophore that can be withdrawn into the body. Contraction of the retractor muscle rapidly withdraws the lophophore, whereas contraction of the muscles encircling the body wall exert pressure on the coelomic fluid, everting the lophophore.

Ectoprocts grow by budding. Thin portions of the body wall grow out as small vesicles or tubes, and contain a complete zooid. The different budding patterns reflect the genetics of the individual animal and such factors as current flow and substrate. The factors determine the colony shape (e.g., thin sheets, convoluted folds, massive coral-like heads, upright tangles) (figure 3*a*). Each colony can contain about 2 million zooids.

Most ectoprocts are monoecious. In some species, heterozooids produce either eggs or sperm in different colonies. In others, simple gonads produce both sperm and eggs in the same autozooid. Sperm enter the coelomic cavity, exit through pores in the tips of the tentacles, and are caught by the tentacles of other colonies. Eggs are fertilized as they are released and are brooded in the coelom; some species have a modified ovicell in which the embryo develops. Marine species have radial cleavage and a free-swimming, ciliated larva. This larva swims for a variable period of time, depending on the species, and then sinks and attaches to a rock or other substrate and grows into a zooid. A colony forms by budding.

Some freshwater ectoprocts produce a dormant stage called a statoblast (figure 3*b*). A statoblast is a hard, resistant capsule containing a mass of germinative cells. Statoblasts are asexually produced and accumulate in the metacoel. They can survive long periods of freezing and drying, enabling a colony to survive many years in seasonally variable lakes and ponds. Some float and are carried downstream, or are blown or carried from pond to pond, spreading ectoprocts over a large area. When environmental conditions become favorable, the statoblasts hatch and give rise to new polypides and, eventually, new colonies.

PHYLUM PHORONIDA: THE PHORONIDS

The Phoronids (fo-ron′ids) consist of about a dozen marine species divided between two genera: *Phoronis* and *Phoronopsis*. These animals live in permanent, chitinous tubes either buried in muddy or sandy sediments, or attached to solid surfaces. A few species bore into mollusc shells or calcareous rock. Generally, only the tentacles extend into the overlying water. Most phoronids are small—less than 20 cm long.

(a)

(b)

FIGURE 3   **Phylum Ectoprocta.** (a) Ectoprocts have a wide variety of shapes. *Philolopora* has lacy, delicate folds. (b) An ectoproct colony forming statoblasts.

The adult phoronid body consists of an anterior lophophore with two parallel rings of long tentacles (figure 4). The tentacles of the lophophore are filled with coelomic fluid that serves as a hydrostatic skeleton to hold them upright. The cilia on the tentacles drive water into the ring of tentacles from the top of the lophophore and out through the narrow spaces between the tentacles. Suspended food particles are directed toward the mouth. A flap of tissue called the epistome (Gr. *epi*, around + *stome*, mouth) covers the mouth.

Some phoronids reproduce asexually by budding and transverse fission; however, the majority are hermaphroditic. The gonads are in the coelom. Gametes pass from the coelom through the nephridiopore to the tentacles. Cross-fertilization is the rule, and the zygotes are either protected among the coils of the lophophore or released into the sea. Cleavage is radial, and a free-swimming larva called the actinotroch develops and feeds on plankton while drifting in the sea. It eventually settles to the bottom, metamorphoses, and begins to grow ventrally to form the body of the sedentary adult. As the animal grows, it burrows into the substrate. The body wall contains gland cells that eventually secrete the chitinous tube

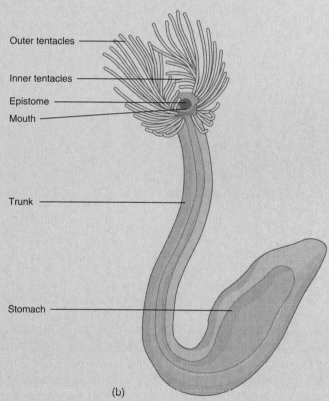

FIGURE 4   **Phylum Phoronida.** (a) Longitudinal view of the internal anatomy of the anterior portion of a phoronid. (b) A phoronid removed from its tube.

NONLOPHOPHORATE PHYLA

The phyla Entoprocta and Cycliophora lack lophophores but share other similarities with the lophophorates. As discussed at the conclusion of this endpaper, some zoologists think that all five phyla —Brachiopoda, Ectoprocta, Phoronida, Endoprocta, and Cycliophora— have evolutionary ties.

Tentacle

Anus

Ganglion

Calyx

Stalk

Vestibule

Mouth

Protonephridium

Gonad

Stomach

FIGURE 5 **Phylum Entoprocta.** Some morphological features of a typical entoproct.

PHYLUM ENTOPROCTA

The entoprocts (en′to-proks) (Gr. *entos*, within + *proktos*, anus) comprise a small phylum of about one hundred species of sedentary marine filter feeders. They are either solitary or colonial, and live in coastal waters. One group is commensalistic on the body surface of various invertebrates. Most entoprocts are microscopic. Entoprocts may form large, matlike colonies on rocks. An individual entoproct consists of a muscular stalk bearing a cup-shaped **calyx** with a crown of ciliated tentacles (figure 5). The stalk is surrounded by a chitinous cuticle and may bear an attachment disk with adhesive glands.

Entoprocts have a small body cavity that most zoologists consider a pseudocoelom. Loose connective tissue, however, fills this body cavity. How this cavity forms and its function are not well known. These uncertainties contribute to questions regarding the phylogenetic position of this group.

Entoprocts are filter feeders, and cilia on the tentacles convey food into the mouth. The filter-feeding apparatus is similar to the lophophore described for three previous phyla. The entoproct feeding structure, however, is not a lophophore because the anus ends with the group of tentacles. Lophophores, by definition, have an anal opening outside their ring of tentacles. The digestive tract forms a U-shaped gut in the calyx. Also in the calyx is a pair of protonephridial tubules that open through a single pore in the mouth. The nervous system consists

of a small, central ganglion and radiating nerves. Gas exchange occurs across the body surface.

Entoprocts reproduce by asexual budding and also sexually. Most entoprocts are monoecious, but eggs and sperm usually are produced at different times in one animal. Sperm are released freely into the water, and fertilization occurs internally. Embryos develop in a brood chamber, from which free-swimming larvae are released. Eventually, larvae settle to the substrate and develop into adults.

PHYLUM CYCLIOPHORA

As mentioned in chapter 16, P. Funch and R. M. Kristensen described the phylum Cycliophora (si″kle-o-for′ah) (Gr. *cyclion*, small wheel + *phora*, to carry) in 1995. It is the most recently described animal phylum. Members of its single species (*Symbion pandora*) are acoelomate, marine, and bilaterally symmetrical. They live in association with the mouthparts of lobsters.

The body of the feeding stage of *Symbion* consists of a buccal funnel, a trunk, and a stalk that ends in an adhesive disk. The disk attaches to a seta on the mouthparts of the lobster host (figure 6; see figure 16.1). The buccal funnel contains the mouth and is surrounded by a ring of compound cilia used in filter feeding A cuticle lines the body on the outside. The mouth leads to a U-shaped gut tract. Protonephridia are used in excretion.

Figure 7 shows the life cycle of *Symbion* that Funch and Kristensen proposed. The asexual feeding stage is about 0.3 mm tall. It can reproduce asexually by producing a larval stage, called the pandora, that is released and settles on the same host. Because of this asexual reproduction, large numbers of *Symbion* can build up on one host. After settling and attachment, the new individual develops a buccal funnel and begins to feed.

Sexual reproduction is apparently correlated to the molt cycle of the lobster. Some cue, possibly hormonal, from the lobster signals *Symbion* that the lobster is about to molt. Male and female stages are produced within the bodies of feeding individuals. When it is mature and filled with sperm, a male escapes from its maternal feeding individual and settles on a feeding individual containing a maturing female. As the female escapes from its maternal feeding individual, fertilization occurs, and the female settles on the lobster's mouthparts. The female contains a single, large fertilized egg. The female dies, leaving a cuticular shell containing a chordoid larva. The chordoid larva is the dispersal stage. It is free-swimming and may settle on the mouth appendages of a new lobster host.

PHYLUM CHAETOGNATHA: THE ARROW WORMS

Members of the phylum Chaetognatha (ke″tog-nath′ah) (Gr. *chaite*, hair or bristle + *gnathos*, jaw) are the arrow worms. The approximately one hundred species in this phylum are distributed throughout the world's oceans. Most are planktonic, 0.5 to 12 cm in length, streamlined, bilaterally symmetrical, and nearly transparent. Their body consists of a head, trunk, and tail. The trunk has paired, lateral fins, and the tail has a single fin. The mouth is

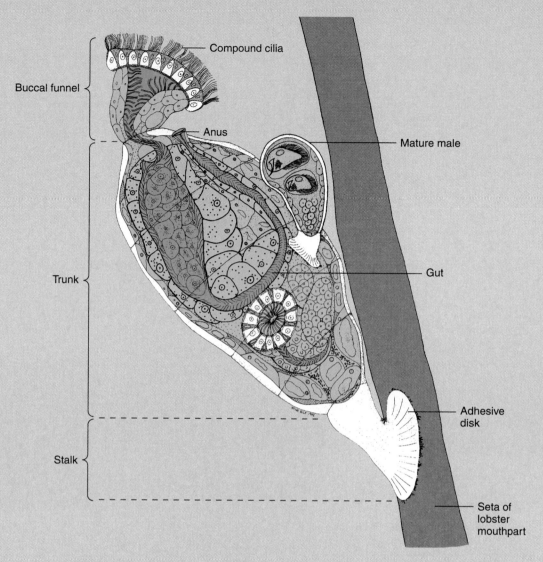

Labels on figure: Compound cilia, Buccal funnel, Anus, Mature male, Gut, Adhesive disk, Seta of lobster mouthpart, Trunk, Stalk

FIGURE 6 *Phylum Cycliophora.* The feeding stage of *Symbion pandora* attaches to the seta of the mouthpart of a lobster. A mature male is shown attached to the feeding stage, which is about 300 μm (0.3 mm) long.

located ventrally on the head. Large, grasping spines are lateral to the mouth, and smaller spines, called teeth, are in front of the mouth (figure 8).

Arrow worms are active swimmers. The near-perfect bilateral symmetry and streamlined shape of arrow worms permit a darting form of locomotion from laterally flexing the body. Their fins stabilize the body during swimming and help prevent sinking during moments of rest.

Arrow worms are active predators. They feed on planktonic crustaceans and small fish. An arrow worm darts forward quickly to grab its prey with mouth spines that inject a neurotoxic venom into the prey. Interestingly, the neurotoxin is not produced by the arrow worm, but by commensalistic bacteria living in the head region. The gut of arrow worms is a simple, straight tube. Although much remains to be learned about arrow worm physiology, circulation, gas exchange, and excretion probably all occur by diffusion. The nervous system consists of a cerebral ganglion in the head and other ganglia associated with sensory organs. Ciliary fans that cover the

body probably detect waterborne vibrations. A single pair of eyes is below the epidermis on the dorsal surface of the head. Arrow worms probably use these photoreceptors to orient to the direction and intensity of light during vertical migrations within the water column.

Chaetognaths are monoecious, with paired ovaries in the trunk and paired testes in the tail. Arrow worms engage in a mating dance during which they deposit sperm in ball-like clusters on the mate's body. These sperm clusters rupture, and sperm migrate to the female gonopore. Fertilization is internal, and zygotes in a jellylike coating float in the sea or sink to the substrate. One genus has a marsupial pouch within which fertilized eggs develop. There is no larval stage or metamorphosis.

PHYLOGENETIC RELATIONSHIPS

The evolutionary relationships among the six phyla described in this endpaper are controversial. The traditional interpretation is

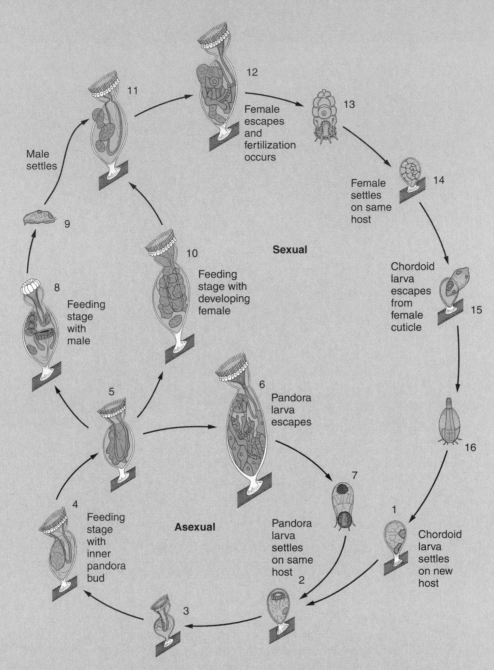

Sexual

Asexual

11

12 — Female escapes and fertilization occurs

13

Male settles

9

14 — Female settles on same host

8 — Feeding stage with male

10 — Feeding stage with developing female

Chordoid larva escapes from female cuticle — 15

5

6 — Pandora larva escapes

16

4 — Feeding stage with inner pandora bud

7

1 — Chordoid larva settles on new host

Pandora larva settles on same host — 2

3

FIGURE 7   **Life Cycle of _Symbion pandora_.** The feeding stage of _Symbion_ undergoes an asexual reproductive phase (1 & 7) that involves the development of a pandora larval stage that escapes from the feeding adult and settles on the mouthparts of the same lobster host. It matures and begins feeding. Prior to a molt by the lobster, feeding individuals form males or females within their body (8-10). When a male matures, it escapes from its feeding parent and attaches to a feeding stage containing a maturing female (9 & 11). When the female matures it escapes from its feeding parent, fertilization occurs, and the female settles on the same lobster host (12). The female then dies, but she leaves her cuticle containing a chordoid larva attached to the lobster mouthpart. When the larva is mature, it breaks out of the cuticle, swims through the water, and may find a new host lobster (13-16).

that the lophophore of the Brachiopoda, Ectoprocta (Bryozoa), and Phoronida represents an evolutionary tie among these three phyla. More recent molecular studies of ribosomal RNA seem to support this view. Other similarities, such as a reduced head, U-shaped digestive tract, and secreted protective covering, correlate with adaptations for a sessile, filter-feeding existence. These common features may represent evolutionary convergence, rather than close evolutionary relationships. This traditional interpreta-

tion would mean that the ectoprocts and cycliophores are more distantly related to the lophophorates. Because of what appears to be a pseudocoelom, the entoprocts are often considered aschelminths.

C. Nielsen has recently suggested that the ectoprocts and entoprocts are closely related. He advocates a superphylum designation, Bryozoa, to reflect this relationship. Funch and Kristensen suggest that the Cycliophora have affinities to these "Bryozoa."

(b)

FIGURE 8   **Arrow Worm.** (*a*) Ventral view of *Parasagitta* (2 to 3 cm). (*b*) Ventral view of the head of *Sagitta setosa*. Notice the large, grasping spines on the lateral margin of the head and the small teeth lateral to the triangular mouth.

They point to such common features as a certain kind of protonephridium (Entoprocta and Cycliophora), budding (Entoprocta, Ectoprocta, and Cycliophora), disapperance of the larval brain at metamorphosis (Entoprocta, Ectoprocta, and Cycliophora), and other common characters as indications of close evolutionary ties. Although this interpretation has not been widely accepted, discussions of the phylogenetic status of these five phyla (Brachiopoda, Ectoprocta, Phoronida, Endoprocta, and Cycliophora) will probably become more frequent and interesting as a result of the discovery of *Symbion*.

Very little is known regarding the phylogenetic relationships of the Chaetognatha. Their embryological development clearly indicates that they are deuterostomes. Their relationships to other deuterostomes are highly speculative.

HEMICHORDATA AND INVERTEBRATE CHORDATES

Concepts

1. Members of the phyla Echinodermata, Hemichordata, and Chordata are probably derived from a common diploblastic or triploblastic ancestor.
2. The phylum Hemichordata includes the acorn worms (class Enteropneusta) and the pterobranchs (class Pterobranchia). Hemichordates live in or on marine substrates, and feed on sediment or suspended organic matter.
3. Animals in the phylum Chordata are characterized by a notochord, pharyngeal slits or pouches, a tubular nerve cord, and a postanal tail.
4. The urochordates are marine and are called tunicates. They are attached or planktonic, and solitary or colonial as adults. All are filter feeders.
5. Members of the subphylum Cephalochordata are called lancelets. They are filter feeders that spend most of their time partly buried in marine substrates.
6. Motile, fishlike chordates may have evolved from sedentary, filter-feeding ancestors as a result of paedomorphosis in a motile larval stage.

Would You Like to Know . . .

1. what acorn worms are? (p. 424)
2. what characteristics all chordates share at some time in their life history? (p. 428)
3. what animals deposit cellulose in their body walls? (p. 429)
4. why sea squirts are classified in the same phylum (Chordata) as humans? (p. 431)
5. why cephalochordates, such as amphioxus, are studied in introductory zoology laboratories? (p. 431)
6. how fishlike chordates could have evolved from filter-feeding ancestors? (p. 432)

This chapter answers these and other useful questions.

This chapter contains evolutionary concepts, which are set off in this font.

EVOLUTIONARY PERSPECTIVE

Some members of one of the phyla discussed in this chapter are more familiar to you than members of any other group of animals. This familiarity is not without good reason, for you yourself are a member of one of these phyla—Chordata. Other members of these phyla, however, are much less familiar. During a walk along a seashore at low tide, you may observe coiled castings (sand, mud, and excrement) at the openings of U-shaped burrows. Excavating these burrows reveals a wormlike animal that is one of the members of a small phylum—Hemichordata. Other members of this phylum include equally unfamiliar filter feeders called pterobranchs.

While at the seashore, you could also see animals clinging to rocks exposed by low tide. At first glance, you might describe them as jellylike masses with two openings at their unattached end. Some live as solitary individuals; others live in colonies. If you handle these animals, you may be rewarded with a stream of water squirted from their openings. Casual observations provide little evidence that these small filter feeders, called sea squirts or tunicates, are chordates. However, detailed studies have made that conclusion certain. Tunicates and a small group of fishlike cephalochordates are often called the invertebrate chordates because they lack a vertebral column (figure 26.1).

PHYLOGENETIC RELATIONSHIPS

Animals in the phyla Hemichordata and Chordata share deuterostome characteristics with echinoderms (figure 26.2). Most zoologists, therefore, believe that ancestral representatives of these phyla were derived from a common, as yet undiscovered, triploblastic ancestor. The chordates are characterized by a dorsal tubular nerve cord, a notochord, pharyngeal slits, and a postanal tail. The only characteristics they share with the hemichordates are pharyngeal slits and, in some species, a dorsal tubular nerve cord. Therefore, most zoologists agree that the evolutionary ties between the chordates and hemichordates are closer than those between echinoderms and either phylum. Chordates and hemichordates, however, probably diverged from widely separated points along the deuterostome lineage. The diverse body forms and lifestyles present in these phyla support this generalization.

PHYLUM HEMICHORDATA

The phylum Hemichordata (hem"i-kor-da'tah) (Gr. *hemi*, half + L. *chorda*, cord) includes the acorn worms (class Enteropneusta) and the pterobranchs (class Pterobranchia) (table 26.1). Members of both classes live in or on marine sediments.

Atrial siphon

Oral siphon

FIGURE 26.1

Phylum Chordata. This tunicate, or sea squirt (*Ciona intestinalis*), is an invertebrate chordate that attaches to substrates in marine environments. Note the two siphons for circulating water through a filter-feeding apparatus.

Characteristics of the phylum Hemichordata include:

1. Marine, deuterostomate animals with a body divided into three regions: proboscis, collar, and trunk; coelom divided into three cavities
2. Ciliated pharyngeal slits
3. Open circulatory system
4. Complete digestive tract
5. Dorsal, sometimes tubular, nerve cord

CLASS ENTEROPNEUSTA

Members of the class Enteropneusta (ent"er-op-nus'tah) (Gr. *entero*, intestine + *pneustikos*, for breathing) are marine worms that usually range in size between 10 and 40 cm, although some can be as long as 2 m. Zoologists have described about 70 species, and most occupy U-shaped burrows in sandy and muddy substrates between the limits of high and low tides. ❶ The common name of the enteropneusts—acorn worms—is derived from the appearance of the proboscis, which is a short, conical projection at the worm's anterior end. A ringlike collar is posterior to the proboscis, and an elongate trunk is the third division of the body (figure 26.3). A ciliated epidermis and gland cells cover acorn worms. The mouth is located ventrally between the proboscis and the collar. A variable number of pharyngeal slits, from a few to several hundred, are positioned laterally on the trunk. Pharyngeal slits are openings between the anterior region of the digestive tract, called the pharynx, and the outside of the body.

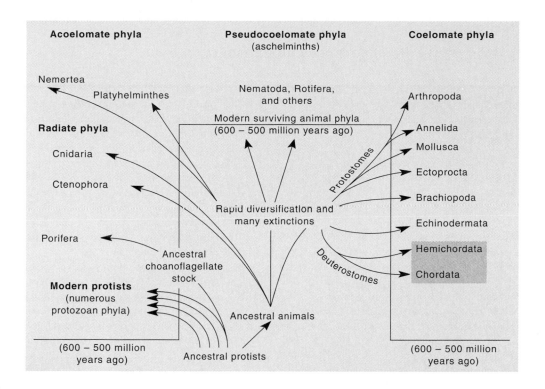

FIGURE 26.2

Phylogenetic Relationships among the Hemichordata and Chordata. Hemichordates and chordates (shaded in orange) are distantly related deuterostomes derived from a common, as yet undiscovered, diploblastic or triploblastic ancestor.

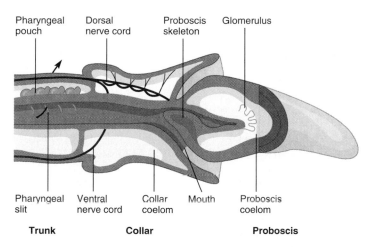

FIGURE 26.3

Class Enteropneusta. Longitudinal section showing the proboscis, collar, pharyngeal region, and internal structures. The black arrow shows the path of water through a pharyngeal slit.

Maintenance Functions

Cilia and mucus assist acorn worms in feeding. Detritus and other particles adhere to the mucus-covered proboscis. Tracts of cilia transport food and mucus posteriorly and ventrally. Ciliary tracts converge near the mouth and form a mucoid string that enters the mouth. Acorn worms may reject some substances trapped in the mucoid string by pulling the proboscis against the collar. Ciliary tracts of the collar and trunk transport rejected material and discard it posteriorly.

The digestive tract of enteropneusts is a simple tube. Food is digested as diverticula of the gut, called hepatic sacs, release enzymes. The worm extends its posterior end out of the burrow during defecation. At low tide, coils of fecal material, called castings, lie on the substrate at burrow openings.

The nervous system of enteropneusts is ectodermal in origin and lies at the base of the ciliated epidermis. It consists of dorsal and ventral nerve tracts and a network of epidermal nerve cells, called a nerve plexus. In some species, the dorsal nerve is tubular and usually contains giant nerve fibers that rapidly transmit impulses. There are no major ganglia. Sensory receptors are unspecialized and widely distributed over the body.

Because acorn worms are small, respiratory gases and metabolic waste products (principally ammonia) probably are exchanged by diffusion across the body wall. In addition, respiratory gases are exchanged at the pharyngeal slits. Cilia associated with pharyngeal slits circulate water into the mouth and out of the body through pharyngeal slits. As water passes through pharyngeal slits, gases are exchanged by diffusion between water and blood sinuses surrounding the pharynx.

TABLE 26.1	CLASSIFICATION OF THE HEMICHORDATA AND CHORDATA

Phylum Hemichordata (hem″i-kor-da′tah)
Widely distributed in shallow, marine, tropical waters and deep, cold waters; soft bodied and wormlike; epidermal nervous system; most with pharyngeal slits.

Class Enteropneusta (ent″er-op-nus′tah)
Shallow-water, wormlike animals; inhabit burrows on sandy shorelines; body divided into three regions: proboscis, collar, and trunk. Acorn worms (*Balanoglossus, Saccoglossus*). About 70 species.

Class Pterobranchia (ter″o-brang′ke-ah)
With or without pharyngeal slits; two or more arms; often colonial, living in an externally secreted encasement. *Rhabdopleura.* About 20 species.

Class Planctosphaeroidea (plank″to-sfer-roi′de-ah)
Spherical body with ciliary bands covering the surface; U-shaped digestive tract; coelom poorly developed; planktonic. Only one species is known to exist (*Planctosphaera pelagica*).

Phylum Chordata (kor-dat′ah) (L. *chorda*, cord)
Occupy a wide variety of marine, freshwater, and terrestrial habitats. A notochord, pharyngeal slits, a dorsal tubular nerve cord, and a postanal tail are all present at some time in chordate life histories. About 45,000 species.

Subphylum Urochordata (u″ro-kor-da′tah)
Notochord, nerve cord, and postanal tail present only in free-swimming larvae; adults sessile, or occasionally planktonic, and enclosed in a tunic that contains some cellulose; marine. Sea squirts or tunicates.

Class Ascidiacea (as-id″e-as′e-ah)
All sessile as adults; solitary or colonial; colony members interconnected by stolons.

Class Appendicularia (a-pen″di-ku-lar′e-ah)
(Larvacea) (lar-vas′e-ah)
Planktonic; adults retain tail and notochord; lack a cellulose tunic; epithelium secretes a gelatinous covering of the body.

Class Sorberacea (sor″ber-as′e-ah)
Ascidian-like urochordates possessing dorsal nerve cords as adults; deep water, benthic; carnivorous. *Octacnemus.*

Class Thaliacea (tal″e-as′e-ah)
Planktonic; adults are tailless and barrel shaped; oral and atrial openings are at opposite ends of the tunicate; muscular contractions of the body wall produce water currents.

Subphylum Cephalochordata (sef″a-lo-kor-dat′ah)
Body laterally compressed and transparent; fishlike; all four chordate characteristics persist throughout life. Amphioxus (*Branchiostoma*). About 45 species.

Subphylum Vertebrata (ver″te-bra′tah)
Notochord, nerve cord, postanal tail, and pharyngeal slits present at least in embryonic stages; vertebrae surround nerve cord and serve as primary axial support; skeleton modified anteriorly into a skull for protection of the brain.

Class Cephalaspidomorphi (sef″ah-las″pe-do-morf′e)
Fishlike; jawless; no paired appendages; cartilaginous skeleton; sucking mouth with teeth and rasping tongue. Lampreys.

Class Myxini (mik′sĭ-ne)
Fishlike; jawless; no paired appendages; mouth with four pairs of tentacles; olfactory sacs open to mouth cavity; 5 to 15 pairs of pharyngeal slits. Hagfishes.

Class Chondrichthyes (kon-drik′thi-es)
Fishlike; jawed; paired appendages and cartilaginous skeleton; no swim bladder. Skates, rays, sharks.

Class Osteichthyes (os″te-ik′the-es)
Bony skeleton; swim bladder and operculum present. Bony fishes.

Class Amphibia (am-fib′e-ah)
Skin with mucoid secretions; possess lungs and/or gills; moist skin serves as respiratory organ; aquatic developmental stages usually followed by metamorphosis to an adult. Frogs, toads, salamanders.

Class Reptilia (rep-til′e-ah)
Dry skin with epidermal scales; amniotic eggs; terrestrial embryonic development. Snakes, lizards, alligators.

Class Aves (a′vez)
Scales modified into feathers for flight; efficiently regulate body temperature (endothermic); amniotic eggs. Birds.

Class Mammalia (mah-ma′le-ah)
Bodies at least partially covered by hair; endothermic; young nursed from mammary glands; amniotic eggs. Mammals.

The circulatory system of acorn worms consists of one dorsal and one ventral contractile vessel. Blood moves anteriorly in the dorsal vessel and posteriorly in the ventral vessel. Branches from these vessels lead to open sinuses. All blood flowing anteriorly passes into a series of blood sinuses, called the glomerulus, at the base of the proboscis. Excretory wastes may be filtered through the glomerulus, into the coelom of the proboscis, and released to the outside through one or two pores in the wall of the proboscis. The blood of acorn worms is colorless, lacks cellular elements, and distributes nutrients and wastes.

Reproduction and Development

Enteropneusts are dioecious. Two rows of gonads lie in the body wall in the anterior region of the trunk, and each gonad opens separately to the outside. Fertilization is external. Spawning by one worm induces others in the area to spawn—behavior that suggests the presence of spawning pheromones. Ciliated larvae, called **tornaria,** swim in the plankton for several days to a few weeks. The larvae settle to the substrate and gradually transform into the adult form (figure 26.4).

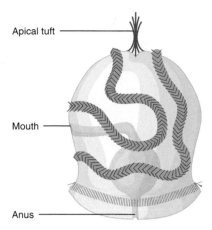

FIGURE 26.4

Tornaria Larva (*Balanoglossus*). When larval development is complete, a tornaria locates a suitable substrate, settles, and begins to burrow and elongate (1 mm).

CLASS PTEROBRANCHIA

Pterobranchia (ter″o-brang′ke-ah) (Gk. *pteron*, wing or feather + *branchia*, gills) is a small class of hemichordates found mostly in deep, oceanic waters of the Southern Hemisphere. A few live in European coastal waters and in shallow waters near Bermuda. Zoologists have described approximately 20 species of pterobranchs.

Pterobranchs are small, ranging in size from 0.1 to 5 mm. Most live in secreted tubes in asexually produced colonies. As in enteropneusts, the pterobranch body is divided into three regions. The proboscis is expanded and shieldlike (figure 26.5). It secretes the tube and aids in movement in the tube. The collar possesses two to nine arms with numerous ciliated tentacles. The trunk is U-shaped.

Maintenance Functions

Pterobranchs use water currents that cilia on their arms and tentacles generate to filter feed. Cilia trap and transport food particles toward the mouth. Although one genus has a single pair of pharyngeal slits, respiratory and excretory structures are unnecessary in animals as small as pterobranchs because gases and wastes exchange by diffusion.

Reproduction and Development

Asexual budding is common in pterobranchs and is responsible for colony formation. Pterobranchs also possess one or two gonads in the anterior trunk. Most species are dioecious, and external fertilization results in the development of a planula-like larva that lives for a time in the tube of the female. This nonfeeding larva eventually leaves the female's tube, settles to the substrate, forms a cocoon, and metamorphoses into an adult.

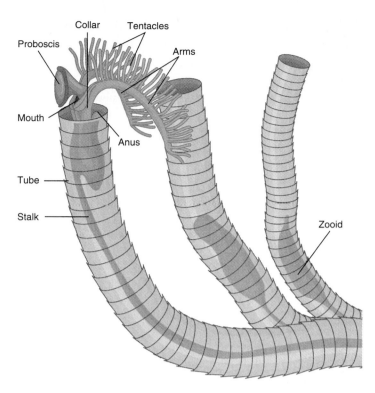

FIGURE 26.5

External Structure of the Pterobranch, *Rhabdopleura*. Ciliated tracts on tentacles and arms direct food particles toward the mouth.

Stop and Ask Yourself

1. What are the three body regions of a hemichordate? What is the function of these regions in acorn worms? What is the function of these regions in pterobranchs?

2. How are the feeding mechanisms of acorn worms and pterobranchs similar?

3. How do respiratory and excretory functions occur in hemichordates?

PHYLUM CHORDATA

Although the phylum Chordata (kor-dat′ah) (L. *chorda*, cord) does not have an inordinately large number of species (about 45,000), its members have been very successful at adapting to aquatic and terrestrial environments throughout the world. Sea squirts, members of the subphylum Urochordata, are briefly described in the "Evolutionary Perspective" that opens this chapter. Other chordates include lancelets (subphylum Cephalochordata) and the vertebrates (subphylum Vertebrata) *(see table 26.1)*. Characteristics of the phylum Chordata include:

1. Bilaterally symmetrical, deuterostomate animals
2. Four unique characteristics present at some stage in development: notochord, pharyngeal slits, dorsal tubular nerve cord, and postanal tail
3. Presence of an endostyle or thyroid gland
4. Complete digestive tract
5. Ventral, contractile blood vessel (heart)

2   The four characteristics listed in number 2 are unique to chordates and are discussed further in the paragraphs that follow *(see figure 10.7a,b)*.

The phylum is named after the **notochord** (Gr. *noton*, the back + L. *chorda*, cord), a supportive rod that extends most of the length of the animal dorsal to the body cavity and into the tail. It consists of a connective-tissue sheath that encloses cells, each of which contains a large, fluid-filled vacuole. This arrangement gives the notochord some turgidity, which prevents compression along the anteroposterior axis. At the same time, the notochord is flexible enough to allow lateral bending, as in the lateral undulations of a fish during swimming. In most adult vertebrates, cartilage or bone partly or entirely replaces the notochord.

Pharyngeal slits are a series of openings in the pharyngeal region between the digestive tract and the outside of the body. In some chordates, diverticula from the gut in the pharyngeal region never break through to form an open passageway to the outside. These diverticula are then called pharyngeal pouches. The earliest chordates used the slits for filter feeding; some living chordates still use them for feeding. Other chordates have developed gills in the pharyngeal pouches for gas exchange. The pharyngeal slits of terrestrial vertebrates are mainly embryonic features and may be incomplete.

The **tubular nerve cord** and its associated structures are largely responsible for chordate success. The nerve cord runs along the longitudinal axis of the body, just dorsal to the notochord, and usually expands anteriorly as a brain. This central nervous system is associated with the development of complex systems for sensory perception, integration, and motor responses.

The fourth chordate characteristic is a **postanal tail.** (A postanal tail extends posteriorly beyond the anal opening.) Either the notochord or vertebral column supports the tail.

Subphylum Urochordata

Members of the subphylum Urochordata (u″ro-kor-dah′tah) (Gr. *uro*, tail + L. *chorda*, cord) are the tunicates or sea squirts. The ascidians comprise the largest class of tunicates *(see table 26.1)*. They are sessile as adults and are either solitary or colonial. The appendicularians and thaliaceans are planktonic as adults (figure 26.6; box 26.1). In some localities, tunicates occur in large enough numbers to be considered a dominant life-form.

(a)

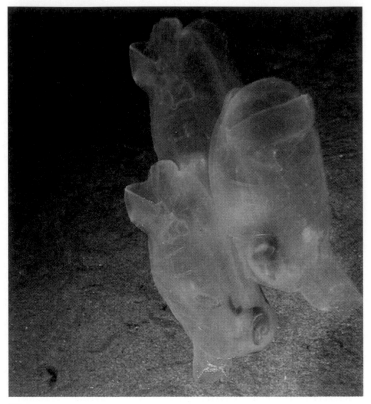

(b)

Figure 26.6

Subphylum Urochordata. *(a)* Members of the class Appendicularia are planktonic and have a tail and notochord that persist into the adult stage. *(b)* The thaliaceans are barrel-shaped, planktonic urochordates. Oral and atrial siphons are at opposite ends of the body, and muscles of the body wall contract to create a form of weak jet propulsion.

Sessile urochordates attach their saclike bodies to rocks, pilings, ship hulls, and other solid substrates. The unattached end of urochordates contains two siphons that permit seawater to circulate through the body. One siphon is the oral siphon, which is the inlet for water circulating through the body and is usually directly opposite the attached end of the ascidian (figure 26.7). It also

BOX 26.1 PLANKTONIC TUNICATES

Although the description of urochordates in this text is based primarily upon attached ascidian tunicates, planktonic species are numerous and important in marine food webs. Dense tunicate swarms, hundreds of kilometers wide and many meters deep, are common in the open ocean. Swarms of larvaceans (*see figure 26.6a*) may contain up to 25,000 animals per cubic meter! Larvaceans filter organisms as small as bacteria (0.1 μm in diameter), and in turn, are fed on by other plankton feeders, such as sardines and herring.

Thaliacean tunicates also occur in large, dense swarms in the open ocean (*see figure 26.6b*). Most are aggregations of solitary individuals; however, some form spectacular luminescent colonies. Pyrosome colonies, such as the one shown in figure 1, are found in many oceans. Colonies 10 m long and 1 m in diameter are common. Individuals are oriented with oral siphons pointed outward and atrial siphons directed toward the center of the colony. Ciliary currents and contractions of body-wall muscles direct water toward a central cavity of the colony and slowly move the entire colony through the water. When chemical or mechanical stimuli stimulate a part of the colony, the part luminesces and ceases ciliary beating.

FIGURE 1 **Planktonic Tunicates.** A pyrosome colony (*Pyrosoma spinosum*).

The luminescence spreads over the entire colony, and the colony stops moving. This behavior may help the colony avoid unfavorable environments or may confuse or frighten predators.

---

serves as the mouth opening. The second siphon, the atrial siphon, is the opening for excurrent water.

③ The body wall of most tunicates (L. *tunicatus*, to wear a tunic or gown) is a connective-tissue-like covering, called the tunic, that appears gel-like but is often quite tough. Secreted by the epidermis, it is composed of proteins, various salts, and cellulose. Some mesodermally derived tissues, including blood vessels and blood cells, are incorporated into the tunic. Rootlike extensions of the tunic, called stolons, help anchor a tunicate to the substrate and may connect individuals of a colony.

Maintenance Functions

Longitudinal and circular muscles below the body wall epithelium help to change the shape of the adult tunicate. They act against the elasticity of the tunic and the hydrostatic skeleton that seawater confined to internal chambers creates.

The nervous system of tunicates is largely confined to the body wall. It forms a nerve plexus with a single ganglion located on the wall of the pharynx between the oral and atrial openings (figure 26.8a). This ganglion is not vital for coordinating bodily functions. Tunicates are sensitive to many kinds of mechanical

and chemical stimuli, and receptors for these senses are distributed over the body wall, especially around the siphons. There are no complex sensory organs.

The most obvious internal structures of the urochordates are a very large pharynx and a cavity, called the atrium, that surrounds the pharynx laterally and dorsally (figure 26.8b). The pharynx of tunicates originates at the oral siphon and is continuous with the remainder of the digestive tract. The oral margin of the pharynx has tentacles that prevent large objects from entering the pharynx. Numerous pharyngeal slits called stigmas perforate the pharynx. Cilia associated with the stigmas cause water to circulate into the pharynx, through the stigmas, and into the surrounding atrium. Water leaves the tunicate through the atrial siphon.

The digestive tract of adult tunicates continues from the pharynx and ends at the anus near the atrial siphon. During feeding, cells of a ventral, ciliated groove, called the **endostyle,** form a mucous sheath (figure 26.8b; box 26.2). Cilia move the mucous sheet dorsally across the pharynx. Food particles, brought into the oral siphon with incurrent water, are trapped in the mucous sheet and passed dorsally. Food is incorporated into a string of mucus that ciliary action moves into the next region of the gut tract. Digestive enzymes are secreted in the stomach, and most absorption

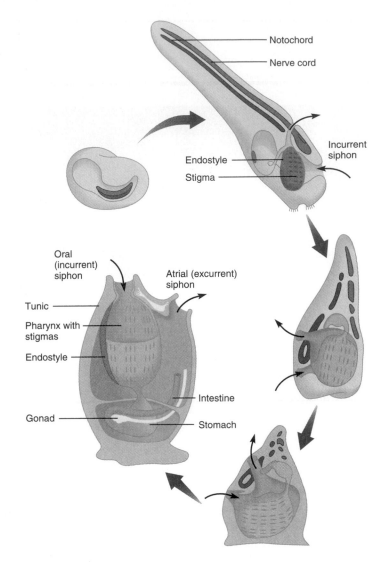

FIGURE 26.7

Tunicate Metamorphosis. Small black arrows show the path of water through the body.

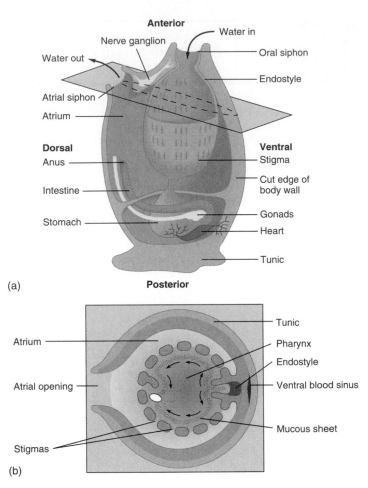

(a)

(b)

FIGURE 26.8

Internal Structure of a Tunicate. (*a*) Longitudinal section. Black arrows show the path of water. (*b*) Cross section at the level of the atrial siphon. Small black arrows show movement of food trapped in mucus that the endostyle produces.

occurs across the walls of the intestine. Excurrent water carries digestive wastes from the anus out of the atrial siphon.

In addition to its role in feeding, the pharynx also functions in gas exchange. Gases are exchanged between water circulating through the tunicate.

The tunicate heart lies at the base of the pharynx. One vessel from the heart runs anteriorly under the endostyle, and another runs posteriorly to the digestive organs and gonads. Blood flow through the heart is not unidirectional. Peristaltic contractions of the heart may propel blood in one direction for a few beats; then the direction is reversed. The significance of this reversal is not understood. Tunicate blood plasma is colorless and contains various kinds of amoeboid cells.

Ammonia diffuses into water that passes through the pharynx and is excreted. In addition, amoeboid cells of the circulatory system accumulate uric acid and sequester it in the intestinal loop. Pyloric glands on the outside of the intestine are also thought to have excretory functions.

Reproduction and Development

Urochordates are monoecious. Gonads are located near the loop of the intestine, and genital ducts open near the atrial siphon. Gametes may be shed through the atrial siphon for external fertilization, or eggs may be retained in the atrium for fertilization and

BOX 26.2 | THE ENDOSTYLE AND THE VERTEBRATE THYROID GLAND

Neither the structure nor the function of the urochordate or cephalochordate endostyle gives any clue to its fate in the vertebrates. Similarly, examinations of adult vertebrates never show a ciliated groove that once functioned to produce a sticky, mucous trap for filter-feeding ancestors. The study of the development of one group of vertebrates, the lampreys, has provided insight into the endostyle's evolutionary fate.

An endostyle is present in larval lampreys, where it produces a mucous filter, just as in the invertebrate chordates. In addition, it binds iodine to the amino acid tyrosine. The significance of this second function is revealed when the larval lamprey metamorphoses to the adult and becomes a predator. Mucus-secreting

functions of the endostyle become secondary, and the secretion of iodine-bound tyrosine derivatives becomes the endostyle's primary function. During larval metamorphosis, the endostyle transforms into an endocrine gland common to all vertebrates, the thyroid gland. The iodine-containing secretions of the vertebrate thyroid gland regulate metamorphosis and metabolic rate.

The development of the thyroid gland of lampreys may reflect evolutionary events leading to the vertebrate thyroid gland. The endostyle of vertebrate ancestors may have had both mucus-secreting and endocrine functions. With the evolution of jaws and a more active, predatory lifestyle, endocrine functions were probably favored.

early development. Although self-fertilization occurs in some species, cross-fertilization is the rule. ④ Development results in the formation of a tadpolelike larva with all four chordate characteristics. Metamorphosis begins after a brief free-swimming larval existence, during which the larva does not feed. The larva settles to a firm substrate and attaches by adhesive papillae located below the mouth. During metamorphosis, the outer epidermis shrinks and pulls the notochord and other tail structures internally for reorganization into adult tissues. The internal structures rotate 180°, positioning the oral siphon opposite the adhesive papillae and bending the digestive tract into a U shape (see figure 26.7).

SUBPHYLUM CEPHALOCHORDATA

Members of the subphylum Cephalochordata (sef″a-lo-kordah′tah) (Gr. kephalo, head + L. chorda, cord) are called lancelets. ⑤ Lancelets clearly demonstrate the four chordate characteristics, and for that reason, are often studied in introductory zoology courses.

The cephalochordates consist of two genera, Branchiostoma (amphioxus) and Asymmetron, and about 45 species. They are distributed throughout the world's oceans in shallow waters that have clean sand substrates.

Cephalochordates are small (up to 5 cm long), tadpolelike animals. They are elongate, laterally flattened, and nearly transparent. In spite of their streamlined shape, cephalochordates are relatively weak swimmers and spend most of their time in a filter-feeding position—partly to mostly buried with their anterior end sticking out of the sand (figure 26.9).

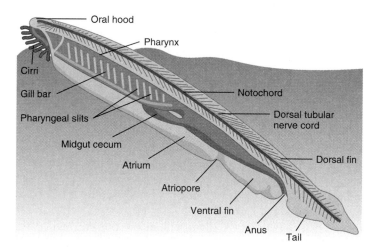

FIGURE 26.9

Subphylum Cephalochordata. Internal structure of *Branchiostoma* (amphioxus) shown in its partially buried feeding position.

The notochord of cephalochordates extends from the tail to the head, giving them their name. Unlike the notochord of other chordates, most of the cells are muscle cells, making the notochord somewhat contractile. Both of these characteristics are probably adaptations to burrowing. Contraction of the muscle cells increases the rigidity of the notochord by compressing the fluids within, giving additional support when pushing into sandy substrates. Relaxation of these muscle cells increases flexibility for swimming.

Muscle cells on either side of the notochord cause undulations that propel the cephalochordate through the water. Longitudinal, ventrolateral folds of the body wall help stabilize cephalochordates during swimming, and a median dorsal fin and a caudal fin also aid in swimming.

An oral hood projects from the anterior end of cephalochordates. Ciliated, fingerlike projections, called cirri, hang from the ventral aspect of the oral hood and are used in feeding. The posterior wall of the oral hood bears the mouth opening that leads to a large pharynx. Numerous pairs of pharyngeal slits perforate the pharynx and are supported by cartilaginous gill bars. Large folds of the body wall extend ventrally around the pharynx and fuse at the ventral midline of the body, creating the atrium, a chamber that surrounds the pharyngeal region of the body. It may protect the delicate, filtering surfaces of the pharynx from bottom sediments. The opening from the atrium to the outside is called the atriopore (figure 26.9).

Maintenance Functions

Cephalochordates are filter feeders. During feeding, they are partially or mostly buried in sandy substrates with their mouths pointed upward. Cilia on the lateral surfaces of gill bars sweep water into the mouth. Water passes from the pharynx, through pharyngeal slits to the atrium, and out of the body through the atriopore. Food is initially sorted at the cirri. Larger materials catch on cilia of the cirri. As these larger particles accumulate, contractions of the cirri throw them off. Smaller, edible particles are pulled into the mouth with water and are collected by cilia on the gill bars and in mucus secreted by the endostyle. As in tunicates, the endostyle is a ciliated groove that extends longitudinally along the midventral aspect of the pharynx. Cilia move food and mucus dorsally, forming a food cord to the gut. A ring of cilia rotates the food cord, dislodging food. Digestion is both extracellular and intracellular. A diverticulum off the gut, called the midgut cecum, extends anteriorly. It ends blindly along the right side of the pharynx and secretes digestive enzymes. An anus is on the left side of the ventral fin.

Cephalochordates do not possess a true heart. Contractile waves in the walls of major vessels propel blood. Blood contains amoeboid cells and bathes tissues in open spaces.

Excretory tubules are modified coelomic cells closely associated with blood vessels. This arrangement suggests active transport of materials between the blood and excretory tubules.

The coelom of cephalochordates is reduced, compared to that of most other chordates. It is restricted to canals near the gill bars, the endostyle, and the gonads.

Reproduction and Development

Cephalochordates are dioecious. Gonads bulge into the atrium from the lateral body wall. Gametes are shed into the atrium and leave the body through the atriopore. External fertilization leads to a bilaterally symmetrical larva. Larvae are free-swimming, but they eventually settle to the substrate before metamorphosing into adults.

FURTHER PHYLOGENETIC CONSIDERATIONS

The evolutionary relationships between the hemichordates and chordates are difficult to document with certainty. The dorsal tubular nerve cord and pharyngeal slits of hemichordates are evidence of evolutionary ties between these phyla (figure 26.10). Questions regarding the homologies of these structures, however, remain. Synapomorphies that distinguish chordates from hemichordates include tadpole larvae, a notochord, a postanal tail, and an endostyle.

Figure 26.10 also shows evolutionary relationships between members of the three chordate subphyla. As discussed in chapter 25, the earliest echinoderms were probably sessile filter feeders. The lifestyle of adult urochordates suggests a similar ancestry (perhaps from a common ancestor with echinoderms) for chordates. The evolution of motile chordates from attached ancestors may have involved the development of a tadpolelike larva. Increased larval mobility is often adaptive for species with sedentary adults because it promotes dispersal. ⑥ The evolution of motile adults could have resulted from paedomorphosis, which is the development of sexual maturity in the larval body form. (Paedomorphosis is well documented in the animal kingdom, especially among amphibians.) Paedomorphosis could have led to a small, sexually reproducing, fishlike chordate that could have been the ancestor of higher chordates.

The largest and most successful chordates belong to the subphylum Vertebrata. Bony or cartilaginous vertebrae that completely or partially replace the notochord characterize the vertebrates. The development of the anterior end of the nerve cord into a brain and the development of specialized sense organs on the head are evidence of a high degree of cephalization. The skeleton is modified anteriorly into a skull or cranium. There are eight classes of vertebrates (*see table 26.1*). Because of their cartilaginous and bony endoskeletons, vertebrates have left an abundant fossil record. Ancient jawless fishes were common in the Ordovician period, approximately 500 million years ago. Over a period of approximately 100 million years, fishes became the dominant vertebrates. Near the end of the Devonian period, approximately 400 million years ago, terrestrial vertebrates made their appearance. Since that time, vertebrates have radiated into most of the earth's habitats. Chapters 27 to 31 give an account of these events.

Stop and Ask Yourself
4. What are four characteristics that all chordates share at some time in their life history?
5. What group of chordates deposit cellulose in their body wall?
6. What is an endostyle? What are its functions in urochordates and in cephalochordates?
7. What is the function of the midgut cecum of cephalochordates?

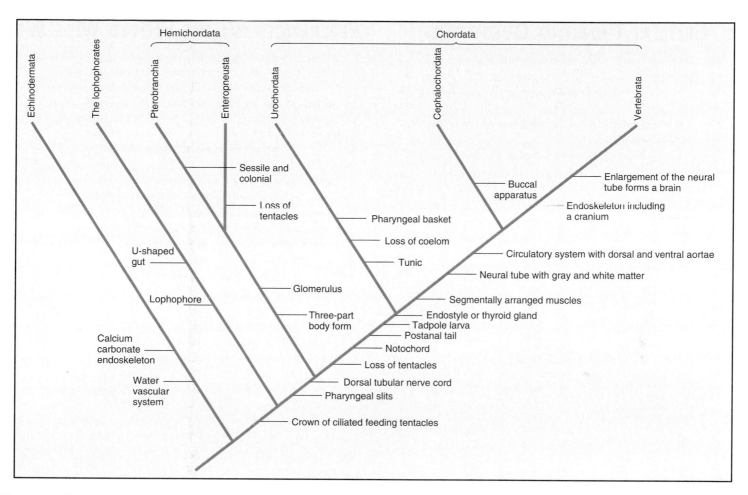

FIGURE 26.10

One Interpretation of Deuterostomate Phylogeny. The dorsal tubular nerve cord and pharyngeal slits are possible synapomorphies that link the Hemichordata and the Chordata. The notochord, postanal tail, and endostyle or thyroid gland are important characters that distinguish the Hemichordata and Chordata. Some of the synapomorphies that distinguish the chordate subphyla are shown.

SUMMARY

1. Echinoderms, hemichordates, and chordates share deuterostome characteristics and are believed to have evolved from a common diploblastic or triploblastic ancestor.

2. Members of the phylum Hemichordata include the acorn worms and the pterobranchs. Acorn worms are burrowing, marine worms, and pterobranchs are marine hemichordates whose collar possesses arms with numerous ciliated tentacles.

3. Chordates have four unique characteristics. A notochord is a supportive rod that extends most of the length of the animal. Pharyngeal slits are a series of openings between the digestive tract and the outside of the body. The tubular nerve cord lies just above the notochord and expands anteriorly into a brain. A postanal tail extends posteriorly to the anus and is supported by the notochord or the vertebral column.

4. Members of the subphylum Urochordata are the tunicates or sea squirts. Urochordates are sessile or planktonic filter feeders. Their development involves a tadpolelike larva.

5. The subphylum Cephalochordata includes small, tadpolelike filter feeders that live in shallow, marine waters with clean sandy substrates. Their notochord extends from the tail into the head and is somewhat contractile.

6. Pharyngeal slits and a tubular nerve cord link hemichordates and chordates to the same evolutionary lineage.

7. Chordates probably evolved from a sessile, filter-feeding ancestor. A larval stage of this sedentary ancestor may have undergone paedomorphosis to produce a small, sexually reproducing, fishlike chordate.

SELECTED KEY TERMS

endostyle (p. 429)
notochord (p. 428)
pharyngeal slits (p. 428)

postanal tail (p. 428)
tubular nerve cord (p. 428)

CRITICAL THINKING QUESTIONS

1. What evidence links hemichordates and chordates to the same evolutionary lineage?
2. What evidence of chordate affinities is present in adult tunicates? In larval tunicates?
3. What is paedomorphosis? What is a possible role for paedomorphosis in chordate evolution?
4. Discuss the possible influence of filter-feeding lifestyles on early chordate evolution.
5. What selection pressures could have favored a foraging or predatory lifestyle for later chordates?

REFERENCES ON THE WORLD WIDE WEB

1. **BIOSIS: Protochordata.**   This site provides links to information on the Hemichordata, Urochordata, and Cephalochordata.
   http://www.york.biosis.org/zrdocs/zoolinfo/grp_prch.htm
2. **Introduction to the Hemichordata.**   This site provides photographs and information on the biology and classification of the hemichordata.
   http://www.ucmp.berkeley.edu/chordata/
3. **Ascidian News.**   This site is an online newsletter concerning the biology of the urochordates. It provides links to other ascidian sites.
   http://nsm.fullerton.edu/~lamberts/ascidian/
4. **Chordata.**   This site provides information on evolutionary relationships among the Chordata and Urochordata.
   http://phylogeny.arizona.edu/tree/eukaryotes/animals/chordata/chord

The Fishes:
Vertebrate Success in Water

Concepts

1. The earliest fossil vertebrates are 510-million-year-old ostracoderms.
2. Members of the superclass Agnatha include extinct ostracoderms, the lampreys, and the hagfishes. Agnathans lack jaws and paired appendages.
3. The superclass Gnathostomata includes the cartilaginous (class Chondrichthyes) and bony (class Osteichthyes) fishes.
4. Aquatic environments have selected for certain adaptations in fishes. These include the abilities to move in a relatively dense medium, to exchange gases with water or air, to regulate buoyancy, to detect environmental changes, to regulate electrolytes (ions) and water in tissues, and to successfully reproduce.
5. Adaptive radiation resulted in the large variety of fishes present today. Evolution of some fishes led to the terrestrial vertebrates.

Would You Like to Know . . .

1. what group of fishes probably gave rise to all other fishes? (p. 436)

2. how a shark's teeth are replaced? (p. 441)

3. what fishes have lungs and breathe air? (p. 442)

4. what fish living today is the closest relative of terrestrial vertebrates? (p. 443)

5. why some sharks never stop moving? (p. 446)

6. how a shark can find a flounder completely covered by sand? (p. 450)

7. what environmental conditions selected for adaptations in fishes that eventually led to terrestrial vertebrates? (p. 453)

This chapter answers these and other useful questions.

This chapter contains evolutionary concepts, which are set off in this font.

EVOLUTIONARY PERSPECTIVE

Water, a buoyant medium that resists rapid fluctuations in temperature, covers over 70% of the earth's surface. Because life began in water, and living tissues are made mostly of water, it might seem that nowhere else would life be easier to sustain. This chapter describes why that is not entirely true.

You do not need to wear scuba gear to appreciate that fishes are adapted to aquatic environments in a fashion that no other group of animals can surpass. If you spend recreational hours with hook and line, visit a marine theme park, or simply glance into a pet store when walking through a shopping mall, you can attest to the variety and beauty of fishes. This variety is evidence of adaptive radiation that began 500 million years ago and shows no sign of ceasing. Fishes dominate many watery environments and are also the ancestors of all other members of the subphylum Vertebrata.

PHYLOGENETIC RELATIONSHIPS

Fishes are members of the chordate subphylum Vertebrata; thus, they have vertebrae that surround their spinal cord and provide the primary axial support. They also have a skull that protects the brain (*see table 26.1*; figure 27.1).

Zoologists do not know what animals were the first vertebrates. Recent cladistic analysis of vertebrate evolution indicates that a group of fishes, called hagfishes, are the most primitive vertebrates known (living or extinct). Fossilized bony fragments indicate that bone was present at least 510 million years ago. These fossils are from bony armor that covered animals called ostracoderms. Ostracoderms were relatively inactive filter feeders that lived on the bottom of prehistoric lakes and seas. They possessed neither jaws nor paired appendages; however, the evolution of fishes resulted in both jaws and paired appendages as well as many other structures. The results of this adaptive radiation are described in this chapter.

Did ancestral fishes live in freshwater or in the sea? The answer to this question is not simple. The first vertebrates were probably marine because ancient stocks of other deuterostome phyla were all marine. Vertebrates, however, adapted to freshwater very early, and much of the evolution of fishes occurred there. Apparently, early vertebrate evolution involved the movement of fishes back and forth between marine and freshwater environments. The majority of the evolutionary history of some fishes took place in ancient seas, and most of the evolutionary history of others occurred in freshwater. The importance of freshwater in the evolution of fishes is evidenced by the fact that over 41% of all fish species are found in freshwater, even though freshwater habitats represent only a small percentage (0.0093% by volume) of the earth's water resources.

SURVEY OF FISHES

The taxonomy of fishes has been the subject of debate for many years. Modern cladistic analysis has resulted in complex revisions

FIGURE 27.1

Fishes. Five hundred million years of evolution have resulted in unsurpassed diversity in fishes. The spines of this beautiful marine lionfish (*Pterois*) are extremely venomous.

in the taxonomy of this group of vertebrates (figure 27.2). The system used in this text divides fishes into two superclasses based on whether they lack jaws and paired appendages (superclass Agnatha) or possess those structures (superclass Gnathostomata) (table 27.1).

SUPERCLASS AGNATHA

Members of the superclass Agnatha (ag-nath'ah) (Gr. *a*, without + *gnathos*, jaw) lack jaws and paired appendages, but possess a cartilaginous skeleton and a notochord that persists into the adult stage. ① **Zoologists believe that ancient agnathans are ancestral to all other fishes** *(see figure 27.2).*

Ostracoderms are extinct agnathans that belonged to several classes. The fossils of predatory water scorpions (phylum Arthropoda [*see figure 23.7*]) are often found with fossil ostracoderms. As sluggish as ostracoderms apparently were, bony armor was probably their only defense. Ostracoderms were bottom dwellers, often about 15 cm long (figure 27.3). Most were probably filter feeders, either filtering suspended organic matter from the water or extracting annelids and other animals from muddy sediments. Some ostracoderms may have used bony plates around the mouth in a jawlike fashion to crack gastropod shells or the exoskeletons of arthropods.

Class Myxini

Hagfishes are members of the class Myxini (mik'sĭ ne) (Gr. *myxa*, slime). Hagfishes live buried in the sand and mud of marine environments, where they feed on soft-bodied invertebrates and scavenge dead and dying fish (figure 27.4). When hagfishes find a suitable fish, they enter the fish through the mouth and eat the con-

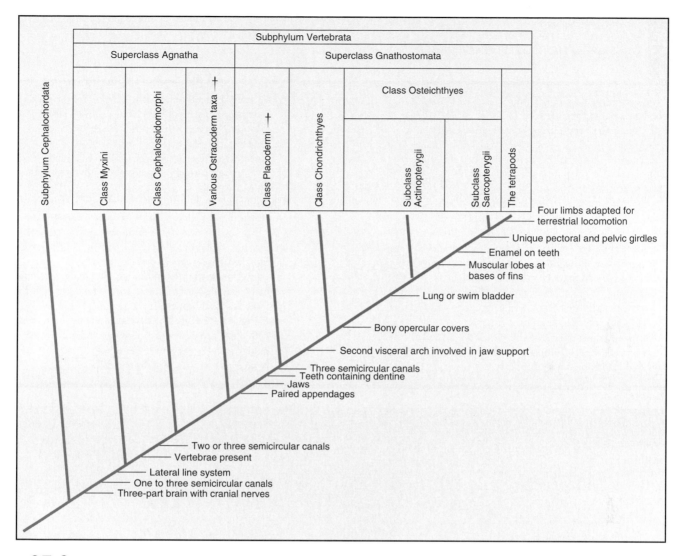

FIGURE 27.2

One Interpretation of the Phylogeny of Fishes. The evolutionary relationships among fishes are unsettled. This cladogram shows few selected ancestral and derived characters. Each lower taxon has numerous synapomorphies that are not shown. The position of the lampreys in fish phylogeny is debated. Recent evidence indicates that both lampreys and ostracoderms are more closely related to jawed vertebrates than to hagfishes. Most zoologists consider the ostracoderms a paraphyletic group (having multiple lineages). Their representation as a monophyletic group is an attempt to simplify this presentation. Daggers (†) indicate groups whose members are extinct.

tents of the body, leaving only a sack of skin and bones. Anglers must contend with hagfishes because they will bite at a baited hook. Hagfishes have the annoying habit of swallowing a hook so deeply that the hook is frequently lodged near the anus. The excessively slimy bodies of hagfishes make all but the grittiest fishermen cut their lines and tie on a new hook. Most zoologists now consider the hagfishes to be the most primitive group of vertebrates.

Class Cephalaspidomorphi

Lampreys are agnathans in the class Cephalaspidomorphi (sef″ah-las″pe-do-morf′e) (Gr. *kephale*, head + *aspidos*, shield + *morphe*,

form). They are common inhabitants of marine and freshwater environments in temperate regions. Most adult lampreys prey on other fishes, and the larvae are filter feeders. The mouth of an adult is suckerlike and surrounded by lips that have sensory and attachment functions. Numerous epidermal teeth line the mouth and cover a movable tonguelike structure (figure 27.5). Adults attach to prey with their lips and teeth, and use their tongue to rasp away scales. Lampreys have salivary glands with anticoagulant secretions and feed mainly on the blood of their prey (box 27.1). Some lampreys, however, are not predatory. Members of the genus *Lampetra* are called brook lampreys. The larval stages of brook lampreys last for about 3 years, and the adults neither feed

TABLE 27.1	CLASSIFICATION OF LIVING FISHES

Subphylum Vertebrata (ver″te-bra′tah)
  Superclass Agnatha (ag-nath′ah)
  Lack jaws and paired appendages; cartilaginous skeleton; persistent notochord; two semicircular canals. (Hagfishes have one semicircular canal that may represent a fusion of two canals.)
    Class Myxini (mik′sĭ-ne)
    Mouth with four pairs of tentacles; olfactory sacs open to mouth cavity; 5 to 15 pairs of pharyngeal slits. Hagfishes.
    Class Cephalaspidomorphi (sef″-ah-las″pe-do-morf′e)
    Sucking mouth with teeth and rasping tongue; seven pairs of pharyngeal slits; blind olfactory sacs. Lampreys.
  Superclass Gnathostomata (na′tho-sto″ma-tah)
  Hinged jaws and paired appendages; vertebral column may have replaced notochord; three semicircular canals.
    Class Chondrichthyes (kon-drik′thi-es)
    Tail fin with large upper lobe (heterocercal tail); cartilaginous skeleton; lack opercula and a swim bladder or lungs. Sharks, skates, rays, ratfishes.

  Subclass Elasmobranchii (e-laz′mo-bran″ke-i)
  Cartilaginous skeleton may be partially ossified; placoid scales or no scales. Sharks, skates, rays.
  Subclass Holocephali (hol″o-sef′a-li)
  Operculum covers pharyngeal slits; lack scales; teeth modified into crushing plates; lateral-line receptors in an open groove. Ratfishes.
  Class Osteichthyes (os′te-ik″the-es)
  Most with bony skeleton; operculum covers single gill opening; pneumatic sacs function as lungs or swim bladders. Bony fishes.
    Subclass Sarcopterygii (sar-kop-te-rij′e-i)
    Paired fins with muscular lobes; pneumatic sacs function as lungs. Lungfishes and coelacanths (lobe-finned fishes).
    Subclass Actinopterygii (ak″tin-op′te-rig-e-i)
    Paired fins supported by dermal rays; basal portions of paired fins not especially muscular; tail fin with approximately equal upper and lower lobes (homocercal tail); blind olfactory sacs. Ray-finned fishes.

FIGURE 27.3

Artist's Rendering of an Ancient Silurian Seafloor. Two ostracoderms, *Pteraspis* and *Anglaspis*, are in the background, and a predatory water scorpion (phylum Arthropoda, class Merostomata) is in the foreground.

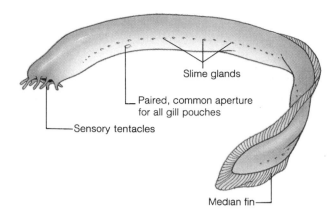

FIGURE 27.4

Class Myxini. Hagfish external structure.

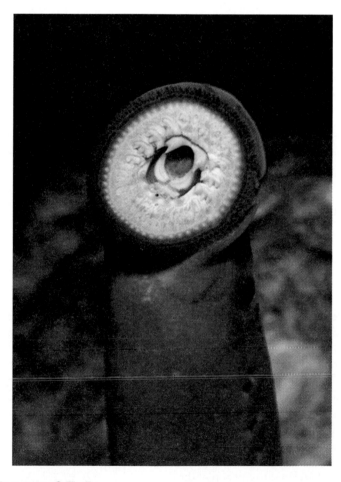

FIGURE 27.5

Class Agnatha. A lamprey *(Petromyzon marinus)*. Note the sucking mouth and teeth used to feed on other fish.

BOX 27.1 LAMPREYS AND GREAT LAKES FISHERIES

Along with many other European immigrants to the United States in the nineteenth century came many Scandinavians. Many of these Scandinavian immigrants fished for a living, and they were understandably attracted to the Great Lakes Region. Through the early part of the twentieth century, fishing was very good. Catches included a variety of smaller fishes that inhabited the shoals and bays of the Great Lakes, but the prize catches were two deep-water predators—lake trout *(Salvelinus namaycush)* and whitefish *(Corygonus clupeaformis)*. The yearly catch of lake trout in each of the Great Lakes in the 1930s exceeded 2,000 metric tons.

These commercial fisheries, however, were doomed. Their fate was sealed years before many immigrants even left their homes in Scandinavia. In 1829, the Welland Canal was completed. It provided a shipping route around Niagara Falls between Lakes Ontario and Erie. Niagara Falls, however, had not only been a barrier to shipping, it had also been a barrier to the sea lamprey. After the Welland Canal was completed, sea lampreys slowly worked their way from Lake Ontario to the other Great Lakes. By 1937, spawning lampreys were recorded in Lake Michigan, and by the early 1940s, Great Lakes fishermen had to work very hard to bring home a single lake trout with a day's catch of predominately smaller fishes. The lamprey, like humans, had a decided preference for the larger, cold-water fish species. In 1944, the annual catch of lake trout from Lake Michigan had been reduced to less than 100 metric tons. In 1953, it was down to a few hundred kilograms!

Although the lamprey invasion into the Great Lakes brought severe economic hardship to many fishermen, it also resulted in an important success story in fishery management. In the 1950s, Canada and the states bordering the Great Lakes instituted an intensive lamprey control program. Control measures involved the use of mechanical weirs that prevented spawning migrations of lampreys into the tributaries of the Great Lakes. Electrical shocking devices were employed in an attempt to kill lampreys in spawning streams. Finally, chemical control measures were employed. Lamprey populations began to decline, and by the mid-1960s, lamprey control measures were considered a success.

A sport fishery has filled the void that the decline of lake trout created. In the late 1960s, Coho *(Concorhynchus kisutch)* and Chinook *(Oncorhynchus tshawytscha)* salmon were stocked in the Great Lakes. Survival and growth of these salmon have been remarkable, and fewer than 5% of the salmon caught are marked by lamprey wounds. Fishermen are catching whitefish and lake trout again. To preserve this fishery, lamprey control measures will be maintained in the future to prevent large-scale growth of lamprey populations. Recently, sterile male lampreys have been released in attempts to reduce reproductive success.

nor leave their stream. They reproduce soon after metamorphosis and then die.

Adult sea lampreys live in the ocean or the Great Lakes. Near the end of their lives, they migrate—sometimes hundreds of miles—to a spawning bed in a freshwater stream. Once lampreys reach their spawning site, usually in relatively shallow water with swift currents, they begin building a nest by making small depressions in the substrate. When the nest is prepared, a female usually attaches to a stone with her mouth. A male uses his mouth to attach to the female's head and wraps his body around the female

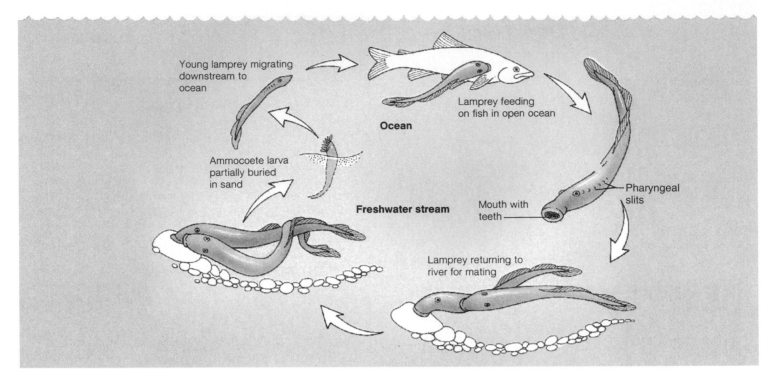

FIGURE 27.6

External Structure and Life History of a Sea Lamprey. Sea lampreys feed in the open ocean and, near the end of their lives, migrate into freshwater streams, where they mate. They deposit eggs in nests on the stream bottom, and young ammocoete larvae hatch in about 3 weeks. Ammocoete larvae live as filter feeders until they attain sexual maturity.

(figure 27.6). Eggs are shed in small batches over a period of several hours, and fertilization is external. The relatively sticky eggs are then covered with sand.

Eggs hatch in approximately 3 weeks into ammocoete larvae. The larvae drift downstream to softer substrates, where they bury themselves in sand and mud and filter feed in a fashion similar to amphioxus (*see figure 26.9*).

Ammocoete larvae grow from 7 mm to about 17 cm over 3 years. During later developmental stages, the larvae metamorphose to the adult over a period of several months. The mouth becomes suckerlike, and the teeth, tongue, and feeding musculature develop. Lampreys eventually leave the mud permanently and begin a journey to the sea to begin life as predators. Adults return only once to the headwaters of their stream to spawn and die.

Stop and Ask Yourself

1. What superclass of vertebrates contains the probable ancestors of all other vertebrates?
2. How are members of the superclass Agnatha characterized?
3. What animals make up the class Myxini?
4. How are the lifestyles of adult and larval lampreys different?

SUPERCLASS GNATHOSTOMATA

Two major developments in vertebrate evolution were the appearance of jaws and paired appendages. These structures are first seen in members of the superclass Gnathostomata (na'tho-sto"ma-tah) (Gr. *gnathos*, jaw + *stoma*, mouth). Jaws are used in feeding and are partly responsible for a transition to more active, predatory lifestyles. Pectoral fins of fishes are appendages usually just behind the head, and pelvic fins are usually located ventrally and posteriorly (figure 27.7). Both sets of paired fins give fish a more precise steering mechanism and increase fish agility.

Two classes of gnathostomes still have living members: the cartilaginous fishes (class Chondrichthyes) and the bony fishes (class Osteichthyes). Another class, the armored fishes, or placoderms, contained the earliest jawed fishes (*see figure 27.2*). They are now extinct and apparently left no descendants. A fourth group of ancient, extinct fishes, the acanthodians, may be more closely related to the bony fishes.

Class Chondrichthyes

Members of the class Chondrichthyes (kon-drik'thi-es) (Gr. *chondros*, cartilage + *ichthyos*, fish) include the sharks, skates, rays, and ratfishes (*see table 27.1*). Most chondrichthians are carnivores or scavengers, and most are marine. In addition to their biting mouthparts and paired appendages, chondrichthians possess epidermal placoid scales and a cartilaginous endoskeleton.

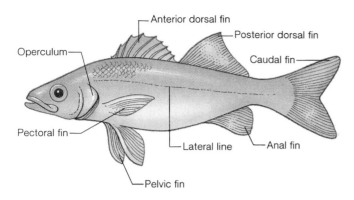

FIGURE 27.7

Paired Appendages. Appendages of a member of the superclass Gnathostomata. These appendages are secondarily reduced in some species.

The subclass Elasmobranchii (e-laz′mo-bran′ke-i) (Gr. *elasmos*, plate metal + *branchia*, gills), which includes the sharks, skates, and rays, has about seven hundred species (figure 27.8). Sharks arose from early jawed fishes midway through the Devonian period, about 375 million years ago. The absence of certain features characteristic of bony fishes (e.g., a swim bladder to regulate buoyancy, a gill cover, and a bony skeleton) is sometimes interpreted as evidence of the primitiveness of elasmobranchs. This interpretation is mistaken, as these characteristics simply resulted from different adaptations in the two groups to similar selection pressures. Some of these adaptations are described later in this chapter.

Tough skin with dermal, placoid scales covers sharks (figure 27.9a). These scales project posteriorly and give the skin a tough, sandpaper texture. (In fact, dried shark skin has been used for sandpaper.) Posteriorly pointed scales also reduce friction with the water as a shark swims.

Shark teeth are actually modified placoid scales. The row of teeth on the outer edge of the jaw is backed up by rows of teeth attached to a ligamentous band that covers the jaw cartilage inside the mouth. ❷ As the outer teeth wear and become useless, newer teeth move into position from inside the jaw and replace them. In young sharks, this replacement is rapid, with a new row of teeth developing every 7 or 8 days (figure 27.9b). Crowns of teeth in different species may be adapted for shearing prey or for crushing the shells of molluscs.

Sharks range in size from less than 1 m (e.g., *Squalus*, the laboratory dissection specimen) to greater than 10 m (e.g., basking sharks and whale sharks). The largest sharks are not predatory but are filter feeders. They have pharyngeal-arch modifications that strain plankton. The fiercest and most feared sharks are the

(a)

(b)

(c)

FIGURE 27.8

Class Chondrichthyes. (*a*) A gray reef shark (*Carcharhinus*). (*b*) A manta ray (*Manta hamiltoni*) with two remoras (*Remora remora*) attached to its ventral surface. (*c*) A bullseye stingray (*Urolophus concentricus*).

(a)

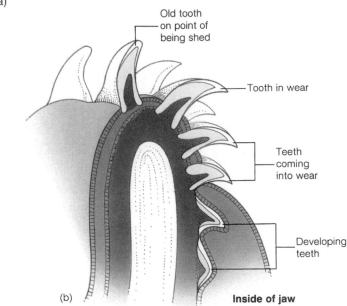

Old tooth
on point of
being shed

Tooth in wear

Teeth
coming
into wear

Developing
teeth

(b)

Inside of jaw

FIGURE 27.9

Scales and Teeth of Sharks. (*a*) Section of shark skin magnified to show posteriorly pointing placoid scales (SEM ×500). (*b*) The teeth of sharks develop as modified placoid scales. Newer teeth that move from the inside to the outside of the jaw continuously replace older teeth.

great white shark (*Carcharodon*) and the mako (*Isurus*). Extinct specimens may have reached lengths of 25 m or more (box 27.2)!

Skates and rays are specialized for life on the ocean floor. They usually inhabit shallow water, where they use their blunt teeth to feed on invertebrates. Their most obvious modification for life on the ocean floor is a lateral expansion of the pectoral fins into winglike appendages. Locomotion results from dorsoventral

muscular waves that pass posteriorly along the fins. Frequently, elaborate color patterns on the dorsal surface of these animals provide effective camouflage (*see figure 27.8c*). The sting ray (*Raja*) has a tail modified into a defensive lash; the dorsal fin persists as a venomous spine. Also included in this group are the electric rays (*Narcine*) and manta rays (*Aetobatus*) (*see figure 27.8b*).

A second major group of chondrichthians, in the subclass Holocephali (hol″o-sef′a-li) (Gr. *holos*, whole + *kephalidos*, head), contains about 30 species. A frequently studied example, *Chimaera*, has a large head with a small mouth surrounded by large lips. A narrow, tapering tail has resulted in the common name "ratfish." Holocephalans diverged from other chondrichthians nearly 300 million years ago. Since that time, specializations not found in other elasmobranchs have evolved, including a gill cover, called an **operculum,** and teeth modified into large plates for crushing the shells of molluscs. Holocephalans lack scales.

Class Osteichthyes

Members of the class Osteichthyes (os′te-ik″the-es) (Gr. *osteon*, bone + *ichthyos*, fish) are characterized by having at least some bone in their skeleton and/or scales, an operculum covering the gill openings, and lungs or a swim bladder. Any group that has 20,000 species and is a major life-form in most of the earth's vast aquatic habitats must be judged very successful from an evolutionary perspective.

The first fossils of bony fishes are from late Silurian deposits (approximately 405 million years old). By the Devonian period (350 million years ago), the two subclasses were in the midst of their adaptive radiations (*see table 27.1; see also figure 27.2*).

Members of the subclass Sarcopterygii (sar-kop-te-rij′e-i) (Gr. *sark*, flesh + *pteryx*, fin) have muscular lobes associated with their fins and usually use lungs in gas exchange. One group of sarcopterygians are the lungfishes. Only three genera survive today, and all live in regions where seasonal droughts are common. ③ When freshwater lakes and rivers begin to stagnate and dry, these fishes use lungs to breathe air (figure 27.10). Some (*Neoceratodus*) inhabit the freshwaters of Queensland, Australia. They survive stagnation by breathing air, but normally use gills and cannot withstand total drying. Others are found in freshwater rivers and lakes in tropical Africa (*Protopterus*) and tropical South America (*Lepidosiren*). They have lost the use of gills for gas exchange and can survive when rivers or lakes are dry by burrowing into the mud. They keep a narrow air pathway open by bubbling air to the surface. After the substrate dries, the only evidence of a lungfish burrow is a small opening in the earth. Lungfishes may remain in aestivation for 6 months or more. (Aestivation is a dormant state that helps an animal withstand hot, dry periods.) When rain again fills the lake or riverbed, lungfishes emerge from their burrows to feed and reproduce.

| BOX | 27.2 | JAWS FROM THE PAST |

Paleontological records can tell scientists much about life-forms from the past. Most is known about ancient animals whose bodies contained hard parts that were resistant to decay and that were more likely to fossilize. The fossil record for fishes that contained substantial quantities of bone is fairly complete. Records of fishes that lack bone are usually harder to find.

In spite of the cartilaginous skeletons of sharks, knowledge of ancient sharks, although not perfect, is more complete than might be expected. Much of what is known of ancient sharks comes from discoveries made in Ohio. Sharks in Ohio may seem surprising at first, but during the upper Devonian (about 350 million years ago), the sea extended southwest from the St. Lawrence River region, across the Great Lakes, and down to Arkansas. The floor of this ocean, in the region now known as Ohio, was made of soft, deep sediments—ideal for fossilization. Some elasmobranch specimens are so well preserved that details of gill structures, and of muscle organization, and even remains of a last meal are sometimes found intact.

Discoveries such as these provide a wealth of information about ancient sharks. The body form of ancient sharks allowed them to become efficient predators, and most modern sharks retain that basic form. The shape of fossilized teeth sometimes identifies the kind of shark they came from. Mineral deposits build up on teeth as they rest on the ocean floor. If mineral deposits accumulate at a constant rate, it is possible to determine how long teeth have been resting on the ocean floor. Assuming that a ratio between tooth size and body size is constant for a given species, scientists can estimate the length of a shark from a fossilized tooth.

Reconstruction of ancient sharks from all available evidence is the job of some museum scientists. The reconstruction in figure 1 is of an ancient shark found in a North Carolina quarry. (Because too few teeth were found to fill out the entire jaw, false teeth were constructed from hard rubber.) They are the teeth of a 30-million-

FIGURE 1   **Ancient Jaws.** These reconstructed jaws of *Carcharodon megalodon* measure 1 m wide by 2 m high.

year-old *Carcharodon megalodon*, which was the ancestor of the great white shark. The largest tooth of this specimen was about 15 cm long. Because 2.5 cm of tooth equals about 3 m of shark, this specimen was estimated to be 18.5 m long! The model shown in figure 1 is on display in the Smithsonian's National Museum of Natural History in Washington, DC.

A second group of sarcopterygians are the coelacanths. The most recent coelacanths fossils are over 70 million years old. In 1938, however, people fishing in deep water off the coast of South Africa brought up fishes that were identified as coelacanths (figure 27.11). Since then, numerous other specimens have been caught in deep water around the Comoro Islands off Madagascar. ④ The discovery of this fish, *Latimeria chalumnae*, was a milestone event because *Latimeria* is probably the closest living fish relative of terrestrial vertebrates. It is large—up to 80 kg—and has heavy scales. Ancient coelacanths lived in freshwater lakes and rivers; thus, the ancestors of *Latimeria* must have moved from freshwater habitats to the deep sea.

A third group of sarcopterygians, called rhipidistians, became extinct before the close of the Paleozoic period. They are believed to have been the ancestors of ancient amphibians.

FIGURE 27.10
Subclass Sarcopterygii. The lungfish, *Lepidosiren paradoxa*, has lungs that allow it to withstand stagnation and drying of its habitat.

FIGURE 27.11

A Sarcopterygian, the Coelacanth. *Latimeria* is the only known surviving coelacanth.

The subclass Actinopterygii (ak″tin-op′te-rig-e-i) (Gr. *aktis*, ray + *pteryx*, fin) contains fishes that are sometimes called the ray-finned fishes because their fins lack muscular lobes. They usually possess **swim bladders,** gas-filled sacs along the dorsal wall of the body cavity that regulate buoyancy. Zoologists now realize that there have been many points of divergence in the evolution of the Actinopterygii. One modern classification system divides the Actinopterygii into two infraclasses.

One group of actinopterygians, the chondrosteans, contains many species that lived during the Permian, Triassic, and Jurassic periods (215 to 120 million years ago), but only 25 species remain today. Ancestral chondrosteans had a bony skeleton, but living members, the sturgeons and paddlefishes, have cartilaginous skeletons. Chondrosteans also have a tail with a large upper lobe.

Most sturgeons live in the sea and migrate into rivers to breed (figure 27.12*a*). (Some sturgeons live in freshwater but maintain the migratory habits of their marine relatives.) They are large (up to 1,000 kg), and bony plates cover the anterior portion of the body. Heavy scales cover the tail. The sturgeon mouth is small, and jaws are weak. Sturgeons feed on invertebrates that they stir up from the sea or riverbed using their snout. Because sturgeons are valued for their caviar (eggs), they have been severely overfished.

(a)

(b)

FIGURE 27.12

Subclass Actinopterygii, the Chondrosteans. (*a*) A shovelnose sturgeon (*Scaphirhynchus platorynchus*). Sturgeons are covered anteriorly by heavy bony plates and posteriorly by scales. (*b*) The distinctive rostrum of a paddlefish (*Polydon spathula*) is densely innervated with sensory structures that are probably used to detect minute electrical fields. Note the mouth in its open, filter-feeding position.

Paddlefishes are large, freshwater chondrosteans. They have a large, paddlelike rostrum that is innervated with sensory organs believed to detect weak electrical fields (figure 27.12*b*). They swim through the water with their large mouths open, filtering crustaceans and small fishes. They are found mainly in lakes and large rivers of the Mississippi River basin and are also known from western North America.

The second group of actinopterygians flourished in the Jurassic period and succeeded most chondrosteans. Two very primitive genera occur in temperate to warm freshwaters of North America. *Lepisosteus*, the garpike, has thick scales and long jaws that it uses to catch fishes. *Amia* is commonly referred to as the dogfish or bowfin. Most living fishes are members of this group and are referred to as teleosts or modern bony fishes. They have a symmetrical caudal fin and a swim bladder that has lost its connection to the digestive tract. After their divergence from ancient marine actinopterygians in the late Triassic period, teleosts experienced a remarkable evolutionary diversification and adapted to nearly every available aquatic habitat (figure 27.13). The number of teleost species exceeds 20,000.

(a)

Stop and Ask Yourself

5. What are characteristics of the superclass Gnathostomata? In what ways are members of this superclass considered more advanced than agnathans?

6. What class of fishes is characterized by jaws, paired appendages, a cartilaginous skeleton, and placoid scales?

7. What class of fishes is characterized by some bone in their skeleton, an operculum, and usually lungs or a swim bladder?

8. What is aestivation? What is its role in the life of some lungfishes?

EVOLUTIONARY PRESSURES

Why is a fish fishlike? This apparently redundant question is unanswerable in some respects because some traits of animals are selectively neutral and, thus, neither improve nor detract from overall fitness. On the other hand, aquatic environments have physical characteristics that are important selective forces for aquatic animals. Although animals have adapted to aquatic environments in different ways, you can understand many aspects of the structure and function of a fish by studying the fish's habitat. This section will help you appreciate the many ways that a fish is adapted for life in water.

(b)

LOCOMOTION

Picture a young girl running full speed down the beach and into the ocean. She hits the water and begins to splash. At first, she lifts her feet high in the air between steps, but as she goes deeper, her legs encounter more and more resistance. The momentum of her upper body causes her to fall forward, and she resorts to labored and awkward swimming strokes. The density of the water makes movement through it difficult and costly. For a fish, however, swimming is less energetically costly than running is for a terrestrial organism. The streamlined shape of a fish and the mucoid

(c)

FIGURE 27.13

Subclass Actinopterygii, the Teleosts. (*a*) Bottom fish, such as this winter flounder (*Pseudopleuronectes americanus*), have both eyes on one side of the head, and they often rest on their side fully or partially buried in the substrate. (*b*) Freshwater teleosts, such as this speckled darter (*Etheostoma stigmaeum*), are common in temperate streams. (*c*) Cichlid fish, including this harlequin cichlid (*Cichlasoma festae*), are common in tropical freshwaters.

secretions that lubricate its body surface reduce friction between the fish and the water. Water's buoyant properties also contribute to the efficiency of a fish's movement through the water. A fish expends little energy in support against the pull of gravity.

Fishes move through the water using their fins and body wall to push against the incompressible surrounding water. Anyone who has eaten a fish filet probably realizes that muscle bundles of most fishes are arranged in a $\lessgtr$ pattern. Because these muscles extend posteriorly and anteriorly in a zigzag fashion, contraction of each muscle bundle can affect a relatively large portion of the body wall. Very efficient, fast-swimming fishes, such as tuna and mackerel, supplement body movements with a vertical caudal (tail) fin that is tall and forked. The forked shape of the caudal fin reduces surface area that could cause turbulence and interfere with forward movement.

NUTRITION AND THE DIGESTIVE SYSTEM

The earliest fishes were probably filter feeders and scavengers that sifted through the mud of ancient seafloors for decaying organic matter, annelids, molluscs, or other bottom-dwelling invertebrates. Fish nutrition dramatically changed when the evolution of jaws transformed early fishes into efficient predators.

Most modern fishes are predators and spend much of their life searching for food. Their prey vary tremendously. Some fishes feed on invertebrate animals floating or swimming in the plankton or living in or on the substrate. Many feed on other vertebrates. Similarly, the kinds of food that one fish eats at different times in its life varies. For example, as a larva, a fish may feed on plankton; as an adult, it may switch to larger prey, such as annelids or smaller fish. Fishes usually swallow prey whole. Teeth capture and hold prey, and some fishes have teeth that are modified for crushing the shells of molluscs or the exoskeletons of arthropods. To capture prey, fishes often use the suction that closing the opercula and rapidly opening the mouth creates, which develops a negative pressure that sweeps water and prey inside the mouth.

Other feeding strategies have also evolved in fishes. Herring, paddlefishes, and whale sharks are filter feeders. Long gill processes, called **gill rakers,** trap plankton while the fish is swimming through the water with its mouth open (*see figure 27.12*b). Other fishes, such as carp, feed on a variety of plants and small animals. A few, such as the lamprey, are external parasites for at least a portion of their life. A few are primarily herbivores, feeding on plants.

The fish digestive tract is similar to that of other vertebrates. An enlargement, called the stomach, stores large, often infrequent, meals. The small intestine, however, is the primary site for enzyme secretion and food digestion. Sharks and other elasmo-branchs have a spiral valve in their intestine, and bony fishes possess outpockets of the intestine, called pyloric ceca, which increase absorptive and secretory surfaces.

CIRCULATION AND GAS EXCHANGE

All vertebrates have a closed circulatory system in which a heart pumps blood, with red blood cells containing hemoglobin, through a series of arteries, capillaries, and veins. The evolution of lungs in fishes was paralleled by changes in vertebrate circulatory systems. These changes are associated with the loss of gills, delivery of blood to the lungs, and separation of oxygenated and unoxygenated blood in the heart.

The vertebrate heart develops from four embryological enlargements of a ventral aorta. In fishes, blood flows from the venous system through the sinus venosus, the atrium, the ventricle, the conus arteriosus, and into the ventral aorta (figure 27.14a). Five afferent vessels carry blood to the gills, where the vessels branch into capillaries. Blood is collected by efferent vessels, delivered to the dorsal aorta, and distributed to the body.

Even though lungfishes are not a transitional group, they provide a good example of how lungs alter the circulatory pattern. Circulation to gills continues, but a vessel to the lungs has developed as a branch off aortic arch VI (figure 27.14b). This vessel is now called the pulmonary artery. Blood returns to the heart through pulmonary veins and enters the left side of the heart. The atrium and ventricle of the lungfish heart are partially divided. These partial divisions help keep unoxygenated blood from the body separate from the oxygenated blood from the lungs. A spiral valve in the conus arteriosus helps direct blood from the right side of the heart to the pulmonary artery and blood from the left side of the heart to the remaining aortic arches. Thus, the lungfishes show a distinction between a pulmonary circuit and a systemic circuit.

Gas Exchange

Fishes live in an environment that contains less than 2.5% of the oxygen present in air. To maintain adequate levels of oxygen in their bloodstream, fishes must pass large quantities of water across gill surfaces and extract the small amount of oxygen present in the water. Most fishes have a muscular pumping mechanism to move the water into the mouth and pharynx, over the gills, and out of the fish through gill openings. Muscles surrounding the pharynx and the opercular cavity, which is between the gills and the operculum, power this pump.

Some elasmobranchs and open-ocean bony fishes, such as the tuna, maintain water flow by holding their mouth open while swimming. This method is called **ram ventilation.**　❺ Elasmo-

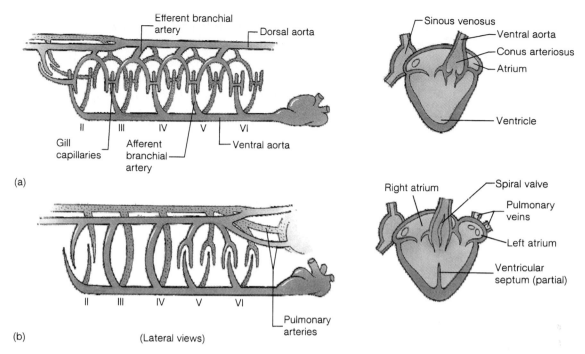

FIGURE 27.14

Circulatory System of Fishes. Diagrammatic representation of the circulatory systems of (*a*) bony fishes and (*b*) lungfishes. Hearts are drawn from a ventral view. Major branches of arteries carrying blood to and from the gills are called branchial arteries (or embryologically, aortic arches) and are numbered with Roman numerals. They begin with II because aortic arch I is lost during embryological development.

branchs do not have opercula to help pump water, and therefore, some sharks must keep moving to survive. Others move water over their gills with a pumping mechanism similar to that just described. Rather than using an operculum in the pumping process, however, these fishes have gill bars with external flaps that close and form a cavity functionally similar to the opercular cavity of other fishes. Spiracles are modified pharyngeal slits that open just behind the eyes of elasmobranchs and are used as an alternate route for water entering the pharynx.

Gas exchange across gill surfaces is very efficient. **Gill (visceral) arches** support gills. **Gill filaments** extend from each gill arch and include vascular folds of epithelium, called **pharyngeal lamellae** (figure 27.15*a,b*). Branchial arteries carry blood to the gills and into gill filaments. The arteries break into capillary beds in pharyngeal lamellae. Gas exchange occurs as blood and water move in opposite directions on either side of the lamellar epithelium. This **countercurrent exchange mechanism** provides very efficient gas exchange by maintaining a concentration gradient between the blood and the water over the entire length of the capillary bed (figure 27.15*c,d*).

Swim Bladders and Lungs

The Indian climbing perch spends its life almost entirely on land. These fishes, as most bony fishes, have gas chambers called **pneumatic sacs.** In nonteleost fishes, a pneumatic duct connects the pneumatic sacs to the esophagus or another part of the digestive tract. Swallowed air enters these sacs, and gas exchange occurs across vascular surfaces. Thus, in the Indian climbing perch, lungfishes, and ancient rhipidistians, pneumatic sacs function(ed) as lungs. In other bony fishes, pneumatic sacs act as swim bladders.

Most zoologists believe that lungs are more primitive than swim bladders. Much of the early evolution of bony fishes occurred in warm, freshwater lakes and streams during the Devonian period. These bodies of water frequently became stagnant and periodically dried. Having lungs in these habitats could have meant the difference between life and death. On the other hand, later evolution of modern bony fishes occurred in marine and freshwater environments, where stagnation was not a problem. In these environments, the use of pneumatic sacs in buoyancy regulation would have been adaptive (figure 27.16).

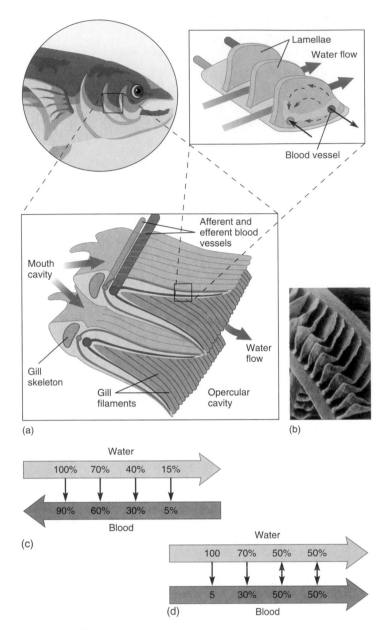

FIGURE 27.15

Gas Exchange at the Pharyngeal Lamellae. (*a*) The gill arches under the operculum support two rows of gill filaments. Blood flows into gill filaments through afferent branchial arteries, and these arteries break into capillary beds in the pharyngeal lamellae. Water and blood flow in opposite directions on either side of the lamellae. (*b*) Electron micrograph of the tip of a trout gill filament, showing numerous lamellae. (*c,d*) A comparison of countercurrent and parallel exchanges. Water entering the spaces between pharyngeal lamellae is saturated with oxygen in both cases. In countercurrent exchange (*c*), this water encounters blood that is almost completely oxygenated, but a diffusion gradient still favors the movement of more oxygen from the water to the blood. As water continues to move between lamellae, it loses oxygen to the blood because it is continually encountering blood with a lower oxygen concentration. Thus, a diffusion gradient is maintained along the length of the lamellae. If blood and water moved in parallel fashion (*d*), oxygen would diffuse from water to blood only until the oxygen concentration in blood equaled the oxygen concentration in water, and the exchange would be much less efficient.

Buoyancy Regulation

Did you ever consider why you can float in water? Water is a supportive medium, but that is not sufficient to prevent you from sinking. Even though you are made mostly of water, other constituents of tissues are more dense than water. Bone, for example, has a specific gravity twice that of water. Why, then, can you float? You can float because of two large, air-filled organs called lungs.

Fishes maintain their vertical position in a column of water in four ways. One way is to incorporate low-density compounds into their tissues. Fishes (especially their livers) are saturated with buoyant oils. A second way fishes maintain vertical position is to use fins to provide lift. The pectoral fins of a shark are planing devices that help to create lift as the shark moves through the water. Also, the large upper lobe of a shark's caudal fin provides upward thrust for the posterior end of the body (*see figure 27.8a*). A third adaptation is the reduction of heavy tissues in fishes. The bones of fishes are generally less dense than those of terrestrial vertebrates. One of the adaptive features of the elasmobranch cartilaginous skeleton probably results from cartilage being only slightly heavier than water. The fourth adaptation is the swim bladder. A fish regulates buoyancy by precisely controlling the volume of gas in its swim bladder. (You can mimic this adaptation while floating in water. How well do you float after forcefully exhaling as much air as possible?)

The pneumatic duct connects the swim bladders of garpike, sturgeons, and other primitive bony fishes to the esophagus or another part of the digestive tract. These fishes gulp air at the surface to force air into their swim bladders.

Most teleosts have swim bladders that have lost a functional connection to the digestive tract. The blood secretes gases (various mixtures of nitrogen and oxygen) into the swim bladder using a countercurrent exchange mechanism in a vascular network called the rete mirabile ("miraculous net"). Gases may be reabsorbed into the blood at the posterior end of the bladder, the ovale (*see figure 27.16c*).

NERVOUS AND SENSORY FUNCTIONS

The central nervous system of fishes, as in other vertebrates, consists of a brain and a spinal cord. Sensory receptors are widely distributed over the body. In addition to generally distributed receptors for touch and temperature, fishes possess specialized receptors for olfaction, vision, hearing, equilibrium and balance, and for detecting water movements.

Openings, called external nares, in the snout of fishes lead to olfactory receptors. In most fishes, receptors are in blind-ending olfactory sacs. In a few fishes, the external nares open to nasal passages that lead to the mouth cavity. Recent research has revealed that some fishes rely heavily on their sense of smell. For example, salmon and lampreys return to spawn in the streams in which they hatched years earlier. Their migrations to these streams often involve distances of hundreds of kilometers, and the fishes' perception of the characteristic odors of their spawning stream guide them.

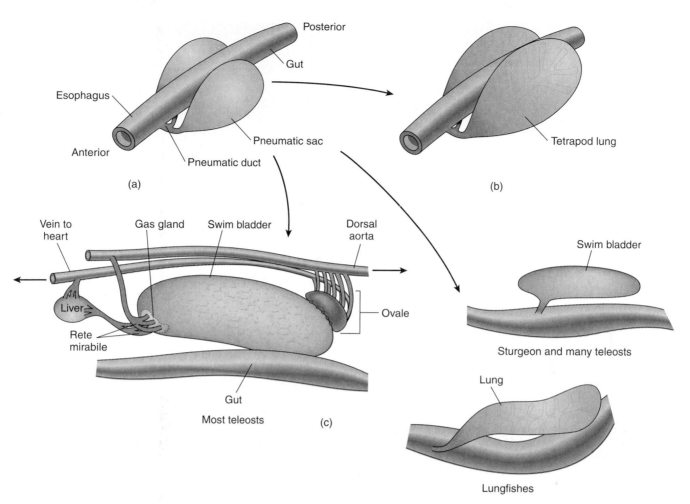

FIGURE 27.16

Possible Sequence in the Evolution of Pneumatic Sacs. (*a*) Pneumatic sacs may have originally developed from ventral outgrowths of the esophagus. Many ancient fishes probably used pneumatic sacs as lungs. (*b*) Primitive lungs developed further during the evolution of vertebrates. Internal compartmentalization increases surface area for gas exchange in land vertebrates. (*c*) In most bony fishes, pneumatic sacs are called swim bladders, and they are modified for buoyancy regulation. Swim bladders are dorsal in position to prevent a tendency for the fish to "belly up" in the water. Pneumatic duct connections to the esophagus are frequently lost, and gases transfer from the blood to the swim bladder through a countercurrent exchange mechanism called a rete mirabile. The ovale, at the posterior end of the swim bladder, returns gases to the bloodstream.

The eyes of fishes are similar in most aspects of structure to those in other vertebrates. They are lidless, however, and the lenses are round. Focusing requires moving the lens forward or backward in the eye. (Most other vertebrates focus by changing the shape of the lens.)

Receptors for equilibrium, balance, and hearing are in the inner ears of fishes, and their functions are similar to those of other vertebrates. Semicircular canals detect rotational movements, and other sensory patches help with equilibrium and balance by detecting the direction of the gravitational pull. Fishes lack the outer and/or middle ear, which conducts sound waves to the inner ear in other vertebrates. As anyone who enjoys fishing knows, however, most fishes can hear. Vibrations may pass from the water through the bones of the skull to the middle ear, and a few fishes have chains of bony ossicles (modifications of vertebrae) that connect the swim bladder to the back of the skull. Vibrations strike the fish, are amplified by the swim bladder, and sent through the ossicles to the skull.

Running along each side and branching over the head of most fishes is a lateral-line system. The **lateral-line system** consists of sensory pits in the epidermis of the skin that connect to canals that run just below the epidermis. In these pits are receptors that are stimulated by water moving against them. Lateral lines are used either to detect water currents, or a predator or a prey that may be causing water movements, in the vicinity of the fish. Fishes may also detect low-frequency sounds with these receptors.

Electric Fishes

A U.S. Navy pilot has just ejected from his troubled aircraft over shark-infested water! What measures can the pilot take to ensure survival under these hostile conditions? The Navy has considered this scenario. One of the solutions to the problem is a polyvinyl bag suspended from an inflatable collar. The polyvinyl bag helps conceal the downed flyer from a shark's vision and keen sense of smell. But is that all that is required to ensure protection?

(a)

(b)

FIGURE 27.17

Electric Fishes. (a) The electrical field of a fish detects the presence of prey and other objects in the fish's murky environment. Currents circulate from electrical organs in the fish's tail to electroreceptors near its head. An object in this electrical field changes the pattern of stimulation of electroreceptors. (b) The electric fish (*Gymnarchus niloticus*).

All organisms produce weak electrical fields from the activities of nerves and muscles. **Electroreception** is the detection of electrical fields that the fish or another organism in the environ-

FIGURE 27.18

Electric Fishes. A lesser electric ray (*Narcine brasiliensis*).

ment generates. Electroreception and/or electrogeneration has been demonstrated in over five hundred species of fishes in seven families of Chondrichthyes and Osteichthyes. These fishes use their electroreceptive sense for detecting prey and for orienting toward or away from objects in the environment.

Nowhere is prey detection with this sense better developed than in the rays and sharks. Spiny dogfish sharks, the common laboratory specimens, locate prey by electroreception. ❻ A shark can find and eat a flounder that is buried in sand, and it will try to find and eat electrodes that are creating electrical signals similar to those that the flounder emits. On the other hand, a shark cannot find a dead flounder buried in the sand or a live flounder covered by an insulating polyvinyl sheet.

Some fishes are not only capable of electroreception, but can also generate electrical currents. An electric fish (*Gymnarchus niloticus*) lives in freshwater systems of Africa. Muscles near its caudal fin are modified into organs that produce a continuous electrical discharge. This current spreads between the tail and the head. Porelike perforations near the head contain electroreceptors. The electrical waves circulating between the tail and the head are distorted by objects in their field. This distortion is detected in changing patterns of receptor stimulation (figure 27.17). The electrical sense of *Gymnarchus* is an adaptation to living in murky freshwater habitats where eyes are of limited value.

The fishes best known for producing strong electrical currents are the electric eel (a bony fish) and the electric ray (an elasmobranch). The electric eel (*Electrophorus*) occurs in rivers of the Amazon basin in South America. The organs for producing electrical currents are in the trunk of the electric eel and can deliver shocks in excess of 500 volts. The electric ray (*Narcine*) has electric organs in its fins that are capable of producing pulses of 50 amperes at about 50 volts (figure 27.18). Shocks that these fishes produce are sufficiently strong to stun or kill prey, discourage large predators, and teach unwary humans a lesson that will never need to be repeated.

Stop and Ask Yourself

9. What are two methods of gill ventilation that fishes use?
10. What is a countercurrent exchange mechanism, and why does it occur in fish gills?
11. Why do some fishes, such as lungfishes, need lungs?
12. What are four mechanisms fishes use to improve their buoyancy?

EXCRETION AND OSMOREGULATION

Fishes, as all animals, must maintain a proper balance of electrolytes (ions) and water in their tissues. This osmoregulation is a major function of the kidneys and gills of fishes. Kidneys are located near the midline of the body, just dorsal to the peritoneal membrane that lines the body cavity. As with all vertebrates, the excretory structures in the kidneys are called **nephrons.** Nephrons filter bloodborne nitrogenous wastes, ions, water, and small organic compounds across a network of capillaries called a **glomerulus.** The filtrate then passes into a tubule system, where essential components may be reabsorbed into the blood. The filtrate remaining in the tubule system is then excreted.

Freshwater fishes live in an environment containing few dissolved substances. Osmotic uptake of water across gill, oral, and intestinal surfaces, and the loss of essential ions by excretion and defecation are constant. To control excess water buildup and ion loss, freshwater fishes never drink and only take in water when feeding. Also, the numerous nephrons of freshwater fishes frequently possess large glomeruli and relatively short tubule systems. Reabsorption of some ions and organic compounds follows filtration. Because the tubule system is relatively short, little water is reabsorbed. Thus, freshwater fishes produce large quantities of very dilute urine. Ions are still lost, however, through the urine and by diffusion across gill and oral surfaces. Active transport of ions into the blood at the gills compensates for this ion loss. Freshwater fishes also get some salts in their food (figure 27.19*a*).

Marine fishes face the opposite problems. Their environment contains 3.5% ions, and their tissues contain approximately 0.65% ions. Marine fishes, therefore, must combat water loss and accumulation of excess ions. They drink water and eliminate excess ions by excretion, defecation, and active transport across gill surfaces. The nephrons of marine fishes frequently possess small glomeruli and long tubule systems. Much less blood is filtered than in freshwater fishes, and water is efficiently, although not entirely, reabsorbed from the nephron (figure 27.19*b*).

Elasmobranchs have a unique osmoregulatory mechanism. They convert some of their nitrogenous wastes into urea in the

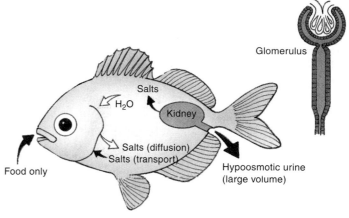

(a) Freshwater teleosts
(hypertonic blood)

(b) Marine teleosts
(hypotonic blood)

FIGURE 27.19

Osmoregulation by (a) Freshwater and (b) Marine Fishes. Large arrows indicate passive uptake or loss of water or electrolytes (ions) through ingestion and excretion. Small, solid arrows indicate active transport processes at gill membranes and kidney tubules. Small, open arrows indicate passive uptake or loss by diffusion through permeable surfaces. Insets of kidney nephrons depict adaptations within the kidney. Water, ions, and small organic molecules are filtered from the blood at the glomerulus of the nephron. Essential components of the filtrate can be reabsorbed within the tubule system of the nephron. Marine fishes conserve water by reducing the size of the glomerulus of the nephron, and thus reducing the quantity of water and ions filtered from the blood. Other ions can be secreted from the blood into the kidney tubules. Marine fishes can produce urine that is isoosmotic with the blood. Freshwater fishes have enlarged glomeruli and short tubule systems. They filter large quantities of water from the blood, and tubules reabsorb some ions from the filtrate. Freshwater fishes produce a hypoosmotic urine.

liver. This in itself is somewhat unusual because most fishes excrete ammonia rather than urea. Even more unusual, however, is that urea is sequestered in tissues all over the body. Enough urea is stored to make body tissues isosmotic with seawater. (That is, the concentration of solutes in a shark's tissues is essentially the same as the concentration of ions in seawater.) Therefore, the problem most marine fishes have of losing water to their environment is much less severe for elasmobranchs. Energy that does not have to be devoted to water conservation can now be used in other ways. This adaptation required the development of tolerance to high levels of urea because urea disrupts important enzyme systems in the tissues of most other animals.

In spite of this unique adaptation, elasmobranchs must still regulate the ion concentrations in their tissues. In addition to having ion-absorbing and secreting tissues in their gills and kidneys, elasmobranchs possess a rectal gland that removes excess sodium chloride from the blood and excretes it into the cloaca. (A **cloaca** is a common opening for excretory, digestive, and reproductive products.)

Diadromous fishes migrate between freshwater and marine environments. Salmon (e.g., *Oncorhynchus*) and marine lampreys (*Petromyzon*) migrate from the sea to freshwater to spawn, and the freshwater eel (*Anguilla*) migrates from freshwater to marine environments to spawn. Diadromous migrations require gills capable of coping with both uptake and secretion of ions. Osmoregulatory powers needed for migration between marine and freshwater environments may not be developed in all life-history stages. Young salmon, for example, cannot enter the sea until certain cells on the gills develop ion-secreting powers.

Fishes have few problems getting rid of the nitrogenous byproducts of protein metabolism. Up to 90% of nitrogenous wastes are eliminated as ammonia by diffusion across gill surfaces. Even though ammonia is toxic, aquatic organisms can have it as an excretory product because ammonia diffuses in the surrounding water. The remaining 10% of nitrogenous wastes are excreted as urea, creatine, or creatinine. These wastes are produced in the liver and are excreted via the kidneys.

REPRODUCTION AND DEVELOPMENT

Imagine, 45 kg of caviar from a single, 450 kg sturgeon! Admittedly, a 450 kg sturgeon is a very large fish (even for a sturgeon), but a fish producing millions of eggs in a single season is not unusual. These numbers simply reflect the hazards of developing in aquatic habitats unattended by a parent. The vast majority of these millions of potential adults will never survive to reproduce. Many eggs will never be fertilized, many fertilized eggs may wash ashore and dry, currents and tides will smash many eggs and embryos, and others will fall victim to predation. In spite of all of these hazards, if only four of the millions of embryos of each breeding pair survive and reproduce, the population will double.

Producing overwhelming numbers of eggs, however, is not the only way that fishes increase the chances that a few of their offspring will survive. Some fishes show mating behavior that helps ensure fertilization, or nesting behavior that protects eggs from predation, sedimentation, and fouling.

Mating may occur in large schools, and one individual releasing eggs or sperm often releases spawning pheromones that induce many other adults to spawn. Huge masses of eggs and sperm released into the open ocean ensure fertilization of many eggs.

FIGURE 27.20

Male Garibaldi *(Hypsypops rubicundus)* Guarding Eggs. The male cultivates a nest of filamentous red algae and then entices a female to lay eggs in the nest. This male is carrying off a bat star that came too close to the nest.

The vast majority of fishes are oviparous, meaning that eggs develop outside the female from stored yolk. Some elasmobranchs are ovoviviparous, and their embryos develop in a modified oviduct of the female. Nutrients are supplied from yolk stored in the egg. Other elasmobranchs, including gray reef sharks and hammerheads, are viviparous. A placenta-like outgrowth of a modified oviduct diverts nutrients from the female to the yolk sacs of developing embryos. Internal development of viviparous bony fishes usually occurs in ovarian follicles, rather than in the oviduct. In guppies (*Lebistes*), eggs are retained in the ovary, and fertilization and early development occur there. Embryos are then released into a cavity within the ovary and development continues, with nourishment coming partly from yolk and partly from ovarian secretions.

Some fishes have specialized structures that aid in sperm transfer. Male elasmobranchs, for example, have modified pelvic fins called claspers. During copulation, the male inserts a clasper into the cloaca of a female. Sperm travel along grooves of the clasper. Fertilization occurs in the female's reproductive tract and usually results in a higher proportion of eggs being fertilized than in external fertilization. Thus, fishes with internal fertilization usually produce fewer eggs.

In many fishes, care of the embryos is limited or nonexistent. Some fishes, however, construct and tend nests (figure 27.20), and some carry embryos during development. Clusters of embryos may be brooded in special pouches attached to some part of the body, or they may be brooded in the mouth. Some of the best-known brooders include the seahorses (*Hippocampus*) and pipefishes (e.g., *Syngnathus*). Males of these closely related fishes carry embryos throughout development in ventral pouches. The male Brazilian catfish (*Loricaria typhys*) broods embryos in an enlarged lower lip.

Most fishes care little, if any, for young after hatching. Sunfishes and sticklebacks, however, provide short-term care of posthatching young. Male sticklebacks assemble fresh plant material into a mass in which the young take refuge. If one wanders too far from the nest, the male snaps it up in its mouth and spits it back into the nest. Sunfish males do the same for young that wander from schools of recently hatched fish. The Cichlidae engage in longer-term care (*see figure 27.13c*). In some species, young are mouth brooded, and other species tend young in a nest. After hatching, the young venture from the parent's mouth or nest but return quickly when the parent signals danger with a flicking of the pelvic fins.

FURTHER PHYLOGENETIC CONSIDERATIONS

Two important series of evolutionary events occurred during the evolution of the Osteichthyes. One of these was an evolutionary explosion that began about 150 million years ago and resulted in the vast diversity of teleosts living today. The last half of this chapter should have helped you appreciate some of these events.

The lungfishes illustrate the second series of events. The lungfishes' lifestyle represents a survival strategy that must have been important for some early Devonian fishes. The current seasonal droughts of tropical South America and Africa must be similar to, but much less geographically extensive than, those in the Devonian period. As in the lungfishes, the ability to breathe air and aestivate must have been present in many freshwater Devo-nian fishes. Distinctive characteristics of the lungfish skeleton lead most zoologists to conclude that the lungfish evolutionary line gave rise to no other vertebrate taxa. Instead, the rhipidistians are thought to be a part of the evolutionary lineage that led to terrestrial vertebrates. Rhipidistians, like lungfishes, had lungs, could breathe air, and may have used their muscular fins to crawl across land looking for water when their own stream dried.

7 Adaptations that favored survival in Devonian streams and lakes may have preadapted some rhipidistians for life that would become increasingly terrestrial. While millions of years would elapse before any vertebrate could be considered terrestrial, brief excursions onto land allowed some vertebrates to exploit resources that for the previous 50 million years had only been available to terrestrial arthropods.

Stop and Ask Yourself

13. Why is osmoregulation, not excretion, the major function of the kidneys of fishes?

14. What osmoregulatory problems does a diadromous fish have?

15. What is viviparity? How does viviparity of some elasmobranchs differ from that of some teleosts?

16. What adaptations to climatic conditions may have preadapted rhipidistian fishes for a partially terrestrial existence?

SUMMARY

1. Ancient members of the vertebrate superclass Agnatha were probably the ancestors of all other vertebrates.

2. Agnathans lack jaws and paired appendages, and include the lampreys, hagfishes, and extinct ostracoderms. Hagfishes are scavengers in marine environments. Lampreys have a life history involving migrations from the open ocean, or large body of freshwater, to freshwater spawning streams.

3. The superclass Gnathostomata includes fishes with jaws and paired appendages. The class Chondrichthyes includes the sharks, skates, rays, and ratfishes. The class Osteichthyes includes the bony fishes.

4. The class Osteichthyes has two subclasses. The subclass Sarcopterygii includes the lungfishes, the coelacanths, and the rhipidistians; and the subclass Actinopterygii includes the ray-finned fishes. In the Actinopterygii, the teleosts are the modern bony fishes. Members of this very large group have adapted to virtually every available aquatic habitat.

5. Fishes show numerous adaptations to living in aquatic environments. These adaptations include an arrangement of body-wall muscles that creates locomotor waves in the body wall; mechanisms that constantly move water across gill surfaces; a countercurrent exchange mechanism to promote efficient gas exchange; buoyancy regulation; well-developed sensory receptors, including eyes, inner ears, and lateral-line receptors; mechanisms of osmoregulation; and mechanisms that help ensure successful reproduction.

6. Two evolutionary lineages in the Actinopterygii are very important. One of these resulted in the adaptive radiation of modern bony fishes, the teleosts. The second evolutionary line probably diverged from the rhipidistians. Adaptations that favored rhipidistian survival in early Devonian streams preadapted some rhipidistians for terrestrial habitats.

SELECTED KEY TERMS

cloaca (p. 452)
countercurrent exchange mechanism (p. 447)
gill (visceral) arches (p. 447)
gill filaments (p. 447)
lateral-line system (p. 449)

operculum (p. 442)
pharyngeal lamellae (p. 447)
pneumatic sacs (p. 447)
ram ventilation (p. 446)
swim bladders (p. 444)

CRITICAL THINKING QUESTIONS

1. What characteristic of water makes it difficult to move through, but also makes support against gravity a minor consideration? How is a fish adapted for moving through water?

2. Could a fish drown? Explain. Would it make a difference if the fish were an open-ocean fish, such as a tuna, or a fish such as a freshwater perch?

3. Why is it a mistake to consider the cartilaginous skeleton of chondrichthians a primitive characteristic?

4. Would swim bladders with functional pneumatic ducts work well for a fish that lives at great depths? Why or why not?

5. What would happen to a deep-sea fish brought rapidly to the surface? Explain your answer in light of the fact that gas pressure in the swim bladders of some deep-sea fishes increases up to about 300 atmospheres.

REFERENCES ON THE WORLD WIDE WEB

1. **National Marine Fisheries Service.** Learn more about marine fishes. This site contains images of fishes, news, information about the Sustained Fisheries Act, a history of fishery science, links to regional NMFS offices, and climatic and oceanographic data.

   http://kingfish.ssp.nmfs.gov/

2. **Reel-Time Archive.** This site contains photographs of North Atlantic fishes and information about North Atlantic fisheries.

   http://www.reel-time.com/arch/archive_top.html

3. **Vertebrate Systematics.** Explore the systematics and natural history of each of the major groups of fishes. Click on photographs for more information about each group. This site also contains links to other fish sites on the web.

   http://www.ucmp.berkeley.edu/vertebrates/vertsy.html

4. **Great Lakes Fishery Commission.** Find information on fishery management in the Great Lakes. This site contains recent information on the lamprey problem in the Great Lakes, as well as information on sport and commercial fishing. It provides a newsletter and information on fisheries research.

   http://www.glfc.org/home.htm

5. **Animal Bytes: Sharks.** This site provides information on the biology and behavior of sharks.

   http://www.bev.net/education/SeaWorld/animal_bytes/sharkab.html

6. **Fishes.** Explore the world of fishes at this site. It contains many links to other fish sites on the web.

   http://muscat.gdb.org/bio/con/medl/browse/B2-493

7. **Fiona's Shark Mania.** This entertaining site provides a variety of information on sharks.

   http://www.oceanstar.com/shark/

8. **FINS.** This site, provided by the Fish Information Service, is an archive of information about aquariums.

   http://www.actwin.com/fish/index.cgi

9. **International Marinelife Alliance.** This organization is dedicated to the protection of marine life and conservation of marine habitats.

   http://www.actwin.com/fish/ima/index.html

10. **Northeast Fisheries Science Center.** This site provides answers to frequently asked questions regarding fish and fisheries. It focuses on fisheries in the Wood's Hole area and all of New England.

    http://www.wh.whoi.edu/noaa.html

11. **Ocean Planet.** This site is an electronic tour of the "Ocean Planet" exhibit on display at the National Museum of Natural History. Visit this fantastic exhibit by clicking on the name of the exhibit room.

    http://seawifs.gsfc.nasa.gov/OCEAN_PLANET/HTML/
    ocean_planet_overview_html

AMPHIBIANS:
THE FIRST TERRESTRIAL VERTEBRATES

Concepts

1. Adaptations that favored survival of fishes during periodic droughts preadapted vertebrates to life on land. There were two lineages of ancient amphibians: one gave rise to modern amphibians, and the other lineage resulted in amniote vertebrates.
2. Modern amphibians belong to three orders. Caudata contains the salamanders, Gymnophiona contains the caecilians, and Anura contains the frogs and toads.
3. Although amphibians are restricted to moist habitats, most spend much of their adult life on land. Virtually all amphibian body systems show adaptations for living on land.
4. Eggs and developmental stages that were resistant to drying probably evolved in some ancient amphibians. This development was a major step in vertebrate evolution because it weakened vertebrate ties to moist environments.

Would You Like to Know . . .

1. how the skeleton of an amphibian is adapted for life on land? (p. 461)
2. how frogs, toads, and some salamanders catch prey with their tongues? (p. 462)
3. why an amphibian's skin is moist? (p. 463)
4. what terrestrial animals lack lungs? (p. 463)
5. how a frog's ear can filter out certain frequencies of sound? (p. 465)
6. what are the functions of a frog's calls? (p. 467)
7. what adaptations permitted life on land? (p. 469)

This chapter answers these and other useful questions.

This chapter contains evolutionary concepts, which are set off in this font.

EVOLUTIONARY PERSPECTIVE

Who, while walking along the edge of a pond or stream, has not been startled by the "plop" of an equally startled frog jumping to the safety of its watery retreat? Or who has not marveled at the sounds of a chorus of frogs breaking through an otherwise silent spring evening? These experiences and others like them have led some to spend their lives studying members of the class Amphibia (am-fib'e-ah) (L. *amphibia*, living a double life): frogs, toads, salamanders, and caecilians (figure 28.1). The class name implies that amphibians either move back and forth between water and land, or live one stage of their life in water and another on land. One or both of these descriptions is accurate for most amphibians.

Amphibians are **tetrapods** (Gr. *tetra*, four + *podos*, foot). The term tetrapod is a nontaxonomic designation that applies to all vertebrates other than fishes, and most tetrapods exhibit adaptations for life on land.

PHYLOGENETIC RELATIONSHIPS

During the first 250 million years of vertebrate history, adaptive radiation resulted in vertebrates filling most aquatic habitats. Prehistoric waters contained many active, powerful predators. Land, however, was free of vertebrates and, except for some arthropods, was free of predators. Animals that moved around the water's edge were not likely to be prey for other animals. With lungs for breathing air and muscular fins for scurrying across mud, these animals probably found ample food in the arthropods that lived there. The major component of the diet of most modern amphibians is arthropods.

Chapter 27 describes the origin of amphibians from ancient sarcopterygians. Adaptive radiation of amphibians resulted in a much greater variety of forms than exists today. Later convergent and parallel evolution and widespread extinction clouded evolutionary pathways. No one knows, therefore, what animal was the first amphibian, but the structure of limbs, skulls, and teeth suggests that *Ichthyostega* is probably similar to the earliest amphibians (figure 28.2). Two lineages of early amphibians from the late Devonian and early Carboniferous periods can be distinguished by how the roof and the posterior portion of the skull attach to each other. One lineage of amphibians became extinct late in the Carboniferous period. An amniotic egg that resisted drying (see figure 10.13), evolved in this group. This lineage, called the **amniote lineage,** left as its descendants the reptiles, birds, and mammals (figure 28.3). A second lineage flourished into the Jurassic period. Most of this lineage became extinct, but not before giving rise to the three orders of living amphibians. This lineage is called the **nonamniote lineage.**

FIGURE 28.1

Class Amphibia. Amphibians, like this tree frog *(Hyla andersoni)*, are common vertebrates in most terrestrial and freshwater habitats. Their ancestors were the first terrestrial vertebrates.

SURVEY OF AMPHIBIANS

Amphibians occur on all continents except Antarctica, but are absent from many oceanic islands. The three thousand modern species are a mere remnant of this once-diverse group. Modern amphibians belong to three orders: Caudata or Urodela, the salamanders; Anura, the frogs and toads; and Gymnophiona, the caecilians (table 28.1).

ORDER CAUDATA

Members of the order Caudata (kaw'dat-ah) (L. *cauda*, tail + Gr. *ata*, to bear) are the salamanders. They possess a tail throughout life, and both pairs of legs, when present, are relatively unspecialized (figure 28.4).

Approximately 115 of the 350 described species of salamanders live in North America. Most terrestrial salamanders live in moist forest-floor litter and have aquatic larvae. A number of

FIGURE 28.2

Ichthyostega: **An Early Amphibian.** Fossils of this early amphibian were discovered in eastern Greenland in late Devonian deposits. The total length of the restored specimen is about 65 cm. Terrestrial adaptations are heavy pectoral and pelvic girdles and sturdy limbs that probably helped lift the body off the ground. Strong jaws suggest that it was a predator in shallow water, perhaps venturing onto shore. Other features include a skull that is similar in structure to ancient sarcopterygian fishes and a finlike tail. Note that bony rays dorsal to the spines of the vertebrae support the tail fin. This pattern is similar to the structure of the dorsal fins of fishes and is unknown in any other tetrapod.

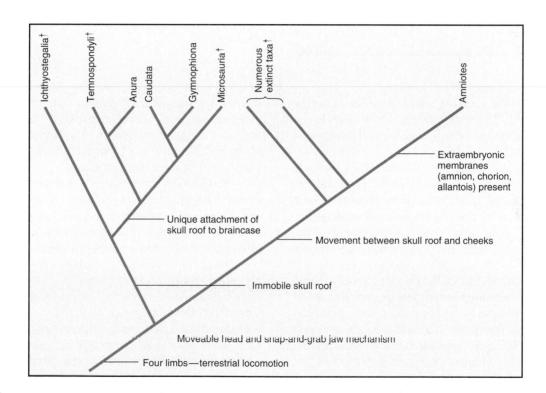

FIGURE 28.3

Evolutionary Relationships among the Amphibians. Earliest amphibians arose during the Devonian period. A nonamniotic lineage gave rise to three classes of modern amphibians and numerous extinct taxa. Some zoologists think that the class Amphibia is a paraphyletic group. If this is true, the three modern classes should be represented as monophyletic taxa. The amniotic lineage of early tetrapods gave rise to reptiles, birds, mammals, and other extinct taxa. Daggers (†) indicate extinct taxa. Synapomorphic characters for lower taxonomic groups are not indicated.

TABLE 28.1	CLASSIFICATION OF LIVING AMPHIBIANS

Class Amphibia (am-fib′e-ah)
Skin with mucoid secretions and lacking epidermal scales, feathers, or hair; larvae usually aquatic and undergo metamorphosis to the adult; two atrial chambers in the heart; one cervical and one sacral vertebra.
    Order Caudata (kaw′dat-ah)
    Long tail, two pairs of limbs; lack middle ear. Salamanders, newts.
    Order Gymnophiona (jim″no-fi′o-nah)
    Elongate, limbless; segmented by annular grooves; specialized for burrowing; tail short and pointed; rudimentary left lung. Caecilians.
    Order Anura (ah-noor′ah)
    Tailless; elongate hindlimbs modified for jumping and swimming; five to nine presacral vertebrae with transverse processes (except the first); postsacral vertebrae fused into rodlike urostyle; tympanum and larynx well developed. Frogs, toads.

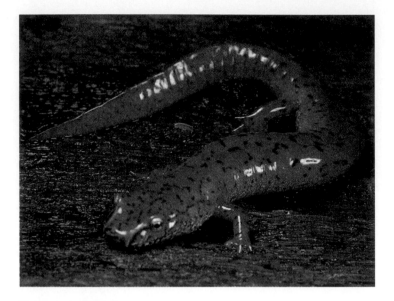

FIGURE 28.4
Order Caudata. The Blue Ridge Spring salamander (*Gyrinophilus danielsi*).

families live in caves, where constant temperature and moisture conditions create a nearly ideal environment. Salamanders in the family Plethodontidae are the most fully terrestrial salamanders in that their eggs are laid on land, and the young hatch as miniatures of the adult. Members of the family Salimandridae are commonly called newts. They spend most of their lives in water and frequently retain caudal fins. Salamanders range in length from only a few centimeters to 1.5 m (the Japanese giant salamander, *Andrias japonicus*). The largest North American salamander is the hellbender (*Cryptobranchus alleganiensis*), which reaches lengths of about 65 cm.

Most salamanders have internal fertilization. Males produce a pyramidal, gelatinous spermatophore that is capped with sperm and deposited on the substrate. Females pick up the sperm cap with the cloaca and store the sperm in a special pouch, the spermatheca. Eggs are fertilized as they pass through the cloaca and are usually deposited singly, in clumps, or in strings (figure 28.5*a*). Larvae are similar to adults but smaller. They often possess external gills, a tail fin, larval dentition, and a rudimentary tongue (figure 28.5*b*). The aquatic larval stage usually metamorphoses into a terrestrial adult (figure 28.5*c*). Many other salamanders undergo incomplete metamorphosis and are paedomorphic (e.g., *Necturus*); that is, they become sexually mature while still showing larval characteristics.

ORDER GYMNOPHIONA

Members of the order Gymnophiona (jim″no-fi′o-nah) (Gr. *gymnos*, naked + *ophineos*, like a snake) are the caecilians (figure 28.6). Zoologists have described about 160 species confined to tropical regions. Caecilians are wormlike burrowers that feed on worms and other invertebrates in the soil. Caecilians appear seg-

mented because of folds in the skin that overlie separations between muscle bundles. A retractile tentacle between their eyes and nostrils may transport chemicals from the environment to olfactory cells in the roof of the mouth. Skin covers the eyes; thus, caecilians are probably nearly blind.

Fertilization is internal in caecilians. Larval stages are often passed within the oviducts, where they scrape the inner lining of the oviducts with fetal teeth to feed. The young emerge from the female as miniature adults. Other caecilians lay eggs that develop into either aquatic larvae or embryos that develop on land.

ORDER ANURA

The order Anura (ah-noor′ah) (Gr. *a*, without + *oura*, tail) includes about 3,500 species of frogs and toads. Anurans live in most moist environments, except in high latitudes and on some oceanic islands. A few even occur in very dry deserts. Adults lack tails, and caudal (tail) vertebrae fuse into a rodlike structure called the urostyle. Hindlimbs are long and muscular, and end in webbed feet.

Anurans have diverse life histories. Fertilization is almost always external, and eggs and larvae are typically aquatic. Larval stages, called tadpoles, have well-developed tails. Their plump bodies lack limbs until near the end of their larval existence. Unlike adults, the larvae are herbivores and possess a proteinaceous, beaklike structure used in feeding. Anuran larvae undergo a drastic and rapid metamorphosis from the larval to the adult body form.

The distinction between "frog" and "toad" is more vernacular than scientific. "Toad" usually refers to anurans with relatively dry and warty skin that are more terrestrial than other members of the order. A number of distantly related taxa have these characteristics. True toads belong to the family Bufonidae (figure 28.7).

(a)

(b)

(c)

FIGURE 28.5

Order Caudata. (*a*) Eggs, (*b*) larva, and (*c*) adult of the spotted salamander, *Ambystoma maculatum*. Larvae are herbivores, and adults feed on worms and small arthropods.

FIGURE 28.6

Order Gymnophiona. A caecilian (*Ichthyophis glutinosus*).

FIGURE 28.7

Order Anura. An American toad (*Bufo americanus*).

BOX 28.1   POISON FROGS OF SOUTH AMERICA

A South American native stalks quietly through the jungle, peering into the tree branches overhead. A monkey's slight movements divulge its presence, and the hunter takes careful aim with what appears to be an almost toylike bow and arrow. The arrow sails true, and the monkey is hit. The arrow seems ineffectual at first; however, after a few moments, the monkey tumbles from the tree. Thousands of years of cultural evolution have taught these natives a deadly secret that makes effective hunting tools out of seemingly innocuous instruments.

All amphibians possess glandular secretions that are noxious or toxic to varying degrees. These glands are distributed throughout the skin and exude milky toxins that help ward off potential predators. Warning (aposematic) coloration often signals to predators the presence of noxious secretions (figure 1).

Four genera of frogs (*Atopophryhnus, Colostethus, Dendrobates,* and *Phyllobates*) in the family Dendrobatidae live in tropical forests from Costa Rica to southern Brazil. South American natives use toxins from these frogs to tip their arrows. They kill the frogs with a stick and hold them over a fire. Granular glands in the skin release their venom, which the natives collect and allow to ferment. Poisons collected in this manner are neurotoxins that prevent nerve impulses from transmitting between nerves and between nerves and muscles. Arrow tips dipped in this poison and allowed to dry contain sufficient toxin to paralyze a bird or small mammal.

In addition to their toxic secretions, members of this family of frogs have interesting reproductive habits. A female lays one to six large eggs in moist, terrestrial habitats. She promptly abandons the

FIGURE 1   A Poison Arrow Frog (*Dendrobates pumilo*). The striking aposematic coloration is a warning to predators.

eggs, but the male visits the clutch regularly and guards the eggs. The eggs hatch after approximately 2 weeks, and the tadpoles wiggle onto the male's back. The male then transports the tadpoles from the egg-laying site to water, where they are left to develop. The tadpoles metamorphose to the adult body form after approximately 6 weeks.

Stop and Ask Yourself

1. What were two ancient lineages of amphibians? What groups of animals are the modern descendants of each lineage?

2. What animals are members of the order Caudata?

3. What order of amphibians is characterized by wormlike burrowing?

4. What order of amphibians is characterized by tail vertebrae fused into a urostyle?

EVOLUTIONARY PRESSURES

Most amphibians divide their lives between freshwater and land. This divided life is reflected in body systems that show adaptations to both environments. In the water, amphibians are supported by water's buoyant properties, they exchange gases with the water, and they face the same osmoregulatory problems as freshwater fishes. On land, amphibians support themselves against gravity, exchange gases with the air, and tend to lose water to the air.

EXTERNAL STRUCTURE AND LOCOMOTION

Vertebrate skin protects against infective microorganisms, ultraviolet light, desiccation, and mechanical injury. As discussed later in this chapter, the skin of amphibians also functions in gas exchange, temperature regulation, and absorption and storage of water.

Amphibian skin lacks a covering of scales, feathers, or hair. It is, however, highly glandular, and its secretions aid in protection. These glands keep the skin moist to prevent drying. They also produce sticky secretions that help a male cling to a female during mating and produce toxic chemicals that discourage potential predators (box 28.1). The skin of many amphibians is smooth, although epidermal thickenings may produce warts, claws, or sandpapery textures, which are usually the result of keratin deposits or the formation of hard, bony areas.

Chromatophores are specialized cells in the epidermis and dermis of the skin, and are responsible for skin color and color changes. Cryptic coloration, aposematic coloration (box 28.1), and mimicry are all common in amphibians.

Support and Movement

Water buoys and supports aquatic animals. The skeletons of fishes function primarily in protecting internal organs, providing points

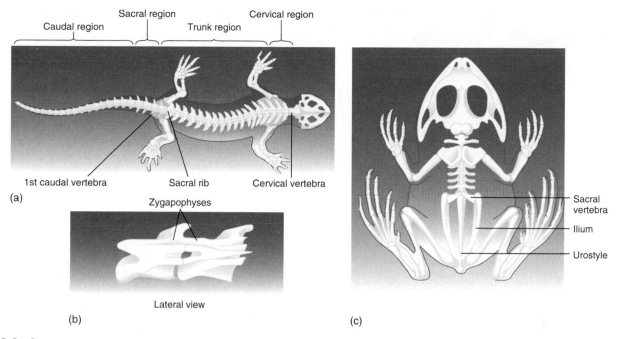

FIGURE 28.8

Skeletons of Amphibians. (*a*) The salamander skeleton is divided into four regions: cervical, trunk, sacral, and caudal. (*b*) Interlocking processes, called zygapophyses, prevent twisting between vertebrae. (*c*) A frog skeleton shows adaptations for jumping. Note the long back legs and the firm attachment of the back legs to the vertebral column through the ilium and urostyle.

of attachment for muscles, and keeping the body from collapsing during movement. In terrestrial vertebrates, however, the skeleton is modified to provide support against gravity and must be strong enough to support the relatively powerful muscles that propel terrestrial vertebrates across land. ❶ The amphibian skull is flattened, is relatively smaller, and has fewer bony elements than the skull of fishes. These changes lighten the skull so it can be supported out of the water. Changes in jaw structure and musculature allow terrestrial vertebrates to crush prey held in the mouth.

The vertebral column of amphibians is modified to provide support and flexibility on land (figure 28.8). It acts somewhat like the arch of a suspension bridge by supporting the weight of the body between anterior and posterior paired appendages. Supportive processes called zygapophyses on each vertebra prevent twisting. Unlike fishes, amphibians have a neck. The first vertebra is a cervical vertebra, which moves against the back of the skull and allows the head to nod vertically. The last trunk vertebra is a sacral vertebra. This vertebra anchors the pelvic girdle to the vertebral column to provide increased support. A ventral plate of bone, called the sternum, is present in the anterior ventral trunk region and supports the forelimbs and protects internal organs. It is reduced or absent in the Anura.

The origin of the bones of vertebrate appendages is not precisely known; however, similarities in the structures of the bones of the amphibian appendages and the bones of the fins of ancient rhipidistian fishes suggest possible homologies (figure 28.9). Joints at the shoulder, hip, elbow, knee, wrist, and ankle allow freedom of movement and better contact with the substrate. The pelvic girdle of amphibians consists of three bones (the ilium, ischium, and

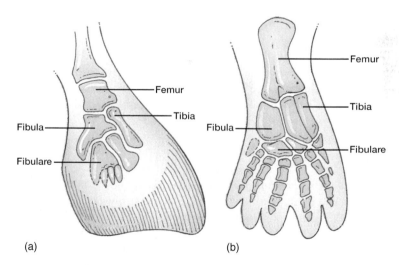

FIGURE 28.9

Origin of Tetrapod Appendages. A comparison of (*a*) the fin bones of a rhipidistian and (*b*) the limb bones of a tetrapod suggests that the basic bone arrangements in tetrapod limbs were already present in primitive fishes.

pubis) that firmly attach pelvic appendages to the vertebral column. These bones, which are present in all tetrapods, but not fishes, are important for support on land.

Tetrapods depend more on appendages than the body wall for locomotion. Thus, body-wall musculature is reduced, and appendicular musculature predominates. (Contrast, for example, what you eat in a fish dinner as compared to a plate of frog legs.)

FIGURE 28.10

Salamander Locomotion. Pattern of leg movement in salamander locomotion. Blue arrows show leg movements.

Salamanders employ a relatively unspecialized form of loco-motion that is reminiscent of the undulatory waves that pass along the body of a fish. Terrestrial salamanders also move by a pattern of limb and body movements in which the alternate movement of appendages results from muscle contractions that throw the body into a curve to advance the stride of a limb (figure 28.10). Caeci-lians have an accordion-like movement in which adjacent body parts push or pull forward at the same time. The long hindlimbs and the pelvic girdle of anurans are modified for jumping. The dorsal bone of the pelvis (the ilium) extends anteriorly and securely attaches to the vertebral column, and the urostyle ex-tends posteriorly and attaches to the pelvis (*see figure 28.8*). These skeletal modifications stiffen the posterior half of the anuran. Long hindlimbs and powerful muscles form an efficient lever sys-tem for jumping. Elastic connective tissues and muscles attach the pectoral girdle to the skull and vertebral column, and function as shock absorbers for landing on the forelimbs.

NUTRITION AND THE DIGESTIVE SYSTEM

Most adult amphibians are carnivores that feed on a wide variety of invertebrates. The diets of some anurans, however, are more diverse. For example, a bullfrog will prey on small mammals, birds, and other anurans. The main factors that determine what amphibians will eat are prey size and availability. Larvae are her-bivorous and feed on algae and other plant matter. Most amphib-ians locate their prey by sight and simply wait for prey to pass by. Olfaction plays an important role in prey detection by aquatic salamanders and caecilians.

Many salamanders are relatively unspecialized in their feed-ing methods, using only their jaws to capture prey. Anurans and plethodontid salamanders, however, use their tongue and jaws in a flip-and-grab feeding mechanism (figure 28.11). A true tongue is first seen in amphibians. (The "tongue" of fishes is simply a fleshy fold on the floor of the mouth. Fish food is swallowed whole and not manipulated by the "tongue.") ➋ The amphibian tongue attaches at the anterior margin of the jaw and folds back over the floor of the mouth. Mucous and buccal glands on the tip of the

FIGURE 28.11

Flip-and-Grab Feeding in a Toad. The tongue attaches at the ante-rior margin of the toad's jaw and flips out to capture a prey on its sticky secretions.

tongue exude sticky secretions. When prey comes within range, an amphibian lunges forward and flicks out its tongue. The tongue turns over, and the lower jaw is depressed. The head tilts on its single cervical vertebra, which helps aim the strike. The tip of the tongue entraps the prey, and the tongue and prey are flicked back inside the mouth. All of this may happen in 0.05 to 0.15 second!

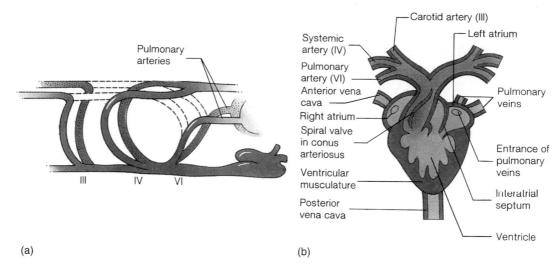

FIGURE 28.12

Diagrammatic Representation of an Anuran Circulatory System. (*a*) The Roman numerals indicate the various aortic arches. Vessels shown in dashed outline are lost during embryological development. (*b*) A ventral view of the heart.

The amphibian holds the prey by pressing it against teeth on the roof of the mouth, and the tongue and other muscles of the mouth push food toward the esophagus. The eyes sink downward during swallowing and help force food toward the esophagus.

CIRCULATION, GAS EXCHANGE, AND TEMPERATURE REGULATION

The circulatory system of amphibians shows remarkable adaptations for a life divided between aquatic and terrestrial habitats. The separation of pulmonary and systemic circuits is less efficient in amphibians than in lungfishes (figure 28.12; *see also figure 27.14*b). The atrium is partially divided in urodeles and completely divided in anurans. The ventricle has no septum. A spiral valve in the conus arteriosus or ventral aorta helps direct blood into pulmonary and systemic circuits. As discussed later, gas exchange occurs across the skin of amphibians, as well as in the lungs. Therefore, blood entering the right side of the heart is nearly as well oxygenated as blood entering the heart from the lungs! When an amphibian is completely submerged, all gas exchange occurs across the skin and other moist surfaces; therefore, blood coming into the right atrium has a higher oxygen concentration than blood returning to the left atrium from the lungs. Under these circumstances, blood vessels leading to the lungs constrict, reducing blood flow to the lungs and conserving energy. This adaptation is especially valuable for those frogs and salamanders that overwinter in the mud at the bottom of a pond.

Adult amphibians have fewer aortic arches than fishes. After leaving the conus arteriosus, blood may enter the carotid artery (aortic arch III), which takes blood to the head; the systemic artery (aortic arch IV), which takes blood to the body; or the pulmonary artery (aortic arch VI).

In addition to a vascular system that circulates blood, amphibians have a well-developed lymphatic system of blind-ending

vessels that returns fluids, proteins, and ions filtered from capillary beds in tissue spaces to the circulatory system. The lymphatic system also transports water absorbed across the skin. Unlike other vertebrates, amphibians have contractile vessels, called lymphatic hearts, that pump fluid through the lymphatic system. Lymphatic spaces between body-wall muscles and the skin transport and store water absorbed across the skin.

Gas Exchange

Terrestrial animals expend much less energy moving air across gas-exchange surfaces than do aquatic organisms because air contains 20 times more oxygen per unit volume than does water. On the other hand, exchanges of oxygen and carbon dioxide require moist surfaces, and exposure of respiratory surfaces to air may result in rapid water loss.

Anyone who has searched pond and stream banks for frogs knows that the skin of amphibians is moist. Amphibian skin is also richly supplied with capillary beds. ③ These two factors permit the skin to function as a respiratory organ. Gas exchange across the skin is called **cutaneous respiration** and can occur either in water or on land. This ability allows a frog to spend the winter in the mud at the bottom of a pond. In salamanders, 30 to 90% of gas exchange occurs across the skin. Gas exchange also occurs across the moist surfaces of the mouth and pharynx. This **buccopharyngeal respiration** accounts for 1 to 7% of total gas exchange.

④ Most amphibians, except for plethodontid salamanders, possess lungs (figure 28.13*a*). The lungs of salamanders are relatively simple sacs. The lungs of anurans are subdivided, increasing the surface area for gas exchange. Pulmonary (lung) ventilation occurs by a **buccal pump** mechanism. Muscles of the mouth and pharynx create a positive pressure to force air into the lungs (figure 28.13*b–e*).

FIGURE 28.13

Amphibian Lung Structure, Buccal Pump, and Buccopharyngeal Ventilation. (*a*) Lung structure of a frog. (*b*) With the opening of the respiratory tract (the glottis) closed, the floor of the mouth lowers, and air enters the mouth cavity. (*c*) The glottis opens, and the elasticity of the lungs and contraction of the body wall force air out of the lungs, over the top of air just brought into the mouth. (*d*) The mouth and nares close, and the floor of the mouth raises, forcing air into the lungs. (*e*) With the glottis closed, oscillations of the floor of the mouth exchange air in the mouth cavity to facilitate buccopharyngeal respiration. Blue arrows show air movements. Red arrows show movements of the lungs and body wall.

Cutaneous and buccopharyngeal respiration have a disadvantage in that their contribution to total gas exchange is relatively constant. The quantity of gas exchanged across these surfaces cannot be increased when the metabolic rate increases. Lungs, however, compensate for this shortcoming. As environmental temperature and activity increase, lungs contribute more to total gas exchange. At 5° C, approximately 70% of gas exchange occurs across the skin and mouth lining of a frog. At 25° C, the absolute quantity of oxygen exchanged across external body surfaces does not change significantly, but because pulmonary respiration increases, exchange across skin and mouth surfaces accounts for only about 30% of total oxygen exchange.

Amphibian larvae and some adults respire using external gills. Cartilaginous rods that form between embryonic pharyngeal slits support three pairs of gills. During metamorphosis, the gills are usually reabsorbed, pharyngeal slits close, and lungs become functional.

Temperature Regulation

Amphibians are ectothermic. (They depend on external heat sources to maintain body temperature [*see chapter 38*].) Any poorly insulated aquatic animal, regardless of how much metabolic heat it produces, loses heat as quickly as it is produced because of the powerful heat-absorbing properties of water. Therefore, when amphibians are in water, they take on the temperature of their environment. On land, however, their body temperatures can differ from that of the environment.

Temperature regulation is mainly behavioral. Some cooling results from evaporative heat loss. In addition, many amphibians are nocturnal and remain in cooler burrows or under moist leaf litter during the hottest part of the day. Amphibians may warm themselves by basking in the sun or on warm surfaces. Body temperatures may raise 10° C above the air temperature. Basking after a meal is common because increased body temperature increases the rate of all metabolic reactions—including digestive functions, growth, and the fat deposition necessary to survive periods of dormancy.

Amphibians' daily and seasonal environmental temperatures often fluctuate widely, and therefore, amphibians have correspondingly wide temperature tolerances. Critical temperature extremes for some salamanders lie between −2 and 27° C, and for some anurans between 3 and 41° C.

Stop and Ask Yourself

5. What are the functions of amphibian skin?

6. What chambers are present in a frog's heart?

7. Under what conditions would blood entering the right atrium of a frog's heart be higher in oxygen than blood entering the left atrium from the lungs?

8. What are four forms of gas exchange in amphibians?

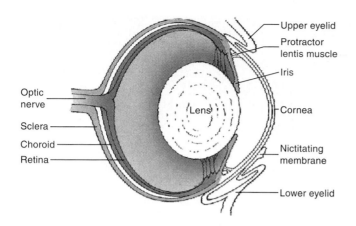

FIGURE 28.14

Amphibian Eye. Longitudinal section of the eye of the leopard frog, *Rana pipiens*.

NERVOUS AND SENSORY FUNCTIONS

The nervous system of amphibians is similar to that of other vertebrates. The brain of adult vertebrates develops from three embryological subdivisions. In amphibians, the forebrain contains olfactory centers and regions that regulate color change and visceral functions. The midbrain contains a region called the optic tectum, that assimilates sensory information and initiates motor responses. The midbrain also processes visual sensory information. The hindbrain functions in motor coordination and in regulating heart rate and the mechanics of respiration.

Many amphibian sensory receptors are widely distributed over the skin. Some of these are simply bare nerve endings that respond to heat, cold, and pain. The lateral-line system is similar in structure to that found in fishes, and it is present in all aquatic larvae, aquatic adult salamanders, and some adult anurans. Lateral-line organs are distributed singly or in small groups along the lateral and dorsolateral surfaces of the body, especially the head. These receptors respond to low-frequency vibrations in the water and movements of the water relative to the animal. On land, however, lateral-line receptors are less important.

Chemoreception is an important sense for many amphibians. Chemoreceptors are in the nasal epithelium and the lining of the mouth, on the tongue, and over the skin. Olfaction is used in mate recognition, as well as in detecting noxious chemicals and in locating food.

Vision is one of the most important senses in amphibians because they are primarily sight feeders. (Caecilians are an obvious exception.) A number of adaptations allow the eyes of amphibians to function in terrestrial environments (figure 28.14). The eyes of some amphibians (i.e., anurans and some salamanders) are on the front of the head, providing the binocular vision and well-developed depth perception necessary for capturing prey. Other amphibians with smaller lateral eyes (some salamanders)

lack binocular vision. The lower eyelid is movable, and cleans and protects the eye. Much of it is transparent and is called the **nictitating membrane.** When the eyeball retracts into the orbit of the skull, the nictitating membrane is drawn up over the cornea. In addition, orbital glands lubricate and wash the eye. Together, eyelids and glands keep the eye free of dust and other debris. The lens is large and nearly round. It is set back from the cornea, and a fold of epithelium called the iris surrounds it. The iris can dilate or constrict to control the size of the pupil.

Focusing, or accommodation, involves bending (refracting) light rays to a focal point on the retina. Light waves moving from air across the cornea are refracted because of the change in density between the two media. The lens provides further refraction. Like the eyes of most tetrapods, the amphibian eye focuses on distant objects when the eye is at rest. To focus on near objects, the protractor lentis muscle must move the lens forward (figure 28.14). Receptors called rods and cones are in the retina. Because cones are associated with color vision in some other vertebrates, their occurrence suggests that amphibians can distinguish between some wavelengths of light. The extent to which color vision is developed is unknown. The neuronal interconnections in the retina are complex and allow an amphibian to distinguish between flying insect prey, shadows that may warn of an approaching predator, and background movements, such as blades of grass moving with the wind.

The auditory system of amphibians is clearly an evolutionary adaptation to life on land. It transmits both substrate-borne vibrations and, in anurans, airborne vibrations. The ears of anurans consist of a tympanic membrane, a middle ear, and an inner ear. The tympanic membrane is a piece of integument stretched over a cartilaginous ring that receives airborne vibrations and transmits them to the middle ear, which is a chamber beneath the tympanic membrane. Abutting the tympanic membrane is a middle-ear ossicle (bone) called the stapes (columella), which transmits vibrations of the tympanic membrane into the inner ear (*see figure 34.9*). High-frequency (1,000 to 5,000 Hz) airborne vibrations are transmitted to the inner ear through the tympanic membrane. Low-frequency (100 to 1,000 Hz) substrate-borne vibrations are transmitted through the front appendages and the pectoral girdle to the inner ear through a second ossicle, called the operculum.

⑤ Muscles attached to the operculum and stapes can lock either or both of these ossicles, allowing an anuran to screen out either high- or low-frequency sounds. This mechanism is adaptive because anurans use low- and high-frequency sounds in different situations. Mating calls are high-frequency sounds that are of primary importance for only a part of the year (breeding season). At other times, low-frequency sounds may warn of approaching predators.

Salamanders lack a tympanic membrane and middle ear. They live in streams, ponds, caves, and beneath leaf litter. They have no mating calls, and the only sounds they hear are probably low-frequency vibrations transmitted through the substrate and skull to the stapes and inner ear.

(a)

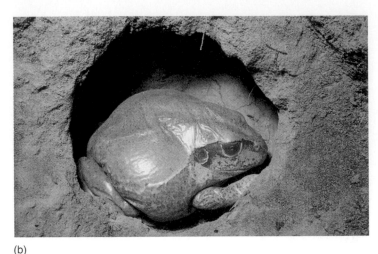

(b)

FIGURE 28.15

Water Conservation by Anurans. (*a*) Daytime sleeping posture of the green tree frog, *Hyla cinerea*. The closely tucked appendages reduce exposed surface area. (*b*) The Australian burrowing frog, *Cyclorana alboguttatus*, in its burrow and water-retaining skin.

The sense of equilibrium and balance is similar to that described for fishes in chapter 27. The inner ear of amphibians has semicircular canals that help detect rotational movements and other sensory patches that respond to gravity and detect linear acceleration and deceleration.

EXCRETION AND OSMOREGULATION

The kidneys of amphibians lie on either side of the dorsal aorta on the dorsal wall of the body cavity. A duct leads to the cloaca, and a storage structure, the urinary bladder, is a ventral outgrowth of the cloaca.

The nitrogenous waste product that amphibians excrete is either ammonia or urea. Amphibians that live in freshwater excrete ammonia. It is the immediate end product of protein metabolism; therefore, no energy is expended converting it into other products. The toxic effects of ammonia are avoided because it rapidly diffuses into the surrounding water. Amphibians that spend more time on land excrete urea that is produced from ammonia in the liver. Although urea is less toxic than ammonia, it still requires relatively large quantities of water for its excretion. Unlike ammonia, urea can be stored in the urinary bladder. Some amphibians excrete ammonia when in water and urea when on land.

One of the biggest problems that amphibians face is osmoregulation. In water, amphibians face the same osmoregulatory problems as freshwater fishes. They must rid the body of excess water and conserve essential ions. Amphibian kidneys produce large quantities of hypotonic urine, and the skin and walls of the urinary bladder transport Na^+, Cl^-, and other ions into the blood.

On land, amphibians must conserve water. Adult amphibians do not replace water by intentional drinking, nor do they have the impermeable skin characteristic of other tetrapods or kidneys capable of producing a hypertonic urine. Instead, amphibians limit water loss by behavior that reduces exposure to desiccating conditions. Many terrestrial amphibians are nocturnal. During daylight hours, they retreat to areas of high humidity, such as under stones, or in logs, leaf mulch, or burrows. Water lost on nighttime foraging trips must be replaced by water uptake across the skin while in the retreat. Diurnal amphibians usually live in areas of high humidity and rehydrate themselves by entering the water. Many amphibians reduce evaporative water loss by reducing the amount of body surface exposed to air. They may curl their bodies and tails into tight coils and tuck their limbs close to their bodies (figure 28.15*a*). Individuals may form closely packed aggregations to reduce overall surface area.

Some amphibians have protective coverings that reduce water loss. Hardened regions of skin are resistant to water loss and may be used to plug entrances to burrows or other retreat openings to maintain high humidity in the retreat. Other amphibians prevent water loss by forming cocoons that encase the body during long periods of dormancy. Cocoons are made from outer layers of the skin that detach and become parchmentlike. These cocoons open only at the nares or the mouth and, in experimental situations, reduce water loss 20 to 50% over noncocooned individuals (figure 28.15*b*).

Paradoxically, the skin—the most important source of water loss—is also the most important structure for rehydration. When an amphibian flattens its body on moist surfaces, the skin, especially in the ventral pelvic region, absorbs water. The skin's permeability, vascularization, and epidermal sculpturing all promote water reabsorption. Minute channels increase surface area and spread water over surfaces not necessarily in direct contact with water.

Amphibians can also temporarily store water. Water accumulated in the urinary bladder and lymph sacs can be selectively reabsorbed to replace evaporative water loss. Amphibians living in very dry environments can store volumes of water equivalent to 35% of their total body weight.

REPRODUCTION, DEVELOPMENT, AND METAMORPHOSIS

Amphibians are dioecious, and ovaries and testes are located near the dorsal body wall. Fertilization is usually external, and because the developing eggs lack any resistant coverings, development is tied to moist habitats, usually water. A few anurans have terrestrial nests that are kept moist by being enveloped in foam or by being located near the water and subjected to flooding. In a few species, larval stages are passed in the egg membranes, and the immatures hatch into an adultlike body. The main exceptions to external fertilization in amphibians are the salamanders. Only about 10% of all salamanders have external fertilization. All others use spermatophores, and fertilization is internal. Eggs may be deposited in soil or water or retained in the oviduct during development. All caecilians have internal fertilization, and 75% have internal development. Amphibian development, which zoologists have studied extensively, usually includes larval stages called tadpoles. Amphibian tadpoles often differ from the adults in mode of respiration, form of locomotion, and diet. These differences reduce competition between adults and larvae.

Interactions between internal (largely hormonal) controls and extrinsic factors determine the timing of reproductive activities. In temperate regions, temperature seems to be the most important environmental factor that induces physiological changes associated with breeding, and breeding periods are seasonal, occurring in spring and summer. In tropical regions, amphibian breeding correlates with rainy seasons.

Courtship behavior helps individuals locate breeding sites, and identify potential mates. It also prepares individuals for reproduction and ensures that eggs are fertilized and deposited in locations that promote successful development.

Salamanders rely primarily on olfactory and visual cues in courtship and mating, whereas male vocalizations and tactile cues are important for anurans. Many species congregate in one location during times of intense breeding activity. Male vocalizations are usually species specific and function in the initial attraction and contact between mates. After that, tactile cues become more important. The male grasps the female—his forelimbs around her waist—so that they are oriented in the same direction, and the male is dorsal to the female (*see figure 10.8a*). This positioning is called **amplexus** and may last from 1 to 24 hours. During amplexus, the male releases sperm as the female releases eggs.

Little is known of caecilian breeding behavior. Males have an intromittent organ that is a modification of the cloacal wall, and fertilization is internal.

Vocalization

6 Sound production is primarily a reproductive function of male anurans. Advertisement calls attract females to breeding areas and announce to other males that a given territory is occupied. Advertisement calls are species specific, and the repertoire of calls for any one species is limited. The calls may also help induce psychological and physiological readiness to breed. Females respond by making reciprocation calls to indicate receptiveness. Release calls inform a partner that a frog is incapable of reproducing. Unresponsive females give release calls if a male attempts amplexus, as do males that have been mistakenly identified as female by another male. Distress calls are not associated with reproduction; either sex produces these calls in response to pain or being seized by a predator. The calls may be loud enough to cause a predator to release the frog. The distress call of the South American jungle frog, *Leptodactylus pentadactylus*, is a loud scream similar to the call of a cat in distress.

The sound-production apparatus of frogs consists of the larynx and its vocal cords. This laryngeal apparatus is well developed in males, who also possess a vocal sac. In the majority of frogs, vocal sacs develop as a diverticulum from the lining of the buccal cavity (figure 28.16). Air from the lungs is forced over the vocal cords and cartilages of the larynx, causing them to vibrate. Muscles control the tension of the vocal cords and regulate the frequency of the sound. Vocal sacs act as resonating structures and increase the volume of the sound.

The use of sound to attract mates is especially useful in organisms that occupy widely dispersed habitats and must come together for breeding. Because many species of frogs often converge at the same pond for breeding, finding a mate of the proper species could be chaotic. Vocalizations help to reduce the chaos.

Parental Care

Parental care increases the chances of any one egg developing, but it requires large energy expenditures on the part of the parent. The most common form of parental care in amphibians is attendance of the egg clutch by either parent. Maternal care occurs in species with internal fertilization (predominantly salamanders and caecilians), and paternal care may occur in species with external fertilization (predominantly anurans). It may involve aeration of aquatic eggs, cleaning and/or moistening of terrestrial eggs, protection of eggs from predators, or removal of dead and infected eggs.

Eggs may be transported when development occurs on land. Females of the genus *Pipa* carry eggs on their back. *Rheobatrachus* females carry developing eggs and tadpoles in their stomach, and the young emerge from the female's mouth (figure 28.17)! Viviparity and ovoviviparity occur primarily in salamanders and caecilians.

Metamorphosis

Metamorphosis is a series of abrupt structural, physiological, and behavioral changes that transform a larva into an adult. A variety of environmental conditions, including crowding and food

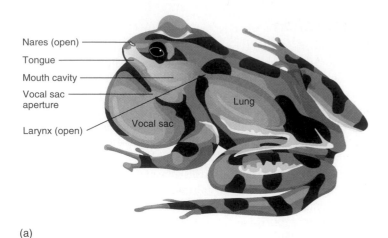

Nares (open)
Tongue
Mouth cavity
Vocal sac aperture
Larynx (open)
Lung
Vocal sac

(a)

(b)

FIGURE 28.16

Anuran Vocalization. (*a*) Generalized vocal apparatus of an anuran. (*b*) Inflated vocal sac of the Great Plains toad, *Bufo cognatus*.

availability, influence the time required for metamorphosis. Most directly, however, metamorphosis is under the control of neurosecretions of the hypothalamus, hormones of the anterior lobe of the pituitary gland (the adenohypophysis), and the thyroid gland (*see figure 35.10*).

Morphological changes associated with metamorphosis of caecilians and salamanders are relatively minor. Reproductive structures develop, gills are lost, and a caudal fin (when present) is lost. In the Anura, however, changes from the tadpole into the small frog are more dramatic (figure 28.18). Limbs and lungs develop, the tail is reabsorbed, the skin thickens, and marked changes in the head and digestive tract (associated with a new mode of nutrition) occur.

The mechanics of metamorphosis explain paedomorphosis in amphibians. Some salamanders are paedomorphic because cells

FIGURE 28.17

Parental Care of Young. Female *Rheobatrachus* with young emerging from her mouth.

fail to respond to thyroid hormones, whereas others are paedomorphic because they fail to produce the hormones associated with metamorphosis. In some salamander families, paedomorphosis is the rule. In other families, the occurrence of paedomorphosis is variable and influenced by environmental conditions.

FURTHER PHYLOGENETIC CONSIDERATIONS

One unresolved controversy concerning amphibian phylogeny is the relationship among the three orders of modern amphibians. Some zoologists place anurans, urodeles, and caecilians into a single subclass, Lissamphibia. This placement implies a common ancestry for modern amphibians and suggests that they are more closely related to each other than to any other group. Supporters of this classification point to common characteristics, such as the stapes/operculum complex, the importance of the skin in gas exchange, and aspects of the structure of the skull and teeth, as evidence of this close relationship. Figure 28.3 depicts this interpretation. Other zoologists think that modern amphibians were derived from at least two nonamniotic lineages. They note that fine details of other structures, such as the vertebral column, are different enough in the three orders to suggest separate origins. If this is true, the class Amphibia is a paraphyletic group and should be divided into multiple monophyletic taxa. This controversy is not likely to be settled soon.

(a)

(b)

(c)

(d)

FIGURE 28.18

Events of Metamorphosis in the Frog, *Rana temporaria.* (*a*) Before metamorphosis. Prolactin secretion, controlled by the hypothalamus and the adenohypophysis, promotes the growth of larval structures. (*b–d*) Metamorphosis. The median eminence of the hypothalamus develops and initiates the secretion of thyroid-stimulating hormone (TSH). TSH begins to inhibit prolactin release. TSH causes the release of large quantities of T_4 and T_3, which promote the growth of limbs, reabsorption of the tail, and other changes of metamorphosis, resulting eventually in a young, adult frog.

The next three chapters focus on descendants of the amniote lineage (*see figure 28.3*). Anthracosaurs are often cited as amphibian ancestors of these animals, but support for this conclusion is weak.

⑦ Three sets of evolutionary changes in amphibian lineages allowed movement onto land. Two of these occurred early enough that they are found in all amphibians. One was the set of changes in the skeleton and muscles that allowed greater mobility on land. A second change involved a jaw mechanism and movable head that permitted effective exploitation of insect resources on land. A jaw-muscle arrangement that permitted rhipidistian fishes to snap, grab, and hold prey was adaptive when early tetrapods began feeding on insects in terrestrial environments. The third set of changes occurred in the amniote lineage—the development of an egg that was resistant to drying. Although the **amniotic egg** is not completely independent of water, the extraembryonic membranes that form during develop-

ment protect the embryo from desiccation, store wastes, and promote gas exchange. In addition, this egg has a leathery or calcified shell that is protective, yet porous enough to allow gas exchange with the environment (*see figure 10.13*). These evolutionary events eventually resulted in the remaining three vertebrate groups: reptiles, birds, and mammals.

Stop and Ask Yourself

9. What region of the amphibian brain integrates sensory information and initiates motor responses?

10. What respiratory and excretory adaptations of amphibians promote life in terrestrial environments?

11. What are four functions of anuran vocalizations?

12. In what ways are amniotic eggs adaptive for life on land?

SUMMARY

1. Terrestrial vertebrates are called tetrapods and probably arose from sarcopterygians. Two lineages of ancient amphibians diverged. The nonamniote lineage gave rise to the three orders of modern amphibians. The amniote lineage gave rise to reptiles, birds, and mammals.

2. Members of the order Caudata are the salamanders. Salamanders are widely distributed, usually have internal fertilization, and may have aquatic larvae or direct development.

3. The order Gymnophiona contains the caecilians. Caecilians are tropical, wormlike burrowers. They have internal fertilization and many are viviparous.

4. Frogs and toads comprise the order Anura. Anurans lack tails and possess adaptations for jumping and swimming. External fertilization results in tadpole larvae, which metamorphose to adults.

5. The skin of amphibians is moist and functions in gas exchange, water regulation, and protection.

6. Skeletal and muscular systems of amphibians are adapted for movement on land.

7. Amphibians are carnivores that capture prey in their jaws or by using their tongue.

8. The circulatory system of amphibians is modified to accommodate the presence of lungs, gas exchange at the skin, and loss of gills in most adults.

9. Gas exchange is cutaneous, buccopharyngeal, and pulmonary. A buccal pump accomplishes pulmonary ventilation. A few amphibians retain gills as adults.

10. Sensory receptors of amphibians, especially the eye and ear, are adapted for functioning on land.

11. Amphibians excrete ammonia or urea. Ridding the body of excess water when in water and conserving water when on land are functions of the kidneys, the skin, and amphibian behavior.

12. Reproductive habits of amphibians are diverse. Many have external fertilization and development. Others have internal fertilization and development. Courtship, vocalizations, and parental care are common in some amphibians. The nervous and endocrine systems control metamorphosis.

13. An egg that is resistant to drying evolved in the amniote lineage, which is represented today by reptiles, birds, and mammals.

SELECTED KEY TERMS

amniote lineage (p. 456)
amplexus (p. 467)
buccal pump (p. 463)
buccopharyngeal respiration (p. 463)

cutaneous respiration (p. 463)
nictitating membrane (p. 465)
nonamniote lineage (p. 456)
tetrapods (p. 456)

CRITICAL THINKING QUESTIONS

1. How are skeletal and muscular systems of amphibians adapted for life on land?

2. Would the buccal pump be more important for an active amphibian or for one that is becoming inactive for the winter? Explain your answer.

3. Why is the separation of oxygenated and nonoxygenated blood in the heart not very important for amphibians?

4. Explain how the skin of amphibians is used in temperature regulation, protection, gas exchange, and water regulation. Under what circumstances might cooling interfere with water regulation?

5. In what ways could anuran vocalizations have influenced the evolution of that order?

REFERENCES ON THE WORLD WIDE WEB

1. **Introduction to the Amphibia.** This site provides links to information on the fossil record, life history, and systematics of the amphibians.
   http://www.ucmp.berkeley.edu/vertebrates/tetrapods/amphibintro.html

2. **Herpetologia-Obscura (TM)—Online Magazine.** This site is dedicated to the publication of obscure, unusual, or trivial herpetological information.
   http://www.xmission.com~gastown/herpmed/obscura

3. **The Electronic Zoo—Amphibians.** This site provides many links to information on the amphibians.
   http://net.vet.wustl.edu/amphib.htm

4. **Frog Calls.** Hear interesting frog vocalizations at this site.
   http://www.oit.itd.umich.edu:80/bio/sounds/Rana_catesbieana.au

5. **Class Lissamphibia.** This site provides more links to information on the modern orders of amphibians. It also provides additional links to sites that have recordings of frog vocalizations.
   http://www.oit.itd.umich.edu:80/bio108/Chordata/Lissamphibia.html

6. **FROGLOG.** This site provides lists of publications regarding amphibians, as well as information on the status of amphibian populations around the world.
   http://acs-info.open.ac.uk/info/newsletters/FROGLOG.html

7. **BIOSIS—Amphibia.** Find general information on amphibians as well as specific information on each of the orders of amphibians.
   http://www.york.biosis.org/zrdocs/zoolinfo/grp_amph.htm

8. **Dendrobatid Frog Page.** This interesting site provides information about poison-arrow frogs.
   http://206.1.0.131/index.html

9. **Interactive Frog Dissection.** This site is designed for high school students about to dissect a frog. It is an interesting review for beginning zoology students or an introduction to frog anatomy for zoology students who did not dissect a frog in high school.
   http://curry.edschool.Virginia.EDU/go/frog/

chapter 29

REPTILES:
THE FIRST AMNIOTES

Concepts

1. Adaptive radiation of primitive amniotes resulted in the three or four lineages of reptiles. These lineages have given rise to four orders of modern reptiles, the birds, and the mammals.
2. The class Reptilia has four orders: Testudines includes the turtles; Rhynchocephalia includes a single species, *Sphenodon punctatus*; Squamata includes the lizards, the snakes, and the worm lizards; and Crocodilia includes the alligators and crocodiles.
3. Many reptiles have adaptations that allow them to spend most of their lives apart from standing or flowing water. These include adaptations for support and movement, feeding, gas exchange, temperature regulation, excretion, osmoregulation, and reproduction.
4. Two reptilian evolutionary lineages gave rise to other vertebrate classes: Aves and Mammalia.

Would You Like to Know . . .

1. what living animals are most closely related to dinosaurs? (p. 472)
2. why turtles are vulnerable to extinction? (p. 476)
3. what animal "walks at both ends"? (p. 478)
4. why a lizard's tail breaks easily? (p. 479)
5. how a chameleon captures prey? (p. 480)
6. why reptiles divert blood away from their lungs? (p. 481)
7. what a median eye is? (p. 483)

This chapter answers these and other useful questions.

This chapter contains evolutionary concepts, which are set off in this font.

Evolutionary Perspective

The earliest members of the class Reptilia (rep-til′e-ah) (L. *reptus*, to creep) were the first vertebrates to possess **amniotic eggs** (figure 29.1). Amniotic eggs have extraembryonic membranes that protect the embryo from desiccation, cushion the embryo, promote gas transfer, and store waste materials (*see figures 10.11 and 10.13*). The amniotic eggs of reptiles and birds also have hard or leathery shells that protect the developing embryo, albumen that cushions and provides moisture and nutrients for the embryo, and yolk that supplies food to the embryo. All of these features are adaptations for development on land. (The amniotic egg is not, however, the only kind of land egg: some arthropods, amphibians, and even a few fishes have eggs that develop on land.) The amniotic egg is the major synapomorphy that distinguishes the reptiles, birds, and mammals from vertebrates in the nonamniote lineage. Even though the amniotic egg has played an important role in vertebrates' successful invasion of terrestrial habitats, it is one of many reptilian adaptations that have allowed members of this class to flourish on land. Living representatives of the class Reptilia include the turtles, lizards, snakes, worm lizards, crocodilians, and the tuatara (table 29.1).

Even though fossil records of many reptiles are abundant, much remains to be learned of reptilian origins. As indicated by the circle at the base of the cladogram in figure 29.2, the ancestral amniote has not yet been discovered. The adaptive radiation of the early amniotes began in the late Carboniferous and early Permian periods. This time coincided with the adaptive radiation of terrestrial insects, the major prey of early amniotes. The adaptive radiation of the amniotes resulted in the lineages described in the paragraphs that follow.

Skull structure, particularly the modifications in jaw muscle attachment, is one way these lineages are distinguished (figure 29.3).

Reptiles in the subclass Anapsida (Gr. *an*, without + *hapsis*, arch) lack openings or fenestrae in the temporal (posterolateral) region of the skull. The turtles represent this lineage today. Recent evidence suggests that the anapsid lineage probably does not have close evolutionary ties to other reptiles. Changes have occurred in their long evolutionary history, but the fundamental form of their skull and shell is recognizable in 200-million-year-old fossils. Evidence of the anapsid lineage has been found in 245-million-year-old rocks from South Africa.

A second group of reptiles are diapsid (Gr. *di*, two). They have upper and lower openings in the temporal region of the skull. Taxonomists debate whether this condition reflects a single lineage (*see figure 29.2*). Some prefer to divide this group into two subclasses. One subclass, the Lepidosauria, includes modern snakes, lizards, and tuataras. A second subclass, Archosauria, underwent extensive evolutionary radiation in the Mesozoic era and includes the dinosaurs. Most archosaurs are now extinct (box 29.1). ① Living archosaurs include the crocodilians and the dinosaurs' closest living relatives— the birds.

Another group of reptiles are synapsid (Gr. *syn*, with). They possess a single dorsal opening in the temporal region of the skull. Although no reptilian descendants of this group survive today, they are important because a group of synapsids, called therapsids, gave rise to the mammals.

Figure 29.1

Class Reptilia. Members of the class Reptilia were the first vertebrates to possess amniotic eggs, which develop free from standing or flowing water. Numerous other adaptations have allowed members of this class to flourish on land. A Nile crocodile (*Crocodylus niloticus*) is shown here.

TABLE 29.1	CLASSIFICATION OF LIVING REPTILES

Class Reptilia (rep-til′e-ah)
Dry skin with epidermal scales; skull with one point of articulation with the vertebral column (occipital condyle); respiration via lungs; metanephric kidneys; internal fertilization; amniotic eggs.

    Order Testudines (tes-tu′din-ez) or Chelonia (ki-lo′ne-ah)
    Teeth absent in adults and replaced by a horny beak; short, broad body; shell consisting of a dorsal carapace and ventral plastron. Turtles.

    Order Rhynchocephalia (rin″ko-se-fa′le-ah)
    Contains very primitive, lizardlike reptiles; well-developed parietal eye. A single species, *Sphenodon punctatus*, survives in New Zealand. Tuataras.

    Order Squamata (skwa-ma′tah)
    Recognized by specific characteristics of the skull and jaws (temporal arch reduced or absent and quadrate movable or secondarily fixed); the most successful and diverse group of living reptiles. Snakes, lizards, worm lizards.

    Order Crocodilia (krok″o-dil′e-ah)
    Elongate, muscular, and laterally compressed; tongue not protrusible; complete ventricular septum. Crocodiles, alligators, caimans, gavials.

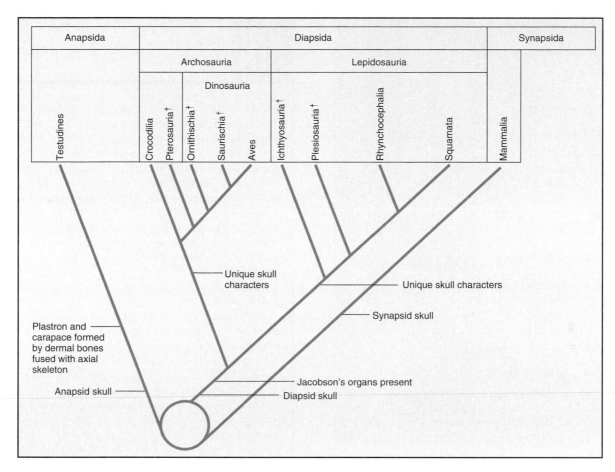

FIGURE 29.2

Amniote Phylogeny. This cladogram shows one interpretation of amniote phylogeny. The circle at the base of the cladogram indicates that the ancestral amniotes are not described. Some researchers believe that the Diapsida is not a single lineage and that the Archosauria and Lepidosauria should be elevated to subclass status. Synapomorphies used to distinguish lower taxa are not shown. Daggers (†) indicate some extinct taxa. Other numerous extinct taxa are not shown.

CLADISTIC INTERPRETATION OF THE AMNIOTIC LINEAGE

Cladistic taxonomic methods have resulted in a reexamination and reinterpretation of the amniotic lineage. As shown in figure 28.3, the amniotic lineage is monophyletic. Figure 29.2 shows that the birds (traditionally the class Aves) and the mammals (traditionally the class Mammalia) share a common ancestor with the reptiles. The rules of cladistic analysis state that all descendants of a most recent common ancestor must be included in a particular taxon. Clearly, that is not the case with the traditional class Reptilia; the birds and mammals are excluded, even though they share a common ancestry with reptiles. According to cladistic interpretations, birds should be classified as "reptiles" with their closest relatives, the dinosaurs. Similarly, cladistic interpretations take into account the close relationships of the mammals and a group of ancient reptiles, the mammal-like reptiles.

Evolutionary systematists disagree with cladists' interpretations. They contend that both the birds and the mammals have important morphological, behavioral, and ecological characteristics (e.g., feathers and endothermy in the birds; hair, mammary glands, and endothermy in mammals) that warrant their assignment to separate classes. In effect, evolutionary systematists weigh these characters and conclude that they are of overriding importance in the taxonomy of these groups.

This text presents the traditional interpretation of amniote classification. This may change in future editions, however, since the disagreements between cladists and evolutionary systematists will probably continue.

SURVEY OF THE REPTILES

Reptiles are characterized by a skull with one surface (condyle) for articulation with the first neck vertebra, respiration by lungs, metanephric kidneys, internal fertilization, and amniotic eggs. Reptiles also have dry skin with keratinized epidermal scales. **Keratin** is a resistant protein found in epidermally derived structures

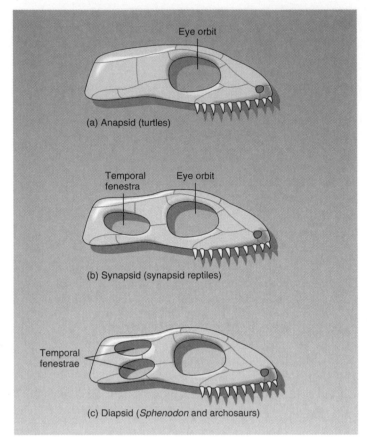

FIGURE 29.3

Amniote Skull Characteristics. Amniotes are classified according to skull characteristics and jaw muscle attachment. (*a*) Anapsid skulls lack openings (fenestrae) in the temporal region. This kind of skull is characteristic of turtles. (*b*) Synapsid skulls have a single temporal opening and are characteristic of the lineage of amniotes leading to mammals. (*c*) Diapsid skulls have two temporal openings. This kind of skull is characteristic of lizards, snakes, worm lizards, the tuatara, and birds.

of amniotes. It is protective, and when chemically bonded to phospholipids, prevents water loss across body surfaces. Members of three of the four orders described here live on all continents except Antarctica. However, reptiles are a dominant part of any major ecosystem only in tropical and subtropical environments. There are 17 orders of reptiles, but members of most orders are extinct. The four orders containing living representatives are described next (*see table 29.1*).

ORDER TESTUDINES OR CHELONIA

Members of the order Testudines (tes-tu′din-ez) (L. *testudo*, tortise), or Chelonia (ki-lo′ne-ah) (Gr. *chelone*, tortise), are the turtles. The approximately 225 species of turtles are characterized by a bony shell, limbs articulating internally to the ribs, and a kera-

BOX 29.1 COLLISION OR COINCIDENCE?

Extinction is the eventual fate of all species. Indeed, 99% of all species ever on the earth are now extinct. Often, the rate of extinction is low; however, on several occasions in earth's history, rates of extinction have increased dramatically, resulting in the total extinction of many formerly successful taxa. For example, at the Permian/Triassic boundary, a mass extinction resulted in the loss of 80 to 90% of all animal species. About 65 million years ago, the dinosaurs, along with 50% of all other animal species, became extinct. This Cretaceous/Tertiary extinction occurred over a period of tens of thousands to several million years. From a geological perspective, these extinctions are "sudden." How the age of the reptiles ended has been the subject of speculation for many years. Various hypotheses involving catastrophic or gradual change have been proposed.

Some scientists have suggested that asteroid impacts or periods of intense volcanic activity are catastrophic events that have caused mass extinctions. Both events may have injected large quantities of dust into the air that shaded the earth's surface, reducing photosynthetic production, and thus, food for animals.

The presence of the element iridium in rock strata from the Cretaceous/Tertiary boundary and other periods of mass extinction is the primary evidence supporting the catastrophic hypotheses. Iridium is a primarily extraterrestrial element that is deposited during asteroid impacts with the earth. Some deposits may also result from volcanic activity. Opponents of the catastrophic hypotheses do not deny that asteroid impacts or periods of volcanic activity resulted in iridium deposits on the earth. They question, however, whether the catastrophes are responsible for mass extinctions. They point out that the paleontological record indicates that extinctions are not as abrupt as implied in catastrophic hypotheses. Extinctions apparently occurred over tens of thousands of years, not tens of years. In addition, catastrophic events would be expected to affect all animal groups more or less equally, which was not the case with the Cretaceous/Tertiary extinction. For example, dinosaurs became extinct, but crocodiles, turtles, birds, and early mammals did not.

Numerous hypotheses propose gradual, selective changes as explanations for mass extinction. Some of these involve climatic changes that continental drift could have induced. In the Cretaceous period, warm, shallow seas covered 70% of the present land area. By the end of the Cretaceous period, these seas were reduced to 15% of the present land area, resulting in the reduction of habitat for shallow-water marine organisms, a decrease in atmospheric temperatures, and dissection of land areas by newly formed rivers. Climatic and habitat changes such as these could have resulted in extinctions over periods of tens of thousands of years.

Regardless of what hypothesis (or hypotheses) of mass extinction is correct, this question is a good example of how interest fueled by controversy stimulates scientific inquiry. The gradualism/catastrophism debate has led to new, innovative ideas on the origin, evolution, and extinction of taxa.

BOX 29.2 BONE AND SCALES

Bone is the primary skeletal tissue of vertebrates. In addition to making up the skeleton, it also is present in the scales of some vertebrates.

Developmentally, bone is derived from two sources. Dermal or membrane bone forms many of the superficial, flat bones of the top (dorsal) portion of the skull and some bones in the pectoral girdle. These bones were especially numerous in the roof of the skull of early vertebrates. Dermal bone forms in the connective tissues of the dermis of the skin. Bone-forming cells called osteoblasts line up along connective-tissue fibers and begin depositing bone. Bony fibers coalesce into the latticework that makes up a flat bone.

Endochondral bone forms many of the long bones and the ventral and posterior bones of the skull. It develops by replacing the cartilage that formed early in development (figure 1a). As the cartilage-based bone develops, osteoblasts lay down a collar of bone around the middle region, the diaphysis. Cartilage cells in the diaphysis break down, beginning the formation of the marrow cavity. Eventually, this cavity fills with bone marrow, in which blood cells form. Bone formation proceeds toward the ends of a bone. The cartilage near the end of the bone, however, continues to grow and results in further bone elongation. Each end of the bone is an epiphysis. In mammals, a secondary ossification center occurs in each epiphysis and forms bony caps on the ends of the bone. However, a cartilaginous plate, the epiphyseal plate, remains between the epiphysis and the diaphysis and is the site of cartilage growth and bone elongation. Bone growth continues until maturity. Except for thin cartilages at the ends of bones that provide gliding surfaces for joints, bone replaces all cartilage at maturity, and growth stops.

Fish scales are composed, in part, of dermal bone. Osteoblasts in the dermis of the skin lay down a core of bone. Other dermal cells lay down a layer of dentine, which is similar to bone, around the bony core. Then, epidermal cells lay down a covering of enamel (figure 1b). Enamel is one of the hardest tissues in the vertebrate body and also occurs on teeth.

The scales of the skin of reptiles and the legs of birds form entirely in the epidermis of the skin and do not contain bone. These scales are composed of many layers of epidermal cells (figure 1c). Keratin and phospholipids are incorporated into the outer, horny layers of a scale to reduce water loss across the skin. As chapter 30 explains, the feathers of birds are modified epidermal scales.

FIGURE 1

Bone and Scales. (a) The formation of endochondral bone. (b) Dermal scales of a fish. (c) Epidermal scales of a reptile.

tinized beak rather than teeth. The dorsal portion of the shell is the **carapace,** which forms from a fusion of vertebrae, expanded ribs, and bones in the dermis of the skin (box 29.2). Keratin covers the bone of the carapace. The ventral portion of the shell is the **plastron.** It forms from bones of the pectoral girdle and dermal bone, and keratin also covers it (figure 29.4). In some turtles, such

as the North American box turtle (*Terrapene*), the shell has flexible areas, or hinges, that allow the anterior and posterior edges of the plastron to be raised. The hinge allows the shell openings to close when the turtle withdraws into the shell. Turtles have eight cervical vertebrae that can be articulated into an S-shaped configuration, that allows the head to be drawn into the shell.

(a)

Hyoid bones

Acromial process

Ulna

Glenoid fossa

Scapula

Dorsal vertebra (10)

Acetabulum

Ilium

Femur

Tibia

Fibula

Metatarsals

Tarsals

(b)

Lower jaw (mandible)

Skull

Cervical vertebrae (8)

Humerus

Radius

Carpals

Phalanges

4th rib

Pubis

Ischium

1st sacral vertebrae

Caudal vertebra

Phalanges

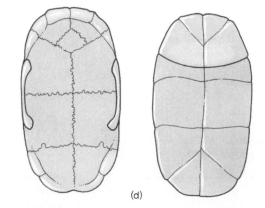

(c)   (d)

FIGURE 29.4

Skeleton of a Turtle. (*a*) Dorsal view of the carapace. (*b*) Ventral view of the carapace and appendicular skeleton. Keratin covers the carapace, which is composed of fused vertebrae, expanded ribs, and dermal bone. (*c*) Dorsal view of the plastron. (*d*) Ventral view of the plastron. The plastron forms from dermal bone and bone of the pectoral girdle. It is also covered by keratin.

Turtles have long life spans. Most reach sexual maturity after 7 or 8 years, and live 14 or more years. Large tortoises of the Galápagos Islands may live in excess of 100 years (*see figure 11.2*). All turtles are oviparous. Females use their hindlimbs to excavate nests in the soil. There they lay and cover with soil clutches of 5 to 100 eggs. Development takes from 4 weeks to 1 year, and the parent does not attend to the eggs during this time. The young are independent of the parent at hatching.

In recent years, turtle conservation programs have been enacted. ❷ Slow rates of growth and long juvenile periods make turtles vulnerable to extinction in the face of high mortality rates. Turtle hunting and predation on young turtles and turtle nests by dogs and other animals have severely threatened some species— in particular, sea turtles that nest on certain beaches year after year. Conservation of sea turtles is complicated by their having ranges of thousands of square kilometers of ocean, so that protective areas must include waters under the jurisdiction of many different nations (figure 29.5).

ORDER RHYNCHOCEPHALIA

The one surviving species of the order Rhynchocephalia (rin″kose-fa′le-ah) (Gr. *rhynchos*, snout + *kephale*, head) is the tuatara (*Sphenodon punctatus*) (figure 29.6). This superficially lizardlike reptile is virtually unchanged from extinct relatives that were present at the beginning of the Mesozoic era, nearly 200 million years ago. Tooth attachment and structure distinguish the tuatara from other reptiles. Two rows of teeth on the upper jaw and a single row of teeth in the lower jaw produce a shearing bite that can decapitate a small bird. Formerly more widely distributed in New Zealand, the tuatara fell prey to human influences and domestic animals. It is now present only on remote offshore islands and is protected by New Zealand law. It is oviparous and shares underground burrows with ground-nesting seabirds. Tuataras venture out of their burrows at dusk and dawn to feed on insects or, occasionally, small vertebrates.

ORDER SQUAMATA

The order Squamata (skwa-ma′tah) (L. *squama*, scale + *ata*, to bear) is divided into three suborders. Ancestral members of these suborders originated in the lepidosaur lineage about 150 million years ago and diverged into numerous modern forms.

Suborder Sauria—The Lizards

About 3,300 species of lizards are in the suborder Sauria (sawr′e-ah) (Gr. *sauro*, lizard). In contrast to snakes, lizards usually have two pairs of legs, and their upper and lower jaws unite anteriorly. The few lizards that are legless retain remnants of a pectoral girdle and sternum. Lizards vary in length from only a few centimeters to as large as 3 m. Many lizards live on surface substrates and retreat under rocks or logs when necessary. Others are burrowers or tree dwellers. Most lizards are oviparous; some are ovoviviparous or viviparous. They usually deposit eggs under rocks, debris, or in burrows.

FIGURE 29.5

Order Testudines. Green sea turtles (*Chelonia mydas*) nest every 2 to 4 years and migrate many miles to nesting beaches in the Caribbean and South Atlantic Oceans.

FIGURE 29.7

Order Squamata. The gila monster (*Heloderma suspectum*) is a poisonous lizard of southwestern North America.

FIGURE 29.6

Order Rhynchocephalia. The tuatara (*Sphenodon punctatus*).

Geckos, commonly found on the walls of human dwellings, are short and stout. They are nocturnal, and unlike most lizards, are capable of clicking vocalizations. Their large eyes, with pupils that contract to a narrow slit during the day and dilate widely at night, are adapted for night vision. Adhesive disks on their digits aid in clinging to trees and walls.

Iguanas have robust bodies, short necks, and distinct heads. This group includes the marine iguanas of the Galápagos Islands and the flying dragons (*Draco*) of Southeast Asia. The latter have lateral folds of skin supported by ribs. Like the ribs of an umbrella, the ribs of *Draco* can expand to form a gliding surface. When this lizard launches itself from a tree, it can glide 30 m or more!

Another group of iguanas, the chameleons, lives mainly in Africa and India. Chameleons are adapted to arboreal lifestyles and use a long, sticky tongue to capture insects. *Anolis,* or the "pet-store chameleon," is also an iguanid, but is not a true chameleon. Chameleons and *Anolis* are well known for their ability to change color in response to illumination, temperature, or their behavioral state.

The only venomous lizards are the gila monster (*Heloderma suspectum*) (figure 29.7) and the Mexican beaded lizard (*Heloderma horridum*). These heavy-bodied lizards are native to southwestern North America. Venom is released into grooves on the surface of teeth and introduced into prey as the lizard chews. Lizard bites are seldom fatal to humans.

Suborder Serpentes—The Snakes

About 2,300 species are in the suborder Serpentes (ser-pen'tez) (L. *serpere,* to crawl). Although the vast majority of snakes are not dangerous to humans, about three hundred species are venomous. Worldwide, 30,000 to 40,000 people die from snake bites each year. Most of these deaths are in Southeast Asia. In the United States, fewer than one hundred people die each year from snake bites.

Snakes are elongate and lack limbs, although vestigial pelvic girdles and appendages are sometimes present. The skeleton may contain more than two hundred vertebrae and pairs of ribs. Joints between vertebrae make the body very flexible. Snakes possess skull adaptations that facilitate swallowing large prey. These adaptations include upper jaws that are movable on the skull, and upper and lower jaws that are loosely joined so that each half of the jaw can move independently. Other differences between lizards and snakes include the mechanism for focusing the eyes and the morphology of the retina. Elongation and narrowing of the body has resulted in the reduction or loss of the left lung and displacement of the gallbladder, the right kidney, and often, the gonads. Most snakes are oviparous, although a few, such as the New World boas and garter snakes, give birth to live young.

FIGURE 29.8
Order Squamata. An amphisbaenian "worm lizard" (*Amphisbaenia alba*), sometimes called a two-headed snake.

Zoologists debate the evolutionary origin of the snakes. The earliest fossils are from 135-million-year-old Cretaceous deposits. Some zoologists believe that the earliest snakes were burrowers. Loss of appendages and changes in eye structure could be adaptations similar to those seen in caecilians (*see figure 28.6*). The loss of legs could also be adaptive if early snakes were aquatic or lived in densely tangled vegetation.

Suborder Amphisbaenia—Worm Lizards

About 135 species are in the suborder Amphisbaenia (am″fis-be′ne-ah) (Gr. *amphi*, double + *baen*, to walk). They are specialized burrowers that live in soils of Africa, South America, the Caribbean, and the Mideast (figure 29.8). Most are legless, and their skulls are wedge or shovel shaped. A single median tooth in the upper jaw distinguishes amphisbaenians from all other vertebrates. The skin of amphisbaenians has ringlike folds called annuli and loosely attaches to the body wall. Muscles of the skin cause it to telescope and bulge outward, forming an anchor against a burrow wall. ❸ Amphisbaenians move easily forward or backward—thus, the suborder name. They feed on worms and small insects and are oviparous.

ORDER CROCODILIA

The order Crocodilia (krok″o-dil′e-ah) (Gr. *krokodeilos*, lizard) has 21 species. Along with dinosaurs, crocodilians are derived from the archosaurs and distinguished from other reptiles by certain skull characteristics: openings in the skull in front of the eye, triangular rather than circular eye orbits, and laterally compressed teeth. Living crocodilians include the alligators, crocodiles, gavials, and caimans.

Crocodilians have not changed much over their 170-million-year history. The snout is elongate and often used to capture food by a sideways sweep of the head. The nostrils are at the tips of the snout, so the animal can breathe while mostly submerged. Air passageways of the head lead to the rear of the mouth and throat, and a flap of tissue near the back of the tongue forms a watertight seal that allows breathing without inhaling water in the mouth. A plate of bone, called the secondary palate, evolved in the archosaurs and separates the nasal and mouth passageways. The muscular, elongate, and laterally compressed tail is used for swimming, offensive and defensive maneuvers, and attacking prey. Teeth are used only for seizing prey. Food is swallowed whole, but if a prey item is too large, crocodilians tear it apart by holding onto a limb and rotating their bodies wildly until the prey is dismembered. The stomach is gizzardlike, and crocodilians swallow rocks and other objects as abrasives for breaking apart ingested food. Crocodilians are oviparous and display parental care of hatchlings that parallels that of birds. Nesting behavior and parental care may be traced back to the common ancestor of both groups.

Stop and Ask Yourself

1. What evolutionary lineages diverged from the earliest amniotes?
2. What order of reptiles has members that lack teeth, have ribs and vertebrae incorporated into a bony shell, and are oviparous?
3. What adaptations for burrowing do worm lizards show?
4. What skull characteristics distinguish between lizards and snakes?

EVOLUTIONARY PRESSURES

The lifestyles of most reptiles reveal striking adaptations for terrestrialism. For example, a lizard common to deserts of southwestern United States—the chuckwalla (*Sauromalus obesus*)—survives during late summer when temperatures exceed 40° C (104° F) and when arid conditions wither plants and blossoms upon which chuckwallas browse (figure 29.9). To withstand these hot and dry conditions, chuckwallas disappear below ground and aestivate. Temperatures moderate during the winter, but little rain falls, so life on the desert surface is still not possible for the chuckwalla. The summer's sleep, therefore, merges into a winter's sleep. The chuckwalla does not emerge until March, when rain falls, and the desert explodes with greenery and flowers. The chuckwalla browses and drinks, storing water in large reservoirs under its skin. Chuckwallas are not easy prey. If threatened, a chuckwalla takes refuge in the nearest rock crevice. There, it inflates its lungs with air, increasing its girth and wedging itself against the rock walls of

FIGURE 29.9

Chuckwalla (*Sauromalus obesus*). Many reptiles, like this chuckwalla, possess adaptations that make life apart from standing or running water possible.

FIGURE 29.10

Secondary Palate. Sagittal section of the skull of a synapsid reptile, showing the secondary palate that separates the nasal and mouth cavities. Extension of the bones of the anterior skull forms the anterior portion of the secondary palate (the hard palate), and skin and soft connective tissues form the posterior portion of the secondary palate (the soft palate).

its refuge. Friction of its body scales against the rocks makes the chuckwalla nearly impossible to dislodge.

The adaptations that chuckwallas display are not exceptional for reptiles. This section discusses some of these adaptations that make life apart from an abundant water supply possible.

EXTERNAL STRUCTURE AND LOCOMOTION

Unlike that of amphibians, the skin of reptiles has no respiratory functions. Reptilian skin is thick, dry, and keratinized. Scales may be modified for various functions. For example, the large belly scales of snakes provide contact with the substrate during locomotion. Although reptilian skin is much less glandular than that of amphibians, secretions include pheromones that function in sex recognition and defense.

All reptiles periodically shed the outer, epidermal layers of the skin in a process called ecdysis. (The term ecdysis is also used for a similar, though unrelated, process in arthropods [see figure 23.5].) Because the blood supply to the skin does not extend into the epidermis, the outer epidermal cells lose contact with the blood supply and die. Movement of lymph between the inner and outer epidermal layers loosens the outer epidermis. Ecdysis generally begins in the head region, and in snakes and many lizards, the epidermal layers come off in one piece. In other lizards, smaller pieces of skin flake off. The frequency of ecdysis varies from one species to another, and it is greater in juveniles than adults.

The chromatophores of reptiles are primarily dermal in origin and function much like those of amphibians. Cryptic coloration, mimicry, and aposematic coloration occur in reptiles. Color and color change also function in sex recognition and thermoregulation.

Support and Movement

The skeletons of snakes, amphisbaenians, and turtles show modifications; however, in its general form, the reptilian skeleton is based on one inherited from ancient amphibians. The skeleton is highly ossified to provide greater support. The skull is longer than that of amphibians, and a plate of bone, the **secondary palate,** partially separates the nasal passages from the mouth cavity (figure 29.10). As described earlier, the secondary palate evolved in archosaurs, where it was an adaptation for breathing when the mouth was full of water or food. It is also present in other reptiles, although developed to a lesser extent. Longer snouts also permit greater development of olfactory epithelium and increased reliance on the sense of smell.

Reptiles have more cervical vertebrae than do amphibians. The first two cervical vertebrae (atlas and axis) provide greater freedom of movement for the head. An atlas articulates with a single condyle on the skull and facilitates nodding. An axis is modified for rotational movements. A variable number of other cervical vertebrae provide additional neck flexibility.

The ribs of reptiles may be highly modified. Those of turtles and the flying dragon were described previously. The ribs of snakes have muscular connections to large belly scales to aid locomotion. The cervical vertebrae of cobras have ribs that may be flared in aggressive displays.

Two or more sacral vertebrae attach the pelvic girdle to the vertebral column. The caudal vertebrae of many lizards possess a vertical fracture plane. ❹ When a lizard is grasped by the tail, caudal vertebrae can be broken, and a portion of the tail is lost. Tail loss, or **autotomy,** is an adaptation that allows a lizard to escape from a predator's grasp, or the disconnected, wiggling piece of tail may distract a predator from the lizard. The lizard later regenerates the lost portion of the tail.

Locomotion in primitive reptiles is similar to that of salamanders. The body is slung low between paired, stocky appendages, which extend laterally and move in the horizontal plane. The limbs of other reptiles are more elongate and slender, and are held closer to the body. The knee and elbow joints rotate posteriorly; thus, the body is higher off the ground, and weight is supported vertically. Many prehistoric reptiles were bipedal, meaning that they walked on hindlimbs. They had a narrow pelvis

FIGURE 29.11

Order Squamata. A chameleon (*Chameleo chameleon*) using its tongue to capture prey. Note the prehensile tail.

and a heavy, outstretched tail for balance. Bipedal locomotion freed the front appendages, which became adapted for prey capture or flight in some animals.

NUTRITION AND THE DIGESTIVE SYSTEM

Most reptiles are carnivores, although turtles will eat almost anything organic. The tongues of turtles and crocodilians are nonprotrusible and aid in swallowing.   ⑤ Like some anurans, some lizards and the tuatara have sticky tongues for capturing prey. The tongue extension of chameleons exceeds their body length (figure 29.11).

Probably the most remarkable adaptations of snakes involve modifications of the skull for feeding. The bones of the skull and jaws loosely join and may spread apart to ingest prey much larger than a snake's normal head size (figure 29.12a). The bones of the upper jaw are movable on the skull, and ligaments loosely join the halves of both of the upper and lower jaws anteriorly. Therefore, each half of the upper and lower jaws can move independently of one another. After a prey is captured, opposite sides of the upper and lower jaws are alternately thrust forward and retracted. Posteriorly pointing teeth prevent prey escape and help force the food into the esophagus. The glottis, the respiratory opening, is far forward so that the snake can breathe while slowly swallowing its prey.

Vipers (family Viperidae) possess hollow fangs on the maxillary bone at the anterior margin of the upper jaw (figure 29.12b).

These fangs connect to venom glands that inject venom when the viper bites. The maxillary bone (upper jaw bone) of vipers is hinged so that when the snake's mouth is closed, the fangs fold back and lie along the upper jaw. When the mouth opens, the maxillary bone rotates and causes the fangs to swing down (figure 29.12c). Because the fangs project outward from the mouth, vipers may strike at objects of any size. Rear-fanged snakes (family Colubridae) possess grooved rear teeth. In those that are venomous, venom is channeled along these grooves and worked into prey to quiet them during swallowing. These snakes usually do not strike, and most are harmless to humans; however, the African boomslang (*Dispholidus typus*) has caused human fatalities. Coral snakes, sea snakes, and cobras have fangs that rigidly attach to the upper jaw in an erect position. When the mouth is closed, the fangs fit into a pocket in the outer gum of the lower jaw. Fangs are grooved or hollow, and contraction of muscles associated with venom glands injects venom into the fangs. Some cobras can "spit" venom at their prey; if not washed from the eyes, the venom may cause blindness.

Venom glands are modified salivary glands. Most snake venoms are mixtures of neurotoxins and hemotoxins. The venoms of coral snakes, cobras, and sea snakes are primarily neurotoxins that attack nerve centers and cause respiratory paralysis. The venoms of vipers are primarily hemotoxins. They break up blood cells and attack blood vessel linings.

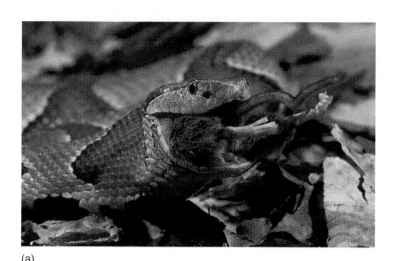

FIGURE 29.12

Feeding Adaptations of Snakes. (*a*) A copperhead (*Ankistrodon*) ingesting a prey. Flexible joints allow the bones of the skull to separate during feeding. Note the pit organ just anterior to the eye. (*b*) The skull of a viper. The hinge mechanism of the jaw allows upper and lower bones on one side of the jaw to slide forward and backward alternately with bones of the other side. Posteriorly curved teeth hold prey as it is worked toward the esophagus. (*c*) Note that the maxillary bone, into which the fang is embedded, swings forward when the mouth opens.

CIRCULATION, GAS EXCHANGE, AND TEMPERATURE REGULATION

The circulatory system of reptiles is based on that of amphibians. Because reptiles are, on average, larger than amphibians, their blood must travel under higher pressures to reach distant body parts. To take an extreme example, the blood of *Brachiosaurus* had to be pumped a distance of about 6 m from the heart to the head—mostly uphill! (The blood pressure of a giraffe is about double that of a human to move blood the 2 m from heart to head.)

Like amphibians, reptiles possess two atria that are completely separated in the adult and have veins from the body and lungs emptying into them. Except for turtles, the sinus venosus is no longer a chamber but has become a patch of cells that acts as a pacemaker. The ventricle of most reptiles is incompletely divided (figure 29.13). (Only in crocodilians is the ventricular septum complete.) The ventral aorta and the conus arteriosus divide during development and become three major arteries that leave the heart. A pulmonary artery leaves the ventral side of the ventricle and takes blood to the lungs. Two systemic arteries, one from the ventral side of the heart and the other from the dorsal side of the heart, take blood to the lower body and the head.

Blood low in oxygen enters the ventricle from the right atrium and leaves the heart through the pulmonary artery and moves to the lungs. Blood high in oxygen enters the ventricle from the lungs via pulmonary veins and the left atrium, and leaves the heart through left and right systemic arteries. ⑥ The incomplete separation of the ventricle permits shunting of some blood away from the pulmonary circuit to the systemic circuit by constriction of muscles associated with the pulmonary artery. This is advantageous because virtually all reptiles breathe intermittently. When turtles withdraw into their shell, their method of lung ventilation cannot function. They also stop breathing during diving. During periods of apnea ("no breathing"), blood flow to the lungs is limited, which conserves energy and permits more efficient use of the pulmonary oxygen supply.

Gas Exchange

Reptiles exchange respiratory gases across internal respiratory surfaces to avoid losing large quantities of water. A larynx is present; however, vocal cords are usually absent. Cartilages support the respiratory passages of reptiles, and lungs are partitioned into spongelike, interconnected chambers. Lung chambers provide a large surface area for gas exchange.

In most reptiles, a negative-pressure mechanism is responsible for lung ventilation. A posterior movement of the ribs and the body wall expands the body cavity, decreasing pressure in the lungs and drawing air into the lungs. Air is expelled by elastic recoil of the lungs and forward movements of the ribs and body wall, which compress the lungs. The ribs of turtles are a part of their shell; thus, movements of the body wall to which the ribs attach

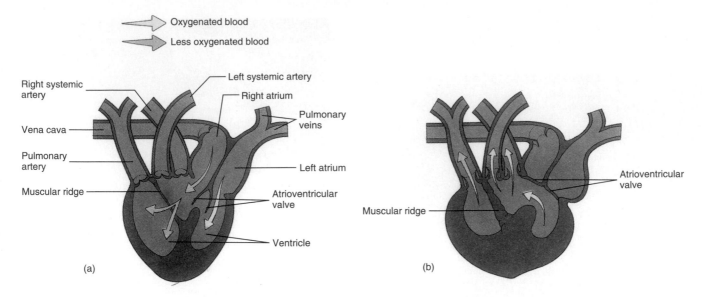

FIGURE 29.13

Heart and Major Arteries of a Lizard. (*a*) When the atria contract, blood enters the ventricle. An atrioventricular valve prevents the mixing of oxygenated and less oxygenated blood across the incompletely separated ventricle. (*b*) When the ventricle contracts, a muscular ridge closes to direct oxygenated blood to the systemic arteries and less oxygenated blood to the pulmonary artery.

are impossible. Turtles exhale by contracting muscles that force the viscera upward, compressing the lungs. They inhale by contracting muscles that increase the volume of the visceral cavity, creating negative pressure to draw air into the lungs.

Temperature Regulation

Unlike aquatic animals, terrestrial animals may face temperature extremes (−65 to 70° C) that are incompatible with life. Temperature regulation, therefore, is important for animals that spend their entire lives out of water. Most reptiles use external heat sources for thermoregulation and are, therefore, ectotherms. Exceptions include monitor lizards and brooding Indian pythons. Female pythons coil around their eggs and elevate their body temperature as much as 7.3° C above the air temperature using metabolic heat sources (box 29.3).

Some reptiles can survive wide temperature fluctuations (e.g., −2 to 41° C for some turtles). To sustain activity, however, body temperatures are regulated within a narrow range, between 25 and 37° C. If that is not possible, the reptile usually seeks a retreat where body temperatures are likely to remain within the range compatible with life.

Most thermoregulatory activities of reptiles are behavioral, and they are best known in the lizards. To warm itself, a lizard orients itself at right angles to the sun's rays, often on a surface inclined toward the sun, and presses its body tightly to a warm surface to absorb heat by conduction. To cool itself, a lizard orients its body parallel to the sun's rays, seeks shade or burrows, or assumes an erect posture (legs extended and tail arched) to reduce conduction from warm surfaces. In hot climates, many reptiles are nocturnal.

Various physiological mechanisms also regulate body temperature. As temperatures rise, some reptiles begin panting, which releases heat through evaporative cooling. (Little evaporative cooling occurs across the dry skin of reptiles.) Marine iguanas divert blood to the skin while basking in the sun and warm up quickly. On diving into the cool ocean, however, marine iguanas reduce heart rate and blood flow to the skin, which slows heat loss. Chromatophores also aid in temperature regulation. Dispersed chromatophores (thus, a darker body) increase the rate of heat absorption.

In temperate regions, many reptiles withstand cold winter temperatures by entering torpor when body temperatures and metabolic rates decrease. Individuals that are usually solitary may migrate to a common site to spend the winter. Heat loss from these groups, called hibernacula, is reduced because the total surface area of many individuals clumped together is reduced compared to widely separated animals. Unlike true hibernators, body temperatures of reptiles in torpor are not regulated, and if the winter is too cold or the retreat is too exposed, the animals can freeze and die. Cold death is an important source of mortality for temperate reptiles.

NERVOUS AND SENSORY FUNCTIONS

The brain of reptiles is similar to the brains of other vertebrates. The cerebral hemispheres are somewhat larger than those of amphibians. This increased size is associated with an improved sense of smell. The optic lobes and the cerebellum are also enlarged, which reflects increased reliance on vision and more refined coordination of muscle functions.

BOX	**29.3**

CHANGING PERCEPTIONS OF ANCIENT LIFESTYLES

Prior to 1960, paleontologists used fossil remains to assemble ancient lineages based on gross anatomical features. Now, they can derive information about the lifestyles of extinct animals from markings of blood vessels, muscles, and tendons present on fossils. In the 1970s, Robert T. Bakker began challenging previous perceptions of dinosaurs as lumbering giants and overgrown lizards. Bakker contended that that view of dinosaurs is difficult to reconcile with fossils, indicating that many dinosaurs were bipedal, or at least held their bodies well off the ground. Reptiles achieved many locomotor advancements long before similar advancements ever appeared in mammals. Unlike modern reptiles, dinosaurs had highly vascular bones, a condition typical of endothermic animals. Many believe it unlikely that very large, strictly ectothermic animals could warm up rapidly enough to maintain high activity levels. Bakker proposed that many, if not all, dinosaurs were endothermic.

Other scientists discount ideas that dinosaurs were endothermic. They maintain that dinosaurs may have been able to maintain active lifestyles, not in spite of their large size, but because of it. As ectotherms increase in size, they resemble endotherms. Large body mass results in slower warming, but it also results in slower heat loss. Further, the climate during the Mesozoic era was considerably warmer than it is now. Even though dinosaurs may have been ectotherms, they could have had stable body temperatures and an active lifestyle. Opponents of the endothermy hypothesis point out that some ectotherms have highly vascular bones. They also note that large endotherms usually have obvious cooling devices (e.g., the ears of an elephant), and these were not found on most large dinosaurs.

There are no clear winners in this debate. The dinosaurs may not have had a single thermoregulatory strategy. The largest dinosaurs could have been ectothermic. Although not swift and agile, they would still have been able to maintain a relatively constant body temperature in a stable, warm climate; find food; and avoid predators. On the other hand, maintenance of speed and agility in smaller dinosaurs that lived in cool climates may have required endothermy.

The complexity of reptilian sensory systems is evidenced by a chameleon's method of feeding. Its protruding eyes swivel independently, and each has a different field of view. Initially, the brain keeps both images separate, but when an insect is spotted, both eyes converge on the prey. Binocular vision then provides the depth perception for determining whether or not the insect is within range of the chameleon's tongue (see figure 29.11).

Vision is the dominant sense in most reptiles, and their eyes are similar to those of amphibians (see figure 28.14). Snakes focus on nearby objects by moving the lens forward. Contraction of the iris places pressure on the gel-like vitreous body in the posterior region of the eye, and displacement of this gel pushes the lens forward. All other reptiles focus on nearby objects when the normally elliptical lens is made more spherical, as a result of ciliary muscles pressing the ciliary body against the lens. Reptiles have a greater number of cones than do amphibians and probably have well-developed color vision.

Upper and lower eyelids, a nictitating membrane, and a blood sinus protect and cleanse the surface of the eye. In snakes and some lizards, the upper and lower eyelids fuse in the embryo to form a protective window of clear skin, called the spectacle. (During ecdysis, the outer layers of the spectacle become clouded and impair the vision of snakes.) The blood sinus, which is at the base of the nictitating membrane, swells with blood to help force debris to the corner of the eye, where it may be rubbed out. Horned lizards squirt blood from their eyes by rupturing this sinus in a defensive maneuver to startle predators.

7 Some reptiles possess a **median (parietal) eye** that develops from outgrowths of the roof of the forebrain (see figure 34.19). In the tuatara, it is an eye with a lens, a nerve, and a retina. In other reptiles, the parietal eye is less developed. Parietal eyes are covered by skin and probably cannot form images. They can, however, differentiate light and dark periods and are used in orientation to the sun.

The structure of reptilian ears varies. The ears of snakes detect substrate vibrations. They lack a middle-ear cavity, an auditory tube, and a tympanic membrane. A bone of the jaw articulates with the stapes and receives substrate vibrations. Snakes can also detect airborne vibrations. In other reptiles, a tympanic membrane may be on the surface or in a small depression in the head. The inner ear of reptiles is similar to that of amphibians.

Olfactory senses are better developed in reptiles than in amphibians. In addition to the partial secondary palate providing more surface for olfactory epithelium, many reptiles possess blind-ending pouches that open through the secondary palate into the mouth cavity. These pouches, called **Jacobson's (vomeronasal) organs,** are in diapsid reptiles; however, they are best developed in the squamates. Jacobson's organs develop in embryonic crocodilians but are not present in adults of this group. Anapsids (turtles) lack these olfactory organs. The protrusible, forked tongues of snakes and lizards are accessory olfactory organs for sampling airborne chemicals. A snake's tongue flicks out and then moves to the Jacobson's organs, which perceive odor molecules. Tuataras use Jacobson's organs to taste objects held in the mouth.

Rattlesnakes and other pit vipers have heat-sensitive **pit organs** on each side of the face between the eye and nostril (see figure 29.12a). These depressions are lined with sensory epithelium and are used to detect objects with temperatures different from the snake's surroundings. Pit vipers are usually nocturnal, and their pits help them locate small, warm-blooded prey.

Stop and Ask Yourself

5. How is the skin of a reptile adapted for preventing water loss?

6. What is a secondary palate? How is a secondary palate adaptive for reptiles?

7. How do reptiles use tongues in feeding? How do they use tongues in sensory perception?

8. How is the heart of a reptile adapted for shunting blood away from the pulmonary circulation? Under what circumstances does this shunting occur?

EXCRETION AND OSMOREGULATION

The kidneys of embryonic reptiles are similar to those of fishes and amphibians. Life on land, increased body size, and higher metabolic rates, however, require kidneys capable of processing wastes with little water loss. A kidney with many more blood-filtering units, called nephrons, replaces the reptilian embryonic kidney during development. The functional kidneys of adult reptiles are called metanephric kidneys. Their function depends on a circulatory system that delivers more blood at greater pressures to filter large quantities of blood.

Most reptiles excrete uric acid. It is nontoxic, and being relatively insoluble in water, it precipitates in the excretory system. The urinary bladder or the cloacal walls reabsorb water, and the uric acid can be stored in a pastelike form. Utilization of uric acid as an excretory product also made possible the development of embryos in terrestrial environments because nontoxic uric acid can be concentrated in egg membranes.

In addition to the excretory system's reabsorption of water, internal respiratory surfaces and relatively impermeable exposed surfaces reduce evaporative water loss. The behaviors that help regulate temperature also help conserve water. Nocturnal habits and avoiding hot surface temperatures during the day by burrowing reduce water loss. When water is available, many reptiles (e.g., chuckwallas) store large quantities of water in lymphatic spaces under the skin or in the urinary bladder. Many lizards possess salt glands below the eyes for ridding the body of excess salt.

REPRODUCTION AND DEVELOPMENT

Vertebrates could never be truly terrestrial until their reproduction and embryonic development became separate from standing or running water. For vertebrates, internal fertilization and the amniotic egg (see figure 10.13) made complete movement to land possible. The amniotic egg, however, is not completely independent of water. Pores in the eggshell permit gas exchange but also allow water to evaporate. Amniotic eggs require significant energy expenditures by parents. Parental care occurs in some reptiles and may involve maintaining relatively high humidity around the eggs. These eggs are often supplied with large quantities of yolk for long developmental periods, and parental energy and time is sometimes invested in posthatching care of dependent young.

Accompanying the development of amniotic eggs is the necessity for internal fertilization. Fertilization must occur in the reproductive tract of the female before protective egg membranes are laid down around an egg. All male reptiles, except tuataras, possess an intromittent organ for introducing sperm into the female reproductive tract. Lizards and snakes possess paired hemipenes at the base of the tail that are erected by being turned inside out, like the finger of a glove.

Gonads lie in the abdominal cavity. In males, a pair of ducts delivers sperm to the cloaca. After copulation, sperm may be stored in a seminal receptacle in the female reproductive tract. Secretions of the seminal receptacle nourish the sperm and arrest their activity. Sperm may be stored for up to 4 years in some turtles, and up to 6 years in some snakes! In temperate latitudes, sperm can be stored over winter. Copulation may take place in the fall, when individuals congregate in hibernacula, and fertilization and development may occur in the spring, when temperatures favor successful development. Fertilization occurs in the upper regions of the oviduct, which leads from the ovary to the cloaca. Glandular regions of the oviduct secrete albumen and the eggshell. The shell is usually tough yet flexible. In some crocodilians, the eggshell is calcareous and rigid, like the eggshells of birds.

Parthenogenesis has been described in six families of lizards and one species of snakes. In these species, no males have been found. Populations of parthenogenetic females have higher reproductive potential than bisexual populations. A population that suffers high mortality over a cold winter can repopulate its habitat rapidly because all surviving individuals can produce offspring. This apparently offsets disadvantages of genetic uniformity resulting from parthenogenesis.

Reptiles often have complex reproductive behaviors that may involve males actively seeking out females. As in other animals, courtship functions in sexual recognition and behavioral and physiological preparation for reproduction. Head-bobbing displays by some male lizards reveal bright patches of color on the throat and enlarged folds of skin. Courtship in snakes is based primarily on tactile stimulation. Tail-waving displays are followed by the male running his chin along the female, entwining his body around her, and creating wavelike contractions that pass posteriorly to anteriorly along his body. Recent research indicates that lizards and snakes also use sex pheromones. Vocalizations are important only in crocodilians. During the breeding season, males are hostile and may bark or cough as territorial warnings to other males. Roaring vocalizations also attract females, and mating occurs in the water.

After they are laid, reptilian eggs are usually abandoned (figure 29.14). Virtually all turtles bury their eggs in the ground or in plant debris. Other reptiles lay their eggs under rocks, in debris, or in burrows. About one hundred species of reptiles have some degree of parental care of eggs. One example is the American alligator, *Alligator mississippiensis* (figure 29.15). The female builds a mound of mud and vegetation about 1 m high and 2 m in diameter. She hollows out the center of the mound, partially fills it with mud and debris, deposits her eggs in the cavity, and then covers the eggs. Temperature within the nest influences the sex of the hatchlings. Temperatures at or below 31.5° C result in female off-

FIGURE 29.14
Reptile Eggs and Young. This young giant Madagascar day gecko (*Phelsuma madagascariensis*) is hatching from its egg.

FIGURE 29.15
Parental Care in Reptiles. A female American alligator (*Alligator mississippiensis*) tending to her nest.

spring. Temperatures between 32.5 and 33° C result in male offspring. Temperatures around 32° C result in both male and female offspring. (Similar temperature effects on sex determination are known in some lizards and many turtles.) The female remains in the vicinity of the nest throughout development to protect the eggs from predation. She frees hatchlings from the nest in response to their high-pitched calls and picks them up in her mouth to transport them to water. She may scoop shallow pools for the young and remain with them for up to 2 years. Young feed on scraps of food the female drops when she feeds and on small vertebrates and invertebrates that they catch on their own.

FURTHER PHYLOGENETIC CONSIDERATIONS

The archosaur and synapsid lineages of ancient reptiles diverged from ancient amniotes about 280 million years ago and are ancestral to animals described in chapters 30 and 31 (see figure 29.2). The archosaur lineage not only included the dinosaurs and gave rise to crocodilians, but also gave rise to two groups of fliers. The pterosaurs (Gr. *pteros*, wing + *sauros*, lizard) ranged from sparrow size to animals with wing spans of 13 m. An elongation of the fourth finger supported their membranous wings, their sternum

was adapted for the attachment of flight muscles, and their bones were hollow to lighten the skeleton for flight. As presented in chapter 30, these adaptations are paralleled by, though not identical to, adaptations in the birds—the descendants of the second lineage of flying archosaurs.

The synapsid lineage eventually gave rise to the mammals. The legs of synapsids were relatively long and held their body off the ground. Teeth and jaws were adapted for effective chewing and tearing. Additional bones were incorporated into the middle ear. These and other mammal-like characteristics developed between the Carboniferous and Triassic periods. The "Evolutionary Perspective" of chapter 31 describes more about the nature of this transition.

Stop and Ask Yourself

9. Why is uric acid an adaptive excretory product for reptiles?
10. What groups of reptiles contain parthenogenetic species?
11. In what group of reptiles are vocalizations an important part of reproductive activities?
12. What reptilian lineage gave rise to the birds? What reptilian lineage gave rise to the mammals?

SUMMARY

1. The earliest amniotes are classified as reptiles. The evolution of the amniotes resulted in lineages leading to the turtles; birds and dinosaurs; squamates (snakes, lizards, and worm lizards) and tuataras; and mammals.
2. The order Testudines contains the turtles. Turtles have a bony shell and lack teeth. All are oviparous.
3. The order Rhynchocephalia contains one species, the tuatara. It is found only on remote islands of New Zealand.
4. The order Squamata contains the lizards, snakes, and worm lizards. Lizards usually have two pairs of legs, and most are oviparous. Snakes lack developed limbs and have skull adaptations for swallowing large prey. Worm lizards are specialized burrowers. They have a single median tooth in the upper jaw, and most are oviparous.

5. The order Crocodilia contains alligators, crocodiles, caimans, and gavials. These groups have a well-developed secondary palate and display nesting behaviors and parental care.

6. The skin of reptiles is dry and keratinized, and provides a barrier to water loss. It also has epidermal scales and chromatophores.

7. The reptilian skeleton is modified for support and movement on land. Loss of appendages in snakes is accompanied by greater use of the body wall in locomotion.

8. Reptiles have a tongue that may be used in feeding. Bones of the skull of snakes are loosely joined and spread apart during feeding.

9. The circulatory system of reptiles is divided into pulmonary and systemic circuits, and functions under relatively high blood pressures. Blood may be shunted away from the pulmonary circuit during periods of apnea.

10. Gas exchange occurs across convoluted lung surfaces. Ventilation of lungs occurs by a negative-pressure mechanism.

11. Reptiles are ectotherms and mainly use behavioral mechanisms to thermoregulate.

12. Vision is the dominant sense in most reptiles. Median (parietal) eyes, ears, Jacobson's organs, and pit organs are important receptors in some reptiles.

13. Because uric acid is nontoxic and relatively insoluble in water, reptiles can store and excrete it as a semisolid. Internal respiratory surfaces and dry skin also promote water conservation.

14. The amniotic egg and internal fertilization permit development on land. They require significant parental energy expenditure.

15. Some reptiles use visual, olfactory, and auditory cues for reproduction. Parental care is important in crocodilians.

16. Descendants of the diapsid evolutionary lineage include the birds. Descendants of the synapsid lineage are the mammals.

SELECTED KEY TERMS

amniotic eggs (p. 472)
Jacobson's organs (p. 483)
keratin (p. 473)
median (parietal) eye (p. 483)
pit organs (p. 483)

CRITICAL THINKING QUESTIONS

1. Explain the nature of the controversy between cladists and evolutionary systematists regarding the higher taxonomy of the amniotes. Do you think that the Reptilia should be retained as a formal class designation? If so, what groups of animals should it contain?

2. What characteristics of the life history of turtles make them vulnerable to extinction? What steps do you think should be taken to protect endangered turtle species?

3. What might explain why parental care is common in crocodilians and birds?

4. List the adaptations that make life on land possible for a reptile. Explain why each is adaptive.

5. The incompletely divided ventricle of reptiles is sometimes portrayed as an evolutionary transition between the heart of primitive amphibians and the completely divided ventricles of birds and mammals. Do you agree with this portrayal? Why or why not?

6. What effect could significant global warming have on sex ratios of crocodilians? Speculate on what long-term effects might be seen in populations of crocodilians as a result of global warming.

REFERENCES ON THE WORLD WIDE WEB

1. **Herpetology Resources on the Internet.** This site is a hypertext of herpetology. It provides an electronic resource covering a wide range of herpetological topics.
   http://www.ttu.edu/~library/subject/bill/biology/herp-hyp.htm

2. **Herp Hotlinks.** This site provides dozens of links to herpetological Web sites.
   http://www.xmission.com/~gastown/herpmed/

3. **The EMBL Reptile Database.** This site provides information on classification of all living reptiles. It includes distribution maps and references, and it allows you to search for any reptile by name.
   http://www.embl-heidelberg.de/uetz/LivingReptiles.html

4. **Reptilia.** This site provides links to all kinds of information on reptiles.
   http://www.bart.nl/~reptilia/links.html

5. **Amphibian and Reptile WWW Sites.** This site contains many links to herpetological sites.
   http://www.flmnh.ufl.edu/natsci/herpetology/mamphrep.htm

6. **Classification of Reptiles.** This site contains information on living and extinct reptiles.
   http://www.embl-heidelberg.de/~uetz/Reptiles.html

7. **Rattlesnakes.** This site contains information on rattlesnakes.
   http://wwwdesertusa.com./may96/du_rattle.html

8. **American Pit Vipers.** This site is devoted to the pit vipers, but most of its information covers rattlesnakes.
   http://www.ncweb.com:80/users/gostanek/

9. **The Electronic Zoo: Reptiles.** This site contains many links to information on the reptiles.
   http://netvet.wustl.edu/reptiles.htm

10. **Endangered Reptiles and Amphibians.** This site provides information on threatened and endangered reptiles and amphibians.
   http://www.pythons.com/end-sp.html

chapter ③⓪

BIRDS:
FEATHERS, FLIGHT, AND ENDOTHERMY

Concepts

1. Fossils of the earliest birds clearly show reptilian features. Fossils of *Archaeopteryx*, *Sinornis*, and *Eoalulavis* give clues to the origin of flight in birds.
2. Integumentary, skeletal, muscular, and gas exchange systems of birds are adapted for flight and endothermic temperature regulation.
3. Large regions of the brain of birds are devoted to integrating sensory information.
4. Birds' complex mating systems and behavioral patterns increase the chances of offspring survival.
5. Migration and navigation allow birds to live, feed, and reproduce in environments favorable to survival of adults and young.

Would You Like to Know . . .

1. what ancient animal is the earliest known bird? (p. 489)
2. how flight evolved in birds? (p. 489)
3. how a bird can sleep without falling from its perch? (p. 492)
4. how wings create enough lift to get a bird off the ground? (p. 493)
5. how an osprey diving for a fish keeps the fish in focus throughout the dive? (p. 498)
6. how birds navigate during migration? (p. 502)

This chapter answers these and other useful questions.

This chapter contains evolutionary concepts, which are set off in this font.

EVOLUTIONARY PERSPECTIVE

Drawings of birds on the walls of caves in southern France and Spain, bird images of ancient Egyptian and American cultures, and the bird images in Biblical writings are evidence that humans have marveled at birds and bird flight for thousands of years. From Leonardo da Vinci's early drawings of flying machines (1490) to Orville Wright's first successful powered flight on 17 December 1903, humans have tried to take to the sky and experience soaring like a bird.

Birds' ability to navigate long distances between breeding and wintering grounds is just as impressive as flight. For example, Arctic terns have a migratory route that takes them from the Arctic to the Antarctic and back again each year, a distance of approximately 35,000 km (figure 30.1). Their rather circuitous route takes them across the northern Atlantic Ocean, to the coast of Europe and Africa, and then across vast stretches of the southern Atlantic Ocean before they reach their wintering grounds.

PHYLOGENETIC RELATIONSHIPS

Birds are traditionally classified as members of the class Aves (a'ves) (L. *avis*, bird). The major characteristics of this class are adaptations for flight, including appendages modified as wings, feathers, endothermy, a high metabolic rate, a vertebral column modified for flight, and bones lightened by numerous air spaces. In addition, modern birds possess a horny bill and lack teeth.

The similarities between birds and reptiles are so striking that birds are often referred to as "glorified reptiles." Like the crocodilians, birds have descended from ancient archosaurs. Other flying reptiles in this evolutionary lineage (e.g., pterosaurs and pterodactyls) are ruled out of bird ancestry because these reptiles lost an important avian feature, the clavicles, long before birds appeared. (The fused clavicles, or "wishbone," is one of the attachment points for flight muscles. Thus, these reptiles could not have been as strong at flying as are modern birds.) In addition, instead of feathered wings, the flight surfaces of the wings of these primitive reptiles were membranous folds of skin. Modern birds are derived from the Saurischian lineage of dinosaurs that also included bipedal carnivorous dinosaurs like *Tyrannosaurus*. According to cladistic interpretations (*see figure 29.2*), the birds can be thought of as modern dinosaurs.

ANCIENT BIRDS AND THE EVOLUTION OF FLIGHT

In 1861, one of the most important vertebrate fossils was found in a slate quarry in Bavaria, Germany (figure 30.2). It was a fossil of a pigeon-sized animal that lived during the Jurassic period, about 150 million years ago. It had a long, reptilian tail and clawed fingers. The complete head of this specimen was not preserved, but imprints of feathers on the tail and on short, rounded wings were the

(a)

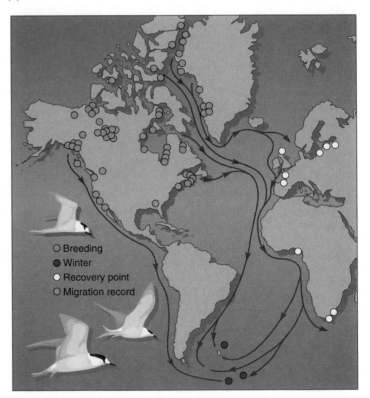

○ Breeding
● Winter
◑ Recovery point
○ Migration record

(b)

FIGURE 30.1

Class Aves. (*a*) The birds were derived from the archosaur lineage of ancient reptiles. Adaptations for flight include appendages modified as wings, feathers, endothermy, a high metabolic rate, a vertebral column modified for flight, and bones lightened by numerous airspaces. Flight has given birds, like this Arctic tern (*Sterna arctica*), the ability to exploit resources unavailable to other vertebrates. (*b*) Migration route of the Arctic tern. Arctic terns breed in northern North America, Greenland, and the Arctic. Migrating birds cross the Atlantic Ocean on their trip to wintering grounds in Antarctica. In the process, they fly about 35,000 km (22,000 mi) each year.

(a)

(b)

FIGURE 30.2

Archaeopteryx, an Ancient Bird. (a) *Archaeopteryx* fossil. (b) Artist's representation. Some zoologists think that *Archaeopteryx* was a ground dweller rather than the tree dweller depicted here.

main evidence that this was the fossil of an ancient bird. It was named *Archaeopteryx* (Gr. *archaios,* ancient + *pteron,* wing). Sixteen years later, a more complete fossil was discovered, revealing teeth in beaklike jaws. Four later discoveries of *Archaeopteryx* fossils have reinforced the ideas of reptilian ancestry for birds. ❶ Most zoologists consider *Archaeopteryx* to be the oldest bird yet discovered and very close to the main line of evolution between the reptiles and birds.

Interpretations of the lifestyle of *Archaeopteryx* have been important in the development of hypotheses on the origin of flight. The clavicles (wishbone) of *Archaeopteryx* were well developed and probably provided points of attachment for wing muscles. The sternum, wing bones, and other sites for flight muscle attachment

were less developed than in modern birds. These observations indicate that *Archaeopteryx* may have primarily been a glider that was capable of flapping flight over short distances.

❷ Some zoologists think that the clawed digits of the wings may have been used to climb trees and cling to branches. A sequence in the evolution of flight may have involved jumping from branch to branch, or branch to ground. At some later point, gliding evolved. Still later, weak flapping supplemented gliding, and finally, wing-powered flight evolved.

Other zoologists note that the hindlimb structure of the earliest birds suggests that they may have been bipedal, running and hopping along the ground. Their wings may have functioned in batting flying insects out of the air or in trapping insects and other prey against the ground. The teeth and claws, which resemble talons of modern predatory birds, may have been used to grasp prey. Wings would have been useful in providing stability during horizontal jumps when pursuing prey, and they would also have allowed flight over short distances. The benefits of such flight may have led eventually to wing-powered flight.

A second ancient bird (*Sinornis*), which was recently discovered in China, fits well with the view that *Archaeopteryx* was closely related to ancestral bird stocks. *Sinornis* fossils are 135 million years old—only 15 million years younger than *Archaeopteryx.* In addition to some primitive dinosaur-like characteristics, *Sinornis* had characteristics similar to modern birds, including a shortened body and tail, and a sternum with a large surface area for flight muscles. The claws were reduced, and the forelimbs were modified to permit the folding of wings at rest. These characteristics all indicate that powered flight was well developed in birds 135 million years ago.

A very recent discovery of a fossil bird from early Cretaceous deposits in Spain provides additional important information on the origin of flight. This bird, *Eoalulavis,* was found in 115-million-year-old deposits and had a wing span of 17 cm (roughly the same as a goldfinch). This fossil showed that *Eoalulavis* had a wing structure called an alula. As described later in this chapter, the alula is present in many modern birds that engage in slow, hovering flight. Its presence in this fossil indicates that complex flight mechanisms associated with slow, hovering, and highly maneuverable flight evolved at least 115 million years ago.

DIVERSITY OF MODERN BIRDS

Archaeopteryx, Sinornis, and *Eoalulavis* provide the only evidence of the transition between reptiles and birds. Zoologists do not know, however, whether or not one of these birds is the direct ancestor of modern birds. A variety of fossil birds for the period between 100 million and 70 million years ago has been found. Some of these birds were large, flightless birds; others were adapted for swimming and diving; and some were fliers. Most, like *Archaeopteryx,* had reptilelike teeth. Most of the lineages that these fossils represent became extinct, along with the dinosaurs, at the end of the Mesozoic era.

TABLE 30.1   CLASSIFICATION OF THE BIRDS

Class Aves (a′ves) (L. *avis*, bird)*
Adaptations for flight include: foreappendages modified as feathered wings, endothermic, high metabolic rate, flexible neck, fused posterior vertebrae, and bones lightened by numerous air spaces. The skull is lightened by a reduction in bone and the presence of a horny bill that lacks teeth. The birds.

Order Sphenisciformes (sfe-nis″i-for′mez)
Heavy bodied; flightless, flipperlike wings for swimming; well insulated with fat. Penguins.

Order Struthioniformes (stroo″the-on-i-for′mez)
Large, flightless birds; wings with numerous fluffy plumes. Ostriches.

Order Rheiformes (re″i-for′mez)
Large, flightless birds; degenerate wings with soft, loose plumes. Rheas.

Order Casuariiformes (kaz″u-ar″e-i-for′mez)
Reduced wings; coarse and hairlike plumage. Cassowaries, emus.

Order Gaviiformes (ga″ve-i-for′mez)
Strong, straight bill; diving adaptations include legs far back on body, bladelike tarsus, webbed feet, and heavy bones. Loons.

Order Podicipediformes (pod″i-si-ped″i-for′mez)
Short wings; soft and dense plumage; feet webbed with flattened nails. Grebes.

Order Procellariiformes (pro-sel-lar-e-i-for′mez)
Tubular nostrils, large nasal glands; long and narrow wings. Albatrosses, shearwaters, petrels.

Order Pelecaniformes (pel″e-can-i-for′mez)
Four toes joined in common web; nostrils rudimentary or absent; large gular sac. Pelicans, boobies, cormorants, anhingas, frigatebirds.

Order Ciconiiformes (si-ko″ne-i-for′mez)
Long neck, often folded in flight; long-legged waders. Herons, egrets, storks, wood ibises, flamingos.

Order Anseriformes (an″ser-i-for′mez)
South American screamers, ducks, geese, and swans; the latter possess a wide, flat bill and an undercoat of dense down; webbed feet; worldwide.

Order Falconiformes (fal″ko-ni-for′mez)
Strong, hooked beak; large wings; raptorial feet. Vultures, secretarybirds, hawks, eagles, ospreys, falcons.

Order Galliformes (gal″li-for′mez)
Short beak; short, concave wings; strong feet and claws. Curassows, grouse, quail, pheasants, turkeys.

Order Gruiformes (gru″i-for′mez)
Order characteristics variable and not diagnostic. Marsh birds, including cranes, limpkins, rails, coots.

Order Charadriiformes (ka-rad″re-i-for′mez)
Order characteristics variable. Shorebirds, gulls, terns, auks.

Order Columbiformes (co-lum″bi-for′mez)
Dense feathers loosely set in skin; well-developed crop. Pigeons, doves, sandgrouse.

Order Psittaciformes (sit″ta-si-for′mez)
Maxilla hinged to skull; thick tongue; reversible fourth toe; usually brightly colored. Parrots, lories, macaws.

Order Cuculiformes (ku-koo″li-for′mez)
Reversible fourth toe; soft, tender skin; Plantaineaters, roadrunners, cuckoos.

Order Strigiformes (strij″i-for′mez)
Large head with fixed eyes directed forward; raptorial foot. Owls.

Order Caprimulgiformes (kap″ri-mul″ji-for′mez)
Owl-like head and plumage, but weak bill and feet; beak with wide gape; insectivorous. Whippoorwills, other goatsuckers.

Order Apodiformes (a-pod″i-for′mez)
Long wings; weak feet. Swifts, hummingbirds.

Order Coraciiformes (kor″ah-si″ah-for′mez)
Large head; large beak; metallic plumage. Kingfishers, todies, bee eaters, rollers.

Order Piciformes (pis″i-for′mez)
Usually long strong beak; strong legs and feet with fourth toe permanently reversed in woodpeckers. Woodpeckers, toucans, honeyguides, barbets.

Order Passeriformes (pas″er-i-for′mez)
Largest avian order; 69 families of perching birds; perching foot; variable external features. Swallows, larks, crows, titmice, nuthatches, and many others.

*Selected bird orders are described.

Some of the few birds that survived into the Tertiary period were the ancestors of modern, toothless birds. The phylogeny of modern birds is controversial. It is sufficient to say that adaptive radiation has resulted in about 9,100 species of living birds, which are divided into about 27 orders (table 30.1). (The number of orders varies, depending on the classification system used.) Characteristic behaviors, songs, anatomical differences, and ecological niches distinguish the orders.

Stop and Ask Yourself

1. What are characteristics of the class Aves?
2. What characteristics of *Archaeopteryx* are reptilelike?
3. What are two hypotheses for the origin of flight in birds? What aspects of the structure of *Archaeopteryx* support each hypothesis?

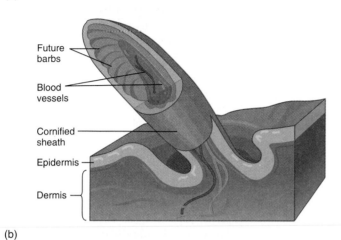

(b)

FIGURE 30.3

Formation of Bird Feathers during Embryonic Development.
(*a*) Feathers form from epidermal evaginations. (*b*) Later in development, the blood supply to the feather is cut off and the feather becomes a dead, keratinized, epidermal structure seated in a feather follicle.

FIGURE 30.4

Anatomy of Selected Feather Types. (*a*) Anatomy of a contour feather, showing enlargements of barbs and barbules. (*b*) Down feather. Various types of down feathers provide insulation for adult and immature birds. (*c*) Contour feather with an aftershaft. (*d*) Filoplume. Filoplume feathers are usually covered by contour feathers and are associated with nerve endings in the skin, thus serving as sensory structures.

EVOLUTIONARY PRESSURES

Virtually every body system of a bird shows some adaptation for flight. Endothermy, feathers, acute senses, long flexible necks, and lightweight bones are a few of the many adaptations described in this section.

EXTERNAL STRUCTURE AND LOCOMOTION

The covering of feathers on a bird is called the plumage. Feathers have two primary functions essential for flight. They form the flight surfaces that provide lift and aid steering, and they prevent excessive heat loss, permitting the endothermic maintenance of high metabolic rates. Feathers also have roles in courtship, incubation, and waterproofing.

Feathers develop in a fashion similar to epidermal scales of reptiles, and this similarity is one source of evidence that demonstrates the evolutionary ties between reptiles and birds (figure 30.3; *see box 29.2*). Only the inner pulp of feathers contains dermal elements, such as blood vessels, which supply nutrients and pigments for the growing feather. As feathers mature, their blood supply is cut off, and the feathers become dead, keratinized, epidermal structures seated in epidermal invaginations of the skin called feather follicles.

The most obvious feathers are **contour feathers,** which cover the body, wings, and tail (figure 30.4*a, c*). Contour feathers consist of a vane with its inner and outer webs, and a supportive shaft. Feather barbs branch off the shaft, and barbules branch off the barbs. Barbules of adjacent barbs overlap one another. The ends of barbules lock with hooklike hamuli (sing., hamulus). Interlocking barbs keep contour feathers firm and smooth. Other types of feathers include **down feathers,** which function as insulating feathers, and **filoplume feathers** (pinfeather), which have sensory functions (figure 30.4*b, d*).

Birds maintain a clean plumage to rid the feathers and skin of parasites. Preening, which is done by rubbing the bill over the feathers, keeps the feathers smooth, clean, and in place. Hamuli that become dislodged can be rehooked by running a feather through the bill. Secretions from an oil gland at the base of the tail of many birds are spread over the feathers during preening to keep the plumage water repellent and supple. The secretions also lubricate the bill and legs to prevent chafing. Anting is a maintenance behavior common to many songbirds and involves picking up ants in the bill and rubbing them over the feathers. The formic acid that ants secrete is apparently toxic to feather mites.

Feather pigments deposited during feather formation produce most colors in a bird's plumage. Other colors, termed

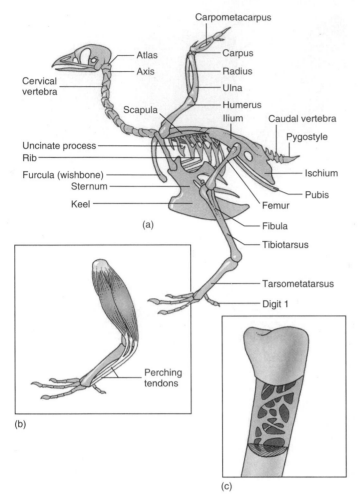

FIGURE 30.5

Bird Skeleton. (*a*) Skeleton of a pigeon. (*b*) Perching tendons run from the toes across the back of the ankle joint, which cause the foot to grip a perch. (*c*) Internal structure of the humerus.

structural colors, arise from irregularities on the surface of the feather that diffract white light. For example, blue feathers are never blue because of the presence of blue pigment. A porous, nonpigmented outer layer on a barb reflects blue wavelengths of light. The other wavelengths pass into the barb and are absorbed by the dark pigment melanin. Iridescence results from the interference of light waves caused by a flattening and twisting of barbules. An example of iridescence is the perception of interchanging colors on the neck and back of hummingbirds and grackles. Color patterns are involved in cryptic coloration, species and sex recognition, and sexual attraction.

Mature feathers receive constant wear; thus, all birds periodically shed and replace their feathers in a process called **molting.** The timing of molt periods varies in different taxa. The following is a typical molting pattern for songbirds. After hatching, a chick is covered with down. Juvenile feathers replace the down at the postnatal molt. A postjuvenile molt in the fall results in plumage similar to that of the adult. Once sexual maturity is attained, a prenuptial molt occurs in late winter or early spring, prior to the breeding season. A postnuptial molt usually occurs be-

tween July and October. Flight feathers are frequently lost in a particular sequence so that birds are not wholly deprived of flight during molt periods. However, many ducks, coots, and rails cannot fly during molt periods and hide in thick marsh grasses.

The Skeleton

The bones of most birds are lightweight yet strong. Some bones, such as the humerus (forearm bone), have large air spaces and internal strutting (reinforcing bony bars), which increase strength (figure 30.5*c*). (Engineers take advantage of this same principle. They have discovered that a strutted girder is stronger than a solid girder of the same weight.) Birds also have a reduced number of skull bones, and a lighter, keratinized sheath called a bill replaces the teeth. The demand for lightweight bones for flight is countered in some birds with other requirements. For example, some aquatic birds (e.g., loons) have dense bones, which help reduce buoyancy during diving.

The appendages involved in flight cannot manipulate nesting materials or feed young. The bill and very flexible neck make these activities possible. The cervical vertebrae have saddle-shaped articular surfaces that permit great freedom of movement. In addition, the first cervical vertebra (the atlas) has a single point of articulation with the skull (the occipital condyle), which permits a high degree of rotational movement between the skull and the neck. (The single occipital condyle is another characteristic that birds share with reptiles.) This flexibility allows the bill and neck to function as a fifth appendage.

The pelvic girdle, vertebral column, and ribs are strengthened for flight. The thoracic region of the vertebral column contains ribs, which attach to thoracic vertebrae. The ribs have posteriorly directed uncinate processes that overlap the next rib to strengthen the rib cage (figure 30.5*a*). (Uncinate processes are also present on the ribs of most reptiles and are additional evidence of their common ancestry.) Posterior to the thoracic region is the lumbar region. The **synsacrum** forms by the fusion of the posterior thoracic vertebrae, all the lumbar and sacral vertebrae, and the anterior caudal vertebrae. Fusion of these bones helps maintain the proper flight posture and supports the hind appendages during landing, hopping, and walking. The posterior caudal vertebrae are fused into a **pygostyle,** which helps support the tail feathers that are important in steering.

The sternum of most birds bears a large, median keel for the attachment of flight muscles. (Exceptions to this include some flightless birds, such as ostriches.) The keel attaches firmly to the rest of the axial skeleton by the ribs. Paired clavicles fuse medially and ventrally into a **furcula** (wishbone).

The appendages of birds have also been modified. Some bones of the front appendages have been lost or fused, and are points of attachment of flight feathers. The rear appendages are used for hopping, walking, running, and perching. Perching tendons run from the toes across the back of the ankle joint to muscles of the lower leg. When the ankle joint is flexed, as in landing on a perch, tension on the perching tendons increases, and the foot grips the perch (figure 30.5*b*). ❸ This automatic grasp helps a bird perch even while sleeping. The muscles of the lower leg can increase the tension on these tendons, for example, when an eagle grasps a fish in its talons.

Muscles

The largest, strongest muscles of most birds are the flight muscles. They attach to the sternum and clavicles, and run to the humerus. The muscles of most birds are adapted physiologically for flight. Flight muscles must contract quickly and fatigue very slowly. These muscles have many mitochondria and produce large quantities of ATP to provide the energy required for flight, especially long-distance migrations. Domestic fowl have been selectively bred for massive amounts of muscle that humans like as food but that is poorly adapted for flight because it contains rapidly contracting fibers with few mitochondria and poor vascularization.

Flight

The wings of birds are adapted for different kinds of flight. However, regardless of whether a bird soars, glides, or has a rapid flapping flight, the mechanics of staying aloft are similar. Bird wings form an **airfoil.** The anterior margin of the wing is thicker than the posterior margin. The upper surface of the wing is slightly convex, and the lower surface is flat or slightly concave. ④ Air passing over the wing travels farther and faster than air passing under the wing, decreasing air pressure on the upper surface of the wing and creating lift (figure 30.6a). The lift the wings create must overcome the bird's weight, and the forces that propel the bird forward must overcome the drag that the bird moving through the air creates. Increasing the angle that the leading edge of the wing makes with the oncoming air (the angle of attack) increases lift. As the angle of attack increases, however, the flow of air over the upper surface becomes turbulent, reducing lift (figure 30.6b). Turbulence is reduced if air can flow rapidly through slots at the leading edge of the wing. Slotting the feathers at the wing tips and the presence of an alula on the anterior margin of the wing reduce turbulence. The **alula** is a group of small feathers that bones of the medial digit support. During takeoff, landing, and hovering flight, the angle of attack increases, and the alula is elevated (figure 30.6c,e). During soaring and fast flight, the angle of attack decreases, and slotting is reduced.

The distal part of the wing generates most of the propulsive force of flight. Because it is farther from the shoulder joint, the distal part of the wing moves farther and faster than the proximal part of the wing. During the downstroke (the powerstroke), the leading edge of the distal part of the wing is oriented slightly downward and creates a thrust somewhat analogous to the thrust that an airplane propeller creates (figure 30.6d). During the upstroke (the recovery stroke), the distal part of the wing is oriented upward to decrease resistance. Feathers on a wing overlap so that, on the downstroke, air presses the feathers at the wing margins together, allowing little air to pass between them, enhancing both lift and propulsive forces. Feathers part slightly on the upstroke, allowing air to pass between them, which reduces resistance during the recovery stroke.

FIGURE 30.6

Mechanics of Bird Flight. (*a*) A bird's wing acts as an airfoil. Air passing over the top of the wing travels farther and faster than air passing under the wing, creating lift. (*b*) Increasing the angle of attack increases lift but also increases turbulence. (*c*) The alula reduces turbulence. (*d*) Wing orientation during a downstroke. (*e*) Note the alula on the wings of this golden eagle (*Aquila chrysaetos*).

BOX 30.1   SAILORS' CURSE—GLIDERS' ENVY

Albatrosses are known by many, not very complimentary names. Dutch sailors called them mollymawks ("stupid gull"), the English call them goonies (another reference to stupidity), and the Japanese call them bakadori ("foul birds"). These names are probably the result of the bird's inexpressive facial features and awkward movements on land. The appearance of an albatross alongside a ship was believed to be a sure sign of changing winds. As the old sailor with "a long grey beard and glittering eye" discovered, killing an albatross brought extremely bad luck (*The Rime of the Ancient Mariner* by Samuel Coleridge, 1798.) His deadly aim with a crossbow caused the winds to die, and all sailors on the becalmed ship, except the mariner, died of thirst. The mariner was forced to sail on alone with the albatross hung around his neck.

> And I had done an hellish thing
> And it would work 'em woe:
> For all averr'd, I had kill'd the Bird
> That made the Breeze to blow.
> Ah wretch! said they, the bird to slay,
> That made the breeze to blow!

The origin of the superstition that associated the albatross with breezes is not difficult to understand. The albatross has relatively poorly developed flight muscles and relies primarily on soaring flight and wind to keep aloft (figure 1). Most species of albatross are found around the Antarctic, where breezes are almost constant and they can launch themselves from cliffs into the air with minimal flapping flight. They soar swiftly downwind, picking up speed and losing altitude. Just above the water's surface, they turn sharply into the wind and use the oncoming wind to soar higher. When air speed drops, they turn again to move downwind. Under favorable winds, an albatross can follow a ship for many miles, zigzagging upwind and downwind, without flapping their long, narrow wings. The sight of a soaring albatross usually does mean a favorable sailing breeze!

FIGURE 1   **Albatross in Flight.** An albatross (*Diomedea irrorata*) uses wind currents to soar around the Southern Hemisphere.

When grounded in calm winds, an albatross experiences great difficulty becoming airborne again. It must run along the ground, flapping its wings, until it reaches air speed adequate for takeoff.

Albatrosses feed on fishes and invertebrates near the ocean's surface and on refuse tossed from ships. After a courtship dance and mating, the female lays a single egg in a mud nest. Incubation may last as long as 85 days and parental care another 3 to 9 months. After leaving the nest, young albatrosses depart the nesting grounds and circle their newly discovered world many times. (For most albatrosses, "their world" is the entire Southern Hemisphere!) Albatrosses reach sexual maturity after about 7 years, and some may live for up to 30 years.

The tail of a bird serves a variety of balancing, steering, and braking functions during flight. It also enhances lift that the wings produce during low-speed flight. During horizontal flight, spreading the tail feathers increases lift at the rear of the bird and causes the head to dip for descent. Closing the tail feathers has the opposite effect. Tilting the tail sideways turns the bird. When a bird lands, its tail deflects downward, serving as an air brake. In the males of some species—for example, sunbirds (*Nectarinia*) and widow birds (*Euplectes*)—tails possess dramatic ornamentation that attracts females and improves reproductive success.

Different birds, or the same bird at different times, use different kinds of flight. During gliding flight, the wing is stationary, and a bird loses altitude. Waterfowl coming in for a landing use gliding flight. Flapping flight generates the power for flight and is the most common type of flying. Many variations in wing shape

and flapping patterns result in species-specific speed and maneuverability. Soaring flight allows some birds to remain airborne with little energy expenditure. During soaring, wings are essentially stationary, and the bird utilizes updrafts and air currents to gain altitude. Hawks, vultures, and other soaring birds are frequently observed circling along mountain valleys, soaring downwind to pick up speed and then turning upwind to gain altitude. As the bird slows and begins to lose altitude, it turns downwind again. The wings of many soarers are wide and slotted to provide maximum maneuverability at relatively low speeds. Oceanic soarers, such as albatrosses and frigate birds, have long, narrow wings that provide maximum lift at high speeds, but they compromise maneuverability and ease of takeoff and landing (box 30.1). Hummingbirds perform hovering flight. They hover in still air by fanning their wings back and forth (50 to 80 beats per second) to remain suspended in front of a flower or feeding station.

FIGURE 30.7

Bird Flight and Feeding Adaptations. This ruby-throated hummingbird (*Archilochus colubris*) hovers while feeding on flower nectar. Hummingbird beaks often match the length and curvature of the flower from which the birds extract nectar.

NUTRITION AND THE DIGESTIVE SYSTEM

Most birds have ravenous appetites! This appetite supports a high metabolic rate that makes endothermy and flight possible. For example, hummingbirds feed almost constantly during the day. In spite of high rates of food consumption, they often cannot sustain their rapid metabolism overnight, and they may become torpid, with reduced body temperature and respiratory rate, until they can feed again in the morning.

Bird bills and tongues are modified for a variety of feeding habits and food sources (figures 30.7 and 30.8). For example, a woodpecker's tongue is barbed for extracting grubs from the bark of trees (*see figure 37.6d*). Sapsuckers excavate holes in trees and use a brushlike tongue for licking the sap that accumulates in these holes. The tongues of hummingbirds and other nectar feeders roll into a tube for extracting nectar from flowers.

In many birds, a diverticulum of the esophagus, called the crop, is a storage structure that allows birds to quickly ingest large quantities of locally abundant food. They can then seek safety while digesting their meal. The crop of pigeons produces "pigeon's milk," a cheesy secretion formed by the proliferation and sloughing of cells lining the crop. Young pigeons (squabs) feed on pigeon's milk until they are able to eat grain. Cedar waxwings, vultures, and birds of prey use their esophagus for similar storage functions. Crops are less well developed in insect-eating birds because insectivorous birds feed throughout the day on sparsely distributed food.

The stomach of birds is modified into two regions. The proventriculus secretes gastric juices that initiate digestion (figure 30.9). The ventriculus (gizzard) has muscular walls to abrade and

(a)

(b)

(c)

FIGURE 30.8

Some Specializations of Bird Bills. (*a*) The bill of a bald eagle (*Haliacetus leucocephalus*) is specialized for tearing prey. (*b*) The thick, powerful bill of this cardinal (*Cardinalis cardinalis*) cracks tough seeds. (*c*) The bill of a flamingo (*Phoenicopterus ruber*) strains food from the water in a head-down feeding posture. Large bristles fringe the upper and lower mandibles. As water is sucked into the bill, larger particles are filtered and left outside. Inside the bill, tiny inner bristles filter smaller algae and animals. The tongue removes food from the bristles.

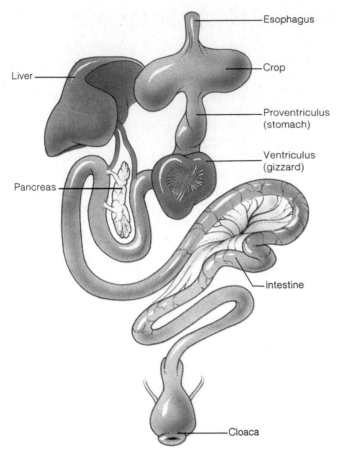

FIGURE 30.9

Digestive System of a Pigeon. Birds have high metabolic rates that require a nearly constant nutrient supply.

crush seeds or other hard materials. Birds may swallow sand and other abrasives to aid digestion. The bulk of enzymatic digestion and absorption occurs in the small intestine, aided by secretions from the pancreas and liver. Paired ceca may be located at the union of the large and small intestine. These blind-ending sacs contain bacteria that aid in cellulose digestion. Birds usually eliminate undigested food through the cloaca; however, owls form pellets of bone, fur, and feathers that are ejected from the ventriculus through the mouth. Owl pellets accumulate in and around owl nests and are useful in studying their food habits.

Birds are often grouped by their feeding habits. These groupings are somewhat artificial, however, because birds may eat different kinds of food at different stages in their life history, or they may change diets simply because of changes in food availability. Robins, for example, feed largely on worms and other invertebrates when these foods are available. In the winter, however, robins may feed on berries.

In some of their feeding habits, birds directly conflict with human interests. Bird damage to orchard and grain crops is tallied in the millions of dollars each year. Flocking and roosting habits of some birds, such as European starlings and redwing blackbirds,

concentrate millions of birds in local habitats, where they devastate fields of grain. Recent monocultural practices tend to aggravate problems with grain-feeding birds by encouraging the formation of very large flocks.

Birds of prey have minimal impact on populations of poultry and game birds, and on commercial fisheries. Unfortunately, the mistaken impression that they are responsible for significant losses has led humans to poison and shoot them.

CIRCULATION, GAS EXCHANGE, AND TEMPERATURE REGULATION

The circulatory system of birds is similar to that of reptiles, except that the heart has completely separated atria and ventricles, resulting in separate pulmonary and systemic circuits. This separation prevents any mixing of highly oxygenated blood with less oxygenated blood. In vertebrate evolution, the sinus venosus has gradually decreased in size. It is a separate chamber in fishes, amphibians, and turtles and receives blood from the venous system. In other reptiles, it is a group of cells in the right atrium that serves as the pacemaker for the heart. In birds, the sinus venosus also persists only as a patch of pacemaker tissue in the right atrium. The bird heart is relatively large (up to 2.4% of total body weight), and it beats rapidly. Rates in excess of 1,000 beats per minute have been recorded for hummingbirds under stress. Larger birds have relatively smaller hearts and slower heart rates. The heart rate of an ostrich, for example, varies between 38 and 176 beats per minute. A large heart, rapid heart rate, and complete separation of highly oxygenated from less oxygenated blood are important adaptations for delivering the large quantities of blood required for endothermy and flight.

Gas Exchange

The respiratory system of birds is extremely complex and efficient. It consists of external nares, which lead to nasal passageways and the pharynx. Bone and cartilage support the trachea. A special voice box, called the **syrinx,** is located where the trachea divides into bronchi. The muscles of the syrinx and bronchi, as well as characteristics of the trachea, produce bird vocalizations. The bronchi lead to a complex system of air sacs that occupy much of the body and extend into some of the bones of the skeletal system (figure 30.10a). The air sacs and bronchi connect to the lungs. The lungs of birds are made of small air tubes called **parabronchi.** Air capillaries about 10 μm in diameter branch from the parabronchi and are associated with capillary beds for gas exchange.

Inspiration and expiration result from increasing and decreasing the volume of the thorax and from alternate expansion and compression of air sacs during flight and other activities. During breathing, the movement of the sternum and the posterior ribs compresses the thoracic air sacs. X-ray movies of European starlings in a wind tunnel show that contraction of flight muscles distorts the furcula. Alternate distortion and recoiling helps

(c)

FIGURE 30.10

Respiratory System of a Bird. (a) Air sacs branch from the respiratory tree. (b) Air flow during inspiration and expiration. Air flows through the parabronchi during both inspiration and expiration. The shading represents the movement through the lungs of one inspiration. (c) Scanning electron micrograph of parabronchi.

compress and expand air sacs between the bone's two shafts. During inspiration, air moves into the abdominal air sacs. At the same time, air already in the lungs moves through parabronchi into the thoracic air sacs (figure 30.10*b*, cycle 1). During expiration, the air in the thoracic air sacs moves out of the respiratory system, and the air in the abdominal air sacs moves into parabronchi (figure 30.10*c*). At the next inspiration (figure 30.10*b*, cycle 2), the air moves into the thoracic air sacs, and it is expelled during the next expiration. It takes two ventilatory cycles to move a particular volume of air through the respiratory system of a bird.

Because of high metabolic rates associated with flight, birds have a greater rate of oxygen consumption than any other vertebrate. When other tetrapods inspire and expire, air passes into and out of respiratory passageways in a simple back-and-forth cycle. Ventilation is interrupted during expiration, and much "dead air" (air not forced out during expiration) remains in the lungs. Because of the unique system of air sacs and parabronchi, bird lungs have a nearly continuous movement of oxygen-rich air over respiratory surfaces during both inspiration and expiration. The quantity of "dead air" in the lungs is sharply reduced, compared with other vertebrates.

This avian system of gas exchange is more efficient than that of any other tetrapod. In addition to supporting high metabolic rates, this efficient gas exchange system probably also explains how birds can live and fly at high altitudes, where oxygen tensions are low. During their migrations, bar-headed geese fly over the peaks of the Himalayas at altitudes of 9,200 m. A human mountain climber begins to feel the symptoms of altitude sickness and must carry auxiliary oxygen supplies above 2,500 m.

Thermoregulation

Birds maintain body temperatures between 38 and 45° C. Lethal extremes are lower than 32 and higher than 47° C. On a cold day, a resting bird fluffs its feathers to increase their insulating properties, as well as the dead air space within them. It also tucks its bill into its feathers to reduce heat loss from the respiratory tract. The most exposed parts of a bird are the feet and tarsi, which have neither fleshy muscles nor a rich blood supply. Temperatures in these extremities are allowed to drop near freezing to prevent heat loss. Countercurrent heat exchange between the warm blood flowing to the legs and feet, and the cooler blood flowing to the body core from the legs and feet, prevents excessive heat loss at the feet. Heat is returned to the body core before it goes to the extremities and is lost to the environment (*see figure* 38.5*b*). Shivering also generates heat in extreme cold. Increases in metabolism during winter months require additional food.

Some birds become torpid and allow their body temperatures to drop on cool nights. For example, whippoorwills allow their body temperatures to drop from about 40° C to near 16° C, and respiratory rates become very slow.

Muscular activity during flight produces large quantities of heat, which birds can dissipate by panting. Evaporative heat loss

FIGURE 30.11

Barn Owl (Tyto alba). A keen sense of hearing allows barn owls to find prey in spite of the darkness of night.

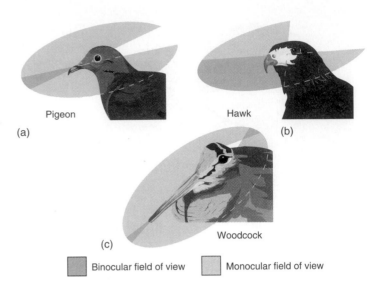

Binocular field of view   Monocular field of view

FIGURE 30.12

Avian Vision. The fields of view of (a) a pigeon, (b) a hawk, and (c) a woodcock. Woodcocks have eyes located far posteriorly and have a narrow field of binocular vision in front and behind. They can focus on predators circling above them while probing mud with their long beaks.

NERVOUS AND SENSORY SYSTEMS

A mouse, enveloped in the darkness of night, skitters across the floor of a barn. An owl in the loft overhead turns in the direction of the faint sounds the tiny feet make. As the sounds made by hurrying feet change to a scratchy gnawing of teeth on a sack of feed, the barn owl dives for its prey (figure 30.11). Fluted tips of flight feathers make the owl's approach imperceptible to the mouse, and the owl's ears, not its eyes, guide it to its prey. Barn owls successfully locate and capture prey in over 75% of attempts! This ability is just one example of the many sensory adaptations of birds.

The forebrain of birds is much larger than that of reptiles due to the enlargement of the cerebral hemispheres, including a region of gray matter, the corpus striatum. The corpus striatum functions in visual learning, feeding, courtship, and nesting. A pineal body on the roof of the forebrain appears to stimulate ovarian development and to regulate other functions influenced by light and dark periods. The optic tectum (the roof of the midbrain), along with the corpus striatum, plays an important role in integrating sensory functions. The midbrain also receives sensory input from the eyes. As in reptiles, the hindbrain includes the cerebellum and the medulla oblongata, which coordinate motor activities and regulate heart and respiratory rates, respectively.

Vision is an important sense for most birds. The structure of bird eyes is similar to that of other vertebrates, but bird eyes are much larger relative to body size than those of other vertebrates (see figure 28.14). The eyes are usually somewhat flattened in an anteroposterior direction; however, the eyes of birds of prey pro-

trude anteriorly because of a bulging cornea. Birds have a unique double-focusing mechanism. Padlike structures (similar to those of reptiles) control the curvature of the lens, and ciliary muscles change the curvature of the cornea.   ⑤ Double, nearly instantaneous focusing allows an osprey or other bird of prey to remain focused on a fish throughout a brief, but breathtakingly fast, descent.

The retina of a bird's eye is thick and contains both rods and cones. Rods are active under low light intensities, and cones are active under high light intensities. Cones are especially concentrated ($1,000,000/mm^2$) at a focal point called the fovea. Unlike other vertebrates, some birds have two foveae per eye. The one at the center of the retina is sometimes called the "search fovea" because it gives the bird a wide angle of monocular vision. The other fovea is at the posterior margin of the retina. It functions with the posterior fovea of the other eye to allow binocular vision. The posterior fovea is called the "pursuit fovea" because binocular vision produces depth perception, which is necessary to capture prey. The words "search" and "pursuit" are not meant to imply that only predatory birds have these two foveae. Other birds use the "search fovea" to observe the landscape below them during flight and the "pursuit" fovea when depth perception is needed, as in landing on a branch of a tree.

The position of the eyes on the head also influences the degree of binocular vision (figure 30.12). Pigeons have eyes located well back on the sides of their head, giving them a nearly 360° monocular field, but a narrow binocular field. They do not have to pursue their food (grain), and a wide monocular field of view helps them stay alert to predators while feeding on the ground. Hawks and owls have eyes farther forward on the head. This increases their binocular field of view and correspondingly decreases their monocular field of view.

Like reptiles, birds have a nictitating membrane that is drawn over the surface of the eye to cleanse and protect the eye.

Olfaction apparently plays a minor role in the lives of most birds. External nares open near the base of the beak, but the olfactory epithelium is poorly developed. Exceptions include turkey vultures, which locate their dead and dying prey largely by smell.

In contrast, most birds have well-developed hearing. Loose, delicate feathers called auriculars cover the external ear opening. Middle- and inner-ear structures are similar to those of reptiles. The sensitivity of the avian ear (100 to 15,000 Hz) is similar to that of the human ear (16 to 20,000 Hz).

EXCRETION AND OSMOREGULATION

Birds and reptiles face essentially identical excretory and osmoregulatory demands. Like reptiles, birds excrete uric acid, which is temporarily stored in the cloaca. Water is also reabsorbed in the cloaca. As with reptiles, the excretion of uric acid conserves water and promotes embryo development in terrestrial environments. In addition, some birds have supraorbital salt glands that drain excess sodium chloride through the nasal openings to the outside of the body (*see box 38.3*). These are especially important in marine birds that drink seawater and feed on invertebrates containing large quantities of salt in their tissues. Salt glands can secrete salt in a solution that is two to three times more concentrated than other body fluids. Salt glands, therefore, compensate for the kidney's inability to concentrate salts in the urine.

Stop and Ask Yourself

8. What evolutionary remnant of the vertebrate sinus venosus is found in the heart of a bird? What is the function of this remnant?

9. How are the lungs of birds adapted to provide continuous, one-way movement of air across gas exchange surfaces?

10. How does a bird cool itself?

11. What is the value of separate "search" and "pursuit" foveae for a bird of prey?

REPRODUCTION AND DEVELOPMENT

Sexual activities of birds have been observed more closely than those of any other group of animals. These activities include establishing territories, finding mates, constructing nests, incubating eggs, and feeding young.

All birds are oviparous. Gonads are in the dorsal abdominal region, next to the kidneys. Testes are paired, and coiled tubules (vasa deferentia) conduct sperm to the cloaca. An enlargement of the vasa deferentia, the seminal vesicle, is a site for temporary storage and maturation of sperm prior to mating. Testes enlarge during the breeding season. Except for certain waterfowl and ostriches, birds have no intromittent organ, and sperm are transferred by cloacal contact when the male briefly mounts the female.

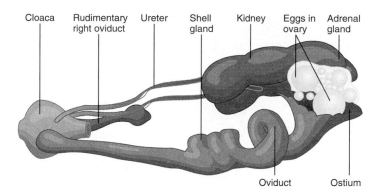

FIGURE 30.13

Urogenital System of a Female Pigeon. The right ovary and oviduct are rudimentary in most female birds.

In females, two ovaries form during development, but usually only the left ovary fully develops (figure 30.13). A large, funnel-shaped opening of the oviduct envelops the ovary and receives eggs after ovulation. The egg is fertilized in the upper portions of the oviduct, and albumen that glandular regions of the oviduct wall secrete gradually surrounds the zygote as it completes its passage. A shell gland in the lower region of the oviduct adds a shell. The oviduct opens into the cloaca.

Many birds establish territories prior to mating. Although size and function vary greatly among species, territories generally allow birds to mate without interference. They provide nest locations and sometimes food resources for adults and offspring. Breeding birds defend their territories and expel intruders of the same sex and species. Threats are common, but actual fighting is minimized.

Mating may follow the attraction of a mate to a territory. For example, male woodpeckers drum on trees to attract females. Male ruffed grouse fan their wings on logs and create sounds that can be heard for many miles. Cranes have a courtship dance that includes stepping, bowing, stretching, and jumping displays. Mating occurs when a mate's call or posture signals readiness. It happens quickly but repeatedly to assure fertilization of all the eggs that will be laid.

Over 90% of birds are **monogamous.** A single male pairs with a single female during the breeding season. Some birds (swans, geese, eagles) pair for life. Frequent mating apparently strengthens the pair bonds that develop. Monogamy is common when resources are widely and evenly distributed, and one bird cannot control access to resources. Monogamy is also advantageous because both parents usually participate in nest building and care of the young. One parent incubates and protects the eggs or chicks while the other searches for food.

Some birds are **polygynous.** Males mate with more than one female, and the females care for the eggs and chicks. Polygyny tends to occur in species whose young are less dependent at hatching and in situations where patchy resource distribution may attract many females to a relatively small breeding area. Prairie chickens are polygynous, and males display in groups called leks. In prairie chicken leks, the males in the center positions are preferred and attract the majority of females (figure 30.14).

FIGURE 30.14

Courtship Displays. A male greater prairie chicken (*Tympanuchus cupido*) displaying in a lek.

A few bird species are **polyandrous,** and the females mate with more than one male. For example, female spotted sandpipers are larger than males, and establish and defend their territories from other females. They lay a clutch of eggs for each male that is attracted to and builds a nest in their territory. If a male loses his eggs to a predator, the female replaces them. Polyandry results in the production of more eggs than in monogamous matings. It is thought to be advantageous when food is plentiful but, because of predation or other threats, the chances of successfully rearing young are low.

Nest construction usually begins after pair formation. The female usually initiates this instinctive behavior. A few birds do not make nests. Emperor penguins, for example, breed on the snow and ice of Antarctica, where no nest materials are available. Their single egg is incubated on the web of the foot (mostly the male's foot), tucked within a fold of abdominal skin.

Nesting Activities

The nesting behavior of birds is often species specific. Some birds choose nest sites away from other members of their species, and other birds nest in large flocks. Unfortunately, predictable nesting behavior has led to the extinction of some species of birds (box 30.2).

The group of eggs laid and chicks produced by a female is called a **clutch.** Clutch size usually varies. Most birds incubate their eggs, and some birds have a featherless, vascularized incubation or brood patch (*see figure 35.13*) that helps keep the eggs at

temperatures between 33 and 37° C. Birds turn the eggs to prevent egg membranes from adhering in the egg and deforming the embryo. Adults of some species sprinkle the eggs with water to cool and humidify them. The Egyptian plover carries water from distant sites in the breast feathers. The incubation period lasts between 10 and 80 days and correlates with egg size and degree of development at hatching. One or two days before hatching, the young bird penetrates an air sac at the blunt end of its egg, inflates its lungs, and begins breathing. Hatching occurs as the young bird pecks the shell with a keratinized egg tooth on the tip of the upper jaw and struggles to free itself.

Some birds are helpless at hatching; others are more independent. Those that are entirely dependent on their parents are said to be **altricial** (L. *altricialis*, to nourish), and they are often naked at hatching (figure 30.15*a*). Altricial young must be brooded constantly at first because endothermy is not developed. They grow rapidly, and when they leave the nest, they are nearly as large as their parents. For example, American robins weigh 4 to 6 g at hatching and leave the nest 13 days later weighing 57 g. **Precocial** (L. *praecoci*, early ripe) young are alert and lively at hatching (figure 30.15*b*). They are usually covered with down and can walk, run, swim, and feed themselves—although one parent is usually present to lead the young to food and shelter.

Young altricial birds have huge appetites and keep one or both parents continually searching for food. They may consume a mass of food that equals their own weight each day. Adults bring food to the nest or regurgitate food stored in the crop or esophagus. Vocal signals or color patterns on the bills or throats of adults initiate feeding responses in the young. Parents instinctively feed gaping mouths, and many hatchlings have brightly colored mouth linings that attract a parent's attention. The first-hatched young is fed first—most often because it is usually the largest and can stretch its neck higher than can its nestmates.

Life is usually brief for birds. About 50% of eggs laid yield birds that leave the nest. Most birds, if kept in captivity, have a potential life span of 10 to 20 years. Natural longevity is much shorter. The average American robin lives 1.3 years, and the average black-capped chickadee lives less than 1 year. Mortality is high in the first year from predators and inclement weather.

MIGRATION AND NAVIGATION

Over 20 centuries ago, Aristotle described birds migrating to escape the winter cold and summer heat. He had the mistaken impression that some birds disappear during winter because they hibernate and that others transmutate to another species. It is now known that some birds migrate long distances. Modern zoologists study the timing of migration, stimuli for migration, and physiological changes during migration, as well as migration routes and how birds navigate over huge expanses of land or water.

BOX 30.2   BRIGHT SKIES AND SILENT THUNDER

No tale in the history of human interactions with wildlife is sadder than that of *Ectopistes migratorius*, the passenger pigeon. Although the full story of the extinction of this bird may never be known, humans are responsible for the excessive slaughter that led to the decline of a vulnerable species.

In the nineteenth century, flocks of passenger pigeons were so vast in eastern North America that their numbers were estimated at up to 2 billion birds. In 1813, the famed naturalist John Audubon watched a flock of passenger pigeons pass overhead for 3 days. He reported that the flock completely darkened the sky by day and that their wings sounded like thunder.

How could a species so abundant become extinct in just a few decades? What made these birds so vulnerable was their social behavior. Passenger pigeons nested, roosted in the evening, and foraged for food in huge aggregations that covered thousands of acres. Trees became so laden with birds that their branches often broke under the weight. One nest site in Wisconsin was 100 miles long! On feeding forays, flocks traveled hundreds of miles and stripped trees of acorns, beechnuts, and other nuts. These colonies were apparently not just convenient associations, but were essential for survival. Highly organized flocks were also an important social stimulus for breeding.

Unfortunately, this behavior made the birds vulnerable. Nesting sites were predictable, and hunters came to them year after year. Professional hunters traveled from nest site to nest site during the nesting season. Birds were blinded at night with lights and knocked out of trees. They were captured in huge nets or choked by burning sulfur. Trees were felled, and the birds in them were harvested. They were shot by the thousands with guns. In 1861, 14,850,000 passenger pigeons were shipped to big-city markets from a single nesting site near Petoskey, Michigan.

How could any bird successfully reproduce and rear young under this onslaught? The single egg tended by a pair of passenger pigeons had little chance for survival during these unfortunate years. Flocks gradually dwindled. By the late 1890s, people began to realize that the passenger pigeons were in trouble. In addition to rampant killing and the resultant breakup of the social organization needed for successful mating, deforestation was contributing to the passenger pigeon's decline. Laws that prohibited further killing were too late. After 1900, no passenger pigeons were seen in the wild. "Martha," the last passenger pigeon in captivity (Cincinnati Zoological Gardens), died on 1 September 1914, after living for 29 years.

(a)

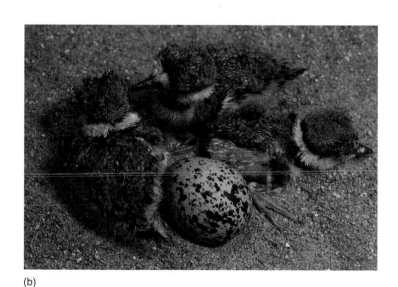

(b)

FIGURE 30.15

Altricial and Precocial Chicks. *(a)* An American robin (*Turdus migratorius*) feeding nestlings. Robins have altricial chicks that are helpless at hatching. *(b)* Killdeer (*Charadrius vociferus*) have precocial chicks that are down covered and can move about.

Migration (as used here) refers to periodic round trips between breeding and nonbreeding areas. Most migrations are annual, with nesting areas in northern regions and wintering grounds in the south. (Migration is more pronounced for species found in the Northern Hemisphere because about 70% of the earth's land is in the Northern Hemisphere.) Migrations occasionally involve east/west movements or altitude changes. Migration allows birds to avoid climatic extremes and to secure adequate food, shelter, and space throughout the year.

Birds migrate in response to species-specific physiological conditions. Innate (genetic) clocks and environmental factors influence preparation for migration. The photoperiod is an important migratory cue for many birds, particularly for birds in temperate zones. The changing photoperiod initiates seasonal changes in gonadal development that often serve as migratory stimuli. Increasing day length in the spring promotes gonadal development, and decreasing day length in the fall initiates gonadal regression. In many birds, the changing photoperiod also appears to promote fat deposition, which acts as an energy reserve for migration. The anterior lobe of the pituitary gland and the pineal body have been implicated in mediating photoperiod responses.

The mechanics of migration are species specific. Some long-distance migrants may store fat equal to 50% of their body weight and make nonstop journeys. Other species that take a more leisurely approach to migration begin their journeys early and stop frequently to feed and rest. In clear weather, many birds fly at altitudes greater than 1,000 m, which reduces the likelihood of hitting tall obstacles. Many birds have very specific migration routes (see figure 30.1).

Navigation

Homing pigeons have served for many years as a pigeon postal service. In ancient Egyptian times and as recently as World War II, pigeons returned messages from the battlefield.

⑥ Birds use two forms of navigation. Route-based navigation involves keeping track of landmarks (visual or auditory) on an outward journey so that those landmarks can be used in a reverse sequence on the return trip. Location-based navigation is based on establishing the direction of the destination from information available at the journey's site of origin. It involves the use of sun compasses, other celestial cues, and/or the earth's magnetic field.

Birds' lenses are transparent to ultraviolet light, and their photoreceptors respond to it, allowing them to orient using the sun, or even on cloudy days. This orientation cue is called a sun compass. Because the sun moves through the sky between sunrise and sunset, birds use internal clocks to perceive that the sun rises in the east, is approximately overhead at noon, and sets in the west. The biological clocks of migratory birds can be altered. For example, birds ready for northward migration can be held in a laboratory in which the "laboratory sunrise" occurs later than the natural sunrise. When released to natural light conditions, they fly in a direction they perceive to be north, but which is really northwest. Night migrators can also orient using the sun by flying in the proper direction from the sunset.

Celestial cues other than the sun can be used to navigate. Humans recognize that in the Northern Hemisphere, the North Star lines up with the axis of rotation of the earth. The angle between the North Star and the horizon decreases as you move toward the equator. Birds may use similar information to determine latitude. Experimental rotations of the night sky in a planetarium have altered the orientation of birds in test cages.

Some zoologists have long speculated that birds employ magnetic compasses to detect the earth's magnetic field, and thus, determine direction. Direct evidence of the existence of magnetic compasses now has been uncovered. Magnets strapped to the heads of pigeons severely disorient the birds. European robins and a night migrator, the garden warbler, orient using the earth's magnetic field. However, no discrete magnetic receptors have been found in either birds or other animals. Early reports of finding a magnetic iron, magnetite, in the head and necks of pigeons did not lead to a greater understanding of magnetic compasses. Further experiments failed to demonstrate magnetic properties in these regions. Magnetic iron has been found in bacteria and a variety of animal tissues. None is clearly associated with a magnetic sense, although the pineal body of pigeons has been implicated in the use of a sun compass and in responses to magnetic fields.

There is redundancy in bird navigational mechanisms, which suggests that under different circumstances, birds probably use different sources of information.

Stop and Ask Yourself

12. Why is monogamy advantageous for most birds?
13. Why are birds with precocial young more likely to be polygynous than birds with altricial young?
14. What environmental cue is important in preparing birds for migration?
15. What is route-based navigation?

SUMMARY

1. Birds are members of the archosaur lineage. Fossils of ancient birds—*Archaeopteryx, Sinornis,* and *Eoalularis* show reptilian affinities and give clues to the origin of flight.

2. Feathers evolved from reptilian scales and function in flight, insulation, sex recognition, and waterproofing. Feathers are maintained and periodically molted.

3. The bird skeleton is light and made more rigid by fusion of bones. Birds use the neck and bill as a fifth appendage.

4. Bird wings form airfoils that provide lift. Tilting the wing during flapping generates propulsive force. Gliding, flapping, soaring, and hovering flight are used by different birds or by the same bird at different times.

5. Birds feed on a variety of foods, as reflected in the structure of the bill and other parts of the digestive tract.

6. The heart of birds consists of two atria and two ventricles. Rapid heart rate and blood flow support the high metabolic rate of birds.

7. The respiratory system of birds provides one-way, nearly constant air movement across respiratory surfaces.

8. Birds are able to maintain high body temperatures endothermically because of insulating fat deposits and feathers.

9. The development of the corpus striatum enlarged the cerebral hemispheres of birds. Vision is the most important avian sense.

10. Birds are oviparous. Reproductive activities include the establishment and defense of territories, courtship, and nest building.

11. Either or both bird parents incubate the eggs, and one or both parents feed the young. Altricial chicks are helpless at hatching, and precocial chicks are alert and lively shortly after hatching.

12. Migration allows some birds to avoid climatic extremes and to secure adequate food, shelter, and space throughout the year. The photoperiod is the most important migratory cue for birds.

13. Birds use both route-based navigation and location-based navigation.

SELECTED KEY TERMS

airfoil (p. 493)
altricial (p. 500)
molting (p. 492)
monogamous (p. 499)
polyandrous (p. 500)
polygynous (p. 499)
precocial (p. 500)

CRITICAL THINKING QUESTIONS

1. Birds are sometimes called "glorified reptiles." Discuss why this description is appropriate.

2. What adaptations of birds promote endothermy and flight? Why is endothermy important for birds?

3. Birds are, without exception, oviparous. Why do you think that is true?

4. What are the advantages that offset the great energy expenditure that migration requires?

5. Compare and contrast the advantages of monogamy, polygyny, and polyandry for birds. In what ways are the advantages and disadvantages of each related to the abundance and utilization of food and other resources?

REFERENCES ON THE WORLD WIDE WEB

1. **Birding on the Web.** This site provides links, answers to frequently asked questions, announcements, links to bird chatlines, information on bird classification, and other information.
   http://www-stat.wharton.upenn.edu/~siler/birding.html

2. **Peterson Online Birds.** This site presents information that helps both the novice or the skilled birder to identify birds. It includes games in bird identification.
   http://www.petersononline.com/birds/index.html

3. **Ornithology.** This site provides links to a variety of information on the birds.
   http://www.environment.sfasu.edu/topics/wildlife/birds.html

4. **The Raptor Center.** The Raptor Center provides medical treatment for injured birds of prey and is dedicated to the preservation of raptors. This site describes the mission of the center, answers frequently asked questions, includes a glossary of terms, and provides information for those interested in the work of The Raptor Center.
   http://www.raptor.cvm.umn.edu/

5. **RSPB Images.** This site catalogs an extensive collection of bird photographs.
   http://www.rspb-images.com/html/homepage.htm

6. **The Birds of North America**. The Academy of Natural Sciences provides this site, where you can look up natural history information on any breeding bird in North America.
   http://www.acnatsci.org/bna/

7. **Links of Interest in Ornithology.** This sites provides links to ornithology journals, societies, meetings, and other information.
   http://www.museum.state.il.us/isas/birdlink.html

8. **The Virtual Birder.** This is an Internet magazine for birders. Learn bird songs by matching the bird to its recording. The site provides many other interesting activities for bird enthusiasts.
   http://magnetolcybersmith.com/vbirder/

9. **Sound and Vision: Online Bird Identification Guide.** Information on many bird species is at this site, including photographs and recordings.
   http://www.uidaho.edu/~scott931/projects/guide.html

10. **Cornell Lab of Ornithology.** This site provides a large amount of information for birders.
    http://www.ornith.cornell.edu/

11. **Vertebrate Flight Exhibit.** This site has an introduction to flight, as well as the physics, evolution, and origin of vertebrate flight.
    http://www.ucmp.berkeley.edu/vertebrates/flight/enter.html

MAMMALS:
SPECIALIZED TEETH, ENDOTHERMY, HAIR, AND VIVIPARITY

Concepts

1. Mammalian characteristics evolved gradually over a 200-million-year period in the synapsid lineage.
2. Two subclasses of mammals evolved during the Mesozoic era—the Prototheria and the Theria. Modern mammals include monotremes, marsupial mammals, and placental mammals.
3. The skin of mammals is thick and protective, and has an insulating covering of hair.
4. Adaptations of teeth and the digestive tract allow mammals to exploit a wide variety of food resources.
5. Efficient systems for circulation and gas exchange support the high metabolic rate associated with mammalian endothermy.
6. The brain of mammals has an expanded cerebral cortex that processes information from various sensory structures.
7. Metanephric kidneys permit mammals to excrete urea without excessive water loss.
8. Complex behavior patterns enhance mammalian survival.
9. Most mammals are viviparous and have reproductive cycles that help ensure internal fertilization and successful development.

Would You Like to Know . . .

1. what group of ancient reptiles is most closely related to mammals? (p. 506)

2. what group of mammals is oviparous? (p. 507)

3. why mammal hair stands on end when a mammal is frightened? (p. 510)

4. how mammalian teeth are specialized for different feeding habits? (p. 513)

5. why the four-chambered hearts of mammals and birds are an example of convergent evolution? (p. 515)

6. why mammals do not have salt glands? (p. 519)

7. why a domestic cat rubs its face on furniture around the house? (p. 520)

This chapter answers these and other useful questions.

This chapter contains evolutionary concepts, which are set off in this font.

Evolutionary Perspective

The beginning of the Tertiary period, about 70 million years ago, was the start of the "age of mammals." It coincided with the extinction of many reptilian lineages, which led to the adaptive radiation of the mammals. Tracing the roots of the mammals, however, requires returning to the Carboniferous period, when the synapsid lineage diverged from other amniote lineages (*see figure 29.2*).

Mammalian characteristics evolved gradually over a period of 200 million years (figure 31.1). The early synapsids were the pelycosaurs. Some were herbivores; others showed skeletal adaptations that reflect increased effectiveness as predators (figure 31.2a). The anterior teeth of their upper jaw were large and were separated from the posterior teeth by a gap that accommodated the enlarged anterior teeth of the lower jaw when the jaw closed. The palate was arched, which strengthened the upper jaw and allowed air to pass over prey held in the mouth. Their legs were longer and slimmer than those of earlier amniotes.

By the middle of the Permian period, other successful mammal-like reptiles had arisen from the pelycosaurs. ① They were a diverse group known as the therapsids. Some were predators, and others were herbivores. In the predatory therapsids, teeth were concentrated at the front of the mouth and enlarged for holding and tearing prey. The posterior teeth were reduced in size and number. The jaws of some therapsids were elongate and generated a large biting force when snapped closed. The teeth of the herbivorous therapsids were also mammal-like. Some had a large space, called the diastema, separating the anterior and posterior teeth. The posterior teeth had ridges (cusps) and cutting edges that were probably used to shred plant material. Unlike other reptiles, therapsids held hindlimbs directly beneath the body and moved them parallel to the long axis of the body. Changes in the size and shape of the ribs suggest the separation of the trunk into thoracic and abdominal regions and a breathing mechanism similar to that of mammals. The last therapsids were a group called the cyncodonts (figure 31.2b). Some of these were as large as a big dog, but most were small and little different from the earliest mammals.

(a)

(b)

FIGURE 31.2

Members of the Subclass Synapsidia. (*a*) *Dimetrodon* was a 3 m long pelycosaur. It probably fed on other reptiles and amphibians. The large sail may have been a recognition signal and a thermoregulatory device. (*b*) *Cynognathus* was a mammal-like reptile that probably foraged for small animals, much like a badger does today. The badger-sized animal was a cynodont within the order Therapsida, the stock from which mammals arose during the mid-Triassic period.

FIGURE 31.1

Class Mammalia. The decline of the ruling reptiles about 70 million years ago permitted mammals to radiate into diurnal habitats previously occupied by dinosaurs and other reptiles. Hair, endothermy, and mammary glands characterize mammals. The lowland gorilla (*Gorilla gorilla graueri,* order Primates) is shown here.

The first mammals were small (less than 10 cm long) with delicate skeletons. Most knowledge of early mammalian phylogeny comes from the study of their fossilized teeth and skull fragments. These studies suggest that the mammals of the Jurassic and Cretaceous periods were mostly predators that fed on other vertebrates and arthropods. A few were herbivores, and others combined predatory and herbivorous feeding habits. Changes in the structure of the middle ear and the regions of the brain devoted to hearing and olfaction indicate that these senses were important during the early evolution of mammals.

Some zoologists speculate that the small size, well-developed olfactory and auditory abilities, and lack of color vision in most mammals suggest that early mammals were nocturnal. This habit may have allowed them to avoid competition with the much larger dinosaurs and the smaller diurnal (day-active [L. *diurnalis,* daily]) reptiles living at the same time. Again, it is speculative, but nocturnal habits could have led to endothermy. Endothermy would have allowed small mammals to maintain body temperatures above that of their surroundings after the sun had set and the air temperature began to fall.

DIVERSITY OF MAMMALS

Hair, mammary glands, specialized teeth, three middle-ear ossicles, and other characteristics listed in table 31.1 characterize modern members of the class Mammalia (mah-ma'le-ah) (L. *mamma,* breast). The extent to which all of these characteristics were developed in the earliest mammals cannot currently be determined. Although zoologists disagree on subclass-level classification, most zoologists consider mid-Cretaceous (about 130 million years ago) mammals to have diverged into two subclasses: the Prototheria and the Theria (figure 31.3). Until recently, monotremes (the duck-billed platypus and the echidna) were classified in the subclass Prototheria (Gr. *protos,* first + *therion,* wild beast). Recent fossil evidence showing monotreme dentition that is characteristic of the subclass Theria has resulted in this group being reassigned to the latter subclass. The Prototheria, therefore, contains only extinct forms.

The subclass Theria diverged into three infraclasses by the late Cretaceous period. The infraclass Ornithodelphia (Gr. *ornis,* bird + *delphia,* birthplace) contains the monotremes (Gr. *monos,* one + *trema,* opening). This name refers to monotremes, unlike other mammals, possessing a cloaca. ② Monotremes are distinguished from all other mammals by being oviparous (figure 31.4a,b). The six species of monotremes are found in Australia and New Guinea.

The infraclass Metatheria (Gr. *meta,* after) contains the marsupial mammals. They are viviparous but have very short gestation periods. A protective pouch, called the marsupium, covers the female mammary glands. The young crawl into the marsupium after birth, where they feed and complete development. About 250 species of marsupials live in the Australian region and the Americas (figure 31.4c; see also figure 31.17).

The other therian infraclass, Eutheria (Gr. *eu,* true), contains the placental mammals. They are usually born at an advanced stage of development, having been nourished within the uterus. Exchanges between maternal and fetal circulatory systems occur by diffusion across an organ called the **placenta,** which is composed of both maternal and fetal tissue. The approximately 3,800 species of eutherians are classified into 17 orders (figures 31.5 and 31.6; see also figures 31.11 and 31.15–31.17).

Stop and Ask Yourself

1. What characteristics of synapsid reptiles are mammal-like?
2. What source has provided the most information about early mammals?
3. Why do some zoologists think that early mammals were nocturnal?
4. What are two subclasses of mammals?

EVOLUTIONARY PRESSURES

Mammals are naturally distributed on all continents except Antarctica and in all oceans. This section discusses the many adaptations that have accompanied their adaptive radiation.

EXTERNAL STRUCTURE AND LOCOMOTION

The skin of a mammal, like that of other vertebrates, consists of epidermal and dermal layers. It protects from mechanical injury, invasion by microorganisms, and the sun's ultraviolet light. Skin is also important in temperature regulation, sensory perception, excretion, and water regulation (see figure 32.9).

Hair is a keratinized derivative of the epidermis of the skin and is uniquely mammalian. It is seated in an invagination of the epidermis, called a hair follicle. A coat of hair, called pelage, usually consists of two kinds of hair. Long guard hairs protect a dense coat of smaller, insulating underhairs.

Because hair is composed largely of dead cells, it must be periodically molted. In some mammals (e.g., humans), molting occurs gradually and may not be noticed. In others, hair loss occurs rapidly and may result in altered pelage characteristics. In the fall, many mammals acquire a thick coat of insulating underhair, and the pelage color may change. For example, the Arctic fox takes on a white or cream color with its autumn molt, which helps conceal the fox in a snowy environment. With its spring molt, the Arctic fox acquires a gray and yellow pelage (see figure 31.6).

Hair is also important for the sense of touch. Mechanical displacement of a hair stimulates nerve cells associated with the hair root. Guard hairs may sometimes be modified into

TABLE 31.1	CLASSIFICATION OF MAMMALS

Class Mammalia (mah-ma′le-ah)
Mammary glands; hair; diaphragm; three middle-ear ossicles; heterodont dentition; sweat, sebaceous, and scent glands; four-chambered heart; large cerebral cortex.

Subclass Prototheria (pro″to-ther′e-ah)
This subclass formerly contained the monotremes. Monotremes have recently been reclassified, and this subclass now contains only extinct species.

Subclass Theria (ther′e-ah)
Technical characteristics of the skull distinguish members of this subclass.

Infraclass Ornithodelphia (or″ne-tho-del′fe-ah)
Technical characteristics of the skull distinguish members of this infraclass. Monotremes.

Infraclass Metatheria (met″ah-ther′e-ah)
Viviparous; primitive placenta; young are born early and often are carried in a marsupial pouch on the female's belly. Marsupials.

Infraclass Eutheria (u-ther′-e-ah)*
Complex placenta; young develop to advanced stage prior to birth. Placentals.

Order Insectivora (in-sec-tiv′or-ah)
Diverse group of small, primitive mammals; third largest mammalian order. Hedgehogs, tenrecs, moles, shrews.

Order Chiroptera (ki-rop′ter-ah)
Cosmopolitan, but especially abundant in the tropics; bones of the arm and hand are elongate and slender; flight membranes extend from the body, between digits of forelimbs, to the hindlimbs; most are insectivorous, but some are fruit eaters, fish eaters, and blood feeders; second largest mammalian order. Bats.

Order Primates (pri-ma′tez)
Adaptations of primates reflect adaptations for increased agility in arboreal (tree-dwelling) habitats; omnivorous diets; unspecialized teeth; grasping digits; freely movable limbs; nails on digits; reduced nasal cavity; enlarged eyes and cerebral hemispheres. Lemurs (Madagascar and the Comoro Islands), tarsiers (jungles of Sumatra and the East Indies), monkeys, gibbons, great apes (apes and humans).

Order Edentata (e″den-ta′tah) or Xenarthra (ze′nar-thra)
Incisors and canines absent; cheek teeth, when present, lack enamel; braincase is long and cylindrical; hindfoot is four toed; forefoot has two or three prominent toes with large claws; limbs are specialized for climbing or digging; xenarthrous lumbar vertebrae. Anteaters, tree sloths, armadillos.

Order Lagamorpha (lag″o-mor′fah)
Two pairs of upper incisors, one pair of lower incisors; incisors are ever-growing and slowly worn down by feeding on vegetation. Rabbits, pikas.

Order Rodentia (ro-den′che-ah)
Largest mammalian order; upper and lower jaws bear a single pair of ever-growing incisors. Squirrels, chipmunks, rats, mice, beavers, porcupines, woodchucks, lemmings.

Order Cetacea (se-ta′she-ah)
Streamlined, nearly hairless, and insulated by thick layers of fat (blubber); no sebaceous glands; forelimbs modified into paddlelike flippers for swimming; hindlimbs reduced and not visible externally; tail fins (flukes) flattened horizontally; external nares (blowhole) on top of skull. Toothed whales (beaked whales, narwhals, sperm whales, dolphins, porpoises, killer whales); toothless, filter-feeding whales (right whales, gray whales, blue whales, and humpback whales).

Order Carnivora (kar-niv′o-rah)
Predatory mammals; usually have a highly developed sense of smell and a large braincase; premolars and molars modified into carnassial apparatus; three pairs of upper and lower incisors usually present, and canines are well developed. Dogs, cats, bears, raccoons, minks, sea lions, seals, walruses, otters.

Order Proboscidea (pro″bah-sid′e-ah)
Long, muscular proboscis (trunk) with one or two finger-like processes at the tip; short skull with the second incisor on each side of the upper jaw modified into tusks; six cheek teeth are present in each half of each jaw; teeth erupt (grow into place) in sequence from front to rear, so that one tooth in each jaw is functional. African and Indian elephants.

Order Sirenia (si-re′ne-ah)
Large, aquatic herbivores that weigh in excess of 600 kg; nearly hairless, with thick, wrinkled skin; heavy skeleton; forelimb is flipperlike, and hindlimb is vestigial; horizontal tail fluke is present; horizontally oriented diaphragm; teeth lack enamel. Manatees (coastal rivers of the Americas and Africa), dugongs (western Pacific and Indian Oceans).

Order Perissodactyla (pe-ris″so-dak′ti-lah)
Skull usually elongate; large molars and premolars; primarily grazers. (The Artiodactyla also have hoofs. Artiodactyls and perissodactyls are, therefore, called ungulates. [L. *ungula*, hoof] Horses, rhinoceroses, zebras, tapirs.

Order Artiodactyla (ar″te-o-dak′ti-lah)
Hoofed; axis of support passes between third and fourth digits; digits one, two, and five reduced or lost; primarily grazing and browsing animals (pigs are an obvious exception). Pigs, hippopotamuses, camels, antelope, deer, sheep, giraffes, cattle.

*Selected eutherian orders are described.

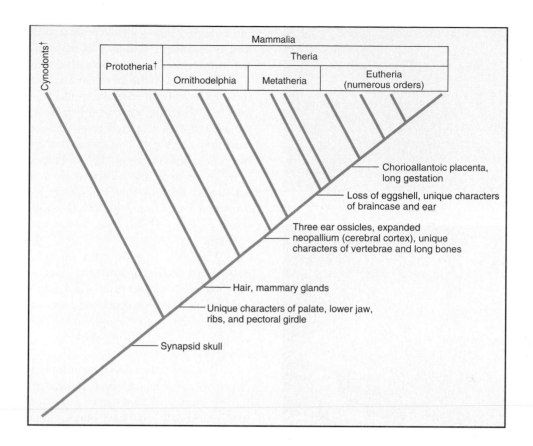

FIGURE 31.3

Mammalian Phylogeny. A cladogram showing the evolutionary relationships among mammals. Selected characters are shown. Daggers (†) indicate some extinct taxa. However, numerous extinct groups have been omitted from the cladogram. The names of the 17 orders of eutherians have also been omitted (*see table 31.1*).

(a)

(b)

(c)

FIGURE 31.4

Representatives of the Mammalian Infraclasses Ornithodelphia and Metatheria. The infraclass Ornithodelphia: (*a*) A duck-billed platypus (*Ornithorhychus anatinus*). (*b*) An echidna or spiny anteater (*Tachyglossus aculeatus*). The infraclass Metatheria: (*c*) The koala (*Phascolarctos cinereus*) feeds on *Eucalyptus* leaves in Australia.

(a)

(b)

FIGURE 31.5

Order Edentata. *(a)* A giant anteater *(Myrmecophaga tridactyla)*. Anteaters lack teeth. They use powerful forelimbs to tear into an insect nest and a long tongue covered with sticky saliva to capture prey. *(b)* An armadillo *(Dasypus novemcinctus)*.

FIGURE 31.6

Order Carnivora. An Arctic fox *(Alopex lagopus)* with its spring and summer pelage. With its autumn molt, the Arctic fox acquires a white or cream-colored coat.

thick-shafted hairs called vibrissae. Vibrissae occur around the legs, nose, mouth, and eyes of many mammals. Their roots are richly innervated and very sensitive to displacement.

Air spaces in the hair shaft and air trapped between hair and the skin provide an effective insulating layer. A band of smooth muscle, called the arrector pili muscle, runs between the hair follicle and the lower epidermis. When the muscle contracts, the hairs stand upright, increasing the amount of air trapped in the pelage and improving its insulating properties. Arrector pili muscles are under the control of the autonomic nervous system, which also controls a mammal's "fight-or-flight" response. ❸ In threatening situations, the hair (especially on the neck and tail) stands on end and may give the perception of increased size and strength.

Hair color depends on the amount of pigment (melanin) deposited in it and the quantity of air in the hair shaft. The pelage of most mammals is dark above and lighter underneath. This pattern makes them less conspicuous under most conditions. Some mammals advertise their defenses using aposematic (warning) coloration. The contrasting markings of a skunk are a familiar example.

Pelage is reduced in large mammals from hot climates (e.g., elephants and hippopotamuses) and in some aquatic mammals (e.g., whales) that often have fatty insulation. A few mammals (e.g., naked mole rats) have almost no pelage.

Claws are present in all amniote classes. They are used for locomotion and offensive and defensive behavior. Claws form from accumulations of keratin that cover the terminal phalanx (bone) of the digits. In some mammals, they are specialized to form nails or hooves (figure 31.7).

Glands develop from the epidermis of the skin. **Sebaceous (oil) glands** are associated with hair follicles, and their oily secretion lubricates and waterproofs the skin and hair. Most mammals also possess **sudoriferous (sweat) glands.** Small sudoriferous glands (eccrine glands) release watery secretions used in evaporative cooling. Larger sudoriferous glands (apocrine glands) secrete a mixture of salt, urea, and water, which microorganisms on the skin convert to odorous products.

Scent or **musk glands** are around the face, feet, or anus of many mammals. These glands secrete pheromones, which may be involved with defense, species and sex recognition, and territorial behavior.

Mammary glands are functional in female mammals and are present, but nonfunctional, in males. The milk that mammary glands secrete contains water, carbohydrates (especially the sugar lactose), fat, protein, minerals, and antibodies. Mammary glands are probably derived evolutionarily from apocrine glands and usually contain substantial fatty deposits.

Monotremes have mammary glands that lack nipples. The glands discharge milk into depressions on the belly, where the young lap it up. In other mammals, mammary glands open via nipples or teats, and the young suckle for their nourishment (figure 31.8).

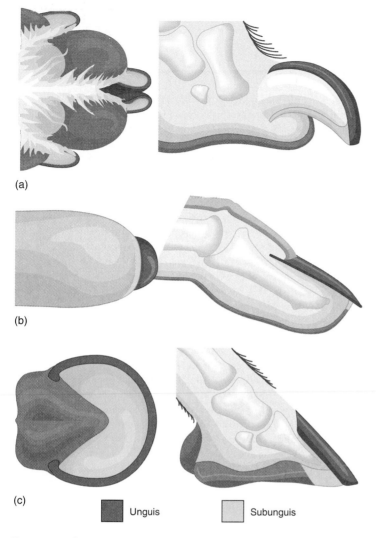

FIGURE 31.7

Structure of Claws, Nails, and Hooves. (*a*) Claws. (*b*) Nails are flat, broad claws found on the hands and feet of primates and are an adaptation for arboreal habits, where grasping is essential. (*c*) Hooves are characteristic of ungulate mammals. The number of toes is reduced, and the animals walk or run on the tips of the remaining digits. The unguis is a hard, keratinized dorsal plate, and the subunguis is a softer ventral plate.

The Skull and Teeth

The skulls of mammals show important modifications of the reptilian pattern (box 31.1). One feature that zoologists use to distinguish reptilian from mammalian skulls is the method of jaw articulation. In reptiles, the jaw articulates at two small bones at the rear of the jaw. In mammals, these bones have moved into the middle ear, and along with the stapes, form the middle-ear ossicles. A single bone of the lower jaw articulates the mammalian jaw.

A secondary palate evolved twice in vertebrates—in the archosaur lineage (*see figure 29.2*) and in the synapsid lineage. In some therapsids, small, shelflike extensions of bone (the hard palate) partially separated the nasal and oral passageways (*see*

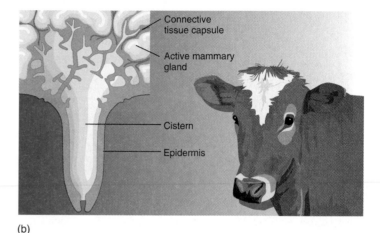

FIGURE 31.8

Mammary Glands. Mammary glands are specialized to secrete milk following the birth of young. (*a*) Many ducts lead from the glands to a nipple. Parts of the duct system are enlarged to store milk. Suckling by an infant initiates a hormonal response that causes the mammary glands to release milk. (*b*) Some mammals (e.g., cattle) have teats that form by the extension of a collar of skin around the opening of mammary ducts. Milk collects in a large cistern prior to its release. The number of nipples or teats varies with the number of young produced.

figure 29.10). In mammals, the secondary palate extends posteriorly by a fold of skin, called the soft palate, which almost completely separates the nasal passages from the mouth cavity. Unlike other vertebrates that swallow food whole or in small pieces, some mammals chew their food. The more extensive secondary palate allows mammals to breathe while chewing. Breathing needs to stop only briefly during swallowing (figure 31.9).

The structure and arrangement of teeth are important indicators of mammalian lifestyles. In reptiles, the teeth are uniformly conical, a condition referred to as **homodont.** In mammals, the teeth are often specialized for different functions, a condition called **heterodont.** Reptilian teeth attach along the top or inside of the jaw, whereas in mammals, the teeth are set into sockets of the jaw. Most mammals have two sets of teeth during their life. The first teeth emerge before or shortly after birth and are called deciduous or milk teeth. These teeth are lost, and permanent teeth replace them.

BOX 31.1 | HORNS AND ANTLERS

Horns were a familiar sight in prehistoric landscapes, 100 million years before they became common in mammals. *Triceratops* had three horns: one nasal horn and two above the eyes. It also had a horny shield along the posterior margin of the head. *Styracosaurus* had a 0.7 m nasal spike. These early reptilian horns probably provided a very effective defense against fierce prehistoric carnivores.

Mammalian horns are a carryover from their reptilian heritage. They are most common in a group of hoofed mammals, the artiodactyls (e.g., cattle, sheep, and goats). A horn is a spike of bone that arises from the frontal bone of the skull and is covered with the protein keratin (figure 1a,b). This bony spike, the "os cornu," grows slowly from youth to adulthood, and its marrow core is highly vascularized. Filaments of keratin arise from follicle-like structures in the skin. Keratin filaments are cemented together and completely cover the os cornu. The outer horn layers have no blood supply.

Horns are defensive structures. They exist in symmetrical pairs and are present in both sexes. As any farmer or rancher knows, horns do not regenerate if cut off. Horns are usually not shed. One exception is the pronghorn antelope (*Antilocapra americana*). Every year, a new horn grows on the os cornu beneath the old horn, and the latter is eventually pushed off.

Another kind of head ornamentation, the antler, is common in deer, elk, moose, and caribou. Antlers are highly branched structures made of bone, but are not covered by keratin. Unlike horns, they are usually present only in males and are shed and reformed every year (figure 1c). Caribou are an exception because antlers are present in both sexes. Antlers are more recent than horns; the earliest records of antlered animals are from the Miocene epoch (mid-Tertiary period), and by the Pleistocene epoch, they had become common.

Seasonal changes in the level of the male hormone testosterone regulate antler development. Antlers of male elk begin to form in April as skin-covered buds from the frontal bone. The primordial cells that initiate antler growth are left behind from the previous year when the antlers were lost. Antlers begin to branch after only 2 weeks. By May, they are well formed, and by August, they are mature. Each year, antlers become more complexly branched. Throughout the spring and summer, they are covered with delicate, vascular tissue called velvet. In August, the bone at the base of the antler becomes progressively more dense and cuts off blood flow to the center of the antler. Later, blood flow to the velvet is cut off, and the velvet begins to dry. It is shed in strips as the antlers are rubbed against the ground or tree branches. Breeding activities commence after the velvet is shed, and the antlers are used in jousting matches as rival males compete for groups of females. (Rarely do these jousting matches lead to severe injury.) Females tend to select males with large antlers, which may explain why antlers can get so large in some species. (Although now extinct, the Giant Stag, *Cervis megaceros*, had antlers with a 3 m spread and a mass of 70 kg.) Later in the fall, or in early winter, the base of the antler weakens as bone is reabsorbed at the pedicels of the frontal bone. Antlers are painlessly cast off when they strike a tree branch or other object.

Other hornlike structures are present in some mammals. Rhinos are the only perissodactyls (e.g., horses, rhinos, and tapirs) to have hornlike structures (*see figure 31.11*). Their "horns" consist of filamentous secretions of keratin cemented together and mounted to the skin of the head. There is no bony core, and thus, they are not true horns. Rhino "horns" are prized in Asian countries for their presumed aphrodisiac and medicinal properties and as dagger handles in certain mideastern cultures. These demands have led to serious overhunting of rhinos; in many regions, they are almost extinct (*see the Wildlife Alert in chapter 3*).

The horns of giraffes are skin-covered bony knobs. Zoologists do not understand their function.

Adult mammals have up to four kinds of teeth. Incisors are the most anterior teeth in the jaw. They are usually chisel-like and used for gnawing or nipping. Canines are often long, stout, and conical, and are usually used for catching, killing, and tearing prey. Canines and incisors have single roots. Premolars are positioned next to canines, and have one or two roots, and truncated surfaces for chewing. Molars have broad chewing surfaces and two (upper molars) or three (lower molars) roots.

Mammalian species have characteristic numbers of each kind of adult tooth. Zoologists use a **dental formula** to characterize taxa. It is an expression of the number of teeth of each kind in one-half of the upper and lower jaws. The teeth of the upper jaw are listed above those of the lower jaw and in the following order: incisors, canine, premolars, and molars. For example:

Human	Beaver
2•1•2•3	1•0•1•3
2•1•2•3	1•0•1•3

Mammalian teeth (dentition) may be specialized for particular diets. In some mammals, the dentition is reduced, sometimes to the point of having no teeth. For example, armadillos and the giant anteater (order Edentata) feed on termites and ants, and their teeth are reduced.

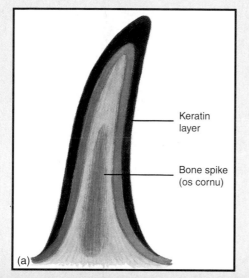

Keratin layer

Bone spike (os cornu)

(a)

(b)

(c)

FIGURE 1

Horns and Antlers. (*a*) The structure of a horn. (*b*) The horn of a male bighorn sheep (*Orvis canadensis*) (order Artiodactyla). (*c*) Development of deer antlers.

④ Some mammals (e.g., humans, order Primates; and pigs, order Artiodactyla) are omnivorous; they feed on a variety of plant and animal materials. They have anterior teeth with sharp ripping and piercing surfaces, and posterior teeth with flattened grinding surfaces for rupturing plant cell walls (figure 31.10*a*).

Mammals that eat plant material often have flat, grinding posterior teeth and incisors, and sometimes have canines modified for nipping plant matter (e.g., horses, order Perissodactyla; deer, order Artiodactyla) or gnawing (e.g., rabbits, order Lagamorpha; beavers, order Rodentia) (figure 31.10*b,c*). In rodents, the incisors grow throughout life. Although most mammals have enamel covering the entire tooth, rodents have enamel only on the front surfaces of their incisors. The teeth are kept sharp by slower wear

in front than in back. A gap called the diastema separates the anterior food-procuring teeth from the posterior grinding teeth. The diastema results from elongation of the snout that allows the anterior teeth to reach close to the ground or into narrow openings to procure food. The posterior teeth have a high, exposed surface (crown) and continuous growth, which allows these teeth to withstand years of grinding tough vegetation.

Predatory mammals use canines and incisors for catching, killing, and tearing prey. In members of the order Carnivora (e.g., coyotes, dogs, and cats), the fourth upper premolars and first lower molars form a scissorlike shearing surface, called the carnassial apparatus, that is used for cutting flesh from prey (figure 31.10*d*).

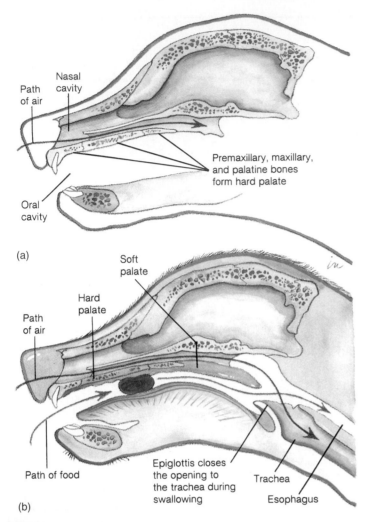

FIGURE 31.9

Secondary Palate. (*a*) The secondary palate (consisting of the hard and soft palates) of a mammal almost completely separates the nasal and oral cavities. (*b*) Breathing stops only momentarily during swallowing.

FIGURE 31.10

Specializations of Teeth. (*a*) An omnivore (*Homo sapiens*). (*b*) An herbivore, the male fallow deer (*Dama dama*). (*c*) A rodent, the beaver (*Castor canadensis*). (*d*) A carnivore, the coyote (*Canis latrans*).

The Vertebral Column and Appendicular Skeleton

The vertebral column of mammals is divided into five regions. As with reptiles and birds, the first two cervical vertebrae are the atlas and axis. Five other cervical vertebrae usually follow. Even the giraffe and the whale have seven neck vertebrae, which are greatly elongate or compressed, respectively. In contrast, tree sloths have either six or nine cervical vertebrae, and the manatee has six cervical vertebrae.

The trunk is divided into thoracic and lumbar regions, as is the case for birds. In mammals, the division is correlated with their method of breathing. The thoracic region contains the ribs. Most ribs connect to the thoracic vertebrae and to the sternum via costal cartilage. Other ribs attach only to the thoracic vertebrae. All ribs protect the heart and lungs. The articulation between the thoracic vertebrae provides the flexibility needed in turning, climbing, and lying on the side to suckle young. Lumbar

vertebrae have interlocking processes that give support, but little freedom of movement.

The appendicular skeleton of mammals rotates under the body so that the appendages are usually directly beneath the body. Joints usually limit the movement of appendages to a single anteroposterior plane, causing the tips of the appendages to move in long arcs. The bones of the pelvic girdle are highly fused in the adult, a condition that is advantageous for locomotion but presents problems during the birth of offspring. In a pregnant female, the ventral joint between the halves of the pelvis—the pubic symphysis—loosens before birth, allowing the pelvis to spread during birth.

Muscles

Because the appendages are directly beneath the body of most mammals, the skeleton bears the weight of the body. Muscle mass

FIGURE 31.11

Order Perissodactyla. This Malayan tapir *(Tapirus indicus)* is an endangered herbivore from Burma, Sumatra.

is concentrated in the upper appendages and girdles. Many running mammals (e.g., deer, order Artiodactyla) have little muscle in their lower leg that would slow leg movement. Instead, tendons run from muscles high in the leg to cause movement at the lower joints.

NUTRITION AND THE DIGESTIVE SYSTEM

The digestive tract of mammals is similar to that of other vertebrates but has many specializations for different feeding habits. Some specializations of teeth have already been described.

The feeding habits of mammals are difficult to generalize. Feeding habits reflect the ecological specializations that have evolved. For example, most members of the order Carnivora feed on animal flesh and are, therefore, carnivores. Other members of the order, such as bears, feed on a variety of plant and animal products and are omnivores. Some carnivorous mammals are specialized for feeding on arthropods or soft-bodied invertebrates, and are often referred to (rather loosely) as insectivores. These include animals in the orders Insectivora (e.g., shrews), Chiroptera (bats), and Edentata (anteaters) (*see figure 31.5a*). Herbivores such as deer (order Artiodactyla) and tapirs (order Perissodactyla) (figure 31.11) feed mostly on vegetation, but their diet also includes invertebrates inadvertently ingested while feeding.

Specializations in the digestive tract of most herbivores reflect the difficulty of digesting food rich in cellulose. Horses, rabbits, and many rodents have an enlarged **cecum** at the junction of large and small intestines. A cecum is a fermentation pouch where microorganisms aid in cellulose digestion. Sheep, cattle, and deer are called ruminants (L. *ruminare,* to chew the cud). Their stomachs are modified into four chambers. The first three chambers are storage and fermentation chambers and contain microorganisms that synthesize a cellulose-digesting enzyme (cellulase). Gases that fermentation produces are periodically belched, and some plant matter (cud) is regurgitated and rechewed. Other microorganisms convert nitrogenous compounds in the food into new proteins.

Stop and Ask Yourself

5. What are the functions of hair in mammals?
6. What are the four kinds of glands in mammals?
7. What is the usefulness of a dental formula?
8. What specializations of teeth and the digestive system are present in some herbivorous mammals?

CIRCULATION, GAS EXCHANGE, AND TEMPERATURE REGULATION

The hearts of birds and mammals are superficially similar. Both are four-chambered pumps that keep blood in the systemic and pulmonary circuits separate, and both evolved from the hearts of ancient reptiles. Their similarities, however, are a result of adaptations to active lifestyles. ⑤ The evolution of similar structures in different lineages is called convergent evolution. The mammalian heart evolved in the synapsid reptilian lineage, whereas the avian heart evolved in the archosaur lineage (figure 31.12).

One of the most important adaptations in the circulatory system of eutherian mammals concerns the distribution of respiratory gases and nutrients in the fetus (figure 31.13a). Exchanges between maternal and fetal blood occur across the placenta. Although maternal and fetal blood vessels are intimately associated, no blood actually mixes. Nutrients, gases, and wastes simply diffuse between fetal and maternal blood supplies.

Blood entering the right atrium of the fetus is returning from the placenta and is highly oxygenated. Because fetal lungs are not inflated, resistance to blood flow through the pulmonary arteries is high. Therefore, most of the blood entering the right atrium bypasses the right ventricle and passes instead into the left atrium through a valved opening between the atria (the foramen ovale). Some blood from the right atrium, however, does enter the right ventricle and the pulmonary artery. Because of the resistance at the uninflated lungs, most of this blood is shunted to the aorta through a vessel connecting the aorta and pulmonary artery (the ductus arteriosus). At birth, the placenta is lost, and the lungs are inflated. Resistance to blood flow through the lungs is reduced, and blood flow to them increases. Flow through the ductus arteriosus decreases, and the vessel is gradually reduced to a ligament. Blood flow back to the left atrium from the lungs correspondingly increases, and the valve of the foramen ovale closes and gradually fuses with the tissue separating the right and left atria (figure 31.13b).

Gas Exchange

High metabolic rates require adaptations for efficient gas exchange. Most mammals have separate nasal and oral cavities and longer snouts, which provide an increased surface area for warming and moistening inspired air. Respiratory passageways are highly

FIGURE 31.12

Possible Sequence in the Evolution of the Vertebrate Heart.
(a) Diagrammatic representation of a bony fish heart. (b) In lungfish, partially divided atria and ventricles separate pulmonary and systemic circuits. This heart was probably similar to that in primitive amphibians and early amniotes. (c) The hearts of modern reptiles were derived from the pattern in (b). (d) The archosaur and (e) synapsid lineages resulted in completely separated, four-chambered hearts.

branched, and large surface areas exist for gas exchange. Mammalian lungs resemble a highly vascular sponge, rather than the saclike structures of amphibians and a few reptiles.

Mammalian lungs, like those of reptiles, inflate using a negative-pressure mechanism. Unlike reptiles and birds, however, mammals possess a muscular **diaphragm** that separates thoracic and abdominal cavities. Inspiration results from contraction of the diaphragm and expansion of the rib cage, both of which decrease the intrathoracic pressure and allow air to enter the lungs. Expiration is normally by elastic recoil of the lungs. Contraction of thoracic and abdominal muscles can produce forceful exhalation.

Temperature Regulation

Mammals are widely distributed over the earth, and some face harsh environmental temperatures. Nearly all face temperatures that require them to dissipate excess heat at some times and to conserve and generate heat at other times.

Heat-producing mechanisms of mammals are divided into two categories. Shivering thermogenesis is muscular activity that generates large amounts of heat but little movement. Nonshivering thermogenesis involves heat production by general cellular metabolism and the metabolism of special fat deposits called brown fat. Chapter 38 discusses these heat-generating processes in more detail.

Heat production is effective in thermoregulation because mammals are insulated by their pelage and/or fat deposits. Fat deposits are also sources of energy to sustain high metabolic rates.

Mammals without a pelage can conserve heat by allowing the temperature of surface tissues to drop. A walrus in cold, arctic waters has a surface temperature near 0° C; however, a few centimeters below the skin surface, body temperatures are about 35° C. Upon emerging from the icy water, the walrus quickly warms its skin by increasing peripheral blood flow. Most tissues cannot tolerate such rapid and extreme temperature fluctuations. Further investigations are likely to reveal some unique biochemical characteristics of these skin tissues.

Even though most of the body of arctic mammals is unusually well insulated, appendages often have thin coverings of fur as an adaptation to changing thermoregulatory needs. Even in winter, an active mammal sometimes produces more heat than is required to maintain body temperature. Patches of poorly insulated skin allow excess heat to be dissipated. During periods of inactivity or extreme cold, however, arctic mammals must reduce heat loss from these exposed areas, often by assuming heat-conserving postures. Mammals sleeping in cold environments conserve heat by tucking poorly insulated appendages and their faces under well-insulated body parts.

Countercurrent heat-exchange systems may help regulate heat loss from exposed areas (figure 31.14). Arteries passing peripherally through the core of an appendage are surrounded by veins that carry blood back toward the body. When blood returns to the body through these veins, heat transfers from arterial blood to venous blood and returns to the body rather than being lost to the environment. When excess heat is produced, blood is shunted away from the countercurrent veins toward peripheral vessels, and excess heat is radiated to the environment.

Mammals have few problems getting rid of excess heat in cool, moist environments. Heat can be radiated into the air from vessels near the surface of the skin or lost by evaporative cooling from either sweat glands or respiratory surfaces during panting.

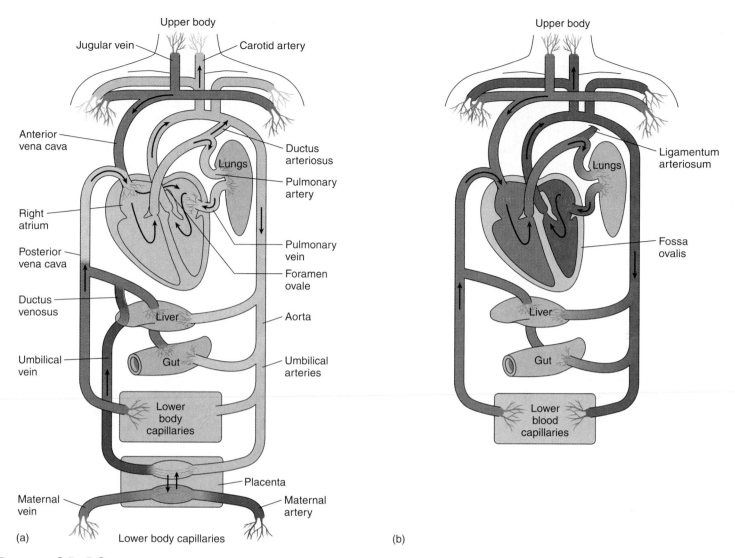

FIGURE 31.13

Mammalian Circulatory Systems. The circulatory patterns of (*a*) fetal and (*b*) adult mammals. Highly oxygenated blood is shown in red, and less oxygenated blood is shown in blue. In fetal circulation, highly oxygenated blood from the placenta mixes with less oxygenated blood prior to entering the right atrium. Thus, most arterial blood of the fetus is moderately oxygenated. The rose color in (*a*) symbolizes this state of oxygenation.

Hot, dry environments present far greater problems because evaporative cooling may upset water balances. Jackrabbits and elephants use their long ears to radiate heat. Small mammals often avoid the heat by remaining in burrows during the day and foraging for food at night. Other mammals seek shade or watering holes for cooling.

Winter Sleep and Hibernation

Mammals react in various ways to environmental extremes. Caribou migrate to avoid extremes of temperature, and wildebeest migrate to avoid seasonal droughts. Other mammals retreat to burrows under the snow, where they become less active but are still relatively alert and easily aroused—a condition called **winter sleep.** For example, bears and raccoons retreat to dens in winter. Their body temperatures and metabolic rates decrease somewhat, but they do not necessarily remain inactive all winter.

Hibernation is a period of winter inactivity in which the hypothalamus of the brain slows the metabolic, heart, and respiratory rates. True hibernators include the monotremes (echidna and duck-billed platypus) and many members of the Insectivora (e.g., moles and shrews), Rodentia (e.g., chipmunks and woodchucks), and Chiroptera (bats). In preparation for hibernation, mammals usually accumulate large quantities of body fat. After a hibernating mammal retreats to a burrow or a nest, the hypothalamus sets the body's thermostat to about 2° C. The respiratory rate of a hibernating ground squirrel falls 100 to 200 breaths per minute to about 4 breaths per minute. The heart rate falls 200 to 300 beats per minute to about 20 beats per minute. During hibernation, a mammal may lose a third to half of its body weight. Arousal from hibernation occurs by metabolic heating, frequently using brown fat deposits, and it takes several hours to raise body temperature to near 37° C.

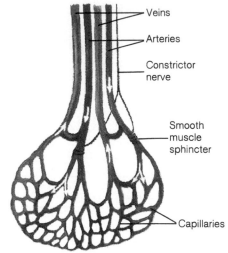

- Veins
- Arteries
- Constrictor nerve
- Smooth muscle sphincter
- Capillaries

Countercurrent vessels

FIGURE 31.14

Countercurrent Heat Exchange. Countercurrent heat exchangers conserve body heat in animals adapted to cold environments. Systems similar to the one depicted here are found in the legs of reindeer (*Rangifer tarandus*) and in the flippers of dolphins. Heat transferred from blood moving peripherally in arteries warms venous blood returning from an extremity. During winter, the lower part of a reindeer's leg may be at 10° C, while body temperature is about 40° C. White arrows indicate direction of blood flow.

NERVOUS AND SENSORY FUNCTIONS

The basic structure of the vertebrate nervous system is retained in mammals. The development of complex nervous and sensory functions goes hand-in-hand with active lifestyles and is most evident in the enlargement of the cerebral hemispheres and the cerebellum of mammals. Most integrative functions shift to the enlarged cerebral cortex (neocortex).

In mammals, the sense of touch is well developed. Receptors are associated with the bases of hair follicles and are stimulated when a hair is displaced.

Olfaction was apparently an important sense in early mammals because fossil skull fragments show elongate snouts, which would have contained olfactory epithelium. Cranial casts of fossil skulls show enlarged olfactory regions. Olfaction is still an important sense for many mammals. Mammals can perceive olfactory stimuli over long distances during either the day or night to locate food, recognize members of the same species, and avoid predators.

Auditory senses were similarly important to early mammals. More recent adaptations include an ear flap (the pinna) and the external ear canal leading to the tympanum that directs sound to the middle ear. The sensory patch of the inner ear that contains receptors for sound is long and coiled and is called the cochlea. This structure provides more surface area for receptor cells and gives mammals greater sensitivity to pitch and volume than is present in reptiles (box 31.2). Cranial casts of early mammals show well-developed auditory regions.

Vision is an important sense in many mammals, and eye structure is similar to that described for other vertebrates. Accommodation occurs by changing the shape of the lens (*see figure 34.18*). Color vision is less well developed in mammals than in reptiles and birds. Rods dominate the retinas of most mammals, which supports the hypothesis that early mammals were nocturnal. Primates, squirrels, and a few other mammals have well-developed color vision.

Stop and Ask Yourself

9. In what way are the hearts of birds and mammals an example of convergent evolution?

10. What are two ways that mammals can generate metabolic heat?

11. How does a reindeer prevent excessive heat loss from its poorly insulated legs?

12. What is the difference between hibernation of a ground squirrel and the winter sleep of a bear?

EXCRETION AND OSMOREGULATION

Mammals, like all amniotes, have a metanephric kidney. Unlike reptiles and birds, which excrete mainly uric acid, mammals excrete urea. Urea is less toxic than ammonia and does not require large quantities of water in its excretion. Unlike uric acid, however, urea is highly water soluble and cannot be excreted in a semisolid form; thus, some water is lost. Excretion in mammals is always a major route for water loss.

In the nephron of the kidney, fluids and small solutes are filtered from the blood through the walls of a group of capillary-like vessels, called the glomerulus. The remainder of the nephron consists of tubules that reabsorb water and essential solutes and secrete particular ions into the filtrate.

BOX 31.2 | MAMMALIAN ECHOLOCATION

Imagine a pool of water so murky that you are only able to see a few centimeters below the surface. Also imagine a clear Plexiglas sheet with a dolphin-sized opening in the middle, dividing the pool in half. At one end of the pool is an eager dolphin; at the other end is a trainer. The trainer throws a dead fish into the water, and on signal, the dolphin unhesitatingly finds its way through the murky water to the opening in the Plexiglas and then finds the fish at the other end of the pool.

Although the dolphin in this account was trained to find the fish, it relied on a sense that it shares with a few other mammals. Toothed whales, bats, and some shrews use the return echoes of high-frequency sound pulses to locate objects in their environment. This mechanism is called **echolocation.**

Zoologists have studied echolocation in bats more completely than in any other group of mammals. Italian scientist Lassaro Spallanzani discovered in the late 1700s that blinded bats could navigate successfully at night, whereas bats with plugged ears could not. Spallanzani believed that bats used echoes of the sounds that beating wings made in echolocation. In 1938, however, ultrasonic bat cries (inaudible to humans) were electronically recorded, and their function in echolocation was described.

Insect-eating bats navigate through their caves and the night sky and locate food by echolocation. During normal cruising flight, they emit ultrasonic (100 to 20 kHz) "clicks" approximately every 50 msec. As bats detect insect prey, the number of clicks per second increases, the duration between clicks decreases, and the wavelength of the sound decreases, increasing directional precision and making small, flying insects easier to detect. On final approach, the sound becomes buzzlike, and the bat scoops up the insect with its wings or in the webbing of its hind legs (figure 1).

Modifications of the bat ear and brain allow bats to perceive faint echoes of their vocalizations and to precisely determine direction and distance. Enlarged ear flaps funnel sounds toward particularly thin eardrums and sensitive ear ossicles. The auditory regions of the bat brain are large, and special neural pathways enhance a bat's ability to determine the direction of echoes.

Bats must distinguish echoes of their own cries from the cries themselves and from other noises. Leaflike folds of the nostrils direct sound emitted from the nostrils forward, rather than in all directions

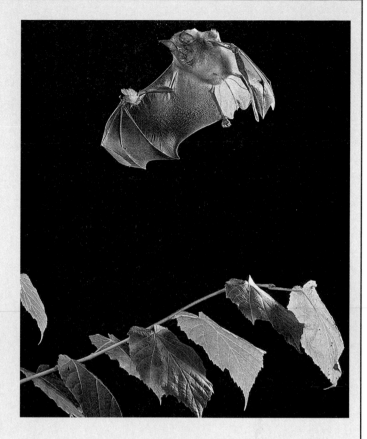

FIGURE 1
Bat Echolocation. A greater horseshoe bat (*Rhinophus*) capturing a moth.

from the head, much like the megaphone of a cheerleader. The ears, therefore, receive little stimulation from direct vocalizations. Fat and blood sinuses surrounding the middle and inner ears reduce transmission of sound from the mouth and pharynx. Some bats temporarily turn off their hearing during sound emission by making the ear ossicles insensitive to sound waves and then turn on their hearing an instant later when the reflected sound is returning.

The primary adaptation of the mammalian nephron is a portion of the tubule system called the loop of the nephron. The transport processes in this loop and the remainder of the tubule system allow mammals to produce urine that is more concentrated than blood. For example, beavers produce urine that is twice as concentrated as blood, while Australian hopping mice produce urine that is 22 times more concentrated than blood. ⑥ This accomplishes the same function that nasal and orbital salt glands do in reptiles and birds.

Water loss varies greatly, depending on activity, physiological state, and environmental temperature. Water is lost in urine, feces, and evaporation from sweat glands and respiratory

surfaces, and during nursing. Mammals in very dry environments have numerous behavioral and physiological mechanisms to reduce water loss. The kangaroo rat, named for its habit of hopping on large hind legs, is capable of extreme water conservation (figure 31.15). It is native to the southwestern deserts of the United States and Mexico, and survives without drinking water. Its feces are almost dry, and its nocturnal habits reduce evaporative water loss. Condensation as warm air in the respiratory passages encounters the cooler nasal passages minimizes respiratory water loss. A low-protein diet, which reduces urea production, minimizes excretory water loss. The nearly dry seeds that the kangaroo rat eats are rich sources of

(a)

(b)

FIGURE 31.15

Order Rodentia. (*a*) The kangaroo rat (*Dipodomys ordii*). (*b*) The long loop of the nephron of this desert animal conserves water, preventing dehydration.

carbohydrates and fats. Metabolic oxidation of carbohydrates produces water as a by-product.

BEHAVIOR

Mammals have complex behaviors that enhance survival. Visual cues are often used in communication. The bristled fur, arched back, and open mouth of a cat communicate a clear message to curious dogs or other potential threats. A tail-wagging display of a dog has a similarly clear message. A wolf defeated in a fight with other wolves lies on its back and exposes its vulnerable throat. Similar displays may allow a male already recognized as being subordinate to another male to avoid conflict within a social group.

Pheromones are used to recognize members of the same species, members of the opposite sex, and the reproductive state of a member of the opposite sex. Pheromones may also induce sexual behavior, help establish and recognize territories, and ward off predators. The young of many mammalian species recognize their parents, and parents recognize their young, by smell. Bull elk smell the rumps of females during the breeding season to recognize those in their brief receptive period. They also urinate on their own belly and underhair to advertise their reproductive status to females and other males. Male mammals urinate on objects in the environment to establish territories and to allow females to become accustomed to their odors. Rabbits and rodents spray urine on a member of the opposite sex to inform the second individual of the first's readiness to mate. Skunks use chemicals to ward off predators.

Auditory and tactile communication are also important in the lives of mammals. Herd animals stay together and remain calm as long as familiar sounds (e.g., bellowing, hooves walking over dry grasses and twigs, and rumblings from ruminating stomachs) are uninterrupted. Unfamiliar sounds may trigger alarm and flight.

Vocalizations and tactile communication are important in primate social interactions. Tactile communication ranges from precopulatory "nosing" that occurs in many mammals to grooming. Grooming helps maintain a healthy skin and pelage, but also reinforces important social relationships within primate groups.

Territoriality

Many mammals mark and defend certain areas from intrusion by other members of the same species. 7 When cats rub their face and neck on humans or on furniture, the behavior is often interpreted as affection. Cats, however, are really staking claim to their territory, using odors from facial scent glands. Some territorial behavior attracts females to, and excludes other males from, favorable sites for mating and rearing young.

Male California sea lions (*Zalophus californianus*) establish territories on shorelines where females come to give birth to young. For about 2 weeks, males engage in vocalizations, displays, and sometimes serious fighting to stake claim to favorable territories (figure 31.16). Older, dominant bulls are usually most successful in establishing territories, and young bulls generally swim and feed just offshore. When they arrive at the beaches, females select a site for giving birth. Selection of the birth site also selects the bull that will father next year's offspring. Mating occurs approximately 2 weeks after the birth of the previous year's offspring. Development is arrested for the 3 months during which the recently born young do most of their nursing. This mechanism is called embryonic diapause. Thus, even though actual development takes about 9 months, the female carries the embryo and fetus for a period of 1 year.

REPRODUCTION AND DEVELOPMENT

In no other group of animals has viviparity developed to the extent it has in mammals. Mammalian viviparity requires a large expenditure

FIGURE 31.16

Order Carnivora. California sea lions (*Zalophus californianus*) on a beach during the breeding season. The adult males in the foreground are vocalizing and posturing.

of energy on the part of the female during development and on the part of one or both parents caring for young after they are born. Viviparity is advantageous because females are not necessarily tied to a single nest site, but can roam or migrate to find food or a proper climate. Viviparity is accompanied by the evolution of a portion of the reproductive tract where the young are nourished and develop. In viviparous mammals, the oviducts are modified into one or two uteri (sing., uterus).

Reproductive Cycles

Most mammals have a definite time or times during the year in which ova (eggs) mature and are capable of being fertilized. Reproduction usually occurs when climatic conditions and resource characteristics favor successful development. Mammals living in environments with few seasonal changes and those that exert considerable control of immediate environmental conditions (e.g., humans) may reproduce at any time of the year. However, they are still tied to physiological cycles of the female that determine when ova can be fertilized.

Most female mammals undergo an **estrus** (Gr. *oistros*, a vehement desire) **cycle,** which includes a time during which the female is behaviorally and physiologically receptive to the male. During the estrus cycle, hormonal changes stimulate the maturation of ova in the ovary and induce ovulation (release of one or more mature ova from an ovarian follicle). A few mammals (e.g., rabbits, ferrets, and mink) are induced ovulators; coitus (copulation) induces ovulation.

Hormones also mediate changes in the uterus and vagina. As the ova are maturing, the inner lining of the uterus proliferates and becomes more vascular in preparation for receiving developing embryos. External swelling in the vaginal area and increased glandular discharge accompany proliferation of vaginal mucosa.

During this time, males show heightened interest in females, and females are receptive to males. If fertilization does not occur, the changes in the uterus and vagina are reversed until the next cycle begins. No bleeding or sloughing of uterine lining usually occurs.

Many mammals are monestrus and have only a single yearly estrus cycle that is sharply seasonal. Wild dogs, bears, and sea lions are monestrus; domestic dogs are diestrus. Other mammals are polyestrus. Rats and mice have estrus cycles that repeat every 4 to 6 days.

The menstrual cycle of female humans, apes, and monkeys is similar to the estrus cycle in that it results in a periodic proliferation of the inner lining of the uterus and correlates with the maturation of an ovum. If fertilization does not occur before the end of the cycle, menses—the sloughing of the uterine lining—occurs. Chapter 39 describes human menstrual and ovarian cycles.

Fertilization usually occurs in the upper third of the oviduct within hours of copulation. In a few mammals, fertilization may be delayed. In some bats, for example, coitus occurs in autumn, but fertilization is delayed until spring. Females store sperm in the uterus for periods in excess of 2 months. This **delayed fertilization** is apparently an adaptation to winter dormancy. Fertilization can occur immediately after females emerge from dormancy rather than waiting until males attain their breeding state.

In many other mammals, fertilization occurs right after coitus, but development is arrested after the first week or two. This **embryonic diapause,** which was described previously for sea lions, also occurs in some bats, bears, martens, and marsupials. The adaptive significance of embryonic diapause varies with species. In the sea lion, embryonic diapause allows the mother to give birth and mate within a short interval, but not have her resources drained by both nursing and pregnancy. It also allows young to be born at a time when resources favor their survival. In some bats, fertilization occurs in the fall before hibernation, but birth is delayed until resources become abundant in the spring.

Modes of Development

Monotremes are oviparous. The ovaries release ova with large quantities of yolk. After fertilization, shell glands in the oviduct deposit a shell around the ovum, forming an egg. Female echidnas incubate eggs in a ventral pouch. Platypus eggs are laid in their burrows.

All other mammals have a placenta through which young are nourished for at least a portion of their development. The maternal bloodstream, not yolk, supplies nutrients.

In marsupials, most nourishment for the fetus comes from "uterine milk" that uterine cells secrete. Some nutrients diffuse from maternal blood into a highly vascular yolk sac that makes contact with the uterus. This connection in marsupials is a primitive placenta. The marsupial **gestation period** (the length of time young develop within the female reproductive tract) varies between 8 and 40 days in different species. The gestation period is short because of marsupials' inability to sustain the production of hormones that maintain the uterine lining. After birth, tiny young crawl into the marsupium and attach to a nipple, where they suckle for an additional 60 to 270 days (figure 31.17).

(a)

(b)

FIGURE 31.17

Order Marsupialia. *(a)* An opossum *(Didelphis marsupialis)* with young. *(b)* Opossum young nursing in a marsupial pouch.

In eutherian mammals, the embryo implants deeply into the uterine wall. Embryonic and uterine tissues grow rapidly and become highly folded and vascular, forming the placenta. Although maternal and fetal blood do not mix, nutrients, gases, and wastes diffuse between the two bloodstreams. Gestation periods of eutherian mammals vary from 20 days (some rodents) to 19 months (the African elephant). Following birth, the placenta and other tissues that surrounded the fetus in the uterus are expelled as "afterbirth." The newborns of many species (e.g., humans) are helpless at birth; others (e.g., deer and horses) can walk and run shortly after birth.

Stop and Ask Yourself

13. What adaptation of the kidney allows mammals to excrete urine that is hypertonic to the blood?

14. What are the advantages of viviparity for mammals? In what way is viviparity costly?

15. What is embryonic diapause?

16. Why is the gestation period of a marsupial so short?

SUMMARY

1. Mammalian characteristics evolved in the synapsid lineage over a period of about 200 million years. Mammals evolved from a group of synapsids called therapsids.

2. Modern mammals include the monotremes, marsupial mammals, and placental mammals.

3. Hair is uniquely mammalian. It functions in sensory perception, temperature regulation, and communication.

4. Mammals have sebaceous, sudoriferous, scent, and mammary glands.

5. The teeth and digestive tracts of mammals are adapted for different feeding habits. Flat, grinding teeth and fermentation structures for digesting cellulose characterize herbivores. Predatory mammals have sharp teeth for killing and tearing prey.

6. The mammalian heart has four chambers, and circulatory patterns are adapted for viviparous development.

7. Mammals possess a diaphragm that alters intrathoracic pressure, which helps ventilate the lungs.

8. Mammalian thermoregulation involves metabolic heat production, insulating pelage, and behavior.

9. Mammals react to unfavorable environments by migration, winter sleep, and hibernation.

10. The nervous system of mammals is similar to that of other vertebrates. Olfaction and hearing were important for early mammals. Vision, hearing, and smell are the dominant senses in many modern mammals.

11. The nitrogenous waste of mammals is urea, and the kidney is adapted for excreting a concentrated urine.

12. Mammals have complex behavior to enhance survival. Visual cues, pheromones, and auditory and tactile cues are important in mammalian communication.

13. Most mammals have specific times during the year when reproduction occurs. Female mammals have estrus or menstrual cycles. Monotremes are oviparous. All other mammals nourish young by a placenta.

SELECTED KEY TERMS

cecum (p. 515)
delayed fertilization (p. 521)
dental formula (p. 512)
diaphragm (p. 516)
embryonic diapause (p. 521)

estrus cycle (p. 521)
gestation period (p. 521)
heterodont (p. 511)
homodont (p. 511)

CRITICAL THINKING QUESTIONS

1. Why is tooth structure important in the study of mammals?
2. What does the evolution of secondary palates have in common with the evolution of completely separated, four-chambered hearts?
3. Why is classifying mammals by feeding habits not particularly useful to phylogenetic studies?
4. Under what circumstances is endothermy disadvantageous for a mammal?
5. Discuss the possible advantages of embryonic diapause for marsupials that live in climatically unpredictable regions of Australia.

REFERENCES ON THE WORLD WIDE WEB

1. **Animal Resources.** This site provides many links to information on a variety of animals. The mammals are featured.
   http://netvet.wustl.edu/ssi.htm

2. **Class Mammalia.** This site includes descriptions of the mammalian orders.
   http://www.vet.ed.ac.uk/tol/chordata/mammalia/

3. **Introduction to the Synapsida.** This site provides much information regarding the ancient synapsid ancestors of the mammals.
   http://www.ucmp.berkeley.edu/synapsids/synapsida.html

4. **Phylogeny of the Mammals.** Click on an icon to find information on the classification and biology of any of the mammalian subclasses and orders.
   http://www.ucmp.berkeley.edu/mammal/mammal.html

5. **Mammalia.** This site lists general characteristics of the class and provides links to information on the mammalian orders.
   http://www.oit.itd.umich.edu/bio108/chordata/mammalia.html

6. **Zoo Animals.** This site provides photographs and information on the mammalian subclasses and orders.
   http://www.science.nussg/~sbs/animal

7. **The Philadelphia Zoo—Mammals!** This site provides general information on the mammals and links to specific information on zoo mammals.
   http://www.phillyzoo.org/pz-mam.htm

8. **Mammal Species of the World.** This site is a database of mammalian taxonomy.
   http://nmnhwww.si.edu/msw/about.html

9. **IMMA.** This site, provided by the International Marine Mammal Association, provides much information on marine mammals in captivity, on fisheries and marine mammals, and on conservation of marine mammals.
   http://www.imma.org/index.html

10. **Wolf Homepage.** This site provides much information on endangered wolf species and on attempts to reintroduce wolves into natural habitats.
    http://www.usa.net.WolfHome/

11. **Yerkes Regional Primate Research Center.** This site provides much information on the primate research being conducted at this center.
    http://www.emory.edy:80/YERKES/

12. **Big Cats Online.** This site contains information on all big cat species.
    http://dialspace.dial.pipex.com/agarman/

13. **Primate Gallery.** This site provides photographs, animations, vocalizations, and links to information on the primates.
    http://www.seky.cin/~bio/PrimateGallery/

SUGGESTED READINGS
BOOKS

Aidley, D. J., ed. 1980. *Animal Migration.* Cambridge: Cambridge University Press.

Baker, R. 1984. *Bird Navigation: The Solution of a Mystery?* New York: Holmes & Meier Publishers.

———, ed. 1981. *The Mystery of Migration.* Minneapolis: Viking Press.

Bakker, R. T. 1986. *The Dinosaur Heresies.* New York: William Morrow.

Barnes, R., Calow, P., and Olive, P. 1993. *The Invertebrates: A New Synthesis.* 2d ed. Boston: Blackwell Scientific.

Bliss, D. E., ed. 1982. *The Biology of Crustacea,* vols. 1–5. San Diego: Academic Press.

Bogitsh, B., and Cheng, T. 1990. *Human Parasitology.* Philadelphia: W. B. Saunders.

Boitani, L., and Bartoli, S. 1983. *Simon and Schuster's Guide to Mammals.* New York: Simon and Schuster.

Borror, D. J., Tripplehorn, C. A., and Johnson, N. F. 1989. *An Introduction to the Study of Insects.* 6th ed. Philadelphia: Saunders College Publishing.

Boss, K. J. 1982. Mollusca. In *Synopsis and Classification of Living Organisms,* vol. 1, edited by S. P. Parker. New York: McGraw-Hill.

Brusca, R. C., and Brusca, G. J. 1990. *Invertebrates.* Sunderland, Mass.: Sinauer Associates.

Chapman, J. A., and Feldhamer, G. A., eds. 1982. *Wild Mammals of North America: Biology, Management, and Economics.* Baltimore: The Johns Hopkins University Press.

Corliss, J. D. 1979. *The Ciliated Protozoa: Characterization, Classification, and Guide to the Literature.* 2d ed. Elmford, N.Y.: Pergamon Press.

Cousteau, J., and Diol'e, P. 1973. *Octopus and Squid, the Soft Intelligence.* Garden City, Mich.: Doubleday.

Dethier, V. G. 1976. *The Hungry Fly.* Cambridge: Harvard University Press.

Duellman, W. E., and Trueb, L. 1986. *Biology of Amphibians.* New York: McGraw-Hill.

Duncan, T., and Stuessy, T. F. 1984. *Cladistics: Perspectives on the Reconstruction of Evolutionary History.* New York: Columbia University Press.

Dunn, D. F. 1982. Cnidaria. In, *Synopsis and Classification of Living Organisms,* vol. 1, edited by S. P. Parker. New York: McGraw-Hill.

Eisenberg, J. F. 1981. *The Mammalian Radiations: An Analysis of Trends in Evolution, Adaptation, and Behavior.* Chicago: University of Chicago Press.

Faaborg, J. 1988. *Ornithology: An Ecological Approach.* Englewood Cliffs, N.J.: Prentice-Hall.

Farmer, J. N. 1980. *The Protozoa: Introduction to Protozoology.* St. Louis: C. V. Mosby.

Feduccia, A. 1980. *The Age of Birds.* Cambridge: Harvard University Press.

Fell, H. B. 1982. Echinodermata. In *Synopsis and Classification of Living Animals,* vol. 2, edited by S. P. Parker. New York: McGraw-Hill.

Fenchel, T. 1987. *Ecology of Protozoa*. New York: Springer-Verlag.

Foelix, R. F. 1982. *Biology of Spiders*. Cambridge: Harvard University Press.

Foreman, R. E., Gorbman, A., Dodd, J. M., and Olsson, R, eds. 1985. *Evolutionary Biology of Fishes*. NATO ASI Series, vol. 103. New York: Plenum Press.

Frangsmyr, T. 1983. *Linnaeus: The Man and His Work*. Berkeley: University of California Press.

Gibson, R. 1972. *Nemerteans*. London: Hutchinson University Library.

———. 1982. *British Nemerteans: Keys and Notes for Identification of the Species*. New York: Cambridge University Press.

Gill, F. B. 1990. *Ornithology*. New York: W. H. Freeman.

Gillot, Cedric. 1980. *Entomology*. New York: Plenum Press.

Goin, C. J., and Goin, O. B. 1978. *Introduction to Herpetology*. 3d ed. San Francisco: W. H. Freeman.

Gould, S. J. 1989. *Wonderful Life: The Burgess Shale and the Nature of the History*. New York: W. W. Norton.

Grell, K. G. 1973. *Protozoology*. Berlin: Springer-Verlag.

Griffiths, M. 1978. *The Biology of Monotremes*. San Diego: Academic Press.

Halstead, L. B. 1968. *The Pattern of Vertebrate Evolution*. San Francisco: W. H. Freeman.

Harbison, G. R., and Madin, L. P. 1982. Ctenophora. In *Synopsis and Classification of Living Organisms*, vol. 1, edited by S. P. Parker. New York: McGraw-Hill.

Hardisty, M. W. 1979. *Biology of the Cyclostomes*. New York: Chapman and Hall.

Hasler, A. D., and Scholz, A. T. 1983. *Olfactory Imprinting and Homing in Salmon*. New York: Springer-Verlag, Zoophysiology Series.

Holldobler, B., and Wilson, E. O. 1990. *The Ants*. Cambridge: Harvard University Press.

Horridge, G. A., ed. 1975. *The Compound Eye and Vision of Insects*. Atlanta, Ga.: Clarendon Group.

Hyman, L. H. 1940. *The Invertebrates*. New York: McGraw-Hill.

———. 1951. *The Invertebrates*, vol. II. *Platyhelminthes and Rhynchocela*. New York: McGraw-Hill.

Jacques, H. E. 1978. *How to Know the Insects*. 3d ed. Dubuque, Iowa: Wm. C. Brown Publishers.

Jahn, T., Bovee, R., and Jahn, F. 1979. *How to Know the Protozoa*. Dubuque, Iowa: Wm. C. Brown Publishers.

Kaston, B. J. 1972. *How to Know the Spiders*. 2d ed. Dubuque, Iowa: Wm. C. Brown Publishers.

King, F. W., and Behler, J. 1979. *The Audubon Society Field Guide to North American Reptiles and Amphibians*. New York: Alfred A. Knopf.

King, P. E. 1973. *Pycnogonids*. New York: St. Martins Press.

Kozloff, E. 1990. *Invertebrates*. Philadelphia: W. B. Saunders.

Laybourn-Parry, J. 1984. *A Functional Biology of Free-Living Protozoa*. Berkeley: University of California Press.

Lee, J., Hunter, S., and Bovee, E. 1985. *An Illustrated Guide to the Protozoa*. Lawrence, Kan.: Allen Press, Society of Protozoologists.

Levandowsky, M., and Hunter, S. H. 1979. *Biochemistry and Physiology of Protozoa*, vols. I–III. New York: Academic Press.

Levi, H. W. 1982. Crustacea. In *Synopsis and Classification of Living Organisms*, vol. 2, edited by S. P. Parker. New York: McGraw-Hill.

Lovtrup, S. 1977. *The Phylogeny of Vertebrata*. New York: John Wiley & Sons.

Margulis, L., and Schwartz, K. V. 1987. *Five Kingdoms: An Illustrated Guide to the Phyla of Life on Earth*. 2d ed. San Francisco: W. H. Freeman.

Matthews, T. W., and Matthews, J. R. 1978. *Insect Behavior*. New York: John Wiley & Sons.

McCafferty, W. P. 1981. *Aquatic Entomology: A Fisherman's and Ecologist's Illustrated Guide to Insects and Their Relatives*. Providence, R.I.: Science Books International.

Meglitsch, P. A., and Schram, F. R. 1991. *Invertebrate Zoology*. 3d ed. New York: Oxford University Press.

Moyle, P. B., and Cech, J. J. 1982. *Fishes: An Introduction to Ichthyology*. Englewood Cliffs, N.J.: Prentice-Hall.

Moynihan, M. H., and Rodaniche, A. F. 1977. Communication, crypsis, and mimicry among cephalopods. In *How Animals Communicate*, edited by T. A. Sebeok. Bloomington: Indiana University Press.

Nelson, J. S. 1984. *Fishes of the World*. 2d ed. New York: John Wiley & Sons.

Nisbet, B. 1984. *Nutrition and Feeding Strategies in Protozoa*. London: Croom Helm.

Pearse, V., Pearse, J., Buchsbaum, M., and Buchsbaum, R. 1987. *Living Invertebrates*. New York: Blackwell Scientific Publications.

Pechenik, J. A. 1996. *Biology of the Invertebrates*. 3d ed. Dubuque, Iowa: Wm. C. Brown Publishers.

Pennak, R. W. 1989. *Freshwater Invertebrates of the United States*. 3d ed. New York: John Wiley & Sons.

Peterson, R. T. 1980. *Field Guide to the Birds*. 2d ed. Boston: Houghton Mifflin.

Pettibone, M. H. 1982. Annelida. In *Synopsis and Classification of Living Organisms*, vol. 2, edited by S. P. Parker. New York: McGraw-Hill.

Poinar, G. O. 1983. *The Natural History of Nematodes*. Englewood Cliffs, N.J.: Prentice-Hall.

Pough, F. H., Heiser, J. B., and McFarland, W. N. 1989. *Vertebrate Life*. 3d ed. New York: Macmillan Publishing.

Rice, M. E., and Todorovic, M. eds. 1975. *Proceedings of the International Symposium on the Biology of the Sipuncula and Echiura*. Washington, D.C.: American Museum of Natural History.

Ridley, M. 1986. *Evolution and Classification: The Reformation of Cladism*. New York: Longman.

Riser, N. W., and Morse, M. P., eds. 1974. *Biology of the Turbellaria*. New York: McGraw-Hill.

Romer, A. S., and Parsons, T. S. 1986. *The Vertebrate Body*. 6th ed. Philadelphia: Saunders College Publishing.

Ruppell, G. 1975. *Bird Flight*. New York: Van Nostrand Reinhold.

Ruppert, E .E., and Barnes, R. D. 1994. *Invertebrate Zoology*. 6th ed. Philadelphia: Saunders College Publishing.

Russell-Hunter, W. D. 1979. *A Life of Invertebrates*. New York: Macmillan Publishing.

Savage, R. J. G., and Long, M. T. 1986. *Mammal Evolution*. New York: Facts on File Publications.

Savory, T. H. 1977. *Arachnida*. 2d ed. San Diego: Academic Press.

Schmidt, G. D., and Roberts, L. S. 1996. *Foundations of Parasitology*. Dubuque, Iowa: Wm. C. Brown Publishers.

Schmidt, K. P., and Inger, R. F. 1975. *Living Reptiles of the World*. New York: Doubleday.

Sleigh, M. 1989. *Protozoa and Other Protists*. New York: Routledge, Chapman, and Hall.

Smith, R. J. F. 1985. *The Control of Fish Migration*. New York: Springer-Verlag, Zoophysiology Series.

Solem, A. 1974. *The Shell Makers: Introducing Mollusks*. New York: John Wiley & Sons.

Stahl, B. J. 1974. *Vertebrate History: Problems in Evolution*. New York: McGraw-Hill.

Steele, R. S. 1985. *Sharks of the World*. New York: Facts on File Publications.

Stonehouse, B., and Gilmore, D., eds. 1977. *The Biology of Marsupials*. New York: Macmillan Publishing.

Terres, J. K. 1980. *The Audubon Society Encyclopedia of North American Birds*. New York: Alfred A. Knopf.

Thomas, R. D. K., and Olson, E. C., eds. 1980. *A Cold Look at the Warm-Blooded Dinosaurs*. AAAS Selected Symposium Series. Boulder, Colo.: Westview Press.

Travola, W. N., Popper, A. N., and Fay, R. R. 1981. *Hearing and Sound Communication in Fishes*. New York: Springer-Verlag.

Tytler, P., and Calow, P. 1985. *Fish Energetics: New Perspectives*. Baltimore: Johns Hopkins University Press.

Vandenbergh, J. G. 1983. *Pheromones and Reproduction in Mammals*. San Diego: Academic Press.

Vaughan, T. A. 1978. *Mammalogy*. Philadelphia: W. B. Saunders.

Walker, W. F. 1987. *Functional Anatomy of the Vertebrates*. Philadelphia: Saunders College Publishing.

Welty, J. C. 1988. *The Life of Birds*. 4th ed. Philadelphia: W. B. Saunders.

Wigglesworth, V. B. 1982. *Principles of Insect Physiology*. 7th ed. New York: John Wiley & Sons.

Wiley, E. O. 1981. *Phylogenetics: The Theory and Practice of Phylogenetic Systematics*. New York: John Wiley and Sons.

Wilford, J. N. 1985. *The Riddle of the Dinosaur*. New York: Alfred A. Knopf.

Wilson, E. O. 1971. *The Insect Societies*. Cambridge: Harvard University Press.

Young, J. Z., and Hobbs, M. J. 1975. *The Life of Mammals: Their Anatomy and Physiology*. 2d ed. New York: Oxford University Press.

Zuckerman, B. M., ed. 1980. *Nematodes as Biological Models*. Vol. II: *Aging and Other Model Systems*. New York: Academic Press.

ARTICLES

Aldhous, P. 1993. Malaria: Focus on mosquito genes. *Science* 261(5121): 546–48.

Alexander, R. M. 1991. How dinosaurs ran. *Scientific American*, April.

Alldredge, A. L., and Madin, L. P. 1982. Pelagic tunicates: Unique herbivores in the marine plankton. *BioScience* 32: 655–63.

Alverez, W., and Asaro, F. 1990. What caused mass extinction—an extraterrestrial impact? *Scientific American*, October.

Bakker, R. T. 1975. Dinosaur renaissance. *Scientific American*, April.

Beard, J. 1992. Warding off bullets by a spider's thread. *New Scientist* 136(1847): 18.

Beebee, T. J. C. 1992. Amphibian decline? *Nature* 355(6356): 120.

Beland, P. 1996. The beluga whales of the St. Lawrence River. *Scientific American*, May.

Birkeland, C. 1989. The faustian traits of the crown-of-thorns starfish. *American Scientist*, 72(2): 154–63.

Birkhead, T. 1996. Mechanisms of sperm competition in birds. *American Scientist*, 84(3): 254–62.

Blaustein, A. R., and Wake, D. B. 1975. The puzzle of declining amphibian populations. *Scientific American*, April.

Bogan, A. E. 1993. Freshwater bivalve extinction (Mollusca: Unionoida): A search for causes. *American Zoologist* 33(6): 599–610.

Borgia, G. 1995. Why do bowerbirds build bowers? *American Scientist*, 83(6): 542–47.

Boycott, B. B. 1965. Learning in the octopus. *Scientific American*, March.

Briggs, D., and Siveter, D. 1996. Soft-bodied fossils from a Silurian volcaniclastic deposit. *Nature* 382(6588): 248.

Brownlee, S. 1987. Jellyfish aren't out to get us. *Discover* 8: 42–52.

Buck, J., and Buck, E. 1976. Synchronous fireflies. *Scientific American*, May.

Calder, W. A., III. 1978. The Kiwi. *Scientific American*, July.

Camhi, J. M. 1980. The escape system of the cockroach. *Scientific American*, December.

Carter, C. S., and Getz, L. L. 1993. Monogamy and the prairie vole. *Scientific American*, June.

Chinsamy, A., and Dodson, P. 1995. Inside a dinosaur bone. *American Scientist* 83(2): 174–80.

Cloney, R. A. 1982. Ascidian larvae and the events of metamorphosis. *American Zoologist* 22: 817–26.

Cole, J. 1984. Unisexual lizards. *Scientific American*, January.

Conniff, R. 1987. The little suckers have made a comeback. *Discover* 8: 84–93.

Corliss, J. 1984. The kingdom Protista and its 45 phyla. *Biosystems* 17: 87–126.

Cortillot, V. 1990. What caused mass extinction?—a volcanic eruption. *Scientific American*, October.

Costa, J. 1997. Caterpillars as social insects. *American Scientist* 85(2): 150–59.

Cox, F. E. G. 1988. Which way for malaria? *Nature* 331: 486–87.

Cracraft, J. 1988. Early evolution of birds. *Nature* 335: 630–32.

Cronin, T., Marshall, N. J., and Land, M. 1994. The unique visual system of the mantis shrimp. *American Scientist* 82(4): 356–65.

Dando, P. R., Southward, A. J., Southward, E. C., Dixon, D. R., Crawford, A., and Crawford, A. 1992. Shipwrecked tube worms. *Nature* 356(6371): 667.

Daves, N. B., and Brooke, M. 1991. Coevolution of the cuckoo and its host. *Scientific American*, January.

Day, S. 1992. A moving experience for sponges. *New Scientist* 136(1847): 15–16.

Deaming, C., and Ferguson, F. 1989. In the heat of the nest. *New Scientist* 121: 33–38.

D'Hondt, J. L. 1971. Gastroticha. *Annual Review Oceanography and Marine Biology* 9: 141–50.

Duellman, W. E. 1985. Systematic zoology: Slicing the Gordian knot with Ockham's razor. *American Zoologist* 25: 751–62.

Dunelson, J., and Turner, M. 1985. How the trypanosome changes its coat. *Scientific American*, February.

Edmunds, P. 1996. Ten days under the sea. *Scientific American*, October.

Erwin, D., Valentine, J., and Jablonski, P. 1997. The origin of animal body plans. *American Scientist* 85(2): 126–37.

Evans, H. E., and O'Neill, K. M. 1991. Beewolves. *Scientific American*, August.

Ewing, T. 1988. Thorny problem as Australia's coastline faces invasion. *Nature* 333: 387.

Fingerman, M. ed. 1992. The complete crab (symposium). *American Zoologist*, 32(2): 359–542.

Fischer, E. A., and Peterson, C. W. 1987. The evolution of sexual patterns in the seabasses. *BioScience* 37: 482–89.

FitzGerald, G. J. 1993. The reproductive behavior of the stickleback (fish). *Scientific American*, April.

Fleming, T. H. 1993. Plant-visiting bats. *American Scientist* 81(5): 460–67.

Forey, P. L. 1988. Golden Jubilee for the coelacanth *Latimeria chalumnae*. *Nature* 336: 727–32.

Franks, N. 1989. Army ants: A collective intelligence. *American Scientist* 77(2): 138–45.

Fricke, Hans. 1988. Coelacanth: The fish that time forgot. *National Geographic* 173(6): 824–38.

Funk, D. H. 1989. The mating of tree crickets. *Scientific American*, August.

Gaffney, E. S., Hutchison, J. H., Jenkings, F. A., Jr., and Meeker, L. J. 1987. Modern turtle origins: The oldest known cryptodire. *Science* 237: 289–91.

Gee, H. 1988. Taxonomy bloodied by cladistic wars. *Nature* 335: 585.

Gerhard, S. 1992. The mammals of island Europe. *Scientific American*, February.

Getz, L., and Carter, C. S. 1996. Prairie-vole partnerships. *American Scientist* 84(1): 56–62.

Gibbons, J. W. 1987. Why do turtles live so long? *BioScience* 37(4): 262–68.

Gilbert, J. J. 1984. To build a worm. *Science* 84(5): 62–70.

Gore, R. 1989. Extinctions. *National Geographic*, June.

Goreau, T. F., Goreau, N. I., and Goreau, T. J. 1979. Corals and coral reefs. *Scientific American*, August.

Gorniak, G. C., and Gans, C. 1982. How does the toad flip its tongue? Test of two hypotheses. *Science* 216: 1335–37.

Gorr, T., and Kleinschmidt, T. 1993. Evolutionary relationships of the coelacanth. *American Scientist* 81(1): 72–82.

Gould, J. L. 1980. The case for magnetic sensitivity in birds and bees (such as it is). *American Scientist* 68: 256–67.

Gould, J. L., and Marler, P. 1987. Learning by instinct. *Scientific American*, January.

Greenwood, J. J. D. 1992. In the pink (snails). *Nature* 357(6375): 192.

Griffiths, M. 1988. The platypus. *Scientific American*, May.

Grimaldi, D. 1996. Captured in amber. *Scientific American*, April.

Grober, M. S. 1988. Brittle-star bioluminescence functions as an aposematic signal to deter crustacean predators. *Animal Behaviour* 36: 493–501.

Gutzke, W. H. N., and Crews, D. 1988. Embryonic temperature determines adult sexuality in a reptile. *Nature* 332: 832–34.

Handel, S. N., and Beattie, A. J. 1990. Seed dispersal by ants. *Scientific American*, August.

Hanken, J. 1989. Development and evolution in amphibians. *American Scientist* 77(4): 336–43.

Harvey, P. H., and Partridge, L. 1988. Of cuckoo clocks and cowbirds. *Nature* 335: 630–32.

Heinrich, B., and Esch, H. 1994. Thermoregulation in bees. *American Scientist* 82(2): 164–70.

Heinrich, B., and Marzluff, J. 1995. Why ravens share. *American Scientist* 83(4): 342–49.

Herbert, S. 1986. Darwin as a geologist. *Scientific American*, May.

Heslinga, G. A., and Fitt, W. K. 1987. The domestication of reef-dwelling clams. *BioScience* 37: 332–39.

Horn, M. H., and Gibson, R. N. 1988. Intertidal fishes. *Scientific American*, January.

Hotez, P., and Pritchard, D. 1995. Hookworm infection. *Scientific American*, June.

Jaeger, R. G. 1988. A comparison of territorial and nonterritorial behaviour in two species of salamanders. *Animal Behavior* 36: 307–400.

Kabnick, K. S., and Peattie, D. A. 1991. *Giardia*: A missing link between prokaryotes and eukaryotes. *American Scientist* 79(1): 34–43.

Kantor, F. S. 1994. Disarming Lyme disease. *Scientific American*, September.

Kanwisher, J. W., and Ridgeway, S. H. 1983. The physiological ecology of whales and porpoises. *Scientific American*, June.

Kelly-Borges, M. M. 1995. Zoology: Sponges out of their depth. *Nature* 273(6512): 284–85.

Kerstitch, A. 1992. Primates of the sea (octupuses). *Discover* 13(2): 34–37.

Kirchner, W. H., and Towne, W. F. 1994. The sensory basis of the honeybee's dance language. *Scientific American*, June.

Klimley, A. P. 1994. The predatory behavior of the white shark. *American Scientist* 82(2): 122–33.

Knoll, A. H. 1991. End of the Proterozoic eon. *Scientific American*, October.

Konishi, M. 1993. Listening with two ears. *Scientific American*, April.

Kristensen, R. M. 1983. Loricifera, a new phylum with Aschelminthes characters from the meiobenthos. *Zeitschrift Zoologie Systumatiks Evolution-Fforschung* 21: 163–80.

Langston, W., Jr. 1981. Pterosaurs. *Scientific American*, February.

Lenhoff, H. M., and Lenhoff, S. G. 1988. Trembly's polyps. *Scientific American*, April.

Lent, C. M., and Dickinson, M. H. 1988. The neurobiology of feeding in leeches. *Scientific American*, June.

Levine, N. D. 1980. A newly revised classification of the protozoa. *Journal of Protozoology* 27: 37–58.

Lizotte, R. S., and Rovner, J. S. 1988. Nocturnal capture of fireflies by lycosid spiders: Visual versus vibratory stimuli. *Animal Behaviour* 36: 1809–15.

Lohman, K. J. 1992. How sea turtles navigate. *Scientific American*, January.

Mackenzie, D. 1991. Where earthworms fear to tread. *New Scientist* 131(1781): 31–34.

Mann, J. 1992. Sponges to wipe away pain. *Nature* 358(6387): 540.

Manzel, R., and Erber, J. 1978. Learning and memory in bees. *Scientific American*, July.

Marshall, L. G. 1988. Land mammals and the great American interchange. *American Scientist* 76(4): 380–88.

Marshall, L. G. 1994. The terror birds of South America. *Scientific American*, February.

Marten, K., Shariff, K., Psarakos, S., and White, D. 1996. Ring bubbles of dolphins. *Scientific American*, August.

May, M. 1991. Aerial defense tactics of flying insects. *American Scientist* 79(4): 316–28.

McClanahan, L. L., Ruibal, R., and Shoemaker, V. H. 1994. Frogs and toads in deserts. *Scientific American*, March.

McMasters, J. H. 1989. The flight of the bumblebee and related myths of entomological engineering. *American Scientist* 72(2): 164–69.

Messing, C. G. 1988. Sea lilies and feather stars. *Sea Frontiers* 34: 236–41.

Miller, J. A. 1984. Spider silk, stretch, and strength. *Science News* 125: 391.

Miller, L. H., Howard, R. J., Carter, R., Good, M. F., Nussenzwieg, V., and Nussenzwieg, R. S. 1986. Research toward malaria vaccines. *Science* 234: 1349–55.

Milne, L. J., and Milne, M. 1978. The social behavior of burying beetles. *Scientific American*, August.

———. Insects of the water surface. 1978. *Scientific American*, April.

Mitchell, T. 1988. Coral-killing starfish meet their mesh. *New Scientist* 120: 28.

Mock, D. W., Drummond, H., and Stinson, H. 1990. Avian siblicide. *American Scientist* 78(5): 438–49.

Moffett, M. W. 1991. All eyes on jumping spiders. *National Geographic* 180(3): 43–63.

Moore, J. 1984. Parasites that change the behavior of their host. *Scientific American*, January.

Morse, A. N. C. 1991. How do planktonic larvae know where to settle? *American Scientist* 79(2): 154–67.

Narins, P. 1995. Frog communication. *Scientific American*, August.

Newman, E. A., and Hartline, P. H. 1982. The infrared "vision" of snakes. *Scientific American*, (March) 246: 116–27.

Nordell, D. 1988. Milking leeches for drug research. *New Scientist* 117: 43–44.

O'Shea, T. 1994. Manatees. *Scientific American*, July.

Osorio, D., Bacon, J., and Whitington, P. 1997. The evolution of arthropod nervous systems. *American Scientist* 85(3): 244–53.

Ostrom, J. H. 1979. Bird flight: How did it happen? *American Scientist* 67: 46–56.

Packer, C., and Pusey, A. 1997. Divided we fall: Communication among lions. *Scientific American*, May.

Partridge, B. L. 1982. The structure and function of fish schools. *Scientific American*, June.

Quicke, D. 1988. Spiders bite their way towards safer insecticides. *New Scientist* 120: 38–41.

Raeburn, P. 1988. Ancient survivor. *National Wildlife* 26(5): 36–38.

Rennie, J. 1993. Insects are forever. *Scientific American*, November.

Reynolds, C. V. 1994. Warm blood for cold water. *Discover* 15(1): 42–43.

Ricciuti, E. R. 1986. A genuine monster. *Audubon* 88: 22–24.

Rinderer, T. E., Oldroyd, B. P., and Sheppard, W. S. 1993. Africanized bees in the U.S. *Scientific American*, December.

Rinderer, T. E., Stelzer, J. A., Oldroyd, B. P., Buco, S. M., and Rubink, W. L. 1991. Hybridization between European and Africanized bees in neotropical Yucatan Peninsula. *Science* 253(5017): 309–11.

Rismiller, P. D., and Seymour, R. S. 1991. The echidna. *Scientific American*, February.

Roberts, L. 1988. Corals remain baffling. *Science* 239: 256.

———. 1990. The worm project. *Science* 248: 1310–13.

Robinson, M. H. 1987. In a world of silken lines, touch must be exquisitely fine. *Smithsonian* 18: 94–102.

Rome, L. C., Swank, D., and Corda, D. 1993. How fish power swimming. *Science* 261(5119): 340–43.

Roper, C. R. E., and Boss, K. J. 1982. The giant squid. *Scientific American*, April.

Russell, D. A. 1982. The mass extinctions of the late Mesozoic. *Scientific American*, January.

Ryan, M. J. 1990. Signals, species, and sexual selection. *American Scientist* 78(1): 46–52.

Schmidt, M. 1996. Working elephants. *Scientific American*, January.

Scott, M. 1996. Communal breeding in burying beetles. *American Scientist* 84(4): 376–82.

Seeley, T. D. 1982. How honeybees find a home. *Scientific American*, October.

———. 1989. The honeybee colony as a superorganism. *American Scientist* 77(6): 546–53.

Shear, W. A. 1994. Untangling the evolution of the web. *American Scientist* 82(3): 256–66.

Shimek, R. B. 1987. Sex among the sessile: With the onset of spring in cool northern Pacific waters, even sea cucumbers bestir themselves. *Natural History* 96: 60–63.

Simmons, L. W. 1988. The calling song of the field cricket, *Gryllus bimaculatus* (De Geer): Constraints on transmission and its role in intermale competition and female choice. *Animal Behaviour* 36: 380–94.

Sitwell, N. 1993. The grub and the Galápagos (sea cucumbers). *New Scientist* 40(1903): 32–35.

Skelly, D. 1997. Tadpole communities. *American Scientist* 85(1): 36–45.

Stanford, C. 1995. Chimpanzee hunting behavior. *American Scientist* 83(3): 256–61.

Stowe, M. K., Tumilinson, J. H., and Heath, R. R. 1987. Chemical mimicry: Bolas spiders emit components of moth prey species sex pheromones. *Science* 236: 964–68.

Stuller, J. 1988. With the gales in their sails. *Audubon* 90: 84–85.

Suga, N. 1990. Biosonar and neural computations in bats. *Scientific American*, June.

Tangley, L. 1987. Malaria: Fighting the African scourge. *BioScience* 37(2): 94–98.

Tattersall, I. 1993. Madagascar's lemurs. *Scientific American*, January.

Taylor, M. 1994. Amphibians that came to stay. *New Scientist* 141(1912): 21–24.

Toner, M. 1992. Spin doctor. *Discover* 13(5): 32–36.

Topoff, H. 1990. Slave-making ants. *American Scientist* 78(6): 520–28.

Tumlinson, J. H., Lewis, W. J., and Vet, L. E. M. 1993. How parasitic wasps find their hosts. *Scientific American*, March.

Tuttle, R. H. 1990. Apes of the world. *American Scientist* 78(2): 115–25.

Verell, P. 1988. The chemistry of sexual persuasion. *New Scientist* 118: 40–43.

Vickers-Rich, P., and Rich, T. H. 1993. Australia's polar dinosaurs. *Scientific American*, July.

Vogel, S. 1988. How organisms use flow-induced pressures. *American Scientist* 76: 92–94.

Vollrath, F. 1992. Spider webs and silks. *Scientific American*, March.

Von Frisch, K. 1974. Decoding the language of the bee. *Science* 185: 663–68.

Ward, P., Greenwald, L., and Greenwald, O. E. 1980. The buoyancy of the chambered nautilus. *Scientific American*, October.

Wellnhofer, P. 1990. *Archaeopteryx*. *Scientific American*, May.

West, M. J., and King, A. P. 1990. Mozart's starling. *American Scientist* 78(2): 106–14.

Wheatley, D. 1988. Whale size quandary. *Nature* 336: 626.

Wicksten, M. D. 1980. Decorator crabs. *Scientific American*, February.

Wilczynski, W., and Brenowitz, E. A. 1988. Acoustic cues mediate inter-male spacing in a neotropical frog. *Animal Behaviour* 36: 1054–63.

Wilkinson, C. R. 1987. Interocean differences in size and nutrition of coral reef sponge populations. *Science* 236: 1654–57.

Wood, R. 1990. Reef-building sponges. *American Scientist* 78(3): 224–35.

Wootton, R. J. 1990. The mechanical design of insect wings. *Scientific American*, November.

Yager, J. 1981. Remipedia, a new class of Crustacea from a marine cave in the Bahamas. *Journal of Crustacean Biology* 1: 328–33.

Yonge, C. M. 1975. Giant clams. *Scientific American*, April.

Zapol, W. M. 1987. Diving adaptations of the Weddell Seal. *Scientific American*, June.

part SIX

FORM AND FUNCTION:
A COMPARATIVE PERSPECTIVE

Is the whole of an animal equal to the sum of its parts? A superficial answer would be "yes." However, the structure and function of an animal are never as simple as this answer implies. A body is composed of many parts (e.g.,

cells, tissues, organs, and organ systems), yet rarely are any of these parts independent of one another. Simple additive relationships fail to describe adequately the interactions between the body's parts. Instead, an animal is the product of many complex interactions. In understanding the structure and function of any system, you only begin to understand the whole animal.

Cells, tissues, organs, and organ systems all interact to maintain a steady homeostatic state compatible with life. Ultimately, you need to look inward to see the genetic potential of the animal, outward to see how environmental constraints limit the fulfillment of that potential, and backward to see the evolutionary pressures that shaped the particular species.

Parts One through Five of this text examine animal life at molecular, cellular, genetic, developmental, behavioral, and taxonomic levels. Throughout, the evolutionary forces and pressures that influenced the development of a vast array of animal life-forms are presented, concluding with five chapters on the vertebrates. Part Six (chapters 32 through 39) continues this coverage of animal life by presenting an overview of the various organ systems: integumentary, skeletal, muscular, nervous and sensory, endocrine, circulatory, lymphatic, respiratory, digestive, urinary, and reproductive.

The major theme in Part Six is that all organ systems are specialized and coordinate with each other and that they constantly adjust to changes inside and outside the animal. Although each system has its own specialized function, none operates without assistance from the others. As you will see, the structure of each system determines its particular function.

chapter 32

PROTECTION, SUPPORT, AND MOVEMENT

Concepts

1. The integumentary system of animals consists of an outer protective body covering called the integument. The integument of most multicellular invertebrates consists of a single layer of cells. The vertebrate integument is multilayered and is called skin. Skin contains nerves and blood vessels, as well as derivatives, such as glands, hair, and nails.

2. Skeletal systems function primarily in movement using antagonistic muscles. Animals have three types of skeletons: fluid hydrostatic skeletons, rigid exoskeletons, and rigid endoskeletons. Many invertebrates have hydrostatic skeletons consisting of a core of liquid wrapped in a tension-resistant sheath containing muscles. Rigid exoskeletons completely surround an animal and are sites for muscle attachment and counterforces for muscle movements. They also offer protection and support. The vertebrate skeletal system is an endoskeleton. It consists mainly of supportive tissue called cartilage and bone.

3. Muscles provide the force for movement in animals from cnidarians to vertebrates. Vertebrates use their endoskeleton in conjunction with muscles to move. In vertebrates, striated skeletal muscles move the body, smooth muscles move material through tubular organs and change the size of tubular openings, and cardiac muscle produces the beating of the heart.

Would You Like to Know . . .

1. how you can determine the age of a fish? (p. 532)

2. what is the function of toad "warts"? (p. 533)

3. why mammals have been able to colonize terrestrial environments? (p. 534)

4. how leather is made and from what source it comes? (p. 534)

5. what "goose bumps" are? (p. 535)

6. what is "animal rubber" and how it functions? (p. 537)

7. where the expression "to clam up" originates? (p. 542)

8. when a heart has time to relax? (p. 542)

9. why insects that jump have relatively long legs? (p. 544)

This chapter answers these and other useful questions.

This chapter contains evolutionary concepts, which are set off in this font.

In animals, structure and function have evolved together. Several results of this evolution are protection, support, and movement. The integumentary, skeletal, and muscular systems are primarily responsible for these functions.

PROTECTION: INTEGUMENTARY SYSTEMS

The **integument** (L. *integumentum*, cover) is the external covering of an animal. It primarily protects against mechanical and chemical injury, and invasion by microorganisms. Many other diverse functions of the integument have evolved in different animal groups. These functions include regulation of body temperature; excretion of waste materials; conversion of sunlight into vitamin D; reception of environmental stimuli, such as pain, temperature, and pressure; locomotion; and movement of nutrients and gases.

THE INTEGUMENTARY SYSTEM OF INVERTEBRATES

Some single-celled protozoa have only a **plasma membrane** for an external covering. This membrane is structurally and chemically identical to the plasma membrane of multicellular organisms (*see figure 3.4*). In protozoa, the plasma membrane has a large surface area relative to body volume, so that gas exchange and removal of soluble wastes occur by simple diffusion. This large surface area also facilitates the uptake of dissolved nutrients from surrounding fluids. Other protozoa, such as *Paramecium*, have a thick protein coat called a **pellicle** (L. *pellicula*, thin skin) outside the plasma membrane. This pellicle offers further environmental protection and is a semirigid structure that transmits the force of cilia or flagella to the entire body of the protozoan as it moves.

Most multicellular invertebrates have an integument consisting of a single layer of columnar epithelial cells (figure 32.1). This outer layer, the **epidermis** (Gr. *epi*, upon + *derm*, skin), rests on a basement membrane. Beneath the basement membrane is a thin layer of connective tissue fibers and cells. Epidermal cells exposed at the surface of the animal may possess cilia. The epidermis of some invertebrates also contains glandular cells, which secrete an overlying, noncellular material that encases part or most of the animal.

Some invertebrates possess **cuticles** (L. *cuticula*, *cutis*, skin) that are highly variable in structure (figure 32.2). For example, in some animals (rotifers), cuticles are thin and elastic, whereas in others (crustaceans, arachnids, insects), cuticles are thick and rigid, and support the body. Such cuticles consist of chitin and proteins in rigid plates that a flexible membrane links. A disadvantage of cuticles is that animals have difficulty growing within them. As a result, some of these invertebrates (e.g., arthropods) periodically shed the old, outgrown cuticle in a process called molting or ecdysis (*see figure 23.5*).

In cnidarians, such as *Hydra*, the epidermis is only a few cell layers thick. Other cnidarians (e.g., the corals) have mucous

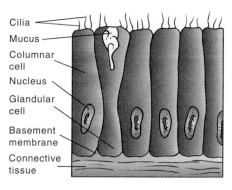

FIGURE 32.1

Integument of Invertebrates. The integument of many invertebrates consists of a simple layer of columnar epithelial cells (epidermis) resting on a basement membrane. A thin layer of connective tissue lies under the basement membrane. Cilia and glandular cells may or may not be present.

glands that secrete a calcium carbonate ($CaCO_3$) **shell.** The outer covering of parasitic flukes and tapeworms is a complex syncytium called a **tegument** (L. *tegumentum*, *tegere*, to cover). Its main functions are nutrient ingestion and protection against digestion by host enzymes. Nematodes and annelids have an epidermis that is one cell thick and secretes a multilayered cuticle. The integument of echinoderms consists of a thin, usually ciliated epidermis and an underlying connective-tissue dermis containing $CaCO_3$. Arthropods have the most complex of invertebrate integuments, in part because their integument is a specialized exoskeleton.

Stop and Ask Yourself

1. How would you define the following terms: (*a*) plasma membrane, (*b*) pellicle, (*c*) cuticle, (*d*) shell, and (*e*) tegument?

2. What is the function of each of the structures in question 1?

3. In what group of organisms would you observe each of the structures in question 1?

THE INTEGUMENTARY SYSTEM OF VERTEBRATES

Skin is the vertebrate integument. It is the largest organ (with respect to surface area) of the vertebrate body and grows with the animal. Skin has two main layers. As in invertebrates, the epidermis is the outermost layer of epithelial tissue and is one to several cells thick. The **dermis** (Gr. *derma*, hide, skin) is a thicker layer of connective tissue beneath the epidermis. A **hypodermis** ("below the skin"), consisting of loose connective tissue, adipose tissue, and nerve endings, separates the skin from deeper tissues.

FIGURE 32.2

Cuticles. The cuticles of (*a*) a crustacean and (*b*) an insect. The underlying epidermis secretes the cuticles of both groups of animals. *From: "A LIFE OF INVERTEBRATES" © 1979 W. D. Russell-Hunter.*

FIGURE 32.3

Skin of Jawless Fishes. The skin of an adult lamprey has a multilayered epidermis with glandular cells and fat storage cells in the hypodermis.

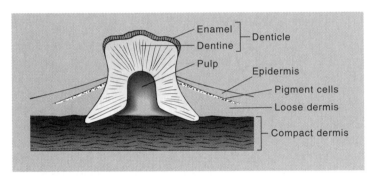

FIGURE 32.4

Skin of Cartilaginous Fishes. Shark skin contains toothlike denticles that become exposed through loss of the epidermal covering. The skin is otherwise fishlike in structure.

The Skin of Jawless Fishes

Jawless fishes, such as lampreys and hagfishes, have relatively thick skin (figure 32.3). Of the several types of epidermal glandular cells that may be present, one secretes a protective cuticle. In hagfishes, multicellular slime glands produce large amounts of mucous slime that covers the body surface. This slime protects the animals from external parasites and has earned hagfishes the descriptive name "slime eels."

The Skin of Cartilaginous Fishes

The skin of cartilaginous fishes (e.g., sharks) is multilayered and contains mucous and sensory cells (figure 32.4). The dermis contains bone in the form of small placoid scales called **denticles** (L. *denticulus*, little teeth). Denticles contain blood vessels and nerves, and are similar to vertebrate teeth. Because cartilaginous fishes grow throughout life, the skin area also increases. New den-

ticles are produced to maintain enough of these protective structures at the skin surface. Like teeth, once denticles reach maturity, they do not grow; thus, they continually wear down and are lost. Since denticles project above the surface of the skin, they give cartilaginous fishes a sandpaper texture.

The Skin of Bony Fishes

The skin of bony fishes (teleosts) contains **scales** (Fr. *escale*, shell, husk) composed of dermal bone. A thin layer of dermal tissue overlaid by the superficial epidermis normally covers scales (figure 32.5). Because scales are not shed, they grow at the margins and over the lower surface. ❶ In many bony fishes, growth lines, which are useful in determining the age of a fish, can often be detected. The skin of bony fishes is permeable and functions in gas exchange, particularly in the smaller fishes that have a large skin surface area relative to body volume. The dermis is richly supplied with capillary beds to facilitate its use in respiration. The epidermis also contains many mucous glands. Mucus production helps

FIGURE 32.5

Skin of Bony Fishes. The skin of a typical bony fish has overlapping scales (two are shown here). The scales are layers of collagenous fibers covered by a thin, flexible layer of bone.

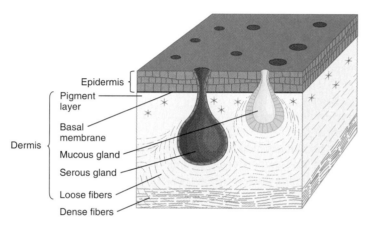

FIGURE 32.6

Skin of Amphibians. Frog skin has a stratified epidermis and several types of glands in the dermis. Notice the pigment layer in the upper part of the dermis.

prevent bacterial and fungal infections, and reduces friction as the fish swims. Some species have granular glands that secrete an irritating—or to some species, poisonous—alkaloid. Many teleosts that live in deep aquatic habitats have photophores that facilitate species recognition or act like lures and warning signals.

The Skin of Amphibians

Amphibian skin consists of a stratified epidermis and a dermis containing mucous and serous glands plus pigmentation cells (figure 32.6). Phylogenetically, amphibians are transitional between aquatic and terrestrial vertebrates. The earliest amphibians were covered by dermal bone scales like their fish ancestors. Three problems associated with terrestrial environments are desiccation, the damaging effects of ultraviolet light, and physical abrasion. During amphibian evolution, keratin production increased in the outer layer of skin cells. (Keratin is a tough, impermeable protein that protects the skin in the physically abrasive, rigorous terres-

FIGURE 32.7

Skin of Reptiles. Lizard skin has the heavily keratinized outer epidermis (scales) characteristic of reptiles. Notice the absence of integumentary glands, making reptilian skin exceptionally dry.

trial environment.) The increased keratin in the skin also protects the cells, especially their nuclear material, from ultraviolet light. The mucus that mucous glands produce helps prevent desiccation, facilitates gas exchange when the skin is used as a respiratory organ, and makes the body slimy, which facilitates escape from predators.

Within the dermis of some amphibians are poison glands that produce an unpleasant-tasting or toxic fluid that acts as a predator deterrent (*see box 28.1*). Sensory nerves penetrate the epidermis as free nerve endings.   ❷ Interestingly, the "warts" of toads seem to be specialized sensory structures since they contain numerous sensory cells.

The Skin of Reptiles

The skin of reptiles reflects their greater commitment to a terrestrial existence. The outer layer of the epidermis (stratum corneum) is thick (figure 32.7), lacks glands, and is modified into keratinized scales, scutes (thick scales) in snakes and turtles, beaks in turtles, rattles on snakes, and claws, plaques, and spiny crests on most other reptiles. This thick, keratinized layer resists abrasion, inhibits dehydration, and protects like a suit of armor. During shedding or molting of the skin of many reptiles (e.g., snakes and lizards), the old outer layer separates from newly formed epidermis. Diffusion of fluid between the layers aids this separation.

The Skin of Birds

The skin of birds shows many typically reptilian features with no epidermal glands (the only epidermal gland of birds is the uropygial or preen gland). Over most of the bird's body, the epidermis is usually thin and only two or three cell layers thick (figure 32.8). Indeed, the term "thin skinned," sometimes applied figuratively to humans, is literal when applied to birds. The outer keratinized

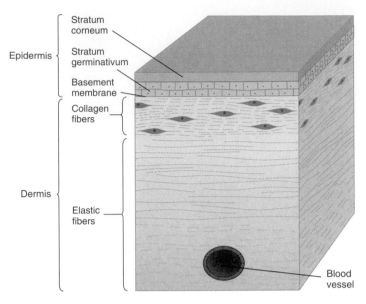

FIGURE 32.8

Skin of Birds. Bird skin has a relatively soft and thin epidermis with no epidermal glands.

layer is often quite soft. The most prominent parts of the epidermis are the feathers. Feathers are derived from the scales of reptilian ancestors and are the most complex of all the derivates of the vertebrate stratum corneum (*see figure 30.4*).

The dermis of birds is similar in structure to that of reptiles and contains blood and lymphatic vessels, nerves, and epidermally derived sensory bodies. Air spaces that are part of the avian respiratory system extend into the dermis. These air spaces are involved in thermal regulation. Associated with the feathers and their normal functioning is an incredibly complicated array of dermal smooth-muscle fibers that control the position of the feathers. Feather position is important in thermal regulation, flying, and behavior. Aquatic birds may also have fat deposits in the hypodermal layer that store energy and help insulate the body.

The Skin of Mammals

The notable features of mammalian skin are: (1) hair; (2) a greater variety of epidermal glands than in any other vertebrate class; (3) a highly stratified, cornified epidermis; and (4) a dermis many times thicker than the epidermis.

The epidermis of mammalian skin is composed of stratified squamous epithelium and consists of several layers of a variety of cells. Rapid cell divisions in the deepest layer of the epidermis push cells toward the surface of the skin. As cells progress toward the surface, they die and become keratinized (contain the protein keratin). Keratinized cells make up the outer skin layer, called the stratum corneum. Because keratin is virtually insoluble in water,

the stratum corneum prevents dehydration and is a first line of defense against many toxic substances and microorganisms. **3** The prevention of dehydration is one of the evolutionary reasons mammals and other animals have been able to colonize terrestrial environments.

The thickest portion of mammalian skin is composed of dermis, which contains blood vessels, lymphatic vessels, nerve endings, hair follicles, small muscles, and glands (figure 32.9). **4** A special tanning process makes leather from the dermal layer of mammalian skin.

The hypodermis underneath the dermis is different from that of other vertebrate classes in that it consists of loose connective tissue, adipose tissue, and skeletal muscles. Adipose tissue stores energy in the form of fat and provides insulation in cold environments. Skeletal muscle allows the skin above it to move somewhat independently of underlying tissues. Blood vessels thread from the hypodermis to the dermis and are absent from the epidermis.

In humans and a few other animals (e.g., horses), the skin regulates body temperature by opening and closing sweat pores and the process of perspiration or sweating. The skin screens out excessive harmful ultraviolet rays from the sun, but it also lets in some necessary rays that convert a chemical in the skin into vitamin D. The skin is also an important sense organ, containing sensory receptors for heat, cold, touch, pressure, and pain. Its many nerve endings keep the animal responsive to potentially harmful factors in the environment.

The skin of humans and other mammals contains several types of glands. **Sudoriferous glands** (L. *sudor*, sweat), also called sweat glands, are distributed over most of the human body surface (figure 32.9). These glands secrete sweat by a process called **perspiration** (L. *per*, through + *spirare*, to breathe). Perspiration helps to regulate body temperature and maintain homeostasis, largely by the cooling effect of evaporation. In some mammals, certain sweat glands also produce pheromones. (A pheromone is a chemical that an animal secretes and that communicates with other members of the same species to elicit certain behavioral responses.) **Sebaceous (oil) glands** (L. *sebum*, tallow or fat) are simple glands connected to hair follicles in the dermis (figure 32.9). They lubricate and protect by secreting **sebum.** Sebum is a permeability barrier, an emollient (skin-softening agent), and a protective agent against microorganisms. Sebum can also act as a pheromone.

Mammalian skin color is due either to pigments or to anatomical structures that absorb or reflect light. Pigments (e.g., melanin in human skin) are within the cells of the epidermal layer, in hair, or in specialized cells called chromatophores. Some skin color is due to the color of blood in superficial blood vessels reflected through the epidermis. Bright skin colors in venomous, toxic, or bad-tasting animals may deter potential predators. Other skin colors may camouflage the animal. In addition, colors serve in social communication, helping members of the same species to identify each other, their sex, reproductive status, or social rank.

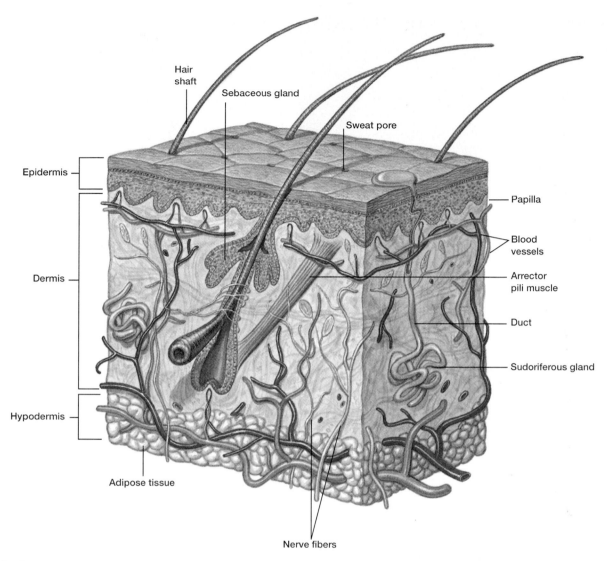

FIGURE 32.9

Skin of Mammals. Notice the various structures in the dermis of human skin.

Hair is composed of keratin-filled cells that develop from the epidermis. The portion of hair that protrudes from the skin is the hair shaft, and the portion embedded beneath the skin is the root (figure 32.9). 5 An arrector pili muscle (smooth muscle; involuntary muscle) attaches to the connective-tissue sheath of a hair follicle surrounding the bulb of the hair root. When this muscle contracts, it pulls the follicle and its hair to an erect position. In humans, this is referred to as a "goose bump." In other mammals, this action helps warm the animal by producing an insulating layer of warm air between the erect hair and skin. If hair is erect because the animal is frightened instead of cold, the erect hair also makes the animal look larger and less vulnerable to attack.

Nails, like hair, are modifications of the epidermis. Nails are flat, horny plates on the dorsal surface of the distal segments of the digits (e.g., fingers and toes of primates). Other mammals have **claws** and hooves (*see figure 31.7*). Other keratinized derivatives of mammalian skin are **horns** (not to be confused with bony antlers; *see box 31.1*) and the **baleen plates** of the toothless whales (*see box 37.2*).

Stop and Ask Yourself

4. What are some functions of skin?
5. What structures are in the dermal layer of mammalian skin? What type of glands are in this layer?
6. What determines the color of skin?

FIGURE 32.10

Hydrostatic Skeletons. (*a*) The hydrostatic skeleton of sea anemones (*Corynactis californic*) allows them to shorten or close when longitudinal muscles contract, or to lengthen or open when circular muscles contract. (*b,c*) How a hydrostatic skeleton changes an invertebrate's shape with only longitudinal muscles. Because the fluid volume is constant, a change (increase) in width must accompany a change (decrease) in length.

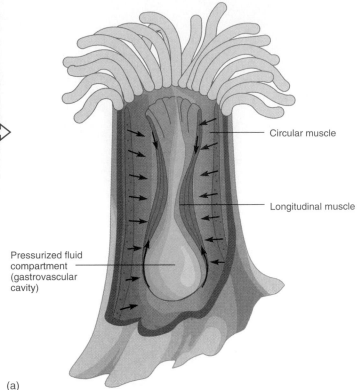

(a)

MOVEMENT AND SUPPORT: SKELETAL SYSTEMS

As organisms evolved from the ancestral protists to the multicellular animals, body size increased dramatically. Systems involved in movement and support evolved simultaneously with the increase in body size.

Four cell types contribute to movement: (1) amoeboid cells, (2) flagellated cells, (3) ciliated cells, and (4) muscle cells. With respect to support, organisms have three kinds of skeletons: (1) fluid hydrostatic skeletons, (2) rigid exoskeletons, and (3) rigid endoskeletons. These skeletal systems also function in animal movement that requires muscles working in opposition (antagonism) to each other.

THE SKELETAL SYSTEM OF INVERTEBRATES

Many invertebrates use their body fluids for internal support. For example, sea anemones (figure 32.10*a*) and earthworms have a form of internal support called the hydrostatic skeleton.

Hydrostatic Skeletons

The **hydrostatic** (Gr. *hydro*, water + *statikos*, to stand) **skeleton** is a core of liquid (water or a body fluid such as blood) surrounded by a tension-resistant sheath of longitudinal and/or circular muscles. It is similar to a water-filled balloon because the force exerted

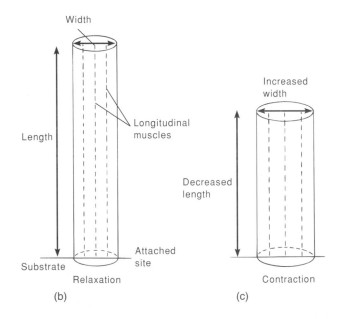

(b)   (c)

against the incompressible fluid in one region can be transmitted to other regions. Contracting muscles push against a hydrostatic skeleton, and the transmitted force generates body movements, as the movement of a sea anemone illustrates (figure 32.10*b,c*). Another example is the earthworm, *Lumbricus terrestris*. It contracts its longitudinal and circular muscles alternately, creating a rhythm that moves the earthworm through the soil. In both of

(a)

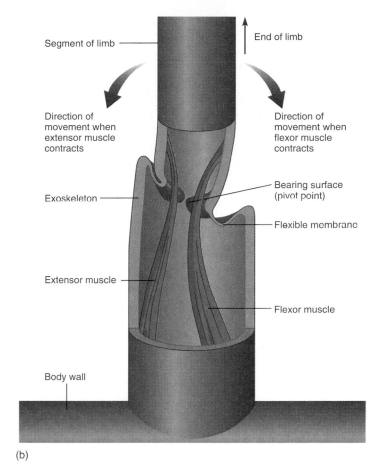

(b)

FIGURE 32.11

Exoskeletons. (*a*) A cicada nymph (*Platypedia*) leaves its old exoskeleton as it molts. This exoskeleton provides external support for the body and attachment sites for muscles. (*b*) In an arthropod, muscles attach to the interior of the exoskeleton. In this articulation of an arthropod limb, the cuticle is hardened everywhere except at the joint, where the membrane is flexible. Notice that the extensor muscle is antagonistic to (works in an opposite direction than) the flexor muscle. (*b*) *Source: After Russell-Hunter.*

these examples, the hydrostatic skeleton keeps the body from collapsing when its muscles contract.

The invertebrate hydrostatic skeleton can take many forms and shapes, such as the gastrovascular cavity of acoelomates, a rhynchocoel in nemertines, a pseudocoelom in aschelminths, a coelom in annelids, or a hemocoel in molluscs. Overall, the hydrostatic skeleton of invertebrates is an excellent example of adaptation of major body functions to this simple but efficient principle of hydrodynamics—use of the internal pressure of body fluids.

Exoskeletons

Rigid **exoskeletons** (Gr. *exo*, outside + skeleton) also have locomotor functions because they provide sites for muscle attachment and counterforces for muscle movements. Exoskeletons also support and protect the body, but these are secondary functions.

In arthropods, the epidermis of the body wall secretes a thick, hard cuticle that waterproofs the body (*see figure 23.3*). The cuticle also protects and supports the animal's soft internal organs.

In crustaceans (e.g., crabs, lobsters, shrimp), the exoskeleton contains calcium carbonate crystals that make it hard and inflexible—except at the joints. Besides providing shieldlike protection from enemies and resistance to general wear and tear, the exoskeleton also prevents internal tissues from drying out. This important evolutionary adaptation contributed to arthropods' successful colonization of land. Exoskeletons, however, limit an animal's growth. Some animals shed the exoskeleton periodically, as arthropods do when they molt (figure 32.11*a*).

Certain regions of the arthropod body have thin, flexible cuticle, and joints (articulations) are usually in these areas (figure 32.11*b*). It is in these areas that pairs of antagonistic muscles function through a system of levers to produce coordinated movement. ⑥ Interestingly, some arthropod joints (e.g., the wing joints of flying beetles and the joints of fleas involved in jumping) possess a highly elastic protein called "animal rubber," or **resilin.** Resilin stores energy on compression and then releases the energy to produce movement (*see figure 32.23*). From an evolutionary perspective, the development of a jointed, flexible exoskeleton that permitted flight is one of the reasons for the success of arthropods.

Endoskeletons

Like the term implies, other body tissues enclose **endoskeletons** (Gr. *endo*, within + skeleton). For example, the endoskeletons of sponges consist of mineral spicules and fibers of spongin that keep the body from collapsing (*see figure 18.5*). Since adult sponges attach to the substrate, they have no need for muscles attached to the endoskeleton. Similarly, the endoskeletons of echinoderms (sea stars, sea urchins) consist of small, calcareous plates called ossicles. The most familiar endoskeletons, however, are in vertebrates and discussed later in the chapter.

Mineralized Tissues and the Invertebrates

Hard, mineralized tissues are not unique to the vertebrates. In fact, over two-thirds of the living species of animals that contain mineralized tissues are invertebrates. Most invertebrates have inorganic calcium carbonate crystals embedded in a collagen matrix. (Vertebrates have calcium phosphate crystals.) Bone, dentin, cartilage, and enamel were all present in Ordovician ostracoderms (*see figure 27.3*).

Cartilage is the supportive tissue that makes up the major skeletal component of some gastropods, invertebrate chordates (amphioxus), jawless fishes such as hagfishes and lampreys, and sharks and rays. Since cartilage is lighter than bone, it affords these predatory fishes the speed and agility that allows them to catch prey. It also provides buoyancy without the need for a swim bladder.

Stop and Ask Yourself

7. How does a hydrostatic skeleton function?
8. What animals have hydrostatic skeletons?
9. How do endoskeletons and exoskeletons differ? What are some examples of animals with exoskeletons? What are some examples of animals with endoskeletons?

THE SKELETAL SYSTEM OF VERTEBRATES

The vertebrate skeletal system is an endoskeleton enclosed by other body tissues. This endoskeleton consists of two main types of supportive tissue: cartilage and bone.

Cartilage

Cartilage is a specialized type of connective tissue that provides a site for muscle attachment, aids in movement at joints, and provides support (*see figure 3.24* h–j). Like other connective tissues, it consists of cells (chondrocytes), fibers, and a cellular matrix.

Bone or Osseous Tissue

Bone (osseous) tissue is a specialized connective tissue that provides a point of attachment for muscles and transmits the force of muscular contraction from one part of the body to another during movement (figure 32.12*a*). In addition, bones of the skeleton support the internal organs of many animals, store reserve calcium and phosphate, and manufacture red blood cells and some white blood cells.

Bone tissue is more rigid than other connective tissues because its homogeneous, organic ground substance also contains inorganic salts—mainly calcium phosphate and calcium carbonate. When an animal needs the calcium or phosphate stored within bones, metabolic reactions (under endocrine control) release the required amounts.

As discussed in chapter 3, **bone cells** (osteocytes) are in minute chambers called lacunae (sing., lacuna), which are arranged in concentric rings around osteonic canals (formerly called Haversian systems) (figure 32.12*b*). These cells communicate with nearby cells by means of cellular processes passing through small channels called canaliculi (sing., canaliculus).

The Skeleton of Fishes

Both cartilaginous and bony endoskeletons first appeared in the vertebrates. Since water has a buoyant effect on the fish body, the requirement for skeletal support is not as demanding in these vertebrates as it is in terrestrial vertebrates. Although most vertebrates have a well-defined vertebral column (the reason they are called "vertebrates"), the jawless vertebrates do not. For example, lampreys only have isolated cartilaginous blocks along the notochord, and hagfishes do not even have these.

Most jawed fishes have an axial skeleton (so named because it forms the longitudinal axis of the body) that includes a notochord, ribs, and cartilaginous or bony vertebrae (figure 32.13). Muscles used in locomotion attach to the axial skeleton.

The Skeleton of Tetrapods

Tetrapods must lift themselves to walk on land. The first amphibians needed support to replace the buoyancy of water. For the earliest terrestrial animals, support and locomotion were difficult and complicated processes. Adaptations for support and movement on land occurred over a period of approximately 200 million years. During this evolution, the tetrapod endoskeleton became modified for support on land (figure 32.14). This added support resulted from the specializations of the intervertebral disks that articulate with adjoining vertebrae. The intervertebral disks help hold the vertebral column together, and also absorb shock and provide joint mobility. Bone replaced cartilage in the ribs, which became more rigid. The various types of connective tissue that connect to the axial skeleton helped keep elevated portions from sagging. Appendages became elongated for support on a hard surface, and changes in the shoulder enabled the neck to move more freely.

(a)

(b)

FIGURE 32.12

Bone. (*a*) Structural organization of a long bone (femur) of mammals. Compact bone is composed of osteons connected together. Spongy bone is latticelike rather than dense. (*b*) Single osteon in compact bone (SEM ×450). (*b*) *From Richard G. Kessel and Randy H. Kardon, Tissues and Organs: A Text-Atlas of Scanning Electron Microscopy, 1979, W.H. Freeman and Company.*

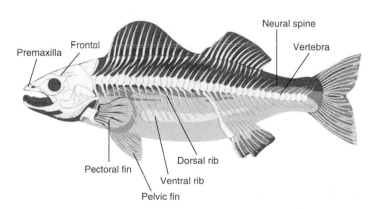

FIGURE 32.13

Fish Endoskeleton. Lateral view of the perch skeleton.

Maxilla

Metacarpal

Carpal

Humerus

Sacral vertebra

Phalanges

Metatarsal

Femur

Tarsals

Nasal

Phalanges

Suprascapula

Radioulna

Ilium

Tibiofibula

Tibiale or astragalus

Fibulare or calcaneus

Ischium

FIGURE 32.14

Tetrapod Endoskeleton. Dorsal view of the frog skeleton.

The Human Endoskeleton

The human endoskeleton has two major parts: the axial skeleton and the appendicular skeleton. The **axial skeleton** is made up of the skull, vertebral column, sternum, and ribs. The **appendicular skeleton** is composed of the appendages, the pectoral girdle, and the pelvic girdles. These girdles attach the upper and lower appendages to the axial skeleton.

Stop and Ask Yourself

10. How are cartilage and bone different?
11. How do the endoskeletons of a fish and a frog differ?
12. What are the two major divisions of the human skeleton?

MOVEMENT: NONMUSCULAR MOVEMENT AND MUSCULAR SYSTEMS

Movement is a characteristic of certain cells, protists, and animals. For example, certain white blood cells, coelomic cells, and protists such as *Amoeba* utilize nonmuscular amoeboid movement. Amoeboid movement also occurs in embryonic tissue movements, in wound healing, and in many cell types growing in tissue culture. Other protists and some invertebrates utilize cilia or flagella for movement. Muscles and muscle systems are found in various invertebrate groups from the primitive cnidarians to the arthropods (e.g., insect flight muscles). In more complex animals, the muscles attach to exo- and endoskeletal systems to form a motor system, which allows complex movements.

NONMUSCULAR MOVEMENT

Nearly all cells have some capacity to move and change shape due to their cytoskeleton (*see figure 3.19*). It is from this basic framework of the cell that specialized contractile mechanisms emerged. For example, protozoan protists move by means of specific nonmuscular structures (pseudopodia, flagella, or cilia) that involve the contractile proteins, actin and myosin. Interactions between these proteins are also responsible for muscle contraction in animals, and the presence of actin and myosin in protozoa and animals is evidence of evolutionary ties between the two groups.

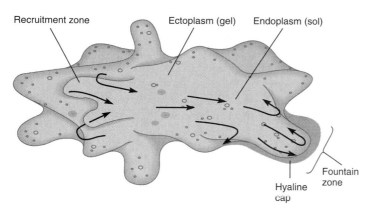

FIGURE 32.15

Mechanism of Amoeboid Movement. Endoplasm (sol) flows into an advancing pseudopodium. At the tip (fountain zone) of the pseudopodium, endoplasm changes into ectoplasm (gel). At the opposite end (recruitment zone) of the amoeba, ectoplasm changes into endoplasm and begins flowing in the direction of movement.

Amoeboid Movement

As the name suggests, **amoeboid movement** was first observed in *Amoeba*. The plasma membrane of an amoeba has adhesive properties since new **pseudopodia** (sing., pseudopodium) (Gr. *pseudes*, false + *podion*, little foot) attach to the substrate as they form. The plasma membrane also seems to slide over the underlying layer of cytoplasm when an amoeba moves. The plasma membrane may be "rolling" in a way that is (roughly) analogous to a bulldozer track rolling over its wheels. A thin fluid layer between the plasma membrane and the ectoplasm may facilitate this rolling.

As an amoeba moves, the fluid endoplasm flows forward into the fountain zone of an advancing pseudopodium. As it reaches the tip of a pseudopodium, endoplasm changes into ectoplasm. At the same time, ectoplasm near the opposite end in the recruitment zone changes into endoplasm and begins flowing forward (figure 32.15).

Ciliary and Flagellar Movement

With the exception of the arthropods, locomotor cilia and flagella occur in every animal phylum. Structurally, **cilia** (sing., cilium) (L. "eyelashes") and **flagella** (sing., flagellum) (L. "small whips") are similar, but cilia are shorter and more numerous, whereas flagella are long and generally occur singly or in pairs.

Ciliary movements are coordinated. For example, in some ciliated protozoa, pairs of cilia occur in rows. Rows of cilia beat slightly out of phase with one another so that ciliary waves periodically pass over the surface of the protozoan (figure 32.16). In fact, many ciliates can rapidly reverse the direction of ciliary beating, which changes the direction of the ciliary waves and the direction of movement.

The epidermis of free-living flatworms (e.g., turbellarians) and nemertines is abundantly ciliated. The smallest specimens (about 1 mm long) lie at the upper end of the size range for effi-

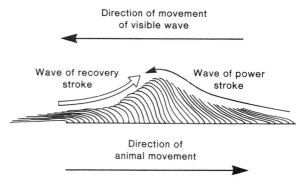

FIGURE 32.16

Ciliary Movement. A metachronal (coordinated) wave passing along a row of cilia.

cient locomotion using cilia. Larger flatworms (e.g., triclads and polyclads) have retained **ciliary creeping** as the principal means of locomotion, and the largest animals to move by ciliary creeping are the nemertines. The muscular activities of the flatworms and nemertines are varied and involve pedal locomotion, peristalsis, or looping movements with anterior and posterior adhesion. Since ciliary and muscular means of movement (locomotion) coexist in some free-living flatworms and nemertines, the transition from ciliary to muscular locomotion is likely to have taken place among the flatworm-like ancestors.

Stop and Ask Yourself

13. Considering protists and animals, where would you find amoeboid movement?
14. What is the major difference between cilia and flagella?
15. How would you describe amoeboid movement? How would you describe ciliary creeping?

AN INTRODUCTION TO ANIMAL MUSCLES

Muscular tissue is the driving force, the power behind movement in most invertebrates and vertebrates. The basic physiological property of muscle tissue is contractility, the ability to contract or shorten. In addition, muscle tissue has three other important properties: (1) excitability (or irritability), the capacity to receive and respond to a stimulus; (2) extensibility, the ability to be stretched; and (3) elasticity, the ability to return to its original shape after being stretched or contracted.

Animals may have one or more of the following types of muscle tissue: smooth, cardiac, and skeletal. The contractile cells of these tissues are called **muscle fibers.**

Smooth muscle is also called involuntary muscle because higher brain centers do not control its contractions. Smooth-muscle fibers have a single nucleus, are spindle shaped, and are arranged in a parallel pattern to form sheets (*see figure 3.24p*).

Smooth muscle maintains good tone (a normal degree of vigor and tension) even without nervous stimulation. It contracts slowly, but can sustain prolonged contractions and does not fatigue (tire) easily.

Smooth muscle is the predominant muscle type in many invertebrates. For example, it forms part of the adductor ("catch") muscles that close the valves of clams and other bivalve molluscs. **7** These smooth muscles give bivalves the ability to "clam up" against predators for days with little or no energy expenditure.

Striated muscle fibers (cells) with single nuclei are common in invertebrates, but occur in adult vertebrates only in the heart, where they are called cardiac muscle. **Cardiac muscle** fibers are involuntary, have a single nucleus, are striated (have dark and light bands), and are branched (see figure 3.24q). This branching allows the fibers to interlock for greater strength during contraction. **8** Hearts do not fatigue because cardiac fibers relax completely between contractions.

Skeletal muscle, also a striated muscle, is voluntary muscle because the nervous system consciously controls its contractions. Skeletal muscle fibers are multinucleated and striated (see figure 3.24o). Skeletal muscles attach to skeletons (both endo- and exoskeletons). When skeletal muscles contract, they shorten. Thus, muscles can only pull; they cannot push. Therefore, skeletal muscles work in antagonistic pairs. For example, one muscle of a pair bends (flexes) a joint and brings a limb close to the body. The other member of the pair straightens (extends) the joint and extends the limb away from the body (see figure 32.11b).

THE MUSCULAR SYSTEM OF INVERTEBRATES

A few functional differences among invertebrate muscles indicate some of the differences from the vertebrate skeletal muscles (discussed next). In arthropods, at least two motor nerves innervate a typical muscle fiber. One motor nerve fiber causes a fast contraction and the other a slow contraction. Another variation occurs in certain insect (bees, wasps, flies, beetles) flight muscles. These muscles are called asynchronous muscles, since the upward wing movement (rather than a nerve impulse) activates the muscles that produce the downstroke. In the midge (a dipteran related to the fly/mosquito), for example, this can happen a thousand times a second.

An understanding of the structure and function of invertebrate locomotion (movement) is crucial to an understanding of the evolutionary origins of the various invertebrate groups. Discussion of several types of invertebrate locomotion that involve muscular systems follows.

The Locomotion of Soft-Bodied Invertebrates

Many soft-bodied invertebrates can move over a firm substratum. For example, flatworms, some cnidarians, and the gastropod molluscs move by means of waves of activity in the muscular system that are applied to the substrate. This type of movement is called **pedal locomotion.** Pedal locomotion can be easily seen by examining the undersurface of a planarian or a snail while it crawls along a glass plate. In the land snail *Helix*, several waves cross the length of the foot simultaneously, each moving in the same direction as the locomotion of the snail, but at a greater rate.

Many large flatworms and most nemertine worms exhibit a muscular component to their locomotion. In this type of movement, alternating waves of contraction of circular and longitudinal muscles generate peristaltic waves, which enhance the locomotion that the surface cilia also provide. This system is most highly developed in the septate coelomate worms, especially earthworms (figure 32.17).

Leeches and some insect larvae exhibit **looping movements.** Leeches have anterior and posterior suckers that provide alternating temporary points of attachment (figure 32.18a). Lepidopteran caterpillars exhibit similar locomotion, in which arching move-

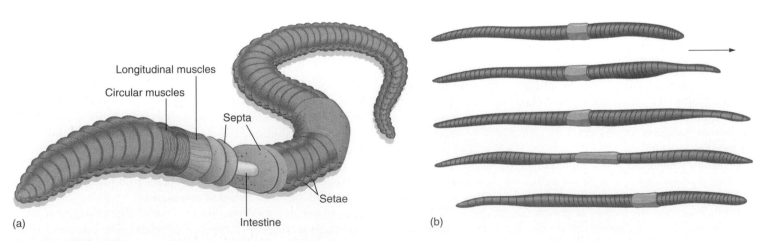

(a)   (b)

FIGURE 32.17

Successive Stages in Earthworm Movement. (a) When the longitudinal muscles contract and the circular muscles relax, the segments of the earthworm bulge and are stationary with respect to the ground. (b) In front of each region of longitudinal muscle contraction, circular muscles contract, causing the segments to elongate and push forward. Contraction of longitudinal muscles in segments behind a bulging region cause those segments to be pulled forward. For reasons of simplification, setae movements are not shown.

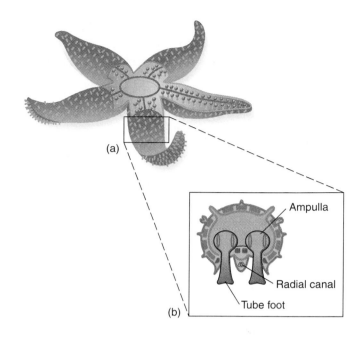

FIGURE 32.18

Looping Movements. *(a)* Leeches have anterior and posterior suckers, which they alternately attach to the substrate in looping movements to move forward. *(b)* Some insect larvae, such as lepidopteran caterpillars, exhibit similar movements. The caterpillar uses arching movements to move forward.

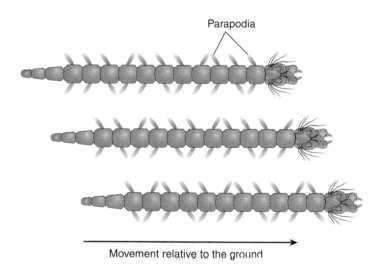

FIGURE 32.19

Locomotion in a Polychaete. When a polychaete (e.g., *Nereis*) crawls slowly, the tips of the multiple limbs (parapodia) move backward relative to the body. Since the tips of the parapodia touch the ground, this moves the body forward. In addition, a coordinated wave of activity in the parapodia passes forward from the tail to the head, with the left and right parapodia being exactly one-half wavelength out of phase. This ensures that each parapodium executes its power stroke without interfering with the parapodium immediately posterior. For simplification, setae movements are not shown.

ments are equivalent to the contraction of longitudinal muscles (figure 32.18*b*).

Polychaete worms move by the alternate movement of multiple limbs (parapodia), the tips of which move backward relative

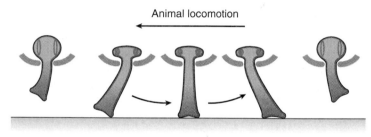

FIGURE 32.20

Water-Vascular System of Echinoderms. *(a)* General arrangement of the water-vascular system. *(b)* Cross section of an arm, showing the radial canal, ampullae, and tube feet of the water-vascular system. *(c)* Stepping cycle of a single tube foot. For simplification, the retractor muscles in the tube foot are not shown.

to the body; however, since the tips attach to the ground, the body of the worm moves forward (figure 32.19).

The **water-vascular system** of echinoderms provides a unique means of locomotion. For example, sea stars typically have five arms, with a water-vascular canal in each. Along each canal are reservoir ampullae and tube feet (figure 32.20*a,b*). Contraction of the muscles comprising the ampullae drives water into the tube feet, whereas contraction of the tube feet moves water into the ampullae. Thus, the tube feet extend by hydraulic pressure and can perform simple steplike motions (figure 32.20*c*).

Terrestrial Locomotion in Invertebrates: Walking

Invertebrates (terrestrial arthropods) living in/on terrestrial environments are much denser than the air in which they live. As a result, they require structural support, and those that move quickly

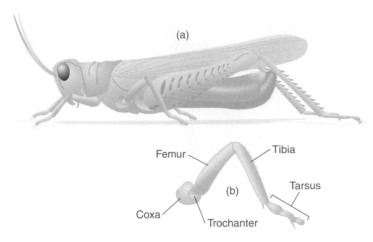

FIGURE 32.21

Typical Arthropod Limb. (a) Notice that most of the muscles are in the basal section. (b) Characteristic projection of the arthropod limb.

make use of rigid skeletal elements that interact with the ground. These elements include flexible joints, tendons, and muscles that attach to a rigid cuticle and form limbs. The walking limbs of the most highly evolved arthropods (Crustacea, Chelicerata, and Uniramia) are remarkably uniform in structure. The limbs are composed of a series of jointed elements that become progressively less massive toward the tip (figure 32.21a). Each joint is articulated to allow movement in only one plane. These limb joints allow extension (a motion that increases the angle of a joint) and flexion (a motion that decreases the angle of a joint) of the limb. The limb plane at the basal joint with the body can also rotate, which is responsible for forward movement. The body is typically carried slung between the laterally projected limbs (figure 32.21b), and walking movements do not involve raising or lowering the body. Depending on the arthropod, the trajectory of each limb is different and nonoverlapping (figure 32.22). Most arthropods walk forward, rotating the basal joint of the limb relative to the body, but crabs walk in a sideways fashion.

Terrestrial Locomotion in Invertebrates: Flight

The physical properties (e.g., strengthening so that the exoskeleton does not deform under muscle contraction) of an arthropod cuticle are such that true flight evolved for the pterygote insects some 200 million years ago. Since then, the basic mechanism of flight has been modified. Consequently, present-day insects exhibit a wide range of structural adaptations and mechanisms for flight (*see figure 24.5*).

Terrestrial Locomotion in Invertebrates: Jumping

Some insects (fleas, grasshoppers, leafhoppers) can jump. Most often, this is an escape reaction. To jump, an insect must exert a force against the ground sufficient to impart a takeoff velocity greater than its weight (figure 32.23). ❾ Long legs increase the

FIGURE 32.22

Walking: Limb Trajectories of Several Arthropods. (a) Crabs walk in a sideways fashion, a movement achieved by extension and retraction of the lower limb joints. Other arthropods, such as (b) the lobster, (c) the spider, and (d) an insect, have nonoverlapping limb trajectories and move forward by rotating the basal joint of the limb relative to their body.

mechanical advantage of the leg extensor muscles. This is why insects that jump have relatively long legs. The mechanical strength of the insect cuticle acting as the lever in this system probably determines the limit to this line of evolution.

Stop and Ask Yourself

16. What are some physiological properties of muscle tissue?

17. What is an asynchronous invertebrate muscle?

18. What invertebrates move by (a) pedal locomotion, (b) looping movements, (c) water-vascular system, (d) walking, and (e) jumping?

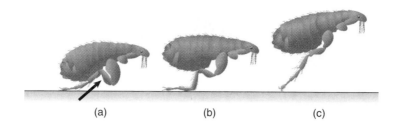

FIGURE 32.23

Jump of Flea. A flea has a jointed exoskeleton. (*a*) When a flea is resting, the femur (black arrow) of the leg (for simplicity, only one leg is shown) is raised, the joints are locked, and energy is stored in the deformed elastic protein ("animal rubber" or resilin) of the cuticle. (*b*) As a flea begins to jump, the relaxation of muscles unlocks the joints. (*c*) The force exerted against the ground by the tibia gives the flea a specific velocity that determines the height of the jump. The jump is the result of the explosive release of the energy stored in the resilin of the cuticle.

FIGURE 32.24

Fish Musculature. (*a*) Skeletal muscles of a bony fish (perch), showing mainly the large muscles of the trunk and tail. These muscles occur in blocks called myomeres separated by connective tissue sheaths. Notice that the myomeres are flexed so that they resemble the letter *W* tipped at a 90° angle. The different colors (red, orange, blue) represent different myomeres. (*b*) Fish movements based on myomere contractions. (*1*) Muscular forces cause the myomere segments to rotate rather than constrict. (*2*) The rotation of cranial and caudal myomere segments bends the fish's body about a point midway between the two segments. (*3*) Alternate bends of the caudal end of the body propel the fish forward.

THE MUSCULAR SYSTEM OF VERTEBRATES

The vertebrate endoskeleton provides sites for skeletal muscles to attach. **Tendons,** which are tough, fibrous bands or cords, attach skeletal muscles to the skeleton.

Most of the musculature of fishes consists of segmental **myomeres** (Gr. *myo,* muscle + *meros,* part) (figure 32.24*a*). My-

omere segments cause the lateral undulations of the trunk and tail that produce fish locomotion (figure 32.24*b*).

The transition from water to land entailed changes in the body musculature. As previously noted, the appendages became increasingly important in locomotion, and movements of the trunk became less important. The segmental nature of the myomeres in the trunk muscles was lost. Back muscles became

(a) One of the arm muscles

(b) Many muscle fibers bundled inside connective tissue sheath make up the arm muscle.

(c) Skeletal muscle fiber

Myofibril

(d) Z line — Sarcomere — Z line — Sarcomere — Z line

Filaments of actin and myosin

H zone

I band — A band — I band — A band

(e) Myosin filaments

Actin filaments

Z line   Z line   Z line

FIGURE 32.25

Structure of Skeletal Muscle Tissue. (*a*) A skeletal muscle in the forearm consists of many muscle fibers (cells) (*b*) bundled inside a connective tissue sheath. (*c*) A skeletal muscle fiber contains many myofibrils, each consisting of (*d*) functional units called sarcomeres. (*e*) The characteristic striations of a sarcomere are due to the arrangement of actin and myosin filaments.

more numerous and powerful. These evolutionary adaptations are well illustrated by comparing what is eaten in a fish dinner to a plate of frog legs.

Skeletal Muscle Contraction

When observed with the light microscope, each skeletal muscle fiber (cell) has a pattern of alternate dark and light bands (*see figure 3.24o*). This striation of whole fibers arises from the alternating dark and light bands of the many smaller, threadlike **myofibrils** in each muscle fiber (figure 32.25*a–c*). Electron microscopy and biochemical analysis show that these bands are due

to the placement of the muscle proteins **actin** and **myosin** within the myofibrils. Myosin occurs as thick filaments and actin as thin filaments. As figure 32.25*c–e* illustrates, the lightest region of a myofibril (the I band) contains only actin, whereas the darkest region (the A band) contains both actin and myosin.

The functional (contractile) unit of a myofibril is the **sarcomere,** each of which extends from one Z line to another Z line. Notice that the actin filaments attach to the Z lines, whereas myosin filaments do not (figure 32.25*e*). When a sarcomere contracts, the actin filaments slide past the myosin filaments as they approach one another. This process shortens the sarcomere. The combined decreases in length of the individual

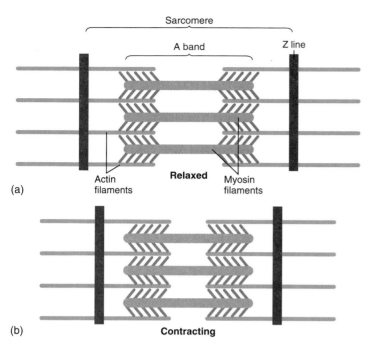

Relaxed

(a)

Actin
filaments

Myosin
filaments

Contracting

(b)

FIGURE 32.26

Sliding-Filament Model of Muscle Contraction. (*a*) A sarcomere in a relaxed position. (*b*) As the sarcomere contracts, the myosin filaments form attachments called cross-bridges to the actin filaments and pull the actin filaments so that they slide past the myosin filaments. Compare the length of the sarcomere in (*a*) to that in (*b*).

sarcomeres account for contraction of the whole muscle fiber, and in turn, the whole muscle. This movement of actin in relation to myosin is called the sliding-filament model of muscle contraction.

A ratchet mechanism between the two filament types produces the actual contraction. Myosin contains globular projections that attach to actin at specific active binding sites, forming attachments called cross-bridges (figure 32.26). Once cross-bridges form, they exert a force on the thin actin filament and cause it to move.

Control of Muscle Contraction

When a motor nerve conducts nerve impulses to skeletal muscle fibers, the fibers are stimulated to contract via a motor unit. A **motor unit** consists of one motor nerve fiber and all the muscle fibers with which it communicates. A space separates the specialized end of the motor nerve fiber from the membrane (**sarcolemma**) of the muscle fiber. The motor end plate is the specialized portion of the sarcolemma of a muscle fiber surrounding the terminal end of the nerve. This arrangement of structures is called a **neuromuscular junction** or cleft (figure 32.27).

When nerve impulses reach the ends of the nerve fiber branches, synaptic vesicles in the nerve ending release a chemical called acetylcholine. Acetylcholine diffuses across the neuromuscular cleft between the nerve ending and the muscle-fiber sarcolemma and binds with acetylcholine receptors on the

Motor neuron fiber

Muscle fiber nucleus

Nerve fiber branches

Motor end plate

Myofibril

Mitochondria

Folded sarcolemma

Synaptic vesicles

Neuromuscular cleft

Motor end plate

FIGURE 32.27

Nerve-Muscle Motor Unit. A motor unit consists of one motor nerve and all the muscle fibers that it innervates. A neuromuscular junction, or cleft, is where the nerve fiber and muscle fiber meet.

FIGURE 32.28

Model of the Calcium-Induced Changes in Troponin That Allow Cross-Bridges to Form between Actin and Myosin. The attachment of Ca^{2+} to troponin moves the troponin-tropomyosin complex, which exposes a binding site on the actin. The myosin cross-bridge can then attach to actin and undergo a power stroke.

sarcolemma. The sarcolemma is normally polarized; the outside is positive, and the inside is negative. When acetylcholine binds to the receptors, ions are redistributed on both sides of the membrane, and the polarity is altered. This altered polarity flows in a wavelike progression into the muscle fiber by conducting paths called transverse tubules. Associated with the transverse tubules is the endoplasmic reticulum (*see figure 3.15*) of muscle cells, called

sarcoplasmic reticulum. The altered polarity of the transverse tubules causes the sarcoplasmic reticulum to release calcium ions (Ca^{2+}), which diffuse into the cytoplasm. The calcium then binds with a regulatory protein called troponin that is on another protein called tropomyosin. This binding exposes the myosin binding sites on the actin molecule that tropomyosin had blocked (figure 32.28). Once the binding sites are open, the myosin filament can form cross-bridges with actin, and power strokes of cross-bridges result in filament sliding and muscular contraction.

Relaxation follows contraction. During relaxation, an active transport system pumps calcium back into the sarcoplasmic reticulum for storage. By controlling the nerve impulses that reach the sarcoplasmic reticulum, the nervous system controls Ca^{2+} levels in skeletal muscle tissue, thereby exerting control over contraction.

Stop and Ask Yourself

19. What is a myofibril?
20. How does the sliding-filament model explain muscle contraction?
21. How do nerves cause skeletal muscles to contract?

ENDANGERED SPECIES

WILDLIFE ALERT 9—AMERICAN CROCODILE (*CROCODYLUS ACUTUS*)

VITAL STATISTICS

Classification: Phylum Chordata, class Reptilia, order Crocodylia, family Crocodylidae
Range: Everglades National Park and the Florida Keys (Key Largo and Turkey Point)
Habitat: Mangrove swamps, salt and brackish water bays, and brackish creeks
Number remaining: 200 to 400
Status: Endangered throughout its range

NATURAL HISTORY AND ECOLOGICAL STATUS

The American crocodile (figure 1) is a large, lizard-shaped reptile, most closely resembling the alligator. Adults may grow to 5 m in length. Their slender build and snout shape differentiate Floridian crocodiles from alligators. The crocodile's snout tapers forward from the eyes, while the alligator's snout is rounded at the end. When the mouth is closed, the fourth bottom tooth on each side of the lower jaw is exposed in the crocodile but concealed in the alligator. As a rule, adult crocodiles feed on any prey item that can be caught and overpowered.

The American crocodile breeds only in the southern portions of the Everglades National Park and outside the park on adjacent Key Largo and Turkey Point (figure 2). Females begin nest construction in April and lay 20 to 60 eggs in late April or May. The eggs hatch in July and August. The female usually opens the nest and

FIGURE 1   The American Crocodile (*Crocodylus acutus*).

assists the young in hatching. Human disturbance of the female while she guards the nest may disrupt this behavioral pattern; thus, freedom from human disturbance during this period may be critical to the crocodile's recovery. Over the last decade, the number of nests produced has increased slightly.

The American crocodile is primarily a coastal species, utilizing mangrove swamps, salt and brackish water bays, and brackish creeks. Crocodiles may also enter coastal canals.

Direct loss of habitat to urbanization causes many crocodile deaths. Other causes include by-products of urbanization, intentional killing, and accidental deaths in commercial fishing nets and on highways. Heavy raccoon predation on crocodile hatchlings is also thought to be hampering crocodile recovery.

The absence of past management programs for the American crocodile makes the crocodile's potential response to specific measures largely unknown. In addition to the currently available state and federal legal protection of the crocodile, a public information program is needed to decrease accidental mortality and to increase public tolerance of large, breeding-sized individuals.

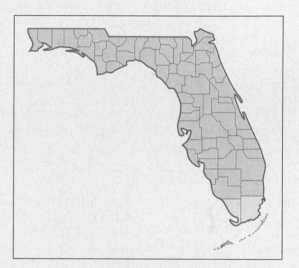

FIGURE **2**   Distribution of the American Crocodile (*Crocodylus acutus*) in Florida.

SUMMARY

1. The integumentary system is the external covering of an animal. It primarily protects against mechanical injury and invasion by microorganisms.

2. Some single-celled protozoa have only a plasma membrane for an external covering. Other protozoa have a thick protein coat, called a pellicle, outside the plasma membrane. Most invertebrates have an integument consisting of a single layer of columnar epithelial cells called an epidermis. Specializations outside of this epithelial layer may be in the form of cuticles, shells, or teguments.

3. Skin is the vertebrate integument. It has two main layers: the epidermis and the dermis. Skin structure varies considerably among vertebrates. Some of these variable structures include scales, hairs, feathers, claws, nails, and baleen plates.

4. The skin of jawless fishes (lampreys and hagfishes) is thick. The skin of cartilaginous fishes (sharks) is multilayered and contains bone in the form of denticles. The skin of bony fishes (teleosts) contains scales. The skin of amphibians is stratified and contains mucous and serous glands plus pigmentation. The skin of reptiles is thick and modified into keratinized scales. The skin of birds is thin and soft and contains feathers. Mammalian skin consists of several layers of a variety of cells.

5. Animals have three types of skeletons: hydrostatic skeletons, exoskeletons, and endoskeletons. These skeletons function in animal movement that requires muscles working in opposition (antagonism) to each other.

6. The hydrostatic skeleton is a core of liquid (water or a body fluid such as blood) surrounded by a tension-resistant sheath of longitudinal and/or circular muscles. Hydrostatic skeletons are found in invertebrates and can take many forms and shapes, such as the gastrovascular cavity of acoelomates, the rhynchocoel in nemertines, a pseudocoelom in aschelminths, a coelom in annelids, or a hemocoel in molluscs.

7. Rigid exoskeletons also have locomotor functions because they provide sites for muscle attachment and counterforces for muscle movements. Exoskeletons also support and protect the body, but these are secondary functions. In arthropods, the epidermis of the body wall secretes a thick, hard cuticle. In crustaceans (crabs, lobsters, shrimp), the exoskeleton contains calcium carbonate crystals that make it hard and inflexible, except at the joints.

8. Rigid endoskeletons are enclosed by other body tissues. For example, the endoskeletons of sponges consist of mineral spicules, and the endoskeletons of echinoderms (sea stars, sea urchins) are made of calcareous plates called ossicles.

9. The most familiar endoskeletons, both cartilaginous and bony, first appeared in the vertebrates. Endoskeletons consist of two main types of supportive connective tissue: cartilage and bone. Cartilage provides a site for muscle attachment, aids in movement at joints, and provides support. Bone provides a point of attachment for muscles and transmits the force of muscular contraction from one part of the body to another.

10. Movement (locomotion) is characteristic of certain cells, protists, and animals. Amoeboid movement and movement by cilia and flagella are examples of locomotion that does not involve muscles.

11. The power behind muscular movement in both invertebrates and vertebrates is muscular tissue. The three types of muscular tissue are smooth, cardiac, and skeletal. Muscle tissue exhibits contractility, excitability, extensibility, and elasticity.

12. The functional (contractile) unit of a muscle myofibril is the sarcomere. Nerves control skeletal muscle contraction.

SELECTED KEY TERMS

amoeboid movement (p. 541)
ciliary creeping (p. 541)
denticle (p. 532)
dermis (p. 531)
endoskeleton (p. 538)
epidermis (p. 531)

exoskeleton (p. 537)
hydrostatic skeleton (p. 536)
integument (p. 531)
neuromuscular junction (p. 547)
skin (p. 531)

CRITICAL THINKING QUESTIONS

1. How does the structure of skin relate to its functions of protection, temperature control, waste removal, water conservation, radiation protection, vitamin production, and environmental responsiveness?

2. How does the epidermis of an invertebrate differ from that of a vertebrate?

3. Give an example of an animal with each type of skeleton (hydro-, exo-, endoskeleton), and explain how the contractions of its muscles produce locomotion.

4. Give one similarity and one difference between vertebrate skeletal muscle and the following: asynchronous insect muscle; the "catch" muscle of molluscs; the movement of cilia; amoeboid movement.

REFERENCES ON THE WORLD WIDE WEB

1. **Frog Skeleton.** This site includes a three-dimensional reconstruction of a frog skeleton.
   http://www.library.wisc.edu.edu/Biotech/demo/frog2/frogskel.mov

2. **Clickable Human Skeleton.** This interactive site features the anatomy of the skeletal system.
   http://www.cs.brown.edu/people/oa/Bin/skeleton.html

3. **Complete Muscle Tables of the Human Body.** This site contains comprehensive information about human muscles.
   http://www.pathway.net/hws/muscles.html

4. **Ultrastructure of the Skin.** This site provides the user with excellent electron micrographs of the epidermis, dermis, and the subcutaneous tissue associated with the skin.
   http://www.medic.mie-u.acjp/derma/anatomy.html

5. **Dermatology in the Cinema.** One of the most intriguing sites on the Internet, this site presents dermatological conditions related to the cinema.
   http://www.skinema.com/

6. **Developmental Biology of the Skin.** This extensive site covers the developmental biology of the skin.
   http://www.hslib.washington.edu/courses/hunio567/

7. **Muscle Physiology and Design.** This site allows you to explore the physiology and design of muscles.
   http://www-neuromus.ucsd.edu/musintro/

8. **Muscle Net.** Rated four stars by Magellan, this site is designed to inform the layperson about muscles.
   http://www.bio.unipd.it/~telethon/

chapter 33

COMMUNICATION I:
NERVES

Concepts

1. The nervous system helps to communicate, integrate, and coordinate the functions of the various organs and organ systems in the animal body.
2. Information flow through the nervous system has three main steps: (1) the collection of information from outside and inside the body (sensory activities), (2) the processing of this information in the nervous system, and (3) the initiation of appropriate responses.
3. Information is transmitted between neurons directly (electrically) or by means of chemicals called neurotransmitters.
4. The evolution of the nervous system in invertebrates has led to elaboration of organized nerve cords and centralization of responses in the anterior portion of the animal.
5. The vertebrate nervous system consists of the central nervous system, made up of the brain and spinal cord, and the peripheral nervous system, composed of the nerves in the rest of the body.
6. Nervous systems evolved through the gradual layering of additional nervous tissue over reflex pathways of more ancient origin.

Would You Like to Know . . .

1. how neurons and electrically active cells maintain an electrical charge? (p. 554)
2. how flea sprays or powders kill fleas but not dogs or cats? (p. 555)
3. how nerve pathways are analogous to a telephone cable? (p. 559)
4. what part of the brain is involved with language, both written and spoken? (p. 561)

This chapter answers these and other useful questions.

This chapter contains evolutionary concepts, which are set off in this font.

The two forms of communication in an animal that integrate body functions to maintain homeostasis are: (1) neurons, which transmit electrical signals that report information or initiate a quick response in a specific tissue; and (2) hormones, which are slower, chemical signals that initiate a widespread, prolonged response, often in a variety of tissues. This chapter focuses on the function of the neuron and the anatomical organization of the nervous system in animals. Chapter 34 presents the senses and the ways in which they collect information and transmit it along nerves to the central nervous system. To conclude the study of communication, chapter 35 examines how hormones affect long-term changes in an animal's body.

NEURONS: THE BASIC FUNCTIONAL UNITS OF THE NERVOUS SYSTEM

The functional unit of the nervous system is a highly specialized cell called the **neuron** (Gr. "nerve"). Neurons are specialized to produce signals that can be communicated over short to relatively long distances, from one part of an animal's body to another. Neurons have two important properties: (1) excitability, the ability to respond to stimuli; and (2) conductivity, the ability to conduct a signal.

The three functional types of neurons are sensory neurons, interneurons, and motor neurons. **Sensory (receptor** or **afferent) neurons** either act as receptors of stimuli themselves or are activated by receptors (figure 33.1a). Changes in the internal or external environments stimulate sensory neurons, which respond by sending signals to the major integrating centers where information is processed. **Interneurons** (figure 33.1c) comprise the integrating centers and receive signals from the sensory neurons and transmit them to motor neurons. **Motor (effector** or **efferent) neurons** (figure 33.1b) send the processed information via a signal to the body's effectors (e.g., muscles), causing them to contract, or to glands, causing them to secrete. Figure 33.2 summarizes the flow of information in the nervous system.

NEURON STRUCTURE: THE KEY TO FUNCTION

Most neurons contain three principal parts: a cell body, dendrites, and an axon (*see figure 33.1*). The **cell body** has a large, central nucleus. The motor neuron in figure 33.1b has many short, threadlike branches called **dendrites** (Gr. *dendron*, tree), which are actually extensions of the cell body and conduct signals toward the cell body. The **axon** is a relatively long, cylindrical process that conducts signals (information) away from the cell body.

FIGURE 33.1

Types of Vertebrate Neurons. (*a*) Sensory neurons transmit information from the environment to the central nervous system. (*b*) Motor neurons transmit information from the central nervous system to muscles or glands, and tend to have short dendrites and long axons. (*c*) Interneurons connect other neurons, permitting integration of information.

(a) **Sensory Neuron**   (b) **Motor Neuron**   (c) **Interneuron**

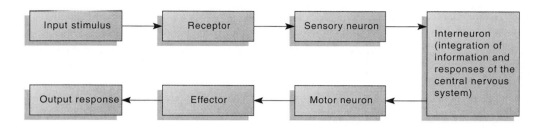

FIGURE 33.2

Generalized Pathway for the Flow of Information within the Nervous System. An input stimulus initiates impulses within some sensory structure (the receptor); the impulses are then transferred via sensory neurons to interneurons. After response selection, nerve impulses are generated and transferred along motor neurons to an effector (e.g., a muscle or gland), which elicits the appropriate output response.

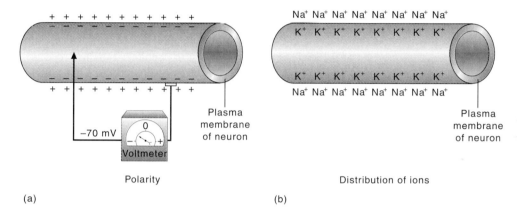

(a)   (b)

FIGURE 33.3

Resting Membrane Potential. (*a*) A voltmeter measures the difference in electrical potential between two electrodes. When one microelectrode is placed inside a neuron at rest, and one is placed outside, the electrical potential inside the cell is −70 mV relative to the outside. (*b*) In a neuron at rest, sodium is more concentrated outside and potassium is more concentrated inside the cell. A neuron in this resting condition is said to be polarized.

The neurons of hydras and sea anemones do not have a sheath covering the axon of the neuron. Other invertebrates and all vertebrates have sheathed neurons. When present, the laminated lipid sheath is called **myelin.** In some neurons, a **neurolemmocyte** (formerly known as a Schwann cell) wraps the myelin sheath in layers. In these neurons, gaps called **neurofibril nodes** (formerly **nodes of Ranvier**) segment the myelin sheath at regular intervals. The neurolemmocyte also assists in the regeneration of injured myelinated neurons.

The nervous system receives data (input stimulus), integrates it, and effects a change (output response) in the animal's physiology. In a given neuron, the dendrites are the receptors, the cell body is the integrator, and the ends of the axon are the effectors.

NEURON COMMUNICATION

The language (signal) of a neuron is the nerve impulse or action potential. The key to this nerve impulse is the neuron's plasma membrane and its properties. Changes in membrane permeability and the subsequent movement of ions produce a nerve impulse that travels along the plasma membrane of the dendrites, cell body, and axon of each neuron.

RESTING MEMBRANE POTENTIAL

A "resting" neuron is not conducting a nerve impulse. The plasma membrane of a resting neuron is polarized; the fluid on the inner side of the membrane is negatively charged with respect to the positively charged fluid outside the membrane (figure 33.3). The difference in electrical charge between the inside and the outside of the membrane at any given point is due to the relative numbers of positive and negative ions in the fluids on either side of the membrane, and to the permeability of the plasma membrane to these ions. The difference in charge is called the **resting membrane potential.** All cells have such a resting potential, but neurons and muscle cells are specialized to transmit and recycle it rapidly.

The resting potential is measured in millivolts (mV). A millivolt is 1/1,000 of a volt. Normally, the resting membrane potential is about −70 mV, due to the unequal distribution of various electrically charged ions. Sodium (Na^+) ions are more highly concentrated in the fluid outside the plasma membrane, and potassium (K^+) and negative protein ions are more highly concentrated inside.

The Na^+ and K^+ ions constantly diffuse through ion channels in the plasma membrane, moving from regions of higher concentrations to regions of lower concentrations. (There are also

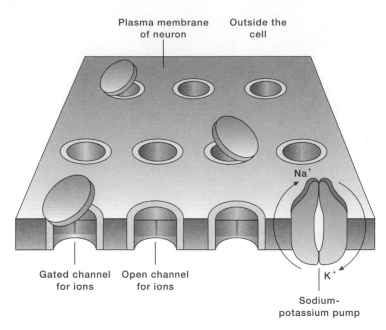

Plasma membrane
of neuron

Outside the
cell

Na⁺

K⁺

Gated channel
for ions

Open channel
for ions

Sodium-
potassium pump

FIGURE 33.4

Ion Channels and the Sodium-Potassium Pump. These mechanisms maintain a balance between the sodium ions and potassium ions on both sides of the membrane and create a membrane potential. Some channels are always open, but others open or close by the position of gates, which are proteins that change shape to block or clear the channel. Whether a gate opens or closes a channel depends on the membrane potential. Such gates are said to be voltage regulated. Some of these membrane channels are specific for sodium ions, and others are specific for potassium ions.

larger Cl^- ions and huge negative protein ions, which cannot move easily from the inside of the neuron to the outside.)   ❶   However, the concentrations of Na^+ and K^+ ions on the two sides of the membrane remain constant due to the action of the **sodium-potassium ATPase pump,** which is powered by ATP (figure 33.4). The pump actively moves Na^+ ions to the outside of the cell and K^+ ions to the inside of the cell. Because it moves three Na^+ molecules out for each two K^+ molecules that it moves in, the pump works to establish the resting potential across the membrane. Both ions leak back across the membrane—down their concentration gradients. K^+ ions, however, move more easily back to the outside, adding to the positive charge there and contributing to the membrane potential of -70 mV.

MECHANISM OF NEURON ACTION: CHANGING THE RESTING MEMBRANE POTENTIAL INTO THE ACTION POTENTIAL (NERVE IMPULSE)

Changing the resting electrical potential across the plasma membrane is the key factor in the creation and subsequent conduction of a nerve impulse. A stimulus that is strong enough to initiate an impulse is called a threshold stimulus. When such a stimulus is applied to a point along the resting plasma membrane, the perme-

ability to Na^+ ions increases at that point. The inflow of positively charged Na^+ ions causes the membrane potential to go from -70 mV toward 0. This loss in membrane polarity is called **depolarization** (figure 33.5). When depolarization reaches a certain level, special Na^+ channels (voltage-gated) that are sensitive to changes in membrane potential quickly open, and more Na^+ ions rush to the inside of the neuron. Shortly after the Na^+ ions move into the cell, the Na^+ gates close, but now voltage-gated K^+ channels open, and K^+ ions rapidly diffuse outward. The movement of the K^+ ions out of the cell builds up the positive charge outside the cell again, and the membrane becomes **repolarized.** This series of membrane changes triggers a similar cycle in an adjacent region of the membrane, and the wave of depolarization moves down the axon as an **action potential.** Overall, the transmission of an action potential along the neuron plasma membrane is a wave of depolarization and repolarization.

After each action potential, there is an interval of time when it is more difficult for another action potential to occur because the membrane has become hyperpolarized (more negative than -70 mV) due to the large number of K^+ ions that rushed out. This brief period is called the **refractory period.** During this period, the resting potential is being restored at the part of the membrane where the impulse has just passed. Afterward, the neuron is repolarized and ready to transmit another impulse.

A minimum stimulus (threshold) is necessary to initiate an action potential, but an increase in stimulus intensity does not increase the strength of the action potential. The principle that states that an axon will "fire" at full power or not at all is the **all-or-none law.**

Increasing the axon diameter and/or adding a myelin sheath increases the speed of conduction of a nerve impulse. Axons with a large diameter transmit impulses faster than smaller ones. Large-diameter axons are common among many invertebrates (e.g., crayfishes, earthworms). The largest are those of the squid (*Loligo*), where axon diameter may be over 1 mm, and the axons have a conduction velocity greater than 36 m/second! (The giant squid axons provide a simple, rapid triggering mechanism for quick escape from predators. A single action potential elicits a maximal contraction of the mantle muscle that it innervates. Mantle contraction rapidly expels water, "jetting" the squid away from the predator.) Most vertebrate axons have a diameter of less than 10 μm; however, some fishes and amphibians have evolved large, unmyelinated axons 50 μm in diameter. These extend from the brain, down the spinal cord, and activate skeletal muscles for rapid escapes.

Regardless of an axon's diameter, the myelin sheath greatly increases conduction velocity. The reason for this velocity increase is that myelin is an excellent insulator and effectively stops the movement of ions across it. Action potentials are generated only at the neurofibril nodes. In fact, the action potential "jumps" from one node to the next node. For this reason, conduction along myelinated fibers is known as **saltatory conduction** (L. *saltare,* to jump). It takes less time for an impulse to jump from node to node along a myelinated fiber than to travel smoothly along an unmyelinated fiber. Myelination allows rapid conduction in small neurons and thus provides for the evolution of nervous systems that do not occupy much space within the animal.

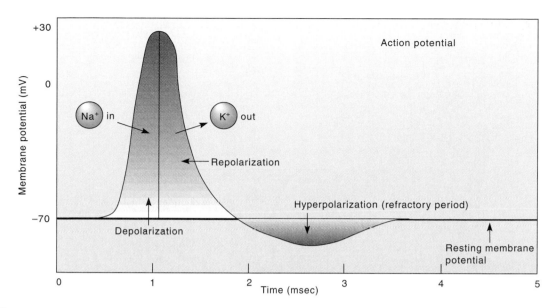

FIGURE 33.5

Action Potential As Recorded on an Oscilloscope. During the depolarization phase of the action potential, sodium (Na^+) ions rush to the inside of a neuron. The repolarization phase is characterized by a rapid increase in potassium (K^+) ions on the outside of the neuron. The action potential is sometimes called a "spike" because of its shape on an oscilloscope screen.

TRANSMISSION OF THE ACTION POTENTIAL BETWEEN CELLS

After an action potential travels along an axon, it reaches the end of a branching axon terminal called the **end bulb.** The **synapse** (Gr. *synapsis,* connection) is the junction between the axon of one neuron and the dendrite of another neuron or effector cell. The space (junction) between the end bulb and the dendrite of the next neuron is the **synaptic cleft.** The neuron carrying the action potential toward a synapse is the presynaptic ("before the synapse") neuron. It initiates a response in the receptive segment of a postsynaptic ("after the synapse") neuron leading away from the synapse. The presynaptic cell is always a neuron, but the postsynaptic cell can be a neuron, muscle cell, or gland cell.

Synapses can be electrical or chemical. In an **electrical synapse,** nerve impulses transmit directly from neuron to neuron when positively charged ions move from one neuron to the next. These ions depolarize the postsynaptic membrane, as though the two neurons were electrically coupled. An electrical synapse can rapidly transmit impulses in both directions. Electrical synapses are common in fishes and partially account for their ability to dart swiftly away from a threatening predator.

In a **chemical synapse,** two cells communicate by means of a chemical agent called a **neurotransmitter,** which the presynaptic neuron releases. A neurotransmitter changes the resting potential in the plasma membrane of the receptive segment of the postsynaptic cell, creating an action potential in that cell, which continues the transmission of the impulse.

When a nerve impulse reaches an end bulb, it causes storage vesicles (containing the chemical neurotransmitter) to fuse with the plasma membrane. The vesicles release the neurotransmitter by exocytosis into the synaptic cleft (figure 33.6). One common neurotransmitter is the chemical **acetylcholine;** another is **norepinephrine** (box 33.1). (More than 50 other possible transmitters are known.)

When the released neurotransmitter (e.g., acetylcholine) binds with receptor protein sites in the postsynaptic membrane, it causes a depolarization similar to that of the presynaptic cell. As a result, the impulse continues its path to an eventual effector. Once acetylcholine has crossed the synaptic cleft, the enzyme acetylcholinesterase quickly inactivates it. Without this breakdown, acetylcholine would remain and would continually stimulate the postsynaptic cell, leading to a diseased state. You have probably created a similar diseased state at the synapses of the fleas on your dog or cat. ❷ The active ingredient in most flea sprays and powders is parathion. It prevents the breakdown of acetylcholine in the fleas, as well as pets and people. However, because fleas are so small, the low dose that immobilizes the fleas does not affect pets or humans.

Stop and Ask Yourself

1. What causes the resting membrane potential in a neuron?
2. How is a resting membrane potential maintained?
3. What are the different phases of an action potential?
4. What is saltatory conduction?
5. How is an action potential transmitted between neurons?

Marshburn

FIGURE 33.6

Chemical Transmission across a Synapse. (*a*) Pre- and postsynaptic neurons with synaptic end bulb. (*b*) Enlarged view of the end bulb containing synaptic vesicles. (*c*) Enlargement of a portion of the end bulb showing exocytosis. The sequence of events in neurotransmitter release is: (*1*) a synaptic vesicle containing neurotransmitter approaches the plasma membrane; (*2*) due to the influx of calcium ions, the vesicle fuses with the membrane; (*3*) exocytosis occurs; and (*4*) the vesicle reforms and begins to fill with more neurotransmitter.

INVERTEBRATE NERVOUS SYSTEMS

All cells respond to some stimuli and relay information both internally and externally. Thus, even when no real nervous system is present, such as in the protozoa and sponges, coordination and reaction to external and internal stimuli do occur. For example, the regular beating of protozoan cilia (*see figure 32.16*) or the response of flagellates to varying light intensities requires intracellular coordination. Only animals that have achieved the tissue level of organization (e.g., the diploblastic and triploblastic animals) have true nervous systems, however. This clearly excludes the protozoa and sponges.

Among animals more complex than sponges, five general evolutionary trends in nervous system development are apparent. The first has been integrated throughout Part Five of this text. More complex animals possess more detailed nervous systems.

Of all animals, the cnidarians (hydras, jellyfishes, and sea anemones) have the simplest form of nervous organization. These animals have a **nerve net,** a latticework that conducts impulses from one area to another (figure 33.7a). In nerve nets, impulse conduction by neurons is bidirectional. Cnidarians lack brains and even local clusters of neurons. Instead, a nerve stimulus anywhere on the body initiates a nerve impulse that spreads across the nerve net to other body regions. In jellyfishes, this type of nervous

BOX 33.1 — NEUROTOXINS

Much of what is known about synaptic transmission has been obtained from chemicals that other animals produce. These chemicals, called **neurotoxins,** block synaptic transmission. For example, symbiotic bacteria in a poison gland of the puffer fish, *Spheroides,* produce tetrodotoxin. Tetrodotoxin blocks sodium channels and prevents an action potential. Humans who eat puffer fish without removing the tissues/organs containing the neurotoxin often die by paralysis. In Japan, where this fish is a delicacy, specially trained chefs remove the organs that contain most of the neurotoxin. In spite of this precaution, about 100 diners die annually from improperly prepared puffer fish.

The dinoflagellates responsible for "red tides" produce a similar neurotoxin, called saxitoxin. Saxitoxin inhibits sodium transport in nerve cells, thus killing the fishes that eat the dinoflagellates. If filter-feeding molluscs consume the dinoflagellates, and humans eat the "shellfish," the humans may suffer from paralytic "shellfish" poisoning (PSP).

Another type of poisoning in humans is called "ciguatera." It results from eating marine fishes (red bass, moray eels, mackerel) that have consumed a dinoflagellate that produces the neurotoxin ciguatoxin. Ciguatoxin also blocks sodium transport.

Batrachotoxin, from the poison-dart frog (*Phyllobates*) of South America, keeps sodium channels open, leading to hyperpolarization and nerve dysfunction. Neurotoxins in the venom of the North African scorpion (*Leiurus*) and from the sea anemone (*Anemonia*) slow the closing of the sodium channels at the end of an action potential.

All of these neurotoxins normally help defend their animal producers against predation. They are also useful tools for experimentation, however, and have helped neurophysiologists to better understand the normal functioning of neurons.

---

system is involved in slow swimming movements and in keeping the body right-side up. At the cellular level, the neurons function in the way discussed earlier in this chapter.

Echinoderms (e.g., sea stars, sea urchins, sea cucumbers) still have nerve nets, but of increasing complexity. For example, sea stars have three distinct nerve nets. The one that lies just under the skin has a circumoral ring and five sets of nerve cords running out to the animal's arms. Another net serves the muscles between the skin plates, called ossicles. The third net connects to the tube feet. This degree of nerve net complexity permits locomotion, a variety of useful reflexes, and some degree of "central" coordination. For example, when a sea star is flipped over, it can right itself.

Animals, such as flatworms and roundworms, that move in a forward direction have sense organs concentrated in the body region that first encounters new environmental stimuli. Thus, the second trend in nervous system evolution involves cephalization, which is a concentration of receptors and nervous tissue in the animal's anterior end. For example, a flatworm's nervous system contains **ganglia** (sing., ganglion), which are distinct aggregations of nerve cells in the head region. Ganglia function as a primitive "brain" (figure 33.7b). Distinct lateral nerve cords (collections of neurons) on either side of the body carry sensory information from the periphery to the head ganglia and carry motor impulses from the head ganglia back to muscles, allowing the animal to react to environmental stimuli.

These lateral nerve cords reveal that flatworms also exhibit the third trend in nervous system evolution: bilateral symmetry. Bilateral symmetry (a body plan with roughly equivalent right and left halves) could have led to paired neurons, muscles, sensory structures, and brain centers. This pairing facilitates coordinated ambulatory movements, such as climbing, crawling, flying, or walking.

In other invertebrates, such as crustaceans, segmented worms, and arthropods, the organization of the nervous system shows further advances. In these invertebrates, axons join into nerve cords, and in addition to a small, centralized brain, smaller peripheral ganglia help coordinate outlying regions of the animal's body. Ganglia can occur in each body segment or can be scattered throughout the body close to the organs they regulate (figure 33.7c,d,e). Regardless of the arrangement, these ganglia represent the fourth evolutionary trend. The more complex an animal, the more interneurons it has. Because interneurons in ganglia do much of the integrating that takes place in nervous systems, the more interneurons, the more complex behavior patterns an animal can perform.

In echinoderms, such as starfishes, the nervous system is divided into several parts (figure 33.7f). The ectoneural system retains a primitive epidermal position and combines sensory and motor functions. A radial nerve extends down the lower surface of each arm. A deeper hyponeural system has a motor function, and the apical system may have some sensory functions.

The fifth trend in the evolution of invertebrate nervous systems is a consequence of the increasing number of interneurons. The brain contains the largest number of neurons, and the more complex the animal, and the more complicated its behavior, the more neurons (especially interneurons) are concentrated in an anterior brain and bilaterally organized ganglia. Vertebrate brains are an excellent example of this trend.

VERTEBRATE NERVOUS SYSTEMS

The basic organization of the nervous system is similar in all vertebrates. Bilateral symmetry, a notochord, and a tubular nerve cord characterize the evolution of vertebrate nervous systems.

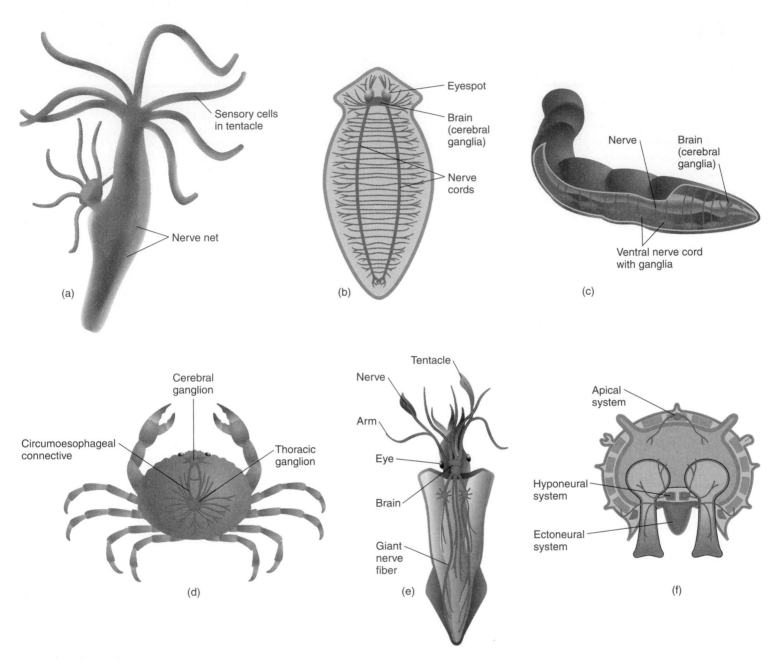

FIGURE 33.7

Some Invertebrate Nervous Systems. (*a*) The nerve net of *Hydra*, a cnidarian, represents the simplest neural organization. (*b*) Brain and paired nerve cords of a planarian flatworm. This is the first nervous system showing differentiation into a peripheral nervous system and a central nervous system. (*c*) Brain, ventral nerve cord, ganglia, and peripheral nerves of the earthworm, an annelid worm. (*d*) A crustacean, showing the principal ganglia and visceral connective nerves. The most primitive crustaceans have nervous systems similar to those of the platyhelminths, whereas (*e*) some cephalopods (such as the squid) have brains and behavior as complex as those of fishes. (*f*) Cross section of a starfish arm. Nerves from the ectoneural system terminate on the surface of the hyponeural system, but the two systems have no contact.

The **notochord** is a rod of mesodermally derived tissue encased in a firm sheath that lies ventral to the neural tube (*see figure 10.7*). It first appeared in marine chordates and is present in all vertebrate embryos, but is greatly reduced or absent in adults. During embryological development in most vertebrate species, vertebrae serially arranged into a vertebral column replace the notochord. This vertebral column led to the development of strong muscles, allowing vertebrates to become fast-moving, predatory animals. Some of the other bones developed into powerful jaws, which facilitated the predatory nature of these animals.

A related character in vertebrate evolution was the development of a single, tubular nerve cord above the notochord. During early evolution, the nerve cord underwent expansion, regional modification, and specialization into a spinal cord and brain. Over time, the

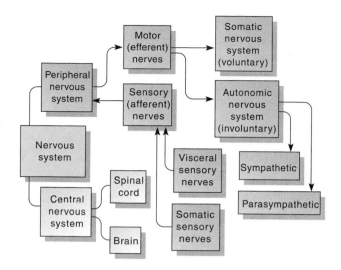

FIGURE 33.8

The Basic Organization of the Nervous System Is Similar in All Vertebrates. This flowchart shows the divisions and nerves of the vertebrate nervous system. Arrows indicate the directional flow of nerve impulses (information).

anterior end thickened variably with nervous tissue and functionally divided into the hindbrain, midbrain, and forebrain. In the sensory world of the fast-moving and powerful vertebrates, the anterior sensory receptors became more complex and bilaterally symmetrical. For example, paired structures, such as eyes and ears, developed to better gather information from the outside environment.

The nervous system of vertebrates has two main divisions (figure 33.8). The **central nervous system** is composed of the brain and spinal cord and is the site of information processing. The **peripheral nervous system** is composed of all the nerves of the body outside the brain and spinal cord. These nerves are commonly divided into two groups: **sensory (afferent) nerves,** which transmit information to the central nervous system; and **motor (efferent) nerves,** which carry commands away from the central nervous system. The motor nerves divide into the **voluntary (somatic) nervous system,** which relays commands to skeletal muscles, and the **involuntary (visceral or autonomic) nervous system,** which stimulates other muscles (smooth and cardiac) and glands of the body. The nerves of the autonomic nervous system divide into **sympathetic** and **parasympathetic** systems.

(3) Nervous system pathways are composed of individual neuronal axons bundled like the strands of a telephone cable. In the central nervous system, these bundles of nerve fibers are called **tracts.** In the peripheral nervous system, they are called **nerves.** The cell bodies from which the axons extend often cluster into groups. These groups are called nuclei if they are in the central nervous system and ganglia if they are part of the peripheral nervous system.

THE SPINAL CORD

The spinal cord serves two important functions in an animal; it is the connecting link between the brain and most of the body, and

it is involved in spinal reflex actions. A reflex is a predictable, involuntary response to a stimulus. Thus, both voluntary and involuntary limb movements, as well as certain organ functions, depend on this link.

The spinal cord is the part of the central nervous system that extends from the brain to near or into the tail (figure 33.9). A cross section shows a neural canal that contains cerebrospinal fluid. The gray matter consists of cell bodies and dendrites, and is concerned mainly with reflex connections at various levels of the spinal cord. Extending from the spinal cord are the ventral and dorsal roots of the spinal nerves. These roots contain the main motor and sensory fibers (axons and/or dendrites), respectively, that contribute to the major spinal nerves. The white matter of the spinal cord gets its name from the whitish myelin that covers the axons.

Three layers of protective membranes called **meninges** (pl. of meninx, membrane) surround the spinal cord. They are continuous with similar layers that cover the brain. The outer layer, the **dura mater,** is a tough, fibrous membrane. The middle layer, the **arachnoid,** is delicate and connects to the innermost layer, the **pia mater.** The pia mater contains small blood vessels that nourish the spinal cord.

SPINAL NERVES

Generally, the number of spinal nerves is directly related to the number of segments in the trunk and tail of a vertebrate. For example, a frog has evolved strong hind legs for swimming or jumping, a reduced trunk, and no tail in the adult. It has only 10 pairs of spinal nerves. By contrast, a snake, which moves by lateral undulations of its long trunk and tail, has several hundred pairs of spinal nerves.

THE BRAIN

Anatomically, the vertebrate brain develops at the anterior end of the spinal cord. During embryonic development, the brain undergoes regional expansion as a hollow tube of nervous tissue forms and develops into the hindbrain, midbrain, and forebrain (figure 33.10). The central canal of the spinal cord extends up into the brain and expands into chambers called ventricles. The ventricles are filled with cerebrospinal fluid.

Hindbrain

The **hindbrain** is continuous with the spinal cord and includes the medulla oblongata, cerebellum, and pons. The **medulla oblongata** is the enlargement where the spinal cord enters the brain. It contains reflex centers for breathing, swallowing, cardiovascular function, and gastric secretion. The medulla oblongata is well developed in all jawed vertebrates, reflecting its ability to control visceral functions and to serve as a screen for information that leaves or enters the brain.

The **cerebellum** is an outgrowth of the medulla oblongata. It coordinates motor activity associated with limb movement, maintaining posture, and spatial orientation. The cerebellum in

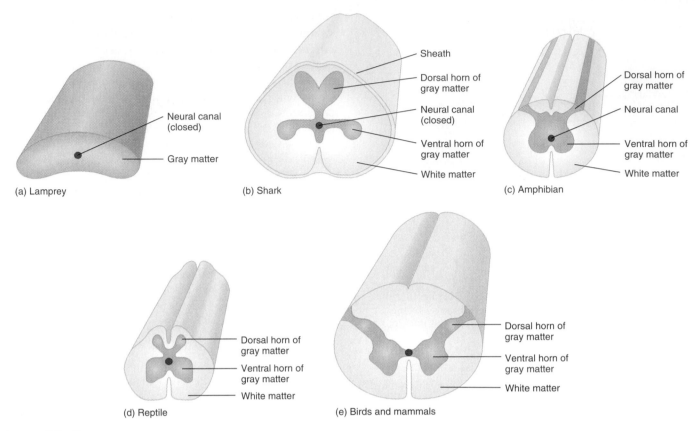

FIGURE 33.9

Spinal Cords of Vertebrates. (a) The spinal cord of a typical agnathan (lamprey) is flattened and possesses no myelinated axons. Its shape facilitates the diffusion of gases, nutrients, and other products. (b,c) In fishes and amphibians, the spinal cord is larger, well vascularized, and rounded. With more white matter, the spinal cord bulges outward. The gray matter in the spinal cord of (d) a reptile and (e) birds and mammals has a characteristic butterfly shape.

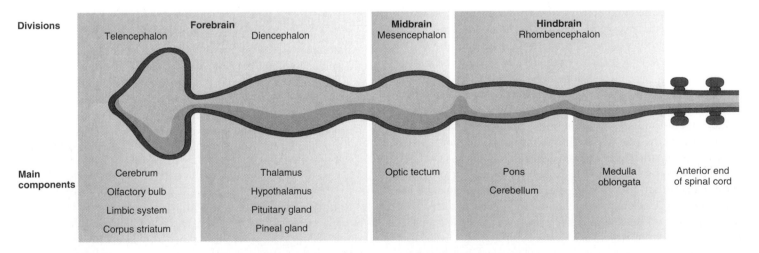

FIGURE 33.10

Development of the Vertebrate Brain. Summary of the three major subdivisions and some of the structures they contain. This drawing is highly simplified and flattened.

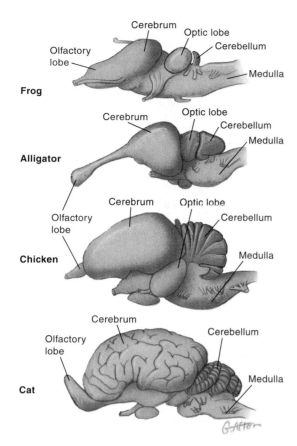

FIGURE 33.11

Vertebrate Brains. Comparison of several vertebrate brains, as viewed from the side. The drawings are not drawn to the same scale. Notice the increase in relative size of the cerebrum from amphibian (frog) to mammal (cat).

cartilaginous fishes has distinct anterior and posterior lobes. In teleosts, the cerebellum is large in active swimmers and small in relatively inactive fishes. Amphibians often have a rudimentary cerebellum, reflecting their relatively simple locomotor patterns (figure 33.11). In tetrapods, the cerebellum is laterally expanded. These expanded lateral lobes provide locomotor control of muscles of the appendages. The cerebellum is much larger in birds and mammals—a reflection of complex locomotor patterns and a common evolutionary history of limb development and phylogeny as terrestrial vertebrates.

The **pons** is a bridge of transverse nerve tracts from the cerebrum of the forebrain to both sides of the cerebellum. It also contains tracts that connect the forebrain and spinal cord in all vertebrates.

Midbrain

The **midbrain** was originally a center for coordinating reflex responses to visual input. As the brain evolved, it took on added functions relating to tactile (touch) and auditory (hearing) input, but it did not change in size. The roof of the midbrain, called the optic tectum, is a thickened region of gray matter that integrates visual and auditory signals.

Forebrain

The vertebrate forebrain has changed a great deal during vertebrate evolution. The **forebrain** has two main parts: the diencephalon and telencephalon (see figure 33.10). The diencephalon lies just in front of the midbrain and contains the pineal gland, pituitary gland, hypothalamus, and thalamus. The **thalamus** relays all sensory information to higher brain centers. The **hypothalamus** lies below the thalamus and regulates many functions, such as body temperature, sexual drive, carbohydrate metabolism, hunger, and thirst. The pineal gland controls some body rhythms. The pituitary is a major endocrine gland, and chapter 35 discusses it in detail.

In fishes and amphibians, the diencephalon processes sensory information. In reptiles and birds, the most important part of the brain is the corpus striatum, which plays a role in their complex behavior patterns (see chapter 30).

As the diencephalon slowly expanded during evolution and handled more and more sensory functions, the telencephalon (the front part of the forebrain) expanded rapidly in both size and complexity.

External to the corpus striatum is the **cerebrum,** which a large groove divides into right and left cerebral hemispheres. The parts of the brain related to sensory and motor integration changed greatly as vertebrates became more agile and inquisitive (figure 33.12). Many functions shifted from the optic tectum to the expanding cerebral hemispheres. The increasing importance of the cerebrum affected many other brain regions, especially the thalamus and cerebellum. In mammals, the outermost part of the cerebrum, called the cerebral cortex, progressively increased in size and complexity. This layer folds back on itself to a remarkable extent, suggesting that evolution of the mammalian cerebrum outpaced enlargement of the skullbones housing it.

Different parts of the cerebrum have specific functions. For example, the cerebral cortex contains primary sensory areas and primary motor areas. ④ Other areas of the cortex are involved in perception of visual or auditory signals from the environment. In humans, this includes the ability to use language—both written and spoken.

Stop and Ask Yourself

6. How is the vertebrate brain related to the spinal cord?
7. What are the three parts of the vertebrate hindbrain?
8. What is the function of the midbrain?
9. What are the different parts of the forebrain and their respective functions?

(a) Bass   (b) Frog   (c) Pit viper   (d) Warbler

(e) Opossum   (f) Bobcat

(g) Macaque   (h) Chimpanzee   (i) Human

FIGURE 33.12

Cerebrum in Different Vertebrate Species. The cerebrum increases in both size and complexity of its neural connections in more advanced groups. (*a*) Fishes and (*b*) amphibians lack cerebral cortices, whereas (*c*) reptiles and (*d*) birds have a small amount of gray matter covering their cerebrums. Most primitive mammals, such as (*e*) the opossum, have smooth cortices. Carnivores, such as (*f*) the bobcat, have larger cerebrums, and the cortex has a few convolutions. (*g,h*) In the primates, the cerebrum is much increased relative to other brain structures, and the cortex is highly convoluted. (*i*) The human cerebrum dominates in brain evolution and is highly convoluted.

CRANIAL NERVES

In addition to the paired spinal nerves, the peripheral nervous system of vertebrates includes paired cranial nerves (table 33.1). Reptiles, birds, and mammals have 12 pairs of cranial nerves. Fishes and amphibians have only the first 10 pairs. Some of the nerves (e.g., optic nerve) contain only sensory axons, which carry signals to the brain. Others contain sensory and motor axons, and are termed mixed nerves. For example, the vagus nerve has sensory axons leading to the brain as well as motor axons leading to the heart and smooth muscles of the visceral organs in the thorax and abdomen.

THE AUTONOMIC NERVOUS SYSTEM

The vertebrate autonomic nervous system is composed of two divisions that act antagonistically (in opposition to each other) to control the body's involuntary muscles (smooth and cardiac) and glands. The **parasympathetic nervous system** functions during relaxation. It contains nerves that arise from the brain and sacral region of the spinal cord, and consists of a network of long efferent nerve fibers that synapse at ganglia in the immediate vicinity of organs, and short efferent neurons that extend from the ganglia to the organs. The **sympathetic nervous system** is responsible for the "fight-or-flight" response. It contains nerves that arise from

TABLE 33.1	FUNCTIONS OF THE CRANIAL NERVES OF REPTILES, BIRDS, AND MAMMALS	
NERVE	**TYPE**	**INNERVATION AND FUNCTION**
I Olfactory	Sensory	Smell
II Optic	Sensory	Vision
III Oculomotor	Primarily motor	Eyelids, eyes, adjustments of light entering eyes, lens focusing (motor)
IV Trochlear	Primarily motor	Condition of muscles (sensory)
		Eye muscles (motor)
V Trigeminal	Mixed	Condition of muscles (sensory)
Ophthalmic division		Eyes, tear glands, scalp, forehead, and upper eyelids (sensory)
Maxillary division		Upper teeth, upper gum, upper lip, lining of the palate, and skin of the face (sensory)
Mandibular division		Scalp, skin of the jaw, lower teeth, lower gum, and lower lip (sensory)
VI Abducens	Primarily motor	Jaws, floor of the mouth (motor)
		Eye muscles (motor)
VII Facial	Mixed	Condition of muscles (sensory)
		Taste receptors of the anterior tongue (sensory)
		Facial expression, tear glands, and salivary glands (motor)
VIII Vestibulocochlear	Sensory	
Vestibular branch		Equilibrium; vestibule
Cochlear branch		Hearing; cochlea
IX Glossopharyngeal	Mixed	Pharynx, tonsils, posterior tongue, and carotid arteries (sensory)
		Pharynx and salivary glands (motor)
X Vagus	Mixed	Speech and swallowing, heart, and visceral organs in the thorax and abdomen (motor)
		Pharynx, larynx, esophagus, and visceral organs of the thorax and abdomen (sensory)
XI Accessory	Motor	
Cranial branch		Soft palate, pharynx, and larynx
Spinal branch		Neck and back
XII Hypoglossal	Motor	Tongue muscles

the thoracic and lumbar regions of the spinal cord. It is a network of short efferent central nervous system fibers that extend to ganglia near the spine, and long efferent neurons extending from the ganglia directly to each organ.

Many organs receive input from both the parasympathetic and sympathetic systems. For example, parasympathetic input stimulates salivary gland secretions and intestinal movements, contracts pupillary muscles in the eyes, and relaxes sphincter muscles. Sympathetic input controls antagonistic actions: inhibition of salivary gland secretions and intestinal movements, relaxation of pupillary muscles, and contraction of sphincters.

Stop and Ask Yourself

10. Name the twelve pairs of cranial nerves found in reptiles, birds, and mammals.

11. How would you describe the parasympathetic nervous system? How would you describe the sympathetic system?

ENDANGERED SPECIES

WILDLIFE ALERT 10—RED-COCKADED WOODPECKER (*PICOIDES BOREALIS*)

VITAL STATISTICS

Classification: Phylum Chordata, class Aves, order Piciformes, family Picidae

Range: Fragmented, isolated populations where southern pines exist in the United States, (Alabama, Arkansas, Georgia, Kentucky, Louisiana, Mississippi, North Carolina, South Carolina, and Tennessee)

Habitat: Open stands of pines with a minimum age of 80 to 120 years

Number remaining: Approximately 4,500 groups, or 10,000 to 12,000 birds

Status: Endangered throughout its range

NATURAL HISTORY AND ECOLOGICAL STATUS

Red-cockaded woodpeckers are 18 to 20 cm long with a wing span of 35 to 38 cm. They have black-and-white horizontal stripes on the back, and their cheeks and underparts are white (figure 1). Males have a small, red spot on each side of their black cap. After the first postfledgling molt, fledgling males have a red crown patch. The diet of these woodpeckers consists mostly of insects and wild fruit.

Eggs are laid from April through June, with females utilizing their mate's roosting cavity as a nest. The average clutch size is three to five eggs. Most often, the parent birds and one or more male offspring from previous nests form a family unit called a group. A group

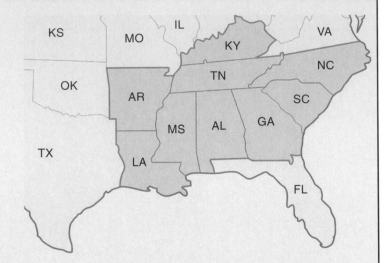

FIGURE 2   Distribution of the Red-Cockaded Woodpecker (*Picoides borealis*).

may include one breeding pair and as many as seven other birds. Rearing the young becomes a shared responsibility of the group.

The range of red-cockaded woodpeckers is closely tied to the distribution of southern pines, with open stands of trees in the 80- to 120-year-old group being the favored nesting habitat (figure 2). Dense stands or hardwoods are usually avoided. The woodpeckers excavate roosting cavities in living pines, usually those infected with a fungus that produces what is known as red-heart disease. The aggregate of cavity trees is called a cluster and may include one to twenty or more cavity trees on 3 to 60 acres. Completed cavities in active use have numerous small resin wells, which exude sap. The birds keep the sap flowing, apparently as a cavity defense mechanism against rat snakes and other predators. The territory for a group averages about 200 acres.

The decline of red-cockaded woodpecker populations is due primarily to the cutting of pine forests with trees that are 80 years or more old and the encroachment of hardwood understories. Recommendations for management and protection include: survey, monitor, and assess the status of individual populations and the species; protect and manage nesting and foraging habitats on federal lands; encourage protection and management on private lands; and inform and involve the public.

FIGURE 1   Red-Cockaded Woodpecker (*Picoides borealis*).

SUMMARY

1. The functional unit of the nervous system is the neuron. Neurons are specialized to produce signals that can be communicated from one part of an animal's body to another. Neurons have two important properties: excitability and conductivity.

2. A typical neuron has three anatomical parts: dendrites, a cell body, and an axon.

3. The language (signal) of a neuron is the nerve impulse or action potential.

4. The plasma membrane of a resting neuron is polarized, meaning that the fluid on the inner side of the membrane is negatively charged with respect to the positively charged fluid outside the membrane. The sodium-potassium ATPase pump and diffusion of ions across membrane channels maintain this polarization.

5. When a threshold stimulus is applied to a resting neuron, the neuron depolarizes, causing an action potential. In myelinated neurons, the action potential jumps from one neurofibril node to the next in a process known as saltatory conduction.

6. Neuronal activity is transmitted between cells at the synapse. Although some animals have electrical synapses that transmit neuronal activity from one neuron to the next, most advanced animals use chemical neurotransmitter molecules.

7. Among animals more complex than sponges, five general evolutionary trends in the nervous system are apparent. That is, the more complex an animal,

   a. the more detailed its nervous system.

   b. the more cephalization concentrates receptors and nervous tissue in an animal's anterior end.

   c. the more bilateral symmetry, which has led to paired nerves, muscles, sensory structures, and brain centers. This pairing facilitates ambulatory movements, such as climbing, crawling, flying, or walking.

   d. the more interneurons it has.

   e. the more complicated its behavior, and the more neurons (especially interneurons) concentrated in an anterior brain and bilaterally organized ganglia.

8. The vertebrate nervous system has two main divisions. The central nervous system is composed of the brain and spinal cord, and the peripheral nervous system is composed of all the nerves (bundles of axons and/or dendrites) outside the brain and spinal cord.

9. The spinal cord of a vertebrate serves two important functions. It is the connecting link between the brain of an animal and most of the body, and it is involved in spinal reflex actions. A reflex is a predictable, involuntary response to a stimulus.

10. The number of spinal nerves is directly related to the number of segments in the trunk and tail of a vertebrate.

11. The vertebrate brain divides into the hindbrain, midbrain, and forebrain. The hindbrain is continuous with the spinal cord and includes the medulla oblongata, cerebellum, and pons.

12. The midbrain is a thickened region of gray matter that integrates visual and auditory signals. The forebrain contains the pineal gland, pituitary gland, hypothalamus, and thalamus. The anterior part of the forebrain expanded during evolution to give rise to the cerebral cortex.

13. In addition to the paired spinal nerves, the vertebrate peripheral nervous system includes 12 pairs of cranial nerves in reptiles, birds, and mammals. Fishes and amphibians have only the first 10 pairs.

14. The autonomic nervous system consists of two antagonistic parts: the sympathetic and parasympathetic divisions.

SELECTED KEY TERMS

action potential (p. 554)   dendrites (p. 552)
axon (p. 552)   medulla oblongata (p. 559)
cell body (p. 552)   neuron (p. 552)
cerebellum (p. 559)   saltatory conduction (p. 554)
cerebrum (p. 561)   synapse (p. 555)

CRITICAL THINKING QUESTIONS

1. What are several ways in which drugs that are stimulants could increase activity of the human nervous system by acting at the synapse?

2. How can a neuron integrate information?

3. Surveying the functions of the evolutionarily oldest parts of the vertebrate brain gives us some idea of the original functions of the brain. Explain this statement.

4. What are the possible advantages and disadvantages in the evolutionary trend toward cephalization of the nervous system?

5. How does an action potential cross a synapse?

REFERENCES ON THE WORLD WIDE WEB

1. **Comparative Mammalian Brain Collection.** This site compares the anatomy of many different mammalian brains.
   http://www.neurophys.wisc.edu/brain/

2. **The Brain and Mind.** This site covers basic neurophysiology.
   http://www.physics.wisc.edu/~shalizi/hyper-weird/brain.html

3. **Shuffle Brain.** This unique site features how the brain and mind work.
   http://www.indiana.edu/~pietsch/home.html

4. **Neurulation and Development of the Nervous System.** This site contains information on the development of the nervous system, one of the most complex and fascinating stories of developmental biology.
   http://www.biology.usu.edu/bio523/nerve96.htm

5. **Living Schwann Cells.** This site presents a light microscope picture of living Schwann cells.
   http://www.ibr.usyd.edu.au/daved/schwann.html

6. **Homeostasis: Animals.** This site provides introductory information on the nervous system, neurons, synapses, and reflex arcs.
   http://bioserve.latrobe.edu.au/vcebiol/cat1/aos2/u3aos22.html

7. **Evolution of the Brain.** Learn more about the evolution of the brain by reading this site.
   http://ursula.uoregon.edu/%ealbates/brain1.html

COMMUNICATION II:
SENSES

Concepts

1. Sensory receptors or organs permit an animal to detect changes in its body, as well as in objects and events in the world around it. Sensory receptors collect information that is then passed to the nervous system, which determines, evaluates, and initiates an appropriate response.
2. Sensory receptors initiate nerve impulses by opening channels in sensory neuron plasma membranes, depolarizing the membranes, and causing a generator potential. Receptors differ in the nature of the environmental stimulus that triggers an eventual nerve impulse.
3. Many kinds of receptors have evolved among invertebrates and vertebrates, and each receptor is sensitive to a specific type of stimulus.
4. The nature of its sensory receptors gives each animal species a unique perception of its body and environment.

Would You Like to Know . . .

① what is the oldest and most universal sense in the animal kingdom? (p. 569)

② why it is so difficult to catch a fly with your hand? (p. 570)

③ how honeybees can recognize particular flowers? (p. 571)

④ what animal has the largest eye and how big the eye is? (p. 571)

⑤ how web-building spiders can sense struggling prey in their webs? (p. 572)

⑥ how certain fishes can detect electrical currents in the surrounding water? (p. 573)

⑦ why dogs can hear the sound from a high-pitched dog whistle while humans cannot? (p. 576)

⑧ what causes motion sickness or seasickness in humans? (p. 576)

⑨ how a sturgeon can taste food before the food reaches its mouth? (p. 580)

This chapter answers these and other useful questions.

This chapter contains evolutionary concepts, which are set off in this font.

About two thousand years ago, Aristotle identified five human senses—sight, hearing, smell, taste, and touch—commonly referred to as the "five senses." Today, zoologists know that animals also have other senses. For example, invertebrates possess an impressive array of sensory receptors through which they receive information about their environment. Common examples include tactile receptors that sense touch; georeceptors that sense the pull of gravity; hygroreceptors that detect the water content of air; proprioceptors that respond to mechanically induced changes caused by stretching, compression, bending, and tension; phonoreceptors that are sensitive to sound; baroreceptors that respond to pressure changes; chemoreceptors that respond to air- and waterborne molecules; photoreceptors that sense light; and thermoreceptors that are influenced by temperature changes.

Most vertebrates have a sense of equilibrium (balance) and a sense of body movement, and are also sensitive to fine touch, touch-pressure, heat, taste, vision, olfaction, audition, cold, pain, and various other tactile stimuli. In addition, receptors in the circulatory system register changes in blood pressure and blood levels of carbon dioxide and hydrogen ions, and receptors in the digestive system are involved in the perception of hunger and thirst.

Overall, an animal's senses limit and define its impression of the environment. In fact, all awareness depends on the reception and decoding of stimuli from the external environment and from within an animal's body. This chapter examines how animals use sensory information to help maintain homeostasis.

SENSORY RECEPTION

Sensory receptors consist of cells that can convert environmental information (stimuli) into nerve impulses. A **stimulus** (pl., stimuli) is any form of energy an animal can detect with its receptors. All receptors are **transducers** ("to change over"); that is, they convert one form of energy into another. Because all nerve impulses are the same, different types of receptors convert different kinds of stimuli, such as light or heat, into a local electrical potential called the **generator potential.** If the generator potential reaches the sensory neuron's threshold potential, it causes channels in the plasma membrane to open and creates an action potential. The impulse then travels along the cell's axon toward a synaptic junction and becomes information going to the central nervous system or brain.

As presented in chapter 33, all action potentials are alike. Furthermore, an action potential is an all-or-none phenomenon; it either occurs or it doesn't. How, then, does a common action potential give rise to different sensations, such as taste, color, or sound, or different degrees of sensation? In those animals that have brains, some nerve signals from specific receptors always end up in a specific part of the brain for interpretation; therefore, a stimulus that goes to the optic center is interpreted as a visual

stimulus. Another factor that characterizes a particular stimulus is its intensity. When the stimulus strength increases, the number of action potentials per unit of time also increases. Thus, the brain can perceive the intensity and type of stimulus from the timing of the impulses and the "wiring" of neurons.

Sensory receptors have the following basic features:

1. They contain sensitive receptor cells or finely branched peripheral endings of sensory neurons that respond to a stimulus by creating a generator potential.
2. Their structure is designed to receive a specific stimulus.
3. Their receptor cells synapse with afferent nerve fibers that travel to the central nervous system along specific neural pathways.
4. In the central nervous system, the nerve impulse is translated into a recognizable sensation, such as sound.

Stop and Ask Yourself

1. What are the five basic senses Aristotle identified about two thousand years ago? What are some additional senses found in different animals?
2. What does it mean to say that receptors function as transducers?
3. What is the difference between a generator potential and an action potential?
4. If all action potentials are alike, how is information regarding the type and intensity of a stimulus conveyed to the central nervous system of an animal?

INVERTEBRATE SENSORY RECEPTORS

An animal's behavior is largely a function of its responses to environmental information. Invertebrates possess an impressive array of receptor structures through which they receive information about their environment. Some common examples are now discussed from a structural and functional perspective.

BARORECEPTORS

Baroreceptors (Gr. *baros*, weight + receptor) sense changes in pressure. However, zoologists have not identified any specific structures for baroreception in invertebrates. Nevertheless, responses to pressure changes have been identified in ocean-dwelling copepod crustaceans, ctenophores, jellyfish medusae, and squids. Some intertidal crustaceans coordinate migratory activity with daily tidal movements, possibly in response to pressure changes accompanying water depth changes.

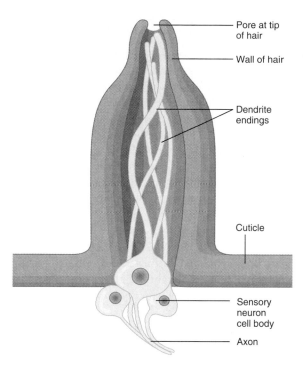

FIGURE 34.1

Invertebrate Chemoreceptor. Cross section through an insect sensillum. The receptor is a projection of the cuticle with a pore at the tip. Each chemoreceptor generally contains four to five dendrites, which lead to sensory neuron cell bodies underneath the cuticle. Each sensory cell has its own spectrum of chemical responses. Thus, a single sensillum with four or five dendrites and cell bodies may be capable of discriminating many different chemicals.

CHEMORECEPTORS

Chemoreceptors (Gr. *chemeia,* pertaining to chemistry) respond to chemicals. Chemoreception is a direct sense in that molecules act specifically to stimulate a response.   ❶ Chemoreception is the oldest and most universal sense in the animal kingdom. For example, protozoa have a chemical sense; they respond with avoidance behavior to acid, alkali, and salt stimuli. Specific chemicals attract predatory ciliates to their prey. The chemoreceptors of many aquatic invertebrates are located in pits or depressions, through which water carrying the specific chemicals may be circulated. In arthropods, the chemoreceptors are usually on the antennae, mouthparts, and legs in the form of hollow hairs (**sensilla;** sing., sensillum) containing chemosensory neurons (figure 34.1).

The types of chemicals to which invertebrates respond are closely associated with their lifestyles. Examples include chemoreceptors that provide information that the animal uses to perform tasks, such as humidity detection, pH assessment, prey tracking, food recognition, and mate location. With respect to mate location, the antennae of male silkworm moths (*Bombyx mori*) can detect one bombykol molecule in over a trillion molecules of air. Female silk moths secrete bombykol as a sex attractant, which enables a male to find a female at night from several miles downwind, an ability that confers obvious reproductive advantage in a widely dispersed species.

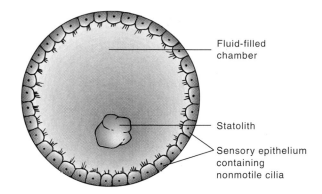

FIGURE 34.2

Invertebrate Georeceptor. A statocyst (cross section) consists of a fluid-filled chamber containing a solid granule called the statolith. The inner lining of the chamber contains tactile epithelium from which cilia associated with underlying neurons project.

GEORECEPTORS

Georeceptors (Gr. *ge,* earth + receptor) respond to the force of gravity. This gives an animal information about its orientation relative to "up" and "down." Most georeceptors are **statocysts** (Gr. *statos,* standing + *kystis,* bladder) (figure 34.2). Statocysts consist of a fluid-filled chamber lined with cilia-bearing sensory epithelium; within the chamber is a solid granule called a **statolith** (Gr. *lithos,* stone). Any movement of the animal changes the position of the statolith and moves the fluid, thus altering the intensity and pattern of information arising from the sensory epithelium. For example, when an animal moves, both the movement of the statolith and the flow of fluid over the sensory epithelium provide information about the animal's linear and rotational acceleration relative to the environment.

Statocysts are found in various gastropods, cephalopods, crustaceans, nemertines, polychaetes, and scyphozoans. These animals utilize information from statocysts in different ways. For example, burrowing invertebrates cannot rely on photoreceptors for orientation; instead, they rely on georeceptors for orientation within the substratum. Planktonic animals orient in their three-dimensional aquatic environment using statocysts. This is especially important at night and in deep water where there is little light.

In addition to having statocysts, a number of aquatic insects detect gravity from air bubbles trapped in certain passageways (e.g., tracheal tubes). Analogous to the air bubble in a carpenter's level, these air bubbles move according to their orientation to gravity. The air bubbles stimulate sensory bristles that line the tubes.

HYGRORECEPTORS

Hygroreceptors (Gr. *hygros,* moist) detect the water content of air. For example, some insects have hygroreceptors that can detect small changes in the ambient relative humidity. This sense enables them to seek environments with a specific humidity or to

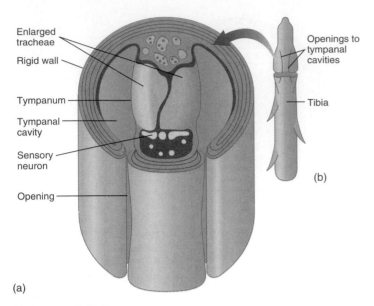

(a)

FIGURE 34.3

Invertebrate Phonoreceptor (Tympanal Organ). (*a*) This organ functions on the drumhead principle. The flattened outer wall (tympanum) of each trachea functions as a "drumhead." As the tympanum vibrates in response to sound waves, pressure changes within the tracheae affect the sensory neuron, causing a generator potential. (*b*) The slit openings on the leg (tibia) of a cricket lead to the tympanal cavities.

modify their physiology or behavior with respect to the ambient humidity (e.g., to control the opening or closing of spiracles). Zoologists have identified a variety of hygrosensory structures on the antennae, palps, underside of the body, and near the spiracles of insects. However, how a hygroreceptor transduces humidity into an action potential is not known.

PHONORECEPTORS

True **phonoreceptors** (Gr. *phone,* voice + receptor) that respond to sound have been demonstrated only in insects, arachnids, and centipedes, although other invertebrates seem to respond to sound-induced vibrations of the substratum. For example, crickets, grasshoppers, and cicadas possess phonoreceptors called **tympanic** or **tympanal organs** (figure 34.3). This organ consists of a tough, flexible tympanum that covers an internal sac that allows the tympanum to vibrate when sound waves strike it. Sensory neurons attached to the tympanum are stimulated and produce a generator potential.

Most arachnids possess phonoreceptors in their cuticle called slit sense organs that can sense sound-induced vibrations. Centipedes have organs of Tomosvary, which some zoologists believe may be sensitive to sound. However, the physiology of both slit sense organs and organs of Tomosvary is poorly understood.

PHOTORECEPTORS

Photoreceptors (Gr. *photos,* light + receptor) are sensitive to light. All photoreceptors possess light-sensitive pigments (e.g., carotenoids, rhodopsin). These pigments absorb photons of light energy and then produce a generator potential. Beyond this basic commonality, the complexity and arrangement of photoreceptors within various animals vary incredibly.

Certain flagellated protozoa (*Euglena*) that contain chlorophyll possess a mass of bright red photoreceptor granules called the **stigma** (pl., stigmata) (figure. 34.4*a*). The granules are carotenoid pigments. The actual photoreceptor is the swelling at the base of the flagellum. The stigma probably serves as a shield, which is essential if the photoreceptor is to detect light coming from certain directions but not from others. Thus, the photoreceptor plus the stigma enable *Euglena* to orient itself so that its photoreceptor is exposed to light. This helps the protozoan maintain itself in the region of the water column where sufficient light is available for photosynthesis.

Some animals, such as the earthworm *Lumbricus*, have simple unicellular photoreceptor cells scattered over the epidermis or concentrated in particular areas of the body. Others possess multicellular photoreceptors that can be classified into three basic types: ocelli, compound eyes, and complex eyes.

An **ocellus** (L. dim of *oculus,* eye) (pl., ocelli) is simply a small cup lined with light-sensitive receptors and backed by light-absorbing pigment (figure 34.4*b*). The light-sensitive cells are called retinular cells and contain a photosensitive pigment. Stimulation by light causes a chemical change in the pigment, leading to a generator potential, which causes an action potential that sensory neurons carry for interpretation elsewhere in the animal's body. This type of visual system gives an animal information about light direction and intensity, but not image formation. Ocelli are common in many phyla (e.g., Annelida, Mollusca, and Arthropoda).

Compound eyes consist of a few to many distinct units called **ommatidia** (Gr. *ommato,* eye + *ium,* little) (sing., ommatidium) (figure 34.4*c*). Although compound eyes occur in some annelids and bivalve molluscs, they are best developed and understood in arthropods. A compound eye may contain thousands of ommatidia, each oriented in a slightly different direction from the others as a result of the eye's overall convex shape. The visual field of a compound eye is very wide, as anyone who has tried to catch a fly knows. Each ommatidium has its own nerve tract leading to a large optic nerve. ❷ The visual fields of adjacent ommatidia overlap to some degree. Thus, if an object within the total visual field shifts position, the level of stimulation of several ommatidia changes. As a result of this physiology, as well as a sufficiently sophisticated central nervous system, compound eyes are very effective in detecting movements and are probably capable of forming an image. In addition, most compound eyes can adapt to changes

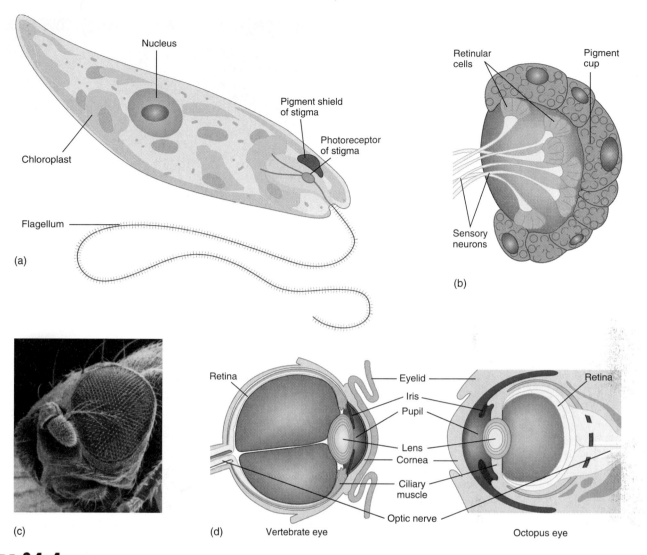

FIGURE 34.4

Invertebrate Photoreceptors. (*a*) Stigma. The protozoan, *Euglena*, contains a mass of bright red granules called the stigma. The actual photoreceptor is the swelling at the base of the flagellum. (*b*) Ocellus. The inverted pigment cup ocellus of a flatworm. (*c*) Compound eye. The compound eye of a fly contains hundreds of ommatidia. Note the eye's convex shape; no two ommatidia are oriented in precisely the same direction (SEM). (*d*) Complex camera eyes. Comparison of a vertebrate eye and an octopus eye (vertical sections).

in light intensities and some provide for color vision. ❸ Color vision is particularly important in active, day-flying, nectar-drinking insects, such as honeybees. Honeybees learn to recognize particular flowers by color, scent, and shape.

The **complex camera eyes** of squids and octopuses are the best image-forming eyes among the invertebrates. ❹ In fact, the giant squid's eye is the largest of any animal's, exceeding 38 cm in diameter. Cephalopod eyes are often compared to those of vertebrates because they contain a thin, transparent cornea, and a lens that focuses light on the retina and is suspended by, and controlled by, ciliary muscles (figure 34.4*d*). However, the complex eyes of squids are different from the vertebrate eye in that the receptor sites on the retinal layer face in the direction of light entering the eye. In the vertebrate eye, the retinal layer is inverted, and the receptors are the deepest cells in the retina. Both eyes are focusing and image-forming, although the process differs in detail. In terrestrial vertebrates, muscles that alter the shape (thickness) of the lens focus light. In fishes and cephalopods, light is focused by muscles that move the lens toward or away from the retina (like moving a magnifying glass back and forth to achieve proper focus), and by altering the shape of the eyeball.

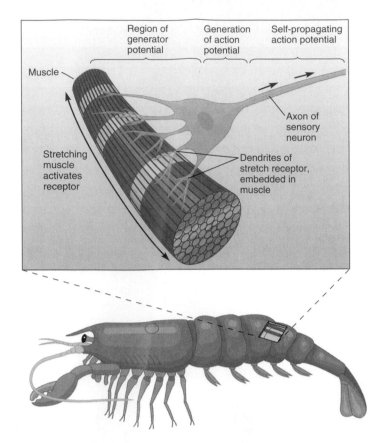

FIGURE 34.5

Invertebrate Proprioceptor. Crayfish stretch receptors are neurons attached to muscles. In this example, when the crayfish arches its abdomen while swimming, the stretch receptor detects the change in muscle length. When the muscle is stretched, so is the receptor. The stretch increases the sodium permeability of the receptor cell plasma membrane by mechanically opening sodium channels. The inflow of sodium ions produces depolarization and a generator potential that evokes an action potential. The axon of the sensory neuron then transmits the action potential to the central nervous system, where it is interpreted.

PROPRIOCEPTORS

Proprioceptors (L. *proprius,* one's self + receptor), commonly called "stretch receptors," are internal sense organs that respond to mechanically induced changes caused by stretching, compression, bending, or tension. These receptors give an animal information about the movement of its body parts and their positions relative to each other. Proprioceptors have been most thoroughly studied in arthropods, where they are associated with appendage joints and body extensor muscles (figure 34.5). In these animals, the sensory neurons involved in proprioception are associated with and attached to some part of the body that is stretched. These parts may be specialized muscle cells, elastic connective-tissue fibers, or various membranes that span joints. As these structures change shape, sensory nerve endings of the attached nerves distort accordingly and initiate a generator potential.

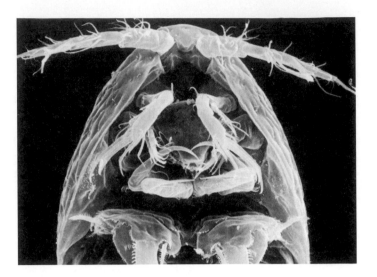

FIGURE 34.6

Invertebrate Tactile Receptor. A copepod, showing the head appendages covered with sensory bristles (SEM ×260).

TACTILE RECEPTORS

Tactile (touch) receptors are generally derived from modifications of epithelial cells associated with sensory neurons. Most tactile receptors of animals involve projections from the body surface. Examples include various bristles, spines, setae, and tubercles (figure 34.6). When an animal contacts an object in the environment, these receptors are mechanically deformed. These deformations activate the receptor, which, in turn, activates underlying sensory neurons, initiating a generator potential.

Most tactile receptors are also sensitive to mechanically induced vibrations propagated through water or a solid substrate. For example, tube-dwelling polychaetes bear receptors that allow them to retract quickly into their tubes in response to movements in their surroundings.   ⑤ Web-building spiders have tactile receptors that can sense struggling prey in webs through vibrations of the web threads.

THERMORECEPTORS

Thermoreceptors (Gr. *therme,* heat + receptors) respond to temperature changes. Some invertebrates can directly sense differences in environmental temperatures. For example, the protozoan *Paramecium* collects in areas where water temperature is moderate, and it avoids temperature extremes. Somehow, a heat-sensing mechanism draws leeches and ticks to warm-blooded hosts. Certain insects, some crustaceans, and the horseshoe crab (*Limulus*) can also sense thermal variations. In all of these cases, however, specific receptor structures have not been identified.

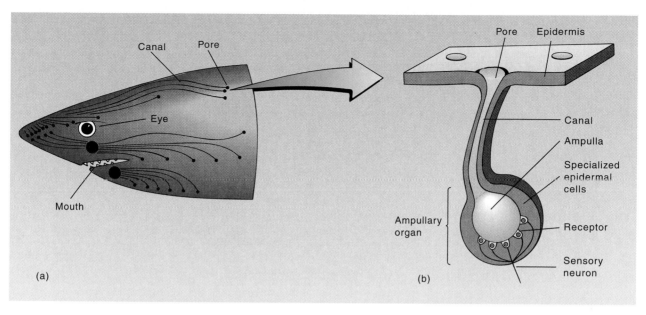

FIGURE 34.7

Lateral-Line System and Electrical Sensing. (*a*) In jawless fishes, jawed fishes, and amphibians, electroreceptors are in the epidermis along the sides of the head and body. (*b*) Pores of the lateral-line system lead into canals that connect to an ampullary organ that functions in electroreception and the production of a generator potential.

Stop and Ask Yourself

5. How does a statocyst function? In what animals do you find statocysts?

6. How does a tympanic or tympanal organ function? What animals possess a tympanic organ?

7. What animals possess (*a*) ocelli, (*b*) compound eyes, and (*c*) complex camera eyes?

8. What is the difference between a proprioceptor and a tactile receptor?

VERTEBRATE SENSORY RECEPTORS

Vertebrate sensory receptors reflect adaptations to the nature of sensory stimuli in different external and internal environments. Each environment has chemical and physical characteristics that affect the kinds of energy and molecules that carry sensory information. For example, your external environment consists of the media that surrounds you: the earth that you stand on and the air that you breathe. Other animals may have different external environments: a trout may be immersed in the cool, clear water of a mountain stream; a turtle may be submerged in the turbid water of a swamp; and a salmon may be swimming in the salty water of the sea.

Each of the previous media contains only certain environmental stimuli. For example, air transmits light very well and conducts sound waves relatively efficiently. But air can carry only a limited assortment of small molecules detectable using the sense of smell and can pass little or no electrical energy. In water, however, sound travels both faster and farther than in air, and water dissolves and carries a wide range of chemicals. Water, especially seawater, is also an excellent conductor of electricity, but it absorbs (and hence fails to transmit) many wavelengths of light. As these examples indicate, vertebrate sensory receptors (organs), like invertebrate sensory receptors, have evolved in ways that relate to the environment in which they must function.

Many underlying similarities unite all vertebrate senses. For each sense, there is a fascinating story of environmental information, the evolutionary adaptation of receptor cells to detect that information, and the processing in the central nervous system of the information so that the animal can use it. What follows is a discussion of particular vertebrate receptors (e.g., lateral-line systems, ears, eyes, skin sensors) that detect changes in the external environment, and of several receptors (e.g., pain, proprioception) that detect changes in the internal environment of some familiar vertebrate animals.

LATERAL-LINE SYSTEM AND ELECTRICAL SENSING

Specialized organs for equilibrium and gravity detection, audition, and magnetoreception have evolved from the lateral-line system of fishes. The **lateral-line system** for electrical sensing is in the head and body areas of most fishes, some amphibians, and the platypus (figure 34.7*a*). It consists of sensory pores in the epidermis of the skin that connect to canals leading into **electroreceptors** called **ampullary organs** (figure 34.7*b*). These organs can sense electrical currents in the surrounding water.   6 Most living organisms

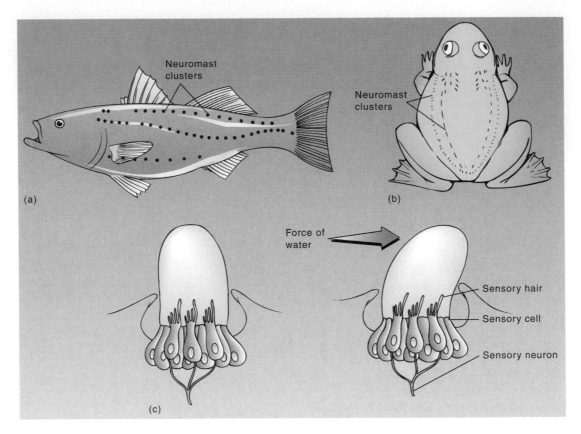

FIGURE 34.8

Lateral-Line System and Mechanoreception. The lateral-line system of (*a*) a bony fish and (*b*) a frog, showing the various neuromast clusters. (*c*) Action of neuromast stimulation. The water movement (blue arrow) forces the cap-like structure covering a group of neuromast cells to bend or distort, thereby distorting the small sensory hairs of the neuromast cells, producing a generator potential. The generator potential causes an action potential in the sensory neuron.

generate weak electrical fields. The ability to detect these fields helps a fish to find mates, capture prey, or avoid predators. This is an especially valuable sense in deep, turbulent, or murky water, where vision is of little use. In fact, some fishes actually generate electrical fields and then use their electroreceptors (electrocommunication) to detect how surrounding objects distort the field. This allows these fishes to navigate in murky or turbulent waters (*see figure 27.17*).

LATERAL-LINE SYSTEM AND MECHANORECEPTION

A **mechanoreceptor** is excited by mechanical pressures or distortions (e.g., sound, touch, and muscular contractions). The lateral-line system of cyclostomes, sharks, some of the more advanced fishes, and aquatic amphibians includes several different kinds of hair-cell mechanoreceptors called **neuromasts.** Neuromasts are in pits along the body, but not in the head region (figure 34.8*a,b*). All neuromasts are responsive to local water displacement or disturbance. When the water near the lateral line moves, it moves the water in the pits and distorts the hair cells, causing a generator potential in the associated sensory neurons (figure 34.8*c*). Thus, the animal can detect the direction and force of water cur-

rents and the movement of other animals or prey in the water. For example, this sense enables a trout to orient with its head upstream.

HEARING AND EQUILIBRIUM IN AIR

Hearing may initially have been important to vertebrates as a mechanism to alert them to either nearby or faraway potentially dangerous activity. It also became important in the search for food and mates, and in communication. Hearing (audition) and equilibrium (balance) are considered together because both sensations are received in the same vertebrate organ—the ear. The vertebrate ear has two functional units: (1) the auditory apparatus is concerned with hearing, and (2) the vestibular apparatus is concerned with posture and equilibrium.

Sound results when pressure waves transmit energy through some medium, such as air or water. Hearing in air poses serious problems for vertebrates, since middle-ear transformers are sound pressure sensors, but in air, sound produces less than 0.1% of the pressure it produces in water. Adaptation to hearing in air resulted from the evolution of an acoustic transformer that incorporates a thin, stretched membrane, called either an eardrum, tympanic membrane, or tympanum, that is exposed to the air.

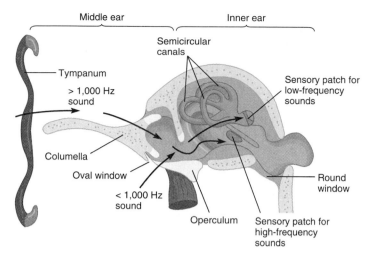

FIGURE 34.9

Ear of an Anuran (Posterior View). Purple arrows show the pathway of low-frequency sounds, via the operculum. Red arrows show the pathway of high-frequency sounds, via the columella (stapes).

The tympanum first evolved in the amphibians. The ears of anurans (frogs) consist of a tympanum, a middle ear, and an inner ear (figure 34.9). The tympanum is modified integument stretched over a cartilaginous ring. It vibrates in response to sounds and transmits these movements to the middle ear, a chamber behind the tympanum. Touching the tympanum is an ossicle (a small bone or bony structure) called the columella or stapes. The opposite end of the columella (stapes) touches the membrane of the oval window, which stretches between the middle and inner ears. High-frequency (1,000 to 5,000 Hz) sounds strike the tympanum and are transmitted through the middle ear via the columella and cause pressure waves in the fluid of the semicircular canals. These pressure waves in the inner ear fluid stimulate receptor cells. A second small ossicle, the operculum, also touches the oval window. Substrate-borne vibrations transmitted through the front appendages and the pectoral girdle cause this ossicle to vibrate. The resulting pressure waves in the inner ear stimulate a second patch of sensory receptor cells that is sensitive to low-frequency (100 to 1,000 Hz) sounds. Muscles attached to the operculum and columella can lock either or both of these ossicles, allowing a frog to screen out either high- or low-frequency sounds. This mechanism is adaptive because frogs use low- and high-frequency sounds in different situations. For example, mating calls are high-frequency sounds that are of primary importance for only part of the year (breeding season). At other times, low-frequency sounds may warn of approaching predators.

Salamanders lack a tympanum and middle ear. They live in streams, ponds, and caves, and beneath leaf litter. They have no mating calls, and the only sounds they hear are probably transmitted through the substratum and skull to the inner ear.

The sense of equilibrium and balance in amphibians involves the semicircular canals. These canals help detect rotational movements and gravity. Since the semicircular canals have a similar function in all vertebrates, they are discussed later in this section in information about the human ear.

The structures of reptilian ears vary. For example, the ears of snakes lack a middle-ear cavity and a tympanum. A bone of the jaw articulates with the stapes and receives vibrations of the substratum. In other reptiles, a tympanum may be on the surface or in a small depression in the head. The inner ear of reptiles is similar to that of amphibians.

Hearing is well developed in most birds. Loose, delicate feathers cover the external ear opening. Middle- and inner-ear structures are similar to those of mammals.

Auditory senses were also important to the early mammals. Adaptations include an ear flap (the auricle) and the auditory tube (external auditory canal), leading to the tympanum that directs sounds to the middle ear. In mammals, the long, coiled, sensory structure of the inner ear that contains receptors for sound is the cochlea. This structure provides more surface area for receptor cells and allows mammals greater sensitivity to pitch and volume than is present in other animals. Since the structure and function of all mammal ears are basically the same, the familiar human ear is a good example.

The human ear has three divisions: the outer, middle, and inner ear. The outer ear consists of the auricle and external auditory canal (figure 34.10). The middle ear begins at the tympanic membrane (tympanum or eardrum) and ends inside the skull, where two small membranous openings, the oval and round windows, are located. Three small ossicles are between the tympanic membrane and the oval window. They include the malleus (hammer), incus (anvil), and stapes (stirrup), so named for their shapes. The malleus adheres to the tympanic membrane and connects to the incus. The incus connects to the stapes, which adheres to the oval window. The auditory (eustachian) tube extends from the middle ear to the nasopharynx and equalizes air pressure between the middle ear and the throat.

The inner ear has three components. The first two, the vestibule and the semicircular canals, are concerned with equilibrium, and the third, the cochlea, is involved with hearing. The semicircular canals are arranged so that one is in each dimension of space. The process of hearing can be summarized as follows:

1. Sound waves enter the outer ear and create pressure waves that reach the tympanic membrane.
2. Air molecules under pressure vibrate the tympanic membrane. The vibrations move the malleus on the other side of the membrane.
3. The handle of the malleus strikes the incus, vibrating it.
4. The vibrating incus moves the stapes back and forth against the oval window.
5. The movements of the oval window set up pressure changes that vibrate the fluid in the inner ear. These vibrations are transmitted to the basilar membrane, causing it to ripple.
6. Receptor hair cells of the organ of Corti that are in contact with the overlying tectorial membrane are bent, causing a generator potential, which leads to an action potential that travels along the vestibulocochlear nerve to the brain for interpretation.
7. Vibrations in the cochlear fluid dissipate as a result of movements of the round window.

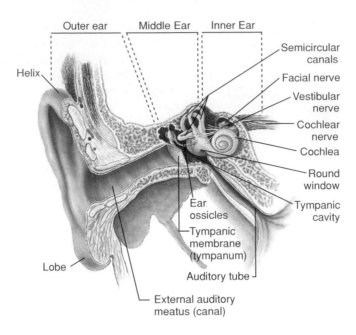

Outer ear   Middle Ear   Inner Ear

Helix

Lobe

External auditory
meatus (canal)

Ear
ossicles

Tympanic
membrane
(tympanum)

Auditory tube

Semicircular
canals

Facial nerve

Vestibular
nerve

Cochlear
nerve

Cochlea

Round
window

Tympanic
cavity

FIGURE 34.10

Anatomy of the Human Ear. Note the outer, middle, and inner regions. The inner ear includes the semicircular canals, which are involved with equilibrium, and the cochlea, which is involved with hearing.

BOX 34.1 | HUNTING WITH SOUND

Zoologists have long wondered how huge whales, such as the sperm whale, catch fishes as small as 4 cm long, and invertebrates as elusive and fast moving as squid. But size is not the only reason that the predatory habits of some of these animals, known as odontocetes (toothed whales), are unusual. The fossil record shows that odontocetes' teeth and beaks have become less, not more, functional over time. Then how do they catch their prey?

Recent evidence indicates that these sea mammals' secret weapon may be sound. Odontocetes immobilize prey with loud vo-

calizations. Zoologists have been able to record the animals' loud hunting bursts, called "bangs," and have found that they are of a different frequency from those used in echolocation, which is the normal form of auditory communication among whales and dolphins. Evidence indicates that when an odontocete emits a "big bang," at least one prey species—anchovies—is stunned, with hemorrhaging in their abdomens as a result of the power of the "bang." Studies are currently measuring the effects of low-frequency "bangs" on locomotion in a variety of other fish.

Humans are not able to hear low-pitched sounds, below 20 cycles per second, although some other vertebrates can (box 34.1). Young children can hear high-pitched sounds up to 20,000 cycles per second, but this ability decreases with age. ⑦ Other vertebrates can hear sounds at much higher frequencies. For example, dogs can easily detect sounds of 40,000 cycles per second. Thus, dogs can hear sounds from a high-pitched dog whistle that seems silent to humans.

The sense of equilibrium (balance) can be divided into two separate senses. Static equilibrium refers to sensing movement in one plane (either vertical or horizontal), and dynamic equilibrium refers to sensing angular and/or rotational movement.

When the body is still, the otoliths in the semicircular canals rest on hair cells (figure 34.11a). When the head or body moves horizontally, or vertically, the granules are displaced, causing the gelatinous material to sag (figure 34.11b). This displacement bends the hairs slightly so that hair cells initiate a generator potential and then an action potential. ⑧ Continuous movement of the fluid in the semicircular canals may cause motion sickness or seasickness in humans.

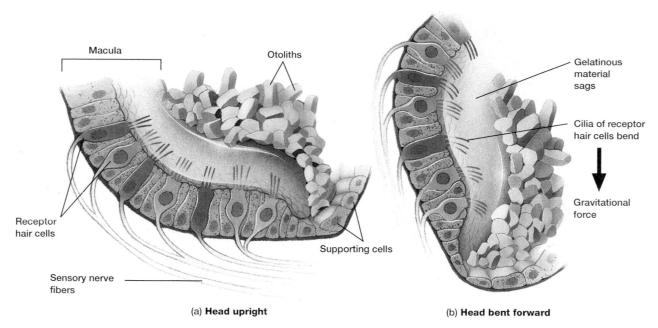

Macula Otoliths

Gelatinous material sags

Cilia of receptor hair cells bend

Receptor hair cells

Gravitational force

Supporting cells

Sensory nerve fibers

(a) **Head upright**   (b) **Head bent forward**

FIGURE 34.11

Static Equilibrium (Balance). Receptor hair cells in the utricle and saccule respond to sideways or up or down movement. (*a*) When the head is upright, otoliths are balanced directly over the cilia of receptor hair cells. (*b*) When the head bends forward, the otoliths shift, and the cilia of hair cells bend. This bending of hairs initiates a generator potential.

HEARING AND EQUILIBRIUM IN WATER

In bony fishes, receptors for equilibrium, balance, and hearing are in the inner ear, and their functions are similar to those of other vertebrates (figure 34.12). For example, semicircular canals detect rotational movements, and other sensory patches help with equilibrium and balance by detecting the direction of gravitational pull. Since fishes lack the outer and/or middle ear found in other vertebrates, vibrations pass from the water through the bones of the skull to the inner ear. A few fishes have chains of bony ossicles (modifications of vertebrae) that pass between the swim bladder and the back of the skull. Vibrations that strike the fishes are thus amplified by the swim bladder and sent through the ossicles to the skull.

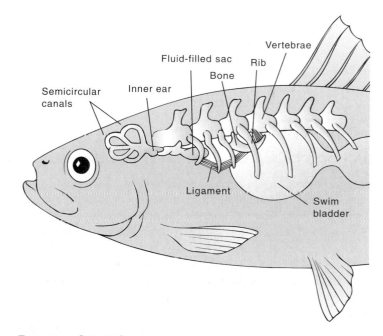

Vertebrae

Fluid-filled sac   Rib

Bone

Semicircular canals   Inner ear

Ligament

Swim bladder

FIGURE 34.12

Inner Ear of a Bony Fish. Sound waves that enter the pharynx are transmitted to gas in the swim bladder, causing it to expand and contract at frequencies and amplitudes corresponding to the incoming sound waves. Contacting the swim bladder is a bone that is suspended by ligaments and vibrates at the same frequency. The vibrations pass forward along a chain of bones (ossicles) and then to a fluid-filled sac connected directly to the inner ear.

Stop and Ask Yourself

9. How do fishes utilize electroreceptors?
10. How do neuromasts function?
11. Why is the tympanic membrane important to life on land?
12. What structures are involved in the sense of equilibrium?
13. Why don't fishes need either an outer or middle ear?

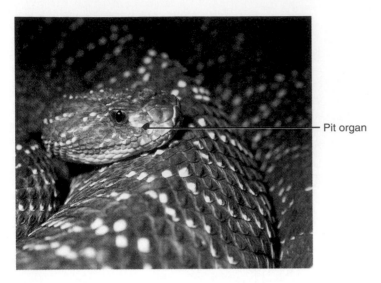

Pit organ

FIGURE 34.13

Thermoreception. A rattlesnake (*Crotalus vergrandis*) has a pit organ between each eye and nostril that detects heat and allows the snake to locate warm prey in the dark.

Skin Sensors of Damaging Stimuli

Pain receptors are bare sensory nerve endings that are present throughout the body of mammals, except for the brain and intestines. These nerve endings are also called **nociceptors** (L. *nocere*, to injure + receptor). Severe heat, cold, irritating chemicals, and strong mechanical stimuli (e.g., penetration) may elicit a response from nociceptors that the brain interprets as pain or itching. Details of the structure and physiology of pain receptors, however, are unknown.

Skin Sensors of Heat and Cold

Sensors of temperature (thermoreceptors) are also bare sensory nerve endings. Thermoreceptors may be present in either the epidermis or dermis. Mammals have a distinctly different distribution of areas sensitive to either cold or warm. These areas are called cold or warm spots. A spot refers to a small area of the skin that, when stimulated, yields a temperature sensation of warmth or cold. Cold receptors in the skin respond to temperatures below skin temperature, and heat receptors respond to temperatures above skin temperature. Materials coming into contact with the skin need not be warm or cold to produce temperature sensations. For example, when metal is placed on the skin, it absorbs heat and you feel a sense of coldness. Wood placed on the skin absorbs less heat and, therefore, feels warmer than metal.

The ability to detect changes in temperature has become well developed in a number of animals. For example, rattlesnakes and other pit vipers have heat-sensitive **pit organs** on each side of

the face between the eye and nostril (figure 34.13). These depressions are lined with sensory epithelium containing receptor cells that respond to temperatures (infrared thermal regulation) different from the snakes' surroundings. Snakes use these pit organs to locate warm-blooded prey.

Skin Sensors of Mechanical Stimuli

Many animals rely on tactile (pertaining to touch) stimuli to obtain information about their environment. Mechanical sensory receptors in vertebrate skin detect stimuli that the brain interprets as light touch, touch-pressure, and vibration.

Light touch is perceived when the skin is touched, but not strongly deformed. Receptors of light touch include **bare sensory nerve endings** and **tactile (Meissner's) corpuscles** (figure 34.14). Bare sensory nerve endings are the most widely distributed receptors in the vertebrate body, and are involved with pain and thermal stimuli, as well as light touch. The **bulbs of Krause** are mechanoreceptors, found in the dermis in certain parts of the body, that respond to some physical stimuli, such as position changes. Other receptors for touch-pressure are **Pacinian corpuscles** and the **organs of Ruffini.**

Many mammals have specially adapted sensory hairs called **vibrissae** (sing., vibrissa) on their wrists, snout, and eyebrows (e.g., cat whiskers). Around the base of each vibrissa is a blood sinus. Nerves that border the sinus carry impulses from several kinds of mechanoreceptors to the brain for interpretation.

Sonar

Bats, shrews, several cave-dwelling birds (oilbird, cave swiftlet), whales, and dolphins can determine distance and depth by a form of echolocation called **sonar (biosonar).** These animals emit high-frequency sounds and then determine how long it takes for the sounds to return after bouncing off objects in the environment. For example, some bats emit clicks that last from 2 to 3 milliseconds and are repeated several hundred times per second. The returning echo created when a moth or other insect flies past the bat can provide sufficient information for the bat to locate and catch its prey. Overall, the three-dimensional imaging achieved with this auditory sonar system is quite sophisticated.

Smell

The sense of smell, or **olfaction** (L. *olere*, to smell + *facere*, to make), is due to olfactory neurons (receptor cells) in the roof of the vertebrate nasal cavity (figure 34.15). These cells, which are specialized endings of the fibers that make up the olfactory nerve, lie among supporting epithelial cells. They are densely packed; for example, a dog has up to 40 million olfactory receptor cells per square centimeter. Each olfactory cell ends in a tuft of cilia containing receptor sites for various chemicals.

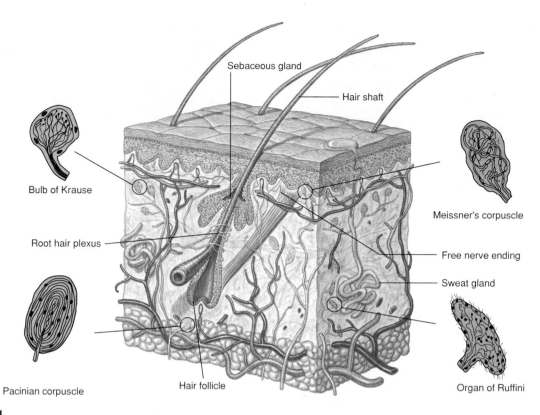

FIGURE 34.14

Different Sensory Receptors to Mechanical Stimuli. Sensory receptors in the skin for light touch (Meissner's corpuscles), touch-pressure (organs of Ruffini and Pacinian corpuscles), position (bulbs of Krause), and pain (free nerve endings).

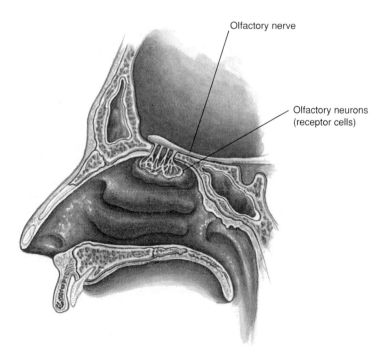

FIGURE 34.15

Smell. Position of olfactory receptors in a human nasal passageway. Columnar epithelial cells support the receptor cells, which have hair-like processes (analogous to dendrites) projecting into the nasal cavity. When chemicals in the air stimulate these receptor cells, the olfactory nerves conduct nerve impulses to the brain.

Several theories have been proposed to explain how odors are perceived. The most likely one is that odor molecules physically interact with protein receptors on the receptor-plasma membrane. Such an interaction somehow alters membrane permeability and leads to a generator potential.

In most fishes, openings (external nares) in the snout lead to the olfactory receptors. Recent research has revealed that some fishes rely heavily on their sense of smell. For example, salmon and lampreys return to spawn in the same streams in which they hatched years earlier. Their migrations to these streams often involve distances of hundreds of miles and are guided by the fishes' perception of characteristic odors of their spawning stream.

Olfaction is an important sense for many amphibians. It is used in mate recognition, as well as in detecting noxious chemicals and locating food.

Olfactory senses are better developed in reptiles than in amphibians. In addition to having more olfactory epithelium, most reptiles (except crocodilians) possess blind-ending pouches that open into the mouth. These pouches, called **Jacobson's (vomeronasal) organs,** are best developed in snakes and lizards (figure 34.16). The protrusible, forked tongues of snakes and lizards are accessory olfactory organs used to sample airborne chemicals. A snake's tongue flicks out and then moves to the Jacobson's organs, which perceive odor molecules. Turtles and the tuatara use Jacobson's organs to taste objects held in the mouth.

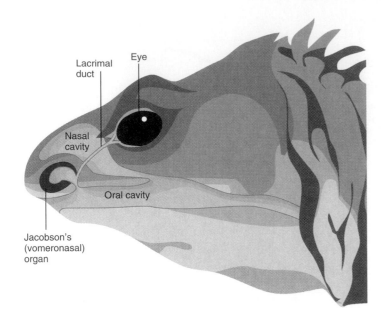

FIGURE 34.16

Smell. Anatomic relationships of Jacobson's (vomeronasal) organ in a generalized lizard. Only the left organ alongside the nasal cavity is shown. Jacobson's organ is a spherical structure, with the ventral side invaginated into a sphere the shape of a mushroom. A narrow duct connects the interior of Jacobson's organ to the oral cavity. In many lizards, fluid draining from the eye via the lacrimal duct may bring odoriferous molecules into contact with the sensory epithelium of Jacobson's organ.

Olfaction apparently plays a minor role in the lives of most birds. External nares open near the base of the beak, but the olfactory epithelium is poorly developed. Vultures are exceptions, in that they locate dead and dying prey largely by smell.

Many mammals can perceive olfactory stimuli over long distances during either the day or night. They use the stimuli to locate food, recognize members of the same species, and avoid predators.

TASTE

The receptors for taste, or **gustation** (L. *gustus*, taste), are chemoreceptors. They may be on the body surface of an animal or in the mouth and throat. For example, the surface of the mammalian tongue is covered with many small protuberances called papillae (sing., papilla). Papillae give the tongue its "bumpy" appearance (figure 34.17*a*). In the crevices between the papillae are thousands of specialized receptors called **taste buds** (figure 34.17*b*). Taste buds are barrel-shaped clusters of chemoreceptor cells called gustatory cells and supporting cells arranged like alternating segments of an orange. Extending from each receptor cell are gustatory hairs that project through a tiny opening called the taste pore. Sensory neurons are associated with the basal ends of the gustatory cells.

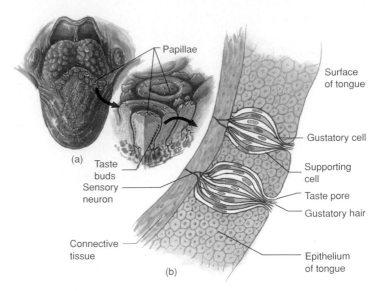

FIGURE 34.17

Taste. (*a*) Surface view of the human tongue, showing the many papillae and the numerous taste buds between papillae. (*b*) Supporting cells encapsulate the gustatory cell and its associated gustatory hair.

The four generally recognized taste sensations are sweet (sugars), sour (acids), bitter (alkaloids), and salty (electrolytes). The exact mechanism(s) that stimulate a chemoreceptor taste cell are not known. One theory is that different types of gustatory stimuli cause proteins on the surface of the receptor-cell plasma membrane to change the permeability of the membrane—in effect, "opening and closing gates" to chemical stimuli and causing a generator potential.

Vertebrates other than mammals may have taste buds on other parts of the body. For example, reptiles and birds do not usually have taste buds on the tongue; instead, most taste buds are in the pharynx. In fishes and amphibians, taste buds may also be found in the skin. ⑨ For example, a sturgeon's taste buds are abundant on its head projection called the rostrum. As the sturgeon glides over the bottom, it can obtain foretaste of potential food before the mouth reaches the food. In other fishes, taste buds are widely distributed in the roof, side walls, and floor of the pharynx, where they monitor the incoming flow of water. In fish that feed on the bottom (catfish, carp, suckers), taste buds are distributed over the entire surface of the head and body to the tip of the tail. They are also abundant on the barbels ("whiskers") of catfish.

VISION

Vision (photoreception) is the primary sense that vertebrates in a light-filled environment use, and consequently, their photoreceptive structures are well developed. Most vertebrates have eyes capable of forming visual images. As figure 34.18 indicates, the eyeball has a lens, a sclera (the tough outer coat), a choroid layer

Superior rectus muscle
Sclera
Choroid
Retina
Fovea centralis
Central artery
Central vein
Optic nerve
Inferior rectus muscle

Conjunctiva
Ciliary body
Posterior chamber
Cornea
Anterior chamber
Pupil
Lens
Iris
Posterior chamber
Suspensory ligament
Vitreous chamber

FIGURE 34.18

Internal Anatomy of the Human Eyeball. Light passes through the transparent cornea. The lens focuses the light on the rear surface of the eye, the retina, at the fovea centralis. The retina is rich in rods and cones.

(a thin middle layer), and an inner retina containing many light-sensitive receptor cells (photoreceptors). The transparent cornea is continuous with the sclera and covers the front of the eyeball. Choroid tissue also extends to the front of the eyeball to form the iris, ciliary body, and suspensory ligaments. The colored iris is heavily endowed with light-screening pigments, and it has radial and circular smooth muscles for regulating the amount of light entering the pupil. A clear fluid (aqueous humor) fills the anterior and posterior chambers, which lie between the lens and the cornea. The lens is behind the iris, and a jellylike vitreous body fills the vitreous chamber behind the lens. The moist, mucous membrane that covers the eyeball is the conjunctiva.

Vertebrates can adjust their vision for light coming from either close-up or distant objects. This process of focusing light rays precisely on the retina is called **accommodation.** Vertebrates rely on the coordinated stretching and relaxation of the eye muscles and fibers (the ciliary body and suspensory ligaments) that attach to the lens for accommodation.

The eyes of fishes are similar in most aspects of structure and function to those in other vertebrates. However, fish eyes are lidless, and the lens is rounded and close to the cornea. Focusing requires moving the lens forward or backward.

Vision is one of the most important senses in amphibians because they are primarily sight feeders. A number of adaptations allow the eyes of amphibians to function in terrestrial environments. For example, the eyes of some amphibians (e.g., anurans, salamanders) are close together on the front of the head and provide the binocular vision and well-developed depth perception necessary for capturing prey. Other amphibians with smaller and more lateral eyes (e.g., some salamanders) lack binocular vision. However, their more laterally placed eyes permit these animals to see

well off to their sides. The transparent **nictitating membrane** (an "inner eyelid") is movable and cleans and protects the eye.

Vision is the dominant sense in most reptiles, and their eyes are similar to those of amphibians. Upper and lower eyelids, a nictitating membrane, and a blood sinus protect and cleanse the surface of the eye. In snakes and some lizards, the upper and lower eyelids fuse in the embryo to form a protective window of clear skin called the spectacle. Some reptiles possess a **median (parietal) eye** that develops from outgrowths of the roof of the optic tectum (midbrain) (figure 34.19). In the tuatara, the median eye is complete with a lens, nerve, and retina. In other reptiles, the median eye is less developed. Skin covers median eyes, which probably cannot form images. They can, however, differentiate light and dark periods and are used in orientation to the sun.

Vision is an important sense for most birds. The structure of the bird eye is similar to that of other vertebrates (*see figure 34.18*). Birds have a unique, double-focusing mechanism. Padlike structures control the curvature of the lens, and ciliary muscles change the curvature of the cornea. Double, nearly instantaneous focusing allows an osprey, or other bird of prey, to focus on a fish throughout a brief, but breathtakingly fast, descent. Like reptiles, birds have a nictitating membrane that is drawn over the eyeball surface to cleanse and protect it.

In all vertebrates, the retina is well developed. Its basement layer is composed of pigmented epithelium that covers the choroid layer. Nervous tissue that contains photoreceptors lies on this basement layer. The photoreceptors are called **rod** and **cone cells** because of their shape. Rods are sensitive to dim light, whereas cones respond to high-intensity light and are involved in color perception.

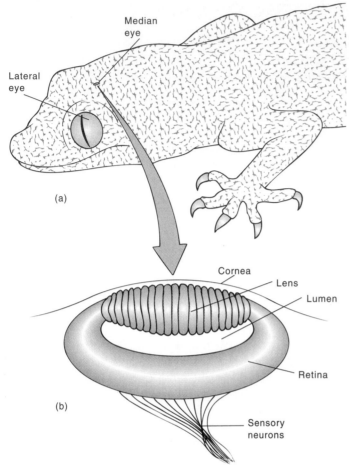

FIGURE 34.19

Median Eye of Reptiles. (*a*) Median eye in a reptile and its relationship to the lateral eyes (dorsal view). (*b*) Sagittal section of the median eye.

When a pigment (**rhodopsin**) in a rod cell absorbs light energy, the energy that this reaction releases triggers the generator potential in an axon and then an action potential that leaves the eyeball via the optic nerve. When the photoreceptor cells are not being stimulated (i.e., in the dark), vitamin A and energy from ATP convert rhodopsin back to its light-sensitive form.

Nineteenth-century poet Leigh Hunt said, "Colors are the smiles of Nature." How does an animal distinguish one smile from another? The answer lies to a great extent in the three types of cone-shaped, color-sensitive cells in the retinas of the eyes of primates, birds, reptiles, and fishes. Each type of cone cell responds differently to light reflected from a colored object, depending on whether the cells have red-, green-, or blue-absorbing pigments. The pigments are light-absorbing proteins that are particularly sensitive to either the long-wavelength (red), intermediate-wavelength (green), or short-wavelength (blue) region of the visible spectrum. The retinal nerves translate the relative amounts of light that each type of cone absorbs into generator potentials that are then transmitted as a nerve impulse to the brain, where the overall pattern evokes the sensation of a specific hue.

Stop and Ask Yourself

14. What is the function of a pit organ?
15. What animals possess a median eye?
16. What is rhodopsin, and how does it function?

ENDANGERED SPECIES

WILDLIFE ALERT 11—KEY DEER (*ODOCOILEUS VIRGINIANUS CLAVIUM*)

VITAL STATISTICS

Classification: Phylum Chordata, class Mammalia, order Artiodactyla, family Cervidae
Range: Restricted to Monroe County, Florida, and the Lower Keys (figure 1)
Habitat: Mostly habitats (islands) with permanent freshwater; 26 islands in the lower Florida Keys
Number remaining: 250 to 300
Status: Endangered throughout its range

NATURAL HISTORY AND ECOLOGICAL STATUS

The Florida Key deer is the smallest North American deer. Adults measure 63 to 76 cm at the shoulder and weigh an average 55 to 75 pounds for males and 45 to 65 pounds for females. The coat of both males and females varies from a deep reddish brown to gray (figure 2). Bucks usually have antlers by age 2 and up to eight points by

age 5. The Key deer's main food source are the leaves of the red mangrove, but many other plants form part of its diet. On the various islands, Key deer browse most plants almost continuously, resulting in stunting and near extirpation of the plants.

Breeding occurs all year, but peaks in September and October. Territorial activity is limited to defending a receptive doe from other bucks. Bucks with full racks are generally the earliest breeders and exclude yearling males and those with lesser racks.

The peak of fawning coincides with the rainy season in April and May. Key deer have a relatively low reproductive rate, averaging 1.08 fawns per doe annually. Longevity records are 8 years for males and 17 years for females. Adult females form loose matriarchal groups with one or two generations of offspring, while bucks feed and bed together only during the nonbreeding season.

The greatest current impact on Key deer is the loss of habitat to development. Anticipated future human population growth implies a further loss of habitat. Other factors include road kills, mortality of young from falling into drainage ditches, and killing by free-roaming dogs.

Recommendations for management include: continuation of a closed hunting season; acquisition of additional refuge habitat of several Keys; prescribed burning in pinelands habitat; maintenance of existing water holes; management of vegetation along select road-ways; providing underpasses for deer to cross safely under U.S. Highway 1; eliminating public feeding, which leads to domestication (enforcement of laws prohibiting feeding and management practices to lure deer away from subdivisions); visitor management; and additional research on all aspects of Key deer biology. The National Key Deer Refuge, headquartered on Big Pine Key, was established in 1957 to preserve the subspecies and its habitat.

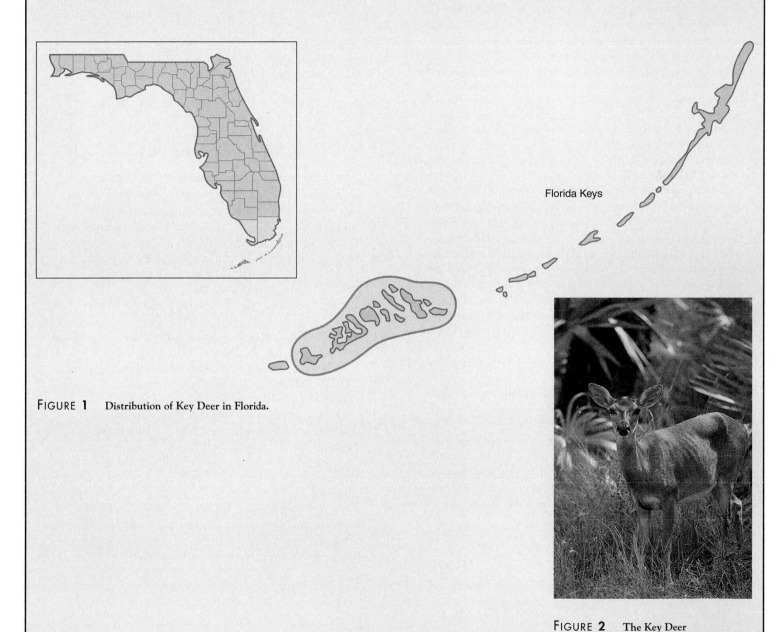

Florida Keys

FIGURE 1   Distribution of Key Deer in Florida.

FIGURE 2   The Key Deer
(*Odocoileus virginianus clavium*).

SUMMARY

1. A stimulus is any form of energy an animal can detect with its receptors. Receptors are nerve endings of sensory neurons or specialized cells that respond to stimuli, such as chemical energy, mechanical energy, light energy, or radiant energy.

2. Receptors transduce energy from one form to another. Stimulation of a receptor initiates a generator potential, which creates an action potential that travels along a nerve pathway to another part of the nervous system, where it is perceived.

3. Invertebrates possess an impressive array of receptor structures through which they receive information about their environment. Examples include chemoreceptors that respond to chemicals in the environment; georeceptors, called statocysts, that respond to the force of gravity; hygroreceptors that detect the water content of air; phonoreceptors, such as tympanic organs, that respond to sound; photoreceptors, such as stigmata, ocelli, compound eyes, and complex camera eyes, that respond to light; proprioceptors that respond to mechanically induced changes caused by stretching; tactile receptors, such as bristles, sensilla, spines, setae, and tubercles, that sense touch; and thermoreceptors that respond to temperature changes.

4. Invertebrate and vertebrate sensory receptors (organs) have evolved in ways that relate to the environment in which they must function.

5. The lateral-line system for electrical sensing is in the head area of most fishes, some amphibians, and the platypus. This system can sense electrical currents in the surrounding water. The lateral-line system of fishes and amphibians also contains neuromasts, which are responsive to local water displacement or disturbances.

6. The vertebrate ear has two functional units: the auditory apparatus is concerned with hearing, and the vestibular apparatus is concerned with posture and equilibrium.

7. Pain receptors (nociceptors) are bare sensory nerve endings that produce a painful or itching sensation.

8. Sensors of temperature (thermoreceptors) are bare sensory nerve endings and the simplest vertebrate receptors. Some snakes have heat-sensitive pit organs on each side of the face.

9. Many vertebrates rely on tactile (pertaining to touch) stimuli to respond to their environment. Receptors include bare sensory nerve endings, tactile (Meissner's) corpuscles, bulbs of Krause, Pacinian corpuscles, organs of Ruffini, and vibrissae.

10. Bats, shrews, whales, and dolphins can determine distance and depth by sonar.

11. The receptors for taste (gustation) are chemoreceptors on the body surface of an animal or in the mouth and throat.

12. The sense of smell is due to olfactory neurons in the root of the vertebrate nasal cavity.

13. Vision (photoreception) is the primary sense that vertebrates in a light-filled environment use. Consequently, their photoreceptive structures are well developed. Most vertebrates have eyes capable of forming visual images.

SELECTED KEY TERMS

accommodation (p. 581)
generator potential (p. 568)
median (parietal) eye (p. 581)
ocellus (p. 570)
pit organs (p. 578)

rhodopsin (p. 582)
sonar (p. 578)
statocysts (p. 569)
stigma (p. 570)
taste buds (p. 580)

CRITICAL THINKING QUESTIONS

1. Why is it correct to compare a vertebrate eye to a camera?

2. Most animals lack cones in their retinas. How then does such an animal view the visual world?

3. Why is the sense of gravity considered a sense of equilibrium?

4. How does vitamin A deficiency result in night blindness?

5. How would you expect your inner ear to behave in zero gravity?

REFERENCES ON THE WORLD WIDE WEB

1. **How We Hear.**   This site contains a discussion of normal and abnormal hearing patterns.
     http://www.siemens-hearing.com/html/how_hear.html

2. **The Eye and Ear Page.**   Perusal of this site will provide you with much information on how the eye and ear function.
     http://rivers.oscs.montana.edu/esg/kla/ta/sight.html

3. **Anatomy and Physiology of the Ear.**   Learn more about the structure and function of the ear at this site.
     http://psych.hanover.edu/classes/hfnotes/sld041.html

4. **Olfactory Connection.**   This site discusses how odors are perceived.
     http://www.frontierherb.com/aromatherapy/aro.olfactory.html

5. **Gustation and Olfaction.**   The senses of taste and smell are discussed at this site.
   http://www.neurosci.pharm.utoledo.edu/neuroscience/lecture13.html

35

COMMUNICATION III:
THE ENDOCRINE SYSTEM
AND CHEMICAL MESSENGERS

Outline

Concepts

1. Chemical messengers are involved in communication, in maintaining homeostasis in an animal's body, and in the body's response to various stimuli. One type of chemical messenger is a hormone. Only those cells that have specific receptors for a hormone can respond to that hormone.
2. Hormones work with nerves to communicate, coordinate, and integrate activities within the body of an animal.
3. Almost every invertebrate produces hormones. However, the physiology of invertebrate hormones is often quite different from that of vertebrate hormones.
4. The major endocrine glands of vertebrates include the hypothalamus, pituitary, thyroid, parathyroids, adrenals, pineal, thymus, pancreas, and gonads. Various other tissues, however, such as the kidneys, heart, digestive system, and placenta also secrete hormones.

Would You Like to Know . . .

1. what causes a crayfish to shed its skin (molt)? (p. 590)
2. what causes brooding behavior in some fishes? (p. 592)
3. why the thyroid gland is in the neck on the ventral side of the pharynx in all vertebrates? (p. 592)
4. what hormones cause a tadpole to metamorphose into a frog? (p. 593)
5. how pigeons and doves produce "milk" to feed their young? (p. 595)
6. why some animals (including humans) possess the "fight-or-flight" response? (p. 600)

This chapter answers these and other useful questions.

This chapter contains evolutionary concepts, which are set off in this font.

Chapters 33 and 34 discuss ways that the nervous and sensory systems work together to rapidly communicate information and maintain homeostasis in an animal's body. In addition, many animals have a second, slower form of communication and coordination—the endocrine system with its chemical messengers.

Some scientists suggest that chemical messengers may initially have evolved in single-celled organisms to coordinate feeding or reproduction. As multicellularity evolved, more complex organs also evolved to govern the many individual coordination tasks, but control centers relied on the same kinds of messengers that were present in the simpler organisms. Some of the messengers worked fairly slowly but had long-lasting effects on distant cells; these became the modern hormones. Others worked more quickly but influenced only adjacent cells for short periods; these became the neurotransmitters and local chemical messengers. Clearly, chemical messengers have an ancient origin and must have been conserved for hundreds of millions of years.

Evolutionarily, new messengers are uncommon. Instead, "old" messengers are adapted to new purposes. For example, some ancient protein hormones are in species ranging from bacteria to humans.

One key to the survival of any group of animals is proper timing of activity so that growth, maturation, and reproduction coincide with the times of year when climate and food supply favor survival. It seems likely that the chemical messengers regulating growth and reproduction were among the first to appear. These messengers were probably secretions of neurons. Later, specific hormones developed to play important regulatory roles in molting, growth, metamorphosis, and reproduction in various invertebrates (as presented in specific chapters in Part Five of this text). Chemical messengers and their associated secretory structures became even more complex with the appearance of vertebrates.

CHEMICAL MESSENGERS

Development of most animals commences with fertilization and the subsequent division of the zygote. Further development then depends on continued cell proliferation, growth, and differentiation. The integration of these events, as well as the communication and coordination of physiological processes, such as metabolism, respiration, excretion, movement, and reproduction, depend on chemical messengers—molecules that specialized cells synthesize and secrete. Chemical messengers can be categorized as follows:

1. **Local chemical messengers.** Many cells secrete chemicals that alter physiological conditions in the immediate vicinity (figure 35.1a). Most of these chemicals act on adjacent cells and do not accumulate in the blood. Vertebrate examples include some of the chemicals called lumones that the gut produces and that help regulate digestion. In a wound, mast cells secrete a substance called histamine that participates in the inflammatory response.

2. **Neurotransmitters.** As presented in chapter 33, neurons secrete chemicals called neurotransmitters (e.g., nitric oxide and acetylcholine) that act on immediately adjacent target cells (figure 35.1b). These chemical messengers reach high concentrations in the synaptic cleft, act quickly, and are actively degraded and recycled.

FIGURE 35.1

Chemical Messengers: Targets and Transport. (*a*) Short-distance local messengers act on an adjacent cell. (*b*) Individual nerve cells secrete neurotransmitters that cross the synaptic cleft to act on target cells. (*c*) Individual nerve cells can also secrete neuropeptides (neurohormones) that travel some distance in the bloodstream to reach a target cell. (*d*) Regulatory cells, usually in an endocrine gland, secrete hormones, which enter the bloodstream and travel to target cells. (*e*) Regulatory cells in exocrine glands secrete pheromones. They leave the body and stimulate target cells in another animal.

3. **Neuropeptides.** Some specialized neurons (called neurosecretory cells) secrete neuropeptides **(neurohormones).** The blood or other body fluids transport neuropeptides to nonadjacent target cells, where neuropeptides exert their effects (figure 35.1c). In mammals, for example, certain nerve cells in the hypothalamus release a neuropeptide that causes the pituitary gland to release the hormone oxytocin, which induces powerful uterine contractions during the delivery of offspring.

4. **Hormones.** Endocrine glands or cells secrete hormones that the bloodstream transports to nonadjacent target cells (figure 35.1d). Many examples are given in the rest of this chapter.

5. **Pheromones.** Pheromones are chemical messengers released to the exterior of one animal that affect the behavior of another individual of the same species (figure 35.1e; *see also table 24.2*).

Overall, scientists now recognize that the nervous and endocrine systems work together as an all-encompassing communicative and integrative network called the **neuroendocrine system.** In this system, feedback systems regulate chemical messengers in their short- and long-term coordination of animal body function to maintain homeostasis.

HORMONES AND THEIR FEEDBACK SYSTEMS

A **hormone** (Gr. *hormaein,* to set in motion or to spur on) is a specialized chemical messenger that an endocrine gland or tissue produces and secretes. The study of endocrine glands and their hormones is called **endocrinology.** Hormones circulate through body fluids and affect the metabolic activity of a target cell or tissue in a specific way. By definition, a **target cell** has receptors to which chemical messengers either selectively bind to or on which they have an effect. Only rarely does a hormone operate independently. More typically, one hormone influences, depends on, and balances another hormone in a controlled feedback network.

BIOCHEMISTRY OF HORMONES

Most hormones are proteins (polypeptides), derivatives of amino acids (amines), or steroids. A few are fatty acid derivatives. For example, most invertebrate neurosecretory cells produce polypeptides called neuropeptides. Hormones that the vertebrate pancreas secretes are proteins; those that the thyroid gland secretes are amines. The ovaries, testes, and cortex of the adrenal glands secrete steroids.

Hormones are effective in extremely small amounts. Only a few molecules of a hormone may be enough to produce a dramatic response in a target cell. In the target cell, hormones help control biochemical reactions in three ways: (1) a hormone can increase the rate at which other substances enter or leave the cell; (2) it can stimulate a target cell to synthesize enzymes, proteins, or other

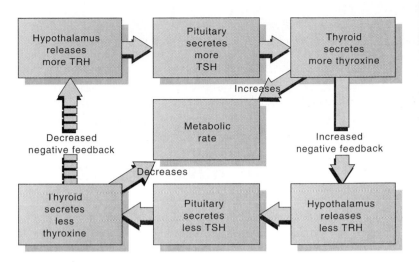

FIGURE 35.2

Hormonal Feedback. Negative feedback system that helps control metabolic rate in a vertebrate such as a dog. (TRH = thyrotropin-releasing hormone; TSH = thyroid-stimulating hormone.)

substances; or (3) it can prompt a target cell to activate or suppress existing cellular enzymes. As is the case for enzymes, hormones are not changed by the reaction they regulate.

FEEDBACK CONTROL SYSTEM OF HORMONE SECRETION

Although hormones are always present in some amount in endocrine cells or glands, they are not secreted continuously. Instead, the glands secrete the amount of hormone that the animal needs to maintain homeostasis. A feedback control system monitors changes in the animal or in the external environment and sends information to a central control unit (such as the central nervous system), which makes adjustments. A feedback system that produces a response that counteracts the initiating stimulus is called a negative feedback system. In contrast, a positive feedback system reinforces the initial stimulus. Positive feedback systems are relatively rare in animals because they usually lead to instability or pathological states.

Negative feedback systems monitor the amount of hormone secreted, altering the amount of cellular activity as needed to maintain homeostasis. For example, suppose that the rate of chemical activity (metabolic rate) in the body cells of a dog slows (figure 35.2). The hypothalamus responds to this slow rate by releasing more thyrotropin-releasing hormone (TRH), which causes the pituitary gland to secrete more thyrotropin, or thyroid-stimulating hormone (TSH). This hormone, in turn, causes the thyroid gland to secrete a hormone called thyroxine. Thyroxine increases the metabolic rate, restoring homeostasis. Conversely, if the metabolic rate speeds up, the hypothalamus releases less TRH, the pituitary secretes less TSH, the thyroid secretes less thyroxine, and the metabolic rate decreases once again, restoring homeostasis.

MECHANISMS OF HORMONE ACTION

Hormones modify the biochemical activity of a target cell or tissue. Two basic mechanisms are involved. The first, the fixed-membrane-receptor mechanism, applies to hormones that are proteins or amines. Because they are water-soluble and cannot diffuse across the plasma membrane, these hormones initiate their response by means of specialized receptors on the plasma membrane of the target cell. The second, the mobile-receptor mechanism, applies to steroid hormones. These hormones are lipid-soluble and diffuse easily into the cytoplasm, where they initiate their response by binding to cytoplasmic receptors.

FIXED-MEMBRANE-RECEPTOR MECHANISM

With the fixed-membrane-receptor mechanism, an endocrine cell secretes a water-soluble hormone that circulates through the bloodstream (figure 35.3a). At the cells of the target organ, the hormone acts as a "first or extracellular messenger," binding to a specific receptor site for that hormone on the plasma membrane (figure 35.3b). The hormone-receptor complex activates the enzyme adenylate cyclase in the membrane (figure 35.3c). The activated enzyme converts ATP into a nucleotide called cyclic AMP, which becomes the "second (or intracellular) messenger." Cyclic AMP diffuses throughout the cytoplasm and activates an enzyme called protein kinase, which causes the cell to respond with its distinctive physiological activity (figure 35.3d). After inducing the target cell to perform its specific function, the enzyme phosphodiesterase inactivates cyclic AMP. In the meantime, the receptor on the plasma membrane loses the first messenger and now becomes available for a new reaction.

MOBILE-RECEPTOR MECHANISM

Because steroid hormones pass easily through the plasma membrane, their receptors are inside the target cells. The mobile-receptor mechanism involves the stimulation of protein synthesis. After being released from a carrier protein in the bloodstream, the steroid hormone enters the target cell by diffusion and binds to a specific protein receptor in the cytoplasm (figure 35.4a,b). This newly formed steroid-protein complex acquires an affinity for DNA that causes it to enter the nucleus of the cell, where it binds to DNA and regulates the transcription of specific genes to form

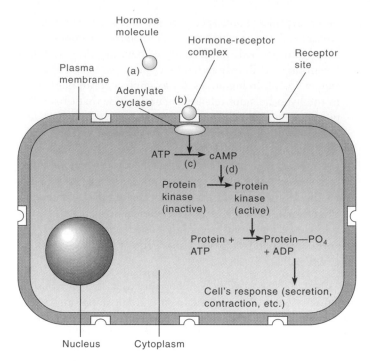

FIGURE 35.3

Steps of the Fixed-Membrane-Receptor Mechanism of Hormonal Action. (*a*) A protein hormone molecule (such as epinephrine) diffuses from the blood to a target cell. (*b*) The binding of the hormone to a specific plasma membrane receptor activates adenylate cyclase (a membrane-bound enzyme system). (*c*) This enzyme system catalyzes cyclic AMP formation (the second messenger) inside the cell. (*d*) Cyclic AMP (cAMP) diffuses throughout the cytoplasm and activates an enzyme called protein kinase, which then phosphorylates specific proteins in the cell, thereby triggering the biochemical reaction, leading ultimately to the cell's response.

messenger RNA (figure 35.4c,d). The newly transcribed mRNA leaves the nucleus and moves to the rough endoplasmic reticulum, where it initiates protein synthesis (figure 35.4e,f). Some of the newly synthesized proteins may be enzymes whose effects on cellular metabolism constitute the cellular response attributable to the specific steroid hormone (figure 35.4g).

FIGURE 35.4

Steps of the Mobile-Receptor Mechanism. (*a*) A steroid hormone molecule (e.g., testosterone) diffuses from the blood to a target cell and then across the plasma membrane of the target cell. (*b*) Once in the cytoplasm, the hormone binds to a receptor that (*c*) carries it into the nucleus. (*d*) This steroid-protein complex triggers transcription of specific gene regions of DNA. (*e*) The messenger RNA transcript is then translated into a gene product via (*f*) protein synthesis in the cytoplasm. (*g*) The new protein then mediates the cell's response.

SOME HORMONES OF INVERTEBRATES

The survival of any group of animals depends on growth, maturation, and reproduction coinciding with the most favorable seasons of the year so that climate and food supply are optimal. Thus, chemicals regulating growth, maturation, and reproduction probably were among the first hormones to appear during the course of animal evolution.

The first hormones were probably neurosecretions. As discusssed next, most of the chemicals functioning as hormones in invertebrate animals are neurosecretions called neuropeptides. Only a few of the more complex invertebrates (e.g., molluscs, arthropods, echinoderms) have hormones other than neurosecretions. What follows is a brief overview of some invertebrate neuropeptides and hormones.

PORIFERA

The porifera (sponges) do not have classical endocrine glands. Since sponges do not have neurons, they also do not have neurosecretory cells.

CNIDARIANS

The nerve cells of *Hydra* contain a growth-promoting hormone that stimulates budding, regeneration, and growth. For example, when the hormone is present in the medium in which fragments of *Hydra* are incubated, head regeneration is accelerated. This so-called "head activator" also stimulates mitosis in *Hydra*.

PLATYHELMINTHS

Zoologists identified neurosecretory cells in various flatworms over 30 years ago. These cells are in the cerebral ganglion and along major nerve cords. The neuropeptides that the cells produce function in regeneration, asexual reproduction, and gonad maturation. For example, neurosecretory cells in the scolex of some tapeworms control shedding of the proglottids or the initiation of strobilization.

NEMERTEANS

Nemerteans have more cephalization than platyhelminths and a larger brain, composed of a dorsal and ventral pair of ganglia connected by a nerve ring. The neuropeptide that these ganglia produce appears to control gonadal development and to regulate water balance.

NEMATODES

Although no classical endocrine glands have been identified in nematodes, they do have neurosecretory cells associated with the central nervous system. The neuropeptide that this nervous tissue produces apparently controls ecdysis of the old cuticle. The neuropeptide is released after a new cuticle is produced and stimulates the excretory gland to secrete an enzyme (leucine aminopeptidase) into the space between the old and new cuticle. The accumulation of fluid in this space causes the old cuticle to split and be shed.

MOLLUSCS

The ring of ganglia that constitutes the central nervous system of molluscs is richly endowed with neurosecretory cells. The neuropeptides that these cells produce help regulate heart rate, kidney function, and energy metabolism.

In certain gastropods, such as the common land snail *Helix*, a specific hormone stimulates spermatogenesis; another hormone, termed egg-laying hormone, stimulates egg development; and hormones from the ovary and testis stimulate accessory sex organs. In all snails, a growth hormone controls shell growth.

In cephalopods, such as the octopus, and squid, the optic gland in the eye stalk produces one or more hormones that stimulate egg development, proliferation of spermatogonia, and the development of secondary sexual characteristics.

ANNELIDS

Since annelids have a well-developed and cephalized nervous system, a well-developed circulatory system, and a large coelom, their correspondingly well-developed endocrine control of physiological functions is not surprising. The various endocrine systems of annelids are generally involved with morphogenesis, development, growth, regeneration, and gonadal maturation. For example, in polychaetes, juvenile hormone inhibits the gonads and stimulates growth and regeneration. Another hormone, gonadotropin, stimulates development of eggs. In leeches, a neuropeptide stimulates gamete development and triggers color changes. Osmoregulatory hormones have been reported in oligochaetes, and a hyperglycemic hormone that maintains a high concentration of blood glucose has been reported for the oligochaete, *Lumbricus*.

ARTHROPODS

The endocrine systems of advanced invertebrates (crustaceans and insects) are excellent examples of how hormones regulate growth, maturation, and reproduction. Much is known about hormones and their functioning in these animals.

The endocrine system of a crustacean, such as a crayfish, controls functions such as ecdysis (molting), sex determination, and color changes. Only ecdysis is discussed here.

X-organs are neurosecretory tissues in the crayfish eye stalks (figure 35.5*a*). Associated with each X-organ is a sinus gland that accumulates and releases the secretions of the X-organ. Other glands, called Y-organs, are at the base of the maxillae.   ❶   X-organs and Y-organs control ecdysis as follows. In the absence of an appropriate stimulus, the X-organ produces molt-inhibiting hormone (MIH), and the sinus gland releases it (figure 35.5*b*). The target of this hormone is the Y-organ. When MIH is present in high concentrations, the Y-organ is inactive. Under appropriate internal and external stimuli, MIH release is prevented, and the Y-organ releases the hormone ecdysone, which leads to molting (figure 35.5*c*).

The sequence of events in insects is similar to that of crustaceans, but does not involve a molt-inhibiting hormone. The presence of an appropriate stimulus to the central nervous system activates certain neurosecretory cells (pars intercerebralis) in the optic lobes of the brain (figure 35.6*a*). These cells secrete the hormone ecdysiotropin, which axons transport to the corpora cardiaca (a mass of neurons associated with the brain). The corpora cardiaca produces thoracotropic hormone, which is carried to the prothoracic glands, stimulating them to produce and release ecdysone, which induces molting (figure 35.6*b*)—in particular, the resorption of some of the old cuticle and the development of a new cuticle.

Other neurosecretory cells in the brain and nerve cords produce the hormone bursicon. Bursicon influences certain aspects of epidermal development, such as tanning (i.e., hardening and darkening of the chitinous outer cuticle layer). Tanning is completed several hours after each molt.

Another hormone, juvenile hormone (JH), is also involved in the morphological differentiation that occurs during the molting of insects. Just behind the insect brain are the paired corpora allata (figure 35.6*a*). These structures produce JH. High concentrations of JH in the blood of an insect inhibit differentiation. In the absence of an appropriate environmental stimulus, the corpora allata decrease JH production, which causes the insect larva to differentiate into a pupa (figure 35.6*c*). The pupa then forms a cocoon to overwinter. In the spring, a final surge of ecdysone, in the absence of JH, transforms the pupa into an adult moth.

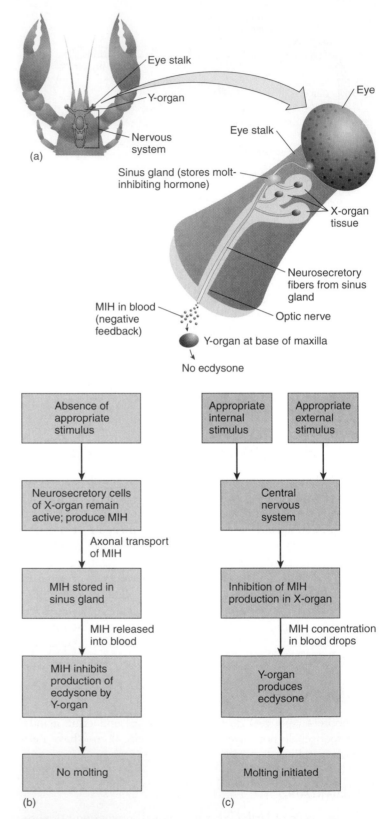

FIGURE 35.5

Hormonal Control of Ecdysis (Molting) in Crustaceans. (*a*) Neurosecretory apparatus in a crustacean eye stalk. (*b*) Flow diagram of the events inhibiting molting and (*c*) causing molting. (MIH = molt-inhibiting hormone.)

(a)

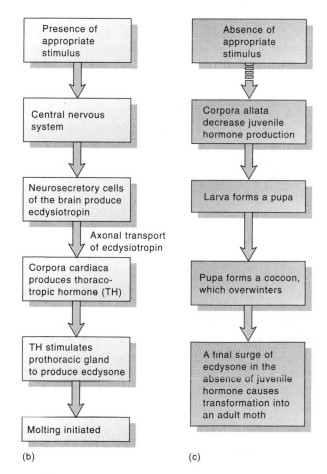

(b)   (c)

FIGURE 35.6

Control of Ecdysis (Molting) and Development (Metamorphosis) in an Insect. (*a*) Anterior end of an insect, showing the location of the brain hormone, juvenile hormone, and ecdysone secretory centers. (*b*) Flow diagram of the events initiating molting in an insect. (*c*) Flow diagram of the events of insect metamorphosis as regulated by a decrease in the production of juvenile hormone.

ECHINODERMS

Since echinoderms are deuterostomes, they are more closely allied to chordates than are the protostome invertebrates. However, the endocrine systems of echinoderms provide few insights into the evolution of chordate endocrine systems because echinoderm hormones and endocrine glands are very different from those of chordates. Zoologists do know, however, that the radial nerves of sea stars contain a neuropeptide called gonad-stimulating substance. When this neuropeptide is injected into a mature sea star, it induces immediate shedding of the gametes, spawning behavior, and meiosis in the oocytes. The neuropeptide also causes the release of a hormone called maturation-inducing substance, which has various effects on the reproductive system.

Stop and Ask Yourself

7. Why were the first hormones probably neurosecretions?

8. How do hormones function in the common land snail, *Helix*?

9. How do the X- and Y-organs of crustaceans control ecdysis?

10. What is the function of juvenile hormone in insects? What is the function of the hormone bursicon?

AN OVERVIEW OF THE VERTEBRATE ENDOCRINE SYSTEM

Since vertebrates have been studied more than invertebrates, vertebrates have the best understood system of hormonal control. As the earliest vertebrates evolved, hormone-producing cells and tissues developed, and came to be controlled in several ways. Sets of nerve cells in the brain direct some endocrine tissues, such as the medullary areas of the adrenal glands. The hypothalamus of the brain and the pituitary gland (hypophysis) control others. Still others function independently of either nerves or the pituitary gland.

Vertebrates possess two types of glands (figure 35.7). One type, **exocrine** (Gr. *exo*, outside + *krinein*, to separate) **glands,** secrete chemicals into ducts that, in turn, empty into body cavities or onto body surfaces (e.g., mammary, salivary, and sweat glands). The second type, **endocrine** (Gr. *endo*, within + *krinein*, to separate) **glands,** have no ducts, and instead secrete chemical messengers, called hormones, directly into the tissue space next to each endocrine cell. The hormones then diffuse into the bloodstream, which carries them throughout the body to their target cells.

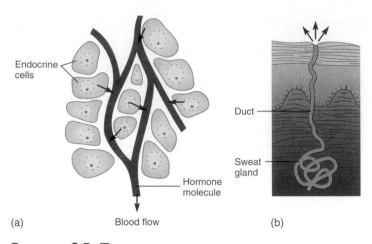

Endocrine
cells

Hormone
molecule

(a)

Blood flow

Duct

Sweat
gland

(b)

FIGURE 35.7

Vertebrate Glands with and without Ducts. (*a*) An endocrine gland, such as the thyroid, secretes hormones into the extracellular fluid. From there, the hormones pass into blood vessels and travel throughout the body. (*b*) An exocrine gland, such as a sudoriferous (sweat) gland, secretes material (sweat) into a duct that leads to a body surface.

ENDOCRINE SYSTEMS OF VERTEBRATES OTHER THAN BIRDS OR MAMMALS

Since this text uses a phylogenetic approach to describe form and function in animals, endocrine regulation in vertebrates other than birds or mammals is now discussed. Birds and mammals are the subject of the last part of this chapter.

Vertebrates other than birds or mammals have somewhat similar endocrine systems, but differences do exist. Recent research has revealed the following three aspects of endocrinology that relate to species differences among these vertebrates:

1. Hormones (or neuropeptides) with the same function in different species may not be chemically identical.
2. Certain hormones are species-specific with respect to their function; conversely, some hormones produced in one species may be completely functional in another species.
3. A hormone from one species may elicit a different response in the same target cell or tissue of a different species.

The examples that follow illustrate these three principles and also present a comparative survey of endocrine function in selected vertebrates.

When more ancient groups of vertebrates are compared with more recent ones, one general tendency surfaces: older groups seem to have simpler endocrine systems. For example, many of the hormones present in mammals are absent in fishes. In fishes, the brain and spinal cord are the most important producers of hormones, with other glands being rudimentary (figure 35.8). In jawed fishes, three major regions secrete neuropeptides. The two in the brain are the **pineal gland** of the epithalamus and

the **preoptic nuclei** of the hypothalamus. The pineal gland produces neuropeptides that affect pigmentation and apparently inhibit reproductive development, both of which are stimulated by light. One specific hormone that the pineal gland produces—**melatonin,** has broad effects on body metabolism by synchronizing activity patterns with light intensity and day length. The preoptic nuclei produce various other neuropeptides that control different functions in fishes (e.g., growth, sleep, locomotion). The third major region of fishes that has neuropeptide function is the urophysis. The **urophysis** (Gr. *oura*, tail + *physis*, growth) is a discrete structure in the spinal cord of the tail. The urophysis produces neuropeptides that help control water and ion balance, blood pressure, and smooth muscle contractions. Other than these functions, little else is known of its functions or the significance of its absence in more complex vertebrates.

In many fishes, amphibians, and reptiles, hormones (e.g., melatonin) from the pineal gland control variations in skin color. When this hormone produced by one species is injected into another species, it can induce dramatic color changes (figure 35.9). This type of experiment indicates that some hormones have a close chemical similarity (point 2 at the beginning of this section), despite the distant evolutionary relationships among the animals producing them. Another example is the hormone prolactin (produced by the **pituitary gland**). Prolactin stimulates reproductive migrations in many animals (e.g., the movement of salamanders to water). **2** Prolactin causes brooding behavior in some fishes. It also helps control water and salt balances, and is essential for certain saltwater fishes to enter freshwater during spawning runs.

3 From an evolutionary perspective, evidence indicates that the thyroid gland in the earliest vertebrates evolved from a pouchlike structure (the endostyle; *see box 26.2*) that carried food particles in the front end of the digestive tract. This explains why the thyroid gland is in the neck on the ventral side of the pharynx in all vertebrates. How did this feeding mechanism turn into an endocrine gland? One possible hypothesis is that as the developing pouch gradually lost all connection with the pharynx, it became independent of the digestive system both functionally and structurally. As a result, a functionally novel structure arose from an ancestral structure with an unrelated function. The shape of the thyroid varies among vertebrates. It may be a single structure (e.g., many fishes, reptiles, and some mammals), or it may have several to many lobes. The major hormones that this gland produces are thyroxine (T_4) and triiodothyronine (T_3), which control the rate of metabolism, growth, and tissue differentiation in vertebrates.

As noted in point 3 at the beginning of this section, the same hormone(s) in different vertebrates may regulate related but different processes. The hormones thyroxine and triiodothyronine are excellent examples of this point. For example, in most animals, thyroxine and triiodothyronine regulate overall metabolism. In amphibians, they play an additional role in metamorphosis (figure 35.10). Specifically timed changes in the concentrations of three hormones—prolactin, thyroxine, and triiodothyronine—

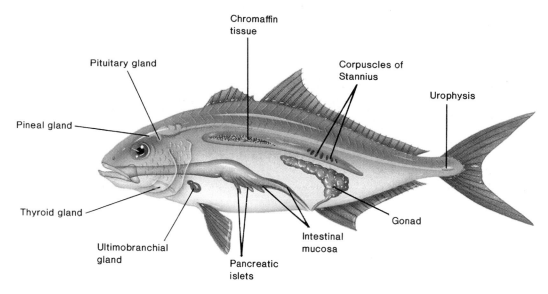

FIGURE 35.8

Approximate Locations of Endocrine Tissues (Glands) in a Bony Fish.

FIGURE 35.9

Hormonal Control of Frog Skin Color. The light-colored frog on the left was immersed in water containing the hormone melatonin. The dark-colored frog on the right received an injection of melanocyte-stimulating hormone.

control metamorphosis in the frog. Low thyroxine and triiodothyronine concentrations and high prolactin concentrations in young tadpoles stimulate larval growth and prevent metamorphosis. As the hypothalamus and pituitary glands develop in the growing tadpole, the hypothalamus releases thyroid-stimulating hormone and prolactin-inhibiting hormone. Their release causes the pituitary gland to release thyroid-stimulating hormone and to cease production of prolactin. ❹ As a result, the concentrations of thyroxine and triiodothyronine rise, triggering the onset

of metamorphosis. Tail resorption and other metamorphic changes follow.

In jawed fishes and primitive tetrapods, several small **ultimobranchial glands** form ventral to the esophagus (*see figure 35.8*). These glands produce the hormone calcitonin that helps regulate the concentration of blood calcium.

Specialized endocrine cells **(chromaffin tissue)** or glands **(adrenal glands)** near the kidneys prepare some vertebrates for stressful emergency situations (figure 35.11). These tissues and glands produce two hormones (epinephrine or adrenaline, and norepinephrine or noradrenaline) that cause vasoconstriction, increased blood pressure, changes in the heart rate, and increased blood glucose levels. These hormones are involved in the "fight-or-flight" reactions.

Stop and Ask Yourself

11. What are some differences between endocrine and exocrine glands?
12. What is the function of the urophysis?
13. What role do thyroxine and triiodothyronine play in amphibian metamorphosis?
14. What is the function of melatonin? What is the function of calcitonin?

ENDOCRINE SYSTEMS OF BIRDS AND MAMMALS

With some minor exceptions, birds and mammals have a similar complement of endocrine glands (figure 35.12). Table 35.1 summarizes the major hormones these vertebrates produce.

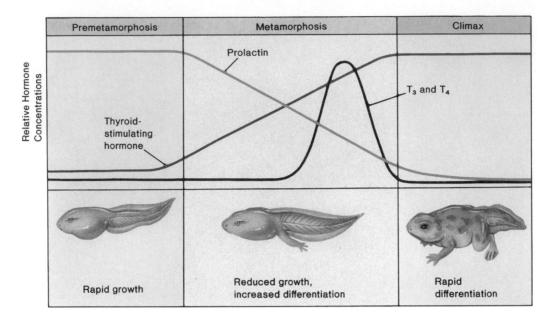

FIGURE 35.10

Frog Tadpole Metamorphosis. The thyroid hormones triiodothyronine (T_3) and thyroxine (T_4) regulate the metamorphosis of an aquatic frog tadpole into a semiterrestrial or terrestrial adult. The anterior pituitary secretes thyroid-stimulating hormone, which regulates thyroid gland activity. During the premetamorphosis (tadpole) stage, the pituitary and thyroid glands are relatively inactive. This keeps the concentration of thyroid-stimulating hormones, T_3 and T_4, at low concentrations. The high prolactin concentration in tadpoles stimulates larval growth and prevents metamorphosis. During metamorphosis, the concentrations of the thyroid hormones markedly increase, and prolactin decreases. These hormonal fluctuations induce rapid differentiation, climaxing in the adult frog.

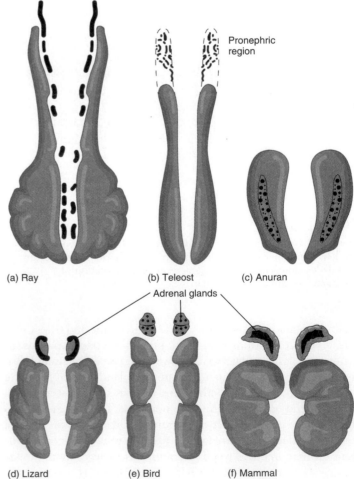

FIGURE 35.11

Chromaffin Tissue and Adrenal Glands in Selected Vertebrates.
The chromaffin tissue (steroidogenic) produces steroid hormones and is shown in gray. The aminogenic tissue that produces norepinephrine and epinephrine is shown in black. The kidneys are shown in brown. Note the reversed location of the two components in lizards and mammals. (*a*) In jawless and cartilaginous fishes (elasmobranchs), aminogenic tissue develops as clusters near the kidneys. (*b*) In teleosts, the chromaffin tissue is generally at the anterior end of the kidney (pronephric region). (*c*) In anurans, the chromaffin tissue is interspersed in a diffuse gland on the ventral surface of each kidney. (*d*) In lizards, the chromaffin tissue forms a capsule around the steroidogenic-producing tissue. (*e*) In birds, the chromaffin tissue is interspersed within an adrenal capsule. (*f*) In most mammals, the chromaffin tissue forms an adrenal medulla, and the steroidogenic tissue forms the cortex.

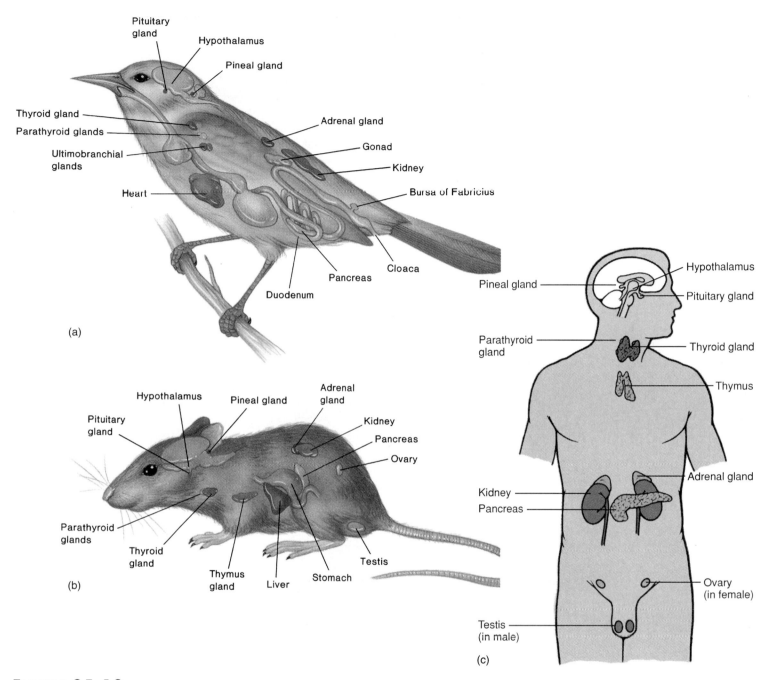

FIGURE 35.12

Endocrine Glands of Birds and Mammals. Locations of the major endocrine glands of (*a*) a bird, (*b*) a rat, and (*c*) a human.

BIRDS

The endocrine glands in birds include the ovary, testes, adrenals, pituitary, thyroid, pancreas, parathyroids, pineal, hypothalamus, thymus, ultimobranchial, and bursa of Fabricius (figure 35.12*a*). Since the hormones that most of these glands produce and their effects on target tissues are nearly the same as in mammals, they are discussed in the next section on mammals. A discussion of some unique hormones and their functions in birds follows.

In some birds (e.g., pigeons and doves), the pituitary gland secretes the hormone prolactin. ⑤ Prolactin stimulates pro-

duction of "pigeon's milk" by desquamation (sloughing off cells) in the pigeon's crop. Prolactin also stimulates and regulates broodiness and certain other kinds of parental behavior, and along with estrogen, stimulates full development of the **brood (incubation) patch** (figure 35.13). The brood patch helps keep the eggs at a temperature between 33 and 37° C.

The bird's thyroid gland produces the hormone thyroxine. In addition to the major vertebrate functions listed in table 35.1, thyroxine regulates normal development of feathers and the molt cycle, and plays a role in the onset of migratory behavior.

TABLE 35.1	MAJOR VERTEBRATE ENDOCRINE TISSUES AND HORMONES	
SOURCE	**HORMONES**	**TARGET CELLS AND PRINCIPAL ACTIONS**
Anterior lobe of pituitary (adenohypophysis)	Somatotropin (STH, or growth hormone [GH])	Stimulates growth of bone and muscle; promotes protein synthesis; affects lipid and carbohydrate metabolism; increases cell division
	Adrenocorticotropic hormone (ACTH)	Stimulates secretion of adrenocortical steroids; is involved in stress response
	Thyrotropin (TSH) or thyroid-stimulating hormone	Stimulates thyroid gland to synthesize and release thyroid hormones concerned with growth, development, metabolic rate
	Endorphins	Decrease pain
	Gonadotropins:	In ovary: Forms corpora lutea; secretes progesterone; probably acts in conjunction with FSH
	Luteinizing or interstitial cell-stimulating hormone (LH or ICSH)	In testis: Stimulates the interstitial cells, thus promoting the secretion of testosterone
	Follicle-stimulating hormone (FSH)	In ovary: Stimulates growth of follicles; functions with LH to cause estrogen secretion and ovulation
		In testis: Acts on seminiferous tubules to promote spermatogenesis
	Prolactin (PRL)	Initiates milk production by mammary glands; acts on crop sacs of some birds; stimulates maternal behavior in birds
Intermediate or posterior lobe of pituitary	Melanocyte-stimulating hormone (MSH)	Expands amphibian melanophores; contracts iridophores and xanthophores; promotes melanin synthesis; darkens the skin; responds to external stimuli
Posterior lobe of pituitary (neurohypophyses) releases these hormones produced by the hypothalamus	Antidiuretic hormone (ADH or vasopressin)	Elevates blood pressure by acting on arterioles; promotes reabsorption of water by kidney tubules
	Oxytocin	Affects postpartum mammary gland, causing ejection of milk; promotes contraction of uterus; has possible action in parturition and in sperm transport in female reproductive tract
Hypothalamus	Thyroid-stimulating hormone (TSH)	Stimulates release of TSH by anterior pituitary
	Adrenocorticotropin-releasing hormone (CRH)	Stimulates release of ACTH by anterior pituitary
	Gonadotropin-releasing hormone (GnRH)	Stimulates gonadotropin release by anterior pituitary
	Prolactin-inhibiting factor (PIF)	Inhibits prolactin release by anterior pituitary
	Somatostatin	Inhibits release of STH by anterior pituitary
Thyroid gland	Thyroxine, triiodothyronine	Affect growth, amphibian metamorphosis, molting, metabolic rate in birds and mammals, development
	Calcitonin	Lowers blood calcium level by inhibiting calcium reabsorption from bone
Parathyroid glands	Parathormone	Regulates calcium concentration
Pancreas, islet cells	Insulin (from beta cells)	Promotes glycogen synthesis and glucose utilization and uptake from blood
	Glucagon (from alpha cells)	Raises blood glucose concentration
Adrenal cortex	Glucocorticoids (e.g., cortisol)	Promote synthesis of carbohydrates and breakdown of proteins; initiates antiinflammatory and antiallergic actions; mediates response to stress
	Mineralocorticoids (e.g., aldosterone)	Regulate sodium retention and potassium loss through kidneys, and water balance
Adrenal medulla	Epinephrine (adrenaline)	Mobilizes glucose; increases blood flow through skeletal muscle; increases oxygen consumption; increases heart rate
	Norepinephrine	Elevates blood pressure; constricts arterioles and venules
Testes	Androgens (e.g., testosterone)	Maintain male sexual characteristics; promotes spermatogenesis
Ovaries	Estrogens (e.g., estradiol)	Maintain female sexual characteristics; promotes oogenesis
Corpus luteum	Progesterone	Maintains pregnancy; stimulates development of mammary glands

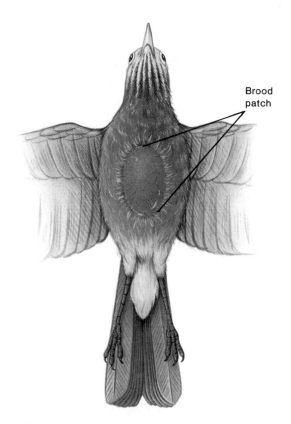

Brood patch

FIGURE 35.13

A Bird's Brood Patch. In this example, a robin's single brood patch appears (due to the effect of the hormone prolactin) a few days before eggs are laid. Prolactin causes the down feathers to drop from the abdomen of the incubating robin, and the bare patch becomes swollen and richly supplied with blood vessels. After laying the eggs, the robin settles on its nest and brings this warm patch in contact with its eggs, thereby transferring heat to the developing embryos.

In male birds, the testes produce the hormone testosterone. Testosterone controls the secondary sexual characteristics of the male, such as bright plumage color, comb (when present), and spurs—all of which strongly influence sexual behavior.

The ultimobranchial glands are small, paired structures in the neck just below the parathyroid glands. They secrete the hormone **calcitonin,** which is involved in regulating blood calcium concentrations.

The **bursa of Fabricius** is a sac that lies just dorsal to the cloaca and empties into it. Although well developed during the bird's embryological development, it begins to shrink soon after hatching. Its tissues produce secretions that are responsible for the maturation of white blood cells (B lymphocytes), which play an important role in immunological reactions.

Stop and Ask Yourself

15. What are several functions of the hormone prolactin in birds?

16. What is the function of the ultimobranchial glands in birds? What is the function of the bursa of Fabricius?

MAMMALS

Zoologists know more about the endocrine organs, hormones, and target tissues of mammals than of any other animal group. This is especially true for the human body. A brief overview of mammalian endocrinology follows.

Pituitary Gland (Hypophysis)

The pituitary gland (also known as the hypophysis) is directly below the hypothalamus (*see figure 35.12c*). The pituitary has two distinct lobes: the anterior lobe (adenohypophysis) and the posterior lobe (neurohypophysis) (figure 35.14). The two lobes differ in several ways: (1) the adenohypophysis is larger than the neurohypophysis; (2) secretory cells called pituicytes are in the adenohypophysis, but not in the neurohypophysis; and (3) the neurohypophysis has a greater supply of nerve endings. Pituicytes produce and secrete hormones directly from the adenohypophysis, whereas the neurohypophysis obtains its hormones from the neurosecretory cells in the hypothalamus, stores them and releases them when they are needed. These modified hypothalamic nerve cells project their axons down a stalk of nerve cells and blood vessels, called the infundibulum, into the pituitary gland, directly linking the nervous and endocrine systems.

The pituitary of many vertebrates (but not in humans, birds, and cetaceans) also has a functional **intermediate lobe (pars intermedia)** of mostly glandular tissue. Its secretions (e.g., melanophore-stimulating hormone) in response to external stimuli induce changes in the coloration of the body surface of many animals.

Hormones of the Neurohypophysis   The neurohypophysis does not manufacture any hormones. Instead, the neurosecretory cells of the hypothalamus synthesize and secrete two hormones, antidiuretic hormone and oxytocin, which move down nerve axons into the neurohypophysis, where they are stored in the axon terminals until released.

Diuretics stimulate urine excretion, whereas antidiuretics decrease urine secretion. When a mammal begins to lose water and becomes dehydrated, antidiuretic hormone (ADH, or vasopressin) is released and increases water absorption in the kidneys so that less urine is secreted. Because less urine is secreted, water is retained. This negative feedback system thus restores water and solute homeostasis.

Oxytocin plays a role in mammalian reproduction by its effect on smooth muscle. It stimulates contraction of the uterus or uteri to aid in expulsion of the offspring and promotes ejection of milk from the mammary glands to provide nourishment for the newborn.

Both ADH and oxytocin are thought to have evolved from a similar ancestral chemical messenger that helped control water loss and, indirectly, solute concentrations. For example, the neurohypophysis is notably larger in animals that live in arid parts of the world, where water conservation is crucial. Also, the structure of the two hormones is similar except for a difference in two of the amino acids.

FIGURE 35.14

Functional Links between the Pituitary Gland and the Hypothalamus. Target areas for each hormone are shown in the corresponding box. The blood vessels that make up the hypothalamic-hypophyseal portal system provide the functional link between the hypothalamus and the adenohypophysis, and the axons of the hypothalamic neurosecretory cells provide the link between the hypothalamus and the neurohypophysis. (TSH = thyroid-stimulating hormone; PRL = prolactin; ACTH = adrenocorticotropic hormone; GH = growth hormone; STH = somatotropin; FSH = follicle-stimulating hormone; LH = luteinizing hormone.)

Hormones of the Adenohypophysis   The true endocrine portion of the pituitary is the adenohypophysis, which synthesizes six different hormones (figure 35.14). All of these hormones are polypeptides, and all but two are true tropic hormones, hormones whose primary target is another endocrine gland. The two nontropic hormones are growth hormone and prolactin.

Growth hormone (GH), or somatotropin (STH), does not influence a particular target tissue; rather, it affects all parts of the body that are concerned with growth. It directly induces the cell division necessary for growth and protein synthesis in most types of cells by stimulating uptake of amino acids, RNA synthesis, and ribosome activity.

Prolactin (PRL) has the widest range of actions of the adenohypophyseal hormones. It plays an essential role in many aspects of reproduction. For example, it stimulates reproductive migrations in many mammals, such as elk and caribou. Prolactin also enhances mammary gland development and milk production in female mammals. (Oxytocin stimulates milk ejection from the mammary glands, but not its production.)

Thyrotropin, or thyroid-stimulating hormone (TSH), stimulates the thyroid gland's synthesis and secretion of thyroxine, the main thyroid hormone.

Adrenocorticotropic hormone (ACTH) stimulates the adrenal gland to produce and secrete steroid hormones called glucocorticoids (cortisol). Secretion of ACTH is regulated by the secretion of corticotropin-releasing factor from the hypothalamus, which, in turn, is regulated by a feedback system that involves such factors as stress, insulin, ADH, and other hormones.

The adenohypophysis produces two gonadotropins (hormones that stimulate the gonads): luteinizing hormone and follicle-stimulating hormone. Luteinizing hormone (LH) receives its name from the corpus luteum, a temporary endocrine tissue in the ovaries that secretes the female sex hormones estrogen and progesterone. In the female, an increase of LH in the blood stimulates ovulation, the release of a mature egg(s) from an ovary. In the male, the target cells of LH are cells in the testes that secrete the male hormone testosterone. In the female, follicle-stimulating hormone (FSH) stimulates the follicular cells in the ovaries to develop into mature eggs and to produce estrogen. In the male, FSH stimulates the cells of the testes to produce sperm.

The pineal gland (or pineal body) is so named because it is shaped like a pine cone. Its distinctive cells evolved from the photoreceptors of lower vertebrates; they synthesize melatonin, and are most active in the dark. Light inhibits the enzymes needed for melatonin synthesis. Because of its cyclical production, melatonin can affect many physiological processes and adjust them to diurnal and seasonal cycles. The use of melatonin by mammals is an evolutionary adaptation to help ensure that periodic activities of mammals occur at a time of the year when environmental conditions are optimal for those activities. In humans, decreased melatonin secretion may help trigger the onset of puberty, the age at which reproductive structures start to mature.

Stop and Ask Yourself

17. What hormones do the neurosecretory cells of the hypothalamus secrete?
18. What hormones does the adenohypophysis secrete?
19. What are the effects of gonadotropins in males and females?
20. What is the function of melatonin?

Thyroid Gland

The **thyroid gland** is in the neck, anterior to the trachea (*see figure 35.12*). Two of its secretions are thyroxine and triiodothyronine, both of which influence overall growth, development, and metabolic rates. Another thyroid hormone, calcitonin, helps control extracellular levels of calcium ions (Ca^{2+}) by promoting deposition of these ions into bone tissue when their concentrations rise. Once calcium returns to its homeostatic concentration, thyroid cells decrease their secretion of calcitonin.

Parathyroid Glands

The **parathyroid glands** are tiny, pea-sized glands embedded in the thyroid lobes, usually two glands in each lobe (*see figure 35.12*). The parathyroids secrete parathormone (PTH), which regulates the concentrations of calcium (Ca^{2+}) and phosphate (HPO_2^{-4}) ions in the blood.

When the calcium concentration in the blood bathing the parathyroid glands is low, PTH secretion increases and has the following effects: It stimulates bone cells to break down bone tissue and release calcium ions into the blood. It also enhances calcium absorption from the small intestine into the blood. Finally, PTH promotes calcium reabsorption by the kidney tubules to decrease the amount of calcium excreted in the urine. Figure 35.15 shows the negative feedback system for parathormone.

Adrenal Glands

In mammals, two adrenal glands rest on top of the kidneys. Each gland consists of two separate glandular tissues. The inner portion is the medulla, and the outer portion, which surrounds the medulla, is the cortex (figure 35.16).

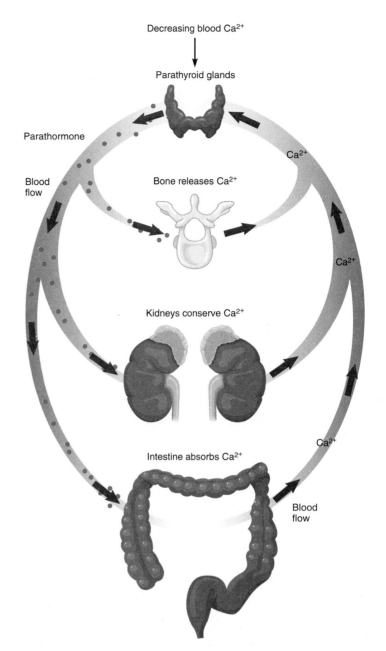

FIGURE 35.15

Hormonal Feedback. The negative feedback mechanism of the parathyroid glands (parathormone). Parathormone stimulates bones to release calcium and the kidneys to conserve calcium. It indirectly stimulates the intestine to absorb calcium. The result increases blood calcium, which then inhibits parathormone secretion.

Adrenal Cortex   The adrenal cortex secretes three classes of steroid hormones: glucocorticoids (cortisol), mineralocorticoids (aldosterone), and sex hormones (androgens, estrogens). The glucocorticoids, such as **cortisol,** help regulate overall metabolism and the concentration of blood sugar. They also function in defense responses to infection or tissue injury. Aldosterone helps maintain concentrations of solutes (such as sodium) in the extracellular fluid when either food intake or metabolic activity changes the amount of solutes entering the bloodstream.

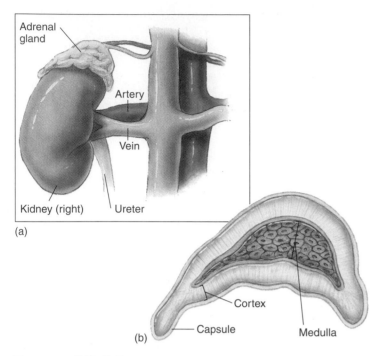

(a)

(b)

FIGURE 35.16

Adrenal Gland of a Mammal. (*a*) An adrenal gland sits on top of each kidney. (*b*) Each gland contains two structurally, functionally, and developmentally distinct regions. The outer cortex is endocrine and produces glucocorticoids (cortisol), mineralocorticoids (aldosterone), and androgens (sex hormones). The inner medulla is nervous tissue that produces epinephrine (adrenaline) and norepinephrine (noradrenaline).

Aldosterone also promotes sodium reabsorption in the kidneys and, thus, water reabsorption; hence, it plays a major role in maintaining the homeostasis of extracellular fluid. Normally, the sex hormones that the adrenal cortex secretes have only a slight effect on male and female gonads. These sex hormones consist mainly of weak male hormones called androgens and lesser amounts of female hormones called estrogens.

Adrenal Medulla

The adrenal medulla is under neural control. It contains neurosecretory cells that secrete epinephrine (adrenaline) and norepinephrine (noradrenaline), both of which help control heart rate and carbohydrate metabolism. Brain centers and the hypothalamus govern the secretions via sympathetic nerves.

⑥ During times of excitement, emergency, or stress, the adrenal medulla contributes to the overall mobilization of the body through the sympathetic nervous system. In response to epinephrine and norepinephrine, the heart rate increases, blood flow increases to many vital organs, the airways in the lungs dilate, and more oxygen is delivered to all cells of the body. This group of events is sometimes called the "fight-or-flight" response and permits the body to react strongly and quickly to emergencies.

Pancreas

The **pancreas** is an elongated, fleshy organ posterior to the stomach (figure 35.17). It functions both as an exocrine (with ducts)

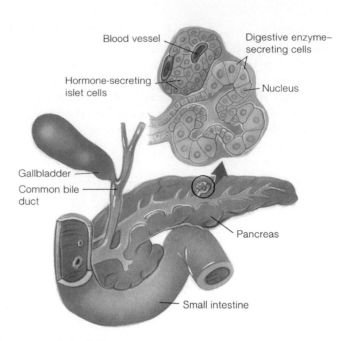

FIGURE 35.17

Pancreas. The hormone-secreting cells of the pancreas are arranged in clusters or islets closely associated with blood vessels. Other pancreatic cells secrete digestive enzymes into ducts.

gland to secrete digestive enzymes and as an endocrine (ductless) gland. The endocrine portion of the pancreas makes up only about 1% of the gland. This portion synthesizes, stores, and secretes hormones from clusters of cells called pancreatic islets.

The pancreas contains 200,000 to 2,000,000 **pancreatic islets** scattered throughout the gland. Each islet contains four special groups of cells, called alpha (α), beta (β), delta (δ), and F cells. The alpha cells produce the hormone glucagon, and beta cells produce insulin. The delta cells secrete somatostatin, the hypothalamic growth-hormone inhibiting factor that also inhibits glucagon and insulin secretion. F cells secrete a pancreatic polypeptide of unknown function that is released into the bloodstream after a meal.

When glucose concentrations in the blood are high, such as after a meal, beta cells secrete insulin. Insulin promotes the uptake of glucose by the body's cells, including liver cells, where excess glucose can be converted to glycogen (a storage polysaccharide; *see figure 2.11*). Insulin and glucagon are crucial to the regulation of blood glucose concentrations. When the blood glucose concentration is low, alpha cells secrete glucagon. Glucagon stimulates the breakdown of glycogen into glucose units, which are released into the bloodstream to raise the blood glucose concentration to the homeostatic level. Figure 35.18 illustrates the negative feedback system that regulates the secretion of glucagon and insulin and maintenance of appropriate blood glucose concentrations (box 35.1).

Gonads

The **gonads** (ovaries and testes) secrete hormones that help regulate reproductive functions. In the male, the testes secrete testosterone, which acts with luteinizing and follicle-stimulating

BOX 35.1   DIABETES

Several disorders classified under the term **diabetes** (Gr. *diabetes*, syphon) are associated with insulin deficiency or with the inability of cells to take up glucose. In type I diabetes (juvenile diabetes), the afflicted person (or other mammal, such as a dog or cat) has little or no insulin because the beta cells have been destroyed. This form of diabetes is relatively uncommon and usually occurs early in life as a result of a genetic susceptibility, viral infection, or an autoimmune response mounted against the beta cells. If insulin is insufficient, glucose accumulates in the blood but does not enter the cells. Because the cells cannot use the accumulated glucose, the body actually begins to starve. Brain, retinal, and gonadal tissues are particularly endangered because glucose is the only nutrient that these tissues can use. The use of fats (to replace glucose) for energy production in other tissues causes acetoacetic acid and keto acids to accumulate in the blood. This buildup leads to acidosis, which can cause coma and death. Survival for type I diabetes depends on regular injections of insulin. (Insulin is a small protein molecule and cannot be taken by mouth because protein-digesting enzymes in the digestive tract would rapidly inactivate it.) Without injections, the person (or other mammal) suffers severe metabolic and urinary disruptions.

In type II (maturity-onset) diabetes, insulin concentrations are nearly normal or even above normal; however, the target cells cannot respond to the hormone. Either the cells have an insufficient number of insulin receptors, or the receptors themselves are abnormal. Diet, exercise, and oral glycemic agents, which facilitate glucose uptake, are used to treat this type of diabetes.

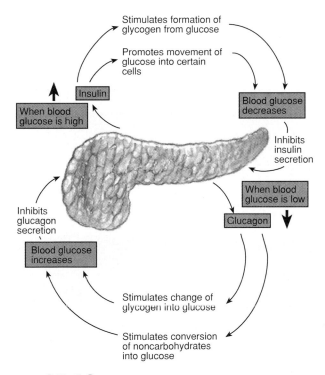

FIGURE 35.18

Two Pancreatic Hormones (Insulin and Glucagon) Regulate the Concentration of Blood Glucose. The negative feedback mechanism for regulating glucagon and insulin secretion helps maintain a relatively stable blood glucose concentration.

hormones that the adenohypophysis produces to stimulate spermatogenesis. Testosterone is also necessary for the growth and maintenance of the male sex organs, promotes the development and maintenance of sexual behavior, and in humans, stimulates the growth of facial and pubic hair, as well as enlargement of the larynx, which deepens the voice.

Three major classes of ovarian hormones help to regulate female reproductive functions. Estrogens (estrin, estrone, and estradiol) help regulate the menstrual and estrus cycles and the development of the mammary glands and other female secondary sexual characteristics. The progestins (primarily progesterone) also regulate the menstrual and estrus cycles, and the development of the mammary glands, and aid in placenta formation during pregnancy. Relaxin, which is produced in small quantities, softens the opening of the uterus (cervix) at the time of delivery.

Thymus

The **thymus gland** is near the heart (*see figure 35.12*). It is large and conspicuous in young birds and mammals, but diminishes in size throughout adulthood. The major hormonal product of the thymus is a family of peptide hormones, including thymopoietin (TP) and alpha$_1$ and beta$_4$ thymosin, that appear to be essential for the normal development of the immune system.

Other Sources of Hormones

In addition to the major endocrine glands, other glands and organs carry on hormonal activity. Table 35.2 summarizes some of these.

Stop and Ask Yourself

21. What effect does parathormone have on blood calcium concentrations?
22. What types of hormones does the adrenal cortex secrete? What types of hormones do the three cell types in the pancreatic islets secrete?
23. How do norepinephrine and epinephrine help an animal respond to stress?
24. How does glucagon function in opposition to insulin?

TABLE 35.2	SOME OTHER MAJOR SOURCES OF VERTEBRATE HORMONES		
GLAND/ORGAN	**HORMONE**	**FUNCTION**	**TARGET AREA**
Placenta	Estrogens, progesterone, human chorionic gonadotropin (hCG)	Maintains pregnancy	Ovaries, mammary glands, uterus
Digestive tract	Secretin	Stimulates release of pancreatic juice to neutralize stomach acid	Cells of pancreas
	Gastrin	Stimulates digestive enzymes and HCl in stomach	Stomach mucosa
	Cholecystokinin (CCK)	Stimulates release of pancreatic enzymes and bile from gallbladder	Pancreas, gallbladder
Heart	Atriopeptin	Lowers blood pressure, maintains fluid balance	Blood vessels, kidneys
Kidneys	Erythropoietin	Stimulates red blood cell production	Bone marrow

ENDANGERED SPECIES

WILDLIFE ALERT 12—INDIANA BAT (*MYOTIS SODALIS*)

VITAL STATISTICS

Classification: Phylum Chordata, class Mammalia, order Chiroptera, family Vespertilionidae

Range: Midwest and eastern United States

Habitat: Limestone caves are used for winter hibernation; summer habitat data are scarce but include under bridges, in old buildings, under bark, and in hollow trees

Number remaining: 500,000

Status: Endangered throughout its range

NATURAL HISTORY AND ECOLOGICAL STATUS

The Indiana bat (also called the Indiana myotis; myotis refers to the mouse-eared bats) is a medium-sized bat with dull gray to chestnut-colored fur (figure 1). The bat's underparts are pinkish to cinnamon-colored. Little is known of the bat's diet beyond it consisting of insects. Families and juveniles forage in the airspace near the foliage of riverbank and floodplain trees. Males usually forage in densely wooded areas at treetop height.

The Indiana bat lives in the Midwest and in the eastern United States, from the western edge of the Ozark region in Oklahoma, to southern Wisconsin, east to Vermont, and as far south as northern Florida (figure 2). In summer, it is absent south of Tennessee; in winter, it is absent from Michigan, Ohio, and northern Indiana, where suitable habitats (caves and mines) are unknown.

The Indiana bat's breeding period is during the first 10 days of October. Mating takes place at night on the ceilings of large rooms

FIGURE 1 Indiana Bat *(Myotis sodalis)*.

near cave entrances. Hibernating colonies disperse in late March, and most of the bats migrate to more northern habitats for the summer. However, some males remain in the hibernating area during this period and wander from cave to cave. Birth occurs in June in widely scattered colonies consisting of about 25 females and their young. Each female bears a single offspring. The young require 25 to 37 days to develop to the flying stage and to feed independently.

Migration to the wintering caves usually begins in August. The bats replace depleted fat reserves from the migration during September. Feeding then declines until mid-November, when the population enters a state of hibernation. The hibernating bats form large, compact clusters. Each individual hangs by its feet from the ceiling. Every 8 to 10 days, hibernating individuals awaken to spend an hour or more flying about before returning to hibernation.

The bats prefer limestone caves with an average temperature of 37° C and a relative humidity around 87% for hibernation.

The decline of the Indiana bat is attributed to commercialization of roosting caves, wanton destruction by vandals, disturbances caused by increased numbers of spelunkers and bat banding programs, the use of bats as laboratory animals, and possibly, insecticide poisoning.

To date, primary conservation efforts have focused on installing gates across cave entrances to control access. Some gating has already been accomplished on federal and state lands. Gating of all seven of the major wintering habitats would protect about 87% of the Indiana bat population. The National Speological Society and the American Society of Mammologists are working together to preserve this species of bat.

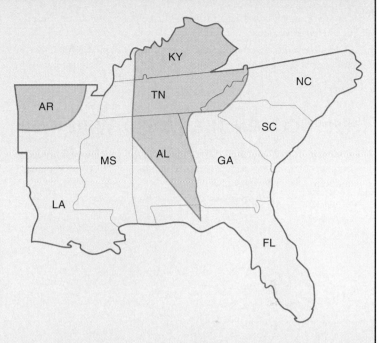

FIGURE 2   Distribution of the Indiana Bat (*Myotis sodalis*).

SUMMARY

1. For metabolic activity to proceed smoothly in an animal, the chemical environment of each cell must be maintained within fairly narrow limits (homeostasis). This is accomplished using negative feedback systems that involve integrating, communicating, and coordinating molecules called messengers.

2. Specialized cells secrete chemical messenger molecules. These chemical messengers can be categorized as local chemical messengers (lumones), neurotransmitters (e.g., acetylcholine), neuropeptides, hormones, and pheromones (e.g., sex attractants).

3. A hormone is a specialized chemical messenger that an endocrine gland or tissue produces and secretes. Hormones are usually steroids, amines, proteins, or fatty acid derivatives. Negative feedback systems often regulate hormone secretion.

4. Hormones modify the biochemical activity of a target cell or tissue (so called because it has receptors to which hormone molecules can bind). Mechanisms of hormone action are the fixed-membrane-receptor mechanism (water-soluble hormones) or the mobile-receptor mechanism (steroid hormones).

5. Most of the chemicals functioning as hormones in invertebrate animals are neurosecretions called neuropeptides. Only a few of the more advanced invertebrates (e.g., molluscs, arthropods, echinoderms) have nonneurosecretory hormones.

6. In all vertebrates, a neuroendocrine control center coordinates communication and integrative activities for the entire body. This center consists of the hypothalamus and pituitary gland.

7. The vertebrate endocrine system consists of several major glands: the hypothalamus, pituitary gland, pineal gland, thyroid gland, parathyroid glands, adrenal glands, pancreas, gonads, and thymus. In addition to these major glands, other glands and organs, including the placenta, digestive tract, heart, and kidneys, carry on hormonal activity.

SELECTED KEY TERMS

endocrinology (p. 587)

hormones (p. 587)

local chemical messengers (p. 586)

neuroendocrine system (p. 587)

neuropeptides (p. 587)

neurotransmitters (p. 586)

pheromones (p. 587)

target cell (p. 587)

CRITICAL THINKING QUESTIONS

1. How do hormones encode information? How do cells "know what to do" in response to hormonal information?

2. Summarize your knowledge of how endocrine systems work by describing the "life" of a hormone molecule from the time it is secreted until it is degraded or used up.

3. All cells secrete or excrete molecules, and all cells respond to certain biochemical factors in their external environments. Could the origin of endocrine control systems lie in such ordinary cellular events? How might the earliest multicellular organisms have evolved some sort of endocrine coordination?

4. Mental states strongly affect the function of many endocrine glands. This mind-body link occurs through the hypothalamus. Can you describe how thoughts are transformed into physiological responses in the hypothalamus?

5. Compared to enzymes and genes, hormones are remarkably small molecules. Would larger molecules be able to carry more information? Explain.

REFERENCES ON THE WORLD WIDE WEB

1. **Endocrinology Web Site.**   The American Association of Clinical Endocrinologists sponsors this site, which has information on many endocrine-related topics.

    http://www.aace.com/other

2. **Endocrine System.**   This site provides an overview of the endocrine system.

    http://www.indiana.edu/~anat215/endo.htm

3. **Reproductive Endocrinology.**   Learn about reproductive endocrinology at this site. It is maintained by Penn State.

    http://www.hmc.psu.edu/depts/obgyn/repend.htm

4. **Endocrines and Reproduction.**   This site includes valuable information on the endocrine system and hormones vital in reproduction.

    http://www.umds.ac.uk/elsewhere/physiology/banks/endorep.html

5. **Human Anatomy On-Line.**   This site provides an abundance of information on the human endocrine system.

    http://www.innerbody.com/

chapter 36

CIRCULATION, IMMUNITY, AND GAS EXCHANGE

Outline

Concepts

1. Animal transport and circulatory systems move substances from one part of the body to another, and between the animal's external environment and extracellular fluid.
2. Some invertebrates have specific transport systems, such as gastrovascular cavities. The circulatory system of more complex animals consists of a central pumping heart, blood vessels, blood, and an ancillary lymphatic system.
3. Invertebrates do not have immune systems with special cells that recognize and destroy specific foreign agents. Vertebrates have both nonspecific and specific mechanisms for defending themselves against microorganisms, foreign matter, and cancer cells.
4. Some invertebrates depend solely on gases, nutrients, and wastes diffusing between body surfaces and individual cells. Others have either open or closed circulatory systems for transporting gases, wastes, and nutrients.
5. Animals have five main types of respiratory systems: simple diffusion across plasma membranes, tracheae, cutaneous (integument or body surface) exchange, gills, and lungs.
6. Gas diffuses between the environment and cells of an animal's body from areas of higher concentration to areas of lower concentration. In large and active animals, respiratory pigments and ventilation—the active movement of air into and out of a respiratory system—increase gas exchange.

Would You Like to Know . . .

1. why a mammalian red blood cell is shaped like a doughnut without a complete hole? (p. 609)
2. if blood in human veins is bluish, why it appears red when you cut a vein and begin to bleed? (p. 609)
3. what a blood pressure reading of 120/80 mm Hg means? (p. 614)
4. why organ and tissue transplants are often rejected except between identical twins? (p. 617)
5. how land snails breathe? (p. 620)
6. how salamanders that do not have lungs breathe? (p. 621)

This chapter answers these and other useful questions.

This chapter contains evolutionary concepts, which are set off in this font.

INTERNAL TRANSPORT AND CIRCULATORY SYSTEMS

All animals must maintain a homeostatic balance in their bodies. This need requires that nutrients, metabolic wastes, and respiratory gases be circulated through the animal's body. Any system of moving fluids that reduces the functional diffusion distance that nutrients, wastes, and gases must traverse is an internal transport or circulatory system. The nature of the system directly relates to the size, complexity, and lifestyle of the animal in question. The first part of this chapter discusses some of these transport and circulatory systems.

TRANSPORT SYSTEMS IN INVERTEBRATES

Because protozoa are small, with high surface-area-to-volume ratios (see figure 3.3), all they need for gas, nutrient, and waste exchange is simple diffusion. In protozoa, the plasma membrane and cytoplasm are the media through which materials diffuse to various parts of the organism, or between the organism and the environment (see figure 36.16a).

Some invertebrates have evolved specific transport systems. For example, sponges circulate water from the external environment through their bodies, instead of circulating an internal fluid (figure 36.1a). Cnidarians, such as *Hydra*, have a fluid-filled internal **gastrovascular cavity** (figure 36.1b). This cavity supplies nutrients for all body cells lining the cavity, provides oxygen from the water in the cavity, and is a reservoir for carbon dioxide and other wastes. Simple body movement moves the fluid.

The gastrovascular cavity of flatworms, such as the planarian *Dugesia*, is more complex than that of *Hydra*. In the planarian, branches penetrate to all parts of the body (figure 36.1c). Because this branched gastrovascular cavity runs close to all body cells, diffusion distances for nutrients, gases, and wastes are short. Body movement helps distribute materials to various parts of the body. One disadvantage of this system is that it limits these animals to relatively small sizes or to shapes that maintain small diffusion distances.

Pseudocoelomate invertebrates, such as rotifers, gastrotrichs, and nematodes, use the coelomic fluid of their body cavity for transport (figure 36.1d). Most of these animals are small, and movements of the body against the coelomic fluids, which are in direct contact with the internal tissues and organs, produce adequate transport. A few other invertebrates (e.g., ectoprocts, sipunculans, echinoderms) also depend largely on the body cavity as a coelomic transport chamber.

Beginning with the molluscs, transport functions occur with a separate circulatory system. A **circulatory** or **cardiovascular system** (Gr. *kardia*, heart + L. *vascular*, vessel) is a specialized system in which a muscular, pumping heart moves the fluid medium called either hemolymph or blood in a specific direction determined by the presence of unidirectional blood vessels.

The animal kingdom has two basic types of circulatory systems: open and closed. In an **open circulatory system,** the heart pumps hemolymph out into the body cavity or at least through parts of the cavity, where the hemolymph bathes the cells, tissues,

and organs. In a **closed circulatory system,** blood circulates in the confines of tubular vessels. The coelomic fluid of some invertebrates also has a circulatory role either in concert with, or instead of, the hemolymph or blood.

The annelids, such as the earthworm, have a closed circulatory system in which blood travels through vessels delivering nutrients to cells and removing wastes (figure 36.1e).

Most molluscs and arthropods have open circulatory systems in which hemolymph directly bathes the cells and tissues rather than being carried only in vessels (figure 36.1f). For example, an insect's heart pumps hemolymph through vessels that open into a body cavity (hemocoel).

CHARACTERISTICS OF INVERTEBRATE COELOMIC FLUID, HEMOLYMPH, AND BLOOD CELLS

As previously noted, some animals (e.g., echinoderms, annelids, sipunculans) use coelomic fluid as a supplementary or sole circulatory system. Coelomic fluid may be identical in composition to interstitial fluids or may differ, particularly with respect to specific proteins and cells. Coelomic fluid transports gases, nutrients, and waste products. It also may function in certain invertebrates (annelids) as a hydrostatic skeleton (see figure 32.10).

Hemolymph (Gr. *haima*, blood + *lympha*, water) is the circulating fluid of animals with an open circulatory system. Most arthropods, ascidians, and many molluscs have hemolymph. In these animals, a heart pumps hemolymph at low pressures through vessels to tissue spaces (hemocoel) and sinuses. Generally, the hemolymph volume is high and the circulation slow. In the process of movement, essential gases, nutrients, and wastes are transported.

Many times, hemolymph has noncirculatory functions. For example, in insects, hemolymph pressure assists in molting of the old cuticle and in inflation of the wings. In certain jumping spiders, hydrostatic pressure of the hemolymph provides a hydraulic mechanism for limb extension.

The coelomic fluid, hemolymph, or blood of most animals contains circulating cells called blood cells or **hemocytes.** Some cells contain a respiratory pigment, such as hemoglobin, and are called erythrocytes or red blood cells. These cells are usually present in high numbers to facilitate oxygen transport. Cells that do not contain respiratory pigments have other functions, such as blood clotting.

The number and types of blood cells vary dramatically in different invertebrates. For example, annelid blood contains hemocytes that are phagocytic. The coelomic fluid contains a variety of coelomocytes (amoebocytes, eleocytes, lampocytes, linocytes) that function in phagocytosis, glycogen storage, encapsulation, defense responses, and excretion. The hemolymph of molluscs has two general types of hemocytes (amoebocytes and granulocytes) that have most of the aforementioned functions as well as nacrecation (pearl formation) in some bivalves. Insect hemolymph contains large numbers of various hemocyte types that function in phagocytosis, encapsulation, and clotting (figure 36.2).

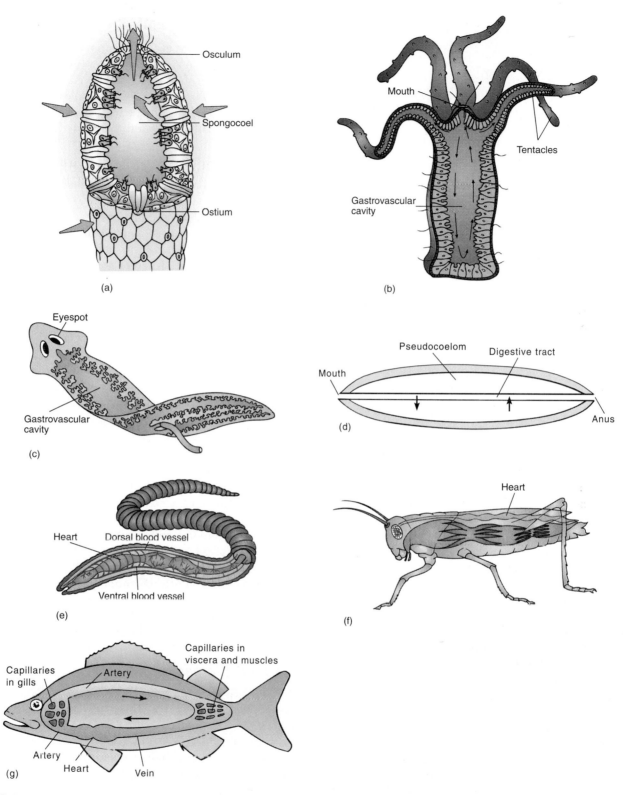

FIGURE 36.1

Some Transport and Circulatory Systems. (*a*) Sponges use water from the environment as a circulatory fluid by passing it through their bodies (blue arrows). (*b*) Cnidarians, such as this *Hydra*, also use water from the environment and circulate it (black arrows) through the gastrovascular cavity. Cells lining the cavity exchange gases and nutrients from the water and release waste into it. (*c*) The planarian's gastrovascular cavity is branched, allowing for more effective distribution of materials. (*d*) Pseudocoelomates use their body cavity fluid for internal transport from and to the digestive tract as the black arrows indicate. (*e*) The circulatory system of an earthworm contains blood that is kept separate from the coelomic fluid. This is an example of a closed circulatory system. (*f*) The dorsal heart of an arthropod, such as this grasshopper, pumps blood through an open circulatory system. In this example, blood and body cavity (hemocoelic) fluid are one and the same. (*g*) Octopuses, other cephalopod molluscs, annelids, and vertebrates, such as this fish, have closed circulatory systems. In a closed system, the walls of the heart and blood vessels are continuously connected, and blood never leaves the vessels. Black arrows indicate the direction of blood flow.

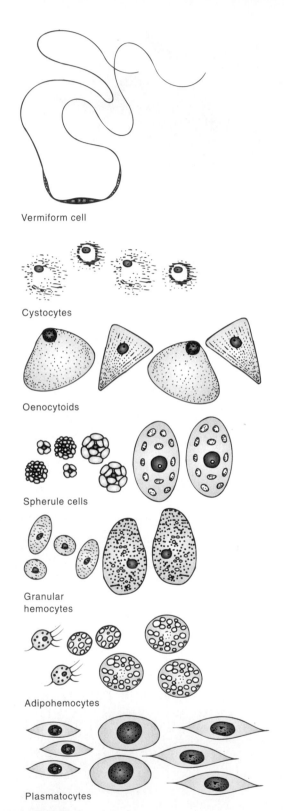

FIGURE 36.2

Examples of Invertebrate Hemocytes. These hemocytes are representative of those found in an insect. The different cells function in phagocytosis, agglutination, nutrient storage, wound repair, formation of connective tissue cells, and lipid transport.

TRANSPORT SYSTEMS IN VERTEBRATES

All vertebrates have a closed circulatory system in which the walls of the heart and blood vessels are continuously contracted, and blood never leaves the blood vessels (figure 36.1g). Blood moves from the heart, through arteries, arterioles, capillaries, venules, veins, and back to the heart. Exchange between the blood and extracellular fluid only occurs at the capillary level.

CHARACTERISTICS OF VERTEBRATE BLOOD AND BLOOD CELLS

Overall, vertebrate blood transports oxygen, carbon dioxide, and nutrients; defends against harmful microorganisms, cells, and viruses; prevents blood loss through coagulation (clotting); and helps regulate body temperature and pH. Because it is a liquid, vertebrate blood is classified as a specialized type of connective tissue. Like other connective tissues, blood contains a fluid matrix called plasma and cellular elements called formed elements.

Plasma

Plasma (Gr., anything formed or molded), is the straw-colored, liquid part of blood. In mammals, plasma is about 90% water and provides the solvent for dissolving and transporting nutrients. A group of proteins (albumin, fibrinogen, and globulins) comprises another 7% of the plasma. The concentration of these plasma proteins influences the distribution of water between the blood and extracellular fluid. Because albumin represents about 60% of the total plasma proteins, it plays important roles with respect to water movement. Fibrinogen is necessary for blood coagulation (clotting), and the globulins include the immunoglobulins and various metal-binding proteins. **Serum** is plasma from which the proteins involved in blood clotting have been removed. The gamma globulin portion functions in the immune response because it consists mostly of antibodies. The remaining 3% of plasma is composed of electrolytes, amino acids, glucose and other nutrients, various enzymes, hormones, metabolic wastes, and traces of many inorganic and organic molecules.

Formed Elements

The **formed-element fraction** (cellular component) of vertebrate blood consists of erythrocytes (red blood cells; RBCs), leukocytes (white blood cells; WBCs), and platelets (thrombocytes) (figure 36.3). White blood cells are present in lower number than are red blood cells, generally being 1 to 2% of the blood by volume. White blood cells are divided into agranulocytes (without granules in the cytoplasm) and granulocytes (have granules in the cytoplasm). The two types of agranulocytes are lymphocytes and monocytes. The three types of granulocytes are eosinophils, basophils, and neutrophils. Fragmented cells are called platelets (thrombocytes). Each of these cell types is now discussed in more detail.

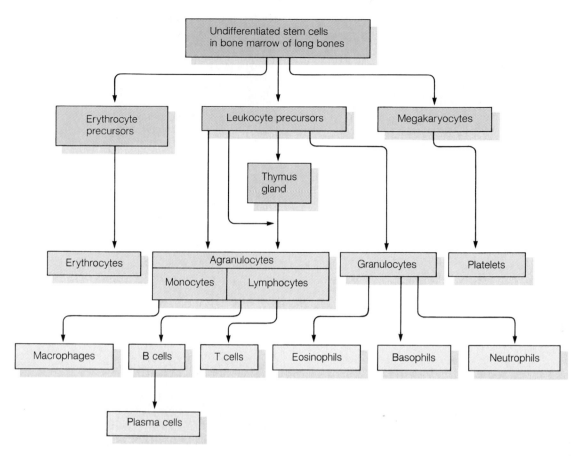

FIGURE 36.3

Cellular Components of Vertebrate Blood. Hematopoiesis is the process of blood cell production. Notice that all blood cells initially begin their lives in the bone marrow of long bones within a vertebrate's body.

Red Blood Cells   Red blood cells (erythrocytes; Gr. *erythros,* red + cells) vary dramatically in size, shape, and number in the different vertebrates (figure 36.4 and 36.5a). For example, the RBCs of most vertebrates are nucleated, but mammalian RBCs are enucleated (without a nucleus). Some fishes and amphibians also have enucleated RBCs. Among all vertebrates, the salamander *Amphiuma* has the largest RBC (figure 36.4a). Avian RBCs (figure 36.4c) are oval-shaped, nucleated, and larger than mammalian RBCs. Among birds, the ostrich has the largest RBC. Most mammalian RBCs are biconcave disks (figure 36.5a); however, the camel (figure 36.4e) and llama have elliptical RBCs. ❶ The shape of a biconcave disk provides a larger surface area for gas diffusion than a flat disk or sphere. Generally, the lower vertebrates tend to have fewer but larger RBCs than the higher invertebrates.

Almost the entire mass of a RBC consists of **hemoglobin** (Gr. *haima,* blood + L. *globulus,* little globe), an iron-containing protein. The major function of an erythrocyte is to pick up oxygen from the environment, bind it to hemoglobin to form **oxyhemoglobin,** and transport it to body tissues. Blood rich in oxyhemoglobin is bright red. As oxygen diffuses into the tissues, blood becomes darker and appears blue when observed through the blood vessel walls. ❷ However, when this less oxygenated blood is exposed to oxygen (such as when a vein is cut and a mammal be-

gins to bleed), it instantaneously turns bright red. Hemoglobin also carries waste carbon dioxide (in the form of **carbaminohemoglobin**) from the tissues to the lungs (or gills) for removal from the body.

White Blood Cells   White blood cells (leukocytes) (Gr. *leukos,* white + cells) are scavengers that destroy microorganisms at infection sites, remove foreign chemicals, and remove debris that results from dead or injured cells. All WBCs are derived from immature cells (called stem cells) in bone marrow by a process called **hematopoiesis** (Gr. *hemato,* blood + *poiein,* to make; *see figure 36.3*).

Among the granulocytes, **eosinophils** are phagocytic, and ingest foreign proteins and immune complexes rather than bacteria (figure 36.5b). In mammals, eosinophils also release chemicals that counteract the effects of certain inflammatory chemicals released during allergic reactions. **Basophils** are the least numerous WBC (figure 36.5c). When they react with a foreign substance, their granules release histamine and heparin. Histamine causes blood vessels to dilate and leak fluid at a site of inflammation, and heparin prevents blood clotting. **Neutrophils** are the most numerous of the white blood cells (figure 36.5d). They are chemically attracted to sites of inflammation and are active phagocytes.

FIGURE 36.4

Comparison of Red Blood Cells from a Variety of Vertebrates.
Light micrographs of (*a*) a nucleated cell from a salamander;
(*b*) nucleated cells from a snake; (*c*) nucleated cells from an ostrich;
(*d*) enucleated cells (biconcave disk) from a red kangaroo; and
(*e*) enucleated cells (ellipsoid) from a camel (bar = 10 μm).

FIGURE 36.5

Blood Cells. (*a*) The biconcave shape of human erythrocytes
(SEM ×1,500). (*b*) Red-staining cytoplasmic granules characterize
an eosinophil. (*c*) Blue-staining granules characterize a basophil.
(*d*) Light-pink granules and a multilobed nucleus characterize a
neotrophil. Cells in *b–d* are also known as granulocytes. The agranulocytes consist of large monocytes (*e*) and lymphocytes (*f*). (*b–f* are
LM ×710.)

The two types of agranulocytes are the **monocytes** and **lymphocytes** (figure 36.5*e,f*). Two distinct types of lymphocytes are B
cells and T cells, both of which are central to the immune response. **B cells** originate in the bone marrow and colonize the
lymphoid tissue, where they mature. In contrast, **T cells** are associated with and influenced by the thymus gland before they colonize lymphoid tissue and play their role in the immune response.
When B cells are activated, they divide and differentiate to produce **plasma cells.**

Platelets (Thrombocytes)   Platelets (so named because of their platelike flatness), or **thrombocytes** (Gr. *thrombus*,
clot + cells), are disk-shaped cell fragments that initiate blood
clotting. When a blood vessel is injured, platelets immediately
move to the site and clump, attaching themselves to the damaged
area, and thereby beginning the process of blood coagulation.

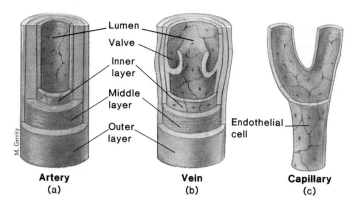

FIGURE 36.6

Structure of Blood Vessels. (*a,b*) The walls of arteries and veins have three layers (tunicae). The outermost layer consists of connective tissue, the middle layer has elastic and smooth muscle tissue, and the inner layer consists of a single layer of smooth endothelial cells (endothelium). Notice that the wall of an artery is much thicker than the wall of a vein. The middle layer is greatly reduced in a vein. (*c*) A capillary consists of a single layer of endothelial cells.

VERTEBRATE BLOOD VESSELS

Arteries are elastic blood vessels that carry blood away from the heart to the organs and tissues of the body. The central canal of an artery (and of all blood vessels) is a lumen. Surrounding the lumen of an artery is a thick wall composed of three layers, or tunicae (L. *tunica*, covering) (figure 36.6*a*).

Most **veins** are relatively inelastic, large vessels that carry blood from the body tissues to the heart. The wall of a vein contains the same three layers (tunicae) as arterial walls, but the middle layer is much thinner, and one or more valves are present (figure 36.6*b*). The valves permit blood flow in only one direction, which is important in returning the blood to the heart.

Arteries lead to terminal **arterioles** (those closest to a capillary). The arterioles branch to form **capillaries** (L. *capillus*, hair), which connect to **venules** and then to veins. Capillaries are generally composed of a single layer of endothelial cells and are the most numerous blood vessels in an animal's body (figure 36.6*c*). An abundance of capillaries makes an enormous surface area available for the exchange of gases, fluids, nutrients, and wastes between the blood and nearby cells.

Stop and Ask Yourself

1. Why don't protozoa need a circulatory system?
2. How does circulation occur in sponges and cnidarians? How does circulation occur in pseudocoelomates?
3. What is the difference between an open and closed circulatory system? What type of cells is in each of these systems?
4. What are the different blood vessels in a vertebrate?

THE HEARTS AND CIRCULATORY SYSTEMS OF BONY FISHES, AMPHIBIANS, AND REPTILES

The heart and blood vessels changed greatly as vertebrates moved from water to land and as endothermy evolved. Examples of these trends are now presented.

The bony fish heart has two chambers—the atrium and ventricle (figure 36.7*a*). Blood leaves the heart via the ventral aorta, which goes to the gills. In the gills, blood becomes oxygenated, loses carbon dioxide, and enters the dorsal aorta. The dorsal aorta distributes blood to all of the body organs, and then blood returns to the heart via the venous system. Because blood only passes through the heart once, this system is called a single circulation circuit. This circuit has the advantage of circulating oxygenated blood from the gills to the systemic capillaries in all organs almost simultaneously. However, the circulation of blood through the gill capillaries offers resistance to flow. Blood pressure and rates of flow to other organs are thus appreciably reduced. This arrangement probably could not support the high metabolic rates present in some birds and mammals.

In amphibians and reptiles, the evolution of a double circulatory circuit, in which blood passes through the heart twice during its circuit through the body, has overcome the slow blood-flow problem. Amphibians and most reptiles have hearts that are not fully divided in two. In amphibians, a single ventricle pumps blood both to the lungs and the rest of the body (figure 36.7*b*). However, because most amphibians absorb more oxygen through their skin than through their lungs or gills, blood returning from the skin also contributes oxygenated blood to the ventricle. The blood pumped out to the rest of the body is thus highly oxygenated.

In the heart of most reptiles, the ventricle is partially divided into a right and left side (figure 36.7*c*). Oxygenated blood from the lungs returns to the left side of the heart via the pulmonary vein and does not mix much with deoxygenated blood in the right side of the heart. When the ventricles contract, blood is pumped out two aortae for distribution throughout the body, as well as to the lungs. The incomplete separation of the ventricles is an important adaptation for reptiles, such as turtles, because it allows blood to be diverted away from the pulmonary circulation during diving and when the turtle is withdrawn into its shell. This conserves energy and diverts blood to vital organs during the time when the lungs cannot be ventilated.

THE HEARTS AND CIRCULATORY SYSTEMS OF BIRDS AND MAMMALS

Even though the physiological separation of blood in left and right ventricles is almost complete in reptiles, the complete anatomical separation of ventricles occurs only in crocodilians, birds, and mammals (figure 36.7*d*). This facilitates the double circulation required to maintain high blood pressure. High blood pressure is important in the rapid delivery of oxygenated nutrient-rich blood to tissues with high metabolic rates.

Gill capillaries

Lung and skin capillaries

Lung capillaries

Lung capillaries

Ventral aorta   Dorsal aorta

Conus arteriosus

Ventricle

Atrium

Sinus venosus

Right atrium   Left atrium

Ventricle

Aorta

Pulmonary artery   Pulmonary vein

Right atrium   Left atrium

Right ventricle   Left ventricle

Right arch   Aorta

Right atrium   Left atrium

Right ventricle   Left ventricle

Aorta

Systemic capillaries

Systemic capillaries

Systemic capillaries

Systemic capillaries

(a) Bony fishes

(b) Amphibians

(c) Most reptiles

(d) Crocodilians, birds, and mammals

FIGURE 36.7

Heart and Circulatory Systems of Various Vertebrates. Oxygenated blood is red; less oxygenated blood is blue; a mixture of oxygenated and less oxygenated blood is purple. (*a*) In bony fishes, the heart's two chambers (atrium, ventricle) pump in series. Respiratory and systemic circulations are not separate. (*b*) The amphibian heart has two atria and one ventricle. Blood from the lungs enters the left atrium, and blood from the body enters the right atrium. The blood from both atria empties into one ventricle, which then pumps it into the respiratory and systemic circulations. (*c*) Most reptiles exhibit a greater degree of anatomical division of the ventricle into two halves. (*d*) In crocodilians, birds, and mammals, the ventricle is completely divided, forming a four-chambered heart, with the blood flow through the lungs completely separated from the flow to other tissues. Black arrows indicate the direction of blood flow.

Blood circulates throughout the avian and mammalian body in two main circuits: the pulmonary and systemic circuits (figure 36.8). The **pulmonary circuit** supplies the blood only to the lungs. It carries oxygen-poor (deoxygenated) blood from the heart to the lungs, where carbon dioxide is removed, and oxygen is added. It then returns the oxygen-rich (oxygenated) blood to the heart for distribution to the rest of the body. The **systemic circuit** supplies all the cells, tissues, and organs of the body with oxygen-rich blood and returns oxygen-poor blood to the heart.

THE HUMAN HEART

The human heart is a hard-working pump that moves blood through the body. It pumps its entire blood volume (about 5 liters) every minute; about 8,000 liters of blood move through 96,000 km of blood vessels every day. The heart of an average adult beats about 70 times per minute—more than 100,000 times per day. In

a 70-year lifetime, the heart beats more than 2.6 billion times without fatiguing.

Most of the human heart is composed of cardiac muscle tissue called myocardium (Gr. *myo*, muscle). The outer protective covering of the heart, however, is fibrous connective tissue called the epicardium (Gr. *epi*, upon). Connective tissue and endothelium form the inside of the heart, the endocardium (Gr. *endo*, inside). (Endothelium is a single layer of epithelial cells lining the chambers of the heart, as well as the lumen of blood vessels; *see figure 36.6*.)

The left and right halves of the heart are two separate pumps, each containing two chambers (figure 36.9). In each half, blood first flows into a thin-walled atrium (L. *antichamber*, waiting room) (pl., atria), then into a thick-walled ventricle. Valves are between the upper (atria) and lower (ventricles) chambers. The tricuspid valve is between the right atrium and right ventricle, and the bicuspid valve is between the left atrium and left ventricle. (Collectively, these are referred to as the AV valves—atri-

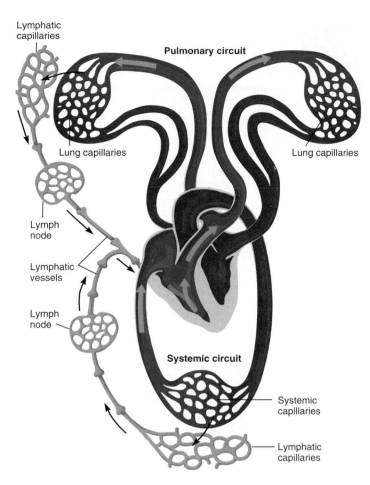

FIGURE 36.8

Circulatory Circuits. The cardiovascular system of a bird or mammal has two major capillary beds and transport circuits: the pulmonary circuit and systemic circuit. The lymphatic system consists of one-way vessels that are also involved in returning tissue fluid, called lymph, to the heart. The black arrows indicate the direction of lymph flow, and the colored (blue and pink) arrows indicate the direction of blood flow.

oventricular valves.) The pulmonary semilunar valve is at the exit of the right ventricle, and the aortic semilunar valve is at the exit of the left ventricle. (Collectively, these are referred to as the semilunar valves.) All of these valves open and close due to blood-pressure changes when the heart contracts during each heartbeat. Like the valves in veins, heart valves keep blood moving in one direction, preventing backflow.

The heartbeat is a sequence of muscle contractions and relaxations called the cardiac cycle. A "pacemaker," a small mass of tissue called the sinoatrial node (SA node) at the entrance to the right atrium, initiates each heartbeat (figure 36.10). (Because the pacemaker is in the heart, nervous innervation is not necessary, which is why a heart transplant without connection to nerves is possible.) The SA node initiates the cardiac cycle by producing an action potential that spreads over both atria, causing them to contract simultaneously. The action potential then passes to the atrioventricular node (AV node), near the interatrial septum. From here, the action potential continues through the atrioventricular bundle (bundle of His), at the tip of the interventricular

FIGURE 36.9

Structures of the Human Heart. Less oxygenated blood from the tissues of the body returns to the right atrium and flows through the tricuspid valve into the right ventricle. The right ventricle pumps the blood through the pulmonary semilunar valve into the pulmonary circuit, from which it returns to the left atrium and flows through the bicuspid valve into the left ventricle. The left ventricle then pumps blood through the aortic semilunar valve into the aorta. The various heart valves are shown in yellow.

FIGURE 36.10

Electrical Conduction System of the Human Heart. The SA node initiates the depolarization wave, which passes successively through the atrial myocardium to the AV node, the atrioventricular bundle, the right and left bundle branches, and the Purkinje fibers in the ventricular myocardium. Black arrows indicate the direction of the electrical current flow.

septum. The atrioventricular bundle divides into right and left branches, which are continuous with the Purkinje fibers in the ventricular walls. Stimulation of these fibers causes the ventricles to contract almost simultaneously and eject blood into the pulmonary and systemic circulations.

The action potential moving over the surface of the heart causes current flow, which can be recorded at the surface of the body as an electrocardiogram (ECG or EKG).

During each cycle, the atria and ventricles go through a phase of contraction called **systole** and a phase of relaxation called **diastole.** Specifically, while the atria are relaxing and filling with blood, the ventricles are also relaxed. As more and more blood accumulates in the atria, blood pressure rises, and the atria contract, forcing the AV valves open and causing blood to rush into the ventricles. When the ventricles contract, the AV valves close, and the semilunar valves open, allowing blood to be pumped into the pulmonary arteries and aorta. After blood has been ejected from the ventricles, they relax and start the cycle anew.

BLOOD PRESSURE

Ventricular contraction generates the fluid pressure, called **blood pressure,** that forces blood through the pulmonary and systemic circuits. More specifically, blood pressure is the force the blood exerts against the inner walls of blood vessels. Although such a force occurs throughout the vascular system, the term blood pressure most commonly refers to systemic arterial blood pressure.

Arterial blood pressure rises and falls in a pattern corresponding to the phases of the cardiac cycle. When the ventricles contract (ventricular systole), their walls force the blood in them into the pulmonary arteries and the aorta. As a result, the pressure in these arteries rises sharply. The maximum pressure achieved during ventricular contraction is called the **systolic pressure.** When the ventricles relax (ventricular diastole), the arterial pressure drops, and the lowest pressure that remains in the arteries before the next ventricular contraction is called the **diastolic pressure.**

③ In humans, normal systolic pressure for a young adult is about 120 mm Hg, which is the amount of pressure required to make a column of mercury (Hg) in a sphygmomanometer (sfig"mo-mah-nom'e-ter) rise 120 mm. Diastolic pressure is approximately 80 mm Hg. Conventionally, these readings are expressed as 120/80.

THE LYMPHATIC SYSTEM

The vertebrate **lymphatic system** begins with small vessels called lymphatic capillaries, which are in direct contact with the extracellular fluid surrounding tissues (*see figure 36.8*). The system has four major functions: (1) to collect and drain most of the fluid that seeps from the bloodstream and accumulates in the extracellular fluid; (2) to return small amounts of proteins that have left the cells; (3) to transport lipids that have been absorbed from the small intestine; and (4) to transport foreign particles and cellular debris to disposal centers called lymph nodes. The small lymphatic capillaries merge to form larger lymphatic vessels called lymphatics. Lymphatics are thin-walled vessels with valves that ensure the one-way flow of lymph. **Lymph** (L. *lympha,* clear water) is the extracellular fluid that accumulates in the lymph vessels. These vessels pass through the lymph nodes on their way back to

	MAJOR STRUCTURAL AND FUNCTIONAL COMPONENTS OF THE LYMPHATIC SYSTEM IN VERTEBRATES
TABLE 36.1	

STRUCTURE	FUNCTION
Lymphatic capillaries	Collect excess extracellular fluid in tissues
Lymphatics	Carry lymph from lymphatic capillaries to veins in the neck, where lymph returns to the bloodstream
Lymph nodes	House the WBCs that destroy foreign substances; play a role in antibody formation
Spleen	Filters foreign substances from blood; manufactures phagocytic lymphocytes; stores red blood cells; releases blood to the body when blood is lost
Thymus gland (in mammals)	Site of antibodies in the newborn; is involved in the initial development of the immune system; site of T-cell differentiation
Bursa of Fabricius (in birds)	A lymphoid organ at the lower end of the alimentary canal in birds; the site of B-cell maturation

the heart. Lymph nodes concentrate in several areas of the body and play an important role in the body's defense against disease.

In addition to the previously mentioned parts, the lymphatic system of birds and mammals consists of lymphoid organs—the spleen and either the bursa of Fabricius in birds or the thymus gland, tonsils, and adenoids in mammals. Table 36.1 summarizes the major components of the lymphatic system. The lymphatic system is also vital to an animal's defense against injury and attack.

Stop and Ask Yourself

5. What is a single circulatory circuit? What is a double circulatory circuit?

6. What is the cardiac cycle? What is blood pressure?

7. What are the four major functions of the lymphatic system?

IMMUNITY

Mechanisms (defenses) have evolved in animals that prevent unwanted cells, microorganisms, or agents from upsetting the animal's homeostasis. This section briefly examines the general innate defenses

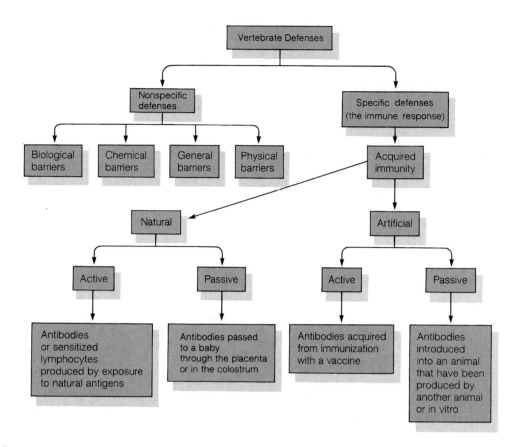

FIGURE 36.11

Various Aspects of the Immune Response: Different Vertebrate Defenses. The details of the vertebrate immune system are astonishingly complex. Many events have been omitted so that the overall organization of the immune response is clear.

of various animals and then the acquired immune response of vertebrates.

Invertebrates do not have immune systems with special cells that recognize and destroy specific foreign agents. However, many do have innate, internal defense mechanisms. For example, molluscs and insects have granulocytes that are highly phagocytic to foreign agents, and in arthropods (primarily insects), these cells can encapsulate foreign agents. Arthropods also possess another type of internal defense mechanism, called melanization, which involves depositing the dark pigment melanin around the foreign agent. Nacrezation, or pearl formation, is another innate defense mechanism of molluscs.

Vertebrates are continuously exposed to microorganisms, foreign macromolecules, or cancer cells that can cause disease. Fortunately, they have an immune system that defends against this exposure. **Immunity** (L. *immunis*, free of burden) refers to the general ability of an animal to resist harmful attack. The immune response is a large and specific complex of defensive elements, widely distributed throughout the body, that helps the animal defend against attack. These defenses can be divided into nonspecific and specific categories (figure 36.11). **Immunology** is the study of these defenses.

NONSPECIFIC DEFENSES

Nonspecific defenses are those general mechanisms that are inherited as part of the innate structure and function of each animal. These mechanisms act in concert as a first line of defense against intruders, before they can cause disease. Nonspecific defenses include biological barriers (inflammation and phagocytosis), chemical barriers (enzymatic action, interferons), general barriers (fever), and physical barriers (skin, mucous membranes).

SPECIFIC DEFENSES: THE IMMUNE RESPONSE

If nonspecific defenses are breached, the specific immune response is called upon for protection. This system consists of a number of immunological mechanisms in which certain white blood cells (lymphocytes) recognize the presence of particular foreign invaders or substances (antigens) and act to eliminate them. Lymphocytes may directly destroy antigens, or specialized proteins (antibodies) may form to either destroy the invader or target it for destruction by other cells (table 36.2).

As an overview, when a foreign invader stimulates B cells, they divide into plasma cells. Plasma cells respond to invaders by

TABLE 36.2	SPECIFIC DEFENSES OF THE VERTEBRATE IMMUNE SYSTEM
DEFENSE	**FUNCTION**
White Blood Cells	
B cells	Lymphocytes that differentiate into plasma cells after stimulation by antigen
Plasma cells	Cells that form from stimulated B cells and secrete antibodies
T cells	Lymphocytes that are produced in bone marrow and mature in the thymus gland
Helper T cells	Stimulate the rapid divisions of lymphocytes and, along with them, mount an attack against foreign invaders
Natural killer cells	Destroy body cells infected with viruses or fungal parasites as well as cancer cells
Suppressor T cells	Slow down or stop the immune response
Memory cells	A portion of the B and T cells produced during a first-time encounter with a specific invader and held in reserve; they make possible a rapid response to subsequent encounters with the same type of invader
Macrophages	Highly phagocytic lymphocytes; alert helper T cells' response to the presence of foreign intruders
Secreted Chemicals	
Antibodies	Receptor molecules that bind specific foreign targets and tag them for destruction by phagocytes or the complement system
Cytokines, interleukins	Secretions by which white blood cells communicate with each other
Perforin-1	A protein that certain T cells secrete and that punches a hole in target cells and kills them

secreting specific proteins (antibodies) into the blood and lymph. These antibodies are specifically directed against proteins (antigens) on the invader that caused their formation. Because antibodies are soluble in blood and lymph, they provide **humoral** (L. *humor*, a liquid) **immunity.** The humoral response defends mostly against bacteria, bacterial toxins, and viruses that enter the animal's various body-fluid systems.

T cells do not secrete antibodies. Instead, they attack host cells that have been infected by microorganisms, tissue cells transplanted from one animal to another, or cancer cells. T cells (e.g., helper T cells) also influence the activity of other components of the immune system. Because T cells must come into close physical contact with foreign cells or infected cells to destroy them, they are said to provide **cell-mediated immunity.**

Acquired Immunity

Acquired immunity refers to the type of specific immunity that develops after exposure to an antigen or is produced after antibodies are transferred from one animal to another. It can be natural or artificial, active or passive (figure 36.11).

Naturally Acquired Naturally acquired active immunity occurs when an animal's immune system comes into contact with an appropriate antigenic stimulus during the course of daily activities. The immune system responds by producing antibodies and sensitized lymphocytes that inactivate the antigen. The immunity produced can be either lifelong (e.g., measles or chicken pox) or last for only a few years (e.g., tetanus).

Naturally acquired passive immunity involves the transfer of antibodies from one host to another. For example, in a pregnant mammal, some of the female's antibodies pass across the placenta to the fetus. Whatever immunity the female has transfers to the newborn. Certain other antibodies pass from the female to her offspring in the first secretions (called colostrum) from the mammary glands. Unfortunately, naturally acquired passive immunity generally lasts only a short time (weeks or months at the most).

Artificially Acquired Artificially acquired active immunity results from immunizing an animal with a vaccine. A **vaccine** consists of a preparation of either killed microorganisms; living, weakened (attenuated) microorganisms; or inactivated bacterial toxins (called toxoids) that is administered to an animal to induce immunity. Such deliberate causing of antibody production is called **immunization.**

Artificially acquired passive immunity results from introducing into an animal antibodies that have been produced either in another animal or by specific in vitro methods. Although this type of immunity is immediate, it is short-lived (about 3 weeks). An example is botulinum antitoxin produced in a horse and given to a human suffering from botulism food poisoning.

Antigens

An elaborate recognition system allows the mammalian immune system to distinguish "self" from "nonself". Prior to birth, the body inventories the proteins and various other large molecules present in the body ("self") and inactivates most of the genetic programming for making antibodies to self-molecules. Subsequently, the body can distinguish self-molecules from foreign, nonself substances, and lymphocytes can produce specific immunological reactions against the foreign material, leading to its removal. Foreign ("nonself") substances (markers) to which lymphocytes respond are called **antigens** (antibody generator). Most

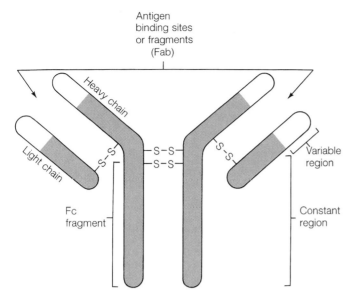

FIGURE 36.12

Antibody Structure. The antibody molecule consists of two identical heavy chains and two light chains joined by disulfide bonds. The five types of the heavy chain give rise to the five types of immunoglobulins (IgG, IgA, IgM, IgD, IgE) with distinct functions. There are antibodies against virtually any potential antigen because the variable regions can form millions of different attachment sites that bind to different antigens.

antigens are large proteins or other complex molecules with a molecular weight generally greater than 10,000.

Antibodies

Plasma cells manufacture **antibodies** (immunoglobulins), a group of recognition glycoproteins present in the blood and tissue fluids of birds and mammals. All antibody molecules have a basic Y structure composed of four chains of polypeptides connected by disulfide bonds (figure 36.12). The arms of the Y contain binding sites or fragments (Fab) for specific invaders (i.e., antigens). The tail of the Y can activate the complement system (20 distinct defensive proteins in serum) or bind to receptors on phagocytic cells.

Antibody-Mediated (Humoral) Immune Response

B cells are of great importance in fighting invading organisms because they produce the antibodies that identify the antigens for destruction. The B cells carry some of their particular antibodies on their plasma membrane. When an antigen comes into contact with a B cell whose antibodies recognize the antigen, the B cell binds to the antigen. When stimulated by one kind of T cell (a helper T cell), the B cell divides many times, producing plasma cells that produce and secrete more of this particular antibody. These antibody molecules are carried through the circulation. If they encounter antigens, the antibodies bind to the antigen mol-

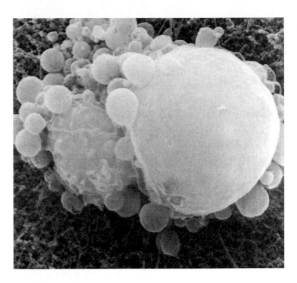

FIGURE 36.13

Natural Killer (NK) Cell Destroying a Cancer Cell. Upon contact with a cancer cell (right), a natural killer cell (left) releases toxic chemicals, such as perforin-1, that punch holes in the cancer cell's plasma membrane, causing the cancer cell to die.

ecules and thus mark them for destruction by other parts of the immune system (e.g., macrophages).

Cell-Mediated Immune Response

Unlike B cells that produce the antibodies that subsequently mark antigens for destruction, T cells are directly involved in destroying invading cells, as well as in regulating other parts of the immune system. T-cell responses are called the cell-mediated immune response.

Natural killer (NK) cells, also called cytotoxic T cells, recognize cell-surface changes on cancer cells, virus-infected cells, fungi, bacteria, protozoa, or helminth parasites (figure 36.13). ④ The action of NK cells is why tissue and organ transplants are rejected in birds or mammals. In the rejection mechanism, NK cells enter the transplanted tissue through the blood vessels, recognize it as foreign, attach to the tissue, and destroy it. However, the body tolerates tissue and organ transplants between identical twins who have identical sets of DNA and, hence, identical self-recognition marker regions.

T cells also regulate the activity of other parts of the immune system. For example, suppose several bacteria penetrate the first line of defense (the skin) through an abrasion or cut. Inflammation occurs, and macrophages phagocytize the bacteria (figure 36.14). The macrophages destroy most of the antigens (bacteria), but some of the antigens are moved to the surface of the plasma membrane of both macrophages and B cells, where they are displayed alongside the self-recognition marker. It is this specific combination of self-recognition marker and antigen that helper T cells recognize.

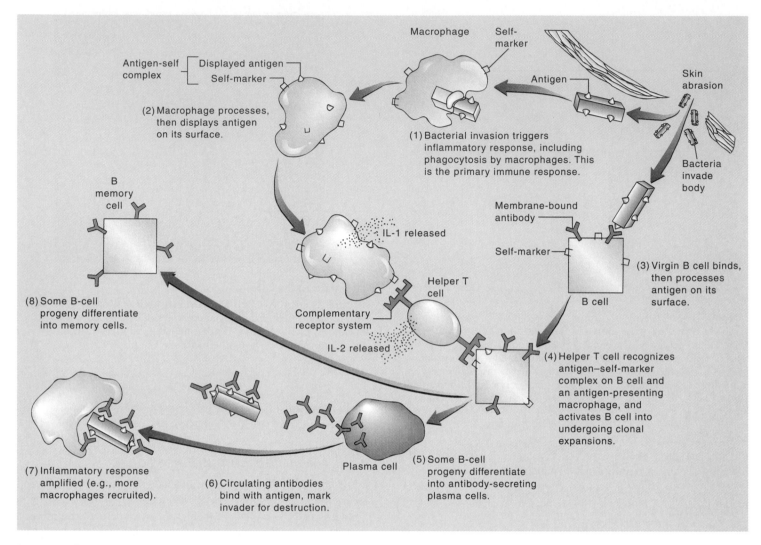

FIGURE 36.14

Cell-Mediated Immune Response. Helper T cells activate B cells to differentiate into plasma cells that produce antibodies. Notice that different cells are involved: macrophages, helper T cells, and B cells. The interaction of these three cells finally causes B cells to differentiate into antibody-producing plasma cells. The self-markers consist of the major histocompatibility complex.

When the macrophage reacts with a helper T cell, it releases interleukin-1 (IL-1). Interleukin-1 stimulates other helper T cells to secrete interleukin-2 (IL-2), which stimulates their (the helper T cells) growth and cell division. Some of the interleukin-2 that helper T cells produce acts on sensitized B cells. Sensitized B cells have recognized and processed the antigen onto their plasma membrane alongside their self-recognition marker (figure 36.14). These stimulated B cells mature and divide into differentiated plasma cells.

Primary and Secondary Immune Responses: Immunological Memory

The **primary immune response** is the response an animal generates during its first encounter with an antigen. During this response, the antigen disappears from the blood because it is either bound to antibodies and/or phagocytized by macrophages.

Most of the B cells producing the antibodies also die. However, if the same antigen enters the body a second time, the body mounts a **secondary immune response** that is faster and more extensive than the primary response (figure 36.15). This rapid response is possible because the immune system has stored a "memory" of the antigen: Some of the original B cells differentiated into **memory cells** (*see figure 36.14*) that remain in the body for life. Memory cells from B-cell clones continually expose antibodies on their plasma-membrane surface. If the antigen invades the body again, these memory cells rapidly produce large numbers of antibody-secreting B cells.

Evolution of the Vertebrate Immune System

The evolution of the vertebrate immune system parallels that of the lymphatic system. Jawless vertebrates (cyclostomes), cartilaginous fishes (chondrichthians), and bony fishes (osteichthians)

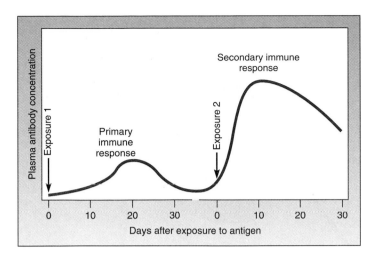

FIGURE 36.15

Primary and Secondary Immune Responses: Immunological Memory. The antibody concentration increases more rapidly during a secondary immune response than during a primary response. Note that the secondary response peaks in 10 days, whereas the primary response does not peak for about 20 days. The magnitude (plasma antibody concentration) of the secondary response is also many times that of the primary response.

have networks of small, blind vessels that accompany the veins and help the capillaries drain the tissues. These vessels developed from veins and empty into them at frequent intervals. They represent the earliest stage in the evolution of the lymphatic system; however, no lymph nodes or lymphocytes are present.

Teleosts and tetrapods have independently evolved lymphatic systems in which lymphatic capillaries help drain most of the tissues of the body. Lymph nodes and lymphocytes occur in a few aquatic birds and are abundant in mammals. Additional aggregations of lymphatic tissue, T cells, and immunoglobulins evolved in birds and mammals, such as the distinct bursa of Fabricius in birds and the thymus gland in mammals (see table 36.1). Both of these organs are particularly large and active in late fetal and young individuals, but gradually regress as the animal matures. They play a functional role in the processing of lymphocytes and the development of immunological maturity.

Stop and Ask Yourself

8. What is the relationship between the lymphatic and immune systems?
9. What is a self-recognition marker? How does it function?
10. How does an antibody differ from an antigen?
11. What is the difference between an antibody-mediated immune response and a cell-mediated immune response?
12. How do NK cells function?
13. How does immunological memory occur?

GAS EXCHANGE

To take advantage of the rich source of energy that earth's organic matter represents, animals must solve two practical problems. First, they must break down and digest the organic matter so that it can enter the cells that are to metabolize it (chapter 37 describes this digestive process). Second, they must provide cells with both an adequate supply of oxygen required for aerobic respiration and a way of eliminating the carbon dioxide that aerobic respiration produces. This process of gas exchange with the environment, also called external respiration, is the subject of the rest of this chapter.

RESPIRATORY SURFACES

Protists and animals have five main types of respiratory systems (surfaces): (1) simple diffusion across plasma membranes, (2) tracheae, (3) cutaneous (integument or body surface) exchange, (4) gills, and (5) lungs. Each of these surfaces is now discussed.

INVERTEBRATE RESPIRATORY SYSTEMS

In single-celled protists, such as protozoa, **diffusion** across the plasma membrane moves gases into and out of the organism (figure 36.16a). Some multicellular invertebrates either have very flat bodies (e.g., flatworms) in which all body cells are relatively close to the body surface or are thin-walled and hollow (e.g., *Hydra*) (figure 36.16b,c). Again, gases diffuse into and out of the animal.

Invertebrates such as earthworms that live in moist environments use **integumentary exchange.** Earthworms have capillary networks just under their integument, and they exchange gases with the air spaces among soil particles (see figure 22.14).

Most aquatic invertebrates carry out gas exchange with **gills.** The simplest gills are small, scattered projections of the skin, such as the gills of sea stars. Other aquatic invertebrates have their gas exchange structures in more restricted areas. For example, marine and annelid worms have prominent lateral projections called parapodia that are richly supplied with blood vessels and function as gills (see figure 22.7).

Crustaceans and molluscs have gills that are compact and protected with hard covering devices (see figure 21.11). Such gills divide into highly branched structures to maximize the area for gas exchange.

Some terrestrial invertebrates (e.g., insects, centipedes, and some mites, ticks, and spiders) have **tracheal systems** consisting of highly branched chitin-lined tubes called tracheae (figure 36.17a). Tracheae open to the outside of the body through spiracles, which usually have some kind of closure device to prevent excessive water loss. Spiracles lead to branching tracheal trunks that eventually give rise to smaller branches called tracheoles, whose blind ends lie close to all cells of the body. Since no cells are more than 2 or 3 μm from a tracheole, gases move between the tracheole and the tissues of the body by diffusion (figure 36.17b). Most insects have ventilating mechanisms that move air into and out of the trachea. For example, contracting flight muscles of

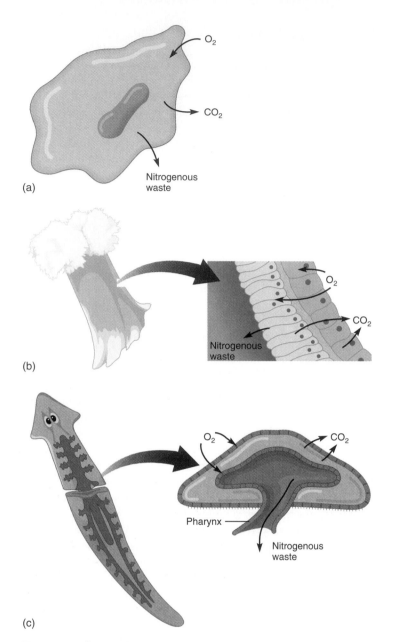

FIGURE 36.16

Invertebrate Respiration: Diffusion through Body Surfaces. The cells of small organisms, such as (a) protozoa, (b) cnidarians, and (c) flatworms, maintain close enough contact with the environment that they have no need for a respiratory system. Diffusion moves gases, as well as waste products, into and out of these organisms.

insects alternately compress and expand the large tracheal trunks and thereby ventilate the tracheae.

Arachnids possess tracheae, book lungs, or both. **Book lungs** are paired invaginations of the ventral body wall that are folded into a series of leaflike lamellae (figure 36.18). Air enters the book lung through a slitlike opening called a spiracle and circulates between lamellae. Respiratory gases diffuse between the hemolymph moving along the lamellae and the air in the air

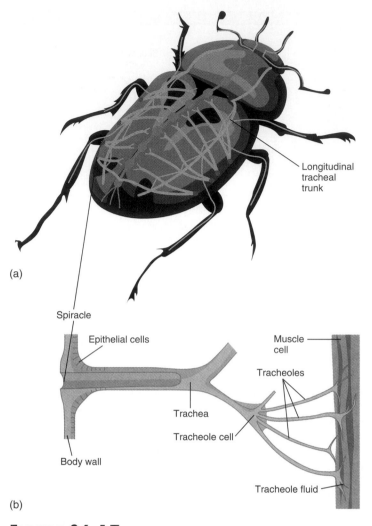

FIGURE 36.17

Invertebrate Respiration: A Tracheal System. (a) Tracheal system of an insect, showing the major tracheal trunks. (b) Tracheoles end at cells, and the terminal portions of tracheoles are fluid filled. The fluid acts as a solvent for gases.

chamber. Some ventilation also results from the contraction of a muscle attached to the dorsal side of the air chamber. This contraction dilates the chamber and opens the spiracle, but most gas movement is still by diffusion.

The only other major group of terrestrial invertebrates whose members have distinct air-breathing structures is the molluscan subclass Pulmonata—the land snails and slugs. ⑤ The gas-exchange structure in these animals is a **pulmonate lung** that opens to the outside via a pore called a **pneumostome** (Gr. *pneumo*, breath + *stoma*, mouth) (figure 36.19). This lung is derived from a feature common to molluscs in general—the mantle cavity—which in other molluscs houses the gills and other organs. Some of the more primitive pulmonate snails are aquatic (freshwater) and close the pneumostome during submergence. When the snail surfaces to breathe air, the pneumostome opens.

FIGURE 36.18

Invertebrate Respiration: A Book Lung. Structure of an arachnid (spider) book lung. Air enters through a spiracle into the air chamber by diffusion and by ventilation due to muscle contraction. Air diffuses from the air chamber into the lamellar spaces; hemolymph circulates through the blood lamellar spaces that alternate with air lamellar spaces. Small, peglike, surface projections hold the lamellae apart. Due to this structural arrangement, air (blue arrows) and blood (purple arrows) move on opposite sides of a lamella in a counter-current flow, allowing the exchange of respiratory gases by diffusion.

Most of the higher pulmonates are terrestrial and rely on their lungs for gas exchange. The lung may be ventilated by arching and then flattening the body, but most gas exchange occurs by diffusion through the pneumostome, which is open most of the time.

VERTEBRATE RESPIRATORY SYSTEMS

Aquatic vertebrates (fish, amphibians, and some reptiles) rely on one, or a combination of, the following surfaces for gas exchange: the cutaneous body surface, external filamentous gills, and internal lamellar gills. **Bimodal breathing** is the ability of an organism to exchange respiratory gases simultaneously with both air and water. A bimodal organism (e.g., some salamanders, crabs, barnacles, bivalve molluscs, and fishes [lungfishes]) uses gills for water breathing and lungs for air breathing. However, some gas exchange is always cutaneous, and some bimodal breathers are actually trimodal (skin, gills, and lungs). Bimodal breathing was an important respiratory adaptation that made possible the evolutionary transition between aquatic and terrestrial habitats. Fundamental changes in the structure and function of the respiratory organs accompanied the transition from water to air breathing. In air-breathing terrestrial vertebrates (reptiles, birds, and mammals) lungs replaced gills. These vertebrate surfaces and transitions are now discussed.

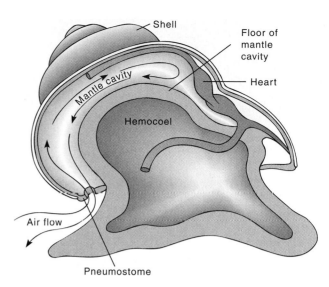

FIGURE 36.19

Invertebrate Respiration: The Pulmonate Lung. The mantle cavity of the pulmonate snail, *Lymnaea*, is highly vascularized and functions as a lung. Downward movement of the floor of the cavity increases the cavity's volume, so that air is drawn into the mantle cavity for respiration. Decreasing the volume of the mantle cavity expels the air. Air flows into and out of the lung through a single pore called the pneumostome. Black arrows indicate the direction of air flow.

CUTANEOUS EXCHANGE

Some vertebrates that have lungs or gills, such as some aquatic turtles, salamanders with lungs, snakes, fishes, and mammals, use **cutaneous respiration** or integumentary exchange to supplement gas exchange. However, cutaneous exchange is most highly developed in frogs, toads, lungless salamanders, and newts.

Amphibian skin has the simplest structure of all the major vertebrate respiratory organs (*see figure 32.6*). In frogs, a uniform capillary network lies in a plane directly beneath the epidermis. This vascular arrangement facilitates gas exchange between the capillary bed and the environment by both diffusion and convection. A slimy mucous layer that keeps amphibian skin moist and protects against injury aids in this gas exchange. **6** Some amphibians obtain about 25% or more of their oxygen by this exchange, and the lungless salamanders carry out all of their gas exchange through the skin and buccal-pharyngeal region.

GILLS

Gills are respiratory organs that have either a thin, moist, vascularized layer of epidermis to permit gas exchange across thin gill membranes, or a very thin layer of epidermis over highly vascularized dermis. Larval forms of a few fishes and amphibians have external gills projecting from their body (figure 36.20). Adult fishes have internal gills.

Gas exchange across internal gill surfaces is extremely efficient (figure 36.21). It occurs as blood and water move in opposite

FIGURE 36.20

Vertebrate Respiration: External Gills. This axolotl (*Ambystoma tigrinum*) has elaborate external gills with a large surface for gas exchange with the water.

directions on either side of the lamellar epithelium. For example, the water that passes over a gill first encounters vessels that are transporting blood with a low oxygen concentration into the body. Because the concentration (partial pressure) of the oxygen is lower in the blood than in the water, oxygen diffuses into the blood. Water then passes over the vessels carrying blood relatively high in oxygen from deep within the body. More oxygen diffuses inward because this blood still has less oxygen than the surrounding water. Carbon dioxide also diffuses into the water because its concentration (pressure) is higher in the blood than in the water. This countercurrent exchange mechanism provides efficient gas exchange by maintaining a concentration gradient between the blood and water over the length of the capillary bed.

LUNGS

A **lung** is an internal sac-shaped respiratory organ. The typical lung of a terrestrial vertebrate comprises one or more internal blind pouches into which air is either drawn or forced. The respiratory epithelium of lungs is thin, well vascularized, and divided into a large number of small units, which greatly increase the surface area for gaseous exchange between the lung air and the blood. This blind-pouch construction, however, limits the efficiency with which oxygen and carbon dioxide are exchanged with the atmosphere because only a portion of the lung air is ever replaced with any one breath. Birds are an exception in that they have very efficient lungs with a one-way pass-through system (*see figure 30.10*). For example, a mammal removes approximately 25% of the oxygen from air with each breath, whereas a bird removes approximately 90%.

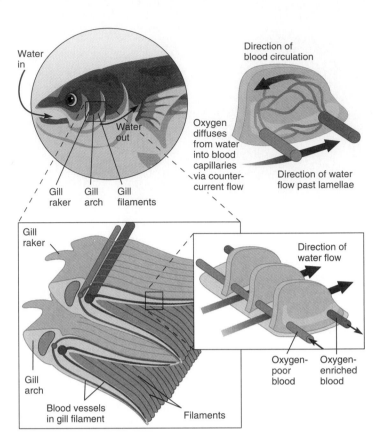

FIGURE 36.21

Vertebrate Respiration: Internal Gills. Removing the protective operculum exposes the feathery internal gills of this bony fish. Each side of the head has four gill arches, and each arch consists of many filaments. A filament houses capillaries within lamellae. Note that the direction of water flow opposes that of blood flow. This countercurrent flow allows the fish to extract the maximal amount of oxygen from the water.

The evolution of the vertebrate lung is related to the evolution of the swim bladder. The swim bladder is an air sac located dorsal to the digestive tract in the body of many modern fishes. Evidence indicates that both lungs and swim bladder evolved from a lunglike structure present in primitive fishes that were ancestors of both present-day fishes and tetrapods (amphibians, reptiles, birds, and mammals). These ancestral fishes probably had a ventral sac attached to their pharynx (*see figure 27.16*). This sac may have served as a supplementary gas-exchange organ when the fishes could not obtain enough oxygen through their gills (e.g., in stagnant or oxygen-depleted water). By swimming to the surface and gulping air into this sac, ancestral fishes could exchange gas through its wall.

Further evolution of this blind sac proceeded in two different directions (*see figure 27.16*). One adaptation is in the majority of modern bony fishes, where the swim bladder lies dorsal to the digestive tract. The other adaptation is in the form of the lungs, which are ventral to the digestive tract. A few present-day fishes and the tetrapods

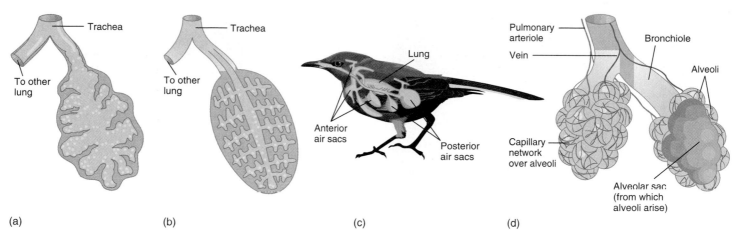

FIGURE 36.22

Vertebrate Respiration: Lungs. Evolution of the vertebrate lung, showing the increased surface area from (a) amphibians and (b) reptiles to (c) birds and (d) mammals. This evolution has paralleled the evolution of larger body size and higher metabolic rates.

FIGURE 36.23

Ventilation in Amphibians. The positive pressure pumping mechanism in a frog (*Rana*). The breathing cycle has several stages. (a) Air is taken into the mouth and pharynx by lowering the floor of the mouth. Notice that the glottis is closed. (b) The glottis is then opened, and air is permitted to escape from the lungs, passing over the air just taken in. (c) With the nostrils and mouth firmly shut, the floor of the mouth is raised. This positive pressure forces air into the lungs. (d) With the glottis closed, fresh oxygenated air can again be brought into the mouth and pharynx. Some gas exchange occurs in the mouth cavity (buccopharyngeal respiration), and frogs may repeat this "mouth breathing" movement several times before ventilating the lungs again. Red arrows indicate body wall movement, and blue arrows indicate air flow.

have ventral lungs. The evolution of the structurally complex lung paralleled the evolution of the larger body sizes and higher metabolic rates of endothermic vertebrates (birds and mammals), which necessitated an increase in lung surface area for gas exchange, compared to the smaller body size and lower metabolic rates of ectothermic vertebrates (figure 36.22).

LUNG VENTILATION

Ventilation is based on several physiological principles that apply to all air-breathing animals with lungs:

1. Air moves by bulk flow into and out of the lungs in the process called ventilation.
2. Oxygen and carbon dioxide diffuse across the respiratory surface of the lung tissue from pulmonary capillaries.

3. At systemic capillaries, oxygen and carbon dioxide diffuse between the blood and interstitial fluid in response to concentration gradients.
4. Oxygen and carbon dioxide diffuse between the interstitial fluid and body cells.

Vertebrates exhibit two different mechanisms for lung ventilation based on these physiological principles. Amphibians and some reptiles use a positive pressure pumping mechanism. They push air into their lungs. Most reptiles and all birds and mammals, however, use a negative pressure system; that is, they inhale (breathe in) by suction.

Figure 36.23 shows the positive pressure pumping mechanism of an amphibian. The muscles of the mouth and pharynx create a positive pressure to force air into the lungs.

Most reptiles (e.g., snakes, lizards, crocodilians) expand the body cavity with a posterior movement of the ribs to ventilate the

0.5 mm

0.5 mm

(a)

(b)

FIGURE 36.24

Gas Exchange Surfaces in Mammals and Birds. (*a*) The gas exchange surfaces in a mammal's lung are in saclike alveoli. Ventilation is by an ebb-and-flow mechanism (arrows), and the air inside the alveoli can never be completely replaced. (*b*) The smallest diameter passages in a bird lung are tubes that are open at both ends. Ventilation is by one-way flow (arrow), and complete replacement of air in the tubes is continuous.

lungs. This expansion decreases pressure in the lungs and draws air into the lungs. Elastic recoil of the lungs and the movement of the ribs and body wall, which compress the lungs, expel air. The ribs of turtles are a part of the shell (*see figure 29.4*); thus, movements of the body wall to which they attach are impossible. Turtles exhale by contracting muscles that force the viscera upward, compressing the lungs. They inhale by contracting muscles that increase the volume of the visceral cavity, creating negative pressure to draw air into the lungs.

Because of the high metabolic rates associated with flight, birds have a greater rate of oxygen consumption than any other vertebrate. Birds also use a negative pressure system to move air into and out of their lungs in an ebb and flow breathing pattern similar to mammals. However, birds also have a special lung ventilation mechanism that permits one-way flow over gas exchange surfaces. This mechanism makes bird lungs more efficient than mammalian lungs (figure 36.24). This is also why bird lungs are smaller than the lungs of mammals of comparable body size. Bird lungs have tunnel-like passages called parabronchi, which lead to air capillaries in which gas exchange occurs. The arrangement and functioning of a system of air sacs make one-way flow possible. These air sacs ramify throughout the body cavity, are collapsible, and open and close as a result of muscle contractions around them. Inhaled air bypasses the lungs and enters the abdominal (posterior) air sacs. It then passes through the lungs into the thoracic (anterior) air sacs. Finally, air is exhaled from the thoracic air sacs. This whole process requires two complete breathing cycles (figure 36.25).

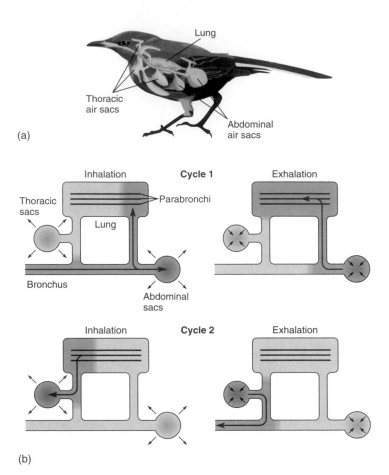

(a)

(b)

FIGURE 36.25

Gas Exchange Mechanism in Birds. (*a*) Birds have a number of large air sacs. Some of them (abdominal) are posterior to the small pair of lungs, and others (thoracic) are anterior to the lungs. The main bronchus (air passageway) that runs through each lung has connections to air sacs, as well as to the lung. In (*b*), abdominal and thoracic air sacs are sketched as single functional units to clarify their relationship to the lung and bronchus. (*b*) Air flow through the bird respiratory system. The darker blue portion in each diagram represents the volume of a single inhalation and distinguishes it from the remainder of the air in the system. Two full breathing cycles are needed to move the volume of gas taken in during a single inhalation through the entire system and out of the body. This system is associated with one-way flow through the gas exchange surfaces in the lungs. Black arrows indicate expansion and contraction of air sacs. Red arrows indicate movement of air.

HUMAN RESPIRATORY SYSTEM

The structure and function of external respiration in humans are typical of mammals. Thus the human respiratory system is used here to describe those principles that apply to all air-breathing mammals.

Air-Conducting Portion

Figure 36.26 shows the various organs of the human respiratory system. Air normally enters and leaves this system through either

Chapter 36 Circulation, Immunity, and Gas Exchange **625**

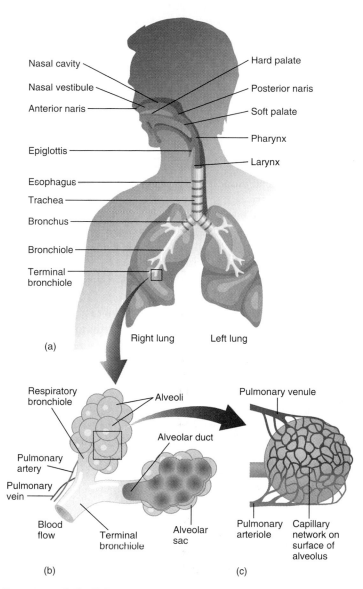

FIGURE 36.26

Organs of the Human Respiratory System. (*a*) Basic anatomy of the respiratory system. (*b,c*) The respiratory tubes end in minute alveoli, each of which is surrounded by an extensive capillary network.

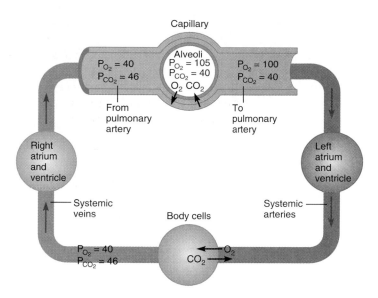

FIGURE 36.27

Gas Exchange between the Lungs and Tissues. Gases diffuse according to partial pressure (P) differences, as the numbers and arrows indicate.

Gas-Exchange Portion

Small tubes called alveolar ducts connect the respiratory bronchioles to grapelike outpouchings called **alveoli** (sing., alveolus) (L. *alveus*, hollow) (figure 36.26*b*). The alveoli cluster to form an alveolar sac. Surrounding the alveoli are many capillaries (figure 36.26*c*). Alveoli are the functional units of the lungs (gas-exchange portion). Passive diffusion, driven by a partial pressure gradient, moves oxygen from the alveoli into the blood and moves carbon dioxide from the blood into the alveoli (figure 36.27). Collectively, the alveoli provide a large surface area for gas exchange. If the alveolar epithelium of a human were removed from the lungs and put into a single layer of cells side by side, the cells would cover the area of a tennis court.

Ventilation

Breathing (also called pulmonary ventilation) has two phases: (1) inhalation, the intake of air; and (2) exhalation, the outflow of air. These air movements result from the rhythmic increases and decreases in thoracic cavity volume. Changes in thoracic volume lead to reversals in the pressure gradients between the lungs and the atmosphere; gases in the respiratory system follow these gradients. The mechanism of inhalation operates in the following way (figure 36.28):

1. Several sets of muscles, the main ones being the diaphragm and intercostal muscles, contract. The intercostal muscles stretch from rib to rib, and when they contract, they pull the ribs closer together, enlarging the thoracic cavity.

2. The thoracic cavity further enlarges when the diaphragm contracts and flattens.

nasal or oral cavities. From these cavities, air moves into the pharynx, which is a common area for both the respiratory and digestive tracts. The pharynx connects with the larynx (voice box) and with the esophagus that leads to the stomach. The epiglottis is a flap of cartilage that allows air to enter the trachea during breathing. It covers the trachea during swallowing to prevent food or water from entering.

During inhalation, air from the larynx moves into the trachea (windpipe), which branches into a right and left bronchus (pl., bronchi). After each bronchus enters the lungs, it branches into smaller tubes called bronchioles, then even smaller tubes called terminal bronchioles, and finally, the respiratory bronchioles, which are part of the gas-exchange portion of the respiratory system.

FIGURE 36.28

Ventilation of Human Lungs As an Example of Breathing in Mammals. (*a*) During inhalation, muscle contractions lift the ribs up and out (upper diagram arrows) and lower the diaphragm. These movements increase the size of the thoracic cavity and decrease the pressure around the lungs. This negative pressure causes more air to enter the lungs. (*b*) Exhalation follows the relaxation of the rib cage and diaphragm muscles, as the increased pressure forces the air out of the lungs. Arrows indicate the direction pressure changes take in the thoracic (lower diagrams) cavity during inhalation and exhalation.

3. The increased size of the thoracic cavity causes pressure in the cavity to drop below the atmospheric pressure. Air rushes into the lungs, and the lungs inflate.

During ordinary exhalation, air is expelled from the lungs in the following way:

1. The intercostal muscles and the diaphragm relax, allowing the thoracic cavity to return to its original, smaller size and increasing the pressure in the thoracic cavity.

2. Abdominal muscles contract, pushing the abdominal organs against the diaphragm, further increasing the pressure within the thoracic cavity.

3. The action in step 2 causes the elastic lungs to contract and compress the air in the alveoli. With this compression, alveolar pressure becomes greater than atmospheric pressure, causing air to be expelled (exhaled) from the lungs.

GAS TRANSPORT

As noted in the previous discussion, oxygen must be transported from the sites of environmental gas exchange to the various cells of an animal's body. Various systems (e.g., tracheae, cutaneous exchange, gills, lungs) help accomplish this transport.

As animals became larger and acquired higher metabolic rates, simple diffusion became increasingly inadequate as a means of delivering oxygen to the tissues. Consequently, in most animals with high metabolic rates and tissues more than a few millimeters from respiratory surfaces, a specialized circulatory system circulates body fluids to aid in the internal distribution of oxygen (box 36.1) (*see figure 36.1*). In general, more active animals have an increased demand for oxygen. However, simply creating a convection of a water-based body fluid does not in itself guarantee internal transport of sufficient oxygen to meet this increased demand. The reason is the low solubility of oxygen in water-based body fluids. Thus, fluid-borne respiratory pigments specialized for reversibly binding large quantities of oxygen evolved in most phyla. Respiratory pigments help the various transport systems satisfy this increased oxygen demand. In addition to oxygen transport, respiratory pigments may also function in short-term oxygen storage.

Respiratory pigments are organic compounds that have either metallic copper or iron that binds oxygen. These pigments may be in solution within the blood or body fluids, or they may be in specific blood cells. In general, the pigments respond to a high oxygen concentration by combining with oxygen and to low oxygen concentrations by releasing oxygen. The four most common respiratory pigments are hemoglobin, hemocyanin, hemerythrin, and chlorocruorin.

Hemoglobin is a reddish pigment that contains iron as the oxygen-binding metal. It is the most common respiratory pigment in animals, being found in a variety of invertebrates (e.g., protozoa, platyhelminths, nemerteans, nematodes, annelids, crustaceans, some insects, and molluscs), and with the exception of a few fishes, in all vertebrates. This wide distribution suggests that hemoglobin evolved very early in the history of animal life. Hemoglobin may be carried within red blood cells (erythrocytes; *see figure 36.5a*) or simply dissolved in the blood or coelomic fluid.

Hemocyanin is the most commonly occurring respiratory pigment in molluscs and certain crustaceans. Hemocyanin contains metallic copper, has a bluish color when oxygenated, and always occurs dissolved in hemolymph. Unlike most hemoglobin, hemocyanin tends to release oxygen easily and to provide a ready source of oxygen to the tissues as long as concentrations of oxygen in the environment are relatively high.

36.1   HOW DEEP-DIVING MARINE MAMMALS ADAPT TO OXYGEN-POOR ENVIRONMENTS

Deep-diving marine animals, such as the sperm whale, have evolved several mechanisms for remaining submerged for up to 1 hour. Most have a large number of red blood cells per milliliter of blood, large quantities of the oxygen-binding pigment **myoglobin** in their muscles, and hemoglobin that releases oxygen much more easily than other mammalian hemoglobin.

The **diving reflex** is an evolutionary adaptation in those mammals that dive (e.g., whales) downward in the sea. In this reflex, blood is shunted away from most regions of the body during a dive and diverted mainly to the heart, brain, and skeletal muscles. Also, the skeletal muscles can incur an **oxygen debt**; they can continue to contract even after all oxygen is depleted. The ATP energy for contraction comes from glycolysis, which forms lactic acid that accumulates in the tissues. When the whale surfaces, it quickly exhales its moist, oxygen-poor air, which condenses to form the "spout." A large amount of carbon dioxide is blown off in the "spout," and oxygen quickly combines with hemoglobin passing through the lungs.

The second part of the diving reflex is the slowing of the heart rate (called bradycardia). This slowing is an adaptation to ensure less rapid depletion of oxygen until the whale can return to the air for more oxygen.

Hemerythrin contains iron and is pink when oxygenated. It is in nucleated cells, rather than free in body fluids or hemolymph. Sipunculans, priapulids, a few brachiopods, and some polychaetes have hemerythrin.

Chlorocruorin also contains iron but is green when associated with low oxygen concentrations and bright red when associated with high oxygen concentrations. Chlorocruorin occurs in several families of polychaete worms.

As just discussed, respiratory pigments raise the oxygen-carrying capacity of body fluids far above what simple transport in a dissolved state would achieve. Similarly, carbon dioxide concentrations in animal body fluids (and in seawater as well) are much higher than would be expected strictly on the basis of its solubility. The reason for this increased transport is that, in addition to being transported bound to hemoglobin and in the dissolved state, most carbon dioxide is transported in the form of carbonic acid (H_2CO_3) and the bicarbonate ion (HCO_3^-) in a series of reversible reactions:

$$CO_2 + H_2O \rightleftharpoons H_2CO_3 \rightleftharpoons H^+ + HCO_3$$

Thus, "tying up" carbon dioxide in other forms lowers its concentration in solution, thereby raising the overall carrying capacity of a body fluid such as blood.

From an evolutionary perspective, the occurrence of respiratory pigments among various taxa has no phylogenetic explanation. Their sporadic distribution suggests that some of the pigments may have evolved more than once through parallel evolution. Interestingly, respiratory pigments are rare in the successful insects. The general absence of respiratory pigments among most insects reflects the fact that most insects do not use blood as a medium for gas transport, but employ extensive tracheal systems to carry gases directly to the tissues (see figure 36.17). In those insects without well-developed trachea, oxygen is simply carried in solution in the hemolymph.

Stop and Ask Yourself

14. What are the five types of respiratory surfaces animals use for external respiration?

15. How do the following accomplish respiration: (a) cutaneous exchange, (b) gills, and (c) lungs?

16. What different parts comprise the air-conducting portion of the mammalian respiratory system?

17. Why are alveoli called the functional units of the respiratory system in mammals?

18. What are four respiratory pigments, and where would you find each one?

SUMMARY

1. Any system of moving fluids that reduces the functional diffusion distance that nutrients, wastes, and gases must transverse is an internal transport system or circulatory system.

2. The two basic types of circulatory systems are open and closed. Open systems generally circulate hemolymph, and closed systems circulate blood.

3. Blood is a type of connective tissue made up of blood cells (red blood cells and white blood cells), plasma, and platelets.

4. The heart pumps blood through a series of vessels in the following order: arteries, arterioles, capillaries, venules, veins, and back to the heart.

5. The action of the heart consists of cyclic contraction (systole) and relaxation (diastole). Systolic contraction generates blood pressure that forces blood through the closed system of vessels.

6. The lymphatic system consists of one-way vessels that help return fluids and proteins to the circulatory system.

7. The vertebrate body uses nonspecific and specific immune defenses to protect itself against the continuous onslaught of microorganisms, foreign invaders, and cancer cells.

8. The nonspecific defenses include biological barriers (inflammation and phagocytosis), chemical barriers (enzymatic action, interferons, the complement system), general barriers (fever), and physical barriers (skin, mucous membranes).

9. The specific immune response is due to the coordinated activity of specialized cells (macrophages and T cells) and antibodies that B cells produce.

10. Acquired immunity can be either active or passive.

11. An immunization is the deliberate provocation of memory lymphocytes by a vaccine.

12. Animals that respire aerobically need a constant supply of oxygen. The process of acquiring oxygen and eliminating carbon dioxide is called external respiration.

13. The exchange of oxygen and carbon dioxide occurs across respiratory surfaces. Such surfaces include gills, cutaneous surfaces, and lungs.

14. The air-conducting portion of the respiratory system of air-breathing vertebrates moves air into (inhalation) and out of (exhalation) this system. This process of air movement is called ventilation.

15. Oxygen and carbon dioxide diffuse from areas of higher concentration to areas of lower concentration.

16. Once in the blood, oxygen diffuses into red blood cells and binds to hemoglobin for transport to the tissues. Carbon dioxide is transported bound to hemoglobin, as well as in the form of the bicarbonate ion and carbonic acid.

17. Respiratory pigments are organic compounds that have either metallic copper or iron that binds oxygen. Examples include hemoglobin, hemocyanin, hemerythrin, and chlorocruorin.

SELECTED KEY TERMS

alveoli (p. 625)   lung (p. 622)
antibodies (p. 617)   lymph (p. 614)
antigens (p. 616)   plasma (p. 608)
bimodal breathing (p. 621)   serum (p. 608)
immunity (p. 615)   vaccine (p. 616)

CRITICAL THINKING QUESTIONS

1. Many invertebrates utilize the body cavity as a circulatory system. However, in humans, the body cavity plays no role whatsoever in circulation. Why?

2. Describe the homeostatic functions of the vertebrate circulatory system. What functions are maintained at relative stability?

3. One of the most important goals of immunological research is developing techniques for transplanting skin between individuals. Why is this so important, and why is it such a difficult problem?

4. The area of an animal's respiratory surface is usually directly related to the animal's body weight. What does this tell you about the mechanism of gas exchange?

5. How can seals and whales stay under water for long periods?

REFERENCES ON THE WORLD WIDE WEB

1. **Blood: Outline.**   This site presents an introduction to blood.
   http://www.mc.vanderbilt.edu/histo/blood/

2. **Cells of the Blood.**   This site has graphics of the different blood cells.
   http://www-micro.msb,le,ac.uk/Imagemap/Bloodmap.html

3. **Blood and Its Components.**   This interesting site explains the components of blood.
   http://www.jsc.nasa.gov/sa/sd/intro/blood.html

4. **The Hematopoietic System.**   This site discusses hematopoiesis of blood.
   http://aeb.cvm.okstate.edu/vpat5315/lymphemo.htm

5. **The Heart: An Online Explosion.**   This site covers a variety of heart-related topics.
   http://sln.fi.edu/biosci/heart.html

6. **Human Anatomy On-Line.**   This site provides a detailed look at the circulatory system.
   http://www.innerbody.com/

7. **Heart: How It Works.**   The American Heart Association has developed this site on the heart.
   http://www.amhrt.org/heartg/heartworkds.html

8. **Immune Explorer.**   This interactive site explores the biology of the immune system.
   http://www-wilson.ucsd.edu/ve/index_noframes.html

9. **Immunology.**   Professor Hedrick developed this extensive site on the immune system.
   http://www-biology,ucsd.edu/others/CBBimmune/Syllabus.95.html

10. **How the Respiratory System Works.**   This site presents an overview of the anatomy and physiology of the respiratory system.
   http://www. physiol.arizona.edu/CELL/Instruct/95BWRS-1/95BWRS-1.html

11. **Respiratory System.**   This NASA site provides you with the basics of the respiratory system.
   http://www.jsc.nasa.gov/sa/sd/intro/resp.html

12. **Structure of the Human Respiratory System.**   This site reviews the structure of the human respiratory system.
   http://www.stemnet.nf.ca/~dpower/resp/struct~1.html

NUTRITION AND DIGESTION

Concepts

1. Animals are heterotrophic organisms that use food to supply both raw materials and energy. Nutrition includes all of those processes by which an animal takes in, digests, absorbs, stores, and uses food to meet its metabolic needs.

2. Digestion is the chemical and/or mechanical breakdown of food into particles that individual cells of an organism can absorb. Digestion can occur either inside a cell (intracellular), outside a cell (extracellular), or in both places.

3. Most animals must work for their nutrients. The number of specializations that have evolved for food procurement (feeding) and extracellular digestion are almost as numerous as the number of animal species. Some examples include continuous versus discontinuous feeding, suspension feeding, deposit feeding, herbivory, predation, surface nutrient absorption, and fluid feeding.

4. Intracellular digestion occurs in some invertebrates (e.g., in sponges); others (e.g., some cnidarians and molluscs) utilize both intracellular and extracellular digestion; and most higher invertebrates (e.g., insects) have evolved variations in extracellular digestion that allow them to exploit different food sources.

5. In primitive, multicellular animals, such as cnidarians, the gut is a blind (closed) sac called a gastrovascular cavity. Its one opening is both entrance and exit; thus, it is an incomplete digestive tract. The development of an anus and complete digestive tract in the aschelminths was an evolutionary breakthrough. The many variations of the basic complete digestive tract correlate with different food-gathering mechanisms and diets.

6. Vertebrate digestive systems have evolved into assembly lines where food is first broken down mechanically and then chemically by digestive enzymes. The simple sugars, fats, triglycerides, amino acids, vitamins, and minerals that result are then taken into the circulatory systems for distribution throughout the animal's body and are used in maintenance, growth, and energy production.

Would You Like to Know . . .

1. why a light beer that is advertised as containing only 95 Calories per 12 oz actually contains 95,000 calories? (p. 630)

2. why a high-fiber diet is good for you? (p. 630)

3. what mammals feed exclusively on blood? (p. 636)

4. why birds do not have teeth? (p. 640)

5. why some snakes have salivary glands that produce venoms? (p. 640)

6. why some birds eat pebbles or stones? (p. 642)

7. why some mice and rabbits eat their own feces? (p. 644)

8. why vomiting causes a burning sensation in your esophagus and mouth? (p. 648)

9. what causes "hunger pangs"? (p. 648)

This chapter answers these and other useful questions.

This chapter contains evolutionary concepts, which are set off in this font.

Nutrition includes all of those processes by which an animal takes in, digests, absorbs, stores, and uses food (nutrients) to meet its metabolic needs. **Digestion** (L. *digestio*, from + *dis*, apart + *gerere*, to carry) is the chemical and/or mechanical breakdown of food into particles that individual cells of an animal can absorb. This chapter discusses animal nutrition, the different strategies animals use for consuming and using food, and various animal digestive systems.

EVOLUTION OF NUTRITION

Nutrients in the food an animal consumes provide the necessary chemicals for growth, maintenance, and energy production. Overall, the nutritional requirements of an animal are inversely related to its ability to synthesize molecules essential for life. The fewer such biosynthetic abilities an animal has, the more kinds of nutrients it must obtain from its environment. Green plants and photosynthetic protists have the fewest such nutritional requirements because they can synthesize all their own complex molecules from simpler inorganic substances; they are **autotrophs** (Gr. *auto*, self + *trophe*, nourishing). Animals, fungi, and bacteria that cannot synthesize many of their own organic molecules and must obtain them by consuming other organisms or their products are **heterotrophs** (Gr. *heteros*, another or different + *trophe*, nourishing). Animals, such as rabbits, that subsist entirely on plant material are **herbivores** (L. *herba*, plant + *vorare*, to eat). **Carnivores** (L. *caro*, flesh), such as hawks, are animals that eat only meat. **Omnivores** (L. *omnius*, all), such as humans, bears, raccoons, and pigs, eat both plant and animal matter. **Insectivores,** such as bats, eat primarily arthropods.

Losses of biosynthetic abilities have marked much of animal evolution. Once an animal routinely obtains essential, complex organic molecules in its diet, it can afford to lose the ability to synthesize those molecules. Moreover, the loss of this ability confers a selective advantage on the animal because the animal stops expending energy and resources to synthesize molecules that are already in its diet. Thus, as the diet of animals became more varied, they tended to lose their abilities to synthesize such widely available molecules as some of the amino acids.

THE METABOLIC FATES OF NUTRIENTS IN HETEROTROPHS

The nutrients that a heterotroph ingests can be divided into macronutrients and micronutrients. **Macronutrients** are needed in large quantities and include the carbohydrates, lipids, and proteins. **Micronutrients** are needed in small quantities and include organic vitamins and inorganic minerals. Together, these nutrients make up the animal's dietary requirements. Besides these nutrients, animals require water.

CALORIES AND ENERGY

The energy value of food is measured in terms of calories or Calories. A **calorie** (L. *calor*, heat) is the amount of energy required to raise the temperature of 1 g of water 1° C. A calorie, with a small c, is also called a gram calorie. A **kilocalorie,** also known as a Calorie or kilogram calorie (kcal), is equal to 1,000 calories. In popular usage, you talk about calories but actually mean Calories because the larger unit is more useful for measuring the energy value of food. ❶ If an advertisement says that a so-called light beer contains 95 calories per 12 oz, it really means 95,000 calories, 95 Calories, or 95 kcal.

Stop and Ask Yourself
1. How do autotrophs and heterotrophs differ?
2. What are some macronutrients? What are some micronutrients?
3. Why have losses in biosynthetic abilities marked much of animal evolution?
4. What is the difference between a calorie and a Calorie?

MACRONUTRIENTS

With a few notable exceptions, heterotrophs require organic molecules, such as carbohydrates, lipids, and proteins, in their diets. Enzymes break down these molecules into components that can be used for energy production or as sources for the "building blocks" of life.

Carbohydrates: Carbon and Energy from Sugars and Starches

The major dietary source of energy for heterotrophs is complex carbohydrates (figure 37.1*a*). Most carbohydrates originally come from plant sources. Various polysaccharides, disaccharides, or any of a variety of simple sugars (monosaccharides) can meet this dietary need. Carbohydrates also are a major carbon source for incorporation into important organic compounds. Many plants also supply cellulose, a polysaccharide that humans and other animals (with the exception of herbivores) cannot digest. Cellulose is sometimes called dietary fiber. ❷ It assists in the passage of food through the alimentary canal of mammals. Cellulose may also reduce the risk of cancer of the colon because the amounts of mutagenic compounds that form during the storage of feces are less if fecal elimination is more frequent.

Lipids: Highly Compact Energy-Storage Nutrients

Neutral lipids (fats) or triacylglycerols are contained in fats and oils, meat and dairy products, nuts, and avocados (figure 37.1*b*).

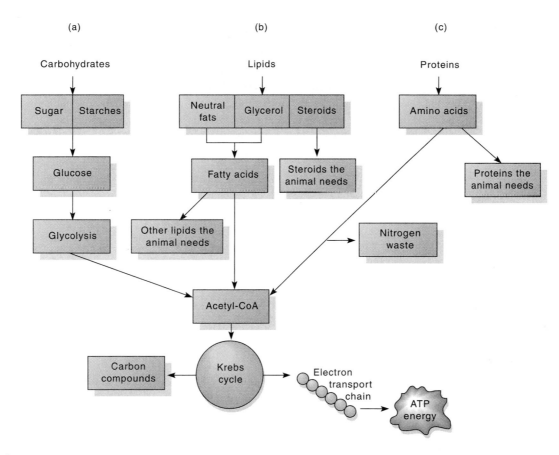

FIGURE 37.1

Macronutrients in the Diet. (*a*) Carbohydrate foods break down to their constituent sugars and starches, and ultimately into glucose. Individual cells use this sugar in glycolysis and aerobic respiration to create new carbon compounds or ATP energy. (*b*) Lipids (fats and oils) in the diet break down to neutral fats, glycerol, and steroids. These molecules can be modified and incorporated into the lipids or steroids the animal needs for storing fat or generating hormones, or they can be converted to acetyl-CoA and enter the Krebs cycle and electron transport chain for ATP production. (*c*) Proteins break down to amino acids, which are incorporated into new proteins or modified to enter the Krebs cycle and electron transport chain to produce ATP energy.

Lipids are the most concentrated source of food energy. They produce about 9 Calories (kcal) of usable energy per gram, more than twice the energy available from an equal mass of carbohydrate or protein (table 37.1).

Many heterotrophs have an absolute dietary requirement for lipids, sometimes for specific types. For example, many animals require unsaturated fatty acids (e.g., linoleic acid, linolenic acid, and arachidonic acid). These fatty acids act as precursor molecules for the synthesis of sterols, the most common of which is cholesterol. The sterols are also required for the synthesis of steroid hormones and cholesterol, which is incorporated into cell membranes. Other lipids insulate the body of some vertebrates and help maintain a constant temperature.

Proteins: Basic to the Structure and Function of Cells

Animal sources of protein include other animals and milk. Plant sources include beans, peas, and nuts. Proteins are needed for their amino acids, which heterotrophs use to build their own body proteins (figure 37.1*c*).

| TABLE 37.1 | THE AVERAGE CALORIC VALUES OF MACRONUTRIENTS |

MACRONUTRIENT	CALORIES PER GRAM
Carbohydrates	4.1
Lipids	9.3
Proteins	4.4

MICRONUTRIENTS

Micronutrients are usually small ions, organic vitamins, inorganic minerals, and molecules that are used repeatedly in enzymatic reactions or as parts of certain proteins (e.g., copper in hemocyanin and iron in hemoglobin). Even though they are needed in small amounts, animals cannot synthesize them rapidly (if at all); thus, they must be obtained from the diet.

TABLE 37.2	PHYSIOLOGICAL ROLES OF THE ESSENTIAL MINERALS (MACROMINERALS) ANIMALS REQUIRE IN LARGE AMOUNTS	
MINERAL	**MAJOR PHYSIOLOGICAL ROLES**	
Calcium (Ca)	Component of bone and teeth; essential for normal blood clotting; needed for normal muscle, neuron, and cellular function	
Chlorine (Cl)	Principal negative ion in extracellular fluid; important in acid-base and fluid balance; needed to produce stomach HCl	
Magnesium (Mg)	Component of many coenzymes; needed for normal neuron and muscle function, as well as carbohydrate and protein metabolism	
Potassium (K)	Major constituent of bones, blood plasma; needed for energy metabolism	
Phosphorus (P)	Major positive ion in cells; influences muscle contraction and neuron excitability; part of DNA, RNA, ATP, energy metabolism	
Sodium (Na)	Principal positive ion in extracellular fluid; important in fluid balance; essential for conduction of action potentials, active transport	
Sulfur (S)	Protein structure; detoxification reactions and other metabolic activity	

TABLE 37.3	SOME PHYSIOLOGICAL ROLES OF TRACE MINERALS (MICROMINERALS) IN ANIMALS	
MINERAL	**PHYSIOLOGICAL ROLES**	
Cobalt (Co)	Component of vitamin B_{12}; essential for red blood cell production	
Copper (Cu)	Component of many enzymes; essential for melanin and hemoglobin synthesis; part of cytochromes	
Fluorine (F)	Component of bone and teeth; prevents tooth decay	
Iodine (I)	Component of thyroid hormones	
Iron (Fe)	Component of hemoglobin, myoglobin, enzymes, and cytochromes	
Manganese (Mn)	Activates many enzymes; an enzyme essential for urea formation and parts of the Krebs cycle	
Molybdenum (Mo)	Constituent of some enzymes	
Selenium (Se)	Needed in fat metabolism	
Zinc (Zn)	Component of at least 70 enzymes; needed for wound healing and fertilization	

Minerals

Some minerals are needed in relatively large amounts and are called essential minerals, or macrominerals. For example, sodium and potassium are vital to the functioning of every nerve and muscle in an animal's body. Animals lose large quantities of these minerals, especially sodium, in the urine every day. Animals that sweat to help regulate body temperature lose sodium in their sweat. A daily supply of calcium is needed for muscular activity and, with phosphorous, for bone formation. Table 37.2 lists the function of the major essential minerals.

Other minerals are known as trace minerals, trace elements, or microminerals. Animals need these in only very small amounts for various enzymatic functions. Table 37.3 lists the function of some trace minerals.

Vitamins

Normal metabolic activity depends on very small amounts of more than a dozen organic substances called vitamins. **Vitamin** (L. *vita*, life) is the general term for a number of chemically unrelated, organic substances that occur in many foods in small amounts and are necessary for normal metabolic functioning. Vitamins may be water soluble or fat soluble. Most water-soluble vitamins, such as the B vitamins and vitamin C, are coenzymes

needed in metabolism (table 37.4). The fat-soluble vitamins have various functions (table 37.5).

The dietary need for vitamin C and the fat-soluble vitamins (A, D, E, and K) tends to be limited to the vertebrates. Even in closely related groups, vitamin requirements vary. For example, among vertebrates, humans and guinea pigs require vitamin C, but rabbits do not. Some birds require vitamin A; others do not.

Stop and Ask Yourself

5. What are some functions of each of the following in vertebrates: (*a*) carbohydrates, (*b*) lipids, and (*c*) proteins?

6. What is the difference between essential minerals and trace minerals?

7. What is a vitamin?

8. What are some water-soluble vitamins? What are some fat-soluble vitamins?

DIGESTION

Recall from chapters 17 and 18 that in some of the simplest forms of life (the protists and sponges), some cells take in whole food particles directly from the environment by diffusion, active transport, and/or endocytosis and break them down with enzymes to obtain nutrients. This strategy is called **intracellular** ("within the cell") **digestion** (figure 37.2*a*). Intracellular digestion circumvents the need for the me-

TABLE 37.4 WATER-SOLUBLE VITAMINS

VITAMIN	CHARACTERISTICS	FUNCTIONS	SOURCES
Thiamin (vitamin B_1)	Destroyed by heat and oxygen, especially in alkaline environment	Part of coenzyme needed for oxidation of carbohydrates, and coenzyme needed in synthesis of ribose	Lean meats, liver, eggs, whole-grain cereals, leafy green vegetables, legumes
Riboflavin (vitamin B_2)	Stable to heat, acids, and oxidation; destroyed by alkalis and light	Part of enzymes and coenzymes needed for oxidation of glucose and fatty acids and for cellular growth	Meats, dairy products, leafy green vegetables, whole-grain cereals
Niacin (nicotinic acid)	Stable to heat, acids, and alkalis; converted to niacinamide by cells; synthesized from tryptophan	Part of coenzymes needed for oxidation of glucose and synthesis of proteins, fats, and nucleic acids	Liver, lean meats, poultry, peanuts, legumes
Vitamin B_6	Group of three compounds; stable to heat and acids; destroyed by oxidation, alkalis, and ultraviolet light	Coenzyme needed for synthesis of proteins and various amino acids, for conversion of tryptophan to niacin, for production of antibodies, and for synthesis of nucleic acids	Liver, meats, fish, poultry, bananas, avocados, beans, peanuts, whole-grain cereals, egg yolk
Pantothenic acid	Destroyed by heat, acids, and alkalis	Part of coenzyme needed for oxidation of carbohydrates and fats	Meats, fish, whole-grain cereals, legumes, milk, fruits, vegetables
Cyanocobalamin (vitamin B_{12})	Complex, cobalt-containing compound; stable to heat; inactivated by light, strong acids, and strong alkalis; absorption regulated by intrinsic factor from gastric glands; stored in liver	Part of coenzyme needed for synthesis of nucleic acids and for metabolism of carbohydrates; plays role in synthesis of myelin	Liver, meats, poultry, fish, milk, cheese, eggs
Folate (folic acid)	Occurs in several forms; destroyed by oxidation in acid environment or by heat in alkaline environment; stored in liver, where it is converted into folinic acid	Coenzyme needed for metabolism of certain amino acids and for synthesis of DNA; promotes production of normal red blood cells	Liver, leafy green vegetables, whole-grain cereals, legumes
Biotin	Stable to heat, acids, and light; destroyed by oxidation and alkalis	Coenzyme needed for metabolism of amino acids and fatty acids and for synthesis of nucleic acids	Liver, egg yolk, nuts, legumes, mushrooms
Ascorbic acid	Closely related to monosaccharides; stable in acids, but destroyed by oxidation, heat, light, and alkalis	Needed for production of collagen, conversion of folate to folinic acid, and metabolism of certain amino acids; promotes absorption of iron and synthesis of hormones from cholesterol	Citrus fruits, citrus juices, tomatoes, cabbage, potatoes, leafy green vegetables, fresh fruits

chanical breakdown of food or for a gut or other cavity in which to chemically digest food. At the same time, however, intracellular digestion limits an animal's size and complexity—only very small pieces of food can be used. Intracellular digestion provides all or some of the nutrients in protozoa, sponges, cnidarians, platyhelminths, rotifers, bivalve molluscs, and primitive chordates.

Larger animals have evolved structures and mechanisms for **extracellular digestion:** the enzymatic breakdown of larger pieces of food into constituent molecules, usually in a special organ or cavity (figure 37.2b). Nutrients from the food then pass into body cells lining the organ or cavity and can take part in energy metabolism or biosynthesis.

TABLE 37.5	FAT-SOLUBLE VITAMINS		
VITAMIN	CHARACTERISTICS	FUNCTIONS	SOURCES
Vitamin A	Occurs in several forms; synthesized from carotenes; stored in liver; stable in heat, acids, and alkalis; unstable in light	Necessary for synthesis of visual pigments, mucoproteins, and mucopolysaccharides; for normal development of bones and teeth; and for maintenance of epithelial cells	Liver, fish, whole milk, butter, eggs, leafy green vegetables, and yellow and orange vegetables and fruits
Vitamin D	A group of sterols; resistant to heat, oxidation, acids, and alkalis; stored in liver, skin, brain, spleen, and bones	Promotes absorption of calcium and phosphorous; promotes development of teeth and bones	Produced in skin exposed to ultraviolet light; in milk, egg yolk, fish-liver oils, fortified foods
Vitamin E	A group of compounds; resistant to heat and visible light; unstable in presence of oxygen and ultraviolet light; stored in muscles and adipose tissue	An antioxidant; prevents oxidation of vitamin A and polyunsaturated fatty acids; may help maintain stability of cell membranes	Oils from cereal seeds, salad oils, margarine, shortenings, fruits, nuts, and vegetables
Vitamin K	Occurs in several forms; resistant to heat, but destroyed by acids, alkalis, and light; stored in liver	Needed for synthesis of prothrombin; needed for blood clotting	Leafy green vegetables, egg yolk, pork liver, soy oil, tomatoes, cauliflower

ANIMAL STRATEGIES FOR GETTING AND USING FOOD

As noted earlier, only a few protists and animals can absorb nutrients directly from their external environment via intracellular digestion. Most animals must work for their nutrients. The number of specializations that have evolved for food procurement (feeding) and extracellular digestion are almost as numerous as the number of animal species. What follows is a brief discussion of the major feeding strategies animals utilize.

CONTINUOUS VERSUS DISCONTINUOUS FEEDERS

One variable related to the structure of digestive systems is whether an animal is a continuous or discontinuous feeder. Many **continuous feeders** are slow-moving or completely sessile animals (they remain permanently in one place). For example, aquatic **suspension feeders,** such as tube worms and barnacles, remain in one place and continuously "strain" small food particles from the water (box 37.1).

Discontinuous feeders tend to be active, sometimes highly mobile, animals. Typically, discontinuous feeders have more digestive specializations than continuous feeders because discontinuous feeders take in large meals that must be either ground up or stored, or both. Many carnivores, for example, pursue and capture relatively large prey. When successful, they must eat large meals so that they need not spend their time in the continuous pursuit of prey. Thus, carnivores have digestive systems that permit storage and gradual digestion of large, relatively infrequent meals.

Herbivores spend more time eating than carnivores do, but they are also discontinuous feeders. They need to move from area to area when food is exhausted and, at least in natural environments, must limit their grazing time to avoid excessive exposure to predators. Thus, their digestive systems permit relatively rapid food gathering and gradual digestion.

SUSPENSION FEEDERS

Suspension feeding is the removal of suspended food particles from the surrounding water by some sort of capture, trapping, or filtration structure. This feeding strategy involves three steps: (1) transport of water past the feeding structure, (2) removal of nutrients from the water, and (3) transport of the nutrients to the mouth of the digestive system. Sponges, ascidians, branchiopods, ectoprocts, entoprocts, phoronids, most bivalves, and many crustaceans, polychaetes, gastropods, and some nonvertebrate chordates are suspension feeders (*see box 37.1*).

DEPOSIT FEEDERS

Deposit feeding involves primarily omnivorous animals. These animals obtain their nutrients from the sediments of soft-bottom habitats (muds and sands) or terrestrial soils. Direct deposit feeders simply swallow large quantities of sediment (mud, soil, sand, organic matter). The usable nutrients are digested, and the remains pass out the anus. Direct deposit feeding occurs in many polychaete annelids, some snails, some sea urchins, and in most earthworms. Other direct deposit feeders utilize tentacle-like structures to consume sediment. Examples include sea cucumbers, most sipunculans, certain clams, and several types of polychaetes.

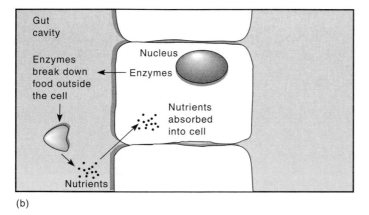

FIGURE 37.2

Intracellular and Extracellular Digestion. (*a*) A simple invertebrate, such as a sponge, has no gut and thus carries out intracellular digestion. Tiny food particles are taken into the body wall cells by endocytosis. Digestive enzymes in the vacuole then break the small particles into constituent molecules. (*b*) A dog, for example, has a gut and so can take in and digest (extracellularly) relatively large food particles. Cells lining the gut cavity secrete enzymes into the cavity. There, the enzymes break down food materials into constituent nutrients, and the nearby cells absorb these nutrients.

HERBIVORY

Herbivory (L. *herba*, herb + *vorare*, to eat) is the consumption of macroscopic plants. This common feeding strategy requires the ability to "bite and chew" large pieces of plant matter (macroherbivory). Although biting and chewing mechanisms evolved within the architectural framework of a number of invertebrate lineages, they are often characterized by the development of hard surfaces (e.g., teeth) that powerful muscles manipulate. Invertebrates that evolved macroherbivory include molluscs, polychaete worms, arthropods, and sea urchins.

Many molluscs have a radula. A radula is a muscularized, belt-like rasp armed with chitinous teeth (*see figure 21.6*). Molluscs use the radula to scrape algae off rocks or to tear the leaves off terrestrial plants. Polychaetes have sets of large chitinous teeth on an eversible proboscis or pharynx that is used to scrape off algae. This toothed pharynx is also suitable for carnivory when plant material is scarce. Macroherbivory is found in almost every group of arthropods. For ex-

ample, insects and crustaceans have large, powerful mandibles capable of biting off plant material and subsequently grinding and chewing it before passing the plant material to the mouth.

PREDATION

Predation (L. *praedator*, a plunderer, pillager) is one of the most sophisticated feeding strategies, since it requires the capture of live prey. Only a few generalizations about the many kinds of predation are presented here; discussions of various taxa are presented in their appropriate chapters.

Predators can be classified by how they capture their prey: motile stalkers, lurking predators, sessile opportunists, or grazers. Motile stalkers actively pursue their prey. Examples include ciliate protozoa, nemerteans, polychaete worms, gastropods, octopuses and squids, crabs, sea stars, and many vertebrates. Lurking predators sit and wait for their prey to come within seizing distance. Examples include certain species of preying mantises, shrimp, crabs, spiders, polychaetes, and many vertebrates. Sessile opportunists usually are not very mobile. They can only capture prey when the prey organism comes into contact with them. Examples include certain protozoa, barnacles, and cnidarians. Grazing carnivores move about the substrate picking up small organisms. Their diet usually consists largely of sessile and slow-moving animals, such as sponges, ectoprocts, tunicates, snails, worms, and small crustaceans.

SURFACE NUTRIENT ABSORPTION

Some highly specialized animals have dispensed entirely with all mechanisms for prey capture, ingestion of food particles, and digestive processes. Instead they directly absorb nutrients from the external medium across their body surfaces. This medium may be nutrient-rich seawater, fluid in other animals' digestive tracts, or body fluids of other animals. For example, some free-living protozoa, such as *Chilomonas*, absorb all of their nutrients across their body surface. The endoparasitic protozoa, cestode worms, endoparasitic gastropods, and crustaceans (all of which lack mouths and digestive systems) also absorb all of their nutrients across their body surface.

A few nonparasitic multicellular animals also lack a mouth and digestive system and absorb nutrients across their body surface. Examples include the gutless bivalves and pogonophoran worms. Interestingly, many pogonophoran worms absorb some nutrients from seawater across their body surface and also supplement their nutrition with organic carbon that symbiotic bacteria fix within the pogonophoran's tissues.

FLUID FEEDERS

The biological fluids of animals and plants are a rich source of nutrients. Feeding on this fluid is called **fluid feeding.** Fluid feeding is especially characteristic of some parasites, such as the intestinal nematodes that bite and rasp off host tissue or suck blood. External parasites (ectoparasites), such as leeches, ticks, mites, lampreys, and

BOX 37.1   SUSPENSION FEEDING IN INVERTEBRATES AND NONVERTEBRATE CHORDATES

MOST suspension feeders are marine rather than freshwater animals because seawater contains an abundance of microscopic food particles. Suspension-feeding invertebrates and some nonvertebrate chordates generally consume bacteria, phytoplankton, zooplankton, and some detritus. To capture food particles from the environment, suspension feeders must either move part or all of their body through the water, or water must be moved past the feeding structures. Relatively few suspension feeders (some ciliate protozoa, certain bivalve molluscs, many tunicates, some large crustaceans) use true filter feeding because driving water through a fine-meshed filter is energetically costly. An analogy would be moving molasses through a fine-meshed filter. Thus, most invertebrates utilize one of the following less energetically costly methods of capturing food particles from the water.

Among some aquatic arthropods, such as the sessile barnacles, certain thoracic appendages are modified with rows of feather-like cirri adapted for generating water currents across parts of the body and removing food from it (figure 1a).

A second method is called "scan and trap." The general strategy here is to move water over all or part of the body, detect suspended food particles, isolate the particles in a small parcel of water, and process only that water by some method of particle extraction. Many copepods, ectoprocts, and a variety of invertebrate larval forms employ this method.

A third suspension-feeding device is the mucous bag or mucous trap. In this method, patches or sheets of mucus trap suspended food particles. A classic example is seen in the annelid worm *Chaetopterus* (figure 1b). This invertebrate lives in a U-shaped tube in sediment and pumps water through the tube and through a mucous net. As the net fills with trapped food particles, it is periodically manipulated and rolled into a ball. The ball is eventually passed to the mouth and swallowed.

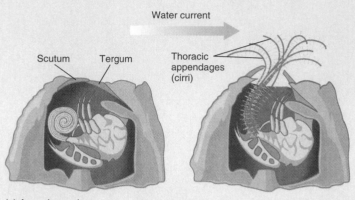

Water current

Scutum   Tergum   Thoracic appendages (cirri)

(a) Acorn barnacle

FIGURE 1   **Suspension Feeding in Invertebrates.** *(a)* In the free-living barnacle, *Balanus* spp. (an acorn barnacle), the scutum and tergum can move apart, allowing the animal to extend cirri into the water currents (blue arrow) and gather food particles. *(b)* In the polychaete, *Chaetopterus* (tube worm), the fanlike parapodia generate water currents. One pair of anterior parapodia is modified for holding a mucous bag, which filters out food particles as water moves through the tube. A food cup holds the bag posteriorly and continuously gathers the food-laden mucus into a ball. Periodically, the ball is released from the rest of the net and passed forward along a ciliated tract to the mouth for ingestion. *(c)* In a typical ascidian (a nonvertebrate chordate; sea squirt), an elongated gland called the endostyle extends along the ventral surface of the pharynx. Mucus secreted by the endostyle is drawn across the pharynx in a thin sheet, so that water passing through the stigmata must pass through the mucous sheet as well. Pharyngeal cilia continually move the particle-laden sheet of mucus to the esophagus for ingestion. *(d)* A crinoid echinoderm (sea lily) collects food by extending the arms (pinnules) and tube feet into the surrounding water current. Food particles in the water become entangled in mucus and are then flicked into the mouth by the cirri. *Sources:* (c) *Modified after Bullough and other sources,* (d) *Modified from Hyman after Clark.*

---

certain crustaceans, use a wide variety of mouthparts to feed on body fluids. For example, the sea lamprey has a funnel structure surrounding its mouth (*see figure 37.6a*). The funnel is lined with over 200 rasping teeth and a rasplike tongue. The lamprey uses the funnel like a suction cup to grip its fish host, and then with its tongue, rasps a hole in the fish's body wall. The lamprey then sucks blood and body fluids from the wound.

Insects have the most highly developed sucking structures for fluid feeding. For example, butterflies, moths, and aphids have tubelike mouthparts that enable them to suck up plant fluids. Blood-sucking mosquitoes have complex mouthparts with piercing stylets.

Most pollen- and nectar-feeding birds have long bills and tongues. In fact, the bill is often specialized (in shape, length, and curvature) for particular types of flowers. The tongues of some birds have a brushlike tip or are hollow, or both, to collect the nectar from flowers. Other nectar-feeding birds have short bills; they make a hole in the base of a flower and use their tongue to obtain nectar through the hole.

3 The only mammals that feed exclusively on blood are the vampire bats, such as *Desmodus*, of tropical South and Central America. These bats attack birds, cattle, and horses, using knife-sharp front teeth to pierce the surface blood vessels, and then lap at the oozing wound. Nectar-feeding bats have a long tongue to extract the nectar from flowering plants, and compared to the blood-feeding bats, have reduced dentition. In like manner, the nectar-feeding honey possum has a long, brush-tipped tongue and reduced dentition.

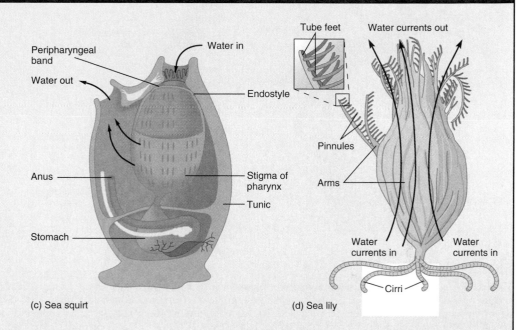

(b) Annelid tube worm

(c) Sea squirt

(d) Sea lily

A fourth type of suspension feeding is the ciliary mucous mechanism. In this mechanism, rows of cilia carry a mucous sheet across some structure while water is passed through or across it. For example sea squirts (ascidians) move a continuous sheet of mucus across their sievelike pharynx while pumping water through it (figure 1c). They secrete fresh mucus from one side of the pharynx, while ingesting the food-laden mucus at the other side using the esophagus.

A fifth type of suspension feeding is tentacle or tube feet suspension feeding. In this strategy, a tentacle-like structure captures larger food particles, with or without the aid of mucus (figure 1d). This food-gathering mechanism is most commonly encountered in the echinoderms (e.g., many brittle stars and crinoids such as the sea lily) and cnidarians (e.g., some sea anemones and corals).

Stop and Ask Yourself

9. How do intracellular and extracellular digestion differ?

10. How do continuous and discontinuous feeding differ?

11. How does suspension feeding occur? How does deposit feeding occur?

12. What are some different types of predation?

13. What protists and animals utilize surface nutrient absorption? What protists and animals are fluid feeders?

DIVERSITY IN DIGESTIVE STRUCTURES: INVERTEBRATES

In primitive, multicellular animals, such as cnidarians, the gut is a blind (closed) sac called a **gastrovascular cavity.** It has only one opening that is both entrance and exit (figure 37.3a); thus, it is an incomplete digestive tract. Some specialized cells in the cavity secrete digestive enzymes that begin the process of extracellular digestion. Other phagocytic cells that line the cavity engulf food material and continue intracellular digestion inside food vacuoles. Some flatworms have similar digestive patterns (figure 37.3b).

The development of the anus and complete digestive tract in the aschelminths was an evolutionary breakthrough (figure 37.3c). A complete digestive tract permits the one-way flow of ingested food without mixing it with previously ingested food or waste. Complete digestive tracts also have the advantage of progressive digestive processing in specialized regions along the system. Food can be digested efficiently in a series of distinctly different steps. The many variations of the basic plan of a complete digestive tract correlate with different food-gathering mechanisms and diets (figure 37.3d). Most of these have been presented in the discussion of the many different protists and invertebrates covered in chapters 17 to 22 and are not repeated in this chapter. Instead, three examples

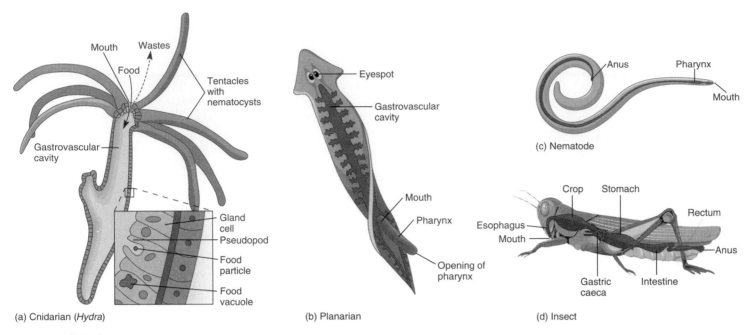

FIGURE 37.3

Various Types of Digestive Structures in Invertebrates. (*a*) The gastrovascular cavity of a cnidarian (*Hydra*) is an incomplete digestive tract because its one opening, a mouth, must serve as the entry and exit point for food and waste. Extracellular digestion occurs in the gastrovascular cavity, and intracellular digestion occurs inside food vacuoles formed when phagocytic cells engulf food particles. (*b*) Even though the gastrovascular cavity in a platyhelminth (planarian) branches extensively, it is also an incomplete digestive tract with only one opening. When a planarian feeds, it sticks its muscular pharynx out of its mouth and sucks in food. (*c*) An aschelminth (*Ascaris*) has a complete digestive tract with a mouth, pharynx, and anus. (*d*) The complete digestive tract of an insect (grasshopper) has an expanded region called a crop that functions as a food storage organ.

further illustrate digestive systems in protozoa and invertebrates: (1) the incomplete digestive system of a ciliated protozoan is an example of an intracellular digestive system; (2) the bivalve mollusc is an example of an invertebrate that has both intracellular and extracellular digestion; and (3) an insect is an example of an invertebrate that has extracellular digestion and a complete digestive tract.

PROTOZOA

As presented in chapter 17, protozoa may be autotrophic, saprozoic, or heterotrophic (ingest food particles). Ciliated protozoa are good examples of protists that utilize heterotrophic nutrition. Ciliary action directs food from the environment into the buccal cavity and cytostome (figure 37.4). The cytostome opens into the cytopharynx, which enlarges as food enters and pinches off a food-containing vacuole. The detached food vacuole then moves through the cytoplasm. During this movement, excess water is removed from the vacuole, the contents are acidified and then made alkaline and a lysosome adds digestive enzymes. The food particles are then digested within the vacuole and the nutrients absorbed into the cytoplasm. The residual vacuole then excretes its waste products via the cytopyge.

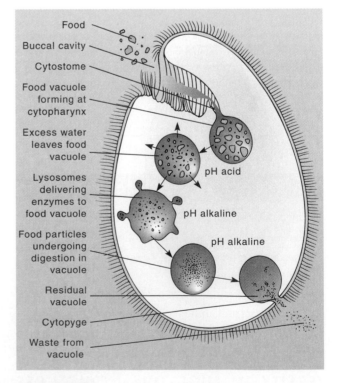

FIGURE 37.4

Intracellular Digestion in a Ciliated Protozoan. Cilia direct food toward the cytostome ("mouth"). The food enters the cytopharynx, where a food vacuole forms and detaches from the cytopharynx. The detached vacuole undergoes acidic and alkaline digestion, and the waste vacuole moves to the cytopyge ("anus") for excretion.

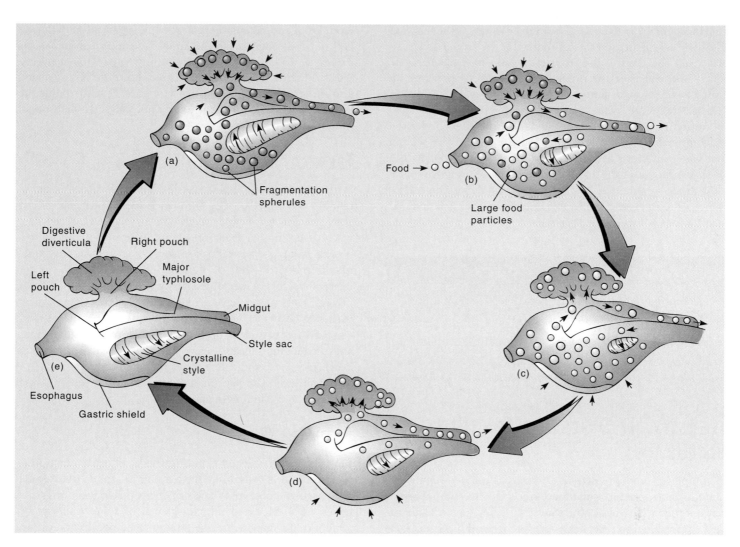

FIGURE 37.5

Extracellular and Intracellular Digestion in a Bivalve Mollusc. (*a*) Extracellular digestion begins before food ingestion by the dissolving of the crystalline style and the formation of fragmentation spherules in the stomach. (*b*) As food enters the stomach, the rotating style and the enzymes released by the gastric shield mechanically and enzymatically break it down. (*c*) The small food particles then move into the digestive diverticulae for intracellular digestion. (*d*) A progressive passage of food particles from the stomach to the digestive diverticulae follows cessation of feeding. (*e*) During this resting phase, the stomach empties and the style re-forms, while intracellular digestion in the diverticulae is completed, and fragmentation spherules begin to form again. The movement of fragmentation spherules starts the next feeding cycle.

BIVALVE MOLLUSCS

Many bivalve molluscs suspension feed and ingest small food particles. The digestive tract has a short esophagus opening into a stomach, midgut, hindgut, and rectum. The stomach contains a crystalline style, gastric shield, and diverticulated region. These diverticulae are blind-ending sacs that increase the surface area for absorption and intracellular digestion. The midgut, hindgut, and rectum function in extracellular digestion and absorption (figure 37.5).

Digestion is a coordination of three cycles: (1) feeding, (2) extracellular digestion, and (3) intracellular digestion. The resting phase is preparative for extracellular digestion. The mechanical and enzymatic breakdown of food during feeding provides the small particles for intracellular digestion. Intracellular diges-

tion releases the nutrients into the blood and produces the fragmentation spherules that are both excretory and lower the pH for optimal extracellular digestion. These three cycles are linked to tidal immersion and emersion of the mollusc.

INSECTS

The grasshopper is a representative insect with a complete digestive tract and extracellular digestion (*see figure 37.3d*). During feeding, the mandibles and maxillae first break up (masticate) the food, which is then taken into the mouth and passed to the crop via the esophagus. During mastication, the salivary glands add saliva to the food to lubricate it for passage through the digestive tract. Saliva also contains the enzyme amylase, which begins the enzymatic digestion of carbohydrates. This digestion continues during food storage in the crop. The midgut secretes other enzymes (carbohydrases, lipases, proteases) that enter the crop. Food passes slowly from the crop to the stomach, where it is mechanically reduced and the nutrient particles sorted. Large particles are returned to the crop for further processing; the small particles enter the gastric cecae, where extracellular digestion is completed. Most nutrient absorption then occurs in the intestine. Undigested food is moved along the intestine and passes into the rectum, where water and ions are absorbed. The solid fecal pellets that form then pass out of the animal via the anus. During this entire feeding process the nervous system, the endocrine system, and the presence of food exert considerable control over enzyme production at various points in the digestive tract.

Stop and Ask Yourself

14. How do incomplete and complete digestive tracts differ?
15. How do heterotrophic protozoa feed?
16. What is the function of diverticulae in bivalve molluscs?
17. Where does digestion begin in an insect?

DIVERSITY IN DIGESTIVE STRUCTURES: VERTEBRATES

The complete vertebrate digestive tract (gut tube) is highly specialized in both structure and function for the digestion of a wide variety of foods. The basic structures of the gut tube include the buccal cavity, pharynx, esophagus, stomach, small intestine, large intestine, rectum, and anus/cloaca. In addition, three important glandular systems are associated with the digestive tract: (1) the salivary glands; (2) the liver, gallbladder, and bile duct; and (3) the pancreas and pancreatic duct.

Because most vertebrates spend the majority of their time acquiring food, feeding is the universal pastime. The oral cavity (mouth), teeth, intestines, and other major digestive structures usually reflect the way an animal gathers food (box 37.2), the type of food it eats, and the way it digests that food. These major digestive structures are now discussed to illustrate the diversity of form and function among different vertebrates.

TONGUES

A tongue or tonguelike structure develops in the floor of the oral cavity in many vertebrates. For example, a lamprey has a protrusible tongue with horny teeth that rasp its prey's flesh (figure 37.6a). Fishes may have a primary tongue that bears teeth that help hold prey; however, this type of tongue is not muscular (figure 37.6b). Tetrapods have evolved mobile tongues for gathering food. Frogs and salamanders and some lizards can rapidly project part of their tongue from the mouth to capture an insect (figure 37.6c). A woodpecker has a long, spiny tongue for gathering insects and grubs (figure 37.6d). Ant- and termite-eating mammals also gather food with long, sticky tongues. Spiny papillae on the tongues of cats and other carnivores help these animals rasp flesh from a bone.

TEETH

With the exception of birds, turtles, and baleen whales, most vertebrates have teeth. ④ Birds lack teeth, probably to reduce body weight for flight. Teeth are specialized, depending on whether an animal feeds on plants or animals, and on how it obtains its food. The teeth of snakes slope backward to aid in the retention of prey while swallowing (figure 37.7a), and the canine teeth of wolves are specialized for ripping food (figure 37.7b). Herbivores, such as deer, have predominantly grinding teeth, the front teeth of a beaver are used for chiseling trees and branches, and the elephant has two of its upper, front teeth specialized as weapons and for moving objects (figure 37.7c–e). Because humans, pigs, bears, raccoons, and a few other mammals are omnivores, they have teeth that can perform a number of tasks—tearing, ripping, chiseling, and grinding (figure 37.7f).

SALIVARY GLANDS

Most fishes lack salivary glands in the head region. Lampreys are an exception because they have a pair of glands that secrete an anticoagulant needed to keep their prey's blood flowing as they feed. ⑤ Modified salivary glands of some snakes produce venom that is injected through fangs to immobilize prey. Because the secretion of oral digestive enzymes is not an important function in amphibians or reptiles, salivary glands are absent. Most birds lack salivary glands, while all mammals have them.

ESOPHAGI

The esophagus (pl., esophagi) is short in fishes and amphibians, but much longer in amniotes due to their longer necks. Grain- and seed-eating birds have a crop that develops from the caudal portion of the esophagus (figure 37.8a). Storing food in the crop ensures an almost continuous supply of food to the stomach and intestine for digestion. This structure allows these birds to reduce the frequency of feeding and still maintain a high metabolic rate.

STOMACHS

The stomach is an ancestral vertebrate structure that evolved as vertebrates began to feed on larger organisms that were caught at less frequent intervals and required storage. Some zoologists believe that

BOX 37.2 FILTER FEEDING IN VERTEBRATES

The baleen, or whalebone whales, include the humpback and gray whales (figure 1a). These are the largest living animals on earth, and because they lack teeth, they have evolved a different approach to feeding. A full-grown blue whale exceeds 30 m in length and weighs as much as 120,000 kg. What food could support the life of such a large animal? The answer is krill. **Krill** (Norw., *kril*, fry or young fish) are small, shrimplike crustaceans.

Baleen whales are named for the fringes of baleen, or whale bone (not true bone), that hang down in "mustachelike" sheets inside their mouths (figure 1b). Baleen is nothing more than hardened, shredded sheets of the gum epithelial layers. When these animals feed, they swim through dense schools of krill, straining huge amounts of water through the baleen meshwork. A large whale's expandable mouth holds 60 m^3, or 60 tons, of water, which it filters in a few seconds. The filtering process allows the smaller plant life (phytoplankton) to escape with the seawater while the krill is retained to be swallowed at leisure. A whale can eat tons of krill in a short time.

Flamingos are also filter feeders. They have fringed filters hanging from the upper bill and a deep-sided, curved lower bill (figure 1c,d). This bill represents a similar evolutionary adaptation to the same problem—removing small particles from a dilute medium.

Flamingos are commonly misportrayed as denizens of lush tropical islands. In fact, many dwell in one of the world's harshest habitats—shallow, hypersaline lakes. Few animals can tolerate the unusual environments of these saline lakes. Those that can, thrive in the absence of competitors and build up their populations to enormous numbers. Hypersaline lakes provide these predators with ideal conditions for filter feeding on small molluscs, crustaceans, and insect larvae.

Flamingos pass water through their bills either by swinging their heads back and forth, permitting water to flow passively through, or by an active pump that a large, powerful tongue maintains. The tongue fills a large channel in the lower beak. The tongue moves rapidly back and forth, up to five times per second, drawing water through the filters on the backward pull and expelling it on the forward drive.

(a)

(b)

(c)

(d)

FIGURE 1 **Vertebrate Filter Feeders.** (*a*) Gray whale (*Eschrichtius robustus*) feeding in a kelp bed. (*b*) Baleen. (*c*) Flamingos (*Phoenicopterus minor*) feeding. (*d*) Filters on the bill of a flamingo.

(a)

(b)

(c)

(d)

FIGURE 37.6

Tongues. (*a*) Rasping tongue and mouth of a lamprey. (*b*) Fish tongue. (*c*) Tongue of a chameleon catching an insect. (*d*) The tongue of a woodpecker extracts insects from the bark of a tree.

the gastric glands and their production of hydrochloric acid (HCl) evolved in the context of killing bacteria and helping preserve food. The enzyme pepsinogen may have evolved later because the stomach is not essential for digestion.

GIZZARDS

Some fishes, some reptiles such as crocodilians, and all birds have a gizzard for grinding up food (figure 37.8*a*). The bird's gizzard develops from the posterior part of the stomach called the ventriculus.   6 Pebbles (grit) that have been swallowed are often retained in the gizzard of grain-eating birds and facilitate the grinding process.

RUMENS

Ruminant mammals—animals that "chew their cud," such as cows, sheep, and deer—show some of the most unusual modifications of the stomach. This method of digestion has evolved in animals that need to eat large amounts of food relatively quickly, but can chew the food at a more comfortable or safer location. More important though, the ruminant stomach provides an opportunity for large numbers of microorganisms to digest the cellulose walls of grass and other vegetation. Cellulose contains a large amount of energy; however, animals generally lack the ability to produce the enzyme cellulase for digesting cellulose and obtaining its energy. Because gut microorganisms can produce cellulase, they have made the herbivorous lifestyle more effective.

FIGURE 37.7

Arrangement of Teeth in a Variety of Vertebrates. (*a*) Snake. (*b*) Wolf. (*c*) Deer. (*d*) Beaver. (*e*) Elephant. (*f*) Human.

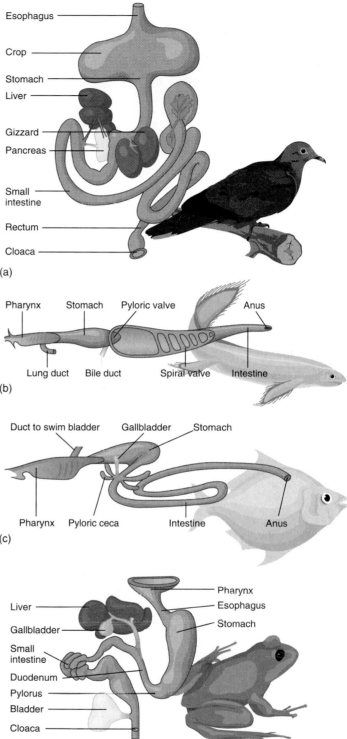

FIGURE 37.8

Arrangement of Stomachs and Intestines in a Variety of Vertebrates. (*a*) Pigeon. (*b*) Lungfish. (*c*) Teleost fish. (*d*) Frog.

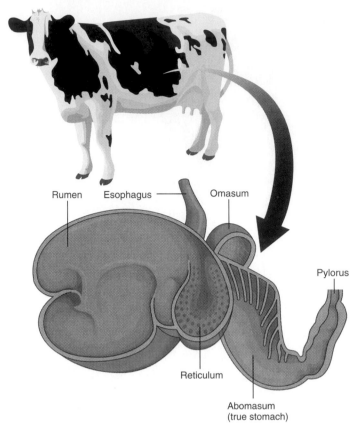

FIGURE 37.9

Ruminant Mammal. Four-chambered stomach of a cow, where symbiotic microorganisms digest cellulose.

In ruminants, the upper portion of the stomach expands to form a large pouch, the rumen, and a smaller reticulum. The lower portion of the stomach consists of a small antechamber, the omasum, with a "true" stomach, or abomasum, behind it (figure 37.9). Food first enters the rumen, where it encounters the microorganisms. Aided by copious fluid secretions, body heat, and churning of the rumen, the microorganisms partially digest the food and reduce it to a pulpy mass. Later, the pulpy mass moves into the reticulum, from which mouthfuls are regurgitated as "cud" (L. *ruminare*, to chew the cud). At this time, food is thoroughly chewed for the first time. When reswallowed, the food enters the rumen, where it becomes more liquid in consistency. When it is very liquid, the digested food material flows out of the reticulum and into the omasum and then the glandular region, the abomasum. Here the digestive enzymes are first encountered, and digestion continues.

CECA

Microorganisms attack the food of ruminants before gastric digestion, but in the typical nonruminant herbivore, microbial action on cellulose occurs after digestion. Rabbits, horses, and rats digest cellulose by maintaining a population of microorganisms in their

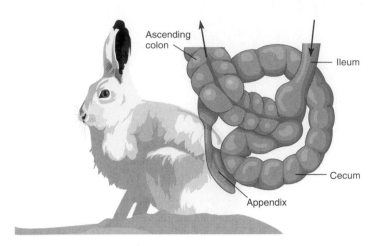

FIGURE 37.10

Extensive Cecum of a Nonruminant Herbivore, Such as a Rabbit. The cecum contains microorganisms that produce digestive enzymes (e.g., cellulase that helps break down cellulose).

unusually large cecum, the blind pouch that extends from the colon (figure 37.10). **7** Adding to this efficiency, a few nonruminant herbivores, such as mice and rabbits, eat some of their own feces to process the remaining materials in them, such as vitamins.

LIVERS AND GALLBLADDERS

In those vertebrates with a gallbladder, it is closely associated with the liver. The liver manufactures bile, which the gallbladder then stores. **Bile** is a fluid containing bile salts and bile pigments. Bile salts play an important role in the digestion of fats, although they are not digestive enzymes. They emulsify dietary fat, breaking it into small globules (emulsification) on the surface of which the fat-digesting enzyme lipase can function. Bile pigments result from phagocytosis of red blood cells in the spleen, liver, and red bone marrow. Phagocytosis cleaves the hemoglobin molecule, releasing iron, and the remainder of the molecule is converted into pigments that enter the circulation. These pigments are subsequently extracted from the circulation in the liver and excreted in the bile as bilirubin ("red bile") and biliverdin ("green bile").

Because of the importance of bile in fat digestion, the gallbladder is relatively large in carnivores and vertebrates, in which fat is an important part of the diet. It is much reduced or absent in bloodsuckers, such as the lamprey, and in animals that feed primarily on plant food (e.g., some teleosts, many birds, rats, and other mammals, such as whales).

PANCREATA

Every vertebrate has a pancreas (pl., pancreata); however, in lampreys and lungfishes it is embedded in the wall of the intestine and is not a visible organ. Both endocrine and exocrine tissues are present, but the cell composition varies. Pancreatic fluid containing many enzymes empties into the small intestine via the pancreatic duct.

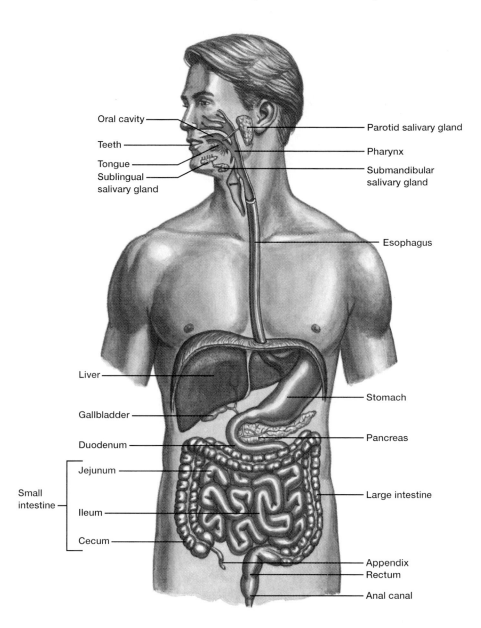

FIGURE 37.11

Major Organs and Parts of the Human Digestive System. Food passes from the mouth through the pharynx and esophagus to the stomach. From the stomach, it passes to the small intestine, where nutrients are broken down and absorbed into the circulatory and lymphatic systems. Nutrients then move to the large intestine, where water is reabsorbed, and feces form. Feces exit the body via the anal canal.

INTESTINES

The configuration and divisions of the small and large intestines vary greatly among vertebrates. Intestines are closely related to the animal's type of food, body size, and levels of activity. For example, cyclostomes, chondrichthian fishes, and primitive bony fishes have short, nearly straight intestines that extend from the stomach to the anus (*see figure 37.8b*). In more advanced bony fishes, the intestine increases in length and begins to coil (*see figure 37.8c*). The intestines are moderately long in most amphibians and reptiles (*see figure 37.8d*) In birds and mammals, the intestines are longer and have more surface area than those of other tetrapods (*see figure 37.8a*). Birds typically have two ceca, and mammals have a single cecum at the beginning of the large intestine. The large intestine is much longer in mammals than in birds, and it empties into the cloaca in most vertebrates.

Stop and Ask Yourself

18. How do vertebrate teeth reflect the eating habits of various animals?
19. How does the stomach of a ruminant function?

THE MAMMALIAN DIGESTIVE SYSTEM

Humans, pigs, bears, raccoons, and a few other mammals are omnivores. The digestive system of an omnivore has the mechanical and chemical ability to process many kinds of foods. The sections that follow examine the control of gastrointestinal motility, the major parts of the alimentary canal, and the accessory organs of digestion (figure 37.11).

FIGURE 37.12

Mammalian Gastrointestinal Tract. Common structural layers of the gastrointestinal tract. The central lumen extends from the mouth to the anus.

The process of digesting and absorbing nutrients in a mammal includes:

1. Ingestion—eating
2. Peristalsis—the involuntary, sequential muscular contractions that move ingested nutrients along the digestive tract
3. Segmentation—mixing the contents in the digestive tract
4. Secretion—the release of hormones, enzymes, and specific ions and chemicals that take part in digestion
5. Digestion—the conversion of large nutrient particles or molecules into small particles or molecules
6. Absorption—the passage of usable nutrient molecules from the small intestine into the bloodstream and lymphatic system for the final passage to body cells
7. Defecation—the elimination from the body of undigested and unabsorbed material as waste

GASTROINTESTINAL MOTILITY AND ITS CONTROL

As with any organ, the function of the gastrointestinal tract is determined by the type of tissues it contains. Most of the mammalian gastrointestinal tract has the same anatomical structure along its entire length (figure 37.12). From the outside inward is a thin layer of connective tissue called the serosa. (The serosa forms a moist epithelial sheet called the peritoneum. This peritoneum lines the entire abdominal cavity and covers all internal organs. The space it encompasses is the coelom.) Next are the longitudinal smooth-muscle layer and circular smooth-muscle layer. Underneath this muscle layer is the submucosa. The submucosa contains connective tissue, blood, and lymphatic vessels. The mucosa faces the central opening called a lumen.

The coordinated contractions of the muscle layers of the gastrointestinal tract mix the food material with various secre-

tions and move the food from the oral cavity to the rectum. The two types of movement involved are peristalsis and segmentation.

During **peristalsis** (Gr. *peri*, around + *stalsis*, contraction), food advances through the gastrointestinal tract when the rings of circular smooth muscle contract behind it and relax in front of it (figure 37.13*a*). Peristalsis is analogous to squeezing icing from a pastry tube. The small and large intestines also have rings of smooth muscles that repeatedly contract and relax, creating an oscillating back-and-forth movement in the same place, called **segmentation** (figure 37.13*b*). This movement mixes the food with digestive secretions and increases the efficiency of absorption.

Sphincters also influence the flow of material through the gastrointestinal tract and prevent backflow. Sphincters are rings of smooth or skeletal muscle at the beginning or ends of specific regions of the gut tract. For example, the cardiac sphincter is between the esophagus and stomach, and the pyloric sphincter is between the stomach and small intestine.

Control of gastrointestinal activity is based on the volume and composition of food in the lumen of the gut. For example, ingested food distends the gut and stimulates mechanical receptors in the gut wall. In addition, digestion of carbohydrates, lipids, and proteins stimulates various chemical receptors in the gut wall. Signals from these mechanical and chemical stimuli travel through nerve plexuses in the gut wall to control the muscular contraction that leads to peristalsis and segmentation, as well as the secretion of various substances (e.g., mucus, enzymes) into the gut lumen. In addition to this local control, long-distance nerve pathways connect the receptors and effectors with the central nervous system. Either or both of these pathways function to maintain homeostasis in the gut. The endocrine cells of the gastrointestinal tract also produce hormones that help regulate secretion, digestion, and absorption.

ORAL CAVITY

A pair of lips protects the **oral cavity** (mouth). The lips are highly vascularized, skeletal muscle tissue with an abundance of sensory nerve endings. Lips help retain food as it is being chewed and play a role in phonation (the modification of sound).

The oral cavity contains the tongue and teeth (figure 37.14). Mammals can mechanically process a wide range of foods because their teeth are covered with enamel (the hardest material in the body) and because their jaws and teeth exert a strong force. The oral cavity is continuously bathed by **saliva,** a watery fluid that at least three pairs of salivary glands secrete. Saliva moistens food, binds it with mucins (glycoproteins), and forms the ingested food into a moist mass called a bolus. Saliva also contains bicarbonate ions (HCO_3^-), which buffer chemicals in the mouth, and thiocyanate ions (SCN^-) and the enzyme lysozyme, which kill microorganisms. It also contributes an enzyme (amylase) necessary for the initiation of carbohydrate digestion.

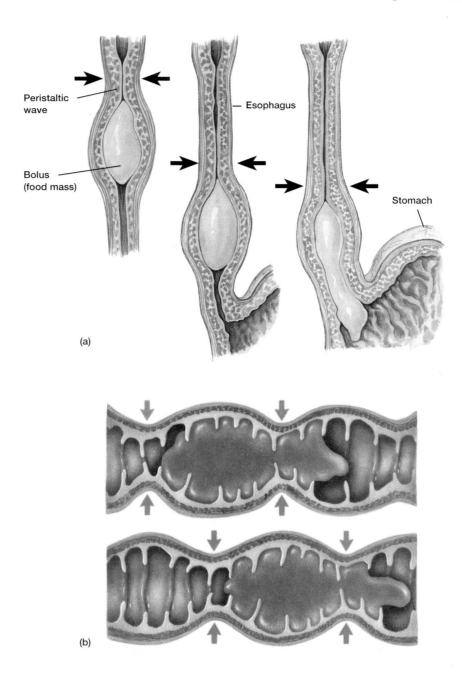

Peristaltic wave

Bolus (food mass)

Esophagus

Stomach

(a)

(b)

FIGURE 37.13

Peristalsis and Segmentation. (*a*) Peristaltic waves move food through the esophagus to the stomach. (*b*) In segmentation, simultaneous muscular contractions of many sections of the intestine (blue arrows) help mix nutrients with digestive secretions.

Stop and Ask Yourself

20. What are the component parts of the mammalian gastrointestinal tract? What are the accessory organs of digestion?

21. How do peristalsis and segmentation differ?

22. How is gastrointestinal motility controlled?

23. What is the function of saliva?

PHARYNX AND ESOPHAGUS

Chapter 36 discusses how both air and swallowed foods and liquids pass from the mouth into the **pharynx**—the common passageway for both the digestive and respiratory tracts. The epiglottis temporarily seals off the opening (glottis) to the trachea so that swallowed food does not enter the trachea. Initiation of the swallowing reflex can be voluntary, but most of the time it is involuntary. When swallowing begins, sequential, involuntary contractions of smooth muscles in the walls of the **esophagus** propel

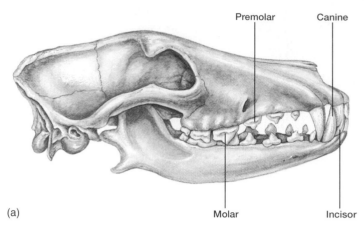

(a)

FIGURE 37.14

Teeth. (*a*) The teeth of a carnivore, such as this wolf, are specialized for slicing, puncturing, tearing, and grinding animal flesh. (*b*) Anatomy of a typical mammalian tooth.

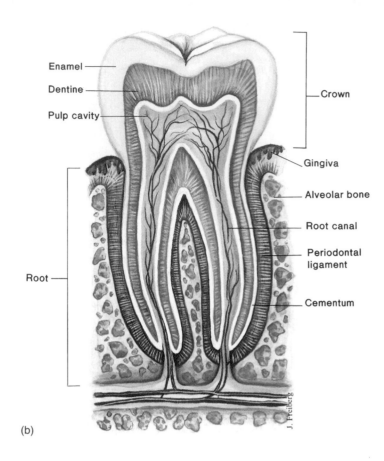

(b)

the bolus or liquid to the stomach. Neither the pharynx nor the esophagus contribute to digestion.

STOMACH

The mammalian **stomach** is a muscular, distensible sac with three main functions. It (1) stores and mixes the food bolus received from the esophagus, (2) secretes substances (enzymes, mucus, and hydrochloric acid [HCl]) that start the digestion of proteins, and (3) helps control the rate at which food moves into the small intestine via the pyloric sphincter (figure 37.15*a*).

The stomach is made up of an inner mucous membrane containing thousands of gastric glands (figure 37.15*b*). Three types of cells are in these glands. **Parietal cells** secrete a solution containing HCl, and **chief cells** secrete pepsinogen, the precursor of the enzyme pepsin. Both of the cells are in the pits of the gastric glands. The surface of the mucous membrane at the openings of the glands contains numerous **mucous cells** that secrete mucus that coats the surface of the stomach and protects it from the HCl and digestive enzymes.   ❽   The surfaces of the upper gastrointestinal tract—the esophagus and mouth—have a much thinner mucous-cell layer than the stomach, which is why vomiting can cause a burning sensation in the esophagus or mouth. Endocrine cells in one part of the stomach mucosa release the hormone gastrin, which travels to target cells in the gastric glands, further stimulating them.

When the bolus of food enters the stomach, it distends the walls of the stomach. This distention, as well as the act of eating, causes the gastric pits to secrete HCl (as H^+ and Cl^-) and pepsinogen. The H^+ ions cause pepsinogen to be converted into the active enzyme pepsin. As pepsin, mucus, and HCl mix with and begin to break down proteins, smooth mucosal muscles contract and vigorously churn and mix the food bolus. About 3 to 4 hours after a meal, the stomach contents have been sufficiently mixed and are a semiliquid mass called **chyme** (Gr. *chymos*, juice). The pyloric sphincter regulates the release of the chyme into the small intestine.

When the stomach is empty, peristaltic waves cease; however, after about 10 hours of fasting, new waves may occur in the upper region of the stomach.   ❾   These waves can cause "hunger pangs" as sensory nerve fibers carry impulses to the brain.

SMALL INTESTINE: MAIN SITE OF DIGESTION

Most of the food a mammal ingests is digested and absorbed in the **small intestine.** The human small intestine is about 4 cm in diameter and 7 to 8 m in length (*see figure 37.11*). It is intermediate in length between the small intestines of typical carnivores and herbivores of similar size, and reflects the human's omnivorous eating habits. The length of the small intestine directly relates to the total surface area available for absorbing nutrients, as determined by the many circular folds and minute projections of the inner gut surface (figure 37.16*a*). On the circular folds, thousands of fingerlike projections called **villi** (L. *villus*, tuft of hair) (sing. villus) project from each square centimeter of mucosa (figure 37.16*b*). Simple columnar epithelial cells, each bearing numerous microvilli cover both the circular folds and villi (figure 37.16*d*). These minute projections are so dense that the inner wall of the human small intestine has a total surface area of approximately 300 m^2—the size of a tennis court.

Loechel

FIGURE 37.15

Stomach. (*a*) Food enters the stomach from the esophagus. (*b*) Gastric glands cover the mucosa of the stomach and include mucous cells, parietal cells, and chief cells. Each type produces a different secretion.

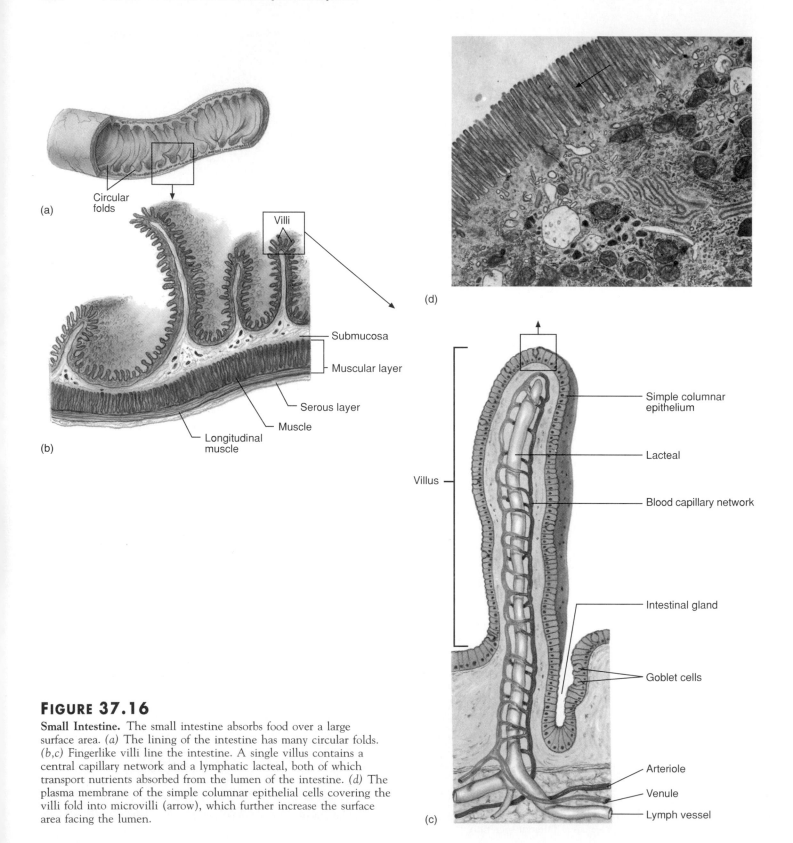

(a) Circular folds

(b) Villi
Submucosa
Muscular layer
Serous layer
Muscle
Longitudinal muscle

(c) Villus
Simple columnar epithelium
Lacteal
Blood capillary network
Intestinal gland
Goblet cells
Arteriole
Venule
Lymph vessel

(d)

FIGURE 37.16

Small Intestine. The small intestine absorbs food over a large surface area. (*a*) The lining of the intestine has many circular folds. (*b,c*) Fingerlike villi line the intestine. A single villus contains a central capillary network and a lymphatic lacteal, both of which transport nutrients absorbed from the lumen of the intestine. (*d*) The plasma membrane of the simple columnar epithelial cells covering the villi fold into microvilli (arrow), which further increase the surface area facing the lumen.

The first part of the small intestine, called the duodenum, functions primarily in digestion. The next part is the jejunum, and the last part is the ileum. Both function in nutrient absorption.

The duodenum contains many digestive enzymes that intestinal glands in the duodenal mucosa secrete. The pancreas secretes other enzymes. In the duodenum, digestion of carbohydrates and proteins is completed, and most lipids are digested. The jejunum and ileum absorb the end products of digestion (amino acids, simple sugars, fatty acids, glycerol, nucleotides, water). Much of this absorption involves active transport and the sodium-dependent ATPase pump. Sugars and amino acids are absorbed into the capillaries of the villi, whereas free fatty acids enter the epithelial cells of the villi and recombine with glycerol to form triglycerides. The triglycerides are coated with proteins to form small droplets called **chylomicrons,** which enter the lacteals of the villi (figure 37.16c). From the lacteals, the chylomicrons move into the lymphatics and eventually into the bloodstream for transport throughout the body.

Besides absorbing organic molecules, the small intestine absorbs water and dissolved mineral ions. The small intestine absorbs about 9 liters of water per day, and the large intestine absorbs the rest.

LARGE INTESTINE

Unlike the small intestine, the **large intestine** has no circular folds, villi, or microvilli; thus, the surface area is much smaller. The small intestine joins the large intestine near a blind-ended sac, the **cecum** (L. *caecum*, blind gut) *(see figure 37.11).* The human cecum and its extension, the **appendix,** are storage sites and possibly represent evolutionary remains of a larger, functional cecum, such as is found in herbivores *(see figure 37.10).* The appendix contains an abundance of lymphoid tissue and may function as part of the immune system.

The major functions of the large intestine include the reabsorption of water and minerals, and the formation and storage of feces. As peristaltic waves move food residue along, minerals diffuse or are actively transported from the residue across the epithelial surface of the large intestine into the bloodstream. Water follows osmotically and returns to the lymphatic system and bloodstream. When water reabsorption is insufficient, diarrhea (Gr. *rhein,* to flow) results. If too much water is reabsorbed, fecal matter becomes too thick, resulting in constipation.

Many bacteria and fungi exist symbiotically in the large intestine. They feed on the food residue and further break down its organic molecules to waste products. In turn, they secrete amino acids and vitamin K, which the host's gut absorbs. What remains—feces—is a mixture of bacteria, fungi, undigested plant fiber, sloughed-off intestinal cells, and other waste products.

ROLE OF THE PANCREAS IN DIGESTION

The **pancreas** (Gr. *pan,* all + *kreas,* flesh) is an organ that lies just ventral to the stomach and has both endocrine and exocrine functions. Exocrine cells in the pancreas secrete digestive enzymes into the pancreatic duct, which merges with the hepatic duct from the liver to form a common bile duct that enters the duodenum. Pancreatic enzymes complete the digestion of carbohydrates and proteins, and initiate the digestion of lipids. Trypsin, carboxypeptidase, and chymotrypsin digest proteins into small peptides and individual amino acids. Pancreatic lipases split triglycerides into smaller, absorbable glycerol and free fatty acids. Pancreatic amylase converts polysaccharides into disaccharides and monosaccharides. Table 37.6 summarizes the major glands, secretions, and enzymes of the mammalian digestive system.

The pancreas also secretes bicarbonate (HCO_3^-) ions that help neutralize the acidic food residue coming from the stomach. Bicarbonate raises the pH from 2 to 7 for optimal digestion. Without such neutralization, pancreatic enzymes could not function.

ROLE OF THE LIVER AND GALLBLADDER IN DIGESTION

The **liver,** the largest organ in the mammalian body, is just under the diaphragm *(see figure 37.11).* In the liver, millions of specialized cells called hepatocytes take up nutrients absorbed from the intestines and release them into the bloodstream. Hepatocytes also manufacture the blood proteins prothrombin and albumin.

In addition, some major metabolic functions of the liver include:

1. Removal of amino acids from organic compounds.
2. Urea formation from proteins and conversion of excess amino acids into urea to decrease body levels of ammonia.
3. Manufacture of most of the plasma proteins, formation of fetal erythrocytes, destruction of worn-out erythrocytes, and synthesis of the blood-clotting agents prothrombin and fibrinogen from amino acids.

TABLE 37.6	MAJOR DIGESTIVE GLANDS, SECRETIONS, AND ENZYMES IN MAMMALS			
PLACE OF DIGESTION	**SOURCE**	**SECRETION**	**ENZYME**	**DIGESTIVE FUNCTION**
Mouth	Salivary glands	Saliva	Salivary amylase	Begins the digestion of carbohydrates; inactivated by stomach HCl
	Mucous glands	Mucus	—	Lubricates food bolus
Esophagus	Mucous glands	Mucus	—	Lubricates food bolus
Stomach	Gastric glands	Gastric juice	Lipase	Digests lipids into fatty acids and glycerol
			Pepsin	Digests proteins into polypeptides
	Gastric mucosa	HCl	—	Converts pepsinogen into active pepsin; kills microorganisms
	Mucous glands	Mucus	—	Lubricates
Small intestine	Liver	Bile	—	Emulsifies lipids; activates lipase
	Pancreas	Pancreatic juice	Amylase	Digests starch into maltose
			Chymotrypsin	Digests proteins into peptides and amino acids
			Lipase	Digests lipids into fatty acids and glycerol (requires bile salts)
			Nuclease	Digests nucleic acids into mononucleotides
			Trypsin	Digests proteins into peptides and amino acids
	Intestinal glands	Intestinal juice	Enterokinase	Digests inactive trypsinogen into active trypsin
			Lactase	Digests lactose into glucose and galactose
			Maltase	Digests maltose into glucose
			Peptidase	Digests polypeptides into amino acids
			Sucrase	Digests sucrose into glucose and fructose
	Mucous glands	Mucus	—	Lubricates
Large intestine	Mucous glands	Mucus	—	Lubricates

4. Synthesis of nonessential amino acids.
5. Conversion of galactose and fructose to glucose.
6. Oxidation of fatty acids.
7. Formation of lipoproteins, cholesterol, and phospholipids (essential cell membrane components).
8. Conversion of carbohydrates and proteins into fat.
9. Modification of waste products, toxic drugs, and poisons (detoxification).
10. Synthesis of vitamin A from carotene, and with the kidneys, participation in the activation of vitamin D.
11. Maintenance of a stable body temperature by raising the temperature of the blood passing through it. Its many metabolic activities make the liver the major heat producer in a mammal's body.
12. Manufacture of bile salts, which are used in the small intestine for the emulsification and absorption of simple fats, cholesterol, phospholipids, and lipoproteins.

13. Main storage center. The liver stores glucose in the form of glycogen, and with the help of insulin and enzymes, converts glycogen back into glucose as the body needs it. The liver also stores fat-soluble vitamins (A, D, E, and K), and minerals, such as iron, from the diet. The liver can also store fats and amino acids, and convert them into usable glucose as required.

The **gallbladder** (L. *galbinus*, greenish yellow) is a small organ near the liver (*see figure 37.11*). The gallbladder stores the greenish fluid called bile that the liver cells continuously produce. Bile is very alkaline and contains pigments, cholesterol, lecithin, mucin, bilirubin, and bile salts that act as detergents to emulsify fats (form them into droplets suspended in water) and aid in fat digestion and absorption. (Recall that fats are insoluble in water.) Bile salts also combine with the end products of fat digestion to form micelles. **Micelles** are lipid aggregates (fatty acids and glycerol) with a surface coat of bile salts. Because they are so small, they can cross the microvilli of the intestinal epithelium.

SUMMARY

1. Nutrition describes all of those processes by which an animal takes in, digests, absorbs, stores, and uses food (nutrients) to meet its metabolic needs. Digestion is the mechanical and chemical breakdown of food into smaller particles that the individual cells of an animal can absorb.

2. Losses of biosynthetic abilities have marked much of animal evolution. This tendency has led to the evolution of the following nutritional types: insectivores, herbivores, carnivores, and omnivores.

3. The nutrients that a heterotroph ingests can be divided into macronutrients and micronutrients. Macronutrients are needed in large quantities and include the carbohydrates, lipids, and proteins. Micronutrients are needed in small quantities and include the vitamins and minerals.

4. Only a few protists and animals can absorb nutrients directly from their external environment. Most animals must work for their nutrients. Various specializations have evolved for food procurement (feeding) in animals. Some examples include continuous versus discontinuous feeding, suspension feeding, deposit feeding, herbivory, predation, surface nutrient absorption, and fluid feeding.

5. The evolution and structure of the digestive system in various invertebrates and vertebrates reflect their eating habits, their rate of metabolism, and their body size.

6. The digestive system of vertebrates is one-way, leading from the mouth (oral cavity), to the pharynx, esophagus, stomach, small intestine, large intestine, rectum, and anus.

7. The coordinated contractions of the muscle layer of the gastrointestinal tract mix food material with various secretions and move the food from the oral cavity to the rectum. The two types of movement involved are segmentation and peristalsis.

8. Most digestion occurs in the duodenal portion of the small intestine. The products of digestion are absorbed in the walls of the jejunum and ileum. In the process of digestion, bile that the liver secretes makes fats soluble. The liver has many diverse functions. It controls the fate of newly synthesized food molecules, stores excess glucose as glycogen, synthesizes many blood proteins, and converts nitrogenous and other wastes into a form that the kidneys can excrete.

9. The large intestine has little digestive or nutrient absorptive activity. It functions principally to absorb water, to compact the material left over from digestion, and to be a storehouse for microorganisms.

SELECTED KEY TERMS

autotrophs (p. 630)
carnivores (p. 630)
digestion (p. 630)
herbivores (p. 630)
heterotrophs (p. 630)
macronutrients (p. 630)

micronutrients (p. 630)
nutrition (p. 630)
omnivores (p. 630)
suspension feeding (p. 634)
vitamin (p. 632)

CRITICAL THINKING QUESTIONS

1. What advantages are there to digestion? Would it not be simpler for a vertebrate to simply absorb carbohydrates, lipids, and proteins from its food and to use these molecules without breaking them down?

2. What might have been some evolutionary pressures acting on animals that led to the internalization of digestive systems?

3. Many digestive enzymes are produced in the pancreas and released into the duodenum. Why, then, has the mammalian stomach evolved the ability to produce pepsinogen?

4. Human vegetarians, unlike true herbivores, have no highly specialized fermentation chambers. Why?

5. Trace the fate of a hamburger from the mouth to the anus, identifying sites and mechanisms of digestion and absorption.

REFERENCES ON THE WORLD WIDE WEB

1. **Digestive Organs.**   This site contains graphics of the digestive organs, as well as information on organ function.

    http://girch301.med.uth.tmc.edu/digestive/organs.html

2. **The Digestive System.**   This site includes useful information for the beginning zoology student.

    http://rivers.oscs.montana.edu/esg/kla/ta/digest.html

3. **Alimentary Tract.**   View the map to develop an understanding of the alimentary tract.

    http://cookie.imcb.osaka-u.ac.jp/bodymap/gallery/alimentary.html

4. **Human Anatomy On-Line.**   This site provides an abundance of information on the human body, including a detailed look at the digestive system.

    http://www.innerbody.com/

5. **Gallbladder.**   This site presents the anatomy and physiology of the gallbladder.

    http://www.jfka.com/alpub/gbflush.htm

6. **Anatomy of the Stomach.**   This site presents the anatomy of the stomach.

    http://www.ee.ualberta.ca/~mintchev/stomach.html

7. **The Large Intestine.**   Learn the structure and function of the large intestine at this site.

    http://gnv.ifas.ufl.edu/~fairsweb/text/ds/2848.html

TEMPERATURE AND BODY FLUID REGULATION

Concepts

1. Thermoregulation is a complex and important physiological process that maintains, to varying degrees, an animal's body temperature, despite variations in environmental temperature. Based on this regulation, animals can be categorized as endotherms or ectotherms, and homeotherms or heterotherms.
2. For osmoregulation, some invertebrates have contractile vacuoles, flame-cell systems, antennal (green) glands, maxillary glands, coxal glands, nephridia, or Malpighian tubules.
3. A vertebrate's urinary system functions in osmoregulation and excretion, both of which are necessary for internal homeostasis. Osmoregulation governs water and salt balance, and excretion eliminates metabolic wastes. In fishes, reptiles, birds, and mammals, the kidneys are the primary osmoregulatory structures.

Would You Like to Know . . .

1. how sweating cools the body? (p. 657)
2. why hummingbirds spend so much more time feeding than larger birds? (p. 658)
3. why bluefin tuna and great white sharks can swim faster than other fishes of a comparable size? (p. 660)
4. why frogs have to live in warm, moist environments? (p. 660)
5. why goose down is traditionally used as an insulator in outdoor vests and jackets? (p. 660)
6. what blubber is? (p. 661)
7. why freshwater fishes usually do not drink much water? (p. 668)
8. why saltwater fishes drink large quantities of water? (p. 668)
9. why a dog's nose is normally cold and wet? (p. 671)
10. how kangaroo rats can live in a desert environment and drink little or no water? (p. 673)

This chapter answers these and other useful questions.

This chapter contains evolutionary concepts, which are set off in this font.

The earth's environments vary dramatically in temperature and amount of water present. In the polar regions, high mountain ranges, and deep oceans, the temperature remains near or below 0° C (32° F) throughout the year. Temperatures exceeding 40° C (103° F) are common in equatorial deserts. Between these two extremes, in the earth's temperate regions, temperatures fluctuate widely. The temperate regions have varying amounts of water, as well as varied habitats—freshwater, saltwater, wetlands, mountains, and grasslands.

Animals have successfully colonized these varied places on earth by possessing homeostatic mechanisms for maintaining a relatively constant internal environment, despite fluctuations in the external environment. This chapter covers three separate but related homeostatic systems that enable animals to survive the variations in temperature, water availability, and salinity (salt concentration) on the earth. The thermoregulatory system maintains an animal's body temperature and/or its responses to shifts in environmental temperature. The osmoregulatory system maintains the level and concentration of water and salts in the body. And the urinary system eliminates metabolic wastes from the body and functions in osmoregulation.

HOMEOSTASIS AND TEMPERATURE REGULATION

As presented in chapters 4 and 5, the temperature of a living cell affects the rate of its metabolic processes. An animal can grow faster and respond to the environment more rapidly if its cells are kept warm. In fact, zoologists believe that the ability of some higher animals to maintain a constant (homeostatic), relatively high body temperature is a major reason for their evolutionary success. This ability to control the temperature of the body is called **thermoregulation** ("heat control") and involves the nervous, endocrine, respiratory, and circulatory systems in higher animals.

THE IMPACT OF TEMPERATURE ON ANIMAL LIFE

Every animal's physiological functions are inexorably linked to temperature because metabolism is sensitive to changes in internal temperature. Thus, temperature has been a strong source of selective pressure on all animals. The rate of cellular respiration increases with temperature up to a point. When the temperature rises above the temperature optima at which enzymes most efficiently catalyze their chemical reactions, the rates decline as the enzymes begin to denature. The chemical interactions holding the enzymes in their three-dimensional shape are also disrupted. Thus, the results of enzyme evolution have frequently been enzymes with temperature optima that reflect an animal's habitat. For example, a digestive enzyme in a trout might function optimally at 10° C, whereas another enzyme in the human body that catalyzes the same reaction functions best at 37° C (*see figure 4.6*). Higher temperatures cause the proteins in nucleic acids to denature, and

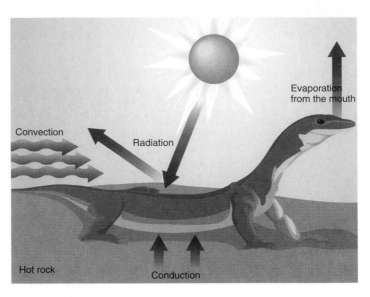

FIGURE 38.1

Heat Gain and Loss for a Terrestrial Reptile in a Typical Terrestrial Environment. Heat is either gained or lost by objects in direct contact with the animal (conduction), by air currents (convection), by exhaled air (evaporation), or by electromagnetic waves (radiation).

lower temperatures may cause membranes to change from a fluid to a solid state, which can interfere with many cellular processes, such as active-transport pumps.

Animals can guard against these damaging effects of temperature fluctuations by balancing heat gains and heat losses with their environment.

HEAT GAINS AND LOSSES

Animals produce heat as a by-product of metabolism and either gain heat from, or lose it to, the environment. The total body temperature is a result of an interaction of these factors and can be expressed as:

Body temperature = heat produced metabolically
+ heat gained from the environment
− heat lost to the environment

Animals use four physical processes to exchange heat with the environment: conduction, convection, evaporation, and radiation (figure 38.1). **Conduction** is the direct transfer of thermal motion (heat) between molecules of the environment and those on the body surface of an animal. This transfer is always from an area of higher temperature to one of lower temperature because heat moves down thermal gradients. For example, when you sit on the cold ground, you lose heat, and when you sit on warm sand, you gain heat.

Convection is the movement of air (or a liquid) over the surface of a body and contributes to heat loss (if the air is cooler than the body) or heat gain (if the air is warmer than the body). On a cool day, your body loses heat by convection because your skin temperature is higher than the surrounding air temperature.

Evaporation is loss of heat from a surface as water molecules escape in the form of a gas. It is useful only to terrestrial animals. For example, humans and some other mammals (chimpanzees and horses) have sweat glands that actively move watery solutions through pores to the skin surface. When skin temperature is high, water at the surface absorbs enough thermal energy to break the hydrogen bonds holding the individual water molecules together, and they depart from the surface, carrying heat with them. ① As long as the environmental humidity is low enough to permit complete evaporation, sweating can rid the mammalian body of excess heat; however, the water must evaporate. Sweat dripping from a mammal has no cooling effect at all.

Radiation is the emission of electromagnetic waves that objects, such as another animal's body or the sun, produce. Radiation can transfer heat between objects that are not in direct contact with each other, as happens when an animal suns itself (figure 38.2).

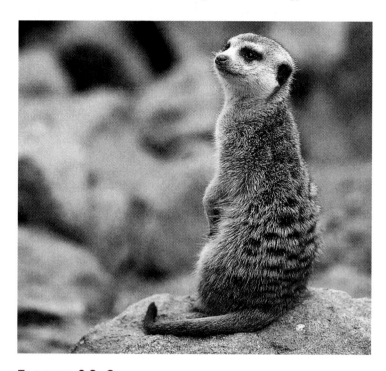

FIGURE 38.2

Radiation Warms an Animal. After a cold night in its den on the Kalahari Desert, a meerkat (*Suricata suricatta*) stands at attention, allowing the large surface area of its body to absorb radiation from the sun.

SOME SOLUTIONS TO TEMPERATURE FLUCTUATIONS

Animals cope with temperature fluctuations in one of three basic ways. (1) They can occupy a place in the environment where the temperature remains constant and compatible with their physiological processes; (2) their physiological processes may have adapted to the range of temperatures in which the animals are capable of living; or (3) they can generate and trap heat internally to maintain a constant body temperature, despite fluctuations in the temperature of the external environment.

Animals can be categorized as ectotherms or endotherms, based on whether their source of body heat is from internal processes or derived from the environment. **Ectotherms** (Gr. *ectos*, outside) derive most of their body heat from the environment rather than from their own metabolism (figure 38.3). They have low rates of metabolism and are poorly insulated. In general, reptiles, amphibians, fishes, and invertebrates are ectotherms, although a few reptiles, insects, and fishes can raise their internal temperature. Ectotherms tend to move about the environment and find places that minimize heat or cold stress to their bodies.

Maximize heat gain

Minimize heat gain

FIGURE 38.3

Heat Gain in an Insect. Postures a dragonfly adopts to either maximize or minimize heat gain.

Birds and mammals are called **endotherms** (Gr. *endos,* within) because they obtain their body heat from cellular processes. A constant source of internal heat allows them to maintain a nearly constant core temperature, despite the fluctuating environmental temperature. ("Core" refers to the body's internal temperature as opposed to the temperature near its surface.)

Most endotherms have bodies insulated by fur or feathers and a relatively large amount of fat. This insulation enables them to retain heat more efficiently and to maintain a high core temperature. Endothermy allows animals to stabilize their core temperature so that biochemical processes and nervous system functions can proceed at steady, high levels. Endothermy allows some animals to colonize habitats denied to ectotherms.

Another way of categorizing animals is based on whether they maintain a constant or variable body temperature. Although most endotherms are **homeotherms** (maintain a relatively constant body temperature), and most ectotherms are **heterotherms** (have a variable body temperature), there are many exceptions. Some endotherms vary their body temperatures seasonally (e.g., hibernation); others vary it on a daily basis.

For example, some birds (e.g., hummingbirds) and mammals (e.g., shrews) can only maintain a high body temperature for a short period because they usually weigh less than 10 g and have a body mass so small that they cannot generate enough heat to compensate for the heat lost across their relatively large surface area. ❷ Hummingbirds must devote much of the day to locating and sipping nectar (a very high-calorie food source) as a constant energy source for metabolism. When not feeding, hummingbirds rapidly run out of energy unless their metabolic rates decrease considerably. At night, hummingbirds enter a sleep-like state, called **daily torpor,** and their body temperature approaches that of the cooler surroundings. Some bats also undergo daily torpor to conserve energy.

Some ectotherms can maintain fairly constant body temperatures. Among these are a number of reptiles that can maintain fairly constant body temperatures by changing position and location during the day to equalize heat gain and loss.

In general, ectotherms are more common in the tropics because they do not have to expend as much energy to maintain body temperature there, and they can devote more energy to food gathering and reproduction. Indeed, in the tropics, amphibians are far more abundant than mammals. Conversely, in moderate to cool environments, endotherms have a selective advantage and are more abundant. Their high metabolic rates and insulation allow them to occupy even the polar regions (e.g., polar bears). In fact, the efficient circulatory systems of birds and mammals can be thought of as adaptations to endothermy and a high metabolic rate.

Stop and Ask Yourself

1. What is thermoregulation?
2. How do temperature extremes affect metabolic reactions?
3. What are three basic ways animals cope with temperature fluctuations?
4. How can animals be categorized according to their source of body heat?

TEMPERATURE REGULATION IN INVERTEBRATES

As previously noted, environmental temperature is critical in limiting the distribution of all animals and in controlling metabolic reactions. Many invertebrates have relatively low metabolic rates and have no thermoregulatory mechanisms; thus, they passively conform to the temperature of their external environment. These invertebrates are termed **thermoconformers.**

Evidence indicates that some higher invertebrates can directly sense differences in environmental temperatures; however, specific receptors are either absent or unidentified. What zoologists do know is that many arthropods, such as insects, crustaceans, and the horseshoe crab (*Limulus*), can sense thermal variation. For example, ticks of warm-blooded vertebrates can sense the "warmth of a nearby meal" and drop on the vertebrate host.

Many arthropods have unique mechanisms for surviving temperature extremes. For example, temperate-zone insects avoid freezing by reducing the water content in their tissues as winter approaches. Other insects can produce glycerol or other glycoproteins that act as an antifreeze. Some moths and bumblebees warm up prior to flight by shivering contractions of their thoracic flight muscles. Most large, flying insects have evolved a mechanism to prevent overheating during flight; blood circulating through the flight muscles carries heat from the thorax to the abdomen, which gets rid of the heat—much as coolant circulating through an automobile engine passes through the radiator. Certain cicadas (*Diceroprocta apache*) that live in the Sonoran Desert have independently evolved the complete repertoire of evaporative cooling mechanisms that vertebrates use. When threatened with overheating, these cicadas extract water from their blood and transport it through large ducts to the surface of their body, where it passes through sweat pores and evaporates. In other words, these insects can sweat.

Body posture and orientation of the wings to the sun can markedly affect the body temperature of basking insects. For example, perching dragonflies and butterflies can regulate their radiation heat gain by postural adjustments (figure 38.3).

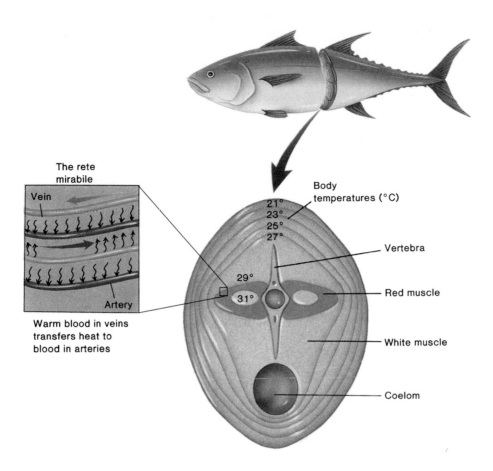

FIGURE 38.4

Thermoregulation in Large, Active Fishes. In the bluefin tuna, the rete mirabile of arteries and veins acts as a countercurrent exchange system that helps reduce the loss of body heat. The cross section through the body shows that the temperature is highest around the red swimming muscles.

To prevent overheating, many ground-dwelling arthropods (*Tenebrio* beetles, locusts, scorpions) raise their bodies as high off the ground as possible to minimize heat gain from the ground. Some caterpillars and locusts orient with reference to both the sun and wind to vary both radiation heat gain and convective heat loss. Some desert-dwelling beetles can exude waxes from thousands of tiny pores on their cuticle. These "wax blooms" prevent dehydration and also are an extra barrier against the desert sun.

Color has a significant effect on thermoregulation since 50% of the radiant energy from the sun is in the visible spectrum. A black surface reflects less radiant energy than a white surface. Thus, many black beetles may be more active earlier in the day because they absorb more radiation and heat faster. Conversely, white beetles are more active in the hotter parts of the day because they absorb less heat.

The previous examples of invertebrate temperature regulation give clues to how thermoregulation may have evolved in vertebrates. The endothermic temperature regulation of active insects apparently evolved because locomotion produced sufficient metabolic heat that thermoregulatory strategies could evolve. An increased locomotor metabolism could well have preceded the evolution of thermoregulation in vertebrates.

TEMPERATURE REGULATION IN FISHES

The temperature of the surrounding water determines the body temperature of most fishes. Fishes that live in extremely cold water have "antifreeze" materials in their blood. Polyalcohols (e.g., sorbitol, glycerol) or water-soluble peptides and glycopeptides lower the freezing point of blood plasma and other body fluids. These fishes also have proteins or protein-sugar compounds that stunt the growth of ice crystals that begin to form. These adaptations enable these fishes to stay flexible and swim freely in a supercooled state (i.e., at a temperature below the normal freezing temperature of a solution).

Some active fishes maintain a core temperature significantly above the temperature of the water. Bluefin tuna and the great white shark have major blood vessels just under the skin. Branches deliver blood to the deeper, powerful, red swimming muscles, where smaller vessels are arranged in a countercurrent heat exchanger called the **rete mirabile** ("miraculous net") (figure 38.4). The heat that these red muscles generate is not lost because it is transferred in the rete mirabile from venous blood passing outward to cold arterial blood passing inward from the body surface.

This arrangement of blood vessels enhances vigorous activity by keeping the swimming muscles several degrees warmer than the tissue near the surface of the fish. This system has been adaptive for these fishes. ③ Their muscular contractions can have four times as much power as those of similar muscles in fishes with cooler bodies. Thus, they can swim faster and range more widely through various depths in search of prey than can other predatory fishes more limited to given water depths and temperatures.

TEMPERATURE REGULATION IN AMPHIBIANS AND REPTILES

Animals, such as amphibians and reptiles, that have air rather than water as a surrounding medium face marked daily and seasonal temperature changes. Most of these animals are ectotherms. They derive heat from their environment, and their body temperatures vary with external temperatures.

Most amphibians have difficulty in controlling body heat because they produce little of it metabolically and rapidly lose most of it from their body surfaces. However, as previously noted, behavioral adaptations enable them to maintain their body temperature within a homeostatic range most of the time. Amphibians have an additional thermoregulatory problem because they must exchange oxygen and carbon dioxide across their skin surface, and this moisture layer acts as a natural evaporative cooling system. ④ This problem of heat loss through evaporation limits the habitats and activities of amphibians to warm, moist areas. Some amphibians, such as bullfrogs, can vary the amount of mucus they secrete from their body surface—a physiological response that helps regulate evaporative cooling.

Reptiles have dry rather than moist skin, which reduces loss of body heat through evaporative cooling of the skin. They also have an expandable rib cage, which allows for more powerful and efficient ventilation. Reptiles are almost completely ectothermic. They have a low metabolic rate and warm themselves by behavioral adaptations. In addition, some of the more sophisticated regulatory mechanisms found in mammals are first found in reptiles. For example, diving reptiles (e.g., sea turtles, sea snakes) conserve body heat by routing blood through circulatory shunts into the center of the body. These animals can also increase heat production in response to the hormones thyroxine and epinephrine. In addition, tortoises and land turtles can cool themselves through salivating and frothing at the mouth, urinating on the back legs, moistening the eyes, and panting.

TEMPERATURE REGULATION IN BIRDS AND MAMMALS

Birds and mammals are the most active and behaviorally complex vertebrates. They can live in habitats all over the earth because they are homeothermic endotherms; they can maintain body temperatures between 35 and 42° C with metabolic heat.

Various cooling mechanisms prevent excessive warming in birds. Because they have no sweat glands, birds pant to lose heat

(a)

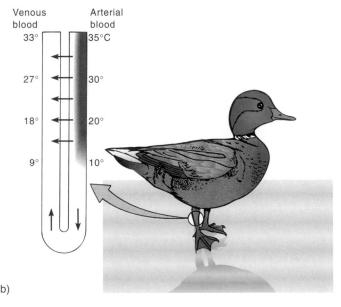

(b)

FIGURE 38.5

Insulation and Countercurrent Heat Exchange. (*a*) A thick layer of down feathers keeps these Chinstrap penguins (*Pygocelis antarctia*) warm. Their covering of short, stiff feathers interlocks to trap air, forming the ornithological equivalent of a diver's suit. (*b*) The countercurrent heat exchanger in a bird foot. Some aquatic birds, such as this duck, possess countercurrent systems of arteries and veins (rete mirabile) in their legs that reduce heat loss. The arteries carry warm blood down the legs to warm the cooler blood in the veins, so that the heat is carried back to the body rather than lost through the feet that are in contact with a cold surface.

through evaporative cooling. Some species have a highly vascularized pouch (gular pouch) in their throat that they can flutter (a process called **gular flutter**) to increase evaporation from the respiratory system.

⑤ Some birds possess mechanisms for preventing heat loss. Feathers are excellent insulators for the body, especially downy-type feathers that trap a layer of air next to the body to reduce heat loss from the skin (figure 38.5*a*). (This mechanism explains

FIGURE 38.6

Temperature Regulation. This antelope jackrabbit (*Lepus alleni*) must get rid of excess body heat. Its huge, thin, highly vascularized ears have a large surface area for heat exchange.

why goose down is such an excellent insulator and is used in outdoor vests and coats for protection from extreme cold.) Aquatic species, who lose heat from their legs and feet, have peripheral countercurrent heat exchange vessels called a rete mirabile in their legs to reduce heat loss (figure 38.5b). Mammals that live in cold regions, such as the arctic fox and barren-ground caribou, also have these exchange vessels in their extremities (e.g., legs, tails, ears, nose). Animals in hot climates, such as jackrabbits, have mechanisms (e.g., large ears) to rid the body of excess heat (figure 38.6).

6 Thick pelts and a thick layer of insulating fat called **blubber** just under the skin help marine animals, such as seals and whales, to maintain a body temperature of around 36 to 38° C. In the tail and flippers, which have no blubber, a countercurrent system of arteries and veins helps minimize heat loss.

Birds and mammals also use behavioral mechanisms to cope with external temperature changes. Like ectotherms, they sun themselves or seek shade as the temperature fluctuates. Many animals huddle to keep warm; others share burrows for protection from temperature extremes. Migration to warm climates and hibernation enable many different birds and mammals to survive the harsh winter months. Others, such as the desert camel, have a multitude of evolutionary adaptations for surviving in some of the hottest and driest climates on earth (box 38.1).

HEAT PRODUCTION IN BIRDS AND MAMMALS

In endotherms, heat generation can warm the body as it dissipates throughout tissues and organs. Birds and mammals can generate heat

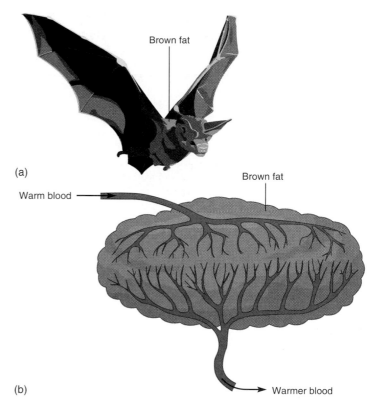

FIGURE 38.7

Brown Fat. (a) Many mammals, such as this bat, have adipose tissue called brown fat between the shoulder blades. (b) The area of brown fat is much warmer than the rest of the body. Blood flowing through the brown fat is warmed.

(thermogenesis) by muscle contraction, ATPase pump enzymes, oxidation of fatty acids in brown fat, and other metabolic processes.

Every time a muscle cell contracts, the actin and myosin filaments sliding over each other and the hydrolysis of ATP molecules generate heat. Both voluntary muscular work (e.g., running, flying, jumping) and involuntary muscular work (e.g., shivering) generate heat. Heat generation by shivering is called **shivering thermogenesis.**

Birds and mammals have a unique capacity to generate heat by using specific enzymes of ancient evolutionary origin—the ATPase pump enzymes in the plasma membranes of most cells. When the body cools, the thyroid gland releases the hormone thyroxine. Thyroxine increases the permeability of many cells to sodium (Na^+) ions, which leak into the cells. The ATPase pump quickly pumps these ions out. In the process, ATP is hydrolyzed, releasing heat energy. The hormonal triggering of heat production is called **nonshivering thermogenesis.**

Brown fat is a specialized type of fat found in newborn mammals, in mammals that live in cold climates, and in mammals that hibernate (figure 38.7). The brown color of this fat comes from the large number of mitochondria with their iron-containing cytochromes. Deposits of brown fat are beneath the ribs and in the shoulders. A large amount of heat is produced when brown fat

BOX 38.1   HOW THE ONE-HUMPED DROMEDARY (CAMEL) OF THE ARABIAN AND AFRICAN DESERTS THRIVES IN SOME OF THE HOTTEST AND DRIEST CLIMATES ON EARTH

During the past 3 million years, various physiological and behavioral mechanisms have evolved in the dromedary or one-humped camel (*Camelus dromedarius*) (figure 1) that enable it to survive on the Arabian and African deserts, where temperatures in the summer can exceed 140° F (60° C). What particularly distinguishes the desert camel is its ability to relinquish strict homeothermy and allow its body temperature to fluctuate with that of the environment. As a result, the difference between a camel's body temperature and that of the environment is never large; thus, the flow of heat from the air to the body is reduced.

Another of the camel's physiological adaptations to heat is its "adjustable" metabolic rate. As the desert temperature increases, the camel's metabolic rate slows. Due to slow dehydration, the amount of thyroxine that the thyroid gland produces drops (*see figure 38.8*). With less thyroxine, the camel's respiratory rate also slows, thereby reducing water loss via breathing.

Camel blood is unusual in two ways: its plasma contains more water than that of other animals, and its oval-shaped red blood cells (*see figure 36.4c*) stay intact even when the plasma surrounding the cells has a high osmolarity (they do not crenate; *see figure 3.11b*). Under similar conditions, the red blood cells of other mammals would crenate, and the blood would cease flowing and transporting body heat outward to the skin, leading to a heatstroke. But even after a camel has lost more than half of its body water, its blood continues to circulate and dissipate heat.

The camel also conserves water by excreting extremely dry feces and recycling water from the kidneys to the stomach and back to the blood. (By contrast, other ruminants [cows and goats] cannot recycle water and lose so much fluid when heat stressed that the alimentary tract and kidneys cease functioning entirely.) A camel, after recycling water for weeks, can drink 40 gallons of water and rehydrate its blood in less than an hour.

To counteract heat and dehydration, the camel also modifies its behavior. When possible, it lies down, thereby reducing the heat

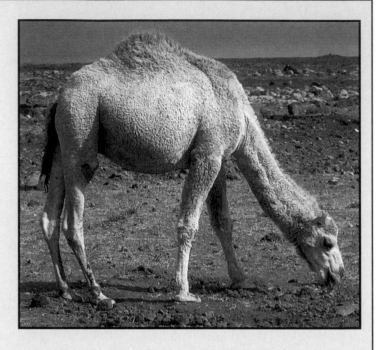

FIGURE 1   The One-humped Camel, (*Camelus dromedarius*).

energy that muscle activity and metabolism produce. Camels also take advantage of the shade cast by other camels and squat close to each other, creating an even larger cooled area. At the same time, each camel faces the sun so that the hump absorbs most of the direct sunlight, and the smallest possible body area is exposed. The hump is a concentration of body fat that acts as a sunscreen, to shield the camel's vital organs. The camel also urinates on its long legs, and evaporation of the urine cools the blood vessels in the legs.

---

cells oxidize fatty acids because little ATP is made. Blood flowing past brown fat is heated and contributes to warming the body.

The basal metabolic rate of birds and mammals is high and also produces heat as an inadvertent but useful by-product (*see figure 4.10*).

In amphibians, reptiles, birds, and mammals, specialized cells in the hypothalamus of the brain control thermoregulation. The two hypothalamic thermoregulatory areas are the heating center and the cooling center. The heating center controls vasoconstriction of superficial blood vessels, erection of hair and fur, and shivering or nonshivering thermogenesis. The cooling center controls vasodilation of blood vessels, sweating, and panting.

Overall, feedback mechanisms (with the hypothalamus acting as a thermostat) trigger either the heating or cooling of the body and thereby control body temperature (figure 38.8). Specialized neuronal receptors in the skin and other parts of the body sense temperature changes. Warm neuronal receptors excite the cooling center and inhibit the heating center. Cold neuronal receptors have the opposite effects.

During the winter, various endotherms (e.g., bats, woodchucks, chipmunks, ground squirrels) go into **hibernation** (L. *hiberna*, winter). During hibernation, the metabolic rate slows, as do the heart and breathing rates. Mammals prepare for hibernation by building up fat reserves and growing long winter pelts.

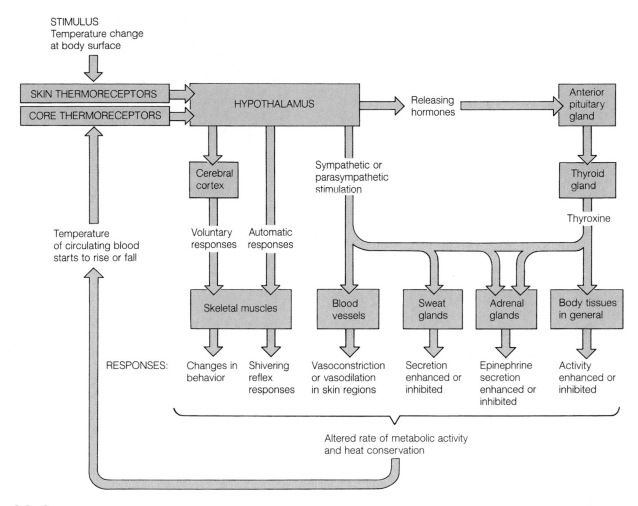

FIGURE 38.8

Thermoregulation. Overview of the feedback pathways that control the core body temperature of a mammal. Arrows show the major control pathways.

All hibernating animals have brown fat. Decreasing day length stimulates both increased fat deposition and fur growth. Another physiological state characterized by slow metabolism and inactivity is **aestivation** (L. *aestivus*, summer), which allows certain mammals to survive long periods of elevated temperature and diminished water supplies.

Some animals, such as badgers, bears, opossums, raccoons, and skunks, enter a state of prolonged sleep in the winter. Since their body temperature remains near normal, this is not true hibernation.

Stop and Ask Yourself

5. What is the function of a rete mirabile?

6. How do amphibians maintain their body temperature?

7. How do birds and mammals generate heat?

8. How do hibernation and aestivation differ?

CONTROL OF WATER AND SOLUTES (OSMOREGULATION AND EXCRETION)

Excretion (L. *excretio*, to eliminate) can be defined broadly as the elimination of metabolic waste products from an animal's body. These products include carbon dioxide and water (which cellular respiration primarily produces), excess nitrogen (which is produced as ammonia from deamination of amino acids), and solutes (various ions). Chapter 36 covers the excretion of respiratory carbon dioxide.

Excretion of nitrogenous wastes is usually associated with the regulation of water and solute (ionic) balance by a physiological process called **osmoregulation.** Osmoregulation is necessary for animals in all habitats. If the osmotic concentration of the body fluids of an animal equals that of the medium (the animal's environment), the animal is an **osmoconformer.** When the osmotic concentration of the environment changes, so does that of the animal's body fluids. Obviously, this type of osmoregulation is not efficient and has limited the distribution of those animals using it. In contrast, an animal that maintains its body fluids at a different osmotic concentration from that of its surrounding environment is an **osmoregulator.**

Animals living in seawater have body fluids with an osmotic concentration that is about a third less (hypoosmotic) than the surrounding seawater, and water tends to leave their bodies continually. To compensate for this problem, mechanisms evolved in these animals to conserve water and prevent dehydration. Freshwater animals have body fluids that are hyperosmotic with respect to their environment, and water tends to continually enter their bodies. Mechanisms evolved in these animals that excrete water and prevent fluid accumulation. Land animals have a higher concentration of water in their fluids than in the surrounding air. They tend to lose water to the air through evaporation and may use considerable amounts of water to dispose of wastes.

The form and function of organs or systems associated with excretion and osmoregulation are related both to environmental conditions (saltwater, freshwater, terrestrial) and to body size (especially the surface-to-volume ratio). Some of the ways animals accomplish excretion and osmoregulation, and the structures involved, are discussed next.

INVERTEBRATE EXCRETORY SYSTEMS

Aquatic invertebrates occur in a wide range of media, from freshwater to markedly hypersaline water (e.g., salt lakes). Generally, marine invertebrates have about the same osmotic concentration as seawater (i.e., they are osmoconformers). This avoids any need to osmoregulate. Most water and ions are gained across the integument, via gills, by drinking, and in food. Ions and wastes are mostly lost by diffusion via the integument, gills, or urine.

Freshwater invertebrates are strong osmoregulators because it is impossible to be isosmotic with dilute media. Any water gain is usually eliminated as urine.

A number of invertebrate taxa have more or less successfully invaded terrestrial habitats. The most successful terrestrial invertebrates are the arthropods, particularly the insects, spiders, scorpions, ticks, mites, centipedes, and millipedes. Overall, the water and ion balance of terrestrial invertebrates is quite different from that of aquatic animals because terrestrial invertebrates face limited water supplies and water loss by evaporation from their integument. Some of the invertebrate excretory mechanisms and systems are now discussed.

CONTRACTILE VACUOLES

Some protists and marine invertebrates (e.g., protozoa, cnidarians, echinoderms, sponges) do not have specialized excretory structures because wastes simply diffuse into the surrounding isoosmotic water. In some freshwater species, cells on the body surface actively pump ions into the animal. Many freshwater species (protozoa, sponges), however, have contractile vacuoles that pump out

FIGURE 38.9

Contractile Vacuoles. A photomicrograph (×100) showing the location of two contractile vacuoles (black arrows) in a stained *Paramecium*. Notice the small tubules surrounding each vacuole. These tubes collect water and deliver it to the contractile vacuole, which expels the fluid through a pore.

excess water. **Contractile vacuoles** are energy-requiring devices that expel excess water from individual cells exposed to hypoosmotic environments (figure 38.9).

PROTONEPHRIDIA

Although a few groups of metazoan invertebrates possess no known excretory structures, most have **nephridia** (Gr. *nephros*, kidney) (sing., nephridium) that serve for excretion, osmoregulation, or both. Probably the earliest type of nephridium to appear in the evolution of animals was the **protonephridium** (Gr. *protos*, first + nephridium).

Among the simplest of the protonephridia are flame-cell systems, such as those in rotifers, some annelids, larval molluscs, and some flatworms (figure 38.10). The protonephridial excretory system is composed of a network of excretory canals that open to the outside of the body through excretory pores. Bulblike **flame cells** are located along the excretory canals. Fluid filters into the flame cells from the surrounding interstitial fluid, and beating cilia propel the fluid through the excretory canals and out of the body through the excretory pores. Flame-cell systems function primarily in eliminating excess water. Nitrogenous waste simply diffuses across the body surface into the surrounding water.

METANEPHRIDIA

A more advanced type of excretory structure among invertebrates is the **metanephridium** (Gr. *meta*, beyond + nephridium;) (pl., metanephridia). Protonephridia and metanephridia have critical structural differences. Both open to the outside, but metanephridia (1) also open internally to the body fluids and (2) are multicellular.

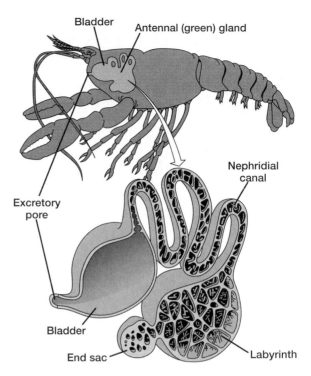

FIGURE 38.10

Protonephridial (Excretory) System in a Turbellarian. (*a*) The system lies in the mesenchyme and consists of a network of fine tubules that run the length of the animal on each side and open to the surface by minute excretory pores called nephridiopores. (*b*) Numerous fine side branches from the tubules originate in the mesenchyme in enlargements called flame cells.

FIGURE 38.12

Antennal (Green) Gland of the Crayfish. The antennal gland, which lies in front of and to both sides of the esophagus, is divided into an end sac, where fluid collects by filtration, and a labyrinth. The labyrinth walls are greatly folded and glandular and appear to be an important site for reabsorption. The labyrinth leads via a nephridial canal into a bladder. From the bladder, a short duct leads to an excretory pore.

FIGURE 38.11

Earthworm Metanephridium. The metanephridium opens by a ciliated nephrostome into the cavity of one segment, and the next segment contains the nephridiopore. The main tubular portion of the metanephridium is coiled and is surrounded by a capillary network. Waste can be stored in a bladder before being expelled to the outside. Most segments contain two metanephridia.

Most annelids (such as the common earthworm) and a variety of other invertebrates have a metanephridial excretory system. Recall that the earthworm's body is divided into segments and that each segment has a pair of metanephridia. Each metanephridium begins with a ciliated funnel, the nephrostome, that opens from the body cavity of a segment into a coiled tubule (figure 38.11). As

beating cilia move the fluid through the tubule, a network of capillaries surrounding the tubule reabsorbs and carries away ions. Each tubule leads to an enlarged bladder that empties to the outside of the body through an opening called the nephridiopore.

The excretory system of molluscs includes protonephridia in larval stages and metanephridia in adults.

ANTENNAL (GREEN) AND MAXILLARY GLANDS

In those crustaceans that have gills, nitrogenous wastes are removed by simple diffusion across the gills. Most crustaceans release ammonia, although they also produce some urea and uric acid as waste products. Thus, the excretory organs of freshwater species may be more involved with reabsorption of ions and elimination of water than with discharge of nitrogenous wastes. The excretory organs in some crustaceans (crayfish, crabs) are **antennal glands** or **green glands** because of their location near the antenna and their green color (figure 38.12). Fluid filters into the antennal gland from the hemocoel. Hemolymph pressure from the heart is the main driving force for filtration. Marine crustaceans have a short nephridial canal and produce urine that is isoosmotic to their hemolymph. The nephridial canal is longer in freshwater crustaceans, which allows more surface area for ion transport.

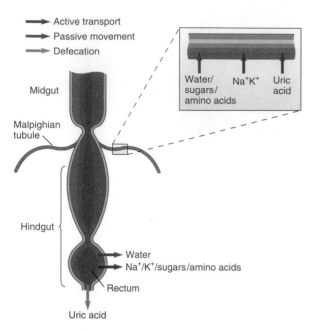

FIGURE 38.13

Malpighian Tubules. Malpighian tubules remove nitrogenous wastes (uric acid) from the hemocoel. Various ions are actively transported across the outer membrane of the tubule. Water follows these ions into the tubule and carries amino acids, sugars, and some nitrogenous wastes along passively. Some water, ions, and organic compounds are reabsorbed in the basal portion of the Malpighian tubules and the hindgut; the rest are reabsorbed in the rectum. Uric acid moves into the hindgut and is excreted.

In other crustaceans (some malacostracans [crabs, shrimp, pillbugs]), the excretory organs are near the maxillary segments and are termed **maxillary glands.** In maxillary glands, fluid collects within the tubules from the surrounding blood of the hemocoel, and this primary urine is modified substantially by selective reabsorption and secretion as it moves through the excretory system and rectum.

MALPIGHIAN TUBULES

Insects have an excretory system made up of the gut and **Malpighian tubules** attached to the gut (figure 38.13). Excretion involves the active transport of potassium ions into the tubules from the surrounding blood and the osmotic movement of water that follows. Nitrogenous waste (uric acid) also enters the tubules. As fluid moves through the Malpighian tubules, some of the water and certain ions are recovered. All of the uric acid passes into the gut and out of the body.

COXAL GLANDS

Coxal (L. *coxa*, hip) **glands** are common among arachnids (spiders, scorpions, ticks, mites). These spherical sacs resemble annelid nephridia (figure 38.14). Wastes are collected from the surrounding hemolymph of the hemocoel and discharged through pores on from one to several pairs of appendages near the proximal

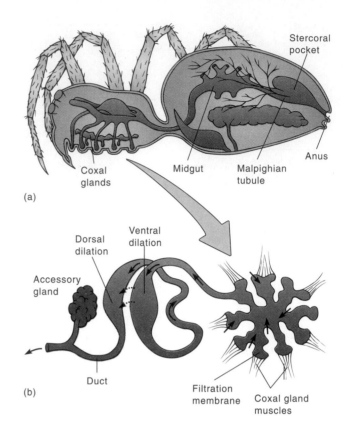

FIGURE 38.14

Coxal Glands in Arachnids. (*a*) The gut and excretory systems of a spider. (*b*) Coxal gland muscles attach to the thin saccular filtration membrane. These muscles promote filtration and fluid flow (black arrows) by contracting and relaxing along the tubular duct. Water and solutes are reabsorbed along the tubular duct.

joint (coxa) of the leg. Recent evidence suggests that the coxal glands may also function in the release of pheromones.

Other arachnid species have Malpighian tubules instead of, or in addition to, the coxal glands. In some of these species, however, Malpighian tubules seem to function in silk production rather than in excretion.

Stop and Ask Yourself

9. How do excretion and osmoregulation differ?
10. What is the function of the contractile vacuole, and where would you find one?
11. How do protonephridia and metanephridia function?
12. How do antennal (green) glands, maxillary glands, and coxal glands function?

VERTEBRATE EXCRETORY SYSTEMS

Vertebrates face the same problems as invertebrates in controlling water and ion balance. Generally, water losses are balanced precisely by water gains (table 38.1). Vertebrates gain water by

TABLE 38.1	AVERAGE WATER GAIN AND LOSS IN A HUMAN AND KANGAROO RAT				
VERTEBRATE	**WATER GAIN (ML)**			**WATER LOSS (ML)**	
Human (daily)	Ingested in solid food	1,200		Feces	100
	Ingested as liquids	1,000		Urine	1,500
	Metabolically produced	350		Skin and lungs	950
	Total	2,550			2,550
Kangaroo rat (over 4 weeks)	Ingested in solid food	6		Feces	3
	Ingested in liquids	0		Urine	13
	Metabolically produced	54		Skin and lungs	44
	Total	60			60

absorption from liquids and solid foods in the small and large intestines, and by metabolic reactions that yield water as an end product. They lose water by evaporation from respiratory surfaces, evaporation from the integument, sweating or panting, elimination in feces, and excretion by the urinary system.

Solute losses also must be balanced by solute gains. Vertebrates take in solutes by absorption of minerals from the small and large intestines, through the integument or gills, from secretions of various glands or gills, and by metabolism (e.g., the waste products of degradative reactions). They lose solutes in sweat, feces, urine, and gill secretions, and as metabolic wastes. The major metabolic wastes that must be eliminated are ammonia, urea, or uric acid.

Vertebrates live in saltwater, freshwater, and on land; each of these environments presents different water and solute problems that vertebrates have solved in different ways. The next section discusses how vertebrates avoid losing or gaining too much water and, in turn, how they maintain a homeostatic solute concentration in their body fluids. The disposal (excretion) of certain metabolic waste products is also coupled with osmotic balance and is discussed with the urinary system (box 38.2).

HOW VERTEBRATES ACHIEVE OSMOREGULATION

A variety of mechanisms have evolved in vertebrates to cope with their osmoregulatory problems, and most of them are adaptations of the urinary system. As presented in chapter 36, vertebrates have a closed circulatory system containing blood that is under pressure. This pressure forces blood through a membrane filter in a kidney, where the following three key functions take place:

1. Filtration, in which blood passes through a filter that retains blood cells, proteins, and other large solutes but lets small molecules, ions, and urea pass through

2. Reabsorption, in which selective ions and molecules are taken back into the bloodstream from the filtrate

3. Secretion, whereby select ions and end products of metabolism (e.g., K^+, H^+, NH_3) that are in the blood are added to the filtrate for removal from the body

VERTEBRATE KIDNEY VARIATIONS

Vertebrates have two kidneys that are in the back of the abdominal cavity, on either side of the aorta. Each kidney has a coat of connective tissue called the renal capsule (L. *renes*, kidney). The inner portion of the kidney is called the medulla; the region between the capsule and the medulla is the cortex.

The structure and function of vertebrate kidneys differ, depending on the vertebrate groups and the developmental stage. Overall, there are three kinds of vertebrate kidneys: the pronephros, mesonephros, and metanephros. The **pronephros** appears only briefly in many vertebrate embryos, and not at all in mammalian embryos (figure 38.15a). In some vertebrates, the pronephros is the first osmoregulatory and excretory organ of the embryo (tadpoles and other amphibian larvae); in others (hagfishes), it remains as the functioning kidney. During embryonic development of amniotes, or during metamorphosis in amphibians, the mesonephros replaces the pronephros (figure 38.15b). The **mesonephros** is the functioning embryonic kidney of many vertebrates and also adult fishes and amphibians. The mesonephros gives way during embryonic development to the **metanephros** in adult reptiles, birds, and mammals (figure 38.15c).

The physiological differences between these kidney types are primarily related to the number of blood-filtering units they contain. The pronephric kidney forms in the anterior portion of the body cavity and contains fewer blood-filtering units than either the mesonephric or metanephric kidneys. The larger number of filtering units in the latter has allowed vertebrates to face the rigorous osmoregulatory and excretory demands of freshwater and terrestrial environments.

38.2 WASTE PRODUCTS OF NITROGEN METABOLISM

Proteins and nucleic acids are the two main sources of nitrogenous wastes. Proteins are the source of over 95% of the total amount of excreted nitrogen; nucleic acids make up the remaining 5%. The major problem is to get rid of the ammonia (NH_3) that forms when amino groups ($-NH_2$) are split from amino acids derived from the metabolized protein or from excess dietary protein. Because ammonia is toxic to most vertebrates, it is kept in low concentrations (0.0001 to 0.003 mg/100 ml) in the blood; higher concentrations can be lethal. For example, a mouse will die if the ammonia concentration in its blood reaches 5 mg/100 ml.

Most vertebrates convert ammonia to a less-toxic form immediately after it forms—thus, allowing it to be retained until it can be excreted. Exceptions are teleost fishes, which excrete almost all of their nitrogen as ammonia through the gills and in the urine. Excretion of most of the nitrogen as ammonia is called **ammonotelic excretion.**

As noted in the text, most mammals need to drink water or eat food containing water to maintain a water balance. Mammals produce only a moderate amount of urine—not the quantities necessary to dilute the toxic ammonia. Most of the ammonia formed from amino acid metabolism is therefore converted to urea, which is less toxic than ammonia. Excretion of urea as the primary nitrogenous waste is called **ureotelic excretion.**

In a third category are animals that, because they inhabit dry habitats or for other reasons of water conservation, excrete a minimal amount of urine that contains little or no water. These animals (e.g., reptiles, some frogs, and birds) convert ammonia to uric acid or another highly insoluble substance. Because the substances are insoluble in water, only small amounts are retained in solution—thus, greatly limiting their toxicity. (For any substance to be toxic and achieve a biological effect, it must be in solution.) Excretion of nitrogen in the form of uric acid is called **uricotelic excretion.** Most uricotelic animals excrete their nitrogenous waste as a solid or semisolid urine, or as uric acid crystals.

Ammonia, urea, and uric acid are the most common nitrogenous waste products, but not the only ones. Some sharks secrete trimethylamine oxide (TMO). A variety of animals also excrete small quantities of creatine and creatinine. Some animals even wastefully excrete some of their excess amino acids.

Because urea, uric acid, and TMO are less toxic than ammonia, why don't more animals excrete most of their nitrogen in these forms? The answer is in the form of biological economics. The synthesis of these compounds from urea requires an expenditure of ATP energy. An animal using energy for an unnecessary function might be selected against during evolution. Therefore, an animal usually excretes its nitrogen in the form requiring the least expenditure of energy, given the environment in which it lives.

A few animals excrete nitrogen that comes from the metabolism of purines (e.g., adenine and guanine). Purines can be broken down to ammonia only if the animal has the enzymes. Most animals excrete purine nitrogen as uric acid or as one or more intermediate products.

What follows is a presentation of how a few vertebrates maintain their water and solute concentrations in different habitats—in the seas, in freshwater, and on land (table 38.2).

Sharks

Sharks and their relatives (skates and rays) have mesonephric kidneys and have solved their osmotic problem in ways different from the bony fishes (figure 38.15b). Instead of actively pumping ions out of their bodies through the kidneys, they have a **rectal gland** that secretes a highly concentrated salt (NaCl) solution. To reduce water loss, they use two organic molecules—urea and trimethylamine oxide (TMO)—in their body fluids to raise the osmotic pressure to a level equal to or higher than that of the seawater.

Urea denatures proteins and inhibits enzymes, whereas TMO stabilizes proteins and activates enzymes. Together in the proper ratio, they counteract each other, raise the osmotic pressure, and do not interfere with enzymes or proteins. This reciprocity is termed the **counteracting osmolyte strategy.**

A number of other fishes and invertebrates have evolved the same mechanism and employ pairs of counteracting osmolytes to raise the osmotic pressure of their body fluids.

Teleost Fishes

Most teleost fishes have mesonephric kidneys. Because the body fluids of freshwater fishes are hyperosmotic relative to freshwater (*see table 38.2*), water tends to enter the fishes, causing excessive hydration or bloating (figure 38.16a). At the same time, body ions tend to move outward into the water. ⑦ To solve this problem, freshwater fishes usually do not drink much water. Their bodies are coated with mucus, which helps stem inward water movement. They absorb salts and ions by active transport across their gills. They also excrete a large volume of water as dilute urine.

Although most groups of animals probably evolved in the sea, many marine bony fishes probably had freshwater ancestors, as presented in chapter 27. ⑧ Marine fishes face a different problem of water balance—their body fluids are hypoosmotic with respect to seawater (*see table 38.2*), and water tends to leave their bodies,

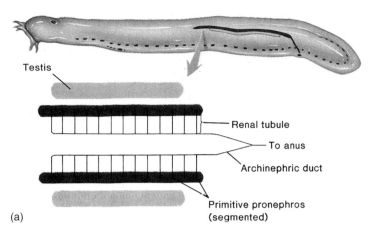

(a)

FIGURE 38.15

Types of Kidneys in Vertebrates and Their Association with the Male Reproductive System. The shaded portions of the drawings represent the mesoderm that forms both the kidneys and gonads. Notice that it extends much of the length of the body during development. (a) The primitive pronephric kidney is found in adult hagfishes and embryonic fishes and amphibians. It is anterior in the body and contains segmental renal tubules that lead from the body of the pronephros to the archinephric duct. Notice that the testes are separated from the kidneys. (b) The mesonephros is the functional kidney in the amniote embryo, adult fishes, and amphibians. It is structurally similar to the nonsegmented opisthonephric (advanced mesonephric) kidney of most nonamniote vertebrates, such as sharks. The anterior portion of the opisthonephros functions in blood cell formation and secretion of sex hormones. Notice that the testes occupy the position of the anterior opisthonephros, and the archinephric duct carries both sperm and urine. (c) The metanephric kidney of adult amniotes (reptiles, birds, and mammals) is the most advanced kidney. Notice the separate ureters (new ducts) for carrying urine. The archinephric duct becomes the ductus deferens for carrying sperm. The kidney is more compact and located more caudally in the body.

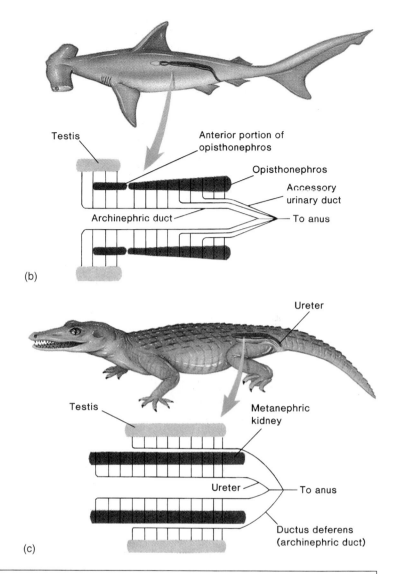

(b)

(c)

TABLE 38.2	HOW VARIOUS VERTEBRATES MAINTAIN WATER AND SALT BALANCE			
ORGANISM	ENVIRONMENTAL CONCENTRATION RELATIVE BODY FLUIDS	URINE CONCENTRATION RELATIVE TO BLOOD	MAJOR NITROGENOUS WASTE	KEY ADAPTATION
Freshwater fishes	Hypoosmotic	Hypoosmotic	Ammonia	Absorb ions through gills
Saltwater fishes	Hyperosmotic	Isoosmotic	Ammonia	Secrete ions through gills
Sharks	Isoosmotic	Isoosmotic	Ammonia	Secrete ions through rectal gland
Amphibians	Hypoosmotic	Very hypoosmotic	Ammonia and urea	Absorb ions through skin
Marine reptiles	Hyperosmotic	Isoosmotic	Ammonia and urea	Secrete ions through salt gland
Marine mammals	Hyperosmotic	Very hyperosmotic	Urea	Drink some water
Desert mammals	No comparison	Very hyperosmotic	Urea	Produce metabolic water
Marine birds	No comparison	Weakly hyperosmotic	Uric acid	Drink seawater and use salt glands
Terrestrial birds	No comparison	Weakly hyperosmotic	Uric acid	Drink freshwater

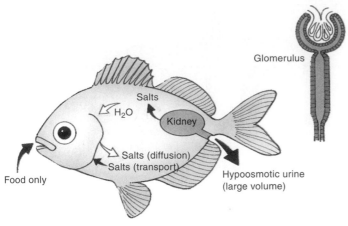

(a) Freshwater teleosts
(hypertonic blood)

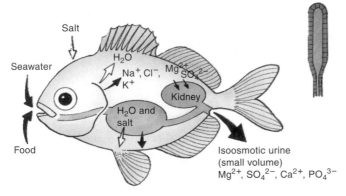

(b) Marine teleosts
(hypotonic blood)

FIGURE 38.16

Osmoregulation. Osmoregulation by (*a*) freshwater and (*b*) marine fishes. Large black arrows indicate passive uptake or loss of water or ions. Small black and white arrows indicate active transport processes at gill membranes and kidney tubules. Insets of kidney nephrons depict adaptations within the kidney. Water, ions, and small organic molecules are filtered from the blood at the glomerulus of the nephron. Essential components of the filtrate can be reabsorbed within the tubule system of the nephron. Marine fishes conserve water by reducing the size of the glomerulus of the nephron, and thus reducing the quantity of water and ions filtered from the blood. Ions can be secreted from the blood into the kidney tubules. Marine fishes can produce urine that is isoosmotic with the blood. Freshwater fishes have enlarged glomeruli and short tubule systems. They filter large quantities of water from the blood, and tubules reabsorb some ions from the filtrate. Freshwater fishes produce a hypoosmotic urine.

resulting in dehydration (figure 38.16*b*). To compensate, marine fishes drink large quantities of water, and they secrete Na^+, Cl^-, and K^+ ions through secretory cells in their gills. Channels in plasma membranes of their kidneys actively transport the multivalent ions that are abundant in seawater (e.g., Ca^{2+}, Mg^{2+}, SO_4^{2-}, and

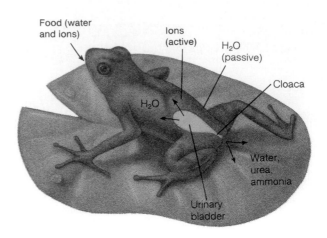

FIGURE 38.17

Water and Ion Uptake in an Amphibian. Water can enter this frog via food, through its highly permeable skin, or from the urinary bladder. The skin also actively transports ions such as Na^+ and Cl^- from the environment. The kidney forms a dilute urine by reabsorbing Na^+ and Cl^- ions. Urine then flows into the urinary bladder, where most of the remaining ions are reabsorbed.

PO_4^{3-}) out of the extracellular fluid and into the nephron tubes. The ions are then excreted in a concentrated urine.

Some fishes encounter both fresh- and saltwater during their life. Newborn Atlantic salmon swim downstream from the freshwater stream of their birth and enter the sea. Instead of continuing to pump ions in, as they have done in freshwater, the salmon must now rid their bodies of salt. Years later, these same salmon migrate from the sea to their freshwater home to spawn. As they do, the pumping mechanisms reverse themselves.

Amphibians

The amphibian kidney is identical to that of freshwater fishes (figure 38.16*a*), which is not surprising because amphibians spend a large portion of their time in freshwater, and when on land, they tend to seek out moist places. Amphibians take up water and ions in their food and drink, through the skin that is in contact with moist substrates, and through the urinary bladder (figure 38.17). This uptake counteracts what is lost through evaporation and prevents osmotic imbalance (*see table 38.2*).

The urinary bladder of a frog, toad, or salamander is an important water and ion reservoir. For example, when the environment becomes dry, the bladder enlarges for storing more urine. If an amphibian becomes dehydrated, a brain hormone causes water to leave the bladder and enter the body fluid.

Reptiles, Birds, and Mammals

Reptiles, birds, and mammals all possess metanephric kidneys (*see figure 38.15c*). Their kidneys are by far the most complex animal kidneys, well suited for these animals' high rates of metabolism.

38.3 EXTRARENAL SECRETION BY AVIAN AND REPTILIAN SALT GLANDS

Salt glands have been described in many species of birds and reptiles, including nearly all marine birds, ostriches, marine iguanas, sea snakes, sea turtles, crocodilians, and many terrestrial reptiles. In general, these animals are subjected to the osmotic stress of a marine or desert environment.

The salt glands of some reptiles and birds occupy shallow depressions in the skull above the eye (figure 1). These glands consist of many lobes, each of which drains via branching secretory tubules, and a central canal into a collecting duct that empties into the nostril. Active secretion takes place across the epithelial cells of the secretory tubules. These cells have a large surface area and many mitochondria. As in other transport epithelia, tight junctions hold adjacent cells together, which prevents the massive leakage of water or solutes past the cells, from one side of the epithelium to another.

The avian salt gland is a countercurrent system that concentrates the secreted salt solution. The capillaries are arranged so that the flow of blood is in the direction opposite to the flow of secretory fluid. This flow maintains a minimum concentration gradient between blood and the tubular lumen along the entire length of the tubule.

FIGURE 1 Salt Glands. (a) The reptilian salt gland is often above the eyes. (b) The many-lobed salt glands of birds empty into the nostril.

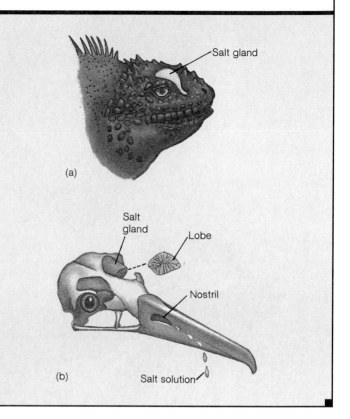

In most reptiles, birds, and mammals, the kidneys can remove far more water than can those in amphibians, and the kidneys are the primary regulatory organs for controlling the osmotic balance of the body fluids. Some desert and marine reptiles and birds build up high salt (NaCl) concentrations in their bodies because they consume salty foods or seawater, and they lose water through evaporation and in their urine and feces. To rid themselves of excess salt, these animals also have salt glands near the eye or in the tongue that remove excess salt from the blood and secrete it as tearlike droplets (box 38.3).

A major site of water loss in mammals is the lungs. To reduce this evaporative loss, many mammals have nasal cavities that act as countercurrent exchange systems (figure 38.18). 🌀 When the animal inhales, air passes through the nasal cavities and is warmed by the surrounding tissues. In the process, the temperature of this tissue drops. When the air gets deep into the lungs, it is further warmed and humidified. During exhalation, as the warm moist air passes up the respiratory tree, it gives up its heat to the nasal cavity. As the air cools, much of the water condenses on the nasal surfaces and does not leave the body. This mechanism explains why a dog's nose is usually cold and moist.

Stop and Ask Yourself

13. How do freshwater fishes osmoregulate? How do saltwater fishes osmoregulate?
14. What is the function of the rectal gland of sharks?
15. How do amphibians conserve water?
16. What is a salt gland?
17. How do nasal cavities help conserve water?

HOW THE METANEPHRIC KIDNEY FUNCTIONS

The filtration device of the metanephric kidney consists of over 1 million individual filtration, secretion, and absorption structures called **nephrons** (Gr. *nephros*, kidney + *on*, neuter) (figure 38.19a). At the beginning of the nephron is the filtration apparatus called the glomerular capsule (formerly Bowman's capsule), which looks rather like a tennis ball that has been punched in

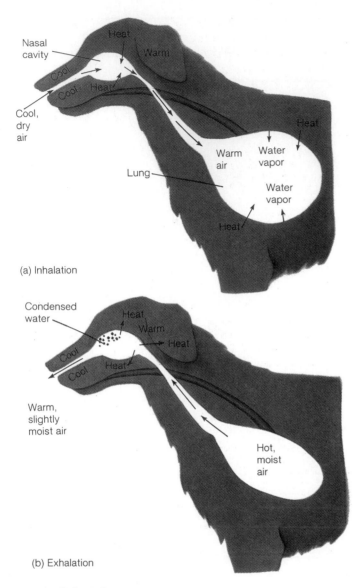

(a) Inhalation

(b) Exhalation

FIGURE 38.18

Water Retention by Countercurrent Heating and Cooling in a Mammal. (*a*) When this animal inhales, the cool, dry air passing through its nose is heated and humidified. At the same time, its nasal tissues are cooled. (*b*) When the animal exhales, it gives up heat to the previously cooled nasal tissue. The air carries less water vapor, and condensation occurs in the animal's nose.

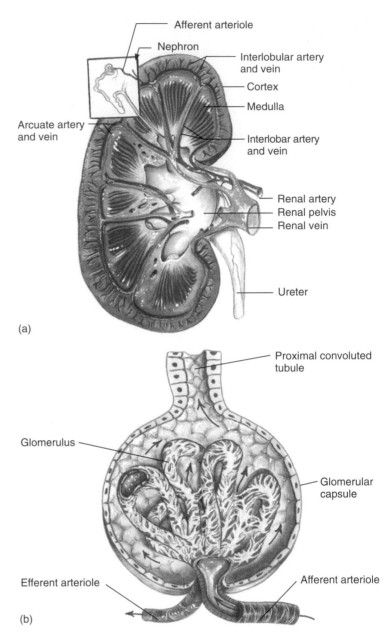

(a)

(b)

FIGURE 38.19

Filtration Device of the Metanephric Kidney. (*a*) Interior of a kidney, showing the positioning of the nephron and the blood supply to and from the kidney. (*b*) Glomerular capsule. Red arrows show that high blood pressure forces water and ions through small perforations in the walls of the glomerular capillaries to form the glomerular filtrate.

on one side (figure 38.19*b*). The capsules are in the cortical (outermost) region of the kidney. In each capsule, an afferent ("going to") arteriole enters and branches into a fine network of capillaries called the **glomerulus.** The walls of these glomerular capillaries contain small perforations called filtration slits that act as filters. Blood pressure forces fluid through these filters. The fluid is now known as glomerular filtrate and contains small molecules, such as glucose, ions (Ca^{2+}, PO_4^{3-}), and the primary nitrogenous waste product of metabolism—urea or uric acid. Because the filtration slits are so small, large proteins and blood cells remain in the blood and leave the glomerulus via the efferent ("outgoing")

arteriole. The efferent arteriole then divides into a set of capillaries called the peritubular capillaries that wind profusely around the tubular portions of the nephron (figure 38.20). Eventually, they merge to form veins that carry blood out of the kidney.

Beyond the glomerular capsule are the proximal convoluted tubule, the loop of the nephron (formerly the loop of Henle), and the distal convoluted tubule. At various places along these structures, the glomerular filtrate is selectively reabsorbed, returning certain ions (e.g., Na^+, K^+, Cl^-) to the bloodstream. Both

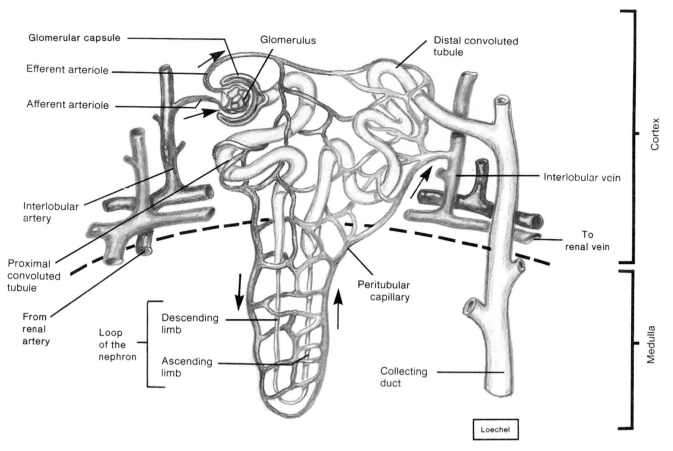

FIGURE 38.20

Metanephric Nephron. The proximal convoluted tubule reabsorbs glucose and some ions. The distal convoluted tubule reabsorbs other ions and water. Final water reabsorption takes place in the collecting duct. Black arrows indicate the direction of movement of materials in the nephron.

active (ATP-requiring) and passive procedures are involved in the recovery of these substances. Potentially harmful compounds, such as hydrogen (H^+) and ammonium (NH_4^+) ions, drugs, and various other foreign materials are secreted into the nephron lumen. In the last portion of the nephron, called the collecting duct, final water reabsorption takes place so that the urine contains an ion concentration well above that of the blood. Thus, the filtration, secretion, and reabsorption activities of the nephron do not simply remove wastes. They also maintain water and ion balance, and therein lies the importance of the homeostatic function of the kidney.

Mammalian, and to a lesser extent avian and reptilian, kidneys can remove far more water from the glomerular filtrate than can the kidneys of amphibians. For example, human urine is 4 times as concentrated as blood plasma, a camel's urine is 8 times as concentrated, a gerbil's is 14 times as concentrated, and some desert rats and mice have urine more than 20 times as concentrated as their plasma. This concentrated waste enables them to live in dry or desert environments, where little water is available for them to drink. Most of their water is metabolically produced

from the oxidation of carbohydrates, fats, and proteins in the seeds that they eat (*see table 38.1*). Mammals, and to a lesser extent, birds achieve this remarkable degree of water conservation by a unique, yet simple, evolutionary adaptation: the bending of the nephron tube into a loop. By bending, the nephron can greatly increase the salt concentration in the tissue through which the loop passes and use this gradient to draw large amounts of water out of the tube.

Countercurrent Exchange

The loop of the nephron increases the efficiency of reabsorption by a countercurrent flow similar to that in the gills of fishes or in the legs of birds, but with water and ions being reabsorbed instead of oxygen or heat. ⑩ Generally, the longer the loop of the nephron, the more water and ions that can be reabsorbed. It follows that desert rodents (e.g., the kangaroo rat) that form highly concentrated urine have very long nephron loops (figure 38.21). Similarly, amphibians that are closely associated with aquatic habitats have nephrons that lack a loop.

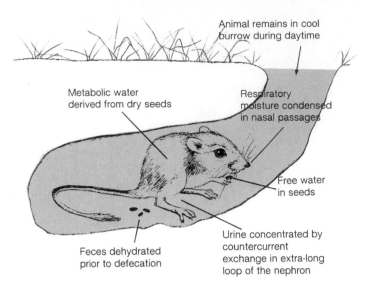

FIGURE 38.21

Kangaroo Rat (*Dipodomys ordii*), a Master of Water Conservation. Its efficient kidneys can concentrate urine 20 times that of its blood plasma. As a result, these kidneys, as well as other adaptations, prevent unnecessary water loss to the environment.

Figure 38.22 shows the countercurrent flow mechanism for concentrating urine. The process of reabsorption in the proximal convoluted tubule removes some salt (NaCl) and water from the glomerular filtrate and reduces its volume by approximately 25%. However, the concentrations of salt and urea are still isosmotic with the extracellular fluid.

As the filtrate moves to the descending limb of the loop of the nephron, it becomes further reduced in volume and more concentrated. Water moves out of the tubule by osmosis due to the high salt concentration (the "brine-bath") in the extracellular fluid.

Notice in figure 38.22 that the highest urea-brine bath concentration is around the lower portion of the loop of the nephron. As the filtrate passes into the ascending limb, sodium (Na^+) ions are actively transported out of the filtrate into the extracellular fluid, with chloride (Cl^-) ions following passively. Water cannot flow out of the ascending limb because the cells of the ascending limb are impermeable to water. Thus, the salt concentration of the extracellular fluid becomes very high. The salt flows passively into the descending loop, only to move out again in the ascending loop, creating a recycling of salt through the loop and the extracellular fluid. Because the flows in the descending and ascending

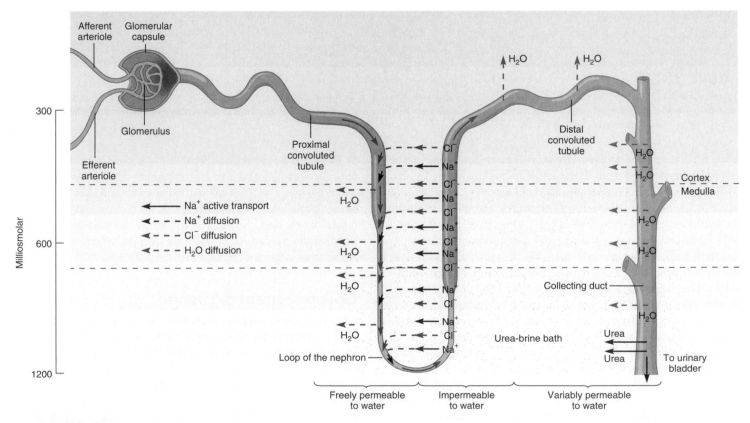

FIGURE 38.22

Countercurrent Exchange. Movement of materials in the nephron and collecting duct. Solid arrows indicate active transport; dashed arrows indicate passive transport. The shading at intervals along the tubules illustrates the relative concentration of the filtrate in milliosmoles.

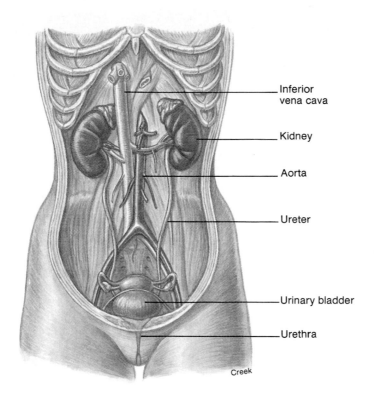

Inferior
vena cava

Kidney

Aorta

Ureter

Urinary bladder

Urethra

Creek

FIGURE 38.23

Component Parts of the Human Urinary System. The positions of the kidneys, ureters, urinary bladder, and urethra.

limbs are in opposite directions, a countercurrent gradient in salt is set up. The osmotic pressure of the extracellular brine bath is made even higher because of the abundance of urea that moves out of the collecting ducts.

Finally, the distal convoluted tubule empties into the collecting duct, which is permeable to urea, and the concentrated urea in the filtrate diffuses out into the surrounding extracellular fluid. The high urea concentration in the extracellular fluid, coupled with the high concentration of salt, forms the urea-brine bath that causes water to move out of the filtrate by osmosis as it moves down the descending limb. Finally, the many peritubular capillaries surrounding each nephron collect the water and return it to the systemic circulation.

The renal pelvis of the mammalian kidney is continuous with a tube called the **ureter** that carries urine to a storage organ called the **urinary bladder** (figure 38.23). Urine from two ureters (one from each kidney) accumulates in the urinary bladder. The urine leaves the body through a single tube, the **urethra,** which opens at the body surface at the end of the penis (in human males)

or just in front of the vaginal entrance (in human females). As the urinary bladder fills with urine, tension increases in its smooth muscle walls. In response to this tension, a reflex response relaxes sphincter muscles at the entrance to the urethra. This response is called urination. The two kidneys, two ureters, urinary bladder, and urethra constitute the urinary system of mammals.

Stop and Ask Yourself

18. How does a vertebrate lose water from its body? How does it gain water?

19. How do vertebrates achieve osmoregulation?

20. What are three functions of the kidneys?

21. What is the anatomy of the nephron?

22. How does the countercurrent flow mechanism in the kidney function?

SUMMARY

1. Thermoregulation is a complex and important physiological process for maintaining heat homeostasis despite environmental changes.

2. Ectotherms generally obtain heat from the environment, whereas endotherms generate their own body heat from metabolic processes.

3. Homeotherms generally have a relatively constant core body temperature, while heterotherms have a variable body temperature.

4. The high, constant body temperature of birds and mammals also depends on insulation, panting, sweating, specific behaviors, vasoconstriction or vasodilation of peripheral blood vessels, and in some species, a rete mirabile system.

5. Thermogenesis involves mainly shivering, enzymatic activity, brown fat, and high cellular metabolism.

6. The hypothalamus is the temperature regulating center that functions as a thermostat with a fixed set point. This set point can either rise or fall during hibernation or torpor.

7. Some invertebrates have contractile vacuoles, flame-cell systems, antennal (green) glands, maxillary glands, coxal glands, nephridia, or Malpighian tubules for osmoregulation.

8. The osmoregulatory system of vertebrates governs the concentration of water and ions; the excretory system eliminates metabolic wastes, water, and ions from the body.

9. Freshwater animals tend to lose ions and take in water. To avoid hydration, freshwater fishes rarely drink much water, have impermeable body surfaces covered with mucus, excrete a dilute urine, and take up ions through their gills.

10. Marine animals tend to take in ions from the seawater and to lose water. To avoid dehydration, they frequently drink water, have relatively permeable body surfaces, excrete a small volume of concentrated urine, and secrete ions from their gills.

11. Amphibians can absorb water across the skin and urinary bladder wall. Desert and marine reptiles and birds have salt glands to remove and secrete excess salt (NaCl).

12. In reptiles, birds, and mammals, the kidneys are important osmoregulatory structures. The functional unit of the kidney is the nephron, composed of the glomerular capsule, proximal convoluted tubule, loop of the nephron, distal convoluted tubule, and collecting duct. The loop of the nephron and the collecting duct are in the kidney's medulla; the other nephron parts lie in the kidney's cortex. Urine passes from the pelvis of the kidney to the urinary bladder.

13. To make urine, kidneys produce a filtrate of the blood and reabsorb most of the water, glucose, and needed ions, while allowing wastes to pass from the body. Three physiological mechanisms are involved: filtration of the blood through the glomerulus, reabsorption of the useful substances, and secretion of toxic substances. In those animals with a loop of the nephron, salt (NaCl) and urea are concentrated in the extracellular fluid around the loop, allowing water to move by osmosis out of the loop and into the peritubular capillaries.

SELECTED KEY TERMS

brown fat (p. 661)
ectotherm (p. 657)
endotherm (p. 658)
heterotherm (p. 658)
hibernation (p. 662)

homeotherm (p. 658)
nephron (p. 671)
osmoconformer (p. 663)
osmoregulation (p. 663)
thermoregulation (p. 656)

CRITICAL THINKING QUESTIONS

1. Reptiles are said to be behavioral homeotherms. Explain what this means.

2. Why do very small birds and mammals go into a state of torpor at night?

3. How does the countercurrent mechanism help regulate heat loss?

4. In endotherms, what controls the balance between the amount of heat lost and the amount gained?

5. If marooned on a desert isle, do not drink seawater; it is better to be thirsty. Why is this true?

REFERENCES ON THE WORLD WIDE WEB

1. **The Kidney.**   This site is from the Department of Cell Biology at Vanderbilt University and contains a wealth of information on the kidney.
   http://vumclib.mc.vanderbilt.edu/~alemanma/kidney-outline.html

2. **Urinary System.**   The urinary system removes waste from the blood and helps regulate body fluids. These functions are covered at this site.
   http://www.aps.uoguel.ph.ca/swatland/html/ch1.4.html

   Normal Anatomy and Physiology.   Learn more about the normal male and female urinary tracts and normal bladder anatomy and physiology at this site.
   http://life-tech.com/uro/urolib/normant.htm

4. **Normal Renal Physiology.**   This site contains information about the nephron—the functional unit of the kidney.
   http://www.ppol.com/brg/brgcambells.html

5. **Control of Sodium, Potassium and Water Balance.**   Learn more about the relationship between sodium, potassium, and fluid balance at this site.
   http://www.physiol.arizona.edu/cell/instruct/95pecgroves/ctrlNaKH20.html

6. **The Basics of the Kidney.**   A good introduction on the basic function of the kidney is presented at this site.
   http://www.clark.net/pub/nhp/med/kidney/basics.html

7. **Acid-Base Homeostasis.**   A discussion of acid-base homeostasis is found at this site.
   http://www.millcomm.com/~arich/outline.html

REPRODUCTION AND DEVELOPMENT

Outline

Concepts

1. All animals have the capacity to reproduce. The simplest form of reproduction is asexual. Asexual reproduction produces new individuals from one parent, but it does not produce new genetic combinations among offspring, as does sexual reproduction.
2. Almost all animals reproduce sexually, at least sometimes. Sexual reproduction involves mechanisms that bring sperm and egg together for fertilization, and ensure that the fertilized egg has a suitable place to develop until the new animal is ready to function on its own.
3. Sexual reproduction evolved in aquatic environments, and its modification for organisms living on dry land entailed evolutionary innovations to prevent the gametes and embryos from drying out.
4. Mammalian fertilization and embryonic development are both internal.
5. Hormones coordinate the reproductive functions in both males and females. In female mammals, hormones also maintain pregnancy, and after childbirth, stimulate the production and letdown of milk from the mammary glands.

Would You Like to Know . . .

1. how the earliest organisms reproduced? (p. 678)
2. how lobsters can reproduce without sperm? (p. 678)
3. what is one of the greatest disadvantages of asexual reproduction? (p. 680)
4. why the human testes are the only abdominal organs that lie outside of the abdominal cavity? (p. 683)
5. what causes an inguinal hernia in humans? (p. 683)
6. why some males are circumcised? (p. 684)
7. what determines the size of a female's breasts? (p. 688)
8. why urine is used to determine if a female is pregnant? (p. 689)
9. when a female is considered pregnant? (p. 690)

This chapter answers these and other useful questions.

This chapter contains evolutionary concepts, which are set off in this font.

Reproduction is a basic attribute of all forms of life. Chapters 6 through 10 describe the general features of animal development and the control processes that allow a genotype to be translated into its phenotype. Although in modern zoology, development is "the center stage" in reproduction, the whole process includes the behavior, anatomy, and physiology of adults—whether protists, invertebrates, or vertebrates. This chapter begins with a comparative focus on the different reproductive strategies observed in protists, invertebrates, and the five major groups of vertebrates. The chapter concludes with a discussion of human reproduction, not only because of the subject's basic interest to everyone, but because scientists know more about the biochemistry, hormones, anatomy, and physiology of human reproduction than they do for any other species.

ASEXUAL REPRODUCTION IN INVERTEBRATES

In the biological sense, reproduction means producing offspring that may (or may not) be exact copies of the parents. Reproduction is part of a life cycle, a recurring frame of events in which animals grow, develop, and reproduce according to a program of instruction encoded in the DNA they inherit from their parents. One of the two major types of reproduction in the biological world is asexual reproduction.

① The first organisms to evolve probably reproduced by pinching in two, much like the simplest organisms that exist today do. This is a form of **asexual reproduction,** which is reproduction without the union of gametes or sex cells. In the first 2 billion years or more of evolution, forms of asexual reproduction were probably the only means by which the primitive organisms could increase their numbers. While asexual reproduction effectively increases the numbers of a species, those species reproducing asexually tend to evolve very slowly because all offspring of any one individual are alike, providing less genetic diversity for evolutionary selection.

Asexual reproduction is common among the protozoa, as well as in lower invertebrates, such as sponges, jellyfishes, flatworms, and many segmented worms. Asexual reproduction is rare among the higher invertebrates. The ability to reproduce asexually often correlates with a marked capacity for regeneration.

In the lower invertebrates, the most common forms of asexual reproduction are fission, budding (both internal and external), and fragmentation. Parthenogenesis, which is comparatively uncommon, also occurs in a few invertebrates.

FISSION

Protists and some multicellular animals (cnidarians, annelids) may reproduce by fission. **Fission** (L. *fissio,* the act of splitting) is the division of one cell, body, or body part into two (figure 39.1a). In this process, the cell pinches in two by an inward furrowing of the plasma membrane. Binary fission is where the division is

equal; each offspring contains approximately equal amounts of protoplasm and associated structures. Binary fission is common in protozoa; for some, it is their only means of reproduction.

In fission, the plane of division may be asymmetrical, transverse, or longitudinal, depending on the species. For example, the multicellular, free-living flatworms, such as the common planarian, reproduce by longitudinal fission (figure 39.1b). Some flatworms and annelids reproduce by forming numerous constrictions along the length of the body; a chain of daughter individuals results (figure 39.1c). This type of asexual reproduction is called multiple fission.

BUDDING

Another method of asexual reproduction found in lower invertebrates is **budding** (L. *bud,* a small protuberance). For example, in the cnidarian *Hydra* and many species of sponges, certain cells divide rapidly and develop on the body surface to form an external bud (figure 39.1d). The bud cells proliferate to form a cylindrical structure, which develops into a new animal, usually breaking away from the parent. If the buds remain attached to the parent, they form a colony. A **colony** is a group of closely associated individuals of one species. Internal budding (as in the freshwater sponges) produces gemmules, which are collections of many cells surrounded by a body wall. When the body of the parent dies and degenerates, each gemmule gives rise to a new individual.

FRAGMENTATION

Fragmentation is a type of asexual reproduction whereby a body part is lost and then regenerates into a new organism. Fragmentation occurs in some cnidarians, platyhelminths, rhynchocoels, and echinoderms. For example, in sea anemones, as the organism moves, small pieces break off from the adult and develop into new individuals (figure 39.1e).

PARTHENOGENESIS

Certain flatworms, rotifers, roundworms, insects, lobsters, some lizards, and some fishes can reproduce without sperm and normal fertilization. ② These animals carry out what is called **parthenogenesis** (Gr. *parthenos,* virgin + *genesis,* production). (However, most parthenogenetic animals also can reproduce sexually at some point in their life history.) Parthenogenesis is a spontaneous activation of a mature egg, followed by normal egg divisions and subsequent embryonic development. In fact, mature eggs of species that do not undergo parthenogenesis can sometimes be activated to develop without fertilization by pricking them with a needle, by exposing them to high concentrations of calcium, or by altering their temperature.

Because parthenogenetic eggs are not fertilized, they do not receive male chromosomes. The offspring would thus be expected to have only a haploid set of chromosomes. In some animals, however, meiotic division is suppressed, so the diploid number is con-

(a)

(b)

(c)

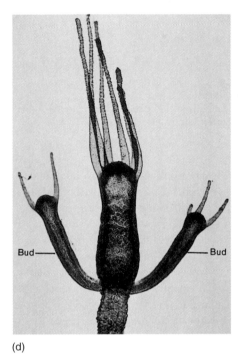

Bud ————   ———— Bud

(d)

FIGURE 39.1

Asexual Reproduction. (*a*) An amoeba (a protist) undergoes fission to form two individual organisms. (*b*) Planarian worms undergoing longitudinal fission. (*c*) The annelid, *Autolysis*, undergoing various constrictions. (*d*) A *Hydra* with developing buds. (*e*) Small sea anemones produced by fragmentation.

(e)

served. In other animals, meiosis occurs, but an unusual mitosis returns the haploid embryonic cells to the diploid condition.

Overall, animals that reproduce parthenogenetically have substantially less genetic variability than do animals with chromosome sets from two parents. This condition may be an advantage for animals that are well adapted to a relatively stable environment. However, in meeting the challenges of a changing environment, parthenogenetic animals may have less flexibility, which may explain why this form of reproduction is relatively uncommon.

Parthenogenesis also plays an important role in social organization in colonies of certain bees, wasps, and ants. In these insects, large numbers of males (drones) are produced parthenogenetically, whereas sterile female workers and reproductive females (queens) are produced sexually.

ADVANTAGES AND DISADVANTAGES OF ASEXUAL REPRODUCTION

The predominance of asexual reproduction in protists and some invertebrates can be partially explained by the environment in which they live. The marine environment is usually very stable. Stable environments may favor this form of reproduction because a combination of genes that matches the relatively unchanging environment is an advantage over a greater number of gene combinations, many of which do not match the environment. In other habitats, asexual reproduction is seasonal. The season during which asexual reproduction occurs coincides with the period when the environment is predictably hospitable. Under such conditions, it is advantageous for the animal to produce asexually a large number of progeny with identical characteristics. A large number of animals, well adapted to a given environment, can be produced even if only one parent is present.

Without the tremendous genetic variability bestowed by meiosis and sexual processes, however, a population of genetically identical animals stands a greatly increased chance of being devastated by a single disease or environmental insult, such as a long drought. A given line of asexually reproducing animals can cope with a changing environment only through the relatively rare spontaneous mutations (alterations in genetic material) that prove to be beneficial. **(3)** Paradoxically, however, most mutations are detrimental or lethal, and herein lies one of the greatest disadvantages of asexual reproduction. All such mutations are passed on to every offspring along with the normal, unmutated genes. Consequently, the typical asexual animal may have only one "good" copy of each hereditary unit (gene); the one on the homologous chromosome may be a mutated form that is nonfunctional or potentially lethal.

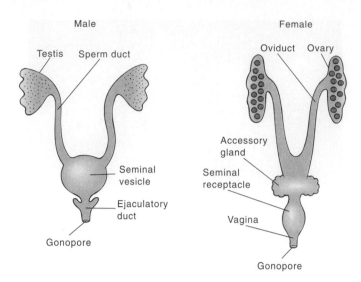

FIGURE 39.2

Stylized Male and Female Reproductive Systems in Invertebrates. Sexual reproduction is possible via these systems.

SEXUAL REPRODUCTION IN INVERTEBRATES

In **sexual** (L. *sexualis,* pertaining to sex) **reproduction,** the offspring have unique combinations of genes inherited from the two parents. Offspring of a sexual union are somewhat different from their parents and siblings—they have genetic diversity. Each new individual represents a combination of traits derived from two parents because syngamy, or fertilization, unites one gamete from each parent.

Sexual reproductive strategies and structures in the invertebrates are overwhelming. What follows is an overview of some principles of reproductive structure and function. The coverage of each invertebrate phylum in chapters 18 through 26 provides more specific details.

EXTERNAL FERTILIZATION

Many invertebrates (e.g., sponges and corals) simply release their gametes into the water in which they live (**broadcast spawning**), allowing external fertilization to occur. In these invertebrates, the gonads are usually simple, often transient structures for releasing the gametes from the body through various arrangements of coelomic ducts, metanephridia, sperm ducts, or oviducts.

INTERNAL FERTILIZATION

Other invertebrates (from flatworms to insects) utilize internal fertilization to transfer sperm from male to female and have structures that facilitate such transfer (figure 39.2).

In the male, sperm are produced in the testes and transported via a sperm duct to a storage area called the seminal vesicle. Prior to mating, some invertebrates (e.g., arrowworms, leeches, some insects) incorporate many sperm into packets termed spermatophores. Spermatophores provide a protective casing for sperm and facilitate the transfer of large numbers of sperm with minimal loss. Some spermatophores are even motile and act as independent sperm carriers. Sperm or the spermatophores are

then passed into an ejaculatory duct to a copulatory organ (e.g., penis, cirrus, gonopore). The copulatory organ is used as an intromittent structure to introduce sperm into the female's system. Various accessory glands (e.g., seminal vesicle) may be present in males that produce seminal fluid or spermatophores.

In the female, ova (eggs) are produced in the ovaries and transported to the oviduct. Sperm move up the oviduct, where they encounter the ova and fertilize them. Accessory glands (e.g., those that produce egg capsules or shells) may also be present in females.

As noted earlier, sexual reproduction usually involves the fusion of gametes from a male and female parent. However, some sexually reproducing animals occasionally depart from this basic reproductive mode and exhibit variant forms of sexual reproduction.

Hermaphroditism (Gr. *hermaphroditos,* an organism with the attributes of both sexes) occurs when an animal has both functional male and female reproductive systems. This dual sexuality is sometimes called the **monoecious** (Gr. *monos,* single + *oikos,* house) condition. Although some hermaphrodites fertilize themselves, most also mate with another member of the same species (e.g., earthworms and sea slugs). When this occurs, each animal serves as both male and female—donating and receiving sperm. Hermaphroditism is especially beneficial to sessile (attached) animals (e.g., barnacles) that may only occasionally encounter the opposite sex.

Another variation of hermaphroditism—**sequential hermaphroditism**—occurs when an animal is one sex during one phase of its life cycle and the opposite sex during another phase. Hermaphrodites are either **protogynous** (Gr. *protos,* first + *gyne,* women) or **protandrous** (Gr. *protos,* first + *andros,* man; **protandry**). In protandry, an animal is a male during its early life history and a female later in the life history. The reverse is true for protogynous animals. A change in the sex ratio of a population is one factor that can induce sequential hermaphroditism, which is common in oysters.

ADVANTAGES AND DISADVANTAGES OF SEXUAL REPRODUCTION

New combinations of traits can arise more rapidly in sexually reproducing animals because of genetic recombinations. The resulting genetic diversity or variability increases the chances of the species surviving sudden environmental changes. Furthermore, variation is the foundation for evolution. In contrast to the way asexually reproducing populations tend to retain mutations, sexually reproducing populations tend to eliminate deleterious and lethal mutations.

Sexual reproduction also has some disadvantages. For example, an animal that cannot reproduce asexually can never bequeath its own exact set of genetic material to its progeny. Sexual reproduction bestows on the progeny a reassortment of maternal and paternal chromosomes. Thus, the same mixing processes that create the adaptive gene combinations in the adult work to dismantle it partially in the offspring. In addition, many of the gametes that are released are not fertilized, leading to a significant waste of metabolic effort.

Stop and Ask Yourself

1. What is the difference between asexual and sexual reproduction?
2. What are some advantages to asexual reproduction in invertebrates? What are some disadvantages?
3. How do each of the following types of asexual reproduction occur in invertebrates: (*a*) binary fission, (*b*) fragmentation, and (*c*) budding?
4. How do hermaphroditism and parthenogenesis differ?
5. What are some advantages and disadvantages of sexual reproduction?

SEXUAL REPRODUCTION IN VERTEBRATES

Since the evolution of the first animals, the basic use of male and female gametes has been preserved. Vertebrate evolution has also given rise to the close link between reproductive biology and sexual behavior. The strong drive to mate or reproduce dominates the lives of many vertebrates, as illustrated by the salmon's fateful spawning run or the rutting of bull elk. Females of most mammal species come into heat or **estrus** (Gr. *oistros*, a most vehement desire; the period of sexual receptivity) about the same time each year. Genetic, hormonal, and nervous system controls usually time estrus so that the young are born when environmental conditions make survival most likely.

SOME BASIC VERTEBRATE REPRODUCTIVE STRATEGIES

Fishes are well known for their high potential fecundity, with most species releasing thousands to millions of eggs and sperm annually. Fish species have reproductive methods, structures, and an attendant physiology that have allowed them to adapt to a great variety of aquatic conditions.

The reproductive strategies in amphibians are much more diverse than those observed in other groups of vertebrates. In each of the three living orders of Amphibia (caecilians, salamanders, anurans) are trends toward terrestriality. The variety of these adaptations is especially noteworthy in anurans. These reproductive adaptations have been viewed as pioneering evolutionary experiments in the conquest of terrestrial environments by vertebrates. Noteworthy is the evolution of direct development of terrestrial eggs, ovoviviparity, and viviparity that have been important in successful invasion of mountainous environments by amphibians.

The reproductive adaptations of reptiles, birds, and early mammals foreshadow changes evident in the reproductive systems of later mammals, including humans. The reptilian system includes shelled, desiccation-resistant eggs. These eggs had the three basic embryonic membranes that still characterize the mammalian embryo, as well as a flat embryo that developed and underwent gastrulation atop a huge yolk mass. The same process of gastrulation is still seen in mammalian embryos, even though the massive yolk mass has been lost.

The mechanisms for maintaining the developing embryo within the female for long periods of time evolved in the early mammals. During **gestation** (L. *gestatio*, from + *gestare*, to bear), the embryo was nourished with nutrients and oxygen, yet it was protected from attack by the female's immune system. After birth, the first mammals nourished their young with milk from the mammary glands, just as primates do today.

Female apes and monkeys are asynchronous breeders. Mating and births can take place over much of the year. Females mate only when in estrus, increasing the probability of fertilization. Human females show a less distinctive estrus phase and can reproduce throughout the year. They can also engage in sexual activity without reproductive purpose; no longer is sexual behavior precariously tied to ovulation. The source of this important reproductive adaptation may be physiological or a result of concomitant evolution of the brain—a process that gave humans some conscious control over their emotions and behaviors that hormones, instincts, and the environment control in other animals. This separation of sex from a purely reproductive function has evolved into the long-lasting pair bonds between human males and females (e.g., marriage) that further support the offspring. This type of behavior has also resulted in the transmission of culture—a key to the evolution and success of the human species.

With this background, the reproductive anatomy and physiology of selected vertebrate classes is now presented.

EXAMPLES OF REPRODUCTION AMONG VARIOUS VERTEBRATE CLASSES

Almost all vertebrates reproduce sexually; only a few lizards and fishes normally reproduce parthenogenetically. Sexual reproduction evolved among aquatic animals and then spread to the land as animals became terrestrial.

FISHES

All fishes reproduce in aquatic environments. In bony fishes, fertilization is usually external, and eggs contain only enough yolk to sustain the developing fish for a short time. After this yolk is consumed, the growing fish must seek food. Although many thousands of eggs are produced and fertilized, few survive and grow to maturity. Some succumb to fungal and bacterial infections, others to siltation, and still others to predation. Thus, to assure reproductive success, the fertilized egg develops rapidly, and the young achieve maturity within a short time.

AMPHIBIANS

The vertebrate invasion of land meant facing for the first time the danger of drying out or desiccating; the tiny gametes were especially vulnerable. The gametes could not simply be released near one another on the land because they would quickly desiccate.

The amphibians were the first vertebrates to invade the land. They have not, however, become adapted to a completely terrestrial environment; their life cycle is still inextricably linked to water. Among most amphibians, fertilization is still external, just as it is among the fishes. Among the frogs and toads, the male grasps the female and discharges fluid containing sperm onto the eggs as she releases them into the water (figure 39.3a).

The developmental period is much longer in amphibians than in fishes, although the eggs do not contain appreciably more yolk. An evolutionary adaptation present in amphibians is the presence of two periods of development: larval and adult stages. The aquatic larval stage develops rapidly, and the animal spends much time eating and growing. After reaching a sufficient size, the larval form undergoes a developmental transition called metamorphosis into the adult (often terrestrial) form.

REPTILES

The reptiles were the first group of vertebrates to completely abandon the aquatic habitat because of adaptations that permitted sexual reproduction on land. A crucial adaptation first found in reptiles is internal fertilization (figure 39.3b). Internal fertilization protects the gametes from drying out, freeing the animals from returning to the water to breed.

Many reptiles are **oviparous** (L. *ovum*, egg + *parere*, to bring forth), and the eggs are deposited outside the body of the female. Others are **ovoviviparous** (L. *ovum*, egg + *vivere*, to live, + *parere*, to bring forth). They form eggs that hatch in the body of the female, and the young are born alive.

The shelled egg and extraembryonic membranes, also first seen in reptiles, constitute two other important evolutionary adaptations to life on land. These adaptations allowed reptiles to lay eggs in dry places without danger of desiccation. As the embryo develops, the extraembryonic chorion and amnion help protect it, the latter by creating a fluid-filled sac for the embryo. The allantois permits gas exchange and stores excretory products. Complete development can occur within the eggshell. When the animal hatches, it has

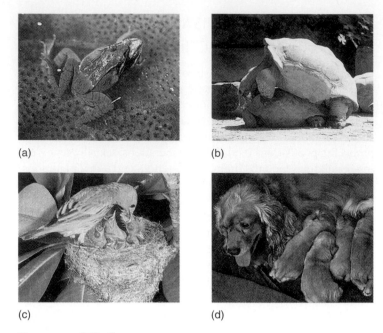

(a)   (b)

(c)   (d)

FIGURE 39.3

Vertebrate Reproductive Strategies. (a) A male wood frog (*Rana sylvatica*) clasping the female in amplexus, a form of external fertilization. As the female releases eggs into the water, the male releases sperm over them. (b) Reptiles, such as these turtles, were the first terrestrial vertebrates to develop internal fertilization. (c) Birds are oviparous. Their shelled eggs have large yolk reserves, and the young develop and hatch outside the mother's body. Birds may show advanced parental care. (d) A placental mammal. This female dog is nursing her puppies.

developed to the point that it can survive on its own or with some parental care.

BIRDS

Birds have retained the important adaptations for life on land that evolved in the early reptiles. With the exception of most waterfowl, birds lack a penis. Males simply deposit semen against the cloaca for internal fertilization. Sperm then migrate up the cloaca and fertilize the eggs before hard shells form. This method of mating occurs more quickly than the internal fertilization that reptiles practice. All birds are oviparous, and the eggshells are much thicker than those of reptiles. Thicker shells permit birds to sit on their eggs and warm them. This brooding, or incubation, hastens embryo development. When many young birds hatch, they are incapable of surviving on their own. Extensive parental care and feeding of young are more common among birds than fishes, amphibians, or reptiles (figure 39.3c).

MAMMALS

The most primitive mammals, the monotremes (e.g., the duck-billed platypus and spiny anteater), lay eggs, as did the reptiles from which they evolved. All other mammals are viviparous.

Mammalian viviparity was another major evolutionary adaptation, and it has taken two forms. The marsupials developed the ability to nourish their young in a pouch after a short gestation inside the female. The other, much larger group—the placentals—retain the young inside the female, where the mother nourishes them by means of a placenta. Even after birth, mammals continue to nourish their young. Mammary glands are a unique mammalian adaptation that permit the female to nourish the young with milk that she produces (figure 39.3d). Some mammals nurture their young until adulthood, when they are able to mate and fend for themselves. As noted at the beginning of this section, mammalian reproductive behavior also contributes to the transmission and evolution of culture that is the key to the evolution of the human species.

Stop and Ask Yourself

6. What reproductive strategy developed in each of the following to increase the chances of survival: (a) bony fishes, (b) amphibians, and (c) reptiles?

7. How do bird eggs and amphibian eggs differ?

8. What reproductive adaptation evolved in humans that is not present in other mammals?

9. What is the advantage and disadvantage of estrus?

THE HUMAN MALE REPRODUCTIVE SYSTEM

The reproductive role of the human male is to produce sperm and deliver them to the vagina of the female. This function requires the following structures:

1. Two testes that produce sperm and the male sex hormone, testosterone.
2. Accessory glands and tubes that furnish a fluid for carrying the sperm to the penis. This fluid, together with the sperm, is called semen.
3. Accessory ducts that store and carry secretions from the testes and accessory glands to the penis.
4. A penis that deposits semen in the vagina during sexual intercourse.

PRODUCTION AND TRANSPORT OF SPERM

The paired **testes** (sing., testis) (L. *testis*, witness; the paired testes were believed to bear witness to a man's virility) are the male reproductive organs (gonads) that produce sperm (figure 39.4). Shortly after birth, the testes descend from the abdominal cavity into the **scrotum** (L. *scrautum*, a leather pouch for arrows), which hangs between the thighs. Because the testes hang outside the body, the temperature inside the scrotum is about 34° C compared to a 38° C core temperature. ④ The lower temperature is necessary for active sperm production and survival. Muscles elevate or lower the testes, depending on the outside air temperature.

Each testis contains over eight hundred tightly coiled **seminiferous tubules** (figure 39.5a,b), which produce thousands of sperm each second in healthy young men (*see figure 6.11a*). The walls of the seminiferous tubules are lined with two types of cells: spermatogenic cells, which give rise to sperm, and sustentacular cells, which nourish the sperm as they form and which also secrete a fluid (as well as the hormone inhibin) into the tubules to provide a liquid medium for the sperm. Between the seminiferous tubules are clusters of endocrine cells, called interstitial cells (Leydig cells), that secrete the male sex hormone testosterone.

A system of tubes carries the sperm that the testes produce to the penis. The seminiferous tubules merge into a network of tiny tubules called the rete testis (L. *rete*, net), which merges into a coiled tube called the epididymis. The epididymis has three main functions: (1) it stores sperm until they are mature and ready to be ejaculated, (2) it contains smooth muscle that helps propel the sperm toward the penis by peristaltic contractions, and (3) it serves as a duct system for sperm to pass from the testis to the ductus deferens. The ductus deferens (formerly called the vas deferens or sperm duct) is the dilated continuation of the epididymis. Continuing upward after leaving the scrotum, the ductus deferens passes through the lower part of the abdominal wall via the inguinal canal. ⑤ If the abdominal wall weakens at the point where the ductus deferens passes through, an inguinal hernia may result. (In an inguinal hernia, the intestine may protrude downward into the scrotum.) The ductus deferens then passes around the urinary bladder and enlarges to form the ampulla (*see figure 39.4*). The ampulla stores some sperm until they are ejaculated. Distal to the ampulla, the ductus deferens becomes the ejaculatory duct. The urethra is the final section of the reproductive duct system.

After the ductus deferens passes around the urinary bladder, several accessory glands add their secretions to the sperm as they are propelled through the ducts. These accessory glands are the seminal vesicles, prostate gland, and bulbourethral glands (*see figure 39.4*). The paired **seminal vesicles** secrete water, fructose, prostaglandins, and vitamin C. This secretion provides an energy source for the motile sperm and helps to neutralize the natural protective acidity of the vagina. (The pH of the vagina is about 3 to 4, but sperm motility and fertility are enhanced when it increases to about 6.) The **prostate gland** secretes water, enzymes, cholesterol, buffering salts, and phospholipids. The **bulbourethral glands** secrete a clear, alkaline fluid that lubricates the urethra to facilitate the ejaculation of semen and lubricates the penis prior to sexual intercourse. The fluid that results from the combination of sperm and glandular secretions is **semen** (L. *seminis*, seed). The average human ejaculation produces 3 to 4 ml of semen and contains 300 to 400 million sperm.

The penis has two functions. It carries urine through the urethra to the outside during urination, and it transports semen through the urethra during ejaculation. In addition to the urethra, the penis contains three cylindrical strands of erectile tissue: two corpora cavernosa and the corpus spongiosum (*see figure 39.4*). The corpus spongiosum extends beyond the corpora cavernosa and becomes the expanded tip of the penis called the glans penis. The loosely fitting skin of the penis folds forward over the glans to form the prepuce or foreskin. **Circumcision** is the removal of the

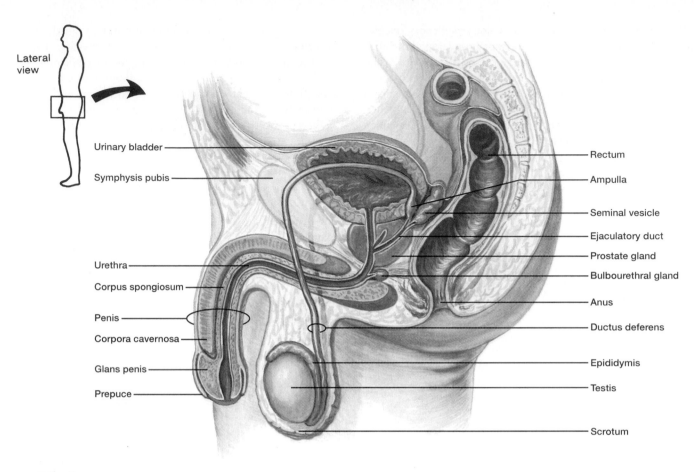

Lateral view

Urinary bladder

Symphysis pubis

Urethra

Corpus spongiosum

Penis

Corpora cavernosa

Glans penis

Prepuce

Rectum

Ampulla

Seminal vesicle

Ejaculatory duct

Prostate gland

Bulbourethral gland

Anus

Ductus deferens

Epididymis

Testis

Scrotum

FIGURE 39.4

Lateral View of the Human Male Reproductive System. There are two each of the following structures: testis, epididymis, ductus deferens, seminal vesicle, ejaculatory duct, and bulbourethral gland.

prepuce for religious or health reasons. ⑥ Today, many circumcisions are performed in the belief that they lessen the likelihood of cancer of the penis.

A mature human sperm consists of a head, midpiece, and tail (figure 39.5c). The head contains the haploid nucleus, which is mostly DNA. The acrosome, a cap over most of the head, contains an enzyme called acrosin that assists the sperm in penetrating the outer layer surrounding a secondary oocyte. The sperm tail contains an array of microtubules that bend to produce whiplike movements. The spiral mitochondria in the midpiece supply the ATP necessary for these movements.

HORMONAL CONTROL OF MALE REPRODUCTIVE FUNCTION

Before a male can mature and function sexually, special regulatory hormones must come into play (table 39.1). Male sex hormones are collectively called **androgens** (Gr. *andros*, man + *gennan*, to produce). The hormones that travel from the brain and pituitary gland to the testes (and ovaries in the female) are called **gonadotropins.** As previously noted, the interstitial cells produce the male sex hormone **testosterone.** Figure 39.6 shows the nega-

tive feedback mechanisms that regulate the production and secretion of testosterone, as well as its actions. When the level of testosterone in the blood decreases, the hypothalamus is stimulated to secrete GnRH (gonadotropin-releasing hormone). GnRH stimulates the secretion of FSH (follicle-stimulating hormone) and LH (luteinizing hormone), also called ICSH (interstitial cell-stimulating hormone), into the bloodstream. (FSH and LH were first named for their functions in females, but their molecular structure is exactly the same in males.) FSH causes the spermatogenic cells in the seminiferous tubules to initiate spermatogenesis, and LH stimulates the interstitial cells to secrete testosterone. The cycle is completed when testosterone inhibits the secretion of LH, and another hormone, inhibin, is secreted. Inhibin inhibits the secretion of FSH from the anterior pituitary. This cycle maintains a constant rate (homeostasis) of spermatogenesis.

Stop and Ask Yourself

10. What are the major constituents of semen?
11. How do LH and FSH function in males?

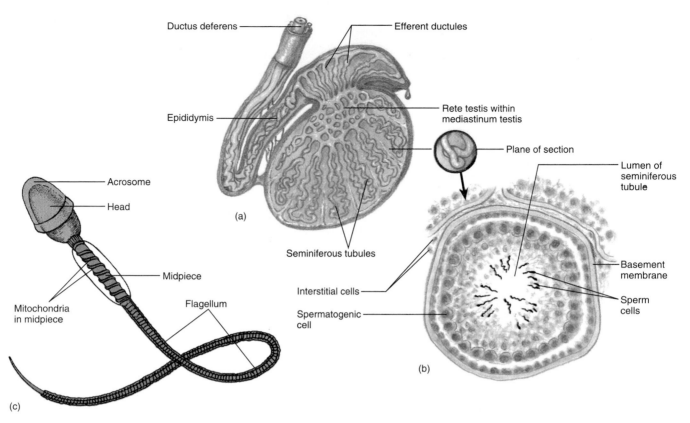

FIGURE 39.5

Human Male Testis. (*a*) Sagittal section through a testis. (*b*) Cross section of a seminiferous tubule, showing the location of spermatogenesis. (*c*) A mature sperm.

TABLE 39.1	MAJOR HUMAN MALE REPRODUCTIVE HORMONES IN AN ADULT	
HORMONE	FUNCTIONS	SOURCE
FSH (follicle-stimulating hormone)	Aids sperm maturation; increases testosterone production	Pituitary gland
GnRH (gonadotropin-releasing hormone)	Controls pituitary secretion	Hypothalamus
Inhibin	Inhibits FSH secretion	Sustentacular cells in testes
LH (luteinizing hormone) or ICSH (interstitial cell-stimulating hormone)	Stimulates testosterone secretion	Pituitary gland
Testosterone	Increases sperm production; stimulates development of male primary and secondary sexual characteristics; inhibits LH secretion	Interstitial cells in testes

THE HUMAN FEMALE REPRODUCTIVE SYSTEM

The reproductive role of human females is more complex than that of males. Not only do females produce gametes (eggs or ova), but after fertilization, they also nourish, carry, and protect the developing embryo. After the offspring is born, the mother may nurse it for a time. Another difference between the sexes is the monthly rhythmicity of the female reproductive system.

The female reproductive system consists of a number of structures with specialized functions (figure 39.7):

1. Two ovaries produce eggs and the female sex hormones estrogen and progesterone.
2. Two uterine tubes, one from each ovary, carry eggs from the ovary to the uterus. Fertilization usually occurs in the upper third of a uterine tube.
3. If fertilization occurs, the uterus receives the blastocyst and houses the developing embryo.

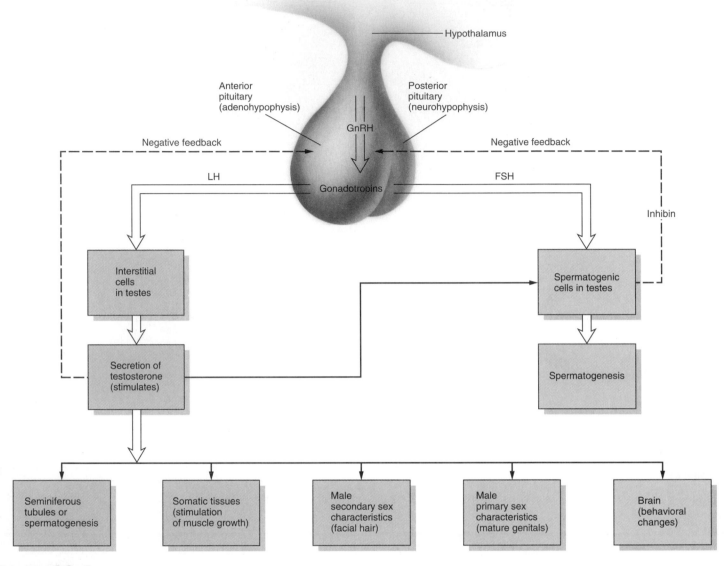

FIGURE 39.6

Hormonal Control of Reproductive Function in Adult Human Males. Negative feedback mechanisms by which the hypothalamus controls sperm maturation and the development of male secondary sexual characteristics. (GnRH=gonadotropin-releasing hormone; LH=luteinizing hormone; FSH=follicle-stimulating hormone.)

4. The vagina receives semen from the penis during sexual intercourse. It is the exit point for menstrual flow and is the canal through which the baby passes from the uterus during childbirth.

5. The external genital organs have protective functions and play a role in sexual arousal.

6. The mammary glands, contained in the paired breasts, produce milk for the newborn baby.

PRODUCTION AND TRANSPORT OF THE EGG

The female gonads are the paired **ovaries** (L. *ovum,* egg), which produce eggs and female hormones. The ovaries are located in the pelvic part of the abdomen, one on each side of the uterus. A cross section of an ovary reveals rounded vesicles called follicles, which are the actual centers of egg production (oogenesis) (figure 39.8). Each follicle contains an immature egg called a primary oocyte, and follicles are always present in several stages of development. After release of a secondary oocyte (commonly called an egg) in the process called **ovulation,** the lining of the follicle grows inward, forming the corpus luteum ("yellow body"), which serves as a temporary endocrine tissue and continues to secrete the female sex hormones estrogen and progesterone.

The paired tubes that receive the secondary oocyte from the ovary and convey it to the uterus are called either the **uterine tubes** or **fallopian tubes** (*see figure 39.7*). Feathery fimbriae fringe the part of the uterine tube that encircles the ovary. Each month, as a secondary oocyte is released, the motion of the fimbriae sweep it across a tiny space between the uterine tube and the ovary into the tube.

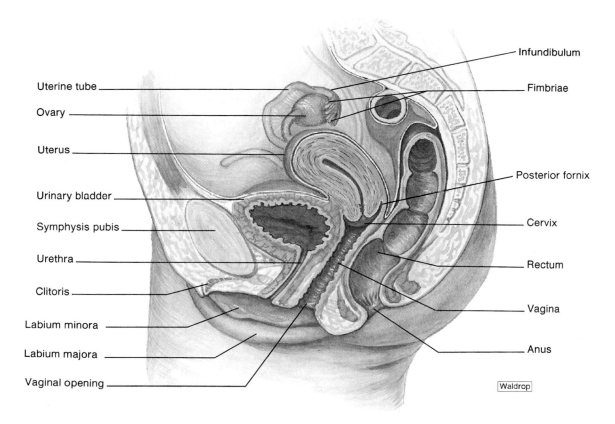

FIGURE 39.7

Lateral View of the Human Female Reproductive System. Two uterine tubes lead into the uterus and two ovaries.

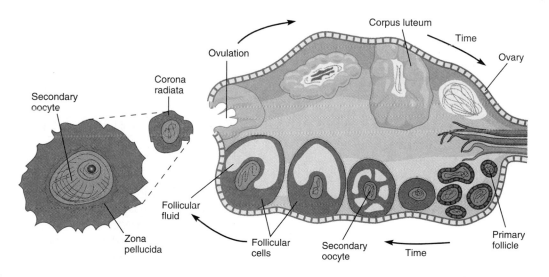

FIGURE 39.8

Cross Section through a Human Ovary. The events in the ovarian cycle proceed from the growth and maturation of the primary follicle, through ovulation (rupture of a mature follicle with the concurrent release of a secondary oocyte), through the formation and maintenance (during pregnancy) or degeneration (no pregnancy) of an endocrine structure called the corpus luteum. The positions of the oocyte and corpus luteum are varied for illustrative purposes only. An oocyte matures at the same site, from the beginning of the cycle to ovulation.

FIGURE 39.9

Cilia Lining the Uterine Tubes. The tiny, beating cilia on the surfaces of the uterine tube cells propel the secondary oocyte downward and perhaps the sperm upward (EM ×1000).

Unlike sperm, the secondary oocyte cannot move on its own. Instead, the peristaltic contractions of the tube and the waving motions of the cilia in the mucous membrane of the tube carry the secondary oocyte along (figure 39.9). Fertilization usually occurs in the uppermost third of the uterine tube. A fertilized oocyte (zygote) continues its journey toward the uterus, where it will implant. The journey takes 4 to 7 days. If fertilization does not occur, the secondary oocyte degenerates in the uterine tube.

The uterine tubes terminate in the **uterus**, a hollow, muscular organ in front of the rectum and behind the urinary bladder (figure 39.10). The uterus terminates in a narrow portion called the cervix, which joins the uterus to the vagina. The uterus has three layers of tissues. The outer layer (perimetrium) extends beyond the uterus to form the two broad ligaments that stretch from the uterus to the lateral walls of the pelvis. The middle muscular layer (myometrium [Gr. *myo*, muscle + *metra*, womb]) makes up most of the uterine wall. The endometrium is the specialized mucous membrane that contains an abundance of blood vessels and simple glands.

The cervix leads to the **vagina**, a muscular tube 8 to 10 cm long. The wall of the vagina is composed mainly of smooth muscle and elastic tissue.

The external genital organs, or genitalia, include the mons pubis, labia majora, labia minora, vestibular glands, clitoris, and

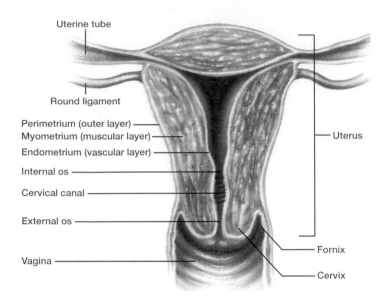

FIGURE 39.10

Human Female Uterus. This frontal section of a uterus shows the three major tissue layers. The outer layer is the perimetrium. The middle myometrium makes up the bulk of the uterine wall. It is composed of smooth muscle fibers. The innermost layer is composed of a specialized mucous membrane called the endometrium, which is deep and velvety in texture. Breakdown of the endometrium comprises part of the menstrual flow.

vaginal opening (*see figure 39.7*). As a group, these organs are called the **vulva**. In most young women, the vaginal opening is partially covered by a thin membrane, the hymen, which may be ruptured during normal strenuous activities or may be stretched or broken during sexual activity.

The **mammary glands** (L. *mammae*, breasts) are modified sweat glands that produce and secrete milk. They contain varying amounts of adipose tissue. ⑦ The amount of adipose tissue determines the size of the breasts, but the amount of mammary tissue does not vary widely from one woman to another.

HORMONAL CONTROL OF FEMALE REPRODUCTIVE FUNCTION

The male is continuously fertile from puberty to old age, and throughout that period, sex hormones are continuously secreted. The female, however, is fertile only during a few days each month, and the pattern of hormone secretion is intricately related to the cyclical release of a secondary oocyte from the ovary.

The cyclical production of hormones controls the development of a secondary oocyte in a follicle (figure 39.11; table 39.2). Gonadotropin-releasing hormone (GnRH) from the hypothalamus acts on the anterior pituitary gland, which releases follicle-stimulating hormone (FSH) and luteinizing hormone (LH) to bring about the oocyte's maturation and release from the ovary. These hormones regulate the **menstrual cycle,** which is the cyclic preparation of the uterus to receive a fertilized egg, and the **ovarian cycle,** during which the oocyte matures and ovulation occurs.

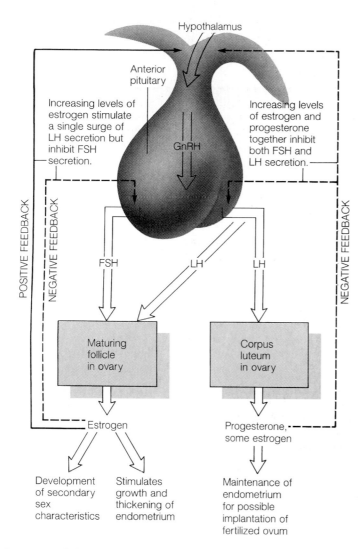

FIGURE 39.11

Hormonal Control of Reproductive Functions in an Adult Human Female. Feedback loops involve the hypothalamus, anterior pituitary, and ovaries. Gonadotropin-releasing hormone (GnRH) stimulates the release of both follicle-stimulating hormone (FSH) and luteinizing hormone (LH). Two negative feedback systems and a positive feedback system (one of the few in the human body) control the ovarian cycle.

This monthly preparation of the uterine lining for the fertilized egg normally begins at puberty. When a female reaches 45 to 55 years of age, the ovaries lose their sensitivity to FSH and LH, they stop making normal amounts of progesterone and estrogen, and the monthly menstrual cycle ceases in what is called the **menopause** (Gr. *men*, month + *pausis*, cessation).

One way to understand the hormonal pattern in the normal monthly cycle is to follow the development of the oocyte and the physical events in the menstrual cycle (figure 39.12; table 39.3). On average, it takes 28 days to complete one menstrual cycle, although the range may be from 22 to 45 days. During this time, the following events take place:

1. The controlling center for ovulation and menstruation is the hypothalamus. It releases, on a regular cycle, GnRH, which stimulates the anterior pituitary to secrete FSH and LH (*see figure 39.11*).

2. FSH promotes the development of the oocyte in one of the immature ovarian follicles.

3. The follicles produce estrogen, causing a buildup and proliferation of the endometrium, as well as the inhibition of FSH production.

4. The elevated estrogen level about midway in the cycle triggers the anterior pituitary to secrete LH, which causes the mature follicle to enlarge rapidly and release the secondary oocyte (ovulation). LH also causes the collapsed follicle to become another endocrine tissue, the corpus luteum.

5. The corpus luteum secretes estrogen and progesterone, which act to complete the development of the endometrium and maintain it for 10 to 14 days.

6. If the oocyte is not fertilized, the corpus luteum disintegrates into a corpus albicans, and estrogen and progesterone secretion cease.

7. Without estrogen and progesterone, the endometrium breaks down, and **menstruation** occurs. The menstrual flow is composed mainly of sloughed-off endometrial cells, mucus, and blood.

8. As progesterone and estrogen levels decrease further, the pituitary renews active secretion of FSH, which stimulates the development of another follicle, and the monthly cycle begins again.

HORMONAL REGULATION IN THE PREGNANT FEMALE

Pregnancy sets into motion a new series of physiological events. The ovaries are directly affected because, as the embryo develops, the cells of the embryo and placenta release the hormone human chorionic gonadotropin (hCG), which keeps the corpus luteum from disintegrating. The progesterone that it secretes is necessary to maintain the uterine lining. After a time, the placenta takes over progesterone production and the corpus luteum degenerates. ⑧ By the end of 2 weeks following implantation, the concentration of hCG is so high in the female's blood, and in her urine as well, that an hCG immunological test can check for pregnancy. As the embryo develops, other hormones are secreted. For example, prolactin and oxytocin induce the mammary glands to secrete and eject milk after childbirth. Oxytocin and prostaglandins also stimulate the uterine contractions that expel the baby from the uterus during childbirth.

Stop and Ask Yourself

12. What is the anatomy of a human uterus?
13. What are the external genital organs in a human female?
14. What events take place in the menstrual cycle?

TABLE 39.2	MAJOR HUMAN FEMALE REPRODUCTIVE HORMONES	

HORMONE	FUNCTIONS	SOURCE
Estrogen	Stimulates thickening of uterine wall, maturation of oocyte and development of female sexual characteristics; inhibits FSH secretion; increases LH secretion	Ovarian follicle, corpus luteum
FSH (follicle-stimulating hormone)	Causes immature oocyte and follicle to develop; increases estrogen secretion; stimulates new gamete formation and development of uterine wall after menstruation	Pituitary gland
GnRH (gonadotropin-releasing hormone)	Controls pituitary secretion	Hypothalamus
hCG (human chorionic gonadotropin)	Prevents corpus luteum from disintegrating; stimulates corpus luteum to secrete estrogen and progesterone	Embryonic membranes and placenta
LH (luteinizing hormone)	Stimulates further development of oocyte and follicle; stimulates ovulation; increases progesterone secretion; aids in development of corpus luteum	Pituitary gland
Oxytocin	Stimulates uterine contractions during labor and milk release during nursing	Pituitary gland
Prolactin	Promotes milk secretion by mammary glands after childbirth	Pituitary gland
Progesterone	Stimulates thickening of uterine wall	Corpus luteum

TABLE 39.3	SUMMARY OF THE MENSTRUAL CYCLE EVENTS	

PHASE	EVENTS	DURATION IN DAYS*
Follicular	Follicle matures in the ovary; menstruation (endometrium breaks down); endometrium rebuilds	1–5
Ovulation	Ovary releases secondary oocyte	6–14
Luteal	Corpus luteum forms; endometrium thickens and becomes glandular	15–28

*Using a 28-day menstrual cycle as an example.

PRENATAL DEVELOPMENT AND BIRTH

This section covers the main event in reproduction—the 9-month pregnancy period, during which time the human female's body carries, nourishes, and protects the embryo as it grows to a full-term baby.

EVENTS OF PRENATAL DEVELOPMENT: FROM ZYGOTE TO NEWBORN

The development of a human being can be divided into prenatal ("before birth") and postnatal ("after birth") periods. During the prenatal period, the developing individual begins life as a zygote, then becomes a ball of cells called a morula, and eventually becomes a blastocyst that implants in the endometrium. From 2 weeks after fertilization until the end of the eighth week of its existence, the individual is called an embryo. From 9 weeks until birth, it is a fetus. During or after birth, it is called a newborn, or baby.

Pregnancy is arbitrarily divided into 3-month periods called trimesters. The first trimester begins at fertilization and is when most of the organs are formed. The next two trimesters are mainly periods of growth for the fetus.

The First Trimester

After fertilization, usually in the upper third of the uterine tube, the zygote goes through several cleavages as it moves down the tube (figure 39.13). It eventually becomes a solid ball of cells called a **morula,** and by the fourth day, it develops into a 50- to 120-cell blastula stage called a **blastocyst.**

The next stage of development occurs when the blastocyst adheres to the uterine wall and implants. During implantation, the outer cells of the blastocyst, called the trophoblast, invade the endometrium. ⑨ Implantation is usually completed 11 to 12 days after fertilization; from then on, the female is considered to be pregnant.

One of the unique features of mammalian development is that most of the cells of the early embryo make no contribution to the embryo's body, giving rise instead to supportive and protective membranes. Only the inner cell mass gives rise to the embryonic body. Eventually, these cells arrange in a flat sheet that undergoes a gastrulation similar to that of reptiles and birds (see figure 10.12).

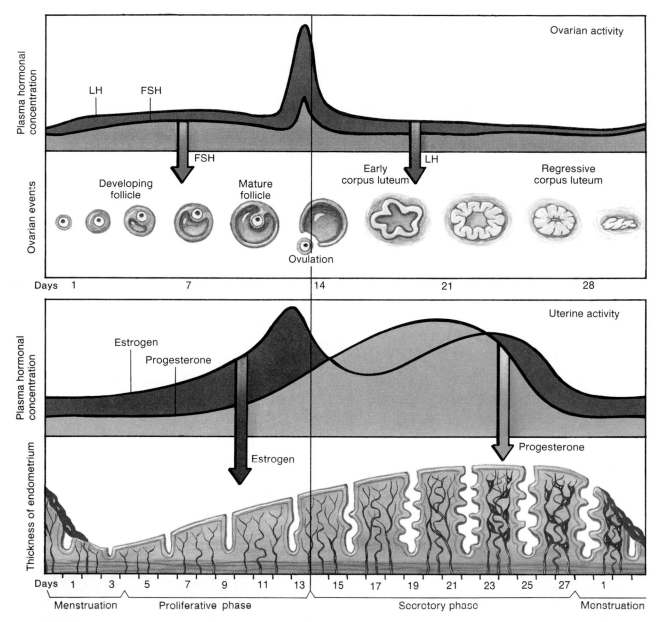

FIGURE 39.12

Major Events in the Female Ovarian and Menstrual Cycles. The two charts correlate the gonadotropins, ovarian hormones, follicle development, ovulation, and changes in uterine anatomy during the cycles.

Once gastrulation is completed, the rest of the first trimester is devoted to organogenesis and growth (figure 39.14). Regulatory events and inductive-tissue interactions shape most of the organ systems. By the middle of the first trimester, all of the major body systems have begun to develop.

The Second Trimester

In the second trimester (fourth month), fetal growth is spectacular. By now, the pregnant mother is aware of fetal movements. The heartbeat can be heard with a stethoscope. During the sixth month, the upper and lower eyelids separate, and the eyelashes form. During the seventh month, the eyes open. During this period, the bones begin to ossify.

The Third Trimester

The third trimester extends from the seventh month until birth. During this time, the fetus has developed sufficiently (with respect to the circulatory and respiratory systems) to potentially survive if born prematurely. During the last month, fetal weight doubles.

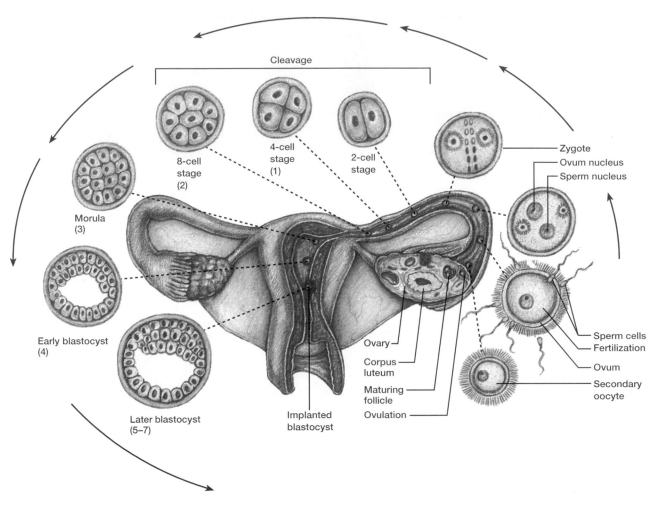

FIGURE 39.13

Early Stages in Human Development. The numbers in parentheses indicate the days after fertilization. The secondary oocyte is fertilized in the upper third of the uterine tube, undergoes cleavage while traveling down the tube, and finally implants in the endometrium of the uterus.

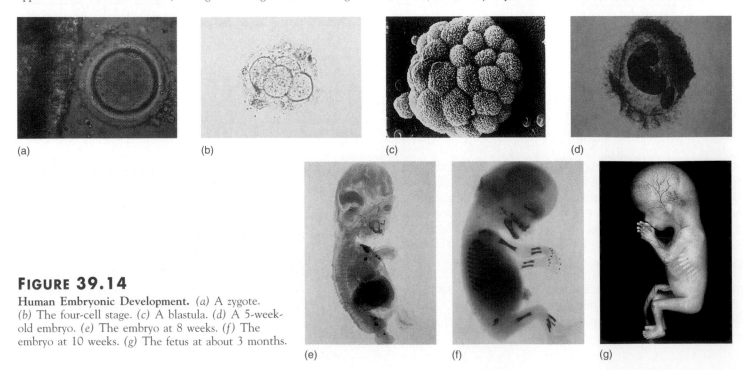

FIGURE 39.14

Human Embryonic Development. (*a*) A zygote. (*b*) The four-cell stage. (*c*) A blastula. (*d*) A 5-week-old embryo. (*e*) The embryo at 8 weeks. (*f*) The embryo at 10 weeks. (*g*) The fetus at about 3 months.

FIGURE 39.15

Fetus and Placenta at Seven Weeks. The circulations of mother and fetus are in close contact at the site of the chorionic villi, but they do not actually mix. Branches of the mother's arteries in the wall of her uterus open into pools near the chorionic villi. Oxygen and nutrients from the mother's blood diffuse into the fetal capillaries of the placenta. The fetal capillaries lead into the umbilical vein, which is enclosed within the umbilical cord. From here, the fresh blood circulates through the fetus's body. Blood that the fetus has depleted of nutrients and oxygen returns to the placenta in the umbilical arteries, which branch into capillaries, from which waste products diffuse to the maternal side.

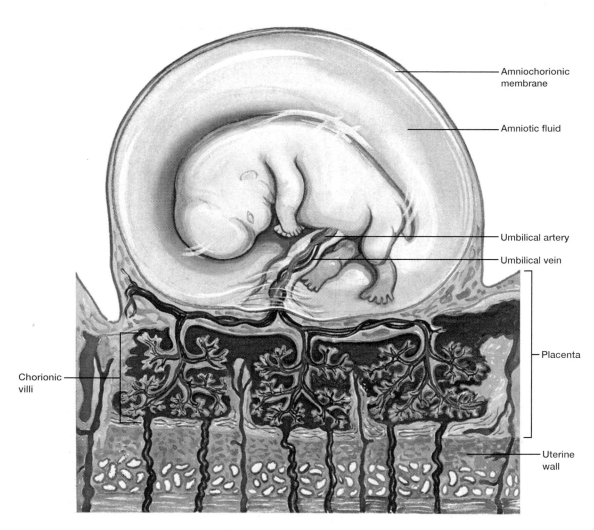

THE PLACENTA: EXCHANGE SITE AND HORMONE PRODUCER

The lengthy pregnancy characteristic of mammals is possible, in part, because of the embryonic membranes that originated in the reptiles: the amnion, yolk sac, chorion, and allantois *(see figure 10.13)*. The latter two gave rise to the embryonic parts of the placenta. The **placenta** is the organ that sustains the embryo and fetus throughout the pregnancy and through which gases, nutrients, and wastes are exchanged between the maternal and fetal systems (figure 39.15). The tiny, fingerlike projections that were sent out from the blastocyst during implantation develop into numerous chorionic villi, which contain embryonic blood vessels. These blood vessels do not merge with those of the mother; the two bloodstreams remain separate throughout the pregnancy. The **umbilical cord** connects the placenta to the abdomen of the fetus. Two fetal umbilical arteries and one fetal umbilical vein spiral about each other in the umbilical cord.

BIRTH: AN END AND A BEGINNING

About 266 days after fertilization, or 280 days from the beginning of the last menstrual period, the human infant is born. The birth process is called **parturition** (L. *parturire*, to be in labor). During

parturition, the mother's uterine muscles begin to contract, and the cervix begins to dilate, or open. The hormone relaxin, produced by the ovaries and placenta, causes the mother's pelvic bones to slightly separate so that the baby can pass through the birth canal.

Changing hormone levels initiate parturition (box 39.1). When it is time for the baby to be born, its pituitary gland secretes adrenocorticotropic hormone (ACTH), which stimulates the adrenal glands to secrete steroids. These steroids stimulate the placenta to produce prostaglandins that, along with the hormone oxytocin from the mother's pituitary, cause the uterus to begin powerful muscular contractions. The contractions build in length and increase in frequency over a period that usually lasts from 2 to 18 hours. During that time, the cervix becomes fully dilated, and the amniotic sac ruptures. Usually within an hour of these events, the baby is expelled from the uterus (figure 39.16*a–c*). After the baby emerges, uterine contractions continue to expel the **afterbirth** (figure 39.16*d*). The umbilical cord is severed, and the newborn embarks on its nurtured existence in the outside world. (In mammals other than humans, the female bites through the cord to sever it.)

MILK PRODUCTION AND LACTATION

Lactation (L. *lactare*, to suckle) includes both milk secretion (production) by the mammary glands and milk release from the

BOX 39.1   THE PARTICIPATION OF THE FETUS DURING CHILDBIRTH

Until recently, scientists thought that the fetus played no active role in its own birth process. Evidence now indicates, however, that the fetus triggers the release of "stress" hormones during parturition that help it survive the arduous process of birth and adjust to life outside the mother's uterus.

In addition to the pressure the fetus feels while passing through the birth canal, it is also periodically deprived of oxygen when powerful uterine contractions compress the umbilical cord and placenta. During these periods of stress, the fetus produces very high levels of epinephrine and norepinephrine, both of which are classified as catecholamines. Catecholamines generally help a person react favorably to incidents of extreme stress. Catecholamine secretions allow the fetus to counteract the periods of low oxygen and other potentially harmful situations throughout most of parturition.

These stress situations are beneficial because the unusually high levels of catecholamines also permit the newborn to adjust to new conditions outside the mother's uterus immediately after birth. Postnatal adjustments include breathing, breaking down fat and glycogen into usable fuel for cells, accelerating the heart rate and cardiac output, and increasing blood flow to the brain, heart, and skeletal muscles.

The surge of catecholamines during parturition also causes the newborn's pupils to dilate, even when strong light is present. This alertness may help the infant form an early bond with its mother.

The production of fetal catecholamines is a direct result of the adrenal glands' response to stress. In adults, however, catecholamine secretions begin with the stimulation of the sympathetic nervous system. It is also of interest that the adrenal glands of the fetus are proportionately larger than those of the adult.

(a) 9-month-old fetus

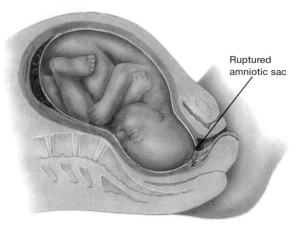

(b) First stage of birth

(c) Second stage of birth

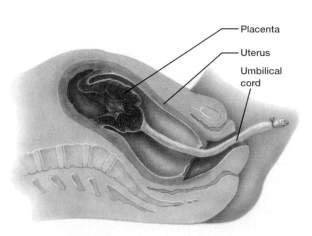

(d) Third stage of birth

FIGURE 39.16

Stages of Labor and Parturition. (*a*) The position of the fetus prior to labor. (*b*) The ruptured amniotic sac and early dilation of the cervix. (*c*) The expulsion stage of parturition. (*d*) Passage of the afterbirth.

breasts. (Mammary glands, a unique characteristic of mammals, evolved from sweat glands in the skin.) During pregnancy, the breasts enlarge in response to increasing levels of the hormone prolactin. Before birth, placental secretions of estrogen and progesterone inhibit milk secretion from the breasts. After the placenta has been expelled from the uterus, the concentrations of estrogen and progesterone drop, and the breasts begin to produce copious amounts of milk.

The mother's breasts do not actually release milk until 1 to 3 days after the baby is born. During these first days, the suckling baby receives **colostrum,** a high-protein fluid present in the breast at birth. Colostrum contains an abundance of maternal antibodies and thus helps strengthen the baby's immune system. It also functions as a laxative, removing fetal wastes, called **meconium,** retained in the intestines. After about 3 days, the prolactin secreted from the pituitary stimulates milk production. The newborn's suckling stim-

ulates the pituitary to release oxytocin as well as prolactin. Oxytocin triggers milk release from the mammary glands.

Stop and Ask Yourself

15. What five stages (cell types) comprise the prenatal period?
16. What are the main events of the first trimester of pregnancy? What are the main events of the second and third trimesters?
17. What is the function of the placenta?
18. What causes parturition to occur?
19. How does lactation occur?

SUMMARY

1. Asexual reproductive processes do not involve the production and subsequent fusion of haploid cells, but rely solely on vegetative growth through mitosis.

2. Sexual reproduction involves the formation of haploid cells through meiosis and the subsequent fusion of pairs of those cells to produce a diploid zygote.

3. The forms of asexual reproduction in invertebrates are binary fission, budding (both external and internal), and fragmentation. Parthenogenesis also occurs in a few invertebrates.

4. Sexual reproductive strategies and structures in the invertebrates are numerous and varied.

5. Sexual reproduction first evolved in aquatic animals. The invasion of land meant facing the danger of the gametes and embryos desiccating. The five major groups of vertebrates have reproductive adaptations for the environment in which they reproduce.

6. The reproductive role of the human male is to produce sperm and deliver them to the vagina of the female. This function requires different structures. The testes produce sperm and the male sex hormone, testosterone. Accessory glands furnish a fluid, called semen, for carrying the sperm to the penis. Accessory ducts store and carry secretions from the testes and accessory glands to the penis. The penis deposits semen in the vagina during sexual intercourse.

7. Before a human male can mature and function sexually, special regulatory hormones (FSH, GnRH, inhibin, LH, and testosterone) must function.

8. The reproductive roles of the human female are more complex than those of the male. Not only do females produce eggs, but after fertilization, they also nourish, carry, and protect the developing embryo. They may also nourish the infant for a time after it is born. The female reproductive system consists of two ovaries, two uterine tubes, a uterus, vagina, and external genitalia. The mammary glands contained in the paired breasts produce milk for the newborn baby.

9. The human female is fertile for only a few days each month, and the pattern of hormone secretion is intricately related to the cyclical release of a secondary oocyte from the ovary. Various hormones regulate the menstrual and ovarian cycles.

10. Pregnancy sets a new series of physiological events into motion that are directed to housing, protecting, and nourishing the embryo.

11. The development of a human may be divided into prenatal and postnatal periods. Pregnancy is arbitrarily divided into trimesters.

12. The placenta is the organ that sustains the embryo and fetus throughout the pregnancy. The birth process is called parturition and occurs about 266 days after fertilization.

13. Lactation includes both milk secretion (production) by the mammary glands and milk release from the breasts.

SELECTED KEY TERMS

asexual reproduction (p. 678)
broadcast spawning (p. 680)
budding (p. 678)
estrus (p. 681)
fission (p. 678)
fragmentation (p. 678)

gestation (p. 681)
parthenogenesis (p. 678)
sequential hermaphroditism (p. 680)
sexual reproduction (p. 680)

CRITICAL THINKING QUESTIONS

1. Is the fertility of a woman affected by the length of a given menstrual cycle or whether the cycles are regular or irregular? Explain.

2. Looking at a variety of animals, what are the advantages to restricting reproduction to a limited time period? Why do so many animals have a sharply defined reproductive season during the year?

3. In most sexual species, males produce far more gametes than do females. Why does this occur when, in most cases, only one male gamete can fertilize one female gamete?

4. Why are the accessory glands of the male so important in reproduction?

REFERENCES ON THE WORLD WIDE WEB

1. **The Continuity of Life, Human.** This site contains a complete review of human reproductive biology.

http://home.ust.hk/~bo_mkc/

2. **The Visible Embryo.** This site provides the user with a detailed look at the first few stages of embryonic development.

   http://visembryo.ucsf.edu/

3. **Fetus.** This site explores the development of the egg from the zygote to birth.

   http://www.innerbody.com/htm/body.html

4. **Reproduction: A Last Hope for Some Endangered Species.** This is a page from the National Zoological Park. It explains the importance of reproductive technologies for some rare animals and the importance of a large gene pool for a population.

   http://www.si.edu/natzoo/zooview/newsserv/artrepro.htmArtificial

5. **Amphibian Embryology Tutorial.** This site contains a wealth of information (movies, photos) on the development of frogs.

   http://www.library.wisc.edu/Biotech/demo/frog2mainmenu.html

6. **Embryo Development Overview.** This site lets you view human development from conception to week 38.

   http://www.med.upenn.edu/embryo_project/overview/overview.html

SUGGESTED READINGS

BOOKS

Allport, S. 1986. *Explorers of the Black Box: The Search for the Cellular Basis of Memory*. New York: W. W. Norton.

Barlow, H. B., and Mollon, J. D. 1982. *The Senses*. Cambridge: Cambridge University Press.

Baulieu, E., and Kelley, P. 1990. *Hormones*. Paris: Hermann Press.

Bruely, D. 1985. *Oxygen Transport to Tissues*. New York: Plenum.

Christian, J. L., and Gregor, J. L. 1985. *Nutrition for Living*. Menlo Park, Calif.: Benjamin Cummings.

Crapo, L. 1985. *Hormones: The Messengers of Life*. New York: W. H. Freeman.

Hadley, M. 1988. *Endocrinology*. Englewood Cliffs, N.J.: Prentice-Hall.

Hancox, N. M. 1972. *Biology of Bone*. Cambridge: Cambridge University Press.

Hochachka, P., and Somero, G. 1984. *Biochemical Adaptations*. Princeton, N.J.: Princeton University Press.

Jones, R. E. 1984. *Human Reproduction and Sexual Behavior*. Englewood Cliffs, N.J.: Prentice-Hall.

Kandel, E., and Schwartz, J. H. 1985. *Principles of Neural Science*. 2d ed. New York: Elsevier.

Margulis, L., and Sagan, D. 1986. *Origins of Sex: Three Billion Years of Genetic Recombination*. New Haven, Conn.: Yale University Press.

Masters, W. H., and Johnson, V. E. 1966. *Human Sexual Response*. Boston: Little, Brown.

Nilsson, L. 1977. *A Child Is Born*. New York: Delacorte Press.

———. 1986. *Behold Man: A Photographic Journey of Discovery Inside the Body*. Boston: Little, Brown.

Rankin, J. C., and Davenport, J. 1981. *Animal Osmoregulation*. New York: John Wiley & Sons.

Ruckenusch, Y., and Thivend, P. 1980. *Digestive Physiology and Metabolism in Ruminants*. Westport, Conn.: AVI Publishing.

Singer, P., and Wells, D. 1985. *Making Babies: The New Science and Ethics of Conception*. New York: Charles Scribner and Sons.

Smith, H. 1961. *From Fish to Philosopher*. New York: Doubleday.

Tregear, R. 1966. *Physical Functions of the Skin*. New York: Academic Press.

ARTICLES

Ada, G., and Nossal, G. 1987. The clonal-selection theory. *Scientific American*, August.

Alexander, R. M. 1991. How dinosaurs ran. *Scientific American*, April.

American Zoologist. 1983. Evolution of endocrine systems in lower vertebrates, a symposium honoring professor Aubrey Gorbman, pp. 595–739.

Atkinson, M., and Macharen, N. 1990. What causes diabetes? *Scientific American*, July.

Avery, M., Wang, N., and Taeusch, W. 1973. The lung of the newborn infant. *Scientific American*, April.

Baldwin, R. L. 1984. Digestion and metabolism of ruminants. *BioScience* 34(4): 244–49.

Barlow, R. 1990. What the brain tells the eye. *Scientific American*, April.

Beaconsfield, P., Birdwood, G., and Beaconsfield, R. 1980. The placenta. *Scientific American*, August.

Berridge, M. 1985. The molecular basis of communication within the cell. *Scientific American*, October.

Binkley, S. 1979. A timekeeping enzyme in the pineal gland. *Scientific American*, April.

Bloom, F. E. 1981. Neuropeptides. *Scientific American*, October.

Bonn, D. 1987. Hormones for healthy bones. *New Scientist*, (February 19): 32–35.

Cantin, M., and Genest, J. 1986. The heart as an endocrine gland. *Scientific American*, February.

Caplan, A. I. 1981. Cartilage. *Scientific American*, October.

Carafoli, F. D., and Penniston, J. T. 1985. The calcium signal. *Scientific American*, November.

Carey, F. G. 1983. Fishes with warm bodies. *Scientific American*, February.

Carmichael, S. W., and Winkler, H. 1985. The adrenal chromaffin cell. *Scientific American*, August.

Cave, L. J. 1983. Brain's unsung cells. *BioScience* 33: 614–21.

Clements, J. A. 1962. Surface tension in the lungs. *Scientific American*, December.

Cohen, L. A. 1987. Diet and cancer. *Scientific American*, November.

Comroe, J. H. 1966. The lung. *Scientific American*, February.

Coutant, C. 1986. Thermal niches of striped bass. *Scientific American*, February.

Cowan, W. 1979. The development of the brain. *Scientific American*, September.

Crews, D. 1979. The hormonal control of behavior in a lizard. *Scientific American*, August.

Crick, F. H. C. 1979. Thinking about the brain. *Scientific American*, September.

Davenport, H. W. 1972. Why the stomach does not digest itself. *Scientific American*, January.

Degabriele, R. 1980. The physiology of the koala. *Scientific American*, July.

Dunant, Y., and Isrel, M. 1985. The release of acetylcholine. *Scientific American*, April.

Eastman, J., and DeVries, A. L. 1986. Antarctic fishes. *Scientific American*, November.

Edelson, R., and Fink, J. 1985. The immunological function of the skin. *Scientific American*, June.

Engelhard, V. 1994. How cells present antigens. *Scientific American*, August.

Epel, D. 1977. The program of fertilization. *Scientific American*, November.

Fedder, M., and Burggren, W. 1985. Skin breathing in vertebrates. *Scientific American*, November.

Fen, W. 1960. The mechanism of breathing. *Scientific American*, June.

Fernstrom, J. D., and Wurtman, R. J. 1974. Nutrition and the brain. *Scientific American*, February.

Finke, R. 1986. Mental imagery of the visual system. *Scientific American*, May.

Flam, F. 1989. Antifreezes in fish work quite similarly. *Science News*, June 30.

French, A. R. 1988. The patterns of mammalian hibernation. *American Scientist* 76(6): 568–75.

Frisch, R. E. 1988. Fatness and fertility. *Scientific American*, March.

Geldard, F. A., and Sherrick, C. E. 1986. Space, time and touch. *Scientific American*, July.

Gibbons, B. 1986. The intimate sense of smell. *National Geographic*, September.

Golde, D. 1991. The stem cell. *Scientific American*, December.

Golde, D., and Gasson, J. 1988. Hormones that stimulate the growth of blood cells. *Scientific American*, July.

Gombrich, E. H. 1972. The visual image. *Scientific American*, September.

Gottlieb, D. I. 1988. GABAergic neurons. *Scientific American*, February.

Grobstein, C. 1979. External human fertilization. *Scientific American*, June.

Guillemin, R., and Burgus, R. 1972. The hormones of the hypothalamus. *Scientific American*, November.

Heatwole, H. 1978. Adaptations of marine snakes. *American Scientist* 66: 594–604.

Heinrich, B. 1989. The raven's feast. *Natural History*, February.

———. 1987. Thermoregulation in winter moths. *Scientific American*, March.

Heinrich, B., and Bartholomew, G. A. 1972. Temperature regulation in flying moths. *Scientific American*, June.

Hoberman, J. 1995. The history of synthetic testosterone. *Scientific American*, February.

Hubel, D. H. 1979. Special issues on neurobiology. *Scientific American*, September.

Hudspeth, A. J. 1983. The hair cells of the inner ear. *Scientific American*, January.

Hume, I. 1989. Reading the entrails of evolution. *New Scientist*, April.

Irving, J. 1966. Adaptations to cold. *Scientific American*, January.

Kalil, R. 1989. Synapse formation in the developing brain. *Scientific American*, December.

Kappas, A., and Alveares, A. P. 1975. How the liver metabolizes foreign substances. *Scientific American*, June.

Keynes, R. 1987. Ion channels in the nerve-cell membrane. *Scientific American*, March.

Kimelberg, H. K., and Norenberg, M. D. 1989. Astrocytes. *Scientific American*, April.

Knudsen, E. I. 1981. The hearing of the barn owl. *Scientific American*, December.

Kolata, G. 1987. Managing the inland sea. *Science* 224: 703–10.

Koretz, J., and Handelman, G. 1988. How the human eye focuses. *Scientific American*, July.

Kretchmer, N. 1972. Lactose and lactase. *Scientific American*, October.

Lagercrantz, H., and Slotkin, A. 1986. The stress of being born. *Scientific American*, April.

Lee, R. E. 1989. Insect cold-hardiness: To freeze or not to freeze. *BioScience* 39: 308–13.

Lester, H. 1977. The response of acetylcholine. *Scientific American*, February.

Liem, K. 1988. Form and function of lungs: The evolution of air breathing mechanisms. *American Zoologist* 28: 739–59.

Linas, R. 1982. Calcium in synaptic transmission. *Scientific American*, October.

Livingston, M. S. 1988. Art, illusion, and the visual system. *Scientific American*, January.

Loeb, G. E. 1985. The functional replacement of the ear. *Scientific American*, February.

Luria, A. R. 1970. The functional organization of the brain. *Scientific American*, March.

Masland, R. H. 1986. The functional architecture of the retina. *Scientific American*, December.

Mcewen, B. 1976. Interactions between hormones and nerve tissue. *Scientific American*, July.

Merton, P. A. 1972. How we control the contraction of our muscles. *Scientific American*, May.

Miller, J. 1990. A matter of taste. *BioScience* 40(2): 78–82.

Mommsen, T., and Walsh, P. 1989. Evolution of urea synthesis in vertebrates. *Science* 243: 72–75.

Montagna, W. 1965. The skin. *Scientific American*, February.

Moog, F. 1981. The lining of the small intestine. *Scientific American*, November.

Morell, P., and Norton, W. 1980. Myelin. *Scientific American*, May.

Murray, J. H., and Weber, A. 1974. The cooperative action of muscles. *Scientific American*, February.

Napier, J. 1967. The antiquity of human walking. *Scientific American*, April.

Nassau, K. 1980. The causes of color. *Scientific American*, October.

Nathan, J., and Greengard, P. 1977. Second messengers in the brain. *Scientific American*, August.

Nathans, J. 1989. The genes for color vision. *Scientific American*, February.

Notkins, A. 1979. The cause of diabetes. *Scientific American*, November.

O'Malley, B., and Schrader, W. 1976. The receptors of steroid hormones. *Scientific American*, February.

Orei, L., Yassalli, J. D., and Perrelet, A. 1988. The insulin factory. *Scientific American*, September.

Oster, G. 1984. Muscle sounds. *Scientific American*, March.

Parker, D. E. 1980. The vestibular apparatus. *Scientific American*, November.

Perutz, M. F. 1964. The hemoglobin molecule. *Scientific American*, November.

Pike, J. E. 1971. Prostaglandins. *Scientific American*, November.

Poggio, T., and Koch, C. 1987. Synapses that communicate motion. *Scientific American*, May.

Rassmussen, H. 1989. The cycling of calcium as an intracellular messenger. *Scientific American*, October.

Rennie, J. 1990. The body against itself. *Scientific American*, December.

Renouf, D. 1989. Sensory function in the harbor seal. *Scientific American*, April.

Robinson, T., Factor, S., and Sonnenblick, E. 1986. The heart as a suction pump. *Scientific American*, June.

Ross, R., and Borstein, P. 1971. Elastic fibers in the body. *Scientific American*, June.

Ruppert, E., and Smith, P. 1988. The functional organization of filtration nephridia. *Biol. Rev.* 63: 231–58.

Sanderson, S., and Wassersug, R. 1990. Suspension-feeding vertebrates. *Scientific American*, March.

Schmidt-Nielsen, B. 1988. Excretory mechanisms as examples of the principle "The whole is greater than the sum of its parts." *Physiol. Zool.* 61: 312–21.

Schmidt-Nielsen, K. 1981. Countercurrent systems in animals. *Scientific American*, May.

———. 1971. How birds breathe. *Scientific American*, December.

———. 1959. Salt glands. *Scientific American*, January.

Schmidt-Nielsen, K., and Schmidt-Nielsen, B. 1953. The desert rat. *Scientific American*, July.

Schnapf, J. L., and Baylor, D. A. 1987. How photoreceptor cells respond to light. *Scientific American*, April.

Scrimshaw, N. S., and Young, V. R. 1976. The requirements of human nutrition. *Scientific American*, September.

Segal, S. J. 1974. The physiology of human reproduction. *Scientific American*, March.

Smith, H. 1953. The kidney. *Scientific American*, January.

Smith, K., and Kier, W. 1989. Trunks, tongues, and tentacles: Moving with skeletons of muscles. *American Scientist* 77: 28–35.

Spector, R., and Johanson, C. 1989. The mammalian choroid plexus. *Scientific American*, November.

Storey, K., and Syorey, V. 1990. Frozen and alive. *Scientific American*, December.

Stryer, L. 1987. The molecules of visual excitation. *Scientific American*, July.

Suga, N. 1990. Biosonar and neural computation in bats. *Scientific American*, June.

Synder, S. 1985. The molecular basis of communication between cells. *Scientific American*, October.

Timmerman, M. 1987. Nerve and muscle: Bridging the gap. *New Scientist* (September 10): 63–66.

Todd, J. T. 1980. The perception of human growth. *Scientific American*, February.

Tonegawa, S. 1985. The molecules of the immune system. *Scientific American*, October.

Triantafyllou, M. 1995. An efficient swimming machine. *Scientific American*, March.

Ulmann, A., Teutsch, G., and Philibert, D. 1990. RU 486. *Scientific American*, June.

Ulvnas-Moberg, K. 1990. The gastrointestinal tract in growth and reproduction. *Scientific American*, July.

von Boehmer, H., and Kisielow, P. 1991. How the immune system learns about self. *Scientific American*, October.

Vonrekesy, G. 1957. The ear. *Scientific American*, August.

Wassarman, P. M. 1988. Fertilization in mammals. *Scientific American*, December.

Webb, P. 1988. Simple physical principles and vertebrate aquatic locomotion. *American Zoologist* 28: 709–25.

Wiggers, C. 1967. The heart. *Scientific American*, May.

Winson, J. 1990. The meaning of dreams. *Scientific American*, November.

Wood, W. 1971. White blood cells versus bacteria. *Scientific American*, February.

Wurtman, R. 1982. Nutrients that modify brain function. *Scientific American*, August.

Young, J., and Cohn, Z. 1988. How killer cells kill. *Scientific American*, January.

Young, V. R., and Scrimshaw, N. S. 1971. The physiology of starvation. *Scientific American*, October.

Zivin, J., and Choi, D. 1991. Stroke therapy. *Scientific American*, July.

Zucker, M. 1980. The functioning of blood platelets. *Scientific American*, June.

glossary

A

abdomen (ab'do-men) 1. The portion of a tetrapod's body between the thorax and pelvic girdle. 2. The region of an arthropod's body behind the thorax. It contains the visceral organs. 384

aboral (ab-or'al) The end of a radially symmetrical animal opposite the mouth. 236

acanthella (a-kan'thel-a) Developing acanthocephalan larva between an acanthor and a cystacanth, in which the definitive organ systems are developed. Develops in the intermediate host. 313

Acanthocephala (a-kan"tho-sef'-a-lah) The phylum of aschelminths commonly called the spiny-headed worms. 313

acanthor (a-kan'thor) Acanthocephalan larva (first larval stage) that hatches from the egg. The larva has a rostellum with hooks that penetrate host tissues. 313

acclimation (ak"li-ma'-shun) The change in tolerance of an animal for a condition in its environment. 192

accommodation (ah-kom"o-da'shun) The adjustment of the eye for various distances. 581

acetabulum (as"e-tab'u-lum) Sucker. The ventral sucker of a fluke. A sucker on the scolex of a tapeworm. 292

Acetospora (ah-sēt-o-spor'ah) The protozoan phylum whose members have multicellular spores. All parasitic in invertebrates. Examples: acetosporans (*Paramyxa*, *Halosporidium*). 245

acetylcholine (as-e-tel-ko'len) A neurotransmitter that certain neurons liberate. It is excitatory at neuromuscular junctions and inhibitory at other synapses. 555

acid A substance that ionizes in water to release hydrogen ions (H⁺). 20

acid deposition The combination of sulfur dioxide and nitrogen oxides with water in the atmosphere. This combination produces acidic precipitation called acid deposition. The burning of fossil fuels is a major contributor to acid deposition. 221

acoelomate (a-se'lah-māt) Without a body cavity. 236

acquired immunity The type of specific immunity that develops after exposure to a suitable antigen or is produced after antibodies are transferred from one individual to another. 616

acrosome (ak-ro-sōm') The enzyme-filled cap on the head of a sperm. Used in egg penetration. 134

actin (ak'tin) A protein in a muscle fiber that, together with myosin, is responsible for contraction and relaxation. 546

action potential The sequence of electrical changes when a nerve cell membrane is exposed to a stimulus that exceeds its threshold. 554

activational effects of hormones Occur when an external stimulus triggers a hormonally mediated response by the organism. 184

active transport A process that requires an expenditure of ATP energy to move molecules across a cell membrane. Usually moved against the concentration gradient with the aid of specific carrier (transport) proteins. 42

adaptation Structures or processes that increase an organism's potential to successfully reproduce in a specified environment. 158

adaptive radiation Evolutionary change that results in the formation of a number of new characteristics from an ancestral form, usually in response to the opening of new habitats. 157

Adenophorea (a-den"o-for'e-ah) The class of nematodes formerly called Aphasmidia. Examples: *Trichinella*, *Trichuris*. 307

adenosine diphosphate (ADP) (ah-dēn'o-sēn di-phos'phate) A nucleotide composed of the pentose sugar D-ribose, adenine, and two phosphates. Formed by hydrolysis of ATP. 65

adenosine monophosphate (AMP) (ah-dēn'o-sēn mon-o-phos'phate) Molecule created when the terminal phosphate is lost from a molecule of adenosine diphosphate. 65

adenosine triphosphate (ATP) (ah-dēn'o-sēn tri-phos'phate) Molecule that stores and releases energy for use in cellular processes. A nucleotide composed of adenine, ribose, and three phosphate groups. 64

adhesive gland Attachment glands in turbellarians that produce a chemical that attaches part of the turbellarian to a substrate. 287

adipose tissue (ad'i-pōs) Fat-storing tissue. 50

adrenal gland (ah-dre'nal) The endocrine gland on top of the kidney. 593

aerobic (a"er-ob'ik) Having molecular oxygen present. An oxygen-dependent form of respiration. 70

aerobic respiration *See also* **cellular respiration.**

aestivation (es'te-va-shun) The condition of dormancy or torpidity during the hot, dry summer months. 194, 663

afterbirth (af'ter-berth) The placental and fetal membranes expelled from the uterus after the birth of a mammal. 693

age structure The proportion of a population that is in prereproductive, reproductive, and postreproductive classes. 221

Agnatha (ag-nath'ah) A superclass of vertebrates whose members lack jaws and paired appendages and possess a cartilaginous skeleton and a persistent notochord. Lampreys and hagfishes. 436

airfoil   A surface, such as a wing, that provides lift by using currents of air it moves through.   493

allantois (ah-lan′tois)   One of the extraembryonic membranes in the embryo of an amniote. Forms as a ventral outgrowth of the gut, enlarges during development, and functions in waste (uric acid) storage and gas exchange.   145

alleles (ah-lēlz′)   Alternate forms of a gene that occur at the same locus of a chromosome. For example, in humans, three alleles (I^A, I^B, and i) that occur at the same locus encode the A, B, and O blood types.   99

allopatric speciation (al″o-pat′rik spe″se-a′shun)   Speciation that occurs in populations separated by geographical barriers.   170

all-or-none law   The phenomenon in which a muscle fiber contracts completely when it is exposed to a stimulus of threshold strength. Also, the principle that states that a neuron will "fire" at full power or not at all.   554

altricial (al-trish′al)   An animal that is helpless at hatching or birth.   500

altruism (al′troo-iz″em)   The principle or practice of unselfish concern for, or devotion to, the welfare of others.   187

alula (al′u-lah)   A group of feathers on the wing of a bird that is supported by the bones of the medial digit. The alula reduces turbulent airflow over the upper surface of the wing.   493

alveolus (al-ve′o-lus)   An air sac of a lung. A saclike structure.   625

ambulacral groove (am″byul-ac′ral)   The groove along the length of the oral surface of a sea star arm. Ambulacral grooves contain tube feet.   404

ametabolous metamorphosis (a″me-tab′a-lus met″ah-mor′fe-sis)   Development in which the number of molts is variable. Immature stages resemble adults, and molting continues into adulthood.   390

amictic eggs (e-mik′tic)   Pertaining to female rotifers that produce only diploid eggs that cannot be fertilized. The eggs develop directly into amictic females.   305

amino acid (ah-me′no)   A relatively small organic compound that contains an amino group ($-NH_2$) and a carboxyl group ($-COOH$). The structural unit of a protein molecule.   24

ammonotelic excretion (ah-mo″no-tel′ik)   Having ammonia as the chief excretory product of nitrogen metabolism. Occurs in freshwater fishes.   668

amnion (am′ne-on)   One of the extraembryonic membranes of the embryos of reptiles, birds, and mammals. The amnion encloses the embryo in a fluid-filled sac.   144

amniote lineage (am′ne-ōt lin′e-ij)   The evolutionary lineage of vertebrates leading to modern reptiles, birds, and mammals.   456

amniotic egg (am″ne-ot′-ik)   The egg of reptiles, birds, and mammals. It has extraembryonic membranes that help prevent desiccation, store wastes, and promote gas exchange. These adaptations allowed vertebrates to invade terrestrial habitats.   472

amoeboid movement (ah-me′boid)   A form of movement similar to that found in amoebae. Fluid endoplasm (plasmasol) flows forward inside the cell and changes state to viscous ectoplasm (plasmagel) on reaching the tip of a pseudopodium. At the opposite end of the cell, ectoplasm changes into endoplasm.   541

Amphibia (am-fib′e-ah)   The class of vertebrates whose members are characterized by skin with mucoid secretions, which serves as a respiratory organ. Developmental stages are aquatic and are usually followed by metamorphosis to an amphibious adult. Frogs, toads, and salamanders.   452

amphid (am′fed)   One of a pair of chemosensory organs on the anterior end of certain nematodes.   308

amplexus (am-plek′sus)   The positioning of a male amphibian dorsal to a female amphibian, his forelimbs around her waist. During amplexus, the male releases sperm as the female releases eggs.   467

ampullary organ (am′pu-la″re)   A receptor that can detect electrical currents. These electroreceptors are found in most fishes, some amphibians, and the platypus. *See* **electroreceptor.**   573

anabolism (an-nab′o-lizm)   Any constructive metabolic process by which organisms convert substances into other components of the organism's chemical architecture. System of biosynthetic reactions in a cell by which large molecules are made from smaller ones   60

anaerobic (an-a″er-o′bik)   The phase of cellular respiration that occurs in the absence of oxygen. Lacking oxygen.   70

analogous (a-nal′a-ges)   Describes structures that have similar functions in two organisms but that have not evolved from a common ancestral form. Analogous structures often arise through convergent evolution.   6

anaphase (an′ah-fāz)   The stage in mitosis and meiosis, following metaphase, in which the centromeres divide and the chromatids, lined up on the mitotic spindle, begin to move apart toward the poles of the spindle to form the daughter chromosomes.   89

anatomy (ah-nat′o-me)   The study of the structure of an organism and its parts.   16

androgen (an′dro-jen)   Any substance that contributes to masculinization, such as the hormone testosterone.   684

aneuploidy (an′u-ploid″e)   An addition or deletion of one or more chromosomes. Aneuploidy may be represented by $2N + 1$, $2N - 1$, etc.   114

animal behavior   Activities animals perform during their lifetime.   179

animal pole   The region of a fertilized egg where meiosis is completed. It contains less yolk and is more metabolically active than the opposite vegetal pole.   136

Animalia (an″i-mal′eah)   The kingdom of organisms whose members are multicellular, eukaryotic, and heterotrophic. The animals.   228

Annelida (ah-nel′i-dah)   The phylum of triploblastic, coelomate animals whose members are metameric (segmented) and wormlike. Annelids have a complete digestive tract and a ventral nerve cord.   340

annuli (an′u-li)   Secondary divisions of each body segment of a leech (phylum Annelida, class Hirudinea).   351

antennal gland (an-ten′al)   The excretory organ in some crustaceans (crayfish). Called antennal gland because of its location near the base of each second antenna and its green color. Also called **green gland.**   665

anterior   The head end. Usually, the end of a bilateral animal that meets its environment.   235

Anthozoa (an″tho-zo′ah)   The class of cnidarians whose members are solitary or colonial polyps. Medusae are absent. Gametes originate in the gastrodermis. Mesenteries divide the gastrovascular cavity. Sea anemones and corals.   274

anthropomorphism (an″thro-po-mor′fizm)   The attribution of human characteristics to nonhuman beings and objects.   179

antibody (an'tĭ-bod"e) A specific substance that cells produce in response to the presence of an antigen. It reacts with the antigen. Also known as an immunoglobulin (Ig). 617

anticodon (an'ti-ko"don) A sequence of three bases on transfer RNA that pairs with codons of messenger RNA to position amino acids during protein synthesis. 124

antigen (an'ti-jen) A foreign (nonself) substance (such as a protein, nucleoprotein, polysaccharide, and some glycolipids) to which lymphocytes respond. Also known as an immunogen because it induces the immune response. 616

antiparallel (an"ti-par'ah-lel") Refers to opposing strands of DNA that are oriented in opposite directions. 121

Apicomplexa (a"pi-kom-plex'ah) The protozoan phylum characterized by members having an apical complex for penetrating host cells. Cilia and flagella are lacking, except in certain reproductive stages. Examples include the gregarines (*Monocystis*), coccidians (*Eimeria, Isospora, Sarcocystis, Toxoplasma*), *Pneumocystis*, and *Plasmodium*. 250

Aplacophora (a"pla-kof'o-rah) The class of molluscs whose members lack a shell, mantle, and foot. Wormlike, burrowing animals with poorly developed head. Some zoologists divide this group into two classes: Caudofoveata and Solengasters. 334

aposematic coloration (ah"pos-mat'ik) Sharply contrasting colors of an animal that warn other animals of unpleasant or dangerous effects. 201

appendicular skeleton (ap"en-dik'u-lar) The bones of the upper and lower extremities. Includes the shoulder and pelvic girdles. 540

appendix (a-pen'diks) Refers to the appendix vermiformis of the colon. 651

Arachnida (ah-rak'nĭ-dah) The class of chelicerate arthropods whose members are mostly terrestrial, possess book lungs or tracheae, and usually have four pairs of walking legs as adults. Spiders, scorpions, ticks, mites, and harvestmen. 365

arachnoid (ah-rak'noid) The weblike middle covering (meninx) of the central nervous system. 559

Archaea (ahr-kay'e-ah) A domain of organisms that includes prokaryotic microbes that live in harsh anaerobic environments. Probably the most primitive life-forms known. 229

archenteron (ar-ken'te-ron") The embryonic digestive tract that forms during gastrulation. 138

Aristotle's lantern The series of ossicles making up the jawlike structure of echinoid echinoderms. 409

arteriole (ar-te're-ōl) A minute arterial branch, especially just proximal to a capillary. 611

artery A vessel that transports blood away from the heart. 611

Arthropoda (ar"thrah-po'dah) The phylum of animals whose members possess metamerism with tagmatization, a jointed exoskeleton, and a ventral nervous system. Includes insects, crustaceans, spiders, and related animals. 360

artificially acquired active immunity The type of immunity that results from immunizing an animal with a vaccine. 616

artificially acquired passive immunity The type of immunity that results from introducing antibodies that have been produced either in another animal or by specific in vitro methods into an animal. 616

aschelminth (ask'hel-minth) Any animal in the phyla Rotifera, Kinorhyncha, Nematoda, Nematomorpha, Acanthocephala, Loricitera, or Priapulida. 302

Ascidiacea (as-id"eas'e-ah) A class of urochordates whose members are sessile as adults, and solitary or colonial. 428

ascon (as'kon) The simplest of the three sponge body forms. Ascon sponges are vaselike, with choanocytes directly lining the spongocoel. 265

asexual reproduction Having no sex, not sexual; not pertaining to sex. Reproduction of an organism without fusion of gametes by fission, budding, or some other method not involving the fertilization of gametes. 678

aster (as'ter) The star-shaped structure in a cell during prophase of mitosis. Composed of a system of microtubules arranged in astral rays around the centrosome. May emanate from a centrosome or from a pole of a mitotic spindle. 87

Asteroidea (as"te-roi'de-ah) The class of echinoderms whose members have rays that are not sharply set off from the central disk, ambulacral grooves with tube feet, and suction disks on tube feet. Sea stars. 404

asymmetry (a-sim'i-tre) Without a balanced arrangement of similar parts on either side of a point or axis. 234

asynchronous flight *See also* **indirect flight.**

atom Smallest particle of an element that has the same properties. The basic unit of an element that can enter into chemical combinations. The smallest unit of matter that is unique to a particular element. 16

atomic mass A mass unit determined by arbitrarily assigning the carbon-12 isotope a mass of 12 atomic mass units. 16

atomic number A value equal to the number of protons in the nucleus of an atom. It differs for each element. 16

ATP *See also* **adenosine triphosphate.**

auricle (aw're-kl) The portion of the external ear not connected within the head. Also used to designate an atrium of a heart. In the class Turbellaria, the sensory lobes that project from the side of the head. 290

autosome (au'te-sōm") Chromosome other than sex chromosomes. 108

autotomy (au-tot'o-me) The self-amputation of an appendage. For example, the casting off of a section of a lizard's tail caught in the grasp of a predator. The autotomized appendage is usually regenerated. 479

autotroph (aw'to-trōf) An organism that uses carbon dioxide as its sole or principal source of carbon and makes its organic nutrients from inorganic raw materials. 630

autotrophic (au"to-trōf'ic) Having the ability to synthesize food from inorganic compounds. 192

Aves (a'vez) A class of vertebrates whose members are characterized by scales modified into feathers for flight, endothermy, and amniotic eggs. The birds. 488

axial filament *See also* **axoneme.**

axial skeleton (ak'se-al) Portion of the skeleton that supports and protects the organs of the head, neck, and trunk. 540

axon (ak'son) A fiber that conducts a nerve impulse away from a neuron cell body. Action potentials move rapidly, without alteration, along an axon. Their arrival at an axon ending may trigger the release of neurotransmitter molecules that influence an adjacent cell. 552

axoneme (ak'so-nēm) The axial thread of the chromosome in which is located the axial combination of genes. The central core of a cilium or flagellum, consisting of a central pair of filaments surrounded by nine other pairs. Also called axial filament. 48

axopodium (ak′se-pōd-eum)   Fine, needle-like pseudopodium that contains a central bundle of microtubules. Also called axopod. Found in certain sarcodine protozoa. Pl., axopodia.   249

B

balanced polymorphism (pol″e-morf′ism)   Occurs when different phenotypic expressions are maintained at a relatively stable frequency in a population.   169

baleen plate (bā-lēn)   A keratined growth in toothless whales.   535

bare sensory nerve endings   Nerve endings that are sensitive to pain.   578

baroreceptor (bar″o-re-sep′tor)   A specialized nerve ending that is stimulated by changes in pressure.   568

Barr body   A heterochromatic X chromosome usually found in the nucleus of female mammals.   112

basal body (ba′sel)   A centriole that has given rise to the microtubular system of a cilium or flagellum, and is located just beneath the plasma membrane. Serves as a nucleation site for the growth of the axoneme.   48

base   A substance that ionizes in water to release hydroxyl ions (OH⁻) or other ions that combine with hydrogen ions.   20

basophil (ba′so-fil)   White blood cell characterized by the presence of cytoplasmic granules that become stained blue-purple by a basophilic dye.   609

Batesian mimicry (bāts′e-an mim′ik-re)   When one species, called the mimic, resembles a second species, the model, that is protected by aposematic coloration.   201

B cell   A type of lymphocyte derived from bone marrow stem cells that matures into an immunologically competent cell under the influence of the bursa of Fabricius in the chicken, and the bone marrow in nonavian species. Following interaction with antigen, it becomes a plasma cell, which synthesizes and secretes antibody molecules involved in humoral immunity. Also called B lymphocyte.   610

Bdelloidea (del-oid′e-ah)   A class of rotifers without males. Anterior end is retractile and bears two disks. Mastax is adapted for grinding. Paired ovaries. Cylindrical body. Example: *Rotaria*.   305

behavioral ecology   The scientific study of all aspects of animal behavior as related to the environment.   179

benthic animal (ben′thik)   Animal that lives in or on the bottom substrate of an ocean, lake, stream, or other body of water.   218

bilateral symmetry (bi-lat′er-al sim′i-tre)   A form of symmetry in which only the midsagittal plane divides an organism into mirror images. Bilateral symmetry is characteristic of actively moving organisms that have definite anterior (head) and posterior (tail) ends.   234

bile (bīl)   A fluid secreted by the liver, stored in the gallbladder, and released into the small intestine via the bile duct. Emulsifies fats.   644

bimodal breathing (bi-mo′del)   The ability of an organism to exchange respiratory gases simultaneously with both air and water, usually using gills for water breathing and lungs for air breathing.   621

binary fission (bi′ne-re fish′en)   Asexual reproduction in protists in which cytoplasmic division follows mitosis to produce two new protists.   243

binomial nomenclature (bi-no′me-al no′men-kla″cher)   A system for naming in which each kind of organism (a species) has a two-part name: the genus and the species epithet.   10

biochemistry   The chemistry of living organisms and of vital processes. Also known as physiological or biological chemistry. The study of the molecular basis of life.   16

biodiversity   The variety of organisms in an ecosystem.   222

biogeochemical cycles   The cycling of elements between reservoirs of inorganic compounds and living matter in an ecosystem.   211

biogeography   The study of the geographic distribution of life on earth. Biogeographers attempt to explain the factors that influence where species of plants and animals live on the earth.   4

biological magnification   The concentration of substances in animal tissues as the substances pass through ecosystem food webs.   222

biology   The study of life.   3

biomass   The part of an ecosystem consisting of living matter.   207

biomes (bi′ōmz)   Distinctive associations of plant and animal populations. Characterized by certain geographical boundaries and specific climatic and geographical features.   214

biosonar   *See also* **sonar.**

biotic potential (bi-ot′ik)   The capacity of a population to increase maximally. Also called **intrinsic rate of growth.**   195

biramous appendages (bi-ra′mus ah-pen′dij-ez)   Appendages having two distal processes that a single proximal process connects to the body.   363

Bivalvia (bi′val ve″-ah)   The class of molluscs whose members are enclosed in a shell consisting of two dorsally hinged valves, lack a radula, and possess a wedge-shaped foot. Clams, mussels, oysters.   325

bladder worm   The unilocular hydatid cyst of a tapeworm. *See also* **cysticercus.**   297

blastocoel (blas′to-sēl)   The fluid-filled cavity of the blastula.   138

blastocyst (blas′to-sist)   An early stage of embryonic development consisting of a hollow ball of cells. The product of cleavage.   690

blastoderm (blas′to-derm)   A small disk of cells at the animal end of a reptile or bird embryo that results from early cleavages.   144

blastomeres (blas′to-merz)   Any of the cells produced by cleavage of a zygote.   137

blastopore (blas′to-por)   The point of invagination at which cells on the surface of the blastula move to the interior of the embryo during gastrulation.   138

blastula (blas′tu-lah)   An early stage in the development of an embryo. It consists of a sphere of cells enclosing a fluid-filled cavity (blastocoel).   138

blood   A type of connective tissue with a fluid matrix called plasma in which blood cells are suspended. The fluid that circulates through the heart, arteries, capillaries, and veins.   50

blood pressure   The force (energy) with which blood pushes against the walls of blood vessels and circulates throughout the body when the heart contracts.   614

blubber (blub′er)   The fat found between the skin and muscle of whales and other cetaceans, from which oil is made. Functions in insulation.   661

bone cells   The hard, rigid form of connective tissue constituting most of the skeleton of vertebrates. Composed chiefly of calcium salts. Also called bone (osseous) tissue.   50, 538

book gill   Modifications of a horseshoe crab's exoskeleton into a series of leaflike plates that are a surface for gas exchange between the arthropod and the water (phylum Arthropoda, class Merostomata).   365

book lung   Modification of the arthropod exoskeleton into a series of internal plates that provide surfaces for gas exchange between the blood and air. Found in spiders.   620

bottleneck effect   Changes in gene frequency that result when numbers in a population are drastically reduced, and genetic variability is reduced as a result of the population being built up again from relatively few surviving individuals.   166

Brachiopoda (bra-ke-op′o-dah)   A phylum of marine animals whose members possess a bivalved calcareous and/or chitinous shell that a mantle secretes and that encloses nearly all of the body. Unlike the molluscs, the valves are dorsal and ventral. Possess a lophophore. Lampshells.   415

broadcast spawning   The release of gametes into the water, for external fertilization.   680

brood patch   The patch of feathers birds use to incubate eggs. Also known as incubation patch.   595

brown fat   Fat deposits with extensive vascularization, mitochondria, and enzyme systems for oxidation. Found in small, specific deposits in a few mammals and used for nonshivering thermogenesis.   661

buccal pump (buk′el)   The mechanism by which lung ventilation occurs in amphibians. Muscles of the mouth and pharynx create positive pressure to force air into the lungs.   463

buccopharyngeal respiration (buk″o-fah-rin′je-al res″pah-ra′shun)   The diffusion of gases across moist linings of the mouth and pharynx of amphibians.   463

budding (bud′ing)   The process of forming new individuals asexually in many different invertebrates. Offspring arise as outgrowths from the parent and are smaller than the parent. When the offspring do not separate from the parent, a colony forms.   243, 678

buffer (buf′er)   A substance that can react with a strong acid or base to form a weaker acid or base and thus resist a change in pH. A buffer accepts H^+ ions from or donates H^+ ions to solutions.   21

bulb of Krause   A sensory receptor in the skin believed to be the sensor for touch-pressure. Also called bulbous corpuscle.   578

bulbourethral gland (bul″bo-u-re′thral)   Gland that secretes a viscous fluid into the male urethra during sexual excitement.   683

bursa (bur′sah)   A membranous sac that invaginates from the oral surface of ophiuroid echinoderms. Functions in diffusion of gases and waste material.   407

bursa of Fabricius (bur′sah of fah-bris′e-us)   The lymphoid organ of birds that, like the thymus, develops as an outpouching of the gut near the cloaca rather than the foregut. It is responsible for the maturation of lymphocytes.   597

C

Calcarea (kal-kar′e-ah)   The class of sponges whose members are small and possess monaxon, triaxon, or tetraaxon calcium carbonate spicules.   265

calcitonin (kal″si-to′nin)   A thyroid hormone that lowers calcium and phosphate levels in the blood. Also called thyrocalcitonin.   597

calorie   A unit used in the measurement of heat energy and the energy value of foods. The amount of heat energy required to raise the temperature of 1 g of water 1° C.   60, 630

Calorie   Amount of heat energy required to raise the temperature of 1,000 g of water 1° C.   630

calyx (ka′liks)   1. A boat-shaped or cuplike central body of an entoproct. The body and tentacles of an entoproct. 2. A cuplike set of ossicles that support the crown of a sea lily or feather star (class Crinoidea, phylum Echinodermata).   411

capillary (kap′i-lar-e)   A small blood vessel that connects an arteriole and a venule. The functional unit of the circulatory system. The site of exchange between the blood and tissue cells.   611

carapace (kar′ah-pās)   The dorsal portion of the shell of a turtle. Formed from a fusion of vertebrae, ribs, and dermal bone.   475

carbaminohemoglobin (kar″bah-me′no-he′mo-glo″bin)   Compound formed by the union of carbon dioxide and hemoglobin.   609

carbohydrate (kahr-bo-hi′drāt)   An organic compound that contains carbon, hydrogen, and oxygen. Carbohydrates consist of simple single-monomer sugars (monosaccharides), disaccharides, or other multi-unit sugars (polysaccharides).   22

cardiac muscle   Specialized type of muscle tissue found only in the heart.   542

cardiovascular system   *See also* **circulatory system.**

carnivore (kar′ne-vor)   One of the flesh-eating animals of the order Carnivora. Also, any organism that eats flesh.   630

carrying capacity   The maximum population size that an environment can support.   195

cartilage (kar′ti-lij)   Type of connective tissue in which cells are within lacunae and separated by a semisolid matrix. Provides a site for muscle attachment, aids in movement of joints, and provides support.   50

caste (kast)   One of the distinct kinds of individuals in a colony of social insects (e.g., queens, drones, and workers in a honeybee colony).   392

catabolism (kah-tă′ bo-lizm)   Metabolic process by which large molecules are broken down into smaller ones. Catabolic metabolism. Intermediates in these reactions are called catabolites.   60

catalysis (kah-tal′i-sis)   An increase in the velocity of a chemical reaction or process produced by the presence of a substance that is not consumed in the net chemical reaction or process.   61

catalyst (kat′ ah-list)   A substance that increases the rate of a chemical reaction but is not permanently altered by the reaction. Enzymes are protein catalysts.   61

Caudofoveata (kaw′do-fo″ve-a″ta)   The class of molluscs characterized by a wormlike, shell-less body and scalelike, calcareous spicules. Lack eyes, tentacles, statocysts, crystalline style, foot, and nephridia. Deep-water marine burrowers. *Chaetoderma*.   334

cecum (se′kum)   1. Each arm of the blind-ending, Y-shaped digestive tract of trematodes (phylum Platyhelminthes). 2. A region of the vertebrate digestive tract where fermentation can occur. It is at the proximal end of the large intestine.   515, 651

cell body   Portion of a nerve cell that includes a cytoplasmic mass and a nucleolus, and from which the nerve fibers extend.   552

cell cycle   The regular sequence of events (including interphase and the mitotic phase) during which a eukaryotic cell grows, prepares for division, duplicates its contents, and divides to form two daughter cells.   85

cell-mediated immunity   Immunity resulting from T cells coming into close physical contact with foreign cells or infected cells to destroy them. It can be transferred to a nonimmune individual by the transfer of cells.   616

cellular respiration   Process by which energy is released from organic compounds within cells. The aerobic process that involves glycolysis, the Krebs cycle, the electron transport chain, and chemiosmosis.   66

central dogma   The relationship among the steps from DNA to the production of a protein. It involves the synthesis of messenger RNA from DNA, and the movement of mRNA out of the nucleus (transcription). Messenger RNA carries the genetic code into the cytoplasm. Within the cytoplasm, ribosomes and transfer RNA convert this genetic code in messenger RNA into a protein (translation).   122

central nervous system   The brain and spinal cord.   559

centriole (sen′tre-ol)   A cellular organelle (composed of microtubules) that organizes the mitotic spindle during mitosis. A pair of centrioles is usually in the center of a microtubule-organizing center in animal cells.   48

centromere (sen′tro-mer)   Constricted region of a mitotic chromosome that holds sister chromatids together. Also, the site on the DNA where the kinetochore forms and then captures microtubules from the mitotic spindle.   86

Cephalaspidomorphi (sef″a-las″pe-do-morf′e)   The class of vertebrates characterized by the absence of paired appendages and the presence of sucking mouthparts with teeth and a rasping tongue. Lampreys.   426

cephalic (se-fal′ik)   Having to do with, or toward, the head of an animal.   236

cephalization (sef″al-iz-a′shun)   The development of a head with an accumulation of nervous tissue into a brain.   235

Cephalocarida (sef″ah-lo-kar′ĭ-dah)   A class of marine crustaceans characterized by uniform, leaflike, triramous appendages.   362

Cephalochordata (sef″a-lo-kor-dat′ah)   The subphylum of chordates whose members possess a laterally compressed, transparent body. They are fishlike and possess all four chordate characteristics throughout life. Amphioxus.   431

Cephalopoda (sef′ah-lop″ o-dah)   The class of molluscs whose members have a foot modified into a circle of tentacles and a siphon. A shell is reduced or absent, and the head is in line with the elongate visceral mass. Octopuses, squid, and cuttlefish.   329

cephalothorax (sef″al-o-thor′aks)   The fused head and thoracic regions of crustaceans and some arachnids.   364

cercaria (ser-kar′e-a)   Juvenile digenetic trematode produced by asexual reproduction within a sporocyst or redia. Cercaria are free-swimming and have a digestive tract, suckers, and a tail. They develop into a metacercaria.   292

cerebellum (ser″e-bel′um)   Portion of the brain that coordinates skeletal muscle movement. Part of the metencephalon, it consists of two hemispheres and a central vermis.   559

cerebrum (sah-re′brum)   The main portion of the brain, occupying the upper part of the cranial cavity. Its two hemispheres are united by the corpus callosum. It forms the largest part of the central nervous system in mammals.   561

Cestoidea (ses-toid′e-ah)   The class of platyhelminthes with members that are all parasitic with no digestive tract. Have great reproductive potentials. Tapeworms.   294

Chaetognatha (ke″tog-nath′ah)   A phylum of planktonic, marine deuterostomes whose body consists of a head, trunk, and tail. Their streamlined shape and darting locomotion are reflected in their common name—arrowworms.   416

chaparral (shap″a-ral′)   A relatively dry biome in the southwestern United States. Plants are low and shrubby, and have tough, waxy leaves. Animals include insects, rodents, rabbits, lizards, snakes, and mule deer.   216

character   Any animal attribute that has a genetic basis and that can be measured. Used by systematists in investigating relatedness among animal groups.   230

chelicerae (ke-lis′er-ae)   One of the two pairs of anterior appendages of arachnids. May be pincerlike or modified for piercing and sucking or other functions.   364

Chelicerata (ke-lis′er-ah″tah)   The subphylum of arthropods whose members have a body that is divided into prosoma and opisthoma. The first pair of appendages are feeding appendages called chelicerae. Spiders, scorpions, mites, and ticks.   364

chemical synapse (sin′apse)   A synapse at which neurotransmitters that one neuron releases diffuse across an extracellular gap to influence a second neuron's activity.   555

chemiosmosis (kem″e-os-mo′sis)   The process whereby electron transport generates a proton gradient and an electrochemical gradient that drive ATP synthesis by oxidative phosphorylation.   66

chemistry   The science dealing with the elements, atomic relations of matter, and various elemental compounds. The study of the properties of substances and how substances react with one another.   16

chemolithoautotroph (kem′o-lith-o-au′te-trof)   An organism that synthesizes organic matter by oxidizing inorganic compounds.   208

chemoreceptor (ke″mo-re-sep′tor)   A receptor that is stimulated by the presence of certain chemical substances.   569

chiasma (ki-as′mah)   A decussation or X-shaped crossing. The places where pairs of homologous chromatids remain in contact during late prophase to anaphase of the first meiotic division. The chiasma indicates where nonsister chromatids have exchanged homologous segments by crossing-over.   91

chief cell   Cell of a gastric gland that secretes various digestive enzymes, including pepsinogen.   648

Chilopoda (ki″lah-pod′ah)   The class of uniramous arthropods whose members have one pair of legs per segment and whose body is oval in cross section. Centipedes.   381

chitin (ki′tin)   The polysaccharide in the exoskeleton of arthropods.   361

chloragogen tissue (klor″ah-gog′en)   Cells covering the dorsal blood vessel and digestive tract of annelids. Functions in glycogen and fat synthesis and urea formation.   350

chlorocruorin (klo″ro-kroo′e-ren)   The greenish iron-containing respiratory pigment dissolved in the blood plasma of certain marine polychaetes.   627

choanocytes (ko-an′o-sitz)   Cells of sponges that create water currents and filter food. 263

Chondrichthyes (kon-drik′thi-es)   The class of vertebrates whose members are fishlike, possess paired appendages and a cartilaginous skeleton, and lack a swim bladder. Skates, rays, and sharks.   426

chordamesoderm (kor″dah-mez′o-derm)   Tissue in the amphibian gastrula that forms between ectoderm and endoderm in the dorsal lip region of the blastopore. Develops into the mesoderm and notochord.   143

Chordata (kor-dat′ah)   A phylum of animals whose members are characterized by a notochord, pharyngeal slits, a dorsal tubular nerve cord, and a postanal tail.   427

chorion (kor′e-on)   The outermost extraembryonic membrane of the embryo of an amniote. Becomes highly vascular and aids in gas exchange.   144

chromaffin tissue (kro′maf-in)   Specialized endocrine cells near the kidneys of various vertebrates. Produces various steroid hormones.   593

chromatid (kro′mah-tid)   One copy of a eukaryotic chromosome formed by DNA replication.   86

chromatin (kro′mah-tin)   Nuclear material that gives rise to chromosomes during mitosis. Complex of DNA, histones, and nonhistone proteins.   49, 108

chromatophores (kro-mah′tah-forz)   Cells containing pigment that, through contraction and expansion, produce temporary color changes.   332

chromosome (kro′mo-sōm)   Rodlike structure that appears in the nucleus of a cell during mitosis. Contains the genes responsible for heredity. Structure composed of a long DNA molecule and associated proteins that carries part (or all) of the hereditary of an organism.   49

chrysalis (kris′ah-lis)   The pupal case of a butterfly that forms from the exoskeleton of the last larval instar.   391

chylomicron (ki″lo-mi′kron)   A particle of the class of lipoproteins responsible for the transport of cholesterol and triglycerides from the small intestine to tissues after meals. 651

chyme (kīm)   Semifluid mass of food materials that passes from the stomach to the small intestine. Consists of partially digested food and gastric juice.   648

cilia (sil′e-ah)   Microscopic, hairlike processes on the exposed surfaces of certain eukaryotic cells. Cilia contain a core bundle of microtubules and can perform repeated beating movements. They are also responsible for the swimming of many single-celled organisms.   48

ciliary creeping   The principal means of nemertine locomotion.   541

Ciliophora (sil″i-of′or-ah)   The protozoan phylum whose members have simple or compound cilia at some stage in their life history. Heterotrophs with a well-developed cytostome and feeding organelles. At least one macronucleus and micronucleus present. Examples: *Paramecium, Stentor, Vorticella, Balantidium.*   253

circadian rhythms (sur-ka′de-an)   Daily cycles of activity. Circadian rhythms are usually based on photoperiods.   194

circulatory system (ser′ku-lah-to″re)   Pertaining to the circulation. *See also* **cardiovascular system.**   606

circumcision (ser″kum-sizh′un)   The removal of all or part of the prepuce or foreskin. 683

cirri (ser′i)   Any of various slender or filamentous, usually flexible appendages, such as one of the compound organelles composed of groups of fused cilia in certain peritrichious ciliate protozoa and used for locomotion. An eversible penis in flatworms. A fingerlike projection of a polychete parapodium.   253

Cirripedia (sir″ĭ-pēd′e-ah)   The class of crustaceans whose members are sessile and highly modified as adults. Enclosed by calcium carbonate valves. Barnacles.   376

citric acid cycle (sit′rik)   A series of chemical reactions in the mitochondrion by which various molecules are oxidized and energy is released. Krebs cycle. TCA or tricarboxylic acid cycle.   73

clade (klād)   A subset of organisms in a phylogenetic group that share a certain synapomorphy (derived character).   232

cladistics (klad-is′tiks)   *See also* **phylogenetic systematics.**

cladogram (klad′o-gram)   Diagram depicting the evolutionary history of taxa. Derived from phylogenetic systematics (cladistics).   232

class   A level of classification between phylum and order.   227

classical conditioning   A type of learning in which positive or negative reinforcement in-

fluences later responses of an animal to a stimulus.   181

claw   The sharp, usually curved, nail on the foot of an animal or insect. The pincerlike extremity of specific limbs of certain arthropods (e.g., lobster claws).   535

cleavage (kle′vij)   The early mitotic and cytoplasmic divisions of an embryo.   137

climax community   A final, relatively stable stage in an ecological succession.   207

clitellum (klĭ-te′lum)   The region of an annelid responsible for secreting mucus around two worms in copula and for secreting a cocoon to protect developmental stages.   348

cloaca (klo-a′kah)   A common opening for excretory, digestive, and reproductive systems. 452

closed circulatory system   A circulatory system in an animal (vertebrates) in which blood is confined to vessels throughout its circuit.   332, 606

clouds of electrons   The distribution of electrons in space around the atomic nucleus. 17

clutch   The number of eggs laid and chicks produced by a female bird.   500

Cnidaria (ni-dar′e-ah)   The phylum of animals whose members are characterized by radial or biradial symmetry, diploblastic organization, a gastrovascular cavity, and nematocysts. Jellyfish, sea anemones, and their relatives.   268

cnidocytes (ni′do-sītz)   The cell that produces and discharges the stinging organelles (nematocysts) in members of the phylum Cnidaria.   268

cocoon   The protective covering of a resting or developmental stage. Sometimes refers to both the covering and the contents.   290, 391

codominance (ko-dom′ah-nens)   An interaction of two alleles such that both alleles are expressed in a phenotype.   103

codon (ko′don)   A sequence of three bases on messenger RNA that specifies the position of an amino acid in a protein.   123

coelom (se′lom)   A fluid-filled body cavity lined by mesoderm.   237

coelomic fluid (se-lom′ic)   The fluid within the body cavity of triploblastic animals.   606

coenzyme (ko-en′zīm)   An organic nonprotein molecule, frequently a phosphorylated derivative of a water-soluble vitamin, that binds with the protein molecule (apoenzyme) to form the active enzyme (holoenzyme). Examples include biotin, NAD$^+$, and coenzyme A.   64

coevolution (ko″ev″ah-lu′shun)   The evolution of ecologically related species such that each species exerts a strong selective influence on the other.   198

cofactor (ko′fak-tor)   A metal ion or inorganic ion with which an enzyme must unite to function. *See also* **coenzymes.**   63

colloblasts (kol′ah-blasts)   Adhesive cells on ctenophoran tentacles for capturing prey.   279

colonial hypothesis   A hypothesis formulated to explain the origin of multicellularity from protist ancestors. Animals may have been derived when protists associated and cells became specialized and interdependent.   260

colony   An aggregation of organisms. Usually a group of closely associated individuals of one species.   678

colostrum (ko-los′trum)   The first secretion of the mammary glands following the birth of a mammal.   695

comb rows   Rows of cilia that are the locomotor organs of ctenophorans.   279

commensalism (kah-men′sal-izm)   Living within or on an individual of another species without harm. The commensal benefits, but the host is unharmed.   244

communication   An act on the part of one organism (or cell) that alters the probability of patterns of behavior in another organism (or cell) in an adaptive fashion. The transfer of information from one animal to another.   184

community   The different kinds of organisms living in an area.   206

community diversity   The number of different kinds of organisms living in an area.   206

comparative anatomy   The study of animal structure to deduce evolutionary pathways in particular animal groups.   6

comparative embryology (em″bre-ol′o-je)   The study of animal development in an attempt to deduce evolutionary pathways in particular animal groups.   318

comparative psychology   Study of the genetic, neural, and hormonal bases of animal behavior.   179

competitive exclusion principle   The idea that two species with identical niches cannot coexist.   197

complete linkage   Two genes positioned so close to one another on the same chromosome that recombination between them does not occur.   111

complex camera eye   The type of image-forming eye found in squids and octopuses.   571

compound   A substance composed of atoms of two or more elements joined by chemical bonds and chemically united in fixed proportions.   18

compound eye   An eye consisting of many individual lens systems (ommatidia). Present in many members of the phylum Arthropoda.   388, 570

Concentricycloidea (kon-sen″tri-si-kloi′de-ah)   The class of echinoderms whose members are characterized by two concentric water-vascular rings encircling a disklike body; no digestive system; and internal brood pouches. Sea daisies.   412

conduction (ken-duk′shun)   The conveyance of energy, such as heat, sound, or electricity. The direct transfer of thermal motion (heat) between molecules of the environment and those on the body surface of an animal.   656

cone cell   A color-sensitive photoreceptor cell concentrated in the retina.   581

conjugation (kon″ju-ga′shun)   A form of sexual union that ciliates use to mutually exchange haploid micronuclei.   254

connective tissue   A basic type of tissue that includes bone, cartilage, and various fibrous tissues. Connective tissue supports and binds.   50

continental drift   The breakup and movement of landmasses of the earth. The earth had a single landmass about 250 million years ago. This mass broke apart into continents, which have moved slowly to their present positions.   160

continuous feeder   Usually slow-moving sessile animals that feed all of the time.   634

contour feathers   Feathers that cover the body, wings, and tail of a bird. Contour feathers provide flight surfaces and are responsible for plumage colors.   491

contractile vacuole (kon-trak′til vak′u-ōl″)   An organelle that collects and discharges water in protists and a few lower metazoa in a cyclical manner to accomplish osmoregulation and some excretion.   242, 664

control group   In a scientific experiment, a control group is treated the same as the experimental group except that the independent variable being tested is omitted. A control group is a basis for comparing the data derived from the experiment.   11

controlled variable   A variable in an experiment that could influence the outcome of the experiment and must be held constant in all treatments.   11

convection (ken-vek′shun)   The act of conveying or transmission. The movement of air (or a liquid) over the surface of a body that contributes to heat loss (if the air is cooler than the body) or heat gain (if air is warmer than the body).   656

convergent evolution   Evolutionary changes that result in members of one species resembling members of a second unrelated (or distantly related) species.   6

Copepoda (ko″pe-pod′ah)   A class of crustaceans characterized by maxillipeds modified for feeding and antennae modified for swimming. The copepods.   376

coracidium (kor″ah-sid′e-um)   Larva with a ciliated epithelium hatching from the egg of certain cestodes. A ciliated, free-swimming oncosphere.   297

coralline algae (kor′ah-lin al′je)   Any red alga that is impregnated with calcium carbonate. Coralline algae often contribute to coral reefs.   277

coral reef   Association of stony coral organisms and algae that forms one of the most highly productive ecosystems in the world.   220

corona (ko-ro′nah)   A crown. An encircling structure. The ciliated organ at the anterior end of rotifers used for swimming or feeding.   304

cortisol (kor′ti-sol)   A glucocorticoid that the adrenal cortex secretes that helps regulate overall metabolism and the concentration of blood sugar.   599

counteracting osmolyte strategy (os-mo-lyt)   An osmolyte (ion) that counteracts another ion.   668

countercurrent exchange mechanism   The passive exchange of something between fluids moving in opposite directions past each other.   447

countershading   Contrasting coloration that helps conceal the animal (e.g., the darkly pigmented top and lightly pigmented bottom of frog embryos).   201

covalent bond (ko-va'lent) Chemical bond created when two atoms share a pair of electrons. 18

coxal glands (koks'el) An organ of excretion in some arthropods (spiders) that empties through a pore near the proximal joint (coxa) of the leg. 366, 666

Crinoidea (krin-oi'de-ah) The class of echinoderms whose members are attached by a stalk of ossicles or are free-living. Possess a reduced central disk. Sea lilies and feather stars. 411

crossing-over The exchange of material between homologous chromosomes, during the first meiotic division, resulting in a new combination of genes. 91

Crustacea (krus-tās'e-ah) The subphylum of mandibulate arthropods whose members are characterized by having two pairs of antennae, one pair of mandibles, two pairs of maxillae, and biramous appendages. Crabs, crayfish, lobsters. 371

cryptic coloration (kript'ik) An animal taking on color patterns of its environment. 201

crystalline style A proteinaceous, rodlike structure in the digestive tract of a bivalve (Mollusca) that rotates against a gastric shield and releases digestive enzymes. 327

Ctenophora (te-nof'er-ah) The phylum of animals whose members are characterized by biradial symmetry, diploblastic organization, colloblasts, and meridionally arranged comb rows. Comb jellies. 278

Cubozoa (ku"bo-zo'ah) The class of cnidarians whose members have prominent cuboidal medusae with tentacles that hang from the corner of the medusa. Small polyp, gametes gastrodermal in origin. *Chironex.* 274

cutaneous respiration (kyoo-ta'ne-us) Gas exchange across thin, moist surfaces of the skin. Also called cutaneous exchange or integumentary exchange. 463, 621

cuticle (ku'tĭ-kel) A noncellular, protective, organic layer secreted by the external epithelium (hypodermis) of many invertebrates. Refers to the epidermis or skin in higher animals and usually consists of cornified dead cells. 303, 343, 531

Cycliophora (si"kle-o-for'ah) A phylum of animals whose members are marine, acoelomate, and bilaterally symmetrical. They live in association with the mouthparts of lobsters. The body consists of a buccal funnel, a trunk, and a stalk that ends in an adhesive disk. The buccal funnel contains the mouth and is sur-

rounded by a ring of compound cilia. It is the most recently described animal phylum. 416

cystacanth (sis'ta-kanth) Juvenile acanthocephalan that is infective to its definitive host. 313

cysticercus (sis"ti-ser'kus) Metacestode developing from the oncosphere in most Cyclophyllidea. Usually has a tail and a well-formed scolex and is characterized by a fluid-filled oval body with an invaginated scolex. Cysticercoid. 297

cytokinesis (si"ta-kin-e'sis) The division of the cytoplasm of a cell into two parts, as distinct from the division of the nucleus (which is mitosis). 85

cytomembrane system (si"to-mem'brān) Organelles, functioning as a system, to modify, package, and distribute newly formed proteins and lipids. Endoplasmic reticulum, Golgi apparatus, lysosomes, and a variety of vesicles and vacuoles are its components 44

cytopharynx (si"to-far'inks) A region of the plasma membrane and cytoplasm of some ciliated and flagellated protists specialized for endocytosis. A permanent oral canal. 243

cytoplasm (si'to-plazm) The contents of a cell surrounding the nucleus. Consists of a semifluid medium and organelles. 34

cytopyge (si'to-pij) A region of the plasma membrane and cytoplasm of some ciliated protists specialized for exocytosis of undigested wastes. 243

cytoskeleton (si"to-skel'e-ton) In the cytoplasm of eukaryotic cells, an internal protein framework of microtubules, microfilaments, and intermediate filaments by which organelles and other structures are anchored, organized, and moved about. 47

cytosol (si'to-sol) Contents of the main compartment of the cytoplasm, excluding membrane-bound organelles. 44

D

daily torpor (tor'por) Daily sluggishness that some animals experience. A period of inactivity that is normally induced by cold. Observed in numerous ectotherms and also endotherms. Often used to describe the specific physiological state of endotherms with a circadian cycle of lowered body temperature and depressed metabolic rate. 658

daughter sporocysts In digenetic trematodes, the embryonic cells that develop from sporocysts and give rise to rediae. 292

deamination reaction (de-am"i-na'shun) A reaction in which an amino group, −NH$_2$, is enzymatically removed from a compound. 74

decomposer Mostly heterotrophic bacteria and fungi that obtain organic nutrients by breaking down the remains or products of other organic compounds. Their activities help cycle the simple compounds back to the autotrophs. 60

definitive host The host in the life cycle of a parasite that harbors the adult stage or sexual stage of the parasite. If no sexual reproduction takes place, then the definitive host is the host in which the symbiont becomes mature and reproduces. 244

degeneracy (de-jen'er-ah-se) The genetic code is said to be degenerate because more than one three-base sequence in DNA can code for one kind of amino acid. 123

delayed fertilization When fertilization of an egg does not occur immediately following coitus but is delayed for weeks or months. 521

deletions The loss of portions of chromosomes, resulting from one or more breaks in a chromosome. 116

deme (deem) A small, local subpopulation. Isolated subpopulations sometimes display genetic changes that may contribute to evolutionary change in the subpopulation. 171

Demospongiae (de-mo-spun'je-e) The class of poriferans whose members have monaxon or tetraaxon siliceous spicules or spongin. Leucon body forms are present and vary in size from a few centimeters to 1 m in height. 265

denaturation (de-na"chur-a'shun) Disruption of bonds holding a protein in its three-dimensional form such that its polypeptide chain(s) unfolds partially or completely. Changes in pH, salt concentration, or environmental temperature can cause denaturation. 63

dendrite (den'drīt) Nerve fiber that transmits impulses toward a neuron cell body. Dendrites compose most of the receptive surface of a neuron. 552

density-dependent factors Environmental parameters that are more severe when population density is high (or sometimes very low) than they are at other densities. Disease, predation, and parasitism are density-dependent factors. 196

density-independent factors Environmental parameters that influence the number of animals in a population without regard to the number of animals per unit space (density). Weather conditions and human influences often have density-independent effects on animal populations. 196

dental formula A notation that indicates the number of incisors, canines, premolars, and molars in the upper and lower jaw of a mammal. 512

denticle (den′ti-kl) A small, toothlike process. 532

deoxyribonucleic acid (DNA) (de-oks′e-ri″bo-nuk-la′ik) A polymer of deoxyribonucleotides in the form of a double helix. DNA is the genetic molecule of life in that it codes for the sequence of amino acids in proteins. Contains nucleotide monomers with deoxyribose sugar and nitrogenous bases adenine (A), cytosine (C), guanine (G), and thymine (T). *See also* **gene.** 26, 120

dependent variable The parameter measured in an experiment to determine the experiment's outcome. 11

depolarization (de-po″lar-i-za′shun) The loss of an electrical charge or polarity on the surface of a membrane. 554

deposit feeding The type of feeding whereby an animal obtains its nutrients from the sediments of soft-bottom habitats (mud or sands) or terrestrial soils. Examples include polychaete annelids, some snails, some sea urchins, and most earthworms. 634

derived character Character that has arisen since common ancestry with an outgroup. *See also* **synapomorphy.** 232

dermal branchiae (der′mal branch′e-ae) Thin folds of the body wall of a sea star that extend between ossicles and function in gas exchange and other exchange processes. 404

dermis (der′mis) The layer of the skin deep to the epidermis, consisting of a dense bed of vascular connective tissue. 531

desert The biome characterized by less than 25 cm of rainfall per year. Cacti and desert shrubs or sagebrush predominate. Animals include birds, rodents, reptiles, and numerous species of arthropods. 216

deuterostomes (du′te-ro-stōms″) Animals in which the anus forms from, or in the region of, the blastopore. Often characterized by enterocoelous coelom formation, radial cleavage, and the presence of a dipleurula-like larval stage. 318

diabetes (di″ah-be′tez) Condition characterized by a high blood glucose level and the appearance of glucose in the urine due to a deficiency of insulin or the inability of body cells to respond to insulin. Diabetes mellitus. 601

diaphragm (di′ah-fram) The domed respiratory muscle between thoracic and abdominal compartments of mammals. 516

diastole (di-as′to-le) Phase of the cardiac cycle during which a heart chamber wall relaxes. *See also* **diastolic pressure.** 614

diastolic pressure (di″ah-stol′ik) The blood pressure measurement during the interval between heartbeats. It is the second number in a blood-pressure reading. 614

differentiation (dif″ah-ren″she-a′shun) The development of embryonic structures from a nondescript form in the early embryo to their form in the adult. 138

diffusion (dĭ-fu′zhun) The random movement of molecules from one location to another because of random thermal molecular motion. Net diffusion always occurs from a region of higher concentration to a region of lower concentration. 619

digestion (di-jest′yun) The process by which mechanical and chemical means break down larger molecules of food into smaller molecules that the digestive system can take up. Hydrolysis. 630

dihybrid cross (di-hi′brid) A mating between individuals heterozygous for two traits. Dihybrid crosses usually result in a phenotypic ratio of 9 dominant, dominant : 3 dominant, recessive : 3 recessive, dominant : 1 recessive, recessive in the offspring. 102

dioecious (di-e′shus) Having separate (male and female) sexes. Male and female organs are in separate individuals. 246

diploblastic (dip″lo-blas′tik) Animals whose body parts are organized into layers that are derived embryologically from two tissue layers: ectoderm and endoderm. Animals in the phyla Cnidaria and Ctenophora are diploblastic. 235

diploid (di′ploid) Having two sets of chromosomes. The 2N chromosome number. 110

Diplopoda (dip″lah-pod′ah) The class of arthropods whose members are characterized by two pairs of legs per apparent segment and a body that is round in cross section. Millipedes. 381

direct (synchronous) flight Insect flight that is accomplished by flight muscles acting on wing bases and in which a single nerve impulse results in a single wing cycle. *See also* **indirect (asynchronous) flight.** 384

directional selection Natural selection that occurs when individuals at one phenotypic extreme have an advantage over individuals with more common phenotypes. 168

disaccharide (di-sak′ah-rīd) A sugar produced by the union of two monosaccharide molecules as a result of a dehydration synthesis. 22

discontinuous feeder An animal that does not feed all the time. Instead, it generally eats large meals sporadically and does not spend time in the continuous pursuit of prey. Most carnivores are discontinuous feeders. 634

disruptive selection Natural selection that occurs when individuals of the most common phenotypes are at a disadvantage. Produces contrasting subpopulations. 169

distal Away from the point of attachment of a structure on the body (e.g., the toes are distal to the knee). 236

diving reflex The reflex certain animals have to stay underwater for prolonged periods of time. 627

domain (do-mān′) The broadest taxonomic grouping. Recent evidence from molecular biology indicates that there are three domains: Archaea, Eubacteria, and Eukarya. 227

dominance hierarchy The physical domination of some members of a group by other members, in relatively orderly and long-lasting patterns. Dominant individuals have greater access to resources, such as food and mates. 187

dominant Describes a gene that masks one or more of its alleles. For a dominant trait to be expressed, at least one member of the gene pair must be the dominant allele. *See also* **recessive.** 99

dominant species A species that exerts an overriding influence in determining the characteristics of a community. 206

dorsal (dor′sal) The back of an animal. Usually the upper surface. Synonymous with posterior for animals that walk upright. 236

down feathers Feathers that provide insulation for adult and immature birds. 491

duplications The presence of two copies of one or more loci in a chromosome. 117

dura mater (du′rah mā′ter)   The outermost and toughest meninx covering the brain and spinal cord.   559

dyad (di′ad)   A double chromosome resulting from the halving of a tetrad in the first meiotic division.   91

E

ecdysis (ek-dis′is)   1. The shedding of the arthropod exoskeleton to accommodate increased body size or a change in morphology (as may occur in molting from immature to adult). 2. The shedding of the cuticle in aschelminths in order to grow. 3. The shedding of the epidermal layers of the skin of a reptile. Also called **molting.**   303, 362

Echinodermata (i-ki′na-dur″ma-tah)   The phylum of coelomate animals whose members are pentaradially symmetrical as adults and possess a water-vascular system and an endoskeleton covered by epithelium. Sea stars, sea urchins, sea cucumbers, sea lilies.   402

Echinoidea (ek″i-noi′de-ah)   The class of echinoderms whose members are globular or disk shaped, possess movable spines, and have a skeleton of closely fitting plates. Sea urchins and sand dollars.   408

Echiura (ek-e-yur′e-ah)   A phylum of protostomate, marine animals whose members burrow in mud or sand or live in rock crevices. They possess a spatula-shaped proboscis and are 15 to 50 cm in length. Spoon worms.   357

echolocation (ek″o-lo-ka′shun)   A method of locating objects by determining the time required for an echo to return and the direction from which the echo returns. As in bat echolocation.   519

ecological niche (ek′o-loj′i-kal nich)   The role of an organism in a community.   206

ecosystem (ek′o-sis″tem)   All of the populations of organisms living in a certain area plus their physical environment.   60, 206

ectoderm (ek′ta-durm)   The outer embryological tissue layer. Gives rise to skin epidermis and glands, also hair and nervous tissues in some animals.   138

ectoplasm (ek′to-plaz-em)   The outer, viscous cytoplasm of a protist. Contrasts with **endoplasm.**   242

Ectoprocta (ek-to-prok′tah)   A phylum of animals whose members are colonial and freshwater or marine. Anus ends outside a ring of tentacles. Lophophore used in feeding. Moss animals or bryozoans.   416

ectotherm (ek′to-therm)   Having a variable body temperature derived from heat acquired from the environment. Contrasts with **endotherm.**   657

egestion vacuole (e-jes′chen vak′u-ol)   Within the cytoplasm of a protist, a membrane-bound vacuole that expels wastes.   243

electrical synapse (sin′aps)   A synapse at which local currents resulting from electrical activity flow between two neurons through gap junctions joining them.   555

electrolyte (e-lek′tro-līt)   A substance that dissociates into ions when fused or in solution and thus becomes capable of conducting electricity. An ionic solute.   20

electron (e-lek′tron)   A small, negatively charged particle that orbits the nucleus of an atom. It has a very low mass. Atoms can gain, lose, or share electrons with other atoms.   16

electron transport chain   In the cristae of a mitochondrial membrane, electron carriers and enzymes positioned in an organized array that enhance oxidation-reduction reactions. Such systems function in the release of energy that is used in ATP formation and other reactions.   73

electroreception (i-lek″tro-re-sep′shun)   The ability to detect weak electrical fields in the environment.   450

electroreceptor (i-lek″tro-re-sep′tor)   A receptor that senses changes in an electrical current, usually in the surrounding water. Also called an **ampullary organ.**   573

element   A basic chemical substance. A substance that cannot be separated into simpler substances by ordinary chemical means. Scientists recognize 92 naturally-occurring elements.   16

elephantiasis (el″e-fan-ti′ah-sis)   A chronic filarial disease most commonly occurring in the tropics due to infection of the lymphatic vessels with the nematode *Wuchereria* spp.   311

embryology (em″bre-ol′a-je)   The study of animal development from the fertilized egg to the formation of all major organ systems.   134

embryonic diapause (em″bre-on′ik di′ah-pauz)   The arresting of early development to allow young to hatch, or be born, when environmental conditions favor survival.   521

endangered species   A species that is in imminent danger of extinction throughout its range.   27

end bulb   A tiny swelling on the terminal end of telodendria at the distal end of an axon. Also called the synaptic bouton.   555

endergonic (end″er-gon′ik)   Characterized by the absorption of energy. Said of chemical reactions that require energy to proceed.   61

endocrine gland (en′do-krin)   Ductless, hormone-producing gland (e.g., pituitary, hypothalamus, thyroid) that is part of the endocrine system.   591

endocrinology (en″do-kri-nol′o-je)   The study of the endocrine system and its role in the physiology of an animal.   587

endocytosis (en″do-si-to′sis)   Physiological process by which substances move across a plasma membrane into the cell via membranous vesicles or vacuoles.   42

endoderm (en′do-durm)   The innermost embryological tissue layer. Gives rise to the inner lining of the gut tract, digestive glands, and the inner lining of the respiratory system.   138

endoplasm (en′do-plaz-em)   The inner, fluid cytoplasm of a protist. Contrasts with **ectoplasm.**   242

endoplasmic reticulum (ER) (en-do-plaz′mic re-tik′u-lum)   Cytoplasmic organelle composed of a system of interconnected membranous tubules and vesicles. Rough ER has ribosomes attached to the side of the membrane facing the cytoplasm, and smooth ER does not. Rough ER functions in protein synthesis, while smooth ER functions in lipid synthesis.   44

endopodite (end-op′o-dīt)   The medial ramus of the biramous appendages of crustaceans and trilobites (phylum Arthropoda).   371

endoskeleton (end″o-skel′e-ton)   A skeleton that lies beneath the surface of the body (e.g., the bony skeleton of vertebrates and the calcium carbonate skeleton of echinoderms).   538

endostyle (en′do-stīl″)   A ciliated tract within the pharynx of some chordates that is used in forming mucus for filter feeding.   429

endosymbiont hypothesis (en″do-sim′bi-ont hi-poth′e-sis)   The idea whereby the eukaryotic cell might have evolved when a large anaerobic amoeboid prokaryote ingested small aerobic bacteria and stabilized them instead of digesting them.   33

endotherm (en′do-therm)   Having a body temperature determined by heat derived from the animal's own metabolism. Contrasts with **ectotherm.**   658

end-product (feedback) inhibition   The inhibition of the first enzyme in a pathway by the end product of that pathway.   75

energy   An ability to cause matter to move, and thus, to do work.   60

energy budget   An accounting of the way in which organisms of an ecosystem process and lose energy from the sun.   192

energy-level shell   The distribution of electrons around the nucleus of an atom.   17

Enteropneusta (ent″er-op-nus′tah)   A class of hemichordates whose members live in burrows in shallow marine water. Their bodies are divided into three regions: proboscis, collar, and trunk. Acorn worms.   424

Entoprocta (en′to-prok-tah)   A phylum of aschelminths commonly called entoprocts.   416

entropy (en′tro-pe)   A measure of the degree of disorganization of a system. How much energy in a system has become so dispersed (usually as heat) that it is no longer available to do work. The higher the entropy, the more the disorder.   61

environmental resistance   The constraints that climate, food, space, and other environmental factors place on a population.   195

enzyme (en′zīm)   A protein that is synthesized by a cell and acts as a catalyst in a specific cellular reaction. The substances that each type of enzyme acts upon are called its substrates.   62

enzyme-substrate complex (ES) (en′zīm sub′strāt)   The binding of a substrate molecule to the active site of an enzyme.   63

eosinophil (e″o-sīn′o-fil)   White blood cells characterized by the presence of cytoplasmic granules that become stained red by an acid dye (eosin).   609

ephyra (e-fi′rah)   Miniature medusae produced by asexual budding of a scyphistoma (class Scyphoza, phylum Cnidaria). Ephyrae mature into sexually mature medusae.   274

epiblast (ep′i-blast)   An outer layer of cells in the embryo of an amniote that forms from the proliferation and movement of cells of the blastoderm.   144

epidermis (ep″i-durm′is)   A sheet of cells covering the surface of an animal's body. In invertebrates, a single layer of ectodermal epithelium.   268, 531

epigenesis (ep″i-jen′i-sis)   The mistaken belief that the egg contains all the materials from which the embryo is constructed.   134

epithelial tissue (ep″i-the′le-al)   The cellular covering of internal and external surfaces of the body. Consists of cells joined by small amounts of cementing substances. Epithelium is classified into types based on the number of layers deep and the shape of the superficial cells.   50

epitoky (ep′i-to″ke)   The formation of a reproductive individual (epitoke) that differs from the nonreproductive (atoke) form of that species.   347

esophagus (e-sof′ah-gus)   The passage extending from the pharynx to the stomach.   647

estrus (es′trus)   The recurrent, restricted period of sexual receptivity in female mammals (other than primates) marked by intense sexual urges. Also known as "being in heat."   681

estrus cycle (es′trus)   A recurrent series of changes in the reproductive physiology of female mammals other than primates. Females are receptive, physiologically and behaviorally, to the male only at certain times in this cycle.   521

estuary (es′choo-er-e)   Body of water where freshwater meets seawater. Estuaries are very productive ecosystems because streams carry nutrients into the estuary, and tidal currents bring nutrients from the ocean.   219

ethology (e-thol′o-je)   The study of whole patterns of animal behavior in natural environments, stressing the analysis of adaptation and the evolution of the patterns.   179

Eubacteria (u″bak-teer′i-ah)   The domain that includes the true bacteria.   229

euchromatic regions (u″kro-mat′ik)   Less densely staining regions of chromosomes that contain active genes.   108

Eukarya (u″kar′e-ah)   The domain that includes all eukaryotic organisms: protists, fungi, plants, and animals.   229

eukaryote (u-kar′e-ōt)   Having a true nucleus. A cell that has membranous organelles, most notably the nucleus. All organisms except bacteria are composed of eukaryotic cells. Compare to **prokaryote.**   32

eutely (u′te-le)   Condition where the body is composed of a constant number of somatic cells or nuclei in all adult members of a species (e.g., rotifers, some nematodes, and acanthocephalans).   303

eutrophication (u-trof″i-ka′shun)   Succession in a lake. The gradual accumulation of nutrients and plant and animal growth that eventually transforms a lake into a marsh and then a forest. The death of a lake.   219

evaporation (e-vap″o-ra′shun)   The act or process of evaporating. Heat that is lost from a surface as water molecules escape in the form of a gas. The conversion of a liquid or solid into a vapor.   657

evolution (ev″o-lu′shun)   Change over time. Organic or biological evolution is a series of changes in the genetic composition of a population over time. *See also* **natural selection** and **punctuated equilibrium model.**   153

evolutionary conservation   The slowness of change in a characteristic of an animal over time. Evolutionary conservation usually indicates that the characteristic is vital for normal functions and that change is not tolerated.   229

evolutionary systematics   The study of the classification of, and evolutionary relationships among, animals. Evolutionary systematists attempt to reconstruct evolutionary pathways based on resemblances between animals that result from common ancestry.   230

excretion (eks-kre′shun)   The act, process, or function of excreting. The elimination of metabolic waste products from an animal's body.   663

exergonic (ek″ser-gon′ik)   Characterized or accompanied by the release of energy. Said of chemical reactions that release energy so that the products have a lower free energy than the reactants.   61

exocrine gland (ek′so-krin)   A gland (e.g., mammary, salivary, sweat) that secretes its product to an epithelial surface, directly or through ducts.   591

exocytosis (eks″o-si-to′sis)   The process by which substances move out of a cell. The substances are transported in the cytoplasmic vesicles, the surrounding membrane of which merges with the plasma membrane in such a way that the substances are dumped outside.   44

exopodite (eks-op′o-dīt)   The lateral ramus of the biramous appendages of crustaceans and trilobites (phylum Arthropoda).   371

exoskeleton (eks″o-skel′e-ton)   A skeleton that forms on the outside of the body (e.g., the exoskeleton of an arthropod).   361, 537

exponential growth (ek″spo-nen′shal)   Population growth in which the number of individuals increases by a constant multiple in each generation.   195

extracellular digestion (eks″tra-sel′u-ler)   Digestion that occurs outside the cell, usually in a special organ or cavity.   633

F

facilitated diffusion (fah-sil′i-tāt″id di-fu′zhun) Diffusion in which a substance is moved across a membrane from a region of higher concentration to a region of lower concentration (down its concentration gradient) by carrier protein molecules. 38

fallopian tube (fal-lo′pe-an) *See also* **uterine tube.**

family The level of classification between order and genus. 227

fermentation (fer″men-ta′shun) Degradative pathway that begins with glycolysis and ends with the electrons being transferred back to one of the breakdown products or intermediates. Does not require molecular oxygen. 72

fertilization membrane A membrane that raises off the surface of an egg after sperm penetration. Prevents multiple fertilization. 136

fibrillar flight muscle (fi′bra-lar) Insect flight muscle responsible for indirect flight. A single nerve impulse results in many cycles of flight muscle contraction and relaxation. 385

fibrocartilage (fi″bro-kar′ti-lij) The type of cartilage made up of parallel, thick, compact bundles, separated by narrow clefts containing typical cartilage cells (chondrocytes). 52

fibrous connective tissue (fi′brus) The tissue made up of densely packed fibers (e.g., tendons and ligaments). 50

filoplume feather (fil′o-ploom) A small, thin feather that probably has sensory functions in birds (pinfeather). 491

filopodium (fi″li-po′de-um) Pseudopodium that is slender, clear, and sometimes branched. Pl., filopodia. 248

filtration (fil-tra′shun) Movement of material across a membrane as a result of hydrostatic pressure. 42

first law of thermodynamics (thur″mo-di-nam′-iks) The total amount of energy in the universe remains constant. More energy cannot be created, and existing energy cannot be destroyed. Energy can only undergo conversion from one form to another. 60

fission (fish′un) Asexual reproduction in which the cell divides into two (binary fission) or more (multiple fission) daughter parts, each of which becomes an individual organism. 678

flagella (flah-jel′ah) Relatively long, motile processes that extend from the surface of a cell. Eukaryotic flagella are longer versions of cilia. Flagellar undulations drive a cell through a fluid medium. Like cilia, flagella have a 9 + 2 arrangement of microtubules covered by the cell's plasma membrane. 48, 541

flame cell Specialized, hollow excretory or osmoregulatory structure consisting of one to several cells containing a tuft of cilia (the "flame") and located at the end of a minute tubule. Flame bulb. 289, 664

flavin adenine dinucleotide (FAD) (fla′vin ad′e-nēn di″nuc′leo-tīd) A coenzyme that is a condensation product of riboflavin phosphate and adenylic acid. It forms the prosthetic group of certain enzymes. 73

fluid feeding The process by which an animal feeds on fluid. Examples include some parasites, leeches, ticks, mites, lampreys, and certain crustaceans. 635

fluke (flook) Any trematode worm. A member of the class Trematoda or class Monogenea. 291

food chain A linear sequence of organisms through which energy is transferred in an ecosystem from producers through several levels of consumers. 60, 207

food vacuole (vak′u-ōl) A cell organelle that functions in intracellular digestion. 243

food web A sequence of organisms through which energy is transferred in an ecosystem. Rather than being linear, a food web has highly branched energy pathways. 207

foraging behavior (for′ij-ing) The process animals use in locating food resources. 185

forebrain (for′brān) Consists of the diencephalon and telencephalon. Also known as the prosencephalon. 561

formed-element fraction The cellular component of vertebrate blood. 608

fossil Any remains, impressions, or traces of organisms of a former geological age. 5

founder effect Changes in gene frequency that occur when a few individuals from a parental population colonize new habitats. The change is a result of founding individuals not having a representative sample of the parental population's genes. 165

fragmentation (frag″men-ta′shun) Division into smaller units. A type of asexual reproduction whereby a body part is lost and then regenerates into a new organism. 678

Fungi (fun′ji) The kingdom of life whose members are eukaryotic, multicellular, and saprophytic (mushrooms, molds). 228

furcula (fur′kyah-lah) The fused clavicles of a bird. The furcula is one point of attachment for flight muscles. The wishbone. 492

G

Galápagos Islands (gah-lah′pe-gos″) An archipelago on the equator in the Pacific Ocean about 900 km west of Ecuador. Charles Darwin's observations of the plant and animal life of these islands were important in the formulation of the theory of evolution by natural selection. 155

gallbladder (gawl′blad-der) The pear-shaped reservoir for bile under the right lobe of the liver. 652

gamete (gam′ēt) Mature haploid cell (sperm or egg) that functions in sexual reproduction. The union of two gametes of opposite sex (fertilization) produces a zygote. 90

gametogenesis (gam″e-to-jen′e-sis) Gamete formation by way of meiosis. 92

gametogony (ga′mēt-o-gony) Multiple fission that forms gametes that fuse to form a zygote. Also called gamogony. Occurs in the class Sporozoea. 251

ganglion (gang′gle-on) A group of nerve cell bodies outside the central nervous system. 557

gastric shield A chitinized plate in the stomach of a bivalve (phylum Mollusca) on which the crystalline style rotates. 327

gastrodermis (gas-tro-derm′is) The endodermally derived lining of the gastrovascular cavity of Cnidaria. 268

Gastropoda (gas-trop′o-dah) The class of molluscs characterized by torsion. A shell, when present, is usually coiled. Snails. 321

Gastrotricha (gas-tro-tri′kah) A small phylum of marine and freshwater species of gastrotrichs that inhabit the spaces between bottom sediments. 298

gastrovascular cavity (gas″tro-vas′ku-lar kav′i-te) The large central cavity of cnidarians and flatworms that receives and digests food. Has a single opening serving as both mouth and anus. 269, 606, 637

gastrozooid (gas″tro-zo′oid) A feeding polyp in a colonial hydrozoan (phylum Cnidaria). 271

gastrulation (gast″ru-la′shun)   The embryological process that results in the formation of the gastrula. Results in the formation of the embryonic gut, ectoderm, and endoderm. 138

gemmule (jem′yool)   Resistant, overwintering capsule formed by freshwater, and some marine, sponges that contains masses of mesenchyme cells. Amoeboid mesenchyme cells are released and organize into a sponge.   266

gene   A heritable unit in a chromosome. A series of nucleotide bases on the DNA molecule that codes for a single polypeptide.   99

gene flow   Changes in gene frequency in a population that result from emigration or immigration.   166

gene insertion   The process by which one or more genes from one organism are incorporated into the genetic makeup of a second organism.   130

gene pool   The sum of all genes in a population.   164

generalists   Animals that are capable of eating a variety of foods or of living in a variety of places.   186

generator potential   A graded potential that travels only a short distance along the plasma membrane of a sensory cell.   568

genetic drift (je-net′ik)   Occurs when chance events influence the frequency of genes (evolutionary change). Also called **neutral selection.**   165

genetic recombination (je-net′ik re-kom-be-na′shun)   Crossing-over. A major source of genetic variation in a population or a given species.   91

genetics (je-net′iks)   The study of the mechanisms of transmission of genes from parents to offspring.   98

genome (je′nōm)   The complete gene complement of an organism, contained in a set of chromosomes in eukaryotes.   85

genotype (je′no-tīp)   The specific gene combinations that characterize a cell or an individual.   99

genotypic ratio (je′no-tip-ik)   The relative numbers of progeny in each genotypic category that a genetic cross produces.   100

genus (je′nus)   The level of classification between species and family.   227

georeceptor (je″o-re-cep′tor)   A specialized nerve ending that responds to the force of gravity.   569

gerontology (jer″on-tol′o-je)   Scientific study of the problems of aging in all their aspects, including clinical, biological, and sociological.   303

gestation (jes-ta′shun)   Period of development of the young in viviparous animals, from the time of fertilization of the ovum until birth.   521, 681

giardiasis (je″ar-di′ah-sis)   A common infection of the lumen of the small intestine with the flagellated protozoan *Giardia lamblia*. Spread via contaminated food and water and by direct person-to-person contact.   248

gill   An aquatic respiratory organ for obtaining oxygen and getting rid of carbon dioxide. Found in fishes, molluscs, and many arthropods.   619

gill arches   Bony or cartilaginous gill support of some vertebrates. Also called **visceral arch.** 447

gill filament   A thin-walled, fleshy extension of a gill arch that contains vessels carrying blood to and from gas exchange surfaces. 447

gill rakers   Processes extending from pharyngeal arches of some fishes that trap food and protect gill filaments from mechanical damage.   446

glochidium (glo-kid′e-um)   A larval stage of freshwater bivalves in the family Unionidae. It lives as a parasite on the gills or fins of fishes.   328

glomerulus (glo-mer′u-lus)   A capillary tuft (coiled mass of capillaries) within the capsule (Bowman's) of a nephron. Forms the glomerular filtrate.   451, 672

glycocalyx (gli′ko-kal′iks)   The glycoprotein and glycolipid covering (cell coat) that surrounds many eukaryotic cells.   38

glycolysis (gli-kol′i-sis)   The conversion of glucose to pyruvic acid (pyruvate) with the release of some energy in the form of ATP. Occurs in the cytosol. Literally, "sugar splitting."   70

Gnathostomata (na′tho-sto″ma-tah)   A superclass of vertebrates whose members possess hinged jaws and paired appendages. A vertebral column may have replaced the notochord.   440

Golgi apparatus (gol′je ap″ah-ra′tus)   The membrane-bound cytoplasmic organelle where the proteins and lipids made in the endoplasmic reticulum are modified and stored. 44

gonad (go′nad)   A gamete-producing gland. Ovary or testis.   600

gonadotropin (go-nad″o-trop′in)   A hormone that stimulates activity in the gonads. 684

gonozooid (gon′o-zo″id)   A polyp of a hydrozoan cnidarian that produces medusae. 271

Gordian worm   *See also* **horsehair worms.**

grasslands   A biome characterized by grasses and a few scattered trees. Grassland animals include numerous insects and other herbivores, such as bison.   215

gravid (grav′id)   Containing developing young. Pregnant.   296

gray crescent   A dark, arching band that forms on the surface of the amphibian zygote opposite the point of sperm penetration. Forms in the region where gastrulation will occur.   136

green gland   *See also* **antennal gland.**

greenhouse effect   The warming of a global climate due to the accumulation of carbon dioxide in the atmosphere from burning fossil fuels.   221

gross primary production   The total energy fixed by autotrophs in an ecosystem.   208

gular flutter (gu′lar)   A type of breathing in some birds. Rapid movement of the throat region promotes evaporative water loss.   660

gustation (gus-ta′shun)   The act of tasting or the sense of taste.   580

H

habitat   The native environment of an organism.   192

habitat selection   The choice of an animal's place to live. Habitat selection involves the interaction of physiological and psychological factors.   185

habituation (hab-bich″u-a′shun)   The gradual decrease in a response to a stimulus or to the environment.   181

hair   A long, slender filament. Applied especially to such filamentous appendages of the skin.   535

haploid (hap′loid)   Having one member of each pair of homologous chromosomes. Haploid cells are the product of meiosis and are often gametes.   110

Hardy-Weinberg equilibrium (har′de wīn′berg e″kwe-lib′re-em)   The condition in which the frequency of genes in a population does not change from one generation to another. The conditions defined by the Hardy-Weinberg equilibrium specify the conditions under which evolution does not occur. 165

head-foot   The body region of a mollusc that contains the head and is responsible for locomotion as well as retracting the visceral mass into the shell.   320

heartworm disease   A parasitic infection in dogs caused by the nematode *Dirofilaria immitis*.   311

hectocotylus (hek″to-kot′i-lus)   A modified arm of some male cephalopods that is used in sperm transfer.   332

hemal system (he′mal)   Strands of tissue found in echinoderms. The hemal system is of uncertain function. It may aid in the transport of large molecules or coelomocytes, which engulf and transport waste particles within the body.   404

hematopoiesis (hem″ah-to-poi-e′sis)   The formation and development of blood cells. 609

hemerythrin (hem″e-rith′rin)   The red iron-containing respiratory pigment in the blood plasma of some polychaetes, sipunculids, priapulids, and brachiopods.   627

Hemichordata (hem″i-kor-da′tah)   The phylum of marine, wormlike animals whose members have an epidermal nervous system and pharyngeal slits. Acorn worms and pterobranchs.   424

hemimetabolous metamorphosis (hem″i-met-ab′ol-us met-ah-morf′a-sis)   A type of insect metamorphosis in which immature insects are different in form and habitats from the adult. It is different from holometabolous metamorphosis in that there is a gradual series of changes in form during the transition from immature to adult.   391

hemizygous (hem″e-zi′gus)   An individual having one member of a pair of genes. Males of most animal species are hemizygous for traits carried on the X chromosome.   111

hemocoel (he′mo-sēl)   Large tissue spaces within arthropods that contain blood. Derived from the blastocoel of the embryo. 366

hemocyanin (he″mo-si′ah-nin)   A non-heme, blue respiratory pigment in the plasma of many molluscs and arthropods. Composed of monomers, each of which contains two atoms of copper and can bind one molecule of oxygen.   626

hemocyte (he′mo-sīt)   Any blood corpuscle or formed element of the blood in animals with an open circulatory system.   606

hemoglobin (he′mo-glo″bin)   An iron-containing respiratory pigment of red blood cells responsible for the transport of oxygen and carbon dioxide. Occurs in vertebrate red blood cells and in the plasma of many invertebrates.   609, 626

hemolymph (he′mo-limf)   The fluid in the coelom or hemocoel of some invertebrates that represents the blood and lymph of higher animals. Found in animals with an open circulatory system.   606

herbivore (her′bi-vor)   A plant-eating animal. Any organism that subsists on plants. 630

herbivory (her-bi′vor-e)   The process of existing by eating macroscopic plants. Examples include molluscs, polychaete worms, arthropods, and sea urchins.   630, 635

hermaphroditism (her-maf′ro-di″tizm)   A state characterized by the presence of both male and female reproductive organs in the same animal. Monecious.   680

heterochromatic regions (het″er-o-chrom-ă′tik)   Having inactive genes. Inactive regions of chromosomes are heterochromatic. 108

heterodont (het′e-ro-dont)   Having a series of teeth specialized for different functions. 511

heterotherm (het′e-ro-therm)   An animal whose body temperature fluctuates markedly. "Cold-blooded." An animal that derives essentially all of its body heat from the environment.   658

heterotrophic (het″er-o-tro′fik)   The type of nutrition in which organisms derive energy from the oxidation of organic compounds either by consumption or absorption of other organisms.   192

heterotrophs (het′er-o-trofs)   Organisms that obtain both inorganic and organic raw materials from the environment to live. Animals, fungi, many protists, and most bacteria are heterotrophs.   630

heterozygous (het″er-o-zi′ges)   Having different expressions of a gene on homologous chromosomes.   99

Hexactinellida (hex-act″in-el′id-ah)   The class of sponges whose members are characterized by triaxon siliceous spicules, which sometimes form an intricate lattice. Cup or vase shaped. Sycon body form. Glass sponges. 265

Hexapoda (hex″sah-pod′ah)   The class of mandibulate arthropods whose members are characterized by having three pairs of legs. Commonly called insects. Hexapods often have wings and a body divided into head, thorax, and abdomen. Insecta has been used as an alternate class name.   384

hibernation (hi″ber-na′shun)   Condition of mammals that involves passing the winter in a torpid state in which the body temperature drops to nearly freezing and the metabolism drops close to zero. May last weeks or months. 193, 517, 662

hindbrain (hīnd′brān)   Includes the medulla oblongata, cerebellum, and pons. Also known as the rhombencephalon.   559

Hirudinea (hi′ru-din″e-ah)   The class of annelids whose members are characterized by bodies with 34 segments, each of which is subdivided into annuli. Anterior and posterior suckers are present. Leeches.   351

holoblastic (hol″o-blas′tik)   Division of a zygote that results in separate blastomeres. 137

holometabolous metamorphosis (hol″o-met-ab′ol-us met-ah-morf′a-sis)   A type of insect metamorphosis in which immatures, called larvae, are different in form and habitats from the adult. The last larval molt results in the formation of a pupa. Radical cellular changes in the pupal stage end in adult emergence. 391

homeostasis (ho″me-o-sta′sis)   A state of equilibrium in which the internal environment of the body of an animal remains relatively constant with respect to the external environment.   38

homeotherm (ho′me-o-therm)   Having nearly uniform body temperature, regulated independently of the environmental temperature. "Warm-blooded."   658

homodont (ho′mo-dont)   Having a series of similar, unspecialized teeth.   511

homologous (ho-mol′o-ges)   Describes structures that have a common evolutionary origin. The wing of a bat and the arm of a human are homologous since each can be traced back to a common ancestral appendage.   6

homologous chromosomes (ho-mol′o-ges kro′mo-sōmz)   Chromosomes that carry genes for the same traits. One of two copies of a particular chromosome in a diploid cell, each copy being derived from a different parent.   91

homozygous (ho″mo-zi′ges)   Having the same expression of a gene on homologous chromosomes.   99

hormone (hor′mōn)   A chemical secreted by an endocrine gland that is transmitted by the bloodstream or body fluids to a target cell or tissue.   184, 587

horn   The paired growths on the head of certain ungulate animals. The median growth of hair on the snout of the rhinoceros.   535

horsehair worms   Pseudocoelomate animals that belong to the phylum Nematomorpha. Also known as Gordian worms or hairworms (Gordius is the name of an ancient king who tied an intricate knot).   312

host   An animal or protist that harbors or nourishes another organism (parasite).   244

humoral immunity (hu′mor-al i-mu′nǐ-te)   The type of immunity that results from the presence of antibodies that are soluble in blood and lymph.   616

hyaline cartilage (hi′ah-līn kar′ti-lij)   The type of cartilage with a glassy, translucent appearance.   52

hydraulic skeleton (hi-dro′lik)   The use of body fluids in open circulatory systems to give support and facilitate movement. Muscles contracting in one part of the body force body fluids into some distant tissue space, thus causing a part of the body to extend or become turgid.   324

hydrocarbon (hi″dro-kar′bon)   An organic molecule that contains only carbon and hydrogen and has its carbons bonded in a linear fashion.   21

hydrogen bond (hi′dro-jen)   A weak to moderate attractive force between a hydrogen atom bonded to an electronegative atom and one pair of electrons of another electronegative atom.   19

hydrological cycle (hi″dro-loj′i-kal)   The cycling of water between reservoirs in oceans, lakes, and groundwater, and the atmosphere.   213

hydrostatic skeleton (hi″dro-stat′ik)   The use of body cavity fluids, confined by the body wall, to give support (e.g., the hydrostatic skeleton of nematodes and annelids). Also called hydroskeleton.   270, 536

hydrothermal vents (hi″dro-thur′mal)   Deep, oceanic regions where the tectonic plates in the earth's crust are moving apart. They are characterized by occasional lava flows and hot water springs. These vents support a rich community by chemolithotrophy.   210

Hydrozoa (hi″dro-zo′ah)   The class of cnidarians whose members have epidermally derived gametes, mesoglea without wandering amoeboid cells, and gastrodermis without nematocysts. Medusae, when present, with a velum. *Hydra, Obelia, Physalia.*   271

hygroreceptor (hi″gro-re-sep′tor)   A receptor in insects that detects the water content of air.   569

hypertonic (hi″per-ton′ik)   A solution having a greater number of solute particles than another solution to which it is compared.   40

hypoblast (hi′po-blast)   An inner layer of cells that results from the proliferation and movement of cells in the blastoderm of an avian or reptilian embryo.   144

hypodermis (hi″po-der′mis)   The layer of integument below the cuticle. The outer cellular layer of the body of invertebrates that secretes the cuticular exoskeleton.   531

hypothalamus (hi″po-thal′ah-mus)   A structure within the diencephalon and below the thalamus, that functions as an autonomic center and regulates the pituitary gland.   561

hypothesis (hi-poth′ĕ-sis)   A tentative explanation of a question. An explanation based on careful observations.   11

hypotonic (hi″po-ton′ik)   A solution having a lesser number of solute particles than another solution to which it is compared.   40

I

immunity (i-myu′nǐ-te)   The state of being immune from or not susceptible to a particular disease.   615

immunization (im″yu-nǐ-za′shun)   The process of making one immune. The induction of protective immunity by administration of either (1) a vaccine or toxoid (active immunization) or (2) preformed antibodies (passive immunization).   616

immunology (im″u-nol′o-je)   The study of the immune system. This study reveals the many phenomena responsible for both acquired and innate immunity. It also includes the use of antibody-antigen reactions in other laboratory work (serology and immunochemistry).   615

imprinting (im′print-ing)   A young animal developing an attachment toward an animal or object.   180

incomplete dominance   An interaction between alleles in which both alleles are expressed more or less equally, and the phenotype of the heterozygote is different from either homozygote.   103

incomplete linkage   Two genes that are carried on the same chromosome but are far enough apart that crossing-over between them occurs.   111

independent variable   The parameter being tested in an experiment. Any experiment should have only one independent variable.   11

indirect (asynchronous) flight   Insect flight accomplished by flight muscles acting on the body wall. Changes in shape of the thorax cause wing movements. A single nerve impulse results in many cycles of the wings. *See also* **direct (synchronous) flight.**   384

induced fit   The precise fit between an enzyme and its substrate.   62

inferior   Below a point of reference (e.g., the mouth is inferior to the nose in humans).   236

inorganic molecules (compounds)   Compounds that are not hydrocarbons or their derivatives. Compounds other than organic compounds.   21

Insecta (in-sekt′ah)   *See also* **Hexapoda.**

insectivore (in-sek′tĕ-vor)   An insectivorous animal or plant. Any mammal of the order Insectivora, comprising the moles, shrews, and Old World hedgehogs.   630

insight learning   The use of cognitive or mental processes to associate experiences and solve problems.   182

instrumental conditioning (in″strĕ-men′tal kon-dish′en-ing)   Trial-and-error learning. The reinforcement of certain behaviors in animals leads to an animal repeating the behavior.   181

integument (in-teg′u-ment)   A covering (e.g., the skin).   531

integumentary exchange (in-teg″u-men′tah-re)   Gas exchange through the integument. Also called cutaneous exchange.   619

intercalated disk (in-ter″kah-lat′ed)   Membranous boundary between adjacent cardiac muscle cells.   54

intermediate filament The chemically heterogeneous group of protein fibers, the specific proteins of which vary with cell type. One of the three most prominent types of cytoskeletal filaments. Made of fibrous proteins. 48

intermediate host The organism in the life cycle of a parasite that harbors an immature stage of the parasite and where asexual reproduction usually occurs. 244

intermediate lobe The area in the pituitary gland between the anterior and posterior lobes. Also called the pars intermedia. Produces melanophore-stimulating hormone. 597

interneuron (in″ter-nu′ron) A neuron between a sensory neuron and a motor neuron. Interneurons function as integrating centers. 552

interphase (in′ter-fāz) Period between two cell divisions when a eukaryotic cell is carrying on its normal functions. Long period of the cell cycle between one mitosis and the next. Includes G_1 phase, S phase, and G_2 phase. DNA replication occurs during interphase. 85

intertidal (littoral) zone (in-ter-ti′del li′teral) The marine ecosystem that extends from the splash zone of ocean waves to the low-tide marks. 219

intracellular digestion Digestion that occurs inside a cell, as in many protozoans, sponges, cnidarians, flatworms, rotifers, bivalve molluscs, and primitive chordates. 632

intraspecific competition Competition among members of the same species for environmental resources. 196

intrinsic rate of growth *See also* **biotic potential.**

introvert (in′tro-vert) The anterior narrow portion that can be withdrawn (introverted) into the trunk of a sipunculid worm, a loriciferan, or a bryozoan. 314

inversion (in-ver′zhen) A rearrangement in the structure of a chromosome in which two breaks occur and a segment of the chromosome flip-flops. Genes in that segment occur in a reverse order. 116

involuntary (visceral or **autonomic) nervous system** Stimulates smooth and cardiac muscle and glands of the body. 559

involution (in″vo-lu′shun) The rolling of superficial cells over the dorsal lip of the blastopore during gastrulation of amphibian embryos. 142

ion (i′on) An atom or group of atoms with an electrical charge. The charged particle formed when a neutral atom or group of atoms gains (negative) or loses (positive) one or more electrons. 19

ionic bond (i-on′ik) An association between ions of opposite charges. The electrostatic force that holds ions together in an ionic compound. 19

isomer (i′so-mer) Organic compounds with the same molecular formula but different structures, functions, and properties. 22

isotonic (i″so-ton′ik) In a comparison of two solutions, both have equal concentrations of solutes. 39

isotope (i′sĕ-tōp) Any of two or more forms of a chemical element having the same number of protons in the nucleus or the same atomic number, but having different numbers of neutrons in the nucleus, or different atomic masses. Isotopes of a single element possess almost identical chemical properties. 17

J

Jacobson's (vomeronasal) organ Olfactory receptor present in most reptiles. Blind-ending sacs that open through the secondary palate into the mouth cavity. Used to sample airborne chemicals. 483, 579

Johnston's organ Mechanoreceptor (auditory receptor) found at the base of the antennae of male mosquitoes and midges. 388

K

karyotyping (kar″e-o-tīp′ing) The determination of the number and structure of chromosomes in an individual. 114

keratin (ker′a-tin) A tough, water-resistant protein found in the epidermal layers of the skin of reptiles, birds, and mammals. Found in hair, feathers, hoofs, nails, claws, bills, etc. 473

keystone species A species upon which several other species depend. Removal of the keystone species leads to the death or disappearance of the dependent species. 206

kilocalorie (kil′o-kal″o-re) A unit of heat equal to 1,000 calories. Used to measure the energy content of food. *See also* **Calorie.** 60, 630

kinetic energy (kĭ-net′ik en′er-je) The energy associated with a body by virtue of its motion. The energy of a mass of matter that is moving. 60

kinetochore (kĭ-nĕ′to-kor) A specialized group of proteins and DNA at the centromere of a chromosome. Is an attachment site for the microtubules of the mitotic spindle and plays an active part in the movement of chromosomes to the pole. 86

kingdom (king′dom) The level of classification above phylum. The traditional classification system includes five kingdoms: Monera, Protista, Fungi, Plantae, and Animalia. Recent evidence from molecular biological studies indicates that these five kingdoms may not be monophyletic lineages. 227

Kinorhyncha (kin″o-rink′ah) The phylum of aschelminths that contains members called kinorhynchs. Small, elongate worms found exclusively in marine environments, where they live in mud and sand. 306

kin selection The idea that natural selection acting on related animals can affect the fitness of an individual. When genes are common to related animals, an individual's fitness is based on the genes the individual passes on and on those common genes that relatives pass on. Kin selection is thought to explain how altruism could evolve in a population. *See also* **altruism.** 188

Krebs cycle *See also* **citric acid cycle.**

krill (kril) Any of the small, pelagic, shrimp-like crustaceans. Krill are an important source of energy in antarctic food webs. 641

K-selected Organisms whose populations are maintained near the carrying capacity of the environment. 196

L

labial palp (la′be-al palp) 1. Chemosensory appendage found on the labium of insects (Arthropoda). 2. Flaplike lobe surrounding the mouth of bivalve molluscs that directs food toward the mouth. 327

labium (la′be-um) The posterior mouthpart of insects. It is often referred to as the "lower lip," is chemosensory, and was derived evolutionarily from paired head appendages (Hexapoda, Arthropoda). 386

lactation (lak-ta′shun) The production of milk by the mammary glands. 693

large intestine That part of the digestive system between the ileocecal valve of the small intestine and the anus. Removes salt and water from undigested food and releases feces through the anus. 651

larva (lar'vah)   The immature feeding stage of an insect that undergoes holometabolous metamorphosis. The immature stage of any animal species in which adults and immatures are different in body form and habitat.   266

Larvacea (lar-vas'e-ah)   The class of urochordates whose members are planktonic and whose adults retain a tail and notochord. With a gelatinous covering of the body.   426

larval instars (lar'val in'starz)   Any of the different immature feeding stages of an insect that undergoes holometabolous metamorphosis.   390

latent learning (lat'ent)   Exploratory learning. Latent learning occurs when an animal makes associations without immediate reinforcement or reward.   182

lateral (lat'er-al)   Away from the plane that divides a bilateral animal into mirror images.   236

lateral-line system (lat'er-al)   1. A line of sensory receptors along the side of some fishes and amphibians used to detect water movement (phylum Chordata). 2. The external manifestation of a lateral excretory canal of nematodes (phylum Nematoda).   449, 573

learning   Changes in the behavior of an individual due to experience.   181

lentic ecosystem (len'tik e'ko-sis"tem)   A freshwater ecosystem with standing water (e.g., lakes or ponds).   218

leucon (lu'kon)   The sponge body form that has an extensively branched canal system. The canals lead to chambers lined by choanocytes.   265

light microscope (LM)   The type of microscope in which the specimen is viewed under ordinary illumination.   36

limiting factor   A nutrient or other component of an organism's environment that is in relatively short supply and, therefore, restricts the organism's ability to reproduce successfully.   192

linkage group (link'kij)   Genes linked to the same chromosome that tend to be inherited together.   110

linked gene   Gene on the same chromosome as another gene.   110

lipid (lip'id)   A fat, oil, or fatlike compound that usually has fatty acids in its molecular structure. An organic compound consisting mainly of carbon and hydrogen atoms linked by nonpolar covalent bonds. Examples include fats, waxes, phospholipids, and steroids that are insoluble in water.   22

liver (liv'er)   A large, dark-red gland that carries out many vital functions, such as the formation of urea, manufacture of plasma proteins, synthesis of amino acids, synthesis and storage of glycogen, and many others.   651

lobopodium (lo"bo-po'de-um)   A blunt, lobelike pseudopodium that is commonly tubular, and is composed of both ectoplasm and endoplasm. Pl., lobopodia.   248

local chemical messenger   A chemical that acts on nearby cells.   586

locus (lo'kus)   The position of a gene in a chromosome.   103

looping movement   The type of locomotion exhibited by leeches and some insect larvae whereby they alternate temporary points of attachment to move forward.   542

loose connective tissue   The type of tissue in which the matrix contains strong, flexible fibers of the protein collagen interwoven with fine, elastic, and reticular fibers.   50

lophophore (lof'a-for)   Tentacle-bearing ridge or arm within which is an extension of the coelomic cavity in lophophorate animals (e.g., brachiopods, ectoprocts, phoronids).   415

lorica (lo-ri'kah)   The protective external case in rotifers and some protozoa. It is formed by a thickened cuticle.   304

Loricifera (lor'a-sif"er-ah)   A phylum of aschelminths. A recent animal phylum to be described. Members are commonly called loriciferans.   314

lotic ecosystems (lo'tik e'ko-sis"temz)   Flowing water ecosystems. They include brooks, streams, and rivers.   218

lung   An organ of the respiratory system in which gas exchange occurs between body fluids (e.g., blood) and air.   622

lymph (limf)   Fluid that the lymphatic vessels transport.   614

lymphatic system (lim-fat'ik)   The one-way system of lymphatic vessels, lymph nodes, and other lymphoid organs and tissues. Drains excess tissue fluid from the extracellular space and provides a site for immune surveillance.   614

lymphocyte (lim'fo-sīt)   A type of white blood cell that provides protection to an animal.   610

lysosome (li'so-sōm)   Cytoplasmic, membrane-bounded organelle that contains digestive and hydrolytic enzymes, which are typically most active at the acid pH found in the lumen of lysosomes.   46

M

macronucleus (mak-ro-nu'kle-us)   A large nucleus found within the Ciliata (Protista) that regulates cellular metabolism. Directly responsible for the phenotype of the cell.   254

macronutrient (mak"ro-noo'tre-ent)   An essential nutrient for which an animal has a large minimal daily requirement (greater than 100 mg). For example, calcium, phosphorus, magnesium, potassium, sodium, and chloride, along with carbohydrates, lipids, and proteins.   630

Malacostraca (mal-ah-kos'trah-kah)   The class of crustaceans whose members are characterized by having appendages modified for crawling along the substrate, as in lobsters, crayfish, and crabs. Alternatively, the abdomen and body appendages may be used in swimming, as in shrimp.   371

Malpighian tubules (mal-pig'e-an tu'būlz)   The blind-ending excretory and osmoregulatory tubules that join the midgut of insects and some other arthropods. Secrete waste products and form urine.   366, 666

Mammalia (mah-ma'le-ah)   The class of vertebrates whose members are at least partially covered by hair, have specialized teeth, and are endothermic. Young are nursed from mammary glands. The mammals.   426

mammary gland (mam'ar-e)   The breast. In female mammals, the mammary glands produce and secrete milk to nourish developing young.   510, 688

mandible (man'dib-el)   1. The lower jaw of vertebrates. 2. The paired, grinding and tearing arthropod mouthparts, derived from anterior head appendages.   372

mantle (man'tel)   The outer fleshy tissue of molluscs that secretes the shell. The mantle of cephalopods may be modified for locomotion.   320

mantle cavity (man'tel kav'i-te)   The space between the mantle and the visceral mass of molluscs.   321

manubrium (mah-nu'bre-um)   A structure that hangs from the oral surface of a cnidarian medusa and surrounds the mouth.   271

mass A measure of the quantity of matter in an object. 16

mastax (mas′tax) The pharyngeal apparatus of rotifers used for grinding ingested food. 305

Mastigophora (mas″ti-gof′o-rah) The protozoan subphylum whose members possess one or more flagella for locomotion. Autotrophic, heterotrophic, or saprozoic. 246

matter Anything that has mass and occupies space. 16

maturation (mach″oo-ra′shun) To complete the natural development of an animal system. The performance of behavior improves as parts of the nervous system and other structures complete development. 179

maxilla (maks′il-ah) One member of a pair of mouthparts just posterior to the mandibles of many arthropods. 372

maxillary gland (mak′si-ler″e) In malacostracan crustaceans, the excretory organ located near the maxillary segments. Helps regulate ion concentrations. 666

mechanoreceptor (mek″ah-no-re-sep′tor) A sensory receptor that is sensitive to mechanical stimulation, such as changes in pressure or tension. 574

meconium (mĭ-ko′ne-um) A dark green mucilaginous material in the intestine of the full-term fetus, being a mixture of the secretions of the intestinal glands and some amniotic fluid. 695

medial (me′de-al) On or near the plane that divides a bilateral animal into mirror images. Also median. 236

median (parietal) eye (me′de-an) A photoreceptor located middorsally on the head of some vertebrates (reptiles). It is associated with the vertebrate epithalamus. 483, 581

medulla oblongata (me-dul′ah ob″lon-gah′tah) Inferior-most portion of the brain stem between the pons and the spinal cord. 559

medusa (me-du′sah) Usually, the sexual stage in the life cycle of cnidarians. The jellyfish body form. 269, 271

meiosis (mi-o′sis) Process of cell division by which egg and sperm cells form, involving a diminution in the amount of genetic material. Comprises two successive nuclear divisions with only one round of DNA replication, which produces four haploid daughter cells from an initial diploid cell. 90

melatonin (mel″ah-to′nin) The hormone that the pineal gland secretes. Regulates photoperiodicity. 592

memory cell A lymphocyte capable of initiating the antibody-mediated immune response upon detection of a specific antigen molecule for which it is genetically programmed. It circulates freely in the blood and lymph, and may live for years. 618

meninges (me-nin′jēz) A group of three membranes that covers the brain and spinal cord. 559

menopause (men′o-pawz) Termination of the menstrual cycle. Period of life in a female during which hormonal changes cause ovulation and menstruation to cease. 689

menstrual cycle (men′stroo-al) The period of regularly recurring physiologic changes in the endometrium that culminates in its shedding (menstruation). 688

menstruation (men″stroo-a′shun) Loss of blood and tissue from the uterus at the end of a female primate's reproductive cycle. 689

meroblastic (mer″ah-blas′tik) The division of a zygote in which large quantities of yolk prevent complete cleavages. 137

merogony (mĕ-rog′ah-ne) Schizogony resulting in the production of merozoites. 251

Merostomata (mer′o-sto″mah-tah) The class of arthropods whose members are aquatic and possess book gills on the opisthosoma. Eurypterids (extinct) and horseshoe crabs. 364

mesenchyme (mez′en-kīm) Undifferentiated mesoderm. It eventually develops into muscle, blood vessels, skeletal elements, and (other) connective tissues. 138

mesenchyme cells (mez′en-kīm) Amoeboid cells within the mesohyl of a sponge. Mesenchyme cells are specialized for reproduction, secreting skeletal elements, transporting food, storing food, and forming contractile rings around openings in the sponge wall. 263

mesoderm (mez′ah-durm) The embryonic tissue that gives rise to tissues between the ectoderm and endoderm (e.g., muscle, skeletal tissues, and excretory structures). 138

mesoglea (mez-o-gle′ah) A gel-like matrix between the epidermis and gastrodermis of cnidarians. 268

mesohyl (mez-o-hīl′) A jellylike layer between the outer (pinacocyte) and inner (choanocyte) layers of a sponge. Contains wandering amoeboid cells. 263

mesonephros (mez″o-nef′rōs) The middle of three pairs of embryonic renal organs in vertebrates. The functional kidney of fishes and amphibians. Its collecting duct is a wolffian duct. 667

mesothorax (mez″o-thor′aks) The middle of the three thoracic segments of an insect. Usually contains the second pair of legs and the first pair of wings. 384

Mesozoa (mes″o-zo′ah) A phylum of animals whose members are parasites of marine invertebrates. Two-layered body organization. Dioecious, complex life histories. Orthonectids and dicyemids. 283

messenger RNA (mRNA) A single-stranded polyribonucleotide. Formed in the nucleus from a DNA template and carries the transcribed genetic code to the ribosome, where the genetic code is translated into protein. 122

metabolism (me-tab′o-lizm) All of the chemical changes and processes within cells. All controlled, enzyme-mediated chemical reactions by which cells acquire and use energy. 60

metacercaria (mě″ta-ser-ka′re-ah) Stage between the cercaria and adult in the life cycle of most digenetic trematodes. Usually encysted and quiescent. 292

metamerism (mět-tam′a-riz″em) A segmental organization of body parts. Metamerism occurs in the Annelida, Arthropoda, and other smaller phyla. 340

metamorphosis (met″ah-mor′fo-sis) Change of shape or structure, particularly a transition from one developmental stage to another, as from larva to adult form. 363

metanephridium (met″ah-ně-frid′e-um) An excretory organ in many invertebrates. It consists of a tubule that has one end opening at the body wall and the opposite end in the form of a funnel-like structure that opens to the body cavity. 346, 664

metanephros (me″tah-nef′rōs) The renal organs of some vertebrates arising behind the mesonephros. The functional kidney of reptiles, birds, and mammals. It is drained by a ureter. 667

metaphase (met′ah-fāz) Stage in mitosis when chromosomes align in the middle of the cell and firmly attach to the mitotic spindle but have not yet segregated toward opposite poles. 89

metathorax (met″ah-thor′aks)   The posterior of the three segments of an insect thorax. It usually contains the third pair of walking legs and the second pair of wings (Arthropoda).   384

micelle (mi-sēl′)   Lipid aggregates with a surface coat of bile salts. A stage in the digestion of lipids in the small intestine.   652

microfilament (mi″kro-fil′ah-ment)   Component of the cytoskeleton. Involved in cell shape, motion, and growth. Helical protein filament formed by the polymerization of globular actin molecules.   48

microfilaria (mi″kro-fi-lar′e-ah)   The prelarval stage of filarial worms. Found in the blood of humans and the tissues of the vector.   311

micronucleus (mi″kro-nu′kle-us)   A small body of DNA that contains the hereditary information of ciliates (Protista). Exchanged between protists during conjugation. It undergoes meiosis before functioning in sexual reproduction.   254

micronutrient (mi″kro-nu′tre-ent)   A dietary element essential in only small quantities. For example, iron, chlorine, copper, and vitamins.   630

microscopy (mi-kros′ko-pe)   Examination with a microscope.   36

Microspora (mi″cro-spor′ah)   The protozoan phylum whose members have unicellular spores. Intracellular parasites in nearly all major animal groups. Example: microsporeans (*Nosema*).   252

microtubule (mi″kro-tu′būl)   A hollow cylinder of tubulin subunits. Involved in cell shape, motion, and growth. Functional unit of cilia and flagella. It is one of three major classes of filaments of the cytoskeleton.   47

microtubule-organizing center (MTOC) (mi″kro-tu′būl)   Region in a cell, such as a centrosome or a basal body, from which microtubules grow.   48

mictic eggs (mik′tik)   Pertaining to the haploid eggs of rotifers. If not fertilized, the egg develops parthenogenetically into a male. If fertilized, mictic eggs secrete a heavy shell and become dormant, hatching in the spring into amictic females.   305

midbrain   The portion of the brain between the pons and forebrain (diencephalon).   561

migration   Periodic round trips of animals between breeding and nonbreeding areas or to and from feeding areas.   502

mimicry (mim′ik-re)   When one species resembles one or more other species. Often, protection is afforded the mimic species.   201

miracidium (mi-rah-sid′e-um)   The ciliated, free-swimming, first-stage larva of a digenean trematode that undergoes further development in the body of a snail.   292

mitochondrion (mi″to-kon′dre-on)   Membrane-bound organelle that specializes in aerobic respiration (oxidative phosphorylation) and produces most of the ATP in eukaryotic cells.   47

mitosis (mi-to′sis)   Nuclear division in which the parental number of chromosomes is maintained from one cell generation to the next. Basis of reproduction of single-cell eukaryotes. Basis of physical growth (through cell divisions) in multicellular eukaryotes.   85

mitotic spindle (mi-tŏ′tic spin′dl)   Collectively, the asters, spindle, centrioles, and microtubules of a dividing cell.   87

modern synthesis   The combination of the principles of population genetics and Darwinian evolutionary theory.   159

molecular biology   The study of the biochemical structure and function of organisms.   6

molecular genetics   The study of the biochemical structure and function of DNA.   120

molecule   A particle composed of two or more atoms bonded together. An aggregate of at least two atoms in a definite arrangement held together by special forces.   18

Mollusca (mol-lus′kah)   The phylum of coelomate animals whose members possess a head-foot, visceral mass, mantle, and mantle cavity. Most molluscs also possess a radula and a shell. The molluscs. Bivalves, snails, octopuses, and related animals.   318

molting   The periodic renewal of feathers of birds by shedding and replacement. In arthropods and other invertebrates, the shedding of the exoskeleton or other body covering is called molting or ecdysis. *See also* **ecdysis**.   303, 492

Monera (mon′er-ah)   The kingdom of life whose members have cells that lack a membrane-bound nucleus, as well as other internal, membrane-bound organelles (they are prokaryotic). Bacteria.   228

monocyte (mon′o-sīt)   A type of white blood cell that functions as a phagocyte and develops into macrophages in tissues. A monocyte has a kidney-shaped nucleus and gray-blue cytoplasm.   610

monoecious (mah-ne′shus)   An organism in which both male and female sex organs occur in the same individual. Hermaphroditic.   680

monogamous (mah-nog′ah-mus)   Having one mate at a time.   499

Monogenea (mon″oh-gen′e-ah)   The class of Platyhelminthes with members that are called monogenetic flukes. Most are ectoparasites on vertebrates (usually on fishes, occasionally on turtles, frogs, copepods, squids). One life-cycle form in only one host. Bear an opisthaptor. Examples: *Disocotyle, Gyrodactylus, Polystoma*.   291

Monogononta (mon″o-go-non′tah)   A class of rotifers with members that possess one ovary. Mastax not designed for grinding. Produce mictic and amictic eggs. Example: *Notommata*.   305

monohybrid cross (mon-o-hi′brid)   A mating between two individuals heterozygous for one particular trait. Monohybrid crosses usually result in a phenotypic ratio of 3 dominant : 1 recessive in the offspring.   100

monophyletic group (mon″o-fi-let′ik)   A group of organisms descended from a single ancestor.   230

Monoplacophora (mon″o-pla-kof′o-rah)   The class of molluscs whose members have a single, arched shell; a broad, flat foot; and certain serially repeated structures. Example: *Neopilina*.   334

monosaccharide (mon″o-sak′ah-rīd)   A simple sugar, such as glucose or fructose, that represents the structural unit of a carbohydrate. Monosaccharides are building blocks of more complex sugars (disaccharides) and polysaccharides.   22

morphogenesis (mor″fo-gen′ĕ-sis)   The evolution and development of form, as the development of the shape of a particular organ or part of the body.   138

morula (mor′u-lah)   A stage in the embryonic development of some animals that consists of a solid ball of cells (blastomeres).   138, 690

mosaic evolution (mo-za′ik ev″ah-loo′shun)   A change in a portion of an organism (e.g., a bird wing) while the basic form of the organism is retained.   173

motor (effector or efferent) neuron or nerve
A neuron or nerve that transmits impulses from the central nervous system to an effector, such as a muscle or gland.   552, 559

motor unit   A motor neuron and the muscle fibers associated with it.   547

mucous cell   A glandular cell that secretes mucus.   648

Müllerian mimicry (mul'er-e-an mim'ik-re) When two similar species are both distasteful to predators.   201

Müller's larva   A free-swimming, ciliated larva that resembles a modified ctenophore. Characteristic of many marine polyclad turbellarians.   290

multiple alleles (mul'tĭ-pl ah-lēlz')   The presence of more than two alleles in a population.   103

multiple fission (mul'tĭ-pl fish'un)   Asexual reproduction by the splitting of a cell or organism into many cells or organisms. *See also* **schizogony.**   243

muscle fiber   The contractile unit of a muscle. A muscle cell.   541

muscle tissue   The type of tissue that allows movement. The three kinds are skeletal, smooth, and cardiac. Tissue made of bundles of long cells called muscle fibers.   50

musk gland   *See also* **scent gland.**

mutation pressure (myoo-ta'shun presh'er) A measure of the tendency for gene frequencies to change through mutation.   168

mutualism (myoo'choo-ah-liz-em)   A relationship between two species that benefits both members. The association is necessary to both species.   200, 244

myelin (mi'ĕ-lin)   Lipoprotein material that forms a sheathlike covering around some nerve fibers.   553

myofibril (mi"o-fi'bril)   Contractile fibers within muscle cells.   546

myoglobin (mi"o-glo'bin)   The oxygen-transporting pigment of muscle tissue.   627

myomere (mi'o-mēr)   The muscle plate or portion of a somite that develops into voluntary muscle.   545

myosin (mi'ah-sin)   A protein that, together with actin, is responsible for muscular contraction and relaxation.   546

myriapods (mir'e-a-podz)   Members of the four noninsect classes of the subphylum Uniramia. Includes centipedes, millipedes, pauropods, and symphylans.   381

Myxini (mik'sĭ-ne)   The class of vertebrates whose members are fishlike, jawless, and without paired appendages, and have four pairs of tentacles around the mouth. Hagfishes.   426

Myxozoa (mix"o-zo'ah)   The protozoan phylum whose members have spores of multicellular origin. The myxozoans.   252

N

naiad (na'ad)   The aquatic immature stage of any hemimetabolous insect.   391

nail   The horny, cutaneous plate of the dorsal surface of the distal end of a finger or toe.   535

natural killer (NK) cell   A lymphocyte present in nonimmunized individuals that exhibits independent cytolytic activity against tumor cells. Also called cytotoxic T cells.   617

natural selection   A theory, conceived by Charles Darwin and Alfred Wallace, of how some evolutionary changes occur. The idea that some individuals in a population possess variations that make them less able to survive and/or reproduce. These individuals die or fail to reproduce. Their genes are less likely to be passed into the next generation. Therefore, the genetic composition of the population in the next generation changes (i.e., evolution occurs).   157, 164

naturally acquired active immunity   The type of immunity that develops when an individual's immunologic system comes into contact with an appropriate antigenic stimulus during the course of normal activities. It usually arises as the result of recovering from an infection.   616

naturally acquired passive immunity   The type of immunity that involves the transfer of antibodies from one individual to another.   616

nematocyst (ni-mat'ah-sist)   An organelle characteristic of the Cnidaria that is used in defense, food gathering, and attachment.   268

Nematoda (nem-a-to'dah)   The phylum of aschelminths that contains members commonly called either roundworms or nematodes. Triploblastic, bilateral, vermiform, unsegmented, and pseudocoelomate.   306

Nematomorpha (nem"a-to-mor'fah)   The phylum of aschelminths commonly called horsehair worms.   312

Nemertea (nem-er'te-ah)   The phylum that has members commonly called the proboscis worms. Elongate, flattened worms in marine mud and sand. Triploblastic. Complete digestive tract with anus. Closed circulatory system.   298

neo-Darwinism (ne"o-dar'wĭ-niz"um)   *See also* **modern synthesis.**

nephridiopore (ne-frid'i-o-por) The opening to the outside of a nephridium. An excretory opening in invertebrates.   289

nephridium (ne-frid'e-um)   The excretory organ of the embryo. The embryonic tube from which the kidney develops. Tubular osmoregulatory and excretory organ of many invertebrates. Functions in excretion, osmoregulation, or both.   664

nephron (nef'ron)   The functional unit of a vertebrate kidney, consisting of a renal corpuscle and a renal tubule.   451, 671

neritic ecosystem (nĕ-rit'ik e'ko-sis-tem) The marine ecosystem that consists of relatively shallow water extending from the littoral zone to the edge of the continental shelves.   219

nerve   A bundle of neurons or nerve cells outside the central nervous system.   559

nerve net   A diffuse, two-dimensional plexus of bi- or multipolar neurons found in cnidarians. The simplest pattern of invertebrate nervous systems.   556

nervous tissue   The type of tissue composed of individual cells called neurons and supporting neuroglial cells.   50

net primary production   The total energy that autotrophs convert into biomass. Net primary production is equal to gross primary production less energy lost in maintenance functions of autotrophs.   208

neuroendocrine system (nur"o-en'do-krīn) The combination of the nervous and endocrine systems.   587

neurofibril node (nur"o-fib'ril nōd)   Regular gaps in a myelin sheath around a nerve fiber. Formerly called **node of Ranvier.**   553

neurohormone (nur"o-hor'mōn)   A chemical transmitter that nervous tissue produces. Uses the bloodstream or other body fluids for distribution to its target site.   587

neurolemmocyte (nur"o-lem'o-sīt)   The cell that surrounds a fiber of a peripheral nerve and forms the neurolemmal sheath and myelin. Formerly called **Schwann cell.**   553

neuromast (nur′o-mast)   The hair-cell mechanoreceptor within pits of the lateral-line system. Used to detect water currents and the movements of other animals.   574

neuromuscular junction (nur″o-mus′ku-lar jungk′shun)   The junction between nerve and muscle. Myoneural junction or neuro-muscular cleft.   547

neuron (nu′ron)   A nerve cell that consists of a cell body and its processes. The basic functional unit of communication in nervous systems.   552

neuropeptide (nur″o-pep′tīd)   A hormone (neurohormone) that secretory nervous tissue produces.   587

neurotoxin (nur″o-tok′sin)   A toxin that is poisonous to or destroys nerve tissue.   557

neurotransmitter (nur″o-trans-mit′er)   Chemical substance that the terminal end of an axon secretes that either stimulates or inhibits a muscle fiber contraction or an impulse in another neuron.   555, 586

neurulation (noor″yah-la′shun)   External changes along the upper surface of a chordate embryo that form the neural tube.   143

neutral selection   See also **genetic drift.**

neutron (nu′tron)   A neutral particle with a mass approximately the same as a proton that exists in atomic nuclei.   16

neutrophil (nu′tro-fil)   A type of phagocytic white blood cell with a multilobed nucleus and inconspicuous cytoplasmic granules.   609

nicotinamide adenine dinucleotide (NAD⁺) (nik″ah-tēn′ah-mīd ad′e-nēn di-nu′kle-o-tīd)   A local electron carrier that transfers hydrogen atoms and electrons within metabolic pathways. A free-moving carrier. Not membrane bound in a transport system.   64

nictitating membrane (nik′tĭ-tāt-ing mem′brān)   The thin, transparent lower eyelid of amphibians and reptiles.   465, 581

nociceptor (no″se-sep′tor)   A sensory receptor responding to potentially harmful stimuli. Produces a sensation of pain.   578

node of Ranvier (nōd ov Ran′ve-a)   A constriction of myelinated nerve fibers at regular intervals at which the myelin sheath is absent and the axon is enclosed only by sheath cell processes. Also known as a **neurofibril node.**   553

nomenclature (no′men-kla-cher)   The study of the naming of organisms in the fashion that reflects their evolutionary relationships.   227

nonamniote lineage (non-am′ne-ōt lin′e-ij)   The lineage of vertebrate tetrapods leading to modern amphibians.   456

nondisjunction (non″dis-junk′shun)   The failure of homologous chromosomes to separate during meiosis. Nondisjunction results in gametes with a deficiency of one chromosome or an extra chromosome.   114

nonpolar covalent bond (non-po′lar co-va′lent)   The bond formed when electrons spend as much time orbiting one nucleus as the other. Thus, the distribution of charges is symmetrical.   19

nonshivering thermogenesis (non-shiv′er-ing ther-mo-gen′esis)   The hormonal triggering of heat production. A thermogenic process in which enzyme systems for fat metabolism are activated, breaking down and oxidizing conventional fats to produce heat.   661

norepinephrine (nor″ep-i-nef′rin)   A catecholamine neurotransmitter released from the axon ends of some nerve fibers. Noradrenaline. Also, an adrenal medulla hormone.   555

northern coniferous forest (ko-nif′er-us)   The biome characterized by cool summers, cold winters, and short growing seasons. Characteristic animals include insects, snowshoe hares, lynx, wolves, caribou, and moose.   215

notochord (no′tah-kord)   A rodlike, supportive structure that runs along the dorsal midline of all larval chordates and many adult chordates.   428, 558

nuclear envelope   Double membrane forming the surface boundary of a eukaryotic nucleus. Consists of outer and inner membranes perforated by nuclear pores.   49

nucleic acid (nu-kle′ik)   A substance composed of bonded nucleotides. DNA and RNA are the two nucleic acids.   26

nucleolus (nu-kle′o-lus)   A small structure within the nucleus of a cell that transcribes ribosomal RNA and assembles ribosomal subunits.   49

nucleosome (nu-kle′ah-sōm)   An association of DNA and histone proteins that makes up chromatin. Many nucleosomes are linked in a chromatin strand.   108

nucleotide (nu′kle-o-tīd)   A component of a nucleic acid molecule consisting of a sugar, a nitrogenous base, and a phosphate group. Nucleotides are the building blocks of nucleic acids.   26

nucleus (nu′kle-us)   1. Cell nucleus. A spheroid body within a cell, contained in a double membrane, the nuclear envelope, and containing chromosomes and one or more nucleoli. The genetic control center of a eukaryotic cell. 2. The cell bodies of nerves within the central nervous system. 3. An atom's central core, containing protons and neutrons.   34

Nuda (nu′dah)   The class of ctenophorans whose members lack tentacles and have a flattened body with a highly branched gastrovascular cavity.   279

numerical taxonomy (nu-mer″ĭ-kal takson′ah-me)   A system of classification that does not attempt to distinguish true and false similarities.   231

nutrition (nu-trī′shun)   The study of the sources, actions, and interactions of nutrients. The study of foods and their use in diet and therapy.   207, 630

nymph (nimf)   The immature stage of a paurometabolous insect. Resembles the adult but is sexually immature and lacks wings (Arthropoda).   391

oceanic ecosystem (o″she-an′ik e′ko-sis-tem)   The marine ecosystem that extends from the continental shelves into the unproductive open ocean.   220

ocellus (o-sel′as)   A simple eye or eyespot in many invertebrates. A small cluster of photoreceptors.   290, 570

odontophore (o-dont′o-for″)   The cartilaginous structure that supports the radula of molluscs.   321

olfaction (ol-fak′shun)   The act of smelling. The sense of smell.   578

Oligochaeta (ol″i-go-kēt′ah)   The class of annelids whose members are characterized by having few setae and no parapodia. Monoecious with direct development. The earthworm (*Lumbricus*) and *Tubifex*.   347

ommatidia (om″ah-tid′e-ah)   The sensory unit of the arthropod compound eye.   388, 570

omnivore (om′nĭ-vor)   Subsisting upon both plants and animals. An animal that obtains its nutrients by consuming plants and other animals.   630

onchosphere (ong′ko-sfēr)   The larva of the tapeworm contained within the external embryonic envelope and armed with six hooks and cilia. Typically referred to as a coracidium when released into the water. 297

oncomiracidium (on″ko-mir-a-sid′e-um) Ciliated larva of a monogenetic trematode. 291

one-gene/one-polypeptide theory The concept that one gene in DNA codes for a sequence of amino acids in a specific polypeptide. 122

Onychophora (on-e-kof′o-rah) A phylum of terrestrial animals with 14 to 43 pairs of unjointed legs, oral papillae, and two large antennae. Onycophorans live in humid, tropical areas of the world. Their ancestor may have been an evolutionary transition between annelids and arthropods. Velvet worms or walking worms. 399

oogenesis (o″o-jen′e-sis) The process by which an egg cell forms from an oocyte. 93

Opalinata (op″ah-li-not′ah) The protozoan subphylum whose members are cylindrical and covered with cilia. Examples: *Opalina*, *Zelleriella*. 245

open circulatory system A circulatory system found in insects and some other invertebrates in which blood is not confined to vessels in part of its circuit. Blood bathes tissues in blood sinuses. 324, 606

operculum (o-per′ku-lum) A cover. 1. The cover of a gill chamber of a bony fish (Chordata). 2. The cover of the genital pore of a horseshoe crab (Meristomata, Arthropoda). 3. The cover of the aperture of a snail shell (Gastropoda, Mollusca). 292, 322, 442

Ophiuroidea (o-fe-u-roi′de-ah) The class of echinoderms whose members have arms sharply set off from the central disk and tube feet without suction disks. Brittle stars. 407

opisthaptor (ah″pis-thap′ter) Posterior attachment organ of a monogenetic trematode. 292

opisthosoma (ah″pis-tho-so′mah) The portion of the body of a chelicerate arthropod that contains digestive, reproductive, excretory, and respiratory organs. 364

oral Having to do with the mouth. The end of an animal containing the mouth. 236

oral cavity The cavity within the mouth. 646

oral sucker The sucker on the anterior end of a tapeworm, fluke, or leech. 292

order The level of classification between class and family. 227

organ A structure consisting of a group of specialized tissues that performs a specialized function. 54

organelle (or″gah-nel′) A part of a cell that performs a specific function. A membrane-bound sac or compartment. 32

organic evolution The change in an organism over time. A change in the sum of all genes in a population. 153

organic molecule A molecule that contains one or more carbon atoms. 21

organizational effects of hormones Changes resulting from the presence of hormones at critical time periods such that specific developmental pathways for specific brain regions and developing gonadal tissues are influenced to become either femalelike or malelike. 184

organ of Ruffini Sensory receptor in the skin believed to be a sensor for touch-pressure, position sense of a body part, and movement. Also known as **corpuscle of Ruffini.** 578

organ system A set of interconnected or interdependent parts that function together in a common purpose or produce results that cannot be achieved by one of them acting alone. 54

osmoconformer (oz″mo-con-form′er) An organism whose body fluids have the same or very similar osmotic pressure as that of its aquatic environment. A marine organism that does not utilize energy in osmoregulation. 663

osmoregulation (oz″mo-reg″u-la′shun) The maintenance of osmolarity by an organism or body cell with respect to the surrounding medium. 663

osmoregulator (oz″mo-reg′u-la-ter) An organism that regulates its internal osmolarity with respect to the environment. 664

osmosis (oz-mo′sis) Net movement of water across a selectively permeable membrane driven by a difference in concentration of solute on either side. The membrane must be permeable to water but not to the solute molecules. 39

Osteichthyes (os-te-ik′the-es) The class of fishes whose members are characterized by a bony skeleton, a swim bladder, and an operculum. Bony fishes. 426

outgroup In cladistic studies, an outgroup is a group outside of a study group that shares an ancestral characteristic with the study group. 232

ovarian cycle (o-va′re-an) The cycle in the ovary during which the oocyte matures and ovulation occurs. 688

ovary (o′var-e) The primary reproductive organ of a female. Where eggs (ova) are produced. 686

oviparous (o-vip′er-us) Organisms that lay eggs that develop outside the body of the female. 368, 682

ovipositor (ov-ĭ-poz′it-or) A modification of the abdominal appendages of some female insects that is used for depositing eggs in or on some substrate (Arthropoda, Hexapoda). 390

ovoviviparous (o′vo-vi-vip′er-us) Organisms with eggs that develop within the female reproductive tract and that are nourished by food stored in the egg. 368, 682

ovulation (ov″vu-la′shun) The release of an egg (female gamete) from a mature ovarian follicle or ovary. 686

oxidation (ok″sĭ-da′shun) The loss of electrons from a compound. 72

oxidation-reduction reaction An electron transfer from one atom or molecule to another. Often, hydrogen is transferred along with the electron(s). 72

oxygen debt The amount of oxygen that must be supplied following physical exercise to convert accumulated lactic acid (lactate) to glucose. 627

oxyhemoglobin (ok″sĭ-he′mo-glo″bin) Compound formed when oxygen combines with hemoglobin. 609

P

Pacinian corpuscle (Pah-sin′e-an kor′pus-l) A sensory receptor in skin, muscles, body joints, body organs, and tendons that is involved with the vibratory sense and firm pressure on the skin. Also called a lamellated corpuscle. 578

paedomorphosis (pe′dah-mor′fo-sis) The development of sexual maturity in the larval body form. 286

pain receptor A modified nerve ending that, when stimulated, gives rise to the sense of pain. 578

paleontology (pa″le-on-tol′o-je) The study of early life-forms on earth. 5

pancreas (pan′kre-as) Glandular organ in the abdominal cavity and behind the stomach that secretes hormones and digestive enzymes. 600, 651

pancreatic islet (pan″kre-at′ic i′let)   An island of special tissue in the pancreas. Secretes insulin or glucagon.   600

parabronchi (par′ah-brong″ke)   The tiny air tubes within the lung of a bird that lead to air capillaries where gases are exchanged between blood and air.   496

parapatric speciation (par″ah-pat′rik spe″she-a′shun)   Speciation that occurs in small, local populations, called **demes.**   171

paraphyletic group (par″ah-fi-let′ik)   A group that includes some, but not all, members of a lineage. Paraphyletic groups result from insufficient knowledge of the group.   230

parapodia (par″ah-pod′e-ah)   Paired lateral extensions on each segment of polychaetes (Annelida). May be used in swimming, crawling, and burrowing.   343

parasitism (par′ah-sĭ″tizm)   A relationship between two species in which one member (the parasite) lives at the expense of the second (the host).   244

parasitoid (par′ah-sĭ″toid)   Animal that deposits eggs or other developmental stages on another animal. Immatures then feed on host tissues and eventually kill the host.   199

parasympathetic nervous system (par″ah-sim″pah-thet′ik ner′vus sis′tem)   Portion of the autonomic nervous system that arises from the brain and sacral region of the spinal cord.   562

parathyroid gland (par″ah-thi′roid)   One of the small glands within a lobe of the thyroid gland. Produces the hormone parathormone.   599

parenchyma (pa-ren′ka-ma)   A spongy mass of mesenchyme cells filling spaces around viscera, muscles, or epithelia in acoelomate animals. Depending on the species, parenchyma may provide skeletal support, nutrient storage, motility, reserves of regenerative cells, transport of materials, structural interactions with other tissues, modifiable tissue for morphogenesis, oxygen storage, and perhaps other functions that have yet to be determined.   287

parietal cell (pah-ri′ĕ-tal)   Cell of a gastric gland that secretes hydrochloric acid and intrinsic factor.   648

parietal eye (pah-ri′ĕ-tal)   *See also* **median eye.**

pars intermedia   *See also* **intermediate lobe.**

parthenogenesis (par″thĕ-no-jen′ĕ-sis)   A modified form of sexual reproduction by the development of a gamete without fertilization, as occurs in some bees, wasps, certain lizards, and a few other animals.   678

parturition (par″tu-rish′un)   The process of childbirth.   693

paurometabolous metamorphosis (por″o-mĕ-tab′a-lus met″ah-morf′a-sis)   A form of insect development in which immatures resemble parents, and molting is restricted to the immature stages.   391

Pauropoda (por″o-pod′ah)   A class of arthropods whose bodies are small, soft, and divided into 11 segments, and who have 9 pairs of legs.   382

pebrine (pa-brēn′)   An infectious disease of silkworms caused by the protozoan *Nosema bombicis*.   252

pedal locomotion (ped′el)   The type of locomotion exhibited by flatworms, some cnidarians, and the gastropod molluscs. This locomotion involves waves of activity in the muscular system, which are applied to the substratum.   542

pedicellariae (ped″e-sel-ar′i-a)   Pincerlike structures found on the body wall of many echinoderms. They are used in cleaning and defense.   404

pedipalps (ped′e-palps)   The second pair of appendages of chelicerate arthropods. These appendages are sensory in function.   364

pellicle (pel′ik-el)   A thin, frequently noncellular covering of an animal (e.g., the protective and supportive pellicle of protists occurs just below the plasma membrane). May be composed of a cell membrane, cytoskeleton, and other organelles.   242, 531

pentaradial symmetry (pen″tah-ra′de-al sim′ĭ-tre)   A form of radial symmetry in the echinoderms in which body parts are arranged in fives around an oral-aboral axis.   402

Pentastomida (pen-tah-stom′id-ah)   A phylum of worms that are all endoparasites in the lungs or nasal passageways of carnivorous vertebrates. Tongue worms.   400

peptide bond   The covalent bond that joins individual amino acids. Formed by dehydration synthesis.   24

peripheral nervous system (pĕ-rif′er-al)   The nerves and ganglia of the nervous system that lie outside of the brain and spinal cord.   559

peristalsis (per″i-stal′sis)   Rhythmic waves of muscular contraction in the walls of various tubular organs that move material through the organs.   646

peristomium (per″i-stom′e-um)   The segment of an annelid body that surrounds the mouth.   343

perspiration (per″spĭ-ra′shun)   Sweating. The function of sweat secretion.   534

phagocytosis (fag″o-si-to′sis)   Process (endocytosis) by which a cell engulfs bacteria, foreign proteins, macromolecules, and other cells and digests their substances. Cellular eating.   42

phagolysosome (fag″o-li′so-sōm)   The organelle that forms when a lysosome combines with a vesicle.   43

pharyngeal lamellae   Thin plates of tissue on gill filaments that contain the capillary beds across which gases are exchanged.   447

pharyngeal slit (far-in′je-al)   One of several openings in the pharyngeal region of chordates. Pharyngeal slits allow water to pass from the pharynx to the outside of the body. In the process, water passes over gills, or suspended food is removed in a filter-feeding mechanism.   428

pharynx (far inks)   The passageway posterior to the mouth that is common to respiratory and digestive systems.   647

phasmid (faz′mid)   Sensory pit on each side near the end of the tail of nematodes of the class Secernentea (formerly Phasmidea).   308

phenotype (fe′no-tīp)   The expression that results from an interaction of one or more gene pairs and the environment.   99

phenotypic ratio (fe″no-tip′ik)   The relative numbers of progeny in each phenotypic category that a genetic cross produces.   100

pheromone (fer′o-mōn)   A chemical that is synthesized and secreted to the outside of the body by one organism and that is perceived (as by smell) by a second organism of the same species, releasing a specific behavior in the recipient.   185, 587

phonoreceptor (fo″no-re-sep′tor)   A specialized nerve ending that responds to sound.   570

Phoronida (fo-ron′ĭ-dah)   A phylum of marine animals whose members live in permanent, chitinous tubes in muddy, sandy, or solid substrates. They feed via an anterior lophophore with two parallel rings of long tentacles.   416

photoautotroph (fo″to-au′tĕ-trōf″)   An organism that synthesizes organic matter using the energy of light.   207

photoreceptor (fo″to-re-sep′tor) A nerve ending that is sensitive to light energy. 570

pH scale The numerical scale that measures acidity and alkalinity, ranging from 0 (most acidic) to 14 (most basic). pH stands for potential hydrogen and refers to the concentration of hydrogen ions (H^+). 20

phyletic gradualism (fi-let′ik graj′oo-el-izm) The idea that evolutionary change occurs at a slow, constant pace over millions of years. 172

phylogenetic systematics (fi-lo-je-net′ik sis-tem-at′iks) The study of the phylogenetic relationships among organisms in which true and false similarities are differentiated. Cladistics. 231

phylum (fi′lum) The level of classification between kingdom and class. Members are considered a monophyletic assemblage derived from a single ancestor. 227

physiology The branch of science that deals with the function of living organisms. 16

Phytomastigophorea (fi″to-mas-ti-go-for′ah) The protozoan class whose members usually have chloroplasts. Mainly autotrophic, some heterotrophic. Examples: *Euglena, Volvox, Chlamydomonas.* 246

pia mater (pi′ah mā′ter) The innermost meninx that is in direct contact with the brain and spinal cord. 559

pilidium larva (pi-lid-e-um lar′va) Free-swimming, hat-shaped larva of nemertean worms characterized by an apical tuft of cilia. 298

pinacocyte (pin″ah-ko′sīt) Thin, flat cell covering the outer surface, and some of the inner surface, of poriferans. 263

pineal gland (pin′e-al) A small gland in the midbrain of vertebrates that converts a signal from the nervous system into an endocrine signal. Also called the pineal body. 592

pinfeather *See also* **filoplume feather.**

pinocytosis (pin″o-si-to′sis) Cell drinking. The engulfment into the cell of liquid and of dissolved solutes by way of small membranous vesicles. A type of endocytosis. 42

pioneer community The first community to become established in an area. 206

pit organ Receptor of infrared radiation (heat) on the head of some snakes (pit vipers). 483, 578

pituitary gland (pǐ-tu′ǐ-tar″e) Endocrine gland that attaches to the base of the brain and consists of anterior and posterior lobes. Hypophysis. 592

placenta (plah-sen′tah) Structure by which an unborn child or animal attaches to its mother's uterine wall and through which it is nourished. 507, 693

placid (plas′id) Plates on the Kinorhyncha. 306

Placozoa (plak″o-zo′ah) A phylum of small, flattened, marine animals that feed by forming a temporary digestive cavity. Example: *Tricoplax adherans.* 283

planktonic (plangk-ton′ik) Describes small organisms that passively float or drift in a body of water. 218

Plantae (plant′a) One of the five kingdoms of life. Characterized by being eukaryotic and multicellular, and having rigid cell walls and chloroplasts. 228

planula (plan′u-lah) A ciliated, free-swimming larva of most cnidarians. The planula develops following sexual reproduction and metamorphoses into a polyp. 271

plasma (plaz′mah) The fluid or liquid portion of circulating blood within which formed elements and various solutes are suspended. 608

plasma cell (plaz′mah) A mature, differentiated B lymphocyte chiefly occupied with antibody synthesis and secretion. A plasma cell lives for only 5 to 7 days. 610

plasma membrane (plaz′mah mem′brān) Outermost membrane of a cell. Its surface has molecular regions that detect changes in external conditions and act as a selective barrier to ions and molecules passing between the cell and its environment. Consists of a phospholipid bilayer in which are embedded molecules of protein and cholesterol. The external covering of a protozoan. 34, 531

plastron (plas′tron) The ventral portion of the shell of a turtle. Formed from bones of the pectoral girdle and dermal bone. 475

platelet (plāt′let) Cytoplasmic fragment formed in the bone marrow that functions in blood coagulation. Also called **thrombocyte.** 610

plate tectonics (tek-ton′iks) The study of the movement of the earth's crustal plates. These movements are called continental drift. 160

Platyhelminthes (plat″e-hel-min′thēz) The phylum of flatworms. Bilateral acoelomates. 287

plerocercoid larva (ple″ro-ser′koid) Metacestode that develops from a procercoid larva. It usually shows little differentiation. 297

pneumatic sacs (nu-mat′ik) Gas-filled sacs that arise from the esophagus, or another part of the digestive tract, of fishes. Pneumatic sacs are used in buoyancy regulation (swim bladders) or gas exchange (lungs). 447

pneumostome (nu′mo-stōm) The outside opening of the gas exchange structure (lung) in land snails and slugs (Pulmonata). 620

Pogonophora (po″go-nof′e-rah) A phylum of protostomate, marine animals that are distributed throughout the world's oceans. Live in secreted, chitinous tubes in cold water at depths exceeding 100 m. Lack a mouth and digestive tract. Nutrients absorbed across the body wall and from endosymbiotic bacteria that they harbor. Beard worms. 358

point mutations A change in the structure of a gene that usually arises from the addition, deletion, or substitution of one or more nucleotides. 125

polar covalent bond (po′-lar co-va′lent) The bond formed by asymmetrically moving electrons. 19

polyandrous (pol″e-an′drus) Having more than one male mate. Polyandry is advantageous when food is plentiful, but because of predation or other factors, the chances of successfully rearing young are low. 500

Polychaeta (pol″e-kēt′ah) The class of annelids whose members are mostly marine and are characterized by a head with eyes and tentacles and a body with parapodia. Parapodia bear numerous setae. Examples: *Nereis, Arenicola.* 343

polygenes (pol′e-gēnz) Genes at multiple loci that influence a trait in a quantitative fashion. 104

polygynous (pah′-lij′ah-nus) Having more than one female mate. Polygyny tends to occur in species whose young are relatively independent at birth or hatching. 499

polyp (pol′ip) The attached, usually asexual, stage of a cnidarian. 269

polyphyletic group (pol-e-fi-let′ik) An assemblage of organisms that includes multiple evolutionary lineages. Polyphyletic assemblages usually reflect insufficient knowledge regarding the phylogeny of a group of organisms. 230

Polyplacophora (pol″e-pla-kof′o-rah)   The class of molluscs whose members are elongate and dorsoventrally flattened, and have a shell consisting of eight dorsal plates.   333

polyploidy (pol′e-ploi-de)   Having more than two sets of chromosomes (3*N*, 4*N*, and so forth).   110

polysaccharide (pol″e-sak′ah-rīd)   A carbohydrate composed of many monosaccharide molecules joined by dehydration synthesis reactions.   22

pons (ponz)   A portion of the brain stem above the medulla oblongata and below the midbrain.   561

population   A group of individuals of the same species that occupy a given area at the same time and share a unique set of genes.   164

population genetics   The study of genetic events in gene pools.   164

Porifera (po-rif′er-ah)   The animal phylum whose members are sessile and either asymmetrical or radially symmetrical. Body is organized around a system of water canals and chambers. Cells are not organized into tissues or organs. Sponges.   262

porocytes (por′o-sītz)   Tubular cells in sponge body wall that create a water channel to an interior chamber.   263

postanal tail (post-an′al)   A tail that extends posterior to the anus. One of the four unique characteristics of chordates.   428

postmating isolation (post-mat′ing i-sah-la′shun)   Isolation that occurs when fertilization and development are prevented, even though mating has occurred.   170

potential energy   The energy matter has by virtue of its position. Stored energy.   60

preadaptation (pre-ă-dap-ta′shun)   Occurs when a structure or a process present in members of a species proves useful in promoting reproductive success when an individual encounters new environmental situations.   366

precocial (pre-ko′shel)   Having developed to a high degree of independence at the time of hatching or birth.   500

predation (pre-da′shun)   The derivation of an organism of elements essential for its existence from organisms of other species that it consumes and destroys. The ingestion of prey by a predator for energy and nutrients.   635

preformation (pre-for-ma′shun)   The erroneous idea that gametes contain miniaturized versions of all of the elements present in an adult.   134

premating isolation (pre-mat′ing i-sah-la′shun)   Isolation that occurs when behaviors or other factors prevent animals from mating.   170

preoptic nuclei   Neurons in the hypothalamus that produce various neuropeptides (hormones).   592

Priapulida (pri′a-pyu-li-da)   A phylum of aschelminths commonly called priapulids.   314

primary consumer   A plant-eating animal (an herbivore) that obtains organic molecules by eating producers (autotrophs) or their products.   60

primary germ layers   Blocks or layers of embryonic cells that give rise to tissues and organs of animals. *See also* **ectoderm, mesoderm,** and **endoderm.**   138

primary immune response   The initial immune response following antigen exposure.   618

primary producer   An autotrophic organism that is able to build its own complex organic molecules from simple inorganic substances (CO_2, H_2O) in the environment.   60

Primates   The order of mammals whose members include humans, monkeys, apes, lemurs, and tarsiers.   508

primitive streak   A medial thickening along the dorsal margin of an amniote embryo that forms during the migration of endodermal and mesodermal cells into the interior of the embryo.   144

principle of independent assortment   One of Mendel's observations on the behavior of hereditary units (genes) during gamete formation. A modern interpretation of this principle is that genes carried in one chromosome are distributed to gametes without regard to the distribution of genes in nonhomologous chromosomes.   102

principle of segregation   One of Mendel's observations on the behavior of hereditary units (genes) during gamete formation. A modern interpretation of this principle is that genes exist in pairs, and during gamete formation, members of a pair of genes are distributed into separate gametes.   99

procercoid larva (pro-ser′koid lar′va)   Cestode developing from a coracidium in some orders. It usually has a posterior cercomer. Developmental stage between oncosphere and plerocercoid.   297

proglottid (pro-glot′id)   One set of reproductive organs in a tapeworm strobila. Usually corresponds to a segment. One of the linearly arranged segmentlike sections that make up the strobila of a tapeworm.   294

prokaryote (pro-kar′e-ōt)   Single-celled organism that has no membrane-bound nucleus or other membrane-enclosed organelles (e.g., bacteria). Found only in the kingdom Monera.   32

pronephros (pro-nef′res)   Most anterior of three pairs of embryonic renal organs of vertebrates. Functional only in larval amphibians and fishes, and in adult hagfishes. Vestigial in mammalian embryos.   667

prophase (pro′fāz)   The stage of mitosis during which the chromosomes become visible under a light microscope. The first stage of mitosis during which the chromosomes are condensed but not yet attached to a mitotic spindle.   87

proprioceptor (pro″pre-o-sep′tor)   A sensory nerve terminal that gives information concerning movements and positions of the body. They occur chiefly in the muscles, tendons, and the labyrinth of the mammalian ear and in the joints of arthropods.   572

prosoma (pro-so′mah)   A sensory, feeding, and locomotor tagma of chelicerate arthropods.   364

prostate gland (pros′tāt)   Gland around the male urethra below the urinary bladder that adds its secretions to seminal fluid during ejaculation.   683

prostomium (pro-stōm′e-um)   A lobe lying in front of the mouth, as found in the Annelida.   343

protandrous (pro-tan′drus)   *See also* **protandry.**

protandry (pro-tan′dre)   The condition in a monoecious (hermaphroditic) organism in which male gonads mature before female gametes. Prevents self-fertilization.   276, 680

protein (pro′tēn)   Nitrogen-containing organic compound composed of amino acid molecules joined by peptide bonds. The unique sequence of amino acids in the protein is the basis for the protein's three-dimensional structure and chemical behavior.   24

prothorax (pro-thor′aks)   The first of the three thoracic segments of an insect. Usually contains the first pair of walking appendages.   384

Protista (pro-tist′ah)   The kingdom whose members are eukaryotic and unicellular or colonial.   228

protogynous (pro-toj′ĭ-nus)   Hermaphroditism in which the female gonads mature before the male gonads.   680

proton (pro′ton)   A positively charged particle in the atomic nucleus. The mass of a proton is about 1,840 times that of an electron. 16

protonephridium (pro-to-ně-frid′e-um) Primitive osmoregulatory or excretory organ composed of a tubule terminating internally with a flame cell or solenocyte. The unit of a flame-cell system. Protonephridia are specialized for ultrafiltration.   289, 664

protopodite (pro″to-po′dīt)   The basal segment of a biramous appendage of a crustacean.   371

protostome (pro′to-stōm″)   Animal in which the embryonic blastopore becomes the mouth. Often possesses a trochophore larva, schizocoelous coelom formation, and spiral embryonic cleavage.   318

protostyle (pro′to-stīl″)   A rotating mucoid mass into which food is incorporated in the gut of a gastropod (phylum Mollusca).   323

protozoa (pro″to-zo′ah)   A subkingdom (formerly a phylum) comprising the simplest organisms called protista. Divided into seven phyla.   242

protozoologist (pro-to-zo-ol′-o-jist)   A person who studies protozoa.   244

proximal (proks′em-al)   Toward the point of attachment of a structure on an animal (e.g., the hip is proximal to the knee).   236

pseudocoel   *See also* **pseudocoelom.**

pseudocoelom (soo″do-se′lom)   A body cavity between the mesoderm and endoderm. A persistent blastocoele that is not lined with peritoneum. Also called **pseudocoel.**   237

pseudocoelomate (soo′do-sēl′o-māt)   Animals having a pseudocoelom, as the aschelminths.   303

pseudopodia (soo-dah-po′de-ah)   Temporary cytoplasmic extensions of amoebas or amoeboid cells that are used in feeding and locomotion. Sing., pseudopodium.   247, 541

Pterobranchia (ter″o-brang′ke-ah)   The class of hemichordates whose members lack gill slits and have two or more arms. Colonial, living in externally secreted encasements. 427

pulmonary circuit (pul′mo-ner″e)   The system of blood vessels from the right ventricle of the heart to the lungs, transporting deoxygenated blood and returning oxygenated blood from the lungs to the left atrium of the heart.   612

pulmonate lung (pul′mon-āt)   The gas exchange structure in the Pulmonata—the land snails and slugs.   620

punctuated equilibrium model (pungk′choo-āt″ed e″kwě-lib′re-ahm)   The idea that evolutionary change can occur rapidly over thousands of years and that these periods of rapid change are interrupted by periods of constancy (stasis).   172

Punnett square   A tool geneticists use to predict the results of a genetic cross. Different kinds of gametes that each parent produces are placed on each axis of the square. Combining gametes in the interior of the square gives the results of random fertilization.   100

pupa (pu′pah)   A nonfeeding immature stage in the life cycle of holometabolous insects. It is a time of radical cellular changes that result in a change from the larval to the adult body form.   391

puparium (pu-par′e-um)   A pupal case formed from the last larval exoskeleton. *See also* **pupa.**   391

purine (pyoor′ēn)   A nitrogen-containing organic compound that contributes to the structure of a DNA or RNA nucleotide. Uric acid is also derived from purines.   120

Pycnogonida (pik″no-gon′ĭ-dah)   The class of chelicerate arthropods whose members have a reduced abdomen and four to six pairs of walking legs. Without special respiratory or excretory structures. Sea spiders.   370

pygostyle (pig′o-stīl)   The fused posterior caudal vertebrae of a bird. Helps support tail feathers that are important in steering.   492

pyramid of biomass   A representation showing the total mass of living matter in each trophic level of an ecosystem.   211

pyramid of energy   A representation showing the total energy in each trophic level of an ecosystem.   211

pyramid of numbers   A representation showing the number of individuals in each trophic level of an ecosystem.   211

pyrenoid (pi-re′noid)   Part of the chloroplast that synthesizes and stores polysaccharides.   246

pyrimidine (pi-rim′i-děn)   A nitrogen-containing organic compound that is a component of the nucleotides making up DNA and RNA.   120

Q

quantitative trait   A genetic trait that is determined by multiple interacting loci, and for which there is a range of phenotypes between phenotypic extremes.   104

R

radial symmetry   A form of symmetry in which any plane passing through the oral-aboral axis divides an organism into mirror images.   234

radiation (ra″de-a′shun)   A form of energy that includes visible light, ultraviolet light, and X rays. Means by which body heat is lost in the form of infrared rays.   657

radioisotope (ra″de-o-i′so-tōp)   An isotope that is radioactive (i.e., has an unstable nucleus), which gives it the property of decay by one or more of several processes. Also called a radioactive isotope.   17

radula (raj′oo-lah)   The rasping, tonguelike structure of most molluscs that is used for scraping food. Composed of minute chitinous teeth that move over a cartilaginous odontophore.   321

ram ventilation   The movement of water across gills as a fish swims through the water with its mouth open.   446

range of optimum   The range of values for a condition in the environment that is best able to support survival and reproduction of an organism.   192

receptor-mediated endocytosis (re-cep′tor-me′de-āt-ed en″do-si-to′sis)   The type of endocytosis that involves a specific receptor on the plasma membrane that recognizes an extracellular molecule and binds with it.   43

recessive   A gene whose expression is masked when it is present in combination with a dominant allele. For a recessive gene to be expressed, both members of the gene pair must be the recessive form of the gene. 99

recombinant DNA (re-kom′bě-nant)   The incorporation of DNA from one organism into that of another organism (usually a bacteria) so that the second organism produces a desired protein.   128

rectal gland (rek′tel)   The excretory organ of elasmobranchs and the coelacanth near the rectum. It excretes a hyperosmotic salt (NaCl) solution.   668

red blood cell (erythrocyte)   The type of blood cell that contains hemoglobin and no nucleus. During their formation in mammals, erythrocytes lose their nuclei. Those of other vertebrates retain the nuclei.   609

redia (re′de-ah)   A larval, digenetic trematode produced by asexual reproduction within a miracidium, sporocyst, or mother redia.   292

redox reaction   *See also* **oxidation-reduction reaction.**

reduction   The gain of electrons by a compound.   72

refractory period (re-frak′ter-e)   Time period following stimulation during which a neuron or muscle fiber cannot respond to a stimulus.   554

regulator genes   Genes that control the activity of other genes that code for enzymes or structural proteins.   125

releaser gland   A gland in turbellarians that secretes a chemical that dissolves the organism's attachment to a substrate.   287

Remipedia (re-mi-pe′de-ah)   A class of crustaceans whose members possess about 30 body segments and uniform, biramous appendages. This class contains a single species of cave-dwelling crustaceans from the Bahamas.   362

renette (re′net)   An excretory structure in some worms.   309

repolarized (re-po′ler-īzd)   The reestablishment of polarity, especially the return of plasma membrane potential to resting potential after depolarization.   554

reproductive isolation   Occurs when individuals are prevented from mating, even though they may occupy overlapping ranges. *See also* **premating** and **postmating isolation.**   170

Reptilia (rep-til′e-ah)   The class of vertebrates whose members have dry skin with epidermal scales and amniotic eggs that develop in terrestrial environments. Snakes, lizards, and alligators.   426

resilin (rez′ĭ-lin)   The elastic protein in some arthropod joints that stores energy and functions in jumping.   537

respiratory pigment   Organic compounds that have either metallic copper or iron with which oxygen combines.   626

respiratory tree   A pair of tubules attached to the rectum of a sea cucumber that branch through the body cavity and function in gas exchange.   411

resting membrane potential   The potential difference that results from the separation of charges along the plasma membrane of a neuron or other excitable cell. The steady voltage difference across the plasma membrane.   553

rete mirabile (re′te ma-rab′a-le)   A network of small blood vessels arranged so that the incoming blood runs countercurrent to the outgoing blood and, thus, makes possible efficient exchange of heat or gases between the two bloodstreams. An extensive countercurrent arrangement of arterial and venous capillaries.   659

reticulopodium (re-tik″u-lo-po′de-um)   A pseudopodium that forms a threadlike branched mesh and contains axial microtubules. Pl., reticulopodia.   248

rhabdite (rab′dīt)   A rodlike structure in the cells of the epidermis or underlying parenchyma in certain tubellarians that discharged in mucous secretions, possibly in response to attempted predation or desiccation.   287

rhodopsin (ro-dop′sin)   Light-sensitive substance in the rods of the retina. Visual purple.   582

rhopalium (ro-pal′e-um)   A sensory structure at the margin of the scyphozoan medusa. It consists of a statocyst and a photoreceptor (phylum Cnidaria).   273

rhynchocoel (ring′ko-sēl)   In nemerteans, the fluid-filled coelomic cavity that contains the inverted proboscis.   298

ribonucleic acid (RNA) (ri″bo-nu-kle′ik)   A single-stranded polymer of ribonucleotides. RNA forms from DNA in the nucleus and carries a code for proteins to ribosomes, where proteins are synthesized. Contains the nitrogenous bases adenine (A), cytosine (C), guanine (G), and uracil (U).   26, 120

ribosomal RNA (rRNA) (ri″bo-sōm′al)   A form of ribonucleic acid that makes up a portion of ribosomes.   122

ribosome (ri′-bo-sōm)   Cytoplasmic organelle that consists of protein and RNA, and functions in protein synthesis.   44

ribozyme (ri′bo-zīm)   An RNA enzyme.   62

rod cell   A type of light receptor that is sensitive to dim light.   581

Rotifera (ro-tif′er-ah)   The phylum of aschelminths that has members with a ciliated corona surrounding a mouth. Muscular pharynx (mastax) present with jawlike features. Nonchitinous cuticle. Parthenogenesis common. Both freshwater and marine species.   304

r-selected   Populations that are maintained below the carrying capacity of the environment.   196

S

saliva (sah-li′vah)   The enzyme-containing secretion of the salivary glands.   646

saltatory conduction (sal′tah-tor-e konduk′shun)   A type of nerve impulse conduction in which the impulse seems to jump from one neurofibril node to the next.   554

salt gland   An orbital gland of many reptiles and birds that secretes a hyperosmotic NaCl or KCl solution. An important osmoregulatory organ, especially for marine species.   671

Sarcodina (sar″ko-din′ah)   The protozoan subphylum whose members have pseudopodia for movement and food gathering. Naked or with shell or test. Mostly free living.   247

sarcolemma (sar″ko-lem′ah)   The plasma membrane of a muscle fiber.   547

Sarcomastigophora (sar″ko-mas-ti-gof′o-rah)   The protozoan phylum whose members possess flagella, pseudopodia, or both for locomotion and feeding. Single type of nucleus.   246

sarcomere (sar′ko-mer)   The contractile unit of a myofibril. The repeating units, delimited by the Z bands along the length of the myofibril.   546

scale   A thin, compacted, flaky fragment. One of the thin, flat, horny plates forming the covering of certain animals (snakes, fishes, lizards).   532

scalid (sca′lid)   A set of complex spines found on the kinorhynchs, loriciferans, priapulans, and larval nematomorphs, with sensory, locomotor, food capture, or penetrant function.   306

scanning electron microscope (SEM)   The type of microscope in which an electron beam, instead of light, forms a three-dimensional image for viewing, allowing much greater magnification and resolution.   36

scanning tunneling microscope (STM) The type of microscope that uses a needle probe and electrons to determine the surface features of specimens. 36

Scaphopoda (ska-fop′o-dah) A class of molluscs whose members have a tubular shell that is open at both ends. Possess tentacles but no head. Example: *Dentalium*. 333

scent gland A gland around the feet, face, or anus of many mammals. Secretes pheromones, which may be involved with defense, species and sex recognition, and territorial behavior. Musk gland. 510

schizogony (skiz-og′on-e) A form of fission (asexual reproduction) involving multiple nuclear divisions and the formation of many individuals from the parental organism. Occurs in the class Sporozoea. *See also* **multiple fission** and **merogony**. 251

Schwann cell *See also* **neurolemmocyte.**

scientific method An objective system of thought and procedure that reflects how a scientist goes about defining and studying a problem. 11

scolex (sko′leks) The attachment or holdfast organ of a tapeworm, generally considered the anterior end. It is used to adhere to the host. 295

scrotum (skro′tum) A pouch of skin that encloses the testes. 683

scyphistoma (si-fis′to-mah) The polyp stage of a scyphozoan (phylum Cnidaria). Develops from a planula and produces ephyrae by budding. 274

Scyphozoa (si″fo-zo′ah) A class of cnidarians whose members have prominent medusae. Gametes are gastrodermal in origin and are released to the gastrovascular cavity. Nematocysts are present in the gastrodermis. Polyps are small. Example: *Aurelia*. 273

sebaceous (oil) gland (se-ba′shus) Gland of the skin that secretes sebum. Oil gland. 510, 534

sebum (se′bum) Oily secretion from the sebaceous gland. 534

Secernentea (ses-er-nen′te-ah) The class of nematodes formerly called Phasmidea. Examples: *Ascaris, Enterobius, Necator, Wuchereria*. 307

secondary consumer An animal that preys on and eats a primary consumer. 60

secondary immune response The immune response that follows a second exposure to a specific antigen. 618

secondary palate (pal′et) A plate of bone that separates the nasal and oral cavities of mammals and some reptiles. 479

second law of thermodynamics (ther″mo-di-nam′iks) Physical and chemical processes proceed in such a way that the entropy of the universe (the system and its surroundings) increases to the maximum possible. The spontaneous direction of energy flow is from organized (high-quality) to less organized (low-quality) forms. 61

segmentation (seg″men-ta′shun) 1. In many animal species, a series of body units that may be externally similar to, or quite different from, one another. 2. The oscillating back-and-forth movement in the small intestine that mixes food with digestive secretions and increases the efficiency of absorption. 646

Seisonidea (sy″son-id′e-ah) A class of rotifers with members that are commensals of crustaceans. Large and elongate body with rounded corona. Example: *Seison*. 305

selection pressure The tendency for natural selection to occur. Natural selection occurs whenever some genotypes are more fit than other genotypes. 168

selective permeability (sĭ-lek′tiv per″me-ah-bil′ĭ-te) The ability of the plasma membrane to let some substances in and keep others out. 38

semen (se′men) The thick, whitish secretion of the reproductive organs in the male; composed of sperm and secretions from the prostate, seminal vesicles, and various other glands and ducts. Fluid containing sperm. 683

seminal receptacle (sem′ĭ-nal rĭ-sep′tah-kl) A structure in the female reproductive system that stores sperm received during copulation (e.g., in many insects and annelids). 350

seminal vesicle (sem′ĭ-nal ves′ĭ-kl) 1. One of the paired accessory glands of the reproductive tract of male mammals. It secretes the fluid medium for sperm ejaculation (phylum Chordata). 2. A structure associated with the male reproductive tract that stores sperm prior to its release (e.g., in earthworms—phylum Annelida). 350, 683

seminiferous tubule (se″mĭ-nif′er-us tu′bŭl) The male duct that produces sperm. Highly convoluted tube in testis. 683

sensilla (sen-cil′ah) Modifications of the arthropod exoskeleton that, along with nerve cells, form sensory receptors. 569

sensory (receptor or afferent) neuron or **nerve** A neuron or nerve that conducts an impulse from a receptor organ to the central nervous system. 552, 559

sequential hermaphroditism (sĭ-kwen′shal her-maf′ro-di-tizm) The type of hermaphroditism that occurs when an animal is one sex during one phase of its life cycle and an opposite sex during another phase. 680

seral stage (ser′al) A successional stage in an ecosystem. 207

sere (ser) An entire successional sequence in an ecosystem (e.g., the sequence of stages in the succession of a lake to a climax forest). 207

serially homologous (ser′e-al-e ho-mol′o-ges) Metameric structures that have evolved from a common form. The biramous appendages of crustaceans are serially homologous. 372

serum (se′rum) The fluid portion of coagulated blood. The protein component of plasma. 608

setae (se′tah) Hairlike modifications of an arthropod's exoskeleton that may be set into a membranous socket. Displacement of a seta initiates a nerve impulse in an associated cell. 343

sex chromosome A chromosome that carries genes determining the genetic sex of an individual. 108

sex-influenced trait Traits that behave as if they are dominant in one sex but recessive in the other sex. 113

sexual reproduction The generation of a new cell or organism by the fusion of two haploid cells so that genes are inherited from each parent. 680

shell The calcium carbonate outer layer of cnidarians, molluscs, and other animals. Produced by mucous glands. 531

shivering thermogenesis (ther″mo-jen′e-sis) The generation of heat by shivering, especially within the animal body. 661

Simphyla (sim-fi′lah) A class of arthropods whose members are characterized by having long antennae, 10 to 12 pairs of legs, and centipede-like bodies. Occupy soil and leaf mold. 382

simple diffusion (dĭ-fu′zhun) The process of molecules spreading out randomly from where they are more concentrated to where they are less concentrated until they are evenly distributed. 38

siphon (si'fon)   A tubular structure through which fluid flows. Siphons of some molluscs allow water to enter and leave the mantle cavity.   324

Sipuncula (si-pun'kyu-lah)   A phylum of protostomate worms whose members burrow in soft marine substrates throughout the world's oceans. Range in length from 2 mm to 75 cm. Peanut worms.   358

sister chromatid (kro'mah-tid)   One of the two identical parts of a duplicated chromosome in a eukaryotic cell. Sister chromatids are exact copies of a long, coiled DNA molecule with associated proteins. Sister chromatids join at the centromere of a duplicated chromosome.   86

skeletal muscle   Type of muscle tissue in muscles attached to skeletal parts.   542

skin   The outer integument or covering of an animal body, consisting of the dermis and the epidermis and resting on the subcutaneous tissues.   531

small intestine   The part of the digestive system consisting of the duodenum, jejunum, and ileum.   648

smooth muscle   Type of muscle tissue in the walls of hollow organs. Visceral muscle.   541

society   A stable group of individuals of the same species that maintains a cooperative social relationship.   186

sociobiology (so"se-o-bi-ol'o-je)   The study of the evolution of social behavior.   179

sodium-potassium ATPase pump   The active transport mechanism that concentrates sodium ions on the outside of a plasma membrane and potassium ions on the inside of the membrane.   554

somatic cell (so-mat'ik)   Ordinary body cell. Pertaining to or characteristic of a body cell. Any cell other than a germ cell or germ-cell precursor.   90

somites (so'mītz)   Segmental thickenings along the side of a vertebrate embryo that result from the development of mesoderm.   143

sonar (so'nar) or **biosonar**   A system that uses sound at sonic or ultrasonic frequencies to detect and locate objects.   578

specialists   Animals that are efficient at utilizing a particular food or other resource.   186

speciation (spe"she-a'shun)   The process by which two or more species form from a single ancestral stock.   170

species   A group of populations in which genes are actually, or potentially, exchanged through multiple generations. Numerous problems with this definition make it difficult to apply in all circumstances.   170, 227

species diversity   *See also* **community diversity.**

spermatogenesis (sper"mah-to-jen'ĕ-sis)   The production of sperm cells.   93

spermatophores (sper-mat'ah-fors)   Encapsulated sperm that a male can deposit on a substrate for a female to pick up or that a male can transfer directly to a female.   332

sphincter (sfingk'ter)   A ringlike band of muscle fibers that constricts a passage or closes a natural orifice. Acts as a valve.   646

spicules (spik'ūlz)   Skeletal elements that some mesenchyme cells of a sponge body wall secrete. May be made of calcium carbonate or silica.   265

spiracle (spi'rah-kel)   An opening for ventilation. The opening(s) of the tracheal system of an arthropod or an opening posterior to the eye of a shark, skate, or ray.   366

spongin (spun'jin)   A fibrous protein that makes up the supportive framework of some sponges.   265

sporocyst (spor'o-sist)   1. Stage of development of a sporozoan protozoan, usually with an enclosing membrane, the oocyst. 2. An asexual stage of development in some digenean trematodes that arises from a miracidium and gives rise to rediae.   292

sporogony (spor-og'ah-ne)   Multiple fission that produces sporozoites after zygote formation. Occurs in the class Sporozoea.   251

stabilizing selection   Natural selection that results in the decline of both extremes in a phenotypic range. Results in a narrowing of the phenotypic range.   169

statocyst (stat'o-sist)   An organ of equilibrium and balance in many invertebrates. Statocysts usually consist of a fluid-filled cavity containing sensory hairs and a mineral mass called a statolith. The statolith stimulates the sensory hairs, which helps orient the animal to the pull of gravity.   271, 569

statolith   *See also* **statocyst.**

steroid (ster'oid)   An organic substance (lipid) whose molecules include four complex rings of carbon and hydrogen atoms. Examples are estrogen, cholesterol, and testosterone.   24

stigma (stig'mah)   1. The mass of bright red photoreceptor granules found in certain flagellated protozoa (*Euglena*) that shields the photoreceptor. 2. The spiracle of certain terrestrial arthropods.   246, 570

stimulus (stim'u-lus)   Any form of energy an animal can detect with its receptors.   568

stimulus filter (stim'u-lus)   The ability of the nervous system to block incoming stimuli that are unimportant for the animal.   182

stomach   The expansion of the alimentary canal between the esophagus and duodenum.   648

strobila (stro-bi'lah)   The chain of proglottids constituting the bulk of the body of adult tapeworms.   295

structural genes   Genes that code for enzymes or structural proteins, rather than proteins that control the function of other genes.   125

substrate (sub'strāt)   The substance or molecule upon which an enzyme acts. A reactant or precursor molecule for a metabolic reaction.   62

substrate-level phosphorylation (sub'strāt-lev'el fos"for-ĭ-la'shun)   ATP generation by coupling strongly exergonic reactions with ATP synthesis from ADP and phosphate.   65

succession   The sequence of community types during the maturation of an ecosystem.   206

sudoriferous gland (su"do-rif'er-us)   A sweat gland.   510, 534

superior   Above a point of reference (e.g., the neck is superior to the chest of humans).   236

suspension feeder   The type of feeding whereby an animal obtains its nutrients by removing suspended food particles from the surrounding water by some sort of capturing, trapping, or filtering structure. Examples include tube worms and barnacles. Also, **suspension feeding.**   634

swim bladder   A gas-filled sac, usually along the dorsal body wall of bony fishes. It is an outgrowth of the digestive tract and regulates buoyancy of a fish.   444

sycon (si'kon)   A sponge body form characterized by choanocytes lining radial canals.   265

symbiosis (sim"bi-o'sis)   The biological association of two individuals or populations of different species, classified as mutualism, commensalism, or parasitism, depending on the advantage or disadvantage derived from the relationship.   198, 244

symmetry (sim′ĭ-tre)   A balanced arrangement of similar parts on either side of a common point or axis.   234

sympathetic nervous system (sim″pah-thet′ik)   Portion of the autonomic nervous system that arises from the thoracic and lumbar regions of the spinal cord. Also called thoracolumbar division.   562

sympatric speciation (sim-pat′rik spe″she-a′shun)   Speciation that occurs in populations that have overlapping ranges.   171

symplesiomorphies (sim-ples″e-o-mor′fēz)   Taxonomic characters that are common to all members of a group of organisms. These characters indicate common ancestry but cannot be used to describe relationships within the group.   232

synapomorphies (sin-ap′o-mor″fēz)   Characters that have arisen within a group since it diverged from a common ancestor. Synapomorphies indicate degrees of relatedness within a group. Also called **shared, derived characters.**   232

synapse (sin′aps)   The junction between the axon end of one neuron and the dendrite or cell body of another neuron or effector cell.   555

synapsis (sĭ-nap′sis)   The time in reduction division when the pairs of homologous chromosomes lie alongside each other in the first meiotic division.   91

synaptic cleft (sĭ-nap′tik)   The narrow space between the terminal ending of a neuron and the receptor site of the postsynaptic cell.   555

synchronous flight   *See also* **direct flight.**

syncytial hypothesis (sin-sit′e-al hi-poth′ĕ-sis)   The idea that multicellular organisms could have arisen by the formation of plasma membranes within a large, multinucleate protist.   260

syngamy (sin′gah-me)   The fertilization of one gamete with another individual gamete to form a zygote. Found in most animals that have sexual reproduction.   90

synsacrum (sin-sak′rum)   The fused posterior thoracic vertebrae, all lumbar and sacral vertebrae, and anterior caudal vertebrae of a bird. Helps maintain proper flight posture.   492

syrinx (sir′ingks)   The vocal apparatus of a bird. Located near the point where the trachea divides into two bronchi.   496

systematics (sis-tem-at′iks)   The study of the classification and phylogeny of organisms. *See also* **taxonomy.**   227

systemic circuit (sis-tem′ik)   The portion of the circulatory system concerned with blood flow from the left ventricle of the heart to the entire body and back to the heart via the right atrium.   612

systole (sis′to-le)   Phase of the cardiac cycle during which a heart chamber wall contracts. *See also* **systolic pressure.**   614

systolic pressure (sis-tol′ik)   The portion of blood pressure measurement that represents the highest pressure reached during ventricular ejection. It is the first number shown in a blood-pressure reading.   614

T

T cell   A type of lymphocyte, derived from bone marrow stem cells, that matures into an immunologically competent cell under the influence of the thymus. T cells are involved in a variety of cell-mediated immune reactions. Also known as a T lymphocyte.   610

tactile (touch) receptor (tak′tīl rĭ-sep′ter)   A sensory receptor in the skin that detects light pressure. Formerly called Meissner's corpuscle.   572

tagmatization (tag″mah-ti-za′shun)   The specialization of body regions of a metameric animal for specific functions. The head of an arthropod is specialized for feeding and sensory functions, the thorax is specialized for locomotion, and the abdomen is specialized for visceral functions.   342

Tardigrada (tar-di-gra′dah)   A phylum of animals whose members live in marine and freshwater sediments and in water films on terrestrial lichens and mosses. Possess four pairs of unsegmented legs and a proteinaceous cuticle. Water bears.   400

target cell   The cell a specific hormone influences.   587

taste bud   The receptor organs in the tongue that are stimulated and give rise to the sense of taste.   580

taxis (tak′sis)   The movement of an organism in a particular direction in response to an environmental stimulus.   192

taxon (tak′son)   A group of organisms that are genetically (evolutionarily) related.   227

taxonomy (tak″son′ah-me)   The description of species and the classification of organisms into groups that reflect evolutionary relation-

ships. *See also* **phylogenetic systematics, evolutionary systematics,** and **numerical taxonomy.** *Also* **systematics.**   227

tegument (teg′u-ment)   The external epithelial covering in cestodes, trematodes, and acanthocephalans. Once called a cuticle.   291, 531

telophase (tel′o-fāz)   Stage in mitosis during which daughter cells become separate structures. The two sets of separated chromosomes decondense, and nuclear envelopes enclose them.   89

temperate deciduous forest (tem′per-it dĭ-sij′oo-es)   An ecosystem that occurs in regions with moderate climate and well-defined seasons. Deciduous trees predominate. Animals include insects, white-tailed deer, and wolves.   215

tendon (ten′den)   A cord or bandlike mass of white, fibrous connective tissue that connects a muscle to a bone or to another muscle.   545

Tentaculata (ten-tak′u-lah-tah)   The class of ctenophorans with tentacles that may or may not be associated with sheaths into which tentacles can be retracted. Example: *Pleurobranchia.*   279

territory   An area defended by an animal. Territories are established to provide food, shelter, or reproductive space.   187

test   A shell or hardened outer covering, typically covered externally by cytoplasm or living tissue.   249

testcross   A cross between an individual of an unknown genotype and an individual that is homozygous recessive for the trait in question to determine the unknown genotype.   102

testis (tes′tis)   Primary reproductive organ of a male. A sperm-cell producing organ.   683

testosterone (tes-tos′tĕ-rōn)   Male sex hormone that the interstitial cells of the testes secrete.   684

tetrad (tet′rad)   A pair of homologous chromosomes during synapsis (prophase I of meiosis). A tetrad consists of four chromatids.   91

tetrapod (tĕ′trah-pod)   A nontaxonomic designation for amphibians, reptiles, birds, and mammals.   456

thalamus (thal′ah-mus)   An oval mass of gray matter within the diencephalon that is a sensory relay area.   561

Thaliacea (tal″e-as′e-ah)   A class of urochordates whose members are planktonic.

Adults are tailless and barrel shaped. Oral and atrial openings are at opposite ends of the tunicate. Water currents are produced by muscular contractions of the body wall and result in a weak form of jet propulsion. 426

theory A generalized statement that accounts for a body of facts and that can be used in a predictive fashion. 12

theory of evolution by natural selection A theory conceived by Charles Darwin and Alfred Russel Wallace on how some evolutionary changes occur. *See also* **natural selection.** 153

theory of inheritance of acquired characteristics The mistaken idea that organisms develop new organs, or modify existing organs, as environmental problems present themselves and that these traits are passed to offspring. 153

thermoconformer (ther″mo-con-form′er) To conform to the temperature of the external environment. 658

thermodynamics (ther″mo-di-nam′iks) The branch of science that deals with heat, energy, and the interconversion of these. The study of energy transformations. 60

thermogenesis (ther″mo-jen′ah-sis) The metabolic generation of heat by muscle contraction or brown fat metabolism. 661

thermoreceptor (ther″mo-re-sep′tor) A sensory receptor that is sensitive to changes in temperature. A heat receptor. 572

thermoregulation (ther″mo-reg″u-la′shun) Heat regulation. Involves the nervous, endocrine, respiratory, and circulatory systems in higher animals. 656

threatened species A species that is likely to become endangered in the near future. *See also* **endangered species.** 27

thrombocyte *See also* **platelet.**

thymus gland (thi′mus) A ductless mass of flattened lymphoid tissue behind the top of the sternum. It forms antibodies in the newborn and is involved in the development of the immune system. 601

thyroid gland (thi′roid) An endocrine gland in the neck of vertebrates and involved with the metabolic functions of the body. Produces thyroxins. 599

tissue (tish′u) A group of similar cells that performs a specialized function. 50

tolerance range The range of variation in an environmental parameter that is compatible with the life of an organism. 192

tonicity (to-nis′ĭ-te) The state of tissue tone or tension. In body fluid physiology, the effective osmotic pressure equivalent. 39

tornaria (tor-nar′e-ah) The ciliated larval stage of an acorn worm (class Enteropneusta, phylum Hemichordata). 426

torpor (tor′per) A time of decreased metabolism and lowered body temperature in daily activity cycles. 193

torsion (tor′shun) A developmental twisting of the visceral mass of a gastropod mollusc that results in an anterior opening of the mantle cavity and a twisting of nerve cords and the digestive tract. 322

tracheae (tra′che-e) The small tubes that carry air from spiracles through the body cavity of an arthropod. Arthropod tracheae are modifications of the exoskeleton. 366

tracheal system *See also* **tracheae.**

tract A bundle of nerve fibers within the central nervous system. 559

transcription (tran-skrip′shun) The formation of a messenger RNA molecule that carries the genetic code from the nucleus to the cytoplasm of a cell. 122

transducer (trans-du′ser) A receptor that converts one form of energy into another. 568

transfer RNA (tRNA) (trans′fer) A single-stranded polyribonucleotide that carries amino acids to a ribosome and positions those amino acids by matching the tRNA anticodon with the messenger RNA codon. 122

transgenic (tranz-gen′ik) An animal that develops from a cell that received a foreign gene. 130

translation (trans-la′shun) The production of a protein based on the code in messenger RNA. 122

translocation (trans-lo-ka′shun) The movement of a segment of one chromosome to a nonhomologous chromosome. 114

transmission electron microscope (TEM) The type of microscope that produces highly magnified images of ultrathin tissue sections or other specimens by using electron beams. 36

Trematoda (trem″ah-to′dah) The class of Platyhelminthes with members that are all parasitic. Several holdfast devices are present. Complicated life cycles involve both sexual and asexual reproduction. 291

trichinosis (trik″ĭ-no′sis) A disease resulting from infection by *Trichinella spiralis* (Ne-

matoda) larvae from eating undercooked meat. Characterized by muscular pain, fever, edema, and other symptoms. 311

trichocyst (trik′o-sist) A protective structure in the ectoplasm of some ciliates. A bottle-shaped extrusible organelle of the ciliate pellicle. 253

Trilobitamorpha (tri″lo-bit″a-mor′fah) The subphylum of arthropods whose members had bodies divided into three longitudinal lobes. Head, thorax, and abdomen were present. One pair of antennae and biramous appendages. Entirely extinct. 363

triploblastic (trip″lo-blas′tik) Animals whose body parts are organized into layers that are derived embryologically from three tissue layers: ectoderm, mesoderm, and endoderm. Platyhelminthes and all coelomate animals are triploblastic. 236

trochophore larva (trok′o-for lar′va) A larval stage characteristic of many molluscs, annelids, and some other protostomate animals. 318

trophic level (trōf′ik) The feeding level of an organism in an ecosystem. Green plants and other autotrophs function at producer trophic levels. Animals function at the consumer trophic levels. 207

tropical rain forest An ecosystem characterized by high rainfall and temperatures between 20 and 25° C. Very diverse life-forms; broad-leaved, nondeciduous trees; and a highly stratified forest are also characteristic. 216

tube feet Muscular projections from the water-vascular system of echinoderms that are used in locomotion, gas exchange, feeding, and attachment. 403

tubular nerve cord A hollow nerve cord that runs middorsally along the back of chordates. One of four unique chordate characteristics. Also called the neural tube and, in vertebrates, the spinal cord. 428

tundra (tun′drah) An ecosystem that exists in far northern reaches of North America or at high altitudes. Mosses, lichens, grasses, and shrubs predominate. Rodents, musk oxen, caribou, owls, foxes, and weasels are common. 214

Turbellaria (tur″bel-lar′e-ah) The class of Platyhelminthes with members that are mostly free living and aquatic. External surface usually ciliated. Predaceous. Possess rhabdites. Protrusable proboscis. Mostly hermaphroditic. Examples: *Convoluta, Notoplana, Dugesia*. 287

tympanic (tympanal) organs (tim-pan'ik) Auditory receptors present on the abdomen or legs of some insects. 388, 570

U

ultimobranchial gland (ul"ti-mo-bronk'e-el) In jawed fishes, primitive tetrapods, and birds, the small gland(s) that forms ventral to the esophagus. Produces the hormone calcitonin that helps regulate calcium concentrations. 593

umbilical cord (um-bil'ĭ-kal) Cordlike structure that connects the fetus to the placenta. 693

umbo (um'bo) The rounded prominence at the anterior margin of the hinge of a bivalve (Mollusca) shell. It is the oldest part of the shell. 325

unicellular (cytoplasmic) organization The life-form in which all functions are carried out within the confines of a single plasma membrane. Members of the kingdom Protista display unicellular organization. Also called **cytoplasmic organization.** 235

uniformitarianism (u"nah-for"mĭ-tar'e-an-ism) The idea that forces of wind, rain, rivers, volcanoes, and geological uplift shape the earth today, just as they have in the past. 155

Uniramia (u"ne-ram'e-ah) The subphylum of arthropods whose members are characterized by a head with one pair of antennae and one pair of mandibles. All appendages are uniramous. 382

ureotelic excretion (u"re-o-tel'ik eks-kre'shun) Having urea as the chief excretory product of nitrogen metabolism. Occurs in mammals. 668

ureter (u-re'ter) The tube that conveys urine from the kidney to the bladder. 675

urethra (u-re'thrah) The tube that conveys urine from the bladder to the exterior of the body. 675

uricotelic excretion (u'ri-ko-tel"ik eks-kre'shun) Having uric acid as the chief excretory product of nitrogen metabolism. Occurs in reptiles and birds. 668

urinary bladder (u'ri-ner"e blad'er) The storage organ for urine. 675

Urochordata (u"ro-kor-da'tah) The subphylum of chordates whose members have all four chordate characteristics as larvae. Adults are sessile or planktonic and enclosed in a tunic that usually contains cellulose. Sea squirts or tunicates. 428

urophysis (u"ro-fi'sis) A discrete structure in the spinal cord of the fish tail that produces neuropeptides (hormones) that help control water and ion balance, blood pressure, and smooth muscle contractions. 592

uterine tube (u'ter-in) The tube that leads from the ovary to the uterus and transports the ovum or egg(s). Also called **fallopian tube.** 686

uterus (u'ter-us) The hollow, muscular organ in female mammals in which the fertilized ovum normally becomes embedded and in which the developing embryo/fetus is nourished. 688

V

vaccine (vak-sēn') A preparation of either killed microorganisms; living, weakened (attenuated) microorganisms; or inactivated bacterial toxins (toxoids) administered to induce development of the immune response and protect the individual against a pathogen or toxin. 616

vacuole (vak'u-ōl) Any small membrane-bound space or cavity formed in the protoplasm of a cell. Functions in either food storage or water expulsion. 49

vagina (vah-ji'nah) Tubular organ that leads from the uterus to the vestibule of the female reproductive tract. Receptacle for the penis during copulation. 688

valves 1. Devices that permit a one-way flow of fluids through a vessel or chamber. 2. The halves of a bivalve (Mollusca) shell. 325

variable A parameter in an experiment that may change, either intentionally or through oversight. 11

vegetal pole (vě'jĕ-tl) The lower pole of an egg. Usually more dense than the animal pole because it contains more yolk. 136

vein A vessel that carries blood toward the heart from the various organs. 611

veliger larva (vel'i-jer lar'va) The second free-swimming larval stage of many molluscs. Develops from the trochophore and forms rudiments of the shell, visceral mass, and head-foot before settling to the substrate and undergoing metamorphosis. 324

ventral The belly of an animal. Usually the lower surface. Synonymous with anterior for animals that walk upright. 236

venule (ven'yūl) A small blood vessel that collects blood from a capillary bed and joins a vein. 611

Vertebrata (ver"te-bra'tah) The subphylum of chordates whose members are characterized by cartilaginous or bony vertebrae surrounding a nerve cord. The skeleton is modified anteriorly into a skull for protection of the brain. 426

vestigial structures (vě-stij'e-al) Visible evidence of a structure that was present in an earlier stage in the evolution of an organism. One of the sources of evidence for evolution. 6

vibrissa (vi-bris'ah) A long, coarse hair, such as those occurring about the nose (muzzle) of a dog or cat. A sensor for mechanical stimuli. 578

villus (vil'us) Tiny, fingerlike projection that extends outward from the inner lining of the small intestine and increases the surface area for absorption. 648

visceral arches *See also* **gill arches.**

visceral mass (vis'er-al) The region of a mollusc's body that contains visceral organs. 320

vitamin An organic substance other than a carbohydrate, lipid, or protein that is needed for normal metabolism but that the body cannot synthesize in adequate amounts. 632

viviparous (vi-vip'er-us) Organisms with eggs that develop within the female reproductive tract and that are nourished by the female. 368

voluntary (somatic) nervous system That part of the nervous system that relays commands to skeletal muscles. 559

vomeronasal organ *See also* **Jacobson's organ.**

vulva (vul'vah) The external genital organs in the female. 688

W

water-vascular system (wah'ter vas'ku-ler) A series of water-filled canals and muscular tube feet in echinoderms. Provides the basis for locomotion, food gathering, and attachment. 403, 543

white blood cell (leukocyte) A type of blood cell involved with body defenses. 609

winter sleep A period of inactivity in which a mammal's body temperature remains near normal and the mammal is easily aroused. 193, 517

work The exertion or effort needed to accomplish something. 60

Y

yolk plug   The large, yolk-filled cells that protrude from beneath the ectoderm at the blastopore of the amphibian gastrula.   142

yolk sac   The stored food reserve (yolk) and its surrounding membranes. Found in embryonic reptiles, birds, and mammals.   144

Z

zonite (zo-'nīt)   The individual body unit of a member of the phylum Kinorhyncha.   306

zooid (zo'oid)   An individual member of a colony of animals, such as colonial cnidarians and ectoprocts, produced by incomplete budding or fission.   290

zoology (zo-ol'-o-je)   The study of animals. 3

Zoomastigophorea (zo″o-mas-ti-go-for'ah) The protozoan class whose members lack chloroplasts. Heterotrophic or saprozoic. Examples: *Trypanosoma, Trichonympha, Trichomonas, Giardia.*   247

zooxanthellae (zo″o-zan-thel'e)   A group of dinoflagellates that live in mutualistic relationships with some cnidarians. They promote high rates of calcium carbonate deposition in coral reefs.   277

zygote (zi'gōt)   Diploid cell produced by the fusion of an egg and sperm. Fertilized egg cell. 90

credits

LINE ART

Chapter 1

1.2: From Ricki Lewis, *Life*, 2d ed. Copyright © 1995 New York, McGraw-Hill. Reprinted by permission of The McGraw-Hill Companies; **1.11:** From Ricki Lewis, *Life*, 2d ed. Copyright © 1995 New York, McGraw-Hill. Reprinted by permission of The McGraw-Hill Companies.

Chapter 3

Box 3.1: Redrawn from T. Uzzell and C. Spolsky, "Origin of the Eukaryotic Cell," *American Scientist* 62:334–343, copyright 1974 Sigma XI, The Scientific Research Society. Used by permission; **Box 3.2c,d:** Thomas D. Brock, *Biology of Microorganisms*, 3rd ed., © 1979, p. 774, 775. Adapted by permission of Prentice Hall, Englewood Cliffs, New Jersey; **3.4** John W. Hole, Jr., *Human Anatomy and Physiology*, 6th ed. New York, McGraw-Hill. Reprinted by permission of The McGraw-Hill Companies; **3.6:** Ricki Lewis, *Life*, 2d ed, New York, McGraw-Hill. Reprinted by permission of The McGraw-Hill Companies; **3.12:** John W. Hole, Jr., *Human Anatomy and Physiology*, 6th ed. New York, McGraw-Hill. Reprinted by permission of The McGraw-Hill Companies; **3.18b:** Eldon D. Enger, et al., *Concepts in Biology*, 7th ed. New York, McGraw-Hill. Reprinted by permission of The McGraw-Hill Companies; **3.21:** Redrawn from N.K. Wessels and J.L. Hopson, *Biology*, 3d ed, New York, McGraw-Hill. Reprinted by permission of The McGraw-Hill Companies.

Chapter 4

4.1: from Mader, *Biology*, 5th ed, New York, McGraw-Hill. Reprinted by permission of The McGraw-Hill Companies; **4.5:** Ricki Lewis, *Life*, 2d ed, New York, McGraw-Hill. Reprinted by permission of The McGraw-Hill Companies; **4.6:** Stuart Ira Fox, *Human Physiology*, 4th ed. New York, McGraw-Hill. Reprinted by permission of The McGraw-Hill Companies.

Chapter 5

5.1: Based on fig. 6.19 from Ricki Lewis, *Life*, 2d ed. New York, McGraw-Hill. Reprinted by permission of The McGraw-Hill Companies; **5.2:** From Kathleen Talaro and Arthur Talaro, *Foundations in Microbiology*. New York, McGraw-Hill. Reprinted by permission of The McGraw-Hill Companies; **5.5:** From Ricki Lewis, *Life*. New York, McGraw-Hill. Reprinted by permission of The McGraw-Hill Companies; **5.6:** Kathleen Talaro and Arthur Talaro, *Foundations in Microbiology*. New York, McGraw-Hill. Reprinted by permission of The McGraw-Hill Companies.

Chapter 6

6.2: Stuart Ira Fox, *Human Physiology*, 4th ed. New York, McGraw-Hill. Reprinted by permission of The McGraw-Hill Companies; **6.5a,b,d:** John W. Hole, Jr., *Human Anatomy and Physiology*, 6th ed. New York, McGraw-Hill. Reprinted by permission of The McGraw-Hill Companies; **6.6:** Used with permission from Scott Gilbert, *Developmental Biology*. Copyright © 1985 Sinauer Associates, Inc., Sunderland, MA.; **6.8:** John W. Hole, Jr., *Human Anatomy and Physiology*, 6th ed. New York, McGraw-Hill. Reprinted by permission of The McGraw-Hill Companies; **6.9a,b:** From Leland G. Johnson, *Biology*, 2d ed. Copyright © 1987 New York, McGraw-Hill. Reprinted by permission of The McGraw-Hill Companies; **6.11:** John W. Hole, Jr., *Human Anatomy and Physiology*, 6th ed. New York, McGraw-Hill. Reprinted by permission of The McGraw-Hill Companies.

Chapter 9

9.6: Used with permission from W.K. Purves and G.H. Orians, *Life: The Science of Biology*. Copyright © 1983 Sinauer Associates, Inc., Sunderland, MA; **9.8:** From Ricki Lewis, *Life*. New York, McGraw-Hill. Reprinted by permission of The McGraw-Hill Companies.

Chapter 11

11.1: From Ricki Lewis, *Life*. New York, McGraw-Hill. Reprinted by permission of The McGraw-Hill Companies.

Chapter 13

13.3: From Benjamin B. Lahey, *Psychology: An Introduction*, 3d ed. New York, McGraw-Hill. Reprinted by permission of The McGraw-Hill Companies; **13.5b:** Ruth & Stephey Bernstein, *Biology*. Copyright © 1996 New York, McGraw-Hill. Reprinted by permission of The McGraw-Hill Companies

Chapter 14

14.1: Richard R. Brewer, *The Science of Ecology*, copyright 1988 Saunders College Publishing; **14.3:** From Knut-Schmidt-Nelson, *Animal Physiology*, 4th ed., copyright 1990 Cambridge University Press; **14.4:** Richard R. Brewer, *The Science of Ecology*, copyright 1988 Saunders College Publishing; **14.5:** Leland G. Johnson, *Biology*, 2d Ed. Copyright © 1987 New York, McGraw-Hill. Reprinted by permission of The McGraw-Hill Companies; **14.7:** From C.C. Lindsey, "Problems in Zoology of the Lake Trout, *Salvelinus namaycush*," *Journal of Fisheries Research Board of Canada*, 21: 977–994, 1964. Used by permission.

Chapter 15

15.3: From Ricki Lewis, *Life*, 2d ed. Copyright © 1995 New York, McGraw-Hill. Reprinted by permission of The McGraw-Hill Companies; **15.6:** From Ricki Lewis, *Life*, 2d ed. Copyright © 1995 New York, McGraw-Hill. Reprinted by permission of The McGraw-Hill Companies; **15.7:** From Ricki Lewis, *Life*, 2d ed. Copyright © 1995 New York, McGraw-Hill. Reprinted by permission of The McGraw-Hill Companies; **15.19:** Robert Leo Smith, *The Ecology of Man*, 2d ed., copyright 1976 Harper & Row, 1976.

Chapter 17

17.3: From: "*A LIFE OF INVERTEBRATES*" © 1979 W. D. Russell-Hunter; **17.9b** Prescott/Harley/Klein *Microbiology*, 3/e New York, McGraw-Hill. Reprinted by permission of The McGraw-Hill Companies; **17.16:** Theodore Jahn, et al., *How to Know the Protozoa*, 3d ed. New York, McGraw-Hill. Reprinted by permission of The McGraw-Hill Companies; **17.22:** Data of Carl R. Woese, *Proceedings of the National Academy of Sciences*, 87:4576-4579, 1990.

Chapter 18

18.19: Charles Lytle and J.E. Wodsedalek, *General Zoology Laboratory Guide*, 11th ed., Complete Version. New York, McGraw-Hill. Reprinted by permission of The McGraw-Hill Companies.

Endpaper 1

1.2: From K.G. Grell, *Zeitung fur Morphologie der Tiere*, 73:297-314, 1972. Copyright Springer-Verlag, Heidelberg. Used by permission.

Chapter 19

19.18: Redrawn from Centers for Disease Control, Atlanta; **19.19:** Redrawn from Centers for Disease Control, Atlanta; **19.20:** Modified from Turbeville and Ruppert, 1983, *Zoomorphology*, 103:103, Copyright 1983, Springer-Verlag, Heidelberg, Germany.

Chapter 20

20.10: Redrawn from Centers for Disease Control, Atlanta; **20.11:** Redrawn from Centers for Disease Control, Atlanta; **20.12:** Redrawn from Centers for Disease Control, Atlanta; **20.13a:** Redrawn from Centers for Disease Control, Atlanta; **20.15:** Redrawn from Centers for Disease Control, Atlanta.

Chapter 21

21.6a: From: "*A LIFE OF INVERTEBRATES*" © 1979 W. D. Russell-Hunter; **21.7:** Redrawn from L. Hyman, *The Invertebrates*, Volume VI. Copyright © 1967 New York, McGraw-Hill. Reprinted by permission of The McGraw-Hill Companies.

Chapter 22

22.4: From R.E. Snodgras: *The Principles of Insect Morphology*. Copyright © by Ellen Burden and Ruth Roach. Used by permission of the publisher, Cornell University Press; **22.6:** From: "*A LIFE OF INVERTEBRATES*" © 1979 W. D. Russell-Hunter; **22.9a–c:** From: "*A LIFE OF INVERTEBRATES*" © 1979 W. D. Russell-Hunter; **22.10:** From: "A

LIFE OF INVERTEBRATES" © 1979 W. D. Russell-Hunter; **22.12:** From: "*A LIFE OF INVERTEBRATES*" © 1979 W. D. Russell-Hunter; **22.17:** From: "*A LIFE OF INVERTEBRATES*" © 1979 W. D. Russell-Hunter.

Chapter 23

23.4: From: "*A LIFE OF INVERTEBRATES*" © 1979 W. D. Russell-Hunter

Chapter 24

24.12: Phototake; **24.13:** Phototake.

Chapter 25

25.9: Redrawn from L. Hyman, *The Invertebrates*, Volume IV. Copyright © 1959 New York, McGraw-Hill. Reprinted by permission of The McGraw-Hill Companies; **27.9b:** Fr. R. Steale, *Sharks of the World*. Copyright © 1985 Cassel PLC, London

Chapter 28

28.13: From N. Heisler, *Journal of Experimental Biology*, 1983. Copyright 1983 The Company of Biologists Limited, Cambridge , UK. Used by permission.

Chapter 29

29.13 from N. Heisler, *Journal of Experimental Biology*, 1983. Copyright 1983 The Company of Biologists Limited Cambridge, UK. Used by permission.

Chapter 32

32.9: From Kent M. Van De Graaff and Stuart Ira Fox, *Human Anatomy and Physiology*, 4th ed. Copyright © 1995 New York, McGraw-Hill. Reprinted by permission of The McGraw-Hill Companies; **32.11b:** After Russell-Hunter; **32.12a:** From John W. Hole, Jr., *Human Anatomy and Physiology*, 6th ed. Copyright © 1993 New York, McGraw-Hill. Reprinted by permission of The McGraw-Hill Companies; **32.16:** After Wells, after Sleigh; **32.17:** Adapted From: "*A LIFE OF INVERTEBRATES*" © 1979 W.D. Russell-Hunter; **32.18a:** Adapted From: "*A LIFE OF INVERTEBRATES*" © 1979 W.D. Russell-Hunter; **32.24b:** From Robert B. Chiasson, *Laboratory Manual of the Perch*, 3rd ed. Copyright © 1980 New York, McGraw-Hill. Reprinted by permission of The McGraw-Hill Companies; **32.25:** John W. Hole, Jr., *Human Anatomy and Physiology*, 6th ed. New York, McGraw-Hill. Reprinted by permission of The McGraw-Hill Companies; **32.26:** John W. Hole, Jr., *Human Anatomy and Physiology*, 6th ed. New York, McGraw-Hill. Reprinted by permission of The McGraw-Hill Companies; **32.27:** Stuart Ira Fox, *Human Physiology*, 4th ed. New York, McGraw-Hill. Reprinted by permission of The McGraw-Hill Companies.

Chapter 33

33.1: From Ricki Lewis, *Life*, New York, McGraw-Hill. Reprinted by permission of The McGraw-Hill Companies; **33.3:** Redrawn from Ricki Lewis, *Life*, New York, McGraw-Hill. Reprinted by permission of The McGraw-Hill Companies; **33.4:** From Ricki Lewis, *Life*, New York, McGraw-Hill. Reprinted by permission of The McGraw-Hill Companies; **33.10:** Redrawn from Cecie Starr and Ralph Taggart, *Biology: The Unity and Diversity of Life*, 4th ed. Copyright © 1987 Wadsworth Publishing Company, Belmont, CA. Used by Permission; **33.12:** From Ricki Lewis, *Life*, New York, McGraw-Hill. Reprinted by permission of The McGraw-Hill Companies.

Chapter 34

34.2: Redrawn with permission from Richard C. and Gary J. Brusca, *Invertebrates*. Copyright © 1990 Sinauer Associates, Inc., Sunderland, MA; **34.10:** John W. Hole, Jr., *Human Anatomy and Physiology*, 6th ed. New York, McGraw-Hill. Reprinted by permission of The McGraw-Hill Companies; **34.11a,b:** John W. Hole, Jr., *Human Anatomy and Physiology*, 6th ed. New York, McGraw-Hill. Reprinted by permission of The McGraw-Hill Companies; **34.14:** From Kent M. Van De Graaff and Stuart Ira Fox, *Human Anatomy and Physiology*, 4th ed. Copyright © 1995 New York, McGraw-Hill. Reprinted by permission of The McGraw-Hill Companies; **34.15:** From Kent M. Van De Graaff, *Human Anatomy*, 4th ed. Copyright © 1995 New York, McGraw-Hill. Reprinted by permission of The McGraw-Hill Companies; **34.17:** John W. Hole, Jr., *Human Anatomy and Physiology*, 6th ed. New York, McGraw-Hill. Reprinted by permission of The McGraw-Hill Companies; **34.18:** From Kent M. Van De Graaff and Stuart Ira Fox, *Human Anatomy and Physiology*, 4th ed. New York, McGraw-Hill. Reprinted by permission of The McGraw-Hill Companies.

Chapter 35

35.1: Barrett/Abramoff/Kumaran/Millington, *Biology*, © 1986, p. 383. Adapted by permission of Prentice Hall, Inc., Englewood Cliffs, New Jersey; **35.3:** John W. Hole, Jr., *Human Anatomy and Physiology*, 6th ed. New York, McGraw-Hill. Reprinted by permission of The McGraw-Hill Companies; **35.4:** John W. Hole, Jr., *Human Anatomy and Physiology*, 6th ed. New York, McGraw-Hill. Reprinted by permission of The McGraw-Hill Companies; **35.7a:** John W. Hole, Jr., *Human Anatomy and Physiology*, 6th ed. New York, McGraw-Hill. Reprinted by permission of The McGraw-Hill Companies; **35.12c:** John W. Hole, Jr., *Human Anatomy and Physiology*, 6th ed. New York, McGraw-Hill. Reprinted by permission of The McGraw-Hill Companies; **35.17:** From Kent M. Van De Graaff and Stuart Ira Fox, *Human Anatomy and Physiology*, 2d ed. Copyright © 1989 New York, McGraw-Hill. Reprinted by permission of The McGraw-Hill Companies; **35.18:** John W. Hole, Jr., *Human Anatomy and Physiology*, 6th ed. New York, McGraw-Hill. Reprinted by permission of The McGraw-Hill Companies.

Chapter 36

36.6: From Ricki Lewis, *Life*, New York, McGraw-Hill. Reprinted by permission of The McGraw-Hill Companies; **36.7:** Redrawn from N. K. Wessels and J. L. Hopson, *Biology*, 3d ed. Copyright © 1988 New York, McGraw-Hill. Reprinted by permission of The McGraw-Hill Companies; **36.27:** From Stuart Ira Fox, *Human Physiology*, 3d ed. Copyright © 1990 New York, McGraw-Hill. Reprinted by permission of The McGraw-Hill Companies.

Chapter 37

37.11: From Kent M. Van De Graaff and Stuart Ira Fox, *Human Anatomy and Physiology*, 4th ed. Copyright © 1989 New York, McGraw-Hill. Reprinted by permission of The McGraw-Hill Companies; **37.13a:** Stuart Ira Fox, *Human Physiology*, 4th ed. New York, McGraw-Hill. Reprinted by permission of The McGraw-Hill Companies; **37.13b:** From Kent M. Van De Graaff and Stuart Ira Fox, *Human Anatomy and Physiology*, 4th ed. Copyright © 1989 New York, McGraw-Hill. Reprinted by permission of The McGraw-Hill Companies; **37.14:** From Ricki Lewis, *Life*, New York, McGraw-Hill. Reprinted by permission of The McGraw-Hill Companies; **37.15:** John W. Hole, Jr., *Human Anatomy and Physiology*, 6th ed. New York, McGraw-Hill. Reprinted by permission of The McGraw-Hill Companies; **37.16:** John W. Hole, Jr., *Human Anatomy and Physiology*, 6th ed. New York, McGraw-Hill. Reprinted by permission of The McGraw-Hill Companies.

Chapter 38

38.1: *ANIMAL PHYSIOLOGY: MECHANISMS AND ADAPTATIONS* 3/E by Eckert, Randall, and Augustine © 1988 by W.H. Freeman and Company. Used with permission; **38.8:** from Starr & Taggert, *BIOLOGY; THE UNITY & DIVERSITY OF LIFE*, 4/e, fig 33.2: 1987 Wadsworth Publishing; **38.12:** Redrawn with permission from W.K. Purves and G.H. Orians, *Life: The Science of Biology*, 2d ed. Copyright © 1987 Sinauer Associates, Inc. Sunderland, MA.; **38.17:** Redrawn from N.K. Wessels and J. L. Hopson, *Biology*, 3d ed. Copyright © 1988 New York, McGraw-Hill. Reprinted by permission of The McGraw-Hill Companies; **38.18:** Redrawn from N. K. Wessels and J. L. Hopson, *Biology*, 3d ed. Copyright © 1988 New York, McGraw-Hill. Reprinted by permission of The McGraw-Hill Companies; **38.19:** John W. Hole, Jr., *Human Anatomy and Physiology*, 6th ed. New York, McGraw-Hill. Reprinted by permission of The McGraw-Hill Companies; **38.20:** John W. Hole, Jr., *Human Anatomy and Physiology*, 6th ed. New York, McGraw-Hill. Reprinted by permission of The McGraw-Hill Companies; **38.21:** *ANIMAL PHYSIOLOGY: MECHANISMS AND ADAPTATIONS* 3/E by Eckert, Randall, and Augustine © 1988 by W.H. Freeman and Company. Used with permission; **38.22:** From Leland G. Johnson, *Biology*, 2d ed. Copyright © 1987 New York, McGraw-Hill. Reprinted by permission of The McGraw-Hill Companies; **38.23:** From Kent M. Van De Graaff and Stuart Ira Fox, *Human Anatomy and Physiology*, 2d ed. Copyright © 1989 New York, McGraw-Hill. Reprinted by permission of The McGraw-Hill Companies.

Chapter 39

39.2: Redrawn with permission from Richard C. Brusca and Gary J. Brusca, *Invertebrates*. Copyright © 1990 Sinauer Associates, Inc., Sunderland, MA; **39.4:** John W. Hole, Jr., *Human Anatomy and Physiology*, 6th ed. New York, McGraw-Hill. Reprinted by permission of The McGraw-Hill Companies; **39.5a:** From Kent M. Van De Graaff, *Human Anatomy* 4th ed. Copyright © 1995 New York, McGraw-Hill. Reprinted by permission of The McGraw-Hill Companies; **39.5b:** From Kent M. Van De Graaff, *Human Anatomy*, 2d ed. Copyright © 1988 New York, McGraw-Hill. Reprinted by permission of The McGraw-Hill Companies; **39.5c:** John W. Hole, Jr., *Human Anatomy and Physiology*, 6th ed. New York, McGraw-Hill. Reprinted by permission of The McGraw-Hill Companies; **39.7:** John W. Hole, Jr., *Human Anatomy and Physiology*, 6th ed. New York, McGraw-Hill. Reprinted by permission of The McGraw-Hill Companies; **39.10:** From Kent M. Van De Graaff, *Human Anatomy*, 4th ed. Copyright © 1995 New York, McGraw-Hill. Reprinted by permission of The McGraw-Hill Companies; **39.12:** John W. Hole, Jr., *Human*

Anatomy and Physiology, 6th ed. New York, McGraw-Hill. Reprinted by permission of The McGraw-Hill Companies; **39.13:** John W. Hole, Jr., *Human Anatomy and Physiology,* 6th ed. New York, McGraw-Hill. Reprinted by permission of The McGraw-Hill Companies; **39.15:** Stuart Ira Fox, *Human Physiology,* 4th ed. New York, McGraw-Hill. Reprinted by permission of The McGraw-Hill Companies; **39.16:** Redrawn from Kent M. Van De Graaff and Stuart Ira Fox, *Human Anatomy and Physiology,* 4th ed. Copyright © 1995 New York, McGraw-Hill. Reprinted by permission of The McGraw-Hill Companies.

PHOTOS

Part Openers

Part 1: Underwater Life/Photogear; **2:** Flowers/Digital Stock; **3:** Undersea Life/Digital Stock; **4:** Underwater Life/Photogear; **5:** Undersea Life/Digital Stock; **6:** Animals/Digital Stock

Chapter 1

1.1: © Ron Austing/Photo Researchers, Inc.; **1.3a:** © Renee Lynn/Photo Researchers, Inc.; **1.3b:** © Gerald and Buff Corski/Tom Stack & Associates; **1.5:** © Sinclair Stammers/SPL/Photo Researchers, Inc.; **1.8a:** © Stephen Dalton/Animals Animals/Earth Scenes; **1.8b:** © Stephen Dalton/Animals Animals/Earth Scenes; **1.9a:** © Doug Wechsler/Animals Animals/Earth Scenes; **1.9b:** © Dr. Nigel Smith/Animals Animals/Earth Scenes.

Chapter 2

2.16c: © Ken Edward/Science Source/Photo Researchers, Inc.

Chapter 3

Box 3.2e: © Ed Reschke/Peter Arnold, Inc.; **Box 3.2f:** © David M. Phillips/Visuals Unlimited; **Box 3.2g:** © David M. Phillips/Visuals Unlimited; **3.11a–c:** © David M. Phillips/Visuals Unlimited; **3.18a:** Dr. Keith Porter; **3.23** © K.G. Murti/Visuals Unlimited; **3.24a:** © Ed Reschke; **3.24b:** © Ed Reschke; **3.24c:** © Manfred Kage/Peter Arnold, Inc.; **3.24d:** © Ed Reschke; **3.24e:** © Fred Hossler/Visuals Unlimited; **3.24f–j:** © Ed Reschke; **3.24k:** © John D. Cunningham/Visuals Unlimited; **3.24l:** © Victor B. Eichler, Ph.D.; **3.24m:** © Ed Reschke; **3.24n:** © Manfred Kage/Peter Arnold, Inc.; **3.24o,p:** © Ed Reschke; **3.24q** © Manfred Kage/Peter Arnold, Inc.; **p.55** © Austin Stevens/Animals Animals/Earth Scenes.

Chapter 4

4.1: © Gallbridge/Visuals Unlimited.

Chapter 5

p. 78: © A. Rider/Photo Researchers, Inc.

Chapter 6

6.5(all): © John D. Cunningham/Visuals Unlimited; **p.95:** © William A. Dyer/Photo Researchers, Inc.

Chapter 7

7.1: © William E. Ferguson.

Chapter 8

8.1a: From D. Olins, A. Olins, "Nucleosomes: The Structural Quantum in Chromosomes," in *American*

Scientist, 66: November 1978; **8.5a:** © Hans Reinhard/OKAPIA/Photo Researchers, Inc.; **8.5b–1:** From Wilson and Foster, *Williams Textbook of Endocrinology,* 7th edition. © W.B. Saunders 1985; **8.5b–2:** From Wilson and Foster, *Williams Textbook of Endocrinology,* 7th edition. © W.B. Saunders, 1985; **8.7b:** © CNRI/SPL/Photo Researchers, Inc.

Chapter 9

9.10a: © Visuals Unlimited; **9.10b–e:** © Dan McCoy/Rainbow; **9.11a–c:** David Dressler/Huntington Potter/Life Magazine, © Time, Inc.

Chapter 10

10.2a: Courtesy Dr. E. William Byrd; **10.2b:** Courtesy of Dr. Gerlad Schatten, Oregon Health Sciences University; **10.2c,d:** Reprinted with permission from M.J. Tegner, "Sea Urchin Sperm: Eggs Instruction Studied with The Electron Microscope," Science, 179:685, February 1973. Copyright 1973 American Association for the Advancement of Science; **10.6a–h:** © Carolina Biological/Visuals Unlimited; **10.6i:** © David M. Phillips/Visuals Unlimited; **10.8a:** © Bill Beatty/Visuals Unlimited; **10.8b, 10.9a, 10.9B, 10.9c, 10.9d:** © Carolina Biological/Visuals Unlimited; **10.9e:** © Nathan Cohen/Visuals Unlimited; **10.9f:** © Joe McDonald/Visuals Unlimited; **p.146: (bottom)** Courtesy of Kevin S. Cummings, Illinois Natural History Survey, Champaign, IL; **p.146(top)** © M.C. Barnhart 1995.

Chapter 11

11.2a: © Walt Anderson/Visuals Unlimited; **11.2b:** © Joe McDonald/Visuals Unlimited; **11.4a:** © Alan L. Deitrick/Photo Researchers, Inc.; **11.4b:** © Walt Anderson/Visuals Unlimited.

Chapter 12

12.2a: © Don W. Fawcett/Visuals Unlimited; **12.3** © Kevin Schafer/Tom Stack & Associates; **12.5a, b:** © Michael Tweedie/Photo Researchers, Inc.

Chapter 13

13.1: Courtesy of Professor Dr. Eibl-Eibesfeldt; **13.2c:** Nina Leen/*Life Magazine,* © Time, Inc.; **13.4:** © Richard Wood/The Picture Cube; **13.5b:** © Tom McHugh/Photo Researchers, Inc.; **13.6:** © C.P. Hickman/Visuals Unlimited; **13.7:** © Mitch Reardon/Photo Researchers, Inc.; **13.8:** © Dwight Kuhn; **13.10:** © Gerard Lacz/Peter Arnold, Inc.

Chapter 14

14.8a: © Robert C. Simpson/Tom Stack & Associates; **14.8b:** © S. Maslowski/Visuals Unlimited; **14.8c:** © Ron Austing/Photo Researchers, Inc.; **14.8d:** © Johann Schumacher/Peter Arnold, Inc.; **14.8e:** © S. Maslowski/Visuals Unlimited; **14.9:** © Anthony Mercieca/Photo Researchers, Inc.; **14.10a:** © Daniel V. Gotshall/Visuals Unlimited; **14.10b:** © Marty Snyderman/Visuals Unlimited; **14.11:** © E.R. Degginer/Color-Pic, Inc.; **14.12:** © Paul Oppler/Visuals Unlimited; **p. 202:** Courtesy of Brent J. Danielson, Department of Animal Ecology, Iowa State University.

Chapter 15

15.2a: © Richard Thom/Visuals Unlimited; **15.2b:** © Tom Ulrich/Visuals Unlimited; **15.2c:** © Joe McDonald/Visuals Unlimited; **Box 15.1b:** © D. Foster/WHOI/Visuals Unlimited; **15.9:** © Steve

McCutcheon/Visuals Unlimited; **15.10:** © Steve McCutcheon/Visuals Unlimited; **15.11:** © Tom Edwards/Visuals Unlimited; **15.12:** © Richard Thom/Visuals Unlimited; **15.13:** © Ron Spomer/Visuals Unlimited; **15.14:** © Glenn M. Oliver/Visuals Unlimited; **15.15:** © Kjell Sandved; **15.16,15.18:** © Dwight Kuhn; **15.20:** © Walt Anderson/Visuals Unlimited

Chapter 16

16.1: Courtesy of Professor Reinhardt Kristensen, University of Copenhagen, Denmark; **16.7:** © Daniel W. Gotshall/Visuals Unlimited; **16.8:** © Dave B. Fleethan/Visuals Unlimited; **p. 238 (both)** Courtesy of Professor Brenda Clark, Southeastern Oklahoma State University

Chapter 17

17.1: © David John/Visuals Unlimited; **17.5a–d:** © Dennis Diener/Visuals Unlimited; **17.6:** © Terry Hazen/Visuals Unlimited; **17.8a:** © James W. Richards/Visuals Unlimited; **Box 17.1, fig. 1:** Courtesy of Dr. Stanley Erlandsen; **17.11a:** © M. Abben/Visuals Unlimited; **17.13:** © A.M. Siegelman/Visuals Unlimited; **17.14a:** © M. Schliwa/Visuals Unlimited; **17.14b:** © G. Shih-R. Kessel/Visuals Unlimited; **17.17a:** © Karl Auffderheide/Visuals Unlimited; **17.18:** © M. Abbey/Visuals Unlimited; **17.19:** © Biophoto Associates/Photo Researchers, Inc.; **17.20:** © D.J. Patterson/OSF/Animals Animals/Earth Scenes

Chapter 18

18.1: © John D. Cunningham/Visuals Unlimited; **18.4a:** © Nancy Sefton/Photo Researchers, Inc.; **18.4b:** © Daniel W. Gotshall/Visuals Unlimited; **Box 18.1, fig. 1:** © The Field Museum of Natural History, #GEO80872C, Chicago; **18.6:** © Carolina Biological/Visuals Unlimited; **18.8d:** From De Vos, L., Rutzler, K., Boury-Esnault, N. Donadey, C. & Vacelet, J., 1991. *Atlas of Sponge Morphology.* Copyright © 1991 by the Smithsonian Institution. Reprinted by permission of the publisher; **18.13a:** © Carolina Biological/Visuals Unlimited; **18.14a:** © Edward Hodgson/Visuals Unlimited; **18.14b:** © N.G. Daniel/Tom Stack & Associates; **18.17:** © Neville Coleman/Visuals Unlimited; **18.18b:** © Heather Angel; **18.21a:** © Daniel W. Gotshall/Visuals Unlimited; **18.21b:** © Mary Snyderman/Visuals Unlimited; **Box 18.2, fig. 1:** © M. Gottschalk/Tom Stack & Associates; **18.22a:** © R. DeGoursey/Visuals Unlimited

Chapter 19

19.1: © Gary R. Robinson/Visuals Unlimited; **19.17b:** © Drs. Kessel and Shih/Peter Arnold, Inc.

Chapter 20

20.1: © Lauritz Jensen/Visuals Unlimited; **20.4a:** © Peter Parks/OSF/Animals Animals/Earth Scenes; **20.13a: (photo)** © Steve Miller; **20.14:** © Science VU-AFIP/Visuals Unlimited; **20.16:** © R. Calentine/Visuals Unlimited; **20.17b** © Lauritz Jensen/Visuals Unlimited.

Chapter 21

21.1: © Gary Miburn/Tom Stack & Associates; **21.6b:** © Science VU-Polaroid/Visuals Unlimited; **21.8a:** © William J. Weber/Visuals Unlimited; **21.9a:** © OSF/Animals Animals Earth Scenes; **21.9b:** © Daniel W. Gotshall/Visuals Unlimited; **21.9c:** © Gerald & Buff Corsi/Visuals Unlimited;

21.15c: © Ed Reschke; 21.16: Courtesy of Dr. William Roston; **Box fig. 21.1:** © Scott Camazine/ Photo Researchers, Inc.; 21.17b: © Carl Roessler/ Animals Animals/Earth Scenes; 21.21a: © Robert A. Ross; 21.22: © Kjell B. Sandved/ Photo Researchers, Inc.; 21.24: © James Cutler/ Visuals Unlimited; **p. 334:** © D. Dennis/Tom Stack & Associates

Chapter 22

22.1: © Marty Snyderman/Visuals Unlimited; 22.5: © R. DeGoursey/Visuals Unlimited; **Box 22.2, fig. 1:** © C.P. Hickman/Visuals Unlimited; **p. 358:** © WHOI/D. Foster/Visuals Unlimited.

Chapter 23

23.1: © Roger Klocek/Visuals Unlimited; 23.6: © John Cancalosi/Tom Stack & Associates; 23.8a: © Francois Gohier/Photo Researchers, Inc.; 23.11a: © Tom McHugh/Photo Researchers, Inc.; 23.13: © Ken Highfill/Photo Researchers, Inc.; **Box 23.1, fig. a:** © S. Masiowski/Visuals Unlimited; **Box 23.1, fig. b:** © Richard Walters/Visuals Unlimited; 23.14: © David Scharf/Peter Arnold, Inc.; 23.15a: © R. Calentine/Visuals Unlimited; 23.15b: © Scott Camazine/Photo Researchers, Inc.; 23.16: © Heather Angel; 23.18: © Andrew J. Martinez/Photo Researchers, Inc.; 23.21a: © John D. Cunningham/ Visuals Unlimited; 23.21b: © William C. Jorgensen/Visuals Unlimited; 23.22a: © David M. Dennis/Tom Stack & Associates; 23.22b: © Alan Desbonnet/ Visuals Unlimited; 23.23: Bruce Russell/ BioMedia Associates; 23.24b: © Tom Stack/ Tom Stack & Associates; **Box 23.2, fig. 1:** © Heather Angel.

Chapter 24

24.1: © Patti Murray/Animals Animals/Earth Scenes; 24.3a: © Bill Beatty/Visuals Unlimited; 24.3b: © Glenn M. Oliver; 24.10a: © S. L. Flegler/Visuals Unlimited; 24.14a–c: © Treat Davidson/Photo Researchers, Inc.; **p. 399:** © Tom J. Ulrich/Visuals Unlimited; **p. 400** (left) Photomicrograph by John Ubelaker; **p. 400** (right) Courtesy Diane R. Nelson, Ph.D.

Chapter 25

25.1: © Carl Roessler/Tom Stack & Associates; 25.3a: © Michael Dispezio; **Box 25.1, fig. 1:** © Daniel W. Gotshall/Visuals Unlimited; 25.8a: © Robert L. Dunne/Photo Researchers, Inc.; 25.8b: © 1998 Harold W. Pratt/Biological Photo Service; 24.10a: © C. McDaniel/Visuals Unlimited; 25.10b: © Bruce Iverson/Visuals Unlimited; 25.12: © Daniel W. Gotshall/Visuals Unlimited; 25.16: Courtesy of the Museum of New Zealand Te Papa Tongarewa, Alan M. Baker, photographer; **p. 416:** © John D. Cunningham/Visuals Unlimited; **3a:** © Daniel W. Gotshall/Visuals Unlimited.

Endpaper 4

fig. 8b: From Q. Bone, et al., *Journal of the Marine Biological Association of the United Kingdom*, Vol. 63:929, 1983. Reprinted with the permission of Cambridge University Press.

Chapter 26

26.1: © Michael DiSpezio; 26.6a: © William C. Jorgenson/Visuals Unlimited; 26.6b: © Daniel W. Gotshall/Visuals Unlimited; **Box 26.:1** © Gary R. Robinson/Visuals Unlimited.

Chapter 27

27.1: © Albert Copley/Visuals Unlimited; 27.5: © Russ Kinne/Photo Researchers, Inc.; 27.8a: © Ed Robinson/Tom Stack & Associates; 27.8b,c: © Daniel W. Gotshall/Visuals Unlimited; 27.9a: © Science VU/NOAA/Visuals Unlimited; **Box 27.2:** © Roger Klocek/Visuals Unlimited; 27.10: © John D. Cunningham/Visuals Unlimited; 27.11: © Tom Stack/Tom Stack & Associates; 27.12a: © Patrice Ceisel/Visuals Unlimited; 27.12b: © Patrice Ceisel/ Visuals Unlimited; 27.13a: © R. DeGoursey/Visuals Unlimited; 27.13b: © Fred Rohde/Visuals Unlimited; 27.13c: © Patrice Ceisel/Visuals Unlimited; 27.15b: © Fred Hossler/Visuals Unlimited; 27.17b: © Tom McHugh/Photo Researchers, Inc.; 27.18, 27.20: © Daniel W. Gotshall/Visuals Unlimited.

Chapter 28

28.1: © Joe McDonald/Visuals Unlimited; 28.4: © John D. Cunningham/Visuals Unlimited; 28.5a,b: © Dwight Kuhn; 28.5c: © Joel Arrington/Visuals Unlimited; 28.6: © Tom McHugh/Photo Researchers, Inc.; 28.7: © John Serrao/Visuals Unlimited; **Box 28.1:** © Dennis Paulson/Visuals Unlimited; 28.15a: © Nada Pecnik/Visuals Unlimited; 28.15b: © Edward S. Ross; 28.16b: © Dan Kline/Visuals Unlimited; 28.17: © M.J. Tyler, The University of Adelaid, South Australia; 28.18a–d: © Jane Burton/Bruce Coleman, Inc.

Chapter 29

29.1: © E.R. Degginger/Photo Researchers, Inc.; 29.5: © Valorie Hoegson/Visuals Unlimited; 29.6: © Nathan W. Cohen/Visuals Unlimited; 29.7: © Joe McDonald/Visuals Unlimited; 29.8: © Thomas Gula/Visuals Unlimited; 29.9: © John D. Cunningham/Visuals Unlimited; 29.11: © Stephen Dalton/Animals Animals/Earth Scenes; 29.12a: © Joe McDonald/Visuals Unlimited; 29.14: © Zigmund Leszczynski/Animals Animals/Earth Scenes; 29.15: © Robert Hernes/Photo Researchers, Inc.

Chapter 30

30.1a: © Tim Hauf/Visuals Unlimited; 30.2a: © John D. Cunningham/Visuals Unlimited; 30.2b: Net .#K-Set3 #29. Courtesy Department of Library Services, American Museum of Natural History.; 30.6e: © Tom McHugh/Photo Researchers, Inc.; **Box 30.1:** © Tim Hauf/Visuals Unlimited; 30.7: © Robert A. Lubeck/Animals Animals/Earth Scenes; 30.8a: © Thomas Kitchin/Tom Stack & Associates; 30.8b: © Kirtley-Perkins/Visuals Unlimited; 30.8c: © Brian Parker/Tom Stack & Associates; 30.10c:Courtesy of Dr. Hans-Rainer Duncker; 30.11: © Karl Maslowski/Visuals Unlimited; 30.14: © John D. Cunningham/Visuals Unlimited; 30.15a: © Karl Maslowski/Visuals Unlimited; 30.15b: © John D. Cunningham/ Visuals Unlimited.

Chapter 31

31.1: © M. Long/Visuals Unlimited; 31.4a: © Tom McHugh/Photo Researchers, Inc.; 31.4b: © J. Alcock/Visuals Unlimited; 31.4c: © Bruce Berg/Visuals Unlimited; 31.5a: © Walt Anderson/Visuals Unlimited; 31.5b: © William J. Weber/Visuals Unlimited; 31.6: © Bruce Cushing/Visuals Unlimited; **Box 31.1b:** © Tom J. Ulrich/Visuals Unlimited; 31.11: © Peter Weimann/Animals Animals/Earth Scenes; **Box 31.2:** © Stephen Dalton/Animals Animals/Earth Scenes; 31.15: © Dennis Schmidt/

Valan Photos; 31.16: © Walt Anderson/Visuals Unlimited; 31.17a, b: © John D. Cunningham/ Visuals Unlimited.

Chapter 32

32.10a: © Gary Robinson/Visuals Unlimited; 32.11a: © Richard Walters/Visuals Unlimited; 32.12b: From Richard G. Kessel and Randy H. Kardon, *Tissues and Organs: A Text-Atlas of Scanning Electron Microscopy*, 1979, W.H. Freeman and Company; **p. 548:** © Peter Weimann/Animals Animals/Earth Scenes.

Chapter 33

p. 564: © C.C. Lockwood/Animals Animals/Earth Scenes.

Chapter 34

34.4c: © Thomas Eisner, Cornell University; 34.6: © C. Bradford Calloway; 34.13: © Milton H. Tierney/Visuals Unlimited; **p. 583:** © Tess Young/Tom Stack & Associates.

Chapter 35

35.9: Courtesy of Dr. Aaron Lerner, Yale University; **p. 602:** © Merlin D. Tuttle, Bat Conservation International.

Chapter 36

36.4: Figure from *Comparative Animal Physiology* by Philip C. Withers, copyright © 1992 by Saunders College Publishing, reproduced by permission of the publisher; 36.5a: © Stanley L. Flegler/Visuals Unlimited; 36.5b–f: © John D. Cunningham/Visuals Unlimited; 36.13: © Andrejs Liepiins/SPL/ Photo Researchers, Inc.; 36.20: © Victor H. Hutchison/Visuals Unlimited.

Chapter 37

37.6a: © R. Calentine/Visuals Unlimited; 37.6b: © Daniel Gotshall/Visuals Unlimited; 37.6c: © Dwight Kuhn; 37.6d: © Science VU/Visuals Unlimited; **Box 37.2, fig. 1a:** © Gary R. Robinson/ Visuals Unlimited; **Box 37.2, fig. 1b:** © Visuals Unlimited; **Box 37.2, fig. 1c:** © Will Troyer/ Visuals Unlimited; **Box 37.2, fig. 1d:** © Visuals Unlimited; 37.16d: © Visuals Unlimited.

Chapter 38

38.2: © Joe McDonald/Visuals Unlimited; 38.5a: © G. Prance/Visuals Unlimited; 38.6: © Dan Kline/Visuals Unlimited; **Box 38.1, fig. 1** © Elisabeth Weiland/Photo Researchers, Inc.; 38.9: © Cabisco/Visuals Unlimited.

Chapter 39

39.1a: © Carolina Biological/Visuals Unlimited; 39.1b: © John D. Cunningham/Visuals Unlimited; 39.1c: © Mike Mulligan/Visuals Unlimited; 39.1d: © John D. Cunningham/Visuals Unlimited; 39.1e: © Daniel W. Gotshall/Visuals Unlimited; 39.3a: © John Serrao/Visuals Unlimited; 39.3b: © A. Gurmankin/Visuals Unlimited; 39.3c: © Karl Maslowski/ Visuals Unlimited; 39.3d: © SIU/Visuals Unlimited; 39.9: © David M. Phillips/Visuals Unlimited; 39.14a: © Petit Format/Nestle/Photo Researchers, Inc.; 39.14b: © A. Tsiaras/Photo Researchers, Inc.; 39.14c: © Petit Format/Nestle/ Photo Researchers, Inc.; 39.14d–f: © Science/Visuals Unlimited; 39.14g: © Carolina Biological/ Visuals Unlimited.